Springer Texts in Business and Economics

More information about this series at http://www.springer.com/series/10099

Efraim Turban • David King
Jae Kyu Lee • Ting-Peng Liang
Deborrah C. Turban

Electronic Commerce

A Managerial and Social Networks Perspective

Eighth Edition, Revised Edition

 Springer

Efraim Turban
University of Hawaii
Honolulu, HI, USA

David King
JDA Software
Scottsdale, AZ, USA

Jae Kyu Lee
Graduate School of Management
Korea Advanced Institute of Science
and Technology (KAIST)
Seoul, Republic of South Korea

Ting-Peng Liang
National Chengchi University (Taipei,
Taiwan) and National Sun Yat-Sen
University (Kaohsiung, Taiwan)

Deborrah C. Turban
Turban Company Inc.
Kihei, HI, USA

ISSN 2192-4333   ISSN 2192-4341 (electronic)
ISBN 978-3-319-10090-6   ISBN 978-3-319-10091-3 (eBook)
DOI 10.1007/978-3-319-10091-3
Springer Cham Heidelberg New York Dordrecht London

Library of Congress Control Number: 2014950448

Printed on acid-free paper

Springer is part of Springer Science+Business Media (www.springer.com)

Preface

There has been a severe recession in the world economy in recent years, yet electronic commerce, the topic of this book, has grown rapidly, with companies like Facebook, Google, Pinterest, Alibaba Group and Amazon.com setting new levels of performance every year.

Electronic commerce (EC) is a business model in which transactions take place over electronic networks, mostly the Internet. It includes the process of electronically buying and selling goods, services, and information. Certain EC applications, such as buying and selling stocks and airline tickets online, are reaching maturity, some even exceeding non-Internet trade volumes. However, EC is not just about buying and selling; it also is about electronically communicating, collaborating, and discovering information. It is about e-learning, customer service, e-government, social networks, and much more. EC is having an impact on a significant portion of the world, affecting businesses, professions, trade, and of course, people.

The most important developments in EC since 2012 are the phenomenal growth of social networks, especially Facebook, Google+, and Twitter, and the trend toward conducting EC via mobile devices. Other major developments are the global expansion of EC, especially in China, where you can find the world's largest EC company. In addition, some emerging EC business models are changing industries (e.g., travel, banking, fashion, and transportation).

In the 8th edition, we bring forth the latest trends in e-commerce, including social businesses, social networking, social collaboration, innovations, and mobility.

Note: Portions of this book were previously published by: Pearson Education, Inc. under the title: *Electronic Commerce 2012: A Managerial and Social Networks Perspective.*

What's New in This Edition?

The following are the major changes in this edition:
- **New chapters**
  Chapter 7 in EC 2012 has been replaced by two chapters. The new Chapter 7 concentrates on social media marketing, social shopping, and social CRM. Chapter 8 focuses on enterprise social networks, crowdsourcing, and other applications of social media.

- **New topics**

  Many new topics were added in all chapters, while obsolete topics were deleted. The major new topics are divided here into the following categories:

  1. **Topics in basic e-commerce and m-commerce**
     - Cyberwars
     - Digital coupons
     - Gamification
     - Global payment systems
     - IBM's Smarter Commerce
     - Mobile apps
     - Mobile banking
     - Mobile shopping/sales
     - Mobile videos and advertising
     - New shopping aid tools (that shoppers must have)
     - New wearable computing applications including smart glasses, cities, and cars

  2. **EC technology**
     - Augmented reality
     - Crowdsourcing
     - Micro payments devices
     - Big data in EC and its analysis
     - E-payments, including Bitcoin
     - Develop your own applications (DYOA)
     - IBM's Pure Data Systems for analytics
     - Internet of Things (IoT)
     - Machine-to-machine (M2M) communications
     - New devices for e-learning
     - 3D printing and EC
     - Wearable devices

  3. **Managerial topics**
     - The issues surrounding Bring Your Own Device (BYOD)
     - Collaborative strategic planning
     - Crowdfunding
     - Innovation and performance improvement
     - Internet sales tax
     - New aspects of online competition
     - Sharing economy (P2P economy)
     - Small retailers going global

  4. **Social media and commerce topics**
     - Collaboration 2.0 (social collaboration)
     - New methods of social networking data collection and analysis
     - Gamification in social networks
     - Innovation and creativity in social commerce
     - P2P lending and other P2P activities
     - Sentiment analysis
     - Shopping for virtual goods

- Social customers
- Social graph
- Social media frameworks, characteristics, and tools
- Social media search engines (social search)
- Social TV and social radio
- Transformation of traditional companies into social businesses

5. **New cases**

The following are some of the new cases:

Starbucks, Pinterest, Cemax of Mexico, P&G, Sony USA, Madagascar's Port, Red Hat, Axon of New Zealand, Yodobuch (Japan), eGovernment in Germany, Korea's multipurpose smart cards, iRobot, Telstra (Australia), Etsy, Del Monte, Polyvore, and I am Hungry (a failure case).

6. **New Features**

In additional to the regular features of the book (discussed later) we added:

- A large number of links to resources, examples, and videos
- Many examples of mobile applications
- Short video cases (as exercises)

7. **Wikipedia and other wiki-based resources**

Given the copyright issues and some uneven quality issues, we eliminated citations from Wikipedia and similar wiki-based sources. Furthermore, these sources are evolving and changing. Yet, we strongly recommend that instructors encourage students to look at these sources. Note that Wikipedia provides information about the completeness and the quality of many of its entries. Therefore, instructors should review the entries before recommending them to students.

- **Online tutorials**

We provide five technology-related online tutorials (instead of 12 in EC 2012).

The following tutorials are not related to any specific chapter. They cover the essentials of EC technologies and provide a guide to relevant resources.

T1 – eCRM

T2 – EC technology: EDI, Extranet, RFID, and cloud computing

T3 – Business intelligence and analytics, data, text, and Web mining

T4 – Competition in cyberspace

T5 – E-collaboration

The tutorials are available at **affordable-ecommerce-textbook.com/turban**

The Book's Learning Objectives (Learning Outcomes)

Upon completion of this book, the reader will be able to:

1. Define all types of e-commerce systems and describe their major business and revenue models.
2. Describe all the major mechanisms that are used in e-commerce.
3. Describe all methods and models of selling products and services online.

4. Understand all online business-to-business activities, including selling, procurement, auctions, and collaboration.
5. Describe EC activities other than selling online, such as e-government, e-learning/training, and e-collaboration.
6. Describe the importance of mobile commerce, its content, and implementation.
7. Describe social networks, social customers, virtual worlds, and social software as facilitators of e-commerce.
8. Describe the landscape of social commerce applications, including social shopping and advertising, social CRM, social entertainment, and crowdsourcing.
9. Describe social enterprise systems.
10. Understand online consumer behavior.
11. Describe marketing and advertising in the Web environment.
12. Describe security issues and their solutions in e-commerce.
13. Describe the use of e-payments, including mobile payments, in e-commerce.
14. Understand order fulfillment in e-commerce and its relationship to supply chain management.
15. Understand e-commerce strategy and describe its process and steps, including justification, planning, implementation, and assessment.
16. Describe the global aspects of e-commerce.
17. Explain the issues of using e-commerce by small- and medium-sized companies.
18. Understand the ethical, legal, social, and business environments within which e-commerce operates.
19. Describe the options of acquiring or building EC systems.

Features of This Book

Several features are unique to this book.

Most Comprehensive EC Textbook

This is the most comprehensive EC textbook available. It covers more topics than any other text and it provides numerous examples and case studies as well as links to resources and references.

Managerial Orientation

E-commerce can be approached from two major perspectives: technological and managerial. This text uses the second approach. Most of the presentations are about EC applications and their implementation. However, we do recognize the importance of the technology; therefore, we present the essentials of security in Chapter 10 and the essentials of infrastructure and systems development in Chapter 16. We also provide some detailed technology material in the five online tutorials on the book's website (**affordable-ecommerce-textbook. com/turban**). Managerial issues are also provided at the end of each chapter.

Experienced Co-authors and Contributors

In contrast to other EC books written by one or two authors who claim to be polymaths, we have a diversified team of authors who are experts in a variety of fields, including a senior vice president of an e-commerce-related company. All contributions were copyedited to assure quality and uniformity.

Real-World Orientation

Extensive, vivid examples from large corporations, small businesses from different industries and services, governments, and nonprofit agencies from all over the world make concepts come alive. These examples, which were collected by both academicians and practitioners, show the students the capabilities of EC, its cost and justification, and the innovative ways corporations are using EC in their operations.

Solid Theoretical Background and Research Suggestions

Throughout the book, we present the theoretical foundations necessary for understanding EC, ranging from consumer behavior to the economic theory of competition. Furthermore, we provide website resources, numerous exercises, and extensive references to supplement the theoretical presentations. At the end of each chapter, we provide a list of online resources with links to their websites.

Most Up-to-Date and Current Topics

This book presents the most current topics relating to EC, as evidenced by the many citations from 2013 to 2014. Finally, we introduce some of the most promising newcomers to e-commerce such as Pinterest, Instagram, Volusion, and Shopify.

Integrated Systems

In contrast to other EC books that highlight isolated Internet-based systems, we emphasize integrated systems that support the entire life cycle of e-commerce. Social network-based systems are highlighted, as are the latest developments in global EC, mobile commerce, and in Web-based Apps.

Global Perspective

The importance of global competition, partnerships, and trade is increasing rapidly. EC facilitates exporting and importing, the management of multinational companies, and electronic trading around the globe. International examples are provided throughout the book. The world's largest e-commerce company, Alibaba Group, is featured in Chapter 4. Our authors and contributors are from the USA, Macau (China), Korea, Germany, Taiwan, Brazil, Australia, and the Philippines. Examples and cases presented are from over 20 countries.

Small- and Middle-Sized Companies

Throughout the book, we provide discussions and examples of small- and middle-sized companies in addition to the large ones.

The Public Sector

In numerous places, we cover the topic of e-commerce in governments and other public and not-for-profit organizations.

Interdisciplinary Approach

E-commerce is interdisciplinary in nature, and we illustrate this throughout the book. Major EC-related disciplines include accounting, finance, information systems, marketing, management, operations management, and human resources management. In addition, some non-business disciplines are touched upon, especially public administration, computer science, sociology, engineering, psychology, political science, and law. Economics also plays a major role in the understanding of EC.

EC Failures and Lessons Learned

In addition to EC success stories, we also present EC failures and, wherever possible, analyze the causes of those failures with lessons learned (e.g., in the opening case to Chapter 16).

Online Support

More than 50 online files are available to supplement text material on a chapter-by-chapter basis. These are available at **affordable-ecommerce-textbook.com/turban**.

User-Friendliness

While covering all major EC topics, this book is clear, simple, and well organized. It provides all the basic definitions of terms as well as logical and conceptual support. Furthermore, the book is easy to understand and is full of real-world examples that keep the reader's interest. Relevant review questions are provided at the end of each section so the reader can pause to digest the new material.

Links, Links, Links

In this book, the reader will find several hundred links to useful resources supplementing all topics and providing up-to-date information. Note: With so many links, some may change over time.

Other Outstanding Features

1. Five to ten topics for individual discussions, seven to twelve class discussion and debate issues are available in each chapter.
2. A class assignment that involves the opening case is available in each chapter.
3. A class assignment that requires watching one or more short videos (3–10 minutes) about a certain technology or a mini case, followed by questions or some other student engagement are included.
4. Videos related to specific topics are suggested in the text, some related to cases.
5. Over 75 real-world examples on specific topics and subtopics are used.
6. Learning objectives for the entire book are provided in this preface.

Organization of the Book

The book is divided into 16 chapters grouped into 5 parts.

Part I – Introduction to E-Commerce and E-Marketplaces

In Part I, we provide an overview of today's business environment as well as the fundamentals of EC and some of its terminology (Chapter 1). A discussion of electronic markets and their impacts is provided in Chapter 2, where special attention is given to EC mechanisms ranging from traditional shopping carts to social networks and social software tools. We also introduce augmented reality, crowdsourcing and virtual worlds as platforms for EC in this chapter.

Part II – E-Commerce Applications

In Part II, we describe EC applications in three chapters. Chapter 3 addresses e-tailing and electronic service industries (e.g., e-travel, e-banking) as they relate to individual consumers. In Chapter 4, we examine the major B2B models, including online auctions, online trading, e-procurement, and online marketplaces. In Chapter 5, we present several non-selling applications, such as e-government, e-learning, e-books, collaborative commerce, and person-to-person EC.

Part III – Emerging EC Platforms

Chapter 6 explores the developing applications in the world of wireless EC (m-commerce, l-commerce, and pervasive computing). In addition, we cover the Internet-of-Things, smart systems and wearables. In Chapter 7, we explore the world of social media marketing and social CRM. Chapter 8 covers enterprise social networks, crowdsourcing, and other social media applications.

Part IV – EC Support Services

There are four chapters in this part. Chapter 9 is dedicated to online consumer behavior, market research and advertising. Chapter 10 begins with a discussion of the need to protect EC systems. It also describes various types of attacks on e-commerce systems and their users, including fraud, and how to minimize these risks through appropriate security programs. The chapter also deals with the various aspects of cyberwars. Chapter 11 describes a major EC support service – electronic payments including mobile payments. Chapter 12 concentrates on order fulfillment, supply chain improvement, and the role of RFID and CPFR.

Part V – E-Commerce Strategy and Implementation

Chapter 13 discusses the process of EC strategy and strategic issues in implementing EC. The chapter also presents global EC and EC for small businesses. Chapter 14 deals with implementation issues, concentrating on justification and cost–benefit analysis, system acquisitions and developments, and the impacts of EC on organizations. Chapter 15 deals with legal, ethical, and societal issues concentrating on regulatory issues, privacy, and green IT. Chapter 16 is unique; it describes how to build an e-business from scratch, as well as how to add e-commerce projects to conventional businesses. It also takes the reader through all the major steps of online store building and provides guidelines for success.

Learning Aids

The text offers the student a number of learning aids:

- **Chapter Outlines.** A listing of the main headings ("Content") at the beginning of each chapter provides a quick overview of the major topics covered.
- **Learning Objectives.** Learning objectives at the beginning of each chapter help students focus their efforts and alert them to the important concepts to be discussed. Additionally, note the newly added learning objectives for the entire book.
- **Opening Cases.** Each chapter opens with a real-world example that illustrates the importance of EC to modern corporations. These cases were carefully chosen to call attention to some of the major topics to be covered in the chapters. Following each opening case is a short section titled "Lessons learned from the case," that relates the important issues in the case to the forthcoming content of the chapter.
- **EC Application Cases.** In-chapter cases highlight real-world problems encountered by organizations as they develop and implement EC. Questions follow each case to help direct the student's attention to the implications of the case material.
- **Real World Examples.** Dozens of examples illustrate how EC concepts and tools are applied. These are usually linked to detailed descriptions.
- **Figures and Tables.** Numerous eye-catching figures and tables extend and supplement the text presentation.
- **Review Questions.** Each section in each chapter ends with a series of review questions about that particular section. These questions are intended to help students summarize the concepts introduced and digest the essentials of each section before moving on to another topic.
- **Glossary and Key Terms.** Each key term is defined in the text when it first appears. In addition, an alphabetical list of key terms appears at the end of each chapter.
- **Managerial Issues.** At the end of every chapter, we explore some of the special concerns managers face as they prepare to do business in cyberspace. These issues are framed as questions to maximize the readers' active participation.
- **Chapter Summary.** The chapter summary is linked one-to-one with the learning objectives introduced at the beginning of each chapter.
- **End-of-Chapter Exercises.** Different types of questions measure the students' comprehension and their ability to apply the learned knowledge. Questions for Discussion by individual students are intended to challenge them to express their thinking about relevant topics. Topics for Class Discussion and Debates promote dialogs and develop critical-thinking skills. Internet Exercises are challenging assignments that require students to surf the Internet and apply what they have learned. Over 250 hands-on exercises send students to interesting websites to conduct research, learn about applications, download demos, or research state-of-the-art technology.

The Team Assignments and Projects are thought-provoking group projects designed to foster teamwork.

- **Closing Cases.** Each chapter ends with a comprehensive case, which is presented somewhat more in depth than the in-chapter EC Application Cases. Questions follow each case relating the case to the topics covered in the chapter.
- **List of Online Resources.** At the end of each chapter, we provide a list of the chapter's online files with a brief description of their content. In addition, we provide a list of Web addresses linked to relevant resources that can be used to supplement the chapter.

Supplementary Materials

The following support materials are also available.
- The **Instructor's Manual**, written by Jon. C. Outland, includes answers to all review and discussion questions, exercises, and case questions.
- **Test bank.** A broad set of multiple-choice, true-false, and essay questions for all chapters. Written by Jon C. Outland.
- The **PowerPoint Lecture Notes**, by Judy Lang, highlight the important areas and are related to the text learning objectives.

Companion Website: (affordable-ecommerce-textbook.com/turban)

The book is supported by a companion website that includes:
- Five online tutorials.
- Bonus EC Application Cases and other features, which can be found in each chapter's online files.

Content Contributors

The following individuals contributed material for this edition.
- Linda Lai updated Chapter 3 and created Chapter 16.
- Fabio Cipriani contributed his eCRM and social CRM slides to Chapters 1 and 7.
- San Murugesan contributed to Chapter 8 and to the Online Tutorials.
- Judy Lang updated material in several chapters and conducted supporting research.
- Ivan C. Seballos II contributed the new illustrations and helped update several chapters.
- Jörg Blankenbach and Christian Hickel contributed to the closing case of Chapter 5: "From Local SDI to E-Government."
- Judy Strauss contributed an example in Chapter 13.

Acknowledgments

Many individuals helped us create this text. Faculty feedback was solicited via written reviews and through individual interviews. We are grateful to them for their contributions.

Several individuals helped us with the research and the administrative work. We thank all these individuals for their dedication and excellent performance shown throughout the project.

We also recognize the various organizations and corporations that provided us with their permission to reproduce material. Last, but not least, we thank Judy Lang, who as coordinator, advisor, and problem solver, contributed innovative ideas and provided the necessary editing and formatting of this text.

We appreciate the assistance provided by the Springer team under the leadership of Neil Levine, Matthew Amboy, and Christine Crigler. We also recognize Ramesh Sharda (Oklahoma State University) for his guidance and advise.

Reviews

The previous editions of the book were reviewed by many professors.

We wish to thank all of them for the valuable comments they provided. We also thank the reviewers of this edition, the anonymous faculty from the following universities: Franklin Pierce University, University of Maryland, California State University, Clark State Community College, and the University of Houston, who provided a very useful and comprehensive reviews.

Contents

Part II   E-Commerce Applications

Part III   Emerging EC Delivery Platforms

Part IV EC Support Services

Part I

Introduction to E-Commerce and E-Marketplaces

Contents

Electronic supplementary material   The online version
of this chapter (doi: 10.1007/978-3-319-10091-3_1)
contains supplementary material, which is available to
authorized users

Learning Objectives

Upon completion of this chapter, you will be able to:

1. Define electronic commerce (EC) and describe its various categories.
2. Describe and discuss the content and framework of EC.
3. Describe the major types of EC transactions.
4. Describe the drivers of EC.
5. Discuss the benefits of EC to individuals, organizations, and society.
6. Discuss e-commerce 2.0 and social media.
7. Describe social commerce and social software.
8. Understand the elements of the digital world.
9. Describe the major environmental business pressures and organizational responses.
10. Describe some EC business models.
11. List and describe the major limitations of EC.

OPENING CASE: HOW STARBUCKS IS CHANGING TO A DIGITAL AND SOCIAL ENTERPRISE

Starbucks is the world's largest coffee house chain, with about 20,800 stores in 63 countries (see Loeb 2013). Many people view Starbucks as a traditional store where customers drop in, enter an order, pay cash or by credit card for coffee or other products, consume their choices in the store, and go on about their business. The last thing many people think about is the utilization of computers in this business. The opposite is actually true. Starbucks is turning itself into a digital and social company (Van Grove 2012).

For a long time Starbucks was known as appealing to young people because the free Wi-Fi Internet access provided in its U.S. and Canada stores. But lately the company embarked on several digital initiatives to become a truly technology-savvy company.

The Problem

Starting in 2007, the company's operating income declined sharply (from over $1 billion in 2007 to $504 million in 2008 and $560 million in 2009). This decline was caused by not only the economic slowdown, but also by the increased competition (e.g., from Green Mountain Coffee Roasters), which intensified even during the recession. Excellent coffee and service helped but only in the short run. A better solution was needed.

Starbucks realized that better interaction with its customers was necessary and decided to solve the problem via digitization.

The Solution: Going Digital and Social

In addition to traditional measures to improve its operation and margin, the company resorted to *electronic commerce*, meaning the use of computerized systems to conduct and support its business. The company appointed a Senior Executive with the title of Chief Digital Officer to oversee its digital activities. It also created the Digital Venture Group to conduct the technical implementation.

The Electronic Commerce Initiatives
Starbucks deployed several e-commerce projects, the major ones are follow.

Online Store
Starbucks sells a small number of products online at **store.starbucks.com**. These offerings include

coffee, tea, and Starbucks equipment and merchandise. The store was in operation for years, using typical shopping cart (called My Bag), but the company completely redesigned the webstore to make shopping more convenient and easy (in August 2011). In addition, customers (individual or companies) can schedule deliveries of standard and special items. Customers can order rare and exquisite coffee that is available only in some U.S. stores. Now customers around the U.S. and the world can enjoy it too. Finally, online customers get exclusive promotions.

The eGift Card Program
Customers can buy Starbucks customized gift cards digitally (e.g., a gift card for a friend's birthday is auto delivered on the desired date). Payments can be made with a credit card or PayPal. The gift card is sent to the recipient via e-mail or postal mail.

The recipients can print the card and go shopping at a Starbucks physical store, transfer the gift amount to their Starbucks' payment card, or to Starbuck Card Mobile.

Loyalty Program
Like airlines and other vendors, the company offers a Loyalty Program (My Starbucks Rewards). Those who reach the gold level receive extra benefits. The program is managed electronically.

Mobile Payments
Customers can pay at Starbucks stores with prepaid (stored value) cards, similar to those used in transportation, or conduct smartphone payments.

Paying from Smartphones
Starbucks customers can also pay for purchases in physical stores with their mobile devices. Payments can be made by each of two technologies:
- *Using Starbucks mobile app.* Shoppers have an app on their mobile device. Payment is made by selecting "touch to pay" and holding up the barcode on the device screen to a scanner at the seller's register. The system is connected automatically to a debit or credit card. The system works only in the company-owned stores.

The Social Media Projects

Starbucks realized the importance of social media that uses Internet-based systems to support social interactions and user involvement and engagement (Chapter 7). Thus, it started several initiatives to foster customer relationships based on the needs, wants, and preferences of its existing and future customers. The following are some representative activities.

Exploiting Collective Intelligence

Mystarbucksidea.com is a platform in which a community of over 300,000 consumers and employees can make improvement suggestions, vote for the suggestions, ask questions, collaborate on projects, and express their complaints and frustrations. The community generated 70,000 ideas in its first year, ranging from thoughts on the company's rewards cards and elimination of paper cups to ways to improve customer service. The site also provides statistics on the ideas generated, by category, as well as their status (under review, reviewed, in the works, and launched). The company may provide incentives for certain generated ideas. For example, in June 2010, Starbucks offered $20,000 for the best idea concerning the reuse of its used coffee cups. This initiative is based on the technology of *collective intelligence* also known as *crowdsourcing* (see Chapters 2 and 8) and it is supported by the following blog.

Starbucks Idea in Action Blog

This blog is written by employees who discuss what the company is doing about ideas submitted to MyStarbucksIdea site.

Starbucks' Activities on Facebook

Fully integrated into Facebook, Starbucks practices several social commerce activities there. The site was built with input from Starbucks customers. The company uploads videos, blog posts, photos, promotions, product highlights, and special deals. The millions of people who like Starbucks on Facebook verify that it is one of the most popular companies on Facebook with about 36 million followers (February 2014),

see current statistics at **starcount.com/chart/wiki/Starbucks/today** and at **facebook.com/Starbucks**. Starbucks offers one of the best online marketing communication experiences on Facebook to date as well as mobile commerce engagements. Starbucks posts information on its Facebook "wall" whether it is content, questions, or updates. The company is also advertising on its Facebook homepage. Note that Starbucks is assessing the cost-benefit of such advertising.

Starbucks' Presence in LinkedIn and Google+

Starbucks has a profile on the LinkedIn site with over 500,000 followers (July 2014). It provides business data about the company, lists new hires in managerial positions, and advertises available managerial jobs. Starbucks is also active on Google+.

Starbucks Actions on Twitter

In February 2015, Starbucks had over 2.7 million followers (Follow@starbucks) on Twitter organized in 18,025 lists (e.g., @starbucks/friends). Each 'list' has its own followers and tweets. Whenever the company has some new update or marketing campaign, the company encourages conversation on Twitter. By October 2013, Starbucks was the number one retailer to follow Twitter. As of November 2013, Starbucks sends $5 gift cards to Twitter friends and followers.

Starbucks' Activities on YouTube, Flickr, Pinterest, and Instagram

Starbucks has a presence on both YouTube (**youtube.com/starbucks** and Flickr (**flickr.com/starbucks**, with a selection of videos and photos for view. It also runs advertising campaigns there. Finally, Starbucks has about 4 million followers on the photo-sharing company-Instagram (**instagram.com/Starbucks**).

Starbucks Digital Network

To support its digital activities the company offers online content using Starbucks Digital Network in partnership with major media providers (e.g., *New York Times*, iTunes). It is designed for all major mobile devices including tablets (e.g., iPad) and smartphones. The network's content features news, entertainment, business, health, and local neighborhood information channels.

Early Adoption of Foursquare: A Failure

Not all Starbucks social media projects were successes. For example, the company decided to be an early adopter of geolocation by working with Foursquare (Chapter 7). The initiative simply did not work, and the project ended in mid-2010 (see Teicher 2010 for an analysis of the reasons). The company experimented in the UK with a similar location company called Placecast. As of fall 2011, Starbucks had a better understanding of the opportunities and the limitations, so it may decide to try geolocation again with Facebook's Places, or it may revive the Foursquare project.

The Results

According to York (2010), Starbucks turned around sales by effectively integrating the digital and the physical worlds. In 2010, its operating income almost tripled ($1.437 billion versus $560 million in 2009) and so did its stock price. In 2011, the operating income reached $1.7 billion. Since then the operating income is increasing rapidly.

The company's social media initiatives are widely recognized. In 2012 it was listed by *Fortune Magazine* as one of top social media stars (Fortune 2012), and in 2008 it was awarded the 2008 Groundswell Award by Forrester Research. The site is very popular on Facebook where it has millions of fans, (sometimes more popular than pop icon Lady Gaga). Starbucks attributes its success to 10 philosophical guidelines that drive its social media efforts (see Belicove 2010 for details).

Sources: Based on Belicove (2010), York (2010), Callari (2010), Van Grove (2012), Loeb (2013), Gembarski (2012), Marsden (2010), Teicher (2010), Walsh (2010), **mystarbucks.**

force.com, and **blogs.starbucks.com** (both accessed May 2014).

LESSONS LEARNED FROM THE CASE

The Starbucks.com case illustrates the story of a large retailer that is converting to be a digital and social enterprise. Doing business electronically is one of the major activities of e-commerce, the subject of this book. The case demonstrates several of the topics you will learn about in this chapter and throughout the book. These are:

1. There are multiple activities in EC including selling online, customer service, and collaborative intelligence.
2. The case shows major benefits both to buyers and sellers. This is typical in EC.
3. The EC capabilities include the ability to offer products and services in many locations, including overseas to many customers, individuals, and businesses. You can do so because online your customer base is huge, and people can buy from anywhere at any time.
4. In a regular store you pay and pick up the merchandise or service. In Starbucks.com and other webstores you order, pay, and the product is shipped to you. Therefore, order fulfillment needs to be very efficient and timely.
5. Being a digital enterprise can be very useful, but a greater benefit can be achieved by extending it to be socially-oriented enterprise. Both approaches constitute the backbone of electronic commerce, the subject of this book.

In this opening chapter, we describe the essentials of EC, some of which were presented in this case. We present some of the drivers and benefits of EC and explain their impact on the technology. Special attention is provided to the emergence of the social economy, social networks, and social enterprises. Finally, we describe the outline of this book.

1.1 ELECTRONIC COMMERCE: DEFINITIONS AND CONCEPTS

As early as 2002, the management guru Peter Drucker (2002) forecasted that e-commerce (EC) would significantly impact the way that business is done. And indeed the world is embracing EC, which makes Drucker's prediction a reality.

Defining Electronic Commerce

Electronic commerce (EC) refers to using the Internet and intranets to purchase, sell, transport, or trade data, goods, or services. For an overview, see Plunkett et al. (2014). Also watch the video titled
   "What is E-Commerce?" at **youtube.com/watch?v=3wZw2IRb0Vg**. EC is often confused with e-business, which is defined next.

Defining E-Business

Some people view the term *commerce* as describing only buying and selling transactions conducted between business partners. If this definition of commerce is used, the term *electronic commerce* would be fairly narrow. Thus, many use the term *e-business* instead. **E-business** refers to a broader definition of EC, not just the buying and selling of goods and services, but conducting all kinds of business online such as servicing customers, collaborating with business partners, delivering e-learning, and conducting electronic transactions within an organization. However, others view e-business only as comprising those activities that do not involve buying or selling over the Internet, such as collaboration and intra-business activities; that is, it is a *complement* of the narrowly defined e-commerce. In its narrow definitions e-commerce can be viewed as a subset of e-business. In this book, we use the broadest meaning of electronic commerce, which is basically equivalent to the broadest definition of e-business. The two terms will be used interchangeably throughout the text.

Major EC Concepts

Several other concepts are frequently used in conjunction with EC. The major ones are as follows.

Pure Versus Partial EC

EC can be either pure or partial depending on the nature of its three major activities: ordering and payments, order fulfillment, and delivery to customers. Each activity can be physical or digital. Thus, there are eight possible combinations as shown in Table 1.1. If all activities are digital, we have pure EC, if none are digital we have no EC, otherwise we have partial EC.

If there is at least one digital dimension, we consider the situation EC, but only partial EC. For example, purchasing a computer from Dell's website or a book from Amazon.com is partial EC, because the merchandise is physically delivered. However, buying an e-book from Amazon.com or a software product from Buy.com is pure EC, because ordering, processing, and delivery to the buyer are all digital. Note that many companies operate in two or more of the classifications. For example, Jaguar has a 3D application for self configuration of cars online, prior to shopping (see Vizard 2013). For a video titled "Introduction to E-Commerce" see **plunkettresearch.com/video/ecommerce**.

EC Organizations

Purely physical organizations (companies) are referred to as **brick-and-mortar** (or **old economy) organizations**, whereas companies that are engaged only in EC are considered **virtual (pure-play) organizations**. **Click-and-mortar (click-and-brick) organizations** are those that conduct

Table 1.1 Classifications of E-Commerce

Activity	1	2	3	4	5	6	7	8
Ordering, Payment	P	D		D	D	D	P	P	P
Order fulfillment	P	D		D	P	P	D	P	D
Delivery (shipment)	P	D		P	P	D	D	D	D
Type of EC	Non EC	Pure EC	Partial EC						

Legend: *P* physical, *D* digital

some EC activities, usually as an additional marketing channel. Gradually, many brick-and-mortar companies are changing to click-and-mortar ones (e.g., GAP, Target).

Electronic Markets and Networks

EC can be conducted in an **electronic market (e-marketplace)**, an online location where buyers and sellers conduct commercial transactions such as selling goods, services, or information. Any individual can also open a market selling products or services online. Electronic markets are connected to sellers and buyers via the Internet or to its counterpart within organizations, an *intranet*. An **intranet** is a corporate or government internal network that uses Internet tools, such as Web browsers and Internet protocols. Another computer environment is an **extranet**, a network that uses Internet technology to link intranets of several organizations in a secure manner (see Online Tutorial T2).

SECTION 1.1 REVIEW QUESTIONS
1. Define EC and e-business.
2. Distinguish between pure and partial EC.
3. Define click-and-mortar and brick-and-mortar organizations.
4. Define electronic markets.
5. Define intranets and extranets.

1.2   THE ELECTRONIC COMMERCE FIELD: GROWTH, CONTENT, CLASSIFICATION, AND A BRIEF HISTORY

According to the U.S. Census Bureau (2013), e-commerce sales in 2011 accounted for 49.3% of total sales of all manufacturing activities in the United States, 24.3% of merchant wholesalers, 4.7% of all retailing, and 2% of all sales in selected service industries. The grand total of EC in 2010 has been $3,545 billion, of which $3,161 billion was B2B (89%) and $385 billion was B2C (11%). The results over 9 years are shown in Figure 1.1.

Notice the sharp increase in manufacturing compared to other sectors. Also note that EC is growing much faster than the total of all commerce by about 16–17% annually. For a more detailed breakdown, see the U.S. Census Bureau (2013) report as well as Plunkett et al. (2014).

There is a clear trend that online retail sales are taking business from traditional retailers. Knight (2013) reported that during the 2009–2013 economic difficulty EC sales reached double-digit growth. For example, Wilfred (2014) reported that during the 2013 holiday shopping season online shopping grew 10% a year versus 2.7% of traditional retailers.

According to *Ecommerce Europe*, September 5, 2012, European online retail sales will double to €323 billion in 5 years (2018).

The Content and Framework of E-Commerce

Classifying e-commerce aids understanding of this diversified field. In general, selling and buying electronically can be either business-to-consumer (B2C) or business-to-business (B2B). Online transactions are made between businesses and individual consumers in B2C, such as when a person purchases a coffee at **store.starbucks.com** or a computer at **dell.com** (see Online File W1.1). In B2B, business transactions are made online with other businesses, such as when Dell electronically buys parts from its suppliers. Dell also collaborates electronically with its partners and provides customer service online e-CRM (see Online Tutorial T1). Several other types of EC will be described later in this chapter.

According to the U.S. Census Bureau (2013), the total EC shipments grew 16.5% in a year, ComScore reported (cited by BizReport 2012) that U.S. retail commerce online increased 17% in QI 2012 as compared to a year earlier. EC is growing in all areas. For example, Leggatt (2012) reported that in the UK Domino's Pizza online sales grew about 1,000% between 2000 and 2012. Similar results can be found in many industries, companies, and countries (e.g., see periodic

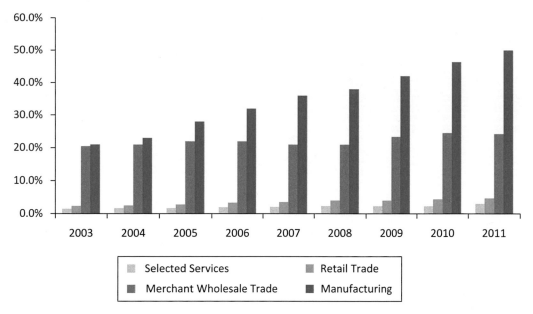

Figure 1.1 E-Commerce as percent of total value: (2003–2011) (Source: Census.gov/estats Accessed February 2014)

reports at ComScore and BizReport) and Ahmad (2014, an Infographic). E-Commerce is exploding globally. According to a press release of **ecommerce-europe.eu/press** of May 23, 2013, European e-commerce grew by 19% in 2012 reaching €312 billion. According to Stanley and Ritacca (2014), e-commerce in China is exploding, reaching $600 billion by the end of 2013. Finally, in several developing countries EC is becoming a major economic asset (e.g., see Maitra 2013 for information on India).

An EC Framework

The EC field is diverse involving many activities, organizational units, and technologies. Therefore, a framework that describes its contents can be useful. Figure 1.2 introduces one such framework.

As shown in the figure, there are many EC applications (top of figure), which will be illustrated throughout the book. To perform these applications, companies need the right information, infrastructure, and support services. Figure 1.2 shows that EC applications are supported by infrastructure and by the following five support areas (shown as pillars in the figure):

1. **People.** Sellers, buyers, intermediaries, information systems and technology specialists, other employees, and any other participants.

2. **Public policy.** Legal and other policy and regulatory issues, such as privacy protection and taxation, which are determined by governments. Included are technical standards and compliance.

3. **Marketing and advertising.** Like any other business, EC usually requires the support of marketing and advertising. This is especially important in B2C online transactions, in which the buyers and sellers usually do not know each other.

4. **Support services.** Many services are needed to support EC. These range from content creation to payments to order delivery.

5. **Business partnerships.** Joint ventures, exchanges, and business partnerships of various types are common in EC. These occur frequently throughout the *supply chain* (i.e., the interactions between a company and its suppliers, customers, and other partners).

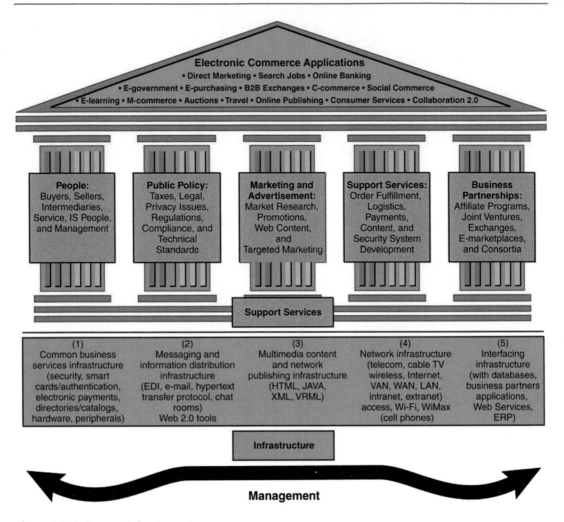

Figure 1.2 A framework for electronic commerce

The infrastructure for EC is shown at the bottom of the figure. *Infrastructure* describes the hardware, software, and networks used in EC. All of these components require good *management practices*. This means that companies need to plan, organize, motivate, devise strategy, and restructure processes, as needed, to optimize the business use of EC models and strategies.

Classification of EC by the Nature of the Transactions and the Relationships Among Participants

Note: Several of the following definitions are similar to those of Katic and Pusara (2004), whose EC terminology is based on the 2003 edition of this book.

A common classification of EC is by the type of the transactions and the transacting members. The major types of EC transactions are listed below.

Business-to-Business (B2B)

Business-to-business (B2B) EC refers to transactions between and among organizations. Today, about 85% of EC volume is B2B. For Dell, the entire wholesale transaction is B2B. Dell buys most of its parts through e-commerce, and sells its products to businesses (B2B) and individuals (B2C) using e-commerce.

Business-to-Consumer (B2C)

Business-to-consumer (B2C) EC includes retail transactions of products or services from businesses to individual shoppers. The typical shopper at Amazon.com is of this type. Since the sellers are usually retailers, we also call this type **e-tailing**.

Business-to-Business-to-Consumer (B2B2C)

In **business-to-business-to-consumer (B2B2C)** EC, a business (B1) sells a product to another business (B2). B2 then sells, or gives away, the product to individuals who may be B2's own customers or employees. An example is **godiva.com**. The company sells chocolates directly to business customers. Those businesses may then give the chocolates as gifts to employees or business partners. Godiva may mail the chocolate directly to the recipients (with compliments of…). Another interesting example of B2B2C can be found at **wishlist.com.au**. Finally, Starbucks sells branded stored value cards to companies to give as gifts to their employees or customers.

Consumer-to-Business (C2B)

In **consumer-to-business (C2B)**, people use the Internet to sell products or services to individuals and organizations. Alternatively, individuals use C2B to bid on products or services. Priceline.com is a well-known organizer of C2B travel service transactions.

Intrabusiness EC

The **intrabusiness EC** category refers to EC transactions among various organizational departments and individuals.

Business-to-Employees (B2E)

The **business-to-employees (B2E)** category refers to the delivery of services, information, or products from organizations to their employees. A major category of employees is *mobile employees*, such as field representatives or repair services that go to customers. EC support to such employees is also called *business-to-mobile employees (B2ME)*.

Consumer-to-Consumer (C2C)

In the **consumer-to-consumer (C2C)** EC category individual consumers sell to or buy from other consumers. Examples of C2C include individuals selling computers, musical instruments, or personal services online. EBay auctions are mostly C2C as are the ads in Craigslist.

Collaborative Commerce

Collaborative commerce (c-commerce) refers to online activities and communications done by parties working to attain the same goal. For example, business partners may design a new product together.

E-Government

In **e-government** EC, a government agency buys or provides goods, services, or information from or to businesses (G2B) or from or to individual citizens (G2C). Governments can deal also with other governments (G2G).

The previous categories are illustrated in Figure 1.3. Many examples of the various types of EC transactions will be presented throughout this book.

A Brief History of EC

The pioneering of e-commerce applications can be tracked to the early 1970s when money was transferred electronically, mostly among financial institutions (known as *electronic funds transfer [EFT]*), whereby funds could be routed electronically from one organization to another. However, the use of these applications was limited to large corporations, financial institutions, and a few other daring businesses. Then came *electronic data interchange (EDI)*, a technology used to enable the electronically transfer of routine documents. EDI later expanded from financial transactions to other types of transactions (see Online Tutorial T2 for more on EDI). More new EC applications followed, ranging from travel reservation systems to online stock trading.

The Internet appeared on the scene in 1969, as an experiment by the U.S. government, and its initial users were mostly academic researchers and other scientists. Some users started to place personal classifieds on the Internet. A major milestone in the development of EC was the appearance of the World Wide Web (The "Web") in the early 1990s. This allowed companies to

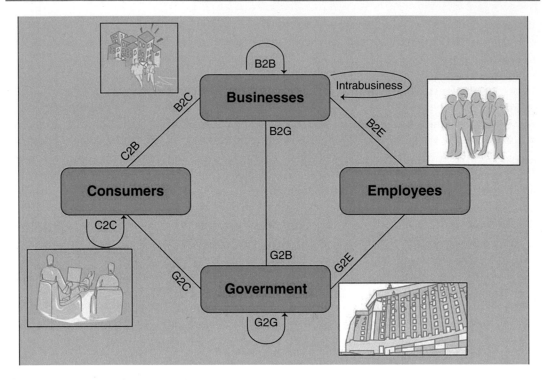

Figure 1.3 Categories of transactions in e-commerce

have a presence on the Internet with both text and photos. When the Internet became commercialized and users began flocking to participate in the World Wide Web in the early 1990s, the term *electronic commerce* was introduced. EC applications rapidly expanded. A large number of so-called dot-coms, or *Internet start-ups*, also appeared. Almost all companies in the developing countries have presence on the Web. Many of these sites contain tens of thousands of pages and links. In 1999, the emphasis of EC shifted from B2C to B2B, and in 2001 from B2B to B2E, c-commerce, e-government, e-learning, and m-commerce. In 2005, social networks started to receive quite a bit of attention, as did m-commerce and wireless applications. As of 2009, EC added social commerce channels. An example is the increasing commercial activities on Facebook and Twitter. Given the nature of technology and Internet usage, EC will undoubtedly continue to grow, add new business models, and change. More and more EC successes are emerging. For a comprehensive ready-reference guide to EC

including statistics, trends, and in-depth profiles of hundreds of companies, see Plunkett et al. (2014) and **en.wikipedia.org/wiki/E-commerce**.

While looking at the history of EC, one must keep in mind the following.

The Interdisciplinary Nature of EC

From just the brief overview of the EC framework and classification, you can probably see that EC is related to several different disciplines. The major academic EC disciplines include the following: *accounting, business law, computer science, consumer behavior, economics, engineering, finance, human resource management, management, management information systems, marketing, public administration*, and *robotics*.

The Google Revolution

During its early years, EC was impacted by companies such as Amazon.com, eBay, AOL, and Yahoo!. However, since 2001 no other company has probably had more of an impact on EC than Google. Google related Web searches to targeted advertisements much better than its competitors did. Today, Google is much more than just a search engine; it employs many innovative EC models, is involved in many EC joint ventures, and impacts both organizational activities and individual lives. For more details, see Levy (2011).

Cyber Monday, Singles' Day

An interesting evidence for the growth of online shopping is the volume of shopping during Cyber Monday in the U.S. and Single Day (11/11) in China. For the magnitude of Single Day in China, in the automotive industry see Li and Han (2013). Also see *Ad Age* Staff (2013).

Social Commerce

The explosion of social media and networks, as well as Web 2.0 tools (e.g., wikis, blogs) resulted in new ways of conducting e-commerce by making it social. Several new and modified EC models were created, rejuvenating the field as described in several chapters in the book especially in Chapters 7 and 8, and in Turban, et al. (2015).

F-Commerce

Given the popularity of Facebook and the rapidly increasing commercial activities conducted on or facilitated by the site, some believe that Facebook is revolutionizing e-commerce especially for small businesses. Thus, they coined the term **f-commerce**, pointing to the increased role of Facebook in the e-commerce field as of 2009 (see Shih 2011).

EC Failures

Starting in 1999, a large number of EC companies, especially e-tailing and B2B exchanges, began to fail. Well-known B2C failures include Drkoop, MarchFirst, eToys, and Boo. Well-known B2B failures include Webvan, Chemdex, Ventro, and Verticalnet. (Incidentally, the history of these pioneering companies is documented by David Kirch in his Business Plan Archive (**businessplanarchive.org**). A survey by Strategic Direction (2005) found that 62% of dot-coms lacked financial skills, and 50% had little experience with marketing. Similarly, many companies failed to have satisfactory order fulfillment and enough inventory to meet the fluctuating and increasing demand for their products. The reasons for these and other EC failures are discussed in Chapters 3, 4, and 14. As of 2008, many start-ups related to Web 2.0 and social commerce started to collapse (see **blogs.cioinsight.com/it-management/startup-deathwatch-20.html**).

Does the large number of failures mean that EC's days are numbered? Absolutely not! First, the dot-com failure rate is declining sharply. Second, the EC field is basically experiencing consolidation as companies test different business models and organizational structures. Third, some pure EC companies, including giants such as Amazon.com and Netflix, are expanding operations and generating increased sales. Finally, the click-and-mortar model seems to work very well, especially in e-tailing (e.g., GAP, Walmart, Target, Apple, HP, and Best Buy).

For supplementary history see **plunkettresearch.com/ecommerce-internet-technology-market-research/industry-and-business-data**.

EC Successes

The last few years have seen the rise of extremely successful EC companies such as eBay, Pandora, Zillow, Google+, Facebook, Yahoo!, Amazon.com, Pay Pal, Pinterest, VeriSign, LinkedIn, and E*TRADE. Click-and-mortar companies such as Cisco, Target, General Electric, IBM, Intel, and Schwab also have seen great success. Additional success stories include start-ups such as Alloy.com (a young-adult-oriented portal), Blue Nile (Chapter 2), Ticketmaster, Net-a-Porter (Case 1.1), Expedia, Yelp, TripAdvisor, and GrubHub (Online File W1.2).

CASE 1.1: NET-A-PORTER: DRESS FOR SUCCESS

Will a woman buy a $2,000 dress online without trying it on? Net-a-Porter (a UK online retailer, known as "the Net") bet on it and proved that today's women will purchase their dresses (for success) online, especially if the luxury clothing and accessories are international brands such as Jimmy Choo or Calvin Klein.

The Opportunity

When talking about e-commerce (EC), most people think about buying online books, vitamins, CDs, or other commodity items. And this indeed was what people bought in the mid-1990s, when EC began. But in 2000, Natalie Massenet, a fashion journalist, saw an opportunity because of the success of luxury online stores such as Blue Nile (see Chapter 2) and the fact that professional women are very busy and willing to do more purchasing online.

The Solution

Natalie decided to open an online business for luxury fashion. She created a comprehensive, socially-oriented e-tailing site, naming it Net-a-Porter.

According to **net-a-porter.com**, Brodie (2009), and Rowe (2010), the company:

- Opened an e-tailing store
- Offered merchandise from over 350 top designers; most offline stores offer few dozen
- Offered its own designs in addition to others
- Arranged global distribution systems to over 170 countries
- Opened physical stores in London and New York to support the online business
- Arranged same day delivery (Chapter 3) in London and New York and overnight delivery elsewhere
- Organized very fast cycle time for producing and introducing new clothes and other products that match customers' preference
- Devised prediction methods of fashion trends based on customer feedback through social media
- Ran online fashion shows
- Developed superb inventory and sales tracking systems based on dashboards (see Chapter 13)

- Offered an online fashion magazine
- Discovered what customers really want via social networks (Chapters 7 and 8) and fulfilled their needs
- Offered large discounts
- Developed a presence on Facebook and app for iPhone
- Has 630,000 followers on Google+ (February 2014)
- Has five million visitors each month (February 2014)
- Experiences 750,000 downloads per month on iPhones
- Started augmented reality shopping windows in several global cities as of 2012 (see **digitalbuzzblog.com/net-a-porter-augmented-reality-shopping-windows**). At this same site you can watch the video "Window Shop" and download the Net-a-Porter iPhone/iPad app.

In 2010, the company started taking advantage of the social media environment that is changing the fashion industry (Rowe 2010).

The Results

Customers now come from over 170 countries and revenue and profits are increasing rapidly. Several million visitors come to the site every week. The 'Net' become profitable after 1 year, a very rare case in e-tailing. During the economic crisis of 2009, the Net's total sales were up 45%, versus a 14% decrease for one of its major competitors (Neiman Marcus; Web and paper catalog sales). The company was so successful that luxury goods company Richemont Corp. purchased a 93% stake in the business. (Since the company is now part of Richemont, there are no separate financial data for the Net.)

In June 2010 when the company celebrated its 10th anniversary, it opened a new website dedicated to menswear. With success comes competition, and the Net's competitors include Bluefly (low prices), Shopbop (an Amazon.com company, but it lacks the Net's prestige), and high-end department stores with their own online stores (Nordstrom, Neiman Marcus). But the Net has the highest prestige and growth rate. A major threat may come from eBay, which has been reaching out to high-end designers about creating their own virtual stores (hosted by eBay) where they can sell at fixed prices and also use auctions. Finally, note that in late 2010, Amazon.com created MYHABIT that offers designer brands at discount. To stay on top of the competition, the Net is planning new ventures and expanding its business model to include children's clothes. Net-a-Porter is an example of the revolution that is occurring in the fashion industry. Another example is Polyvore whose case is presented in Chapter 7. For details on these new business models see **businessoffashion.com/2012/01/e-commerce-week-the-rise-of-new-business-models.html**.

Sources: Based on Brodie (2009), Rowe (2010), **en.wikipedia.org/wiki/Net-a-Porter**, and **net-a-porter.com**(both accessed February 2014).

Questions

1. Why would you buy (or not buy) from Net-a-Porter?
2. Watch the video "The Future of Shopping" (**youtube.com/watch?v=_Te-NCAC3a4**). How would you integrate this development with Net-a-Porter?
3. List both the advantages and disadvantages of the Net's physical stores?
4. It is said that the Net is playing a significant role in transforming how designers reach customers. Explain why.
5. Read the benefits of EC to customers (Section 1.3). Which ones are most relevant here?
6. What EC capabilities are helping the Net and its designers?
7. Analyze the competition in the high-end fashion market.
8. What is the importance of globalization in this case?
9. Imitators are springing up on all sides. Even eBay and Amazon.com are expanding their fashion e-tailing efforts. What strategy do you suggest for the Net? (Hint: Read Brodie 2009 to get some ideas.)

SECTION 1.2 REVIEW QUESTIONS
1. List the major components of the EC framework.
2. List the major transactional types of EC.
3. Describe the major landmarks in EC history.
4. List some EC successes and failures.

1.3 DRIVERS AND BENEFITS OF E-COMMERCE

The tremendous explosion of EC can be explained by its drivers and characteristics, benefits, and by changes in the business environment.

The Drivers of E-Commerce

Although EC is only about 20 years old it is expected to have non-stoppable growth and expand consistently into new areas of our life. The question is why? What drives EC?

The Major Drivers of EC

EC is driven by many factors depending on the industry, company, and application involved. The major drivers are shown in the self-explanatory Figure 1.4, together with the section and/or chapter where details are presented.

The Benefits of E-Commerce

There are many benefits of EC and they continue to increase with time. We elected to organize them in three categories:

EC provides benefits to *organizations, individual customers*, and *society*. These benefits are summarized in Table 1.2.

Opportunities for Entrepreneurs

A major benefit of EC is the creation of opportunities to start a business in an unconventional ways. The new business models permit entrepreneurs to open businesses with little money and

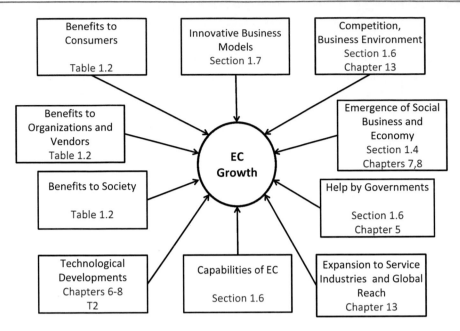

Figure 1.4 The major drivers of e-commerce growth

experience and grow them rapidly. Many entrepreneurs are making money some big money online.

Example: Fish Flops
Madison Robinson was a 15-year old ninth grader when she opened the business, both online and offline. She designs the footwear herself. Madison is doing lots of tweeting about Fish Flops. After only 2 years of operation the business became profitable enough to pay Madison's college expenses. For details see Burke (2013).

EC as a Provider of Efficiency, Effectiveness, and Competitive Advantage
The benefits of EC may result in significant changes in the way business is conducted. These changes may positively impact corporate operations resulting in a competitive advantage for the firms using EC (e.g., see Khosrow-Pour 2013) as well as more efficient governments and nonprofit organizations.

SECTION 1.3 REVIEW QUESTIONS
1. List the major drivers of EC.
2. List five benefits each to customers, organizations, and society.

3. From your knowledge describe some technological developments that facilitate EC.
4. Identify additional benefits to society.

1.4   E-COMMERCE 2.0: FROM SOCIAL COMMERCE TO VIRTUAL WORLDS

The first generation of EC involved mainly trading, e-services, and corporate-sponsored collaboration. Currently, we are moving into the second generation of EC, which we call E-Commerce 2.0. It is based on Web 2.0 tools, social media, social networks, and virtual worlds – all the offspring of social computing.

Social Computing

Social computing refers to a computing system that involves social interactions and behaviors. It is performed with a set of tools that includes blogs, wikis, social network services, and other *social software tools,* and social marketplaces (see Chapter 7). Whereas traditional computing systems concentrate on business processes particularly cost reduction and increases in productivity,

Table 1.2 Benefits of e-commerce

Benefit	Description
Benefits to Organizations	
Global reach	Quickly locating customers and/or suppliers at reasonable cost worldwide
Cost reduction	Lower cost of information processing, storage, and distribution
Facilitate problem solving	Solve complex problems that have remained unsolved.
Supply chain improvements	Reduce delays, inventories, and cost
Business always open	Open 24/7/365; no overtime or other costs
Customization/personalization	Make order for customer preference
Ability to innovate, use new business models	Facilitate innovation and enable unique business models
Lower communication costs	The Internet is cheaper then VAN private lines
Efficient procurement	Saves time and reduces costs by enabling e-procurement
Improved customer service and relationship	Direct interaction with customers, better CRM
Help SME to compete	EC may help small companies to compete against large ones by using special business models
Lower inventories	Using customization inventories can be minimized
Lower cost of distributing digitizable product	Delivery online can be 90% cheaper
Provide competitive advantage	Innovative business models
Benefits to Consumers	
Inventory	Huge selection to choose from (vendor, products, styles)
Ubiquity	Can shop any time from any place
Self configuration	Can self-customize products
Find bargains	Use comparison engine
Real time delivery	Download digital products
No sales tax	Sometimes; changing
Enable telecommuting	Can work or study at home or any place
Social interaction	In social networks
Find unique items	Using online auctions, collectible items can be found
Comfortable shopping	Shop at your leisure without pushy sales clerks bothering you
Benefits to Society	
Enable telecommuting	Facilitate work at home; less traffic, pollution
More public services	Provided by e-government
Improved homeland security	Facilitate domestic security
Increased standard of living	Can buy more and cheaper goods/services
Close the digital divide	Allow people in rural areas and developing countries to use more services and purchase what they really like

social computing concentrates on improving collaboration and interaction among people and on user-generated content. In social computing and commerce, people work together over the Internet, consult with specialists, and locate goods and services recommended by their friends.

Example: Social Computing Helps Travel

Advances in social computing impact travel operations and decisions. Travelers can share good travel experiences or warn others of bad experiences using sites such as **tripadvisor.com**.

Special social networks such as WAYN (Chapter 3) are very popular among travelers.

In social computing, information is produced by individuals and is available to all, usually for free. The major implementation tools of social computing are Web 2.0 and social media.

Web 2.0

The term *Web 2.0* was coined by O'Reilly Media in 2004. **Web 2.0** is the second generation of

Internet-based tools and services that enables users to easily generate content, share media, and communicate and collaborate, in innovative ways. (For more details see Edwards 2013.)

O'Reilly divided Web 2.0 into four levels and provided examples of each. For details see Colby (2008). Karakas (2009) views Web 2.0 as a new digital ecosystem, which can be described through five C's: creativity, connectivity, collaboration, convergence, and community.

The major characteristics of Web 2.0 are presented in Online File W1.3. The major tools of Web 2.0 are described in Chapter 2, and the applications are described in most chapters. Also, browse **enterpriseirregulars.com/author/dion** for an open forum about the Internet, society, collective intelligence, and the future. For Web 2.0 definitions, explanations, and applications see Shelly and Frydenberg (2010).

Social Media

The term **social media** has many definitions. A popular definition is that social media involves user generated online text, image, audio, and video content that are delivered via Web 2.0 platforms and tools. The media is used primarily for social interactions and conversations such as sharing opinions, experiences, insights, and perceptions and to collaborating online. Therefore, it is a powerful force for socialization. A key element is that users produce, control, and manage content. Additional definitions, descriptions, and references, and a framework are provided in Chapters 2 and 7 and in Turban et al. (2015).

The Difference Between Social Media and Web 2.0

Note that the concept of Web 2.0 is related to the concept of social media, many people equate the two terms and use them interchangeably; however, others see a difference. While social media uses Web 2.0 and its tools and technologies, the social media concept includes the philosophy of connected people, the interactions among them,

the social support provided, the digital content that is created by users, and so forth.

Example: How Oprah Is Using Social Media to Build Her Business

According to Smith (2012), Oprah Winfrey is integrating social media activities with everything she does, to encourage interactions of people with different platforms (e.g., Facebook, Twitter). Oprah is rewarding people based on their engagement (e.g., posting comments). She is using Facebook polls, and getting bloggers involved. Oprah is also actively using Twitter to interact with her followers.

Social Networks and Social Network Services

The most interesting e-commerce application in recent years has been the emergence of social and enterprise social networks. Originating from online communities (Chapter 2), these networks are growing rapidly and providing many new EC initiatives, revenue models, and business models (see **sustainablebrands.com/news_and_views/ blog/13-hot-business-model-innovations-follow-2013**).

A **social network** is a social entity composed of nodes (which are generally individuals, groups, or organizations) that are connected by links such as hobbies, friendship or profession. The structures are often very complex.

In its simplest form, a social network can be described by an image of the nodes and links. The network can also be used to describe Facebook's *social graph* (see description at Facebook.com).

Social Networking Services

Social networking services (SNSs), such as LinkedIn and Facebook, provide and host a Web space for people to build their homepages for free. SNSs also provide basic support tools for conducting different activities and allow many vendors to provide apps. Social networks are people oriented.

For example, a 15-year-old Filipino singer named Charice Pempengco and Justin Bieber were discovered on YouTube. Initially, social networks were used solely for social activities. Today, corporations have a great interest in the business aspects of social networks (e.g., see **linkedin.com**, a network that categorizes businesses by geography, functions, industry, and areas of interest).

The following are examples of representative social network services:

- **Facebook.com**: The most visited social network website.
- **YouTube.com** and **metacafe.com**: Users can upload and view video clips.
- **Flickr.com**: Users share and comment on photos.
- **LinkedIn.com**: The major enterprise-oriented social network.
- **Hi5.com**: A popular global social network.
- **Cyworld.nate.com**: Asia's largest social networking website.
- **Habbo.com**: Entertaining country-specific sites for kids and adults.
- **Pinterest.com**: Provides a platform for organizing and sharing images (see the opening case in Chapter 2).
- **Google+**: A business-oriented social network.
- **MySpace.com**: Facilitates socialization and entertainment for people of all ages.

Social Networking

We define **social networking** as the execution of any Web 2.0 activity, such as blogging or having a presence in a social network. It also includes all activities conducted in social networks.

Enterprise Social Networks

Business-oriented social networks can be public, such as LinkedIn.com. As such, they are owned and managed by an independent company. Another type of business-oriented social network is private, owned by corporations and operated inside them. These are known as *enterprise social networks* (e.g., MyStarbucks Idea). These can be directed toward customers or company employees.

Example: A Customer-Oriented Enterprise Social Network

Carnival Cruise Lines sponsors a social networking site (**carnival.com/funville**) to attract cruise fans. Visitors use the site to exchange opinions, organize groups for trips, and much more. It cost the company $300,000 to set up the site, but the initial cost was covered by increased business within a year.

Social Commerce

E-commerce activities that are conducted in social networks by using social software (i.e., Web 2.0 tools) are referred to as **socialcommerce**). Since 2009, social commerce has been rapidly increasing (see Webster 2010). We will return to social commerce in Chapters 7 and 8.

The following are some examples of social commerce.

- Dell Computer claims to have made $6.5 million by selling computers on Twitter in 2 years (Nutley 2010). Also, Dell generates ideas from community members at its *Idea Storm* site.
- Procter & Gamble sells its Max Factor brand cosmetics through Facebook.
- Disney allows people to book certain tickets on Facebook without leaving the social network.
- PepsiCo gives live notification when its customers are close to physical stores (grocery, restaurants, gas stations) that sell Pepsi products. Then PepsiCo sends them coupons and discount information using Foursquare (see Chapter 7).
- Starbucks is using extensive promotions on Facebook including generating ideas from the members via its My Starbucks Idea website (see the opening case for details).

- Mountain Dew attracts video game lovers and sport enthusiasts via Dewmocracy contests. The company also uses the most dedicated community members to contribute ideas. The company used Facebook, Twitter, and YouTube to interact with consumers and engage them.
- In 2010, Target used Twitter to promote their fall fashion show in New York with videos and ads. The show was streamed live on Facebook.
- Levi's advertises on Facebook based on 'what people think their friends would like.'
- Wendy's uses Facebook and Twitter to award $50 gift cards to people who have the funniest and quirkiest responses to Wendy's published challenges online.

Overall, the vast majority of U.S. companies have a presence on Facebook (see **emarketer. com** for periodic reports). For more applications see Chapters 7 and 8, Turban et al. (2015), and Simply Zesty (2011).

Virtual Worlds and Second Life

A special class of social networking is the *virtual world*. A **virtual world**, also known as a *metaverse,* has several definitions. Our working definition is that it is a 3-D computer-based simulated environment built and owned by its residents. In addition to creating buildings, people can create and share cars, clothes, and many other items. Community members inhabit virtual spaces and interact and socialize via *avatars.* The essentials of virtual worlds and the prime example, Second Life (**secondlife.com**), are presented in Chapters 2 and 7.

Until 2007, virtual worlds were most often limited to 3-D games, including massive multiplayer online games. More recently, they have become a new way for people to socialize, and even do business (see Chapter 7). For example,

there.com focuses more on social networking activities, such as chatting, creating avatars, interacting, playing, and meeting people.

How Students Make Money in a Virtual World

If you cannot get a summer (or other) job, try a job in a virtual world. Examples of such jobs and the names of the young entrepreneurs who use their computer skills to develop these jobs are provided by Alter (2008).

The Major Tools of Web 2.0

Web 2.0 uses dozens of tools such as wikis, RSS feeds, blogs, and microblogs (e.g., Twitter). With microblogging you can transmit short messages (up to 140 characters) to a list of recipients via the Internet and wireless or wireline devices. As of 2009, Twitter became a major Web 2.0 tool with diversified business applications. Web 2.0 tools are described in Edwards (2013).

SECTION 1.4 REVIEW QUESTIONS
1. Define social computing and list its characteristics.
2. Define Web 2.0 and list its attributes.
3. Define social networks.
4. Describe the capabilities of social network services (SNSs).
5. Describe Facebook. Why is it so popular?
6. What is an enterprise social network?
7. Define social commerce.
8. Define virtual worlds and list their major characteristics.

1.5　THE DIGITAL AND SOCIAL WORLDS: ECONOMY, ENTERPRISES, AND SOCIETY

E-Commerce, including E-Commerce 2.0 is facilitated by developments in the digital and social economy as well as enterprises.

The digital revolution is upon us. We see it every day at home and work, in businesses, schools, hospitals, on the roads, in entertainment, and even wars (see Daugherty 2014 for details). Next, we describe three elements of the digital world: economy, enterprises, and society.

The Digital Economy

The **digital economy**, also known as the *Internet economy*, is an economy based on online transactions, mostly e-commerce. It includes digital wireline or wireless communication networks (e.g., the Internet, intranets, extranets, and VANs), computers, software, and other related information technologies. This digital economy displays the following characteristics:

- Many digitizable products – books, databases, magazines, information, electronic games, and software – are delivered over a digital infrastructure anytime, anywhere in the world, interconnected by a global grid (see Bisson et al. 2010). We are moving from analog to digital, even the media is going digital (TV as of February 2009).
- Information is transformed into a commodity.
- Financial transactions are now digitized and chips are embedded in many products (e.g., cameras, cars). Knowledge is codified.
- Work and business processes are organized in new and innovative ways.
- Disruptive innovation is occurring in many industries (see Manyika et al. 2014 and Daugherty 2014).

Table 1.3 summarizes the major characteristics of the digital economy.

The digital revolution also enables many innovations, and new ones appear almost daily, improving business processes and productivity. The digital revolution provides the necessary technologies for EC and creates major changes in the business environment, as described in Section 1.6.

Table 1.3 Major characteristics of the digital economy

Area	Description
Globalization	Global communication and collaboration; global electronic marketplaces and competition
Digitization	Music, books, pictures, software, videos, and more are digitized for fast and inexpensive storage and distribution
Speed	A move to real-time transactions, thanks to digitized documents, products, and services. Many business processes are expedited by 90% or more
Information overload and intelligent search	Although the amount of information generated is accelerating, intelligent search tools can help users find what people need
Markets	Markets are moving online. Physical marketplaces are being replaced or supplemented by electronic markets; new markets are being created, increasing competition
Business models and processes	New and improved business models and processes provide opportunities to new companies and industries
Innovation	Digital and Internet-based innovations continue at a rapid pace. More patents are being granted than ever before
Obsolescence	The fast pace of innovation creates a high rate of obsolescence
Opportunities	Opportunities abound in almost all aspects of life and operations
Fraud	Criminals employ a slew of innovative schemes on the Internet. Cybercons are everywhere
Wars	Conventional wars are changing to cyberwars or are complemented by them
Organizations	Organizations are moving to digital enterprises and social businesses

Sharing Economy

Sharing economy refers to an economic system constructed around the concept of sharing goods and services among the participating people. Also known as 'collaborative consumption' and 'collaborative economy' such systems appear in different forms and frequently use information technologies in their operations. A well known example is car sharing. The essentials of this concept are described by Buczynski (2013).

The major benefits for participants are cost reduction for buyers and the ability to sell more for sellers. Societal benefits include reduction of carbon footprint (e.g., in ride sharing), increase recycling, and increase social interactions. For a comprehensive coverage see **en.wikipedia.org/wiki/sharing_economy.**

Sharing Economy and E-Commerce

Several EC models and companies are based on the concept of the sharing economy. Examples include Uber (for ride sharing), Yerdle (a sharing economy free marketplace), Kickstarter (for crowdfunding), Krrb (a P2P marketplace), and Knok and Love Home Swap for home swapping. Vacation rental is a large area where home and condo owners provide short term rentals possibly for an exchange (e.g., see Airbnb, HomeAway, and VRBO).

The Social Impact

The digital revolution is accompanied by social impacts that resulted in part by improved communication and collaboration tools offered by social media. For example, smartphones reduce the digital divide. Also people change their behavior. Both individuals and organizations are impacted. In addition to productivity improvement in the economy, one can see some major social changes, such as the mass participation in social networks. According to Chui et al. (2012), social technologies unlock value and increase productivity in businesses.

The Apps Society

New apps change the way that people communicate, work and play. People are looking for apps for thousands of new uses.

Example: Swedish Farmers Go Online

According to Willgren (2013) small farmers in Sweden created a social network called 'Min Farm (My Farm).' The network allows communication between the farmers and their customers. It also allows people that grow their own food to tell their stories and ask for advice. Customer can visit farms and do some shopping there; they can also order online. The network promotes self-sustainability.

The Digital Enterprise

One of the major impacts of EC is the creation of the digital enterprise concept that accompanies the social enterprise.

The term *digital enterprise* has several definitions. It usually refers to an enterprise, such as Amazon.com, Google, Facebook, or Ticketmaster, which uses computers and information systems to automate most of its business processes. The **digital enterprise** is a new business model that uses IT to gain competitive advantage by increasing employee productivity, improving efficiency and effectiveness of business processes, and better interactivity between vendors and customers. The major characteristics of a digital enterprise are listed in Table 1.4, where they are compared with those of a traditional enterprise.

Note that the term *enterprise* refers to any kind of organization, public or private, small or large. An enterprise can be a manufacturing plant, a hospital, a university, a TV network, or even an entire city. They are all moving toward being digitized.

A digital enterprise uses networks of computers in EC to facilitate the following:

- All business partners are reached via the Internet, or a group of secured intranets, called an extranet, or value-added private communication lines.
- All internal communication is done via an intranet, which is the counterpart of the Internet inside the company.

Most companies' data and EC transactions are done via the Internet and extranets. Many companies employ a **corporate portal**, which is a gateway for customers, employees, and partners to reach corporate information and to communicate with the company.

A key concern of many companies today is how to change themselves into digital (or at least partially digital) enterprises so that they

Table 1.4 The digital versus brick-and-mortar company

Brick-and-mortar organizations	Digital organizations (enterprises)
Selling in physical stores	Selling online
Selling tangible goods	Selling digital goods online as well
Internal inventory/ production planning	Online collaborative inventory forecasting
Paper catalogs	Smart electronic catalogs
Physical marketplace	Electronic marketplace
Use of telephone, fax, VANs, and traditional EDI	Use of computers, smartphones, the Internet, and extranets and EDI
Physical auctions, infrequently	Online auctions, everywhere, any time
Broker-based services, transactions	Electronic infomediaries, value-added services
Paper-based billing and payments	Electronic billing and payments
Paper-based tendering	Electronic tendering (reverse auctions)
Push production, starting with demand forecasting	Pull production, starting with an order (build-to-order)
Mass production (standard products)	Mass customization, build-to-order
Physical-based commission marketing	Affiliated, virtual marketing
Word-of-mouth, slow and limited advertisement	Explosive viral marketing, in particular in social networks
Linear supply chains	Hub-based supply chains
Large amount of capital needed for mass production	Less capital needed for build-to-order; payments can be collected before production starts
Large fixed cost required for plant operation	Small fixed cost required for smaller and less complex plant operation
Customers' value proposition is frequently a mismatch (cost > value)	Perfect match of customers' value proposition (cost <= value)

can take part in the digital economy. For example, Harrington (2006) describes why and how, as a CEO, he transformed the Thomson Corp. from a traditional $8 billion publishing business into an electronic information services provider and a publisher. In 5 years, revenue increased over 20% and profit increased by more than 65%.

The concept of the digital enterprise is related to the smart and intelligent enterprise systems.

Smart and Intelligent Enterprise Systems

IBM is a leading force in developing smart (or intelligent) computing systems (other companies include SAP, Intel, Oracle, Google, and Microsoft) . IBM provides software and knowledge to digital enterprises (including cities). See **ibm.com/ smarterplanet/us/en/smarter_commerce/ overview/index.html**.

Smart Computing and Integrated Expertise

A major part of IBM's project is based on cloud computing (see Online Tutorial T2). The project created software for efficient, easy to use and flexible computing systems that include a built-in pattern of expertise. The integrated systems are known as 'IBM PureFlex' and 'IBM PureApplication.' For details see **ibm.com/pure-systems**. These systems per IBM, are changing the economics of computing by:

- Helping reduce time-to-market
- Conserving resources and reducing costs
- Consolidating diverse computer system components and applications
- Improving security and reducing human error

All of these contribute to IBM's Smarter Commerce efforts.

The Social Business (Enterprise)

The concept of social business has several definitions and characteristics. We present only a few of them.

The Social Business Forum

The concept of social business was developed decades ago and was not related to computers. Today, the Social Business Forum defines **social business** as "an organization that has put in place the strategies, technologies and processes to systematically engage all the individuals of its ecosystem (employees, customers, partners, suppliers) to maximize the co-created value." See **socialbusinessforum.com/social-business-manifesto**. The Forum also discusses the implication of this definition and its relevance inside, across and outside organizations. Note that the efficient creation of value using technology is emphasized. The Forum conducts annual conferences.

IBM's Approach

IBM has been recognized by the research company IDC as the market share leader in social software platform providers. IBM and IDC include in their joint definition the following characteristics: use of emerging technologies such as social software, social-oriented organizational culture, and improvements of business processes. The IBM effort also concentrates on improved collaboration. The basic idea is that social media networks and social customers require organizations to drastically change the way they work to become a social businesses that can exploit the opportunities created by the digital and social revolutions. IBM is helping organizations become social businesses. (For an example, see **ibm.com/social-business/us/en** and **ibm.com/smarterplanet/global/files/us__ en_us__socialbusiness__epw14008usen.pdf**). For a white paper titled "The Social Business: Advent of a New Age" (2011). IBM has an extensive 'social business video library,' two interesting videos are recommended for better understanding of the concept.

1. "How Do You Become a Social Business" – by Sandy Carter from IBM (3:50 minutes) at **youtube.com/watch?v=OZy0dNQbotg**.
2. "Social Business @ IBM" – An Interview with Luis Suarez (8:50 minutes) at **youtube. com/watch?v=enudW2gHek0**.

   (Also, see slide shows embedded in Taft (2012a) and Taft (2012b) used in Team Assignments #4 at the end of this chapter. Both are useful for understanding of the concept).

Social Business by Design

The Dachis Group, a consulting a company on social business sponsored a book on transformative social business strategies (by Hinchcliffe et al. 2012). The book is based on research done by Dachis Group and experience collected from major companies that implemented a social business strategy (e.g., SAP, IBM, Ford, Miller Coors and Procter & Gamble). The strategy.

methodologies, and tactics suggested in the book are called 'Social Business by Design.'

The Social Enterprise

The concept of social business is frequently equated to and sometimes confused with the term *social enterprise*. Many use the two terms interchangeably. The main goal of a **social enterprise** is to focus on social issues. These enterprises generate revenue. The profits do not go to owners and shareholders, but are put back into the company and used toward building positive social change. The Social Enterprise Alliance provides details at **se-alliance.org/why**. It seems that the above definition emphasizes the social goals.

Example

The Children's Medical Center of Dallas is going social. According to Cerrato (2012) the hospital created a patient and family social network, a patient portal, and provided for social collaboration. For more on the social enterprise see Chui et al. (2013).

The Digital Revolution and Society

The final, and perhaps most important, element of the *digital world* is people and the way they work and live. Clearly, the digital revolution has changed almost any activity one can think of – work, play, shopping, entertainment, travel, medical care, education, and much more. Just think about your digital phone, camera, TV, car, home, and almost anything else. It is only natural that people are utilizing technology and EC at an increasing rate. Let's take a look at some examples:

- Google has developed cars that drive themselves automatically in traffic (autonomous vehicles). The cars are being tested in several states, including California, and were approved in the state of Nevada as of summer 2012. In May 2012 these cars were tested in California without people in them. For a comprehensive discussion see Neil (2012). For an overview and potential benefits, including safety, see Cook (2012). By 2014 self-driving cars are running in several cities. For details see Thomas (2014). Also see Chapter 6.

- Billionaire Jack Ma, the founder of Alibaba.com (Chapter 4) is determined to transform China to a better country with an improved environment. Alibaba's sales now exceed those of eBay and Amazon combined. For details see Anderlini (2013).

- As of 2008, high school girls are able to solicit feedback from their friends regarding dozens of different prom dresses that have been displayed by Sears on Facebook.

- Dryers and washers in some college dorms are controlled via the Internet. Students can sign in at **esuds.net** or use their smartphone to check the availability of laundry machines. Furthermore, they can receive e-mail or SMS alerts when their wash and dry cycles are complete. Some systems can even inject premeasured amounts of detergent and fabric softener at the right cycle time.

- Hailing a taxi in New York and other major cities is much easier today. As of August 2012 you can e-hail taxi if you have a smartphone with GPS. Using an application by ZABCAB (**zabcab.com**) all you have to do is to push one button. Your exact location (on a map) will appear automatically on the portable device screen of all subscribing taxi drivers; the cost is $14.95/month for the driver, free for the user. (Note; This application has been temporarily halted due to some internal politics in New York City).

- Over 500 million active users download songs, games and videos at Apple's iTune store. (A selection of over 30 mil-

lion). The store also serves 350 million mobile devices. Total revenue is estimated to reach $9 billion in 2014. The store is considered the most popular music store in the world. Since its inception in 2003 it sold over 28 billion songs by fall 2013. At the same time the iPhone store has had over 1 million apps.

- Ford Company is using 'My Ford Touch' system to calculate the fastest, shortest, and most fuel-efficient way to get to a destination. The system charts a route that avoids congestion (based on historical and real-time traffic data). Results are shown on a dashboard. Initial deployment was in the 2012 model of the Ford Focus.

- Super Bowl XLVI (2012) has served its fans via a social media command center staffed by 50 employees who monitored over 300 keywords during the game. For details see Chaney (2012).

- As of 2014, guests in several Starwood Hotels & Resorts can enter their rooms by using a smartphone as a room key.

- An international research project is developing a computerized system that enables monitoring patients at home in real time, conducting a diagnosis, and providing medical advice. The objective is to reduce traffic to medical facilities while increasing the quality of care. The project is managed in Israel with collaboration of experts from several European countries. For details see **haifa.ac.il**: Search for 'global medical systems.'

- Union Pacific, the largest U.S. railroad company is using a large number of sensors on their trains and other equipment to collect data that is transmitted via wireless and wireline networks to a data center. There an analysis is performed to determine optimal preventive maintenance by using predictive analytics. Over 10 billion data items were collected in

2011 increasing annual revenue by $35–40 million. For details see Murphy (2012).

- Water loss involving many influencing variables in the Valley of the Moon Water District in California has been considerably reduced by using smart analytical computing from IBM.
- Supermarket shoppers in Finland are using camera-equipped smartphones that can scan the bar code of an item to find its ingredients, nutrient value, and exercise time needed to burn the consumed calories.
- Bicycle computers (by Bridgestone Cycle Co.) can automatically keep track of your travel distance, speed, time, and calorie consumption. For cycling communities see **bikewire.net** and **cycling-forum.com**.
- Champions of the World Series of Poker used to be people in their 50s and 60s who spent years playing the game to gain the experience needed to win. But in 2009, Joe Cada from the U.S. won the main event at the World Series of Poker, at the age of 21. To gain experience quickly, Cada plays extensively online. Ryan Riess won in 2013 at the age of 23.

The above list can be extended to hundreds or even thousands of items. For some extreme applications see Pepitone (2012).

Disruptive Impacts

Digital technologies in general and EC and related technologies such as m-commerce and social commerce, may have a disruptive impact on economies, industries, business models, and people (see the 'Disruptive Technologies' video of 2013 at **mckinsey.com/insights/high_tech_telecoms_internet/disruptive_technologies**, and Daugherty (2014). For a

2014 video interview of MIT's Andrew McAfee and McKinsey's James Manyika titled "Why Every Leader Should Care about Digitization and Disruptive Innovation," see **mckinsey.com/insights/business_technology/why_every_leader_should_care_about_digitization_and_disruptive_innovation**.

The Social Customer

An important component in the digital society is the *social customer*. **Social customers** (sometimes called *digital customers*) are usually members of social networks who share opinions about products, services, and vendors, do online social shopping, and understand their rights and how to use the wisdom and power of social communities to their benefit. The number of social customers is increasing exponentially due to wireless shopping and new online shopping models and opportunities (Chapter 7). The highlights of the social customers are shown in Figure 1.5.

As the figure illustrates, social customers expect better service, are willing to provide feedback, product reviews, and connect with like-minded peers. This new behavior pattern requires a new strategy for both marketing communication, and customer service. The social customer is participatory, and has active involvement in the shopping process both as a buyer and as an influencer. Individuals are influenced by friends, friends of friends, and friends of friends of friends. Merchants must understand how these consumers differ from conventional customers, and therefore use appropriate e-commerce marketing strategy as well as superb customer service (e.g., see Turban et al. 2015). For an extensive discussion of today's social customer, see Shih (2011). Procedures, guidelines, and software are publically available for social CRM (e.g., see Smith et al. 2011).

Taft (2012a) explains the reasons IBM's Smarter Commerce initiative is focusing on the digital customer (see the slide show embedded in the article). IBM is developing new software

Being connected, customers realized that they could ask more from companies and share opinions about products and services

Web 2.0 stimulated fundamental changes in consumer behavior

Interactions between customer and brands starting earlier and never ending

New behavior patterns demand a new strategy, better segmentation, new channels and targeted messages and review of current customer facing business processes

Figure 1.5 The social customer (Source: Courtesy of F. Cipriani, "Social CRM: Concept, Benefits, and Approach to Adopt," November 2008. slideshare.net/fhcipriani/ social-crm-presentation-761225 (Accessed June 2014). Used with permission)

and services that deliver intelligence-guided customer experience (e.g., personalization and targeted advertising based on cloud computing analytics).

SECTION 1.5 REVIEW QUESTIONS
1. Define the digital revolution and list its components.
2. List the characteristics of the digital economy.
3. What is the social economy?
4. Define a digital enterprise and relate it to social business.
5. Describe the social enterprise.
6. Compare traditional and digital enterprises.
7. Describe the digital society.
8. Describe the social customer.
9. Visit **packdog.com** and **dogtoys.com**. Compare the two sites and relate their contents to the digital society.

1.6   THE CHANGING BUSINESS ENVIRONMENT, ORGANIZATIONAL RESPONSES, AND EC AND IT SUPPORT

EC is driven by many technological, economic, and social factors. These are frequently related to global competition and rapid changes in the business environment. For predictions about the technological changes see *Enterprise Innovation* Editors (2013).

The Changing Business Environment

Economic, legal, societal, and technological factors and the trend for globalization have created a very competitive business environment. The environmental factors can change quickly, vigorously, and sometimes in an unpredictable manner. For example, the financial crisis of 2008–2012 has resulted in many companies going out of business or being acquired by other companies. These business environment changes impact the manner in which companies operate, and as a result, many firms have restructured their business processes as well as their EC initiatives.

Let's see how all of these impact organizational performance.

Performance, Business Pressures, and Organizational Responses and EC Support

Most people, sports teams, and organizations are trying to improve their *performance*. For some, it is a challenge; for others, it is a requirement for survival. Yet for others it is the key to improved quality of life, profitability, or reputation.

Most organizations measure their performance periodically, comparing it to some metrics and to the organization's mission, objectives, and plans. Unfortunately, in business, performance often depends not only on what you do but also on what others are doing, as well as on what is happening in the business and physical environments.

The Business Environment and Performance Impact Model

The model shown in Figure 1.6 illustrates how the business environment (left) creates pressures, problems, and opportunities that drive what organizations are doing in their business processes (the "Our Company" circle). Other drivers are the organization's mission, goals, strategy, and plans. Business processes include competencies, activities, and responses to the environmental pressures that we call *critical response activities* or *solutions*. The business processes and activities result in measurable performance, which provides solutions to problems/opportunities, as

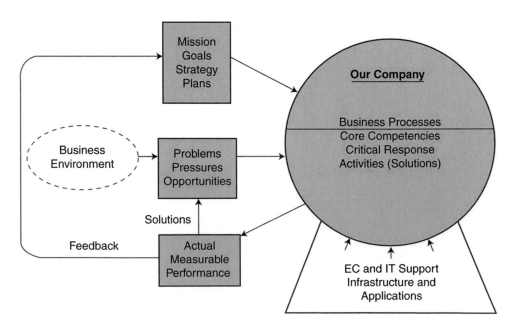

Figure 1.6 The business environment and performance model

Table 1.5 Major business pressures

Market and economic pressures	Societal pressures	Technological pressures
Intense global competition	The nature (and composition) of the workforce is changing	Increasing innovations and new technologies
Global economy and markets	Government deregulation, leading to more competition	Rapid technological obsolescence
Regional trade agreements (e.g., NAFTA)	Compliance with regulations is needed (e.g., Sarbanes-Oxley Act)	Increases in information overload
Extremely low labor costs in some countries	Shrinking government subsidies	Rapid decline in technology cost versus labor cost (technology becomes more and more attractive)
Regular and important changes in markets	Politics drives government regulations	
Increased power of consumers	Increased importance of ethical and legal issues	
Political and government Interventions in markets	Increased social responsibility of organizations	
	Rapid political changes	
	Terrorism is on the rise	

well as feedback to the attainment of the mission, strategy, goals, and plans.

Notice that in Figure 1.6 EC and IT provide support to organizational activities and to the resultant performance, countering the business pressures. Now, let us examine the two major components of the model: business pressures and organizational responses.

Business Pressures

In this text, business pressures are divided into the following categories: market (economic), societal, and technological. The main types of business pressures in each category are listed in Table 1.5. (Note that some of the business environment conditions create opportunities.)

Organizational Response Strategies

How can organizations operate in such an environment? How can they deal with the threats and the opportunities? To begin with, many traditional strategies are still useful in today's environment. However, because some traditional response activities may *not* work in today's turbulent and competitive business environment, some of the old solutions may not work and need to be modified or supplemented. Alternatively, new responses can be devised. Critical response

activities can take place in some or all organizational processes, from payroll processing to a merger. A response activity can be a reaction to a specific pressure already in existence, or it can be a scheme that will protect an organization against future pressures. It can also be an activity that exploits an opportunity created by changing conditions as shown in Case 1.1, Net-a-Porter (p. 13).

Representative response activities are provided in Table 1.6.

The Support of EC

Many response activities can be greatly facilitated by EC, and this fuels the growth of the field. In some cases, EC is the *only* solution to certain business pressures. The reasons for this are related to the capabilities of EC.

The Major Capabilities of E-Commerce

EC initiatives play an increasing role in supporting innovations and strategies that help companies compete and flourish, especially companies that want to be proactive and introduce changes rather than be reactive and respond to them. What makes EC suitable for such a role is a *set of*

Table 1.6 Innovative organizational responses

Response strategy	Descriptions
Strategic systems	Strategic advantage in industry improved
Agile systems	Ability to adapt to changes and flexibility increased
Continuous improvements and business process management	Business processes improved through Use of enterprise systems
Customer relationship management	Use of Internet and EC models to introduce programs for improvement of customer relationships
Business alliances and partner relationship management (PRM)	Win-win situations – even with competitors created through joint ventures, partnerships, e-collaboration, and virtual corporations
Electronic markets	Increased efficiency and effectiveness through the use of both private and public electronic markets
Cycle time reduction	Speed of operation increased and time to market reduced
Empowering employees, especially on the front line (interacting with customers, partners)	Employees make quick decisions on their own with computerized decision aids provided by company
Mass customization in a build-to-order system	Quickly produce customized products (services) at reasonable cost to many customers (mass) as Dell does
Intrabusiness use of automation	Improvement of many intrabusiness activities (e.g., sales force automation, inventory management using e-commerce and m-commerce)
Knowledge management	Increased productivity, agility, and competitiveness through appropriate creation, storage, and dissemination of knowledge using electronic systems
Customer selection, loyalty, and service	Retain customer loyalty by identifying customers with the most profit potential and increasing chances that they will want the product or service offered
Human capital	Choose the top employees for particular tasks or jobs, at particular payment levels
Quality of products and services	Minimize quality problems through early detection.
Financial performance	Recognize the drivers of financial performance and the effects of nonfinancial factors involved
Research and development	Quality, effectiveness, and, where applicable, safety of products and services improved
Social networking	Innovative marketing, advertising, collaboration, and innovation using the power of the crowd

capabilities and *technological developments*; some of which were listed in Figure 1.4 (p. 16).

The essential capabilities that drive EC are the ability to:

- Provide efficient and effective business transactions.
- Provide global reach for selling, buying, or finding business partners.
- Conduct business anytime, from anywhere, in a convenient way. For example, there were more than 300 million wireless subscribers in the U.S. and over 600 million in China in 2013 (see Peterson 2014).
- Disseminate information rapidly, frequently in real time.
- Enable price comparisons.
- Customize products and personalize services.
- Use rich media in advertisement, entertainment, and social networking.
- Receive expert and other user advice quickly.
- Collaborate in different ways, both internally and externally.
- Share information and knowledge.
- Increase productivity and performance, reduce costs, and compress time within the supply chain (e.g., by having smarter applications).
- Easily and quickly find information about vendors, products, and competitors.

Because EC technology is improving over time and decreasing in cost, its comparative advantage is continuously increasing, further contributing to the growth of EC.

SECTION 1.6 REVIEW QUESTIONS
1. List the components of the business environment and the performance model and explain the model.
2. List the major factors in today's business environment.
3. List some of the major response activities taken by organizations.
4. List and briefly discuss five capabilities of EC.

1.7   ELECTRONIC COMMERCE BUSINESS MODELS

One of the major characteristics of EC is that it facilitates the creation of new business models. A **business model** describes the manner in which business is done to generate revenue and create value. This is accomplished by attaining organizational objectives. A key area is attracting enough customers to buy the organization's products or services. Note: The January–February 2011 issue of *Harvard Business Review* is dedicated to business model innovations (5 articles), including several topics related to e-commerce. Several different EC business models are possible, depending on the company, the industry, and so on. Business models can be found in existing businesses as well as in proposed ones.

The Structure and Properties of Business Models

A comprehensive business model (for a proposal company) may include some or all of the following components illustrated in Figure 1.7.

- A description of the *customers* to be served and their *value proposition*. Also, how these customers can be reached and supported.

- A description of all *products* and *services* the business plans to deliver. Also, what the differentiating aspects of the products are.
- The company's growth strategies.
- A description of the required *business process* and the distribution infrastructure (including human resources).
- A list of the *resources* required, their cost and availability (including human resources).
- A description of the organization's *supply chains*, including *suppliers* and other *business partners*.
- The value chain structure.
- The relevant markets with a list of the major competitors and their market share. Also, market strategies and strengths/weaknesses of the company.
- The competitive advantage offered by the business model including pricing and selling strategies.
- The anticipated organizational changes and any resistance to change.
- A description of the revenues expected (*revenue model*), sources of funding, and the *financial viability*.

Models also include a *value proposition,* which is a description of the benefits of using the specific model (tangible and intangible), both to the customers and to the organization. A detailed discussion and examples of business models and their relationship to business plans is presented at **en.wikipedia.org/wiki/Business_model**.

This chapter presents two of the models' elements: *revenue models* and *value propositions*.

Revenue Models

A revenue model specifies how the organization, or the EC project, will generate revenue. For example, the revenue model for Net-a-Porter shows revenue from online sales of luxury dresses. The major revenue models are:

A company uses its *revenue model* to describe how it will generate revenue and its *business model* to describe the *process* it will use to do so.

Figure 1.7 The major
components of a business
model

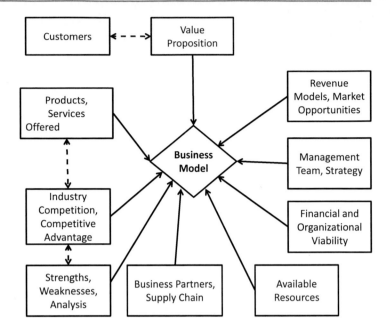

Sales. Companies generate revenue from selling products or services on their websites. An example is when Net-a-Porter, Starbucks, Amazon.com, or Godiva sells a product online.

Transaction Fees. Commissions are based on the volume of transactions made. For example, when a home owner sells a house, he or she typically pays a transaction fee to the broker. The higher the value of the sale, the higher the total transaction fee. Alternatively, transaction fees can be levied *per transaction*. With online stock trades, for example, there is usually a fixed fee per trade, regardless of the volume.

Subscription Fees. Customers pay a fixed amount, usually monthly, to get some type of service. An example would be the fee you pay to an Internet access provider (fixed monthly payments).

Advertising Fees. Companies charge others for allowing them to place a banner on their sites (see Chapter 4).

Affiliate Fees. Companies receive commissions for referring customers to certain websites. A good program is available at Amazon.com.

Licensing Fees. Another revenue source is licensing fees (e.g., see **progress.com/products/datadirect**). Licensing fees can be assessed as an annual fee or a per usage fee. Microsoft receives fees from each workstation that uses Windows NT, for example.

Other Revenue Sources. Some companies allow people to play games for a fee or to watch a sports competition in real time for a fee (e.g., see **espn.go.com**).

Innovative Revenue Models for Individuals

The Internet allows for innovative revenue models, some of which can be utilized even by individuals, as demonstrated by the following example.

- *Example: Buy Low–Sell High.* This strategy has been known for generations, but now you have a better chance. How about buying stuff cheap on Craigslist (or other online classified ad sites) and resell it for a 50–200% profit in an auction on eBay? Try it, you might make money. Some people make it even bigger. The person who bought the domain name *pizza.com* for $20 in 1994 sold it for $2.6 million in April 2008 (one of the many he purchased). The revenue model can be part of the value proposition or it may supplement it.

Value Proposition

Business models also include a value-proposition statement. A **value proposition** refers to the benefits, including the intangible ones that a company hopes to derive from using its business model. In B2C EC, for example, the *customer value proposition* defines how a company's product or service fulfills the needs of customers. In other words, it describes the total benefits to the customer. The *value proposition* is an important part of the marketing plan of any product or service. For 50 value propositions in B2C e-commerce see CPC Andrew (2012).

Functions of a Business Model

Business models have the following major functions or objectives:

- Describe the supply and value chains.
- Formulate the venture's competitive strategy and its long-range plans.
- Present the customer value proposition.
- Identify who will use the technology for what purpose; specify the revenue-generation process; where the company will operate.
- Estimate the cost structure and amount and profit potential.

Typical EC Business Models

There are many types of EC business models. Examples and details of EC business models can be found throughout this text, and in Rappa (2010). The following are five common models. Additional models are listed in Online File W1.4.

1. **Online direct marketing.** The most obvious EC model is that of selling products or services online. Sales may be from a *manufacturer* to a customer, eliminating intermediaries or physical stores (e.g., Dell), or from *retailers* to consumers, making distribution more efficient (e.g., Net-a-Porter, Walmart online). This model is especially efficient for digitizable products and services (those that can be delivered electronically). This model has several variations (see Chapters 3 and 4) and uses different mechanisms (e.g., auctions). It is practiced in B2C (where it is called *e-tailing*) and in some B2B types of EC.

2. **Electronic tendering systems.** Large organizational buyers usually make large-volume or large-value purchases through a **tendering (bidding) system,** also known as a *reverse auction.* Such tendering can be done online, saving time and money. Pioneered by General Electric Corp., e-tendering systems are gaining popularity. Indeed, many government agencies mandate that most of their procurement must be done through e-tendering. (Details are provided in Chapter 4.)

3. **Electronic marketplaces and exchanges.** Electronic marketplaces existed in isolated applications for decades (e.g., stock and commodities exchanges). But as of 1996, hundreds of e-marketplaces (old and new) have introduced new methods and efficiencies to the trading process. If they are well organized and managed, e-marketplaces can provide significant benefits to both buyers and sellers. Of special interest are vertical marketplaces that concentrate on one industry. For details see Chapter 4.

4. **Viral marketing.** According to the viral marketing model (see Chapter 7, people use e-mail and social networks to spread word-of-mouth advertising. It is basically Web-based *word-of-mouth* advertising, and is popular in social networks.

5. **Group purchasing.** Group purchasing is a well-known offline method, both in B2C and B2B. It is based on the concept of quantity discounts ("cheaper by the dozen"). The Internet model allows individuals to get together, so they can gain the large-quantity advantage. This model was not popular in B2C until 2010 when Groupon introduced a modified model in which people are grouped around special deals, as illustrated in Chapter 7.

Note that a company may use several EC models as demonstrated in Starbucks opening case, the NFL closing case, and the Dell case (Online File W1.1).

Classification of Business Models in E-Commerce

Rappa (2010) classified the EC business models into eight categories:
1. Brokerage: Market makers that charges fee for their services.
2. Advertising: Websites that provide content and charge advertisers for related ads.
3. Infomediary: Provide information and/or infrastructure that help buyers and/or sellers and charge for their services.
4. Merchant: Retailers (such as Walmart or Amazon): These buy the products and sell them at profit.
5. Direct model: Sell without intermediaries.
6. Affiliate: Paying website owners to place banners. Share fees received from advertisers.
7. Community: A social media-based model that utilizes Web 2.0 tools, social networks, and the characteristics presented in Chapter 7.

Rappa (2010) provides examples of each plus their revenue models. Also he presents the major varieties in each category.

SECTION 1.7 REVIEW QUESTIONS
1. What is a business model? Describe its functions and properties.
2. Describe a revenue model and a value proposition. How are they related?
3. Describe the following business models: direct marketing, tendering system, electronic exchanges, viral marketing, and social networking/commerce.
4. Identify some business models related to buying and those related to selling.
5. Describe how viral marketing works.

1.8   THE LIMITATIONS, IMPACTS, AND THE FUTURE OF E-COMMERCE

As indicated in Section 1.2 there are some limitations and failures in EC.

The Limitations and Barriers of EC

Barriers to EC are either non-technological or technological. Representative major barriers are listed in Table 1.7.

Van Toorn et al. (2006) classified the barriers into sectorial barriers (e.g., government, private sector, international organizations), internal barriers (e.g., security, lack of technical knowledge, and lack of time and resources), external barriers (e.g., lack of government support), cultural differences, organizational differences, incompatible B2B interfaces, international trade barriers, and lack of standards. These limitations are diminishing with time but still need to be addressed when implementing EC. One important area that may limit some EC project is ethics.

Ethical Issues
Ethical issues can create pressures or constraints on EC business operations. Yet some ethical sites increase trust and help EC vendors. **Ethics** relates to standards of right and wrong. Ethics is a difficult concept, because what is considered ethical by one

Table 1.7   Limitations of electronic commerce

Technological limitations	Non-technological limitations
Need for universal standards for quality, security, and reliability	Security and privacy concerns deter customers from buying
The telecommunications bandwidth is insufficient, especially for m-commerce, videos, and graphics	Lack of trust in sellers, in computers, and paperless faceless transactions hinders buying
Software development tools are still evolving	Resistance to change
It is difficult to integrate Internet and EC software with some existing (especially legacy) applications and databases	Many legal and public policy issues are not resolved or are not clear
Special Web servers are needed in addition to the network servers, which add to the cost of EC	National and international government regulations sometimes get in the way
Internet accessibility is still expensive and/or inconvenient	It is difficult to measure some of the costs and benefits of EC
Large-scale B2C requires special automated warehouses for order fulfillment	Not enough customers. Lack of collaboration along the supply chain

person may seem unethical to another. Likewise, what is considered ethical in one country may be unethical in another. For further discussions of EC ethical issues see Gaskin and Evans (2010).

Implementing EC use may raise ethical issues ranging from monitoring employee e-mail to invasion of privacy of millions of customers whose data are stored in private and public databases. In implementing EC, it is necessary to pay attention to these issues and recognize that some of them may limit, or even prohibit, the use of EC. An example of this can be seen in the attempted implementation of RFID tags (Online Tutorial T2) in retail stores due to the potential invasion of buyers' privacy.

Overcoming the Barriers

Despite these barriers, EC is expanding rapidly. As experience accumulates and technology improves, the cost-benefit ratio of EC will increase, resulting in even greater rates of EC

adoption. For suggestions on how to lesson some of the barriers via appropriate strategy see Chapters 13 and 14 and **powerhomebiz.com/vol103/implement.htm**.

Why Study E-Commerce?

The major reason to study e-commerce is that it is a rapidly growing field. The percentage of EC of total commerce is increasing rapidly and some predict that most future commerce will be online. Thus, any business person or a business student should learn about this field.

This is why the academic area of e-commerce that started around 1995 with only a few courses and textbooks is growing rapidly. Today, many universities offer EC courses and complete programs in e-commerce or e-business (e.g., majors in e-commerce, minors in e-commerce and certificate programs; see University of Virginia, University of Maine, University of Arkansas). Recently, e-commerce topics have been integrated into all functional fields (e.g., Internet marketing, electronic financial markets). The reason for this proliferation is that e-commerce is penetrating more and more into business areas, services, and governments. Finally, it is fascinating field with its innovative business models.

However, there are also some very tangible benefits to increased knowledge of EC. First, your chances of getting a good (or better) job are higher. The demand for both technical and managerial EC skills is growing rapidly, and so are the salaries (e.g., see salary comparison sites such as salary.com and **cbsalary.com**. Hundreds of well paying open positions are available in areas related to social media, social networking, and social commerce. Second, your chances for promotion could be higher if you understand EC and know how to seize its opportunities. Finally, it gives you a chance to become a billionaire, like the founders of Google, Facebook, YouTube, Amazon.com, and Yahoo!, or to make a great deal of money on eBay (see Joyner 2007). Even if you are not so lucky you can still make good money in Second Life (see Rymaszewski, et al. 2008) or simply by selling on eBay, Yahoo!, Facebook, Craigslist, or your own website. And you can do it while you are a student. (See the case of Jetpens as described by Blakely 2007). Even some teenagers practice successful EC. An example is Diane Keng, an entrepreneur from Cupertino Monte Vista High School in California, who initiated three Web 2.0 successful start-up companies, making substantial money (see Fowler 2010).

There are many other opportunities for young people to make money from EC in addition to the examples in this book and selling on eBay. Hunt (2010) suggests the following ways to earn extra cash online: (1) sell your craft; (2) make money from your talent; (3) be a nurse on call; (4) write, edit, or proofread; (5) design graphics and websites; (6) tutor kids or adults; (7) give advice; (8) provide customer service; (9) launch a blog; (10) give your opinion (for a fee); (11) search the Internet; and (12) do online tasks. Hunt also provides examples, URLs, and advice regarding scams. For 55 ways to make money online see Pantic (2013). Also see **shop.com**. Finally, for how to make money on the Internet using EC see Bates and Money Online (2014).

Web 2.0 also creates many opportunities for full-time jobs. For a list and discussion, see Tice (2010).

The Future of EC

Several economic, technological, and societal trends impact EC and shape its direction. For example, most experts agree that the shift from EC to mobile commerce is inevitable. Also, many believe in the future of social commerce, as a major component of e-commerce (e.g., see Turban et al. 2015). There will be a surge in the use of e-commerce in developing countries (mostly thanks to smartphones and tablets as well as e-payment systems). E-commerce will win its battle against conventional retailing (see the Amazon vs. Best Buy discussion in Chapter 3). Finally, e-commerce will increase its global reach.

EC will impact some industries more than others. This impact is changing with time. For example, major impacts in the past 5 years were felt in

travel, retail, stock brokering, and banking. Next, according to Hiner (2011) are: movies: healthcare, book publishing, and electronic payments. For an interesting review see Solis (2012).

Today's predictions about the future size of EC, provided by respected analysts such as ComScore, eMarketer.com, and Forrester, vary. For a list of sites that provide such predictions and other statistics on EC, see Table 3.1 (p. 108).

The number of Internet users worldwide was estimated to be around 2.6 billion in winter 2014, up from 2.4 billion in 2012 (see **internetworldstats.com**). With more people on the Internet EC will increase.

EMarketer forecasted that almost 73% of all Internet users in the US would shop online in 2011 (eMarketer 2011). The estimate for February 2014 is over 85. EC growth would come not only from B2C, but also from B2B and from newer applications such as e-government, e-learning, B2E, social commerce, and c-commerce. The total volume of EC has been growing every year by 10–16% in spite of the failures of individual companies and initiatives and the economic slowdown.

The rising price of petroleum, along with repercussions of the 2008–2012 financial meltdown, has motivated people to shop online and look for bargains where price comparison is easy and fast (e.g., try to find the price of an item on Amazon.com). Another important factor is the increase in mobile devices and especially smartphones. According to Mashable (2012), soon there will be more than smartphones than humans on the planet.

According to Gartner Inc. (2012), smartphone sales rose more than 42% in the 2nd quarter of 2012; this trend is forecasted to continue through the next few years.

Gartner Inc. (2011) also predicts that by 2015, companies will generate 50% of Web sales through their social presence and mobile applications.

The future of EC depends on technological, organizational, and societal trends. Piastro (2010) lists the top 10 trends that are shaping the future of e-commerce and Gartner Inc., publishes a list of the "Top 10 Strategic Technology Trends' every year. See **gartner.com/newsroom/id/**

2603623 for the 2014 list that includes several EC topics (e.g., mobile apps, Internet of Things).

SECTION 1.8 REVIEW QUESTIONS
1. List the major technological and non technological barriers and limitations to EC.
2. Describe some of the benefits of studying EC.
3. How can EC help entrepreneurship?
4. Summarize the major points involved with the future of e-commerce.

1.9 OVERVIEW OF THIS BOOK

This book is composed of 16 chapters grouped into five parts, as shown in Figure 1.8. Additional content, including online supplemental material for each chapter, is available online on the book's website.

The specific parts and chapters of this textbook are as follows:

Part I: Introduction to E-Commerce and E-Marketplaces

This section of the book includes an overview of EC and its content, benefits, limitations, and drivers, which are presented in Chapter 1. Chapter 2 presents electronic markets and their mechanisms, such as electronic catalogs and auctions. This chapter also includes a presentation of Web 2.0 tools of social networks and virtual worlds.

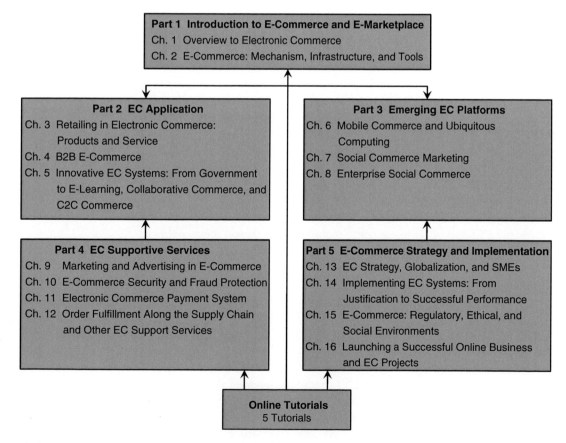

Figure 1.8 The plan of the book

Part II: EC Applications

This section includes three chapters. Chapter 3 describes e-tailing (B2C), including some of its most innovative applications for selling products online. It also describes the delivery of services, such as online banking, travel, and insurance. In Chapter 4, we introduce B2B EC and describe company-centric models (one buyer–many sellers, one seller–many buyers) as well as electronic exchanges (many buyers and many sellers). E-government, e-learning, knowledge management, and C2C are the major subjects of Chapter 5.

Part III: Emerging EC Delivery Platforms

In addition to traditional EC delivery platforms, described in Part II we present in the three chapters of Part III the following topics: Chapter 6 covers the area of mobile commerce and ubiquitous computing. In Chapter 7 we cover the area of social commerce and social media marketing. The part concludes with enterprise social commerce (Chapter 8).

Part IV: EC Support Services

Part IV examines issues involving the support services needed for EC applications in four chapters. Chapter 9 explains consumer behavior in cyberspace, online market research, and Internet advertising. Chapter 10 delves into EC security and fraud protection. Chapter 11 discusses electronic payments, and Chapter 12 deals with order fulfillment.

Part V: EC Strategy and Implementation

Part V includes four chapters. Chapter 13 examines e-strategy and planning, including going global and the impact of EC on small businesses. Chapter 14 deals mostly with justification and

economics of EC. In Chapter 15 we cover ethical, legal, and societal issues. Chapter 16 deals with creating, operating, and maintaining an Internet company. It also discusses initiating EC initiatives and creating EC content. Chapter 16 also addresses EC application development processes and methods.

Online Mini Tutorials

Five tutorials are available at the book's website (**affordable-ecommerce-textbook.com/turban**).
T1 e-CRM
T2 EC Technology: EDI, Extranet, RFID, and Cloud Computing
T3 Business Intelligence, Data, Text, and Web Mining
T4 Competition in Cyberspace
T5 E-Collaboration

Online Supplements

A large number of online files organized by chapter number support the content of each chapter.

They are available at **affordable-ecommerce-textbook.com/turban**.

MANAGERIAL ISSUES

Some managerial issues related to this introductory chapter are as follows.

1. **Why is B2B e-commerce so essential and successful?** B2B EC is essential for several reasons. First, some B2B models are easier to implement than B2C models. The volume and value of transactions is larger in B2B than in B2C, and the potential savings are larger and easier to justify in contrast to B2C, which has several major problems, ranging from channel conflict with existing distributors to fraud to a lack of a critical mass of buyers. Many companies can start B2B by simply buying from existing online stores and B2B exchanges or

selling electronically by joining existing marketplaces or an auction house. The problem is determining *what* and *where* to buy or sell.

2. **Which EC business model should I choose?** Beginning in early 2000, the news was awash with stories about the failure of many dotcoms and EC projects. Industry consolidation often occurs after a "gold rush." About 100 years ago, hundreds of companies tried to manufacture cars, following Ford's success in the United States; only three survived. The important thing is to learn from the successes and failures of others, and discover the right business model for each endeavor. For lessons that can be learned from EC successes and failures, see Chapters 3 and 14.

3. **How can we exploit social commerce?** There are major possibilities here. Some companies even open their own social networks. Advertising is probably the first thing to consider. Recruiting can be a promising avenue as well. Offering discounted products and services should also be considered. Providing customer services and conducting market research can be a useful activity as well. Finally, the ultimate goal is associating the social network with commerce so that revenue is created.

4. **What are the top challenges of EC today?** The top 10 technical issues for EC (in order of their importance) are security, adequate infrastructure, virtualization, back-end systems integration, more intelligent software, cloud computing, data warehousing and mining, scalability, and content distribution. The top 10 managerial issues for EC are justification, budgets, project deadlines, keeping up with technology, privacy issues, unrealistic management expectations, training, reaching new customers, improving customer ordering services, and finding qualified EC employees. Most of these issues are discussed throughout this book.

SUMMARY

In this chapter, you learned about the following EC issues as they relate to the chapter's learning objectives.

1. **Definition of EC and description of its various categories.** EC involves conducting transactions electronically. Its major categories are pure versus partial EC, Internet versus non-Internet, and electronic markets versus company-based systems.

2. **The content and framework of EC.** The applications of EC, and there are many, are based on infrastructures and are supported by people; public policy and technical standards; marketing and advertising; support services, such as logistics, security, and payment services; and business partners – all tied together by management.

3. **The major types of EC transactions.** The major types of EC transactions are B2B, B2C, C2C, m-commerce, intrabusiness commerce, B2E, c-commerce, e-government, social commerce, and e-learning.

4. **The drivers of EC.** EC is a major product of the digital and technological revolutions, which enables companies to simultaneously increase both growth and profits. These revolutions enables digitization of products, services, and information. A major driver of EC is the changing business environment. The rapid change is due to technological breakthroughs, globalization, societal changes, deregulation, and more. The changing business environment forces organizations to respond. Many traditional responses may not be sufficient because of the magnitude of the pressures and the pace of the changes involved. Therefore, organizations must frequently innovate and reengineer their operations. EC, due to its characteristics is a necessary partner for this process.

   Finally, EC is driven due to its ability to provide a much needed strategic advantage so organizations can compete better.

5. **Benefits of EC to organizations, consumers, and society.** EC offers numerous benefits to all participants. Because these benefits are substantial, it looks as though EC is here to stay and cannot be ignored. Also, organizations can go into remote and global markets for both selling and buying at better prices. Organizations can speed

time-to-market to gain competitive advantage. They can improve the internal and external supply chain as well as increase collaboration. Finally, they can better comply with government regulations.

6. **E-commerce 2.0 and social media.** This refers to the use of social computing in business, often through the use of Web 2.0 tools (such as blogs, wikis) with its social media framework, as well as the emergence of enterprise social networking and commercial activities in virtual worlds. Social and business networks attract huge numbers of visitors.

7. **Describe social commerce and social software.** Companies are beginning to exploit the opportunity of conducting business transactions in social networks and by using social software such as blogs. Major areas are advertising, shopping, customer service, recruiting, and collaboration.

8. **The elements of the digital world.** The major elements of the digital world are the digital economy, digital enterprises, and digital society. They are diversified and expanding rapidly.

   The digital world is accompanied by social businesses and social customers.

9. **Business pressures.** The major pressures include: market and economic factors (e.g., competition, globalization, product innovation), societal pressures (e.g., regulations, social customers, social responsibility), and technological pressures (e.g., new products, obsolescence, cheaper technologies). Organizational responses can be traditional (e.g., niche market, cost reduction, CRM) and technology based (innovations, automation, e-commerce).

10. **The major EC business models.** The major EC business models include online direct marketing, electronic tendering systems, name-your-own-price, affiliate marketing, viral marketing, group purchasing, online auctions, mass customization (make-to-order), electronic exchanges, supply chain improvers, finding the best price, value-chain integration, value-chain providers, information brokers, bartering, deep discounting, and membership.

11. **Limitations of e-commerce.** The major limitations of EC are the resistance to new technology, fear from fraud, integration with other IT systems may be difficult, costly order fulfillment, privacy issue, unclear regulatory issues, lack of trust in computers, and unknown business partners, difficulties to justify EC initiatives, and lack of EC skilled employees.

KEY TERMS

Brick-and-mortar (old economy) organizations
Business model
Business-to-business (B2B)
Business-to-business-to-consumer (B2B2C)
Business-to-consumer (B2C)
Business-to-employees (B2E)
Click-and-mortar (click-and-brick) organizations
Collaborative commerce (c-commerce)
Consumer-to-business (C2B)
Consumer-to-consumer (C2C)
Corporate portal
Digital economy
Digital enterprise
E-business
E-government
Electronic commerce (EC)
Electronic market (e-marketplace)
E-tailing
Ethics
Extranet
F-commerce
Intrabusiness EC
Intranet
Sharing economy
Social business
Social commerce
Social computing
Social (digital) customer
Social enterprise
Social media
Social network
Social networking

Social networking services (SNSs)
Tendering (bidding) system
Value proposition
Virtual (pure-play) organizations
Virtual world
Web 2.0

DISCUSSION QUESTIONS

1. Compare brick-and-mortar and click-and-mortar organizations.
2. Why is buying with a smart card from a vending machine considered EC?
3. Explain how EC can reduce cycle time, improve employees' empowerment, and facilitate customer service.
4. Compare and contrast viral marketing with affiliate marketing.
5. Identify the contribution of Web 2.0. What does it add to EC?
6. Discuss the reasons companies embark on social commerce.
7. Distinguish an enterprise social network from a public one such as Facebook.
8. Carefully examine the non-technological limitations of EC. Which are company-dependent and which are generic?
9. Why are virtual worlds such as Second Life related to EC?
10. Relate the social customer to social business.

TOPICS FOR CLASS DISCUSSION AND DEBATES

1. How can EC be both a business pressure and an organizational response to other business pressures?
2. Debate: Does digital business eliminate the "human touch" in trading? And if "yes," is it really bad?
3. Why do companies frequently change their business models? What are the advantages? The disadvantages?
4. Debate: EC eliminates more jobs than it creates. Should we restrict its use and growth?

5. Debate: Will online fashion hurt traditional fashion retailers?
6. Search for information on the enterprise of the future. Start with **ibm.com**.In one or two pages, summarize how the enterprise of the future differs from today's enterprise.
7. Read McDonald's activities at P&G (McDonald 2011). Discuss the various e-commerce and other digital activities. Discuss the need for such a revolution.
8. Investigate why the one day sales during Singles' Day in China generated more than twice the money generated on Cyber Monday in the U.S. (see Wang and Pfanner 2013).

INTERNET EXERCISES

1. Enter **excitingcommerce.com** and find recent information about emerging EC models and the future of the field.
2. Visit **amazon.com** and locate recent information in the following areas:
   (a) Find the five top-selling books on EC.
   (b) Find a review of one of these books.
   (c) Review the personalized services you can get from Amazon.com and describe the benefits you receive from shopping there.
   (d) Review the products directory.
3. Visit **priceline.com** and **zappos.com** and identify the various business revenue models used by both. Discuss their advantages.
4. Go to **nike.com** and design your own shoes. Next, visit **office.microsoft.com** and create your own business card. Finally, enter **jaguar.com** and configure the car of your dreams. What are the advantages of each activity? The disadvantages?
5. Try to save on your next purchase. Visit **pricegrabber.com**, **kaboodle.com**, **yub.com**, and **buyerzone.com**. Which site do you prefer? Why?
6. Enter **espn.go.com**, **123greetings.com**, and **facebook.com** and identify and list all the revenue sources on each of the companies' sites.

7. Enter **philatino.com, stampauctioncentral. com**, and **statusint.com**. Identify the business model(s) and revenue models they use. What are the benefits to sellers? To buyers?

8. Go to **zipcar.com**. What can this site help you do?

9. Enter **digitalenterprise.org**. Prepare a report regarding the latest EC models and developments.

10. Visit some websites that offer employment opportunities in EC (such as **execunet.com** and **monster.com**). Compare the EC salaries to salaries offered to accountants. For other information on EC salaries, check *Computerworld*'s annual salary survey and **salary.com**.

11. Visit **bluenile.com, diamond.com**, and **jewelryexchange.com**. Compare the sites. Comment on the similarities and the differences.

12. Visit **ticketsonline.com, ticketmaster.com, ticketonline.com**, and other sites that sell event tickets online. Assess the competition in online ticket sales. What services do the different sites provide?

13. Enter the Timberland Company (**timberland.com**) and design a pair of boots. Compare it to building your own sneakers at **nike.com**. Compare these sites to **zappos.com/shoes**.

14. Examine two or three of the following sites: **prosper.com, paperbackswap.com, bigvine.net**, etc. Compare their business and revenue models.

TEAM ASSIGNMENTS AND PROJECTS

1. Read the opening case and answer the following questions:
   (a) In what ways you think Starbucks increases its brand recognition with its EC initiatives?
   (b) Some criticize My Starbucks Idea as an ineffective "show off." Find information about the pros and cons of the program. (See Starbucks Ideas in Action Blog).
   (c) Starbucks initiates discussions on Facebook about non-business topics such as the marriage equality bill, Why?
   (d) Discuss how customers are being kept involved and engaged in the various EC initiatives.
   (e) Starbucks believes that its digital and social initiatives are "highly innovative and cause dramatic changes in consumer behavior." Discuss.
   (f) View the video available at Stelzner (2010), (8 minutes) and answer the following:
      1. How does Starbucks uses video marketing in social media?
      2. How does the company listen to their customers?
      3. What are some tips for success and for things to avoid?
      4. Enter **facebook.com/Starbucks**. Summarize your impressions of the site.

2. Each team will research two EC success stories. Members of the group should examine companies that operate solely online and some that extensively utilize a click-and-mortar strategy. Each team should identify the critical success factors for their companies and present a report to the other teams.

3. Watch the video *Part 1-E-Commerce* (8 minutes) at **youtube.com/watch?v=OY2tcQ574Ew.**
   (a) Update all the data shown in the video.
   (b) What fundamental change is introduced by EC?
   (c) What is the first mover advantage discussed in the video?
   (d) Amazon.com and other companies that lost money during the time the video was made are making a lot of money today; find out why.
   (e) Identify all the EC business models discussed in the video.
   (f) How can one conduct an EC business from home?
   (g) EC is considered a disruptor. In what ways?

4. Conduct a search on 'social business.' Start at **eweek.com**. Divide the work between several

teams, each team covers one topic and each team writes a report.

5. Research the status of self-driven cars. Start by reading Neil (2012). Outline the pro and con points. Why this is considered an EC. Make a presentation.

6. Find the recent report on 'HBR/McKinsey M-Prize for Management Innovation at **mixprize.org/m-prize/innovating-innovation**. Identify the e-commerce cases among the 20 finalists. What is unique in each case?

7. Compare Net-a-Porter with Myhabit from Amazon and other sites that discount designer items. Also, see what Groupon offers in this area. Analyze the competitive advantage of each. Write a report.

CLOSING CASE: E-COMMERCE AT THE NATIONAL FOOTBALL LEAGUE (NFL)

Professional sports are multibillion-dollar businesses in the United States and they are growing rapidly in many other countries. The National Football League (NFL), which consists of 32 teams, is a premier brand of the most popular sport in the United States – football. The NFL uses e-commerce and other information technologies extensively to run its business efficiently. The following are some examples of e-commerce activities the NFL conducts both at the corporate level and the individual team level.

Selling Online

In addition to the official store (**nflshop.com**) and the individual team stores, (e.g., the Atlanta Falcons), there are dozens of independent stores that sell authentic as well as replicas of jerseys, hats, shirts, and other team merchandise. Most of these sales are done online, which enables you to buy your favorite team's items from anywhere; you can also save with coupons. It is basically a multibillion-

dollar B2C business, supported by search and shopping tools (see Chapter 2), including price comparisons (e.g., compare prices at **bizrate.com/ electronics-cases-bags**).

Several online stores sell tickets for NFL events, including resale tickets. For example, see **ticketsnow.com/nfl-tickets**.

Selling in China

In October 2013, the NFL opened its official online store in China (**nfl.tmall.com**). To embark on this venture the NFL used two partners: Export Now to handle all the administration of the transactions, and Tmall.com (China's leading EC seller with over 500 million registered members).

Information, News, and Social Networks

The NFL is on Facebook where there is a company description and many posts by its fans. It is also on Twitter where you can find information on upcoming NFL events, and be one of its 4,000,000+ followers. You can also get local news including real-time sports scores texted to your smartphone. The popularity of social media used by players created a need for a policy regarding the use of social networks before and after (but not during) games. For the policy, see the article titled "Social Media Before, After Games" at **sports.espn.go.com/nfl/news/story?id= 4435401**.

Videos and Fantasy Games

Madden NFL 11 is a video game available across all major consoles with an adaptation for iPhone and iPad versions of the game. For details see **en.wikipedia.org/wiki/Madden_ NFL_11**. Related to these games are the NFL fantasy games that are available for free at **fantasy.nfl.com**.

Smartphone Experience

Smartphones, and especially iPhones, now allow users to go online to view games in real time (some are costly). You can also use the iPhone to view photos in the stadium that are projected on TV, and much more (e.g., for many applications see McCafferty 2008).

Wireless Applications in Stadiums

Several stadiums are equipped with state-of-the-art wireless systems. One example is the University of Phoenix Stadium, which is the home of the Arizona Cardinals. Fans can access many high-definition TVs in real time. Fans with smartphones can get real-time scores or purchase food and other merchandise. The system also enables employees to process ticket sales quickly. Also, fans can watch the game while buying food in the stadium. The Cardinal's marketing department can advertise the forthcoming games and other events on the system. It also delivers data to coaches as needed during games. A similar system (used in the Sun Life Stadium, home of the Miami Dolphins) enables personalized replay during games (see the video about a special portable device titled "Miami Dolphins Transform Sun Life Stadium into Entertainment Destination for Fans" at **youtube.com/watch?v=t2qErS7f17Y**). Also, you can order food online, have it delivered to your seat, and pay for it electronically. Finally, you can play fantasy games while in the stadium. These EC applications are designed to make fans happy and to generate revenue.

Other Applications

The NFL uses many other EC applications for the management of transportation to the Super Bowl, security implementation, procurement (B2B), providing e-CRM, and much more.

    Sources*: Based on McCafferty (2008), Hickins (2009), and material collected on Facebook, and Twitter (accessed February 2014).

Questions

1. Identify all applications related to B2C in online stores.
2. Identify all B2C applications inside the stadium.
3. Identify all B2E applications inside the stadium.
4. Relate online game playing to EC at NFL.
5. Compare the NFL information available on Facebook and on Twitter.
6. Find additional NFL-related applications not cited in this case.
7. Enter **www.ignify.com/Atlanta_Falcons_eCommerce_Case_Study.html**. Read the case "Atlanta Falcons E-Commerce Case Study," then go to the Falcons' online store and describe all major EC models that are used there.
8. Find information on ball tracking technology that can be used by the NFL.
9. Compare *Madden NFL 11* with NFL fantasy games.

ONLINE RESOURCES
available at **affordable-ecommerce-textbook.com/turban**

ONLINE FILES

W1.1 Application Case: Dell – Using E-Commerce for Success

W1.2 Application Case: Campusfood.com – Student Entrepreneurs

W1.3 Major Characteristics of Web 2.0

W1.4 Representative EC Business Models

COMPREHENSIVE EDUCATIONAL WEBSITES

ecommercebusinessjournal.com: Source for news, events, etc., about e-commerce.

dictionary.reference.com: Just enter the topic of your interest.

libguides.rutgers.edu/ecommerce: The Electronic Resource Guide offers resources and links to Internet statistics – see ClickZ Stats, Nielsen/NetRatings, U.S. Census Bureau, and comScore.

ecommerce-europe.eu: A source of e-commerce news in Europe.

webopedia.com: Online encyclopedia dedicated to computer technology.

whatis.techtarget.com: Detailed definitions of most e-commerce and other technological topics.

digitalintelligencetoday.com: A comprehensive resources for social commerce activities.

GLOSSARY

Brick-and-mortar (old economy) organizations Purely physical organizations (corporations) doing business offline.

Business model The manner in which business is done to generate revenue and create value.

Business-to-business (B2B) All transactions take place between and among organizations.

Business-to-consumer (B2C) Retail transactions of products or services from businesses to individual shoppers.

E-tailing Online retailing, usually B2C.

Business-to-business-to-consumer (B2B2C) A business (B1) sells a product to another business (B2). B2 then sells or gives away the product to individuals who may be B2's own customers or employees.

Business-to-employees (B2E) The delivery of services, information, or products from organizations to their employees.

Click-and-mortar (click-and-brick) organizations Organizations that conduct some e-commerce activities, usually as an additional marketing channel.

Collaborative commerce (c-commerce) Refers to online activities and communications done by parties working to attain the same goal.

Consumer-to-business (C2B) People use the Internet to sell products or services to individuals and organizations. Alternatively, individuals use C2B to bid on products or services.

Consumer-to-consumer (C2C) E-commerce category in which individual consumers sell to or buy from other consumers.

Corporate portal A gateway for customers, employees, and partners to reach corporate information and to communicate with the company.

Digital economy An economy that is based on online transactions, mostly e-commerce. Also called the *Internet economy.*

Digital enterprise A new business model that uses IT to gain competitive advantage by increasing employee productivity, by improving efficiency and effectiveness of business processes and by better interactivity between vendors and customers.

E-business A broader definition of EC, not just the buying and selling of goods and services, but conducting all kinds of business online such as servicing customers, collaborating with business partners, delivering e-learning, and conducting electronic transactions within an organization.

E-government A government agency buys or provides goods, services, or information from or to businesses (G2B) or from or to individual citizens (G2C). Governments can deal also with other governments (G2G).

Electronic commerce (EC) Using the Internet and intranets to purchase, sell, transport, or trade data, goods, or services.

Electronic market (e-marketplace) An online location where buyers and sellers conduct commercial transactions such as selling goods, services, or information.

Ethics Standards of right and wrong.

Extranet A network that uses Internet technology to link intranets of several organizations in a secure manner.

F-commerce Rapidly increasing commercial activities conducted on or facilitated by Facebook.

Intrabusiness EC E-commerce category that refers to EC transactions among various organizational departments and individuals.

Intranet An internal corporate or government network that uses Internet tools, such as Web browsers, and Internet protocols.

Sharing economy An economic system constructed around the concept of sharing goods and services among the participating people.

Social business "An organization that has put in place the strategies, technologies and processes to systematically engage all the individuals of its ecosystem (employees, customers, partners, suppliers) to maximize the co-created value." (Social Business Forum 2012)

Social commerce The e-commerce activities conducted in social networks by using social software.

Social computing Computing systems that involve social interactions and behavior.

Social (digital) customers Members of social networks who share opinions about products, services, and vendors, do online social shopping, and understand their rights and how to use the wisdom and power of social communities to their benefit.

Social enterprise These organizations embrace the main goal of focusing on social issues. The enterprises generate revenue. The profits do not go to owners and shareholders, but are put back into the company and used toward building positive social change.

Social media Involves user generated online text, image, audio, and video content that are delivered via Web 2.0 platforms and tools. The media is used primarily for social interactions and conversations such as to share opinions, experiences, insights, and perceptions and to collaborate, all online.

Social networking The execution of any Web 2.0 activity, such as blogging or having a presence in a social network. It also includes all activities conducted in social networks.

Social network A social entity composed of nodes (which are generally individuals, groups, or organizations) that are connected by links such as hobbies, friendship or profession. The structures are often very complex.

Social networking service (SNS) A service that builds online communities by providing an online space for people to build free homepages and that provides basic communication and support tools for conducting different activities in the social network.

Tendering (bidding) system System through which large organizational buyers make large-volume or large-value purchases (also known as a *reverse auction*).

Value proposition Refers to the benefits, including the intangible ones that a company hopes to derive from using its business model.

Virtual (pure-play) organizations Organizations that conduct their business activities solely online.

Virtual world A 3-D computer-based simulated environment built and owned by its residents. In addition to creating buildings, people can create and share cars, clothes, and many other items. Community members inhabit virtual spaces and interact and socialize via *avatars*.

Web 2.0 The second generation of Internet-based tools and services that enables users to easily generate content, share media, and communicate and collaborate, in innovative ways.

REFERENCES

Ad Age Staff. "How Western Brands Are Tapping into China's Crazy-Big E-Commerce Holiday." *Ad Age #Protips*, November 4, 2013.

Ahmad, I. "100 Most Startling Tech Facts, Figures, and Statistics from 2013 [Infographic]." January 2, 2014. **socialmediatoday.com/irfan-ahmad/2033741/100-most-startling-tech-facts-figures-and-statistics-2013-infographic** (accessed February 2015).

Alter, A. "My Virtual Summer Job." May 16, 2008. **online.wsj.com/news/articles/SB121088619095596515** (accessed February 2015).

Anderlini, J. "The Billionaire Determined to Transformed His Country." *Financial Times*, December 17, 2013.

Bates, D., and Money Online. *Making Money Online: Making Your First Thousand Dollars from the Internet has Never Been this Easy! Generate a Huge Monthly Passive Income from Home. Start...to Make Money Online with Proven Methods!* [Kindle Edition], Seattle, WA: Amazon Digital Services, 2014.

Belicove, M. "How Starbucks Builds Meaningful Customer Engagement via Social Media." April 1, 2010. **openforum.com/articles/how-starbucks-builds-meaningful-customer-engagement-via-social-media-1** (accessed February 2015).

Bisson, P., E. Stephenson, and S. P. Viguerie. "The Global Grid." *McKinsey Quarterly*, June 2010.

BizReport. "More People Using Online Tools, Platforms to Shop." May 10, 2012. **bizreport.com/2012/05/more-people-using-online-tools-platforms-to-shop.html** (accessed February 2015).

Blakely, L. "Making Their Point." *Business 2.0*, April 23, 2007.

Brodie, J. "The Amazon of Fashion." *Fortune*, September 14, 2009.

Buczynski, B. *Sharing is Good: How Save Money, Time and Resources through Collaborative Consumption*. Gabriola Island, BC Canada: New Society Publishers, 2013.

Burke, A. "How a 15-Year-Old Entrepreneur Got Her Product into Nordstrom." December 23, 2013. **news. yahoo.com/blogs/profit-minded/15-old-entrepreneur-got-her-product-nordstrom-233738356.html** (accessed February 2015).

Callari, R. "Starbuck's Social Media Menu Adds Exclusive Content and Happy Hours?" October 10, 2010. **inventorspot.com/articles/starbucks_social_media_menu_adds_exclusive_content_happy_hours** (accessed February 2015).

Cerrato, P. "Children's Medical Center Dallas Gets Social." *Information Week*, September 17, 2012.

Chaney, P. "Super Bowl XLVI Gets Its Game on with First-Ever Social Media Command Center." February 3, 2012. **digitalintelligencetoday.com/super-bowl-xlvi-gets-its-game-on-with-first-ever-social-media-command-center-screenshots** (accessed February 2015).

Chui, M., M. Dewhurst, and L. Pollak. "Building the Social Enterprise." *McKinsey Quarterly*, November 2013.

Chui, M., J. Manyika, J. Bughin, R. Dobbs, C. Roxburgh, H. Sarrazin, G Sands, and M. Westergren. "The Social Economy: Unlocking Value and Productivity through Social Technologies." *McKinsey Quarterly*, July 2012.

Colby, K. L. "Web 2.0 Technology for the New Generation. Simplify. Simplify. Simplify. (TECHNOLOGY)." *Alaska Business Monthly*, December 2008.

Cook, S. "Google's Self-Driving Cars, and How Society Copes with New Technology." September 7, 2012. **geek.com/news/googles-self-driving-cars-and-how-society-copes-with-new-technology-1492453** (accessed February 2015).

CPC Andrew. "50 Value Propositions for Ecommerce Retailers." *CPC Strategy*, July 12, 2012. **cpcstrategy. com/blog/2012/07/50-value-propositions-for-ecommerce-retailers** (accessed May 2014).

Daugherty, P. "From Digitally Disrupted to Digital Disrupter." 2014. **accenture.com/microsite/it-technology-trends-2014/Documents/TechVision/Downloads/Accenture_Technology_Vision_2014. pdf** (accessed May 2014).

Drucker, P. *Managing in the Next Society*. New York: Truman Talley Books, 2002.

Edwards, S., *Web 2.0 Guide- Tools and Strategy for the New Internet Wave*, [Kindle] Amazon Digital Services, 2013.

eMarketer. "Quick Stat: 72.6 Percent of Internet Users Will Buy Online in 2011." July 26, 2011. **scoop.it/t/ retail/p/324190325/quick-stat-72-6-of-internet-users-will-buy-online-in-2011-the-emarketer-blog** (accessed February 2015).

Enterprise Innovation Editors. "A Whole Host of Predictions for 2014 and Beyond." December 31, 2013. **enterpriseinnovation.net/article/whole-host-predictions-2014-and-beyond-1771618066** (accessed May 2014).

Fortune. "Top 10 Social Media Stars." May 3, 2012. **money.cnn.com/galleries/2012/fortune/1205/ gallery.500-social-media.fortune** (accessed February 2015).

Fowler, G. "Report Card? How About that Annual Report?" May 6, 2010. **online.wsj.com/news/articles/SB1000142405274870434260457522209364123 7212** (accessed February 2015).

Gartner Inc. "Gartner Says Companies Will Generate 50 Percent of Web Sales via Their Social Presence and Mobile Applications by 2015." October 19, 2011. **gartner.com/newsroom/id/1826814** (accessed February 2015).

Gartner Inc. "Gartner Says Worldwide Sales of Mobile Phones Declined 2.3 Percent in Second Quarter of 2012." August 14, 2012. **gartner.com/newsroom/ id/2120015** (accessed February 2015).

Gaskin, S., and A. Evans. *Go! With Ethics in Cyberspace Getting Started*. Upper Saddle River, NJ: Pearson Prentice Hall, 2010.

Gembarski, R. "How Starbucks Built an Engaging Brand on Social Media." February 6, 2012. **brandingpersonality.com/how-starbucks-built-an-engagin-brand-on-social-media** (accessed February 2015).

Harrington, R. "The Transformer" (an e-mail interview with *Baseline*'s editor-in-chief, J. McCormick). *Baseline*, April 2006.

Hickins, M. "Arizona Cardinals Score Technology Touchdown." *IT Infrastructure*, March 11, 2009.

Hinchcliffe, D., et al. *Social Business by Design: Transformative Social Media Strategies for the Connected Company*. Hoboken, NJ: Jossey-Bass/ Wiley, 2012.

Hiner, J. "Four Industries about to be Transformed by the Internet." September 6, 2011, **techrepublic.com/blog/ tech-sanity-check/four-industries-about-to-be-transformed-by-the-internet** (accessed February 2015).

Hunt, M. "Make Money Online." *Womansday.com*, October 1, 2010.

IBM, "Social Business: The Advent of a New Age," A White Paper, April 2011. Available for download at **informationweek.com/whitepaper/Internet/the-social-business-advent-of-a-new-age-wp136687905 5?articleID=191708356** (accessed November 2014).

Joyner, A. *The eBay Billionaire's Club*. Hoboken, NJ: Wiley Publications, 2007.

Karakas, F. "Welcome to World 2.0: The New Digital Ecosystem." *Journal of Business Strategy*, 3, no. 4 (2009).

Katic, M. and K. Pusara. "Adoption of eCommerce Terminology." Proceedings of the 17th Bled eCommerce Conference eGlobal, Bled, Slovenia, June 21–23, 2004.

Knight, K. "ComScore: Desktop Spending Up." *BizReport*, May 21, 2013.

Khosrow-Pour, M., *E-Commerce for Organizational Development and Competitive Advantage*, Hershey, PA: IGI Global, 2013.

Leggatt, H. "UK: Half of Domino's Pizza Sales Online." February 16, 2012. **bizreport.com/2012/02/uk-almost-half-of-dominos-pizza-sales-online.html** (accessed February 2015).

Levy, S. *In The Flex: How Google Thinks, Works, and Shapes Our Lives*. New York: Simon and Schuster, 2011.

Li, F., and T. Han. "Singles' Day Spurs Industry Rally." *China Daily Hong Kong Edition*, November 25, 2013.

Loeb, W. "Starbucks: Global Coffee Giant Has New Growth Plans." *Forbes* January 31, 2013.

Maitra, D. "E-Commerce Is a New Dream for India Inc." *Deccan Herald*, April 14, 2013.

Manyika, J., Y. Chen, M. Chui, S. Lund, and J. Remes. "Disruptive Technologies: Advances That Will Transform Life, Business, and the Global Economy." McKinsey Global Institute. May (2014). **mckinsey.com/insights/business_technology/disruptive_technologies** (accessed May 2014).

Marsden, P. "Starbucks F-Commerce + M-Commerce = New Gold Standard." May 7, 2010. **digitalintelligencetoday.com/starbucks-f-commerce-m-commerce-new-gold-standard** (accessed February 2015).

Mashable. "There Will Be More Smartphones Than Humans on the Planet by Year's End." [video] February 14, 2012. **mashable.com/2012/02/14/more-smartphones-than-humans** (accessed February 2015).

McCafferty, D. "How the NFL Is Using Business Technology and Information Technology Together." *Baseline*, August 8, 2008.

McDonald, R. "Inside P&G's Digital Revolution." *McKinsey Quarterly*, November 2011.

Murphy, C. "The Internet of Things." *Information Week*, August 13, 2012.

Neil, D. "Who's Behind the Wheel? Nobody." *The Wall Street Journal*, September 24, 2012.

Nutley, M. "Forget E-Commerce; Social Commerce Is Where It's At." July 28, 2010. **marketingweek.co.uk/forget-e-commerce-social-commerce-is-where-its-at/3016388.article** (accessed February 2015).

Pantic, M. "How to Make Money from a Website – 55 Ways to Bring in the Cash." August 31, 2013. **business2community.com/online-marketong/make-money-website-55-ways-bringing-in-the-cash-0601137** (accessed February 2015).

Pepitone, J. "7 Craziest Things Connected to the Internet." September 18, 2012, **money.cnn.com/gallery/technology/2012/09/18/internet-of-things/4.html** (accessed February 2015).

Peterson, A. "China Has Almost Twice as Many Internet Users as the U.S. Has People." January 31, 2014. **washingtonpost.com/blogs/the-switch/wp/2014/01/31/china-has-almost-twice-as-many-internet-users-as-the-u-s-has-people** (accessed February 2015).

Piastro, M. "The Top 10 Trends Shaping the Future of Ecommerce." November 8, 2010. **imediaconnection.com/content/27969.asp** (accessed February 2015).

Plunkett, J. W., et.al. (eds.), *Plunkett's E-Commerce & Internet Business Almanac 2014 (Plunkett's E-Commerce and Internet Business Almanac)*, Houston, TX: Plunkett Research Ltd., 2014.

Rappa, M. "Business Models on the Web." January 17, 2010. **digitalenterprise.org/models/models.html** (accessed February 2015).

Rowe, R. "Facebook and Twitter Impact Fashion Industry." May 19, 2010. **goshtv.com/2010/05/19/facebook-and-twitter-impact-fashion-industry** (accessed February 2015).

Rymaszewski, M., et al. *Second Life: The Official Guide*. Indianapolis, IN: Wiley Publishers, Inc., 2008.

Shelly, G. B., and M. Frydenberg. *Web 2.0: Concepts and Applications*. Independence, KY: Course Technology, 2010.

Shih, C. *The Facebook Era: Tapping Online Social Networks to Market, Sell and Innovate*, 2nd ed. Upper Saddle River, N.J.: Prentice Hall, 2011.

Simply Zesty. "The 50 Best Examples of Social Commerce in Action." September 19, 2011. **simplyzesty.com/Blog/Article/September-2011/The-50-Best-Examples-Of-Social-Commerce-In-Action-An-eBook** (accessed February 2015).

Smith, B. "The Oprah Guide to Using Social Media to Build Her Business." April 8, 2012. **socialmediatoday.com/content/oprah-guide-using-social-media-build-her-business**. Accessed Nov 2014.

Smith, N., R. Wollan, and C. Zhou. *The Social Media Management Handbook*. Hoboken, NJ: Wiley, 2011.

Solis, B. *The End of Business As Usual: Rewire the Way You Work to Succeed in the Consumer Revolution*. Hoboken, NJ: Wiley, 2012.

Stanley, T. and R. Ritacca. "E-Commerce in China: Driving a New Consumer Culture." *KPMG Report*, January 2014.

Stelzner, M. "How Starbucks Engages Millions of Facebook Fans." May 20, 2010, **socialmediaexaminer.com/how-starbucks-engages-millions-of-facebook-fans** (accessed February 2015).

Strategic Direction. "DotCom Boom and Bust: The Secrets of E-Commerce Failure and Success." February 2005.

Taft, D. K. "Enterprise Applications: IBM Goes Social: 25 Examples of Big Blue Becoming a Social Business." January 19, 2012a. **eweek.com/c/a/Enterprise-Applications/IBM-Goes-Social-25-Examples-of-Big-Blue-Becoming-a-Social-Business-601979** (accessed February 2015).

Taft, D. K. "Enterprise Applications: Why IBM Smarter Commerce Focuses on the Digital Customer." September 10, 2012b. **eweek.com/it-management/slideshows/Why-IBM-Smarter-Commerce-Focuses-on-the-Digital-Customer** (accessed February 2015).

Teicher, D. "What Marketers Can Learn from Starbucks' Foursquare Stumble." *Advertising Age*, July 27, 2010.

Thomas, J. "Google's Self-Driving Car, the Justin Bieber of The Car World." *San Jose Mercury News*, January 21, 2014.

Tice, C. "Emerging Jobs in Social Media." 2010. **humboldt.edu/career/tips/735** (accessed February 2014).

Turban, E., J. Strauss, and L. Lai. *Social Commerce*. New York: Springer, 2015.

U.S. Census Bureau. "E-Stats." May 23, 2013. **census.gov/econ/estats** accessed February 2014).

Van Grove, J. "How Starbucks Is Turning Itself into a Tech Company." *Social*, June 12, 2012. **venturebeat.com/2012/06/12/starbucks-digital-strategy** (accessed February 2015).

Van Toorn, C., D. Bunker, K. Yee, and S. Smith. "The Barriers to the Adoption of E-Commerce by Micro Businesses, Small Businesses and Medium Enterprises." *Sixth International Conference on Knowledge, Culture, and Change in Organisations*, Prato, Tuscany, Italy, July 11–14, 2006.

Vizard, M. "Jaguar Launches Virtual Shopping Experiences." *CIO Insight*, June 5, 2013.

Walsh, M. "Starbucks Surpasses 10 Million Fans, Closing in on Lady Gaga." July 14, 2010. **mediapost.com/appy-awards/article/131970/starbucks-surpasses-10-million-fans-closing-in-on.html** (accessed February 2015).

Wang, S., and E. Pfanner. "Online Shopping Marathon Zooms Off the Blocks in China." *The New York Times*, November 11, 2013.

Webster, K. "S-Commerce- A Fourth Retail Channel: An Overview of Social Commerce and What's Fueling Its Growth." November 20, 2010, **pymnts.com/business-wire/2010/s-commerce-a-fourth-retail-channel-an-overview-of-social-commerce-and-what-s-fueling-its-growth** (accessed February 2015).

Wilfred, M. "Struggling Retailers Report Change in Shopping Trends." February 2, 2014. **sproutwired.com/struggling-retailers-report-change-in-shopping-trends/185173** (accessed February 2015).

Willgren, S. "Farmers Online: Old Traditions, Modern Technology." *The Epoch Times* (Toronto, Canada), June 20–26, 2013.

York, E. B. "Starbucks Gets Its Business Brewing Again with Social Media." February 22, 2010. **adage.com/article/special-report-digital-alist-2010/digital-a-list-2010-starbucks-brewing-social-media/142202** (accessed February 2015).

E-Commerce: Mechanisms, Platforms, and Tools

2

Contents

Electronic supplementary material The online version
of this chapter (doi: 10.1007/978-3-319-10091-3_2)
contains supplementary material, which is available to
authorized users

Learning Objectives

Upon completion of this chapter, you will be able to:
1. Describe the major electronic commerce (EC) activities and processes and the mechanisms that support them.
2. Define e-marketplaces and list their components.
3. List the major types of e-marketplaces and describe their features.
4. Describe electronic catalogs, search engines, and shopping carts.
5. Describe the major types of auctions and list their characteristics.
6. Discuss the benefits and limitations of e-auctions.
7. Describe bartering and negotiating online.
8. Describe virtual communities.
9. Describe social networks as EC mechanisms.
10. Understand virtual worlds and their use in EC.
11. Describe the emerging technologies of augmented reality and crowdsourcing.
12. Describe Web 3.0 and define Web 4.0.

OPENING CASE: PINTEREST: A NEW KID ON THE E-COMMERCE BLOCK

An e-commerce site talked about a great deal since 2011 is Pinterest.

The Opportunity

Pinterest is a social bookmarking website where users "pin" images on a virtual "pinboard." The social bookmarking of images has been practiced on the Internet all over the world, for several years. The company's founders saw the business potential and the success of similar companies in Brazil and China. Furthermore, they succeeded in attracting initial venture capital (see Chapter 16) to expand the business. For a guide, see Leland (2013), and for statistics, see Smith (2014).

The Solution

Pinterest is a company that provides virtual pinboards that allow users to organize and share images found on the Web (referred to as "pins"). The pinned images ("boards") are organized by any category the user wants and placed on a virtual pinboard, just like on a real bulletin board. For example, one can collect pictures of sailboats and pin them on one pinboard, with appropriate text explanation. You can collect decorations for your home on another pinboard, while you collect Chinese recipes on a third pinboard. Millions of people create pinboards and anyone can search and view them. You can also add friends to your account and "follow" them. According to their website, 'Pinterest is a tool for collecting and organizing the things that inspire you' (see **about.pinterest.com/**). For more about what Pinterest is and how it works, see **sheknows.com/living/articles/852875/pinterest-what-it-is-how-to-use-it-and-why-youll-be-addicted**.

Having many visitors and a rapid growth rate are necessary but not sufficient for EC success. Viable business and revenue models are also needed.

The Business and Revenue Models

Pinterest does not have a formal revenue model. (The company is privately held and it does not have to report about such a model to the public.) It looks as though the company's current priority is growth, as expressed in its mission statement. Nevertheless, many people speculate about (or suggest) revenue opportunities for the company, some of which are provided next.

Yang's Suggestions

Quora Corporation posted a question on its website: "How does Pinterest generate revenue?" One of the most comprehensive answers received was provided by "Avid Pinterest User" Yang (2012) who presented 13 *potential* monetization opportunities in four categories: charging advertisers (e.g., see Dembosky 2013), charging e-commerce partners, charging users, and charging other B2B partners. Most of these opportunities have existed in EC for years (e.g., charging for premium services, creating an online retail shop, using an affiliate program, and building a comprehensive advertisement scheme).

Selling Data for Market Research and Analysis

Brave (2012) suggested selling customer data available on Pinterest to retailers who can use analytics, including data mining, to conduct market research using this data. Customer data may reveal important statistical associations and relationships between consumer behavior, content (e.g., product recommendations, personalization, ads), and services and products provided. These associations can be used for one-to-one relationships and segmentation, as well as for marketing promotions and advertisements. Retailers can use *affinity modeling* and analysis to ascertain relationships so retailers can better understand consumer purchasing behavior. This enables optimal marketing *communication strategies*. Brave also noted that by pinning and re-pinning at Pinterest, consumers show their affinity to certain themes or specific products. Brave provided the following types of affinity data: connection between products and themes, segmenting people based on their affinity to products, or to a collection of products in specific themes.

Other Suggestions for Doing Business on Pinterest

- Hemley (2012) provides 26 different suggestions in an A-Z guide (e.g., A=Add a Pinterest "Follow" and/or "Pin it" Button; B=Brands and Pinterest; C=Crowdsourcing and so forth)
- Hub Spot (**hubspot.com**) offers a free e-book titled "How to Use Pinterest for Business" (**offers.hubspot.com/how-to-use-pinterest-for-business**). It includes information such as

how to create a Pinterest business account and how Pinterest works.

- Mitroff (2012) suggested using the approach of Zappos Corporation. This approach, which is called *PinPointing*, involves product recommendations based on what customers pin. Pinterest may collaborate with retailers such as Zappos to jointly create product recommendations. (See **pinpointing.apps.zappos.com/**.)
- Wikipedia lists several potential revenue sources at **en.wikipedia.org/wiki/Pinterest**.
- For more suggestions see **business.pinterest.com/en/pinterest-guides**.

Using Pinterest for Advertising and Marketing

Most of the suggestions cited above, as well as suggestions by others, concentrate on advertising and marketing opportunities. For comprehensive coverage, see Cario (2013), Hayden (2012), and Miles and Lacey (2012). For how retailers can use Pinterest, see Jopson and Kuchler (2013).

Results and Managerial Issues

Pinterest is the fastest growing social network ever, and according to a marketing service (Experian 2012), Pinterest is the third most popular social network on the Web, behind Facebook and Twitter (up from 7th place in November 2011). As of July 2013, the total number of Pinterest users worldwide was 70 million (**smallbusiness.yahoo.com/advisor/30-reasons-market-business-pinterest-2014-infographic-184545665.html**).

Similar reports on this amazing growth rate and popularity are provided by comScore and other reporting companies. This growth has attracted over $200 million in venture capital in 2012/2013 and generated many suggestions on money-making possibilities with Pinterest (e.g., see Carr 2012; Loren and Swiderski 2012).

In January 2014, the valuation of Pinterest was about $3.8 billion. Should the company be able to generate significant revenue, it probably will go to the IPO route, in which case the valuation may be much higher. Let us look now at some managerial issues facing the company. Representative managerial issues are:

Legal Concerns

Many people collect images from the Internet to build their pinboards (and possibly a brand) without asking permission from the content creators, giving them an attribute, or compensating them. Some of the collected material is formally copyrighted; other material may be considered copyrighted. A similar problem exists with material used on Facebook or by bloggers. According to Pinterest's 'Terms of Use,' members are "solely responsible for what they pin and repin." Furthermore, users must have explicit permission from the owners of contents to post them. According to Shontell (2012), one lawyer deleted all her Pinterest boards out of fear of copyright violation. Note that Pinterest places all blame and potential legal fees on its users (who may have to pay the legal fees incurred by Pinterest also). Pinterest has taken several steps to alleviate the legal concerns of users (e.g., see Hempel 2012). The company is continuously adding measures to minimize the legal problems. For example, in May 2012, the company added a feature that facilitates the attribution of credit to content creators. For a discussion, see Hornor (2012). Finally, legal concerns may include dealing with the spammers who are busy on the site.

The Competition

The popularity of Pinterest has resulted in many attempts to clone the company. Since the core concept is basically image sharing, it may not be patentable; therefore, competitors try to jump into niche markets. For example, TripAdvisor (**tripadvisor.com**) concentrates on travel. We Heart It (**weheartit.com**) is a Brazilian company (operating in the U.S.) that is very similar to Pinterest. An emerging competitor is Fancy (**fancy.com**), which partnered with Google+ in 2013. Several companies concentrate on adult entertainment and pornography. Indirect competitors are several Chinese companies that operate in a culturally different environment (see McKenzie 2012). Companies such as Facebook and Google may initiate a competitive service. Some believe that Pinterest may take business away from both Facebook and Twitter due to its better match with the business world.

Conclusion

According to Hempel (2012), Pinterest is more business oriented than Facebook or Twitter and visitors tend to buy more from there, although the latter companies drive more visitors to their sites. It seems that Pinterest has some potential benefits for small businesses (e.g., designers). Many companies already use Pinterest to derive benefits (e.g., see the Etsy case in Chapter 3 and Volpe 2012). However, these applications do not currently provide any revenue to Pinterest. The success of Pinterest will be determined by its revenue model and the company's profitability.

Sources: Based on Brave (2012), Carr (2012), Hempel (2012), Jopson and Kuchler (2013), Loren and Swiderski (2012), Yang (2012), and Volpe (2012).

LESSONS LEARNED FROM THE CASE

Pinterest is a social network that connects people who find interesting images on the Web. At the same time, Pinterest is a platform on which several activities of EC can be supported. For example, companies can build pinboards that promote their brands. Pinterest can be used as a platform for facilitating innovations via idea-generation and sharing. Pinterest is a derivative of Web 2.0 and social media and as such, it is a new mechanism for supporting EC. Other social media mechanisms that are covered in this chapter are social networks and virtual worlds; different types of social media tools such as blogs, microblogs, and wikis, are discussed in Online File W2.1. This chapter also covers the traditional mechanisms of EC such as marketplaces, merchant software, and auctions.

2.1 ELECTRONIC COMMERCE MECHANISMS: AN OVERVIEW

The many EC models and types of transactions presented in Chapter 1 are enabled by different mechanisms. To begin with, most B2C applications are conducted on the Internet. In addition, the generic enablers of any information system including databases, networks, security, software and server software, operating systems, hardware (Web servers), and hosting services need to be established. Added to the above are the specific EC mechanisms presented in this chapter, such as electronic markets, shopping carts, e-catalogs, and support services such as payment and order fulfillment. In addition to of all of the above, there are different methods for executing EC, such as buying at a fixed price or at an auction, and each method has a different support mechanism. Finally, there are the Web 2.0-based collaboration and communication mechanisms (e.g., Twitter) and special platforms such as the one used by Pinterest. In this chapter, we describe the major EC mechanisms so that you will be able to understand their uses in the forthcoming chapters.

EC Activities and Support Mechanisms

EC activities are divided into six categories, which are listed on the left side of Figure 2.1. Each activity is supported by one or more EC mechanisms, which are shown on the right side of Figure 2.1, along with the section number in this chapter where they are presented. Additional mechanisms exist for special activities, such as payment (Chapter 11), security (Chapter 10), and order fulfillment (Chapter 12). Also, standard IT technologies such as RFID, EDI, and extranets are described in Online Tutorial T2.

In the next section, we describe online markets. Before we do this, however, we will describe what happens during a typical purchasing process.

EC Activities   **EC Mechanism**

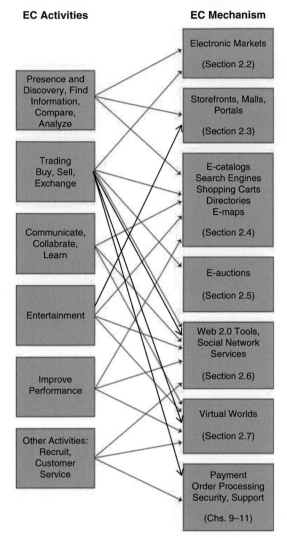

Figure 2.1   The EC activities–mechanism connection

The Online Purchasing Process

Customers buy goods online in different ways. The most common is purchasing from catalogs at fixed prices. Sometimes prices may be negotiated or discounted. Another way to determine price is *dynamic pricing*, which refers to non-fixed prices such as those in auctions or stock (commodity) exchanges.

The process starts with a buyer logging on to a seller's website, registering (if needed), and entering an online catalog or the buyer's "My Account." E-catalogs can be very large, so using a search engine may be useful. Buyers usually like to compare prices; therefore, an online price comparison service can be useful (now available on smartphones). Some sellers (e.g., American Airlines, Amazon.com) provide price comparisons showing competitors. If not satisfied, the buyer may abandon the seller's site. If satisfied, the buyer will place the chosen item in a virtual *shopping cart* (or bag). The buyer may return to the seller's catalog to choose more items. Each selected item is placed in the shopping cart. When the item selection is completed, the buyer goes to a checkout page, where a shipment option is selected from a menu (e.g., standard, next day). Finally, a payment option is selected. For example, **newegg.com** allows you to pay by credit card, PayPal, check after billing, in installments, and so on. After checking all the details for accuracy, the buyer *submits* the order. This process is illustrated in Figure 2.2.

The major mechanisms that support this process are described in Sections 2.3 and 2.4 of this chapter. The place where buying and selling occurs is called an *e-marketplace,* which we introduce next.

SECTION 2.1 REVIEW QUESTIONS
1. List the major EC activities.
2. List the major EC mechanisms.
3. Describe the online purchasing process

2.2   E-MARKETPLACES

Electronic markets play a central role in the digital economy, facilitating the exchange of information, goods, services, and payments. In executing the trading process, e-marketplaces create economic value for buyers, sellers, market intermediaries, as well as for society at large.

Markets (electronic or otherwise) have four major functions: (1) enabling transactions to occur by providing a meeting place for buyers and sellers; (2) enabling the flow of relevant information; (3) providing services associated with market transactions, such as payments and escrow; and (4) providing auxiliary services such as legal, auditing, and security (see Table 2.1).

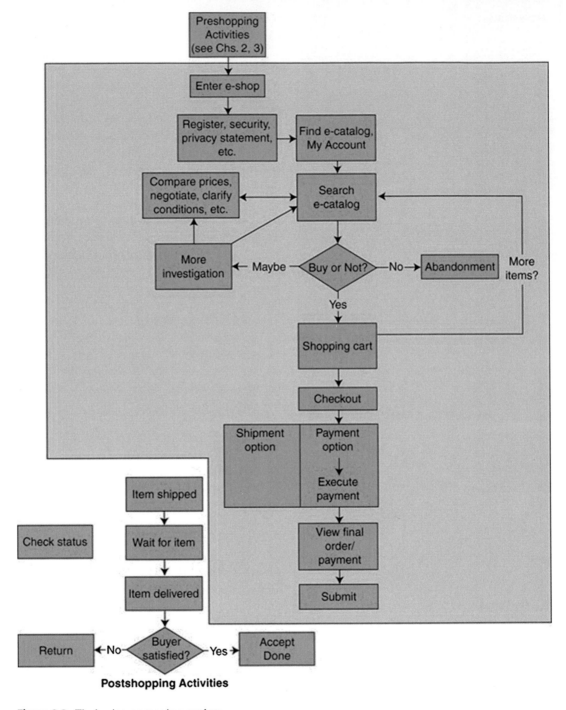

Figure 2.2 The buying process in e-markets

Electronic Markets

The *electronic market* is the major venue for conducting EC transactions. An **e-marketplace** (also called *e-market, virtual market,* or *marketspace*), is an electronic space where sellers and buyers meet and conduct different types of transactions. Customers receive goods and services for money (or for other goods and services, if bartering is used). The functions of an e-market are the same as those of a physical marketplace; however, computerized systems tend to make electronic markets much more efficient by providing more updated information and various support services, such as rapid and smooth executions of transactions.

EC has increased market efficiency by expediting and or improving the functions listed in Table 2.1. Furthermore, EC has been able to significantly decrease the cost of executing these functions.

The emergence of *electronic marketplaces*, especially Internet-enabled ones, has changed several of the processes used in trading and supply chains. In many cases, these changes, driven by technology, have frequently resulted in:

- Lower the search time for information and cost to buyers
- Reduced information misunderstanding between sellers and buyers
- Possible reduction in the time gap between purchase and possession of physical products purchased online (especially if the product can be digitized)
- The ability of market participants to be in different locations while trading online
- The ability to conduct transactions at any time (24/7) from any place.

Components of and the Participants in E-Marketplaces

The major components and players in a *marketspace* are customers, sellers, products and services (physical or digital), infrastructure, a front end, a back end, intermediaries and other business partners, and support services such as security and payments. A brief description of each follows:

- **Customers.** More than 2 billion Internet users worldwide are potential buyers of goods and services offered on the Internet. These consumers are looking for bargains, customized items, collectors' items, entertainment, socialization, and more. The social customers have more power than regular customers. They can search for detailed information, compare prices, bid, and sometimes negotiate. Buying organizations are also customers, accounting for more than 85% of EC volume and value activities.
- **Sellers.** Millions of webstores are advertising and offering a huge variety of items. These stores are owned by companies, government agencies, or individuals. Every day it is possible to find new offerings of products and services. Sellers can sell directly from their websites or from public e-marketplaces.
- **Products and services.** One of the major differences between the *marketplace* and the *marketspace* is the possible digitization of products and services in a marketspace. Although both types of markets can sell physical products, they can also sell **digital products**, which are goods that can be transformed into a digital format. However, in marketspaces, buyers can buy digitized products online, anytime and from any place in seconds, and receive the purchased goods instantly. In addition to the digitization of software, music, and airline tickets, it is possible to digitize dozens of other products and services, as shown in Online File W2.2. Digital products have different cost curves than those of physical products. In digitization, most of the costs are fixed, and variable costs are very low. Thus, profits

will increase rapidly as volume increases, once the fixed costs are paid.

- **Infrastructure.** The marketspace infrastructure includes electronic networks, databases, hardware, software, and more.
- **Front end.** Customers interact with a marketspace via a **front end.** The major components of the front end can include the seller's portal, electronic catalogs, a shopping cart, a search engine, an auction engine, a payment gateway, and all other activities related to placing orders.
- **Back end.** All the activities that are related to order aggregation and fulfillment, inventory management, purchasing from suppliers, accounting and finance, insurance, payment processing, packaging, and delivery are done in what is termed the **back end** of the business.

- **Intermediaries.** In marketing, an **intermediary** is typically a third party that operates between sellers and buyers. Intermediaries of all kinds offer their services on the Web. Some intermediation is done manually; many kinds are done electronically. The role of these electronic intermediaries is frequently different from that of regular intermediaries (such as wholesalers or retailers), as will be seen throughout the text, especially in Chapters 3 and 4. For example, online intermediaries create and manage the online markets. They help match buyers and sellers, provide escrow services, and help customers and/or sellers complete transactions. Physical intermediaries may be eliminated and their jobs be computerized (fully or partially) as described next.

Table 2.1 Functions of a market

Matching of buyers and sellers	Facilitation of transactions	Institutional infrastructure
• Determination of product offerings. Product features offered by sellers Aggregation of different products	• Communication Posting buyers' requests Posting RFQs	• Legal Commercial code, contract law, dispute resolution, intellectual property protection
• Search (buyers for sellers, and sellers for buyers) Price and product information Organizing bids and bartering Matching the seller's offerings with the buyer's preferences	• Mechanisms: provide catalogs, etc.	• Regulatory Rules and regulations, compliance, monitoring, enforcement
• Price discovery Process determination of prices Enabling price comparisons	• Logistics Delivery of information, goods, or services to buyer	• Discovery Provides market information (e.g., about competition, government regulations)
• Others Providing sales leads Providing W2.0 tools Arranging auction	• Settlement Transfer of payments to sellers Escrow services	
	• Trust Credit system, reputations, rating agencies such as *Consumer Reports* and the BBB, special escrow and online trust agencies	

Sources: Based on Bakos (1998), *E-Market Services* (2006), and the authors' experiences

Disintermediation and Reintermediation

Intermediaries usually provide three types of services: (1) they provide relevant information about demand: supply, prices, and trading requirements. (2) they help match sellers and buyers; and/or (3) they offer value-added services such as transfer of products, escrow, payment arrangements, consulting, or assistance in finding a business partner. In general, the first and second types of services can be fully automated, and thus it is likely to be assumed by e-marketplaces, info-mediaries, and portals that provide free or low-fee services. The third type requires expertise, such as knowledge of the industry, the market, the products, and the technological trends, and therefore can only be partially automated.

Intermediaries that provide only (or mainly) the first two types of services may be eliminated; this phenomenon is called **disintermediation**. An example is the airline industry and its push for selling electronic tickets directly by the airlines. Most airlines require customers to pay $25 or more per ticket processed by an employee via telephone. This results in the *disintermediation* of many travel agents from the purchasing process. In another example, discount stockbrokers that only execute trades manually are disappearing. However, brokers who manage electronic intermediation are not only surviving but may also be prospering (e.g., **priceline.com** and **expedia.com** in the travel industry and **tdameritrade.com** in stock trading). This phenomenon, in which disintermediated entities or newcomers take on new intermediary roles, is called *reintermediation* (see Chapter 3).

Disintermediation is more likely to occur in supply chains involving several intermediaries, as illustrated by Case 2.1.

CASE 2.1: EC APPLICATION: HOW BLUE NILE INC. IS CHANGING THE JEWELRY INDUSTRY

Blue Nile Inc. (**bluenile.com**), a pure-play online e-tailer that specializes in diamonds and jewelry, capitalized on online diamond sales as a dot-com start-up in 1999. The company is a textbook case of how EC fundamentally changes the way that an industry conducts its business. For information about the company, see **quotes.wsj.com/NILE/company-people**.

The Opportunity

Using the B2C EC model – eliminating the need for physical stores – Blue Nile was able to offer discounts of 35%, yet it became profitable in a short time. (The cost of operating online stores is very low.)

What are the critical success factors of the company? First, they offer large discounts. For example, you can purchase a $6,000 diamond for $4,000, which attracts more customers. Second, Blue Nile offers a huge selection of diamonds online and provides more information about diamonds than many physical jewelry stores can offer. In May 2012, Blue Nile offered about 60,000 round diamonds that could be used to build a customized engagement rings. No physical store can offer so many diamonds. Third, the company provides educational guides as well as independent (and trusted) quality ratings for every stone. A customer can look over a rating scale for cut, clarity, color, and so on, and then compare prices using Bizrate (**bizrate.com**) and other online stores. Note that there usually is a 30-day 100% money-back guarantee (now an online industry standard). This provides customers with a comfort level of trust against fraud and gives Blue Nile a competitive edge against stores that take the stones back but charge a fee. The site provides live chat, payment options, build-your-own engagement ring, gift ideas, and much more. The company has a mobile app for iPhone and Android users (**m.bluenile.com**).

The Results

Blue Nile's sales reached $129 million in 2003 (a 79% increase over 2002), with a net income of $27 million. In 2013, net sales were $450 million (**marketwatch.com/story/blue-nile-announces-**

fourth-quarter-and-full-year-2013-financial-results-2014-02-06 and **investor.bluenile.com/releasedetail.cfm?ReleaseID=823747**). The company became the eighth-largest specialty jewelry company in the United States and went public in 2004 (one of the most successful IPOs of that year). While sales fell during the economic downturn in 2008, in 2009 and 2010 the company rallied again with a 2.3% growth.

In order to sell $450 million in jewelry in 1 year, a traditional retail chain needs over 300 stores and over 3,000 employees. Blue Nile does it with one 10,000-square-foot warehouse and 193 employees. The company also bypasses the industry's complex supply chain, in which a diamond may pass through five or more middlemen before reaching a retailer. Because they are a large buyer, they can deal directly with original suppliers.

As a result, some 465 small jewelry stores closed in 2003 alone. The survivors specialize in custom-crafted pieces. Large traditional companies compete with Blue Nile by offering online merchandise, becoming click-and-brick multi-channel organizations, and by streamlining their supply chain and customer service.

The future seems to be clear, as can be seen in Bloomberg (2004), in the case of Roger Thompson, a small jeweler in Lambertville, New Jersey, who said, "Anyone with half a brain who wants a diamond engagement ring will go to the Internet." In the meantime, grooms who propose with Blue Nile rings can save $3,000 to $5,000.

Note that, the competition in the jewelry business is very intense, not only from jewelry retailers (both offline and online, e.g., **bidz.com**; that now also sell fashion and apparel, fine art, and accessories), but also from general e-tailers such as **overstock.com** and **amazon.com**.

Sources: Based on Rivlin (2007), Bloomberg (2004), *BusinessWeek Online* (2006), **en.wikipedia.org/wiki/Blue_Nile_Company**, and **bluenile.com/about-blue-nile** (both accessed March 2015).

Questions

1. Using the classification of EC (Section 1.2, Chapter 1), how would you classify the Blue Nile's business?
2. In what ways is the company changing its industry?
3. What are the critical success factors of the company?
4. Research Blue Nile's affiliate marketing programs. Write a report. Include how this program helps Blue Nile.
5. Competition between Blue Nile and Amazon.com will continue to increase. In your opinion, which one will win? (Visit their websites and see how they sell jewelry.)
6. Compare the following three sites: **diamond.com**, **ice.com**, and **bluenile.com**.
7. Follow the performance of Blue Nile's stock since 2003 (symbol: NILE, go to **money.cnn.com**). Compare it to the performance of the market average. What is your conclusion?
8. Find the payment options at Blue Nile when you shop there.

Types of E-Marketplaces

The term *marketplace* differs once it referred to the Web. It is sometimes refers to as e-marketplace or marketspace. We distinguish two types of e-marketplaces: private and public.

Private E-Marketplaces

Private e-marketplaces are those owned and operated by a single company. **Starbucks.com**, **dell.com**, **target.com**, and **united.com** sell from their websites. Private markets are either sell-side or buy-side. In a **sell-side e-marketplace**, a company, (e.g., **net-a-porter.com** or **cisco.com**) will sell either standard or customized products to individuals (B2C) or to businesses (B2B); this type of selling is considered to be *one-to-many*. In a **buy-side e-marketplace,** a company purchases from many potential suppliers; this type of purchasing is considered to be *many-to-one*, and it is a B2B activity. For example, some hotels buy their supplies from approved vendors that come to its e-market. Walmart (**walmart.com**) buys goods from thousands of suppliers. Private marketplaces can be open only to selected members and are not publicly regulated. We will return to the topic of private e-marketplaces in Chapters 3 (B2C) and 4 (B2B).

Public E-Marketplaces

Public e-marketplaces are in many cases B2B markets. They often are owned by a third party (not a seller or a buyer) or by a group of buying or selling companies (referred to as a *consortium*), and they serve many sellers and many buyers. These markets also are known as *exchanges* (e.g., a stock exchange). They are open to the public and usually are regulated by the government or the exchange's owners. Public e-marketplaces (for B2B) are discussed in detail in Chapter 4.

SECTION 2.2 REVIEW QUESTIONS

1. Define e-marketplace and describe its attributes.
2. What is the difference between a physical marketplace and an e-marketplace (marketspace)?
3. List the components of a marketspace.
4. Define a digital product and provide five examples.
5. Describe private versus public e-markets.

2.3 CUSTOMER SHOPPING MECHANISMS: WEBSTORES, MALLS, AND PORTALS

Several kinds of interactions exist among sellers, buyers, and e-marketplaces. The major B2C mechanisms are *webstores (storefronts)* and *Internet malls*. Let us elaborate on these, as well as on the gateways to e-marketplaces – portals.

Webstores

A **webstore** (or **storefront**) refers to a single company's (or individual seller's) website where products and services are sold.

Webstores may target an industry, a location, or a niche market (e.g., **cattoys.com**). The webstore may belong to a manufacturer (e.g., **geappliances.com** and **dell.com**), to a retailer (e.g., **amazon.com** and **wishlist.com.au**), to individuals selling from home, or to another type of business. Note that companies that sell services (such as insurance) may refer to their webstores as *portals*.

A webstore includes tools known as *merchant software* (available in a suite), that are necessary for conducting online sales. The most common tools are an *electronic catalog*; a *search engine* that helps the consumer find products in the catalog; an *electronic shopping cart* for holding items until checkout; *e-auction facilities* where auctions take place; a *payment gateway* where payment arrangements can be made; a *shipment center* where shipping arrangements are made; and *customer services*, which include product and warranty information and CRM.

Microsites

A *microsite* is a webpage(s) that acts as a supplement to a primary website, but is external to it. It expands on the content by adding editorial, commercial, or educational material.

Electronic Malls

In addition to shopping at individual webstores, consumers can shop in electronic malls (e-malls). Similar to malls in the physical world, an **e-mall (online mall)** is an online shopping location where many stores present their catalogs. The mall charges commission from the sellers based on their sale volume. For example, the Emall of Maine (**emallofmaine.com**) is an e-mall that aggregates products, services, and providers in the state of Maine. It contains a directory of vacation services and product categories and the vendors in each category. When a consumer indicates the category he or she is interested in, the consumer is transferred to the appropriate independent *webstore*. This kind of mall does not provide any shared services; it is merely a directory. Other malls, such as **choicemall.com**, or **etsy.com** (see

Chapter 3) do provide some shared services. Both **yahoo.com** and **ebay.com** operate electronic malls.

Web (Information) Portals

A *portal* is an information gateway that is used in e-marketplaces, webstores, and other types of EC (e.g., in e-collaboration, intrabusiness, and e-learning). A **Web (information) portal** is a single point of access, through a Web browser, to critical business information located inside and outside of organizations. This information is aggregated and is accessed and presented in a consistent way. Many Web portals personalize for users. Note that wireless devices are becoming portals for both enterprise and Internet access. A schematic view of a portal is shown in Figure 2.3. Information sources (external and internal) are shown on the left side, and integrated and process data are shown as output on the monitor's screen. Web portals offer some generic services such as e-mail, news, stock prices, entertainment, shopping capabilities, and so forth.

Types of Portals

Portals can assume many shapes. One way to distinguish among them is to look at their content, which can vary from narrow to broad, and their community or audience, which also can differ. The major types of portals are as follows:

- **Commercial (public) portals.** These popular portals offer content for anyone. Although they can be customized by the user, they are still intended for broad audiences and offer fairly routine content, some in real time (e.g., a stock ticker and news). Examples of such sites are **yahoo.com**, **google.com**, and **msn.com**.
- **Corporate (private) portals.** Corporate portals provide organized access to internal corporate information. These also are known as *enterprise portals* or *enterprise information portals*. Corporate portals appear in different forms and are described in detail in Chapters 4 and 5. Examples of e-commerce portals can be found at **ibm.com/software/products/en/websphere-portal-family**.
- **Patient Portals.** Several companies offer patient portals. For example, Quality Systems, Inc. (**qsii.com**) and **mypop.healthcarepartners.com**. Quality Systems provides software for health care providers so they can offer information for their patients (in English, Spanish and Chinese) via a portal. Patients have access to their personal information. The portal also allows communication between patients and their caregivers. Called 'Next Gen Patient Portal the portal increases patients' engagement in their healthcare.
- **Publishing portals.** These portals are intended for communities with specific interests and involve relatively little customization of content; however, they provide extensive online search features and some interactive capabilities. Examples of such sites are **techweb.com** and **zdnet.com**.
- **Mobile portals.** Mobile portals are portals that are accessible from mobile devices (see Chapter 6 for details). An increasing number of portals are accessible via mobile devices. One example of such a mobile portal is i-mode, which is described in Chapter 6.
- **Voice portals.** Voice portals are websites, usually portals, with audio interfaces. This means that they can be accessed by a standard telephone or a cell phone. AOLbyPhone (**aolbyphone.com**) is an example of a service that allows users to retrieve e-mail, news, and other content from AOL via telephone. It uses both speech recognition and text-to-speech technologies. Products by

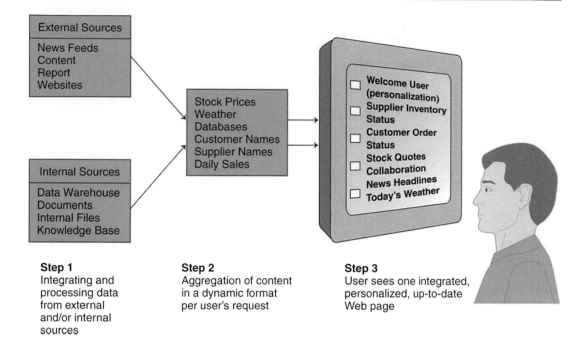

Step 1
Integrating and processing data from external and/or internal sources

Step 2
Aggregation of content in a dynamic format per user's request

Step 3
User sees one integrated, personalized, up-to-date Web page

Figure 2.3 How a portal works

companies such as Microsoft's Tellme (**tmaa.com/microsoftand247inc.html**) and Nuance OnDemand (**nuance.com/for-business/by-solution/customer-service-solutions/solutions-services/hosted-contact-center-solutions/index.htm**) offer access to the Internet from telephones, as well as tools to build voice portals. Voice portals are especially popular for 1–800 numbers (enterprise 800 numbers) that provide self-service to customers with information available in Internet databases (e.g., finding your balance or last deposit made at your bank).

- **Knowledge portals.** Knowledge portals enable easy access to knowledge by knowledge workers and facilitate collaboration.
- **Communities' portals.** These are usually parts of online communities. They are dedicated to some theme and may be sponsored by a vendor such as Sony.
- An example is 17173.co-- portal for gamers in China.

The Roles and Value of Intermediaries in E-Marketplaces

Intermediaries, such as brokers, play an important role in commerce by providing value-added activities and services to buyers and sellers. There are several types of intermediaries. The most well-known intermediaries in the physical world are wholesalers and retailers.

The two major types of *online intermediaries* are brokers and infomediaries.

Brokers

A *broker* in EC is a person or a company that facilitates transactions between buyers and sellers. The following are different types of brokers:

- **Trading.** A company that aids online trading (e.g., E*TRADE or eBay).
- **Organization of online malls.** A company that organizes many online stores in one place (e.g., Yahoo! Shopping and Alibaba.com).
- **Comparison agent.** A company that helps consumers compare prices, encourages

user comments, and provides customer service at different stores (e.g., Bizrate for a great diversity of products and Hotwire, Inc. for travel-related products and services.

- **Shopping aids provider.** A company that helps online shopping by providing escrow, payments, shipping, and security (e.g., PuntoMio, Inc.).
- **Matching services.** These services match entities such as jobs to applicants, and buyers to sellers.

Distributors in B2B

A special type of intermediary in e-commerce is the B2B *e-distributor*. These intermediaries connect manufacturers with business buyers (customers), such as retailers (or resellers in the computer industry). **E-distributors** aggregate product information from many manufacturers, sometimes thousands of them, in the e-distributor's catalog. An example is W.W. Grainger (**grainger. com**). The distributor buys the products and then sells them, as supermarkets do.

SECTION 2.3 REVIEW QUESTIONS

1. Describe webstores and e-malls.
2. List the various types of webstores and e-malls.
3. What are Web (information) portals? List the major types.
4. Describe e-distributors.

2.4   MERCHANT SOLUTIONS: ELECTRONIC CATALOGS, SEARCH ENGINES, AND SHOPPING CARTS

To enable selling online, a website usually needs *EC merchant server software.* Merchant software includes several tools and platforms. Such software offers basic tools that include electronic catalogs, search engines, and shopping carts; all are intended to facilitate the electronic trading process.

One example of such software is osCommerce, which is open-source software (see **oscommerce.com**). Another example can be seen at **smallbusiness.yahoo.com/ecommerce**.

Electronic Catalogs

Catalogs have been printed on paper for generations. Recently, electronic catalogs on a DVD (or CD-ROM) and on the Internet have gained popularity. **Electronic catalogs (e-catalogs)** consist of a product database, directory, and a presentation function. They are the backbone of most e-commerce sales sites. For merchants, the objective of e-catalogs is to advertise and promote products and services. For the customer, the purpose of such catalogs is to locate information on products and services. E-catalogs can be searched quickly with the help of search engines. Some offer tools for interactions. For an example, see Infinisys 'Change My Image' for Microsoft Windows at **en.infinisys.co.jp/product/cmimage**, and for Macintosh at **en.infinisys. co.jp/product/cmimage_mac**. This product permits a buyer to insert his/her photo and then change the hairstyle and color in the photo, so the buyer can see his/her look with a new hairstyle. E-catalogs can be very large; for example, Amazon.com's catalog contains millions of products.

Most early online catalogs were static presentations of text and messages from paper catalogs. However, online catalogs have evolved to become more dynamic, customizable, and integrated with selling and buying procedures, shopping carts, order taking, and payment. E-catalogs may include video clips. The tools for building them are being integrated with merchant software suites and Web hosting tools (e.g., see **smallbusiness.yahoo.com/ecommerce**). Examples of a simple product catalog can be seen at JetPens (**jetpens.com** and Starbucks Store (**store.starbucks.com**).

Although used only occasionally in B2C commerce, customized catalogs are used frequently in B2B e-commerce.

EC Search Activities, Types, and Engines

Search activities are popular in EC, and many tools for conducting searches are available. A study by Stambor (2010) published in *Internet Retailer* revealed that 94% of shoppers conduct research online before making any purchase, and 61% use a search engine when shopping online. Consumers may search inside one company's catalog to find a product or service, or use Google or Bing to find companies that sell the product they need. Here we describe only the essentials for EC search. For a video illustration, see "Google Commerce Search" (2009) by Google+ Your Business (2:15 minutes) at **youtube.com/watch?v=gj7qrotOmVY**. To read publications on electronic research and e-commerce at the Research at Google website, see **research.google.com/pubs/EconomicsandElectronic Commerce.html**. Let us now look at three major types of searches.

Types of EC Searches

The three major types of EC searches are *Internet/Web search, enterprise search,* and *desktop search.*

> **Internet/Web Search.** This is the most popular search that involves looking for any documents on the Web. According to Pew Research Internet Project (**pewinternet.org**) and other statistical sites (e.g., see **infoplease.com/ipa/A0921862.html**), finding information is one of the most frequent activities done on the Web.
>
> **Enterprise Search.** An **enterprise search** describes the search for information *within* the files and databases of an organization. For example, Google has a powerful Enterprise Search Appliance (known as GSA).
>
> **Desktop Search.** A **desktop search** involves a search of a user's own com-

> puter files (e.g., using **copernic.com** or **windows.microsoft.com/en-us/windows7/products/features/windows-search**). Searching for documents is done by looking through all the information that is available on the user's PC. A simple example is the ability to search all files related to your e-mail archive. A search also can be extended to photos, USB ports, and Word documents. For details, see **pcmag.com/encyclopedia/term/41175/desktop-search**.

All search types discussed above are accomplished by using search software agents.

Search Engines

Customers tend to ask for information (e.g., requests for product information or pricing) in similar ways. This type of request is repetitive, and answering such requests manually is costly. Search engines deliver answers economically and efficiently by matching questions with frequently asked question (FAQ) templates, which respond with "canned" answers. In general, a **search engine** is a computer program that can access databases of Internet or intranet resources, search for specific information or keywords, and report the results.

Google and Bing are the most popular search engines in the U.S. Baidu is the primary search engine in China. Portals such as Yahoo! and MSN have their own search engines. Special search engines organized to answer certain questions or search in specified areas include **ask.com**, **mamma.com**, and **looksmart.com**. Thousands of different public search engines are available (see **searchengineguide.com**). Each of these tools excels in one area. These can be very specialized with different capabilities. In addition, many companies have their own enterprise search engines. For example, Endeca Commerce from Oracle (**oracle.com/technetwork/apps-tech/commerce/endeca-commerce/index.html**) is a special search engine for online catalogs. For more information about training in Oracle Endeca Commerce, see **education.oracle.com/pls/web_prod-plq-dad/ou_product_category.getPage?p_cat_id=338**.

Voice-Powered Search

To ease searching, especially when using a smartphone, Google introduced a voice-powered tool (Google Voice Search; **google.com/insidesearch/features/voicesearch/index-chrome.html**) that allows you to skip the keyboard altogether. The first product was included as part of iPhone's mobile search application. It allows you to talk into your phone, ask any question, and the results of your query are provided on your iPhone. In addition to asking questions by talking into your iPhone, you can also listen to search engine results. For an example of Apple's intelligent personal assistant, "Siri," see **apple.com/ios/siri** and **imore.com/siri**.

Video and Mobile Search

There are dozens of dedicated search tools and sites that will search for videos and other images. Some of them, such as **bing.com/videos** will search across multiple sites; others, such as YouTube will search only for their own content. For a list of over 40 sites (compiled in 2010) see **thesearchenginelist.com/video-search**. For another example, the search engine Bing has a search feature that allows you to listen to more than 5 million fulllength songs.

Mobile Search

Several search engines are adapted to mobile search. Notable are Google, Yippy, and Yahoo!

Visual Shopping Search Engine

Visual search means looking for information that is presented visually (photos, images, etc.) For an overview, see **scholarpedia.org/article/Visual_search**. This technology can be used to support e-commerce. For example, **google.com/shopping** provides a visual search engine based on machine learning and computer vision that focuses on consumer products.

The technology lets users see what terms like "red high-heeled pumps" mean. It also created algorithms that evaluate how well red pumps match specific clothing the consumer plans to buy. Visual search is popular when conducted on mobile devices.

Social Network Search Engines

Social network search, also known as *social search* is a class of online search engines that help people find material about social networking activities, such as in user generated content, discussion groups, or recommendations. Like all search engines, these organize, prioritize, and filter search results. Examples of such search engines are: **socialmention.com** – 'real time social media search and analysis,' **yoname.com** – 'people search across social networks, blogs, and more,' **bing.com/explore/social**. For an overview, see the blog "Social is the Next Search" available at **info.gigya.com/rs/gigya/images/Gigya-Social-The-Next-Search.pdf**. For a discussion of the benefits and concerns, see **en.wikipedia.org/wiki/Social_search**.

Shopping Carts

An **electronic shopping cart** (also known as *shopping bag* or *shopping basket*) is software that allows customers to accumulate items they wish to buy before they arrange payment and check out, much like a shopping cart in a supermarket. The electronic shopping cart software program automatically calculates the total cost, and adds tax and shipping charges when applicable. Customers can review and revise their shopping list before finalizing their purchase by clicking on the "submit" button.

Shopping carts for B2C are fairly simple (visit **amazon.com** to see an example), but for B2B, a shopping cart may be more complex. Shopping cart software is sold or provided free to store builders as an independent component outside a merchant suite (e.g., see **networksolutions.com/e-commerce/index-v3.jsp** – 'create an online store now, **zippycart.com**, and **easycart. com**). It also is embedded in merchants' servers, such as **smallbusiness.yahoo.com/ecommerce**. Free online shopping carts (trials and demos) are available at **volusion.com** and **1freecart.com**; powered by MyFreeCommerce.com. For shopping cart applications for Facebook, see **ecwid. com/facebook-app.html** and the Ecwid app page on Facebook at **facebook.com/ecwid**.

Product Configuration (Self Customization)

A key characteristic of EC is the ability to self-customize products and services, as done by **dell.com**, **nike.com**, or **jaguarusa.com**. Manufacturers like to produce customized products in economical and rapid ways so that the price of their products will be competitive.

Questions and Answers Online

Intelligent search engines can answer users' questions. A leading engine is **ask.com**, a subsidiary of IAC. As of 2009, Ask.com had over 300 million questions and answers in its database (see **billhartzer.com/pages/askcom-unveils-database-of-300-million-questions-and-answers**). The Q&A service matches answers from the database to questions users ask. For details, see **ask.com** and **answers.ask.com**. A competing engine is **answers.com**, a question and answer (Q&A) site, which comprises **wikianswers.com**. Wiki Answers is a community-generated social knowledge Q&A platform available in several languages. People ask questions on the platform and the community answers them. Another similar platform is **answers. wikia.com/wiki/Wikianswers**.

SECTION 2.4 REVIEW QUESTIONS

1. List and briefly describe the dimensions by which electronic catalogs can be classified.
2. List the benefits of e-catalogs.
3. Describe an electronic shopping cart.
4. Describe voice- and vision-related search engines.
5. What is self-customization?

2.5 AUCTIONS, BARTERING, AND NEGOTIATING ONLINE

One of the most interesting market mechanisms in e-commerce is the electronic auction. Auctions are used in B2C, B2B, C2C, G2B, and G2C.

Definition and Characteristics

An *online auction* is an electronic space where sellers and buyers meet and conduct different types of transactions. This market mechanism uses a competitive process where a seller solicits consecutive bids from buyers (forward e-auctions) or a buyer solicits bids from sellers (reverse e-auctions). A wide variety of online markets qualify as auctions using this definition. Prices are determined dynamically by the bids. Auctions, an established method of commerce for generations, deal with products and services when conventional marketing channels are ineffective or inefficient. For example, e-auctions can expedite the clearance of items that need to be liquidated or sold quickly. Rare coins, stamps, and other collectibles are frequently sold at e-auctions.

There are several types of auctions, each with its own specialties and procedures. (For coverage, see **en.wikipedia.org/wiki/Online_auction_business_model**.) Auctions can be conducted on *public* auction sites, such as **ebay.com**, or on *private* auction sites, which may be by invitation only. For example, the state of New York periodically auctions old vehicles from its fleet on eBay.

Dynamic Pricing

One major characteristic of auctions is that they are based on dynamic pricing. **Dynamic pricing** refers to prices that are not fixed, but are allowed to fluctuate, and are determined by supply and demand. In contrast, catalog prices are fixed, as are prices in department stores, supermarkets, and most webstores.

Dynamic pricing appears in several forms. Perhaps the oldest forms are negotiation and bargaining, which have been practiced for many generations in open-air markets. The most popular today are online auctions.

Traditional Auctions Versus E-Auctions

Traditional, physical auctions are still very popular. However, the volume traded on e-auctions is significantly larger and continues to increase. In addition, person-to-person auctions are done mostly online.

Limitations of Traditional Offline Auctions

Traditional offline auctions, regardless of their type, have several limitations. They usually last only a few minutes, or even seconds, for each item sold. This rapid process may give potential buyers little time to make a decision, so they may decide not to bid. Therefore, sellers may not get the highest possible price; bidders may not get what they really want, or they may pay too much for the items. Additionally, in many cases, the bidders do not have much time to examine the goods before placing a bid. Bidders have difficulty learning about auctions and cannot compare what is offered at each location. Bidders must usually be physically present at auctions; thus, many potential bidders are excluded.

Similarly, it may be difficult for sellers to move goods to an auction site. Commissions are fairly high because a physical location must be rented, the auction needs to be advertised, and an auctioneer and other employees need to be paid. Electronic auctioning removes these drawbacks.

Electronic Auctions

The Internet provides an infrastructure for executing auctions electronically at lower cost, with a wide array of support services, and with many more participating sellers and buyers than physical auctions. Individual consumers and corporations can both participate in this rapidly growing and very convenient form of e-commerce. According to an IBISWorld report, e-commerce and Internet auction industry sales are expected to increase to 10% to $278 billion in the U.S. in 2013 (from $219 billion in 2011). The annual growth rate of the industry is expected to increase at a rate of 11.6% in the 5 years to 2013 (between 2007 and 2012 was 10.4%) (IBISWorld 2012, 2013).

Electronic auctions (e-auctions) are similar to offline auctions except that they are conducted online. E-auctions (or online auctions) have been in existence since the 1980s over LANs (e.g., for flowers; see Saarinen et al. 2006). Host sites on the Internet, which were started in 1995, serve as brokers, offering services for sellers to post their goods for sale and enabling buyers to bid on those items.

Major online auction sites, such as eBay (see Online File W2.3), offer consumer products, electronic parts, artwork, vacation packages, airline tickets, and collectibles, as well as excess supplies and inventories that are being auctioned off by businesses. Another type of B2B online auction is used to trade special types of commodities, such as electricity transmission capacities and gas and energy options (e.g., see **energyauctionexchange.com**). Furthermore, conventional business practices that traditionally have relied on contracts and fixed prices increasingly are converted into auctions with bidding for online procurements.

For a comparison of 10 online auction sites (2014), see **online-auction-sites.toptenreviews.com**.

Types of Auctions

It is customary to classify auctions into the following major types based on how many buyers and sellers are involved.

One Buyer, One Seller

In this configuration, one can use negotiation, bargaining, or bartering. The resulting price will be determined by each party's bargaining power, supply and demand in the item's market, and (possibly) business environment factors.

One Seller, Many Potential Buyers

In this configuration, the seller uses a **forward auction**, which is an auction where a seller entertains bids from multiple buyers. (Because forward auctions are the most common and traditional form, they often are simply called *auctions*.) The four major types of forward auctions are *English* and *Yankee* auctions, in which bidding prices increase as the auction progresses, and *Dutch* and *free-fall* auctions, in which bidding prices decline as the auction progresses. Each of these can be used for either liquidation or for market efficiency.

Example: Warren Buffet's Annual Power Lunch Auctions

Every year, Warren Buffet, the famous U.S. investment guru, has an auction with the prize being a lunch with him; the winner may also bring along up to seven friends. The winner pays big money for the honor. The money is donated to a charity called the Glide Foundation, which helps the poor and homeless in San Francisco. In the past, Buffett charged $30,000 per group. Since July 2003, Buffett has placed the invitation on an online auction (eBay). In

2003, bidders pushed the bid from $30,000 to $250,100. The highest winning bid was in 2012, by an anonymous bidder, in the record-setting amount of $3,456,789. However, in 2014, the highest bid was $2.2million. In addition to benefiting the needy, the auction provides an opportunity for people (with money) to meet Mr. Buffett.

One Buyer, Many Potential Sellers

Two popular types of auctions in which there is one buyer and many potential sellers are reverse auctions (tendering) and name-your-own-price auctions.

Reverse Auctions

When there is one buyer and many potential sellers, a **reverse auction** (**bidding** or **tendering system**) is in place. In a reverse auction, the buyer places an item he or she wants to buy for a bid (or *tender*) on a *request for quote* (RFQ) system. Potential suppliers bid on the item, reducing the price sequentially (see Figure 2.4). In electronic bidding in a reverse auction, several rounds of bidding may take place until the bidders do not reduce the price any further. The winning supplier

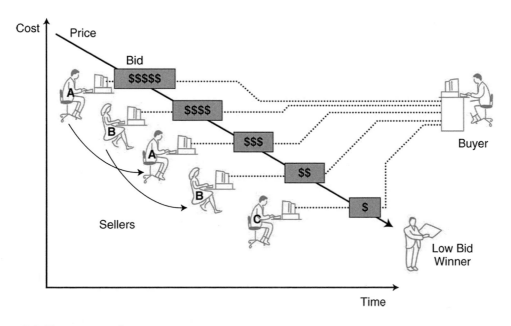

Figure 2.4 The reverse auction process

is the one with the lowest bid (assuming that only price is considered). Reverse auctions are primarily a B2B or G2B mechanism. (For further discussion and examples, see Chapter 4, including its opening case).

The Name-Your-Own-Price Model

Priceline.com pioneered the **name-your-own-price model**. In this model, a would-be buyer specifies the price (and other terms) that he or she is willing to pay to any willing and able seller. For example, Priceline.com (**priceline.com**) presents consumers' requests to sellers, who fill as much of the guaranteed demand as they wish at prices and terms requested by buyers. The sellers may come up with counter offers managed by Priceline. Alternatively, Priceline.com searches its own database that contains the participating vendors' lowest prices and tries to match supplies with requests. Priceline.com asks customers to guarantee acceptance of the offer if it is at or below the requested price by giving a credit card number. This is basically a C2B model, although some businesses also use it.

Many Sellers, Many Buyers

When there are many sellers and many buyers, buyers and their bidding prices are matched with sellers and their asking prices based on the quantities on both sides. Stocks and commodities markets are typical examples of this configuration. Buyers and sellers may be individuals or businesses. Such an auction is also called a **double auction**.

Penny Auctions

A *bidding fee auction*, also called a **penny auction**, is a new type of online forward auction in which participants must pay a small nonrefundable fee each time they place a bid (usually in small increments above the previous bid). When the time expires, the last participant to have placed a bid wins the item and also pays the final bid price, which is usually significantly lower than the retail price of the item. For a tutorial, see the video titled "BidBidSold Penny Auction Site Tutorial" (2:23 minutes) at **youtube.com/watch?v=ngr2kJcnAr4**.

Because most bidders will receive nothing in return for their paid bids, some observers have stated that the fee spent on the bid is actually equivalent to a lottery or wager. The auctioneer receives income both in the form of the fees collected for each participant bidder as well as in the form of a commission for the winning bid. Examples of penny auction companies are **us.madbid.com** and **quibids.com/en**. At **100auctionsites.com**, you can find a list of several penny auction companies. Some companies allow the auction's unsuccessful bidders to use all their bidding fees toward a purchase of items at regular or slightly discounted prices. Users need to be careful of scams. For additional information, see **en.wikipedia.org/wiki/Bidding_fee_auction**.

Several other innovative auctions are available.

Benefits and Limitations of E-auctions

E-auctions are becoming important selling and buying channels for many companies and individuals. E-auctions enable buyers to access goods and services anywhere auctions are conducted. Moreover, almost perfect market information is available about prices, products, current supply and demand, and so on. These characteristics provide benefits to all.

Benefits of E-Auctions

The auction culture seems to revolutionize the way customers buy, sell, and obtain what they want. A listing of the benefits of e-auctions to sellers, buyers, and e-auctioneers is provided in Table 2.2.

Limitations of E-Auctions

E-auctions have several limitations. The most significant limitations are minimal security, the possibility of fraud, and limited participation.

Minimal Security

Some of the C2C auctions conducted on the Internet are not secure because they are done in an unencrypted (or poorly protected) environment. This means that credit card numbers can be stolen during the payment process. Payment methods such as PayPal (**paypal.com**) can be

Table 2.2 Benefits of e-auctions

Benefits to sellers	Benefits to buyers	Benefits to E-auctioneers
• Increased revenues from broadening bidder base and shortening cycle time. Can sell anywhere globally	• Opportunities to find unique items and collectibles	• Higher repeat purchases. **marketresearch.com** found that auction sites, such as eBay, tend to garner higher repeat-purchase rates than the top B2C sites, such as Amazon.com
• Opportunity to bargain instead of selling at a fixed price. Can sell at any time and conduct frequent auctions	• Entertainment. Participation in e-auctions can be entertaining and exciting (e.g. virtual live auction site **tophatter.com**)	• High "stickiness" to the Web site (the tendency of customers to stay at sites longer and come back more often). Auction sites are frequently "stickier" than fixed-priced sites. Stickier sites generate more ad revenue for the e-auctioneer
• Optimal price setting determined by the market (more buyers, more information)	• Convenience. Buyers can bid from anywhere, even using a mobile device; they do not have to travel to a physical auction place	• Easy expansion of the auction business
• Sellers can gain more customer dollars by offering items directly (saves on the commission to intermediaries; also, physical auctions are very expensive compared to e-auctions)	• Anonymity. With the help of a third party, buyers can remain anonymous	
• Can liquidate large quantities quickly. • Improved customer relationship and loyalty (in the case of specialized B2B auction sites and electronic exchanges)	• Possibility of finding bargains, for both individuals and organizations	

used to solve the problem (see Chapter 10). In addition, some B2B auctions are conducted over highly secure private lines.

Possibility of Fraud

In many cases, auction items are unique, used, or antique. Because the buyer cannot see and touch the items, the buyer may receive something different than she (or he) had in mind. In addition, products may be defective. Buyers may also commit fraud (e.g., by receiving goods or services without paying for them). Thus, the fraud rate in e-auctions is relatively high. For a discussion of e-auction fraud and fraud prevention, see **fraud.org/scams/internet-fraud/online-auctions**. For information

on internet fraud in general, see **fraud.org/learn/internet-fraud** and for information for sellers, see **fraud.org/component/content/article/2-uncategorised/62-seller-beware**. Lately, several people have warned about fraud on penny auctions sites. For examples of scams, see **tomuse.com/penny-auction-fraud-scam-cheat-bidders**.

Limited Participation

Some auctions are by invitation only; others are open only to dealers. Limited participation may be a disadvantage to sellers, who usually benefit from as large a pool of buyers as possible. Buyers also may be unhappy if they are excluded from participation.

Impacts of Auctions

Because the trade objectives and contexts for auctions are very diverse, the rationale behind auctions and the motives of the different participants for setting up auctions are quite different. The following are some representative impacts of e-auctions.

Auctions as a Mechanism to Determine a Price

Given their characteristics, auctions create a market where prices are determined. This is especially true in markets for unique or rare items. Typical examples are fine art or rare stamp auctions. For example, wine collectors can find a global wine auction site at **winebid.com**.

Auctions and Social Networks

Some social networks enable auctions (e.g., see Internet Exercise #3).

Online Bartering

Bartering, the exchange of goods and services, is the oldest method of trade. Today, it is done primarily between organizations. The problem with bartering is that it is difficult to match trading partners. Businesses and individuals may use classified ads to advertise what they need and what they offer in exchange, but they still may not be able to find what they want. Intermediaries may be helpful, but they are expensive (20–30% commissions) and very slow.

E-bartering (electronic bartering) – bartering conducted online – can improve the matching process by attracting more partners to the barter. In addition, matching can be done faster, and as a result, better matches can be found. Items that are frequently bartered online include office space, storage, and factory space; unused facilities; and labor, products, and banner ads. (Note that e-bartering may have tax implications that need to be considered.)

E-bartering is usually done in a **bartering exchange**, a marketplace where an intermediary arranges the transactions. These exchanges can be very effective. Representative bartering websites include **u-exchange.com** – 'Trade anything, Pay nothing,' **swapace.com** – 'Swap anything for anything,' and **barterdepot.com**. The typical bartering process works like this: First, the company tells the bartering exchange what it wants to offer. The exchange then assesses the value of the company's products or services and offers it certain "points" or "bartering dollars." The company can use the "points" to buy the things it needs from a participating member in the exchange.

Bartering sites must be financially secure; otherwise, users may not have a chance to use the points they accumulate. (For further details, see **virtualbarter.net** and **barternews.com**.)

Online Negotiating

Dynamic prices also can be determined by *negotiation*. Negotiated pricing is commonly used for expensive or specialized products. Negotiated prices also are popular when large quantities are purchased. Much like auctions, negotiated prices result from interactions and bargaining among sellers and buyers. Negotiation also deals with terms, such as the payment method, timing, and credit. Negotiation is a well-known process in the offline world (e.g., in real estate, automobile purchases, and contract work). A simple peer-to-peer (P2P) negotiation can be seen at **ioffer.com**. For more on negotiation in P2P money lending, see the ZOPA and Prosper cases in Online File W7.1. *Online (electronic) negotiation* may be more effective and efficient than offline negotiation.

SECTION 2.5 REVIEW QUESTIONS
1. Define auctions and describe how they work.
2. Describe the benefits of e-auctions over traditional (offline) auctions.
3. List the four major types of auctions.
4. Distinguish between forward and reverse auctions.
5. Describe the "name-your-own-price" auction model.
6. Describe penny auctions.
7. List the major benefits of auctions to buyers, sellers, and auctioneers.

8. What are the major limitations of auctions?
9. List the major impacts of auctions on markets.
10. Define bartering and describe the advantages of e-bartering.
11. Explain the role of online negotiation in EC.

2.6 VIRTUAL COMMUNITIES AND SOCIAL NETWORKS

A *community* is a group of people with common interests who interact with one another. A **virtual community** is one where the interaction takes place over a computer network, mainly the Internet. Virtual communities parallel typical physical communities, such as neighborhoods, clubs, or associations, but people do not meet face-to-face. Instead, they meet online. Virtual communities offer several ways for members to interact, collaborate, and trade (see Table 2.3 for types of virtual communities).

Characteristics of Traditional Online Communities and Their Classification

Most virtual communities are Internet-based, known also as *Internet communities*.

Hundreds of thousands of communities exist on the Internet, and the number is growing rapidly. Pure-play Internet communities may have thousands, or even hundreds of millions of members. By early 2014 (its 10th anniversary), Facebook had grown to about 1.23 billion members around the world (see **businessweek.com/articles/2014-01-30/facebook-turns-10-the-mark-zuckerberg-interview**). This is one major difference from traditional purely physical communities, which usually are smaller. Another difference is that offline communities frequently are confined to one geographic location, whereas only a few online communities are geographically confined. For images of virtual communities, do a Google search.

Table 2.3 Types of virtual communities

Community type	Description
Transaction and other business activities	Facilitate buying and selling Combines an information portal with an infrastructure for trading. Members are buyers, sellers, intermediaries, etc., who are focused on a specific commercial area (e.g., fishing)
Purpose or interest	No trading, just exchange of information on a topic of mutual interest. Examples: Investors consult The Motley Fool (**fool.com**) for financial advice; music lovers go to **mp3.com**
Relations or practices	Members are organized around certain life experiences. Examples: **ivillage.com** caters to women and **seniornet.com** is for senior citizens. Professional communities also belong to this category. Examples: **aboutus.org/Isworld.org** is a space for information systems faculty, students, and professionals
Fantasy/role playing	Members share imaginary environments. Examples: sports fantasy teams at **espn.com** see **games.yahoo.com**, **horseracegame.com**
Social networks	Members communicate, collaborate, create, share, form groups, entertain, and more. Facebook is the leader
Virtual worlds	Members use avatars to represent themselves in a simulated 3-D environment where they can play games, conduct business, socialize, and fantasize about whatever they like

Classifications of Virtual Communities

Virtual communities can be classified in several ways.

Public Versus Private Communities

Communities can be designated as *public*, meaning that their membership is open to anyone. The owner of the community may be a privately held corporation (e.g., Twitter), public for profit, or non-profit organizations. Many of the large social networks, including Facebook, belong to the public for profit category.

In contrast, *private* communities belong to a company, an association, or a group of companies and their membership is limited to people who meet certain requirements (e.g., work for a particular employer or work in a particular profession). Private communities may be internal (e.g., only employees can be members), or external (for customers).

Classification Categories

Another option is to classify the members as *traders, players, just friends, enthusiasts*, or *friends in need*. A more common classification recognizes six types of Internet communities: (1) transaction, (2) purpose or interest, (3) relations or practices, (4) fantasy, (5) social networks, and (6) virtual worlds.

The most popular type of virtual community today is the social network, the subject of our next section.

Online Social Networks and Social Network Sites

Let us first define social networks and then look at some of the services they provide and capabilities.

A Definition and Basic Information

As you may recall, in Chapter 1 we defined a *social network* site as a company, such as Facebook, that provides free Web space and tools for its community members to build profiles, interact, share, connect, and create and publish content.

A list of the characteristics and capabilities of social networks was provided in Section 1.3 of Chapter 1.

Social Network Services

Social network services (or sites) are companies that host social communities. They are also known as *social networks*.

Social networks appear in a variety of forms; the most well-known, mostly social-oriented net-work is Facebook. LinkedIn is a business-oriented network.

The Size of Social Network Sites

Social network sites are growing rapidly, with some having over 100 million members. For example, in late 2013, Pinterest had 70 million members. The typical annual growth of a successful site is 40–50% in the first few years and 15–25% thereafter. For a list of the major sites (including user counts), see **leveragenewagemedia.com/blog/social-media-infographic** and **en.wikipedia.org/wiki/List_of_social_networking_websites**.

A Global Phenomenon

Although Facebook, Pinterest, Twitter, Google+, and other social networks attract the majority of media attention in the United States, they also have many members in other countries. Other country-based social network sites are proliferating and growing in popularity worldwide. For example, **renren.com**, **weixin.qq.com** and **us.weibo.com** are large communities in China; **mixi.jp** has been widely adopted in Japan; and **vk.com** in Europe (primarily in Russia). Dutch users have embraced **hyves.nl**; and Nasza Klasa (**nk.pl**) has captured Poland. **Hi5.com**, a social network (now part of Tagged) has been popular in Latin America, the U.S., South America, and Europe. **Migente.com** is an English language site geared toward the Hispanic community. Additionally, previously popular communication and community services have begun implementing social networking features. For example, the Chinese instant messaging service **qq.com** became one of the largest social networking services in the world once it added profiles and made friends visible to one another. Finally, Cyworld conquered the Korean market by adding 'buddies.' Note that, international entrepreneurs, inspired by the success of the largest social network sites and their capabilities, have created their own local clones of successful U.S. companies. Information about the magnitude of social networks is changing rapidly; therefore, to get the most up-to-date data, go to **alexa.com** and **comscore.com**.

Representative Capabilities and Services Provided by Social Network Sites

Social network sites provide many capabilities and services such as:

- Users can construct a Web page where they present their profile to the public.
- Users can create a circle of friends who are linked together.
- The site provides discussion forums (by subgroup, by topic).
- Photo, video, and document viewing and sharing (streaming videos, user-supplied videos) are supported.
- Wikis can be used to jointly create documents.
- Blogs can be used for discussion, dissemination of information, and much more.
- These sites offer community e-mail and instant messaging (IM) capabilities.
- Experts can be made available to answer member queries.
- Consumers can rate and comment on products and services.
- Online voting may be available to poll member opinions.
- The site may provide an e-newsletter.
- The site supports conference (group) chatting, combined with document and image sharing.
- Message and bulletin board services are available for posting information to groups and individuals on the website.
- The site provides storage for content, including photos, videos, and music.
- Users can bookmark self-created content.
- Users can find other networks, friends, or topics of interest.

These capabilities can make social networks user-friendly.

Business-Oriented Public Social Networks

Business-oriented social networks, also known as *professional social networks*, are social networks whose primary objective is to facilitate business. The prime example here is **linkedin.com**, which provides business connections and enables recruiting and finding jobs. Another example is **craigslist.org**, the largest classified ad site, which offers many social-oriented features (see Case 2.2 later in this section). Another example is The Brain Yard, a place for executives to find news, knowledge and contacts. Finally, **doximity.com** is a medical network for U.S. physicians and health care professionals. Businesses are using business social networks to advertise their brands as well as making and enhancing contacts globally.

Example of a Business-Oriented Social Network

Originating in Germany, **xing.com** is a business network that attracts millions of executives, sales representatives, and job seekers from over 200 countries (2014 data). The site offers secure services in 16 languages. According to **xing.com** and the authors' experiences, users can visit the site to:
- Establish new business contacts and find sales trends.
- Promote themselves professionally to employers.
- Identify experts that can give their advice on problems and opportunities (for a fee or for free).
- Participate in or organize meetings and events.
- Develop and grow a network of contacts.
- Control the level of privacy and ensure that their personal data are protected.
- Keep up-to-date with industry groups.

Some Capabilities of Business-Oriented Networks

With Web 2.0 tools, companies can engage users in new innovative ways (for an example, see Online File W2.4). More direct communication is achieved by offering additional ways for consumers to engage and interact among themselves and with organizations. For example, a company can:

- Encourage consumers to rate and comment on products and services.
- Allow consumers to create their own topic areas and build communities (forums) around shared interests possibly related to a company's products.
- Hire bloggers or staff editors who can lead discussions about customer feedback.
- Provide incentives such as sweepstakes and contests for customers to get involved in new product (service) design and marketing campaigns.
- Encourage user-made videos about products/services and offer prizes for winning video ads.
- Provide interesting stories in e-newsletters.

An interesting business-oriented company that uses classified ads is **craigslist.org**, which is described in Case 2.2.

CASE 2.2: EC APPLICATION: CRAIGSLIST: THE ULTIMATE ONLINE CLASSIFIED COMMUNITY

If you want to find (or offer) a job, housing, goods and services, social activities, romance, advice, and much more in over 700 local sites in 13 languages, and in more than 70 countries worldwide (2014 data), go to Craigslist (**craigslist.org**). The site has much more information than you will find in newspapers. According to their website, Craigslist receives 80 million new classified ads every month. Each month there are more than 60 million visitors to the site in the United States alone (see **craigslist.org/about/factsheet**).

Finally, there are over 50 billion page views per month. For more statistics, see **alexa.com/siteinfo/craigslist.org** and **siteanalytics.compete.com/craigslist.com/#.Uw27nfmICm4**. According to Alexa.com, Craigslist is the eleventh most visited site in the United States.

In addition, Craigslist features over 100 topical discussion forums with more than 200 million user postings. Every day, people from 700 local sites in 70 countries worldwide check classified ads and interact on forums. Craigslist is considered by many as one of the few websites that could change the world because it is simply a free social-oriented, popular, and useful notice site. Although many other sites offer free classifieds, no other site comes close to Craigslist.

- It gives people a voice.
- It is consistent and champions down-to-earth values.
- It illustrates simplicity.
- It has social-networking capabilities.
- It can be used for free in most cases (you can post free ads, except for business; for rent, or for sale ads in a few large cities; some employment ads; and for adult and therapeutic services).
- It is effective and well visited.

For more information, see **craigslist.org/about/factsheet**.

Users cite the following reasons for the popularity of Craigslist:

As an example of the site's benefits, we provide the personal experience of one of the authors, who needed to rent his condo in Long Beach, California. The usual process to get the condo rented would take 2–4 weeks and $400 to $700 in newspaper ads, plus ads in local online sites for rental services. With Craigslist, it took less than a week at no cost. As more people discover Craigslist, the traditional newspaper-based classified ad industry will probably be the loser;

ad rates may become lower, and fewer ads will be printed.

In some cities, Craigslist charges for "help wanted" ads and apartments listed by brokers. In addition, Craigslist may charge for ads with rich media features.

Concerns About Craigslist

Critics charge that some users post illegitimate or false ads on the site and the Craigslist staff are unable to effectively monitor this practice. Some users have complained about questionable ads and scams being posted. Craigslist also attracts criminals seeking to commit fraud by paying with bad checks. The anonymity of Craigslist's users as well as the lack of ratings encourages unlawful acts.

Another concern is that adult services make up a significant portion of the total traffic on the site and may involve illegal activities, especially concerning minors. With the sheer volume of users and ads posted per day, such monitoring is not possible given the modest workforce of only 40 plus that the site employs (data of 2014). (As of September 8, 2010, Craigslist has been trying to control such activities.)

On the other side, many supporters contend that attempts to control Craigslist may simply cause users to use other, less-regulated sites.

In China, a company called 58.com Inc. (**58. com**) is modeled after Craigslist and provides similar information and generates sizeable revenue and profits. The company is listed in the NYSE under the symbol WUBA.

Sources*: Based on Clark (2008), Liedtke (2009), and **craigslist.org** (accessed May 2014).

Questions

1. Identify the business model used by Craigslist.
2. Visit **craigslist.org** and identify the social network and business network elements.
3. What do you like about the site? What do you dislike about it?
4. Why is Craigslist considered by some as a site that "could change the world?"

5. What are some of the risks and limitations of using this site?

Private (or Enterprise) Social Networks

In addition to public-oriented business social networks such as LinkedIn and Craigslist, there are many private social networks (also called enterprise networks) within an organization. An example is the opening case in Chapter 1 (Starbucks). Other companies with notable internal networks for employees only include Northwestern Mutual. According to the company, they have an internal blog ("Mutualblog") and a Yammer account internally, which is used by over 1,000 employees to dialog and make connections on non-proprietary topics. Private networks are for employees, business partners, and customers.

Business Models and Services Related to Social Networking

Social networking sites provide innovative business models, ranging from customer reviews of food and night life in India (**burrp.mumbai. com**), to users who dress up paper dolls that look like celebrities (**stardoll.com**). New revenue models are being created almost daily. Although some generate limited revenue, others succeed. Lately, the Pinterest model has become popular, as described in Chapter 7.

Many communities attract advertisers. For example, **vivapets.com** attracts pet lovers with wiki contributions in its attempt to catalog all pet breeds. The site attracts hundreds of thousands of unique visitors per month. Obviously, pet food-related vendors are interested in placing ads there.

Some of the popular social-oriented services are:
1. **Xanga.com** hosts blogs, photoblogs, and social networking profiles. Users of Xanga are referred to as "Xangans." Xanga was originally launched as a site for sharing book and music

reviews. Today it is one of the most popular blogging and networking services, with an estimated 10,000,000–100,000,000 million users worldwide. Xanga has a very popular blogring in Hong Kong, Macao, and Singapore. (A *blogring* links together a number of blogs that share mutual interests and can be searched by subject matter). In 2013 the company was planning to get involved in online gambling.

2. **Digg.com** is a community-based website that takes short reports from members on podcasts, news articles, and videos, which are then voted on by other participants. Digg is available on a website, iPhone app, and daily e-mail.

Mobile Social Commerce

Mobile computing is growing faster than any other type of EC computing. According to Bent (2014), mobile data traffic grew 81% (from 820 petabytes per month in 2012 to 1.5 exabytes per month in 2013). This clearly boosts mobile commerce. According to The Retail Bulletin (2012), 64% of smartphone consumers used them to shop online. In subsequent chapters, we will discuss many mobile applications. Here we present the basic definitions, technologies, and a few examples.

Mobile Social Networking

Mobile social networking refers to social networking where members chat and connect with one another using any mobile device. Most major social networking websites now offer mobile services. According to Protalinski (2012), in July 2012 the number of mobile subscribers accessing Facebook was 543 million out of a total membership of 955 million. By Q4 2013, Facebook had 945 million mobile users out of a total 1.23 billion million monthly active users (see **techcrunch.com/2014/01/29/facebook-is-a-mobile-ad-company** and **newsroom.fb.com/Company-info**). Some social networking sites offer mobile-only services (e.g., **path.com** and **javagala.ru**).

Mobile social networking is especially popular in Japan, South Korea, and China, generally due to better data pricing (flat rates are widespread in Japan). In Japan and South Korea, where 4G networks offer more bandwidth, the leaders in social networking are **mixi.jp** and Mobage by Dena (**mbga.jp**). Numerous other mobile social networking sites have been launched in Japan. For statistics on the exponential growth of mobile social networks, see **comscore.com**.

Experts predict that mobile social networks will experience explosive growth, as evidenced in 2012. For how social platforms are powering mobile commerce see Gupta (2011).

Mobile Enterprise Networks

Several companies have developed (or fully sponsor) mobile-based social networks. For example, Coca-Cola has a social network that can only be accessed by mobile devices. There Coca-Cola employees attempt to influence young people to buy its products.

Examples of Social Mobile Commerce Applications

There are several types of social mobile applications. Illustrative examples are provided next.

Example 1

Coca-Cola created a social network under its Sprite brand (Sprite Yard), which is only accessible via cellphones. The network was aimed at the youth market, and members could set profiles, meet friends, share photos and so on. The idea was to use the site mainly for promoting the brand. To attract visitors, the company offered free content (music and video clips). However, the free access requires a PIN code found under Coca-Cola bottle lids. This service was discontinued in 2013.

Example 2

IBM is a leader in social commerce adoption on mobile devices. Following are some examples of IBM's initiatives according to Taft (2011).

- IBM Mobile Connect (formerly IBM Lotus Mobile Connect) (social media and social networks building software, abbreviated as Connect) is popular in industry.. Customers can get immediate access to blogs, wikis, and other tools. They can also share photos, videos, and files on major mobile devices (e.g., Android, BlackBerry, iOS).

- IBM Connections allows people to generate and vote on ideas at work (see **ibm.com/connections/blogs/SametimeBlog/?lang=en**).
- The capabilities in IBM Connections 4.0, such as Moderations, or Ideation Blogs, enabled workers to embrace networks of engaged people.

Example 3

A poll conducted by **travelclick.com** in October 2011 revealed that half of the participating hoteliers around the globe are investing in mobile technologies to support social commerce (see **bizreport.com/2011/10/travelclick-hotels-to-invest-more-in-mobile-social-marketing.html**).

With the current technology, we also see a trend toward sophisticated interactions of Internet social networks with images, voice, and videos. This is expected to be a powerful managerial and marketing feature in the near future.

Recent Innovative Tools and Platforms for Social Networking

A large number of software tools and platforms are available for social networking. Well known tools are blogs, microblogs, and wikis, which are described in Online File W2.1. Note that the capabilities of these tools are changing continuously. Here we provide a representative list of recent innovative tools:

- **Snapchat.com** – A mobile photo messaging service for "chatting" with friends through photos, videos, and captions "like 'texting' with pictures or videos" (see **webtrends.about.com/od/Iphone-Apps/a/What-Is-Snapchat.htm**).
- **Whatsapp.com** – According to its website, WhatsApp is a cross-platform free mobile messaging app for smartphones. Users can form groups, send each other unlimited images, video and audio media messages. The company was acquired by Facebook in 2014 for around $19 billion.
- **Ortsbo.com** – Enabler of real-time conversational translation mainly in social media.
- **Droid Translator (droid-translator.tiwinnovations.com)** – Translates phone calls, video chats (e.g., Skype), and text conversations into 29 different languages. (For more information, see Petroff 2014).
- **Tagged.com** – A maker of *social discovery* products that enable people to meet and socialize with other people through playing games, browsing features, shared interests, and more. You can share tags, browse profiles, and exchange virtual gifts.
- **Viber.com, line.me/en, etc**. – Companies that provide free voice and video calling, etc. for mobile devices and desktops (e.g. Viber for Desktop).
- **Instagram.com** – A free platform for sharing photos and videos. As a social network, it allows for creation of reviews, etc. (Acquired by Facebook in 2012.)
- **Hshtags.com**; ('A social media search engine dedicated to hashtags') –Enables users to see in real-time, all public content related to any keyword and join any related public conversation in real time (see **digitaltrends.com/social-media/new-search-engine-like-google-social-web**).

Mobile Community Activities

In many mobile social networks, devices can be utilized to conduct the same activities that are performed in a non-mobile configuration. Customers can even create their own mobile community.

Mobile video sharing, which sometimes is combined with photo sharing, is a new technological and social trend. Mobile video-sharing portals are becoming popular (e.g., see **myubo. com**). Many social networking sites offer mobile features.

SECTION 2.6 REVIEW QUESTIONS

1. Define virtual communities and describe their characteristics.
2. List the major types of virtual communities.
3. Define social network.
4. Describe mobile social commerce.
5. List some major social network sites.
6. Describe the global nature of social networks.
7. Describe social networking.
8. Describe mobile social networking and commerce

2.7   VIRTUAL WORLDS AS AN ELECTRONIC COMMERCE PLATFORM

A **virtual world** is a site for online communities in a computer-generated setting, where users socialize and work with one another through the use of avatars. The creation of objects, jobs, homes, and businesses in the 3D environment, which are owned by their residents, is the foundation of these worlds. It is an interactive environment, which is fun and satisfying. Virtual worlds (also referred to as *digital worlds* or *Metaverse*), usually structured as interactive 3-D virtual environments, are created for users to inhabit and interact in. Users feel as if they are actually within the environment because they have the ability to control certain features of the virtual world. Virtual worlds, according to Wikipedia, initially appeared in massively multiplayer online games; however, they are not limited to games. Players can create a character that travels between buildings, towns, and even planets and stars as well as conducting activities there. In a virtual world, you can be anyone you want. You can build a dream house, decorate it, have a job, or fly a spaceship. For a comprehensive overview, see Malaby (2009). For research directions, see Wasko et al. (2011). To learn more about Second Life, see **wiki.secondlife.com/wiki/Video_Tutorials**, and

the video titled "Philip Rosedale: Second Life, Where Anything Is Possible" (28:31 minutes) at **youtube.com/watch?v=lHXXsEtE3b4**.

Major Features

There are several different types and purposes of virtual worlds; however all share the following features (compiled from The Virtual Policy Network's 'A Virtual Worlds Primer' at **virtualpolicy.net/resources/virtual-worlds-primer**), and the authors' experiences:

- The worlds can be used by many users who access them via online interface
- The interface is mostly 3D, which is more engaging than 2D.
- All interactions are in real time from anywhere.
- Most of the content is user-generated. It is facilitated by tools provided on the sites.
- The virtual world is always in motion, regardless of the presence of its residents.
- Socialization is encouraged. Tools are provided for engagement and for creating groups and socially-oriented activities.

Additional features are:
- Communication among users can include text, graphical icons, visual gestures, video clips, sound, and so forth.
- Use of avatars is a common way to represent the residents of the virtual worlds.

Avatars

Residents of virtual worlds can represent themselves by 2-D or 3-D images known as avatars. **Avatars** are interactive, animated, computerized "characters" that are graphical images designed to look like humans and are programmed to exhibit people's behavior. Avatars have unique names and can move around. Advanced avatars can "speak" and display behaviors such as emotions, gestures, and facial expressions. They can be fully automated to act like robots. Avatars are designed to gain the trust of users. Then, they can be programmed to perform human tasks. Many companies use avatars as tour guides or to staff virtual reception desks. For a demonstration of avatars in action, see **meez.com**.

The purpose of avatars is to make the human–computer interface more realistic. Thus, they are sometimes referred to as interactive *conversational characters*. They are being used extensively to support users' Internet chat with companies (e.g., Live Chat), representing the company's people. A popular use is the live chat with avatars. You ask questions and the avatar, using natural language processing, attempts to understand your question. Then, the avatar matches an answer from a database. For an example, see "Ted", at **tdameritrade.com**. Instant-messaging programs such as **google.com/hangouts** use avatars (e.g., see **hangoutapps.com**). Avatars can improve customer satisfaction and retention by offering personalized, one-to-one service. They also can help companies get to know their customers in order to better design promotions. For more on avatars you must see the 2009 movie *Avatar*.

Example 1: Jetstar Airways

According to Business Wire (2013), Nuance Communications, Inc., announced that Jetstar "has launched a new virtual assistant called 'Ask Jess,' which is based on Nuance Nina Web, an intelligent virtual assistant that delivers a human-like, conversational customer service experience. Customers simply type their request to Jess, and Jess provides the answers. Jetstar is the first airline to deploy Nuance Nina Web virtual assistant for customer service. The new Ask Jess virtual assistant draws on Nuance Nina, an intelligent virtual assistant that leverages innovative technology for natural language understanding and deliv-

ers a conversational interface to web visitors which stimulates human conversation. Nuance's Natural Language Understanding (NLU) technology allows applications like Ask Jess to understand a customer's intent through an interactive, text-based chat experience. By understanding what customers want, Ask Jess makes getting information on booking, baggage and seating easier than navigating pages on a Web site. Jetstar's Ask Jess virtual assistant is also fully integrated with the company's existing live chat service, delivering a seamless handover to human support when required." (To ask Jess a question, see **jetstar.com/au/en/customer-service**.)

Example 2: American TESOL

The American TESOL, Teaching English to Speakers of Other Languages Institute (**americantesol. com/blogger/p=1367**) teaches and certifies qualified individuals to teach English worldwide. The company deploys multiple avatars throughout its website. The avatars provide tips for ESL (English as a Second Language) students to help them improve their conversational abilities. Other activities are:

- Engaging students with talking avatars
- Students introducing their avatars in Second Life
- Using avatars in text-to-movie and much more.

For more information see **sanako.com**.

Business Activities and Value in Virtual Worlds

Virtual worlds provide an interesting platform for business activities. Businesses compete in virtual worlds, just like they do in the real world. Many companies and organizations now incorporate virtual worlds as a new form of advertising and sales.

There are several types of business activities in virtual worlds:

- Creating and managing a virtual business (see Terdiman 2008 for guidelines on how to do this)

- Conducting regular business activities (e.g., advertising, marketing, collaboration) within the framework of the virtual world
- Providing services for those who build, manage, or make money with virtual properties

For additional business activities, see Mahar and Mahar (2009) and Chapter 8.

In a cover story in *Businessweek Magazine*, Hof (2006) discusses the various opportunities for conducting business in Second Life. Specifically, he introduces seven residents who make substantial amounts of money. These include the Anshe Chung avatar, known as the "Rockefeller of Second Life." Her successful company buys virtual land from Second Life, "develops" it, and sells or rents it globally.

For more on business applications for virtual worlds, see **knowledge.wharton.upenn.edu/?s= virtual+worlds**.

Following is an example of how companies use virtual worlds in businesses:

Example: Market Research

Starwood Hotels constructed a prototype of its Aloft brand hotels before they were built in 2008. People using Second Life were asked to view the prototype and give the company their opinions on the model. Then, using the feedback, the company completed the design and built the hotel.

Using virtual worlds gives companies a chance to receive and examine feedback about new products or services. This can be crucial because it gives the companies insight into what the market and customers really want from new products. The 3D presentation helps users better understand products; thus giving companies a competitive edge. For other potential activities, see Mahar and Mahar (2009), Stinton (2013), and the closing case of this chapter. There is an increased use of avatars in help desks.

Example

Avatars guide and advise passengers in airports. As of 2012 you can see avatars acting as greeters in many airports in Europe (e.g., Paris) and the U.S. (New York), that are there to help passengers by giving them information about ground transportation, etc. (see **abcnews.go.com/ Travel/york-airports-introduce-avatars- assist-passengers/story?id=16957584**). The avatars are human sized. For a demonstration of the avatars in the New York airports, watch WNYC's video titled "Airport Avatar Demonstration" (47 seconds) at **youtube.com/ watch?v=tI3YBf36twk**. Advanced avatars can conduct vocal conversations with passengers (sometimes in several languages). Similar avatars act as guides in some companies, universities, and tourist attractions. New York airports are working on developing avatars that will allow customers to ask questions about the airport (see **digitaltrends.com/cool-tech/new-york- airports-are-installing-virtual-avatars-to- help-visitors**).

Virtual Shopping

You can go shopping with friends while each shopper is located at his or her individual home. You enter a virtual store in the virtual mall and find jeans on sale. Your avatar tries on the jeans (the avatar's body's size is the same as yours) and displays it to your friends. If you like it, you may buy the pants online or visit the physical store later. Virtual shopping is gaining popularity (see Turban et al. 2015, and Chapter 7).

One type of virtual shopping is described next.

Trading Virtual Properties

As you will see in the closing case, trading virtual properties is a very popular activity in Second Life. **Habbo.com** (formerly known as Habbo Hotel), a Finnish social networking site for teenagers, sells more virtual furniture worldwide than the giant Swedish retailer IKEA sells actual furniture. The virtual furniture is designed by teens on the site who decorate their Habbo rooms with the furnishings. The teen users are buying not only furniture but also clothes, bags, etc., for their avatars.

SECTION 2.7 REVIEW QUESTIONS

1. Define virtual worlds.
2. Describe avatars. Why do we use them?

3. List some business activities in virtual worlds. Categorize them by type.
4. Describe virtual shopping.

2.8   EMERGING EC PLATFORMS: AUGMENTED REALITY AND CROWDSOURCING

Several technologies are used as platforms that enable innovative EC applications. Here we present two.

Augmented Reality

An increasing number of business applications use the technology of *augmented reality* (AR). See Marcom on a Dime (2010) for more details. The term AR has several definitions depending on its field of applications. According to Wikipedia, **augmented reality** is "a live or indirect view of a physical, real-world environment whose elements are *augmented* (or supplemented) by computer-generated sensory input such as sound, video, graphics or GPS data" (see **en.wikipedia.org/wiki/Augmented_reality**). Such an arrangement helps people enhance the sensory perception of reality. The computerized layer can be seen through an application on mobile devices such as smartphones, webcams, or 3D glasses (including 3D TV). Google developed Augmented Reality (AR) glasses called 'Google Glass' (see Chapter 6 and Bilton 2012). For how AR works, see Bonsor (2001). Bonsor also explains the relationship of AR to *virtual reality*.

Applications in E-Commerce

The major applications in e-commerce are in the areas of advertising and marketing (for details, see Rorick 2012), as will be described in Chapter 9. An application in real estate is described in Chapter 3. There are potentially many other areas of applications. For example, Hayes (2009) describes 16 business applications, while iPhoneness (2010) and Elliott (2009) describe more

potential applications. Finally, Wikipedia lists many e-commerce related applications of AR.

Example 1: Net-a-Porter

This innovative company (Chapter 1) is using an iPhone/iPad app to view an AR 'shopping window.' As can be seen in the video "Net-A-Porter Augmented Reality Shopping Windows" (1:37 minutes) available at **digitalbuzzblog.com/ net-a-porter-augmented-reality-shopping-windows**, customers at the company's physical store can point the mobile device camera at a clothing display (e.g., in the stores or store windows), and see a 360 degree view of the clothes. They also can see presentations at fashion shows, price, availability, and other relevant information. Furthermore, the window shoppers can immediately buy the clothing online using their mobile device (for the download, see **itunes.apple.com/ ne/app/net-a-porter/id318597939?mt=8**).

Example 2: IKEA

IKEA uses AR to show how its furniture can fit in your house. For details on this mobile phone app, see Truong (2013) and watch the video "Place IKEA Furniture in Your Home with Augmented Reality" at **youtube.com/watch? v=vDNzTasuYEw**.

Crowdsourcing

Another platform for e-commerce is crowdsourcing. Crowdsourcing is a platform for collective intelligence in e-commerce and social commerce (see the industry website **crowdsourcing.org**). Here we present the essentials of the technology. In Chapter 8 we present the applications that are based on this technology.

Definitions and Major Concepts

The term *crowd* refers to any group of people such as a group of consumers, employees of a corporation, or members of a social network who offer expertise. A *crowd* is frequently referred to a large group.

Figure 2.5 The elements of crowdsourcing

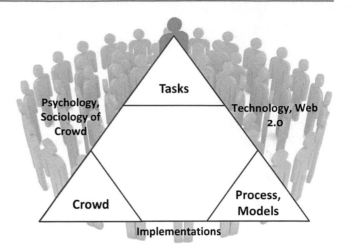

Applications in Social Gaming

AR is already used in several applications. According to **t-immersion.com/augmented-reality/use-cases/social-augmented-reality-games**, social AR gaming is a superb tool for generating marketing leads and brand recognition because of the huge number of players engaged in games connected with a product.

Crowdsourcing utilizes crowds to collectively execute tasks such as solving problems, innovating, or getting large projects completed by dividing the work among many people. The term was coined by Jeff Howe in June 2006 (Howe 2008). In the crowdsourcing process, the initiator recruits a crowd (e.g., customers) to create content, a cumbersome task (e.g., translating Wikipedia articles), or in research and development. This is based on the idea that two heads are better than one. The collective intelligence of large groups is assumed to be able to solve complex problems at low cost (Sherman 2011; Brabham 2013).

The basic elements of crowdsourcing are illustrated in Figure 2.5. Three elements are involved: the task(s) to be carried out, the crowd, which is used to work on the task and the models and processes used by the crowd (to execute the task). These elements are connected by features related to the tasks and the crowd (such as the psychology of the crowd), the technologies used (such as idea generation and voting), and imple-

mentation issues such as incentives paid to the participants.

The Process of Crowdsourcing

Crowdsourcing can be viewed as a collective problem-solving or work sharing process, and usually is conducted as a Web-based activity. In a typical use of crowdsourcing, problems are broadcast either to a known crowd (e.g., employees or business partners) or to an *unknown* group of participants (e.g., expert problem solvers or consumers). The communication usually starts as an open call for solutions (see first step in Figure 2.6). The members of the crowd are organized as online communities, and members submit individual solutions. The crowd may also discuss the solutions and may vote for a final short list. Alternatively, the short list is then prioritized (e.g., ranked). The final selection can be made by the crowd or by management (Figure 2.6). The winning individuals in the crowd are well compensated, either monetarily or with special recognition. In other cases, the only rewards may be the satisfaction with a job well done. The use of crowdsourcing can yield results from amateurs or unrecognized professionals.

Example

In 2008, Starbucks introduced My Starbucks Idea (**mystarbucksidea.force.com**), a social media site designed to solicit ideas and feedback from

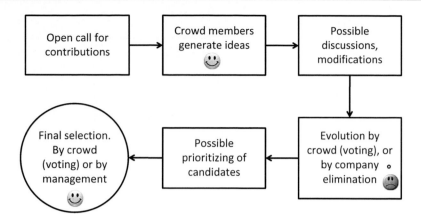

Figure 2.6   A typical crowdsourcing process

its customers (see opening case in Chapter 1). The site was built around four key themes: (1) ideas are user generated; (2) users can vote to short list ideas, discussing them before and/or after the vote; and (3) company employees act as "idea partners," providing answers to questions and leading discussions.

The process is visible to the entire Starbucks community. The members can see the status of each proposal.

Note that crowdsourcing focuses on innovation, creativity, and the problem-solving capabilities of a crowd organization. An overview of crowdsourcing is provided in BrightSightGroup's video titled "Jeff Howe - Crowdsourcing" (3:20 minutes) at **youtube.com/watch?v=F0-UtNg3ots**, also see **crowdsourcing.org**, Sherman (2011) and Crowdsortium (**crowdsortium.org**). These specialists have developed best practices for the industry.

Benefits of Crowdsourcing

The major perceived benefits of crowdsourcing include the following:

- Problems can be analyzed or solved at comparative little cost. (Payment can be determined by the results; however, sometimes there is no monetary payment, just praise or accolades).
- Solutions can be reached quickly since many people work on the needed

research project simultaneously. Also, designs of products may be expedited.
- The contributing crowd may reside within the organization; therefore, talents may be discovered.
- By listening to the crowd, organizations gain first hand insight into the desires of their customers (or employees). There is built-in market research when the crowd is composed of customers.
- Crowdsourcing can tap into the global world of ideas. The crowd may include business partners, customers, academicians, etc., and the members of the crowd can reside in different countries.
- Customers tend to be more loyal if they participate in a company's problem solving project (see the opening case in Chapter 1).

For additional benefits to crowdsourcing, see Sherman (2011).

Uses of Crowdsourcing in E-Commerce

There are several EC applications of crowdsourcing – notable is the creation of Wikipedia. Sherman (2011) presents many successful applications; the major ones are described in Chapter 8.

SECTION 2.8 REVIEW QUESTIONS
1. Define augmented reality.
2. Describe how AR can facilitate EC.
3. Define crowdsourcing.
4. List the elements of crowdsourcing.
5. Describe the process of crowdsourcing.
6. What are the major benefits of crowdsourcing?
7. How is crowdsourcing used in EC?

2.9 THE FUTURE: WEB 3.0, WEB 4.0 AND WEB 5.0

Web 2.0 is here. What's next? The answer is a still-unknown entity referred to as *Web 3.0*, the future wave of Internet applications. Some of the desired capabilities of Web 3.0 will be discussed later in this section. In general, there is optimism about the future of the use of the Web 3.0 to facilitate EC (see **siliconangle.com/blog/2013/08/02/the-future-of-ecommerce-with-web-3-0**).

Web 3.0: What Does the Future Hold?

Web 3.0 is projected to deliver a new generation of business applications that will see business and social computing converge. Web 3.0 could change the manner in which people live and work as well as the organizations where they work, and it may even revolutionize social networking (see Laurent 2010; Aghaei et al. 2012).

According to several experts, Web 3.0 could have the following capabilities:

- Make current applications smarter by introducing new intelligent features
- Provide easier and faster interaction, collaboration and user engagement
- Facilitate intelligent-based powerful search engines
- Provide more user-friendly application-creation and human-computer interaction capabilities
- Increase the wisdom and creativity of people

- Enable smarter machines (Gartner 2014)
- Enable much wider bandwidth
- Enable better visualization including 3-D tools
- Simplify the use of mobile computing and mobile commerce

For additional capabilities see Patel (2013).

Web 3.0 and the Semantic Web

One of the major possible platforms of Web 3.0 technologies is the *Semantic Web.*. The term was presented by the inventor of the Web, Tim Berners-Lee, who visualized the Semantic Web as the platform for making the Web smarter. There is no standard definition of **Semantic Web**. It is basically a group of methods that focus on machines (in contrast with Web 2.0 that focuses on people). The technology attempts to enable computers to understand the semantics (i.e., the meaning) of information, by using natural language understanding tools. For a video titled "Evolution Web 1.0, Web 2.0 to Web 3.0" (3.58 minutes) see **youtube.com/watch?v=bsNcjya56v8**.

A similar view regarding the role of the Semantic Web is expressed by Borland (2007), who believes that new Web 3.0 tools (some of which are already helping developers put together complex applications) will enhance and automate database searches, assist people in choosing vacation destinations, and make sorting through complicated financial data more efficient.

An experimental Semantic Web browser has been in use lately. This browser enables users to display data, draw graphs, and make browsing more interactive. (e.g., see **w3.org/standards/semanticweb**). Another example would be "friend-of-a-friend" networks, where individuals in social networks provide data in the form of links between themselves and friends.

For a video titled "Web 3.0" (14:25 minutes) see **youtube.com/watch?v=CG9cPtIYy8Y**.

Concerns

The following are a few concerns regarding the implementation of Web 3.0 and the future of EC.

- **Future Threats.** According to Stafford (2006), Laurent (2010), and the authors' experiences, the following trends may slow the growth of EC and Web 3.0, and may even cripple the Internet.
  - **Security concerns.** Shoppers, as users of e-banking and other services, and members of social networks, worry about online security. The Web needs to be made safer.
  - **Lack of Net neutrality.** If the big telecommunications companies are allowed to charge companies for a guarantee of faster access, critics fear that small innovative Web companies could be demolished by the big companies that can afford to pay more for efficient Internet usage. (see Chapter 15).
  - **Copyright complaints.** The legal problems of YouTube, Craigslist, Wikipedia, and others may result in a loss of originality, dedication, and creativity of user-generated content.
  - **Insufficient connectivity.** Upstream bandwidths are still constraining applications, making uploading of video files a time-consuming task.
- **Language Fitness.** There will be a need to reconsider the existing spoken languages with Web 3.0 taxonomies and schemes.
- **Standards.** There will be a need for architectural standards for Web 3.0.

Therefore, some believe that the Semantic Web will never work (see the 91 minute video at **youtube.com/watch?v=oKiXpO2rbJM**).

Despite these concerns, Web 3.0 and e-commerce could thrive due to several innovations in the technological environment.

The Technological Environment

The future of EC and the Semantic Web is dependent on how far the relevant information technol-ogy advances (e.g., see Gartner 2014). Of the many predictions, we cite two here.

McKinsey & Company's Prediction

According to this prediction (Bughin et al. 2010), there are 10 tech-enabled business trends to watch. These include the developments in the global information grid, new collaboration technologies, and pervasive computing (Chapter 6).

Definitions, details, and discussions are provided by Bughin et al. (2010). Also, see Gartner's annual reports about Strategic Technology Trends at **gartner.com/technology/research**.

Nicholas Carr's Predictions

In his free e-book, Nicholas Carr (2008) discusses the following trends:

1. More intelligent computers
2. Larger and more efficient data centers based on cloud computing
3. Use of virtualization in computing infrastructure that will enable the running of any application on an external computing grid
4. Parallel processing grids that will cut processing costs by 90%
5. Utility and cloud computing will become the norm

Web 4.0

Web 4.0 is the Web generation after Web 3.0. It is still an unknown entity. It is known as Symbiotic Web (see Aghaei et al. 2012 for a description). However, Coleman and Levine (2008) envision it as being based on islands of intelligence and on being ubiquitous. For the evolution from Web 1.0 to Web 4.0 see Aghaei et al. (2012). For a discussion, see Koren (2013).

Web 5.0

According to Patel (2013), "Web 5.0 is still an underground idea in progress and there is no exact definition of how it would be. Web 5.0 can be considered as a Symbionet Web, decentralized." Patel provides some technical information.

SECTION 2.9 REVIEW QUESTIONS

1. What is Web 3.0, and how will it differ from Web 2.0?

2. Define Semantic Web.
3. List the major potential inhibitors and concerns of e-commerce and Web 3.0.
4. What are the major influencing computing and IT trends?
5. What are Web 4.0 and Web 5.0?

5. **Shall we take part in virtual worlds?** For many companies and applications, the technology is still immature and cumbersome. A good strategy is observing what other companies, especially in the same industry, are doing in Second Life.

MANAGERIAL ISSUES

Some managerial issues related to this chapter are as follows.

1. **Should we use auctions for selling?** A major strategic issue is whether to use auctions as sales channels. Auctions do have some limitations, and forward auctions may create conflicts with other distribution channels. If a company decides to use auctions, it needs to select auction mechanisms and determine a pricing strategy. These decisions determine the success of the auctions and the ability to attract and retain visitors on the selling site. Auctions also require support services. Decisions about how to provide these services and to what extent to use business partners are critical to the success of high-volume auctions.

2. **Should we barter?** Bartering can be an interesting strategy, especially for companies that lack cash, need special material or machinery, and have surplus resources. However, the valuation of what is bought or sold may be hard to determine, and the tax implications in some countries are not clear.

3. **How do we select merchant software?** There are many products and vendors on the market. Small businesses should consider offers from Yahoo! or eBay since the software is combined with hosting and offers exposure to the vendor-managed e-market. The functionalities of the software as well as the ease of building webstores need to be examined (see discussion in Chapter 13).

4. **How can we use Facebook and other social networks in our business?** There are many possibilities that are presented in Chapter 7, mostly in marketing and advertising. Any progressive organization should examine and experiment with social networking.

SUMMARY

In this chapter, you learned about the following EC issues as they relate to the chapter's learning objectives.

1. **Activities and mechanisms.** The major activities are information dissemination and presence, online trading, collaboration, entertainment, and search. The major mechanisms are marketplaces, webstores, shopping carts, catalogs, search engines, Web 2.0 tools, and virtual worlds.

   Most of the activities are between sellers and buyers. However, there also are collaboration activities among supply chain members as well as among people within organizations. EC attempts to automate the interaction process for the above activities.

2. **E-marketplaces and their components.** An e-marketplace or marketspace, is a virtual market that does not suffer from limitations of space, time, or borders. As such, it can be very efficient and effective. Its major components include customers, sellers, products (some digital), infrastructure, front-end processes, back-end activities, electronic intermediaries, other business partners, and support services.

   The role of intermediaries will change as e-markets develop: Some will be eliminated (disintermediation); others will change their roles and prosper (reintermediation). In the B2B area, for example, e-distributors connect manufacturers with buyers by aggregating e-catalogs of many suppliers. New value-added services that range from content creation to syndication are mushrooming.

3. **The major types of e-marketplaces.** In the B2C area, there are webstores and e-malls. In the B2B area, there are private and public e-marketplaces, which may be vertical

(within one industry) or horizontal (across different industries). Exchanges are the platform for many buyers and sellers to meet and trade. Different types of portals provide access to e-marketplaces.

4. **Electronic catalogs, search engines, and shopping carts.** The major mechanisms in e-markets are e-catalogs, search engines, software (intelligent) agents, and electronic shopping carts. These mechanisms, which are known as merchant suites, facilitate EC by providing a user-friendly and efficient shopping environment.

5. **Types of auctions and their characteristics.** In forward auctions, bids from buyers are placed sequentially, either in increasing mode or in decreasing mode. In reverse auctions, buyers place an RFQ and suppliers submit offers in one or several rounds. In name-your-own-price auctions, buyers specify how much they are willing to pay for a product or service, and an intermediary tries to find a supplier to fulfill the request. Penny auctions are forward auctions where a small fee is paid each time a bid is made. The final member to bid wins the auction when the designated time is up.

6. **The benefits and limitations of auctions.** The major benefits for sellers are the ability to reach many buyers, sell quickly, and save on intermediary commissions. Buyers have excellent access to auctions, and a chance to obtain bargains and collectibles while shopping from their homes. The major limitation is the possibility of fraud.

7. **Bartering and negotiating.** Electronic bartering can greatly facilitate the swapping of goods and services among organizations, thanks to improved search and matching capabilities, which is managed by bartering exchanges. Software agents can facilitate online negotiation.

8. **The structure and role of virtual communities.** Virtual communities create new types of business opportunities. They bring people with similar interests together at one website. (Such groups are a natural target for advertis-

ers and marketers.) Using chat rooms, discussion spaces, and so forth, members can exchange opinions about certain products and services. Of special interest are communities of transactions, whose interest is the promotion of commercial buying and selling. Virtual communities can foster customer loyalty. This may increase sales of products made by vendors that sponsor communities, and facilitate customer feedback for improving service and business operations.

9. **Social networks as EC mechanisms.** These are very large Internet communities that enable the sharing of content, including text, videos, and photos, and promote online socialization and interaction. Hundreds of social networks, are emerging around the world, competing for advertising money. Millions of corporations advertise, entertain, and even sell on social networks.

Business-oriented communities concentrate on business issues, both in one country and around the world (e.g., recruiting, finding business partners). Social marketplaces meld social networks and some aspects of business. Notable business-oriented social networks are LinkedIn and XING. Some companies are active in public social networks such as Facebook. Other companies own and operate their own social networks within the company, which are known as enterprise social networks. Their members are usually employees and retirees. They are used mainly for collaboration, knowledge creation and preservation, training, and socialization. Many large companies have such networks (e.g., IBM, Wells Fargo, Northwestern Mutual).

10. **Virtual worlds.** These environments provide entertainment, trading of virtual property, discussion groups, learning, training, and much more. Everything is simulated, animated, and supported by avatars. Many companies have established presences in virtual worlds, especially in Second Life, mainly offering dissemination of information and advertising.

11. **Augmented Reality (AR) and crowdsourcing.** These emerging technologies facilitate two types of EC activities. AR blends visual aspects of computer and physical worlds. Thus, it can facilitate advertisement and presentation of information. It works by pointing a mobile device (e.g., smartphone) to a product or building and adds information to what you see (e.g., 360 degree view, price tag). Crowdsourcing solicits the wisdom of the crowd for idea-generation or problem solving. It also is used to divide a large task among many people, each of whom is executing a different, small subtask.

12. **Web 3.0 and Web 4.0.** Web 3.0, the next generation of the Web, will combine social and business computing. It will be more portable and personal, with powerful search engines, increased clout, and greater connectivity with the wireless environment and on-demand applications. Knowledge management will be one of its main pillars. The Semantic Web will play a major role in Web 3.0 applications. Web 3.0 and its applications will depend on IT trends such as the developments in cloud computing, utility computing, parallel processing, and machine intelligence. Web 4.0 is a futuristic Web that will be built on ubiquitous and intelligent systems. It will connect "islands" of intelligence from different sources.

KEY TERMS

Augmented reality
Avatar
Back end
Bartering
Bartering exchange
Business-oriented social network
Buy-side e-marketplace
Crowdsourcing
Desktop search
Digital products
Disintermediation
Double auction

Dynamic pricing
E-bartering (electronic bartering)
E-distributor
Electronic auction (e-auction)
Electronic catalog (e-catalog)
Electronic shopping cart
E-mall (online mall)
E-marketplace
Enterprise search
Forward auction
Front end
Intermediary
Mobile portal
Mobile social network
Name-your-own-price model
Penny auction
Reverse auction (bidding or tendering system)
Search engine
Sell-side e-marketplace
Semantic Web
Virtual community
Virtual world
Voice portal
Web 3.0
Web 4.0
Web (information) portal
Webstore (storefront)

DISCUSSION QUESTIONS

1. Compare physical marketplaces with marketspaces. What are the advantages and limitations of each?
2. Discuss the competitive advantage Craigslist has using classified ads.
3. Discuss the value of a virtual world as an EC environment. Why does it attract users? Why does it attract companies? How can it provide a competitive advantage to a company that has a presence there? What are its limitations?
4. Discuss the need for portals in EC.
5. How do business-oriented networks differ from regular social networks such as Facebook?
6. Why are social marketplaces considered to be a Web 2.0 application?

7. Discuss the following statement: "Technically, you can put together a portal in a weekend, but culturally there are a slew of things to consider; therefore it takes much longer."

8. Discuss the pros and cons of selling cars via auctions.

9. Discuss the pros and cons of using avatars in help desks. What are the benefits? The limitations?

TOPICS FOR CLASS DISCUSSION AND DEBATES

1. Compare and contrast the efficiency of traditional markets with that of digital markets.

2. Some claim that social networking, especially microbloging and social network sites, displace the traditional electronic bulletin board systems. Discuss.

3. Discuss the advantages of dynamic pricing strategy over fixed pricing. What are the potential disadvantages of dynamic pricing?

4. Enter Facebook and search for companies that do auctions on the site. Identify the different types of auctions on the site.

5. What is the advantage of a business using eBay instead of conducting auctions from its own site? Distinguish between C2C and B2B cases.

6. Debate: Should companies build in-house social networks for external activities or use existing public social networks? (e.g., see Roberts 2008).

7. Debate: Should Craigslist and YouTube monitor and control what users publish there? Who will pay the cost?

8. Debate: Social network services can provide good security to enterprise social networks. However, security may limit users' creativity and disrupt the business. Should a company use such a service?

9. Debate: Some research suggests that the use of public social networks by employees during work hours can be good for a business because employees develop relationships and share information, which increases productivity and innovation. Others say it is a waste of time and ban the use of Facebook, YouTube, and other such sites at work.

10. Debate the business value of social networking. To start, read Tom Davenport's blog of October 2007 titled "Where's the 'Working' in Social Networking?" at **blogs.hbr. org/2007/10/wheres-the-working-in-social-n**.

11. Debate: Facebook and Twitter compete for advertisers' money. Which one has a better chance to get more ad money and why? (Consult Mangalindan 2010.)

12. Some of the largest social media networks exist in China (**qq.com, qzone.qq.com, us. weibo.com, weixin.qq.com** and **renren. com**). Find information about these networks and list their properties. How do they differ from U.S. social networks?

INTERNET EXERCISES

1. Enter **droid-translator.tiwinnovations.com** and **tranzactive.com** and compare their translation capabilities.

2. Examine how bartering is conducted online at **tradeaway.com, barterquest.com,** and **u-exchange.com**. Compare and contrast the functionalities and ease of use of these sites.

3. Enter **volusion.com** and identify all specific e-commerce mechanisms (or solutions) provided by the company.

4. Enter **respond.com** and request a product or a service. Once you receive replies, select the best deal. You have no obligation to buy. Write a short report based on your experience.

5. Enter **dtsearch.com** and find its capabilities. What type(s) of search does it conduct (e.g., desktop, enterprise, general)?

6. Enter **cars.com**. List all services available to both sellers and buyers of cars. Compare it to **carsdirect.com**. Finally, identify the revenue sources of both sites.

7. Enter **ups.com**.
   (a) Find out what information is available to customers before they send a package.
   (b) Find out about the "package tracking" system; be specific.
   (c) Compute the cost of delivering a $10'' \times 20'' \times 15''$ box, weighing 40 pounds, from your hometown to Long Beach, California. Compare the cost for the fastest delivery option with to the lowest possible delivery cost.
   (d) Prepare a spreadsheet using Excel for two different types of calculations available on the UPS site. Enter data to solve for two different calculations.

8. Register at Second Life, and enter the site.
   (a) Find what three corporations are doing on the site.
   (b) Find out what three universities are doing on the site.
   (c) Write a report on your findings.

9. Create an avatar on Second Life. Let your avatar interact with avatars of some companies. Why do we consider an avatar a mechanism for EC? Write a report.

10. Enter **ibm.com** and **oracle.com**. Prepare a list of the major products available for building corporate portals.

11. Enter **go.sap.com/index.html** and find the key capabilities of its enterprise portals. List the benefits of using five of the capabilities of SAP's portals.

12. Enter **networksolutions.com**. View the shopping cart demo. What features impress you the most and why? What related services does it provide? Compare it to **storefront. net**, **nexternal.com** and **ecwid.com**.

13. Enter the website of a social network service of your choice. Build a homepage. Add a chat room and a message board to your site using the free tools provided. Describe the other capabilities available. Make at least five new friends.

14. Enter **vivapets.com** and **dogster.com** and compare their offerings.

15. Enter **w3.org**. Find material about Semantic Web (SW); check their RDF/FAQ and search for some applications. Write a report.

16. Enter **secondlife.com** and find the commercial activities of the following avatars: Fizik Baskerville, Craig Altman, Shaun Altman, FlipperPA Peregrine, and Anshe Chung. Briefly describe what they represent.

17. Enter **zippycart.com** and read the article "13 Ecommerce Link Building Tactics for Your Online Store" at **zippycart.com/ecommerce-news/1430-13-ways-to-gain-inbound-links-to-your-online-store.html**. Write a brief summary.

TEAM ASSIGNMENTS AND PROJECTS

1. **Assignments Related to the Opening Case**
   (a) Why is Pinterest considered a social network?
   (b) What are the company's business and revenue models?
   (c) How can manufacturers advertise on Pinterest?
   (d) Compare Pinterest and We Heart It. Pay attention to the business models.
   (e) Pinterest has a large amount of money. How does it use this money on its website to increase its competitive advantage?

2. Assign each group a large e-tailer (e.g., Amazon.com, Walmart.com, Target.com, Dell.com, Apple.com, and HP.com). Trace the purchasing process. Look at the catalogs, search engines, shopping carts, Web 2.0 features, and any other mechanisms that improve e-shopping. Prepare a presentation that includes recommendations for improving the existing process.

3. Build your own business in Second Life (SL). This can be done by each member or each group. Determine what business you want to build. Then read Terdiman's book (2008), Mahar and Mahar's book (2009), or a similar book. Register at SL and begin to work. In your project, do the following:
   (a) Select a business category and develop a business strategy.
   (b) Develop a business plan and model for your virtual enterprise.

(c) Choose where (island or property) to establish a business. Explain your choice.

(d) Conduct a budget and cash flow analysis (see Appendix B in Terdiman 2008).

(e) Buy virtual land and other virtual properties.

(f) Develop marketing and advertising plans (examine the competition).

(g) Look for any possible revenues; make a pricing decision.

(h) Plan all support services using the SL tools.

(i) Watch for legal issues and other risks; plan their mitigation.

(j) Build the business (using the SL tools).

(k) Build a supporting blog. How would you use it for viral marketing?

4. Watch the O'Reilly Media video titled "Online Communities: The Tribalization of Business" (Part 1 is 6:15 minutes; Parts 2 and 3 are optional) at **youtube.com/watch?v=qQJvKyytMXU** and answer the following questions:

(a) Why is the term tribalization used in the video?

(b) What are virtual communities?

(c) How can traditional businesses benefit from online communities?

(d) What is the value of communities for the customers?

(e) Compare social vs. marketing frameworks.

(f) How are virtual communities aligned with the businesses?

(g) Discuss the issues of measurements, metrics, and CSFs.

(h) Optional: View Part 2 (**youtube.com/watch?v=U0JsT8mfZHc#t=15**) and Part 3 (**youtube.com/watch?v=AeE9VWQY9Tc**) (6:50 and 10:24 minutes respectively), and summarize the major topics discussed.

5. The team's mission is to analyze Pinterest's U.S. and global competition, including similar companies in China and Brazil. Start by reading McKenzie (2012) about the Chinese social sites Meilishuo and Mogujie and compare them to Pinterest. Do the same for **weheartit.com**. Look at another country of your choice. Comment on the cultural differences. Write a report.

CLOSING CASE: MADAGASCAR'S PORT MODERNIZES CUSTOMS WITH TRADENET

Madagascar is an island-state in Africa whose port is critical to its trade activities and the overall economy. The country's customs operations play an essential part in the port operations.

The Problem

The trade administration process in this underdeveloped country used to be cumbersome and slow. This limited the trade volume and the customs revenue. Madagascar's 'Trading Across Borders' indicator position was one of the world's lowest (143rd ranking). The country's Logistics Performance Index was also low (120th place).

The Business Process

According to CrimsonLogic (2014), "Everyone exporting to Madagascar must first register and fill in an electronic form, called Advance Cargo Information – ACI…, for each consignment. The exporter attaches copies of the trade documents, such as the commercial invoice, bill of lading and certificate of origin to the BSC and these are then transmitted electronically to the Customs in Madagascar to be verified for consistency and risk profiling."

Once completed, the importer or customs broker can submit the customs declaration electronically.

Once submitted, the approval process begins. It may involve several government agencies, port container terminal management, commercial banks, and the country's Central Bank and Treasury. While the submission portion was computerized and fairly efficient, the approval process was not. Overall, the cargo clearance took over 15 days.

The Solution

Originally, Customs had been using ASYCUDA++ (a legacy computerized system designed by the United Nations Conference on Trade and Development). This system helped with the submission, but the overall process was still slow due to lack of integration of all participants' subsystems. The port had difficulties competing with other ports in the area that offered faster and more efficient customs management systems. Therefore, the Medagasy Community Network Services ("GasyNet") saw the need to create a single online platform to connect the entities in the trade community. They relied on a new system, which is an integration of TradeNet, an electronic data exchange, and ASYCUDA++.

What Is TradeNet?

TradeNet is an electronic data interchange (EDI) system (see Online Tutorial T2) developed in Singapore in 1989. It is now administered, operated, and maintained by CrimsonLogic of Singapore. TradeNet, which initially operated only in Singapore, is used today in several ports around the world, including Madagascar. The current system also includes Windows-based and Web-based portions. Using the TradeNet-based system the trading community can submit electronically all the forms needed by the Customs administration. The system then routes the applications for processing. Approved permits are then returned electronically to the senders via ASYCUDA++. The process starts before ships even enter the port. For an overview of TradeNet, see **customs.gov.sg/leftNav/trad/ TradeNet/An+Overview+of+TradeNet.htm**, and the United Nations Economic Commission for Europe (**unece.org/energy.html**).

The Integrated System

In order to improve the flow of information and provide an efficient trade environment, the TradeNet system was integrated with ASYCUDA++. The importers input their customs declarations data into GasyNet, which in turn transmits the data to TradeNet, which enables all involved partners to share data and transmit results. The results that are returned to TradeNet are transferred to GasyNet and then to the importers. To use TradeNet, users need to buy special software from TradeNet Frontend Solution. The software enables data entry by the users (e.g., the customs declarations) from PC's or mobile devices. The system provides permit status information, company billing inquiries, ability to retrieve lost permits, acknowledgement notification, an audit trail, permit listings and more.

The system links the multiple partners in the trade by creating a single point of transaction for all the standard documents involved.

The Results

The system is an efficient platform for the B2B customs-related transactions. It reduced the cargo clearance time from more than 15 days to less than five days for sea shipments, which resulted in increased trade volume. In addition, customs revenue more than doubled in 5 years (accounting for around half of Madagascar's total income). Other recorded benefits include: elimination of unnecessary bureaucracy and cost reduction due to paperless processes.

Finally, Madagascar's 'Trading Across Borders' indicator improved from 143rd to 109th place, and their Logistics Performance Index ranking improved from 120th to 84th.

Sources: Based on Fjeldsted (2009), Crimson Logic (2014), and Singapore Customs (2014).

Questions
1. Describe the role of GasyNet in the process.
2. Describe the contribution of TradeNet.
3. What is the role of EDI in this system?
4. The TradeNet system is a typical B2B platform. Explain why.
5. Relate the content of this chapter to the case.

ONLINE FILES
available at **affordable-ecommerce-textbook.com/turban**

W2.1 Social Software Tools: From Blogs to Wikis to Twitter

W2.2 Examples of Digital Products

W2.3 Application Case: eBay: The World's Largest Auction Site

W2.4 Application Case: Social Media at Eastern Mountain Sports

COMPREHENSIVE EDUCATIONAL WEBSITES

wiki.secondlife.com: Learn SL in a fun, easy way. Look for videos and tutorials.

vectec.org/resources: The Virginia Electronic Commerce Technology Center offers special reports, e-business news, and statistics.

allthingsweb20.com: Reference for locating the top social marketing sites.

informationweek.com: Large collection of EC-related material.

cioinsight.com: A comprehensive collection of all type of resources.

bloombergmarketing.blogs.com: A comprehensive Marketing Blog.

zdnet.com/blog/hinchcliffe: Dion Hinchcliffe's compendium of articles, reviews, galleries, videos, podcasts, and downloads about Enterprise 2.0.

awarenesstechnologies.com: A collection of webinars on social media, Web 2.0, ROI, and marketing.

GLOSSARY

Augmented reality "A live, copy, view of a physical, real-world environment whose elements are *augmented* (or supplemented) by computer-generated sensory input such as sound, video, graphics, or GPS data" (see **en.wikipedia.org/wiki/Augmented_reality**).

Avatar Interactive, animated, computerized characters designed to look like humans and are programmed to exhibit people's behavior.

Back end Where activities that are related to order aggregation and fulfillment, inventory management, purchasing from suppliers, accounting and finance, insurance, payment processing, packaging, and delivery.

Bartering The exchange of goods and services.

Bartering exchange A marketplace where an intermediary arranges barter transactions.

Business-oriented social network A social network whose primary objective is to facilitate business.

Buy-side e-marketplace Where a company purchases from many potential suppliers; this type of purchasing is considered to be *many-to-one*, and it is a B2B activity.

Crowdsourcing Utilizing crowds to collectively execute tasks such as solving problems, innovating, or getting large projects done by dividing the work among many people.

Desktop search The search of a user's own computer files. The search is done by looking through all the information that is available on the user's PC.

Digital products Goods that can be transformed to digital format.

Disintermediation Elimination of intermediaries between sellers and buyers because they offer only services that can be fully automated.

Double auction An auction in which multiple buyers and their bidding prices are matched with multiple sellers and their asking prices, considering the quantities on both sides.

Dynamic pricing Prices that are not fixed but that are allowed to fluctuate, and are determined by supply and demand.

E-bartering (electronic bartering) Bartering conducted online, usually in a bartering exchange.

E-distributor An entity that basically aggregates product information from many manufacturers, sometimes thousands of them, in the e-distributor's catalog.

E-mall (online mall) An online shopping center where many online stores present their catalogs.

E-marketplace An electronic space where sellers and buyers meet and conduct different types of transactions.

Electronic auction (e-auction) An auction conducted online.

Electronic catalog (e-catalog) The presentation of product information in electronic form; the backbone of most e-selling sites.

Electronic shopping cart Software that allows customers to accumulate items they wish to buy before they arrange payment and check out.

Enterprise search The search for information *within* the files and databases of an organization.

Forward auction An auction where a seller entertains bids from multiple buyers.

Front end The place where customers interact with a marketspace. The major components of the front end can include the seller's portal, electronic catalogs, a shopping cart, a search engine, an auction engine, a payment gateway and all other activities related to placing orders.

Intermediary A third party that operates between sellers and buyers.

Mobile portal A portal accessible via a mobile device.

Mobile social networking Social networking where members converse and connect with one another using any mobile device.

Name-your-own-price model Auction model in which a would-be buyer specifies the price (and other terms) he or she is willing to pay to any willing and able seller. It is a C2B model that was pioneered by Priceline.com.

Penny auction A new type of forward auction in which participants must pay a small nonrefundable fee each time they place a bid (usually in small increments above the previous bid). When time expires, the last participant to have placed a bid wins the item and also pays the final bid price.

Reverse auction (bidding or tendering system) Auction in which the buyer places an item for bid (tender) on a request for quote (RFQ) system, potential suppliers bid on the job, with the price reducing sequentially, and the lowest bid wins; primarily a B2B or G2B mechanism.

Search engine A computer program that can access databases of Internet resources, search for specific information or keywords, and report the results.

Sell-side e-marketplace A place where a company sells either standard or customized products to individuals (B2C) or to businesses (B2B); this type of selling is considered to be one-to-many.

Semantic Web A group of methods that focuses on machines (in contrast with Web 2.0 that focuses on people), trying to enable machines to understand the semantics (i.e., the meaning) of information using natural language understanding tools.

Virtual community A community where the interaction takes place over a computer network, mainly the Internet.

Virtual world A site for online communities in a computer-generated setting where users socialize and work with one another through the use of avatars. The creation of objects, jobs, homes, and businesses in the 3D environment is the foundation of these worlds and is fun and satisfying.

Voice portal A portal with audio interfaces that can be accessed by telephone or cell phone.

Web 3.0 A term used to describe the future of the World Wide Web. It is projected to deliver a new generation of business applications that will see business and social computing converge.

Web 4.0 The Web generation after Web 3.0. It is still an unknown entity. However, it is envisioned as being based on islands of intelligence and as being ubiquitous.

Web (information) portal A single point of access, through a Web browser, to critical business information located inside and outside organizations.

Webstore (storefront) A single company's (or individual seller's) website where products or services are sold.

REFERENCES

Aghaei, S., M. A. Nematbakhsh, and H. K. Farsani. "Evolution of the World Wide Web: From Web 1.0 to Web 4.0." *International Journal of Web & Semantic Technology (IJWesT)*, January 2012.

Bakos, Y. "The Emerging Role of Electronic Marketplaces on the Internet." *Communications of the ACM* (Volume 1, Issue 4, August 1998).

Bent, K. "Mobility Revolution: 8 Shocking Stats From Cisco's 2014 Mobile Traffic Forecast." February 20, 2014. **crn.com/slide-shows/mobility/300071779/mobility-revolution-8-shocking-stats-from-ciscos-2014-mobile-traffic-forecast.htm/pgno/0** (accessed May 2014).

Bilton, N. "Google Begins Testing Its Augmented-Reality Glasses." April 4, 2012. **bits.blogs.nytimes.com/2012/04/04/google-begins-testing-its-augmented-reality-glasses/** (accessed March 2014).

Bloomberg. "Jewelry Heist." Special Report E-Biz, May 9, 2004. **businessweek.com/stories/2004-05-09/jewelry-heist** (accessed March 2014).

Bonsor, K. "How Augmented Reality Works." February 19, 2001. **howstuffworks.com/augmented-reality.htm** (accessed March 2014).

Borland, J. "A Smarter Web: New Technologies Will Make Online Search More Intelligent – And May Even Lead to a 'Web 3.0'." *MIT Technology Review*, March–April 2007. **technologyreview.com/featured-story/407401/a-smarter-web/** (accessed March 2014).

Brabham, D. C. *Crowdsourcing*, Cambridge, MA: The MIT Press, 2013.

Brave, S. "Pinterest, We've Got a Business Model for You." March 24, 2012. **gigaom.com/2012/03/24/pinterest-weve-got-a-business-model-for-you/** (accessed March 2014).

Bughin, J., M. Chui, and J. Manyika. "Clouds, Big Data, and Smart Access: Ten Tech-Enabled Business Trends to Watch." *McKinsey Quarterly*, August 2010. **mckinsey.com/insights/high_tech_telecoms_internet/clouds_big_data_and_smart_assets_ten_tech-enabled_business_trends_to_watch** (accessed March 2014).

Business Wire. "Jetstar Seeks Nuance's Nina Web for 'Ask Jess' Virtual Assistant." December 16, 2013. **businesswire.com/news/home/20131216005468/en/Jetstar-Selects-Nuance's-Nina-Web-"Ask-Jess"#.Uw_OzPmICm4** (accessed March 2014).

BusinessWeek Online. "Hot Growth Special Report 2006 [Blue Nile]." June 2006. **businessweek.com/hot_growth/2006/company/10.htm** (accessed March 2014).

Cario, J. E. *Pinterest Marketing: An Hour a Day*. Hoboken, NJ: Sybex, 2013.

Carr, K. *Pinterest for Dummies*. Hoboken, NJ: Wiley, 2012.

Carr, N. "IT in 2018: From Turing's Machine to Computing Cloud." *Internet.com IT Management eBook,* New York: Jupitermedia Corp., 2008.

Clark, K. "Discover the Best-of-Craigslist." *L'Atelier*, March 10, 2008. **atelier.net/en/trends/articles/discover-best-craigslist** (accessed March 2014).

Coleman, D., and S. Levine. *Collaboration 2.0: Technology and Best Practices for Successful Collaboration in a Web 2.0 World*. Cupertino, CA: Happy About Info., 2008.

CrimsonLogic. "Madagascar TradeNet." Case Study. 2014 **crimsonlogic.com/Documents/pdf/resourceLibrary/brochures/tradeFacilitation/Madagascar_TradeNet_Case_Study.pdf** (accessed May 2014).

Davenport, T. "Where's the 'Working' in Social Networking?" October 29, 2007. **blogs.hbr.org/2007/10/wheres-the-working-in-social-n/** (accessed March 2014).

Dembosky, A. "Pinterest Takes a Track with Advertising Launch." *Financial Times*, September 20, 2013.

Elliott, A. "10 Amazing Augmented Reality iPhone Apps.", December 5, 2009. **mashable.com/2009/12/05/augmented-reality-iphone/** (accessed March 2014).

E-Market Services. "Why Use E-Marketplaces?" 2006. **emarketservices.com/start/Knowledge/eMarket-Basics/Why-use-eMarkets/index.html** (accessed March 2014).

Experian. "The 2012 Digital Marketer Trend and Benchmark Report." 2012. **experian.com/hitwise/digital-marketer-2012.html** (free registration for download) (accessed March 2014).

Fjeldsted, K. "Madagascar Trade" in *Celebrating Reform 2009: Doing Business Case Studies*. Washington, D.C.: World Bank. **doingbusiness.org/reports/case-studies/2009/trade-reform-in-madagascar** (accessed May 2014).

Gartner. "Top 10 Strategic Technology Trends for 2014." **gartner.com/technology/research/top-10-technology-trends** (accessed June 2014).

Gupta, A. "How Social Platforms are Powering Mobile Commerce." September 1, 2011. **socialmediatoday.com/achintya-gupta/348719/how-are-social-networks-powering-mobile-commerce** (accessed March 2014).

Hayes, G. "16 Top Augmented Reality Business Models." September 14, 2009. **personalizemedia.com/16-top-augmented-reality-business-models** (accessed March 2014).

Hayden, B. *Pinfluence: The Complete Guide to marketing your Business with Pinterest*. Hoboken, NJ: Wiley, 2012.

Hemley, D. "26 Tips for Using Pinterest for Business." *Social Media Examiner,* February 27, 2012. **socialmediaexaminer.com/26-tips-for-using-pinterest-for-business/** (accessed March 2014).

Hempel, J. "Is Pinterest the next Facebook?" March 22, 2012. **tech.fortune.cnn.com/2012/03/22/pinterest-silbermann-photo-sharing/** (accessed March 2014).

Hof, R. D. "My Virtual Life." April 30, 2006. **businessweek.com/stories/2006-04-30/my-virtual-life** (accessed March 2014).

Hornor, T. "Pinterest Legal Concerns: What is Lawful to Pin?" June 26, 2012. **socialmediatoday.com/tara-hornor/565706/pinterest-legal-concerns-what-lawful-pin** (accessed March 2014).

Howe, J. *Crowdsourcing: Why the Power of the Crowd is Driving the Future of Business*. New York: Crown Business, 2008.

IBISWorld. "E-Commerce and OnlineAuctions in the U.S.: Market Research Report." March 13, 2012.

prweb.com/releases/2012/3/prweb9277980.htm (accessed March 2014).

IBISWorld. "E-Commerce and Online Auctions in the U.S. Industry Market Research Report Has Been Updated." October 5, 2013. prweb.com/releases/2013/10/prweb11199325.htm (accessed March 2014).

iPhoneness. "40 Best Augmented Reality iPhone Apps." September 2010. iphoneness.com/iphone-apps/best-augmented-reality-iphone-applications (accessed March 2014).

Jopson, B., and H. Kuchler. "Pinterest Hopes to Bridge the Retail Divide." *Financial Times*, November 27, 2013.

Koren, J. "From Web 4.0 and Beyond." *Integrating Educational Technology and Digital Learning* January 20, 2013. slideshare.net/joh5700/educational- technology-and-digital-learning-16077621 (accessed March 2014).

Laurent, W. "Interface: Where We're Headed with Web 3.0." July 1, 2010. information-management.com/issues/20_4/where-were-headed-with-web-3.0-10018222-1.html (accessed March 2014) (free registration necessary to read).

Leland, K. *Ultimate Guide to Pinterest for Business (Ultimate Series).* Irvine, CA: Entrepreneur Press, 2013.

Liedtke, M. "Study: Craigslist Revenue to Climb 23 Pct to $100M." June 10, 2009. thestreet.com/story/10511645/1/study-craigslist-revenue-to-climb-23-pct-to-100m.html (accessed March 2014).

Loren, J., and E. Swiderski. *Pinterest for Business: How to Pin Your Company to the Top of the Hottest Social Media Network (Que Biz-Tech).*Indianapolis, IN: Que Publishing, 2012.

Mahar, S. M., and J. Mahar. *The Unofficial Guide to Building Your Business in Second Life Virtual World: Marketing and Selling Your Product, Services, and Brand In-World.* New York: AMACOM, 2009.

Malaby, T. M. *Making Virtual Worlds: Linden Lab and Second Life.* New York: Cornell University Press, 2009.

Mangalindan, J. P. "Twitter's Business Model: A Visionary Experiment." July 9, 2010. money.cnn.com/2010/07/09/magazines/fortune/Twitter_business_model.fortune/index.htm (accessed March 2014).

Marcom on a Dime. "Augmented Reality: Business Uses 2010." marcomonadime.com/?p=699 (accessed March 2014).

McKenzie, H. "Here's a Social Shopping Site that Could Undermine Pinterest." May 22, 2012. pando.com/2012/05/22/heres-a-social-shopping-site-that-could-undermine-pinterest/ (accessed March 2014).

Miles, J.G., and K. Lacey, *Pinterest Power: Market Your Business, Sell Your Product, and Build Your Brand on the World's Hottest Social Network*, New York: McGraw Hill, 2012.

Mitroff, S. "How Zappos Could Help Pinterest Pin Down a Business Model." August 30, 2012. wired.com/business/2012/08/pinterest/ (accessed March 2014).

Patel, K. "Incremental Journey for World Wide Web: Introduced with Wen 1.0 to Recent Web 5.0- A Survey Paper." *International Journal of Advanced Research in Computer Science and Software Engineering*, 3(10), October 2013.

Petroff A. "Want to Chat in 29 Languages?" *CNN Money*, January 2, 2014. money.cnn.com/2014/01/02/technology/translation-service-app/ (accessed March 2014).

Protalinski, E. "Facebook: Over 955 Million Users, 543 Million Mobile Users." July 26, 2012. news.cnet.com/8301-1023_3-57480950-93/facebook-over-955-million-users-543-million-mobile-users (accessed March 2014).

Rivlin, G. "When Buying a Diamond Starts with a Mouse." January 7, 2007. nytimes.com/2007/01/07/business/yourmoney/07nile.html?pagewanted=all&_r=0 (accessed March 2014).

Roberts, B. "Social Networking at the Office." *HR Magazine*, March 2008, Volume 53, No. 3.

Rorick, S. "Why Marketers Should Care about Augmented Reality." *iMedia Connection*, March 13, 2012. imediaconnection.com/content/31213.asp (accessed March 2014).

Saarinen, T., M. Tinnilä, and A. Tseng, (Eds.). *Managing Business in a Multi-Channel World: Success Factors for E-Business.* Hershey, PA: Idea Group, Inc., 2006.

Sherman, A. *The Complete Idiot's Guide to Crowdsourcing.* New York: Alpha, 2011.

Shontell, A. "A Lawyer Who Is Also a Photographer just Deleted All Her Pinterest Boards Out of Fear." February 28, 2012. businessinsider.com/pinterest-copyright-issues-lawyer-2012-2 (accessed March 2014).

Singapore Customs. "An Overview of TradeNet." (Last reviewed April 29, 2014.) customs.gov.sg/leftNav/trad/TradeNet/An+Overview+of+TradeNet.htm (accessed May 2014).

Smith, C., "(January 2014) By the Numbers: 50 Amazing Pinterest Stats", *Digital Marketing Ramblings (DMR)*, January 18, 2014. expandedramblings.com/index.php/pinterest-stats/#.UwV9JfldWSo (accessed March 2014).

Stafford, A. "The Future of the Web." October 2, 2006. pcworld.com/article/126855/article.html (accessed March 2014).

Stambor, Z. "61% of Shoppers Use a Search Engine When They Shop Online, Study Says." March 2, 2010. internetretailer.com/2010/03/02/61-of-shoppers-use-a-search-engine-when-they-shop-online-study (accessed March 2014).

Stinton, N., *Working in a Virtual World: A Practical Guide to Working with Virtual Clients, Managers and Team Members, and Becoming More Connected, Efficient and Productive*, Singapore: Marshall Cavendish International (Asia) Pte. Ltd., 2013.

Taft. D. K. "Cloud Computing: IBM's Top 12 Tech Trends for 2012 Include Cloud, Analytics, Mobile." *eWeek*, December 5, 2011.

Terdiman, D. *The Entrepreneur's Guide to Second Life: Making Money in the Metaverse.* Indianapolis, IN: Wiley & Sons, 2008.

The Retail Bulletin. "M-Commerce Quadruples in Two Years." May 24, 2012. **theretailbulletin.com/news/ mcommerce_quadruples_in_two_years_24-05-12** (accessed May 2014).

Truong, A. "Today's Most Innovative Company: IKEA Uses Augmented Reality to Show How Furniture Fits in a Room." July 26, 2013, **fastcompany.com/3014930/ most-innovative-companies/todays-most-innova- tive-company-ikea-uses-augmented-reality-to- show** (accessed March 2014).

Turban, E., et al. Social Commerce, New York: Springer 2015.

Volpe, M. "7 Examples of Brands that Pop on Pinterest." *Social Media Today*, February 3, 2012. **socialmedia- today.com/mikevolpe/559222/7-examples-brands- pop-pinterest** (accessed March 2014).

Wasko, M., R. Teigland, D. Leidner, and S. Jarvenpaa. "Stepping into the Internet: New Ventures in Virtual Worlds." *MIS Quarterly (Special Issue)*, September 2011, Vol. 35, No. 3.

Yang, J. "Pinterest: How Does Pinterest Generate Revenue?" February 23, 2012 [Updated]. **quora.com/Pinterest/ How-does-Pinterest-generate-revenue-What-is-the- companys-business-model** (accessed March 2014).

Part II

E-Commerce Applications

Retailing in Electronic Commerce: Products and Services

3

Contents

Learning Objectives

Upon completion of this chapter, you will be able to:

1. Describe electronic retailing (e-tailing) and its characteristics.
2. Classify the primary e-tailing business models.
3. Describe how online travel and tourism services operate and how they influence the industry.
4. Discuss the online employment market, including its participants and benefits.
5. Describe online real estate services.
6. Discuss online stock-trading services.
7. Discuss cyberbanking and online personal finance.
8. Describe on-demand delivery of groceries and similar perishable products and services related to them.
9. Describe the delivery of digital products such as online entertainment.
10. Discuss various online consumer aids, including price comparison sites.
11. Describe the impact of e-tailing on retail competition.
12. Describe disintermediation and other B2C strategic issues.

Electronic supplementary material The online version of this chapter (doi: 10.1007/978-3-319-10091-3_3) contains supplementary material, which is available to authorized users

OPENING CASE: AMAZON.COM: THE KING OF E-TAILING

The Problem

In the early 1990s, entrepreneur Jeff Bezos saw an opportunity rather than a business problem. He decided that books were the most logical product for selling online. In July 1995, Bezos started Amazon.com (**amazon.com**) and began selling books online. Over the years, the company has continually improved, expanded, changed its business model, and expanded its product selection, improving customer experience, and adding new products and services and business alliances. The company also recognized the importance of order fulfillment and warehousing early on. It has invested billions of dollars building physical warehouses and distribution centers designed for shipping packages to millions of customers. In 2012, the company started same day delivery from its new distribution centers. After 2000, the company added information technology products and services, notably the Kindle e-reader family as well as Web Services (cloud technologies). Amazon.com's challenge was, and still is, to profitably sell many consumer products and services online.

The Solution: Innovations and Reaching Out to Customers

In addition to its initial electronic bookstore, Amazon.com has expanded its offerings to include millions of products and services. A unique example of a service they offer is Mechanical Turk (**mturk.com**), a marketplace for crowdsourcing work that requires human intelligence in dozens of categories (see Chapter 8). Key features of Amazon.com are easy browsing, searching, and ordering; useful product information, reviews, recommendations, and other personalization techniques; a very large selection of products, the ability to compare prices; low prices; secure payment system; efficient order fulfillment; and an easy product return arrangement.

The Amazon.com website has a number of useful services, some provided by its companies. For example, its & "Gift Finder and Wish Lists" section (**amazon.com/gp/gift-finder**) suggests gifts for all occasions and seasons, categorized by relationship, price, and more. Author Central (**author-central. amazon.com**) is a page where customers can read about authors (such as their biography and speaking events) and even connect with some of them. Authors can discuss their work and answer readers' questions via tweeting.

Amazon.com also offers support services. Amazon Services **services.amazon.com** hosts webstores for a small monthly fee, offering small businesses the opportunity to have customized storefronts supported by Amazon.com's payment and order-fulfillment system (see **services. amazon.com/content/sell-on-amazon**). Customers can use mobile devices to shop. Amazon Prime (**amazon.com/prime**) offers unlimited free shipment for a modest annual fee. In 2013, Amazon announced that they had been researching the idea of using drones for fast package shipment, via their Amazon Prime Air service (**amazon.com/b?node=8037720011**). This idea has lots of legal and regulatory obstacles. For more information see **forbes.com/sites/stevebanker/2013/12/19/amazon-drones-here-is-why-it-will-work**, **geekwire.com/2014/drone-pilot-beat-faa-regs-says-amazon-delivery-long-way**, and Chapter 12.

Amazon.com is also recognized as an online leader in providing personalized services and CRM. When a customer revisits Amazon.com, a cookie file (see Chapter 9) identifies the user and says, for example, "Welcome back, Sarah Shopper," and then proceeds to recommend new books on topics similar to past purchases. You may receive recommendations for cheaper products. For example, a customer who buys printer toner for $30 a unit regularly might be directed to a vendor that sells four units for a total of $65. Amazon also provides detailed product descriptions and ratings to help consumers make informed purchase decisions. The site has an efficient search engine and other shopping aids. Amazon.com has a state-of-the-art warehousing system that gives the company an advantage over the competition.

Amazon.com is known for its business strategy and the acquisition of its successful competitors in niche markets (e.g., **kivasystems.com**, **zappos. com**). The company also acquired supplementary companies such as **alexa.com**, **junglee.com**, and Digital Photography Review (**dpreview.com**). (See also **crunchbase.com/organization/amazon**, and Distinguin 2011.) To read about the possibility of Amazon's future acquisitions, see **recode.net/2014/01/31/after-amazons-smallest-acquisition-year-since-2007-will-it-gobble-up-competitors-in-2014**.

Customers can personalize their accounts and manage orders online with the patented "1-Click" ordering feature. 1-Click includes an electronic digital wallet (see Chapter 11), which enables shoppers to save time paying for their orders, since all the shopping information, including preferred method of payment and default address, is stored online.

In 1997, Amazon.com started an extensive associates program (a method of affiliate marketing; see Chapter 9). The company has millions of affiliates worldwide that refer customers to Amazon.com (see **affiliate-program.amazon. com**). These associates can earn up to a 15% referral fee if the referral ends with a sale. Amazon.com also is becoming a Web fulfillment contractor (**services.amazon.com/content/fulfillment-by-amazon.htm**), even for large competitors. Other services Amazon offers include: AmazonFresh (**fresh.amazon.com**; a grocery delivery service); Amazon MP3 store (**amazon.com/MP3-Music-Download/b?node=163856011**; music downloads, some free, others for 69¢ per song); and Prime Instant Video (**amazon.com/Prime-Instant-Video/b?node=2676882011**; thousands of movies and TV episodes available for purchase, rental, and streaming).

Amazon.com offers many Web 2.0 social shopping features (e.g., customer reviews). It acquired Woot! (**woot.com**), a social networking company known for its daily deals. Amazon is continuously adding innovative services. In 2011, the company introduced Price Check (to be described later), which enables customers to compare prices in physical stores with a smartphone app. Notable in 2012 are the same day delivery initiative, the **myhabit.com** clothing site (designer brands at reduced prices), and the

ability to use mobile devices while you are inside a physical store to compare prices using the Price Check app. The Amazon strategy is to provide the best customer satisfaction, make large investments in the short run at the expense of profit, and promote innovations (see **businessinsider. com/amazons-profits-what-people-dont-understand-2013-10**).

The Results

In 1999, *Time* magazine named Bezos "Person of the Year." In January 2002, Amazon.com declared its first profit – for the 2001 fourth quarter. Since then, the company has remained profitable despite its huge investments in distribution centers and other initiatives. Amazon.com reported that despite adverse U.S. and global economic conditions, its annual profit for 2011 had doubled from 2007, with a 41% revenue increase in one year. Revenues continue to rise every quarter.

In 2012, *Fortune* magazine selected Bezos as the "businessperson of the year" (see **fortune. com/2012/11/16/business-person-of-the-year. fortune/2.html**). Annual sales increased consistently by 30–40% each year due to the addition of more products and services, going global, and the increased volume purchased by existing customers. Amazon offers about 20 million books, music, and DVD/video titles to millions of customers. In 2012, Amazon had over 1 million e-books for sale. Finally, its investors are rewarded with rapidly increasing stock prices. Data from 2014 show Amazon.com as #12 on Alexa (global rank) and #5 (U. S. rank). It has over 23 million "Likes" and over 84,000 "Talking about this" on Facebook (see **facebook.com/Amazon**). As of February 2014, Amazon has 1.01 million followers on Twitter (**twitter.com/amazon**). For the "Amazing Amazon Story – Jeff Bezos Full Speech," watch the video (17:59 minutes) at **youtube.com/watch?v=YlgkfOr_GLY**.

Despite increased competition from thousands of e-tailers in the online market, Amazon.com has been holding its place as the number one B2C e-tailer and money-making EC site in the world (some Chinese sites are getting closer to Amazon, but they are not competitors). Due to its order fulfillment system, Amazon.com can offer very low prices. Add this to high customer satisfaction and the selection of quality products, one can understand why Amazon.com sells more than three times the products compared to its nearest U.S. competitor.

Amazon.com also offers several features for international customers, including over 1 million Japanese-language books. Amazon.com operates in 12 countries but it can ship its products to other countries. Each country has a website in its own language (for example, Amazon China **amazon. cn**). Amazon.com generated revenues of about $75 billion in 2013, with an operating income of over $745 million (see **digitalbookworld. com/2014/amazon-booms-in-2013-with- 74-45-billion-in-revenue**). As of Q4 2013, the company employs over 117,000 full-time and part-time employees. Amazon.com is considered as the "king of e-tailers." The company has been ranked by the U.S. National Retail Federation, as the #1 fastest-growing large retail organization in the U.S. with a 42.5% sales growth in 2011 (Groth and Cortez 2012). For a comprehensive slide show about Amazon.com, see Distinguin (2011). See also Stone (2013).

Sources: Based on Distinguin (2011), Brandt (2011), Stone (2013), Groth and Cortez (2012), Kain (2011), and **amazon.com** (accessed May 2014).

LESSONS LEARNED FROM THE CASE

The case of Amazon.com, the most recognized name of all e-tailers in the world, demonstrates the evolution of e-tailing, some of the problems encountered by e-tailers, and the solutions that a company can employ to expand its business. It also is indicative of some key trends in Internet retailing. For example, there is fierce competition online. Amazon.com is successful because of its size, innovations, personalization, order fulfillment and customer service. The biggest online retailer is still growing and becoming more dominant. E-tailing, as demonstrated by the Amazon.com case, continues its double-digit, year-over-year growth rate despite the global economic downturn. This is, in part, because sales are shifting away from physical stores. In this chapter, we look at the delivery of both products and services online to individual customers. We also discuss e-tailing successes and failures.

3.1 INTERNET MARKETING AND B2C ELECTRONIC RETAILING

The Amazon.com case illustrates how commerce can be conducted on the Internet. Indeed, the amount and percentage of goods and services sold on the Internet is increasing rapidly, despite the failure of many dot-com companies. According to Grau (2011), approximately 71% of adult U.S. Internet users shop online and 94% conduct research online about a product before purchasing the item, whether online or in a physical store. Similar figures are reported in several Western countries, as well as in Taiwan, Malaysia, Australia, and New Zealand. **Internetworldstats. com** estimates that there are over 2.67 billion Internet users worldwide and over 273 million in North America as of March 2014 (see **internet-worldstats.com/stats.htm**). For "A Day in the Life of the Internet [Infographic]," see **adweek. com/socialtimes/internet-24-hours/499019**. Forrester Research estimates that U.S. shoppers will spend $327 million online in 2016, a 62% increase over 2012 (reported by Rueter 2012). Experts estimate the global B2C to be over 1 trillion in 2014, especially due to the growth in China. Some think that as the number of Internet users reaches saturation, the rate of increase of online shopping may slow down. However, this may not be the case. In fact, the rise of social and mobile shopping seems to have accelerated the pace of B2C. In addition, the economic downturn may increase online shopping as a means of saving money (e.g., save on gas if you do not need to drive to a physical store). Finally, global B2C is still increasing rapidly. Therefore, one of the challenges facing e-tailers is increasing the amount of money each person spends online.

As discussed in Chapter 1, companies have many benefits from selling their goods and services online. Innovative marketing models and strategies and a better understanding of online consumer behavior (Chapter 9) are critical success factors in B2C. For statistics on EC in general and retail trade in particular, see **census.gov/econ/estats**.

This chapter presents an overview of Internet retailing, its diversity, prospects, and limitations. Retailing, especially when conducted in a new medium, must be supported by an understanding of consumer buying behavior, market research, and advertising, topics that will be presented in Chapter 9. Let us begin our discussion of EC products and services with an overview of electronic retailing.

Overview of Electronic Retailing

A retailer is a sales *intermediary* between manufacturers and customers. Even though many manufacturers sell directly to consumers, they usually do so to supplement their major sales through wholesalers and retailers. In the physical world, retailing is done in stores (or factory outlets) that customers must visit physically in order to make a purchase, although sometimes customers may order by phone. Companies that produce a large number of products for millions of customers, such as Procter and Gamble, must use retailers for efficient product distribution. However, even if a company sells relatively few different types of products (e.g., Apple Computers), it still might need retailers to reach a large number of customers who are scattered in many locations.

Catalog (mail-order) sales offer companies the opportunity to reach more customers and give customers a chance to buy from home. Catalog retailers do not need a physical store with staff; online shopping has created the need for electronic catalogs. Retailing conducted over the Internet is called **electronic retailing (e-tailing)**, and sellers who conduct retail business online are called **e-tailers**, as illustrated in the opening case. E-tailing can be conducted through catalogs that have fixed prices as well as online via auctions. E-tailing helps manufacturers (e.g., Dell) sell directly to customers. This chapter examines the various types of e-tailing and related issues.

Note that the distinction between B2C and B2B EC may be unclear. For example, Amazon.com sells to both individuals and to organizations. Walmart (**walmart.com**) sells to both individuals and businesses (via Sam's Club). Dell sells its computers to both consumers and businesses from **dell.com**, Staples sells to both markets at **staples.com**, and insurance sites sell to both individuals and corporations.

Size and Growth of the B2C Market

B2C e-commerce is growing rapidly, especially in developing countries (e.g., China, Russia, Brazil and India).

The statistics for the volume of B2C EC sales, including forecasts for future sales, come from many sources. Reported amounts of online sales *deviate substantially* based on how the numbers are derived, and thus it is often difficult to obtain a consistent and accurate picture of the growth of EC. Some of the variation stems from the use of different definitions and classifications of EC. Another issue is how the items for sale are categorized. Some sources combine certain products and services; others do not or use different methods. Some sources include online travel sales in the statistics for EC retail; others do not. Sometimes different time periods are used in the measurement. Therefore, when reading data about B2C EC sales, it is important that care is taken in interpreting the figures.

The sites listed in Table 3.1 provide statistics on e-tailing as well as on other Internet and EC activities. Typical statistics used in describing e-tailing and consumer behavior include Internet usage by demographic (online sales by age, gender, country, etc.), online sales by item, online sales by vendor, and online purchasing patterns of customers.

Table 3.1 Representative sources of EC statistics

BizRate (**bizrate.com**)	InternetRetailer (**internetretailer.com**)
Business 2.0 (**money.cnn.com/magazines/business2/**)	Nielsen Online (**nielsen-online.com**)
Emarketer (**emarketer.com**)	Shop.org (**shop.org**)
comScore (**comscore.com**)	Adobe SiteCatalyst (**adobe.com/solutions/digital-analytics/sitecatalyst.html?promoid=KIVFD**)
ClickZ (**clickz.com**)	Pew Research Internet Project (**pewinternet.org**)
emarket (**emarket.com**)	Yankee Group (**yankeegroup.com**)
Forrester Research (**forrester.com**)	U.S. Census Bureau (**census.gov/econ/estats/**)
Gartner (**gartner.com**)	

What Sells Well on the Internet

Despite the inconsistency of the data, it is clear that B2C is growing at least 15% each year. This is due both to more shoppers and to more money spent online.

With approximately 189 million shoppers online in the United States in 2013, e-tailers realized the opportunity to sell large quantities of products (see **cpcstrategy.com/blog/2013/08/ecommerce-infographic** for infographics and statistics on online shopping). Millions of different items are available on the Web from numerous vendors. Online File W3.1 shows the major categories of goods that are selling well online.

Developments in B2C E-Commerce

The first-generation of B2C e-commerce sold books, software, and music – simple to understand small items (known as commodity items) that were easily shipped to consumers. The second wave of online growth started in 2000, as consumers started researching and buying complex products such as furniture, large appliances, and expensive clothing (see Case 1.1 on Net-a-Porter, p. 13). Today consumers research product information and purchase online from categories such as bedding, spas, expensive jewelry, designer clothes, appliances, cars, flooring, big-screen TVs, and building supplies. Consumers are also buying many services such as college educations and insurance policies.

Characteristics and Advantages of Successful E-Tailing

Many of the same success factors that apply to physical retailing also apply to e-tailing. In addition, a scalable and secure infrastructure is needed. However, e-tailers can offer special consumer services not offered by traditional retailers. For a comparison of e-tailing and retailing, including advantages, see Table 3.2.

Goods with the following characteristics are expected to sell the most:

- Brand name recognition (e.g., Apple, Dell, Sony). A service guarantee provided by well-known vendors (e.g., Amazon.com, BlueNile.com). For example, return policies and expedited delivery; free shipping.
- Digitized format (e.g., software, music, e-books, or videos).
- Relatively inexpensive items (e.g., office supplies, vitamins).
- Frequently purchased items (e.g., books, cosmetics, office supplies, prescription drugs).
- Commodities for which physical inspection is not necessary (e.g., books, CDs, airline tickets).
- Well-known packaged items that you normally do not open in a physical store (e.g., canned or sealed foods, chocolates, vitamins).

Table 3.2 Retailing versus e-tailing

Factor	Retailers	E-Tailers
Increase of sales volume	• Expansion of locations, stores, and space	• Going out of their regular area and even globally to find customers
More visitors, but less revenue	• Expand marketing efforts to turn "window shoppers" into active shoppers	• Expand marketing communications to turn viewers into shoppers
Use of technology	• Automation store technologies such as POS, self-check, and information kiosks	• Ordering, payments, and fulfillment systems. • Comparisons and customer testimonials • Instant delivery of digital products
Customer relations and handling of complaints	• Face-to-face, stable contacts	• Anonymous contacts, less stability
	• More tolerance of disputes due to face-to-face contacts	• More responsiveness to complaints due to potential negative publicity via social media platforms (e.g., Facebook, Twitter).
Competition	• Local competition • Fewer competitors	• More competitors • Intense due to comparisons and price reductions • Global competition
Customer base	• Local area customers • Lack of anonymity • High increase of customer loyalty	• Wide area (possibly global) customers • Anonymity most of the time • Easy to switch brands (less loyalty)
Supply chain cost	• High cost, interruptions	• Lower cost, more efficient
Customization and personalization	• Expensive and slow • Not very popular	• Fast, more efficient • Popular
Price changing	• Expensive and slow, not done often	• Inexpensive, can be done anytime
Adaptability to market trends	• Slow	• Rapid

Sources: Based on Lee and Brandyberry (2003), Kwon and Lennon (2009), Ha and Stoel (2009), and authors' experiences

Advantages of E-Tailing

E-tailing provides advantages to both sellers and buyers. The advantages of e-commerce, described in Chapter 1, also apply here.

The major advantages to sellers are:

- Lower product cost, thus increasing competitive advantage.
- Reach more customers, many outside the vendor's region, including going global. For example, some Chinese and Taiwanese e-tailers operate sites that sell electronic products all over the world (e.g., E-Way Technology Systems Corp. [ewayco.com]).

- Change prices and catalogs quickly, including the visual presentation. Such flexibility increases competitive advantage.
- Lower supply chain costs (see Chapter 12).
- Provide customers with a wealth of information online as a self-service option, thus saving customer service costs.
- React quickly to customer needs, complaints, tastes, and so forth.
- Provide customization of products and services, self configuration, and personalization of customer care.
- Enable small companies to compete with larger companies.
- Better understand customers and interact with them.

- Sell specialized items country-wide, or even worldwide (e.g., surfing-related merchandise by the Australian company **surfstitch.com**).
- Engage customers in interesting search, comparison, and discussion activities.
- Contact customers who are not reachable by traditional methods of communication.

The major benefits to the buyers are to:

- Pay less than in traditional or even discount stores.
- Find products/services not available in local stores.
- Shop globally: compare prices and services.
- Shop anytime and from anywhere.
- Find it unnecessary to go to the store wasting time and gasoline, and being pressured by salespeople.
- Create their own designs and products (e.g., see **spreadshirt.com**).
- Find collectors' items.
- Buy in groups: buy with friends and engage in social shopping.

The next section examines the major business models that have proven successful in e-tailing.

SECTION 3.1 REVIEW QUESTIONS

1. Describe the nature of B2C EC.
2. What sells well in B2C?
3. What are the characteristics of high-volume products and services?
4. Describe the major trends in B2C.
5. Why is B2C also called e-tailing?
6. List the major characteristics of B2C.
7. What are the benefits of B2C for both buyers and sellers?

3.2   E-TAILING BUSINESS MODELS

In order to understand e-tailing better, let us look at it from the point of view of a retailer or a manufacturer that sells to individual consumers (see Figure 3.1). The seller has its own organization and must also buy materials, goods, and services from others, usually businesses (B2B in Figure 3.1). As also shown in the figure, e-tailing, which is basically B2C (right side of the figure), is done between the seller (a retailer or a manufacturer) and an individual buyer. The figure shows other EC transactions and related activities that may affect e-tailing. Retailing businesses, like other businesses, are driven by a business model. A **business model**, as defined in Chapter 1, is a description of how an organization intends to generate revenue through its business operations.

In this section, we will look at the various B2C models and their classifications.

Classification of Models by Distribution Channel

E-tailing business models can be classified in several ways. For example, some classify e-tailers by the nature of the business (e.g., general purpose versus specialty e-tailing) or by the scope of the sales region covered (global versus regional), whereas others use classification by revenue sources. Here we classify the models by the distribution channel used, distinguishing five categories:

1. **Traditional mail-order retailers that also sell online.** For example, QVC and Lands' End also sell on the Internet.
2. **Direct marketing by manufacturers.** Manufacturers such as Dell, LEGO, and Godiva market directly online from their webstore to customers, in addition to selling via retailers.
3. **Pure-play e-tailers.** These e-tailers sell only online. Amazon.com is an example of a pure-play e-tailer (see opening case).

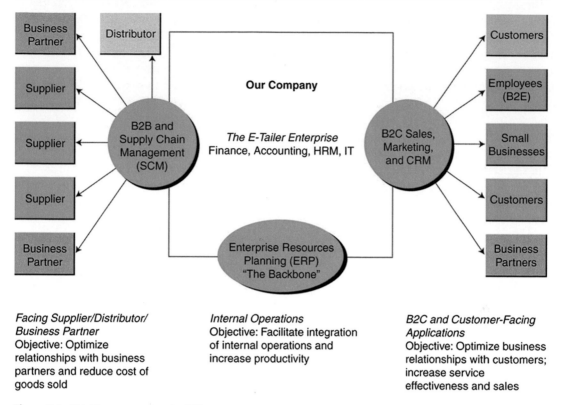

E-tailing as an enterprise EC system

4. **Click-and-mortar ("brick-and-click") retailers.** These are retailers that open webstores to supplement their regular business activities (e.g., **walmart.com** and **homedepot.com**). For details, see **en.wikipedia.org/wiki/Bricks_and_clicks**. However, we are now seeing a reverse trend: Some pure play e-tailers are creating physical storefronts. For example, Apple opened physical stores and Dell sells its products at partner store locations, such as Best Buy and Staples. Expedia. com opened physical kiosks in tourist areas, and Net-a-Porter has two physical stores. The idea of selling both online and offline is part of a model or strategy known as a **multichannel business model**. Using this strategy, the company offers several options for the customer to shop, including over the Internet. This strategy gives customers the opportunity to select the marketing channel with which

they are most comfortable. For discussions and an illustrative case, see Greene (2010) and Lewis (2010).

5. **Internet (online) malls.** As described in Chapter 2, these malls include many stores on one website.

Note that, in direct marketing of any type, sellers and buyers have a chance to interact directly and better understand each other.

6. **Flash sales.** In any of the above categories, sellers can offer steep discounts via an intermediary or directly to the consumers. These discounts exist in several varieties.

Our examination of each of these distribution channel categories follows.

Direct Marketing by Mail-Order Companies

In a broad sense, **direct marketing** describes marketing that takes place without physical stores.

Direct marketers take orders directly from consumers, frequently bypassing traditional intermediaries. Sellers can be retailers or manufacturers.

Direct Sales by Manufacturers and Make-to-Order

Many manufacturers are selling directly to customers. Dell, HP, and other computer manufacturers use this method. It is usually combined with self-configuration of products (customized, build to order). Online File W3.2 describes the process by which customers can configure and order cars online from manufacturers. The major success factor of this model is the ability to offer customized products at a reasonable cost.

Virtual (Pure-Play) E-Tailers

Virtual (pure-play) e-tailers are companies with direct online sales that do not need physical stores. Amazon.com is a prime example of this type of e-tailer. Virtual e-tailers have the advantage of low fixed costs. However, one drawback can be a lack of an efficient order fulfillment system. Virtual e-tailers can be *general-purpose* (such as Amazon.com, or Rakuten.com) or *specialized* e-tailers (such as Dogtoys.com).

Note that a general store may be composed of specialty stores. For example, **hayneedle.com** includes over 200 specialty stores such as furniture, seasonal gifts, yard and garden, and so forth. General-purpose pure-play companies can be very large. Amazon.com is one example. Another example is Rakuten Ichiba, Japan's largest online mall that offers more than 50 million products made by over 33,000 merchants. In May 2010, the Japanese company acquired U.S.-based Buy.com (which is now known as Rakuten.com Shopping). The combined company offers more than 90 million products made by over 35,000 merchants worldwide. The company had over 64 million registered members in Japan in 2009. In 2010, there were about 80 million registered members and sales approached $4 billion (statistics reported by Clearlake Capital 2010 and **rakuten.com/ct/aboutus.aspx**). Thousands of other companies operate as pure play e-tailers. Examples are Australian companies **dealsdirect.com.au** and **asiabookroom.com**.

Specialty e-tailers, such as CatToys.com (**cattoys.com**), can operate in a very narrow market (see Online File W3.3). Blue Nile (Chapter 2) is another example. Such specialized businesses would find it difficult to survive in the physical world because they would not have enough customers and could not hold a large variety of stock.

Click-and-Mortar Retailers and Multichanneling

This is probably the most commonly used model of e-tailing competing with pure play e-tailers. Examples are Walmart.com, Target.com, and thousands of other retailers that offer products and services online as an additional sales channel. This strategy is gaining momentum, but it is not always successful for large companies. A prime example is Best Buy (see Section 3.9).

A **click-and-mortar retailer** is a combination of both the traditional retailer and a webstore.

A **brick-and-mortar retailer** conducts business exclusively in the physical world. In some cases, sellers also might operate a traditional mail-order business.

In today's digital economy, *click-and-mortar* retailers sell via stores, through phone calls, over the Internet, and via mobile devices. A firm that operates both physical stores and an online e-tail site is a click-and-mortar business selling in a *multichannel business model*. Examples of retailers going from brick-and mortar only to brick-and-click are department stores, such as Macy's (**macys.com**) and Sears (**sears.com**), as well as discount stores, such as Walmart (**walmart.com**) and Target (**target.com**). It also includes supermarkets and all other types of retailing.

Lately, there is a trend to open stores on Facebook and other social network sites, in addition to selling from their own sites.

Retailing in Online Malls

There are two types of online malls: referring directories and malls with shared shopping services.

Referring Directories

This type of virtual mall contains a directory organized by product type. Banner ads at the mall site advertise the products or vendors. When users click on the product and/or a specific store, they are transferred to the webstore of the seller, where they can complete the transaction. Examples of referring directories can be found at **bedandbreak fast.com**. The stores listed in a directory either own the directory collectively, or they pay a subscription fee or a commission to the organizing third party for maintaining the site and advertising their products. This type of e-tailing is a kind of affiliate marketing (see **virtualshoppingmall.weebly.com/affiliate-referral-sites.html**).

Malls with Shared Services

In online malls with shared services, a consumer can find a product, order and pay for it, and arrange for shipment. The hosting mall provides these services.

Ideally, the customer would like to go to different stores in the same mall, use one shopping cart, and pay only once. This arrangement is possible, for example, in Yahoo! Small Business (see **smallbusiness.yahoo.com/ecommerce**). Other examples of malls with shared services are **firststopshops.com** and **bing-shop.com**.

Other B2C Models and Special Retailing

Several other business models are used in B2C. They are discussed in various places throughout the book and by Wieczner and Bellstrom (2010). Some of these models also are used in B2B, B2B2C, G2B, and other types of EC.

B2C Social Shopping

Social shopping activities are facilitated by new or improved business models, (e.g., see Turban et al. 2015; Shih 2011; Singh and Diamond 2012). For example, B2C sites such as **amazon. com** and **netflix.com** provide consumers with extensive social context and engagement opportunities, such as product ratings. Using blogs, wikis, discussion groups, and Twitter, retailers can help customers find and recommend shopping opportunities. Typical new or improved models created by social media tools are summarized below and described in Chapter 7.

Flash Deals (Deals of the Day)
These are sales in which companies offer heavily discounted products to consumers for a limited time (usually 24–72 hours), directly or via intermediaries such as Groupon. The discounts are so large that the sellers hope that people will spread the news to their friends. For details see Chapter 7.

Online Group Buying
In these depressed economic times, more people are using the Internet as a smart way to save money. Using online *group buying*, it is easy to join a group of buyers to get volume discounts (see Chapter 7 for details). There are several start-ups in this market: **yipit.com**, and **livingsocial. com**. Other sites that used pure group buy are now concentrating on flash deal sales. For example see Groupon, **dealradar.com**; and **myhabit.com**.

Personalized Event Shopping
Event shopping is the B2C model in which sales are designed to meet the needs of special events (e.g., a wedding, Black Friday). This model may be combined with group purchasing (to lower the customers' cost). For details, see Wieczner and Bellstrom (2010). Two variations of this online model are *private shopping clubs* and *group gifting online*.

Private Shopping Clubs
An online **private shopping club**, like an offline shopping club (e.g., Costco), enables members to shop at a discount, frequently for short periods of time (just few hours or days). Members may need to register before they are invited to see the special offers. To assure quality, many clubs buy directly from the manufacturers.

Examples of such clubs are Gilt (**gilt.com**) in the U.S. (see Wieczner and Bellstrom 2010) and KupiVIP (**kupivip.ru**) in Russia.

Private shopping clubs can be organized in different ways (e.g., see **beststreet.com**). For details, see Chapter 7 and **en.wikipedia.org/wiki/Private_shopping_club**.

Group Gifting Online

In many cases, a group of friends can collaborate on gifts for events such as a wedding. To help coordinate the group activities and select the gifts, one can use sites like **frumus.com** and **socialgift.com**.

Location-Based E-Commerce

Location-based e-commerce (l-commerce) is a wireless-based technology used by vendors to send advertisements relevant to the location where customers are at a given time by using GPS. The technology is a part of mobile commerce (Chapter 6). The model was unsuccessful until social networking emerged. Today, companies such as Foursquare provide l-commerce services.

Shopping in Virtual Worlds

B2C in virtual worlds is also available. The objective is to foster user interaction with one another and the products in the virtual world, hopefully leading to purchases in the real world.

Virtual Visual Shopping

Many consumers embrace virtual shopping because they get interesting products they would never have bought without seeing them.

According to *Baseline* (2007), one advantage of 3-D is its ability to make things online look more realistic. For example, if you want to see how a new sofa will look in your living room, all you have to do is move a virtual 3D picture of the sofa into an image of a similar living room that is illustrated in 3D. Such an experience can be extended to appliances, decorating rooms, or improving structures.

SECTION 3.2 REVIEW QUESTIONS

1. List the B2C distribution channel models.
2. Describe how traditional mail-order firms are transforming or adding online options.
3. Describe the direct marketing model used by manufacturers.
4. Describe virtual e-tailing.
5. Describe the click-and-mortar approach. Compare it to a pure e-tailing model.
6. Describe the different types of e-malls.
7. Describe flash sales (daily deals).
8. Describe B2C social shopping models.
9. Describe visual virtual shopping.

3.3 ONLINE TRAVEL AND TOURISM (HOSPITALITY) SERVICES

Online services are provided by many travel vendors. Some major travel-related websites are **expedia.com**, **travelocity.com**, **tripadvisor.com**, and **priceline.com**. All major airlines sell their tickets online. Other services are vacation packages (e.g., **blue-hawaii.com**), train schedules and reservations (e.g., **amtrak.com**), car rental agencies (e.g., **autoeurope.com**), hotels (e.g., **marriott.com**), commercial portals (e.g., **cnn.com/TRAVEL**), and tour companies (e.g., **atlas-travelweb.com**). Publishers of travel guides such as **lonelyplanet.com**, **fodors.com**, and **tripadvisor.com** provide considerable amounts of travel-related information on their websites, as well as selling travel services. The competition is fierce, but there is also collaboration. For example, in 2012, TripAdvisor helped New Orleans hotels to attract more guests.

Example: TripAdvisor

According to comScore Media Matrix (December 2013), TripAdvisor (**tripadvisor.com**) is the world's largest travel site. The company provides trip advice generated from actual travelers. This is a global site with more than 260 million visitors a month (per Google Analytics, July 2013). For history, features, and more facts, see **tripadvisor.com/PressCenter-c4-Fact_Sheet.html**.

Example: Qunar.com

Qunar (**qunar.com**) is the world's largest Chinese-language travel platform. The site provides services similar to those provided by TripAdvisor, such as travel information, travel arrangements, and in-depth search (see **www.qunar.com/site/zh/Qunar.in.China_1.2.shtml**).

Characteristics of Online Travel

Online travel services generate income from com-missions, advertising fees, lead-generation pay-ments, subscription fees, site membership fees, etc.

With rapid growth and increasing success, the online travel industry is very popular, although online travel companies cite revenue loss due to fraud as their biggest concern (see **tnooz.com/ article/travel-companies-highlight-revenue-loss-as-biggest-concern-in-online-fraud**). Consumers themselves can fall prey to online travel fraud (see **telegraph.co.uk/travel/travel-news/9446395/Warning-over-online-holiday-fraud.html**). However, competition among online travel e-tailers is intense and has low mar-gins. In addition, customer loyalty and difference in prices make it more difficult to survive. Thus, guaranteed best rates and the provision of loyalty programs are becoming a necessity.

Three important trends will drive further changes in the online travel industry. First, online travel agents may try to differentiate themselves by providing superior customer-service. Second, they provide easy search capabilities (e.g., for best prices). Third, online travel companies are likely to use social media tools to provide content to travelers and would-be travelers (see the dis-cussion later in this section and Chapter 7).

Services Provided

Online travel agencies offer almost all the same services delivered by conventional travel agen-cies, from providing general information to reserving and purchasing travel accommodations and event tickets. In addition, they often provide services that most conventional travel agencies do not offer, such as travel tips and reviews pro-vided by other travelers, fare tracking (free e-mail alerts on low fares), expert opinions, detailed driving maps and directions (see **infohub.com** and **airbnb.com**; a website that connects travel-ers and lists accommodations around the world, chat rooms and bulletin boards). In addition, some offer other innovative services, such as online travel auctions (e.g. **skyauction.com**). Almost all services are available both on desktop and on wireless devices. (For a list of apps for last minute travel, see France 2013.)

Special Online Travel Services

Many online travel services offer travel bargains. Consumers can go to specialty sites, such as those offering standby opportunities and last-minute bargain tickets. For example, **lastminutetravel. com** offers low airfares and discounted accommo-dation prices to fill otherwise-empty airline seats and hotel rooms. Last-minute trips also can be booked on **americanexpress.com**, sometimes at a steep discount. Special vacation destinations can be found at **priceline.com** and **greatrentals.com**. **Flights.com** offers cheap airline tickets and Eurail passes. Travelers can access **cybercaptive.com** for a list of thousands of Internet cafés around the world. Similar information is available via many portals, such as Yahoo! and MSN. Search engines such as Google or Bing can also be helpful.

Example: HomeAway.com, Inc.

HomeAway, Inc. (**homeaway.com**) is a market-place for the vacation rental industry. This online marketplace hosts 890 paid listings offering vaca-tion rental homes in 190 countries (April 2014 data). The basic idea is to offer travelers vacation homes at affordable prices. For example, you can rent a whole vacation house at less than half price of a hotel. The site connects property managers and owners with travelers. Besides the U.S., the company has subsidiaries in several countries, such as the UK, France, and Spain. It has both short and longer stay rentals. The company also operates **bedandbreakfast.com**. The company has an extensive affiliate program (**homeaway. com/info/affiliate-program**) too. The company is very profitable and its stock price is increasing rap-idly (in 2014). For details, see **homeaway.com**.

Also of interest are sites that offer medical advice and services for travelers. This type of information is available from the World Health Organization (**who.int**), governments (e.g., **cdc. gov/travel**), and private organizations (e.g., **medicalert.org** and **webmd.com**).

Other special services include:

- **Wireless services.** Many airlines (e.g., Cathay Pacific, Delta, and Qantas) allow passengers to access the Internet during flights with mobile devices (usually for a fee).

- **Advance check-in.** Most airlines provide advance online check-in. You can print your boarding pass within 24 hours prior to departure. Alternatively, you can use a smartphone (or a tablet) to download the boarding pass to your cell phone and then submit your phone to security with your ID. The security department has electronic scanners that read the boarding pass from your smartphone and let you board the plane.
- **Direct marketing.** Airlines sell electronic tickets (or "e-tickets") over the Internet. When customers purchase electronic tickets online (or by phone), all they have to do is print the boarding pass or enter their credit card at an *electronic kiosk* to get a boarding pass there.
- **Alliances and consortia.** Airlines and other travel companies are creating alliances with one another (e.g., **staralliance.com**) to increase sales or reduce purchasing costs for purchases made over the Internet.

Using Mobile Devices

The use of these is increasing rapidly, with hundreds of apps related to comparing prices, making reservations, looking at travel reviews, and finding the best travel deals available (see Knight 2012 for the use of mobile devices by travelers and **travel.cnn.com/explorations/shop/50-ultimate- travel-apps-so-far-353352** for a list of 50 ultimate travel apps).

Social Travel Networks

Travelers are using sites like Facebook, YouTube, Twitter, Gogobot, Flickr, Foursquare, and TripAdvisor to plan their trips and share experiences (both good and bad) afterward. For example, all major airlines have pages on Facebook that provide information and news about their airline and offer their customers a community to meet other travelers and share experiences (e.g., see **facebook.com/AmericanAirlines**).

Several social networks have travel channels that cater to travelers. Examples of such networks are **wikitravel.org** and **world66.com**, which features a travel channel that uses a wiki allowing any Internet reader to create, update, edit, and illustrate *any* article on the website ("the travel guide you write"). For a comprehensive resource on travel, see **tripad-**

visor.com. Other social networks available exclusively for travelers are Trip Wolf, Trip Hub (a blog dedicated to group travel), Trip Advisor, Virtual Tourist, BootsnAll, and Lonely Planet (see discussion by O'Neill 2011). Case 3.1 shows an example of a social network for travelers.

For an HVS Sales and Marketing Services slideshow presentation on how hotels are using social commerce, see **slideshare.net/VisitKissimmee/examples-of-how-hotels-are-using-social-media-a-guide-for-getting-started-4606358.**

CASE 3.1: EC APPLICATION: WAYN: A LIFESTYLE AND TRAVEL SOCIAL NETWORK

WAYN (**wayn.com**), which stands for "Where Are You Now?" is a social network website with a goal of uniting travelers globally, allowing them to share experiences, describe problems, participate in forums, and find friends. WAYN, a UK company, has grown from 45,000 members in 2005 to over 22.4 million in 2014. Approximately 2 million members are based in the United Kingdom. WAYN is popular in most major developed countries.

The capabilities of the site are similar to that of Facebook and other major social networks. Travelers can search for contacts and visually locate them on countries' maps. The goal is for travelers to keep their friends informed of where they are while traveling and, in turn, to be able to locate their friends ("find who is around").

In addition, users can send SMSs to any of their contacts worldwide and chat online using WAYN's Instant Messenger. Utilizing WAYN, users can create discussion groups, make friends, plan trips, and ask for recommendations.

As of April 2014, WAYN is available in 193 countries, becoming a global and profitable brand. WAYN is followed on Facebook and Twitter. To survive, the company sells travel deals, and provides advertising opportunities to service providers (see **wayn.com/advertising**). WAYN can be accessed on the go via several downloadable mobile applications (see **wayn.com/mobileapps**). The site also provides an opportunity to meet like-minded people and make friends. For a comprehensive description, see **tnooz.com/article/wayn-social-travel-revenue-gains** (posted February 2014). To read an interview with the CEO of WAYN, see **travelblather.com/2013/01/the-future-for-social-travel-websites-an-interview-with-wayn-ceo-pete-ward.html**.

Sources: Based on Butcher (2008) and **wayn.com** (accessed May 2014).

Questions

1. Visit **wayn.com**. What options do you find most exciting on the site?
2. Enter **wayn.com** and identify all advertising options. List them and discuss three that would work best for you as a traveler.
3. Identify the mobile capabilities on the site.
4. Why has WAYN been so successful even though the site requires subscription fees for some of its services?

Benefits, Limitations, and Competition in Online Travel Services

The benefits of online travel services to travelers and travel providers are extensive. The amount of free information is voluminous, and is accessible at any time from any place. Shoppers can find the lowest prices. Travel providers also benefit by eliminating commissions and selling otherwise-empty spaces. Finally, processing fees are reduced. For tips on the limitations and hazards of the use of social travel, see Barish (2010).

Online travel services do have some limitations. First, complex trips are difficult to arrange and may not be available on some sites because they require complicated arrangements. Therefore, the need for travel agents as intermediaries remains, at least for the time being.

Competition in Online Travel

The competition in online travel is intense. In addition to well-known pure players such as Expedia (**expedia.com**), Priceline (**priceline.com**), and Hotels.com (**hotels.com**), there are thousands of travel-related sites online. Many service providers have their own sites, related websites advertise travel sites, and tourist guides sell services or direct users to them. In such a competitive environment, online businesses may fail (e.g., TravelTicker folded in September 2012).

Corporate Travel

The corporate travel market is huge and its online portion has been growing rapidly in recent years. Corporations can use all the online travel services mentioned earlier where they may receive special services. Companies can enable employees to plan and book their own trips to save time and money. Using online optimization tools provided by travel companies, such as those offered by American Express (**amexglobalbusinesstravel.com**), companies can try to reduce travel costs even further. Expedia via Egencia TripNavigator (**egencia.com**), Travelocity (**travelocity.com**), and Orbitz (**orbitzforbusiness.com**) also offer software tools for corporate planning and booking. TripAdvisor for Business (**tripadvisor.com/Owners**) provides information to the tourism and hospitality industries. TripAdvisor TripConnect offers a way for businesses to compete for bookings and generate new business by bringing visitors directly to their online booking pages. For more on how TripConnect works, watch the video guide (2:57 minutes) on **tripadvisor.com/TripConnect**.

Example: American Express's Business Travel Helps URS Corp. to Survive Hurricanes

In order to repair the damage caused by Hurricane Katrina, URS Corporation (a large engineering and architectural design firm) realized that they needed an automated system to identify travelers in need of immediate assistance. A solution was found by implementing American Express Business Traveler's TrackPoint system (**trackpoint.americanexpress.com**), which "enables companies to quickly interface impacted travelers, pinpoint their locations, and review their itineraries" (see **business travel.americanexpress.com/se/files/**

2011/11/CS_URSCorp-US.pdf). For details, see American Express Business Travel (2011).

For details, see the Association of Corporate Travel Executives (**acte.org**).

SECTION 3.3 REVIEW QUESTIONS

1. What travel services are available online that are not available offline?
2. List the benefits of online travel services to travelers and to service providers.
3. How do social networks facilitate travel?
4. Describe corporate online travel services.
5. Describe the competition in online travel services.

3.4 EMPLOYMENT AND THE ONLINE JOB MARKET

The online job market connects job seekers with potential employers. An online job market is now very popular with both job seekers and employers. In addition to job ads posted online and placement services available through specialized websites (such as **careerbuilder.com**), larger companies are building career portals on their corporate websites as a way of reducing recruitment costs and expediting the time to fill vacancies. Advantages of the online job market over the traditional one are listed in Table 3.3.

The Internet Job Market

The Internet offers a comprehensive and large environment for job seekers and for recruiters. Nearly all *Fortune 500* companies now use the Internet for some of their recruitment activities. Online resources are the most popular recruitment option for many companies. Since 2000, online job recruitment revenues and volume significantly overtook print ad classifieds. Tens of thousands of job-related sites are active in the United States alone. Note that many sites provide free lists of available positions. For example, see **jobsearch.money.cnn.com**. The U.S. market is dominated by several major players, especially Monster that acquired Yahoo! HotJobs in August 2010, and CareerBuilder. However, socially-oriented sites such as Craigslist, LinkedIn, Twitter, and Facebook are becoming very important online recruitment sites (see **askingsmarter-questions.com/how-to-recruit-online-finding-talent-with-facebook-twitter-study**).

Note: Jobs searches and finding applicants is going mobile with increasing apps and activities in this direction.

Online Job Markets on Social Networks

According to McCafferty (2012), 58% of recruiters agree that social networking is the 'next big thing' in recruiting. Specifically, 86% already use LinkedIn, 51% use Facebook and 27% use Google+. Facebook has many features that help

Table 3.3 Traditional versus online job markets

Characteristic	Traditional job market	Online job market
Cost	Expensive, especially in prime space	Can be very inexpensive
Life cycle	Short	Long
Place	Usually local and limited if global	Global
Context updating	Can be complex, expensive	Fast, simple, inexpensive
Space for details	Limited	Large
Ease of search by applicant	Difficult, especially for out-of-town applicants	Quick and easy
Ability of employers to find applicants	May be very difficult, especially for out-of-town applicants	Easy
Matching of supply and demand	Difficult	Easy
Reliability	Low, material can get lost in mail	High
Communication speed between employees and employers	Can be slow	Fast
Ability of employees to compare jobs	Limited	Easy, fast

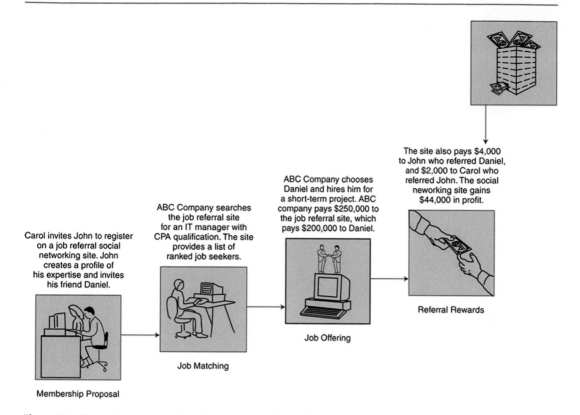

The site also pays $4,000 to John who referred Daniel, and $2,000 to Carol who referred John. The social neworking site gains $44,000 in profit.

ABC Company chooses Daniel and hires him for a short-term project. ABC company pays $250,000 to the job referral site, which pays $200,000 to Daniel.

ABC Company searches the job referral site for an IT manager with CPA qualification. The site provides a list of ranked job seekers.

Carol invites John to register on a job referral social networking site. John creates a profile of his expertise and invites his friend Daniel.

Referral Rewards

Job Offering

Job Matching

Membership Proposal

Figure 3.2   The referral power of social networks in job matching

people find jobs and help employers find candidates. One such feature is Jobcast (**jobcast.net**), which is an app for companies to place on their Facebook page to recruit candidates. The app, which has different types of plans (free and paid), offers social sharing to LinkedIn and Twitter, as well as to Facebook. Their app on Facebook is for jobseekers and employers to connect, and they also have interesting articles regarding the job market. (See **facebook.com/jobcastnet**.) Another way for employers and jobseekers to connect via Facebook is through a company called FindEmployment (**facebook.com/findemployment**), which also offers tips and suggestions for job seekers. A similar service is provided by **linkedin.com/job**. Craigslist, for example, claims more than 1 million new job listings every month. For an overview and examples of finding jobs on Twitter, see Dickler (2009). The LinkedIn search engine can help employers find appropriate candidates quickly. For more on social networking activities in recruiting, see Chapter 8 and Masud (2012).

In addition, *job referral social networking* sites solve the need for finding the right people for the job (e.g., **jobster.com**). These sites provide job seekers opportunities to promote themselves and their areas of expertise, as well as help them be discovered by employers. The referral process is illustrated in Figure 3.2. The site's algorithms enable headhunters to analyze qualified applicants by different criteria. When a job offer is made, the job referral site receives referral fees. Lately, the use of Twitter as an aid for job searches has increased. Bortz (2014) provides a strategy for job seekers and for how to use Twitter to access recruiters and increase job seekers' visibility. For more about recruiting online using Twitter, see **askingsmarterquestions.com/how-to-recruit-online-finding-talent-with-facebook-twitter-study**. TwitJobSearch (**twitjobsearch.com**) is a job search engine allowing employers to post job ads on Twitter. Its features include posting jobs, having the company post jobs for the recruiters, and job seekers being "tweeted" daily from major companies and job boards. According to LinkedIn, "TwitJobSearch scours twitter; indexing tweets that are jobs, and filtering out the rest. Thus providing jobseekers with the tools necessary to find meaningful, relevant job opportunities amongst the noise" (see **linkedin.com/company/1913098/twitjobsearch-com-260783/product**). To sign up or follow TwitJobSearch, go to **twitter.com/TwitJobSearch**.

The following are examples of activities in social networks:

- Search for posted positions
- Track people in your field
- Learn from the experts
- Engage and communicate with people and ask for help
- Make connections
- Note: Lately, companies use gamification (Chapter 8) to help recriters (see Meister 2012).

Global Online Portals for Job Placement

The Internet is very helpful for anyone looking for a job in another country. An interesting global site for placing/finding jobs in different countries is **xing.com**. The electronic job market may increase employee turnover and its costs. Finally, recruiting online is more complicated than most people think, mainly because there are so many résumés online. To facilitate recruitment, top recruiters are seeking the benefits of using new tools like video conferencing to interview and connect with candidates from remote locations.

Virtual Job Fairs

Virtual job fairs as well as recruiting via social networks are becoming popular for expeditiously finding qualified candidates at a reduced cost. Such job fairs use special 3D hosting environments in virtual worlds, social networks, or the employers' websites. They are similar to 'trade fairs' (Chapter 4). These are done on virtual world sites, social networks, employers' websites, or special vendor sites (e.g., **expos2.com**, **brazencareerist.com**).

Example

According to Weinstein (2009), KPMG, which operates in over 150 countries, is using job fairs to globally find and reach job applicants by allowing them to study their particular global office's opportunities and requirements in virtual booths at online fairs. Visitors can then submit a résumé online. For details, see Weinstein (2009), **big4.com/news/kpmg-48-hour-virtual-world-jobs-fair-to-directly-connect-with-job-seekers**, and **brazenconnect.com/event/kpmg_may_2014**.

Components and Hosting

Virtual job fairs are becoming popular. According to Commuiqué Conferencing, Inc. (**virtualjobfairhosting.com**), a virtual job fair hosting service, some virtual job fair features they offer are:

- *Main Hall*: Visitors enter the showroom and watch the video greeting. Visitors may then go to the Auditorium, Exhibit Hall, etc.
- *Exhibitor Booth*: These can be personalized for each exhibitor.
- *Lounge or Communication Center*: Contains professional networking features from message boards to forums and group chat.
- *Resource Center*: Contains demos, webcasts, and documents.

The hosting company of generic fairs also runs private fairs for major corporations such as Time Warner, Nike, and Ford.

Another company that hosts virtual communications and job fairs is ON24, Inc. (**on24.com**). For how IBM used ON24 to find qualified employees for their operations in Africa, read the case study at **on24.com/case-studies/ibm-job-fair**.

For a video titled "Virtual Job Fair Tutorial – Job Seeker" (6:02 minutes) see **youtube.com/watch?v=ZY5-NV5ExJ4**.

Benefits and Limitations of the Electronic Job Market

The online job market has many benefits for both job seekers and recruiters. The major advantages are shown in Table 3.4. For more on the advantages of attending job fairs, see **onlinemba.com/blog/how-to-attend-and-get-the-most-out-of-a-virtual-job-fair**. For benefits of virtual recruiting, see **smallbusiness.chron.com/advantages-virtual-recruitment-16632.html**.

Table 3.4 Advantages of the electronic job market for job seekers and employers

Advantages for job seekers	Advantages for employers
Can discover a large number of job openings	Can reach a large number of job seekers
Can communicate directly and quickly with potential employers	Can reduce recruitment costs
Can market themselves quickly to appropriate employers (e.g., **quintcareers.com**)	Can reduce application-processing costs by using electronic application forms
Can post résumés for large-volume distribution (e.g., at **careerbuilder.com**, **brassring.com**)	Can provide greater equal opportunity for job seekers
	Opportunity of finding highly skilled employees who match the job requirements
Can search for available positions any time	Can describe positions in great detail
Can obtain several support services at no cost (e.g., **careerbuilder.com** and **monster.com** provide free career-planning services)	Can interview candidates online (e.g., using video teleconferencing)
Can determine appropriate salaries in the marketplace (e.g., use **salary.com** and **rileyguide.com**; look for salary surveys)	Can arrange for testing online
	Can view salary surveys for recruiting strategies
Can learn how to behave in an interview (**greatvoice.com**)	
Can access social network groups dedicated to electronic job markets	

Sources: Based on Dixon (2000), Wanarsup and Pattamavorakun (2008), Williams (2000), and the authors' experiences

The electronic job market also has a few limitations. One major limitation is the fact that some people do not use and do not have access to the Internet, although this problem is declining substantially. One solution to the problem of limited access is the use of in-store Internet kiosks, as used by companies such as Home Depot or Macy's. Computers are also available in libraries and other public places. Mobile job search apps such as iPQ Career Planner and Pocket Resume are becoming popular.

Security and privacy are other limitations. Posted résumés and employer-employee communications are usually not encrypted. Thus, confidentiality and data protection cannot be guaranteed. It is also possible that someone at a job seeker's current place of employment (e.g., his or her boss) could find out that that person is job hunting. LinkedIn, for example, provides privacy protection, enabling job seekers to determine who can see their résumé online.

For tips on how to protect your privacy while job hunting, see **guides.wsj.com/careers/how-to-start-a-job-search/how-to-protect-your-privacy-when-job-hunting**.

SECTION 3.4 REVIEW QUESTIONS

1. What are the driving forces of the electronic job market?

2. What are the major advantages of the electronic job market to the candidate? To employers?
3. Why is LinkedIn so useful for job seekers and for employees? List the specific tools provided by EC to job seekers.
4. List the specific tools provided by recruiters.
5. What are the limitations of electronic job markets?

3.5   ONLINE REAL ESTATE, INSURANCE, AND STOCK TRADING

Online infrastructures enable additional marketing channels, new business models, and provide new capabilities. The infrastructures provide a different way of delivering products and services. Some major services are presented in this and the following section.

Real Estate Online

Changes in online real estate information search and transactions significantly impact the way that business is conducted.

To get some idea of the changes, see **realtor.org/research-and-statistics** and for statistics on the growth of the online and offline real estate markets, see **realtor.org/research-and-statistics/research-reports**. For example, in 2012, 74% of all realtors used social media tools regularly. Additional studies by the National Association of Realtors (NAR) have shown that over 36% of real estate buyers begin their searches for properties on the Internet, and 89% of all recent buyers used the Internet at some point in their home search (National Association of Realtors® 2010).

E-commerce and the Internet are slowly but surely having an ever-increasing impact on the real estate industry. For example, despite the changes that are beginning to emerge, real estate agents have not been disintermediated. Home buyers today tend to use both real estate agents and the Internet. One possible impact is declining commissions that sellers pay agents.

Zillow, Craigslist, and Other Web 2.0 Real Estate Services

Craigslist (**craigslist.org**) and Zillow (**zillow.com**) are examples of Web 2.0 free real estate services. Both reduce the use of newspaper classified advertising, and allow buyers to find housing information and do price and location comparisons on their own.

Zillow operates the "Make Me Move" (**zillow.com/make-me-move**) service (free) that allows you to see for what price you would be willing to sell your home without actually putting it on the market (**zillow.com/wikipages/What-is-Make-Me-Move**). Homeowners may be motivated to sell when they see the price they can get when they list their homes (anonymously). Sellers can see prices of similar homes. Buyers can contact the sellers via anonymous e-mail. The company also provides free listings (including photos). Users can also participate in a blog or wiki, start a discussion, and engage in other social-oriented activities. Zillow also offers mortgage calculators and current loan rates. Zillow makes money from advertisers and was listed on the stock market in 2012. Zillow has several competitors (e.g., **ziprealty.com** and **listingbook.com**). Zillow offers its brand via more than a dozen

websites (e.g., **zillow.com/homes/for_rent**, and **agentfolio.com**). Zillow generates revenue by selling ads on its companion websites (**zillow.com/agent-advertising** and **vator.tv/news/2013-12-27-how-does-zillow-make-money**). For additional information, see **zillow.com/corp/About.htm**.

Craigslist has a major classifieds section for real estate ('for sale' and 'for rent' listings). Listings are free except in some large cities, where brokers must pay a fee for placing ads. For more about real estate applications and services offered online, see National Association of Realtors® (**realtor.com**), CRE Online, Inc. (**real-estate-online.com**), and Auction.com (**auction.com**).

Insurance Online

An increasing number of companies use the Internet to offer standard insurance policies, such as auto, home, life, or health, at a substantial discount, mostly to individuals. Furthermore, third-party aggregators offer free comparisons of available policies. Several large insurance and risk-management companies offer comprehensive insurance contracts online (e.g., **allstate.com**, **ensurance.com**, **statefarm.com/insurance**, **progressive.com/insurance-choices**, **geico.com**). Although many people do not trust the faceless insurance agent, others are eager to take advantage of the reduced premiums. A visit to **insurance.com** will show a comparison of a variety of different policies. For example, customers and businesses can compare car insurance on **answerfinancial.com/Auto-Insurance** and then purchase a policy on their site. At TFB Global Travel Insurance (**globaltravelinsurance.com**), customers can purchase travel insurance. Another popular insurance site is **insweb.com**. Many insurance companies use a dual strategy, using sales agents in the field but also selling online. (e.g., advertising on e-mails and Google searches.) Like real estate brokers, insurance brokers send unsolicited e-mails to millions of people. The stiff competition will probably reduce the commission for the surviving agents.

Example

The insurance industry has seen that 70–80% of potential insurance customers are researching and gathering information on the Internet. Thus, insurance companies are trying to capitalize on this trend. For example, by attempting to profile the online customers and understand their needs, they can match Web advertisements and offerings to the meet those needs (*eMarketer* 2011).

Purchasing insurance online may involve several issues. For example, one needs to check the laws regarding electronic signatures on documents.

For a discussion and examples of how social networks drive insurers' marketing and advertising strategies, see Chordas (2010).

Online Stock Trading and Investments

The commission for an online trade is between $1 and $15 ("dirt cheap brokers") to $15–$30 ("mid-priced discount brokers"), compared with an average fee of $100–$200 per trade from a full-service broker (see **investopedia.com/university/broker/broker1.asp**). With online trading, there are no busy telephone lines, and the chance to err is small, because there is no oral communication in a frequently noisy environment. Orders can be placed from anywhere, at any time, and there is no biased broker to push a sale. Furthermore, investors can find a considerable amount of free research information about specific companies or mutual funds. Many services provided to online traders include online statements, tax-related calculations, extensive research on industries, real-time news, and even tutoring on how to trade (e.g., check **etrade.com** or **google.com/finance**).

Several discount brokerage houses initiated extensive online stock trading, notably Charles Schwab in 1995. Full-service brokerage companies, such as Merrill Lynch, followed suit during 1998–1999. As of 2011, 96% of stock trades in the United States are executed via electronic communications networks including the Internet (Krantz 2012).

How does online trading work? Let us say an investor has an account with Charles Schwab. The investor accesses Schwab's website (**schwab.com**), enters an account number and password, and clicks on "stock trading." Using a menu, the investor enters the details of the order (buy, sell, margin or cash, price limit, or market order). The computer tells the investor the current (real-time) "ask" and "bid" prices, just as a broker would do over the telephone, and the investor can approve or reject the transaction. The flow chart of this process is shown in Figure 3.3.

Some companies, including Schwab, are now also licensed as exchanges. This allows them to match the selling and buying orders of their own customers for many securities in one to two seconds. Some well-known companies that offer online trading are E*TRADE, TD Ameritrade, Scottrade, and ShareBuilder.

E*TRADE (**us.etrade.com**) is expanding into several countries, enabling global stock trading. In 2009, E*TRADE started allowing customers to trade online in seven different countries, taking care of payments using the appropriate currencies.

With the rapid pace of adoption of mobile computing, mobile stock trading is becoming more and more popular (e.g., see the mobile offering from E*TRADE). For example, users can pay bills and purchase stocks (see details in Chapter 11).

The SEC is working on new regulations for online trading because of the May 2010 "flash crash" of the New York Stock Exchange. For details, see the FTC and SEC report regarding the market events of May 6, 2010 (**sec.gov/news/studies/2010/marketevents-report.pdf**, **businessinsider.com/the-flash-crash-report-is-out-heres-what-you-need-to-know-2010-10**, and **en.wikipedia.org/wiki/2010_Flash_Crash**). For details on SEC regulations, see **counselworksllc.com** and **sec.gov**.

Online Investments

In addition to the stock market, there are many other online investment opportunities.

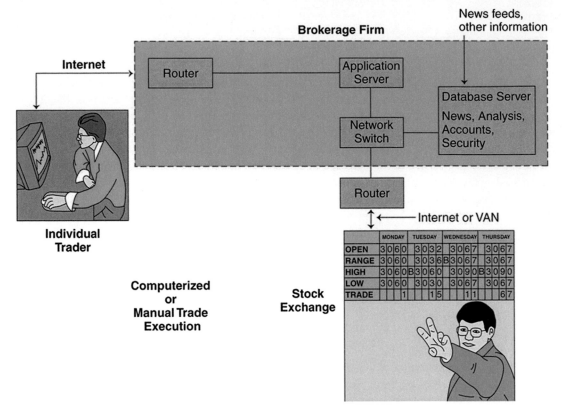

Figure 3.3 Online electronic stock trading

Example: Investments in China

Feng (2013) discusses the opportunities in what he calls e-finance in China. He provides as an example Yu'E Bao, an Alibaba company that pioneered online financial services in China with great success.

The Risk of Online Stock Trading and Other E-Finance Activities

The major risk of online trading is security. Although all trading sites require users to have an ID and password, problems may still occur. Problems of this nature (e.g., security breaches) also can occur when conducting online banking, our next topic.

SECTION 3.5 REVIEW QUESTIONS

1. List the major online real estate applications.

2. What are the advantages of selling insurance online?
3. What are the advantages of online stock trading?

3.6 ONLINE BANKING AND PERSONAL FINANCE

Electronic (online) banking (e-banking), also known as *cyberbanking*, and *virtual banking*, refers to conducting banking activities online. Consumers can use e-banking to check their accounts, pay bills online, secure a loan, transfer money, and much more. Sixty-one percent of U.S. adult Internet users bank and pay bills online (RenWeb 2011). See also **thefinanser.co.uk/fsclub/2013/08/61-of-us-internet-users-bank-online.html**, and for the results of a 2013 Pew

Research Center Study on online banking, see **pewinternet.org/files/old-media/Files/Reports/ 2013/PIP_OnlineBanking.pdf**. Several sites have tools that can help you with personal finance and budgeting. Examples are **mint.com**, **geezeo. com**, and **kiplinger.com**. In general, the e-finance field is taking off rapidly (e.g., see Joshi 2010). One area is e-banking.

E-Banking

E-banking saves users time and money. For banks, it offers a rapid and inexpensive strategy to acquire out-of-the-area customers. In addition, the banks may need fewer branches or employees. Many physical banks now offer online banking services, and some use EC as a major competitive strategy. For details, see **en.wikipedia.org/wiki/Online_banking**.

Online banking in general has been embraced worldwide, including developing countries. For example, online banking in China is increasing rapidly in popularity, especially among China's new educated middle class who live in the more developed cities. It is facilitated by the use of smartphones and other mobile devices. (See **hsbc.com. cn/1/2/personal-banking/e-banking/personal-internet-banking** and Bank of China **boc.cn/en**.)

Online Banking Capabilities

Banking applications can be divided into the following categories: informational, administrative, transactional, portal, and others. In general, the larger the bank, the more services are offered online.

Online banking offers several of the generic EC benefits listed in Chapter 1, both to the banks (expanding the bank's customer base and saving on administrative and operational costs) and to the customers (convenience and possibly lower fees).

Pure Virtual Banks

Virtual banks have no physical location and conduct only online transactions. Security First

Network Bank (SFNB) was the first such bank to offer secure banking transactions on the Web. Amid the consolidation that has taken place in the banking industry, SFNB has since been purchased and now is a part of RBC Bank (**rbcbank. com**). Other representative virtual banks in the United States are First Internet Bank (**firstib. com**) and Bank of Internet USA (**bankofinternet.com**). For a list of online banks, see **mybanktracker.com/best-online-banks**. Virtual banks exist in many other countries (e.g., **bankdirect. co.nz**). In some countries, virtual banks are also engaging in stock trading, and some stockbrokers offer online banking (e.g., see **us.etrade.com/ banking**). However, more than 97% of the hundreds of pure-play virtual banks failed by 2003 due to a lack of financial viability. Many more failed during 2007–2012. The most successful banks seem to be of the click-and-mortar type (e.g., Wells Fargo, City Corp, HSBC).

Virtual banking can be done with new business models, one of which is P2P lending.

P2P Lending

The introduction of online banking enables the move of personal loans to the Web in what is called *online person-to-person money lending*, or in short *P2P lending*. This model allows people to lend money and to borrow from each other via the Internet. For how P2P loans work, see **banking.about.com/od/peertopeerlending/a/peer-topeerlend.htm**.

Examples

An emerging innovation in online banking is peer-to-peer (P2P) online lending. Two examples are Zopa Limited in the United Kingdom (**zopa. com**) and Prosper Marketplace in the United States (**prosper.com**), which offer P2P online lending (see **en.wikipedia.org/wiki/Zopa** and **en.wikipedia.org/wiki/Prosper_Marketplace**), respectively. Note that, despite the global credit crunch of 2008–2012 and the fact that neither has a government-backed guarantee, both Zopa and Prosper are enjoying solid growth. For example, as of April 2014, Zopa's 50,000 active members had lent more than £528 million at negotiated rates to UK customers, mainly for car payments, credit card debts, and home improvements (Zopa Press Office 2011). The default rate of these P2P lenders is very low (e.g., Zopa's historical bad debt is 0.19% since 2010) since money is lent only to the most credit-worthy borrowers. For Prosper's company overview, see **prosper.com/about**.

A word of caution about virtual banking, including P2P lending: Before sending money to any cyberbank, especially one that promises high interest rates for your deposits, make sure that the bank is a legitimate one. Several cases of fraud already have occurred. For a discussion, see Nguyen (2010).

International and Multiple-Currency Banking

International banking and the ability to handle trades in multiple currencies are critical for international finance. Although some international retail purchasing can be done by providing a credit card number, other transactions may require international banking support. Examples of such cross-border support include the following:

- Bank of America (**bankofamerica.com**) and most other major banks offer cash management, trades and services, foreign exchange, risk management investments, merchant services, and special services for international traders.
- FX Alliance (**fxall.com**) is a multi-dealer foreign exchange service that enables faster and cheaper foreign exchange transactions. Special services are being established for stock market traders who need to pay for foreign stocks (e.g., at Charles Schwab, Fidelity Finance, or E*TRADE).

Online Financial Transaction Implementation Issues

As one would expect, the implementation of online banking and online stock trading can be interrelated. In many instances, one financial institution offers both services. The following are some other implementation issues for online financial transactions.

Securing Financial Transactions
It is imperative that financial transactions for home banking and online trading are secure. In Chapter 10, we discuss the details of secure EC payment systems. In Case 3.2, we give an example of how a bank provides security and privacy to its customers. For examples, look at the *security resources* on the websites of all major banks (e.g., **chase.com/resources/privacy-security**).

CASE 3.2: EC APPLICATION: SECURITY FOR ONLINE BANK TRANSACTIONS

Banks provide extensive security measures to their customers. The following describes some of the safeguards provided.

Customers accessing a bank system online must go through encryption provided by SSL (Secure Socket Layer) and digital certificate verification (see Chapters 10 and 11). The verification process assures users each time they sign on that they are indeed connected to their specific bank. The customer inquiry message then goes through an external firewall. Once the logon screen is reached, a user ID and a password are required. This information flows through a direct Web server and then goes through an internal firewall to the bank's application server. This process is illustrated in Figure 3.4.

Information is shared among a bank's business partners only for legitimate business purposes.

Banks do not capture information provided by customers when conducting hypothetical scenarios using planning tools (to ensure privacy). Many banks use cookies to learn about their customers; however, customers can control both the collection and in some cases the use of such information. In addition, most banks provide suggestions on how users can increase security (e.g., by using a browser that supports 128-bit encryption).

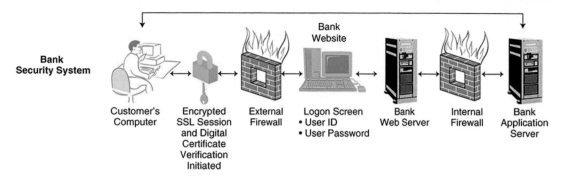

Figure 3.4 Security for online banking transactions

With the increased use of mobile devices, the threat of security risks has increased. Banks are creating innovative solutions. For example, in January 2009, Bank of America introduced "SafePass," a feature that can generate a six-digit, one-time passcode that is necessary to complete an online transaction. The passcode is delivered via text message to your mobile device. (See **bankofamerica.com/privacy/online-mobile-banking-privacy/safepass.go**.) A similar device is offered by other financial institutions.

Sources: Based on the authors' consulting experiences and from the various security statements of online banking websites, including **co-operativebank.co.uk/internetbanking** and **anz.com/auxiliary/help/help/website-security-privacy** (both accessed May 2014). For more information on the safe use of Internet banking, see **fdic.gov/bank/individual/online/safe.html**.

Questions

1. Why is security so important for a bank?
2. Why is there a need for two firewalls?
3. Who is protected by the bank's security system – the customer, the bank, or both? Elaborate.
4. What might be the limitations of such a security system?

Banks can enhance security by adding more steps in the account access procedures.

Example

Some banks have multi-stage security systems. For example, Central Pacific Bank (**centralpaci-ficbank.com**) asks you to log in (with your ID)

and then answer security questions to which you previously provided the answers. You then see an image on the screen that you pre-selected. If you do not recognize the image and a pre-established phrase, you know you have not accessed the real bank. If all answers are provided satisfactorily, you provide a password to enter your account.

Imaging Systems

Many financial institutions (e.g., Bank of America, Wells Fargo, and Citibank) allow customers to view images of all of their processed checks, and other related material online.

Fees for Online Versus Fees for Offline Services

Computer-based banking services are offered free by some banks, whereas others charge $5 to $10 a month, which may be waived if there is a minimum balance in the account. In addition, some banks charge fees for individual transactions (e.g., fee per check, per transfer, and so on). Many banks charge more for offline services in order to encourage customers to go online.

Risks

Online banks, as well as click-and-mortar banks, might carry some risks and problems, especially in international banking. The first is the risk of hackers accessing their accounts. In addition, some believe that virtual banks carry a *liquidity* risk (the risk of not having sufficient funds to pay obligations as they become due) and could be more susceptible to panic withdrawals. Regulators are grappling with the safeguards that need to be imposed on e-banking.

According to Nguyen (2010), online banking fraud in the United Kingdom alone exceeded $100 million in 2009 (an increase of 15% over 2008).

Online Billing and Bill Paying

The popularity of e-payments is growing rapidly. The number of checks the U.S. Federal Reserve System processes has been decreasing while the volume of commercial Automated Clearing House (ACH) transactions has been increasing. Many people prefer online payments of monthly bills such as mortgage payments, car loans, telephone, utilities, rent, credit cards, cable, TV, and so on. The recipients of such payments are equally eager to receive money online because online payments are received much more regularly and timely and have lower processing costs.

Another method for paying bills via the Internet is electronic billing or electronic bill payment and presentment (EBPP). With this method, the consumer makes payments at each biller's website, either with a credit card or by giving the biller enough information to complete an electronic withdrawal directly from the consumer's bank account. The biller sends the invoice to the customer via e-mail or a hosting service site. The customer then authorizes and initiates a payment via an automatic authorization, e-check, and so forth. See Chapter 11, **searchcio.techtarget. com/definition/EBPP**, and **investopedia.com/ terms/e/electronic-billpayment-presentment. asp** for more about EBPP.

This section has focused largely on B2C services that help consumers save time and payees save on processing fees. However, B2B services can save businesses about 50% of billing administrative costs as wells as expediting the payment cycle.

Taxes
One important area in personal finance is advice about and computation of taxes. Dozens of sites are available to help people with their federal tax preparations. Many sites will help people legally reduce their taxes. The following list offers some sites worth checking:

- **irs.gov**: The official website of the Internal Revenue Service.
- **taxsites.com**: A massive directory of tax-related information, research, and services.
- **fairmark.com**: A tax guide for investors.
- **taxaudit.com**: IRS tax audit help and audit assistance.

For a list of the 200 best money websites (2012) in most of the areas discussed in Sections 3.5 and 3.6, see **money.msn.com/shopping-deals/ the-102-best-money-websites-liz-weston.** For a list of the 15 best financial sites and apps (2014), see **money.cnn.com/gallery/pf/2013/12/11/best-financial-apps**.

Mobile Banking
Mobile banking is a system that enables people to conduct financial transactions from a smartphone or other wireless mobile device. Many of the recent developments are in the area of mobile banking (presented in Chapters 6 and 11). Topics such as payments from smartphones and handling micropayments have revolutionized the financial systems (Chapter 11). The need for an improved banking and financial system is clear. E-finance in general, and mobile finance in particular, lead the change in this area. For more information see **en.wikipedia.org/wiki/ Mobile_banking**. For an example of services available at Bank of America, including mobile banking, see **promo.bankofamerica. com/mobilebanking**.

SECTION 3.6 REVIEW QUESTIONS
1. List the capabilities of online banking. Which of these capabilities would be most beneficial to you?
2. How are banks protecting customer data and transactions?
3. Define a P2P loan system.
4. How are banking transactions protected?
5. List and briefly describe other major personal finance services available online.
6. What is mobile banking?

3.7   ON-DEMAND DELIVERY OF PRODUCTS, DIGITAL ITEMS, ENTERTAINMENT, AND GAMING

This section examines B2C delivery issues related to on-demand items, such as perishable products, as well as the delivery of digitizable items, entertainment, and games.

On-Demand Delivery of Products

Most e-tailers use third party logistics carriers to deliver products to customers. They might use the postal system within their country or they might use private shippers such as UPS, FedEx, or DHL. Deliveries can be made within days or overnight. Customers are frequently asked to pay for expedited shipments (unless they have a "premium" subscription, such as Amazon.com Prime [**amazon.com/Prime**]).

Some e-tailers and direct marketing manufacturers own a fleet of delivery vehicles in order to provide faster service or cut delivery costs to the consumer. According to Mark Sebba, CEO of Net-a-Porter (**net-a-porter.com**), the company prefers "to do as much as possible in-house, which includes operating their own delivery vans for customers in London and Manhattan" (see **net-a-porter-brand.blogspot.com/2013/05/some-more-current-content.html**). Such firms provide either regular deliveries or will deliver items on demand (e.g., auto parts). They might also provide additional services to increase the value proposition for the buyers. An example in this category is an online grocer, or *e-grocer*. An **e-grocer** is a grocer that takes orders online and provides deliveries on a daily or other regular schedule or within a very short period of time, sometimes within an hour. Home delivery of food from restaurants or pizza parlors is another example. In addition, office supply stores, repair parts distributors (e.g., for cars), and pharmaceutical suppliers promise speedy, same day delivery. As of 2014, Amazon.com offers same day delivery (via their Local Express Delivery) in over 11 cities such as Baltimore, Las Vegas, and New York. (Other online e-tailers have similar services.)

An express delivery option is referred to as an **on-demand delivery service**. In such a case, the delivery must be done quickly after an order is received. A variation of this model is same-day delivery. According to this model, delivery is done faster than "overnight," but slower than the 30–60 minutes expected with on-demand delivery of pizzas, fresh flowers, or auto repair parts. E-grocers often deliver using the same-day delivery model.

The Case of E-Grocers

In the United States, online grocery sales are expected to reach $25 billion, or 2% of total grocery sales in 2014 (Nielsen Company 2011). It is a very competitive market, and margins are very thin. Many e-grocers are click-and-mortar retailers that operate in the countries where they have physical stores, such as Woolworths Supermarkets in Australia (**woolworths.com.au**) and Safeway, Inc. in the United States (**shop.safeway.com**). AmazonFresh (**fresh.amazon.com**), a subsidiary of Amazon.com, is an online grocery service in Seattle and certain cities in California. Delivering fresh foods is becoming fashionable (e.g., see **thefreshdiet.com**).

Despite its potential advantages, retailers are cautious about the idea (see Zwiebach and Hamstra 2013). An interesting case is that of WunWun, a delivery service in New York.

Today, it is possible to shop for groceries from smartphones and tablets (e.g., iPhone, iPad). For images of e-grocers, do a Google search for 'images e-grocery.'

One innovative company is Instacart (**instacart.com**), a San Francisco-based start-up that, according to its founder, will 'buy all your groceries from your favorite stores and deliver them within an hour or two' (see **wired.com/2014/02/next-big-thing-missed-future-groceries-really-online**). Instacart delivers from Whole Foods, Costco, and other local stores and is available in certain cities, including San Francisco, New York, and Boston. As of April 2014, Instacart will be available in Los Angeles (**latimes.com/business/la-fi-instacart-grocery-20140403,0,3795439.**

story#axzz2xyqVNdTL). For more about Instacart and its expansion, see **mercurynews. com/business/ci_24986836/startup-instacart-hopes-dominate-grocery-delivery**.

Speed of Delivery

Speed of delivery is critical not only for groceries and perishable items but also for other on-demand and large items. For example, **uber.com** is an on-demand travelers delivery service. In 2013, they partnered with Home Depot to deliver Christmas trees (Rodriguez 2013). See also **blog.uber.com/ UberTREE**.

The fastest delivery in the future may be by drones (see Chapter 12). Amazon.com, UPS, and Google are exploring this phenomenon. In 2014, Facebook decided to "jump on the bandwagon" with the purchase of drone maker Titan Aerospace for $60 million (see **forbes.com/ sites/briansolomon/2014/03/04/facebook-follows-amazon-google-into-drones-with-60-million-purchase**).

Online Delivery of Digital Products, Entertainment, and Media

Certain goods, such as software, music, or news stories, can be distributed in physical format (such as hard copy, CD-ROM, DVD, and newsprint), or they can be digitized and delivered over the Internet. Online delivery is much cheaper and saves sellers storage room, handling, and distribution costs.

Online Entertainment

Online entertainment is growing rapidly and is now the most popular medium in the United States among young people between the ages of 8 and 17. There are many kinds of Internet entertainment. It is difficult to categorize them precisely because there is a mixture of entertainment types, delivery modes, and personal taste. All these must be considered when deciding whether something is entertainment or not, and what kind of entertainment it is. Some online entertainment is interactive, in that the user is engaged in it.

PricewaterhouseCoopers (2013) predicts that the global entertainment and media industry spending will reach $2.2 trillion in 2017. This includes online gaming, streaming videos, and audio (streaming media refers to multimedia that is constantly presented to users in real time).

All forms of traditional entertainment are now available over the Internet. However, some have become much more popular in the new environment due to the capabilities of technology. For example, Facebook's online games attract millions of players. For information on entertainment in the Web 2.0 environment and social networks, see Chapter 8.

iTunes

iTunes (**apple.com/itunes**) is a media management software by Apple that includes an online store for buying music and other media. The program also enables you to organize and play the digital items you downloaded. For its features, see **apple.com/itunes/features**. Note that iTunes and similar services have basically crushed the music industry (see **money.cnn.com/2013/04/25/ technology/itunes-music-decline**), similar to the way **netflix.com** has impacted the sale of DVDs and CDs. A 2014 study by Asymco found at **asymco.com/2014/02/10/fortune-130**, discovered that iTunes is more profitable than Xerox and Time Warner Cable (see **wallstcheatsheet. com/stocks/study-itunes-is-more-profitable-than-xerox-and-time-warner-cable.html/?a= viewall**).

Online Ticketing

This popular service enables customers to buy tickets for events (e.g., sports, music, theater) by using a computer or mobile device. Companies such as Ticketmaster, Inc. are active in this area. Fandango is a company that sells movie theater tickets.

Internet TV and Internet Radio

Two similar streaming technologies are popular on the Web: Internet TV and Internet Radio.

Internet TV

Internet TV is the delivery of TV content via the Internet by video streaming technologies. The content includes TV shows, sporting events, movies, and other videos. Several video-on-demand and subscription services, such as **netflix.com, hulu.com** and **hulu.com/plus**, as well as **amazon. com/Prime-Instant-Video/b?node=2676882011** offer this service. For a comprehensive description of Internet TV, see **wisegeek.org/what-is-internet-tv.htm**. The major advantage is the ability to select what and when to view content and the ability to do so from computers, tablets, smartphones, Blue-Ray consoles, Apple TV (**apple.com/appletv**), Roku (**roku.com**), Google Chromecast (**google.com/intl/en/chrome/devices/chromecast**), Aereo (**aereo.com**), and so forth In order to compete with other channels, such as HBO (**hbo. com**). In 2012, Netflix began to air its own original programming (see **techradar.com/us/news/ internet/netflix-begins-broadcasting-first-original-series-1061339**). As of February 2014, Netflix is showing 10 new and returning original series (see **uproxx.com/tv/2014/02/10-original-series-coming-netflix-2014**). Since Internet TV can be streamed at low or no cost, the issue of copyright is of major concern. In January 2014, the U.S. Supreme Court decided to hear the case of *ABC Television Stations* vs. *Aereo*. For details, see Vaughan-Nichols (2014) and **abcnews. go.com/blogs/politics/2014/01/supreme-court-will-hear-tv-broadcasters-against-aereo**.

Internet Radio

Known by several other names, **Internet radio** refers to audio content transmitted live via the Internet. It is a broadcasting service that enables users to listen online to thousands of radio stations (e.g., over 4,000 in Europe, see **listenlive.eu**). The service can broadcast anything that is on the radio stations plus broadcasts from organizations, governments, and even individuals. For details, see Beller (2001) and **radio.about.com/od/ listentoradioonline/qt/bl-InternetRadio.htm**. Internet radio has the same copyright issues as those of Internet TV. Note that, in many cases, there is an agreement between the content creators and the distributors (e.g., Warner Music and

Apple reached an iTunes Radio deal in 2013; see **cnet.com/news/apple-reaches-iradio-deal-with-warner-music-suggesting-wwdc-launch** and **apple.com/itunes/itunes-radio**).

Pandora Radio

Pandora is a leading free Internet radio that delivers music not only from radio stations but also from many other sources. The core of the service is the *Music Genome Project*. According to **pandora.com/about**, the project is an inclusive analysis of thousands of musical pieces. All the music in the project is available on Pandora for your listening pleasure.

Pandora is actually a music streaming and automated music recommendation service that in 2014 is available only in the U.S., Australia, and New Zealand. Users can create up to 100 personalized stations that play pre-arranged selections. In February 2014, the company opened up its content submission process to independent artists (see **submit.pandora.com, help.pandora.com/ customer/portal/articles/24802-information-for-artists-submitting-to-pandora** and Hockenson 2014). For Pandora's Help Center, see **help.pandora.com**.

Various e-tailers offer songs for sale to Pandora's listeners. You can access Pandora through many streaming media devices. You can enjoy Pandora for free on the Web, on home-listening devices, and most mobile devices. Pandora One (**pandora.com/one**) has a monthly fee, but the benefits include ad-free service and higher quality audio. Pandora is a profitable business. Its subscriber base continues to grow; in March of 2014, it had 75.3 million active listeners (**investor.pandora.com/phoenix.zhtml?c= 227956&p=irol-newsArticle&ID=1915496&hi ghlight=**).

Social Television (TV)

Social TV is an emerging social media technology that enables several TV viewers who are in different locations to interactively share experiences such as discussions, reviews, and recommendations while watching the same show simultaneously. According to WhatIsSocial Television.com (**whatissocialtelevision.com**), social TV is "the union of television and social media" and refers to "the phenomenon of people communicating with each other while watching a TV show or discussing with each other about television content using the Internet as a medium of communication." The communication can be done via texting in social networks, smartphones, tablets, etc. Social TV combines broadcast television programs and user-generated content with rich social media. *Social TV* was listed by *MIT Technology Review* (reported by Evangelista 2011) as one of the 10 most important emerging technologies of 2010. The editor of *Wired Magazine* named social TV as number three of six important technology trends for 2011.

Characteristics of Social TV

Social TV has several unique characteristics:

- The possibility of discovering new video content and sharing this discovery with friends.
- Most social TV activities are done in real time by watching content and commenting on it to others, even if the viewers are in different locations.
- Social TV allows people to connect in a unique way, with other people who share the same interests.

Social TV is attracting an ample number of viewers. (The number of traditional television viewers is declining due to Internet viewing.)

Technology and Services of Social TV

Large numbers of social TV tools and platforms are emerging. According to Rountree (2011), there are three major types of social TV:

1. Using a second screen (such as a smartphone, tablet, etc.) while watching TV or using another communication device.
2. Using an on-screen experience where information is displayed directly on the TV.

3. Using a personal computer or mobile device to watch TV shows.

These options are not pure social media tools, but they facilitate social interaction revolving around TV programs.

Rountree (2011) and Media Bistro's Lost Remote (**lostremote.com/social-tv-companies**) provide a list of startups in the field (e.g., Kwarter **kwarter.com**) and Youtoo Interactive TV (**youtoo.com**). Each startup and tool has a different capability for activities that are related to each specific TV program.

Vendors are interested in social TV mainly as an emerging tool for marketing communication strategies such as increasing brand awareness or conducting market research.

Example

The Pepsi Sound Off is a social TV venture, where fans of "The X-Factor" (the talent competition reality show) can meet online to chat about the contestants and the judges. Interactions occur mostly in real time.

Adult Entertainment

Online adult entertainment is probably the most profitable B2C model (usually with no or little advertisement; viewers pay subscription fees) and it accounts for a large percentage of Internet use. Adult content sites are popular because they provide a large and vivid selection, low fees (even free), and anonymity for those who watch. This popularity may cause a problem for some companies. According to the Nielsen Company (reported by Montopoli 2010), in October 2010 approximately 29% of U.S. employees visited Internet porn sites during working hours. According to reports by market research firms that monitor the industry, such as Forrester Research, IDC, Datamonitor, Mediabistro Inc. and Nielsen viewers are willing to pay substantial fees to view adult sites.

ICANN, (the Internet Corporation of Assigned Names and Numbers, which approves Web addresses), approved the .xxx domain name. The adult entertainment industry uses the .xxx suffix (upper level), similar to .com domain names used by other companies. Supporters of this decision feel that it will make it easier for people to filter or block unwanted adult content, as well as assist with the self-regulation of the Web pornography industry.

Internet Gaming

Internet gaming is comprised of all forms of gaming such as arcade gaming, lotteries, casino gaming, and promotional incentives. Between 2008 and 2010, online gambling revenue continued to increase despite the bad economy. The global online gambling industry grew 12% during 2010 to reach $30 billion. According to Statistica.com (2014), the online gaming market will reach almost $41.5 billion in 2015. The ease of access and use of broadband services throughout the world in recent years has been vital to the expansion of online gaming.

Legal Aspects

Online gambling is booming despite the fact that it is illegal in almost all U.S. states. In 2013, Delaware and Nevada were the first U.S. states to allow some online gambling, followed by New Jersey (in October 2013, Delaware became the first state to allow a "full suite" of Internet gambling). In February 2014, both Delaware and Nevada signed a deal to allow interstate online gambling. Delaware estimated about $8 million revenue in 2013. Note that Federal Law limits online gambling to players while they are physically within a given state. (This can be verified by using geolocation software.) Therefore, if one state allows online gambling, you can play only when you are in that state. Online gambling is legal in other countries (e.g., Australia). By 2013, at least 8 U.S. states had pending legislation that would legalize online gambling. *Source*: Based on Zernike (2013) and Fox News (2014). For a list of top online casino sites for 2014, see **onlinecasinobluebook.com**.

A special case is that of poker. Companies such as PokerStars (**pokerstars.net**) provide online opportunities to gamblers (available now on Facebook **apps.facebook.com/pokerstarsplay**). Unfortunately, there were charges of fraud in 2011; however, these were settled. More interesting is the fact that according to Berzon (2012), a federal judge in New York ruled that poker is a game of skill more than that of chance. This may help to legalize poker games both online and offline.

SECTION 3.7 REVIEW QUESTIONS

1. Describe on-demand delivery services.
2. Explain how e-grocers operate.
3. What are the difficulties in conducting an online grocery business? Describe some solutions.
4. Describe digital goods and their delivery process(es).
5. What are the benefits and limitations of digital delivery of software, music, and so forth?
6. What are the major forms of online entertainment?
7. Describe Internet TV, social TV, and Internet radio.
8. Describe Internet gambling and its challenges.

3.8 OTHER B2C SERVICES: FROM DATING SERVICES TO WEDDING PLANNING

This section describes only a few of the hundreds of types of B2C businesses.

Online Dating Services

Online dating enables people to identify potential mates and contact them, usually via the service's e-mail or chat functions. Sites such as **eharmony.com** and **match.com** attempt to match applicants with potential partners based on participants' profiles and answers to questionnaires. Online dating services, which have many advantages (e.g., Atik 2012 and **bestdatingwebsite.org/advantages**), are the third largest attractors of "for fee" Internet users (behind music and games). Spark Networks (**spark.net**) owns and operates more than 20 online personals sites such as JDate.com, BlackSingles.com, and ChristianMingle.com. These are known as "niche" dating sites (see **spark.net/about-us/company-overview**). In 2011, the online dating industry revenue was more than $1 billion with a projected 3% annual revenue increase through 2016 (Donnelly 2011). Despite its popularity and millions of success stories, there are risks and scams. For an overview and advice on safety, see Bernstein (2011) and **health.howstuff-works.com/relationships/dating/risks-and-rewards-of-online-dating.htm**. For further information, see **en.wikipedia.org/wiki/Online_dating_service**. According to comScore (**com-score.com**), in 2011, over 14 million people worldwide were using *mobile dating apps* and the time spent on mobile dating sites is rapidly increasing (reported by 1888 Press Release 2011). Online dating sites (e.g., **match.com**) also provide dating articles and advice, success stories, and relationship tips.

Planning a Wedding

The wedding planning business is going online also. A large number of companies are active in online wedding planning. Mywedding.com, for example, helps with collecting ideas and planning, assists in budgeting, finds vendors, creates registries and helps in honeymoon planning and travel (watch their video on the home page). WeddingWire, Inc. (**weddingwire.com**) connects couples with event vendors. The most comprehensive site is probably **theknot.com**; now part of the XO Group, Inc.

What About After the Wedding?
Theknot.com offers two additional channels:

Thenest.com
Created by The Knot, TheNest.com is a "new home for newlyweds," to learn about what to do after the wedding, from buying furniture for the home, selecting décor, getting a pet and even relationship advice.

Thebump.com
The Bump is a site for parents-to-be that gives advice on fertility, birth, pregnancy, babies, and much more.

Buying Cars Online

For many, the idea of buying cars online seems crazy. However, today, more and more cars are being sold online; or at least some of the steps in the purchasing process are completed online. Initially, online car sales alienated dealers. However, according to Levin (2014), a change is coming. About 7,000 car dealers in the U.S. use a company called TrueCar (**truecar.com**) to sell their cars at anonymous reverse auctions. Nearly 3% of all car transactions are sold via reverse auctions. (2014 data). Like Edmunds.com (**edmunds.com**) and Kelley Blue Book Co. (**kbb.com**), TrueCar also provides consumer information. TrueCar earns commissions from the sellers. The company is offering new digital tools to dealers. The dealers save money on traditional advertising.

There are several ways to sell cars online. For example, GM's tool 'Shop-Click-Drive' (**shopclickdrive.com**), allows shoppers to buy cars online without going to dealers' showrooms (see **edmunds.com/car-news/gm-dealers-embrace-shop-click-drive-online-shopping-tool.html**).

According to their website, Autobytel, Inc. (**autobytel.com**) is a pioneer in online car transactions (they launched their website in 1995). Autobytel helps dealers sell new (including built-to-order) and used automobiles via the Internet. The company ("Your lifetime automotive advisor") offers car buying tips, dealer locators, car pictures, car reviews, and much more. The company offers tools like Mygarage.com ("everything you need to manage your vehicle").

Selling-Build-to-Order Cars Online

As more people like to configure their cars, the use of online configuration has become more and more popular. Such services save time for both sellers and buyers. People configure their PC's online (e.g., at HP, Dell), so why not do the same with cars? This way, they can compare prices as well. Luxury car companies, such as Jaguar (**jaguarusa.com**), usually sell build-to-order-cars (see **jaguarusa.com/build-yours/index. html**). Here is where online configuration is most useful.

Example

Jaguar offers virtual shopping for cars. Jaguar buyers have been able to custom configure their dream cars online since 2005. Jaguar cars are usually built-to-order. However, customers like to see how the cars will look like before they buy them. There are hundreds of thousands of possible configurations of Jaguar cars. Initially, the system offered a view of the dream cars with all the desired options and the price. Customers were able to rotate the cars, change the configuration, simulate any desired options, and then place orders online.

As of 2013, the system became more effective, interactive, and engaging. The "Jaguar Land Rover Virtual Experience" provides exceptional customer experience. The 3D based system includes motion detecting technology, which is offered in the dealers' showroom. Built in collaboration with IBM Interactive, a selected car is projected on a screen. Customers can browse vehicles, options and features, customize a car to their specifications, and interact with the "car of their dreams" (see **asmarterplanet. com/blog/2014/01/smarter-commerce.html**). According to Vizard (2013), "Motion-sensing technology enables the customer to use his or her body to control the image of the car and inspect its features, such as opening the driver's door to examine the interior. Want to hear how the engine sounds? Just push a button."

The highly portable system can be displayed in auto shows. The system generates volumes of data that can be mined for learning about customer preferences. Furthermore, car designers can learn how to improve their next generation design. For example, a designer can see how certain add-on options impact the overall look and feel of a car even before a prototype is built.

Other Online Services

There are hundreds of unique services available online. Here we present only a short representative list:

- **Online pharmacies are all over the Internet**. Large companies such as CVS (**cvs.com**) offer prescription refills online for home delivery. Buying in the USA from Canadian pharmacies can save you 50% (make sure it is a legitimate pharmacy – many are not). For details, see **en. wikipedia.org/wiki/Online_pharmacy**.
- **Stamps online**. There is no need to go to the post office; **stamps.com** provides Internet-based postage and shipping services. Stamps. com allows customers to personalize their stamps with its PhotoStamp. Companies such as Zazzle, Inc. (**zazzle.com**) offer similar services.
- **Online flower delivery.** Many companies, including **1800flowers.com**, allow customers to order flowers and related items from online catalogs and arrange for delivery to just about anywhere in the world.
- **Online food ordering**. Customers search catalogs of local restaurants (e.g., from **grubhub. com**) and order food to be delivered to their homes or workplaces. Major pizza chains offer delivery services online in addition to their phone delivery service. (See **en.wikipedia.org/wiki/Online_food_ordering**.)
- **Virtual farmers' marketplaces are becoming popular in many countries**. One example is the San Francisco-based online delivery service **goodeggs.com** (see Chea 2013). In addition to eggs, the company delivers all kinds of fresh, locally produced food to consumers, which is ideal for people who want to support the local producers and community.

SECTION 3.8 REVIEW QUESTIONS

1. What are the advantages and limitations of online dating?
2. List all the services offered by wedding planning sites (consult 'The Knot'). Can you add some more?

3. What are the business models for selling cars online? What are the benefits to buyers? To sellers?
4. Would you use Jaguar's Land Rover virtual experience system? Why or why not?
5. Find five more online services not cited here and describe them briefly.

3.9 ONLINE PURCHASING DECISION AIDS

Many sites and tools are available to help consumers with online purchasing decisions. Some sites offer price comparisons as their primary tool (e.g., **pricerunner.co.uk** and **shopzilla.com**); others evaluate services, trust, quality, and other factors. Shopping portals, shopping robots ("shopbots"), business ratings sites, trust verification sites, friends' advice in social networks, and other shopping aids are available also. The major types are discussed next.

Shopping Portals

Shopping portals are gateways to webstores and e-malls. Specifically, they host many online stores simultaneously. Like any other portal, they can be comprehensive or niche-oriented. Comprehensive, or general-purpose, portals have links to many different sellers, and present and evaluate a broad range of products. An example of a comprehensive portal is eCOST.com (**ecost. com**). Several public portals also offer shopping opportunities and comparison aids. Examples are **shopping.com**; (part of the eBay Commerce Network), **shopping.yahoo.com**, and **price-grabber.com**. eBay (**ebay.com**) is a shopping portal also because it offers shopping at fixed prices as well as auctions. Several of these evaluation companies have purchasing shopbots or other, smaller shopping aids, and have incorporated them into their portals.

Some shopping portals offer specialized items with links to certain products (e.g., books, phones) or services (universities, hospitals). Such portals also help customers conduct research. Examples include **zdnet.com/topic-reviews** and **shopper.cnet.com** for computers, appliances, and electronics. The advantage of niche shopping portals is their ability to specialize in a certain line of products.

For a comprehensive site with information on e-retailers, B2B, marketing, etc., see Internet Retailer (**internetretailer.com**).

Helping Communities

Social communities can be very helpful for their members, as shown in several examples in this book (e.g., see Chapter 7).

Price and Quality Comparison by Shopbot Software Agents

Savvy Internet shoppers may want to find bargain shopping. **Shopping robots** (**shopping agents, shopbots**) are search engines that look for the lowest prices or other search criteria. Different shopbots use different search methods. For example, mySimon (**mysimon.com**) searches the Web to find the best prices and availability for thousands of popular items.

Google Enterprise Search and Enterprise Search Appliance
Google Enterprise Search helps companies search all internal and public-facing information.

Search is facilitated by a powerful server called Enterprise Search Appliance which enables many flexible search options including the search of some foreign languages.

A similar service is offered by Search Spring **searchspring.net**.

"Spy" Services
In this context, "spy" services are not the CIA or MI5. Rather, they are services that visit websites for customers, at their direction, and notify them of their findings. Web surfers and shoppers constantly monitor sites for new information, special sales, ending times of auctions, stock market updates, and so on, but visiting the sites to monitor them is time consuming. Several sites will track stock prices or airline special sales and send

e-mails accordingly. For example, **money.cnn.com**, **pcworld.com**, **expedia.com**, and alerts at **google.com/alerts** will send people personalized e-mail alerts.

Of course, one of the most effective ways to "spy" on Internet users is to introduce cookies and spyware to their computers (see Chapter 9 for details).

Ratings, Reviews, and Recommendation Sites

Ratings and reviews by friends, even by people that you do not know (e.g., experts or independent third-party evaluators), are usually available for social shoppers. In addition, any user has an opportunity to contribute reviews and participate in relevant discussions. The tools for conducting ratings and reviews, which are presented next, are based on Marsden (2011), Gratton and Gratton (2012), **bazaarvoice.com/solutions/conversations**, and the authors' experiences. The major types of tools and methods are:

- **Customer ratings and reviews.** Customer ratings are popular; they can be found on product (or service) pages or on independent review sites (e.g., TripAdvisor) and/or in customer news feeds (e.g., Amazon.com, Buzzillions, and Epinions). Customer ratings can be summarized by votes or polls.
- **Customer testimonials.** Customer experiences are typically published on vendors' sites, and third party sites such as TripAdvisor. Some sites encourage discussion (e.g., Bazaarvoice Connections; **bazaarvoice.com/solutions/connections**).
- **Expert ratings and reviews.** Ratings or reviews can also be generated by domain experts and appear in different online publications.

- **Sponsored reviews.** These reviews are written by paid bloggers or domain experts. Advertisers and bloggers can find each other by searching through websites such as **sponsoredreviews.com**, which connects bloggers with marketers and advertisers.
- **Conversational marketing.** People communicate via e-mail, blog, live chat, discussion groups, and tweets. Monitoring conversations may yield rich data for market research and customer service. An example of a conversational marketing platform is Adobe Campaign (**adobe.com/solutions/campaign-management.html**; formerly Neolane).
- **Video product review.** Reviews can be generated by using videos. YouTube offers reviews that are uploaded, viewed, commented on, and shared.
- **Bloggers post reviews.** This is a questionable method, however, since some bloggers are paid and may use a biased approach. However, many bloggers have reputations as unbiased sources. For a list of 50 product review blogs, see Sala (2012).

Many websites rate various e-tailers and online products based on multiple criteria. Bizrate (**bizrate.com**), and Consumer Reports Online (**consumerreports.org**) are well-known rating sites. Bizrate.com organized a network of shoppers that reports on various sellers and uses the compiled results in its evaluations. Note that different rating sites provide different rankings. Alexa Internet, Inc. (**alexa.com**; an Amazon.com company) computes Web traffic rank, see **alexa.com/pro/insight**.

Recommendations from Other Shoppers and Friends and Family

Prior to making a purchase, customers tend to collect information online that can help them make a decision. Online customers can get information such as what brand to buy, from which vendor, and at what price, by using shopping aids (e.g., price comparison sites) (e.g., **nextag.com**), looking at sites such as Epinions (**epinions.com**), and researching other sources. Examining and participating in social networking forums is another way to compare prices as well as reading product and service reviews. According to Gartner, Inc. (reported by Dubey 2010; see also **gartner.com/newsroom/id/1409213**), the majority of online customers already rely on social networks to guide them in purchase decisions.

In marketing, a **referral economy** describes the practice of receiving recommendations from buyers (e.g., in social networks or blogs). For how to use social media to build a referral economy, see **socialmediatoday.com/jkriggins/2121281/how-use-social-media-build-referral-economy**.

Example: Kaboodle

Kaboodle (**kaboodle.com**) is a social shopping community site that allows users to find, recommend, and share product information via product lists, blogs, and so forth while communicating with friends. For details, see Chapter 7 and **kaboodle.com/zm/about**.

Comparison Shopping Websites

A large number of websites provide price comparisons for products and services (e.g., online tickets, cruises). Online retailers such as Amazon.com also provide price comparisons and so do many other sites (e.g., **nextag.com**, **pricegrabber.com**, **mysimon.com**). FreePriceAlerts.com (**freepricealerts.com**) is a price comparison app.

Trust Verification Sites

With so many sellers online, many consumers are not sure whom they should trust. A number of companies evaluate and verify the trustworthiness of various e-tailers. One such company is TRUSTe (**truste.com**). The TRUSTe seal appears at the bottom of each TRUSTe-approved e-tailer's website. E-tailers pay TRUSTe for the use of the seal (which they call a "trustmark"). TRUSTe's 1,300-plus members hope that consumers will use the seal as an assurance and as a proxy for actual research into their conduct of business, privacy policy, and personal information protection. Trust sites grant a *trust seal* for a business to display, demonstrating to customers the level of quality. For types see Trust Seal in Wikipedia. TRUSTe now offers a service for mobile devices, called TRUSTed apps (**truste.com/products-and-services/enterprise-privacy/TRUSTed-apps**), which provide ongoing monitoring and safeguarding of brands to ensure that merchants' mobile apps are trusted by consumers.

Some comprehensive trust verification sites are Symantec Corporation's VeriSign (**verisign.com**) and BBBOnline (**bbb.org**). VeriSign tends to be the most widely used. Other sources of trust verification include Secure Assure (**secureassure.co.uk**), which charges yearly fees. In addition, Ernst & Young, the global public accounting firm, has services for auditing e-tailers in order to offer some guarantee of the integrity of their business practices. Other sites are **trust-guard.com** and **trust-verified.org**. For the results of a 2013 survey on which site seal people trust the most (conducted using Google Consumer Surveys, and reported at **baymard.com/blog/site-seal-trust**).

Concerns About Reviews, Ratings, and Recommendations

Some people raise the issue of how accurate reported reviews and recommendations are. On some sites, fake reviews and claims are suspected to encompass 30–40% of the total reviews. In 2012, however, Yelp unveiled its Consumer Alerts, which shows warnings to users when they find businesses who have paid for reviews (see **webpronews.com/just-how-bad-is-yelps-fake-review-problem-2014-01**). As of mid-January 2014, Yelp has issued almost 300 Consumer Alerts. (For an example of a Consumer Alert, see **searchengineland.com/yelp-turns-up-the-heat-285-consumer-alerts-issued-over-fake-reviews-181706**.) There is also a concern about businesses paying money to bloggers for producing reviews. Some claim that such reviews may be biased. Another concern is that in cases of a small number of reviewers, a bias (positive or negative) may exist. Finally, it is wise to look at bloggers' review sites. (For a list of the top 50 review blogs, see Sala 2012.) As a side note, Amazon.com has compiled a list of the "Funniest Reviews" posted on their site, on products ranging from banana slicers to horsehead masks (see **amazon.com/gp/feature.html?ie=UTF8&docId=1001250201**).

Other Shopping Assisting Tools

Other digital intermediaries assist buyers or sellers, or both, with research and purchase processes. For example, escrow services (e.g., **escrow.com** and **abnamro.com/en**) assist buyers and sellers with the exchange of items and money. A trusted third party frequently is needed to facilitate the proper exchange of money and goods, or to verify information. (Remember that trading partners usually do not even see each other.) Escrow sites may also provide payment-processing support, as well as letters of credit (see Chapter 11).

- Similar to Craigslist, Angie's List (**angieslist.com**) helps its members find high quality service companies and health care professional services in over 700 categories. Although there is a fee, its advantage over free review sites is there are no anonymous reviews and their data is certified "so you get the whole story" (see **angieslist.com/how-it-works.htm**). **Angieslist.com** also provides a complaint resolution service and discounts from highly-rated service companies. They also offer live support through a call center.
- To organize store information in a standard, easy to see, and understandable format, vendors can use tools such as **thefind.com**. Shoppers can use the same tools to search once and compare products at every store, finding the best deals.

Must-Have Shopping Tools

Brownell (2013) lists the following must-have online tools for shoppers:
- Price Rewind (price protection)
- Free Price Alerts (last minute bargaining)
- RedLaser (bar code scanning apps)
- Honey (coupon code finder)
- Shop Advisor (price drop tracker)
- Decide (price drop predictor)
- Google Shopping and Price Grabber (price comparisons)

Other decision aids include summaries of advice and opinions provided by consumers about products and e-tailers. These aids are known as *mass reviews*. One site that provides such summaries is **epinions.com**, which has searchable recommendations on thousands of products. **Pricewatch.com** is a price-comparison engine, **pricegrabber.com** is a comparison shopping tool that covers millions of products, and **onlineshoes.com** is a review and shopping site that specializes in all types of shoes.

Layar (**layar.com**) offers another type of tool called the Layar Creator. The company uses a mobile augmented reality device that can activate printed pages containing information about certain products (including videos). For details about Layar Creator, see **realareal.com/layar-creator-welcome-to-interactive-print**.

Another shopping tool is a *wallet* – in this case, an *electronic wallet*, which is a program that contains the shopper's information. To expedite online shopping, consumers can use electronic wallets so that they do not need to reenter the information each time they shop. Although sites such as Amazon.com offer their own specialized wallets, Microsoft Passport has two services, "a Single Sign-On service that allows members to use a single name and password to sign on to a growing number of participating websites, and a Wallet service that members can use to make fast, convenient online purchases" (see Microsoft Passport FAQ at **support.microsoft.com/kb/277759**) and Chapter 11 for details). For more on shopping aids, see Strauss and Frost (2012). Shopping aids are now expanding to social networking sites as shown in the following example.

Example: Yelp

Yelp (**yelp.com**) is a search engine whose mission is to help people find local (in a specific city) qualified services ranging from mechanics to restaurants to hairstylists based on recommendations of fellow locals. It connects people with businesses. Community members, known as "Yelpers," write reviews of the businesses and then rate them. Yelpers also find events and special offers and can connect with each other by posting "conversations" on different topics (for example, to "talk" with someone from Los Angeles, see **yelp.com/talk/la**). For details, see **yelp.com/faq** and Chapter 7.

Aggregators

These are sites that aggregate information from many other sites and bring them to one place. Yipit (**yipit.com**) is a free "e-mail based daily aggregator" that gathers deals ("every deal in your city") on products from daily deal sites such as Groupon, Living Social, etc. Tell Yipit what you want, and they will alert you when there are deals that match, usually at a fraction of the retail price (**yipit.com/about**).

Barcode Readers for Price Comparisons

It is now common behavior for e-commerce shoppers to gather information in physical stores and then buy online. Capitalizing on this behavior to make the search faster and easier, Amazon. com and other vendors provide smartphone apps of mobile bar scanners. Shoppers enter physical stores and take a picture of a bar code. The photo is transmitted to the vendor who provides them with an immediate price comparison. Leading apps are RedLaser (**redlaser.com**) from eBay (which is also used to support location-based ads, see Chapter 7), and Price Check from Amazon. com (see Kain 2011), and Quick Scan.

Digital Coupons

Shoppers are introduced to a new generation of coupons, which can be described as "no clip and no print." This is how it works. You register, for example, with the 'Just-For-U' program at Safeway. You click on the special sale items, or on the coupon of a product you want. When you go into Safeway and buy any of the products you clicked on (if they are available), you automatically receive a 10–20% discount. SavingStar Inc. (**savingstar.com**) offers a similar nationwide service in the U.S.

Self Service

One of the major benefits of EC is that it facilitates self-service. By providing tools that enhance self-service, customers can improve their online shopping experience. Examples of self-service tools are: configuration tools, calculators (e.g., for cost), FAQs, virtual online real time assistants, application tools, and site searches.

Virtual Visual Shopping

Many consumers embrace impulse buying when they see interesting or new products in physical stores. Theoretically, online shoppers in 3-D environments might also make such purchases.

One aspect of 3D is its ability to put items into a more physical view than 2D does. A 3D view of a house interior could help in visualizing whether a large dining table would fit in the intended space. Consumers can experiment with the location of the virtual table and see how it will fit into their home before they buy it. 3-D platforms could take the guesswork out of buying many types of products online, ranging from furniture to clothes.

Example

Can you imagine looking at a computer screen where you can see yourself wearing a piece of clothing you have selected, exactly as you can in the fitting room of a physical clothing store? Now wave your hand and the color of the outfit changes; wave your hand again and a dress will be shorter or longer. Another wave of your hand and another dress is on your "virtual body." A dream? Not really, it is coming! To learn about this "try-on" system, see Facecake Marketing Technology's "Swivel" **facecake.com/swivel**. For an illustration, watch the video titled "Tobi Virtual Dressing Room" (1:14 minutes) at **dailymotion.com/video/xcg18d_tobi-virtual-dressing-room_tech**.

For more information, see **workspaces. codeproject.com/nayan-zawar/virtual-3d-shopping-mall** and **virtwayworld.com/EN_products_3d_virtual_shop.php**.

Mobile Apps

Several mobile apps (Chapter 6) are available to assist shoppers who use smartphones or tablets both online and offline. For example, customers can shop and pay from their mobile devices. Most of the decision aids listed in this section are available today on mobile devices.

Wireless Shopping Comparisons

Users of **mysimon.com**, **slickdeals.net**, and other comparison sites can use mobile devices to access shopping comparisons and receive deal alerts. With the AT&T Code Scanner, shoppers can scan barcodes from their smartphone and compare prices anytime from anywhere, including from any physical store, newspaper ads, and even when the ads are online. Comparisons can be accessed from smartphones. For more about the Code Scanner and the downloading process, see **wireless.att.com/businesscenter/solutions/mobile-marketing/products/index.jsp**. For a slideshow of the 10 best shopping apps for comparing prices (2012 data), see **pcmag.com/slideshow/story/290959/the-10-best-shopping-apps-to-compare-prices**.

Note: Descriptions of social media-based shopping aids are provided in Chapter 7.

SECTION 3.9 REVIEW QUESTIONS

1. Define shopping portals and provide two examples.
2. What are shopbots?
3. Explain the role of business and website ratings, reviews, recommendations, and site verification tools in the purchase-decision process.
4. Why are escrow services useful for online purchases? Describe "spy" services in B2C EC.
5. How can a site motivate people to contribute their opinions on products and vendors?
6. Describe digital coupons.
7. What is virtual visual shopping?

3.10 THE NEW FACE OF RETAIL COMPETITION: RETAILERS VERSUS E-TAILERS

The introduction of B2C intensified the competition in the retail market. As we illustrated in the Blue Nile case in Chapter 2, prices are declining, while companies are disappearing or changing. For example, many retailers are adding an online channel to their offline offerings, or adding Internet only options. Adding an online retail channel helps, but many well-known retailers such as Best Buy, J.C. Penney, Radio Shack, Sears, Staples, and Office Depot still are forced to close numerous physical stores and are struggling to survive (e.g., see **usatoday.com/story/money/business/2014/03/12/retailers-store-closings/6333865** and Schoon 2014). Let us first look at an overview of the competition.

The Online Versus Offline Competition: An Overview

The Oxford Handbook of the Digital Economy from **oxfordhandbooks.com** provides a comprehensive study by Lieber and Syverson (2012), which describes the nature of the competition as well as the interplay of online and offline retail markets. They also look at the characteristics of online shoppers and the changes in both the demand and supply. The major variables studied in the Oxford handbook are:

- **Customers' search cost.** With today's shopping search and comparison engines and the use of mobile devices, the search cost to customers is very low and its importance in the competition is probably declining.
- **Delivery time.** Order fulfillment in physical stores is usually immediate for physical goods. However, online companies are constantly reducing the time between purchase and consumption. Sometime in the future, delivery will be by drones (see Chapter 12 and the opening case to this chapter). In the meantime, e-tailers are developing efficient same day delivery

services, at least in the large metropolitan areas. Additionally, in 2013 Amazon.com partnered with the U.S. Postal Service for Sunday delivery to Los Angeles and New York metropolitan areas, with service to extend to other cities in 2014 (see **usatoday.com/story/tech/2013/11/11/amazon-Sunday-delivery-usps/3479055**). Google Shopping Express (**google.com/shopping/express**) is a same-day delivery service in the San Francisco and San Jose areas, challenging similar services offered by Amazon.com and eBay (see Hsu 2014). In 2013, eBay launched a local delivery service called eBay Now (**ebay.com/now**). According to **ebay.com/now/faq.html**, they offer the delivery of "thousands of local products from hundreds of local retailers…usually in 1–2 hours!" This service is only available in select cities, including the San Francisco Bay area, New York, and Dallas. eBay plans to expand same-day delivery service to 25 cities in 2014 (see **cnet.com/news/ebay-to-expand-same-day-delivery-to-25-cities-in-2014**). For how eBay Now works, see **ebay.com/now/faq.html**.

Obviously the delivery time of digitizable products is very fast in e-tailing. This is an important factor since prices and the quality of products sold online are getting to be similar in different stores, so delivery time becomes an important factor.

- **Distribution costs.** Traditional retailers need to spend money to build (or rent) stores, have inventory, advertise, etc. On the other hand, e-tailers need to pay for packing and shipments, but their advertising costs and inventory costs are lower. These costs vary, depending on the products, the geographical location and more. The distribution costs can be an important factor in the competition.
- **Tax differences.** The advantage of online shopping is diminishing as the trend is to levy a tax on out of state online products. This topic is discussed in Chapter 15.
- **Price.** Not only do online vendors offer lower prices on the same goods, but they also may create a price conflict within click-and-mortar companies (see Section 3.11).
- **Information available to buyers.** While buyers cannot physically examine goods they buy

online, they can use the Internet to obtain considerable information on what they plan to purchase. In general, this is not a major factor in most transactions.
- **Other influencing factors.** Several other factors are important in the competition. For example, who the sellers are, who the buyers are, the distribution channels used, consumer satisfaction, level of consumer loyalty and the relationship between the sellers' online and offline marketing channels are all important. Finally, the shopping trends clearly indicate that more people are shopping online and spending more money doing so (e.g., see Moseti 2014). Younger people especially are turning to so-called "showrooming," meaning that shoppers go to a physical store to examine goods and check prices. Then they buy online at a lower price (see Isidore 2014), Shoppers are using apps on their mobile devices to compare prices (see Motorola Solutions 2013, and for some of the apps used, see **verizonwireless.com/news/article/2014/01/showrooming-trend.html**). Customers in general prefer to "touch and feel" items before they purchase them online (see **cnbc.com/id/100597529**).

Global Competition

As of 2010, we are seeing an increase in online global competition. For example, several Chinese companies are offering consumer electronic products at a discount when compared to what you can get at Amazon.com. After acquiring Buy.com, Japanese company Rakuten (**rakuten.com**) is competing in the U.S. market by offering their website in English.

Retailers Versus E-Tailers

Since the beginning of EC in the mid 1990s, it has become clear that in certain industries, e-tailing will hurt brick and mortar retailers. In Chapter 2, we introduced Blue Nile as an example of disrupting the jewelry industry. Stock brokerages and travel agents also have become victims to pure play competitors. Amazon.com initially concentrated on books, eliminating bookstores such as Borders. Today, Amazon.com is competing with thousands of retailers, including giants such as Walmart (see O'Connor 2013). *Encyclopedia Britannica,* and many others no longer have printed editions. The initial line of defense for traditional retailers was to become a 'click and brick,' namely adding an online distribution channel to their physical presence. This helped some department stores and specialty stores, but not all.

Examples of Click-and-Brick Retailers

Most large retailers have already migrated to be click-and-brick companies. Let us look at several examples:

Gap Inc.

The Gap (**gap.com**), a global clothing and accessories retailer, opened an independent online unit (Gap Inc. Direct). According to their website, Gap Inc. Direct is the e-commerce division of Gap, Inc. (known as "Growth Innovation Detail" or "GID") which "operates as a small business unit creating and managing the websites and fulfillment systems for some of the most powerful retail brands in the world. GID commerce brands include **gap.com**, **oldnavy.com**, **bananarepublic.com**, **athleta.com**, and **piperlime.com** in the U.S., as well as e-commerce sites in Canada, Europe and Japan" (see **gap.com/browse/info. do?cid=80004**). The company allows customers to order items online from different Gap Stores (Gap, Banana Republic, and Old Navy) and pay, all in a single transaction, Customers can also order online and pick up their purchases in its physical stores. Sales in Gap's online store are growing 15% per year. Gap's strategy is a mix of online and offline. For example, Athleta (**athleta. gap.com**) used to be a pure direct marketer. But in 2011, Gap started to build physical Athleta stores, and in 2012, Piperlime, which used to be online-only, opened a store in New York. Gap's online sales spiked 21% in FY 2013; more than 80% of the store's overall sales came from the Web (see **internetretailer.com/2014/02/27/ online-sales-spike-215-gap-fiscal-2013**). Overall, e-commerce revenue at GAP reached over $2 billion in 2013.

Best Buy

Best Buy, like Walmart, Target and others, added an online marketing channel. However, in contrast with GAP, Best Buy was not successful. One reason is that the company operates large scale stores. Consumers come to the stores, examine the products and go home and order them online ("showrooming") on Amazon.com because it is much cheaper. In summer 2012, Best Buy reduced its prices to match those of Amazon. com. The result was that in August 2012, Best Buy, which is one of the world's largest electronic retailers, saw its profit going down 91% in one year. Thus, the company decided to close 50 of its stores, and also is moving to smaller stores to cut expenses. The future of Best Buy, which was one of the most successful electronic retailers just a few years ago, is improving but still uncertain as of April 2014. Because of customers engaging in "showrooming," in early 2013, Best Buy decided to price match not only all local retail competitors but also 19 "major online competitors." The price matching initiative was temporary during the 2012 holiday season, but due to its popularity, Best Buy decided to make it permanent (see **businessinsider.com/best-buy-new-price-matching-policy-2013-2**).

SM Chain of Malls in the Philippines

According to Magdirila (2014), this huge chain (over 230 malls and supermarkets across the Philippines) is preparing for full-scale online operations by 2016.

HHGregg

Appliance and electronics retailer HHGregg (**hhgregg.com**) also suffers from its online competitors. Sales and profits are declining. Besides major appliances, HHGregg also sells big screen TV's, computers, and home furniture. However, nowadays, people buy these products at lower prices on Amazon (or other e-tailers), and the products are delivered free of charge to the purchasers' homes. HHGregg is increasing its marketing and advertising efforts, but is still losing market share (see **blogs.marketwatch.com/behindthestore-front/2014/01/06/hhgregg-sees-sales-plummet-in-first-holiday-season-report-card**).

Eventually, it may go out of business. As a marketing strategy, in 2013, HHGregg looked to expanding its major appliances and furniture assortment for higher sales and profits (**twice.com/article-type/news/hhgregg-looks-furniture-appliances-profits/107090**).

Niche Markets

A popular strategy for competing in the online retail environment is to go to a niche market, which targets consumers in smaller markets (e.g., one product, one industry). The logic is that it is difficult for large e-tailers to identify specialized consumer needs for many products; therefore, they usually address niche markets inadequately.

Examples: CatToys (**cattoys.com**) and DogToys (**dogtoys.com**)

These webstores have a huge variety of specialized cat and dog-related items that a physical store cannot afford to carry. If you are pet lover, try it – your pet may like it.

Example: Ivy's Garden (**ivysgardenfood. com**)

This company sells gluten-free, home-style Asian food dishes. For the story of this company see Quick (2013).

Example: Zulily (**zulily.com**)

This company focuses on merchandise from specialized vendors, using a flash sale strategy. The company is very successful and debuted on the NASDAQ stock exchange in November 2013. The company's focus is on high-quality apparel for moms, babies, and children.

Other Strategies

According to VOA News (2013), many retailers are providing apps that help shoppers locate items while they are inside physical stores. The retailers can also provide digital discount coupons and make it easier for shoppers to place online orders for out-of-stock merchandise. For more on these strategies, see Krupnik (2013).

What Can Traditional Retailers Do?

In addition to opening online channels and closing the least profitable stores, traditional companies have a few strategies to defend themselves. Here are representative examples:

Can Small Businesses Survive?

While large retailers such as Best Buy and HHGregg may go out of business, some small businesses may survive. We discuss this issue in Chapter 13. Small businesses such as **dogtoys.com** and **hothothot. com** were pioneers of e-commerce and are still doing well. It seems that the success of small e-tailers is related to a strategy that includes:

- Niche markets. Products that cannot be produced in mass production (e.g., non-commodities) should be considered by a small business (e.g., provide custom-made and specialized products).
- Faster delivery than Amazon. Uniquely distributed products in local markets are ideal for small companies. (However, now Amazon offers same day delivery in select cities via its "Local Express Delivery" service.)
- Protect privacy. Amazon tracks customers' movements on the Web.
- Concentrate on local markets.
- Provide outstanding customer service.
- Prices should be competitive.
- Maintain their reputation using such strategies as many small companies have done; either pure play, brick-and-mortar, or click-and-brick can survive and succeed.

Going Global

Some small companies (e.g. Hothothot.com) have many global customers. Big companies, like Amazon.com are also very active globally. For example, according to Brohan (2012), Amazon. com is Europe's largest online retailer. Large companies acquire local EC companies or need to enter into joint ventures with them.

Examples

Ralph Lauren Corporation (**ralphlauren.com**), apparel designer, manufacturer and retailer, is selling aggressively online in Europe. In 2013, it started to sell online in Japan. Online sales increased about 30% in FY 2012 (**internetre-tailer.com/2012/05/25/ralph-lauren-sees-more-global-e-commerce-coming-soon**). A similar global expansion was done by Baccarat, a large French manufacturer of jewelry, crystal, and stemware products. For details on how Baccarat is growing its online sales, see Enright (2012). For more on companies going global, see Chapter 13.

Conclusion

According to Isidore (2014) and many others, the future of brick-and-mortar retail does not look good. Many stores already have gone out of business. In addition, many retailers will go out of business sooner or later. Note that the online business is becoming more diversified. For example, Amazon.com is experimenting with the same day delivery of vegetables and fruits, and China's e-commerce companies are moving on to banking (see Riley et al. 2014).

SECTION 3.10 REVIEW QUESTIONS

1. What are the major advantages of e-tailers over retailers?
2. Why is offline retailing in bad shape?
3. Discuss some strategies for SMEs to survive and succeed.
4. Why do e-tailers go global? What are their CSFs?

3.11 ISSUES IN E-TAILING AND LESSONS LEARNED

The following are representative issues and problems (and some lessons learned from them) that need to be addressed when conducting B2C EC. These and others are discussed by Laseter et al. (2007).

Disintermediation and Reintermediation

Disintermediation refers to the removal of an intermediary that is responsible for certain activities between trading partners (usually in a supply chain). As shown in part B of Figure 3.5, a manufacturer can bypass wholesalers and retailers, selling directly to consumers. Thus, B2C may drive regular retailers out of business. According to Lieber and Syverson (2012), half of the U.S. travel agencies went out of business between 1997 and 2007 due to online competition. For a vivid case of such disintermediation, see the Blue Nile case in Chapter 2. For bypassing intermediaries see Miller and Clifford (2013).

However, consumers might have problems selecting an online vendor, vendors might have problems delivering goods to customers, and both might need an escrow service to ensure the transactions. Thus, new types of intermediaries might be needed, and services might be provided by new or by traditional intermediaries. This new activity is called **reintermediation**. It is pictured in part C of Figure 3.5. An example of a company that provides these new roles of intermediation is Edmunds (**edmunds.com**), which provides consumers with information about cars (e.g., price comparisons, ratings, and the dealer costs). Another example would be travel agents who can arrange complicated trips, provide longer periods for holding reservations, arrange special tours and spot deals. Such new role playing companies can grow rapidly while traditional intermediaries decline.

Resistance to Change

Intermediaries that may be eliminated, or their status and pay may decrease, might resist the change. One example is the computerization of the Chicago Mercantile Exchange (CME) and the Chicago Board of Trade (CBOT). The resistance by brokers there has been going on for a long time. For an interesting discussion, see Ingwersen and Saphir (2011).

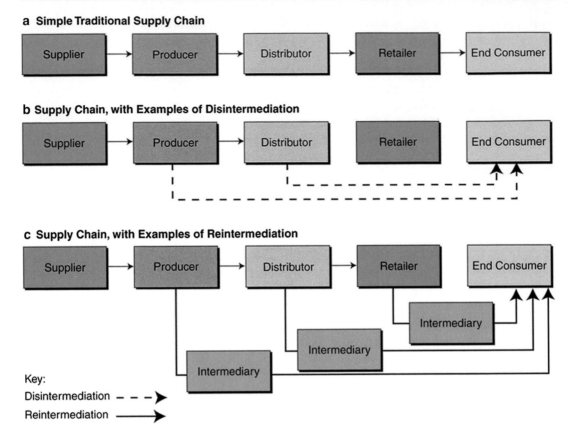

Figure 3.5 Disintermediation and reintermediation in the B2C supply chain

Channel Conflict

Many traditional retailers establish a supplemental marketing channel when they start selling online. (For a discussion about a practice known as *multichannel* marketing, see Kline 2010.) Similarly, some manufacturers have instituted direct marketing initiatives parallel with their established channels of distribution, such as retailers or dealers. In such cases, *channel conflict* can occur. **Channel conflict** refers to the case in which online sales damage the well being of an existing channel partner. The extent of this conflict varies according to the nature of the industry and the characteristics of particular firms, but sometimes a move to sell online can damage old, valued relationships between trading partners. Channel conflict may occur when a move to online trading simply shifts a company's customers from their traditional stores to an online environment, thus cannibalizing the sales from the former, and potentially negatively affecting the traditional outlets by rendering them less profitable. One model that can solve the conflict is to allow ordering and payment online, but the item is delivered to a physical store for pickup. For details on how to manage multichannel situations, see Kline (2010).

Possibility of a Price Conflict and Determining the Right Price by Sellers

Pricing a product or service on the Internet, especially by a click-and-mortar company, is complicated. One reason is that prices need to be competitive both on the Internet and in the physical stores. Today's comparison engines show consumers the prices of the same goods or services at many stores, for almost all commodity (or standard) products. In such a case, the click-and-brick e-tailer may be forced to offer online prices, which are lower than what the company charges in its physical store (e.g., some airlines direct you online to find special low price flights). On the other hand, prices are determined by the corporate policy on profitability and, in a click-and-brick company, in line with the offline channel's pricing strategy. To avoid such internal price conflicts, some companies have created independent online subsidiaries, some even with different names. For example, **allstate.com** created the online site **ensurance.com**.

Product and Service Customization and Personalization

The Internet also allows for easy self-configuration ("design it your way"). This creates a large demand for customized products and services. Manufacturers can meet that demand by using a *mass customization* strategy (see **en.wikipedia.org/wiki/Build_to_order**). As indicated earlier, many companies offer customized products on their websites (e.g., see the Dell case in Online File W1.1).

In conclusion, e-tailing is growing rapidly as an additional marketing channel. In other words, the *click-and-brick model is* a successful one regardless of the conflicts cited. For more about e-tailing and multi-channeling retailing, see **dmsretail.com/etailing.htm**.

Fraud and Other Illegal Activities

A major problem in B2C is the increasing rate of online fraud. This can cause losses both to buyers and sellers. For a more detailed and thorough discussion of online fraud and how to minimize it, see Chapter 10.

Lessons Learned from Failures and Lack of Success of E-Tailers

As in the physical world, companies can also fail when doing business online. Online File W3.4 provides some samples of failed B2C companies. Some lessons learned from failures are discussed next.

Although thousands of companies have evolved their online strategies into mature websites with extensive interactive features that add value to the consumer purchasing process, many other sites remain simple "brochureware" sites with limited interactivity. Many traditional companies are in a transitional stage. Mature transactional systems include features for payment processing, order fulfillment, logistics, inventory management, and a host of other services. In most cases, a company must replicate each of its physical business processes and design several more that can be performed online only. Today's environment includes sophisticated access to order information, shipping information, product information, and more through Web pages, touch-tone phones, Web-enabled smartphones, and tablets over wireless networks. Faced with all of these variables, the challenges to profitably in implementing EC can be daunting.

A traditional brick-and-mortar store with a mature website that uses a successful click-and-mortar strategy such as those used by Target, Walmart, and Staples, can create a successful multi-channel business whose benefits can be enjoyed by customers who like to have options on how to buy.

SECTION 3.11 REVIEW QUESTIONS
1. Define disintermediation.
2. Describe reintermediation.
3. Describe channel conflict and other conflicts that may appear in e-tailing.
4. Describe price determination in e-tailing. Under what circumstances might there be a conflict?
5. Explain personalization and customization opportunities in e-tailing. What are their benefits to customers?
6. What makes click-and-mortar companies successful?

MANAGERIAL ISSUES

Some managerial issues related to this chapter are as follows.

1. **What are the limitations of e-tailing? Where is e-tailing going?** In Korea, Internet retailing has become the second most important distribution channel, exceeding the national sales volume of all department stores. In many countries, B2C is the fastest growing form of retailing. The question is what will be the limits of e-tailing? The market concentration has already begun, setting a high bar for new e-tailers. However, small businesses can easily start their online channel as part of a stable e-mall service platform when they find a niche opportunity.

   Because many easy sources of funding have dried up and revenue models are being scrutinized, vendor consolidation will continue until greater stability within the e-tailing sector occurs. Ultimately, there will likely be a smaller number of larger sellers with comprehensive general sites (e.g., Amazon.com) and many smaller, specialized niche sites (e.g., Net-a-Porter, Blue Nile).

2. **How should we introduce wireless shopping?** In some countries (e.g., Japan, Korea, Finland, USA), shopping from smartphones is already very popular. In other countries, mobile shopping is not popular yet, although the platform itself may be available. Alternative channels (multichannel marketing) and a culture of a variety of communication channels is developing in many countries, facilitating mobile strategies. In addition, because the younger generation prefers the mobile platform, strategies for the younger generation need to be considered. Offering mobile shopping might not be simple or appropriate to all businesses, but it certainly will be dominant in the future.

3. **Do we have ethics and privacy guidelines?** Ethical issues are extremely important online, just as they are offline. In traditional systems, people play a significant role in ensuring the ethical behavior of buyers and sellers. Will online ethics and the rules of etiquette be sufficient to guide behavior on the Internet? Only time will tell. For example, as job-applicant information travels over the Internet, security and privacy become even more important. It is management's job to make sure that information from applicants is secure. Moreover, e-tailers need to establish guidelines for protecting the privacy of customers who visit their websites. Security and privacy must be priorities.

4. **How will intermediaries act in cyberspace?** The role of online intermediaries has become more and more important. In the banking, stock trading, job market, travel industry, and book sales sectors, the Internet has become an essential service channel. These intermediary services create new business opportunities for sellers and intermediaries.

5. **Should we try to capitalize on social networks?** Many organizations and individuals began advertising or selling products and services on Facebook and other social networks. Although large companies currently are concentrating on advertising, some are experimenting with B2C sales (see Chapter 7). Social commerce may become an extremely important marketing channel and should be at least experimented with by retailers.

6. **How should we manage multichannel marketing to avoid channel and/or price conflicts?** Managing multichannels requires a strategy on handling different types of transactions in the most appropriate and cost-effective way. Changing channels needs to be done together with appropriate conflict management (see Kline 2010 for approaches).

7. **What are the major potential limitations of the growth of B2C EC?** First, the limitations depend on market demands for online products. The saturation effect may be strong. Second, the cost and availability of Internet access may influence growth. Third, cultural differences and habits may deter or slowdown e-shopping. Fourth, the ease of B2C shopping is important, and fifth, the availability of payments and order fulfillment infrastructure are critical success factors.

8. **How to deal with "big data"?** A large amount of data is collected in B2C and is growing rapidly. It is necessary to extract valuable information and knowledge from this data. The technologies that are used belong mostly to the category of business intelligence (BI); they range from data and Web mining to several other analytical tools. An example of an analytical tool is WebSphere Commerce from IBM (**ibm.com/software/products/en/web-sphere-commerce**). For details on BI, see **cio.com/article/40296/Business_Intelligence_Definition_and_Solutions** and Online Tutorial T3.

SUMMARY

In this chapter, you learned about the following EC issues as they relate to the chapter's learning objectives.

1. **The scope and characteristics of e-tailing.** E-tailing, the online selling of products and services, is growing rapidly. Computers, software, and electronics are the major items sold online. Books, CDs, toys, office supplies, and other standard commodities also sell well. Even more successful are services that are sold online, such as airline tickets and travel services, stock trading, and some financial services.

2. **Classify e-tailing business models.** The major e-tailing business models can be classified by distribution channel – a manufacturer or mail-order company selling directly to consumers, pure-play (virtual) e-tailing, a click-and-mortar strategy with both online and traditional channels, and online malls that provide either referring directories or shared services. Social commerce facilitates group buying and location shopping.

3. **How online travel/tourism services operate.** Most services available through a physical travel agency also are available online. However, customers can get additional information more quickly using online resources. Customers can even submit bids to travel providers (e.g., using the C2B business model).

Finally, travelers can compare prices, participate in online activities, read other travelers' recommendations, and view user-generated videos. Lately, social travel is becoming popular, with travelers learning from each other and organizing trips accordingly.

4. **The online employment market and its benefits.** The online job market is growing rapidly. The major benefits for employers are the ability to quickly reach a large number of job seekers at a low cost, conduct remote video interviews, and even conduct pre-employment qualification tests. Finally, résumés can be checked and matched against job requirements. Millions of job offers posted on the Internet help job seekers, who also can post their résumés for recruiters. Recruiting in social networks, especially LinkedIn and Facebook, is growing rapidly.

5. **The electronic real estate marketplace.** In most cases, the online real estate marketplace supports traditional operations. However, both buyers and sellers can save time and effort by using the electronic markets. Buyers can purchase properties in several locations much more easily than without the Internet, and in some situations they have access to less expensive services (insurance, mortgages, etc.). Eventually, agents' commissions on regular transactions are expected to decline as a result of the electronic market for real estate, as more online sales directly by owner become popular.

6. **Online trading of stocks and bonds.** One of the fastest growing online businesses is the online trading of securities. It is inexpensive, convenient, and supported by a tremendous amount of financial and advisory information. Trading is very fast and efficient, almost fully automated, and is moving toward 24/7 global trading. However, security breaches are more possible, so good security protection is essential.

7. **Cyberbanking and online personal finance.** Branch banking is on the decline due to less expensive, more convenient online banking as the world becomes more accustomed to and trusting in cyberbanking. Today, most

routine banking services can be done from anywhere. Banks can reach customers in remote places, and customers can conduct transactions with banks outside their community. This makes the financial markets more efficient. Online personal finance applications, such as bill paying, monitoring of accounts, and tax preparation, also are very popular.

8. **On-demand delivery service.** On-demand delivery service is needed when items are perishable or when delivering medicine, express documents, or urgently needed supplies. One example of on-demand delivery is e-groceries; these may be ordered online and are shipped or ready for store pickup within 24 hours or less.

9. **Delivery of digital products.** Anything that can be digitized can be successfully delivered online. Delivery of digital products such as music, software, e-books, movies, and other entertainment online has been a success. Some print media, such as electronic versions of magazines or electronic books (see Chapter 5), also are successful when digitized and delivered electronically.

10. **Aiding consumer purchase decisions.** Purchase decision aids include shopping portals, shopbots and comparison agents, business rating sites, recommendations (including electronic ones), trust verification sites, and other tools. Tools include real-time mobile devices and extensive support from social networks.

11. **The new face of retail competition.** The surge in B2C has resulted in pressure on traditional retailers to add online channels and reduce prices. Even large companies such as Best Buy are struggling. The online retail giants, Amazon.com and eBay, are becoming more aggressive and competitive (e.g., adding same day delivery) so their consumers are enjoying lower prices and better service. Traditional retailers also need a strategy to deal with the intense competition. New competition is also coming from Chinese and other foreign online vendors.

12. **Disintermediation and other B2C strategic issues.** Direct electronic marketing by manufacturers results in disintermediation by removing wholesalers and retailers. However, online reintermediaries provide additional services and value, such as helping consumers select among multiple vendors. Traditional retailers may feel threatened or pressured when manufacturers decide to sell directly to customers online; such direct selling can cause channel conflict. Pricing of online and offline products and services is also an issue that frequently needs to be addressed.

KEY TERMS

Brick-and-mortar retailer
Business model
Channel conflict
Click-and-mortar retailer
Direct marketing
Disintermediation
E-grocer
Electronic (online) banking (e-banking)
Electronic retailing (e-tailing)
E-tailers
Event shopping
Internet Radio
Internet TV
Location-based e-commerce (l-commerce)
Multichannel business model
On-demand delivery service
Private shopping club
Referral economy
Reintermediation
Shopping portals
Shopping robots (shopping agents, shopbots)
Social TV
Virtual (pure-play) e-tailers

DISCUSSION QUESTIONS

1. Discuss the importance of comparison tools, product reviews, and customer ratings in online shopping.

2. Discuss the advantages of a specialized e-tailer, such as DogToys.com (**dogtoys.com**). Could such a store survive in the physical world? Why or why not?

3. Use Google to find the benefits of travel-related social networking sites. Discuss five of them.

4. Discuss the benefits of **salary.com**. Are there any disadvantages?

5. Why are online travel services a popular Internet application? Why do so many websites provide free travel information?

6. Compare the advantages and disadvantages of online stock trading with offline trading.

7. Compare the advantages and disadvantages of distributing digitizable products electronically versus physical delivery.

8. Do you trust your personal data on social networks such as **linkedin.com** or **facebook.com**? How do you protect your privacy?

9. Many companies encourage their customers to buy products and services online, sometimes "pushing" them to do so. Why?

10. Would you use **monster.com** or **linkedin.com** for recruiting, or would you rather use a traditional agency? Why?

11. Travel social network WAYN (**wayn.com**) says that it is a bridge between two social sites: Facebook and TripAdvisor. Discuss.

TOPICS FOR CLASS DISCUSSION AND DEBATES

1. Discuss the advantages of established click-and-mortar companies such as Walmart over pure-play e-tailers such as Amazon.com. What are the disadvantages of click-and-brick retailers as compared with pure-play e-tailers? Also debate: Competition between pure play e-tailers (e.g., Amazon.com, Blue Nile) and traditional retailers such as HP, Walmart, and other department stores that have added the Web as a part of a multichannel business model (e.g., see O'Connell 2009). Who may win? Under what assumptions?

2. Online employment services make it easy to change jobs; therefore, turnover rates may increase. This could result in total higher costs for employers because of increased costs for recruiting and training new employees, and the need to pay higher salaries and wages to attract or keep existing employees.

What can companies do to minimize this problem?

3. Discuss each of the following as limiting factors on the growth of B2C EC: (a) Too much competition, (b) expensive technology, (c) people need desktop computers to shop online (but smartphones are changing this situation), (d) people need the social interaction of face-to-face shopping, (e) many people cannot afford Internet access, (f) the fear of fraud and security breaching.

4. Debate: Some employers ask job applicants permission to log into their Facebook account during an in-person interview; others ask for complete, unfiltered access to the entire Facebook account. Some U.S. states propose legislation (several already have passed laws) banning employers (and universities) from using a prospective employee's Facebook content as selection criteria.

5. In April 2012, TripAdvisor announced on its website that it is the world's largest social travel site. Some people say that WAYN is the only truly social travel network. Compare the social networking activities of both sites. Debate the issue.

6. Debate: Should online sales be an independent division in a click-and-mortar firm?

7. Debate: What is the future of Amazon.com?

8. Discuss the benefits and limitations of recruiting with the help of social games.

9. Read Berzon's 2012 article and find more information about online poker. Then debate: Is poker a game of skill or it is just gambling?

10. Some love digital coupons, others say the idea is waste of time since coupons are not available for the products they want to buy. Research the topic and debate the value of digital versus paper coupons.

11. Investigate the impact of online casinos on physical ones. Discuss.

INTERNET EXERCISES

1. Many consumer portals offer advice and ratings on products or e-tailers. Identify and examine two separate general-consumer

portals that look at sites and compare prices or other purchase criteria. Try to find and compare prices for some digital cameras, microwave ovens, and MP3 players. Visit **yippy.com**. How can this site help with your shopping? Summarize your experience. Comment on the strong and weak points of such shopping tools.

2. Visit **landsend.com** and prepare a customized order for an item of clothing. Describe the process. Do you think this will result in better-fitting clothes? Do you think this personalization feature will lead to greater sales volume for Lands' End?

3. Make your résumé accessible to millions of people. Consult **asktheheadhunter.com** or **careerbuilder.com** for help rewriting your résumé. See **monster.com** for ideas about planning your career. Get prepared for an online job interview and look at **monstertronics.com** for interesting capabilities. Use the Web to determine what salary you can get in the city of your choice for the kind of job you want.

4. Visit **move.com**, **decisionaide.com**, or a similar site and compute the monthly mortgage payment on a 30-year loan at 5.5% fixed interest. Also check current interest rates. Estimate your closing costs on a $200,000 loan. Compare the monthly payments of the fixed rate with that of an adjustable rate for the first year. Finally, compute your total payments if you take the loan for 15 years at the going rate. Compare it with a 30-year mortgage. Comment on the difference.

5. Access the Virtual Trader game at **virtualtrader.co.uk** and register for the Internet stock game. You will be bankrolled with a virtual £100,000 in a trading account every month. You can play other investment games at **investopedia.com/simulator** or find and create a free stock market game at **marketwatch.com/game**. Comment on your experiences.

6. Compare the price of a specific Sony digital camera at **shopping.com**, **mysimon.com**, **bizrate.com**, and **pricegrabber.com**. Which site locates the best deal? Where do you get the best information?

7. Enter **vineyardvines.com**. Identify all multichannels used in their retail operations. List the benefits to the company. Consult Greene (2010).

8. Enter **bazaarvoice.com** and find how consumers can engage in a dialog. Look at its Q&A functionality in both "Conversations" and "Connections." Write a report based on your findings.

9. Enter **couchsurfing.org** and examine how they connect potential travelers with hosts. Discuss the things that you like and the limitations of this service. Compare with home swapping sites such as **homeexchange.com**.

10. Enter **zillow.com/corp/ZillowPortfolio.htm** and see Zillow's portfolio. Examine their capabilities and the benefits to consumers. Write a report.

11. How can LinkedIn and Facebook help job seekers? How can they help employers? Relate your answers to what you can find on **indeed.com**.

12. Compare the sites **yelp.com** and **epinions.com**.

13. Visit **hayneedle.com**. What kind of a mall is this?

14. Enter **layar.com**. Find information about Layar Creator and other products that can support B2C shopping. Write a report.

15. Enter **play.google.com/store**. Relate the offerings of this site to topics in this chapter.

TEAM ASSIGNMENTS AND PROJECTS

1. **Assignment for the Opening Case**
   Read the opening case and answer the following questions.
   (a) What are Amazon.com's critical success factors? Is its decision to offer a much broader selection of items a good marketing strategy? With the increased services and diversification, do you think the company will be able to concentrate on its core competency of enhancing the Amazon.com brand? What about their long term vs. short term strategy?

(b) Amazon.com operates Zappos (**zappos. com**) as a separate entity. Does this make sense? Why or why not?

(c) Visit **amazon.com** and identify at least three specific elements of its personalization and customization features. Browse specific books on one particular subject, leave the site, and then go back and revisit the site. What do you see? Are these features likely to encourage you to purchase more books in the future from Amazon.com? Check the 1-Click feature and other shopping aids provided. List the features and discuss how they may lead to increased sales.

(d) With what type(s) of companies does Amazon.com have alliances? Why?

(e) Check all the personalization features on Amazon.com. List their advantages.

(f) Find the technology-oriented activities at Amazon.com (e.g., Mechanical Turk; making e-readers). List the major ones and discuss the logic of such offerings.

(g) Find some recent material on Amazon.com's marketing strategy and discuss your findings.

(h) Examine social networking activities on Amazon.com. What are their purposes?

2. Each team will investigate the services of two online car-selling sites (from the following list or other sites). When the teams have finished, they should bring their research together and discuss their findings.

(a) Buying new cars through an intermediary (**autobytel.com** or **carsdirect.com**).

(b) Buying used cars **autotrader.com**.

(c) Buying used cars from auto dealers (**manheim.com**)

(d) Automobile rating sites (**carsdirect.com** and **fueleconomy.gov**)

(e) Car-buying portals **thecarportal.com** and **cars.com**

(f) Buying collector cars **classiccars.com** and **antiquecar.com**

3. Each team (or team member) will review two or three travel-oriented social networks (e.g., **world66.com**, **virtualtourist.com**, **bootsnall.com**, **tripadvisor.com**, **travel.tripcase.com**, Lonely Planet's Thorn Tree travel forum **lonelyplanet.com/thorntree**, **wayn.com**, and **budgetglobetrotting.com**). Compare their functionalities. Then read Carey et.al. (2012) and examine the various issues raised in this paper including the surfing strategy. Write a report.

4. Each team will represent a broker-based area (e.g., real estate, insurance, stocks, employment). Each team will find a new development that has occurred within the assigned area over the most recent three months. Look for vendor announcements on these sites, and search for new happenings in each area. In addition, examine the relevant business news at **bloomberg.com**. After completing your research, as a team, prepare a report on disintermediation in your assigned area.

5. Plan a "geek style" wedding entirely online. First, make a chart of the process. Do not forget the groom's proposal, buying the rings, getting music, etc. Finally, explore the use of a self-managed DJ. You want to save money and use guest-generated content (consider using Facebook and Twitter for your wedding plans). You can start by looking at weddings 'going geek' at **itworld.com/offbeat/68244/wedding-20-when-weddings-go-geek**, getting 100 geeky wedding ideas at **trendhunter.com/slideshow/geeky-wedding**, and by googling 'geek wedding.'

6. Watch the video "Internet Marketing and E-Commerce with Tom Antion Part One" (9:06 minutes) at **youtube.com/watch?v=tc1u9eqpf68**. (Part Two at **youtube.com/watch?v=7jmK0_QTguk** is optional.) and answer the following questions:

(a) What revenue sources are cited?

(b) What B2C revenue sources that you are aware of are not cited?

(c) What are the two "affiliate" models? Compare these two models.

(d) Why is eBay so great for selling?

(e) Comment on the suggestions for products/services you can sell from your home.

(f) What problems and limitations do you see for conducting business from your home?

7. View some videos about future retail shopping (both offline and online). Discuss what

B2C e-commerce may look like in the future, considering future shopping innovations (e.g., see Microsoft's future vision on retailing and several videos offered by Metro AG in Europe on future shopping).

8. Your mission is to help people find jobs online. Each team evaluates several job sites and lists their capabilities and shortcomings. (Starting list: **craigslist.org**, **careerbuilder.com**, **dice.com**, **glassdoor.com**, **linkedin.com**, **mediabistro.com**, **monster.com**, **simplyhired.com**, and **tweetmyjobs.com**.) In addition, check virtual job fairs such as 'Monster Virtual Job Fair' (**virtualjobfair.be**).

9. The team(s) investigates Pandora Radio (**pandora.com**). Concentrate on:
   (a) All sources of music they can stream.
   (b) All devices that can be used to access Pandora.
   (c) Their business model and competitiveness.
   (d) Present your findings.

10. E-commerce, including B2C, is growing very rapidly in China. Investigate the major Chinese B2C sites, starting with **tmall.com**, **taobaofocus.com**, and **aliexpress.com**. Present your findings.

CLOSING CASE: ETSY – A SOCIAL-ORIENTED B2C MARKETPLACE

Etsy is online marketplace where designers across the world sell unique hand-crafted jewelry, clothing, vintage items (20 years or older), art, prints and posters, handmade goods, craft supplies, and more. According to its website, Etsy has created a community of sellers, each with a virtual storefront. The sellers are usually independent designers who sell small quantities of unique handcrafted goods. Etsy can be viewed as a designer's virtual fair where creators have their own virtual store with an "about" link so buyers can learn about the shop, read reviews, and contact the seller with any questions. Each seller may offer a link to their Facebook or Instagram page, so potential buyers can see products available to purchase. This is how Etsy emphasizes its social presence. For tips on

social networking success on Etsy, see **blog.etsy.com/en/tags/etsy-success-social-networking**.

The Company's Mission

According to **etsy.com/about**, the company's mission is "to re-imagine commerce in ways that build a more fulfilling and lasting world." In 2012, Etsy became a "Certified B Corporation," which is "a new kind of company that uses the power of business to solve social and environmental problems" (see **blog.etsy.com/news/2012/etsy-joins-the-b-corporation-movement**).

The Community

According to **etsy.com/community**, Etsy is more than a marketplace. It is a community of artists, creators, collectors, thinkers, and doers. Members are encouraged to share ideas, attend events (in your area), and join streaming workshops. Community members can post comments and stories. Etsy describes itself as "the marketplace we make together."

Etsy uses several social media tools and networks. For example, in April 2009, it organized an "Etsy Day" promotion on Twitter. In March 2011, the company introduced a Facebook-type social networking system called 'People Search,' a tool for people to search through all Etsy buyers and sellers and add people to their 'Circle.' This addition resulted in criticism regarding privacy (e.g., see Cheng 2011), and subsequently to the protection of such personal information on Etsy's site. For more details, see **huffingtonpost.com/2011/03/15/etsy-privacy-debacle-site_n_836277.html**.

The Business and Revenue Models

Etsy is a for-profit private company. Although there is no membership fee, Etsy charges 20¢ for each item listed for four months, or until that item sells. There is an additional fee of 3.5% of the sale price of that item once that item is sold, and if the seller uses the site's payment system (called Direct Checkout), there is an additional 3% fee (or more, depending on location of bank account) per transaction. Etsy declared that the company is profitable and intends to go public.

Competition

Many of Etsy's direct competitors are located outside the U.S. (e.g., German-based DaWanda; **en.dawanda.com**, Swiss-based Ezebee.com; **ezebee.com**). See details at **en.wikipedia.org/wiki/Etsy**. In the U.S., many handcraft creators sell on eBay and Amazon.com. Some competing websites sell only selected items (e.g., clothes, jewelry). Etsy has an official blog (see **blog.etsy.com/en**). It has a presence on Facebook (**facebook.com/Etsy**) and Twitter (**twitter.com/etsy**). As of early 2014, the company has over 409,000 followers on Pinterest (see **pinterest.com/etsy**) where there are thousands of pins about Etsy merchandise organized on almost 100 boards.

Conclusion

In addition to the 'People Search' privacy issue, the company was criticized for insufficient fraud detection efforts. For example, only original creations are allowed to be sold on Etsy, while reselling items is forbidden. Etsy is now insisting on transparency from all of its vendors, and will continue to investigate all shops "flagged" for possible violations (see **blog.etsy.com/news/2013/a-frank-conversation-about-resellers/?ref=about_blog_title**). Despite the criticism, the company is growing rapidly. Etsy now operates in Germany, France, and Australia, and plans expansion to other countries.

Sources: Based on Cheng (2011), Chow (2014), Feldmann (2014), Walker (2007), **en.wikipedia.org/wiki/Etsy**, and **etsy.com/blog/news** (both accessed April 2014).

Questions

1. Explain why the company has been compared to a cross between Amazon.com, eBay, and a grandma's basement.
2. Examine the mission of the company and explain what the company is doing to attain its mission.
3. The sellers in this case are mostly small businesses. As such, Etsy is considered a B2C company. However, it can also be viewed as an enabler of P2P. Explain.
4. Compare and contrast similar transactions conducted on Etsy and on eBay.
5. Enter **storenvy.com** and look at their markets. Compare this site with Etsy. Write a report.
6. Investigate the connection between Pinterest and Etsy. Start with Feldmann (2014). Write a report.

ONLINE FILES
available at **affordable-ecommerce-textbook.com/turban**

W3.1 What Sells Well on the Internet?

W3.2 Applications Case: Selling Cars Online – Build-to-Order

W3.3 Application Case: CatToys.com – A Specialty E-Tailer

W3.4 Lessons Learned from E-Tailing Failures

COMPREHENSIVE EDUCATIONAL WEBSITES

investopedia.com: Resources for investment education (tutorials, videos, white papers).

techrepublic.com/resource-library: White papers, Webcasts, and other resources on B2C e-commerce.

marketresearch.com/Technology-Media-c1599/E-Commerce-IT-Outsourcing-c88/B2C-c622/: B2C market research reports on e-commerce.

managementhelp.org/computers/e-commerce.htm: A basic guide to e-commerce.

bitpipe.com/data/tlist?b=ka_bp_ecommerce: A comprehensive site for information on most topics in this chapter.

wikinvest.com: An investment portfolio manager.

internetretailing.net: A very comprehensive site about Europe's multichannel retailers.

employmentguide.com: An easy search tool for finding jobs.

linkedin.com/company/onlinemarketing-group: An online marketing group at LinkedIn that focuses on digital marketing covering a number of specialties in the field.

dmsretail.com: Information, resources, articles, tips, and advice about retail management

GLOSSARY

Brick-and-mortar retailer A retailer that conducts business exclusively in the physical world.

Business model A description of how an organization intends to generate revenue through its business operations.

Channel conflict Refers to the case in which online sales damage the wellbeing of existing channel partner.

Click-and-mortar retailer A combination of both the traditional retailer and an online store.

Direct marketing Describes marketing that takes place without physical stores. Selling takes place directly from manufacturer to customer.

Disintermediation The removal of an intermediary that is responsible for certain activities (usually in a supply chain) between trading partners.

E-grocer A grocer that takes orders online and provides deliveries on a daily or other regular schedule or within a very short period of time, sometimes within an hour.

E-tailers Sellers who conduct retail business online.

Electronic (online) banking or e-banking Conducting banking activities online.

Electronic retailing (e-tailing) Retailing conducted over the Internet.

Event shopping A B2C model in which sales are designed to meet the needs of special events (e.g., a wedding, black Friday).

Internet TV The delivery of TV content via the Internet by video streaming technologies.

Internet Radio Audio content transmitted live via the Internet.

Location-based commerce (l-commerce) A wireless-based technology used by vendors to send advertisements relevant to the location where customers are at a given time by using GPS.

Multichannel business model The model or strategy of selling both online and offline.

On-demand delivery service An express delivery option.

Private shopping club Enables members to shop at discount, frequently for short periods of time (just few days).

Referral economy Describes the practice of receiving recommendations from buyers (e.g., in social networks or blogs).

Reintermediation The new intermediation that provides valuable help services.

Shopping portals Gateways to webstores and e-malls.

Shopping robots (shopping agents or shop-bots) Search engines that look for the lowest prices or for other search criteria.

Social TV An emerging social media technology that enables several TV viewers who are in different locations to interactively share experiences such as discussions, reviews, and recommendations while watching the same show simultaneously.

Virtual (pure-play) e-tailers Companies with direct online sales that do not need physical stores.

REFERENCES

1888 Press Release. "Top 10 Mobile Dating Apps in 2011." September 21, 2011. **1888pressrelease.com/cyber-dating-expert-announces-top-10-best-mobile-dating-apps-pr-336451.html** (accessed April 2014).

American Express Business Travel. "Automated Tool Improves Global Traveler Security and Peace of Mind for Relief Agency Contractor." 2011 **businesstravel.americanexpress.com/se/files/2011/11/CS_URSCorp-US.pdf** (accessed April 2014).

Atik, C. "10 Reasons Why It's Time to Bite the Bullet and Try Online Dating (Even If You Swore You Never Would)." May 28, 2012. **glamour.com/sex-love-life/blogs/smitten/2012/05/10-reasons-its-time-to-bite-th.html** (accessed April 2014).

Barish, M. "Social Networking and Travel: Do's & Don'ts." April 21, 2010. **gadling.com/2010/04/21/social-networking-and-travel-dos-and-donts** (accessed April 2014).

Baseline. "E-Commerce's New Dimension." November 30, 2007. **baselinemag.com/c/a/Projects-Supply-Chain/Ecommerces-New-Dimension** (accessed April 2014).

Beller, D., "How Internet Radio Works." March 27, 2001. **electronics.howstuffworks.com/internet-radio.htm** (accessed April 2014).

Bernstein, E. "Online, is Dream Date a Scam?" May 4, 2011. **online.wsj.com/news/articles/SB10001424052 748703834804576300973195520918** (accessed April 2014).

Berzon, A. "U.S. Judge Gives Poker a Break." August 23, 2012. **online.wsj.com/news/articles/SB10000872396 390444082904577607661262270108** (accessed April 2014).

Bortz, D. "Tweet Yourself to a New Job." February 6, 2014. **money.cnn.com/2014/01/01/pf/twitter-job. moneymag** (accessed April 2014).

Brandt, R. *One Click: Jeff Bezos and the Rise of Amazon. com.* USA: Portfolio Hardcover, 2011.

Brohan, M. "Amazon Dominates Europe." March 21, 2012. **internetretailer.com/2012/03/21/amazon-dominates-europe** (accessed April 2014).

Brownell, M. "Get the Best Prices, Period: 10 Must-Have Tools for Every Shopper." January 9, 2013. **dailyfinance.com/2013/01/09/best-prices-apps-tools-comparison-shopping-showrooming/** (accessed April 2014).

Butcher, M. "WAYN Said to Be Close to Sale. The Price? $200m. The Buyer? AOL." January 16, 2008. **techcrunch.com/2008/01/16/wayn-said-to-be-close-to-sale-the-price-200m-the-buyer-aol/** (accessed April 2014).

Carey, R., D. Kang, and M. Zea. "The Trouble with Travel Distribution." February 2012. **mckinsey.com/insights/ travel_transportation/the_trouble_with_travel_distribution** (accessed April 2014).

Chea, T., "Tech startups create virtual farmers markets." December 23, 2013. **finance.yahoo.com/news/tech-startups-create-virtual-farmers-152714415.html** (accessed April 2014).

Cheng, J. "Etsy Users Irked After Buyers, Purchases Exposed to the World." March 14, 2011. **arstechnica. com/business/2011/03/etsy-users-irked-after-buyers-purchases-exposed-to-the-world/** (accessed April 2014).

Chordas, L. "Strength in Numbers." *Best's Review*, January 2010.

Chow, C., "The website Etsy.com a virtual craft shop for designers and shoppers alike." *San Jose Mercury News*, February 5, 2014. **mercurynews.com/camp-bell/ci_25072351/website-etsy-com-virtual-craft-shop-designers-and** (accessed April 2014).

Clearlake Capital. "Clearlake Capital Group Portfolio Company Buy.com Sold to Global Online Retailer Rakuten." May 21, 2010. **clearlakecapital.com/news/25-052110-buy_dot_com.html** (accessed April 2014).

Dickler, J. "I Found My Job on Twitter." May 12, 2009. **money.cnn.com/2009/05/12/news/economy/social_networking_jobs/** (accessed April 2014).

Distinguin, S. "Amazon.com: The Hidden Empire." *faberNovel*, May 2011. [Updated 2013.] **slideshare.net/ faberNovel/amazoncom-the-hidden-empire** (accessed March 2014).

Dixon, P. *Job Searching Online for Dummies*, 2nd ed., New York: For Dummies, 2000.

Donnelly, T. "Online Dating and Matchmaking." April 11, 2011. **inc.com/best-industries-2011/online-dating-and-matchmaking.html** (accessed May 2014).

Dubey, K. "Gartner Analyzes Social Networking Influence on Purchase Decisions." July 31, 2010. **techshout.com/internet/2010/31/gartner-analyzes-social-networking-influence-on-purchase-decisions** (accessed April 2014).

eMarketer. "Insurers Slowly Move to the Web." January 14, 2011. **emarketer.com/Article/Insurers-Slowly-Move-Web/1008174** (accessed April 2014).

Enright, A. "Baccarat Makes a Second Attempt at U.S. E-Commerce." *Internet Retailer* March 21, 2012. **internetretailer.com/2012/03/21/baccarat-makes-second-attempt-us-e-commerce** (accessed April 2014).

Evangelista, B. "How Social Television Is Gaining in Popularity." January 24, 2011. **sfgate.com/business/ article/How-social-television-is-gaining-in-popularity-2531128.php** (accessed April 2014).

Feldman, A. "Etsy Expands Reach and Sales for Its Seller Community." *Pinterest for Business*, 2014. **business. pinterest.com/case-study-etsy** (accessed May 2014).

Feng, Z. "The Future Points to E-Finance." November 29, 2013. **africa.chinadaily.com.cn/weekly/2013-11/29/ content_17140982.htm** (accessed April 2014).

Fox News. "Nevada, Delaware Sign Deal to Allow Interstate Online Gambling." February 25, 2014. **foxnews.com/politics/2014/02/25/raising-stakes-nevada-and-delaware-sign-agreement-to-allow-interstate-online** (accessed May 2014).

France, J. "10 Terrific Apps for Last-Minute Travel." April 18, 2013. **itworld.com/software/353027/10-terrific-apps-last-minute-travel** (accessed April 2014).

Gratton, S-J. and D. A. Gratton. *Zero to 100,000: Social Media Tips and Tricks for Small Businesses.* Upper Saddle River, NJ: Pearson Education and Que, 2012.

Grau, J. "U.S. Retail E-Commerce Forecast: Growth Opportunities in a Maturing Channel." *eMarketer,* April 2011. (No longer available online.)

Greene, M.V. "Many Channels, One Customer: Vineyard Vines Sees Its Shoppers through a Single Lens." June 2010. **stores.org/stores-magazine-june-2010/many-channels-one-customer** (accessed April 2014).

Groth, A., and S. Cortez. "The 15 Fastest-Growing Retailers in America." *Business Insider*, July 10, 2012. **businessinsider.com/fastest-growing-retailers-in-america-2012-7?op=1** (accessed April 2014).

Ha, S., and L. Stoel. "Consumer E-Shopping Acceptance: Antecedents in a Technology Acceptance Model." *Journal of Business Research*, May 2009.

Hockenson, L. "Updated: Pandora Opens Submission Process to Independent Artists." February 7, 2014. **gigaom.com/2014/02/07/Pandora-opens-submission-process-to-independent-artists/** (accessed April 2014).

Hsu, T. "Google Expands Same-Day Delivery Test to Southern California." January 23, 2014. **latimes.com/business/money/la-fi-mo-google-delivery-los-angeles-20140123,0,190849.story#axzz2yN0AT1zE** (accessed April 2014).

Ingwersen, J., and A. Saphir, "Chicago Traders Revolt at Change in CME Rules." December 12, 2011 **reuters.com/article/2011/12/12/markets-cbot-settlements-idUSL1E7NC90020111212** (accessed April 2014).

Isidore, C. "Everything Must Go: There's a Flood of Store Closings." March 7, 2014. **money.cnn.com/2014/03/07/news/companies/retail-store-closings** (accessed April 2014).

Joshi, V.C. *E-Finance: The Future Is Here*, 2nd ed., Thousand Oaks, CA: Sage, 2010.

Kain, E. "Amazon Price Check May Be Evil but It's the Future." December 14, 2011. **forbes.com/sites/erikkain/2011/12/14/amazon-price-check-may-be-evil-but-its-the-future** (accessed April 2014).

Kline, C. "Delivering Exceptional Customer Experience in a Multichannel World." July 12, 2010. **crmbuyer.com/story/70386.html** (accessed April 2014).

Knight, K. "Why Travel Advertisers Need to Think Mobile." May 9, 2012. **bizreport.com/2012/05/why-travel-advertisers-need-to-think-mobile.html** (accessed April 2014).

Krantz, M. *Investing Online For Dummies*. New York: For Dummies, 2012.

Krupnik, Y., "Can Brick-and-Mortar Still Compete with Online Retailers?" August 13, 2013. **retailtouchpoints.com/executive-viewpoints/2779-can-brick-and-mortar-still-compete-with-online-retailers/** (accessed April 2014).

Kwon, W. S., and S. J. Lennon. "What Induces Online Loyalty? Online Versus Offline Brand Images." *Journal of Business Research,* May 2009.

Laseter, T. M., E. Rabinovich, K. K. Boyer, and M. J. Rungtusanatham. "3 Critical Issues in Internet Retailing." (Spring 2007). **sloanreview.mit.edu/article/critical-issues-in-internet-retailing** (accessed April 2014).

Lee, S.C., and A.A. Brandyberry, "The E-tailer's Dilemma", *ACM SIGMIS Database*, Vol. 34, No. 2, Spring 2003.

Levin, D., "How TrueCar Won Auto Dealers Over." January 21, 2014. **features.blogs.fortune.cnn.com/2014/01/21/truecar** (accessed April 2014).

Lewis, L. "Open-Shelf Solution: New E-Commerce Platform Driving Sales for the Container Store." March 2010. **stores.org/stores-magazine-march-2010/open-shelf-solution** (accessed April 2014).

Lieber, E., and C. Syverson. *Online versus Offline Competition: The Oxford Handbook of the Digital Economy.* New York: Oxford University Press, 2012. (Note: Paper prepared for the Oxford Handbook of the Digital Economy (January 2011); a free version is available online at **faculty.chicagobooth.edu/chad.syverson/research/onlinevsoffline.pdf** (accessed April 2014).

Magdirila, P. "After Creating Biggest Chain of Malls in Philippines, SM Plans to Conquer E-Commerce." February 27, 2014. **techinasia.com/Philippines-sm-malls-preparing-huge-ecommerce-entry** (accessed April 2014).

Marsden, P. "Commerce Gets Social: How Your Networks Are Driving What You Buy." January 6, 2011. **socialcommercetoday.com/speed-summary-wired-feb-2011-cover-story-on-social-co** (accessed May 2014).

Masud, S. "The Social Media Recruitment Survival Guide." August 18, 2012. **mashable.com/2012/08/18/social-media-recruitment-survival-guide** (accessed April 2014).

McCafferty, D. "Social Networks Surge as Recruiting Tools." July 11, 2012. **baselinemag.com/careers/slideshows/Social-Networks-Surge-as-Recruiting-Tools** (accessed April 2014).

Meister, J. "Gamification: Three Ways to Use Gaming for Recruiting, Training, and Health and Wellness." May 21, 2012. **forbes.com/sites/jeannemeister/2012/05/21/gamification-three-ways-to-use-gaming-for-recruiting-training-and-health-amp-wellness** (accessed May 2014).

Miller, C. C., and S. Clifford, "E-Commerce Companies Bypass the Middlemen." March 31, 2013. **nytimes.com/2013/04/01/business/e-commerce-companies-bypass-middlemen-to-build-premium-brand.html?_r=0** (accessed April 2014).

Montopoli, B. "29% Accessed Porn on Work Computers Last Month." April 23, 2010. **cbsnews.com/news/29-accessed-porn-on-work-computers-last-month/** (accessed April 2014).

Moseti, Wilfred M. "Struggling Retailers Report Change in Shopping Trends." February 2, 2014. **sproutwired.com/struggling-retailers-report-change-in-shopping-trends/185173** (accessed April 2014).

Motorola Solutions. "What's Driving Tomorrow's Retail Experiences?" March 19, 2013. **enterpriseinnovation.net/whitepaper/whats-driving-tomorrows-retail-experiences** (accessed April 2014). White Paper available for (free) download at **motorolasolutions.com/web/Business/Products/_Documents/White_Paper/Static_Files/MT_White_Paper.pdf** (accessed April 2014).

National Association of Realtors. "Market Challenges, New Technologies Converge to Change Realtor®-Consumer Relationship." November 6, 2010. **marketwired.com/press-release/market-challenges-tnew-technologies-converge-to-change-realtorr-consumer-relationship-nasdaq-move-1348328.htm** (accessed April 2014).

Nguyen, A. "Online Banking Fraud Losses Rise to Nearly £60: Criminals Use Malware to Target Customers." March 10, 2010. **computerworlduk.com/news/security/19299/online-banking-fraud-losses-rise-to-nearly-60-million** (accessed April 2014).

Nielsen Company. "Five Things to Know about Online Grocery Shopping." May 31, 2011. **nielsen.com/us/en/newswire/2011/five-things-to-know-about-online-grocery-shopping.html** (accessed April 2014).

O'Connell, V. "Saks Challenges Web Discounters." *Wall Street Journal*, October 29, 2009. **online.wsj.com/**

news/articles/SB2000142405274870357460457 4501 741691272378 (accessed April 2014).

O'Connor, C. "Wal-Mart vs. Amazon: World's Biggest E-Commerce Battle Could Boil Down to Vegetables." April 23, 2013. **forbes.com/sites/clareoconnor/2013/04/23/wal-mart-vs-amazon-worlds-biggest-e-commerce-battle-could-boil-down-to-vegetables** (accessed April 2014).

O'Neill, S. "What's the Best Social Network for Travel?" *Budget Travel*, January 11, 2011. **budgettravel.com/blog/whats-the-best-social-network-for-travel,11619/** (accessed April 2014).

PricewaterhouseCoopers. "Global Entertainment and Media Outlook: 2013–2017."2013. **pwc.com/us/en/industry/entertainment-media/publications/global-entertainment-media-outlook.jhtml** (accessed May 2014).

Quick, B. "Ivy's Garden: Growing a Gluten-Free Asian Food Business Online." May 9, 2013. **smallbusiness.yahoo.com/advisor/ivy's-gardeDOUBLEHY-PHENrowing-a-gluten-free-asian-food-business-onlinDOUBLEHYPHEN81900556.html** (accessed April 2014).

RenWeb. "Did You Know that 61% of American Adults Use Online Banking and Bill Pay?" September 22, 2011. **renweb.com/Blog/EntryId/133/Did-You-Know-That-61-Percent-of-American-Adults-Use-Online-Banking-and-Bill-Pay.aspx** (accessed April 2014).

Riley, C., Y. Yang, and P. Chiou. "China's Big Tech Moves onto Banks' Turf." February 27, 2014 **money.cnn.com/2014/02/27/news/economy/china-alibaba-bank** (accessed April 2014).

Rodriguez, S. "Uber to Deliver Some Christmas Trees on Demand Thursday." December 4, 2013. **articles.latimes.com/2013/dec/04/business/la-fi-tn-uber-christmas-trees-home-depot-20131204** (accessed April 2014).

Rountree, E. "Social TV 101—The Apps, Tools and Blogs You Need to Know." August 4, 2011. **socialmediaweek.org/blog/2011/08/social-tv-101-the-apps-tools-and-blogs-you-need-to-know/#.UuwOyfldWSq** (accessed April 2014).

Rueter, T. "E-Retail Spending to Increase to 62% by 2016." February 27, 2012. **internetretailer.com/2012/02/27/e-retail-spending-increase-45-2016** (accessed April 2014).

Sala, K. "Top 50 Product Review Blogs." June 25, 2012. **blog.us.cision.com/2012/06/top-50-product-review-blogs/** (accessed April 2014).

Schoon, R. "RadioShack Announces It's Closing 1000's of Stores: Mistakes and E-Commerce Competition to Blame." March 5, 2014. **latinpost.com/articles/8316/20140305/radioshack-announces-its-closing-1000s-of-stores-mistakes-and-e-commerce-competition-to-blame.htm** (accessed April 2014).

Shih, C. *The Facebook Era: Tapping Online Social Networks to Market, Sell, and Innovate*, 2nd ed., Upper Saddle River, NJ: Pearson Education, 2011.

Singh, S., and S. Diamond. *Social Media Marketing for Dummies*, , 2nd edition. Hoboken, NJ: Wiley, 2012.

Statistica.com. "Size of Online Gaming Market from 2003 to 2015." 2014. **statista.com/statistics/270728/market-volume-of-online-gaming-worldwide** (accessed May 2014).

Strauss, J., and R. Frost. *E-Marketing, 6th edition*. Upper Saddle River, NJ: Prentice Hall, 2012.

Stone, B. *The Everything Store: Jeff Bezos and the Age of Amazon*. New York: Little, Brown and Company, 2013.

Turban, E., J. Strauss, and L. Lai. *Social Commerce*. New York: Springer, 2015.

Vaughan-Nichols, S. J. "Supreme Court to Decide the Future of Internet TV." January 10, 2014. **zdnet.com/supreme-court-to-decide-the-future-of-internet-TV-7000025039/** (accessed April 2014).

Vizard, M. "Jaguar Launches Virtual Shopping Experience." June 5, 2013. **cioinsight.com/it-news-trends/jaguar-launches-virtual-shopping-experience** (accessed April 2014).

VOA News. "Retailers Find New Ways to Compete with Online Sales." *Voice of America*, November 21, 2013. **voanews.com/content/retailers-find-new-way-to-compete-with-online-sales/1795214.html** (accessed April 2014).

Walker, R. "Handmade 2.0." December 16, 2007. **nytimes.com/2007/12/16/magazine/16Crafts-t.html?pagewanted=all** (accessed April 2014).

Wanarsup, W. and S. Pattamavorakun. "Intelligent Personalization Job Web Site." Proceedings of the 9th ACIS International Conference on Software Engineering, Artificial Intelligence, Networking, and Parallel/Distributed Computing (SNPD), Phuket, Thailand, August 6–8, 2008.

Wieczner, J., and K. Bellstrom. "The Mall Goes High-Tech." *SmartMoney*, November 2010.

Weinstein, M. "Virtual Handshake." *Training.com*, September 2009. **nxtbook.com/nxtbooks/nielsen/training0909/index.php?startid=18#/20** (accessed April 2014).

Williams, K. "Online Recruiting: A Powerful Tool." *Strategic Finance*, December 2000.

Zernike, K. "New Jersey Now Allows Gambling via Internet." November 26, 2013. **nytimes.com/2013/11/27/nyregion/new-jersey-opens-up-for-online-gambling.html?_r=1**& (accessed May 2014).

Zopa Press Office. "Key Facts." November 13, 2011. **zopa.com/about-zopa/press-office** (accessed April 2014).

Zwiebach, E., and M. Hamstra ."Retailers Cautious on E-Grocery." December 16, 2013. **supermarketnews.com/online-retail/retailers-cautious-e-grocery** (accessed April 2014).

Business-to-Business E-Commerce

4

Contents

Learning Objectives

Upon completion of this chapter, you will be able to:
1. Describe the B2B field.
2. Describe the major types of B2B models.
3. Discuss the models and characteristics of the sell-side marketplace, including auctions.
4. Describe sell-side intermediaries.
5. Describe the characteristics of the buy-side marketplace and e-procurement.
6. Explain how reverse auctions work in B2B.
7. Describe B2B aggregation and group purchasing models.
8. Define exchanges and describe their major types.
9. Describe B2B portals.
10. Describe third-party exchanges.
11. Describe how B2B can benefit from social networking and Web 2.0.
12. Provide an overview of the major B2B support services.

OPENING CASE: ALIBABA.COM: THE WORLD'S LARGEST B2B MARKETPLACE

Alibaba Group is a collection of Internet-based e-commerce companies, some of which are B2B (notably Alibaba.com); the others are B2C and EC services (e.g., payments). For a company overview, see **alibabagroup.com/en/about/overview**. The company started as a portal for connecting

---

Electronic supplementary material The online version of this chapter (doi: 10.1007/978-3-319-10091-3_4) contains supplementary material, which is available to authorized users

Chinese manufacturers with buyers from other countries. By 2014, Alibaba Group became the world's largest e-commerce enterprise. Its B2B operation (Alibaba.com) is the world's largest marketplace. The fascinating story of the company is described by Charles (2014) and by Schepp and Schepp (2009).

The Opportunity

The Alibaba Group was started in 1999 by Jack Ma and his partners. Ma envisioned an opportunity to connect foreign buyers with Chinese manufacturers, especially the small ones. These companies wanted to go global but did not know how to do it. The initial business was Alibaba.com, a B2B portal, which later on developed into a comprehensive B2B marketplace. The Alibaba Group also added a consumer-to-consumer (C2C) marketplace called Taobao (**taobao.com**). In 2004, Alibaba added the "Alipay Cross-Border E-Payment Service" (**alipay.com**). In 2007, the Alibaba Group founded Internet-based business management software company Alisoft (**alisoft.com**), followed by Tmall.com (**tmall.com**), a giant B2C platform. The company established a cloud computing platform and restructured over time.

In 2014 Alibaba Group had an IPO in the USA to raising over $20 billion. This case concentrates on Alibaba.com, the B2B company (herein "Alibaba.com").

The Solution

In 2014, Alibaba.com was an online marketplace composed of a platform for buyers, a platform for sellers, a community, and B2B (business-to-business) services. The company's mission is to provide all the necessary support for buyers, suppliers and traders. The components and role of the company are illustrated in Figure 4.1.

- **Suppliers:** Post their catalogs, company information, special promotions, etc. on the suppliers' space. Alibaba.com helps to reach international buyers. Suppliers can get free online training.
- **Buyers:** Search for potential products and suppliers and also have the option to post what they need (requests) on the buyers' space and get quotes from suppliers. Buyers can verify the suppliers' worthiness. (See a video about suppliers' assessment at **sa.alibaba.com**). Alibaba.com provides inspection services with reliable experts. Buyers can compare prices and terms of service as well.

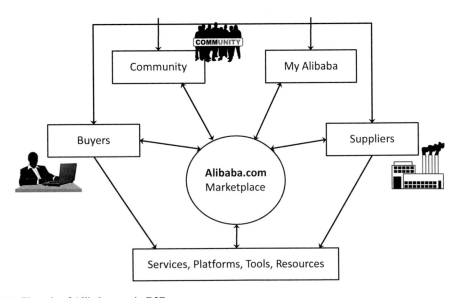

Figure 4.1 The role of Alibaba.com in B2B

- **Services for Buyers and Suppliers:** Alibaba.com helps to communicate, negotiate, and assist in reaching a deal. They also arrange the payment process, insurance, and delivery details. Alibaba.com provides all the technology necessary to support the activities on its site. It also provides services such as escrow and handling customer complaints.
- **My Alibaba:** A personal communication and trade management tool on Alibaba.com. It is now separated for buyers and suppliers.
- **Tools and Resources:** Alibaba.com provides information and tools for export and import. It also provides a tradeshow channel.
- **Alibaba Cloud Computing and Other Infrastructure:** The company is a developer of cloud computing services. The company is committed to supporting the growth of Alibaba Group companies and providing a comprehensive suite of Internet-based EC-oriented computing services, which include e-commerce data mining, high-speed massive e-commerce data processing capabilities, and data customization.
- **Alipay** (**alipay.com**) is a cross-border online payment platform, mainly used by buyers and sellers engaging in e-commerce transactions. It offers an easy, safe, and secure way for millions of individuals and businesses to make and receive payments on the Internet. By the end of 2013, Alipay had 300 million registered users who made over 12.5 billion payments; mobile users, through Mobile Alipay, made over 2.78 billion in payments. Mobile Alipay is now the largest mobile platform in the world (2014 data). See **chinainternetwatch.com/6183/alipay-the-largest-mobile-payments-platform-in-the-world**.
- Alibaba.com Secure Payment (an escrow service; **alibaba.com/escrow/buyer.html**) is a service that holds the payment to the seller until both parties have confirmed that the transaction is complete. Alibaba Escrow Service also has a Dispute and Refund process if the buyer does not receive the goods or is unhappy with the delivery. For more information about the Escrow Service and the Dispute and Refund process, see **alibaba.com/help/safety_security/products/escrow/faq.html**.

Alipay also offers an online global payment solution to help buyers or sellers outside China to do business in China. Alipay supports transactions in 12 major foreign currencies.

The Database

The center of Alibaba.com is its huge database, which is basically horizontal information organized into dozens of industry categories, including agriculture, apparel and fashion, automobiles, and toys. Each industry category is further divided into subcategories (over 800 in total). For example, the toy category includes items such as dolls, electronic pets, and wooden toys. Each subcategory includes classified postings organized into four groups: sellers, buyers, agents, and cooperation. Each group may include many companies and products. (Some categories have thousands of product postings.) A powerful search engine helps navigate the database.

Community Services

Alibaba.com provides the following major features all related to import and export: free e-mail, help center, 24-hour online intelligent robot to assist with answering questions, tutorials for traders, Trade Alert free updates to your inbox, news, tradeshow information, legal information, arbitration, forums and discussion groups, trade trends, and so on. In addition, a supplier can create a personalized company Web page as well as a "product showroom;" members also can post their own marketing leads (where to buy and sell). Alibaba.com also offers the TradeManager mobile app (**trademanager.alibaba.com**), which is their Instant Messaging tool. TradeManager can be used to chat with buyers in real time, get real-time translation, easily search for buyers and suppliers, and get the latest trade results. The TradeManager app is provided in multiple languages and at relatively low fees (the IM is free). For details, see Charles (2014) and **alibaba.com/help/features-trademanager.html**.

According to DYC Software Studio (**chat-translator.com**), DYC sells translation software called ChatTranslator for TradeManager, which is available in 20 languages. It can translate and send messages in any foreign language and translate replies from one language into the user's language. (For information about features and to purchase and download the software, see **chat-translator.com/products/chat-translator-trademanager.html** and **download.cnet.com/Chat-Translator-for-TradeManager/3000-20424_4-75212643.html**). To see the new features of TradeManager, see **trademanager.alibaba.com/features/introduction.htm**. To see more about the tools and features Alibaba offers to help buyers and sellers, see **alibaba.com/help/alibaba-features.html**.

The Competition

Many companies are attempting to rival Alibaba. For example, JD.com (**jd.com**, which merged with Tencent) is China's second largest e-commerce company. (It is used for both B2B and B2C.) **Trade.gov.cn/product.html** is a comprehensive e-commerce platform, used mainly to promote domestic and overseas trade, and Made-in-China.com (**made-in-china.com**), another world leading B2B portal, is another competitor. In the international market, companies such as TradeBanq (**tradebanq.com**), EC21 (**ec21.com**), Hubwoo (**hubwoo.com**), and Allactiontrade.com (**allactiontrade.com**) are all competing.

The Results

By 2014, Alibaba.com covered over 5,000 product categories and had about 5 million registered users in its international marketplace (outside China), as well as around 25 million registered users in China. The company conducts business in over 240 countries and regions and its employs more than 25,000 people.

According to Chen and Gill (2014), the pre-issue valuation of the company was $168 billion.

Sources: Based on Chen and Gill (2014), Lai (2010), Schepp and Schepp (2009), **crunchbase.com/organization/alibaba**, **buyer.alibaba.com**, and **seller.alibaba.com** (all accessed April 2014).

Note: For seven things to know about Jack Ma, see **upstart.bizjournals.com/entrepreneurs/hot-shots/2013/09/25/meet-jack-ma-things-to-know-about.html**.

LESSONS LEARNED FROM THE CASE

B2B e-commerce, which constitutes over 85% of all EC volume, is composed of different types of marketplaces and trading methods. The opening case illustrates a marketplace for many buyers and sellers to make transactions. The case presents the technology support provided for the B2B marketplace. In addition, the case describes information about support services (e.g., escrow services). The case illustrates the services provided for sellers (which are discussed in more detail in Sections 4.2 through 4.3) and the services for buyers (described in Sections 4.4, 4.5, and 4.6). The case also demonstrates the role of marketplaces (Sections 4.7 and 4.8). All the major EC buying and selling B2B methods as well as types of B2B marketplaces and portals are described in this chapter. Finally, we relate B2B to social networking and other support services.

4.1　CONCEPTS, CHARACTERISTICS, AND MODELS OF B2B E-COMMERCE

B2B EC has some special characteristics as well as specific models, components, and concepts. The major ones are described next.

Basic B2B Concepts and Process

Business-to-business e-commerce (B2B EC), also known as *eB2B* (*electronic B2B*), or just B2B, refers to transactions between businesses conducted electronically over the Internet, extranets, intranets, or private networks. Such transactions may take place between a business and its supply chain partners, as well as between a business and a government, and with any other business. In this context, a *business* refers to any organization, private, public, for profit, or nonprofit. In B2B, companies aim to computerize trading transactions and communication and collaboration processes in order to increase efficiency and effectiveness. B2B EC is very different and more complex than B2C. It is much more difficult to sell to a company than to individuals. For a comprehensive discussion, see Wirthwein and Bannon (2014).

Key business drivers for electronic B2B (some of which were shown in the opening case) are the need to reduce cost, the need to gain competitive advantage, the availability of a secure Internet platform (i.e., the extranet), and the private and public B2B e-marketplaces. In addition, there is the need for collaboration between business partners, the need to reduce transaction time and delays along the supply chain, and the emergence of effective technologies for interactions and systems integration. Several large companies have developed efficient B2B buying and selling systems. An example is 'Dell PremierConnect' that is illustrated in the video "Dell PremierConnect—The Efficiency of B2B (a Punchout Demo)" at **youtube.com/watch?v=OGgecp0uH9k**.

The Basic Types of B2B Transactions and Activities

The number of sellers and buyers and the form of participation used in B2B determine the five basic B2B transaction activity types:

1. **Sell-side.** One seller to many buyers.
2. **Buy-side.** One buyer from many sellers.
3. **Marketplaces or Exchanges.** Many sellers to many buyers.
4. **Supply chain improvements**.
5. **Collaborative commerce** (presented in Chapter 5).

The last two categories include activities other than buying or selling inside organizations and among business partners. They include, for example, removing obstacles from the supply chain, communicating, collaborating, sharing information for joint design and planning, and so forth.

Figure 4.2 illustrates these five B2B types. A brief explanation follows.

The Basic Types of B2B E-Marketplaces and Services

The following are the descriptions of the basic types of B2B e-marketplaces.

One-to-Many and Many-to-One: Private E-Marketplaces

In one-to-many and many-to-one markets, one company does either all the selling (*sell-side market*) or all the buying (*buy-side market*). Because EC is focused on a single company's buying or selling needs, this type of EC is also referred to as **company-centric EC**. Company-centric marketplaces—both sell-side and buy-side—are discussed in Sections 4.2, 4.3, 4.4, 4.5, and 4.6.

In company-centric marketplaces, the company has complete control over all transactions and supporting information systems. The owner of the market may restrict and control its trading parties. Thus, these marketplaces are essentially *private*. They may be on the sellers' or buyers' websites or hosted by a third party (intermediary).

Many-to-Many: Public Exchanges (or E-Marketplaces)

In many-to-many e-marketplaces, many buyers and many sellers meet electronically to trade with one another. There are different types of such *e-marketplaces*, which are also known as **exchanges** (**trading communities** or **trading exchanges**). We will use the term *exchanges* in this book. Exchanges are usually marketplaces owned and run by a third party or by a consortium. They are described in more detail in Section 4.7. **Public e-marketplaces** are open to all interested parties (sellers and buyers). Alibaba. com is an example of an exchange.

Supply Chain Improvers and Collaborative Commerce

B2B transactions are conducted frequently along segments of the supply chain. Therefore, B2B initiatives need to be examined in light of other supply chain activities such as procurement of raw materials, fulfilling orders, shipments, and logistics (see Chapter 12). For example, Liz

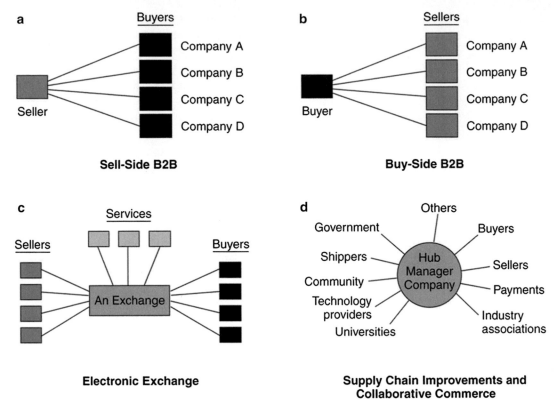

Figure 4.2 Five types of B2B e-commerce

Claiborne, Inc. (retail fashion company) digitized its entire supply chain, reaping substantial results (see case study at **gxs.com/assets/uploads/pdfs/caseStudies/CS_L_Claiborne_GXS.pdf**).

Collaboration

Businesses deal with other businesses for purposes beyond just selling or buying. One example is that of *collaborative commerce*, which includes communication, joint design, planning, and information sharing among business partners (see Chapters 5 and 12).

Market Size and Content of B2B

The U.S. Census Bureau estimates B2B online sales to be about 40% of the total B2B volume depending on the type (e.g., 49% in manufacturing). Chemicals, computer electronics, utilities, agriculture, shipping and warehousing, motor vehicles, petrochemicals, paper and office products, and food are the leading items in B2B. According to the authors' experience and several sources, the dollar value of B2B comprises at least 85% of the total transaction value of all e-commerce, and in some countries, it is over 90% for a total of about $20 trillion worldwide.

The B2B market, which went through a major consolidation in 2000–2002, is growing rapidly. Note that different B2B market forecasters use different definitions and measurement methodologies. Because of this, predictions frequently change and statistical data from different sources often differ. Therefore, we will not provide any more estimates here. Data sources that can be checked for the latest information in the B2B market are provided in Chapter 3 (Table 3.1).

B2B EC is now in its sixth generation, as shown in Figure 4.3. This generation includes collaboration with suppliers, buyers, government, and other business partners via extensive use of mobile com-

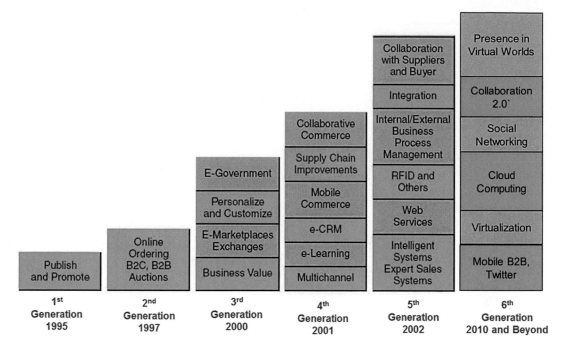

Figure 4.3 Generations of B2B e-commerce

puting; use of blogs, wikis, and other Web 2.0 tools; deployment of in-house social networks; use of public social networks such as LinkedIn and Facebook; and presence in virtual worlds. In addition, the sixth generation is capitalizing on mobile computing, especially tablets and smartphones. Note that the older generations coexist with the new ones. Furthermore, some companies are still using only EC from early generations. This chapter focuses on topics from the second and third generations. Topics from the fourth and fifth generations are presented in Chapter 8.

The B2B field is very diverse, depending on the industry, products and services transacted, volume, method used, and more. The diversity can be seen in Figure 4.4 where we distinguish five major components: Our company, which may be manufacturer, retailer, service provider, and so forth, is shown in the center. It has suppliers (on the left) and retailers (on the right). Our company operations are supported by different services (bottom), and we may work with several intermediaries (top of Figure 4.4). The solid lines show the flow of information.

B2B Components

Next, we present various components of B2B commerce.

Parties to the Transaction: Sellers, Buyers, and Intermediaries

B2B commerce can be conducted *directly* between a *customer* and a *manufacturer* or it can be conducted via an *online intermediary*. An **online intermediary** is a third-party entity that brokers the transactions between the buyer and seller; it can be either virtual or click-and-mortar. Some of the electronic intermediaries for individual consumers mentioned in Chapter 3 also can be used for B2B by replacing the individual consumers with business customers. Aggregations of buyers or sellers are typical B2B activities conducted by intermediaries.

Types of Materials Traded: What Do Firms Buy?

Two major types of materials and supplies are traded in B2B markets: *direct* and *indirect*. **Direct**

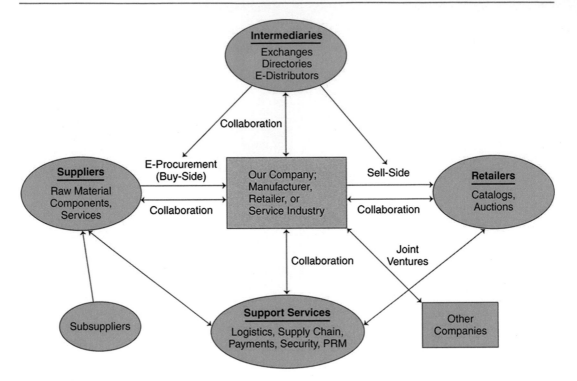

Figure 4.4 The components of B2B

materials are materials used in making products, such as steel in a car or paper in a book.

Indirect materials are items, such as office supplies or light bulbs, which support operation and production. They normally are used in **maintenance, repair, and operation (MRO)** activities. Collectively, they are also known as *nonproduction materials*.

B2B Marketplaces and Platforms

B2B transactions are frequently conducted in marketplaces such as Alibaba.com. B2B marketplaces can be classified as *vertical* or *horizontal*. **Vertical marketplaces** are those for one particular industry or industry segment. Examples include marketplaces specializing in electronics, cars, hospital supplies, steel, or chemicals. **Horizontal marketplaces** are those in which trading is in a service or a product that is used in many types of industries. Examples are office supplies, cleaning materials, or paint. Alibaba.com is an example of a horizontal marketplace.

The types of materials traded and the types of B2B transactions are used to define the B2B marketplaces. One way of classifying these markets is:
- *Strategic (systematic) sourcing* and indirect materials = MRO hubs (horizontal markets for MRO)
- Systematic sourcing and direct materials = Vertical markets for direct materials
- *Spot buying* and indirect materials = Horizontal markets for spot sourcing
- Spot sourcing and direct materials = Vertical markets

The various characteristics of B2B transactions are presented in summary form in Table 4.1.

Service Industries Online in B2B

In addition to trading products between businesses, services also can be provided electronically in B2B. Just as service industries such as travel, banking, insurance, real estate, and stock trading can be conducted electronically for

Table 4.1 Summary of B2B characteristics

Parties to transactions	Types of transactions
Direct, seller to buyer or buyer to seller	Spot buying
Via intermediaries	Strategic sourcing
B2B 2C: A business sells to a business, but delivers to individual consumers	
Types of materials sold	**Direction of trade**
Direct materials and supplies	Vertical
Indirect (MROs)	Horizontal
Number and form of participation	**Degree of openness**
One-to-many: sell-side (e-storefront)	Private exchanges, restricted
Many-to-one: buy-side	Private exchanges, restricted
Many-to-many: exchanges	Public exchanges, open to all
Many, connected: collaborative, supply chain	Private (usually), can be public

individuals (as discussed in Chapter 3), they also can be conducted electronically for businesses. The major B2B services are:

- **Travel and hospitality services.** Many large corporations arrange their travel electronically through corporate travel agents. For instance, American Express Global Business Travel offers several tools to help corporate travel managers plan and control their employees' travel. In addition to traditional scheduling and control tools, American Express offers the following EC-based tools (**amexglobalbusinesstravel.com/total-program-management**):
  - *TrackPoint* enables locating a traveler in real time.
  - *Travel Alert* provides travel advisories and updates, such as weather conditions and delays.
  - *Info Point* (**businesstravel.american-express.com/info-point**) is a website that includes detailed information about countries and cities around the world.
  - *Meetings and Events* (**amexglobal-businesstravel.com/meetings-and-events**) assists in managing meetings, including searching for venues.
  - *American Express* has a presence on social networks (e.g., Facebook, Twitter, YouTube).

- *Egencia LLC* (**egencia.com/en**) (an Expedia company) partners with organizations to optimize the organizations' total travel activities by providing advice and travel management software. For details, see (**egencia.com/en/about-egencia**).
- Expedia (**expedia.com**), Travelocity (**travelocity.com**), Orbitz (**orbitz.com**), and other online travel services provide similar services for both B2C and B2B.
- **Real estate.** Commercial real estate transactions can be large and complex. Therefore, the Web might not be able to replace existing human agents completely. Instead, the Web can help businesses find the right properties, compare properties, and assist in negotiations. Some government-run foreclosed real estate auctions are open to dealers only and are conducted online.
- **Financial services.** Internet banking can be an efficient way of making business payments, transferring funds, or performing other financial transactions. For example, electronic funds transfer (EFT), which provides for electronic payments, is popular with businesses, as are electronic letters of credit. Transaction fees over the Internet are less costly than any other alternative method. To see how payments work in B2B, see Chapter 11. Businesses can

also purchase insurance online, from both pure online insurance companies and from click-and-mortar ones.

- **Banking and online financing.** Business loans can be solicited online from lenders. Because of the economic downturn, it is difficult for some business owners (even those with excellent credit scores) to obtain loans; therefore, they may turn to companies like Biz2Credit (**biz-2credit.com**), a company that helps small businesses grow. Biz2Credit is an online credit marketplace that matches loan applicants with over 1,200 lenders (see **biz2credit.com/about** and **cnbc.com/id/101009116**). Several sites, such as Garage Technology Ventures, LLC (**garage.com**), provide information about venture capital. Institutional investors use the Internet for certain trading activities.
- **Other online services.** Consulting services, law firms, medical services, and others sell enterprise knowledge and special services online. Many other online services, such as the purchase of electronic stamps (similar to metered postage, but generated on a computer), are available online (see **stamps.com**). Recruiting and staffing services can also be done online.

Partner and Supplier Relationship Management

Successful e-businesses need to coordinate and collaborate with business partners along the relevant supply chains. For benefits and methods, see Chopra and Meindl (2012). There are many tools to do just that electronically. The use of such tools supports customer relationship management (CRM) and partner relationship management (PRM).

Corporate customers may require more services than individual customers need. For example, corporate customers may need to have access to the supplier's inventory status report so they know what items a supplier can deliver quickly. Suppliers also may want to see their historical purchasing records of individual items by specific buyers, and they may need private online showrooms and online trade rooms to interact with buyers. Large numbers of vendors are available for designing and building appropriate B2B relationship solutions. The strategy of providing such comprehensive, quality e-services for business partners is sometimes called **partner relationship management (PRM)**.

Software for PRM is provided by companies such as **netsuite.com**, **channeltivity.com**, **relayware.com**, and **salesforce.com**.

The Benefits and Limitations of B2B

The benefits of B2B are for buyers, sellers, or for both, and they depend on which model is used. In general, though, the major benefits of B2B (the beneficiaries are marked after each benefit: S = seller, B = buyer, J = joint) are that it:

- Creates new sales opportunities (S)
- Eliminates paper and reduces administrative costs (J)
- Expedites processing and reduces trading cycle time (J)
- Lowers search costs and time for buyers to find products and vendors (B)
- Increases productivity of employees dealing with buying and/or selling (J)
- Reduces errors and improves quality of service (J)
- Makes product configuration easier (B)
- Reduces marketing and sales costs (S)
- Reduces inventory levels and costs (J)
- Reduces purchasing costs by cutting down on use of intermediaries (B)
- Enables customized e-catalogs with different prices for different customers (J)
- Increases production flexibility, permitting on demand delivery (S)

- Reduces procurement costs (B)
- Facilitates customization via self-configuration (J)
- Provides for efficient customer service (B)
- Increases opportunities for collaboration (J)
- Web-based EC is more affordable than traditional EDI (J)
- Allows more business partners to be reached than with EDI (J)
- Reaches a more geographically dispersed customer base (S)
- Provides a better means of communication with other media (J)
- Provides 24/7 coverage of the shop front (J)
- Helps equalize small enterprises (B)

B2B EC development has limitations as well, especially regarding channel conflict and the operation of public exchanges. Furthermore, personal face-to-face interactions may be needed but are unavailable.

Implementing e-B2B might eliminate the distributor or the retailer, which could be a benefit to the seller and the buyer (though not a benefit to the distributor or retailer). In previous chapters, such a phenomenon is referred to as *disintermediation* (Chapter 3). The benefits and limitations of B2B depend on such variables as who buys what items, and in what quantities; who are the suppliers; how often a company buys, and so forth.

SECTION 4.1 REVIEW QUESTIONS

1. Define B2B.
2. Discuss the following: spot buying versus strategic sourcing, direct materials versus indirect materials, and vertical markets versus horizontal markets.
3. What are company-centric marketplaces? Are they public or private?
4. Define B2B exchanges.
5. Relate the supply chain to B2B transactions.
6. List the benefits and limitations of B2B.

4.2 ONE-TO-MANY: SELL-SIDE E-MARKETPLACES

A major portion of B2B is selling in what is known as B2B marketing. A variety of methods exist.

Sell-Side Models

In the B2C model, a manufacturer or a retailer electronically sells directly to consumers from a *storefront* (or *webstore*). In a B2B **sell-side e-marketplace**, a business sells products and services to business customers electronically, frequently over an extranet. The seller can be a raw material producer selling to manufacturers, or a manufacturer selling to an intermediary such as a wholesaler, a retailer, or an individual business. Intel (**intel.com**), Exxon (**exxon.com**), Cisco Systems, Inc. (**cisco.com**), and Dell (**dell.com**) are examples of such sellers. Alternatively, the seller can be a distributor selling to retailers or businesses (e.g., W.W. Grainger, Inc. (**grainger.com**), discussed in Section 4.2). In either case, sell-side e-marketplaces involve one seller and many potential buyers. In this model, both individual consumers and business buyers might use either the same private sell-side marketplace (e.g., **dell.com**), or a public marketplace.

The one-to-many model has three major marketing methods: (1) selling from *electronic catalogs* with fixed prices; (2) selling via *forward auctions*; and (3) one-to-one selling, usually under a *negotiated* long-term contract. Such one-to-one negotiation is familiar: The buying company negotiates the price, quantity, payments, delivery, and quality terms with the selling company. We describe the first method in this section and the second method in Section 4.3.

B2B Sellers

Sellers in the sell-side marketplace may be click-and-mortar manufacturers or intermediaries (e.g., distributors or wholesalers). The intermediaries may even be pure online companies (e.g., Alibaba.com.com).

Customer Service

Online sellers can provide sophisticated customer service. For example, General Electric (**ge.com**) receives over 20 million calls a year regarding appliances. Although most of these calls come from individuals, many come from businesses. By using the Internet and automatic-response software programs (autoresponders), GE has reduced the cost of handling such calls from $5 per call when done by phone to 20¢ per electronically answered call. Today, autoresponders can provide real-time responses in live chat with avatars. In this case, the cost can be even lower.

We now turn our attention to the most common sell-side method—selling online from a company's e-catalog.

Sales from Catalogs: Webstores

Companies can use the Internet to sell directly from their online catalog. A company might offer one catalog for all customers or a *customized catalog* for each large customer (possibly both). For example, Staples (**staples.com**), an office-supply vendor, offers its business customers a personalized software catalog of about 100,000 products at different pricing schemes (see their ordering site at **order.staplesadvantage.com**).

Many companies use a multichannel marketing strategy where one channel is e-commerce.

In selling online to business buyers, manufacturers might encounter a similar problem to that of B2C sellers, namely conflict with the regular distribution channels, including corporate dealers (channel conflict). To avoid conflicts, some companies advertise online, but sell only in physical stores. An example is Gregg's Cycle (**greggscycles.com**). The company sells only peripheral products, such as parts and accessories, to individual consumers online. In addition, Gregg's Cycles provides a locator where customers can buy its core product—bicycles—at brick-and-mortar stores.

Distributors' Catalogs

Webstores are used by manufacturers (e.g., Gregg's Cycles) or by *distributors*. Distributors

in B2B are similar to retailers in B2C. They can be general (like W.W. Grainger, see Section 4.2) or they can concentrate on one area, much like Toys "R" Us (**toysrus.com**) in B2C.

Example

Stone Wheel (**stonewheel.com**) distributes over 100,000 different auto parts from 15 warehouses serving over 3,500 independent repair shops in the Midwest region of the U.S. They deliver within 30 minutes, using their own vehicles. Using the e-catalog, customers can order the exact part, saving time and minimizing misunderstandings and errors.

Self Service Portals

Portals are used for several purposes, one of which is to enable business partners to conduct self-service, as is shown in the following example.

Example: Whirlpool B2B Trading Portal

Whirlpool (**whirlpool.com**) is a large global manufacturer of home appliances (about 69,000 employees in 2013 and annual sales of $19 billion). The company needs to operate efficiently to survive in an extremely competitive market. It must collaborate with its business partners along the selling segments of the supply chain and provide them with outstanding customer support.

The company sells its products via all types of retailers and distributors (25% of which are small), located in over 170 countries. Until 2000, the small retailers had entered their orders from Whirlpool manually. This process was slow, costly, and error prone.

Therefore, Whirlpool developed a B2B trading partner portal (for the small retailers), which enabled self-ordering, therefore reducing the transaction cost considerably.

The system was tested with low-volume items and then extended to larger volume items. In addition, more features were added. Adding the portal has increased Whirlpool's competitive advantage.

For additional information, see IBM (2000) and **whirlpoolcorp.com**.

For a comprehensive case, see Course Hero (2013).

Benefits and Limitations of Online Sales from Catalogs

Successful examples of the B2B online direct sales model include manufacturers, such as Dell, Intel, IBM, and Cisco, and distributors, such as Ingram Micro (**ingrammicro.com**) that sells to value-added retailers; the retailer adds some service along with the product. Sellers that use this model can be successful as long as they have a solid reputation in the market and a large enough group of loyal customers.

While the benefits of direct online sales are similar to that of B2C, there are limitations also. One of the major issues facing direct sellers is finding buyers. Many companies know how to advertise using traditional channels, but are still learning how to contact would-be business buyers online. In addition, B2B sellers may experience channel conflicts with their existing distribution systems. Another limitation is that if traditional electronic data interchange (EDI)—the computer-to-computer direct transfer of business documents—is used, the cost might be passed on to the customers, and they could become reluctant to go online. The solution to this problem is transferring documents over extranets and using an Internet-based EDI (see Online Tutorial T2). Finally, the number of business partners online must be large enough to justify the system infrastructure and operation and maintenance expenses.

Comprehensive Sell-Side Systems

Sell-side systems must provide several essential functionalities that enable B2B vendors to execute sales efficiently, provide outstanding customer service, allow integration with existing IT systems, and provide integration with non-Internet sales systems. For an example of such a system provided by Sterling Commerce (an IBM Company), see **ibm.com/software/info/sterling-commerce**.

Selling via Distributors and Other Intermediaries

Manufacturers can sell directly to other businesses, and they do so if the customers are large buyers. However, manufacturers frequently use intermediaries to distribute their products to a large number of smaller buyers. The intermediaries buy products from many other manufacturers and aggregate those products into one catalog from which they sell to customers or to retailers. Many of these distributors also are selling online via webstores.

Some well-known online distributors for businesses are Sam's Club (**samsclub.com**), Avnet (**avnet.com**), and W.W. Grainger (**grainger.com**). Many e-distributors sell in horizontal markets, meaning that they sell to businesses in a variety of industries. However, some distributors sell to businesses that specialize in one industry (vertical market), such as Boeing PART Page (see **boeing.com/assets/pdf/commercial/aviationservices/brochures/MaterialsOptimization.pdf**). Most intermediaries sell at fixed prices; however, some offer quantity discounts, negotiated prices, or conduct auctions.

SECTION 4.2 REVIEW QUESTIONS

1. What are buy-side and sell-side transactions? How do they differ?
2. List the types of sell-side B2B transaction models.
3. Describe customer service in B2B systems.
4. Describe the direct online B2B sales process from catalogs.
5. Discuss the benefits and limitations of direct online B2B sales from catalogs.
6. What are the advantages of using intermediaries in B2B sales?
7. Compare an e-distributor in B2B to Amazon.com. What are the similarities? What are the differences?

4.3   SELLING VIA E-AUCTIONS

Auctions are gaining popularity both as B2B buying and as sales channels. Some major B2B auction issues are discussed in this section.

The Benefits of Auctions on the Sell Side

Many companies use *forward auctions* to liquidate their surplus products or capital assets. In such a situation, items are usually displayed on an auction site (private or public) for quick clearance. Forward auctions offer the following benefits to B2B sellers:

- **Revenue generation.** Forward auctions support and expand online and overall sales. Forward auctions also offer businesses a new venue to quickly and easily dispose of excess, obsolete, and returned products (e.g., see **liquidation. com**).
- **Cost savings.** In addition to generating new revenue, conducting e-auctions reduces the costs of selling the auctioned items, which helps increase the seller's profits.
- **Increased "stickiness."** Forward auctions give websites increased "stickiness," namely, potential buyers stay there longer. *Stickiness* is a characteristic that measures customer loyalty to a site that eventually results in higher revenue.
- **Member acquisition and retention.** Registered members of auctions can invite their business contacts. In addition, auction software aids enable sellers to search and report on virtually every relevant auction activity. Such information can be analyzed and used for business strategy.

Forward auctions can be conducted in two ways. A company can conduct its forward auctions from its own website or it can sell from an intermediary auction site, such as **liquidation. com** or **ebay.com**. Let us examine these options.

Auctioning from the Company's Own Site

For large and well-known companies that frequently conduct auctions, it makes sense to build an auction mechanism on the company's own website. Why should a company pay a commission to an intermediary if the intermediary cannot provide the company with added value? Of course, if a company decides to auction from its own site, it will have to pay for infrastructure, and operate and maintain the auction site. Note that, if the company already has an electronic marketplace for selling from e-catalogs, the additional cost for conducting auctions might not be too high.

Using Intermediaries in Auctions

Several intermediaries offer B2B auction sites (e.g., see **assetnation.com** and **liquidation. com**). Some companies specialize in government auctions while others focus on surplus stock auctions (e.g. **govliquidation.com**). An intermediary can conduct private auctions either from the intermediary's or the seller's sites. Alternatively, a company can conduct auctions in a public marketplace, using an intermediary (e.g., eBay, which has a special "business exchange" for small companies).

Using an intermediary to conduct auctions has many benefits. The first is that no additional resources (e.g., hardware, bandwidth, engineering resources, or IT personnel) are required. There are no hiring costs for using corporate resources. B2B auction intermediary sites also offer fast time-to-market as they are capable of running the auction immediately. Without the intermediary, it can take weeks for a company to prepare an auction site in-house.

Another benefit of using intermediaries relates to payments, which are handled by the intermediary.

For an example of using an intermediary in B2B auction services, see Liquidity Services Inc. (**liquidityservicesinc.com**). For an example of a company that helped liquidate old equipment in the Commonwealth of Pennsylvania, see Case 4.1.

For more about B2B online auctions, see **vasthouse.com/b2b-online-auctions.php** and **liz. petree.tripod.com/test_2/auctions.html**.

For more about B2B online auctions, see Parente (2007).

CASE 4.1: EC APPLICATION: HOW THE COMMONWEALTH OF PENNSYLVANIA SELLS SURPLUS EQUIPMENT

For many years, the Pennsylvania Department of Transportation (DOT) (**dot.state.pa.us**) used a traditional offline auction process. Beginning in October 2003, the state held online auctions to sell its surplus heavy equipment. At his fifth monthly radio address, Pennsylvania then-Governor Ed Rendell stated, "The old, live-in-person auction system generated about $5 million a year. Using the Internet, we're on pace for a 20% revenue increase."

The initial online sale of surplus DOT items consisted of 77 items (including 37 dump trucks). On-site inspection was available twice during the 2-week bidding period. The online sale allowed the Commonwealth of Pennsylvania to obtain an average price increase of 20%, while reducing labor costs related to holding a traditional on-site sale. On high-value specialty items (i.e., a bridge inspection crane and a satellite van), results exceeded the estimated sale prices by over 200%.

The auction was conducted by AssetAuctions (**assetnation.com**). The results of the auction were as follow:
- Total sales: $635,416.03.
- Half of the bidding activity occurred in the final 2 days.
- Every lot received multiple bids.
- Overtime bidding occurred in 39 lots.
- 174 bidders from 19 states and Mexico made about 1,500 bids in 5 days.
- 47 different buyers participated.

The Commonwealth of Pennsylvania now sells surplus equipment and properties using both Auctions by Gov and eBay. Many other states and city governments use auctions to sell their surplus equipment.

Sources: Based on **assetnation.com** (accessed November 2014), the Commonwealth of Pennsylvania (2006), and *PR Newswire* (2003).

Questions

1. Why is heavy equipment amenable to such auctions?
2. Why did the Commonwealth generate 20% more in revenue with the online auction?
3. Why do you need an intermediary to conduct such an auction?

In 2006, Governor Rendell went a step further and signed into law legislation that would permit the use of electronic and reverse auction bidding in the local governments (e.g., municipalities, school districts) of Pennsylvania (see **americancityand county.com/resource-center/legislation-permits- use-electronic-bidding-and-reverse-auctions- local**).

Examples of B2B Forward Auctions

The following are examples of B2B auctions:
- Whirlpool Corp. sold $20 million in scrap metal in a single auction via **asset-auctions. assetnation.com;** the sale price received was 15% higher than prior e-auctions.
- Sam's Club (**samsclub.com**) auctions thousands of items (especially electronics) at Sam's Club Auctions (**auctions.samsclub. com**). Featured auctions include the current bid, the number of bids, and the open and close date. They liquidate overstock items, returns, and out of style goods.
- Yahoo! conducts both B2C and B2B auctions in Hong Kong, Taiwan, and Japan.

To learn more about B2B auctions, see **vasthouse.com**.

SECTION 4.3 REVIEW QUESTIONS

1. List the benefits of using B2B auctions for selling.
2. List the benefits of using auction intermediaries.
3. What are the major purposes of forward auctions, and how are they conducted?
4. Comment on the number of bidders and bids using an online auction as compared to using an offline auction.

4.4   ONE-FROM-MANY: E-PROCUREMENT AT BUY-SIDE E-MARKETPLACES

The term *procurement* refers to the purchase of goods and services by organizations. Procurement is usually done by *purchasing agents*, also known as *corporate buyers*.

The buyer's purchasing department sometimes has to enter the order information manually into its own corporate information system. Furthermore, manually searching webstores and e-malls to find and compare suppliers and products can be slow and costly. As a solution, large buyers can open their own marketplaces called **buy-side e-marketplaces**, and invite sellers to browse and offer to fulfill demand.

Inefficiencies in Traditional Procurement Management

Procurement management refers to the process of planning, organizing, and coordinating of all the activities pertaining to the purchasing of the goods and services needed by an organization. It involves the B2B purchase and sale of supplies and services, as well as the flow of required information. Approximately 80% of an organization's purchased items, mostly MROs, constitute 20–25% of the total purchase value. In this case, much of the buyers' time is spent on clerical activities, such as entering data and correcting errors in paperwork.

The procurement process may be lengthy and complex due to the many activities performed. The following are the major activities that may be included in a single purchase:

- *Search for items* using search engines, catalogs, virtual fairs and showrooms, and sellers' sales presentations.
- *Learn details of items and buying terms* using comparison engines and quality reports, and research industry report and vendors' information.
- *Negotiate or join group purchasing* using software support (if available).
- *Determine when and how much to order each time.* Authorize corporate buyers.
- *Join business-oriented social networks* such as **linkedin.com**.
- *Sign agreements or contracts* using e-contract management (e.g., from Ariba, Inc. **ariba.com**; a SAP company); arrange financing, escrow insurance, etc.
- *Create specific purchasing order(s)* using a computerized system.
- *Arrange packing, shipments, and deliveries* using electronic tracking, RFID, etc.
- *Arrange invoicing, payments, expense management, and purchasing budgetary control* using software packages (e.g., from **ariba.com**).

An example of the traditional procurement process that is often inefficient is shown in Figure 4.5. For high-value items, purchasing personnel need to spend considerable time and effort on procurement activities. However, the purchasers may not have time to do a quality job since they are busy with the many items of small value such as MROs.

Other inefficiencies, ranging from delays in deliveries to the high cost of rush orders, also may occur in conventional procurement. This situation is called **maverick buying**, which occurs when a buyer makes unplanned purchases of items needed quickly, resulting in buying at non-pre-negotiated, and usually higher, prices.

To correct the situation(s) that may result from traditional procurement, companies must reengineer their procurement systems, implement new purchasing models, and, in particular, introduce e-procurement. Let us elaborate on the generic procurement methods first.

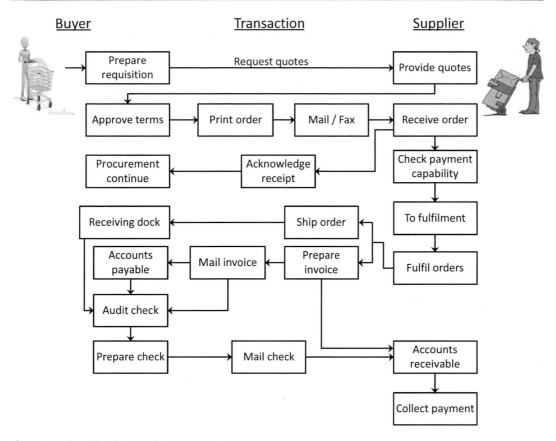

Figure 4.5 Traditional (manual) procurement process

Procurement Methods

Companies use different methods to procure goods and services depending on factors such as what and where they buy, the quantities needed, and how much money is involved. Each method has its own process benefits and limitations. To minimize the inefficiencies described earlier, companies automate activities in the process. This is the major objective of e-procurement. Examples of companies utilizing efficient methods are Walmart (**walmart.com**), Dell (**dell.com**), and Starbucks (**starbucks.com**) to name a few. The major procurement methods include the following:

- Buy directly from the catalogs of manufacturers, wholesalers, or retailers, and possibly by negotiation (Sections 4.2 and 4.3).

- Buy at private or public auction sites in which the buying organization is one of many (Section 4.5).
- Conduct bidding in a reverse auction system where suppliers compete against each other. This method is used for high value items or when large quantities are involved (Section 4.5).
- Buy from the catalog of an intermediary (e-distributor) that aggregates sellers' catalogs (Section 4.6).
- Buy from the company's own internal buyer catalog. Such catalogs usually include agreed-upon prices of items from many suppliers. This is part of *desktop purchasing*, which allows the users to bypass the procurement department (Section 4.6).

- Join a group-purchasing system that aggregates participants' demands, creating a large volume. Then the group may negotiate prices or initiate a tendering process (Section 4.6).
- Buy at an exchange or industrial mall (Section 4.7).

E-Procurement Concepts

E-procurement (electronic procurement) is the online purchase of supplies, materials, energy, work, and services. It can be done via the Internet or via a private network such as an electronic data exchange (EDI). For the different types of EDI and the trading community, see **edibasics.com/ types-of-edi**.

Some activities done by e-procurement include enabling buyers to search for suppliers, facilitating reverse auctions for buyers, and automating paperwork and documentation.

Some of these activities are done in private marketplaces, others in public exchanges.

The Goals and Process of E-Procurement

As stated earlier, e-procurement frequently automates activities in the purchasing process from multiple suppliers via the Web for better execution and control.

Improvements to procurement have been attempted for decades, usually by using information technologies. Using e-procurement results in a major improvement. For comprehensive coverage and case studies, see **zdnet.com**.

Essentially, e-procurement automates the process of auctions, contract management, vendor selection, and management, etc.

For an overview of e-procurement goals and processes, see **plenitude-solutions.com/index. php?option=com_content&view=article&id= 54&Itemid=62**.

The general e-procurement process (with the exception of tendering) is shown in Online File W4.1. For a free e-book on e-procurement, see Basware (2011).

Example: Volvo's E-Procurement

Volvo is a premium Swedish car manufacturer (now owned by a Chinese company). The company operates in dozens of countries worldwide. The company has more than 30 purchasing centers on six continents. In the past, this has resulted in inconsistent purchasing practices, lack of collaboration among the centers, and inefficient and inconsistent procurement processes. To overcome the problems, management decided to use a unified e-procurement system. They selected Ariba's Sourcing and Ariba's Contract Management solutions (Ariba is a B2B SAP company). The system assures standardization of the purchasing processes, sharing of best practices activities, and streamlining of the contracting process and its management. All these systems are digital. The e-procurement resulted in a greater cohesion among the sourcing centers, better use of best practices, and reduced cost of procurement while its effectiveness increases.

Types of E-Procurement

Four major methods of e-procurement are available: (1) Buy at own website, (2) buy at sellers' store, (3) buy at exchanges, and (4) buy at others' e-market sites. Each method includes several activities, as illustrated in Figure 4.6. Some of these will be described in Sections 4.7 through 4.8.

The seven main types of e-procurement are as follows: (1) e-sourcing, (2) e-tendering, (3) e-reverse auctioning, (4) e-informing, (5) Web-based ERP (enterprise resource planning), (6) e-market sites, and (7) E-MRO (maintenance, repair, and operating).

The Benefits and Limitations of E-Procurement

E-procurement has the ability of improving supply chain management, and providing real-time information on what is going on in the supply chain (known as *visibility* of the supply chain), starting with the customers' needs.

The Benefits of E-Procurement

By automating and streamlining the procurement process, corporate purchasing buyers can focus on more strategic activities that result in:

- Increasing the productivity of purchasing agents, providing them with more non-routine time and reducing job pressures, possibly reducing purchasing departments' overhead.
- Lowering purchase per item prices through activities such as product standardization, reverse auctions, volume discounts, and consolidation of purchases from fewer suppliers.
- Improving information flow and its control (e.g., price comparisons).
- Reducing the frequency and cost of maverick buying.
- Improving the payment process, and sellers' savings due to expedited payment cycle.
- Establishing more efficient and collaborative partner relations due to information sharing.
- Improving the manufacturing process for the suppliers.

- Ensuring delivery on time and fewer stock outs.
- Reducing the skill requirements and training needs of purchasing agents.
- Reducing the number of suppliers.
- Streamlining and expediting the purchasing process.
- Controlling inventories more effectively at the buyers' end.
- Streamlining invoice reconciliation and dispute resolution.
- Reducing the administrative processing cost per order by as much as 90% by reducing purchasing overheads and intermediary fees.
- Finding new suppliers that can provide goods and services faster and/or less expensively (e.g., by going global and use online price comparisons).
- Integrating budgetary controls into the procurement process (e.g., **ariba.com**).
- Minimizing human errors in the buying or shipping processes.

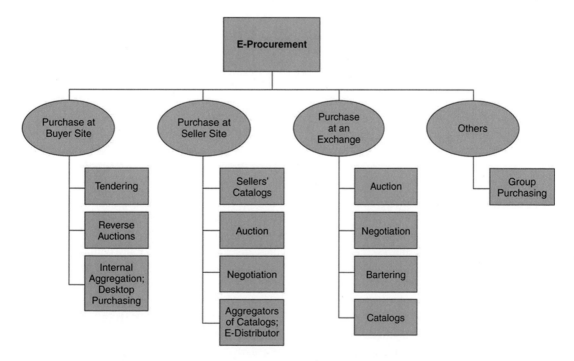

Figure 4.6 E-procurement methods

For more on the benefits of e-procurement and on implementation issues, see the video titled "eProcurement Case Study: Oldcastle Materials" (3:16 minutes) at **youtube.com/watch?v=PPVC_CaG1S4**.

The Limitations and Challenges of E-Procurement

Unfortunately, e-procurement practices have some limitations and risks such as:

- The total cost (TCO) may be too high.
- It may be subject to hacker attacks.
- It may be difficult to get suppliers to cooperate electronically.
- The system may be too complex (e.g., when it uses a traditional EDI; see Online Tutorial T2).
- It may be difficult to have internal and external integration (sometimes it involves different standards).
- The technology may change frequently.

For software issues, see **eprocurement software.org**. For an example of how procurement is used in government, see NC E-Procurement (**eprocurement.nc.gov**). Governments frequently use reverse auctions for procurement, which we present next.

Procurement is an extremely important success factor for many companies. Therefore, it is important to learn about the future of e-procurement as well. For ideas about procurement in 2020, see Oka et al. (2011). To learn about Shoplet's platform for e-procurement, see Regal (2014) and **shoplet.com/about**.

E-Procurement and Strategic Sourcing

E-procurement is frequently used as a component in *strategic sourcing* which is a comprehensive procurement process that continuously improves and re-evaluates all the purchasing activities of an organization. The objective is to smooth the process and increase efficiency and profitability. For a comparison of strategic sourcing and traditional procurement, see the 17 minute video at **youtube.com/watch?v=AdMXNK7yLH4**.

SECTION 4.4 REVIEW QUESTIONS

1. Define the procurement process.
2. Describe the inefficiencies of traditional procurement.
3. List the major procurement methods.
4. Define e-procurement and list its goals.
5. List the major e-procurement methods and list some activities in each.
6. List the major benefits of e-procurement.

4.5 REVERSE AUCTIONS AT BUY-SIDE E-MARKETPLACES (E-TENDERING)

A major method of e-procurement is using reverse auctions. A **reverse auction** is a process in which many sellers (suppliers) compete to fulfill orders requested by one buyer. Recall from our earlier discussion, that a *reverse auction* is a tendering system where suppliers are invited to bid on the fulfillment of an order, and the lowest bid wins. In B2B usage of a reverse auction, a buyer may open an e-market on its own server (or use an independent auctioneer such as eBay) and invite potential suppliers to bid on the items. This "invitation" to such reverse auctions is a form or document called a **request for quote (RFQ)**. Traditional tendering usually implies one-time sealed bidding, whereas an e-reverse auction opens the process to competing *sequential bidding*. For a comprehensive overview of reverse auctions, see **reverseauctions.com**, **epiqtech.com/reverse_auctions-Overview.htm**, and **reverseauctions.gsa.gov**.

Governments and large corporations frequently mandate reverse auctions, which may provide considerable savings because more suppliers are participating in a more competitive process. The electronic process is faster and administratively much less expensive. It also can benefit suppliers in finding RFQs. Reverse auctions are very important B2B mechanisms in e-procurement. The opening case to this chapter describes a supplier's point of view, while the closing case of this chapter describes a buyer's point of view.

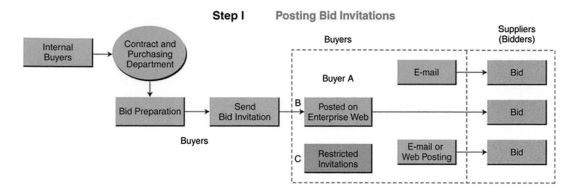

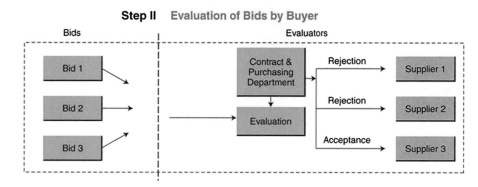

Figure 4.7   The reverse auction process

The Major Benefits of Reverse Auctions

The major benefits of the technology to a buyer are: (a) lower cost of items purchased, (b) reduction of administrative costs of procurement, (c) reduction of corruption and bribes, and (d) decrease in time to receive the goods, which may result from the suppliers' ability to produce their products and services faster (see closing case).

For suppliers, as seen in the opening case, savings comes from a reduction in: (a) time required to find customers, (b) administrative costs, and (c) time needed by managers to conduct manual bids.

Note that some question the value of reverse auctions (e.g., see Rockwell 2013).

Conducting Reverse Auctions

As the number of reverse auction sites increases, suppliers may not be able to monitor all relevant open RFQs manually. This problem has been addressed with the introduction of online directories that list open RFQs. Another way to solve this problem is through the use of monitoring software agents. Software agents also can aid in the bidding process itself. Examples of agents that monitor and support the bidding process are **auctionsniper.com** and **auctionflex.com**.

Alternatively, third-party intermediaries may run the electronic bidding, as they do in forward auctions (e.g., see Opentext Corporation [**opentext.com**]). Auction sites such as **ebay.com**, and **liquidation.com** also belong to this category. Conducting reverse auctions in B2B can be a fairly complex process. This is why using an intermediary may be beneficial.

The reverse auction process is demonstrated in Figure 4.7. As shown in the figure, the first step for the would-be buyer is to post bid invitations. When bids arrive, contract and purchasing personnel for the buyer evaluate the bids and decide which one(s) to accept.

An example of e-tendering is provided in Case 4.1.

CASE 4.2: EC APPLICATION: BRANAS ISAF COMPETES BY USING E-TENDERING

Branas Isaf is a small UK company that provides therapeutic care for children who exhibit harmful behavior. A central part of the company is its education department, which provides several types of training.

The Problem

The company has grown rapidly since 2005 and has doubled in size to 25 employees. The company serves both the private and the public sectors in the UK.

Branas Isaf's major competitive advantages are: (1) competitive fees, (2) provision of customized training, and (3) provision of on-site training. These advantages enable the company to compete with large training institutions such as colleges.

Branas Isaf frequently bids on jobs, especially in the public sector where tendering is mandatory. Many of its 1,000 customers began using electronic tendering over the Internet. Thus, to maintain its competitive advantage, Branas Isaf decided to participate in e-tendering also. This case describes Branas's experience with its first electronic bid.

The Solution

The UK government mandated that all bids for government-related jobs must be done via the eTendering (also called e-tendering) system, including the Government Work Based Learning Programme, on which Branas bids on as a supplier. Branas followed these steps on the eTendering portal, where requests for bids are posted:

1. Electronically submitted a pre-qualification questionnaire.
2. Accepted the terms and conditions of BravoSolution eTraining System.
3. Downloaded online supplier guidance material.
4. Created a user name; received a password.
5. Found the specific invitation to tender (ITT) on which it wanted to bid online.
6. Pressed the "Express Interest" button—moved automatically to "My ITTs."
7. Downloaded all the necessary documents for the specific bid.
8. Made a decision to bid and pressed the "Reply" button.
9. Accessed the project's details; found and filled out a questionnaire.
10. Submitted the tender electronically and uploaded all necessary attachments. (It is possible to update or change the documents until the deadline is reached.)

Sending and receiving messages are embedded in the portal with e-mail alerts. Acceptance notification is done in the same manner. Once the bid is accepted by the system, a "winner" icon is displayed.

The Results

Since its inception in late 2006, the practice of e-tendering at Branas has grown rapidly. Branas employees have become experts in using the computerized system. While the cost to Branas declined only slightly, the opportunity for such a small company to compete with very large competitors increased significantly.

Furthermore, since most nonprofit organizations and many for-profit ones mandate e-tendering, bidders have no choice but to use the system. In addition, Branas understands that e-tendering is clearly more beneficial for its customers as well as being a more sustainable way of doing business. Overall, Branas has been able to maintain its competitive advantage and continue to grow rapidly.

Sources*: Based on eProc.org (2010), **branas. co.uk**, and **etenderwales.bravosolution.co.uk** (both accessed March 2014).

Questions

1. Discuss the drivers of e-tendering for Branas.
2. Given the small size of the company, was it an advantage or disadvantage to participate?
3. Is the process of e-tendering simple or complex? Explain.
4. Why do buyers choose e-tendering instead of regular tendering?
5. What are the benefits of e-tendering for a small company such as Branas?

E-Tendering by Governments

Most governments must conduct tendering when they buy or sell goods and services. Doing this manually is slow and expensive. Therefore, many governments are moving to e-reverse auctions for their purchasing. The opening case demonstrates e-tendering from a seller's point of view; the closing case demonstrates e-tendering from a buyer's perspective.

Group Reverse Auctions

To increase their bargaining power and get price discounts, companies, like individuals, can buy in a group, and the group can use a reverse auction to get an even better deal than a quantity discount.

B2B reverse auctions can be done in a private exchange or at an aggregator's site for a group of buying companies. Such *group reverse auctions* are popular in South Korea and usually involve large conglomerates. For example, the LG Group operates the LG MRO Auction for its member companies, and Samsung Group operates the Samsung iMarketKorea (**imarketkorea.com**), which provides procurement services and MRO goods. Samsung's iMarketKorea's revenue comes primarily from B2B transactions (see Online File W4.2). This practice is popular in the healthcare industry in the United Kingdom, the United States, and other countries where hospitals are banding together to buy their supplies at a quantity discounted low prices.

4.6   OTHER E-PROCUREMENT METHODS

Other innovative e-procurement methods have been implemented by companies. Some common ones are described in this section.

Desktop Purchasing

Desktop purchasing refers to purchasing by employees without the approval of supervisors and without the involvement of a procurement department. This usually is done by using a *purchasing card (P-card)* (see Chapter 11). Desktop purchasing reduces the administrative cost and the cycle time involved in purchasing urgently needed or frequently purchased items of small dollar value. This approach is especially effective for MRO purchases.

The desktop purchasing approach can be implemented by collaborating with external private exchanges. For instance, Samsung Electronics of South Korea, a huge global manufacturer, and its subsidiaries, have integrated its iMarketKorea (**imarketkorea.com**) exchange (see Online File W4.2) with the e-procurement systems of its buying agents. This platform can also be linked easily with *group purchasing*, which is described next.

Group Purchasing

Many companies, especially small ones, are moving to *group purchasing*. With **group purchasing**, orders from several buyers are aggregated so that better prices due to larger quantities purchased can be negotiated. This model is similar to the one we described for B2C. Two sub-models are in use: internal aggregation and external (third-party) aggregation.

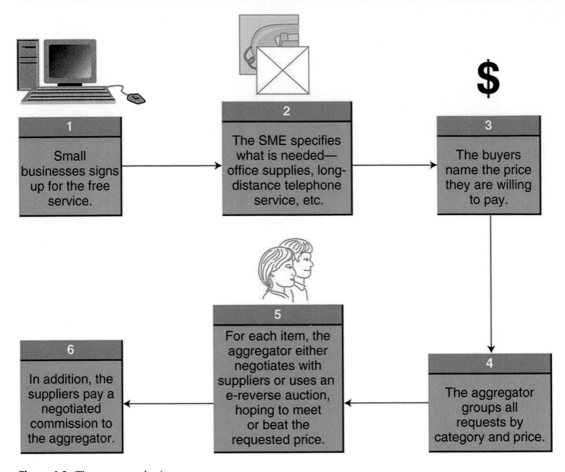

Figure 4.8 The group purchasing process

Internal Aggregation of Purchasing Orders

Large companies, such as GE, spend many millions of dollars on MROs every year. These companies aggregate the orders from their subsidiaries and various departments (sometimes there are hundreds of them) for quantity discounts. They can cut administrative and item costs by 90%.

External Aggregation for Group Purchasing

Many SMEs would like to enjoy quantity discounts but have difficulty finding others to join a group purchasing organization to increase the procurement volume. Finding partners can be accomplished by an external third party such as BuyerZone (**buyerzone.com**), the Healthcare Supply Chain Association (**supplychainassociation.org**), or the United Sourcing Alliance

(**usa-llc.com**). The idea is to provide SMEs with better prices, larger selections, and improved services by aggregating demand online and then either negotiating with suppliers or conducting reverse auctions. The external aggregation/group purchasing process is shown in Figure 4.8.

Several large companies, including large CPA firms and software companies such as EDS Technologies (**edstechnologies.com**) and Ariba, Inc. (**ariba.com**), provide external aggregation services, mainly to their regular customers. Yahoo! and AOL also offer such services. A key to the success of these companies is a critical mass of buyers. An interesting strategy is for a company to outsource aggregation to a third party. For example, ECNG Energy (**ecng.com**) provides group buying in the energy industry. Web 2.0 companies serve businesses as well.

Buying from Other Sources

Section 4.2 described how companies use e-distributors as sales channels. When buying small quantities, purchasers often buy from an e-distributor. Another option for e-procurement is to buy at a B2B exchange using one of several available methods. In all of these options, one may automate some actions in the process, such as the generation of a purchasing order (e.g., see **esker.com** and **ariba.com**), which is a major provider of e-procurement software and services.

Acquisition Via Electronic Bartering

Bartering is the exchange of goods or services without the use of money. The basic idea is for a company to exchange its surplus for something that it needs. Companies can advertise their surpluses in classified ads and may find a partner to make an exchange, but in many cases, a company will have little success in finding an exact match on its own. Therefore, companies usually ask an intermediary to help.

A bartering intermediary can use a manual search-and-match approach or it can create an electronic bartering exchange. With a **bartering exchange**, a company submits its surplus to the exchange and receives points of credit, which the company can then use to buy items that it needs. Popular bartering items are office spaces, idle facilities and labor, products, and even banner ads. For examples of bartering companies, see U-Exchange (**u-exchange.com**) and Itex (**itex.com**).

Selecting an Appropriate E-Procurement Solution

Having many procurement methods, consultants, and software makes the selection of the right method(s) difficult. Ariba, Inc. (**ariba.com**) provides an innovative score sheet that companies use to evaluate vendors based on the described success factors. The success factors are grouped by cost reduction, increased agility, managing complete commerce, and fulfilling tactical requirements.

When organizations make such decisions, these decisions may be influenced by factors such as: Who is buying? What are you buying? How much information do you need to make the decisions? What is the reputation of the vendor(s)? What testimonials are available?

SECTION 4.6 REVIEW QUESTIONS
1. Describe a buyer-operated procurement marketplace and list its benefits.
2. Describe the benefits of desktop purchasing.
3. Discuss the relationship of desktop purchasing with group purchasing.
4. Explain the logic of group purchasing and how it is organized.
5. How does B2B bartering work?
6. What are the major considerations for selecting an e-procurement vendor and solution?

4.7 B2B EXCHANGES (E-MARKETPLACES): DEFINITIONS AND CONCEPTS

The term *B2B exchange*, or simply *exchange*, implies the existence of many potential buyers and many potential sellers in B2B e-marketplaces. In addition to being online trading venues, many exchanges provide support services such as payments and logistics software and consulting services. They also act as industry portals.

Exchanges are known by a variety of names: *e-marketplaces, trading exchanges*, *trading communities, exchange hubs, Internet exchanges, Net marketplaces*, and *B2B portals*. We will use the term *exchange* in this book to describe the general many-to-many e-marketplaces, but we will use some of the other terms in more specific contexts (e.g., see **epiqtech.com/others-B2B-Exchanges.htm**.

Despite their variety, all exchanges share one major characteristic: Exchanges are electronic trading-community meeting places for many sellers and many buyers, and possibly for other business partners, as shown in Figure 4.9. At the

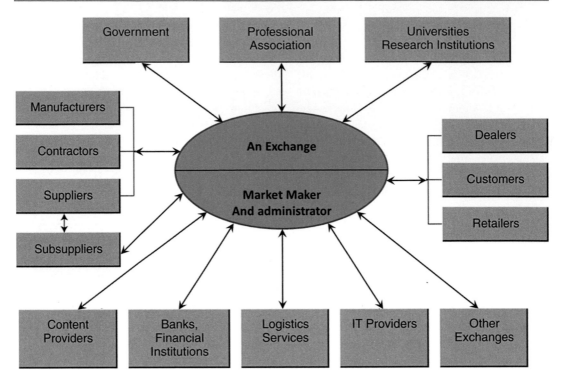

Figure 4.9 The community of an exchange: flow and access to information

center of every exchange, there is a market maker that operates the exchange and, in some cases, may also own it.

Exchanges can be horizontal, serving many industries (e.g., **ariba.com** or **alibaba.com**), or vertical, serving one or a few connected industries (e.g., see **supplyon.com** for automotive; and **oceanconnect.com** for refineries and shipping services). In an exchange, just as in a traditional open-air marketplace, buyers and sellers can interact and negotiate prices and quantities.

Functions of and Services Provided by Exchanges

Exchanges have the following four major sets of functions: (1) Matching and connecting buyers and sellers, (2) facilitating transactions, (3) developing and maintaining exchange policies and infrastructure, and (4) providing services to buyers and sellers. Details of these functions are provided next.

Functions and Services of B2B Exchanges

The following are the major functions of B2B exchanges (compiled from Tumolo (2001), E-Commerce Wiki (2013), and the authors' experiences):

1. Matching buyers and sellers. The matching of buyers and sellers includes such activities as:
   - Presentation of product offering (e.g., the company's catalogs)
   - Aggregating and posting different products for sale – to meet buyers' need
   - Providing price comparisons
   - Organizing bids (bartering) and (auctions)
   - Providing sellers' profiles and product information
   - Matching suppliers' offerings with buyers' requests
   - Supporting negotiations between buyers and sellers
   - Providing directories of sellers
   - Maintaining security, privacy, and anonymity

2. Facilitating transactions. Facilitating transactions by optimizing the purchasing and sales processes, including the following activities:
   - Allowing for efficient trading between participants
   - Providing for B2B auctions
   - Providing the trading platform with mechanisms such as arranging payment, insurance, order fulfillment and security
   - Providing escrow services
   - Arranging for group (volume) purchasing and other discounts
   - Defining terms and other transaction values, including negotiation
   - Inputting searchable information, including industry news
   - "Grant[ing] exchange access to users and identify[ing] company users eligible to use exchange" (Tumolo 2001)
   - Collecting transaction fees and providing the necessary software and its integration with buyers and/or sellers systems, including EDI, XML, etc.
   - Providing analysis and statistics of products' transactions
   - "[R]egistering and qualifying buyers and suppliers" (Tumolo 2001)
3. Maintaining exchange policies and infrastructure. Per Tumolo (2001), maintaining institutional infrastructure involves the following activities:
   - "Ascertaining compliance with commercial code, contract law, export and import laws, [and] intellectual property law [law for transactions made within the exchange]
   - Maintaining technological infrastructure to support volume and complexity of transactions [providing auction management]
   - Providing interface capability to standard systems of buyers and suppliers
   - Obtaining appropriate site advertisers and collecting advertising and other fees"
4. Services provided by an exchange. Exchanges provide many services to buyers and sellers including:
   - Sourcing – RFQ bid coordination (product configuration, negotiation)

- Security, anonymity
- Software: groupware, workflow
- Integration with members' back-office systems
- Support services (financing, order tracking)

The types of services provided by an exchange depend on the nature of the exchange. For example, the services provided by a stock exchange are completely different from those provided by a steel or food exchange or by an intellectual property or patent exchange. However, most exchanges provide the services illustrated above. Note that, some B2B exchanges may have individuals as either sellers or buyers, in addition to corporations. An example is **localdirt.com**, an online marketplace that connects thousands of farmers with many buyers, promoting efficient trading of local produce.

Ownership of B2B Exchanges

Exchanges, portals, and directories are usually owned by a third-party operator. Both sellers and buyers prefer such an arrangement. Alternatively, exchanges may be owned by a few very large sellers or buyers. This kind of arrangement is referred to as a *consortium*.

Third-Party Independent Exchanges

Third-party exchanges are electronic intermediaries. The intermediary not only presents catalogs, but also tries to *match* buyers and sellers and encourages them to make transactions by providing electronic trading tools and rooms.

Third-party exchanges are characterized by two contradicting properties. On the one hand, they are *neutral* (they do not favor either sellers or buyers). On the other hand, they sometimes have difficulty attracting enough buyers and/or sellers to be profitable. Therefore, to increase their financial viability, these exchanges try to team up with partners, such as large sellers or buyers, financial institutions that provide payment schemes or logistics companies that fulfill orders.

Example 1: Intercontinental Exchange Group (ICE)

Intercontinental Exchange (**theice.com**) is an Internet-based global network of B2B exchanges (17 regulated exchanges and 6 central clearing houses (2014 data)) that operates marketplaces that trade commodities contracts and over-the-counter (OTC) energy and commodity features as well as related financial products. While the company's original focus was energy products, recent acquisitions have expanded its activity into "soft" commodities (grains, sugar, cotton, and coffee), foreign exchange, and equity index features. For details, see **intercontinentalexchange.com/about**.

ICE is linked electronically to all its customers (members). Trading is global and is done 24/7. Currently, ICE is organized into three business lines:

- **ICE Markets.** Futures, options, and OTC markets. Energy futures are traded via ICE Futures Europe; soft commodity futures/options are handled by ICE Futures U.S.
- **ICE Services.** Electronic trade confirmations and education.
- **ICE Data.** Electronic delivery of market data, including real-time trades, historical prices, and daily indices.

ICE offers market participants a range of trading and risk management services globally:

1. Benchmark futures contracts
2. Risk management via a global central counterparty clearinghouse
3. Integrated access to global derivatives markets
4. Leading electronic trading platform
5. Transparency and regulation
6. Independence governance

Intercontinental Exchange owns several pioneering exchanges such as ChemConnect.

Example 2: The Receivables Exchange.

The *Receivables Exchange* is a website where businesses seeking financing can sell their receivables to those who are willing to loan them money. (The receivables are used as collateral for the loans.) The process involves auctions and is managed by The Receivables Exchange, LLC. (**recx.com**). A demo is available on the site.

For a list of exchanges all over the world, see **internetworldstats.com/links2.htm**.

Example 3: SolarExchange.com

SolarExchange.com is a global *solar marketplace* facilitating B2B online *auctions* for solar-related materials and finished goods. This exchange is a global community where suppliers collaborate with buyers from anywhere in the world.

According to the company, their service portfolio "spans the solar supply chain, delivering procurement management, risk management, online auctions, price indexes, human resource sourcing and a knowledge base serving the solar industry."

The major benefits, according to the company, are:

- "Connect with the global solar trading community
- Reduce costs by automating solar procurement and sale activities
- React rapidly to changing market conditions for greater competitive advantage
- Extend your market reach through access to new trading partners and suppliers
- Accelerate sales cycles and minimize inventory risk
- Lower operating costs and improve margins
- Promote your brand to increase awareness and drive commerce activities
- Source global talent"

(see **solarexchange.com/solarxpages/Static AboutUs.aspx**).

For how this exchange works and the bidding process, see **solarexchange.com/solarxpages/StaticGetStarted.aspx** and **solarexchange.com/solarxpages/StaticBiddingProcess.aspx**.

Consortium Trading Exchanges (CTE)

A **consortium trading exchange (CTE)** is an exchange formed and operated by a group of major companies in one industry. They can be suppliers, buyers, or both. The major declared goal of CTEs (also called consortia) is to provide services that support trading activities. These services include links to the participants' back-end processing systems as well as collaborative planning and design services. Examples of consortia exchanges are **avendra.com** in the hospitality industry and OceanConnect **oceanconnect.com** in the shipping industry.

Note that some consortia have hundreds of members in the same industry.

Dynamic Pricing in B2B Exchanges

The market makers in both vertical and horizontal exchanges match supply and demand in their exchanges, and this matching determines prices, which are usually *dynamic* and are based on changes in supply and demand. **Dynamic pricing** refers to the rapid movement of prices over time and possibly across customers. Stock exchanges are a prime example of dynamic pricing. Another good example of dynamic pricing occurs in auctions, where prices vary all the time.

The typical process that results in dynamic pricing in most exchanges includes the following steps:

1. A company posts a bid to buy a product or an offer to sell one.
2. An auction (forward or reverse) is activated.
3. Buyers and sellers can see the consecutive bids and offers but usually do not see who is making them. Anonymity often is a key ingredient of dynamic pricing (e.g., in stock markets).
4. Buyers and sellers interact with bids and offers in real time.

5. Sometimes buyers join together to obtain a volume discount price (group purchasing).
6. A deal is struck when there is an exact match between a buyer and a seller on price, volume, delivery date, and other variables, such as location or quality.
7. The deal is finalized, and payment and delivery are arranged.

Advantages, Limitations, and the Revenue Model of Exchanges

Exchanges have several benefits, for buyers and sellers, including making markets more efficient, providing opportunities for sellers and buyers to find new business partners, reducing the administrative costs of ordering MROs, and expediting trading processes. They also facilitate global trade and create communities of informed buyers and sellers.

Despite these benefits, beginning in 2000, exchanges started to collapse, and both buyers and sellers realized that they faced the risks of exchange failure or deterioration. The potential benefits and risks of B2B exchanges for buyers and for sellers are summarized in Table 4.2. As the table shows, the benefits outnumber the risks.

Table 4.2   Potential gains and risks in B2B exchanges

	For buyers	**For sellers**
Potential gains	One-stop shopping, huge	New sales channel
	Search and comparison shopping	No physical store is needed
	Volume discounts	Reduced ordering errors
	24/7 ordering from any location	Sell 24/7
	Make one order from several suppliers	Community participation
	Huge, detailed information	Reach new customers spending only little cost
	Access to new suppliers	Promote the business via the exchange
	Status review and easy reordering	An outlet for surplus inventory
	Community participation	Can go global more easily
	Fast delivery	Efficient inventory management
	Less maverick buying	Better partner relationship management
	Better partner relationship management	Loss of direct CRM and PRM
Potential risks	Unknown vendors; may not be reliable	More price wars
	Loss of customer service quality (inability to compare all services)	Competition for value-added services
		Must pay transaction fees; possible loss of customers to competitors

Revenue Models

Exchanges, like all organizations, require revenue to survive. Therefore, an exchange's owners, whoever they are, must decide how they will earn revenue. The potential sources of revenue for exchanges are similar to those discussed in Chapter 1. They include transaction fees, membership fees, service fees, advertising fees, and auction fees (paid by the sellers and/or buyers). In addition, for a fee, exchanges offer software, computer services, management consultation, and so forth.

SECTION 4.7 REVIEW QUESTIONS

1. Define B2B exchanges and list the various types of exchanges.
2. List the major functions of exchanges and the services they provide.
3. What is dynamic pricing? How does it work?
4. List the potential advantages, gains, limitations, and risks of exchanges to buyers.
5. List the major advantages and limitations to sellers.
6. List the major ownership types in B2B exchanges.
7. Define consortium trading exchanges.

4.8   B2B PORTALS AND DIRECTORIES

B2B marketplaces tend to have two complementary facilities: portals and directories.

B2B Portals: An Overview

Portals, as defined in Chapter 2, are gateways to information.

B2B portals are information portals for businesses. They usually include lists of products offered by each seller, lists of potential buyers and what they want to buy, and other industry or general information. Buyers then visit sellers' sites to conduct their transactions. The portal may receive a commission for referrals, or derive revenue from advertisements. Thus, information portals sometimes have a difficult time generating sufficient revenues. Because of this, many information portals are beginning to offer additional services that support trading, such as escrow and shipments for a fee. An example of a B2B portal is **myboeing-fleet.com**, which is a Web portal for Boeing's airplane owners, operators, and MRO suppliers.

Like exchanges, information portals may be horizontal (e.g., Alibaba.com, described in the opening case), offering a wide range of information about different industries. Alternatively, they may be vertical, focusing on a single industry or industry segment. Vertical portals often are referred to as **vortals**. Portals can be limited to directory services, as will be described later in this chapter. Let us look at the various types of corporate portals first.

Corporate (Enterprise) Portals

Corporate portals facilitate collaboration with suppliers, customers, employees, and others. This section provides in-depth coverage of corporate portals, including their support of collaboration and business process management.

Corporate Portals: An Overview

A **corporate (enterprise) portal** is a gateway to a corporate website and other information sources that enables communication, collaboration, and access to company information. In contrast with public commercial portals such as Yahoo! and MSN, which are gateways to general information on the Internet, corporate portals provide a single point of access to information and applications available on the intranets and extranets of a specific organization. Companies may have separate portals for outsiders and for insiders. Through the portal, viewers can have structured and personalized access to information across large, multiple, and disparate enterprise information systems, including the Internet. For the top 10 B2B websites and trading portals in 2013, see **directory.tradeford.com/b2b**.

Types of Corporate Portals

The following five generic types of business portals can be found in organizations.

Portals for Suppliers and Other Partners

These portals facilitate relationships with business partners. For example, suppliers can manage the current inventories of the products that they sell to each specific customer online. Suppliers can see the inventory levels of their customers and reorder material and supplies when they note that an inventory level of any specific item is low, using a *vendor-managed inventory* system (see Chapter 5); they can also collaborate with corporate buyers and other staff members.

Customer Portals

Portals for customers serve businesses' customers. Customers can use these customer-facing portals to view products and services and to place orders, which they can later track. They can view their own accounts and see what is going on almost in real time. They can pay for products and services, arrange for warranties and deliveries, and much more. These portals include a personalized section (e.g., under "My account").

Employee Portals

Such portals are used for training, dissemination of company news and information, discussion groups, and more. Employee portals also are used for self-service activities, mainly in the human resources area (e.g., reporting address changes, filing expense reports, registering for classes, and requesting tuition reimbursement). Employee portals are sometimes bundled with supervisor portals in what are known as *workforce portals.*

Executive and Supervisor Portals

These portals enable managers and supervisors to control the entire workforce management process—from budgeting to workforce scheduling. For example, Pharmacia (a Pfizer company) built a portal for its executives and managers worldwide, called the Global Field Force Action Planner, which provides a single, worldwide view of the company's finances and performance.

Mobile Portals

Mobile portals are portals accessible via mobile devices, especially cell phones, smartphones, tablets, and so forth. Many mobile portals contain no corporate information, such as in NTT DOCOMO's i-Mode. Large corporations have mobile corporate portals or they offer access to their regular portals from wireless devices.

The Functionalities of Portals

Whoever their audience, the functionalities of portals range from simple **information portals** that store data and enable users to navigate and query those data, to sophisticated **collaborative portals** that enable and facilitate collaboration.

Corporate Portal Applications and Issues

Typical portal applications include knowledge bases and learning tools; business process support; customer-facing (frontline) sales, marketing, and services; collaboration and project support; access to data from disparate corporate systems; personalized pages for various users; effective search and indexing tools; security applications; best practices and lessons learned; directories and bulletin boards; identification of industry experts; news; and Internet access.

Directory Services and Search Engines

One of the most useful features of B2B is the directory that is displayed in the corporate portal or is offered by an independent, third-party company. For a comprehensive list of directories, see **internetworldstats.com/links2.htm**. A list of about 500 B2B global websites is provided at **b2bbyte.com/b2b/b2btrade.html**.

The B2B landscape is huge, with hundreds of thousands of companies online. Therefore, specialized search engines are becoming a necessity. The most useful search engines are those concentrating on vertical searches. Examples of vertical search engines and their services can be found on GlobalSpec (**globalspec.com**). In contrast to vertical searches, products such as Google Search provide search capabilities on many topics within one enterprise or on the Web in general. However, search engines by themselves may not be sufficient. Directories contain vast amounts of information that can be searched manually or by using the directory search engine. For example, **local.com** is a local-search engine for finding companies in any designated area--it contains over 16 million listings. See **local.com/faq.aspx**.

Directory services are available on many B2B sites (e.g., see GlobalSpec's Directory of Suppliers at **globalspec.com/SpecSearch/SuppliersByName/Suppliers_A.html**). Also, download the free e-market services handbook titled 'E-Markets and Online Directories: A Handbook for Small Businesses' at **emarketservices.com/clubs/ems/artic/HandbookEnglish.pdf**. Directory services help find products, vendors, services, and potential partners. In addition, the Daily Deal Media sells an *Ecommerce & Internet Business Directory*, which contains about 75,000 company records. For details, see **dailydealmedia.com/report/?ecommerce-internet-businesses-directory**.

Finally, TradeB2B **tradeb2b.net** provides information in dozens of B2B categories, including 'B2B Auctions and commodities.'

International Trade Directories

E-commerce provides an extraordinary opportunity to engage in global trade, mostly in import and export. Companies are buying, selling, working jointly, advising, opening branches, and much more on a global basis. The opportunities are much larger and diverse than one can find in just one country alone. The important topic of global trading is described in Chapter 13. Here we touch on one topic: how to find business opportunities and partners globally.

Millions of businesses, and even more products and services, exist globally. Several of the directories described earlier cover, in part, international business as well as some of the search engines. In 2014, the largest company in this field was Alibaba.com (see opening case).

SECTION 4.8 REVIEW QUESTIONS

1. Define B2B portals.
2. Distinguish a vortal from a horizontal portal.
3. List the major types of corporate portals.
4. Describe some directory services in B2B.

4.9   B2B IN WEB 2.0 AND SOCIAL NETWORKING

Although a large number of companies conduct social networking activities that target individual consumers (B2C), there also is increasing activity in the B2B arena. However, the potential in B2B is large, and new applications are added daily. The opportunities of B2B social networking depends on the companies' goals and the perceived benefits and risks involved (for more information see **adage.com/article/btob/social-media-increasingly-important-b-b-marketers/291033**).

E-Communities in B2B

B2B applications may involve many participants: buyers and sellers, service providers, industry associations, and others. In such cases, the B2B market maker needs to provide community services, such as chat rooms, bulletin boards, and possibly personalized Web pages.

E-communities connect employees, partners, customers, and any combination of the three. E-communities offer a powerful resource for e-businesses to leverage online discussions and interactions in order to maximize innovation and responsiveness. It is therefore beneficial to study the tools, methods, and best practices of building and managing B2B e-communities. Although the technological support of B2B e-communities is basically the same as for any other online community (see Chapter 2), the nature of the community itself and the information provided by the community are different.

B2B e-communities are mostly communities of transactions and, as such, members' major interests are trading and business-related information gathering. Many of the communities are associated with vertical exchanges; therefore, their needs may be specific. Communities also support partner-to-partner collaboration and networking. For example, see **partners.salesforce.com** for partnership software. However, it is common to find generic services such as classified ads, job vacancies, announcements, industry news, and so on. For B2B social communities, see Brooks et al. (2013).

Communities promote collaboration. The newest variation of these communities is the business-oriented or professional social network such as **linkedin.com**, presented in Chapter 8.

The Opportunities of Social Commerce in B2B

Companies that use B2B social networking may experience the following advantages:

- Use the network to advertise to large audiences and create brand awareness.
- Discover new business partners and sales prospects.
- Enhance their ability to learn about new technologies, competitors, customers and the business environment.
- Generate sales leads via 'contacts,' especially on **linkedin.com** and by tweeting (**twitter.com**), or engaging on **facebook.com**.
- Post questions and facilitate discussions on **linkedin.com** by searching the "Help Center," asking the community a question through the "Help Forum," or by using the posting module on your homepage to ask your network a question. Post questions on the question and answer forums on other social networks.
- Improve participation in industry association activities (including lobbying).
- Create buzz about upcoming product releases.
- Drive traffic to their Facebook page and other social sites and engage visitors there (e.g., provide games, prizes, competitions, etc.). Word of mouth also may increase traffic.
- Create social communities to encourage discussions among business partners (e.g., customers and suppliers) about their products.
- Use social networks, such as **facebook.com** and **linkedin.com** to recruit new talent.

For more opportunities using **linkedin.com**, see Prodromou (2012).

More uses of B2B social networking are seen in *enterprise social networking,* which are private social networks within enterprises (see Chapter 8).

The Use of Web 2.0 Tools in B2B

More companies are using blogs, microblogs, wikis, RSS feeds, video ads, podcasts, and other tools in B2B EC. For example, Eastern Mountain Sports (**ems.com**) uses blogs (**blog.emsoutdoors.com**), RSS feeds, and wikis to communicate and collaborate with their suppliers and distributors. Thousands of other companies are using (or experimenting with) these tools. For a study on using YouTube for B2B, see **scgpr.com/41-stories/youtube-for-b2b-marketers**; and on using Twitter, see Maddox (2010). For comprehensive coverage, see Bodnar and Cohen (2012).

Example

Orabrush Inc. (**orabrush.com**) is a startup company that makes tongue cleaners that reduce bad breath. The company created funny YouTube videos targeting Walmart employees. In a short time, the company had over 160,000 subscribers on YouTube, and more than 39 million views. In addition, the company advertised on Facebook at a cost of $28, resulting in 300,000 fans. This publicity convinced some Walmart buyers to try the product, and Orabrush landed a huge contract with Walmart. For details, see Neff (2011).

B2B Games (Gamification)

Virtual games, or **gamification**, refer to virtual games designed to support B2B training and decision making. Players compete against each other and make market predictions. For details, see DiMauro (2012).

Virtual Trade Shows and Trade Fairs

Virtual trade shows and fairs are gaining popularity. They are primarily B2B in nature.

Virtual trade shows are an application of virtual worlds. A **virtual trade show**, also known as a *virtual trade fair*, is the online analogy of a physical trade show. These are temporary or permanent showplaces where exhibitors present their new products to potential customers. For a detailed description of virtual trade shows, see Online File W4.3 and Lindner (2009).

For a large number of screen shots of virtual trade show conduct a Google search for 'Virtual Trade Show.'

Example: MarketPlace365

MarketPlace365 (**marketplace365.com**) is a vendor that gives companies tools to build virtual trade shows and attract traffic to the shows. For details, see **marketplace365.com** and **marketplace365.com/Marketing/features.aspx**.

Note: Social media can be used to support exhibits even in physical trade shows. For more on using social media at trade shows, see Patterson (2012) and download his free 'Social Media Tradeshow Marketing Checklist' at **tradeshowguyblog.com/downloads/Social-Media-Tradeshow-Marketing-Checklist.pdf**.

Social Networking in B2B

Businesses can use B2B social networking to improve knowledge sharing, collaboration, and feedback. Furthermore, social networking sites may also prove beneficial in aiding troubleshooting and problem-solving efforts. Companies (especially small ones) are using social networks and Yahoo! Answers (**answers.yahoo.com**) and specialized groups within LinkedIn; for example, for problem solving. B2B participants need to look into social networking as part of their overall EC strategy, otherwise they may miss an opportunity to reach the B2B audience and differentiate themselves from the competition.

By the end of 2013, social networking was playing a much more important role in B2B. According to a 2010 study by Regus (reported by Leggatt 2010), both small and large businesses are using social networks quite successfully to find and retain new business. A few highlights of the study include:
- 50–75% of companies globally use social networks for various networking functions.
- "40% of businesses globally have found new customers via social networks" (Leggatt 2010).
- 27% of companies include social networking activity to both acquire and retain customers in the marketing budget.

The main uses of social networks are keeping in contact with business contacts; meeting with special interest groups; learning useful business intelligence; and organizing, managing, and connecting with customer groups.

For some interesting statistical data see Karr (2013).

According to a survey by Pardot (2011; a Salesforce company), social media use among B2B marketers is already very high. However, 30% are not calculating the return on investment for social media. The survey also ranked Twitter as the most popular social media channel. In 2013, Twitter and LinkedIn were the most-used social networks in B2B (see **spiral16.com/blog/2013/10/how-b2b-companies-are-using-social-media-infographic/**).

Using Twitter in B2B
Twitter is used extensively in B2C mainly as a communication tool for customer service advertising campaigns, customer engagement platforms, CRM, and market research. Similar uses are evidenced in B2B. Schaffer (2009) provides four examples of companies that use Twitter in B2B. The applications include the monitoring of conversations for identifying business opportunities, enabling small businesses to engage with potential customers, making contacts with potential customers and customers discovering potential suppliers.

Examples of Other Activities of B2B Social Networks

The following are examples of some social network–oriented B2B activities:
- **Location-based services.** These are getting popular in B2C (see Chapter 6) and they

may provide opportunities for B2B (see Zwilling 2011).

- **Corporate profiles on social networks.** LinkedIn and Facebook include substantial information on companies and their individual employees. In fact, employee profiles can be part of a company's brand. For example, in early 2012, IBM had approximately 280,000 employees registered on LinkedIn; Microsoft had approximately 134,000 as of early 2014. In addition, some sites feature company profiles, with comments by employees and customers.

Success Stories

BtoB's Interactive Marketing Guide (available periodically at **btobonline.com**) provides examples of successful B2B implementation (e.g., look for Cisco systems, Arketi Group and Hewlett Packard Co.). Note: Now part of Adage.

For case studies, read Simply Zesty's eBook titled '50 Brilliant Social Media B2B Case Studies' (available for purchase at **simplyzesty.com/Blog/Article/June-2011/50-Brilliant-Social-Media-B2B-Case-Studies**).

Wiebesick (2011) provides a slide show of these four examples of success stories:

- Kinaxis (**kinaxis.com**): Increased traffic and leads by creating funny and entertaining videos and using a blog.
- Archer Technologies: Created an enterprise social network for customers for interactions and idea generation
- Indium Corp. (**indium.com**): Engineers shared blogs among themselves and with the industry.
- Cree, Inc. (**cree.com**): Created an enterprise social network site for engagement, including blogging, YouTube videos, and photo contests.

Strategy for B2B Social Networking

Bhutani (2008) made several strategy implementation suggestions, organized into three categories: participate, monitor, and use existing applications.

Eventually, companies will be able to use social networking more efficiently. Success stories of five companies—SAP, United Linen (a small laundry service), Forrester Research,

Kinaxis, and Expert Laser Services—are discussed by Pergolino (2010).

The Future of B2B Social Networking

Marketing users are developing social media and search tools. Products such as Google's OpenSocial may increase interest in social networking.

Businesses must embrace social networking in order to better understand their customers and business partners.

B2B marketing, which is discussed in Online File W4.4, refers to marketing by manufacturers and wholesalers along the sell-side of the supply chain.

SECTION 4.9 REVIEW QUESTIONS

1. List some of the opportunities for corporations to use social networking in B2B EC.
2. What are some of the benefits of social networking for B2B EC?
3. List some Web 2.0 social software for B2B applications.
4. Describe some of the applications of B2B in social networks.
5. Discuss the strategies for B2B social networking.
6. Define e-communities in B2B.

4.10   SOME B2B SUPPORT MECHANISMS

Implementing B2B can be difficult due to the large number and volume of transactions and products, the potential large numbers of buyers and suppliers, and the need for transporting large quantities of goods. In this section, we cover several representative topics.

Major differences exist between B2B and B2C EC with respect to the nature of demand and supply and the trading process. Here we discuss the corporate purchaser's buying behavior and some of the marketing and advertising methods used in B2B EC. There is more discussion about this topic in **blog.marketo.com**, which provides tutorials

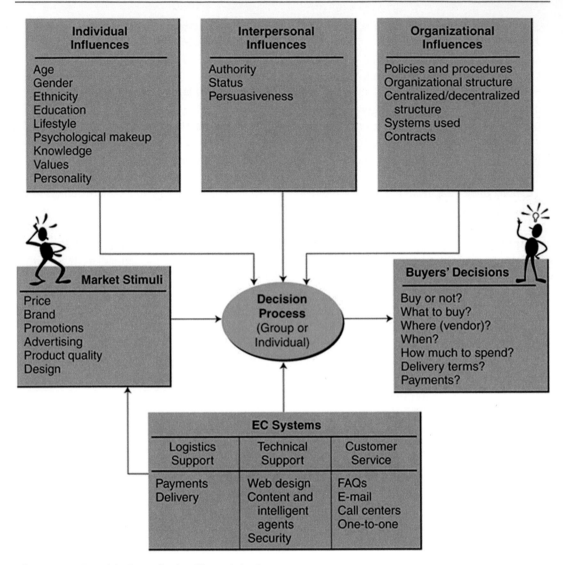

Figure 4.10   A model of organizational buyer behavior

and tips as a guide to both successful B2B social marketing and B2B marketing optimization.

Organizational Buyer Behavior

Although the number of organizational buyers is much smaller than the number of individual consumers, their transaction volumes are by far larger, and the terms of negotiations and purchasing are more complex. In addition, the purchasing process itself usually is more complex than the purchasing

process of an individual customer. Likewise, the organization's buyer may be a group. In fact, decisions to purchase expensive items are usually made by a group. Therefore, factors that affect individual consumer behavior and organizational buying behavior are quite different.

A Behavioral Model of Organizational Buyers

The behavior of an organizational buyer is illustrated by the model shown in Figure 4.10. A B2B module includes the organization's purchasing guidelines and constraints (e.g., contracts with certain suppliers) and the purchasing system used. Interpersonal influences, such as authority, and the possibility of group decision making must be considered.

The Marketing and Advertising Processes in B2B

B2B marketing refers to marketing and sales made by manufacturers and wholesalers along the sell-side of the supply chain.

The marketing and advertising processes for businesses differ considerably from those used for selling to individual consumers. For example, traditional (offline) B2B marketers use methods such as physical trade shows, advertisements in industry magazines, utilization of paper catalogs, and salespeople who visit existing customers and potential buyers.

In the digital world, these approaches may not be effective, feasible, or economical. Therefore, organizations use a variety of online methods to reach business customers. Popular methods include online directory services, matching services, the marketing and advertising services of exchanges, co-branding or alliances, affiliate programs, online virtual trade shows, online marketing services, or social networks. Several of these methods are discussed next.

Methods for B2B Online Advertising and Marketing

When a B2C niche e-tailer seeks to attract for example, its audience of cat or dog lovers, or travelers, the e-tailer may advertise in traditional media targeted to those audiences, such as magazines, newspapers, or television shows, or use Google's or Facebook's Internet ads. The same is true in B2B, where marketers use trade magazines and directories, which can be digital. In addition, as in B2C, B2B advertisers try to target their customers.

Targeting Customers

A B2B company, whether a provider of goods or services, an operator of a trading exchange, or a provider of digital real-time services, can contact all of its targeted customers individually when they are part of a well-defined group. For example, to attract companies to an exchange for auto supplies, one might use information from industry trade association records or industry magazines to identify potential customers.

Several of the advertising methods that will be presented in Chapter 9 are applicable both to B2C and B2B. For example, video ads can be used to target customers in B2B.

Affiliate Programs

Here we briefly examine one popular method: affiliate programs.

B2C affiliate services were introduced in Chapter 1 and will be described in Chapter 9. There are several types of affiliate programs. The simplest type, which is used extensively in B2C EC, is where an affiliate posts a banner display ad of a selling vendor, such as Amazon.com, on its own website. When a consumer clicks on the banner, the consumer is directed to that vendor's website, and a commission is paid to the affiliate if the customer makes a purchase (or sometimes just for clicking on the vendor's banner). The same method works in B2B.

For more on B2B affiliate programs, see Peters (2014) and **quicksprout.com/the-beginners-guide-to-online-marketing-chapter-9**.

B2B Market Research

One of the major objectives of market research is to provide tactics and strategies for EC advertising, as described in Chapter 9. The data collected in market research can be voluminous. To analyze it, one can use data and text mining. For the use of data mining in B2B market research, see Chapter 9.

A final note: In marketing, we use the classical 4Ps (product, price, place, and promotion). Dunay (2010) argues that the 4Ps are good mostly for B2C. For B2B, he proposes 4Cs: content, connection, communication, and conversion.

Other B2B Support Mechanisms

Similar to B2C, there are several support services in B2B. Representative examples follow.

Collaboration Networks and Supply Chain Facilities

The collaboration process is critical for the success of B2B and supply chain management. Despite the importance of collaboration, only 14% of respondents to the Aberdeen Group survey published in June 2011 indicated they had the ability to collaborate with trading partners online (Aberdeen Group 2011). The survey shows the needs and the potential benefits and concludes that collaboration is a necessity. Collaboration is about the relationships among organizations. Many companies provide tools that facilitate collaboration.

Example: IBM Sterling Commerce

This is a cloud-based value added network that helps to reduce costs and increase productivity, quality, and customer satisfaction. For a description and more benefits, see **ibm.com/software/info/sterling-commerce**.

Example: NTE B2B Collaboration

This solution provides: easy connections with trading partners, EDI translation (see Online Tutorial T2), unrestricted protocols used for communication, and collaboration modules. For details, see **nte.com/technology/b2b-collaboration**.

Example: Ariba Network

Ariba, Inc. (**ariba.com**) is a global supplier network that finds, connects, and collaborates with a huge community of trading partners. For details, see **ariba.com/community/the-ariba-network**.

Supply Chain Facilitators

Several companies concentrate on improving B2B supply chains. For example, SupplyON (**supplyon.com**) monitors logistics in several industries (e.g., automotive, aerospace, railways). NeoGrid (**neogrid.com**) is another company that facilitates improvements along the supply chains of several industries. **Alibaba.com**, **ec21.com**, and **ziliot.com** are examples of marketplaces that facilitate supply chain management for global trading. Finally, AmazonSupply (**amazonsupply.com**) is an emerging service in this area.

Payments

Payments for B2B transactions differ from those of B2C. While credit cards are used for smaller purchases, larger purchases are paid for by other methods (e.g., letters of credit). For details, see Chapter 11. For a video titled "How to Use PayPal for Your Business" (9:38 minutes), see **youtube.com/watch?v=Z-Qd_nWuugM**.

Standards and RosettaNet

It is necessary to establish standards for processing and sharing B2B information, especially in global trade. The most common standard for this purpose in the U.S. is that of RosettaNet. For an overview on using RosettaNet, see **public.dhe.ibm.com/software/commerce/doc/sb2bi/si51/stds70/Stds70_Using_RosettaNet.pdf**. A similar standard is UN/EDIFACT (The United Nations Rules for Electronic Data Interchange for Administration, Commerce and Transport), which is popular in Europe. Many of the large technology companies are members of RosettaNet (e.g., IBM, Microsoft, Intel). This organization defines about 100 B2B transaction processes, and standardizes them.

The Future of B2B

In B2B, as in B2C, there is a trend to add socially-oriented activities and strategies. IBM calls this trend *community marketing*. The major advantage is to foster collaboration with and among customers by using social networks (e.g., for discussion and feedback). This enables marketers to use the best practices borrowed from B2C. B2B suppliers will need to provide B2B buyers with many of the features that B2B sellers provide to their customers. IBM provides Elite Starter Store software to facilitate interactions in its WebSphere Commerce suite (**ibm.com/software/products/en/websphere-commerce**). Overall, B2B is expected to grow even faster as smaller companies are joining the B2B movement. For the future of B2B marketplaces, see Wertz (2013).

SECTION 4.10 REVIEW QUESTIONS

1. Distinguish between organizational buyers and individual consumers.
2. Describe B2B EC marketing and advertising methods.
3. Explain how affiliate programs work in B2B EC.
4. What can market research do to help in B2B?
5. Why is collaboration important in B2B?

MANAGERIAL ISSUES

Some managerial issues related to this chapter are as follows.

1. **Which B2B model(s) should we use for e-procurement?** When evaluating the various upstream B2B models, we need to match the suitable e-procurement goals with solution strategies depending upon whether the purchases are direct material or indirect material. Four typical goals that should be distinguished are organizational operational efficiency, minimum price, minimum inventory and stock-outs, and low administrative costs. For each of these goals, the appropriate solution and system should be designed accordingly. Managing many small and medium suppliers that do not have sophisticated systems is a challenging goal.

2. **Which B2B model(s) should we use for online B2B sales?** A key issue for B2B sales is how to reconcile with the multiple buyers who adopt different EDI and ERP systems. The Enterprise Application Integration (EAI) solution transforms the internal data of multiple EDI formats used by different buyers. The integration of various types of EDI standards with ERP solutions is another challenge to overcome. In addition to contract management, B2B marketers use auctions, liquidations, and social networks to increase sales.

3. **Which solutions and vendor(s) should we select?** Vendors normally develop and deploy B2B applications, even for large organizations. Two basic approaches to vendor selection exist: (1) Select a primary vendor such as IBM (**ibm.com**), Microsoft (**microsoft.com**),

or Oracle (**oracle.com**). This vendor will use its software and procedures and add partners as needed. (2) Use an integrator that will mix and match existing products and vendors to create "the best of breed" for your needs.

4. **What is the organizational impact of B2B?** The B2B system will change the role of the procurement department by redefining the role and procedures of that department. The function of the procurement department may be completely outsourced. A procurement policy portfolio is necessary to balance strategic sourcing items, spot purchasing items, and design a supply relationship management system.

5. **What are some ethical issues in B2B?** Because B2B EC requires the sharing of proprietary information, business ethics are necessary. Employees should not be able to access unauthorized areas in the trading system, and the privacy of trading partners should be protected.

6. **Which type of social network should we use—private (proprietary) or public?** There are successes and failures in both types. Some large companies have both types (e.g., **northwesternmutual.com**). In most cases, it is better to use public networks such as **linkedin.com** and **facebook.com**.

7. **Which business processes to automate?** It depends on the company, industry and value chain. However, as illustrated in this chapter, selling and purchasing and other activities along the supply chains are the prime targets. These include payments (financial supply chains). Also important are logistics, shipments, and inventory management.

SUMMARY

In this chapter, you learned about the following EC issues as they relate to the chapter's learning objectives.

1. **The B2B field.** The B2B field comprises e-commerce activities between businesses. B2B activities account for 77 to 95% of all EC. B2B e-commerce can be done by using different models.

2. **The major B2B models.** The B2B field is quite diversified. It can be divided into the following segments: sell-side marketplaces (one seller to many buyers), buy-side marketplaces (one buyer from many sellers), and trading exchanges (many sellers to many buyers). Each segment includes several business models. Intermediaries play an important role in some B2B models.

3. **The characteristics and models of sell-side marketplaces.** Sell-side B2B EC is the online direct sale by one seller (a manufacturer or an intermediary) to many buyers. The major technology used is electronic catalogs, which also allow for efficient customization, configuration, and purchase by customers. In addition, forward auctions are becoming popular, especially for liquidating surplus inventory. Sell-side auctions can be conducted from the seller's own site or from an intermediary's auction site. Sell-side activities can be accompanied by extensive customer service. E-commerce allows customization of products and services in personalized catalogs.

4. **Sell-side intermediaries.** The primary role of intermediaries in B2B is to provide value-added services for manufacturers and business customers. Intermediaries can also support group buyers, conduct auctions, and aggregate catalogs of many sellers.

5. **The characteristics of buy-side marketplaces and e-procurement.** Today, companies are moving to e-procurement to expedite purchasing, save on item and administrative costs, and gain better control over the purchasing process. Major procurement methods are reverse auctions (bidding systems), buying from webstores and catalogs, negotiation, buying from an intermediary that aggregates sellers' catalogs, internal marketplaces and group purchasing, desktop purchasing, buying in exchanges or industrial malls, and e-bartering. E-procurement offers the opportunity to achieve significant cost and time savings.

6. **B2B reverse auctions.** A reverse auction is a tendering system used by buyers to get better prices from suppliers competing to fulfill the buyers' needs. Auctions can be done on a company's website or on a third-party auction site. Reverse auctions can lower buyers' costs dramatically, both in product costs and in the time and cost of the tendering process.

7. **B2B aggregation and group purchasing.** Increasing the bargaining power and efficiency of companies can be done by aggregating either the buyers or the sellers. Aggregating suppliers' catalogs into a buyer's catalog, for example, gives buying companies better control of purchasing costs. In desktop purchasing, employees are empowered to buy up to a certain limit without the need for additional approval. Employees view internal catalogs with pre-agreed-upon prices with the approved suppliers and then buy within their budget. Industrial malls or large distributors specialize in one industry (e.g., computers) or in industrial MROs. They aggregate the catalogs of thousands of suppliers. A purchasing agent can place an order for parts or materials and shipping is arranged by the supplier or the mall owner. Buyer aggregation through group purchasing is very popular because it enables even SMEs to get better prices on their purchases. In addition to direct purchasing, items can be acquired via bartering.

8. **Exchanges defined and the major types of exchanges.** Exchanges are e-marketplaces that provide a trading platform for conducting business among many buyers, many sellers, and other business partners. Types of public e-marketplaces include B2B third-party trading exchanges and consortium trading exchanges. Exchanges may be vertical (industry oriented) or horizontal.

9. **B2B portals.** B2B portals are gateways to B2B community-related information. They are usually of a vertical structure, in which case they are referred to as *vortals*. Some B2B portals offer product and vendor information and even tools for conducting trades, sometimes making it difficult to distinguish between B2B portals and trading exchanges.

10. **Third-party exchanges.** Third-party exchanges are owned by an independent company and usually are operated in highly

fragmented markets. They are open to anyone and, therefore, are considered public exchanges. They try to maintain neutral relations with both buyers and sellers.

11. **B2B in Web 2.0 and social networks.** Although considerable B2C social networking activities exist, B2B activities are just beginning. A major success has been seen in the use of blogs and wikis to collaborate with suppliers and customers. Large companies use social networking to create and foster business relationships. Smaller companies use social networking for soliciting expert opinions. Other companies use it for finding business partners, cultivating business opportunities, recruiting employees, and finding sales leads.

12. **B2B Internet marketing and other support services.** Marketing methods and marketing research in B2B differ from those of B2C. A major reason for this is that the buyers must observe organizational buying policies and frequently conduct buying activities as a group (committee). Organizations use modified B2C methods such as affiliate marketing. The purchasing is controlled by rules and constraints as well as by the purchasing agent's behavior.

KEY TERMS

B2B marketing
B2B portals
Bartering exchange
Business-to-business e-commerce (B2B EC)
Buy-side e-marketplace
Collaborative portals
Company-centric EC
Consortium trading exchange (CTE)
Corporate (enterprise) portal
Desktop purchasing
Direct materials
Dynamic pricing
E-procurement (electronic procurement)
Exchanges (trading communities or trading exchanges)
Gamification
Group purchasing
Horizontal marketplaces
Indirect materials
Information portals
Maintenance, repair, and operation (MRO)
Maverick buying
Mobile portals
Online intermediary
Partner relationship management (PRM)
Procurement management
Public e-marketplaces
Request for quote (RFQ)
Reverse auction
Sell-side e-marketplace
Vertical marketplaces
Virtual trade shows
Vortals

DISCUSSION QUESTIONS

1. Explain how a catalog-based sell-side e-marketplace works and describe its benefits.
2. Discuss the advantages of selling through online auctions over selling from catalogs. What are the disadvantages?
3. Discuss and compare all of the mechanisms that group-purchasing aggregators can use.
4. Should desktop purchasing only be implemented through an internal marketplace?
5. Compare and contrast a privately owned exchange with a private e-marketplace.
6. Compare external and internal aggregation of catalogs.
7. Relate social commerce to B2B group buying.
8. Compare an organizational buyer to an individual consumer.

TOPICS FOR CLASS DISCUSSION AND DEBATES

1. Discuss B2B opportunities in social networking.
2. Discuss the risks in B2B social networking.
3. Discuss how globalization is related to B2B.
4. Relate B2B to the four Ps of marketing (product, pricing, placement, and promotion) and the four Cs (content, connection, communication, and conversion).

5. Discuss potential channel conflicts in B2B.
6. What is the contribution of B2B directories such as Alibaba.com to global trade? What are the potential limitations?
7. Debate: Some say that exchanges must be owned by a third-party intermediary and that consortiums should not be allowed.
8. Discuss why **facebook.com** is not as good as **linkedin.com** in generating sales leads.
9. In class, watch the video "B2B Marketing in a Digital World" (4:11 minutes) at **youtube.com/watch?v=−nTkBhsUIRQ**. Discuss the implications for a progressive marketing manager.
10. Research companies that conduct liquidations. Concentrate on: **liquidation.com**, **govliquidation.com**, and **govdeals.com**. Examine the similarities and uniquenesses in the services provided. Discuss the value added to the companies that use these services.

ducting various types of e-procurement. List and analyze each tool.
8. Enter **navigatorhms.com/gpo**, and two other group purchasing sites. Report on B2B group buying activities available at each site.
9. Enter **blog.marketo.com** and find eight recent successful applications of social B2B. Prepare a list of topics covered at the site. Write a brief summary about the content, including tips and guides, and lessons learned.
10. Enter **business.yahoo.com/category/business_to_business**. Prepare a list of resources about exchanges and B2B directories.
11. Enter **smallbusiness.yahoo.com/ecommerce** and summarize one of the 'Success Stories.'
12. Enter **eprocurement.nc.gov**. What e-procurement methods does it provide? What are the benefits of each method?
13. Enter **equinix.com** and identify the B2B services they provide.

INTERNET EXERCISES

1. **Tripadvisor.com** launched a B2B division in 2010. Find information about the benefits to a company using it and to its business customers.
2. Examine the following sites: **ariba.com**, **ibm.com**, and **ibxplatform.com**. Review their products and services. How do they support mobile marketing and social commerce?
3. Match a B2B business model with the services on each site listed in the previous question.
4. Visit **ebay.com** and identify all of the activities related to its small business auctions. What services are provided by eBay? Then, enter eBay Business & Industrial area at **ebay.com/rpp/business-industrial**. What kind of e-marketplace is this? What are its major capabilities?
5. Enter **ondemandsourcing.com** and use the free registration to view the product demo. Prepare a list of benefits to small and medium-sized organizations.
6. Enter **bitpipe.com** and find recent B2B vendor reports related to e-procurement. Identify topics not covered in this chapter.
7. Visit **iasta.com** and **cognizant.com**. Examine the major tools they sell for con-

TEAM ASSIGNMENTS AND PROJECTS

1. **Assignment for the Opening Case**
   Read the opening case and answer the following questions.
   (a) What directory services are provided by Alibaba.com?
   (b) Identify the revenue sources of Alibaba.com.
   (c) Find information about the 2014 IPO. Do you think that the company valuation is realistic?
   (d) Enter **slideshare.net/yanhufei/case-study-alibaba-final-v-11** and review the Alibaba.com case study. Expand on the answers to questions which are designated by your teacher.
   (e) Describe Alibaba's business model.
   (f) Enter **sa.alibaba.com** and watch the video about supplier assessment at Alibaba.com (3:31 minutes); summarize its content.
   (g) Watch the video titled 'e-Riches 2.0: − The Best Online Marketing Book by Scott Fox' (6:18 minutes) at **youtube.com/watch?v=6O747UHN9Mw**.
   What did you learned from this video?

2. Each team should explore a different social networking B2B activity and prepare a summary paper for a class presentation. The paper should include the following about the activity or method:
   (a) The mechanisms and technologies used
   (b) The benefits to buyers, suppliers, and others (if applicable)
   (c) The limitations to buyers, suppliers, and others (if applicable)
   (d) The situations for which each method is recommended
   Hint: Look at Leake et al. (2012), and vendors' products.
3. Each team finds a global B2B intermediary that competes with **alibaba.com** (e.g., **globalsources.com**). Prepare a list of services available to sellers and to buyers from both Alibaba.com and your chosen competitor.
4. Do a Google search and find the "10 Great B-to-B Sites" for the last 3 years. Read the comments and visit these sites. Each team prepares a statement of why they think five of these sites are superior.
5. Enter **ariba.com** and find out what its software solutions such as Ariba Commerce Cloud can do to facilitate inter-enterprise commerce. Also examine the company's solution for sourcing, procurement, and contract management. Present your findings to the class.
6. View the slide presentation "Vision 2020: Ideas for Procurement in 2020 by Industry-Leading Procurement Executives" by Oka and 13 other procurement executives (2011) available at **slideshare.net/Ariba/vision2020-thefutureofprocurement**. Each team analyzes the ideas of several contributors and presents the highlights to the class.
7. Watch the video titled "eProcurement Case Study: HOYER Group" (3:44 minutes) at **youtube.com/watch?v=BFaJPeDQyIs&noredirect=1**. Answer the following questions.
   (a) What problems did the Hoyer Group face?
   (b) What were some of the software requirements?
   (c) How did they evaluate the software? What criteria did they use?
   (d) What have you learned from the video?
8. The class researches Ariba's supplier network and compares it to several similar networks (e.g., to IBM Sterling B2B Collaboration Network). Each team examines one comparison and makes a presentation to the class.

CLOSING CASE: THE UNIVERSITY OF SHEFFIELD'S E-TENDERING SYSTEM

The University of Sheffield in Sheffield, England **sheffield.ac.uk** is a leading large public teaching and research institute with over 25,000 registered students and over 5,300 staff (see **sheffield.ac.uk/about/facts**).

The University's research output is recognized all over the world. Despite its excellent reputation, it operates on a tight budget. One area where the university saved a considerable amount of money in procurement.

Due to its research activities, the university purchases over £110 million of supplies a year from about 12,000 suppliers, of which 4,500 are regular. The university needed an electronic system in order to minimize procurement delays, standardize processes across all departments, and reduce potential errors. In addition, the administrative expenditures (e.g., postal cost, employees' time, photocopying) were very high. As of 2005, the university has enhanced an e-tendering system as part of its government mandated e-procurement system.

The E-Tendering Initiative

The objective of the procurement department, which initiated the e-tendering initiative, was and still is, to support the university in attaining its mission. The initiative must also comply with public procurement regulations. The system was built with software called *in-Tend* (a standard European Union tendering tool) in collaboration with users, suppliers, the staff of the procurement department, and the IT development team.

The E-Tendering Process

The procurement department communicates with the participants via the portal In-Tend Ltd.

(**in-tend.co.uk**). In-Tend Ltd. provides policy and open tendering information, including historical bidding data, contracts, and the tendering process to registered suppliers. This portal is very user friendly, allowing small suppliers to participate in biddings. The system is highly secured. (For features of the portal, see **tendernotification.co.uk/features.aspx**.)

The Process

The university has dozens of departments that need to purchase materials and supplies. The requirements are submitted to the central Procurement Office (PO) that arranges the reverse auctions. The PO started the project by standardizing the ordering process and examining all related existing information systems. After extensively testing and training the staff, a small scale tendering job was tested with the local suppliers. Once satisfied, the PO deployed the system, which is used for about 200 tenders each year. The tenders are both for goods and for services.

Bidders can download all the needed documents and upload their bids electronically. The electronic processes resulted in financial savings as well, with an improved level of support to potential bidders.

The PO facilitated connections with the local business community, in order to induce the local businesses to submit bids (e.g., promoting pre-qualification and facilitating the finding of current opportunities).

Sources: Based on CIPS Knowledge Works (2006); **sheffield.ac.uk/procurement**, **www.sheffield.ac.uk/finance/regulations/p_flowchart**, and **in-tendhost.co.uk/sheffield/aspx/Home** (all accessed March 2014).

Questions

1. Why does a public university need to comply with government regulations that may reduce its efficiency?
2. Find information on the software In-Tend at **in-tend.co.uk**. Why is it so popular?
3. Examine the information available to suppliers on the portal. How does the tendering provide a fair chance for bidders?
4. Trace the flow of information in an e-tender at the university. Write a report.

5. What procurement services are provided to the internal staff? What services are provided to suppliers and other external companies or individuals (e.g., stockholders)?

ONLINE FILES
available at **affordable-ecommerce-textbook.com/turban**

W4.1 The E-Procurement Process: The Buyers View
W4.2 Application Case: iMarketKorea
W4.3 Virtual Trade Shows and Trade Fairs
W4.4 B2B Internet Marketing

COMPREHENSIVE EDUCATIONAL WEBSITES

optimizeandprophesize.com: Jonathan Mendez's blog covering many topics including analytics, applications, landing page optimization, and social media.
techrepublic.com: Case studies, publications.
business.com: Resources including guides, blogs, and newsletters on B2B, procurement, and more.
internet.com: Technology news, product reviews, technical advice.
blog.marketo.com: A comprehensive blog site on B2B marketing.
b2bmarketing.net: A dedicated B2B marketing resource, including industry news, training events, and blogs.
b2b-today.com: "World's largest B2B website." Comprehensive information and resources for online trade and promotion services to businesses in China and abroad.
btobonlinedirectory.com: A list of companies and services for your business.

GLOSSARY

B2B marketing   Marketing and sales made by manufacturers and wholesalers along the sell-side of the supply chain.
B2B portals   Information portals for businesses.
Bartering exchange   A company submits its surplus to the exchange and receives points of

credit, which the company can then use to buy items that it needs.

Business-to-business e-commerce (B2B EC) Transactions between businesses conducted electronically over the Internet, extranets, intranets, or private networks.

Buy-side e-marketplace An e-marketplace owned by large buyers that invites sellers to browse and offers to fulfill orders.

Collaborative portals Portals that enable and facilitate collaboration.

Company-centric EC One-to-many and many-to-one markets where one company does either all the selling (*sell-side market*) or all the buying (*buy-side market*).

Consortium trading exchange (CTE) An exchange formed and operated by a group of major companies in one industry. They can be suppliers, buyers, or both.

Corporate (enterprise) portal A gateway to a corporate website and other information sources that enables communication, collaboration, and access to company information.

Desktop purchasing Purchasing done by employees without the approval of supervisors and without the involvement of a procurement department.

Direct materials Materials used in making products, such as steel in a car or paper in a book.

Dynamic pricing The rapid movement of prices over time and possibly across customers.

E-procurement (electronic procurement) The online purchase of supplies, materials, energy, work, and services. It can be done via the Internet or via a private network such as EDI.

Exchanges (trading communities or trading exchanges) Many-to-many e-marketplaces where many buyers and many sellers meet electronically to trade with one another.

Gamification Virtual games designed to support B2B training and decision making.

Group purchasing Orders from several buyers are aggregated so that better prices due to larger quantities purchased can be negotiated.

Horizontal marketplaces Markets in which trading is in a service or a product that is used in many types of industries. Examples are office supplies, PCs, or travel services.

Indirect materials Items, such as office supplies or light bulbs, which support operation and production.

Information portals Portals that store data and enable users to navigate and query those data.

Maintenance, repair, and operation (MRO) Indirect materials used in activities that support production.

Maverick buying A buying situation that occurs when a buyer makes unplanned purchases of items needed quickly, resulting in buying at non-pre-negotiated, and usually higher, prices.

Mobile portals Portals accessible via mobile devices, especially cell phones, smartphones, tablets, and other handheld devices.

Online intermediary A third-party entity that brokers the transactions between the buyer and seller and can be either a virtual or a click-and-mortar intermediary.

Partner relationship management (PRM) The strategy of providing comprehensive, quality e-services for business partners.

Procurement management The process of planning, organizing, and coordinating of all the activities pertaining to the purchasing of the goods and services needed by an organization.

Public e-marketplaces Third-party exchanges open to all interested parties (sellers and buyers).

Request for quote (RFQ) A form or document used as an "invitation" to take part in a reverse auction.

Reverse auction The auction process in which many sellers (suppliers) compute to fulfill orders requested by one buyer.

Sell-side e-marketplace The model in which a business sells products and services to business customers electronically, frequently over an extranet.

Vertical marketplaces Markets for one industry or one industry segment. Examples include marketplaces specializing in electronics, cars, hospital supplies, steel, or chemicals.

Virtual trade show Temporary or permanent showplaces where exhibitors present their new products to potential customers.

Vortals Vertical portals focusing on a single industry or industry segment.

REFERENCES

Aberdeen Group. "B2B Integration and Collaboration: Strategies for Building a ROI Business Case." Research Brief, June 27, 2011. **aberdeen.com/Aberdeen-Library/7260/RB-business-integration-collaboration.aspx** (must register (free) to download) (accessed March 2014).

Basware. "7 Golden Rules for e-Procurement Success." *Basware eBook*, December 16, 2011. **basware.com/knowledge-center/basware-ebook-7-golden-rules-for-e-procurement-success** (accessed March 2014; free registration to access free download).

Bhutani, N. "Social Media Stepping Up as Source for Connecting B2B Networks." June 8, 2008. **demandgenreport.com/industry-topics/archives/feature-articles/89-social-media-stepping-up-as-source-for-connecting-b2b-networks.html#.UxrSP_mtmSo** (accessed November March 2014).

Bodnar, K., and J. L. Cohen. *The B2B Social Media Book: Become a Marketing Superstar by Generating Leads with Blogging, LinkedIn, Twitter, Facebook, Email and More.* Hoboken, NJ: Wiley, 2012.

Brooks, M., J.J. Lovett, and S. Creek, *Developing B2B Social Communities: Keys to Growth, Innovation, and Customer Loyalty*, New York: Apress, 2013.

Charles, M. *China Wholesale Trader Secrets- The Rise of Alibaba.com and New Entrepreneurs [Kindle Edition]*, Seattle, WA: Amazon Digital Services, 2014.

Chen, L.Y., and S. Gill. "Alibaba Valuation Rises to $168 Billion After Earnings." April 17, 2014. **bloomberg.com/news/2014-04-17/alibaba-valuation-rises-to-168-billion-after-eearnings.html** (accessed April 2014).

Chopra, S., and P. Meindl. *Supply Chain Management: Strategy, Planning, and Operation*, 5th ed. Upper Saddle River, NJ: Pearson/Prentice-Hall, 2012.

CIPS Knowledge Works. "The University of Sheffield e-Tendering Case Study." January 2006. **globalpublicprocurement.org/Documents/Resources/White-Papers/Successful-e-tendering.pdf** (accessed April 2014).

Commonwealth of Pennsylvania. "Department of General Services: Supplies and Surplus Operations." 2006. Search at **portal.state.pa.us/portal/server.pt/community/state_surplus_property_program** (accessed April 2014).

Course Hero, "Whirlpool B2B Trading Portal." **coursehero.com** (accessed March 2014; must request free access).

DiMauro, V. "Let the B2B Games Begin!" June 27, 2012. **socialmediatoday.com/vanessa-dimauro/567122/let-b2b-games-begin** (accessed March 2014).

Dunay, P. "The 4 C's of B2B Marketing." *Marketing Darwinism*, January 19, 2010. **pauldunay.com/4-cs-of-b2-marketing** (accessed March 2014).

E-Commerce Wiki. "B2B Exchanges." (Last modified by R. Pfont: June 2, 2013). **en.ecommercewiki.info/fundamentals/market_places/exchanges** (accessed March 2014).

eProc.org. "Sustainable Electronic Procurement Case Study: Branas Isaf Training." 2010. **eproc.org** (no longer available online).

IBM. "Whirlpool's B2B Trading Portal Cuts Per Order Costs Significantly." G325-6693-00, 2000. White Plains, NY: IBM Corporation Software Group, Pub. 2000.

Lai, L. S.-L. "Chinese Entrepreneurship in the Internet Age: Lessons from Alibaba.com." *World Academy of Science, Engineering and Technology*, Volume 48, 2010.

Leake, W., et al. *Complete B2B Online Marketing.* San Francisco, CA: Sybex, 2012.

Leggatt, H. "Survey: Small Businesses Find Success with Social Networking." July 9, 2010. **bizreport.com/2010/07/survey-small-businesses-find-success-with-social-networking.html** (accessed March 2014).

Karr, D. "B2B Marketing Strategies for 2013 and Beyond: An Infographic." August 12, 2013. **socialmediatoday.com/douglaskarr/1661106/b2b-marketing-strategies-2013-and-beyond-infographic** (accessed May 2014).

Lindner, M. "How to Tackle A Virtual Trade Show." July 28, 2009. **forbes.com/2009/07/28/virtual-trade-show-steps-entrepreneurs-technology-tradeshow.html** (accessed March 2014).

Maddox, K. "Twitter Debuts New Ad Platform." May 3, 2010. **adage.com/article/btob/twitter-debuts-ad-platform/280747/?btob=1** (accessed March 2014).

Neff, J. "How Orabrush Got National Walmart Deal with YouTube Videos, $28 in Facebook Ads: Telling Walmart Employees They Have Bad Breath Leads to Distribution in 3,500 Stores." September 20, 2011. **adage.com/article/news/orabrush-national-walmart-deal-youtube-videos/229914** (accessed March 2014).

Oka, A., et al. "Vision 2020: Ideas for Procurement in 2020 by Industry-Leading Procurement Executives." 2011. **ariba.com/resources/library/vision-2020-the-future-of-procurement** (accessed March 2014).

Pardot. "Many Marketers Don't Measure Social Media Impact." November 3, 2011. **pardot.com/press/many-marketers-dont-measure-social-media-impact/** (accessed March 2014).

Parente, D. H. *Best Practices for Online Procurement Auctions (Premier Reference Source).* Hershey PA: IGI Global, 2007.

Patterson, T. "Top Eleven Reasons to Use Social Media at your Next Tradeshow Appearance." June 27, 2012. **socialmediatoday.com/timpatterson/566327/top-eleven-reasons-use-social-media-your-next-trade-show-appearance** (accessed March 2014).

Pergolino, M. "5 B2B Social Media Success Stories." May 16, 2010. **blog.marketo.com/2010/05/b2b-social-media-success.html** (accessed March 2014).

Peters, J. *Affiliate Marketing for Beginners- A No-Nonsense Guide on How to Make Money Online*, [Kindle Edition], Seattle, WA: Amazon Digital Services, 2014.

Prodromou, T. *Ultimate Guide to LinkedIn for Business: How to Get Connected With 150 Million+ Customers in 10 Minutes*, Irvine, CA: Entrepreneur Press, 2012.

PR Newswire. "Pennsylvania Governor Rendell Delivers December Radio Address." News release, December 6, 2003. **prnewswire.com/news-releases/pennsylvania-governor-rendell-delivers-december-radio-address-73229672.html** (accessed March 2014).

Regal, D. *Revolutionizing the Checkout Process: Shoplet's E-Procurement [Kindle Edition]*. Amazon Digital Services, Seattle, WA: 2014.

Rockwell, M. "Experts Debate Value of Reverse Auctions." December 11, 2013. **fcw.com/articles/2013/12/11/experts-debate-value-of-reverse-auctions.aspx** (accessed May 2014).

Schaffer, N. *The Windmill Networking Approach to Networking: Understanding, Leveraging, and Maximizing LinkedIn.* Scotts Valley, CA: BookSurge Publishing, 2009.

Schepp, B., and D. Schepp. *The Official Alibaba.com Success Guide: Insider Tips and Strategies for Sourcing Products from the World's Largest B2B Marketplace.* Hoboken, NJ: Wiley, 2009.

Tumolo, M. "Business-to-Business Exchanges." *Information Systems Management*, Volume 18, Issue 2, Spring 2001.

Wertz, B. "Alibaba Is Just the Beginning: How B2B Marketplaces Will Thrive (For Real, This Time)." June 30, 2013. **gigaom.com/2013/06/30/alibaba-is-just-the-beginning-how-b2b-marketplaces** (accessed March 2014).

Wiebesick, C. "Four B2B Social Media Success Stories: How B2B Companies Can (and Should) Use Social Media." May 24, 2011. **slideshare.net/cwiebesick/four-b2b-social-media-success-stories-how-b2b-companies-can-and-should-use-social-media** (accessed March 2014).

Wirthwein, C., and J. Bannon. *The People Powered Brand: A Blueprint for B2B Brand and Culture Transformation.* Ithaca, NY: Paramount Market Publishing, Inc., 2014.

Zwilling, M. "Smartphone Location Tracking Apps Next Wave is B2B." September 3, 2013. **blog.startupprofessionals.com/2013/09/smartphone-location-tracking-apps-next.html** (accessed March 2014).

Innovative EC Systems: From E-Government to E-Learning, Collaborative Commerce, and C2C Commerce

5

Contents

Electronic supplementary material The online version
of this chapter (doi: 10.1007/978-3-319-10091-3_5)
contains supplementary material, which is available to
authorized users

Learning Objectives

Upon completion of this chapter, you will be able to:
1. Describe various e-government initiatives.
2. Describe e-government activities and implementation issues including government 2.0 and m-government.
3. Describe e-learning, virtual universities, and e-training.
4. Describe e-books and their readers.
5. Describe knowledge management and dissemination as e-commerce.
6. Describe and discuss online advisory systems.
7. Describe collaborative commerce.
8. Describe C2C activities in e-commerce.

OPENING CASE: COMPASS GROUP TURNS MANAGERS INTO DETECTIVES TO ENHANCE E-TRAINING

Compass Group (**compass-group.com**) is a UK-based major provider of food and support services worldwide. The support services include security, janitorial services, building operations and maintenance, and project management. (See **compass-group.com/Support-Services-wwd.htm** and **compass-group.com/about-us.htm**.) According to their financial statement, the company's annual revenue was £17,557 million (in 2013). (For more on the company's financial information, see **ar13.compass-group.com/ assets/pdfs/Compass-AR-2013-Financial- Statements.pdf**, and **ar13.compass-group.com/ our-business/our-regions**.) Their clients include major UK corporations such as Marks & Spencer and Tesco.

The Problem

The company's regional managers used financial performance software to analyze trends and review statistical data available in financial statements related to their functional areas. By defining the causes of problems and explaining unusual financial deviations from budgets, corrections could be planned. However, the company found that the managers had difficulty using the software. Therefore, Compass Group decided to partner with City & Guilds Kineo to train the managers using the financial software from Kineo Learning Solutions (**kineo.com/solutions**). However, some managers were skeptical about e-training (an application of e-learning), so in order to alleviate concerns and secure collaboration and use, it was necessary to convince them of the program's usefulness.

The Solution

To train the regional managers, Compass Group decided to use an attractive approach that would enable rapid mass training at low cost. They decided on e-training.

The implementation team created the "Compass Detective Board Game." The participating managers played the role of "detectives" in the game. Each detective needed to analyze performance and find solutions to problems ("crimes"). Each player had an adaptation to her/his functional area, based on real-life situations. The players received assistance in problem solving so they could gain experience. The players were able to come up with answers to questions such as how to react to a price cut by a competitor or how to determine when a budget deviation is significant. (Read the case study at **kineo.com/case-studies/process-and- technical/compass-group-systems-training**.)

The Results

In the first six months of its existence, the project had some outstanding successes:
- *Improved perceived performance:* Most participants agreed that their performance was likely to improve thanks to the training.
- *Train large numbers of people, quickly:* The e-learning enabled training many more managers rather than using conventional training (at the same cost and time frame).
- *Cost reduction:* The Compass Group saved £495,000 in 6 months, compared with the costs for conventional training.

Sources: Based on City & Guilds Kineo (2011), Training Press Releases (2011), and **compass-group.com** (accessed April 2014).

LESSONS LEARNED FROM THE CASE

E-learning (and e-training) is an EC application that helps organizations electronically teach a large number of students or employees, who are frequently in different locations, to ensure that they can grow and handle their jobs effectively. E-training at Compass Group is based in part on making sure that employees know why training is important to their business, clients, and customers. By creating an e-training program that engaged the trainees, the company not only reduced training costs and successfully trained the employees, it also motivated many employees to embrace e-training. E–learning and e-training are major topics in this chapter. Other innovative systems described in this chapter are e-government, e-books, and consumer-to-consumer EC.

5.1 E-GOVERNMENT: AN OVERVIEW

Electronic government, also known as *e-government* or *digital government* is a growing e-commerce application that encompasses many topics. This section presents the major ones.

Definition and Scope

E-government refers to the use of information technology in general, and e-commerce in particular, to improve the delivery of government services and activities in the public sector, such as: providing citizens with more convenient access to information and services, and providing effective delivery of government services to citizens and businesses as well as improving the performance of government employees. It also is an efficient and effective way for governments to interact with citizens, businesses, and other entities and to improve governmental business transactions (such as buying and selling goods), and to operate effectively within the governments themselves. E-Government includes a large number of activities, as can be seen in the New Zealand case (Online File W5.1) and in **en.wikipedia.org/wiki/E-Government**. For details, see Shark and Toporkoff (2008). For resources, see **w3.org/egov**.

Note that e-government also offers an opportunity to improve the efficiency and effectiveness of the internal operation of a government.

E-government includes the following major categories: government-to-citizens (G2C), government-to-business (G2B), government-to-government (G2G), internal efficiency and effectiveness (IEE), and government-to-employees (G2E). The major activities of the first four categories are provided in Table 5.1 (also see Digital Government Strategy 2012 and Egov 2003). For a description of the range of e-government activities in the United States, see Digital Government Strategy (2012) and **whitehouse. gov/omb/e-gov**. For examples of e-government in Singapore, see **egov.gov.sg**.

Example: The European Commission

The European Commission's Digital Agenda website (**ec.europa.eu/digital-agenda/welcome-digital-agenda**) is an example of a comprehensive e-government system. It is one of the European Union's seven flagships for achieving its 10-year growth strategy. The site is divided into several topics—notably, life and work, public services, ongoing studies, smart cities, and e-health and aging. For details, see **ec.europa.eu/digital-agenda/welcome-digital-agenda**.

The above categories are based on different entities with whom the government is interacting. However, these entities are also interconnected, as shown in the broken lines of Figure 5.1.

The following is a brief description of the major activities conducted between the government and each major entity.

Government-to-Citizens

The **government-to-citizens (G2C)** category includes all the interactions between a government and its citizens that take place electronically. G2C can involve dozens of different initiatives. The basic idea is to enable citizens to interact electronically with the government from anywhere and at any time. G2C applications enable citizens to ask questions of government agencies and receive answers, pay taxes, receive payments and documents, and schedule services, such as employment interviews and medical appointments. For example, in many U.S. states, residents can renew driver's licenses, pay traffic tickets, and make appointments for vehicle emission inspections and driving tests—all online. Governments also can disseminate information on the Web, conduct training, help citizens find employment, administer surveys, and much more. Government services to citizens are provided via citizen portals. The services will vary depending on the country, and on the governmental level (city, county, state country).

The major features of government websites are: information on how to contact the government,

Table 5.1 Representative categories of e-government performance objectives

G2C	G2B
• Reduce the time needed to interact with the government	• Increase the ability for businesses to find, view, and comment on rules and regulations
• Create a friendly single point access to government services for individuals	• Reduce the burden on businesses by enabling online filing of taxes and other documents
• Reduce the time spent in finding federal jobs	• Reduce the time to fill out export forms and locate related information
• Reduce the average time for citizens to find benefits and determine eligibility • Increase the number of citizens who use the Internet to find information on recreational opportunities • Meet the high public demand for information • Improve the value of government services to its citizens • Expand access to information for people with disabilities • Make obtaining financial assistance from the government easier, cheaper, quicker, and more comprehensible	• Reduce the time for businesses to comply with government regulations
G2G	**IEE**
• Decrease time needed to respond to emergency incidents by government agencies	• Increase availability of training programs for government employees
• Reduce the time to verify public records	• Reduce the average time to process clearance forms
• Increase the number of grant programs available for electronic applications	• Increase use of e-travel services within each agency
• Increase efficiency of communication between federal, state, local, and tribal governments	• Reduce time and overhead costs to purchase goods and services throughout the federal government
• Improve collaboration with foreign partners, including governments and institutions	• Plan IT investments more effectively.
• Automate internal processes to reduce costs within the federal government by disseminating the best practices across agencies	• Secure better services at a lower cost
	• Cut government operating costs

Sources: Based on Egov (2003), InfoDev/World Bank (2009), and the authors' experience

Figure 5.1 E-government
categories of activities

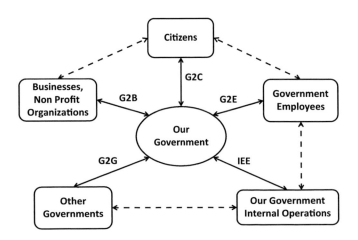

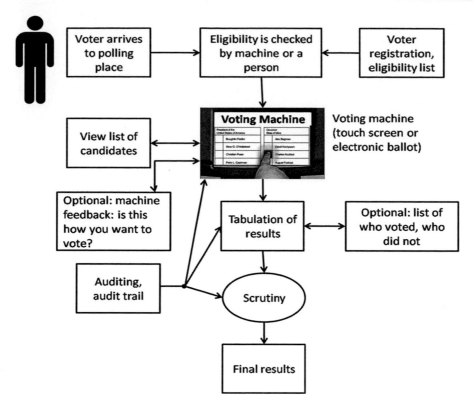

Figure 5.2   The process of using a voting machine

public notices to citizens, links to other sites, educational material, publications, statistics, legal notes, and databases. The major areas of such G2C activities are social services, tourism and recreation, public safety, research and education, downloadable forms, discovery of government services, tax filing, information about public policy, and advice about health and safety issues. G2C is now available on mobile/wireless devices in many countries and local governments.

Another area of G2C activity takes place by solving citizens' problems. The government (or a politician) can use CRM-type software to assign inquiries and problem cases to appropriate staff members (as shown on **ict.govt.nz**). Subsequently, workflow CRM software can be used to track the progress of the problems' resolution.

Note that over 20 countries block some websites for political, social, or other reasons (e.g., China, Iran, Syria). For more on G2C, see **usa.gov/Citizen/Topics/All-Topics.shtml**. For an overview of major citizens' groups and the

services provided to them by the U.S. Department of Labor, see **dol.gov/_sec/e_government_plan/ p41-43_appendixe.htm**.

Two popular examples of G2C are provided next.

Electronic Voting

Voting processes may be subject to errors, manipulation, and fraud. In many countries, there are attempts to "rig" the votes; in others, the losers want a recount. Voting may result in major political crises, as has happened in several countries. Problems with the U.S. 2000 and 2004 presidential elections have accelerated the trend toward electronic voting.

The voting process encompasses a broad spectrum of technological and social activities from voter registration and voter authentication to the casting of ballots and subsequent tallying of results. For an example of this process, see Figure 5.2. Electronic voting automates some or all steps in the process.

Fully electronic voting systems have raised considerable controversy because of a variety of relevant factors, such as the proprietary nature of the software. Typical issues are the difficulties in selling the systems to voters, complex auditing, and the lack of experience in some steps of the process.

From a technology point of view, election fraud could be committed, for example, by directing a computer program to count votes twice for a specific candidate, or to not count votes for another candidate. Therefore, security and auditing measures are key success factors of e-voting. However, considering the amount of fraud that occurs with traditional, manual voting systems and the fact that e-security is improving, e-voting eventually could be the norm. For more information on e-voting, see **en.wikipedia.org/wiki/Electronic_voting** and the Electronic Frontier Foundation (**eff.org**).

Electronic Benefits Transfer

One e-government application that is not new is the electronic benefits transfer (EBT). It has been available since the early 1990s and is now in use in many countries. The U.S. government transfers billions of dollars in benefits to many of its citizens on a regular basis. Beginning in 1993, an attempt was made to deliver benefits to recipients' bank accounts. However, more than 20% of payments go to citizens who do not have a bank account. To solve this problem, the government initiated the use of smart cards (see Chapter 11). Benefit recipients can load the money they receive onto the cards and use the cards at automated teller machines (ATMs), point-of-sale locations, and grocery and other stores, just like other prepaid value cards. The advantage is not only the reduction in processing costs (from about 50¢ per paper check to 2¢ for electronic payment) but also the reduction of fraud. With biometrics (see Chapter 10) coming to smart cards and PCs, officials expect a substantial reduction in fraud. EBT has been implemented in all states since 2004. For more information on EBT in government, see **fns. usda.gov/apd/electronic-benefits-transfer-ebt** and **fns.usda.gov/ebt/general-electronic-benefit-transfer-ebt-information**.

Government-to-Business

Governments seek to automate their interactions with businesses. Although we call this category **government-to-business (G2B)**, the relationship works two ways: government-to-business and business-to-government. Thus, G2B refers to activities where the government sells products to businesses or provides businesses with services and vice versa. Two key G2B activities are e-procurement and the auctioning of government surpluses. For other U.S. G2B initiatives for businesses and nonprofits, see **usa.gov/Business/Business-Gateway.shtml**.

Government E-Procurement

Governments buy large amounts of MROs (maintenance, repair, and operations; Chapter 4) and other materials directly from suppliers. In many cases, RFQ (or tendering) systems are mandated by law. For years, these RFQs were done manually; the systems are now moving online. These systems utilize reverse (buy-side) auction systems, such as those described in Chapter 4. Governments provide all the support for such tendering systems. For additional information about such reverse auctions, see GSA Auctions (**gsaauctions.gov**). For an overview of and to watch a video about GSA auctions, see **gsa.gov/ portal/content/100747?utm_source= FAS&utm_medium=print-radio&utm_term= gsaauctions&utm_campaign=shortcuts**. In the United States, for example, the local housing agencies of HUD (Housing and Urban Development), which provides housing to low-income residents, are moving to e-procurement (see U.S. Department of Housing and Urban Development 2009).

Example 1: Procurement at GSA

The U.S. General Services Administration (**gsa. gov**) uses technologies such as demand aggregation and reverse auctions to buy items for various units of the federal government (see also **government auctions.org** and **liquidation.com**).

Example 2: The U.S. SBA

The Procurement Marketing and Access Network of the Small Business Administration (**sba.gov**) has developed a service called PRO-Net (**pro-net.sba.gov**). It is a searchable database that contracting officers in various U.S. government units can use to find products and services sold by small, disadvantaged businesses, or businesses owned by women.

Group Purchasing

Many government agencies also utilize online group purchasing, which was described in Chapters 1 and 3. A related aspect is *quantity discount*, where suppliers post prices that get lower as quantities of orders increase. A similar method occurs when government buyers initiate group purchasing by posting product requests that other buyers may review and then join the group(s).

Forward E-Auctions

Many governments auction equipment surpluses or other goods, ranging from vehicles to foreclosed real estate. These auctions are now moving to the Internet. Governments can auction from a government website or they can use third-party auction sites such as **ebay.com**, **bid4assets.com**, or **governmentauctions.org**. The U.S. General Services Administration (GSA) in the United States operates a property auction site online (see **gsaauctions.gov**), where real-time auctions for surplus and seized goods are conducted. Some of these auctions are restricted to dealers; others are open to the public (see **governmentauctions.org**).

Government-to-Government

The **government-to-government (G2G)** category consists of EC activities between different units of governments, including those within one governmental body. Many of these are aimed at improving the effectiveness and the efficiency of government operations. Here are a few G2G examples from the United States:

- **Intelink.** Intelink (**intelink.gov**) is an intranet that contains classified information that is shared by the numerous U.S. intelligence agencies. It is a U.S. Government computer system that is provided only for authorized U.S. government use.
- **Federal Case Registry (Department of Health and Human Services).** This service helps state governments locate information about child support, including data on paternity and enforcement of child-support obligations. See the Office of Child Support Enforcement (**acf.hhs.gov/programs/css**) and the Office of Child Support Enforcement Federal Case Registry Overview (**acf.hhs.gov/programs/css/resource/overview-of-federal-case-registry**). For more examples of G2G services, see **govexec.com**, **socialsecurity.gov**, and the New Zealand e-government case in Online File W5.1).

Government-to-Employees and Internal Efficiency and Effectiveness

Governments are introducing various EC initiatives internally. Two areas are illustrated next.

Government-to-Employees (G2E)

Governments are just as interested, as private-sector organizations are, in providing services and information electronically to their employees. **Government-to-employees (G2E)** applications refers to e-commerce activities between the government and its employees. Such activities may be especially useful in enabling efficient e-training of new employees, e-learning for upgrading skills and communication and collaboration activities. Other typical services are: e-payroll, e-human resources management, and e-recruiting.

Examples of G2E services are provided in Online File W.5.1.

Internal Efficiency and Effectiveness (IEE)

Governments have to improve the efficiency and effectiveness of their operations in order to stay within their budgets and avoid criticism. Unfortunately, not all governments (or units within governments) are efficient or effective. Automation, including e-commerce, provides an opportunity to significantly improve operations.

The following example illustrates some e-commerce applications for improving IEE.

Example

The U.S. Office of Management and Budget (OMB) (**whitehouse.gov/omb**) provides a list of activities related to IEE in their FY 2011 'Report to Congress' (see Office of Management and Budget 2012).

This list includes topics such as:

- Federal Cloud Computing Program Management
- Innovative Wireless and Mobile Apps Platform
- FedSpace (a collaborative platform for Federal employees)
- Federal Data Center Consolidation Initiative
- Small Business Dashboard
- IT Dashboard (also available via mobile devices)
- Performance.gov (website with information about performance improvement activities)

In addition, there are traditional IEE-related initiatives such as: e-payroll, e-record management, e-training, integrated acquisition, and e-HRM.

Implementing E-Government

Like most other organizations, government entities want to become digital. Therefore, one can find a large number of EC applications in government organizations. For many examples, see Foley and Hoover (2011) and the government innovators network at **innovations.harvard.edu**.

This section examines some of the trends and issues involved in implementing e-government (see Chan et al. 2011 for an overview). Note that one of the major implementation inhibitors is the desire of many governments to maintain control over the use and dissemination of data and knowledge.

The Transformation to E-Government

The transformation from traditional delivery of government services to full implementation of e-government may be a lengthy process. The business consulting firm Deloitte & Touche conducted a study that identified six stages in the transformation from traditional to e-government. These stages do not have to be sequential, but frequently are, with a seventh stage added by the authors, as shown in Online File W5.2.

All major software companies provide tools and solutions for conducting e-government. One example is Cognos (an IBM Company; see **ibm.com/software/analytics/cognos**). The company also provides free white papers.

E-Government 2.0 and Social Networking

By employing social media tools, new business models, and embracing social networks and user participation, government agencies can raise the effectiveness of their online activities to meet users' needs at a reasonable cost. Such initiatives are referred to as **Government 2.0**. For extensive coverage of content and applications of this topic, see NIC Inc. (2010), Hartley (2011), and McLoughlin and Wilson (2013). Government agencies around the world are now experimenting with social media tools as well as with their own pages and presence on public social network sites. Governments are using Web 2.0 tools mainly for collaboration, dissemination of information, e-learning, and citizen engagement.

Example

Ali (2010) provides an example of how the U.S. Coast Guard uses YouTube, Twitter, and Flickr to disseminate information and discuss their rescue operations. Notable is FEMA's Twitter feed (previously 'FEMA in Focus'), a channel that provides dissemination of FEMA-related information (see **twitter.com/fema**). Law enforcement agencies use social media (such as Facebook and Twitter) to hunt for criminals. (For some examples, see **digitaltrends.com/social-media/**

the-new-inside-source-for-police-forces-social-networks.) For more on how government agencies are expanding their use of social media, see **federalnewsradio.com/445/3547907/Agencies-open-the-door-to-innovative-uses-of-social-media**.

The Potential of E-Government 2.0

Many governments are embarking on government 2.0 initiatives. Several examples are provided in Online File W.5.1.

For an extensive list of resources on social networks in governments, including reports, applications, and policies see **adobe.com/solutions/government.html?romoid=DJHAZ**. E-government software and solutions are provided by most large software vendors (e.g., see Adobe.com's government white papers; **cisco.com/web/strategy/us_government/index.html**; **ibm.com/software/analytics/government**; and **microsoft.com/government/en-us/Pages/default.aspx**). For extensive coverage of e-government, see **wisegeek.com/what-is-e-government.htm**.

M-Government

Mobile government (m-government) is the implementation of e-government applications using wireless platforms. It is done mostly in G2C (e.g., see Government of Canada Wireless Portal (**mgovworld.org**). M-government uses wireless Internet infrastructure and devices. It is a value-added service, because it enables governments to reach a larger number of citizens (e.g., via smartphone or Twitter) and it can be more cost-effective than wireline-based EC platforms. It is very useful in disasters (e.g., emergency notifications), is fast (e.g., in conducting surveys and polls), and it is convenient for citizens as well. In addition, governments employ large numbers of mobile workers who are supported by wireless devices.

Example: Public Buses in Honolulu

An example of a mobile government project is the city government–run bus location system (an app) in Honolulu, Hawaii called 'DaBus' (**honolulu.gov/mobile**). Using your cell phone, you can find the estimated arrival time of any of the buses at

more than 4,000 bus stops. Buses are equipped with GPS devices (Chapter 6) that transmit the bus's location in real time. The system then calculates the estimated arrival time for each stop. Similar systems exist in many other places (e.g., in Singapore 'IRIS'; in the U.S. 'NextBus,' and in the UK 'JourneyPlanner' apps).

M-government can help make public information and government services available anytime and anywhere. See **en.wikipedia.org/wiki/M-government, fiercemobilegovernment.com** and **usa.gov/mobileapps.shtml**. A specific example of e-government would be texting a mass alert to the public in the event of a major disaster.

The Benefits of M-Government

The major benefits of m-government are:

- More citizens and employees can be reached (anyplace, anytime)
- Cost reduction (e.g., by increasing productivity of employees; reduced budgets)
- Modernizing the operations of the government (e.g., employ mobile devices)
- Employees can bring their own mobile devices to work, saving hardware and software costs.
- Providing quality, flexible services to the public.
- Increasing the reach and speed for public dissemination of information.

In addition, many of the generic benefits of m-commerce (Chapter 6) are valid in m-government too.

Some Implementation Issues

Representative issues of implementing m-government are:

- An expensive infrastructure may be needed to supplement the existing traditional infrastructure. More infrastructures are needed for the wireless systems as well as for the increased volume of information flow.
- It may be difficult to maintain security and privacy of information on public mobile networks.

- For many citizens, mobile devices are too small or complex to use.
- In many countries there is a lack of standards and legislation regarding the use of data delivered wirelessly.

Applications

Several wireless applications suitable for e-government are presented in Chapter 6. Notable are G2E applications, especially for field employees, and G2C information discovery, such as the U.S. Department of Transportation's (DOT) 511 (see **fhwa.dot.gov/trafficinfo/511.htm**). Another example is the city of Bergen, Norway, which provides extensive wireless portable tourism services (see **visitnorway.com/us/games-and-more/free-app-from-visit-norway**). For a comprehensive list of emerging applications, see Trimi and Sheng (2008), **howto.gov/mobile**, and **apps.usa.gov**.

For other implementation issues, success stories, applications, benefits, and so forth, see MedLibrary (2010), Mobile Government Consortium International (**mgovernment.org**), and **m-government.info**.

SECTION 5.1 REVIEW QUESTIONS

1. Define e-government.
2. What are the four major categories of e-government services?
3. Describe G2C.
4. Describe how e-voting works.
5. Describe the two main areas of G2B activities.
6. How does government use EC internally and when dealing with other governments?
7. Describe e-government social networking activities. What are some potential benefits?
8. Describe m-government and its implementation issues.

5.2   E-LEARNING, E-TRAINING, AND E-BOOKS

The topic of e-learning is gaining much attention, especially because first-rate universities such as MIT, Harvard, and Stanford in the United States and Oxford in the United Kingdom are implementing it. Figure 5.3 shows the forces that are driving the transition from traditional education to online learning. E-learning also is growing as a method for training and knowledge creation in the business world and is becoming a major e-business activity. In this section, we will discuss several topics related to e-learning.

The Basics of E-Learning: Definitions and Concepts

There are several definitions of e-learning. A working definition of **e-learning** is the use of online delivery of educational materials and methods using information technologies, for the purposes of learning, teaching, training, or gaining knowledge at any time, and at many different locations (see **people.howstuffworks.com/elearning1.htm**, **en.wikipedia.org/wiki/E-learning**, and **webopedia.com/TERM/E/e_learning.html**). For a free comprehensive guide to e-learning, see Naidu (2003).

E-learning is also broader than the term *online learning*, which generally refers exclusively to Web-based learning. E-learning includes *m-learning* (or *mobile learning*) that is used when the material is delivered wirelessly to smartphones, tablets, or other mobile devices (description to follow). E-learning is synonymous with *computer-based instruction*, *computer-based training*, *online education*, and other terms.

E-learning can be useful as both an environment for facilitating learning at schools as well as an environment for efficient and effective corporate training. It appears in a variety of electronically supported learning and teaching activities, ranging from virtual classrooms to mobile conferences. For an overview on how e-learning works, including its major concepts, tools, delivery systems, and benefits, see Garrison (2011). For a theory of e-learning, see Harasim (2011). E-learning includes a variety of methods of computer-facilitated learning ranging from self study with DVDs to online degrees offered by universities. E-learning may also include the use of Web-based teaching materials and hypermedia, multimedia CD-ROMs, learning and teaching portals, discussion boards, collaborative software, e-mail, blogs, wikis, chat rooms, computer-aided assessments, educational animation, simulations, games, learning management software, electronic voting systems, and more (possibly a few of these combined).

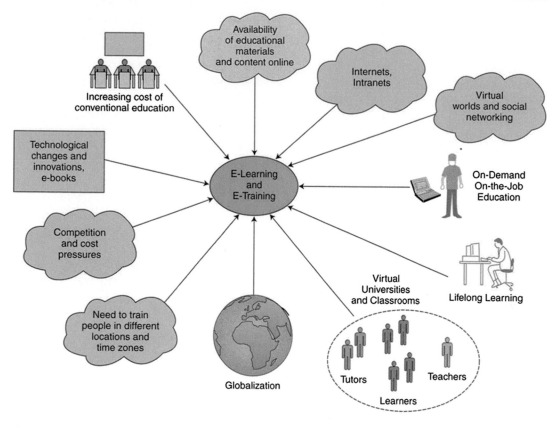

Figure 5.3   The drivers of e-learning

An interesting school without classrooms is the Hellerup School in Denmark. Students there 'learn by doing' and even determine the best way they can learn. For how the school operates, see **theguardian.com/smart-class-2025/denmark-hellerup-schoop-learning-by-doing** and Millar (2013). For details, see **en.wikipedia.org/wiki/E-learning** and Horton (2011). For a community and resources for e-learning professionals, see **elearningguild.com**.

M-Learning

A special category of e-learning is **m-learning**, or mobile learning, which refers to e-learning or other forms of education using mobile devices. Thus, one can learn at any place where a mobile device works. M-learning deals with communication and teaching in wireless environments. Special attention is given to situations where the instructors and the teaching materials are mobile. This technology enables learners to work and collaborate more easily than in offline situations. An example is MobileLearn (**waldenu.edu/about-walden/mobilelearnsm-walden-university-online**), an online learning program offered by Walden University (**waldenu.edu**), an online university that extensively uses m-learning. Some offline universities are using mobile learning as well. One such university is Abilene Christian University (**acu.edu**); faculty are focused on using iPad learning and teaching in their curriculum (see **acu.edu/technology/mobilelearning**). For further details including case studies and resources, see **m-learning.org** and **en.wikipedia.org/wiki/M-learning**. See also a slide presentation titled "What is M-Learning" at **slideshare.net/aurionlearning/what-is-mlearning**.

Benefits and Drawbacks of E-Learning

E-learning has many benefits both to the teaching institutions and to the learners. However, it also has several drawbacks, thus making it a controversial topic.

Benefits of E-Learning

In the Internet age, skills and knowledge need to be *continually updated* and refreshed (lifetime learning) to keep up with today's fast-paced business and technological changes. This means that more people need to learn and frequently do so in non-traditional ways. E-learning supports such learning due to the following capabilities and benefits (based in part on Garrison 2011; Agarwal et al. 2010; and Horton 2011):

- **Education.** Students can learn at home and keep their regular jobs while in school. Busy homemakers can earn degrees.
- **Learning and training time reduction.** E-learning can expedite training time by up to 50%.
- **Cost reduction.** The cost of providing a learning experience can be reduced by 50 to 70% when classroom lectures are replaced by e-learning sessions. This includes reduced faculty cost, no classrooms, less or no travel time.
- **Large number and diversity of learners.** E-learning can provide training to a large number of people from diverse cultural backgrounds and educational levels, even though they are at different locations in different time zones. Large companies such as Cisco Systems, Inc. (**cisco.com**) provide online training courses to a large number of employees, customers and business partners.
- **Innovative teaching.** Ability to provide innovative teaching methods such as special engagements, interaction with experts, interaction with learners in other countries, and so forth.
- **Measurement and assessment of progress.** Ability to assess progress in real time, find areas of difficulties, and design remedial work.
- **Self-paced and motivation learning.** E-learning students usually are self-paced and self-motivated. These charac-

teristics may result in higher content retention (25 to 60% higher than with traditional lecture-based training).
- **Richness and quality.** E-learning enables the use of top instructors as well as employing rich multimedia support. This may make learning more enjoyable. Difficult content can be made interesting and easy to understand. Overall, the quality of learning may increase.
- **Flexibility.** E-learners are able to adjust the time, location, content, and speed of learning according to their own personal schedules.
- **Updated and consistent teaching material.** It is almost impossible to economically update the information in textbooks more frequently than every 2 or 3 years; e-learning can offer real time access to the most updated knowledge. Delivery of e-learning may be more consistent than that of material presented in traditional classroom learning, because variations among teachers and teaching materials are minimized.
- **Ability to learn from mobile devices.** This helps learning in any place and at any time as well as providing support to learners by teachers and peers.
- **Expert knowledge.** In contrast with the knowledge of a single instructor in the classroom, e-learning may include the knowledge of several experts, each of whom prepares a teaching module in his or her area of expertise.
- **Fear-free environment.** E-learning can facilitate learning for students who may not wish to join a face-to-face group discussion to interact with peers or teachers.

E-learning can be very useful in developing countries. For an example of positive results in Jamaica, see Thompson (2014). For the top 10 e-learning statistics in 2014 with an infographic, see **elearningindustry.com/top-10-e-learning-statistics-for-2014-you-need-to-know**.

Drawbacks and Challenges of E-Learning

Despite the numerous benefits for both the learners and the teaching organizations, e-learning does have some drawbacks, such as the following:

- **Need for instructor retraining.** Some instructors do not have the knowledge to teach by electronic means and may require training, which costs money.
- **Equipment needs and support services.** Additional funds are needed (by the teaching institute) to purchase e-learning systems that supplement traditional ones. These are needed for e-learning creation, use, and maintenance.
- **Lack of face-to-face interaction and campus life style.** Many feel that the intellectual stimulation that takes place through interaction in a classroom with "live" instructors and peers cannot fully be replicated with e-learning.
- **Assessments and examinations.** In the higher education environment, one criticism is that professors may not be able to adequately assess student work completed through e-learning. There is no way of knowing, for example, who actually completed the assignments or exams. (Nevertheless, the same is true for any homework done outside the classroom).
- **Maintenance and updating.** Although e-learning materials are easier to update than traditionally published materials, there are practical difficulties (e.g., cost, instructors' time) in keeping e-learning materials current. The content of e-learning material can be difficult to maintain due to the lack of ownership of, and accountability for, website material. The developers of online content might not be those who update it.
- **Protection of intellectual property.** It is difficult and expensive to control the transmission of copyrighted works downloaded from the e-learning platform.
- **Student retention.** Without some human feedback and intervention, it may be difficult to keep certain students engaged and energetic.

According to Rossett and Marshall (2010), the top constraints for corporate e-learning are: (1) too costly to create and maintain; (2) difficulties persuading people to learn in new ways; (3) insufficient technological support; (4) employee hesitation to contribute to social learning; and (5) learners may prefer traditional classroom instruction. For a business case on e-learning, see Agarwal et al. (2010). For a practical guide on how to teach online, see Ko and Rossen (2010).

Advanced technologies can reduce some of the above and other drawbacks and constraints. For example, some online software products have features that help stimulate student thinking. Biometric controls can be used to verify the identity of students who are taking examinations from home. However, these features add to the costs of e-learning.

For more about the disadvantages of e-learning, see **peoplelearn.homestead.com/ELearning/Introduction/Disadvantages.html**.

Distance Learning and Online Universities

The term **distance learning**, also known as *distance education*, refers to education conducted from home or other place, anytime. In such a case, the student is separated from a classroom by distance and possibly time. Sometimes students meet once or twice at a physical location in order to get to know each other, meet the instructor or coordinator, or take examinations. Distance learning is becoming widely used in universities and learning institutions around the globe. Major universities offer courses and degrees via this mode, which is becoming more recognized and acceptable. For details, see **onlineeducation.org**.

Virtual Universities—Real Degrees

The concept of **virtual universities**, online universities where students take classes from home via the Internet, is expanding rapidly. Hundreds of thousands of students in many countries, from the United Kingdom to Israel to Thailand, are taking online classes. A large number of existing universities, including Stanford University and other top-tier universities, offer online education of some form; for example, MIT offers thousands of their courses online (see courses at **ocw.mit. edu**). Millions of independent learners from all over the world (students, professors, self-learners) log on to the MIT OpenCourseWare site each year (see **ocw.mit.edu/about** and **ocw.mit. edu/about/site-statistics**). Some universities, such as University of Phoenix (**phoenix.edu**), National University (**nu.edu**), and the University of Maryland (**umuc.edu**), offer hundreds of courses and dozens of degrees online to students worldwide. The California Virtual Campus (**cvc. edu**) provides a directory and links to thousands of courses and online degree programs offered by colleges and universities in California (see **cvc. edu/students/courses**). For information about distance learning resources and online universities, see **distancelearn.about.com**. For a list of the top online MBA programs in the world, see **onlinemba.com/rankings**. According to Chubb and Moe (2012), "online technology promises historic improvements in the quality of and access to higher education." For practical advice on taking classes online, see Sparkman (2012).

Innovations in E-Learning

There are many innovations in e-learning, one of which is shown in the following example.

Example: E-Learning Via Robots

In December 2010, the city of Daegu in South Korea, introduced 29 robots into 19 elementary schools. Each robot, about 3.2-feet tall, was designed to teach English to the students. Developed by the Korea Institute of Science and Technology (KIST), the robots roll around on wheels and ask questions in English (see Figure 5.4). (For details see **cnet.com/news/ korean-schools-welcome-more-robot-teachers**.)

The robots can be moved around the classroom by the instructor (via remote control), which facilitates the interaction of teachers with students. The robots can read books to the students and even "dance" to music. The robots display the face of a Caucasian "teacher" as an avatar. The tutoring is actually provided by experienced teachers in the Philippines, who are paid much less than Korean teachers. The robots are programed to use the most effective and current teaching methods (e.g., using multimedia games).

Cameras detect the Filipino teachers' facial expressions and instantly reflect them on the robot's avatar face. The students participate more actively, especially the shy ones who are afraid of speaking out loud. The robots are also used in remote rural areas where English teachers are in short supply.

For more examples on educational robotic teachers, see **intorobotics.com/advanced-robots-designed-for-educational-use-in-schools-and-kindergartens**. For more on robotic telepresence for distance education, watch the 2 minute video and see the text at **verizon.com/powerfulanswers/ solutions/education**.

Online Corporate Training

Like educational institutions, a large number of business organizations are using e-learning on a large scale. Many companies, such as Cisco Systems (**cisco.com**), offer online training. A 2008 study by the American Society for Training & Development found that nearly one-third of corporate training content was delivered electronically (reported by Rossett and Marshall 2010).

Corporate training is driven by multiple factors and is often done via intranets and corporate portals. However, the students use the Internet as well. It has several variations, one of which is *on-demand online training*, which is offered by software companies such as Citrix Systems (**citrix. com**). However, in large corporations with multiple sites, and for studies from home, the Internet is used to access the online material. Vendors'

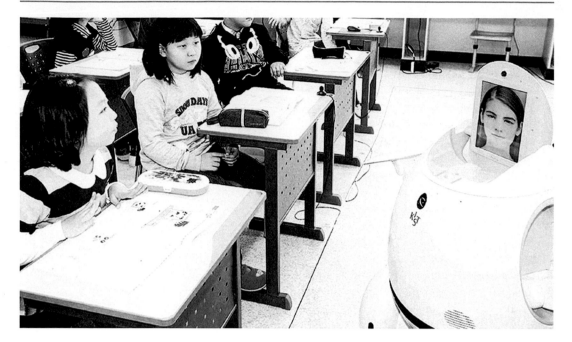

Figure 5.4 The Engkey – Robot English teacher (Source: The Korea Advanced Institute of Science and Technology.) Used with permission

success stories of online training and educational materials can be found at **adobe.com/resources/learning** and at **brightwave.co.uk**. For a comprehensive guide to online training, see Kaattari and Trottier (2013). For how e-learning helps in training new employees, see Robb (2012).

Example

Dresser-Rand is a global U.S. corporation that makes compression equipment. It has over 5,500 employees in 50 different locations in 26 countries that speak 14 different languages. The company needs to do extensive training due to growth and employee retirement. Previously, the company used over 600 training vendors to conduct training. A major challenge was the update of the teaching material due to technological changes. Using the learning management system (LMS) from Coastal eLearning (**training.dupont.com**; now a part of DuPont Sustainable Solutions), the company deployed a comprehensive online training program via Dresser-Rand University,

saving over $1 million per year. To read the case study, see **training.dupont.com/pdf/case-study/dresser-rand-v1211.pdf** .

Using Computer Games for Training Current and New Employees

There is an emerging trend to use computer simulation games for recruitment and training.

Example

Marriott International developed a game "My Marriott Hotel," available on Facebook for help in recruiting and training. According to Berzon (2011), the players learn how hotels and their restaurants operate. Initially, Marriott developed a game for the kitchen. The players needed to choose what ingredients to use for different foods (based on price and quality). The players also learned how to select employees from a pool of candidates and make decisions about equipment purchasing. They also learned about food quality.

Social Networks and E-Learning

Since its inception, social networking has been interrelated with learning (e.g., see Mason and Rennie 2008; Kidd and Chen 2009). A new term, **social learning**, also known as *e-learning 2.0*, has been coined to describe the learning, training, and knowledge sharing in social networks and/or facilitated with social software tools (see Bingham and Conner 2010 and Cobb 2011). Social environments facilitate high-tech based training, making it possible for learners to share their experiences with others. Thus, several companies already are using social networking for training and development purposes (e.g., see **advancinginsights.com** and Wang and Ramiller 2009). Social learning is based on *social learning theory,* which was developed by Bandura (1969). For details, see **en.wikipedia.org/wiki/Social_learning_theory**.

Some students use Facebook, LinkedIn, Pinterest, Twitter, and so forth to connect with other pupils. For example, learners can study together, discuss topics or brainstorm online. Unfortunately, the distractions found on these networks can make it difficult to focus on learning. Some companies use social media to engage employees in group learning via knowledge sharing (see Zielinski 2012).

Several social networks (or communities) are dedicated to learning and training (e.g., see **e-learning.co.uk**). An example of a social network for learning is LearnHub (**learnhub.com**), which is dedicated to international education. Some scholars believe that the future of e-learning is social learning (e.g., see Hart 2009).

According to Derven (2009) and the authors' experiences, social networking technology possesses the following capabilities that may facilitate learning:

- *Connect learners in a learning project.* It enables people to connect in real time for discussion, collaboration, and problem solving.

- *Make 'social' part of the company's learning strategy.*
- *Build the know-how of experts.*
- *Enable learners to engage.* Generation X and Millennial workers use Web 2.0 tools extensively for interacting among themselves and with others. Organizations can reach out to this group and use social networks for training.
- *Use platforms such as Pinterest to develop creativity in design and to use images to sharpen some learning skills.*
- *Provide relevant content prior to offline meetings for voting, or requesting supplements.* This can enrich and facilitate classroom delivery.
- *Link learners to relevant resources and let them rate and share opinions.*
- *Quickly identify the training needs and implementation issues of individuals and groups.*
- *Have learners provide social support to each other.*
- *Improve and expedite learning-related communication (e.g., via Twitter).*

Many universities combine e-learning and social networking; also, numerous professors have blogs and wikis for their classes and encourage communication and collaboration via Facebook.

Bingham and Conner (2010) explain why and how social media can provide solutions to some of the most pressing educational challenges.

For more about the definition of social learning, see Marcia Conner's blog at **marciaconner.com/blog/defining-social-learning**.

Learning in Virtual Worlds and Second Life

A number of interesting learning initiatives have been implemented in virtual worlds, especially in Second Life (SL). Users can participate in simulations, role-plays, construction projects, and social events. Learners can use virtual worlds to explore places they cannot afford to visit otherwise, as well as fantasy worlds.

Many people see SL and other virtual worlds as an opportunity to carry out learning projects that would be impossible in the real world because of constraints such as geography or cost (e.g., experiment with imaginary environments and processes). Others see virtual worlds as a place and opportunity to engage a younger generation of learners, many of whom are impatient or unsatisfied with traditional forms of education and training. Therefore, many refer to SL as an important classroom of the future. For more about education in Second Life, see **secondlife. com/destinations/learning** and **wiki.secondlife. com/wiki/Second_Life_Education**.

Learning in virtual worlds also offers the possibility of collaboration. For example, managerial training is no longer a matter of listening to lectures in a classroom, or at best, interacting with a learning program. Now learners can interact and collaborate with each other as well with people in social networks around the globe. Learning a foreign language, team building, and leadership all can benefit from online group interaction in virtual worlds.

Learning in virtual worlds in general, and in SL in particular, is growing slowly. Some universities created campuses in SL where instructors meet students, interact with them, and even conduct formal classes. For example, Indiana University conducted a demonstration of the university's Second Life island (see **uits.iu.edu/ page/bbcn** and **world.secondlife.com/place/ ad50ecb7-4f76-091c-3187-7706eb19e0fc**). For a comprehensive list of resources, see **secondlife. com/wiki/Second_Life_Education**.

Visual Interactive Simulation

An effective technology for e-training and e-learning is *visual interactive simulation* (VIS), which uses computer graphic displays to present the impact of evaluating alternative solutions to problems. It differs from regular graphics in that the user can manipulate the decision-making process and see the results of the interventions. Some

learners respond better to graphic displays, especially when they are interactive. For example, VIS was used to examine the operations of a physician clinic environment within a physician network in an effort to provide high-quality medical care. The simulation system identified the most important input factors that significantly affected performance. These inputs, when properly managed, led to lower costs and a higher level of medical care.

VIS systems provide the following major potential benefits:

- Shorten learning time.
- Aid in teaching how to operate complex equipment.
- Enable self-paced learning, any place, any time.
- Aid in memorization.
- Lower overall training costs.
- Record an individual's learning progress and improve on it.

Visual interactive simulation can facilitate learning on-demand.

Learning On Demand

A newly emerging learning trend is **learning on-demand** or "*just-in-time learning.*" The basic idea is that learners can study anywhere whenever they are ready. Several universities already offer such programs (e.g., see Kentucky Community & Technology College System; **learnondemand. kctcs.edu**). In a learning on-demand environment, courses or other learning materials are available whenever and wherever a learner needs them.

For a comprehensive discussion of learning on-demand, see **en.wikipedia.org/wiki/Demand-side_learning** and the survey done by Allen and Seaman (2009). See also **ondemand.blackboard. com** and **strategicmodularity.com/2013/09/ learning-on-demand**. Software for learning on-demand is provided by major vendors such as SAP (SAP Learning Hub; see **sapappsdevelop-mentpartnercenter.com/en/build/sap-learn-ing-hub**), Adobe (**adobe.com**), IBM (**ibm.com**), and Citrix (**citrix.com**). For a virtual training demo and case studies go to **infozone.clomedia. com/unifair**.

Also, see **gotomeetings.com**.

E-Learning Management Systems

A **learning management system (LMS)** (also known as a course management system) consists of software applications for managing e-training and e-learning programs including content, scheduling, delivery tips, and so forth. According to Ellis (2009), Dvorak (2011), Capterra Inc. Learning Management System Software (**capterra.com/learning-management-system-software**) and the authors' experiences, a robust LMS should be able to:

> - Provide effective student-instructor interactions.
> - Centralize and automate program administration.
> - Enable the use of self-service and self-guided e-learning services.
> - Create and rapidly deliver learning content modules.
> - Provide a single point of access to all e-learning online materials.
> - Help manage compliance requirements.
> - Consolidate training initiatives on a scalable Web-based platform.
> - Support the portability of systems.
> - Increase the efficiency and effectiveness of e-learning.
> - Personalize content and enable knowledge reuse.

Many companies (e.g., Saba Software, Inc.; **saba.com/us/lms**, SumTotal Systems; **sumtotal systems.com**) provide methodologies, software, hardware, and consultation about e-learning and its management. For examples, see Clark and Mayer (2011). For more on LMS, see **en.wikipedia.org/wiki/Learning_management_system** and watch the video titled "What is a Learning Management System?" (2:51 minutes) at **proprofs.com/c/category/lms**.

Note that it is possible to control what the students are doing when they self study. For example, according to Streitfeld (2013), teachers can find out when students are skipping pages, not bothering to take notes, or failing to highlight significant passages.

One of the most effective tools for learning management is Blackboard Inc. (**blackboard.com**; now combined with WebCT). A brief description follows.

Example 1: Blackboard

Blackboard Inc. (**blackboard.com**) is the world's largest supplier of course management system software for educational institutions. How do Blackboard products work? A textbook publisher places a book's content, teaching notes, quizzes, and other materials on a Blackboard in a standardized format. Instructors can access modules and transfer them on to their university's Blackboard sites, which can be accessed by their students.

A professor can easily incorporate a book's content into Blackboard's software. As of 2009, Blackboard also delivers corporate and government employee training programs worldwide which increases productivity and reduces costs. For details, see **blackboard.com** and **en.wikipedia.org/wiki/Blackboard_Inc.**.

Example 2: Moodle

An alternative to Blackboard is a mostly free open source system called Moodle (see **moodle.org** and Dvorak 2011).

Electronic Books (E-Books)

An **electronic book (e-book)** is a book in digital format that can be read on a computer screen, mobile device (e.g., a tablet, iPhone), or on a dedicated device known as an *e-reader*. A major event in electronic publishing occurred in 2000, when Stephen King's book *Riding the Bullet* was published exclusively online. For $2.50, readers were able to purchase the e-book on Amazon.com and other e-book providers. Several hundred thousand copies were sold in a few days. However, hackers broke the security protection, copied the book and distributed free copies of the book online. (See **bookbusinessmag.com/article/after-riding-bullet-12555/1#**.)

Publishers of e-books have since become more sophisticated, and online publishing has become more secure. Today there are several types of e-books that can be delivered and read in various ways:

- **Via a dedicated reader.** The book must be downloaded to an e-reader such as Amazon's Kindle.
- **Via Web access.** Readers can locate a book on the publisher's website and read it there. The book cannot be downloaded.
- **Via Web download and smart phones.** Readers can download the book to a PC.
- **Via a general-purpose reader.** The book can be downloaded to a mobile device such as an iPad or iPhone.
- **Via a Web server.** The contents of a book are stored on a Web server and downloaded for print-on-demand (which is discussed later in this book).

Most e-books require some type of payment. Readers either pay before they download a book from a website, such as buying a Kindle copy on Amazon.com, or they pay when they order the special CD-ROM edition of a book. Today, Amazon.com offers hundreds of thousands of e-books, e-newspapers (including international ones), and other digital products. All are cheaper than the hard-copy version (e.g., new release books may cost $10 or less). There are many free e-books as well (e.g., **free-ebooks.net** and **onlinebooks.library.upenn.edu**).

Devices for Reading E-Books

The major device used to read an e-book is an e-reader. Most e-readers are lightweight (about 10 ounces) and are convenient to carry. The major e-readers and tablets are listed and compared at **the-ebook-reader.com**. Between 2010 and 2012 there was a price war among all the main e-reader manufacturers.

Several other aids are available to help readers who want to read a large amount of material online. For example, Microsoft ClearType (**microsoft.com/typography/ClearTypeInfo.mspx**) and CoolType from Adobe (**adobe.com**) can be used to improve screen display, colors, and font sizes. Glowing screens can help you read in the dark (e.g., Kindle Touch and the Kindle Fire have a built-in light).

Combining E-Readers and Tablets

The trend today is to combine e-readers with tablet computers as was initiated with Amazon's Kindle Fire. The 7-inch portable devices allow people to read books, magazines, and documents, and listen to audio books. Users can play games, listen to music, watch movies and TV shows, and much more. Kindle has Internet access via Wi-Fi, so social network access and e-mail is available also. Finally, with Amazon's Kindle Owner's Lending Library, Kindle owners who have Amazon Prime can choose from a selection of more than 500,000 books to borrow, for free with no due dates.

Note: Tablet manufacturers also offer a combination of e-readers and tablets. The difference is that e-reader-based products such as Kindle Fire have less computing capabilities, while tablets such as iPad, have a less capable e-reader and are more expensive (see Falcone 2012 for a comparison).

Advantages and Limitations of E-Books

For e-books to make an impact, they must offer advantages to both readers and publishers. Otherwise, there would be little incentive to change from traditional books. Indeed, e-book sales are exploding due to the following advantages:

- Ability to store hundreds of books on a small mobile device (7″ to 10″). (External storage can hold much more.)
- Lower cost to buyers. The simple e-reader model costs less than $75; the tablet-based less than $200.

- Searchable text—you can show links and connect easily to the Web.
- Instant delivery via downloads from anywhere. The tablet-based models provide you with many of the capabilities of other types of mobile computers.
- Portability—they go where you go.
- Easy integration of content from several sources.
- Durability—they are built stronger than a traditional book (but they can break if you are not careful). Also, readers tend not to lose them (again, you need to be careful).
- Ability to enlarge the font size for easy reading and to add light if needed.
- Media rich (audio, color, video, etc.).
- Minimal cost for printing out a hard copy.
- Good readability in bright sunlight (able to read books outdoors).
- Easy updating of content.
- Almost no wear and tear.
- Easy to find out-of-print books.

The primary advantage that e-books offer publishers is lower production, marketing, and distribution (shipment) costs, which have a significant impact on the price of books (e-textbooks are about 50% cheaper than print versions). Other advantages for publishers are lower updating and reproduction costs, the ability to reach many readers, and the ease of combining chapters from several books to create customized textbooks, so professors can use materials from different books (usually by the same publisher) in one course.

A number of schools are experimenting with eliminating textbooks altogether and using an Internet-based curriculum (they lend iPads to all students). Finally, the light weight of the tablet can eliminate the back pain that people, especially school children, have from carrying backpacks full of heavy books.

Of course, e-books have some limitations: They require hardware and software that may be too expensive for some readers; some people have difficulty reading large amounts of material on a relatively small computer screen; batteries may run out; and there are multiple, competing software and hardware standards to choose from, confusing the buyers. Several of these obstacles may lessen in time.

A Final Note: Is This the End of Printed Books?

According to Amazon.com, in 2011, the sales of e-books on their site considerably exceeded the sales of hardcover and paperback books. (See **nytimes.com/2011/05/20/technology/20amazon.html** and Leggatt 2012).

Despite the limitations, e-books have become very popular, especially due to sophisticated e-readers. For example, even the Harry Potter books are now available in electronic format and they are not encrypted, so that readers can move the books between mobile devices and even to a PC. For a comparison between e-books and printed books, see **thrall.org/docs/ebooksand-books.pdf** and **en.wikipedia.org/wiki/E-book** .

The question is: Will most printed books be eliminated? The trend is very clear. Sales of printed books are on the decline, while e-books are up. With Amazon's free loan of Kindle books to their Prime members, we expect even more people reading e-books. Are paper books going to disappear? (See discussion by Vaughan-Nichols 2012). For the advantages of e-books versus traditional books, see **online-bookstores-review.toptenreviews.com/the-advantages-of-ebooks-versus-traditional-books.html**.

SECTION 5.2 REVIEW QUESTIONS

1. Define e-learning and describe its drivers and benefits.
2. List some of the major drawbacks of e-learning and describe how they can be prevented.
3. Describe virtual universities and distance learning.
4. Define e-training and describe how it is done.

5. Describe the connection between e-learning and social networking.
6. Describe learning in virtual worlds.
7. List some e-learning tools, and describe Blackboard and visual interactive simulation (VIS).
8. Describe e-books.
9. What is an e-reader? What are its major capabilities?
10. List the major advantages and limitations of e-books to their users.

5.3   KNOWLEDGE MANAGEMENT, ADVISORY SYSTEMS, AND ELECTRONIC COMMERCE

The term *knowledge management* is frequently mentioned in discussions about e-learning. Why is this? To answer this question, you first need to understand what knowledge management is.

An Overview of Knowledge Management

Knowledge management and e-learning are both centered on knowledge. Whereas e-learning uses knowledge to enhance individual learning, knowledge management is essential for improving the operation of individuals' organizations, or teams. Knowledge is one of the most important assets in any organization, and thus it is important to capture, store, secure, and reuse (share) it. These are the major purposes of knowledge management. Thus, **knowledge management (KM)** refers to the process of capturing or creating knowledge, storing and protecting it, updating it constantly, disseminating it, and using it whenever necessary (see **en.wikipedia.org/wiki/Knowledge_management** and Bahal 2011).

Knowledge in organizations is collected from both external and internal sources. It is then examined, interpreted, refined, and stored in what is called an *organizational knowledge base,* the repository for the enterprise's knowledge. A major purpose of an organizational knowledge base is to allow for *knowledge sharing.*

Knowledge Management Types and Activities

Organizational knowledge is embedded in the following key resources: (1) human capital, which includes employee knowledge, competencies, intelligence, and creativity; (2) organizational capital, which includes stored organizational experiences (e.g., best practices, patents, manuals, teaching materials); and (3) customer and partner capital, which includes the experience of working with customers and business partners.

This organizational knowledge must be managed properly and leveraged through sharing and dissemination. This is the major purpose of KM, which has the following major tasks:

- **Create knowledge.** Knowledge is created as people gain more experience (e.g., trial-and-error) and education. Sometimes, external knowledge is brought in (e.g., provided by vendors and consultants).
- **Capture knowledge.** Existing knowledge must be identified and assembled. Remember that, a considerable amount of knowledge is not documented, and just dwells in people's memory.
- **Refine knowledge.** New knowledge must be placed in context so that it is actionable. This is why human insights (tacit qualities) must be captured along with explicit facts.
- **Store knowledge.** Useful knowledge must be stored into an easily retrievable format in a secured knowledge repository.
- **Update knowledge.** The knowledge must be kept current. It must be reviewed to verify that it is relevant and accurate; if not, it must be updated.
- **Disseminate knowledge.** Knowledge must be made available in a useful format to anyone in the organization who needs it, and who is authorized to access it.

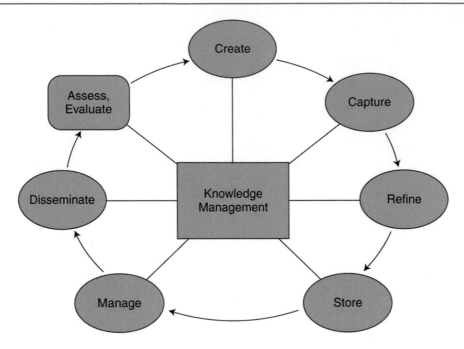

Figure 5.5 The knowledge management system cycle

These tasks can be viewed as a cyclical process, as shown in Figure 5.5. The objective of e-commerce is to automate KM activities as well as help in using the stored knowledge.

For a comprehensive list of KM activities and tools, see **en.wikipedia.org/wiki/Knowledge_management**, **kmworld.com**, FinRM Financial Risk Management (**riskmanagement.finrm.com**), and Awad and Ghaziri (2010).

Knowledge Sharing

Knowledge is of limited value if not updated and shared. The ability to share and then distribute knowledge decreases its cost per user and increases its effectiveness. Shared knowledge can also decrease risk and uncertainty and facilitate problem solving. An example of a knowledge-sharing system at Infosys Technologies is provided in Case 5.2.

CASE 5.1: EC APPLICATION: KNOWLEDGE MANAGEMENT AT INFOSYS TECHNOLOGIES

The Problem

Infosys Technologies (**infosys.com**), a software services company based in India (with over 158,000 employees as of December 2013), provides outsourcing and consulting services worldwide. Infosys develops IT solutions for some of the largest corporations in the world. Between 1997 and 2010, Infosys had experienced an annual growth rate of 30%. Therefore, the company faced a challenge of keeping its large employee base up-to-date, and staying ahead of its competitors by ensuring that the best practices were available to its employees anytime from anywhere, so that employees could reuse the accumulated knowledge. The company uses mottos like "Learn once, use anywhere." However, how does such a large organization do this?

The Solution

Infosys started its KM in the early 1990s and it continues to this day. The initial KM initiative, known as *'bodies of knowledge (BOK),'* encouraged employees to document their best practices by cataloging them according to subjects. These best practices were then shared companywide (by hard copy and later via the intranet). This early effort turned into the formal KM program. In 1999, Infosys began to consolidate the various knowledge initiatives. A central *knowledge portal* was created, called KShop, and the corporate KM group updated and expanded the KM infrastructure, while the local KM groups were directed to manage their own content on KShop. According to the company's 2012–2013 Sustainability Report, 2.5 million activities were recorded from 100,000 employees in FY 2013 (see **infosys.com/sustainability/Documents/infosys-sustainability-report-2012-13.pdf**). For a presentation on Infosys and KShop, watch the video titled 'Infosys KShop" (4:29 minutes) at **youtube.com/watch?v=Z7WzJjKyBeE**.

To encourage usage and contribution by employees, a reward program was initiated that in the beginning, included prizes and cash.

In 2007, the company introduced an automated tool called Infosys KMail; employees can send queries to KMail and a search engine tries to match responses from the knowledge base (reported by Mehta et al. 2007). According to the company's 2012–2013 Sustainability Report, over 800,000 activities were recorded from 18,000 employees in FY 2013 (see **infosys.com/sustainability/Documents/infosys-sustainability-report-2012-13.pdf**).

The Results

As the volume of content increased, so did the difficulty finding and reviewing the needed content for quality control. The KM group therefore developed a new and more lucrative incentive program that includes the need for justification content (e.g., usefulness to users). By 2014 there were 75,000 knowledge assets stored in the central knowledge repository.

The company has filed a patent for its KM mechanism called *Knowledge Currency Unit*. The KM project has enabled the company to sustain its competitiveness and market leadership (see Suresh and Mehesh 2008).

For more on the Global Delivery Model of KM, see **infosys.com/global-sourcing/global-delivery-model/Pages/knowledge-management.aspx**.

Sources: Based on **infosys.com** (accessed April 2014), Mehta et al. (2007), Bahal (2011), Suresh and Mehesh (2008), Tariq (2011), and Rao (2010).

Questions

1. Why are consulting organizations such as Infosys interested in KM?
2. Identify the benefits of KM to the company.
3. Identify the KM cycle and activities in this case.
4. Why is a reward system beneficial? Compare the old and new reward systems.

Software Tools for Knowledge Sharing

There are many software knowledge-sharing tools. Some call these "knowledge-sharing technologies." In this chapter and book, we cover the following:

- Expert and expertise location systems (Section 5.3)
- Knowledge management systems (Section 5.3)
- Social networks and Web 2.0 tools (Chapters 2 and 7)
- Collaborative commerce tools (Section 5.4)

How Is Knowledge Management Related to E-Commerce?

Organizations need knowledge, which is provided by KM, in order to better perform their tasks.

Core KM activities for companies engaging in EC should include the following: creation, capture and codification, classification, distribution, and utilization. *Knowledge creation* involves using various computer-based tools and techniques to analyze transaction data and generate new ideas (e.g., Group Support Systems [GSS], crowdsourcing, and blogs). *Knowledge capture and codification* includes gathering new knowledge and storing it in a machine-readable format. *Knowledge classification* organizes knowledge using the appropriate classification related to its use. *Knowledge distribution* is sharing relevant information with other employees, suppliers, and consumers, and other internal and external stakeholders through electronic networks—both public and private. *Knowledge utilization* involves the appropriate application of knowledge to problem solving by exploiting opportunities and improving employees' skills. Intuitively, KM is related to e-learning (e.g., see Lytras et al. 2013). Finally, *knowledge evolution* entails updating knowledge as time progresses.

In the past KM and EC initiatives were dealt with independently; however, they can be used together for mutual benefit.

Examples

According to Britt (2013), "E-commerce retailers are using knowledge management solutions to pull together order, inventory, sales and other transaction information, as well as to improve customer feedback and to enhance the overall e-commerce experience." Britt provides the following examples:

- Dog is Good Inc. (a merchant of "'canine-themed apparel'") is using KM to help in the integration of EC subsystems (ordering, inventory, order fulfillment, accounting, and EC stores) using the offerings from NetSuite.
- Ideeli, Inc., an online daily flash retailer, uses KM analytics (ForeSee Satisfaction Analytics) to learn about customer experiences from collected feedback.
- Ideeli, Inc. also uses KM analytics (ForeSee's mobile analytics solution) to identify the needs of frequent visitors (by segments on mobile devices). As a result, the company modified its e-commerce strategies.

- Retina-X Studios provides tracking and monitoring of activities on mobile phones, computing devices, etc. The KM system is used to improve the handling of EC chargebacks due to cancellation. The company turned to Avangate's e-commerce solution that cut costs and improved customer service.

Some managers believe that a major EC-related role of KM is linking EC and business processes. Specifically, knowledge generated in EC contributes to the enhancement of three core processes: CRM, SCM, and product development management. For more on KM-enabling technologies and how they can be applied to business unit initiatives, see **kmworld.com**, **riskmanagement.finrm.com**, and **knowledgestorm.com**.

KM and Social Networks

A major place of knowledge creation is in online communities, including social networks. This is done by *crowdsourcing* and customer and employee discussions and feedback. This area has several variations. One variety is limited within a single company (see the Knowledge Network in the Caterpillar Online File W5.3). Knowledge can also be created in *user-generated content* (see Chapter 7) and in the "answer" function of some social networks, or KMail at Infosys.

Web 2.0 applications help aggregate corporate knowledge, facilitate communication and collaboration, and simplify the building of repositories of best practices, as demonstrated by the following example.

Example: IBM Jam Events

Since 2001, IBM has been using communities for online brainstorming sessions, idea generation, and problem solving. These sessions are called "Jam Events." According to their page, "IBM's Jams and other Web 2.0 collaborative mediums are opening up tremendous possibilities for collaborative innovation…" (**collaborationjam.com**). Each Jam has a different topic. In 2006 the largest IBM online brainstorming session ever held, called the *Innovation Jam*, brought a community of over 150,000 employees from 104 countries and 67 companies to launch new IBM businesses (see Bjelland and Wood 2008 and **collaborationjam.com/**).

Virtual meetings where IBM employees can participate in Innovation Jam launches were conducted in SL. IBM's former CEO even created an avatar to represent himself. Besides business, recent topics that have been explored by IBM Jams include social issues. See **collaboration jam.com/IBMJam**. Other topics that have been explored are new technologies for water filtration, 3-D Internet, and branchless banking. For more on IBM's Jams—the process, examples of topics, and results, as well as the use of virtual worlds, see Bjelland and Wood (2008), **ibm.com/ibm/jam/index3.shtml**, **blogs.hbr.org/2013/01/learning-how-to-jam**, **en.wikipedia.org/wiki/Knowledge_management**, and **ibm.com/developerworks/webservices/library/ws-virtualspaces**. For the history of IBM Jams, see **collaborationjam.com/IBMJam**.

Deploying KM Technologies

Knowledge management as it relates to EC and IT is not easy to implement. Bahal (2011) lists 8 critical success factors for KM including strategy, leadership, integration, and technical infrastructure. Currier (2010) lists the following reasons by declining order of importance: ROI difficult to measure; difficulties in training end-users; insufficient budget; poorly defined or executed strategies; employee resistance; difficulty in finding the right KM software and vendors; need to ensure security; customization is too difficult; maintaining quality of output can be costly; lack of upper management commitment; implementation is disruptive; lack of IT commitment; and employee privacy protection issues.

Finding Expertise and/or Experts Electronically and the Use of Expert Location Systems

Expert advice can be provided within an organization in a variety of ways. Human expertise is rare; therefore, companies attempt to preserve it electronically, *as expert systems*, in corporate knowledge bases. Users may look for human

experts to answer their questions or they may search the knowledge bases for expertise.

People who need help may post their inquiries internally on corporate intranets (e.g., using special Q&A platforms, like KMail of Infosys, or discuss their issue in forums or blogs), or on public social networks such as Yahoo! Answers (**answers.yahoo.com**), that have a "search answers" feature. Similarly, companies may ask for advice on how to solve problems or exploit an opportunity and offer incentives to participate. Answers may generate hundreds of useful ideas within a few days. This is a kind of brainstorming.

Answers Provided by People on Social Networks or Portals

Several social networks (e.g., **linkedin.com**), or Internet portals (e.g., **answers.yahoo.com**) offer free Q&A capabilities.

Example

Yahoo! Answers (**answers.yahoo.com**) allows you to post a question, for free.

One of the authors of this book posted the following question on Yahoo! Answers.

Question: "My Yahoo! e-mail has been hijacked. The spammer sends requests for money in my name to all the people on my contact list. What should I do?" Answer (Anonymous): (Best answer-chosen by voters): "The spammer could have obtained your password with phishing spam. Change your password. While you are in your account settings, check for tampering with your alternate e-mail contact address. That could be used to obtain new passwords. Also, abstain from clicking on links within your spam. That spammer's webpage can run a malicious script. This runs within your browser and can tell webmail currently logged in within that browser to send spam."

The answers provided by Yahoo! are usually generated manually by volunteers for free. Sometimes the answers are generated automatically, as described in the next section.

Automated Question-Answer Systems

In addition to advice provided by humans, an increasing number of applications attempt to provide automated answers to users' questions. The expert finding system described in the following section is an example of such a system. The user asks a question and the computer tries to find an answer that best matches the question. The goal of an **automated question-answer (Q&A) system** is to find answers that match questions asked in a natural language (e.g., English, Chinese).

Example: Search Engine Advice

Answers.com and Ask.com belong to a special category of search engines containing a massive collection of questions, each with pre-generated answers. The engine tries to match a question asked in a natural language with a standard question within its matched answer.

A *Q&A system* differs from *frequently asked questions (FAQ)* in that the content of an FAQ is fairly structured and limited in its size, concentrating on "frequently asked questions." In addition, an FAQ posts questions to choose from while in a Q&A forum, users ask unstructured questions in a natural language.

To begin, the computer needs to understand the questions (e.g., by using natural language understanding software); then, the computer can search for matching answers. There are several methods for computers to find the answers to such questions. One method is based on the use of Artificial Intelligence (AI) by using intelligent agents such as expert systems. Trying to reason automatically from historical cases is another popular approach. Note that automated Q&A concentrates mostly on automated problem solving and is not related to Web search.

Example: IBM PureSystems

IBM PureSystems are an Expert Integrated System family of intelligent computer systems designed to help companies solve IT challenges. They are based on Cloud Computing. For details, see **ibm.com/ibm/puresystems/us/en/index.html**.

Live Chat with Experts

Live chats with experts are becoming popular. For example, you can chat with physicians practicing different specialties. You can do the same with many other professionals. Many companies provide live chat (similar to Yahoo Messenger or AOL IM). The waiting time for replies is usually short.

Chat with Avatars

You can chat with avatars that use a collection of preprogrammed Q&A. Such a service is very inexpensive (but may be not too accurate). The quality of the answers is increasing as the knowledge base increases and as the ability of the computer to understand natural language improves. For example, see Ted, the Virtual Investment Consultant at TD Ameritrade (**tdameritrade.com/virtualclient/about.html**). More discussion is provided in Chapter 2.

Expert Location Systems

Expert/expertise location systems (ELS) are interactive computerized systems that help employees locate experts within their organization in order to get help in solving specific, critical business or technical problems in a short time. Expertise location systems are designed to:

- Identify experts in specific domain areas inside organizations.
- Link people to information about such experts and enable contacts with them.
- Assist employees with advice on career development.
- Provide support for teamwork and groups in social networks.

Software for such systems is made by companies such as IBM and RightNow Technologies (now an Oracle company). For benefits, features, and demonstrations, see Hivemine AskMe (**hivemine.com/products/askme_difference.html**) and AskMe's Product Data Sheet (**hivemine.com/realcom/whse/Hivemine_AskMe_Datasheet.pdf**). Most expert location systems work in a similar manner, exploring knowledge bases for either an answer to the problem (if it exists there) or for locating qualified experts. The general process is shown in Figure 5.6.

The four steps of the process are:
1. An employee submits a question to the ELS.
2. The software searches its database to see if an answer to the question already exists.

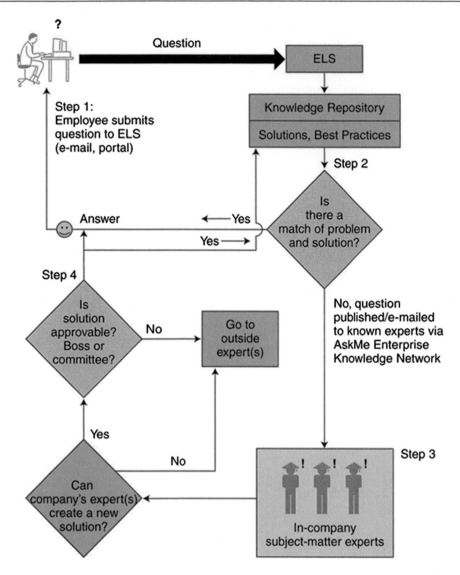

Figure 5.6 AskMe's expert location system

If it exists, the information (research reports, spreadsheets, etc.) is returned to the employee. If not, the software searches documents and archived communications for an expert in the domain area.

3. Once an expert candidate is located, the system asks if he or she is able to answer the question. If so, the expert submits a response. If the expert is unable to respond, he or she can elect to reroute the question to the next appropriate expert until one responds.

4. After an answer to the question is found, it is reviewed for accuracy by a corporate advisor and sent to the person who made the query. At the same time, the question and its response are added to the knowledge repository to be used in future similar situations.

Example: How the U.S. Department of Commerce Uses Expert Location Systems

The U.S. Commercial Service Division at the Department of Commerce (DOC) conducts approximately 200,000 counseling sessions a year involving close to $40 billion in trade. The division employs many specialists who frequently need to do research or call on experts to answer a complex question posed by a U.S. corporation.

For example, according to D'Agostino (2004), a DOC specialist was approached for advice regarding the tax legitimacy of a U.S. transaction with a Polish company. The employee did not know the answer, so he looked for an expert within the agency using an expert location system (from India's AskMe). In a short time, he found 80 experts and transferred the query to six of them. In one day, he had enough information to formulate the answer. Previously, it would have taken up to three days to obtain the information needed for a similar answer by phone.

The employee estimates that he now uses the system for roughly 40% of the work he does.

For details, see D'Agostino (2004).

Seeking Expertise in Social Networks

Seeking expertise (and experts) is becoming a very popular social activity. People post their queries on bulletin boards, forums, and blogs and wait for responses. One of the features of LinkedIn is the free "Help Forum," where users can post questions to get help from forum members or start a discussion.

SECTION 5.3 REVIEW QUESTIONS

1. Define knowledge management.
2. Discuss the relationship between KM and EC.
3. Describe online advisory services.
4. Describe expert location systems and their benefits.
5. Relate social networks to providing advice.

5.4   COLLABORATIVE COMMERCE

Collaborative commerce is an e-commerce technology that can be used to improve collaboration within and among organizations, frequently in supply chain relationships.

Essentials of Collaborative Commerce

Collaborative commerce (c-commerce) refers to electronic support for business collaboration. It enables companies to collaboratively plan, design, develop, manage, and research products, services, and innovative business processes, including EC applications. An example would be a manufacturer who is collaborating electronically with an engineering company that designs a product or a part for the manufacturer. C-commerce implies communication, information sharing, and collaborative planning done online by using tools such as groupware, blogs, wikis, and specially designed EC collaboration tools. Many collaboration efforts are done along the supply chain where the major benefits are cost reduction, increased revenue, fewer delays, faster movement of goods, fewer rush orders, fewer stockouts, and better inventory management. C-commerce is strongly related to **e-collaboration**, which is collaboration using digital technologies among people for accomplishing a common task.

The Elements and Processes of C-Commerce

The elements of the processes of c-commerce vary according to situations. For example, in many cases, c-commerce involves a manufacturer (or an assembler) who collaborates with its suppliers, designers, and other business partners, as well as with its customers and possibly the government. The major elements of the collaboration process are illustrated in Figure 5.7. Notice that the collaboration process is based on the analysis of internal and external data that are made visible via a visualization portal. On the lower left side of the figure, we show the cyclical process of c-commerce. The people involved in this cycle use the information in the displays as well as the interactions among the major groups of participants (shown on the right side of the figure).

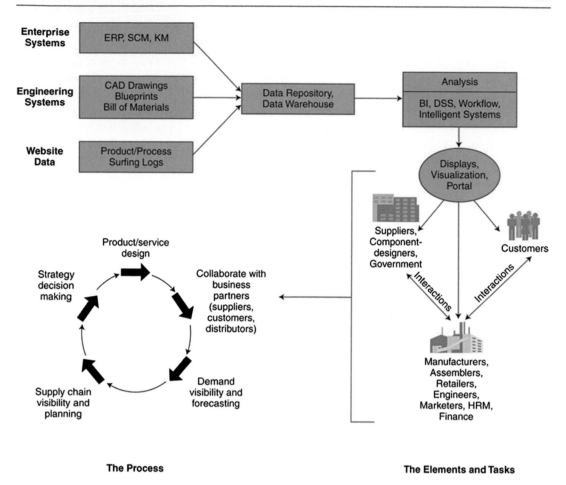

Figure 5.7   Elements and process of c-commerce systems

The elements of c-commerce can be arranged in different configurations, one of which is a hub.

Collaboration Hubs

A popular form of c-commerce is the *collaboration hub*, which is often used by the members of a supply chain. A **collaboration hub (c-hub)** is the central point of interaction and of a company's supply chain (see Figure 12.4, pg. 582). A single e-hub can host multiple *collaboration spaces* in which trading partners transact, collaborate, communicate, and share information. For the collaboration life-cycle, see Wishom (2012).

Improving Collaborative Commerce

C-commerce can be divided into two major categories: internal and external. *Internal collaboration* refers to inter-departmental collaboration such as collaboration among organizational employees and collaboration of departments with their mobile employees. It also refers to collaboration among teams and individual employees who are off premises. *External collaboration* refers to any collaboration between an organization and others in the external environment.

A large number of electronic tools is available to improve collaboration, starting with e-mail and wikis and ending with collaborative spaces and comprehensive tools such as Microsoft SharePoint (**office.microsoft.com/en-us/sharepoint**), Salesforce Chatter (**salesforce.com/ap/chatter/overview**), and Jive Software (**jivesoftware.com**). For example, Fox (2012) points to SAP Inc., which provides a social-based layer of software products that optimizes collaboration.

A large number of publications is available on how to improve c-collaboration. Examples are Siebdrat et al. (2009), who provide a comprehensive coverage of managing virtual teams, McCafferty (2011), who suggests eight improvement methods, and Strom (2011) who compares collaboration tools from Cisco (WebEx), Citrix (Go To tools), DokuWiki (wiki software), Google Apps and more. Note that collaboration tools can be either same time (synchronous) or different times (a-synchronous).

Representative Examples of Collaborative Commerce

Leading technology companies such as Dell, Cisco, and HP use collaborative commerce mostly for supply chain improvement such as e-procurement. Other collaboration EC initiatives are used to increase efficiency and effectiveness of operation as can be seen in the following examples.

Vendor-Managed Inventory Systems

Vendor-managed inventory (VMI) refers to a process in which retailers make their suppliers responsible for monitoring the inventory of each item they supply, and determining when to order each item, and how much to order each time. Then the orders are generated electronically and fulfilled by the vendors. (A third-party logistics provider (3PL) can also be involved in VMI by organizing the shipments as needed.) The retailer provides the supplier with real-time usage (depletion) information (e.g., point-of-sale data), inventory levels, and the threshold below which orders need to be replenished. With this approach, the retailer is no longer involved with inventory management, and the demand forecasting becomes the responsibility of the supplier who can calcu-

late the need for an item before the item is depleted. In addition, instead of sending purchase orders, customers electronically send daily information to the supplier, who generates the replenishment orders for the customer based on this demand information (see **datalliance.com/whatisvmi.html**). Thus, administrative costs are reduced, inventories are kept low, and stock-outs become rare. A VMI also can be conducted between a supplier and its sub suppliers. For more information, see **en.wikipedia.org/wiki/Vendor-managed_inventory**, **vendormanagedinventory.com**, and Spychalska (2010). Representative VMI software solutions are provided by Vecco International (**veccoint.com**) and JDA Software Group, Inc. (**jda.com**).

Example: VMI and Information Sharing Between a Retailer (Walmart) and a Supplier (P&G)

Walmart provides P&G access to sales information on every item P&G sells to Walmart. The sales information is collected electronically by P&G on a daily basis from every Walmart store. By monitoring the inventory level of its items, P&G knows when the inventories fall below the threshold that triggers an automatic order fulfillment and a shipment. Everything is done electronically. The benefit for P&G is accurate demand information; the benefit for Walmart is adequate inventory, and both enjoy reduced administrative costs (minimum paper orders and manual work). P&G has similar agreements with other major retailers; Walmart has similar agreements with other major suppliers.

Retailer-Supplier Collaboration

In addition to VMI, retailers and the suppliers can collaborate in other areas as illustrated in the following example.

Example: Target Corporation

Target Corporation (**corporate.target.com**) is a large retail conglomerate. It conducts EC activities with tens of thousands of trading partners. The company has an extranet-based system for those partners who are not connected to its value-added network (VAN)–based EDI

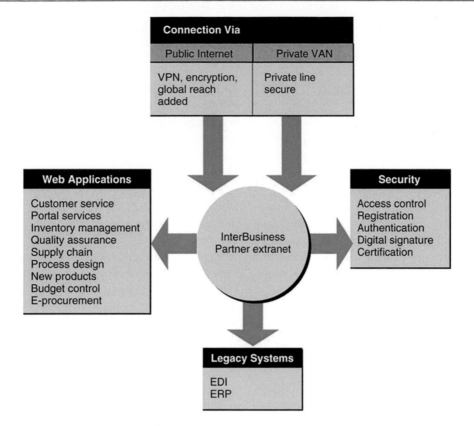

Figure 5.8 Target's extranet

(see Online Tutorial T2). The extranet enables the company not only to reach many more partners but also to use many applications not available on the traditional EDI. The system enables the company to streamline its communication and collaboration with suppliers. It also allows the company's business customers to create personalized Web pages, as shown in Figure 5.8. Target now has a business website called Partners Online (**partnersonline.com**), which it uses to communicate with business partners, providing them with valuable information.

Reducing Transportation and Inventory Costs

Cost reduction in shipping and inventory can be achieved through collaboration. An example is the collaboration between Amazon.com (**amazon. com**) and shippers such as UPS (**ups.com**).

Amazon.com delivers millions of items every week from its distribution centers. Rapid delivery is critical and collaboration with the shippers is essential.

Reduction of Design Cycle Time

The following examples demonstrate cycle time reduction through c-collaboration.

Example 1: Clarion Malaysia

Clarion Malaysia (**clarion.com/my/en/top.html**), a subsidiary of the global car-audio electronics company Clarion Group, manufactures audio electronic systems for cars.

Using computerized technologies provided by IBM, such as computer aided design (CAD) and product cycle management, the two companies reduced the time-to-market by about 40%, while at the same time improving the design of the products because engineers were able to spend more time creating innovative designs. In addition, closer interaction with Clarion's customers is easier now throughout the design process. Finally, there is also a reduction in tooling preparation time.

Example 2: Caterpillar, Inc

Caterpillar, Inc. (**caterpillar.com**) is a multinational, heavy-machinery manufacturer. In the traditional mode of operation, cycle time along the supply chain was lengthy because the process involved the distribution of paper documents among managers, salespeople, and technical staff. To solve the problem, Caterpillar connected its engineering and manufacturing divisions with its suppliers, dealers, distributors, overseas factories, and customers through an extranet-based global e-collaboration hub. By using the collaboration system, a customer can order a specialized part from any place in the world by transmitting the order electronically to a local Caterpillar dealer. The order quickly gets to the appropriate designers or engineers. Customers also can use an extranet (accessible with wireless devices) to track the order status (see details in Online File W5.3).

Elimination of Channel Conflict: Collaboration with Dealers and Retailers

As discussed in Chapters 3 and 4, a conflict between manufacturers and their distributors, including retailers and/or dealers, may arise when customers order online directly from the manufacturer. One solution mentioned earlier is to order from the manufacturer and pick up the merchandise from a local retailer or dealer instead. This requires collaboration between the manufacturer and the local vendor. One company that provides the support for such collaborative EC is JG Sullivan Interactive, Inc. (see **jgsullivan.com/our-platform**). Their product allows manufacturers to sell online with minimal channel conflict. Another example is Cisco Systems (see **cisco.com/c/en/us/solutions/collaboration/index.html**).

Companies such as Commerce Guys (**commerceguys.com**) offer a socially-oriented collaboration platform (e.g., see **drupalcommerce.org**).

Example: Whirlpool Corp

Whirlpool (**whirlpool.com**) is another company that experienced the problem of channel conflict. Consumers prefer to buy appliances (sometimes customized) online, directly from Whirlpool. Whirlpool's nationwide network of dealers was not happy with the direct ordering. Note that, some appliances (e.g., a dishwasher, a washing machine) need to be installed, a job usually organized by the dealers.

JG Sullivan's system for Whirlpool was then used globally. The system was designed to enable direct online ordering, and at the same time manage the delivery, installation, warranty, and services by the local dealers. This made customers as well as dealers happy, since marketing and sales expenses decreased significantly. Also, the direct contact with customers allowed Whirlpool to know their customers better.

Barriers to C-Commerce

Despite the many potential benefits, and with the exception of some very large companies, c-commerce adaptation is moving ahead slowly. Reasons cited in various studies include technical factors involving a lack of internal integration and standards. Other reasons include network security and privacy concerns, and some distrust over who has access to and control of information stored in a partner's database. Internal resistance to information sharing and to new approaches and lack of company skills to conduct c-commerce are also possible factors. Gaining agreement on how to share costs and benefits can also prove problematic.

Finally, global collaboration may be complicated by additional barriers ranging from language and cultural misunderstandings to insufficient budgeting. For a detailed list and discussion see Currier (2010).

Overcoming Barriers to C-Collaboration

Specialized c-commerce software tools may lessen some of the barriers to c-commerce. In addition, as companies learn more about the major benefits of c-commerce—such as smoothing the supply chain, reducing inventories and operating costs, and increasing customer satisfaction--it is expected that more companies will implement c-commerce. New approaches, such as the use of cloud computing and its variants and the use of Web Services could significantly lessen the implementation problem. The use of collaborative Web 2.0 tools based on open source, could help as well. Finally, it is essential to have a collaborative culture within and among organizations. One area related to c-commerce is consumer-to-consumer (C2C) e-commerce, which is presented in the next section.

Collaboration Processes and Software

A large number of proprietary methods and supportive communication and collaborative software are available to support c-commerce.

SECTION 5.4 REVIEW QUESTIONS

1. Define c-commerce.
2. List the major types and characteristics of c-commerce.
3. Describe some examples of c-commerce.
4. Describe the elements and processes of c-commerce.
5. List some major barriers to c-commerce. How can a company overcome these limitations?

5.5   CONSUMER-TO-CONSUMER ELECTRONIC COMMERCE

Consumer-to-consumer (C2C) EC, which is sometimes called *peer-to-peer (P2P)* e-commerce, refers to electronic transactions completed between and among individuals. These transactions can also include intermediaries, such as eBay (**ebay.com**) or social network sites that organize, manage, and facilitate the C2C networks. C2C activities may include transactions resulting from classified ads, music and file sharing, career and job matching (e.g., at **linkedin.com** and **careerone.com.au**), and personal matchmaking services (e.g., **match.com**).

C2C EC has given online shopping and trading a new dimension. Although this sort of trading is prevalent in the offline world (classified newspaper ads, garage sales, etc.), it was not expected to succeed online because of problems regarding trust due to the anonymity of the traders, especially those who are in different locations. This problem was solved by using a third-party payment provider (e.g., **paypal.com**) and escrow or insurance services provided by eBay and others. One advantage of C2C EC is that it reduces the administrative and commission costs for both buyers and sellers. It also gives many individuals and small business owners a low-cost way to sell their goods and services.

Social networks have become a popular place for C2C activities such as selling products and services via classified ads at **craigslist.org** or **facebook.com** and other social networks. People are sharing or selling music, bartering, selling virtual properties, and providing personal services.

E-Commerce: C2C Applications

Many websites facilitate C2C activities between individuals. We cover several representative applications next.

C2C Auctions

A very successful example of a C2C application is participation in auctions. In dozens of countries, selling and buying on auction sites is growing rapidly. Most auctions are managed by intermediaries (the most well-known intermediary is eBay). Consumers can visit auctions at general sites such as **ebay.com** or **auctionanything.com**; or they can use specialized sites. In addition, many individuals conduct their own auctions with the use of special software. For example, ProcurePort.com (see **procureport.com/reverse-auction-services.html**) provides software to create C2C reverse auction communities online.

Selling and Buying in C2C

In addition to auctions, eBay enables individuals to sell goods to other individuals at fixed prices. Amazon.com and Etsy (Chapter 3) do the same. Hundreds of other sites facilitate C2C trading including those that use classified ads.

Person-to-Person Money Lending

As described in Chapters 3 and 7, people use the Internet for direct person-to-person money lending. For an overview, see Dachille (2014).

Classified Ads

Internet-based classified ads have several advantages over newspaper classified ads. They cover a national, rather than a local, audience, and can be updated quickly and easily. Most of them are free or charge very little. This greatly increases the supply of goods and services available and the number of potential buyers. One of the most successful sites of C2C classified ads is **craigslist. org** as seen in Chapter 2. Classified ads also include apartments for rent and corporate housing across the U.S. (powered by **forrent.com**). **Freeclassifieds.com** allows you to buy or sell anything for free. Many newspapers also offer their classified ads online. In some cases, placing an ad in the classified section of one website automatically directs it into the classified sections of numerous partners (known as cross-posting). This increases ad exposure at no additional cost. To help narrow the search for a particular item, some sites offer shoppers search engines.

Classified ads appear on thousands of websites including popular social networks such as **facebook.com/free.classified** and **linkedin.com**.

Personal Services

Numerous personal services are available on the Internet (lawyers, handy helpers, tax preparers, investment clubs, dating services). Some are located in the classified ad section, but others are listed on specialized websites (e.g., **hireahelper. com**) and directories. Some are offered free; others charge a fee.

Note: Be very careful before looking for any personal services online. Fraud or crime could be involved (e.g., a lawyer online may not be an expert in the area professed or may not even be a lawyer at all).

File-Sharing Utilities:
Napster and Others

It all started in 1999. By logging onto services such as Napster, people were able to download files that others were willing to share for free. Such *P2P*

networks enabled users to search other members' hard drives for a particular file, including data files created by users or copied from elsewhere. Digital music and games were the most popular files accessed. Movies, TV shows, and videos followed shortly thereafter. Napster had over 60 million members in 2002 before it was forced to stop its service due to copyright violations.

The Napster server, and others that followed, functioned as a directory that listed the files being shared by other users. Once logged onto the server, users could search the directory for specific songs and locate the file owner. They could then directly access the owner's computer and download the songs they had chosen. Napster also included chat rooms to connect its millions of users.

However, a U.S. federal court found Napster to be in violation of copyright laws because it enabled people to obtain music files without paying royalties to the creators of the music. Following this ruling, in March 2002, Napster was forced to shut down and filed for Chapter 11 bankruptcy. In 2011, Napster was acquired by Rhapsody (**rhapsody.com**), a subscription-based music downloading site. For a history of Napster, see **theguardian.com/music/2013/feb/24/napster-music-free-file-sharing**.

A number of free file-sharing programs still exist. For example, an even purer version of P2P is BitTorrent (**bittorrent.com**), software that makes downloading files fast. To access games over P2P networks, try TrustyFiles (**trustyfiles. com**). See also the Pirate Bay case in Chapter 15. Despite the temptation to get "something for nothing," remember that downloading copyrighted materials for free is usually against the law.

C2C Activities in Social Networks
and Trading Virtual Properties

C2C activities in social networks include the sharing of photos, videos, music, and other files; trading of virtual properties; and conducting other activities. Trading virtual properties is very popular in virtual worlds, especially in Second Life (**secondlife.com**).

SECTION 5.5 REVIEW QUESTIONS
1. Define C2C e-commerce.
2. Describe the benefits of C2C e-commerce.

3. Describe the major e-commerce applications.
4. Define file sharing.
5. How is C2C practiced in social networking?
6. Describe file sharing and the legal issues involved (see the Pirate Bay case in Chapter 15).

MANAGERIAL ISSUES

Some managerial issues related to this chapter are as follows.

1. **How do we design the most cost-efficient government e-procurement system?** Several issues are involved and questions may be raised in planning e-government: How much can the governmental e-procurement system save on procurement costs? How can the system be used for procuring small quantities? How do you deal with bidders from outside your country? How can illegal bribery be prevented? What criteria besides cost need to be considered? How should the online and offline procurement systems be designed? How do you advertise RFQs online? How should the portfolio of auctions and desktop purchasing be constructed? Can the government use commercial B2B sites for procurement? Can businesses use the government procurement system for their own procurement? All these must be considered in an effective design.

2. **How do we design the portfolio of e-learning knowledge sources?** There are many sources of e-learning services. The e-learning management team needs to design the portfolio of the online and offline training applications, and the internal and external knowledge sources, (paid and nonpaid sources). The internal knowledge management system is an important source of training materials for large corporations, whereas external sources could be more cost-effective for small organizations. Obviously, justification of each item in the portfolio is needed, which is related to vendor selection. For illustrative case studies, see **brightwave.co.uk**.

3. **How do we incorporate social networking-based learning and services in our organization?** With the proliferation of social networking initiatives in the enterprise comes the issue of how to integrate these with the enterprise system, including CRM, KM, training, and other applications and business processes. One issue is how to balance the quality of knowledge with the scope of knowledge in e-learning and training programs.

4. **What will be the impact of the e-book platform?** If the e-book is widely adopted by readers, the distribution channel of online book sales may be disruptive. This new platform may cannibalize the offline book retail business. Additionally, there is the need for the protection of intellectual property of digital contents since it is easy to copy and distribute electronic files (see Chapter 15). In general, more e-books will be published and read.

5. **How difficult is it to introduce e-collaboration?** Dealing with the technological aspects of e-collaboration may be the easy part. Tackling the behavioral changes needed within an organization and its interactions with the trading partners may be the greater challenge. Change management may be needed for the newly created collaborations, to deal with issues such as the resistance to change. In addition, the responsibilities of the collaborative partners must be articulated with the business partners. Finally, e-collaboration costs money and needs to be economically and organizationally justified; however, justification may not be an easy task due to the intangible risks and benefits involved.

6. **How much can be shared with business partners? Can they be trusted?** Many companies are sharing forecast data and actual sales data. However, when it comes to allowing real-time access to product design, inventory, and interface to ERP systems, there may be some hesitation. It is basically a question of security and trust. The more information that is shared, the better the collaboration. However, sharing information can lead to accidently giving away some trade secrets. In some cases, there is an organizational cultural resistance against sharing (some employees do not like to share information, even within their own organization). The business value of sharing needs to be assessed carefully against its risks.

7. **Who benefits from vendor-managed inventory?** When VMI systems are deployed, both sellers and retailers reap benefits. However, small suppliers may not have the ability to systematically monitor and manage inventory of their business customers. In this case, the large buyer will need to support the inventory management system on behalf of its suppliers. Sensitive issues must be agreed upon when initiating VMI. One such issue is how to deal with item shortages created in the system.

SUMMARY

In this chapter, you learned about the following EC issues as they relate to the chapter's learning objectives.

1. **E-government activities.** Governments, like any other organization, can use EC applications for great savings and increased effectiveness. Notable applications are e-procurement using reverse auctions, e-payments to and from citizens and businesses, auctioning of surplus goods, and electronic travel and expense management systems. Governments also conduct electronic business with other governments. As a result, governments can do a better job with less money.

2. **Implementing e-government to citizens, businesses, and its own operations.** Governments worldwide are providing a variety of services to citizens over the Internet. Such initiatives increase citizen satisfaction and decrease government expenses for providing citizens' service applications, including electronic voting. Governments also are active in electronic trading with businesses. Finally, EC can be conducted within and between governments. E-government's growth can be strengthened by the use of wireless systems in what is described as mobile or m-government. Also, e-government 2.0 is becoming increasingly popular with tools such as wikis, blogs, social networks and Twitter.

3. **E-learning and training.** E-learning is the delivery of educational content through electronic media via the Internet and intranets. Degree programs, lifelong learning topics, and corporate training are delivered online by thousands of organizations worldwide. A growing area is distance learning via online university offerings; and virtual universities are becoming quite popular. Some are virtual; others are delivered as a combination of online and offline offerings. Online corporate training is increasing also, and is sometimes conducted at formal corporate learning centers. Implementation is done in steps starting with just an online presence and ending with activities on social networks. New e-readers contain easy-to-read text, search capabilities, rich media as well as other functions. Add to this the low cost of e-books and the capability of storing hundreds of books on a single e-reader, and you can understand the increased popularity of these devices.

4. **E-books and their readers.** There is an increased interest in e-books due to their many benefits (Amazon.com sells more e-books than hardcover ones). There is intense competition among e-reader and tablet manufacturers, and the products' capabilities are increasing while their prices are declining. E-books are used both for pleasure reading and for studying. E-books can be read on several portable devices including tablets.

5. **Knowledge management and dissemination.** Knowledge has been recognized as an important organizational asset. It needs to be properly captured, stored, updated, and shared. Knowledge is critical for many e-commerce tasks. Knowledge can be shared in different ways; experts can provide knowledge to non-experts (for a fee or free) via a knowledge portal, e-mail, or chatting and discussion tools, and through social networks (e.g., via user generated videos or text).

6. **Online advisory systems.** Online advisory systems of all kinds are becoming popular. Some are free although most charge fees. Users must be careful about the quality of the advice they receive. Social networks and portals provide a variety of advisory services of different qualities.

7. **C-commerce.** Collaborative commerce (c-commerce) refers to a planned use of digital technology by business partners. It includes

planning, designing, researching, managing, and servicing various partners and tasks, frequently along the supply chain. C-commerce can be conducted between different pairs of business partners or among many partners participating in a collaborative network. Collaboration with Web 2.0 tools and in social networks adds a social dimension that could improve communication, participation, and trust. There are many new tools, some of which are being added to traditional collaboration tools. Better collaboration may improve supply chain operation, knowledge management, and individual and organizational performance.

8. **C2C activities.** C2C consists of individual consumers conducting e-commerce with other individual consumers, mainly in auctions (such as at eBay), classified ads, matching services, specialty webstores at Amazon.com, and file sharing.

KEY TERMS

Automated question-answer (QA) system
Collaboration hub (c-hub)
Collaborative commerce (c-commerce)
Consumer-to-consumer (C2C) EC
Distance learning
E-collaboration
E-government
E-learning
Electronic book (e-book)
Expert/expertise location systems (ELS)
Government 2.0
Government-to-business (G2B)
Government-to-citizens (G2C)
Government-to-employees (G2E)
Government-to-government (G2G)
Knowledge management (KM)
Learning management system (LMS)
Learning on-demand
Mobile government (m-government)
M-learning
Social learning (e-learning 2.0)
Vendor-managed inventory (VMI)
Virtual universities

DISCUSSION QUESTIONS

1. Discuss the advantages and disadvantages of e-government using social networking versus the traditional e-government portal.
2. Discuss the advantages and shortcomings of e-voting.
3. Discuss the advantages and disadvantages of e-books.
4. Discuss the advantages of e-learning in the corporate training environment.
5. In what ways does KM support e-commerce?
6. Some say that B2G is simply B2B. Explain.
7. Compare and contrast B2E with G2E.
8. Which e-government EC activities are intra-business activities? Explain why they are categorized as intrabusiness.
9. Identify the benefits of G2C to citizens and to governments.
10. Relate IBM's Jams to KM and social networks.
11. Relate KM to learning, to e-publishing, and to C2C.
12. It is said that c-commerce signifies a move from a transaction focus to a relationship focus among supply chain members. Discuss.

TOPICS FOR CLASS DISCUSSION AND DEBATES

1. Discuss the advantages and disadvantages of e-learning for an undergraduate student and for an MBA student.
2. Discuss the advantages of expert/expertise location systems over corporate databases that contain experts' information and knowledge. What are the disadvantages? Can expert location systems and corporate databases be combined? How?
3. Discuss the benefits of using virtual worlds to facilitate learning. What are the limitations? The disadvantages?
4. One of the major initiatives of many governments (e.g., European Commission) is Smart Cities (see Chapter 6 for the technology).

Discuss the content of such initiatives and explain why they are a part of e-government.

5. Debate: E-books will replace traditional books.

6. Debate: Why aren't all firms embracing KM?

7. Debate: Analyze the pros and cons of electronic voting.

8. Enter **en.wikipedia.org/wiki/E-Government** and find the 'controversies of e-Government' section. Discuss the advantages and disadvantages. Write a report.

9. Differentiate between e-learning and m-learning.

10. Discuss the content and benefits of the UN E-Government Development Database (**unpan3.un.org/egovkb**).

11. Angry Birds of Rovio Entertainment became a very popular mobile game. Read about its success and find some educational and learning aspects. Write a report.

INTERNET EXERCISES

1. Enter **e-learningcentre.co.uk**, **elearnmag. acm.org**, and **elearningpost.com**. Identify current discussion issues and find two articles related to the effectiveness of e-training. Write a report. Also prepare a list of the resources available on these sites.

2. Enter **adobe.com** and find the tutorials and tools it offers for e-learning, knowledge management, and online publishing. Prepare and give a presentation on your findings.

3. Identify a difficult business problem in your or another organization. Post the problem on **elance.com**, **linkedin.com**, **answers.yahoo. com**, and **answers.com**. Summarize the information you received to solve the problem.

4. Enter **blackboard.com** and also view **en. wikipedia.org/wiki/Blackboard_Inc.**. Find the major services provided by the company, including its community system. Write a report.

5. Enter **fcw.com** and read the latest news on e-government. Identify initiatives not covered in this chapter. Then enter **gcn.com**. Finally, enter **egovstrategies.com**. Compare the information presented on the three websites.

6. Enter **procurement.org** and **govexec.com**. Identify recent e-government procurement initiatives and summarize their unique aspects.

7. Enter **hivemine.com** and look at their products, solutions, news, and blogs. Do you agree with the company's motto: "Socialize your knowledge and thrive?" Explain your answer.

8. Enter **amazon.com**, **barnesandnoble.com**, and **sony.com** and find the latest information about their e-readers. Compare their capabilities and write a report. (Consult **ebook-reader.com**.)

9. Enter **kolabora.com** or **mindjet.com**. Find out how collaboration is supported there. Summarize the benefits of the site to the participants.

10. Enter **opentext.com** or **kintone.cybozu. com/us**. Read the company vision for collaborative commerce and view the demo. Explain in a report how the company facilitates c-commerce.

11. Enter **guru.com** and **elance.com** and compare their offerings. Which one would you prefer to post your skills on and why?

12. Find two companies that enable C2C (or P2P) e-commerce (such as **egrovesys.com**). Comment on their capabilities.

13. Enter **collaborativeshift.com** or other c-collaborative sites, and read about recent issues related to e-collaboration. Prepare a report.

14. The U.S. government opened a virtual embassy in Iran. Find information about the service and the reaction of the Iranian government. Write a report.

TEAM ASSIGNMENTS AND PROJECTS

1. **Assignment for the Opening Case**
   Read the opening case and answer the following questions.

(a) What were the primary and secondary problems that Compass Group faced with training its managers?

(b) How did the company overcome the skeptics of e-training?

(c) How did the company approach the complexity of systems training?

(d) What were the outcomes of the new e-training?

(e) In your opinion, what are the most important aspects in e-training implementation?

2. New York City is known for its extensive e-government initiatives that were sponsored by Mayor Bloomberg between 2002 and 2013. Find information about these initiatives, their benefits to the public, and their fate after Bloomberg completed his term. Each team will concentrate on one area. Write a report.

3. Create four teams, each representing one of the following: G2C, G2B, G2E, and G2G. Each team will prepare a description of the activities in the assigned area (e.g., G2C) in a small country, such as Holland, Denmark, Finland, or Singapore. A fifth team will deal with the coordination and collaboration of all e-government activities in each of the four countries chosen. Prepare a report.

4. View the video "Panel Discussion on Collaborative Commerce (Pt.1) @ Ariba LIVE 2011" (12:36 minutes) at **youtube.com/watch?v=bucxXpDvWDI**. (Part 2 (11:11 minutes) at **youtube.com/watch?v=dV_KUJ0eVuE** is optional.) Answer the following questions:

(a) What benefits do the buyers see? Relate these benefits to collaborative commerce.

(b) How is EC used to support c-commerce?

(c) How can buyer/supplier relationships be fostered with c-commerce?

(d) Run a similar panel discussion in class. If possible, ask large buyers to attend and take part.

(e) How is bringing business partners online accomplished?

(f) What role does Ariba play? (Check its website **ariba.com**.)

(g) What have you learned from this video about the benefits of c-commerce and e-commerce?

5. View the video "E-Learning Debate 2010 - Highlights" (4:51 minutes) at **youtube.com/watch?v=Q42f1blFnck**. Debate the pros and cons regarding the value of e-learning.

(a) List all the pro and con statements from the video.

(b) For each statement, have two teams (or individuals) explain why each agrees or disagrees with the statement.

(c) Add several pro and con statements from what you learned in class or discovered on the Web.

(d) For each added statement, have two teams (or individuals) explain why each agrees or disagrees with the statement.

(e) Jointly prepare a summary. The use of a wiki is advisable.

6. Have each team represent one of the following sites: **netlibrary.net**, and **ebooks.com**. Each team will examine the technology, legal issues, prices, and business alliances associated with its site. Each team will then prepare a report answering the question, "Will e-books succeed?"

7. Each team is assigned a question-and-answer company (e.g., **answers.com**, **ask.com**). Check the company's offerings, including social networking/games. Present your findings.

CLOSING CASE: FROM LOCAL SDI TO E-GOVERNMENT

Case Study in Municipalities in the South of Hesse (Germany)

Introduction

The increase of e-government solutions associated with spatial data is one of the main goals of the European Union. The citizens should gain access to spatially related services provided by all administrative levels. This poses a substantial challenge, especially for small municipalities that are some of the main producers and owners of spatial data. The process of capacity building even in the superordinate administrative levels has to be established first to launch the use of geospatial data online. Based on a project of the German federal state Hesse, the cooperation between administrative bodies has been found with a high degree of financial self-sufficiency.T extension from desktop computer his case presents the technical requirements as well as the concept and implementation of Spatial Data Infrastructures (SDI) by means of the service chain to discover a land-use plan as the first step to a Service Oriented Architecture (SOA) for geospatial data in a municipality. The existing project guides to the exploration of related projects in municipalities using SDI to develop user-oriented offers in planning and administrative processes. The capabilities of Web 2.0 enable the move from traditional publishing in the Web to social collaboration, in combination with SDI which causes participation to become a common option in the communication between citizens and governments.

Based on the latest geostandards and map viewers out of the Web 2.0 sphere, user-friendly SDI-applications can be developed. A case in point is a service for citizens in the city of Wiesbaden. This example also demonstrates the potentialities in extending services and the access via mobile interfaces.

Local SDI in Hesse

Hesse, whose state capital is Wiesbaden, is one of the 16 federal states of Germany. The SDI activities in the state are initiated and supported by the network of "GDI-Hessen" as part of the federal administration for Land Management and Geoinformation (HVBG). Based on this framework, the pilot project "GDI-Südhessen" (GDI-Südhessen 2014) has been deployed to build the foundation for a local SDI in the south of Hesse. The aim of the project is the collaborative use of geospatial data by creating a network based on the idea of the European INSPIRE directive (Directive 2007/2/EC).

In this context, the cooperation focused on the organizational and technical structures and capacity building to encourage the cost-efficient integration and use of SDI-based services in the administrative daily work. To increase the technical knowledge in terms of SDI, the workflow to discover a binding land-use plan was chosen (see Figure 5.9). The implemented service chain combines SDI components like Web Feature Services (WFS), metadata search via Catalogue Services (CSW), Web Map Services (WMS), and Map Viewer following the standards of the OGC (cf. OGC 2014). For further details see (Hickel and Blankenbach 2012).

SDI-Based Citizen Service for Improved Participation

In cooperation with the city of Wiesbaden, the project began with the development of prototyped applications using a local SDI as part of the future municipal e-government portal.As a first application, an e-participation service had been implemented to enable Wiesbaden´s citizens to inform the city administration about infrastructural problems (e.g., with lamps, roads, and trees).

Unlike existing applications with similar functionalities (e.g. see Mängelmelder 2014), the idea was to incorporate Web 2.0 concepts with the local SDI to optimize citizen services (Blankenbach and Schaffert 2010). As result, a citizen service, called "Bürgerservice," became an integral part of the municipal SDI within the city's e-government structures by the use of OGC geo standards (OGC 2014). Figure 5.10 shows the architecture of the citizen's service as an application of the local SDI.

The idea is to enable citizens to report infrastructural problems online using a Web application. Besides the descriptive report information, an integrated map viewer is used to show the exact geolocalization and provide a pictorial view. The OGC interface of the local SDI enables submitting and storage of the reported data as well as direct access to the report database from the city´s GIS applications (see Figure 5.10). By merging the report with specific municipal geospatial data, the reported problems can be solved faster and more efficiently by the administrative staff.

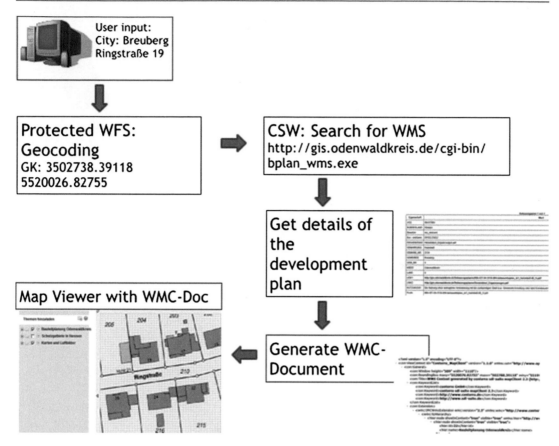

Figure 5.9 Technical workflow: discover a land-use plan (Source: Hickel and Blankenbach 2012.) Used with permission

A standardized OGC-interface enables the extension from desktop and laptop computers to mobile access. Thus, the citizens are able to report the problem directly on-site using a smartphone. For further details, see Hickel and Blankenbach (2012). The users are provided with mobile access to the platform. This enables them to use a mobile phone to bring a malfunction in the street to the municipality´s attention. Currently, the mobile interface is implemented through a client application running on almost every smartphone. Similar to the "stationary" desktop version, the users can select a topical category and enter free text. The reported geocoding and its picture documentation is aimed to be done seamlessly using the smartphone´s embedded sensors, in this case, a GPS-receiver with its camera. For further details, see Blankenbach and Hickel (2013).

Conclusion

To achieve a high acceptance of SDI-supported applications in e-government, it is essential to consider several aspects during the development and use of the applications. The nature of SDI results in several different players encountering the SDI components. This includes the IT department for the technical provisioning of applications, the experts for legal issues and the political decision-makers. The collaboration between all departments involved is an essential aspect to success. The users want applications with high usability, especially in terms of ease of use. In this case, the usability is provided by other Web 2.0 applications like Google Maps for handling spatial information or by using Twitter to send short messages from any device and from any

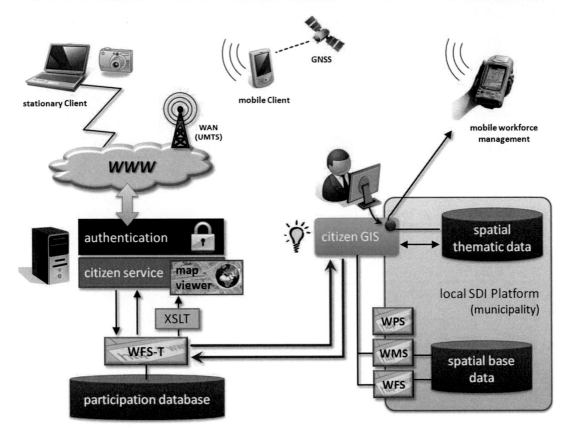

Figure 5.10 Ideal architecture of the citizen service as an application of a local SDI (Source: Blankenbach and Schaffert 2010.) Used with permission

location. To meet these requirements, the socio-technical criteria in terms of social acceptability, usefulness, and usability have to be considered (Macintosh and Whyte 2008).

Throughout the project, several problems and challenges were discovered and pointed out, and based on this experience, several independent new services have been installed and are offered to the citizens.

This citizen service represents an example of value-added applications of local SDI for municipalities. Several other areas of applications (e.g., in municipal planning tasks) are also possible. The system is currently (April 2014) being eval-uated by the city's personnel and is going to be used first for internal municipal tasks. The citizens as well as the administration can benefit from the SDI based applications.

Sources: Blankenbach and Hickel (2013), Blankenbach and Schaffert (2010), Directive 2007/2/EC (2007), GDI-Südhessen (2014), Hickel and Blankenbach (2012), Macintosh and Whyte (2008), OGC (2014), and Mängelmelder (2014).

Review Questions
1. What are the key features of such successful e-government solutions?
2. What are the main challenges for the SDI?

3. Describe how an administration could provide other SDI-based e-government solutions for citizens.

4. What are the essential features that enable parallel mobile access to the e-government infrastructure?

ONLINE FILES available at **affordable-ecommerce-textbook.com/turban**

W5.1 E-Government Social Media Activities in New Zealand

W5.2 The Stages of E-Government Transformation

W5.3 Application Case: Knowledge Sharing as a Strategic Asset at Caterpillar Inc.

COMPREHENSIVE EDUCATIONAL WEBSITES

e-learningcentre.co.uk: A vast collection of selected and reviewed links to e-learning resources.

mgovernment.org: A mobile government consortium.

tools.kmnetwork.com: A portal for KM tools and techniques.

astd.org: American Society for Training and Development: "The world's largest professional association dedicated to the training and development field."

portal.brint.com: A portal for KM.

kmworld.com: A collection of KM solutions.

vic.gov.au: The official Victorian Government website (Australia).

zdnet.com: Search site for 'e-government' in white papers, case studies, technical articles, and blog posts.

forums.e-democracy.org: A portal focused on e-democracy.

whitehouse.gov/omb/e-gov: The official e-government and information technology site of the U.S. government.

knowledgemanagement.wordpress.com: A comprehensive source of KM-related material (2006–2008).

icl-conference.org: Annual conferences on e-learning.

the-ebook-reader.com: All about e-readers (e.g., comparisons, software, free e-books).

igi-global.com/journal/international-journal-collaboration-ijec/1090: *The International Journal of E-Collaboration*

ec.europa.eu/digital-agenda/egovernment-going-studies: Digital agenda for Europe. Information on current studies, publications, and news.

GLOSSARY

Automated question-answer (Q&A) System used to find answers that match questions asked in a natural language (e.g., English, Chinese).

Collaborative commerce (c-commerce) Electronic support for business collaboration. It enables companies to collaboratively plan, design, develop, manage, and research products, services, and innovative business processes, including EC applications.

Collaboration hub (c-hub) The central point of interaction and of a company's supply chain. A single e-hub can host multiple *collaboration spaces* in which trading partners trade, collaborate, communicate, and share information.

Consumer-to-consumer (C2C) EC Electronic transactions completed between and among individuals.

Distance learning Education conducted from home or other place, anytime.

E-collaboration The use of digital technologies among people for accomplishing a common task.

E-government The use of information technology in general, and e-commerce in particular, to improve the delivery of government services and activities in the public sector, such as: providing citizens and organizations with more convenient access to government information and services, and to providing effective delivery of public services to engage citizens and businesses partners, as well as improving the performance of government employees.

E-learning The online delivery of educational materials and methods using information technologies, for the purposes of learning, teaching, training, or gaining knowledge at any time, and at many different locations.

Electronic book (e-book) A book in digital format that can be read on a computer screen, including mobile devices (e.g., a tablet, iPhone), or on a dedicated device known as an *e-reader*.

Expert/expertise location systems (ELS) Interactive computerized systems that help employees locate experts within their organization in order to get help in solving specific, critical business or technical problems in a short time.

Government 2.0 The employment of social media tools, new business models, and embracing social networks and user participation, government agencies can raise the effectiveness of their online activities to meet users' needs at a reasonable cost.

Government-to-business (G2B) E-government category that works both ways: government-to-business and business-to-government. Thus, G2B refers to activities where the government sells products to businesses or provides businesses with services and vice versa.

Government-to-citizens (G2C) E-government category that includes all the interactions between a government and its citizens that take place electronically.

Government-to employees (G2E) E-government category that includes activities between the government and their employees.

Government-to government (G2G) E-government category that includes EC activities between different units of governments, including those within one governmental body. Many of these are aimed at improving the effectiveness and the efficiency of the government operation.

Knowledge management (KM) The process of capturing or creating knowledge, storing it, updating it constantly, disseminating it, and using it whenever necessary.

Learning on-demand The trend where learners can study anywhere whenever they are ready.

Learning management system (LMS) Software applications for managing e-training and e-learning programs including content, scheduling, delivery tips, and so forth.

M-learning (mobile learning) Refers to e-learning or other forms of education using mobile devices.

Mobile government (m-government) The implementation of e-government applications using wireless platforms.

Social learning Learning, training, and knowledge sharing in social networks and/or facilitated by social software tools.

Vendor-managed inventory (VMI) A process in which retailers make their suppliers responsible for monitoring the inventory of each item they supply, and determining when to order each item.

Virtual university Online universities where students take classes from home via the Internet.

REFERENCES

Agarwal, A., A. Thomas, R. Gupta, and T. Mandal. "E-Learning: Tomorrow's Technology Today." April 5, 2010, **scribd.com/doc/219630151/29418813-e-Learning-White-Paper** (accessed April 2014).

Ali, T. "How Social Media is Changing Government Agencies." May 19, 2010. **mashable.com/2010/05/19/government-agencies-social-media** (accessed March 2014).

Allen, I. E., and J. Seaman. "Learning on Demand: Online Education in the United States." 2009. **sloanconsortium.org/publications/survey/learning_on_demand_sr2010** (accessed April 2014).

Awad, E. M., and H. Ghaziri. *Knowledge Management*, 2nd ed., Hershey, PA: International Technology Group, 2010.

Bahal, A. "Knowledge11: Pragmatic Approach to Knowledge Management." 2011. **infosys.com/newsroom/events/Documents/pragmatic-approach-knowledge-management.pdf** (accessed April 2014).

Bandura, A. "Social-Learning Theory of Identificatory Processes." in *Handbook of Socialization Theory and Research* by David A. Goslin, Ed., New York: Rand McNally & Co., 1969.

Berzon, A. "Enough with 'Call of Duty,' Answer the Call in Room 417." June 6, 2011. **online.wsj.com/news/articles/SB10001424052702304432304576367493214200856** (accessed April 2014).

Bingham, T., and M. Conner. *The New Social Learning: A Guide to Transforming Organizations Through Social*

Media. Alexandria, VA: American Society for Training & Development, 2010.

Bjelland, O. M., and R. C. Wood. "An Inside View of IBM's Innovation Jam." (Fall 2008). **sloanreview.mit.edu/article/an-inside-view-of-ibms-innovation-jam** (accessed April 2014).

Blankenbach, J., and C. Hickel. "With INSPIRE from SDI to Mobile E-Government." *Proceedings of the International Conference SDI&SIM 2013 FIG-COM3, FIG-TH-PH & GeoSEE*, Skopje, (FYROM) Macedonia, November 13–16, 2013.

Blankenbach, J., and M. Schaffert. "A SDI and Web 2.0 Based Approach to Support E-Participation in Municipal Administration and Planning Strategies." *Proceedings of the XXIV FIG International Congress*. Sydney, Australia, April 11–16, 2010.

Britt, P. "E-Commerce Buys into KM." October 2013. **kmworld.com/Articles/Editorial/Features/E-commerce-buys-into-KM-92023.aspx** (accessed April 2014).

Chan, C. M. L., R. Hackney, S. L. Pan, and T. C. Chou. "Managing e-Government System Implementation: A Resource Enactment Perspective." *European Journal of Information Systems,* vol. 20, 2011.

Chubb, J. E., and T .M. Moe. "Chubb and Moe: Higher Education's Online Revolution." May 30, 2012. **online.wsj.com/news/articles/SB10001424052702304019404577416631206583286** (accessed April 2014).

City & Guilds Kineo. "Compass Group Systems Training."2011.**kineo.com/case-studies/process-and-technical/compass-group-systems-training** (accessed March 2014).

Cobb, J. "Defining Social Learning." July 31, 2011. **tagoras.com/2011/07/31/define-social-learning** (accessed April 2014).

Clark, R. C., and R. E. Mayer. *e-Learning and the Science of Instruction*, 3rd ed. San Francisco: Pfeiffer/Wiley & Sons, 2011.

Currier, G. "Sharing Knowledge in the Corporate Hive." *Baseline*, May/June 2010.

Dachille, D. "How to Rate the Risks of Peer-to-Peer Lending, The Newest Bubble." January 1, 2014. **pbs.org/newshour/making-sense/how-to-rate-the-risks-of-peer-to-peer-lending-the-newest-bubble** (accessed April 2014).

D'Agostino, D. "Expertise Management: Who Knows About This?" *CIO Insight*, July 1, 2004.

Derven,M. "Social Networking: A Force for Development?" *Training and Development*, July 16, 2009.

Digital Government Strategy. "Building a 21st Century Platform to better serve the American People." A Whitehouse Report, 2012. **whitehouse.gov/sites/default/files/omb/egov/digital-government/digital-government.html** (accessed April 2014).

Directive 2007/2/EC: Directive 2007/2/EC of the European Parliament and of the Council of 14 March 2007 Establishing an Infrastructure for Spatial Information in the European Community (INSPIRE), *Official Journal L 108 Volume 50,* April 25, 2007.

Dvorak, R. *Moodle for Dummies.*, New York: For Dummies, 2011.

Egov. "E-Government Strategy: Implementing the President's Management Agenda for E-Government." April 2003. **whitehouse.gov/sites/default/files/omb/assets/omb/egov/2003egov_strat.pdf** (accessed April 2014).

Ellis, R. K. (Ed.). "A Field Guide to Learning Management Systems." A guide published by the American Society for Training and Development (ASTD), 2009. **cgit.nutn.edu.tw:8080/cgit/PaperDL/hclin_091027163029.PDF** (accessed April 2014).

Falcone, J. P. "Kindle vs. Nook vs. iPad: Which E-Book Reader Should You Buy?" July 6, 2010 [Updated December 17, 2012]. **cnet.com/news/kindle-vs-nook-vs-ipad-which-e-book-reader-should-you-buy** (accessed April 2014).

Foley, J., and J. N. Hoover. "Government Innovators." *InformationWeek*, September 19, 2011.

Fox, M. "SAP's Social Layer: Making Collaboration Real." June 25, 2012. **socialmediatoday.com/maggiefox-social-media-group/565356/sap-s-social-layer-making-collaboration-real** (accessed April 2014).

Garrison, D. R. *E-Learning in the 21st Century: A Framework for Research and Practice*, 2nd edition, New York: Routledge, 2011.

GDI-Südhessen (2014): Website of the Cooperation GDI-Südhessen, **gdi-suedhessen.de** (access February 2014).

Harasim, L. *Learning Theory and Online Technology.* New York: Routledge, 2011.

Hart, J. "The Future of E-Learning is Social Learning." May 2, 2009. **slideshare.net/janehart/the-future-of-elearning-is-social-learnng** (accessed April 2014).

Hartley, H. "Government 2.0: Examining Government in World 2.0." June 2, 2011. **gov2.wordpress.com/author/quepol** (accessed April 2014).

Hickel, C., and J. Blankenbach, J. "From Local SDI to E-Government, Case Study in Municipalities in the South of Hesse." *FIG Working Week 2012*, Rome, Italy, 6–10 May 2012.

Horton, W. *e-Learning by Design*, 2nd edition, Hoboken, NJ: Pfeiffer, 2011.

InfoDev/World Bank. *e-Government Primer.* Washington, DC, 2009. **infodev.org/infodev-files/resource/InfodevDocuments_821.pdf** (accessed April 2014).

Kaattari, J., and V. Trottier. "Guide to Effective Technologies for Online Learning [Kindle Edition]." Ontario, Canada, Community Literacy of Ontario, 2012 (revised and updated October 2013).

Kidd, T. T., and I. L. Chen. *Wired for Learning: An Educator's Guide to Web 2.0*, Charlotte, NC: Information Age Publishing, 2009.

Ko, S., and S. Rossen. *Teaching Online: A Practical Guide*, 3rd ed., New York: Routledge, 2010.

Leggatt, H. "Ebooks Now Outsell Hardbacks." *BizReport*, June 21, 2012. **bizreport.com/2012/06/ebooks-now-outsell-hardbacks.html** (accessed April 2014).

Lytras, M. D., et.al. (Eds.) *Information Systems, E-Learning, and Knowledge Management Research.* - 4th World Summit on the Knowledge Society, WSKS 2011, Mykonos, Greece, September 21–23, 2011. Revised Selected Papers. Springer 2013 Communications in

Computer and Information Science, New York: Springer, 2013.

Macintosh, A., and A. Whyte. "Towards an evaluation framework for eParticipation." *Transforming Government: People, Process & Policy*, vol. 2 no. 1, 2008.

Mängelmelder. "Portal to Report Defects in a City." **maengelmelder.de** (accessed February 2014).

Mason, R., and F. Rennie. *E-Learning and Social Networking Handbook: Resources for Higher Education*. New York: Routledge, 2008.

McCafferty, D. "Eight Ways to Improve Collaboration." July 18, 2011. **baselinemag.com/c/a/IT-Management/ Eight-Ways-To-Improve-Collaboration-730615** (accessed April 2014).

McLoughlin, I., and R. Wilson. *Digital Government at Work: A Social Informatics Perspective*, New York: Oxford University Press, 2013.

MedLibrary. "M-Government." December 1, 2010. **medlibrary.org/medwiki/M-government** (accessed March 2015).

Mehta, N., S. Oswald, and A. Mehta. "The Knowledge Management Program of Infosys Technologies." *Journal of Information Technology,* Vol. 22, November 26, 2007.

Millar, E. "No Classrooms and Lots of Technology: A Danish School's Approach." June 20, 2013. **theglobe-andmail.com/report-on-business/economy/canada-competes/no-classrooms-and-lots-of-technology-a-danish-schools-approach/article12688441** (accessed April 2014).

Naidu, S. "E-Learning: A Guidebook of Principles, Procedures and Practices." *Commonwealth of Learning*, June 2003. (See also 2nd Revised Edition at **cemca.org.in/ckfinder/userfiles/files/e-learning_ guidebook.pdf** (accessed April 2014).

NIC Inc. "Gov 2.0 – eGovernment Social Media Platform Deployments and Future Opportunities." A White Paper, February 8, 2010. **slideshare.net/egov/gov-20-egovern-ment-social-media-platform-deployments-and-future-opportunities** (accessed April 2014).

Office of Management and Budget. "FY 2011 Report to Congress on the Implementation of the E-Government Act of 2002." March 7, 2012. **whitehouse.gov/sites/ default/files/omb/assets/egov_docs/fy11__e-gov_ act_report.pdf** (accessed April 2014).

OGC. Open Geospatial Consortium. **opengeospatial.org** (accessed February 2014).

Rao, M. "Knowledge Management: Frameworks and Case Studies." August 9, 2010. **km.techsparks. com/?p=129** (accessed April 2014).

Robb, D. "Welcome Onboard." *HR Magazine*, May 2012.

Rossett, A., and J. Marshall. "E-Learning: What's Old Is New Again." *American Society for Training & Development*, January 14, 2010. **astd.org/Publications/Magazines/TD/ TD-Archive/2010/01/E-Learning-WhatS-Old-Is-New-Again** (accessed April 2014).

Shark, A., and S. Toporkoff. *Beyond e-Government and e-Democracy: A Global Perspective*. Scotts Valley, CA: BookSurge Publishing, 2008.

Siebdrat, F., M. Hoegl, and H. Ernst. "How to Manage Virtual Teams." Summer 2009. **sloanreview.mit.edu/ article/how-to-manage-virtual-teams** (accessed April 2014).

Sparkman, R.P. *So, You Want to Take a Class Online: Practical Advice for the Digital Classroom* [Kindle Edition]. Amazon Digital Services, Seattle, 2012.

Spychalska, D. *Vendor Managed Inventory: Exploring Objectives, Benefits and Shortcomings of the Business Concept*. Saarbrucken, Germany: Lambert Academic Publishing, 2010.

Streitfeld, D. "Teacher Knows if You've Done the E-Reading." April 8, 2013. **nytimes.com/2013/04/09/ technology/coursesmart-e-textbooks-track-students-progress-for-teachers.html?pagewanted=all&_r=0** (accessed April 2014).

Strom, D. "Choosing the Right Collaboration Tools." June 16, 2011. **baselinemag.com/c/a/IT-Management/ Choosing-the-Right-Collaboration-Tools-391600** (accessed April 2014).

Suresh, J. K., and K. Mahesh. "Managing the Knowledge Supply Chain at Infosys." *Knowledge Management Review* (November/December 2008).

Tariq, S. "Knowledge Management at Infosys." June 29, 2011. **slideshare.net/shuhabtrq/knowledge-man-agement-at-infosys-8462891** (accessed April 2014)

Thompson, K., "Managers of E-Learning Project Tout Positive Results." February 13, 2014. **jamaicaobserver. com/news/Managers-of-e-learning-project-tout-positive-results_16006381** (accessed April 2014).

Training Press Releases. "Kineo and Compass Group Create Award-Shortlisted Systems Training E-Learning." October 26, 2011. **trainingpressre-leases.com/news/kineo/2011/kineo-and-compass-group-create-award-shortlisted-systems-training-e-learning-** (accessed April 2014).

Trimi, S., and H. Sheng. "Emerging Trends in M-Government." *Communications of the ACM*, (May 2008).

U.S. Department of Housing and Urban Development. *Performance and Accountability Report Fiscal Year 2009*. **portal.hud.gov/hudportal/documents/ huddoc?id=hudfy2009par.pdf** (accessed April 2014).

Vaughan-Nichols, S. J. "Good-Bye Books, Hello E-Books." December 27, 2012. **zdnet.com/good-bye-books-hello-e-books-7000009208** (accessed April 2014).

Wishom, L. "Flexing your Collaboration Muscle in 3 Easy Phases- Part 1." August 9, 2012. **highachieving-women.biz/growth-success-acceleration/flexing-your-collaboration-muscle-in-3-easy-phases-part-1** (accessed April 2014).

Wang, P., and N. C. Ramiller. "Community Learning in Information Technology Innovation." *MIS Quarterly* (December 2009): 709–734. **terpconnect.umd. edu/~pwang/Wang&Ramiller2009.pdf** (accessed April 2014).

Zielinski, D. "Group Learning." May 2012. **shrm.org/pub-lications/hrmagazine/editorialcontent/2012/0512/ pages/0512zielinski.aspx** (accessed April 2014).

Part III

Emerging EC Delivery Platforms

Mobile Commerce and Ubiquitous Computing

Contents

Learning Objectives

Upon completion of this chapter, you will be able to:

1. Discuss the value-added attributes, benefits, and fundamental drivers of m-commerce.
2. Describe the mobile computing infrastructure that supports m-commerce (devices, software, and services).
3. Describe the four major types of wireless telecommunications and networks.
4. Discuss m-commerce applications in banking and financial services.
5. Describe enterprise mobility applications.
6. Describe consumer and personal applications of m-commerce, including entertainment.
7. Understand the technologies and potential applications of location-based m-commerce.
8. Define and describe ubiquitous computing and sensory networks.
9. Describe wearable Google Glass, driverless cars, and mobile apps.
10. Describe the major implementation issues from security and privacy to barriers of m-commerce.

Electronic supplementary material The online version of this chapter (doi: 10.1007/978-3-319-10091-3_6) contains supplementary material, which is available to authorized users

E. Turban et al., *Electronic Commerce: A Managerial and Social Networks Perspective*,
Springer Texts in Business and Economics, DOI 10.1007/978-3-319-10091-3_6,
© Springer International Publishing Switzerland 2015

OPENING CASE: HERTZ GOES MOBILE ALL THE WAY

The Problem

The car rental industry is very competitive, and Hertz Corporation (**hertz.com**), the world's largest car rental company, competes against hundreds of companies in approximately 10,400 locations in 150 countries. The strong competition negatively impacted profits. For Hertz Global Holdings, Inc. business profile and statistics, see **hoovers.com/company-information/cs/company-profile.Hertz_Global_Holdings_Inc.7b9c49d62787624c.html**. Hertz needs to constantly maintain a mobile presence. Customers can easily connect with the company through its mobile site. The Hertz mobile app is available for iPhone, iPad, Android, and Windows phone.

The Solution

Hertz pioneered several mobile commerce applications to increase its competitiveness. Mobile commerce is now embedded in the company's national wireless network. This information is needed to reserve a car, confirm or change reservations, and other customer-related services (e.g., review rental history, direct credit mileage to the proper loyalty program, etc.).

Here are some of Hertz's mobile services:

- **Easy and quick rentals.** Reservations can be made by phone, e-mail, and on the website (via smartphone, tablet, or desktop). Confirmations are e-mailed (or texted) within seconds of making the reservation. Upon arrival in a city, the renter receives a text message pinpointing the car's location in Hertz's parking area. In many rental locations, the cars are equipped with an RFID system. In such a case, the renter sweeps the Hertz key-fob/card over the RFID reader to unlock the doors. Alternatively, in some locations, Hertz's curbside attendant confirms the reservation on a handheld device, and transmits the arrival information wirelessly to the rental booth.

This in return reveals the location of the car. All the renter needs to do is go to the slot where the car is parked and drive away. For interesting new features see Elliott (2013).

- **Instant returns (eReturn).** There is no longer any need to wait in line in Hertz's office to return the car. An attendant with a handheld device connected to the wireless system enters the return time, and the system calculates the cost of the rental and prints a receipt. The checkout time takes about a minute, right in the parking lot.

- **NeverLost® GPS Navigation System.** Many Hertz cars are equipped with the Hertz NeverLost® GPS system (**neverlost.com**) that includes a display screen and voice prompts (e.g., when to make a turn). A map (either Google Maps or MapQuest) shows the routes and business information (e.g., public and consumer services, such as the location of the nearest hospitals, gas stations, and eateries displayed). Hertz also offers the MyExplore™ NeverLost® Mobile Companion app (see **neverlost.com/Products/ProductDetail?ProductName=myexplore**). This app allows you to plan your trip on your smartphone and use the app to navigate selected cities such as Washington, D.C. and New York. Some of the app's features include augmented reality (turn your camera phone into a live map); social media integration (share your experiences on social networks such as Facebook and Twitter); and weather information (get live weather information and five day forecasts).

  For new functionalities see **finance.yahoo.com/news/navigation-solutions-hertz-neverlost-r-221503204.html**.

- **Additional customer services.** In addition to the location guide, the NeverLost® system provides driving directions, emergency telephone numbers, city maps, shopping guides, customer reviews of hotels, restaurants, and other consumer services. This content also is available to Hertz's club members at home, where they can print the information or load it into their mobile devices.

- **Car locations.** Hertz is experimenting with a GPS-based tracking system, which enables the company to find the location of a rental car at any given time. Furthermore, the system may be able to report in real time th*e speed at which the* car is being driven. Although the company promises to keep the collected information secure, many view it as an *invasion of privacy*. However, some renters may feel safer knowing that they are being tracked at all times. Note: Currently, (May 2014) Hertz is using the system only to track stolen cars and to find when cars are returned.

- **Hertz 24/7 (with on demand technology).** According to their website, Hertz 24/7 with on demand technology offers self-service access to a rental vehicle for a short period of time (by the hour, or a day), competing with car sharing company Zipcar Inc. (**zipcar.com**). The Hertz 24/7 mobile app is available for download at **hertz.com/rentacar/productservice/index.jsp?targetPage=hertzmobilesite.jsp** and can be used to find car rental locations. This application is available on PCs and mobile devices (**hertz247.com/NewYork/en-US/About/Mobile**). The application includes ride sharing (e.g., rate comparisons of public transportation versus car rental).
- **Wi-Fi connection.** Free high-speed Internet access is available in Hertz's offices in all major Hertz locations in the United States, Canada, and some other countries.
- **Hertz mobile apps.** With the Hertz apps, which are available for iPhone, iPad, Windows, and Android, you can make reservations, search for store locations, enjoy special offers, and much more. See the Hertz Mobile page at **hertz.com/rentacar/productservice/index.jsp?targetPage=hertzmobilesite.jsp**. For recent mobile apps see *PR Newswire* (2014).

The Results

Despite the economic problems of 2008–2012, Hertz has retained the number one position in the car rental industry. Its earnings, which declined in 2008 and 2009, rebounded between 2010 and 2014. Hertz did better than most of its competitors. Its stock market share price, which bottomed out in 2009, more than tripled in 2010 and continued to climb from 2011 to 2014. The company is expanding its operations and maintaining an excellent reputation among customers, due in part to its mobile applications.

Sources: Based on **hertz.com** (accessed May 2014), Goodwin (2010), and Kahn et al. (2010).

LESSONS LEARNED FROM THE CASE

The Hertz case illustrates several mobile applications in the transportation industry that can help improve both customer service and the company's operations. The applications are run on mobile devices and supported by a wireless network. (Both topics are discussed in Section 6.2.) The mobile technology is based on a set of unique attributes (Section 6.1) that enable the use of many applications (Sections 6.3, 6.4, 6.5, 6.6 and 6.7).

The Hertz case is only one example of the impact of emerging mobile and wireless technologies on business and electronic commerce (EC). In this chapter, we explore a number of these emerging mobile and wireless technologies as well as their potential applications in the commercial and societal arenas. The chapter also deals with the mobile enterprise, location-based services, and ubiquitous computing, which are cutting-edge technologies.

6.1   MOBILE COMMERCE: CONCEPTS, LANDSCAPE, ATTRIBUTES, DRIVERS, APPLICATIONS, AND BENEFITS

As described in Chapter 1, businesses are becoming digital (Accenture Technology Vision 2014). In addition, many enterprises are going borderless and the need for mobile communication is increasing rapidly. According to GSMA (2013), the mobile industry is already a major contributor to the global economy. More than half of the world's population already own mobile phones, many of which are smartphones. Obviously, all the above are drivers of mobile commerce.

Mobile commerce has its own framework, attributes landscape, concepts, and terminology. These provide many benefits. For an overview, see the 2:45 minute video titled "What is M-Commerce" at **youtube.com/watch?v=QtpTTpgpELg**.

One of the clearest trends in computing and e-commerce is that mobile computing is increasing exponentially. Each year, Gartner Inc. compiles a list of the top ten strategic technology trends that have the potential to offer numerous benefits to individuals, businesses, and IT organizations during the following 3 years. The 2014 list (**gartner.com/technology/research/top-10-technology-trends**) includes four topics, 40% of which are related to mobile computing, and are discussed later in this chapter.

Basic Concepts, Magnitude, and the Landscape

Mobile commerce (m-commerce), also known as *m-business*, refers to conducting e-commerce by using mobile devices and wireless networks. Activities include B2C, B2B, m-government, and m-learning transactions, as well as the transfer of information and money. Like regular EC applications, m-commerce is an electronic transaction conducted by using mobile devices via the Internet, corporate intranets, private communication lines, or over other wireless networks. For example, paying for an item in a vending machine or pay taxes with an iPhone is considered m-commerce. M-commerce provides an opportunity to deliver new services to existing customers and to attract new customers to EC anytime, anywhere. Initially, the small screen size and slow bandwidth limited the usefulness to consumers. However, this situation is changing rapidly due to the widespread use of smartphones and tablet computers. In addition, now consumers are more accepting of the handheld culture. Furthermore, the adoption of m-com-

merce is accelerating due to the spread of 3G and 4G networks. Finally, free Wi-Fi Internet access in many locations helps. As a result, smartphones now account for almost 60% of all mobile phones in the U.S. The *strategic value* of mobile systems is increasing significantly.

Note that m-commerce is quite different from traditional e-commerce and frequently uses specialized business models (see **mobilinfo.com/Mcommerce/differences.htm**). This results in many new applications and a change in the relationship between buyers and sellers (see **ibm.com/software/genservers/commerce/mobile**).

The Magnitude of M-Commerce
According to a 2013 eMarketer study, by 2017, approximately 25% of all online retail transactions in the U.S. will take place on mobile devices (reported by **mashable.com/2013/04/24/mcommerce-sales-forecast**). Forrester Research forecasts that m-commerce will top $38 billion in 2014 (reported by Fiegerman 2014 at **mashable.com/2014/05/12/mobile-commerce-sales**). A 2014 InMobi report found that 83% of customers plan to conduct mobile commerce in 2014, a 15% increase from the previous year. The full report can be downloaded from **inmobi.com/company/press/inmobi-report-finds-83-of-consumers-plan-to-conduct-mobile**.

Knight (2012a) provides some statistics that show the explosive growth of mobile commerce. For mobile marketing statistics (2012), see **snaphop.com/2012-mobile-marketing-statistics**. In addition, according to Leggatt (2012), m-commerce has quadrupled from April 2010 to May 2012. For more statistics see **snaphop.com/2013-mobile-marketing-statistics**.

In this chapter, we consider some of the distinguishing attributes and key drivers of m-commerce, some technical issues relevant to m-commerce, and some of the major m-commerce applications.

The Landscape of M-Commerce
The overall landscape of m-commerce is summarized in Figure 6.1.

Note that in the figure, the enabling technologies (e.g., devices, networks) are on the left side

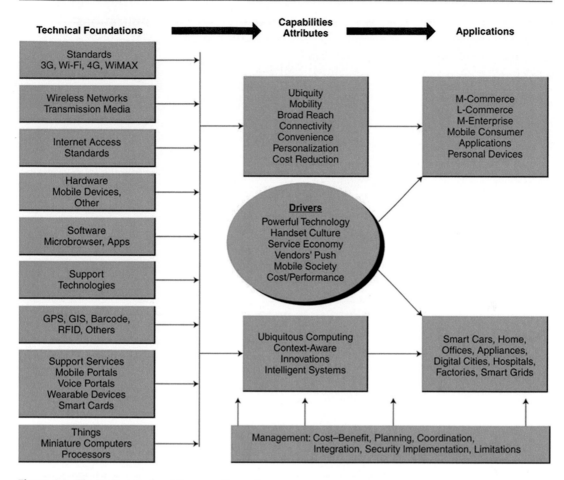

Figure 6.1 The landscape of mobile computing and m-commerce

and the resulting capabilities and attributes are in the middle. These provide the foundation for the applications that are shown on the right side of the figure. In this section, we describe the attributes and provide an overview of the applications. In Section 6.2, we present the essentials of the major technologies.

Mobile and Social: A Powerful EC Combination

M-commerce is a very powerful platform, but it can be even more powerful when combined with social commerce, as we will describe in Chapters 7 and 8. This combination will shape the future of e-commerce and could be its major facilitator in the future. The so-called mobile social networking application field is already growing rapidly (126% in 2011; see Eler 2011).

Example: The 2012 London Olympics

Mueller (2012) provides an interesting description of the use of a combination of mobile and social environments in the 2012 Olympic Games in London.

The Attributes of M-Commerce

Many of the EC applications described in this book also apply to m-commerce. For example, online shopping, e-travel, e-learning, e-entertainment, and online gaming are all gaining popularity in mobile B2C. Auction sites use m-commerce to send messages to bidders during the auction process, governments encourage m-government (Chapter 5), and wireless collaborative commerce in B2B EC is on the rise. Some key attributes that enable new applications are possible only in the mobile environment. The major attributes include:

> - **Ubiquity.** *Ubiquity* means being everywhere, especially at the same time. It is facilitated by wireless computing. Given that Wi-Fi access is available in more and more places, and that about half of all mobile phones are smartphones, we have easier ubiquity.
> - **Convenience and capabilities.** Having a mobile device increases the convenience of communication. The functionality and usability of mobile devices is increasing while their physical size remains small and the cost is affordable. Unlike traditional computers, mobile devices connect to the Internet almost instantly.
> - **Interactivity.** Mobile systems allow for fast and easy interactions (e.g., via Twitter, tablets, or smartphones).
> - **Personalization.** Mobile devices are personal devices. While several people may share the same PC, a specific mobile device is usually used by one person.
> - **Localization.** Knowing where a user is physically located in real time provides an opportunity to offer him or her relevant mobile advertisements, coupons, or other services. Such services are known as location-based m-commerce (see Section 6.6). Localization may be for the entire public (e.g., an announcement about an emergency) or it can be personalized for an individual.

Mobile vendors differentiate themselves from wireline vendors by offering unique services based on the above attributes. The drivers of m-commerce are illustrated in Figure in 6.2 and discussed in Online File W6.1.

An Overview of the Applications of M-Commerce

There are thousands of different m-commerce applications. Many of these are similar to those in a wireline environment, as described in Chapters 3 and 4. Others are available for mobile devices only.

To simplify our presentation, we divided the applications in this chapter into the following categories, adding consumer applications to the framework:

> - Banking and financial services – Section 6.3
> - Mobile enterprise applications – Section 6.4
> - Consumer services (including shopping) and entertainment – Section 6.5
> - Location-based mobile commerce – Section 6.6
> - Ubiquitous computing – Section 6.7
> - Emerging applications: Wearables, Google Glass, smart grid, and driverless cars – Section 6.8
> - Mobile shopping is covered in Chapter 7
> - Mobile marketing and advertising are covered in Chapter 9
> - Mobile payment is introduced in Chapter 11

We categorized the *enterprise-related applications* by the framework used by Motorola Corp. See **motorolasolutions.com/US-EN/enterprise+ mobility**. Note: Zebra Tech. acquired Motorola Solutions Enterprise Business in April 2014.

According to this framework, *enterprise applications* are created to meet specific business needs. These needs have some generic aspects as well as industry-specific aspects (see Figure 6.3). The four needs are:

1. **Field mobility** – the support of the mobile workforce
2. **Fleet mobility** – the support of vehicles in order to minimize downtime and increase effectiveness, efficiency, and utilization

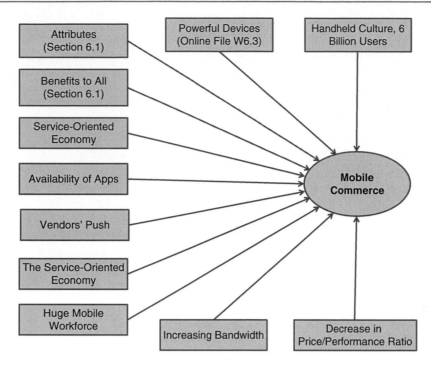

Figure 6.2 The drivers of m-commerce

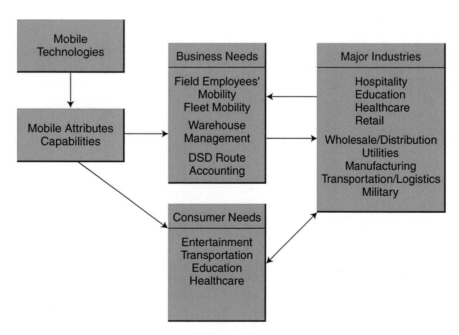

Figure 6.3 M-commerce applications and their classifications

3. **Warehouse management** – the improvement of the operations inside warehouses
4. **Direct store delivery (DSD) route accounting** – the increased usefulness by conducting pre-delivery activities (e.g. by texting information about a new shipment from the shipper to the receiver).

These needs can exist in any industry, and drive the use of m-commerce. The major industries that use m-commerce are hospitality, education, health care, retail, wholesale and distribution, utilities, manufacturing, transportation, and logistics. Each of these industries and its needs can be divided into 3 to 10 subcategories for which Motorola (and other vendors) provide specific solutions.

This chapter, as well as Olariu and Tiliute (2011), discuss the techniques and applications in the m-commerce field from a managerial point of view. A related application, ubiquitous computing, will be discussed in Section 6.7.

Also of interest is the emerging field of *mobile intelligence* (see Saylor 2012).

The Benefits of M-Commerce

M-commerce has many benefits to organizations, individuals, and society. As a result, many believe that the future of EC is mobile applications (watch the 5:06 minute video titled "The Future of E-Commerce Is: Mobile Applications" at **youtube.com/watch?v=kYSMP_RH67w**).

Benefits for Organizations

- Increases sales due to ease of ordering by customers from anywhere, anytime.
- Allows location-based commerce for more sales and revenue (Section 6.6).
- Provides an additional channel for advertising and distribution of coupons (wider reach).
- Increases customers' loyalty.
- Improves customer satisfaction through real-time apps.

- Enables many enterprise applications (Section 6.4).
- Facilitates CRM and collaboration.
- Reduces employee training time and help desk resources.
- Improves time utilization and productivity of mobile employees.
- Expedites information flow to and from mobile employees.
- Delivers digitized products and services directly to mobile devices.
- Reduces order lead-time and fulfillment cycle.
- Allows for lower, competitive pricing.

Benefits for Individuals and Customers

- Allows e-commerce from any place, anytime.
- Assists in shopping by providing real time information and other shopping aids.
- Helps organization of and communication while travelling.
- Expedites banking and financial services.
- Provides rich media entertainment anytime and anywhere.
- Facilitates the finding of new friends and whereabouts of existing ones.
- Provides a choice of mobile devices for transactions.
- Expedites communication (e.g., locate people; get fast answers to queries; compare prices while in physical stores or via shopping comparison sites/apps).
- Increases affordability over the cost of using desktop computing in some countries.

Benefits to Society

There are many benefits to society. For example, self-driving cars can reduce accidents; smart cities can benefit the population. Contributions are in almost any field, from medical care and education to law enforcement. Significant reductions in energy expenses are achieved by using smart grids. Traffic jams can be reduced by using wireless sensors and much more.

There are also limitations to m-commerce, which are discussed in Section 6.9.

Other Benefits

In addition to the benefit of ubiquity, m-commerce enables true personalization, reduces costs, increases time available to employees, expedites business processes, and much more, as will be shown throughout this book.

SECTION 6.1 REVIEW QUESTIONS

1. Define m-commerce.
2. Briefly describe the five value-added attributes of m-commerce.
3. List and briefly describe eight major drivers of m-commerce (see Online File W6.1) and Figure 6.2.
4. Describe the framework of m-commerce applications.
5. What are the major categories of m-commerce applications?
6. Describe the landscape of m-commerce.
7. What are the major benefits of m-commerce?
8. Describe the major online enterprise applications.

6.2   THE ENABLING INFRASTRUCTURE: COMPONENTS AND SERVICES OF MOBILE COMPUTING

The technology that supports m-commerce is very diversified. Here we concentrate on some major technology items.

Overview of Mobile Computing

In the traditional computing environment, users were confined to desktop computers in fixed locations. A solution to this situation is **wireless mobile computing** (**mobile computing**), where

computing is done by using mobile devices at any place connected to a wireless network. According to TechTarget Bitpipe, wireless mobile computing, also known as nomadic computing, is the use of portable computing devices (such as laptops and handheld computers) in conjunction with mobile communications technologies to enable users access to the Internet and data on their home or work computers from anywhere in the world (see **bitpipe.com/tlist/Wireless-Computing.html**).

An extensive hardware and software infrastructure enables mobile computing. First, there are mobile devices (e.g., tablets, smartphones, wearables, and hand held computers) that connect users wirelessly to networks and to other devices. Next, there are those features that provide the wireless connection, (e.g., network access points and Wi-Fi), as well as parts of the infrastructure that support the delivery of services over the connection (e.g., GPS locators). Finally, there are those components that support m-commerce activities in the same way they support typical e-commerce activities (e.g., a Web server, payment gateway, database server, and enterprise application server).

This section briefly discusses the major technologies of mobile computing systems. For an extensive list of related terms, see **mobileinfo.com/ Glossary** and **webopedia/Mobile_computing**. For the importance and magnitude of mobile computing, see Gannes (2013), who presents the relevant highlights from Meeker's 2013 Internet Trends. For the introduction and history of mobile computing, see Livingston's (2013) presentation at **slideshare.net/davidjlivi/introduction-history-of-mobile-computing**.

Mobile Devices

Mobile devices come in all shapes and sizes – laptops, thin-and-light notebooks, tablet computers, smartphones, ultra portables, and ultra-mobile PCs (UMPCs). What distinguishes one type of mobile computer from another are its different capabilities, such as physical dimensions, shape, and the executions of the capabilities. Most of the major computer manufacturers (HP, Apple, Dell,

ASUS, Toshiba, ACER, and Lenovo) produce thin laptops and ultra portables.

A few years ago, portable computers, cell phones, and other mobile devices were different from each other and had unique features. Today, all of these devices are converging so that it is sometimes difficult to tell them apart (from a functional perspective).

Mobile devices can be large. Several manufacturers offer 17″ laptops or mobile workstations (e.g., Dell, HP and Lenovo). Tablets are available in a 7″ or 10″ screen. Smartphones come in a variety of sizes.

Smartphones

A **smartphone** is a mobile phone with Internet access and PC-like functionality (such as iPhone).

There is a wide range and variety of smartphone manufacturers. Note that smartphones get "smarter" with time and add features and capabilities. There is also a wide variety of operating systems, including Symbian, Google Apps, Android, Palm OS, Windows Mobile, Apple OS/X, RIM BlackBerry, and Google's Chrome OS. Like PDAs, smartphones have small screens, keyboards, memory, and storage. Most smartphones have built-in cameras and some are GPS-enabled.

Tablets

A fast growing category of mobile devices is the *tablet computer.* Tablet computers received a major boost in 2010 with the introduction of the Apple iPad and its competitors, all with a virtual keyboard (but a portable physical keyboard can be attached). Since then, many companies are manufacturing tablets. Notable are Amazon.com, Samsung, HP, Dell, Microsoft, HTC and Google. Like laptops, tablets can access the Web via Wi-Fi hotspots. The *iPad* weighs about 1 pound (in between a smartphone and a small laptop), and its screen measures 7.87 (the iPad mini, which weighs .73 pounds) or 9.5 (larger sizes coming soon). Tablets are replacing PCs and laptops in enterprises and schools. Tablets are also replacing hardcover textbooks in many schools. Tablets can be used as e-readers and can be used to access the Internet. Note that the price of tablets is declining while their capabilities are increasing. In India, for instance, Aakash students can buy tablets for as little as $35.

Tablets are becoming popular in enterprises as well. For example, Waste Management Inc. (**wm. com**) provides 7″ tablets to their truckers for finding optimal routes. For a comprehensive description, see Murphy (2012), **informationweek.com/ mobile.asp**, and **apple.com/ipad**. A Yankee Group report found that "[t]ablets lead enterprises into a mobile computing transformation" (Lund and Signorini 2011). The enterprise tablets are used mostly by mobile professionals and field force employees. McCafferty (2012) reports that "tablets are changing how employees work."

A major use of a tablet is to facilitate communication and collaboration.

Example

Mydin is a large Malaysian retailer that operates 100 stores all over the country for budget-oriented consumers. The competition is fierce in this industry and the profit margin is low. Therefore, making faster informed decisions is critical for the company's success. To make timely decisions, managers needed appropriate communication and effective collaboration tools. In 2012, Mydin's managers began using a real-time telepresence solution from U.S.-based conferencing solutions provider Vidyo. According to Malik Murad Ali, Mydin's IT director, "Immediate benefits included enhanced real-time collaboration between staff, which has raised our quality standards with the accelerated decision-making during the course of the day's business." For Mydin's success story, see **cio-asia.com/resource/applications/mobile- telepresence-trims-costs-for-major-malaysian- retailer/?page=1** and the case study at **vidyo. com/wp-content/uploads/2013/10/vidyo_case_ study_MYDIN.pdf**.

Google's Smart Glasses

In 2012, Google introduced its *Project Glass*, which takes the major functionalities of a smartphone and embeds them into a wearable device that looks like virtual reality glasses. Google Glass has a smartphone-like display, allowing you to take basic smartphone features (messaging, e-mail) and making them hands free. For more on the features of Google Glass, see **gizmag.com/ google-glass-review/30300**. The Google Glass Field Trip app can now be activated by voice commands (**mashable.com/2014/04/29/field-trip- google-glass-update**) (see Section 6.8).

Personal Digital Assistants: Enterprise Tablets

Originally called a **personal digital assistant (PDA)**, or *palmtop computer*, the early version of the device was a stand-alone handheld computer that provided access to a user's address book and calendar and supported calculations and some desktop applications, such as word processing and spreadsheets. PDAs were used mostly for enterprise applications. Most of the original PDAs had the ability to be synchronized with a user's desktop computer. This enabled a user to read e-mails offline. Over time, most PDAs have added support for wireless connectivity to the Internet through Wi-Fi. Most PDAs also provide multimedia support for audio and video. Today, PDAs are very similar to enterprise tablets. Most vendors changed the name PDA to tablets. An example is the Blackberry PlayBook. Another example is Motion Computing's CL910.

Wearable Devices

The smallest mobile devices are wearable. Notable are many devices used in the enterprise (e.g., mounted on the arm, head, or body and carried by employees). Samsung's Galaxy Gear SmartWatch, which was released in 2013, is one example. In April 2014, Samsung released its Gear Fit device, a "fitness tracker-smartwatch hybrid"(see**mashable.com/2014/04/08/samsung- gear-fit-review**). Apple iWatch is already in production and is scheduled to debut in the latter part of 2014. For more about wearable devices, see Section 6.8.

Other Mobile Devices

There are other kinds of mobile devices as well. For example, Microsoft offers a tablet with an attachable keyboard and Dell offers a foldable tablet with a keyboard, combining the capabilities of a laptop and a tablet. A representative list of mobile devices is available in Online File W6.2.

Radio-Frequency Identification (RFID)

Radio-Frequency Identification (RFID) enables the transfer of data wirelessly (non-contact), usually for the purpose of automatically identifying and tracking tags attached to objects. RFID does this by employing radio-frequency electromagnetic fields (see Online Tutorial T2). Most of the enterprise applications relate to logistics and inventory control. For details, see Chapter 12. Also related to EC is the use of RFID to enable mobile payments. For images of RFID applications, conduct a Google Images search for 'RFID applications.' For a comprehensive guide to RFID (e.g., white papers, case studies, definition), see the RFID technology Primer at **impinj.com/guide-to-rfid/what-is-rfid.aspx**. Finally, for 100 uses of RFID, see **rfid.thingmagic. com/ 100-uses-of-rfid**.

Mobile Computing Software and Services

Mobile devices offer some capabilities that desktops do not. These capabilities provide a foundation for newer applications such as location-based services.

Mobile Portals and Content Providers

A **mobile portal** is a gateway to the Internet from mobile devices. It combines content from several sources and can be personalized for mobile users. These portals offer services similar to those of desktop portals (see **gartner.com/it-glossary/ mobile-portal** and **ehow.com/facts_7631652_ definition-mobile-portal.html** for an additional discussion of mobile portals). An example of a pure mobile portal is Zed (**zed.com**; a wholly owned subsidiary of Finnish telecommunication company Sonera) headquartered in Spain. Japan's largest mobile provider, with over 60 million customers, is i-mode from NTT DOCOMO (see **nttdocomo.co.jp/english/service/imode** for the capabilities of i-mode).

The services provided by mobile portals are similar to those provided by desktop portals (e.g., news, health, sports, and downloading music). Mobile portals sometimes charge for their services.

Short Message Service

Short message service (SMS), frequently referred to as *text messaging*, or simply *texting*; the technology supports the transmittal of short text messages (up to 140 or 160 characters) between wireless devices. The cost of texting is very low compared to the charge per minute to talk on cell phones. The limited message length makes users use acronyms to convey standard messages. Examples of such acronyms include "how are you" becoming "HOW RU," or "HRU," and "in my opinion" becoming "IMO." Texting is popular worldwide due to the use of smartphones and microblogging (e.g., Twitter).

Multimedia Messaging Services (MMS)

Multimedia messaging service (MMS) is the new type of wireless messaging, delivering rich media content, such as videos, images, and audio to mobile devices. MMS is an extension of SMS (no extra charge with an SMS "bundle"). It allows for longer messages than with SMS.

For the difference between SMS and MMS and their benefits for mobile marketing, see **blog.mogreet.com/understanding-mobile-marketing-what-is-sms-mms-message-marketing**.

Location-Based Services

Retailers who use location-based services use the *global positioning system (GPS)* or other positioning techniques, to find a customer's location and then deliver services, such as ads for products and services, and coupons in real time. GPS also is used in emergency services, traffic management, and other applications (see Section 6.6).

Voice-Support Services

The most natural mode of human communication is voice. Voice recognition and voice synthesizing in m-commerce applications offer advantages such as hands- and eyes-free operation, better operation in dirty or moving environments, faster input (people talk about two-and-a-half times faster than they type), and ease-of-use for disabled people.

IVR Systems

Voice support applications such as **interactive voice response (IVR) systems** enable users to interact by telephones (of any kind) with a computerized system to request and receive information. These systems have been around since the 1980s but are now becoming more capable and widespread as artificial intelligence–based voice-recognition capabilities continue to evolve.

Voice Portals

A **voice portal** is a website with an audio interface that can be accessed through a telephone call. A user requests information by speaking, and the voice portal finds the information on the Web, transforms it into a computer-generated voice reply, and provides the answer by voice. For example, Bing Tell voice assistant (**bing.com/dev/speech**; a Microsoft company) allows callers to request information ranging from weather to current traffic conditions. IVR and voice portals are likely to become important ways of delivering m-commerce services over audio. Popular applications are used for banking, hospitals, airlines, government services, and online entertainment. A similar service, called Siri, is available on iPhones where you can place commands by voice, including sending messages asking questions, and receiving answers.

Wireless Telecommunications Networks

Wireless Application Protocol (WAP) is the technology protocol that enables Internet browsing using mobile devices. All mobile devices need to connect with a telecommunications network. How they do this depends on the purpose of the connection, the capabilities and location of the devices, and what connection options are in use. The major systems are:

- **Personal area networks.** A **personal area network (PAN)** provides very short-range device-to-device wireless connections (a distance up to 60 feet). The most common way to establish a PAN is with Bluetooth technology. **Bluetooth** is a set of wireless technologies standards for exchanging data between devices over a short range. For additional information, see **bluetooth.com** and the Bluetooth Special Interest Group (**bluetooth.org**).
- **Wireless local area networks and Wi-Fi.** As its name implies, a **wireless local area network (WLAN)** acts wirelessly (similar to how a wired LAN acts). Most WLANs run on a telecommunications standard known as *IEEE 802.11* (e.g., 802.11g), which is known as **Wi-Fi**. Figure 6.4 explains how Wi-Fi works by presenting the processes and components. Users need to find *access points* (or hotspots) to connect to the Internet. A wireless network card installed on your PC, for example, supports the connectivity throughout your house. The access point connects to the Internet in a similar manner as a wired LAN cable does. Wi-Fi access is now available almost everywhere: in many hotels, airlines, long distance bus services, shopping centers, trains, airports, university campuses, restaurants, coffee shops, cruise ships, libraries, and other public places. Google is bringing free Wi-Fi to several cities, including parts of New York City. Comcast Corp. is planning a similar service. The Comcast Wi-Fi network is projected to reach 8 million hotspots in select cities across the country by the end of 2014, with 325,000 hotspots installed in Chicago as of April 2014 (see **articles.chicagotribune.com/2014-04-30/business/chi-comcast-wif-otspot-rollout-20140430_1_own-xfinity-credentials-chicago-area-wi-fi-network-neighborhood-hot-spots-initiative** and Channick 2014).
- **Municipal Wi-Fi networks (WMAN).** A large number of connected hotspots can create a wireless campus or city. This is known as a *city-wide* or *municipal Wi-Fi network*. For example, Google created a network of 380 access points posted on light poles throughout the city of Mountain View, California, giving the city's residents free Wi-Fi access. The company also provides such service in parts of New York City. WMANs also are known as *grid* or *mesh networks*. Throughout the United States, there have been a number of municipal Wi-Fi projects, many of which, like Philadelphia, Pennsylvania's "Wireless Philadelphia" project, have experienced cost and schedule overruns, and were forced to close or limit the service area.
- **WiMAX.** Instead of relying on a mesh or grid of many access points, **WiMAX** (Worldwide Interoperability for Microwave Access) provides relatively fast (e.g., 75 Mbps to several GHz) broadband access over an area of up to 31 miles (50 kilometers). The usefulness of WiMAX is still uncertain. The WiMAX Forum (**wimaxforum.org**) provides detailed information about WiMAX capabilities and usage.
- **Wireless wide area networks.** A **wireless wide area network (WWAN)** offers the broadest wireless coverage. WWANs rely on the same network technologies as cell phones. For details, see **wireless.att.com/businesscenter/business-programs/mid-large/wireless-network**, **searchenterprisewan.techtarget.com/definition/wireless-WAN**, and **pcmag.com/category2/0,2806,2354098,00.asp**. For images of WWAN, do a Google Images search for 'wireless wide area network.'
- **LTE (Long Term Evolution).** This developing technology is supposed to replace the WiMAX. See **mashable.com/2012/06/12/4g-explained-what-is-lte**.

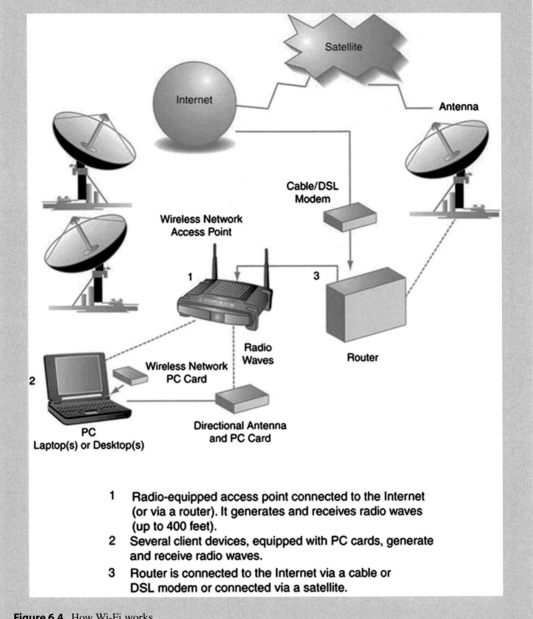

1   Radio-equipped access point connected to the Internet
    (or via a router). It generates and receives radio waves
    (up to 400 feet).
2   Several client devices, equipped with PC cards, generate
    and receive radio waves.
3   Router is connected to the Internet via a cable or
    DSL modem or connected via a satellite.

Figure 6.4 How Wi-Fi works

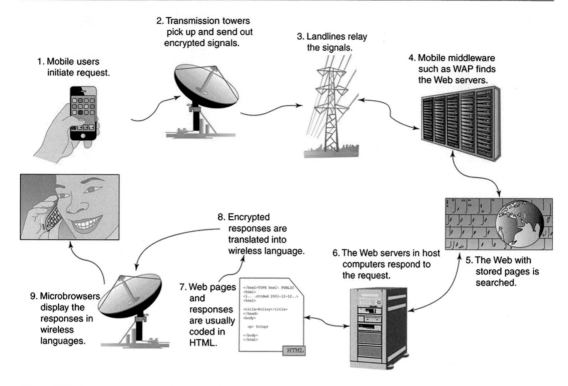

1. Mobile users initiate request.

2. Transmission towers pick up and send out encrypted signals.

3. Landlines relay the signals.

4. Mobile middleware such as WAP finds the Web servers.

5. The Web with stored pages is searched.

6. The Web servers in host computers respond to the request.

7. Web pages and responses are usually coded in HTML.

8. Encrypted responses are translated into wireless language.

9. Microbrowsers display the responses in wireless languages.

Figure 6.5   An m-commerce system at work

Note: Some companies are trying to connect to the Internet by sending signals from high in the sky and even from outer space (e.g., watch the video titled "Beaming the Internet from Outer Space" (1:36 minutes) at **money.cnn.com/video/ technology/2014/02/26/t-beaming-internet- from-space-outernet-cubesat.cnnmoney**).

Putting It All Together

The previously mentioned software, hardware, and telecommunications are connected by a management system to support wireless electronic trading, as shown in Figure 6.5. The figure, which is self-explanatory, shows the flow of information from the user (Step 1) to the conclusion of the transaction (Step 9).

SECTION 6.2 REVIEW QUESTIONS
1. Briefly describe some of the key differences and similarities among the major mobile devices.
2. Briefly describe the types of messaging services offered for mobile devices.
3. Define mobile portal and voice portal.
4. Distinguish between MMS and SMS.
5. Define IVR.
6. What are the distinguishing features of PANs, WLANs, WMAN, LTE, and WWANs?

6.3   MOBILE FINANCIAL APPLICATIONS

Most mobile financial services are mobile versions of their wireline counterparts. However, they can be used anytime, anywhere. We divided these services into two broad categories: mobile banking and other mobile financial services. Mobile payments are described in Chapter 11.

Mobile Banking

Mobile banking (m-banking) describes the conducting of banking activities via a mobile device (mostly via smartphones, tablets, texting, or mobile website). The influx of smartphones and tablets, especially iPhones and iPads, has led to an increased utilization of mobile banking. For details, a conceptual model, and challenges for mobile banking solutions, see Krishnan (2014) and Nicoletti (2014).

Throughout the world, more and more banks are offering mobile-based financial and accounting information.

Examples

Most banks deploy mobile services through a variety of channels, although the Internet and SMS are the most widely used. A blog written by Brandon McGee (**bmcgee.com**) provides links to a number of banking websites throughout the world that provide comprehensive wireless financial services. The Chase Mobile app and other mobile banking services offered by J.P. Morgan Chase Bank at **chase.com**, enable customers to access their accounts via smartphones and send text messages to request and receive account information.

In February 2014, mBank (**mbank.pl/en**) launched a mobile banking platform in Poland. The app allows access to the banking services, such as checking an account balance or a credit card limit (see **telecompaper.com/news/mbank-launches-new-mobile-banking-app-in-Poland**). For a case study on people in developing countries who have no need for a physical bank but do need access to financial services (e.g., to transfer money home to their families), see Nobel (2011).

Historically, the use of mobile banking has been relatively low. This situation is changing. Much of the change is being driven by the world economic crisis of 2008–2013. Bank and financial services' customers are utilizing their smartphones and cell phones to obtain current financial information and perform real time transactions. For comprehensive coverage, see Paulsen (2013) and Knowledge@Wharton and Ernst & Young (2013); Graham (2014) predicts some mobile banking trends for 2014.

Finally, *mobile payments*, including payments withdrawn from bank accounts via mobile devices, have become very popular (see Chapter 11).

Other Mobile Finance Applications

There are several other mobile finance applications (search Google for 'future of mobile finance'). Two applications follow.

Mobile Stock Trading

Several brokerage companies offer extensive mobile services and stock trading mobile tools.

Examples: E*TRADE Mobile

With *E*TRADE Mobile Pro for the iPad*, customers are able to trade anytime and anywhere using their smartphone. iPad users can:

- Get real-time news, quotes, and charts.
- Trade stocks (regular market sessions and extended hours).
- Check personalized stock watch lists and portfolios.
- Access and manage accounts.
- Prepare year-end tax documents.
- Stream live CNBC TV financial programs.

For about $10 (starting price), you can buy iMoblife.com's MobFinance software app for Symbian and BlackBerry that enables real time stock price monitoring, stock market research, and portfolio management, from 57 stock exchanges all over the world (including the United States, China, Germany, and Australia).

Free services are also available from Google (Realtime Stock Quotes app) and Yahoo! (Yahoo! Finance app). Both employ a search engine that provides real-time stock market information and financial news and research data. Similar services are available from TD Ameritrade (see **tdameritrade.com/tools-and-platforms/mobile-trading.page**). For the future of mobile finance, see **mint.com/blog/trends/the-future-of-mobile-finance**.

Real Estate Mobile Transactions

The real estate market can be an ideal place for mobile commerce since real estate brokers and buyers and sellers are constantly on the move. Most realtors offer a photo gallery for each property on your desktop or mobile device; but m-commerce can do more than that. Let us look at two examples.

Example 1: Mobile Video Marketing Platform at Partners Trust

According to *PR Newswire* (2010), Partners Trust Estate is a brokerage firm in the high-end real estate market. In 2010, the company launched an interactive mobile campaign to help buyers find their dream properties, using Mogreet's video platform. The mobile marketing video platform from Outspoken (**outspoken.com**) delivers informative mobile video tours to be viewed by potential buyers. The service enables brokers to better interact with customers any place, any time and gives consumers the tools for finding properties. For details, see *PR Newswire* (2010).

Example 2: Using Augmented Realty

Using augmented reality (see Chapter 2), some companies in Europe and the U.S. allow you to point your smartphone at certain buildings in a city (e.g., Paris) and then see the property value superimposed on the image of the particular building (Macintosh 2010). This technology is combined with a GPS to let the system know your location. HomeScan is an iPhone and McIntosh application developed by California-based ZipRealty.com that allows prospective real estate customers to find, see, and download properties in a mobile environment. For more about the HomeScan app, see **ziprealty.com/iphone**. A more generic application is available from HomeSpotter.

Several other mobile real estate applications are available or being developed, combining Google Maps and Google Earth with mobile applications. Note that some people object to other people taking photos of their houses on the basis that it is an invasion of privacy.

For a list of the top 20 AR apps of 2013 for iPhone/iPad and Android, videos, and an infographic, see **deepknowhow.com/2013/04/04/top-20-augmented-reality-apps-for-android-and-iphoneipad-users**.

SECTION 6.3 REVIEW QUESTIONS

1. Describe some of the services provided by mobile banking.
2. List some of the benefits derived from e-banking.
3. Describe mobile stock trading applications.
4. Describe mobile applications in real estate.

6.4 MOBILE ENTERPRISE SOLUTIONS: FROM SUPPORTING THE WORKFORCE TO IMPROVING INTERNAL OPERATIONS

Although B2C m-commerce gets considerable publicity in the media, for most organizations the greatest benefit from m-commerce is likely to come from applications within the enterprise. These applications mostly support the mobile workforce employees who spend a substantial part of their workday away from the corporate premises.

The majority of enterprise mobile applications are included in **enterprise mobility** or *mobile enterprise* (Fitton et al. 2012). Enterprise mobility includes the people and technology (e.g., devices and networks) that enable mobile computing applications within the enterprise. Enterprise mobility is one of the top 10 items in Gartner's 2013 and 2014 strategic technology lists. For the 2014 list see Cearley (2014).

Defining Mobile Enterprise (Enterprise Mobility)

Mobile technology is rapidly proliferating in the enterprise. In the previous sections, we introduced several business-oriented examples, in what we survey "mobile enterprise applications" or in short, "mobile enterprise." This term refers to mobile applications in enterprises (to distinguish from consumer-oriented applications, such as mobile entertainment). Obviously, there are many mobile enterprise applications; examples are illustrated in Section 6.1, Figure 6.3 (p. 263).

A Working Definition of Mobile Enterprise

Mobile enterprise refers to mobile applications used by companies to improve the operations of the employees, facilities, and relevant supply chains within the enterprise and with its business partners. For a comprehensive description of mobile enterprise including guidelines for implementation, best practices, and case studies, see

Fitton et al. (2012). The term is also known as *enterprise mobility.*

For details see **searchconsumerization.techtarget.com/definition/Enterprise-mobility**, and Mordhorst (2014). For a large collection of enterprise mobility and enterprise mobility applications, conduct a Google search. Finally, for a comprehensive guide to enterprise mobility, see Sathyan et al. (2013). Also do a Google images search for 'enterprise mobility.' For Gartner's analysis (with figures) of enterprise mobility and the impact on IT, see **gartner.com/doc/1985016/enterprise-mobility-impact-it**.

Many companies and experts believe that mobility can transform businesses. For a comprehensive presentation see SAP (2012) and Fonemine (2014).

The Framework and Content of Mobile Enterprise Applications

In addition to Motorola's framework that we introduced in Section 6.1, there are several other proprietary frameworks used by other vendors. For example, AT&T Enterprise Business provides categories such as vertical industry, healthcare, mobility, mobile productivity, at **business.att.com**.

Mobile Collaboration
Mobile collaboration refers to collaboration activities conducted on smartphones, tablets, and other mobile devices, enabling users to improve their performance. According to Schadler (2011), the major mobile collaboration software vendors who "lead the pack" in this area are Adobe, Box, Cisco, IBM, Salesforce, SugarSync, Skype, and Yammer.

Mobile Workers

A **mobile worker** is usually defined as any employee who is away from his or her primary work space at least 10 hours a week (or 25% of the time). In 2014, there were more than 150 million workers in the United States, of which approximately 50 million, or one-third, could be classified as mobile. This figure is growing rapidly. Using the definition of mobile workers, International Data Corporation (IDC) estimated that the number of mobile workers in 2013 was 1.2 billion.

Examples of mobile workers include members of sales teams, travelling professionals and managers, telecommuters, and repair people or installation employees who work off the company's premises. These individuals need access to the same office and work applications and data as those who work at the office. Online File W6.3 presents examples of mobile devices that support mobile workers in different areas including salesforce automation, along with issues that arise in providing this support. The major categories covered are *salesforce automation* (SFA) and *field force automation* (FFA). In addition, Online File W6.3 describes fleet and transportation management and warehouse management. For additional details, see Motorola (2007).

Other Enterprise Mobile Applications

Hundreds of other mobile applications exist. For examples, see Motorola Solutions Enterprise Mobility (**motorolasolutions.com/US-EN/Enterprise+Mobility**; now Zebra).

An example of a popular mobile application in the field of medical care is the use of communication devices in clinics, physicians' offices, and hospitals. For an interesting case study on Maryland's Frederick Memorial Hospital and their use of Panasonic laptops, see **mobileenterprise.edgl.com/news/Panasonic-Laptops-A-Key-Player-in-Hospital-s-Goals60630**.

Transportation Management
Another popular mobile application area is that of transportation management (e.g., trucks, forklifts, buses, vans, and so forth). In this area, mobility is used in communication with drivers, use of control systems, surveillance, and dispatching. Examples of these applications can be seen in the Hertz Corp. opening case. Mobile devices are used extensively in airports and by airlines, traffic control systems, public bus

systems, and more (see the NextBus case in Online File W6.4).

iPad in the Enterprise

Apple's iPad is now moving to the enterprise. Initially, the iPad was used as a communication and collaboration device connected to existing systems. However, many companies are using iPads for diversity of business applications especially in hotels, financial services, construction, and manufacturing. In addition, the iPad is replacing paper menus in restaurants. For example, sandwich and pastry chain Au Bon Pain uses iPads for taking customers' sandwich orders. In a collaboration between food and beverage provider OTG and Delta airlines, airports in certain cities (LaGuardia in NY, Pearson in Toronto, and Minneapolis-St. Paul International) are installing iPads so that customers can have free Wi-Fi, real-time flight access, and order food from a selection of restaurants and have it delivered to them at the gate (see **eatocracy. cnn.com/2012/12/21/ipad-ordering-becoming-the-new-norm-at-airport-restaurants**). Payment can be made via the iPad as well. For further descriptions, see **apple.com/ipad/business**. As of February 2014, Concessions International is providing the Atlanta airport with iPads for tabletop ordering (see **qsrmagazine.com/news/ci-launches-ipad-ordering-atlanta-airport**).

Trends for 2015 and Beyond

It is clear that the number of applications and their benefits is increasing. The large global software company Infosys ("Building Tomorrow's Enterprise") provides a paper titled "Trends 2014: The Mobility Collection" (see **infosys. com/mobility/pages/mobility-2014.aspx**). The website describes the challenges and opportunities of enterprise mobility as well as provides a large collection of mobility related resources (e.g., case studies, white papers).

SECTION 6.4 REVIEW QUESTIONS
1. Define mobile enterprise.
2. Describe the content of mobile enterprise applications.
3. Define mobile workers.
4. List the major segments of the mobile workforce.
5. What are some of the common benefits of mobile SFA, FFA, and CRM? (Consult Online File W6.3).

6.5   MOBILE ENTERTAINMENT, GAMING, CONSUMER SERVICES, AND MOBILE SHOPPING

Mobile entertainment applications have been around for years, but only recently they have expanded rapidly due to developments in wireless devices and mobile technology. Consumer applications started in the 1990s, but really soared after 2000. This section mainly describes mobile entertainment and briefly discusses some other areas of consumer services.

Overview of Mobile Entertainment

There is some debate about what actually constitutes mobile entertainment and which of its segments is really m-commerce. For example, assume you purchase a song from the Web and download it to your PC, and then download it to your MP3 player. Is this a form of mobile entertainment? What if you copy the song to a smartphone rather than to an MP3 player? What if you buy the song and download it directly from the Web to your smartphone? There are many similar "what ifs." A popular definition is: **mobile entertainment** refers to entertainment delivered on mobile devices over wireless networks or that interacts with mobile service providers.

According to a 2013 report by Juniper Research, it was estimated that the global market for mobile entertainment would jump from worldwide revenues of approximately $39 billion in 2013 to $75 billion in 2017 (Juniper Research 2013). For example, the National Basketball Association (NBA) offers the NBA League Pass (**nba.com/leaguepass**), which allows fans to watch games in real time on iPhones and other smartphones for a fee of $50 per season. There are a large number of entertainment related apps; many are free. For the top free entertainment apps offered by Google Play, see **play.google.com/store/apps/category/ENTERTAINMENT/collection/topselling_free**. For *PC Magazine*'s list of the 100 top paid (some free) iPad apps of 2014, see **pcmag.com/article2/0,2817,2362576,00.asp**.

This section discusses some of the major types of mobile entertainment, including mobile music and video, mobile gaming, mobile gambling, and mobility and sports. Mobile entertainment in social networks is covered in Chapter 8.

Mobile Streaming Music and Video Providers

Apple is the clear leader in the digital distribution of music and video. Since 2001, Apple has offered consumers the ability to download songs and videos from the Apple iTunes store. iTunes customers purchase billions of songs annually. For example, in 2010, Apple's customers were downloading videos at the rate of 70,000 a day. According to Groth and Cortez (2012), Apple's annual sales in iTunes stores increased 36.9% in 2011 to $18.4 billion, becoming the third fastest growing retailer in the U.S. At the end of 2007, Amazon.com launched their Amazon MP3 and Amazon Video on Demand, a digital download service for music and video, respectively. Other major Internet music providers are **spotify.com**, **youtube.com**, **myspace.com**, and **facebook.com/FreeOnlineMp3**. Note that, cell phones today can display analog TV (popular in developing countries). Smartphones can display any programs offered on the Internet. For details, see **venturebeat.com/2010/12/01/telegent-ships-100mth-chip-for-tv-on-mobile-phones**. Note that with their Dish Anywhere mobile app, Dish Network works anywhere customers can access the Internet through their smartphone or tablet, and with their Sling Technology, customers can watch live TV or DVR content on their iPhone, iPad, Android, and Kindle Fire (see **dish.com/technology/dish-anywhere**). Netflix has a free app for its subscribers to watch TV shows and movies streaming from Netflix on their mobile

device (e.g., iPhone, iPad, Android). See **get.it/netflix**.

Entertainment in Cars

Entertainment is coming to cars directly from the Internet. For example, in March 2014, Apple announced that it is teaming up with a major car maker for its *CarPlay* system. The system enables iPhones to plug into cars so drivers can request music with voice commands or with a touch on a vehicle dashboard screen. For details, see Liedtke (2014). JVC ("Experience Apps in a New Mobile Way") allows you to connect an iPod to a JVC receiver and "watch it come alive with your favorite apps." The JVC feature works with compatible car receivers and apps only. For more about JVC and its mobile features for cars, see **jvckenwood.com/english/car/applink**. Future opportunities include car diagnosis, driver health monitoring, usage-based insurance and even parental alerts. Some car brands already provide communication, telematics, social networking, and mobile commerce.

Mobile Games

A wide range of mobile games have been developed for different types of players. According to Knight (2012b), 46% of gamers play more on mobile devices than on PCs. The vast majority of players use smartphones. Many computer games can be played on mobile devices. For example, trading card games like "Magic: The Gathering" are online or plan to be (see **accounts.online-gaming.wizards.com**). Mobile games can be classified according to:

- **Technology.** Embedded, SMS/MMS, Web browsing, J2ME, BREW, native OS
- **Number of players.** Solo play or multiplay (from few to many players)
- **Social network-based.** Using smartphones, people can play games available in social networks, such as FarmVille on Facebook.

Several blogs provide information and discussions about the current state of the mobile gaming market, including various game offerings, as well as the technologies and platforms used to develop the games. One of the best is **blog.mobilegames-blog.com**.

According to Soh and Tan (2008), and our authors' experience, the drivers of the popularity of mobile games are:

- Increasing spread of mobile devices. The more people use smartphones, the more people will play e-games.
- The inclusion of games in social networks, and particularly on Facebook.
- The streaming of quality videos is improving.
- The support for the gamification movement.
- The ability of vendors to generate money from ads attached to games.
- Technological improvements for downloading complex games.

The potential size and growth of the overall online gaming market is enormous. This explains the large number of companies involved in creating, distributing, and running mobile games.

Hurdles for Growth

Although the market is growing rapidly, game publishers (especially in China and India), are facing some major hurdles. For example, there is a lack of standards, unavailability of many different types of software and hardware, and increasing costs. The newest generation of games requires advanced capabilities available only in higher-end mobile devices and with at least 3G networks. The ad spending in mobile games has remained low, but it is growing.

To address these hurdles, game publishers are focusing their attention on Apple's iPhone and iPad and on similar popular devices.

Mobile Gambling

Unlike some of the other forms of mobile entertainment, the mobile gambling market has a high demand but also some unique hurdles. First, mobile gambling requires two-way financial transactions. Second, online gambling sites face major trust issues. Gamblers and bettors have to believe that the site is trustworthy and fair. Finally, while the legislative and regulatory picture is very restrictive, it is also unclear and keeps changing.

Online gambling is booming despite the fact that it is illegal in almost all U.S. states. In 2013, Delaware and Nevada were the first U.S. states to allow some online gambling, followed by New Jersey (in October 2013, Delaware became the first state to allow a "full suite" of Internet gambling). In February 2014, both Delaware and Nevada signed a deal to allow interstate online gambling. Note that Federal Law limits online gambling to players while they are physically present within each state. (This can be verified by using geolocation software.) Therefore, if one state allows online gambling, you can play only when you are in that state. As of February 2014, 10 states were considering legalizing or expanding online gambling (**washingtonpost.com/blogs/govbeat/wp/2014/02/05/at-least-10-states-expected-to-consider-allowing-online-gambling-this-year**). However, in March of 2014, a bill was introduced in Congress to outlaw any Internet gambling, including in the states where it is already legal (**reviewjournal.com/news/new-bill-would-prohibit-internet-gambling-including-where-already-legal**).

Mobility and Sports

There are many sports mobile applications (e.g., see the closing case about the NFL in Chapter 1).

Here are some representative examples of unique sports mobile applications:

- Nike and Apple introduced an iPod shoe called Nano (a best seller), which can calculate how many calories are burned during workouts. This is done via wireless sensors. In addition to calories burned, users can get information about the distance they run. The data collected by the sensors are transmitted to the runner's iPod and headphones. In addition, the Nike+iPod system delivers music and voice entertainment, including podcasts on different sports topics. For details, see Frakes (2010).

- Personalized live sport events can be viewed on mobile devices. The user can select the event to watch. In the future, systems will be able even to predict users' preferred events during several simultaneous live sports competitions. Streaming live sports to mobile devices is becoming very popular. Unfortunately, there may a fee to enjoy this.
- In 2006, Levi Strauss featured the RedWire DLX iPod-compatible jeans. The $250 jeans come complete with all the necessary hardware.
- ESPN's SportsCenter offers WatchESPN, is a system where subscribers can watch ESPN on a desktop or on a mobile device. For details, see **espn.go.com/watchespn/index**.
- Eventbrite **eventbrite.com** is a company that provides several applications for event management online (e.g., creating tickets, promoting events, managing event entry).

Service Industry Consumer Applications

A large number of mobile applications are used in different service industries. Here are two examples.

Healthcare
Mobile devices are everywhere in the field of healthcare, as illustrated next:

- Using a handheld device, a physician can submit a prescription directly to participating pharmacies from her office or patient bedside. In addition, your physician can order tests, access medical information, scan billable items, and check costs and fees for services.
- Remote devices not only monitor patient vital signs while he/she is at home, but also can adjust operating medical equipment. This is done by using sensors.
- To reduce errors, mobile devices can validate the managing, tracking, and verifying of blood collected for transfusions. Promises Treatment

Centers (alcohol and drug rehabilitation) uses a free mobile app (iPromises for iPhone; **ipromises.org**) that works as a virtual recovery tool (e.g., list of AA meetings in the U.S. and Canada, add friends, track progress, etc.) While the iPromises Recovery Companion does not generate revenue for the company, "it is aimed at bolstering Promises' reputation among patients and doctors" (see Del Rey 2010 for details).

For more applications, see **motorolasolutions.com/US-EN/Business+Solutions/Industry+Solutions/Healthcare** (now Zebra).

Hospitality Management
Many applications exist from travel reservations to ensuring safety in hotel rooms. Examples are: two-way radio communication, wireless hotspot solutions, food safety checks, parking lot management, asset location and management, guest services, safety and security on the premises, entertainment, inventory management, and much more. For details, see **motorolasolutions.com/en_us/solutions/hospitality.html**. One area in hospitality that benefits from a wireless system is restaurant operations.

Example 1: Dolphin Fast Food
Dolphin Fast Food Inc. operates 19 Burger King franchises in Minnesota (reported by *Baseline*, June 28, 2010). The company uses a wireless system to streamline operations, control costs, increase staff and customer satisfaction, and comply with regulations. The system includes free Wi-Fi access both in the restaurants and in a corporate management wireless network. The company realized that customers can use their mobile devices while waiting and during dining. Managers use mobile devices to increase effectiveness. The wireless system is also used for improved security on the premises (e.g., video surveillance). The secure Internet access is protected by a VPN (see Chapter 10) and it can block inappropriate content. The wireless system also operates the payment gateways and the POS terminals. For the deployment of the system and the security tools used, see Dolphin (2010).

For more recent material see **sonicwall.com/ downloads/CS_BurgerKing_US.pdf**.

Note: In many full-service restaurants, there are several additional applications such as customers placing orders on handheld devices, where the orders go directly to the kitchen and to the cashiers, and mobile devices for advising waiting customers to come in when their tables are ready. A vendor that provides mobile programs for tablets for menus, food ordering, entertainment, and payments is Ziosk.

Example 2: Tablets and Other Mobile Devices in Restaurants

Several restaurants worldwide are introducing tablets or smartphones as a substitute to paper menus. For example, as mentioned earlier, Au Bon Pain is using iPads in several of their locations. One option is to provide the servers with an iPad with a built-in menu. This way they can submit the order directly to the kitchen. Another one is to loan tablets to those customers that do not have one while dining in the restaurant. Using the tablets, customers can order food by themselves and provide their credit card information. It seems that the use of tablets also facilitates customer relationships since self-ordering expedites the service and reduces errors in ordering. The tablets can supplement or replace paper menus. Some restaurants provide portable devices for playing games or ordering movie tickets while waiting for the food. For details, see Nassauer (2012).

Public Safety and Crime Prevention

There are many mobile devices and methods for improving public safety. For example, in Vietnam and in Australia, mobile cameras identify unregistered cars by reading license plate numbers from a distance, and then comparing these numbers to those in a database. Another example is using digital cameras in Vietnam and Australia to find illegal taxi operators, and in Singapore to photograph speeding vehicles. (For information about new "average speed" cameras implemented in Singapore, see **therealsingapore.com/content/ singapore-trialling-new-average-speed-speed-cameras.**)

Other Industries

Mobile systems and applications can be found in almost all industries. For example, extensive applications can be found in m-government and m-learning (see Chapter 5). Two interesting application are provided in the Motorola closing case to this chapter (hospitals and manufacturing). The Department of Homeland Security applies many devices, as do the transportation industry and the military. In agriculture, wireless devices can even guide tractors to work at night.

Mobile Shopping and Advertising

Online shopping can be easier when done from your smartphone or tablet. For shopping, one needs a mobile shopping platform such as the one provided by ADCentricity Corporation (**adcentricity. com**; acquired by Bee Media Inc.), or by adMobile Corp. (**admobile.com**). Many apps for iPhones facilitate advertising and shopping. For example, you can download the Costco Mobile App for easy coupon redemption (see **costco. com/costco-app.html**). For a list of smartphone applications for business, see the iPhone apps and Del Rey (2010). Wishpond Technologies Ltd. (2014) shows how smartphone shoppers use their devices for different shopping-related activities (e.g., checking prices, searching for reviews).

Example: Delta Airlines

Delta offers in-flight Wi-Fi connection on many of its flights (called *Delta Connect*). With Delta Connect, there is free access to many shopping and entertainment sites, including eBay. For a nominal fee, you can purchase a Wi-Fi Mobile Pass and be able to connect to the Internet via your smartphone, and send and receive mobile messages, check your e-mail, and browse the Web. For more about Delta Connect and Wi-Fi Mobile Pass, see **delta.com/content/www/en_ US/traveling-with-us/in-flight-services/ amenities-information/in-flight-wi-fi.html#.** Other airlines offer similar capabilities.

In addition, consumers use mobile devices to locate stores, compare prices, and place orders.

For more, see 'mobile marketing' in Chapter 9. For example, Chinese consumers can make purchases from inside WeChat (Millward 2014). China's largest e-tailers, Taobao and T.mall offered special discounts in 2014, in order to encourage shoppers to buy from their smart phones. Finally, using text messages greatly facilitates recommendations and advice for shoppers, especially in social networks (see Chapter 7 and Butcher 2011). To see how mobile shopping is done, visit Amazon. com, JCPenney, Target, REI, and Crate & Barrel to download their shopping apps.

Example

METRO Group (AG) is offering an application for high-capacity mobile phones to use in its Future Store in Rheinberg, Germany. According to their site, the Mobile Shopping Assistant (MSA) "is a software package which allows customers to scan items independently, receive current pricing information and a quick overview of the value of their goods." An MSA provides online access to product descriptions and pictures, pricing information, and store maps. It also enables scanning items before they are placed in the cart, calculating the total cost of the items. At checkout, the MSA allows a shopper to "pay in passing" by using the MSA to pass scanned data to a payment terminal. For more about METRO's Future Store Initiative and functionalities of the MSA, see **future-store. org/internet/site/ts_fsi/node/25216/Len/index. html**. METRO has measured the reactions and satisfaction of the Future Store shoppers. The results indicate that customers are more satisfied and visit the store more often than before. In addition, the percentage of new customers has increased, and customers spend 45 more euros per month. Metro AG, like Food Lion and other grocers, are experimenting with RFID, which can be used for supply chain logistics and more.

SECTION 6.5 REVIEW QUESTIONS

1. Briefly describe the growth patterns of the various segments of mobile entertainment.
2. Discuss the basic components of the mobile music market.
3. What are some of the key barriers to the growth of the mobile games market?

4. Discuss some of the key legal issues impeding the growth of mobile gambling.
5. Describe the use of mobility in sports and in restaurants.
6. Describe some hospitality management mobile applications.
7. Describe mobile shopping and advertising.

6.6 LOCATION-BASED MOBILE COMMERCE AND MOBILE SOCIAL NETWORKS

Location-based m-commerce (l-commerce) (or LBC), refers to the use of location finding systems such as GPS-enabled devices or similar technologies (e.g., triangulation of radio- or cell-based stations) to find where a customer with a mobile device, or an object, are located and provide them with relevant services, such as an advertisement or vehicle route optimization. According to TechTarget, LBS is "a software application for a IP-capable mobile device that requires knowledge about where the mobile device is located" (see **searchnetworking.techtarget.com/definition/ location-based-service-LBS**). L-commerce them with involves context-aware computing technology (Section 6.7). For images, search Google for 'images of location-based commerce.' L–commerce offers convenient services to consumers such as connections with friends, the ability to receive relevant and timely sales information, safety features (e.g., emergency assistance), and convenience (a user can locate what facility needed is nearby without consulting a directory or a map). Sellers get the opportunity to advertise and provide or meet a customer's needs in real time. In essence, LBC is the delivery of m-commerce transactions to individuals who are in a known specific location, at a specific time. Foursquare (**foursquare.com**) is a company that makes LBC apps (see Chapter 7).

Basic Concepts in L–Commerce

Location-based m-commerce mainly includes five possible activities, all done in real time:

1. **Location.** Finding where a person (with a smartphone) or a thing (e.g., a truck) are located.
2. **Navigation.** Finding and illustrating a route from one location to another (e.g., as done by Google maps)
3. **Tracking.** Monitoring the movements and whereabouts of people or objects (e.g., a truck, airplane)
4. **Mapping.** Creating maps of certain geographical locations with super-imposed data if needed (e.g., GIS, Google maps)
5. **Timing.** Determining arrival or departure time of something at a specific location (e.g., arrival of a bus to a specific bus stop, or an airplane to an airport).

For example, WeatherBug (**weather.weatherbug.com**) and Send Word Now (**sendwordnow.com**) have combined some of these five services to ensure the safety of customers, employees, and stores during severe weather and other emergencies.

A recent development of l-commerce is known as **real-time location systems (RTLS)**, which are used to track and identify the location of objects in real time (see Malik 2009). For an overview, see **searchmobilecomputing.techtarget.com/definition/real-time-location-system-RTLS** and **computerlearningcentre.blogspot.com/2014/04/l-commerce.html**.

L-Commerce Infrastructure

L-commerce is based on an infrastructure. The components depend on the applications. However, the following usually exist:

1. **Location finder (positioning) component.** A GPS (or other device) that finds the location of a person or a thing.
2. **Mobile Positioning Center.** This includes a server that manages the location information received from the location finder.
3. **User.** The user can be a person or thing (e.g., a vehicle).
4. **Mobile devices.** The user needs a mobile device (e.g., a smartphone) that includes a GPS or other feature that locates the position of something or someone.
5. **Mobile communication network.** The network(s) that transfers user requests to the service providers, and then transmits the reply to the user.
6. **Service or application providers.** Providers are responsible for servicing a user's request. They may use applications such as GIS.
7. **Data or content provider.** Service providers usually need to acquire (e.g., buy) geographic, financial, or other data in order to provide a reply to requests. Data may include maps and GIS information.
8. **Geographical Information System (GIS).** This includes maps, location of businesses, and more (described later).
9. **Opt-in application.** In the U.S. and some other countries, LBC can be used only with people's permission (opt-in). This requires an additional software app.

These components work together as illustrated in Figure 6.6.

For additional components, see **gps.gov/technical/icwg** and TeleCommunication Systems, Inc. (2010).

Here is how the LBS system works (see Figure 6.6):

1. The user expresses his or her wish by clicking on a function (e.g., "find me the nearest gas station").

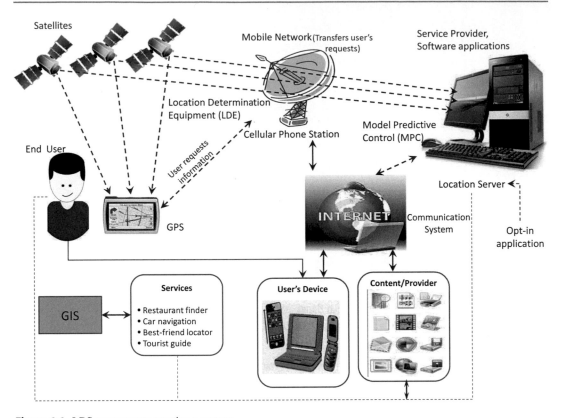

Figure 6.6 LBS components creating a system

2. The mobile network service finds where the user is located using satellite and GPS.
3. The request is transferred via a wireless network to the service provider software application that activates a search for the needed data.
4. The server goes to a database, to find for example, the nearest requested business and check if it is open, what it serves, and so forth.
5. Using a GIS, the service delivers the reply to the user, including a map and driving directions if necessary.

A similar system can be used for vehicle or asset location. A GPS is then attached to the object.

Musil (2013) reported that by combining conventional GPS signals with data from sensors, one can pinpoint the location of a car within six feet of its location.

Geolocation

LBS is related to the concept of *geolocation*. **Geolocation** refers to the ability to find the location of a user who is connected to the Web via a mobile device. Geolocation works with all Web browsers.

L-commerce is distinguished from general m-commerce by the *positioning component*, the compulsory opt-in, and the mash up with GIS or other data sources.

The GPS: Positioning Component

The major device in l–commerce is a global positioning system (GPS). Here is how it works:

According to GPS.gov (2014), "the **Global Positioning System (GPS)** is a U.S.-owned utility that provides users with positioning, navigation, and timing (PNT) services. This system consists of three segments: the space segment, the control segment, and the user segment."

The U.S. government describes these segments as follows:

Space Segment. The space segment consists of 24 satellites that transmit signals. The signals designate the satellites' positions at any given time (using an atomic clock). Each satellite orbits the earth once every 12 hours at an altitude of 10,900 miles.

Control Segment. The control segment includes a global monitoring system and control station to monitor the satellites.

User Segment. The user's equipment, which is the GPS receiver, receives information from the satellites and calculates the user's position at the given time.

In recent years, GPS locators have become a part of the consumer electronics market. They are available in many smartphones, and today are used widely for business and recreation. Online File W6.4 provides an example of the use of GPS for tracking buses. See Garmin Ltd. (**garmin. com**) for examples of GPS devices, and Trimble Navigation Limited (**trimble.com/gps_tutorial/ whatgps.aspx**) for tutorials on different GPS-related topics.

Note: The European Union (EU) and the European Space Agency are constructing an alternative global navigation satellite system called *Galileo*, which will be under civilian control. Galileo, which will consist of 30 orbiting satellites, has been given a budget of €7 billion to fund the system from 2014 to 2020. Four operational satellites were dispatched in 2011 and 2012. For more information about Galileo (history, benefits, application, etc.), see the European Global Navigation Satellite Systems Agency (**gsa. europa.eu/galileo-0**) and **ec.europa.eu/enterprise/policies/satnav/galileo/index_en.htm**. For further details, see **navipedia.net/index.php/ Galileo** and **navipedia.net/index.php/Galileo_ General_Introduction**, respectively.

Note: GPS dating applications let you sort through lists of people you may want to date based on their location at any given time (see applications such as Skout (**skout.com**; "the global network for meeting new people"). For an example of a success story, see Sutter (2010).

Location-Based Data

Location-based services (LBS) and l-commerce are based on a series of location-based questions or queries.

Using Data Collections

GPS-enabled smartphones and other devices help in collecting large amounts of data, which can be used in decision making to save millions of dollars (see Feldman 2010).

Locating Customers in Physical Stores

When shoppers equipped with smartphones are in physical stores, it is possible to track their movements in specific stores and malls. The information collected may give retailers ideas about the customers' shopping habits. The companies that collect the information say that it is anonymous. The tracking is done via the smartphone's MAC address (the smartphone's unique identifier code). Any smartphone that is connected to Wi-Fi sends signals with the MAC address, which a store can capture. Smartphone users can opt-out of the use of their MAC address by going to the Smart Store Privacy website at **smartstoreprivacy.org**. For a discussion, see Kerr (2014). For more information on what happens to the information collected on your smartphone and disabling "geotagging" (locating geographic information), see **bctnv.com/what-happens-to-the-gps-location-information-collected-on-your-smartphone.html**.

Geographical Information Systems

Some data, information, and processes that are needed to answer location-based queries are usually handled by a *geographical information system (GIS)*. According to USGS (2007), a **geographical information system (GIS)** is a computer-based system whose function is to capture, store, analyze, and display geographically-related data. For example, suppose a person is using his or her mobile phone to ask an online directory service to provide a list of Italian restaurants that are close by. In order to service this query, the directory service would need access to a GIS containing information about local restaurants by geographical coordinates and type. For more on GIS, see **en. wikipedia.org/wiki/Geographic_information_**

system, USGS (2007), Heywood et al. (2012), and **esri.com/what-is-gis/overview**.

Geographical information systems are frequently combined with GPS, as shown next.

Example: Hailing Taxis from a Smartphone

As discussed in Chapter 1, hailing taxis from smartphones is spreading slowly around the globe. ZabCab (**zabcab.com**; "connecting taxicabs and passengers") provides an app by which a user with a GPS-enabled smartphone can push a button and GPS technology identifies their location. An icon with a map appears on the mobile devices of participating taxi drivers, letting the driver know the location of the passenger who needs to be picked up. Currently (2014), ZabCab is only available in certain cities in New York. The HAIL A CAB™ app (**hailacabapp.com**), a product of Yellow Cab, offers the taxi-hailing service in several cities in Texas (Austin, Houston, San Antonio, and Galveston), with more locations forthcoming. The Alibaba Group also offers a cab-hailing app in Beijing (see **online.wsj.com/news/articles/SB1000142405270230328780457944 2993327079748**).

Note: Taxi company Comfort Transportation, located in Singapore, offers a taxi-booking system in which the booking is done by SMS (see **cdgtaxi.com.sg/commuters_services_booking. mvn**). They also offer taxi-booking apps and online taxi booking. It is not location–based, but it solves the problem of busy telephone lines. Finally, GetTaxi (**gett.com**), available in New York and other major cities worldwide (e.g., Moscow, London, Tel Aviv), offers a free app that allows you to order taxis directly from your smartphone. What differentiates GetTaxi is that they are the only taxi company that has: game-changing technology, unbelievable customer service, and transparent and attractive practices (see **gett.com/about.html**).

Location-Based Services and Applications

A **location-based service (LBS)** is a mobile device–based computerized service, which

Table 6.1 Location-based applications and services

Category	Examples
Advertising	Banners, advertising alerts (e.g., promotions, coupons)
Billing and payments	Road tolling, location-sensitive billing
Emergency	Emergency calls, automotive assistance
Games	Mobile games, geocaching
Information	Entertainment services, mobile yellow pages, shopping guides
Leisure and travel	Buddy finder, instant messaging, social networking, travel guides, travel planner
Management	Facility, infrastructure, fleet, security, environmental
Navigation	Directions, indoor routing, car park guidance, traffic management
Tracking	People/vehicle tracking, product tracking

Sources: Based on Steiniger et al. (2006), **geoawesomeness.com/knowledge-base/location-based-services** (accessed May 2014), and the authors' experiences.

utilizes information about the geographical position of a user's mobile device (e.g., mobile phone tracking) for delivering a service (e.g., advertisers can target ads to specific location), to the user.

There are a large number of LBS applications. The major categories of these are shown in Table 6.1. For a list of location-based services (applications), see **geoawesomeness.com/knowledge-base/location-based-services/location-based-services-applications**.

Location-based services can be used in marketing, operations, services, finance, and so forth. LBS technologies determine the location of a person (or an object), and act upon this information. LBS also work in asset tracking (e.g., of parcels at USPS or FedEx) and in vehicle tracking (see Online File W6.4 and the Tracking section at **geoawesomeness.com/knowledge-base/location-based-services/location-based-services-applications**). LBS also include location-based games.

Other examples of location-based services are:

- Recommending public events in a city to tourists and residents.
- Asset recovery, for example, finding stolen cars.
- Pointing a user to the nearest business (e.g., a gas station) to his (her) location.
- Providing detailed navigation from any place to any address (sometimes with voice prompts).
- Locating things (such as trucks) and displaying them on the mobile devices' map.
- Inventory tracking in warehouses.
- Delivering alerts, such as notification of a real time sale in a specific store.

RFID technologies wirelessly track objects in warehouses (see Tutorial T2).

Personnel Tracking

Different technologies are used by managers and employees for tracking personnel on the company premises and while they are off premises.

Social Location-Based Marketing

Social location-based marketing occurs when users share their location with vendors in real time (opt–in), usually within social media environments. The vendors then deliver targeted ads, coupons, or rebates to the users. In addition, the vendors may conduct market research about the user's preferences and collect feedback about product quality. For more information, see the video titled "The Future of M-Commerce - Did You Know?" (4:30 minutes) at **youtube.com/watch?v=F58q6yUAsHE**.

The major LBS 'check in' services in 2014 were Foursquare, Facebook Places, and Plyce (in France). Technology vendors include AT&T, IBM and Telecomsys. Retailers that use such systems include Best Buy ("check-in" app).

Barriers to Location-Based M-commerce

The following are some factors that are slowing down the widespread use of location-based m-commerce:

- **Lack of GPS in some mobile phones.** In 2014, only about 35% of regular mobile phones were sold with GPS. Without GPS, it is difficult to use LBS. However, GPS-enabled phones are increasing in popularity. Also, the use of cellphone towers helps.
- **Accuracy of devices.** Some of the location-finding tools are not too accurate. A good, but expensive, GPS provides accuracy of 10 feet. Less accurate locators provide accuracy of about 1,500 feet.
- **The cost–benefit justification.** The benefits of location-based services may not justify the cost. For customers, it may be inconvenient to utilize the service. As you may recall from Chapter 1, Starbucks discontinued LBS.
- **Limited network bandwidth.** Wireless bandwidth is still limited. As bandwidth improves with 4G and 5G, applications will expand, which will increase the use of the technology.
- **Invasion of privacy.** Many people are reluctant to disclose their whereabouts and have their movements tracked (see Yun et al. 2013 and Chapter 15 for a discussion).

SECTION 6.6 REVIEW QUESTIONS
1. Describe the key elements of the l-commerce infrastructure.
2. What is GPS? How does it work?
3. What are some of the basic questions addressed by location-based services?
4. Define geographical information systems. How do they relate to LBS?

5. List the services enabled by LBS.
6. Describe social location-based marketing.
7. List the major barriers to LBS.

6.7   UBIQUITOUS (PERVASIVE) COMPUTING AND SENSORY NETWORKS

Many experts believe that the next major step in the evolution of computing will be *ubiquitous computing (ubicom)*. In a ubiquitous computing environment, almost every object in the system has a processing power (i.e., microprocessor) and a wireless or wireline connection to a network (usually the Internet or intranets). This way the objects can both communicate and process information. This section provides an overview of ubiquitous computing and briefly examines a number of related applications in the areas of sensor network technologies. (Note: The words *ubiquitous* and *pervasive* mean "existing everywhere.")

Overview of Ubiquitous Computing

Ubiquitous computing is a comprehensive field that includes many topics (e.g., see **en.wikipedia.org/wiki/Ubiquitous_computing** and Krumm 2009). Here we present only the essentials that are related to EC.

Definitions and Basic Concepts
Ubiquitous computing (ubicom), also known as *pervasive computing*, has computing capabilities embedded into a relevant system, usually not visible, which may be mobile or stationary. It is a form of human-computer interaction. In contrast, mobile computing is usually represented by visible devices (e.g., smartphones) possessed by users. Ubiquitous computing is also called *embedded computing*, *augmented computing*, or *pervasive computing*. Sometimes a distinction is made between pervasive and ubiquitous computing. The distinction revolves around the notion of mobility. **Pervasive computing** is embedded in the environment but typically is not mobile. In contrast, ubiquitous computing possesses a high degree of mobility. Therefore, for example, most

smart appliances in a smart home represent wired, *pervasive computing*, while mobile objects with embedded computing, such as in clothes, cars, and personal communication systems, represent *ubiquitous computing*. In this chapter, however, we treat pervasive and ubiquitous as equivalent terms, and we use them interchangeably.

Context-Aware Computing
Context-aware computing is a technology that is capable in predicting people's needs and providing fulfillment options (sometimes even before a request by the end user is made). The system is fed with data about the person, such as location and preferences. Regardless of the types of the end user, the system can sense the nature of personalized data needed for different environments. In its 2014 predictions, cited earlier, Gartner, Inc. cited context-awareness as one of the top 10 futuristic technologies. Context awareness technologies are related to LBS, but the technology can also be used without LBS.

In general, the technology is expected to increase productivity and result in many new applications. Carnegie Mellon University is a leader in the research of business applications in this technology.

Internet of Things (IoT)
The **Internet of Things (IoT)** is an evolving term with several definitions. In general, The IoT refers to a situation where many objects (people, animals, items) with embedded microprocessors are connected mostly wirelessly to the Internet. That is, it uses ubiquitous computing. Analysts predict that by the year 2020, there will be more than 50 billion devices connected to the Internet, creating the backbone of the IoT. The challenges and opportunities of this disruptive technology are discussed in an interview with Peter Utzschneider, vice-president of product management for Java at Oracle (see Kvita 2014). Note that the more 'things' are connected to the Internet the more security issues are anticipated (Vogel 2014).

Embedding mobile devices into items everywhere and connecting all devices to the Internet permits extensive communication between users and items. This kind of interaction adds a unique perspective to collaboration. For business applications of the Internet of Things, see Nazarov (2009). In addition, check the "Internet of Things Consortium" (**iofthings.org**) and their annual conference. For the technology see Holler et al. (2014).

Machine-to-Machine Technology.

An integral part of IoT is machine-to-machine (M2M) communication. According to **whatis. techtarget.com**, M2M is a "technology that supports wired or wireless communication between machines. An example of M2M technology might be a set of devices that monitor traffic in a city and communicate the information to the city's traffic lights in order to regulate the flow of traffic. M2M is used in telemetry, data collection, remote control, robotics, remote monitoring, status tracking, road traffic control, offsite diagnostics and maintenance, security systems, logistics services, fleet management, and telemedicine." For more see Holler et al. (2014).

For more on the IoT (e.g., definition, history), see **whatis.techtarget.com/definition/Internet-of-Things**.

The IoT will include many everyday things, ranging from smart grids to smart homes, clothes, cities and many others, all being networked. For more about the Internet of Things (smart cities, smart cars, and so forth), see the 2013 presentation from van Geest at **wired.com/2013/04/ the-internet-of-things-quantified-self-iot-smart-cities-smart-cars-smart-clothes**.

Smart Application: Grid, Homes, Cars, and More

An example of a simple application of pervasive computing is the use of smart meters for measuring electricity use. With smart meters there is no need to go from house to house to read the meter. Also, electricity consumption can be optimized. According to the Pacific Gas and Electric (PG&E) 'SmartMeter' Web page, current benefits include: more reliable service (two-way communication between PG&E and the grid, thus eliminating the need for workers to go to houses to read the meter); tracking energy use online in real time; getting alerts about usage; and much more. Future benefits

include better usage of renewable power – using energy from solar and wind sources. For more details on PG&E's SmartMeter see **pge.com/en/ myhome/customerservice/smartmeter/index. page**.

Pervasive computing technology is the key to many smart applications. Some examples are presented next.

According to the U.S. Department of Energy, a **smart grid (smartgrid.gov)** is an electricity network managed by utilizing digital technology. Like the Internet, the Smart Grid consists of controls, computers, automation, and new technologies and equipment working together, but in this case, these technologies work with the electrical grid to improve usage by responding to the quickly changing electric demand.

The Smart Grid represents an unprecedented opportunity to move the energy industry into a new era of reliability, availability, and efficiency that will contribute to our economic and environmental health. The benefits associated with the Smart Grid include:

- More efficient transmission of electricity
- Quicker restoration of electricity after power disturbances
- Reduced operations and management costs for utilities, and ultimately lower power costs for consumers
- Reduced peak demand, which will also help lower electric rates
- Increased integration of large-scale renewable energy systems
- Better integration of customer-owner power generation systems, including improved security of renewable energy systems
- Goal of zero carbon emissions

The U.S. Department of Energy (DOE) Office of Electricity Delivery and Energy Reliability provides substantial information about the smart grid (see **energy.gov/oe/technology-development/ smart-grid**). According to the DOE, the smart grid devices have sensors to gather data and two-way digital communication between the device in

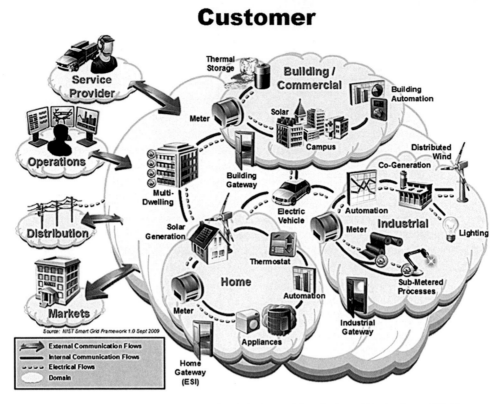

Figure 6.7 Smart grid environment (Source: National Institute of Standards and Technology, U.S. Department of Commerce *nist.gov/smartgrid/upload/FinalSGDoc2010019-corr010411-2.pdf* accessed July 2014)

the field and the network operations' center. The essentials of the grid are shown in Figure 6.7 and in the "Smart Grid Basics" infographic at **edf.org/energy/infographic-smart-grid-basics**.

The U.S. Department of Energy proposes that the following four types of technologies will drive the advancement of smart grids:

1. Integrated, automated communication between components of the electric grid.
2. Sensing and measurement technologies.
3. Automated controls for distribution and repairs.
4. Improved management dashboards and decision support software.

The major features of the grid include: smart meters for measuring electricity usage, self-healing ability from power malfunction incidents, and engagement by consumers. The meter reading is used for pricing strategy aimed at reducing consumption during peak demand. For more information, see **en.wikipedia.org/wiki/**

Smart_grid. Smart grids enable the use of smart homes and appliances. For more see **edf.org/climate/smart-grid-overview** and **smartgrid.gov**.

Smart Homes and Appliances

In a smart home, the home appliances such as computers, refrigerators, washers, dryers, televisions, and security systems are interconnected and can be controlled remotely by smartphone or via the Internet. For an overview see **smarthomeenergy.co.uk/what-smart-home**.

In the United States, thousands of homes are connected to such systems and other countries are warming to the idea. Currently, smart home systems support a number of different tasks:

- **Lighting.** Users can manage their home lighting from wherever they are.
- **Energy management.** A remote home heating and cooling system can be controlled via remote to adjust the thermostat in the house.

- **Water control.** WaterCop (**watercop.com**) is a system that reduces water damage by monitoring leaking water via a sensor, which sends a signal to the valve, causing the valve to close.
- **Home and senior communities security and safety.** Home security and safety systems can be programmed to alert you to a security related event on your property. Home security can also be supported by cameras, so you can remotely view your property in real time. Sensors can be used at home to detect intruders, keep an eye on working appliances and much more.
- Security measures are common in assisted living facilities and in senior communities, and for seniors who live independently. For example, the iHealthHome Touchscreen system collects data and communicates with the company's software. According to their website, it is a comprehensive monitoring and communication system for professional caregivers and independent living communities. Family caregivers and physicians are given remote access to the patient's health data. Using this technology, the iHealthHome program reminds seniors of their daily appointments, makes the Internet useful, keeps their mind occupied, and much more. iHealthHome also reminds seniors to take their medicine, monitor their blood pressure, and stay in touch with their caregiver. See **ihealthhome.net** for more information.
- **Home entertainment.** Audio and video equipment can be programmed to respond to a remote control device. For instance, the remote control for a stereo system located in the family room can command the system to play on speakers installed anywhere else in the house. Home automation performs for the user all from one remote and all from one button.
- **Smart appliances.** According to **smartgrid. gov**, a smart appliance is "an appliance that includes the intelligence and communications to be automatic or remote-controlled based on user preferences or external signals from a utility or third party energy service provider. A *smart appliance* may utilize a *Home Area Network* to communicate with other devices in

the customer's premise, or other channels to communicate with utility systems."

For more about home automation, see **smarthome.com/sh-learning-center-what-can-i-control.html**. To see the various apps used for home control, see **smarthome.com/android_apps.html**.

Smart and Driverless Cars

The average automobile today already contains 30–50 invisible microprocessors that control many functions such as the air conditioning. This is only the beginning of this revolution. In Section 6.8, we describe smart cars in more detail.

Smart Cities

Smart grids, homes, cars, and other things lead to smart cities (see Section 6.8).

Wireless Sensor Networks

A question facing many companies that are interested in becoming more efficient is "How can we sense the important or changing events in the real world and quickly respond more effectively?" *Real-world awareness* is a concept used to describe the ability of a company to access real-time information, allowing them to respond more effectively. For how RFID devices can be used for this purpose, see the SAP Press Release at **global.sap.com/press.epx?pressID=4143**.

Sensor Network Basics

A **sensor network** is a group of sensors distributed throughout a particular space (e.g., a manufacturing plant or an orange grove) that monitors and records environmental conditions and analyzes the collected data. Each individual sensor is called a "node." Most sensor networks are wireless. Each node consists of (1) a sensor that monitors and records environmental conditions (e.g., temperature), (2) a microprocessor that collects and processes information, and (3) a device that receives and sends data. For an overview of wireless sensor networks, see **intechopen.com/books/wireless-sensor-networks-technology-and-protocols/overview-of-wireless-sensor-net-**

work. When nodes with embedded intelligence are inserted into physical items, the items are called *smart items* or *smart objects*. RFIDs that are combined with a sensing device can be used as nodes in a sensor network; however, most sensor networks use other technologies. Advanced sensor systems can measure almost anything. For a video titled "This Sensor Measures Almost Anything" (2:06 minutes) on advanced sensor systems see (**money.cnn.com/video/technology/ 2013/01/15/t-ces-node-sensor.cnnmoney.index. html**).

Smart Sensor Applications

Connected World magazine (**connectedworldmag. com**) covers machine-to-machine communication. It has constructed a list of more than 180 applications of sensor networks. In addition to this list, *M2M Magazine* (**machinetoma- chinemagazine.com**) also provides a listing of the major sensor network vendors, as well as key resources for sensor networking. For an application in traffic flow, see Case 6.1. For an example of how sensors are used in Amtrak's high-speed trains, see Rash (2014).

CASE 6.1: EC APPLICATION: SENSORS AT INRIX HELP PEOPLE AVOID TRAFFIC JAMS

INRIX (**inrix.com**) provides a free app called INRIX Traffic, which enables drivers to get real-time traffic information (they also offer a premium service for a fee). The predictive analysis used is based on a large amount of data obtained from consumers, the environment (e.g., road construction, accidents), and government sources. Such sources include:

- Real-time traffic flow and accident information collected in real time by driver services (e.g., radar)
- Flow of traffic collected by participating delivery companies and by over 100 million anonymous volunteer drivers that have GPS–enabled smartphones, reporting in real time
- Road weather conditions and forecasts
- Traffic congestion (e.g., road maintenance).

INRIX processes the collected information with proprietary analytical tools and formulas. The processed information is used to make traffic predictions. For example, it creates a picture of anticipated traffic flows and delays for the next 15–20 minutes, the next few hours, and the next few days. This enables drivers to plan their optimal routes. As of 2014, INRIX offers global coverage in 37 countries and in major cities, and they analyze traffic information from over 100 sources. This service is combined with digital maps. In Seattle, traffic information is disseminated via smartphones and color codes on the freeways. Smartphones also display estimated times for the roads to be either clear or become jammed. By 2014, the company covered 4,000,000 miles of highways in 37 countries, delivering the best routes to drivers in real-time.

The Inrix system provides recommendations for decisions such as:

- Optional route for delivery vehicles
- Best time to go to work or other places
- How to reroute a trip to avoid an incident that just occurred
- Fees to be paid on highways, which are based on traffic conditions
  The technologies used are:
- Magnetic sensing detectors embedded under the road surface
- Closed-circuit TV cameras and radar monitoring traffic conditions
- Public safety and traffic information
- Information about free access and departure flows
- Toll collection queues.

According to their website, INRIX has partnered with Clear Channel Radio to broadcast real-time traffic data directly to vehicles via in-car or portable navigation systems, broadcast media, and wireless and Internet-based services. Clear Channel's Total Traffic Network is available in more than 125 metropolitan areas in 4 countries. See **inrix.com/partners.asp** for more about INRIX's partners and their services.

The INRIX Traffic app (available for download at **inrixtraffic.com**) is available for all smartphones and supports 10 languages, including English, French, Spanish, and Hungarian.

For the INRIX Traffic free features, see **inrix-traffic.com/features**.

Sources: Based on Jonietz (2005/2006), **inrix.com**, **inrix.com/inrix-traffic-app**, and **inrix.com/why-inrix/customers-partners** (all accessed May 2014).

Questions

1. Why is this service considered m-commerce?
2. What role do sensors play in the systems?
3. What is the revenue model of the company?
4. Enter the company's website and find additional services provided.

Implementation Issues in Ubiquitous Computing

For ubiquitous systems to be widely deployed, it is necessary to overcome many of the technical, ethical, and legal barriers associated with mobile computing (Section 6.9), as well as a few barriers unique to ubiquitous, invisible computing. Poslad (2009) provides a comprehensive list of technical and nontechnical issues.

Among the nontechnical issues, the possible loss of individual privacy seems to be at the forefront. There is a concern about "Big Brother" watching. In some cases, privacy groups have expressed a concern that the tags and sensors embedded in items, especially retail items, make it possible to track the owners or buyers of those items. A larger problem is that the information processed by tags, sensors, and other devices may be misused or mishandled.

With ubiquitous computing, the privacy issue is sometimes complex, since in many cases the data are collected in an invisible fashion. When no opt out is possible, individual privacy could be in jeopardy. However, using sensors can be very beneficial. For example, equipping the elderly or impaired people with wearable devices for monitoring movement, vital signs, usage of facilities and equipment, etc., and transmitting this information regularly over a sensor network can help people to live with minimal assistance.

SECTION 6.7 REVIEW QUESTIONS

1. Define pervasive computing.
2. What is the Internet of Things (IoT)?
3. Describe the smart grid and the role of sensors there.
4. Describe a smart home.
5. Describe machine-to-machine (M2M) technology.
6. Describe sensor networks. What are some of their benefits?
7. In what ways can pervasive computing impinge on an individual's right to privacy?

6.8 EMERGING TOPICS: FROM WEARABLES AND GOOGLE GLASS TO SMART CITIES

In this section, we will briefly describe several emerging issues related to wireless computing.

Wearable Computing Devices

Wearable computing devices have been used in industry since the mid 1990s. Typical devices were wireless computers tied to people's wrists, digital cameras mounted on the head, mobile devices attached to a belt, and much more. These became popular in the consumer market when Samsung came out with a computer mounted on a watch (smart watch), and Apple planned to released its Apple Watch in April 2015. In March 2014, Google decided to enter the smart watch market. In 2014, Google is planning to release a Nexus-like platform for wearables, called Android Wear (see **cnet.com/news/google-unveils-android-wear-its-modified-os-for-wearables** and for a developer preview, see **developer.android.com/wear/index.html?utm_source=ausdroid.net**).

Wearables are getting popular. For example, medical tracking of patients with chronic diseases is on the increase, and for $130 you can place a device on your dog's collar to track its movements.

Albanesius (2013) reported on Meeker's Internet trend assessment of the forthcoming trend of wearable technology. Also see Toh (2013). Regarding "Wearable Worries," Vijayan (2014) stated, "Wearable computers, like fitness bands, digital glasses, medical devices, and smart phones promise to radically transform the manner in which information is collected, delivered, and used by, and about, people. Many of the emerging technologies promise significant, and potentially revolutionary, user benefits. But as with most Internet-connected devices, the growing proliferation of wearables has spawned both privacy and security concerns." Vijayan presents seven devices and their hidden dangers. These devices are: digital glasses (e.g., eyewear like Google Glass), wearable/embedded medical devices, police cameras (wearable "cop cams"), smart watches, smart clothing, and fitness bands/activity monitors.

Dale (2014) describes a wearable headband that can read the brain's activity. The Canadian company Interaxon developed the device, called Muse (see **interaxon.ca/muse**). In 2014, Amazon opened a special store for wearable devices (Morphy 2014).

State of the Art

Japan is one of the leaders in developing wearable devices. For example, Patrizio (2014) reports the following: "A Japanese university has shown off a tiny personal computer that is worn on the ear and isn't much larger than many Bluetooth headsets, but it can be controlled with the blink of an eye or the click of a tongue."

The 17 gram device, creatively called 'Earclip-type Wearable PC,' is the creation of Kazuhiro Taniguchi of Hiroshima City University and made by NS West, a machinery company. "The device has Bluetooth and comes with a GPS, compass, gyrosensor, battery, barometer, speaker, and microphone. It can be connected to a smartphone or other gadget and allows the user to navigate through software programs using facial expressions, such as a raised eyebrow, tongue, nose, or mouth movement."

This device is expected to compete with Google Glass.

Google Glass

Of all the wearable devices, the one that has attracted much attention and debates in 2013/2014 is Google Glass. **Google Glass** is a wearable Android-powered mobile device controlled by voice and built like a pair of glasses. According to Petroff (2013), Google Glass (and other "smart glasses") may save companies $1 billion a year by 2017 due to increased productivity of employees, especially those who need to use both hands to perform complex tasks (e.g., by surgeons, technicians). Also known as smart glasses, the devices can be used, for example, by insurance agents to video damaged property while simultaneously checking on the costs of replacement. Several of the benefits of smart glasses are the same as those of all wearable devices.

Some people love the glasses; others hate them. In February 2014, a woman was attacked in San Francisco for wearing the device in a bar. A similar attack was reported in a McDonald's in Paris in April 2013. Several bars in San Francisco and a café in Seattle have placed a ban on Google Glass. Other cities are following suit, with Google Glass being banned in strip clubs and casinos in Las Vegas, and they are banned in most movie theatres (see **huffingtonpost. com/2013/04/10/google-glass-banned_ n_3039935.html#slide=2314456**). A 2014 poll, conducted by the research firm Toluna, found that 72% of Americans did not want to wear Google Glass due to privacy and security issues (see **mashable.com/2014/04/07/google-glass-privacy**). Google is trying to counter what they call 'the 10 myths about Google glass.'

The renowned tech blogger Robert Scoble likes it so much that he said he "he's never taken them off." However, he complained about the price of $1,500 and suggested a fair price of $200. For details and resources of Google Glasses, see Rosenblatt (2013).

Other companies in the U.S., Japan, and Korea are also experimenting or coming up with smart glasses. Note that Google Glass is getting more stylish by adopting the look of Ray-Ban and Oakley eye glasses' top brands.

Smart Cities

The idea of smart cities took off around 2007 when IBM launched their Smart Planet project and Cisco began its Smart Cities and Communities program. The idea is that in smart cities, digital technologies (mostly mobile-based) facilitate better public services for citizens, better utilization of resources, and less negative environmental impact. For resources, see **ec.europa.eu/digital-agenda/en/about-smart-cities**. Townsend (2013) provides a broad historical look and current coverage of the technologies. In an overview of his book, he provides the following examples: "In Zaragosa, Spain, a 'citizen card' can get you on the free city-wide Wi-Fi network, unlock a bike share, check a book out of the library, and pay for your bus ride home. In New York, a guerrilla group of citizen-scientists installed sensors in local sewers to alert you when storm water runoff overwhelms the system, dumping waste into local waterways." Campbell (2012) looks at smart cities from the point of view of learning and innovation.

SECTION 6.8 REVIEW QUESTIONS
1. Describe wearable computing devices.
2. What are the benefits of wearable devices?
3. What are smart glasses? Why do some people have issues with them?
4. Define smart cities. What are their major objectives?

6.9 IMPLEMENTATION ISSUES IN MOBILE COMMERCE: FROM SECURITY AND PRIVACY TO BARRIERS TO M-COMMERCE

Many issues need to be considered before applying mobile applications (for a list, see Finneran 2011a). Here, we discuss only a few of them.

Despite the vast potential for mobile commerce to change the way many companies do business, several barriers are slowing down the deployment of m-commerce applications. The major barriers to m-commerce are security, performance, availability, cost–benefit, lack of clear strategy, difficulty in integrating with in-house IT, and difficulty in customizing applications. In this section, we examine only some of these barriers, starting with the issue of security. For more on implementation issues, see the three-part video series on Mobile Commerce. Part 1 is titled "Mobile Commerce: Part 1: Where Are We Now?" (8:03 minutes), available at **youtube.com/watch?v=a--5yhJCg**. Part 2 is titled "Mobile Commerce: Part 2, The Evolution" (8:51 minutes), available at **youtube.com/watch?v=fBlLxVeCouo**. Part 3 is titled "Mobile Commerce: Part 3, How to Make mCommerce Work" (8:23 minutes), available at **youtube.com/watch?v=DsDGNLjYPxQ**.

M-commerce Security and Privacy Issues

In 2004, Cabir became the first known wireless worm that infects mobile phones. It spreads through Bluetooth devices. Since then, attacks on phones, including smartphones, have increased rapidly. For more on the Cabir worm, see **technewsworld.com/story/34542.html** and **f-secure.com/v-descs/cabir.shtml**.

Most Internet-enabled cell phones in operation today have basic software embedded in the hardware. This makes programming malware difficult. However, as the capabilities of smartphones and tablets improve, the threat of malware attacks increases. The widespread use of smartphones opens up the possibility of viruses coming from Internet downloads. Although m-commerce shares some of the same security issues as general e-commerce (see Chapter 10), there are some differences between the two.

The basic security goals of confidentiality, authentication, authorization, and integrity (Chapter 10) are just as important for m-commerce as they are for e-commerce, but they are more difficult to ensure. Specifically, m-commerce transactions usually pass through several networks, both wireless and wired. An appropriate level of security must be maintained on each network, despite the fact that interoperability among the various networks is difficult. For details, see Currier (2009). According to Finneran (2012), an *InformationWeek* 2012 security survey shows that mobile security problems are increasing, and there is gap in the measures used to combat the problem. Finneran (2012) provides some recommendations for increasing security.

Another area is that of identity fraud. A 2011 Javelin Strategy and Research Study showed that smartphone users (as well as social media users) could easily become victims of identity fraud (reported by Rashid 2012). See discussion in Chapter 10. The research study also found that people who use social networks (mainly Facebook and Twitter) were more likely to become victims of identity fraud.

In general, many of the defense mechanisms used in IT and e-commerce security are also used in m-commerce. However, given the unique nature of mobile security, additional defense methods may be needed. For example, there are many anti-theft apps that can help you find your phone and keep your personal data safe from identity theft.

Technological Barriers to M-commerce

The navigation systems for mobile applications have to be fast in order to enable rapid and easy search and shopping. Similarly, the information content needs to meet the user's needs. Other technical barriers related to mobile computing technology include limited battery life and transmission interference with home appliances. These barriers and others are listed in Table 6.2. Note that with the passage of time the technological barriers are decreasing.

Failures in Mobile Computing and M-commerce

As with many new technologies, there have been many failures of m-commerce initiatives as there are entire m-commerce companies that collapse. It is important to anticipate and plan for possible failures and to learn from those failures.

Table 6.2 Technical limitations of mobile computing

Limitation	Description
Insufficient bandwidth	Sufficient bandwidth is necessary for widespread mobile computing, and it must be inexpensive. It will take a few years until 4G and LTE are the norm in many places. Wi-Fi solves some of the problems for short-range connections
Security standards	Universal standards are still under development. It may take few more years for sufficient standards to be in place
Power consumption	The longer the life of a battery, the better the devices are (constantly improving)
Transmission interferences	Weather and terrain, including tall buildings, can limit reception. Microwave ovens, cordless phones, and other devices are free, but crowded. 2.4 GHz range may interfere with Bluetooth and Wi-Fi 802.11b transmissions
GPS accuracy	Tall buildings may limit the use of location-based m-commerce
Potential health hazards	Potential health damages (e.g., cancer) from cellular radio frequency emission are under investigation. Known health hazards include cell phone addiction, thumb-overuse syndrome, and accidents caused by people using cell phones (e.g., texting) while driving
Human-computer interface	Some people, especially the elderly or those with vision problems, may have difficulty using a small monitor and keypad in cell phones
Complexity	Many add-ons and features may make the device difficult to use

For mistakes that CIOs can avoid while encouraging enterprise mobility, see Goldschlag (2008).

Ethical, Legal, Privacy, and Health Issues in M-commerce

The increasing use of mobile devices in business and society raises new ethical, legal, and health issues that individuals, organizations, and society will have to resolve.

One workplace issue is the isolation that mobile devices can impose on a workforce. Some workers have had difficulty adjusting to the m-commerce environment since there is less need for face-to-face interactions that some people prefer.

The personal nature of mobile devices also raises ethical and legal issues. Most employees have desktop computers both at home and at work, and they can easily separate business and personal work accordingly. However, it is not so easy to separate work and personal life on a cell phone, unless one carries two phones. The concept of "bring your own device" (BYOD) is spreading rapidly, introducing issues of management, monitoring, and security. For example, if an organization has the right to monitor e-mail communications on its own network, does it also have the right to monitor voice communications on a company-owned or on a BYOD smartphone? BYOD will be discussed later.

A widely publicized but unproven potential risk is the potential health problems (e.g., cancer) from cellular radio frequency emissions. Cell phone addiction also is a problem.

Other ethical, legal, and health issues include the ethics of monitoring staff movements. Finally, there is the issue of privacy infringement and protection while implementing some m- commerce applications.

Privacy

Invasion of privacy is one of the major issues related to the use of mobile computing technologies, especially LBS, tracking, RFID, and context aware applications (see Chapter 15 for a discussion of privacy issues).

For three suggested steps for developing a strategic plan for mobility, see AT&T (2010).

Enterprise Mobility Management

According to TechTarget, *enterprise mobility management* (EMM) is "an all-encompassing approach to securing and enabling business workers' use of smartphones and tablets."

It includes data and access security, physical device tracking and configuration, and application management (see **i.zdnet.com/whitepapers/SAP_Enterprise_Mobility_for_Dummies_Guide.pdf**). Since more workers are bringing smartphones and tablets and using them in the enterprise, it is necessary to support these devices. This is where enterprise mobility management enters the picture. With an increasing number of people using mobile devices for many applications, mobility management has become a significant and challenging task. For example, Greengard (2011) suggests organizing mobility management under the security and control of IT, concentrating on data rather than on devices and employees. For guidelines on device management strategy, see Dreger and Moerschel (2010).

Mobility management can be divided into the following areas:

- **Mobile Device Management (MDM)**. Some companies allow their IT department to have full control over all mobile devices. Others allow users to maintain their devices mostly on their own (see a discussion on BYOD later in this section). Special software can help companies with their MDM.
- **Mobile Application Management (MAM)**. Similar to MDM, MAM attempts to control all applications in a company.
- **Mobile Information Management (MIM)**. This is a newer area that deals with cloud computing.

For details on these types of mobile management, see Madden (2012). Related to these are two specific areas: Bring your own device ("BYOD") and mobile apps. These are briefly described next.

The BYOD Issue

The proliferation of mobile devices in the enterprise raises the issue of "Bring Your Own Device" (BYOD). Many employees like to use their personal devices for work-related activities (e.g., their iPhones for corporate mail, travel reservations, etc.). They bring their devices to their workplace and use those devices to access the company's network. BYOD may save the company money. On the other hand, there are many implementation issues ranging from security to reimbursement policy to technical support (for a discussion, see Reisinger 2013; Finneran 2011b). Also see Cisco's 'BYOD Smart Solution' (**cisco.com/web/solutions/trends/byod_smart_solution/index.html**).

There are many suggestions regarding the management and control of BYOD. See Fiberlink (2012) for the "Ten Commandments of BYOD." Major consulting companies such as Gartner, Inc. (**gartner.com**) and Forrester Research, Inc. (**forrester.com**) provide free white papers, webinars, and reports on BYOD.

Mobile Apps and their Management

According to WhatIs.com, a **mobile app** "is a software application developed specifically for use on small, wireless computing devices, such as smartphones and tablets, rather than desktop or laptop computers. Mobile apps are designed with consideration for the demands and constraints of the devices and also to take advantage of any specialized capabilities they have. A gaming app, for example, might take advantage of the iPhone's accelerometer" (**whatis.techtarget.com/definition/mobile-app**).

Mobile applications are very popular for both consumers and use inside the enterprise. For example, as of 2013, Apple had about 1 million approved applications in its app store. McKendrick (2014) proposes six ways to bring more mobile apps into the enterprise.

Build (or Bring) Your Own App (BYOA)

BYOA is an increasing trend towards the creation of applications by users rather than by software developers. Unfortunately, BYOA creates security challenges. For a practical guide to affordable mobile app development, see Salz and Moranz (2013).

Other Managerial Issues

Several other issues are related to mobility management. For example, Currier (2009) cites the issues of ROI measurement, determining the mobility platform, training, budget and cost control, and justification. Other issues are integration, collaboration, and communication (Finneran

2011a), tablet management (Murphy 2012), data management (Greengard 2011), and mobility strategy (AT&T 2010).

SECTION 6.9 REVIEW QUESTIONS

1. How is m-commerce security similar to e-commerce security? How is it different?
2. Discuss a few of the technical limitations of m-commerce.
3. Describe the potential impact of mobile devices on organizational, health, and privacy issues.
4. Describe mobility management.
5. Define BYOD and its challenges.
6. Describe mobile apps. Why are they so popular?

MANAGERIAL ISSUES

Some managerial issues related to this chapter are as follows.

1. **What is your m-commerce strategy?** M-commerce is composed of these elements: support for internal business processes; an extension of existing e-business customer services, availability of suppliers and other business partners; and an extension of Web-based services to smartphone and tablet users. The key to success in the m-commerce world is to define your overall e-commerce and m-commerce business strategy, determine which segments are critical to the strategy and the order in which they need to be addressed, and which of the available mobile technologies will support the strategy and the critical segments (consult AT&T 2010).
2. **Are there any clear technical winners?** Among mobile devices, the answer is yes. Many like the all-in-one devices, such as smartphones or tablets. There still is a confusing multiplicity of standards, devices, and supporting hardware. The key is to select a suitable platform and infrastructure that can support the existing needs of most users. While m–commerce is becoming very popular in marketing, payments, manufacturing, and services, l–commerce applications are still in their infancy.

3. **How should BYOD be managed?** Device management becomes a complex issue since employees started to bring and use their mobile devices at work. Mobile devices are made by different manufacturers and use different operating systems. Add to this the thousands of apps and you need a good system and policies to manage BYOD. For a comprehensive strategy for managing BYOD, see **cisco.com**: search for Cisco's "BYOD Smart Solutions" and Reisinger (2013).

4. **Is it wise to embark on l–commerce?** While l-commerce is still emerging and there is not much evidence of mega success, it is wise to at least experiment with the technology. Given that several of its driving factors are growing rapidly and so are its potential benefits, users need to conduct a preliminary feasibility study to find the most promising applications and then go ahead with small scale experimentation.

5. **Which applications should be implemented first**? Although there is little interest associated with various m–commerce applications, especially location–based services, mobile applications must be judged like any other business technology – by ROI, cost-benefit analysis, potential cost reductions, and improved efficiency. Enterprise applications such as supporting the mobile workforce, fleets, and warehouses have resulted in the highest returns. Implementers need to remember that the m–commerce platform is the platform most preferred by younger generations. It is also important to understand why Japan and Korea have a much higher penetration rate in m–commerce while other countries with the same level of mobile telecommunication infrastructure do not have a similar level of penetration. Implementation includes the topic of mobile device management (see Oliver 2008).

SUMMARY

In this chapter, you learned about the following EC issues as they relate to the chapter's learning objectives.

1. **What is m-commerce, its value-added attributes, and fundamental drivers?** M-commerce is any e-commerce activity conducted with mobile devices over a wireless telecommunications network. M-commerce complements e-commerce. M-commerce can help a business improve its value proposition to customers by utilizing its unique attributes: ubiquity, convenience, interactivity, personalization, and localization. Currently, m-commerce is driven by the large number of users of mobile devices; a developing "smartphone culture" among youth; demands from service-oriented customers; vendor marketing; declining prices; an increase in size of the mobile workforce; improved ratio of performance to price; and the increasing bandwidth.

2. **What is the mobile computing environment that supports m-commerce?** The mobile computing environment consists of three key elements: mobile devices, wireless networks, and services. Although mobile computing devices vary in size and functionality, they are rapidly moving toward an all-in-one device that is overcoming some of the limitations associated with poor usability, such as small screen size, limited bandwidth, and restricted input capabilities. Even with their limitations, mobile devices offer a series of support services, principally SMS, voice, and location-based services, which differentiate m-commerce from e-commerce.

3. **Which types of networks support mobile devices?** Mobile devices connect wirelessly to networks or other devices at personal, local, metropolitan, or wide area levels. Bluetooth (personal), cellular phone networks (WWAN), and wireless LANs (like Wi-Fi) are well-known technologies that are well established in the wireless marketplace. In contrast, municipal and WiMAX (metropolitan) are less well-known.

4. **Financial and banking applications.** Many EC applications in the financial services industries (such as e-banking) can be conducted with wireless devices. Most mobile

financial applications are simply wireless versions of their wireline counterparts, and they are conducted via SMS or the mobile Web system. Mobile banking and mobile payments are examples of this activity. More and more, banks throughout the world are enabling their customers to use mobile devices to make payments, view paid checks, compare bank services, transfer funds, and locate branches.

5. **Enterprise mobility applications.** The major application is that of supporting the various types of workforce (e.g., salespeople, repair people, and field force). Other areas are mobile CRM, inventory management, and wireless job dispatch. These applications offer high return on investment, even in the short run. Additional areas are fleet and transportation management and applications in warehouses.

6. **Consumer and personal applications and mobile entertainment.** One of the fastest growing markets in m-commerce is mobile entertainment. Mobile entertainment encompasses mobile music, games, gambling, adult entertainment, and specialized user-generated content. Among these, mobile music is the largest segment, but mobile video is the fastest growing. Mobile gambling is also growing rapidly despite the legal restrictions by various government bodies. Also growing are mobile sports applications. Service industries using mobile applications include health care, hospitality, public safety, crime prevention, and homeland security.

7. **Location-based commerce.** Location-based commerce (l-commerce) refers to the use of positioning devices, mostly GPS, to find a customer's location and deliver products and services based on the user's location. The services provided by companies using l-commerce tend to focus on one or more of the: location, navigation, tracking, mapping, and timing. These services include five basic components: mobile devices, communication networks, positioning components, service and application providers, and data or content providers. Among these, the position and data components, especially geographical information systems (GIS), are critical. Even though l-commerce has a large potential, several factors impede its widespread use, including the accuracy of the location finding devices, the cost of many applications in relation to the benefits, the limited network bandwidth, and potential invasion of privacy.

8. **Ubiquitous computing and sensory systems.** The *Internet of Things (IoT)* is upon us, and so are cutting-edge and futuristic systems that involve many embedded and invisible processors. These systems appear in several formats, notably those that are context aware, and they enable intelligent and useful applications. They are interrelated with sensory systems and provide for smart applications such as smart electric grids, smart homes, smart buildings, smart cars, and much more.

9. **Google Glass, driverless cars, and mobile apps.** Wearables are getting more important as they relate to the Internet of Things and to improved productivity in the enterprise. Wearables improve business processes and communication. They free people's hands so business processes can be improved. They can be controlled by voice and even by the brain. Most benefits are derived when the wearables are connected to the Internet. A wearable device that gets lots of publicity is Google Glass (and similar smart glasses). On one hand these can increase productivity, but on the other hand many fear the potential of invasion of privacy. Wearables and other mobile devices are important components in smart cities. Designers of smart cities aim to improve both government services to citizens and the dwellers quality of life.

10. **Security and other implementation issues.** Even though the potential benefits of m-commerce applications may be substantial, their implementation faces a number of challenges, including technical interruptions and gaps in network coverage; performance problems created by slow mobile networks and applications; managing and securing mobile devices; and managing mobile network bandwidth. The mobile computing

environment offers special challenges for security, including the need to secure transmission over the open air and through multiple connecting networks. The biggest technological challenges relate to the usability and technological changes of mobile devices. Finally, privacy concerns, such as legal, ethical, and health issues, that can arise from the use of m-commerce, especially in the workplace, need to be considered.

KEY TERMS

Bluetooth
Context-aware computing
Enterprise mobility
Geographical information system (GIS)
Geolocation
Global positioning system (GPS)
Google Glass
Interactive voice response (IVR) system
Internet of Things (IoT)
Location-based m-commerce (l-commerce)
Location-based services (LBS)
Mobile app
Mobile banking (m-banking)
Mobile commerce (m-commerce;
   m-business)
Mobile enterprises
Mobile entertainment
Mobile portal
Mobile worker
Multimedia messaging service (MMS)
Personal area network (PAN)
Personal digital assistant (PDA)
Pervasive computing
Radio Frequency identification (RFID)
Real-time location systems (RTLS)
Sensor network
Short message service (SMS)
Smart Grid
Smartphone
Social location-based marketing
Ubiquitous computing (ubicom)
Voice portal
Wi-Fi (wireless fidelity)
WiMAX
Wireless local area network (WLAN)

Wireless mobile computing
   (mobile computing)
Wireless wide area network (WWAN)

DISCUSSION QUESTIONS

1. Discuss how m-commerce can expand the reach of EC.
2. Which of the m-commerce limitations listed in this chapter do you think will have the biggest near-term negative impact on the growth of m-commence? Which ones will be minimized within 5 years? Which ones will not?
3. Discuss the advantages and limitations of self–driven cars.
4. Discuss the factors that are critical to the overall growth of mobile banking.
5. Why are many of the more popular mobile gambling sites located in small island countries?
6. How are GPS and GIS related?
7. Discuss the advantages of m-commerce over wired EC.
8. Why must location-based services, by law, be permission-based?

TOPICS FOR CLASS DISCUSSION AND DEBATES

1. Discuss the potential benefits and drawbacks of conducting m-commerce on social networks.
2. Discuss the strategic advantage of m-commerce.
3. Google acquired AdMob (**google.com/ads/admob**) partly to compete with Apple's iAd. Discuss the strategic implications of AdMob versus iAd.
4. Debate the issue of tracking the whereabouts of employees. Related to this is the privacy issue of tracking people and cars. Discuss the pros and cons.
5. Debate the issue of a company's right to check all employee's e-mail and voice communications, done on either their own, or on the company's devices during work hours.
6. Examine the use of mobile devices in restaurants and debate the possibility of the elimination of paper menus. (Start by reading Nassauer 2012.)

7. Read Sutter (2010). Discuss the advantages and risks of GPS-based dating.

8. Find information about EcoRebate's incentive programs (see **ecorebates.com**). Explain their relationship to LBS. Write a report.

9. Research the evolvement of Google Glass. Write a report. Start with the evolution of Google Glass at **redmondpie.com/the-evolution-of-google-glass-in-two-years-since-its-inception-image**. What will be the benefits of the device to users? (See **golocal-worcester.com/business/smart-benefits-vision-coverage-for-google-glass-is-clear**.)

10. Find information on IBM's "smarter cities." What are the benefits of the initiative to the residents of such cities? (See **ibm.com/smarterplanet/us/en/smarter_cities/overview**.)

11. Find information about Cisco's "BYOD smart solution." Examine the benefits and discuss the possibility of using this solution in medium or small companies. (See **cisco.com/web/solutions/trends/byod_smart_solution/index.html**.)

12. Find the latest applications of the "Internet of Things" and discuss their usability.

13. In-store mobile tracking of shoppers in brick-and-mortar retailers is increasing. Examine the benefits and the necessary protection of the customers (e.g., choice to opt-out). Under what circumstances would you allow customer tracking?

INTERNET EXERCISES

1. Research the status of 4G. You can find information on 4G by conducting a Google search and by going to Verizon Wireless (see **verizonwireless.com/wcms/consumer/4g-lte.html**). Prepare a report on the status of 4G based on your findings.

2. You have been asked to assemble a directory of Wi-Fi hotspots in your local area. There are a number of sites, such as **hotspot-locations.com** that offer search capabilities for finding hotpots in a specific area. Make a list of locations that offer this feature.

3. Juniper Research has created a variety of white papers dealing with different segments of the mobile entertainment market (e.g., mobile games). Go to Juniper Research (**juniperresearch.com**) and download a white paper regarding one of these market segments. Use the white paper as a guide to write a summary of the market segment you selected – the size of the market, the major vendors, the factors encouraging and impeding its growth, and the future of the market segment.

4. Enter **gpshopper.com**. Find the products/services they provide for LBS. Then enter **jiwire.com/advertisers/ad-solutions/compass-audience**. Compare the products and services it provides with those offered by GPShopper. Write a report.

5. Find information about Google Maps for mobile devices. Also review the capabilities of Google SMS and other related Google applications. Write a report on your findings.

6. Enter **mobile.fandango.com** and find the services they offer to mobile customers. Write a report.

7. Enter IBM's Smarter Cities Challenge (**smartercitieschallenge.org**). Find the recent activities related to IBM's initiatives about smarter cities. Then check MIT Media Lab Initiative City Science (**cities.media.mit.edu**) and find their latest smart cities projects. Finally, enter European Smart Cities (**smart-cities.eu**). Write a report on the major current projects related to smart cities.

8. Enter **ehow.com** and find information on "how to locate a cell phone with GPS." Why does a mobile device need to have this capability?

9. Conduct a Google search for comparisons on tablets vs. PCs. Write a report.

TEAM ASSIGNMENTS AND PROJECTS

1. **Assignment for the Opening Case**
   Read the opening case and answer the following questions.
   (a) Do you really need the NeverLost GPS (fee of $13.99/day) when you can get almost the same information with a smartphone like the iPhone (or iPad) and a portable GPS? Why or why not?

(b) Which one of Hertz's mobile applications can be considered a mobile enterprise and which one can be considered a mobile customer service?

(c) Identify finance and marketing-oriented applications in this case.

(d) What are the benefits of offering mobile apps to Hertz?

(e) As a customer, how do you feel about Hertz knowing where you are at all times?

(f) Find information about the competition between Hertz Fleet with Eileo and Zipcar. Provide a summary. Start by reading **trefis.com/stock/zip/articles/112405/ is-hertz-fleet-with-eileo-a-big-trouble-for-zipcar/2012-06-29**.

2. Each team should examine a major vendor of enterprise-oriented mobile devices (Nokia, Kyocera, Motorola; a Google company, BlackBerry, etc.). Each team will research the capabilities of the devices offered by each company and then present the findings to the class. The objective of the presentation is to convince the rest of the class to buy that company's products.

3. Each team should explore the commercial applications of m-commerce in one of the following areas: financial services (including banking); stocks; insurance; marketing and advertising; travel and transportation; human resources management; public services; restaurants; and health care. Each team will present a report to the class based on their findings. (Start with **sociomine.eu**).

4. Each team should choose one of the following areas – homes, cars, appliances, or other consumer goods, such as clothing – and investigate how embedded microprocessors are currently being used. How will they be used in the future to support consumer-centric services? Each team will present a report to the class based on its findings.

5. There are many applications of tablets in the enterprise. Investigate the major applications as well as the IT requirements, support, necessary security, development efforts, and so forth. Begin by reading Carr (2010).

6. Indiana University, with 8 campuses, has over 110,000 students and over 18,000 employees, including faculty and support staff. The information systems include the use of many BYOD mobile devices. Enter **citrix.com/products/ enterprise-mobility.html** and read the story about Indiana University. Watch the 2:28 minute video titled "Indiana University Customer Story" and conduct an additional search regarding how the university controls mobile device security. Write a report. (Start with the university's IT services at **uits.iu.edu/page/bcnh**.)

7. Wireless cities and communities can improve people's lives and even reduce the digital divide. Find information on the research and applications of wireless (or smart) cities. Use this as a class project where different teams cover different topics.

8. Watch the video titled "Technology Advances Fuelling M-Commerce Today" (7:43 minutes) at **youtube.com/watch?v=398EztRwPiY** and answer the following questions:

(a) What EC services are provided by m-commerce?

(b) Discuss the role of m-commerce in retailing.

(c) Discuss the lack of m-commerce strategy vs. its wide acceptance.

(d) Why is m-commerce such a fragmented market?

(e) Why do retailers spend much of their IT budget on m-commerce?

(f) Discuss the impact of m-commerce on competition among retailers.

(g) What are the difficulties in managing mobile technology?

(h) What are the advantages of mobile payments?

(i) Research the major methods and vendors of m-payments.

CLOSING CASE: MOTOROLA ENTERPRISE: WIRELESS SOLUTIONS FOR A HOSPITAL AND A MANUFACTURER

Motorola (**motorola.com**) is one of the world's largest enterprise mobility companies. The company's diverse operations are classified next.

Products and Services

The Major Enterprise Products

In 2014 Motorola's major enterprise products included: barcode scanners, interactive kiosks, mobile computers, tablets, RFID products, original equipment manufacturer (OEM) products, two-way radios and pagers, enterprise voice and data services, and wireless LAN (described next).

For details, benefits, and case studies, see Motorola Solutions Enterprise (**motorolasolutions.com/US-EN/Enterprise+Mobility**; Note: acquired by Zebra.com).

The Major Wireless Solutions

In 2014, the major wireless solutions offered by Motorola were: indoor location, remote access, voice over wireless, mobile application services, BYOD, cloud wireless, video over wireless, and mobile data offload.

The wireless LAN products are: access, management, and security.

For details, benefits, and case studies, see Motorola Solutions Wireless LAN (**motorolasolutions.com/US-EN/Business+Product+and+Services/Wireless+LAN**).

The Industries Services

Motorola serves many major industries, including: manufacturing, retail, hospitality, health care, education, utilities, petrochemical, transportation and logistics, and wholesale distribution.

A Health Care Example: North York General Hospital of Toronto, Canada

This hospital, which is affiliated with the University of Toronto, is a three-site community teaching hospital with 5,000 staff, physicians, and volunteers. To improve quality of care (e.g., ensuring that patients receive the correct medication), the hospital introduced an electronic health system which includes significant wireless subsystems.

The system, known as eCare, is based on wireless network and advanced electronic mobile points of care. For example, it includes a computerized provider of order entries, a high speed electronic medication administration system, communication, and secured network access features. All these have increased patient safety and quality of care. The system facilitated teamwork of the staff in the hospital. To read the case study, see **motorolasolutions.com/web/Business/Solutions/Industry%20Solutions/Healthcare/documents/static_files/MOT_North_York_General_Hospital_CaseStudy_EN_073012.pdf**. See also Motorola Solutions for health care (**motorolasolutions.com/US-EN/Business+Solutions/Industry+Solutions/Healthcare**).

A Supply Chain Example: Yodobashi Camera of Japan

The company is one of Japan's largest retailers of electronic goods. It has 19 stores with more than 850,000 items and new products arriving almost every day. The products are supplied by hundreds of manufacturers and distributors. Inventory levels must be sufficient to meet customer demands and avoid lost sales. The effective management of the supply chain, the warehouse, and the inventory is a critical success factor.

The company is using Motorola's RFID-based warehouse management solution, which operates in real time. RFID tags are pasted on all product boxes arriving from the suppliers. They are detected at the entry gate by the RFID readers and the information is transmitted automatically to the warehouse management system. The result is reduced cost of warehousing operation, flow of real-time information, minimization of inventory-related problems, and increased customer satisfaction and sales.

Sources: Extracted from Motorola's website. The cases are condensed versions of:

"Electronic TLC: Toronto Hospital Increases Patient Safety with eCare Project" and "Yodobashi Camera Deploys RFID Warehouse Management." (All materials accessed May 2014.)

Questions

1. Enter **motorolasolutions.com** and **zebra.com** and find case studies similar to the above that are related to restaurants, cruise ships, salesforce automation, and education. Relate the wireless system to the benefits for each case.

2. Yodobashi Camera uses tags attached to boxes and containers. Conduct a Google search to find other companies that tag individual items.
3. In what ways has patient safety increased in Toronto's North York General Hospital?
4. Find any enterprise applications that are provided by Motorola's competitors. Write a report.

ONLINE FILES
available at **affordable-ecommerce-textbook.com/turban**

W6.1 Drivers of M-Commerce
W6.2 Representative List of Mobile Devices
W6.3 Mobile Workforce and M-Commerce Support
W6.4 Application Case: NextBus – Superb Customer Service

COMPREHENSIVE EDUCATIONAL WEBSITES

bitpipe.com: A collection of white papers, videos, and case studies on information technology and m-commerce.

bmcgee.com: Brandon McGee's blog on m-banking and e-payment systems.

ecommercetimes.com/perl/section/m-commerce: A vast collection of articles on m-commerce.

iab.net: Interactive Advertising Bureau – standards, guidelines, and standards and practices of interactive advertising.

ipso-alliance.org: Technical information, resource library, news, and events on enabling the Internet of Things.

juniperresearch.com/mobile_commerce: A collection of reports, white papers, and data on m-commerce.

theemf.org: Enterprise Mobility Foundation—Mobility success stories, latest research, news and events, and much more.

mobilecommercepress.com: Comprehensive site dedicated to many m-commerce topics.

mobilemarketer.com: News, resources, and articles on mobile marketing, media, and commerce.

mobilemarketingwatch.com: "The Pulse of the Mobile Marketing Community"—Best practices and industry guidelines on mobile computing.

searchmobilecomputing.techtarget.com/resources: News, articles, white papers, blogs, and tutorials on mobile computing.

trimble.com/gps_tutorial: A tutorial on GPS technology designed to give a basic understanding of the principles behind GPS.

wimaxforum.org: An industry-led organization that represents the entire mobile Internet ecosystem, committed to the global adoption of 4G mobile broadband.

wsnmagazine.com: *Wireless Sensor Networks Magazine*--All about wireless sensor networks, including technical articles, news, and events.

GLOSSARY

Bluetooth A set of wireless technology standards for exchanging data between devices over a short range.

Context-aware computing A technology that is capable in predicting people's needs and providing fulfillment options (sometimes even before a request by the end user is made).

Enterprise mobility The people and technology (e.g., devices and networks) that enable mobile computing applications within the enterprise.

Geographical information system (GIS) A computer-based system whose function is to capture, store, analyze, and display geographically-related data.

Geolocation The ability to find the location of a user who is connected to the Web via a mobile device.

Global positioning system (GPS) "A U.S.-owned utility that provides users with positioning, navigation, and timing (PNT) services. This system consists of three segments: the space segment, the control segment, and the user segment." (Per GPS.gov; last modified February 2014)

Google Glass   A wearable Android-powered mobile device controlled by voice and built like a pair of glasses.

Interactive voice response (IVR)   A voice support application system that enables users to interact by telephone (of any kind) with a computerized system to request and receive information.

Internet of Things (IoT)   A situation where many objects (people, animals, items) with embedded microprocessors are connected mostly wirelessely to the Internet.

Location-based m-commerce (l-commerce)   The use of location finding systems such as GPS-enabled devices or similar technologies (e.g., triangulation of radio- or cell-based stations) to find where a customer or an object is located and provide relevant services, such as an advertisement or vehicle route optimization.

Location-based service (LBS)   A mobile device–based computerized service, which utilizes information about the geographical position of a user's mobile device (e.g., mobile phone tracking) for delivering a service (e.g., advertisers can target ads to specific location), to the user.

Mobile app   A software application developed specifically for use on small, wireless computing devices, such as smartphones and tablets, rather than desktop or laptop computers.

Mobile banking (m-banking)   A term used to describe the conducting of banking activities via a mobile device (mostly by texting, or via mobile website).

Mobile commerce (m-commerce; m-business)   Conducting e-commerce by using mobile devices and wireless networks.

Mobile enterprise   Mobile applications conducted by enterprises to improve the operations of the employees, facilities, and relevant supply chains, within the enterprise and with its business partners.

Mobile entertainment   Any entertainment delivered on mobile devices over wireless networks or that interacts with mobile service providers.

Mobile portal   A gateway to the Internet from mobile devices.

Mobile worker   Any employee who is away from his or her primary work space at least 10 hours a week (or 25% of the time).

Multimedia messaging service (MMS)   The new type of wireless messaging, delivering rich media content, such as video, images, and audio to mobile devices. MMS is an extension of SMS (no extra charge with an SMS "bundle"). It allows for longer messages than with SMS.

Personal area network (PAN)   A network that provides very short-range device-to-device wireless connections (a distance up to 60 feet).

Personal digital assistant (PDA)   A stand-alone handheld computer that provides access to a user's address book and calendar and supports calculations and some desktop applications, such as word processing and spreadsheets. New versions of the PDA also provide multimedia support for audio and video.

Pervasive computing   Computing capabilities that are embedded in the environment but typically are not mobile.

Radio frequency identification (RFID)   A short-range radio frequency communication technology for wirelessly identifying and tracking tags attached to objects.

Real-time location systems (RTLS)   Systems used to track and identify the location of objects in real time.

Sensor network   A group of sensors distributed throughout a particular space (e.g., a manufacturing plant or an orange grove) that monitors and records environmental conditions and analyze the collected data.

Short message service (SMS)   A service that supports the transmittal of short text messages (up to 140 to 160 characters) between wireless devices.

Smartphone   A mobile phone with Internet access and PC-like functionality.

Smart grid   An electricity network managed by utilizing digital technology.

Social location-based marketing   Marketing that occurs when users share their location with vendors (opt–in) in real time, usually within social media environments.

Ubiquitous computing (ubicom)   Computing capabilities embedded into a relevant system, usually not visible, which may be mobile or stationary.

Voice portal A website with an audio interface that can be accessed through a telephone call.

Wi-Fi The common name used to describe a wireless networking technology known as IEEE 802.11 (e.g., 802.11g).

WiMAX Worldwide Interoperability for Microwave Access is a wireless communications standard that provides relatively fast (e.g., 75 Mbps to several GHz) broadband access over a medium-sized area of up to 31 miles (50 kilometers).

Wireless Application Protocol (WAP) The technology protocol that enables Internet browsing using mobile devices.

Wireless local area network (WLAN) A telecommunications network that acts wirelessly, similar to a wired LAN.

Wireless mobile computing (mobile computing) A computing solution where computing is done using mobile devices at any place connected to a wireless network.

Wireless wide area network (WWAN) A telecommunications network that offers the broadest wireless coverage. WWANs rely on the same network technologies as cell phones.

REFERENCES

Accenture Technology Vision 2014. "From Digitally Disrupted to Digital Disrupter." A White Paper, 2014. **accenture.com/microsite/it-technology-trends-2014/Documents/TechVision/Downloads/Accenture_Technology_Vision_2014.pdf** (accessed May 2014).

Albanesius, C., "Meeker: Expect Wearable Tech, More Internet Oversharing." May 29, 2013. **pcmag.com/article2/0,2817,2419630,00.asp** (accessed May 2014).

AT&T. "Three Steps for Creating a Mobility Strategy." White paper AB-1500-01, September 21, 2010. **business.att.com/content/whitepaper/3-steps-for-creating-a-mobile-strategy.pdf** (accessed May 2014).

Butcher, D. "Guide to Smart SMS Marketing." A Mobile Marketer Presentation. White Paper (2011). **neustar.biz/enterprise/docs/whitepapers/digital-marketing/how-retailers-can-use-sms-to-drive-sales.pdf**; (Updated 2013 by Neustar, Inc. **usshortcodes.com/docs/whitepapers/guide-to-smart-sms-marketing.pdf**) (both accessed May 2014).

Campbell, T. *Beyond Smart Cities: How Cities Network, Learn and Innovative.* Florence, KY: Taylor & Francis, 2012.

Carr, D. F. "iPad Hit the Enterprise" *Information Week,* December 2, 2010.

Channick, R. "Comcast Turning Chicago Homes into Public Wi-Fi Hot Spots." March 5, 2014. **articles.chicagotribune.com/2014-03-05/business/chi-chicago-public-wifi-comcast-20140304_1_xfinity-wi-fi-moffettnathanson-public-wi-fi-hot-spots** (accessed May 2014).

Cearley, D. "Gartner: Top 10 Strategic Technology Trends for 2014." 2014. **gartner.com/technology/research/top-10-technology-trends** (accessed May 2014).

Currier, G. "Orchestrating Enterprise Mobility." May 5, 2009. **baselinemag.com/c/a/Mobile-and-Wireless/Orchestrating-Enterprise-Mobility-602379** (accessed May 2014).

Dale, B. "This Wearable Device Reads Your Brain Waves. Is There a Market for It?" February 10, 2014. **tech.fortune.cnn.com/2014/02/10/this-wearable-device-reads-your-brain-waves-is-there-a-market-for-it** (accessed May 2014).

Del Rey, J. "Does Your Business Need an App?: How a Smartphone Application Can Supercharge Your Business." December 1, 2010 (Last update). **inc.com/magazine/20101201/does-your-business-need-an-app.html** (accessed May 2014).

Dolphin, G. "Will There Be WiFi with That?" May/June 2010. **baselinemag.com/infrastructure/Wireless-Infrastructure-Boosts-Business-Results/** (accessed May 2014).

Dreger, R., and G. Moerschel. "Watch Out." *Information Week,* May 3, 2010. Available for download in .pdf format at **reports.informationweek.com/abstract/18/6706/Mobility-Wireless/Information Week-Full-Issue:-May-3,-2010.html** (accessed May 2014).

Eler, A. "ComScore: Mobile Social Networking App Audience Grows 126% in past Year." October 20, 2011. **readwrite.com/2011/10/20/comscore_mobile_social_networking_app_audience_grows_126_in_past_year#awesm=~oCWXFGIjmyiYbN** (accessed May 2014).

Elliott, C. "What Will Your Next Rental Car Know about You? Everything." August 14, 2013. **elliott.org/blog/what-will-your-next-rental-car-know-about-you-everything** (accessed May 2014).

Feldman, J. "Location Data: More Valuable, Easier to Access." October 28, 2010. **informationweek.com/mobile/location-data-more-valuable-easier-to-access-/d/d-id/1093716** (accessed May 2014).

Fiberlink. *The Ten Commandments of BYOD,* a MaaS 360 free e-book (2012). Available for download at **trials.maas360.com/forms/register_service_m.php?id=332&A=StumbleUpon** (accessed May 2014).

Fiegerman, S. "Report: U.S. Mobile Commerce to Hit $144 Billion This Year." May 12, 2014. **mashable.com/2014/05/12/mobile-commerce-sales** (accessed May 2014).

Finneran, M. "A New Approach for Mobile: 8 Elements of a Complete Mobile App Environment." *Information Week,* August 15, 2011a.

Finneran, M. "Survive the BYOD Revolution." *Information Week*, October 19, 2011b. **informationweek.com/mobile/mobile-devices/survive-the-byod-revolution/d/d-id/1100848** (accessed May 2014).

Finneran, M. "Mobile Security Gaps Abound." May 1, 2012. **reports.informationweek.com/abstract/21/8837/Security/mobile-security-gaps-abound.html** (accessed May 2014).

Fitton, C., et al. *Enterprise Mobility for Dummies*. Ontario, Canada: John Wiley, 2012. (A free download is available from SAP).

Fonemine. "Can Mobility Transform Your Business?" *MobileForce*, March 24, 2014. **corp.fonemine.com/mobility-transform-business** (accessed May 2014).

Frakes, D. "iPod Nano (Sixth Generation, Late 2010)." September 7, 2010. **macworld.com/article/1153921/6G_iPod_nano.html** (accessed May 2014).

Gannes, L. "The Best of Mary Meeker's 2013 Internet Trends Slides." May 29, 2013. **allthingsd.com/20130529/the-best-of-mary-meekers-2013-internet-trends-slides** (accessed May 2014).

Goldschlag, D. "How CIOs Can Encourage Innovative Enterprise Mobility—Top Mistakes to Avoid." August 25, 2008. **eweek.com/c/a/Mobile-and-Wireless/How-CIOs-Can-Encourage-Innovative-Enterprise-MobilityTop-Mistakes-to-Avoid** (accessed May 2014).

Goodwin, A. "Hitting the Road with Hertz's NeverLost GPS." August 18, 2010. **cnet.com/news/hitting-the-road-with-hertzs-neverlost-gps/** (accessed May 2014).

GPS.gov. "The Global Positioning System." (Last modified February 2014). **gps.gov/systems/gps** (accessed May 2014).

Graham, B. "Mobile Banking Trends for 2014." February 20, 2014. **banktech.com/architecture-infrastructure/mobile-banking-trends-for-2014/240166190** (accessed May 2014).

Greengard, S. "Can IT Manage Mobility?" *Baseline*, January/February 2011.

Groth, A., and S. Cortez. "The 15 Fastest-Growing Retailers in America." *Business Insider*, July 10, 2012. **businessinsider.com/fastest-growing-retailers-in-america-2012-7?op=1#!HKYjc** (accessed May 2014).

GSMA. "Mobile Industry: Major Contributor to the Global Economy." A Mobile Economy White Paper, *Enterprise Innovation*, March 12, 2013. **enterpriseinnovation.net/whitepaper/mobile-industry-major-contributor-global-economy** (accessed May 2014).

Heywood, I., et al. *An Introduction to Geographical Information Systems*, 4th ed. Upper Saddle River, NJ: Prentice-Hall, 2012.

Holler, J., et al. *From Machine-to-Machine to the Internet of Things: Introduction to a New Age of Intelligence*, Salt Lake City, UT: Academic Press, 2014.

Jonietz, E. "Traffic Avoidance." *MIT Technology Review*, December 2005/January 2006. **technologyreview.com/article/405043/traffic-avoidance** (accessed May 2014).

Juniper Research. "Press Release: Global Mobile & Tablet Entertainment Revenues to Reach Almost $75 Billion by 2017, Finds Juniper." December 10, 2013. **juniperresearch.com/viewpressrelease.php?pr=417** (accessed May 2014).

Kahn, M. A., G. Tsirulnik, D. Butcher. "Hertz Breaks Multichannel Location-Based Campaign to Increase Car Rentals." November 23, 2010. **mobilemarketer.com/cms/news/advertising/8206.html** (accessed May 2014).

Kerr, J. C. "Stores Can See Where You Go by Tracking Your Phone." *AP News*, February 19, 2014. **bigstory.ap.org/article/stores-can-track-where-you-go-using-your-phone** (accessed May 2014).

Knight, K. "How Mobile Is Impacting Online Commerce." February 22, 2012a. **bizreport.com/2012/02/how-mobile-is-impacting-online-commerce.html** (accessed May 2014).

Knight, K. "Report: Gamers Playing More on Mobiles." January 9, 2012b. **bizreport.com/2012/01/report-gamers-playing-more-on-mobiles.html** (accessed May 2014).

Knowledge@Wharton and Ernst & Young. *Mobile Banking: Financial Services Meet the Electronic Wallet* [Kindle edition with Audio/Video]. Philadelphia, PA: Knowledge@Wharton, 2013.

Krishnan, S. *The Power of Mobile Banking: How to Profit from the Revolution in Retail Financial Services*. Hoboken, NJ: Wiley, 2014.

Krumm, J. *Ubiquitous Computing Fundamentals*. London: Chapman & Hall/CRC, 2009.

Kvita, C. "Navigate the Internet of Things." January/February 2014. **oracle.com/technetwork/issue-archive/2014/14-jan/o14interview-utzschneider-2074127.html** (accessed May 2014).

Leggatt, H. "M-Commerce Quadruples in Past Two Years." May 29, 2012. **bizreport.com/2012/05/m-commerce-quadruples-in-past-two-years.html** (accessed May 2014).

Liedtke, M. "Apple Hopes Carplay Will Drive Further Success." March 5, 2014. **irishexaminer.com/ireland/apple-hopes-carplay-will-drive-further-success-260832.html** (accessed May 2014).

Lund, D., and G. Signorini. "Creating the Enterprise-Class Tablet Environment." A White Paper. *Yankee Group Research, Inc.*, October 2011.

Macintosh, R. S. "Portable Real Estate Listings—But with a Difference." March 25, 2010. **nytimes.com/2010/03/26/greathomesanddestinations/26iht-rear.html?pagewanted=all&_r=0** (accessed May 2014).

Madden, B., "What Is MDM, MAM, and MIM? (And What's the Difference?)" May 29, 2012. **brianmadden.com/blogs/brianmadden/archive/2012/05/29/what-is-mdm-mam-and-mim-and-what-s-the-difference.aspx** (accessed May 2014).

Malik, A. *RTLS for Dummies*. Hoboken, NJ: Wiley & Sons, 2009.

McCafferty, D. "Tablets Are Changing How Employees Work." December 19, 2012. **baselinemag.com/mobility/slideshows/tablets-are-changing-how-employees-work** (accessed May 2014).

McKendrick, J. "6 Ways to Bring Mobile Apps into the Enterprise Fold." January 13, 2014. **zdnet.com/6-ways-to-bring-mobile-apps-into-the-enterprise-fold-7000025091** (accessed May 2014).

Millward, S. "Starting Today, Chinese Consumers Will Be Able to Buy Almost Anything Inside WeChat." March 5, 2014. **techinasia.com/wechat-adds-payment-support-for-brands-and-retailers** (accessed May 2014).

Mordhorst, M. *How to Help Enterprises Going Mobile: Investigation on Influences and Requirements of Business Apps within Enterprise Mobility.* Hamburg, Germany: Anchor Academic Pub., 2014.

Morphy, E. "Amazon Opens Wearable Tech Outpost." May 6, 2014. **technewsworld.com/story/emerging-tech/80375.html** (accessed May 2014).

Motorola. "Synchronizing the Distribution Supply Chain with Mobility." White paper, 2007. **enterprisemobilitynetwork.com/wp-content/uploads/2012/01/motorola-synchronising-the-distribution-supply-chain.pdf** (accessed May 2014).

Murphy, C. "March of the Tablets." February 1, 2012. **reports.informationweek.com/abstract/18/8665/Mobility-Wireless/march-of-the-tablets.html** (accessed May 2014).

Mueller, K. "The Olympics in the Social/Mobile Age." July 3, 2012. **socialmediatoday.com/kenmueller/579151/olympics-socialmobile-age** (accessed May 2014).

Musil, S. "Researchers Develop a More Accurate Car Navigation System." February 13, 2013. **cnet.com/news/researchers-develop-a-more-accurate-car-navigation-system** (accessed May 2014).

Nassauer, S. "Screens Get a Place at the Table." May 30, 2012 (Updated). **online.wsj.com/news/articles/SB10001424052702303552104577436233174389816** (accessed May 2014).

Nazarov, A. R. "The Internet of Things." *Internet Evolution*, September 5, 2009. Available for download in .pdf format at **netlingo.com/more/Internet_of_Things.pdf** (accessed May 2014).

Nicoletti, B., *Mobile Banking: Evolution or Revolution?* Houndmills, UK: Palgrave Pivot, 2014.

Nobel, C. "Mobile Banking for the Unbanked" *Harvard Business School Cases*, June 13, 2011 **hbswk.hbs.edu/item/6729.html** (accessed May 2014).

Olariu, S., and D. E.Tiliute. *Handbook of Mobile Commerce.* New York: Chapman & Hall, 2011.

Oliver, M. *Mobile Device Management for Dummies (An e-Book).* New York: Wiley & Sons, 2008. (Available in .pdf format at **energycentral.com/download/products/Mobile_Device_Management_for_Dummies_05012008.pdf** (accessed May 2014).

Patrizio, A. "Japan Produces Its Own Wearable PC." March 5, 2014. **itworld.com/mobile-wireless/408274/japan-produces-its-own-wearable-pc** (accessed May 2014).

Paulsen, S., (ed.) *Mobile Financial Services: Consumer Use of Mobile Payments and Banking*, Happauge, New York: Nova Science Pub., Inc., 2013.

Petroff, A. "Google Glass May Save Firms $1 Billion." November 11, 2013. **money.cnn.com/2013/11/11/technology/google-glass-report/index.html?iid=s_mpm** (accessed May 2014).

Poslad, S. *Ubiquitous Computing: Smart Devices, Environments and Interactions.* Hoboken, NJ: Wiley & Sons, May 2009.

PR Newswire. "Hertz Debuts A Redesigned and Improved Mobile App." January 21, 2014. **ir.hertz.com/2014-01-21-Hertz-Debuts-A-Redesigned-And-Improved-Mobile-App** (accessed May 2014).

PR Newswire. "Partners Trust Real Estate Brokerage & Acquisitions Launches Mogreet's Mobile Video Marketing Platform to Enable Home Buyers to See Mobile Video Tours." December 6, 2010. **prnewswire.com/news-releases/partners-trust-real-estate-brokeragDOUBLEHYPHENcquisitions-launches-mogreets-mobile-video-marketing-platform-to-enable-home-buyers-to-see-mobile-video-tours-111378279.html** (accessed May 2014).

Rash, W. "Amtrak's New Siemens Locomotive with Digital Controls Cruises Rails." February 14, 2014. **eweek.com/mobile/slideshows/amtraks-new-siemens-locomotive-with-digital-controls-cruises-rails.html** (accessed May 2014).

Rashid, F. Y. "Identity-Fraud Victims Are Smartphone, Social Media Users: Report." February 23, 2012. **eweek.com/c/a/Security/Identity-Fraud-Victims-are-Smartphone-Social-Media-Users-Report-187247** (accessed May 2014).

Reisinger, D. "BYOD: A Cost-Saving Must-Have for Your Enterprise." February 11, 2013. **cioinsight.com/it-strategy/tech-trends/slideshows/byod-a-cost-saving-must-have-for-your-enterprise-02** (accessed May 2014).

Rosenblatt, S. "OK, Glass: Show Me What's Next for Google." December 28, 2013. **cnet.com/news/ok-glass-show-me-whats-next-for-google** (accessed May 2014).

SAP. "How Mobility Can Transform Your Business." 2012. **slideshare.net/sapmobile/how-mobility-can-transform-your-business** (accessed May 2014).

Salz, P. A., and J. Moranz. *The Everything Guide to Mobile Apps: A Practical Guide to Affordable Mobile App Development for your Business.* Avon, MA: Adams Media, 2013.

Sathyan, J., et.al. *A Comprehensive Guide to Enterprise Mobility.* Boca Raton, FL: Taylor and Francis Group, 2013. (a CRC Press publication)

Saylor, M., *The Mobile Wave: How Mobile Intelligence Will Change Everything*, New York: (Da Capo Press, a Member of the Perseus Books Group)/Vanguard Press Edition, 2012.

Schadler, T. "The Forrester Wave™: Mobile Collaboration, Q3 2011." *Forrester Research Inc.*, August 5, 2011. Available in .pdf format for free download at **i.zdnet.com/whitepapers/Forrester_mobile_collaboration_2011.pdf** (accessed May 2014).

Soh, J. O. B., and B. C. Y. Tan. "Mobile Gaming." *Communications of the ACM*, 51, no. 3 (March 2008).

Steiniger, S., M. Neun, and A. Edwardes. "Foundation of Location Based Services: Lesson One: CartouCHe – Lecture Notes on LBS, V. 1.0." 2006. Available for download in .pdf format at **sourceforge.net/projects/jump-pilot/files/w_other_freegis_documents/articles/lbs_lecturenotes_steinigeretal2006.pdf/download** (accessed May 2014).

Sutter, J. D. "With New GPS Dating Apps, It's Love the One You're Near." August 6, 2010. **cnn.com/2010/TECH/innovation/08/06/gps.dating.apps/** (accessed May 2014).

TeleCommunication Systems, Inc. "Location-Based Services: An End-to-End Perspective." A White Paper. February 2010. **cdn2.hubspot.net/hub/51409/file-14400282-pdf/docs/telecommunication-systems-whitepape-lbs-end-to-end-perspective-msb020910v5.pdf** (accessed May 2014).

Toh, P.K. *The New Age of Consumer Wearables: Internet of Smart Things (Wearable Computers.)* CreateSpace Independent Publishing Platform, 2013.

Townsend, A.M. *Smart Cities: Big Data, Civic Hackers, and the Quest for a New Utopia.* New York: W.W. Norton & Company, 2013.

USGS. "Geographic Information Systems." (Last modified February 22, 2007). **egsc.usgs.gov/isb//pubs/gis_poster** (accessed May 2014).

Vijayan, J. "7 Hidden Dangers of Wearable Computers." February 25, 2014. **itworld.com/slideshow/142017/7-hidden-dangers-wearable-computers-406874** (accessed May 2014).

Vogel, P. S. "The Tangled Web of IoT Security." May 6, 2014. **technewsworld.com/story/80400.html** (accessed May 2014).

Wishpond Technologies Ltd. "New Trends of Mobile Users and Their Shopping Behaviour." A White Paper. 2014. **corp.wishpond.com/mobile-marketing-resources/new-trends-of-mobile-users-and-their-shopping-behaviour** (accessed May 2014).

Yun, H., D. Han, and C. C. Lee. "Understanding the Use of Location-Based Service Applications: Do Privacy Concerns Matter?" *Journal of Electronic Commerce Research*, vol. 14, no. 3, 2013. **csulb.edu/web/journals/jecr/issues/20133/Paper2.pdf** (accessed May 2014).

Social Commerce: Foundations, Social Marketing, and Advertising

7

Contents

Learning Objectives

Upon completion of this chapter, you will be able to:

1. Define social commerce and describe its roots and evolution.
2. Describe the scope, drivers, and content of the social commerce field.
3. Summarize the benefits and limitations of social commerce.
4. Describe the major models of social shopping.
5. Explain how advertising and promotions are conducted in social networking environments.
6. Describe how social networking can facilitate customer service, customer support, and CRM.

OPENING CASE: HOW SONY USES SOCIAL MEDIA FOR IMPROVING CRM

Sony, the giant consumer electronics producer, has been struggling during the last few years.

Now, by using social media, improvement is in sight.

The Problem

Sony Corporation (**sony.com**) faces fierce competition from Samsung (**samsung.com/us**), Sharp Electronics (**sharpusa.com**), LG Electronics (**lg.com/us**), and other large, global companies.

Electronic supplementary material The online version of this chapter (doi: 10.1007/978-3-319-10091-3_7) contains supplementary material, which is available to authorized users

E. Turban et al., *Electronic Commerce: A Managerial and Social Networks Perspective*,
Springer Texts in Business and Economics, DOI 10.1007/978-3-319-10091-3_7,
© Springer International Publishing Switzerland 2015

This competition has intensified during the economic slowdown in recent years. As a result, total revenues for Sony have declined every year from 2008 until 2012. The company suffered heavy losses in 2009 and 2012, causing its share price to drop from $35/share in 2010 and 2011 to $9.57 in late 2012. In 2013, the stock rose mostly due to the recovery in Tokyo's stock exchange. Consumer electronic products are fairly mature, so the differences in quality and prices are not substantial. Therefore, the competitors in the field are promoting their customer service as a strategic differentiator. Sony is trying to do this with the help of their social media communities and initiatives.

The Solution: Social Media Projects

Sony Corporation embarked on social CRM as a vehicle for improving customer service. According to Jack (2013), Sony combined a customer support and direct marketing program, mostly using social channels. The various initiatives are managed by Sony's Customer Experience Management Team. The team organized *Sony's Community Site* (**community.sony.com**), which is a central hub for customer information and support. It includes *idea boards, discussion groups, blogs, Twitter feeds*, and other content-generating channels. The site is used also for marketing campaigns.

The following are representative activities, many of which are done at Sony Europe (see Taylor 2013).

- Active social communities; some are for specific products, others are general for the entire Sony brand. The company's staff members and consumers are involved in these communities. Members of these communities are helping each other and providing feedback. Customer service employees are "listening" to the feedback and using the information to improve service.
- YouTube videos provide training for customers on the use of Sony's products.
- Using Lithium Social Web software (a SAP company), relevant sites are monitored for reviews and comments (positive and negative). This allows Sony to improve operations, resolve problems, and capitalize on opportunities.
- There is a special "Customer Relations" tab located on Sony's Community site, the company's central social network, for easy communication.
- The company created a 'Facebook Support Community' within their Facebook page (**facebook.com/sony**), Twitter 'Sony Support USA' (**twitter.com/sonysupportusa**), Tumblr Support (**sony.tumblr.com**), and a YouTube Sony Support Channel 'Sony Listens' (**youtube.com/user/SonyListens**).
- In the communities, the company's staff demonstrates how problems are resolved quickly and efficiently. For example, there is an "Experts" tab for "How To" videos and technical support, etc. See **community.sony.com/t5/Meet-Our-Experts/bg-p/experts**.
- Sony is using all its social media channels, including LinkedIn, to proactively engage users and provide customer service in a timely fashion.
- Sony Electronic integrates Pinterest (**pinterest.com/sonyprousa**) to send information about its products to community members (see details at Eckerle 2013 and **ohsopinteresting.com/lessons-from-sony-on-pinterest**).

According to Holland (2011), Sony monitors social media conversations and conducts sentiment analysis (Chapter 10) to improve customer service and product improvement and design. Note that Sony is using social media campaigns for customer engagement (e.g., 2011 'CatchTheTablet' contest, see **atomicpr.com/results/sony-catch-the-tablet**). Finally, software from Reevoo.com helps Sony to automatically translate reviews from one language to another.

The Results

Significant results are expected in 2014 after the deployment of most SC initiatives. However, some improvements have already materialized. For example, according to Jack (2013), the improved communication resulted in a 22% increase in 'clicks' (over 100% in some cases). Other results are:

- Customer trust in Sony increased (Jack 2013).
- Page views, conversation rates, and engagement activities (e.g., posting) increased by 100% (Jack 2013).

- Customer service was combined with marketing promotions, which resulted in new sources of revenue for Sony.
- In March 2014, PlayStation had about 2.5 million followers on Twitter and 35 million fans on Facebook.

Sources: Based on Jack (2013), Taylor (2013), Eckerle (2013), and Reevoo.com (2014).

LESSONS LEARNED FROM THE CASE

The Sony case illustrates that a company can use social media to not only advertise and sell, but also to provide outstanding customer service. Operating in a highly competitive market, customer service can be an important strategic tool. Sony has supplemented their traditional customer service with social networks, blogs (e.g., Twitter, and a Facebook fan page). They have concentrated on improving communication and interactions with customers. The customer service provided by social media tools and platforms is more interactive, timely, and direct. Furthermore, the system fosters a truly conversation-based communication. This kind of service is important to customers, and contributes to the company's success. In this chapter we introduce social commerce fundamentals and describe its content and benefits. We also describe three major areas: social shopping, social advertising, and social CRM.

7.1   SOCIAL COMMERCE: DEFINITIONS AND EVOLUTION

As it is a new field that involves several academic and professional disciplines, there is no agreed-upon definition or description of the content and boundaries of the social commerce field. Next, we will provide some working definitions.

Definitions and Characteristics

Social commerce (SC), also known as *social business,* refers to e-commerce transactions delivered via social media. Social commerce is considered a subset of e-commerce by some. More specifically, it is a combination of e-commerce, e-marketing, the supporting technologies, and social media content. This definition is illustrated in Figure 7.1. The figure shows that social commerce is created from the integration of e-commerce and e-marketing using Web 2.0/ social media applications. The integration is supported by theories such as social capital, social psychology, consumer behavior, and online

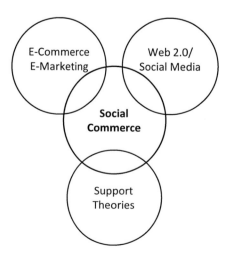

Figure 7.1 The foundation of social commerce

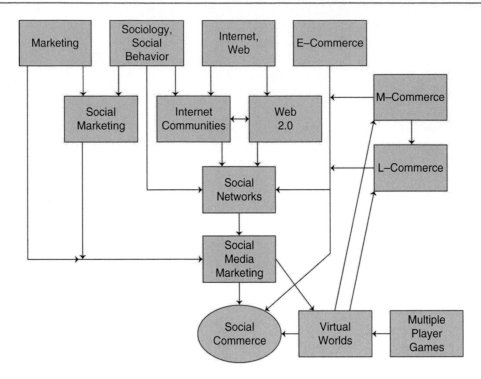

Figure 7.2 The major roots of social commerce

collaboration, resulting in a set of useful applications that drive social commerce.

The field of social commerce is growing rapidly; between 2011 and 2015, it is projected to rise six-fold to $30 billion in revenues, according to Booz & Co. (reported by Cuccureddu 2011). For the impact of the technology, see Shopsocially (2013). The magnitude of the field can be seen in Bennett's infograhic (2013).

Wang and Zhang (2012) provide a list of 11 definitions, including that of Stephen and Toubia (2010), who define SC as "a form of Internet-based social media that allows people to participate actively in the marketing and selling of products and services in online marketplaces and communities. "They distinguish *social shopping* that connects customers from *social commerce* that connects sellers." Dennison et al. (2009) provide an IBM definition, "social commerce is the concept of *word of mouth* applied to e-commerce." Marsden (2009a) collected 24 different definitions of SC that include several of SC's properties (such as word of mouth, trusted advice, and buying with the opinion and assistance of friends).

For additional discussion, see **bazaarvoice. com/research-and-insight/social-commerce-statistics** and Baekdal (2011).

The Evolution of Social Commerce

In Figure 7.1, we illustrated the essential idea of social commerce. Let us look at this idea in more detail.

Social commerce emerged from the integration of several fields, which are shown in Figure 7.2. For example, Marsden and Chaney (2012) show how social media contributes to sales, making it a social commerce application.

A major origin of social commerce (SC) was the development of Web 2.0 technologies, as previously mentioned. With these came commercial applications, which included activities in social networks and the use of social software such as blogs and wikis. A major driver of SC is the globalization of business. This prompted the need for collaboration of employees, partners, and customers, sometimes worldwide. Web 2.0

Table 7.1 The major differences between e-commerce and social commerce

Property	E-commerce	Social commerce
Major objective	Transactions	Social interactions
Major activity	Publishing	Engagement
Content	Company generated	User generated
Problem solving	Company experts, consultants	Crowdsourcing
Collaboration	Traditional, unified communications	Web 2.0 tools
Product information	Product descriptions on websites	Peer product reviews
Marketplaces	E-tailers (e.g., Amazon.com) and direct from manufacturers' stores (Dell)	Social networks (f-commerce), collaborative markets
Targeting	Mass marketing, segmentation	Behavioral targeting, micro segmentation
CRM	Seller/manufacturer support	Social support by peers and by vendors and employees
Online marketing strategy	Website selling	Multi-channel, direct at social network sites
Integration	System integration	Mashups and system integration
Data management	Reports and analytics	Analytics

applications created an efficient and effective platforms for such collaboration.

The development and rapid growth of mobile computing and smartphones have also facilitated social commerce. Mobile commerce is the basis for SC models such as location-based applications, virtual communities, virtual worlds, and consumer/company networking. Social commerce also relies on communication and collaboration theories.

A major emphasis of SC is its marketing orientation. Traditional marketing activities were applied to Internet marketing in the mid-1990s, when companies began building websites and using e-mail to advertise their products for sale offline. As the Web developed, marketers applied the Internet to facilitate e-commerce *transactions*. Until that point, marketers controlled brand messages and continued their advertising and other communication monologues to customers and potential buyers (prospects). With the emergence of social media, marketing communication changed to a dialog with Internet users, and many marketing strategies evolved or completely transformed to support social commerce.

Note: The original term *social marketing* referred to the application of marketing strategies and tactics to social causes, such as the American Heart Association. This concept was not related to marketing activities in social media. Today, however, many practitioners and academicians use the term *social marketing* to describe *social media marketing*.

Marketing, technology, and consumer and management evolution paved the way for SC, just as they prompted e-commerce development. The major differences between social commerce and e-commerce are illustrated in Table 7.1.

For a chronicle presentation and an infographic of historical milestones in the development of social commerce, see **socialtimes.com/social-commerce-infographic-2_b84120**.

SECTION 7.1 REVIEW QUESTIONS

1. Define social commerce and list its major characteristics.
2. Trace the evolution of social commerce.
3. Describe the major differences between e-commerce and social commerce.

7.2 THE CONTENT OF THE SOCIAL COMMERCE FIELD

The content of the SC field is very diversified (e.g., see Solis 2010).

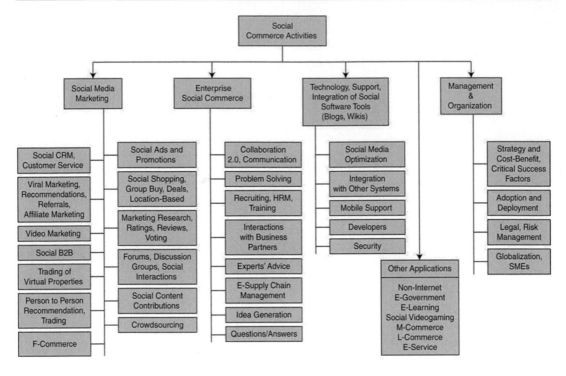

Figure 7.3 The major dimensions of social commerce

The Landscape and Major Components of the Field

The landscape of social commerce is multidisciplinary (see slide presentation by Marsden (2010a) and Liang and Turban (2011/2012)). Most of the activities center around e-marketing conducted with social media, particularly marketing communication, techniques of advertising, sales promotions, and public relations usually expressed as *social media marketing* activities (e.g., see Solis 2010). However, several other areas are emerging in the field, especially activities within organizations that are referred to as *social enterprise* or *Enterprise 2.0*. Liang and Turban (2011/2012) illustrate the social commerce landscape in Figure 7.3 and an infographic describe only some of the areas here. Discussions of the other activities of the figure are provided throughout the book. The major social networking tools are listed in Table 7.2. Additional software tools and development platforms are listed in Table 7.3.

For additional descriptions of some SC elements, see "The 2010 Social Business Landscape" at **enterpriseirregulars.com/23628/ the-2010-social-business-landscape**. For a detailed discussion, see Marsden (2010b) and his slide presentation "Social Commerce Opportunities for Brands" at **digitalinnovationtoday.com/ new-presentation-social-commerce-opportu- nities-for-brands**. For statistics about social commerce and its use see "Social Commerce Statistics" at **bazaarvoice.com/research-and- insight/social-commerce-statistics**. The two major elements in social commerce, social media marketing and Enterprise 2.0, are described next.

Social Media Marketing

Social media marketing (SMM) is the application of marketing communication and other marketing tools using social media. Social media marketing facilitates social commerce, builds brands, repairs brand reputation damage in social media, and fosters long-term customer relationships, among other things (per McAfee 2009).

Table 7.2 Social networking software tools

Tools for online communication	Emerging technologies
• Instant messaging	• Peer-to-peer social networks
• VoIP and Skype	• Virtual presence
• Text chat	• Mobile tools for Web 2.0
• Collaborative real-time editors	**Tools for individuals**
• Internet forums	• Personalization
• Blogs, vlogs, microblogs (Twitter)	• Customization
• Wikis	• Search
• Collaborative real-time editor	• Clipping tools
• Prediction markets	• RSS feeds
Types of services	• File-sharing tools
• Social network services	**Web 2.0 development tools**
• Commercial and professional social networks	• Mashups
• Social network search engines	• Web services
• Enterprise social networks	
• Social guides	
• Media sharing (YouTube) and Photos (Flickr)	
• Social bookmarking	
• Social citations	
• Social libraries	
• Virtual worlds and massively multiplayer online games (MMOGs)	
• Nongame worlds	
• Other specialized social applications	
• Social games (Zynga, Electronic Arts)	
• Politics and journalism	
• Content management tools	

Sources: Compiled from **en.wikipedia.org/wiki/social_software,   en.wikipedia.or/wiki/list-of-social-software** (accessed June 2014), and authors' experience

Table 7.3 Social networking software tools and services

Tools for online communication
• Blogs, vlogs, microblogs (Twitter)
• Wikis
• Instant messaging and VoIP
• Internet forums
• Text chat
• Collaborative real-time editors
Platforms and applications for support
• Social network general services
• Commercial and professional social networks
• Social search engines
• Enterprise social networks
• Social guides
• Multiemedia sharing sites (YouTube) and Photos (Flickr)
• Article sharing
• Social bookmarking
• Social citations
• Social libraries
• Social cataloging

(continued)

Table 7.3 (continued)

• Virtual worlds and massive multiplayer online games (MMOGs)
• Crowdsourcing and idea generation
• Social games in networks (Zynga, Electronic Arts)
• Content management tools
Emerging technologies
• Peer-to-peer social networks for selling and bartering
• Virtual presence
• Mobile tools for Web 2.0
Tools for individual users
• Personalization tools
• Customization
• Search in blogs, in all types of media
• Clipping tools
• RSS
• File-sharing tools
Web 2.0 devleopment tools
• Mashups
• Web services

Note: For descriptions and examples, see the 'social software' entry on Wikipedia

Today, integrated marketing communication applies the traditional marketing tools in innovative ways in social media activities, such as in viral marketing. The emergence of Web 2.0 allows marketers to connect directly with increasingly smaller target markets, including a single individual. For example, savvy marketers now build brands and respond to questions and complaints in social networks instead of (or in addition to) sending press releases to traditional journalists. They can also build social interactions with customers and conduct market research. The various topics of social media marketing communication are described in Chapters 4, 5, 6, 7 and by Singh and Diamond (2012).

For an infographic see Wood (2014).

Enterprise 2.0

The second major type of social commerce is *Enterprise 2.0*, also known as *Social Media-based Enterprise*, which is used by an increasing number of companies to conduct several social media and social commerce activities inside the enterprises (e.g., idea generation, problem solving, joint design, and recruiting).

There are several definitions of **Enterprise 2.0**. The term "Enterprise 2.0" was first coined by McAfee (2006). The initial definition connected the term to Web 2.0 and to collaboration. McAfee revised the definition several times. A refined definition is "…the use of social software platforms within companies, or between companies and their partners or customers" McAfee (2009).

Note: For more definitions and concepts of Enterprise 2.0 technology, see the slide presentation "What is Enterprise 2.0?" at **slideshare.net/norwiz/what-is-enterprise-20**. Several Enterprise 2.0 conferences are held every year, some providing additional definitions that may even change with time (e.g., see **e2conf.com**). This organization provided a white paper in which it compared Enterprise 2.0 to Enterprise 1.0, listing the following as characteristics of Enterprise 2.0: ease of information flow, agility, flexibility, user-driven content, bottom up communication, global teams, fuzzy boundaries, transparency, folksonomies (rather than taxonomies), open standards, and on-demand (rather than scheduled) activities. Also important are flat organizations (rather than hierarchical) and short time-to-market cycles.

For other characteristics of Web 2.0, see IBM (2011a). For a comprehensive article on the social enterprise, see **worldlibrary.org/Articles/ Social enterprise?&Words=social enterprise**.

For more on Enterprise 2.0, see Chapter 8, and Chui et al. (2013).

Examples of Social Enterprise Applications
Some examples of social enterprise applications include the following:

- Dell, Sony, IBM, and many other companies solicit ideas from large groups of employees, customers, and business partners on how to improve their business operations (e.g., Dell's IdeaStorm site).
- More than 50% of medium and large corporations use LinkedIn and Facebook to announce available positions and to find potential employees.
- Best Buy provided state-of-the-art customer service via a Twitter-based system where thousands of employees used to answer customers' questions, sometimes within minutes.

For a comprehensive study on the benefits and inhibitors of social commerce in the enterprise, see Forrester Consulting (2010).

SECTION 7.2 REVIEW QUESTIONS
1. Describe the major components of social commerce.
2. What is social media marketing?
3. Describe Enterprise 2.0.

7.3   THE BENEFITS AND LIMITATIONS OF SOCIAL COMMERCE

According to many practitioners and researchers, social commerce is making significant impacts on organizations and industries (e.g., Shopsocially 2013). A major impact has been seen in the fashion industry (e.g., see Little 2013).

Several surveys (e.g., Leggatt 2010) have confirmed that social commerce results in significant monetary and strategic benefits to businesses. Also see success stories at IBM (2011b) and 67 case studies at **barnraisersllc.com/2010/10/33-case-studies-prove-social-media-roi**.

SC benefits fall, in general, into three categories: benefits to customers, benefits to retailers, and benefits to other types of enterprises. Some are illustrated in Table 7.2, others are described in the following section.

Benefits to Customers

The success of social commerce depends on its benefits to customers. The major benefits appear in the following list:

- It is easy to get recommendations from friends and other customers (e.g., via Twitter, in social networks discussion groups, and on product review sites). Recommendations result in more confidence and trust helping customers decide about purchasing products and services.
- Customers are exposed to special deals (e.g., via Groupon) for large savings.
- Purchases are better matched with specific needs, wants, tastes, and wishes of customers (e.g., see the Netflix case in Chapter 9); this increases satisfaction and reduces product choice decision time.
- It is easy for customers to use the SC technology.

- Social commerce fits the mobile device lifestyle well.
- Increased trust in vendors is developed (via closer relationships).
- Social commerce allows customers to help other customers (social support).
- Customers can get better customer service from vendors.
- Customers can meet new friends (e.g., for travel) and socialize online.
- Customers can get rich social context and relevancy during their purchase decisions.
- Customers can connect with individuals and businesses who otherwise are inaccessible to them.

Benefits to Retailers

Retailers are major benefactors of social commerce. For example, over 40% of businesses globally find new customers via social networks (Leggatt 2010). In addition, over 27% of companies invest in social networking in order to acquire and retain customers (Leggatt 2010).

Retailers may benefit from social commerce in the following ways:

- Consumers can provide feedback on market communication strategy and on product (service) design.
- Vendors get free word-of-mouth marketing (see Chapters 3 and 4).
- Increased website traffic (recall the Sony opening case), which increases revenue and sales.
- Increased sales as collaborative filtering and other social influence methods are used (see Chapters 3 and 4 and **trendwatching.com/trends/TWINSUMER.htm**).

Note that the concept of "twinsumer" is related to these benefits. The twinsumer trend involves consumers looking for the best of the best, the first of the first, and the most relevant products and services, by viewing people with similar tastes. For more on benefits to retailers, see the video titled "Social Media a Powerful Tool for Online Retailers" (4:08 minutes) at **youtube.com/watch?v=1ByDmQICXs4**.

Example

Beretta Inc. increased its revenue in 2013 by 15% by introducing social commerce into its e-commerce store using ShopSocially's SC platform. For details see the December 23, 2013 press release "Popular Firearms Manufacturer Beretta Hits the Bullseye on Social Commerce with a 15% Revenue Uplift" at **digitaljournal.com/pr/1655392**.

For a comprehensive presentation of social commerce effects on retailing, see Dennison et al. (2009).

Benefits to Other Types of Enterprises

In addition to increased sales and revenue, enterprises can benefit from social commerce in several ways (see Chapter 8):

- Conduct faster and less costly recruitment with a larger reach to large number of candidates.
- Reduce costs via innovative methods such as using the collective intelligence of employees and business partners (see Crowdsourcing in Chapter 8).
- Foster better external relationships; for example, with partners and channel distribution members.
- Increase collaboration and improve communication within the enterprise and with business partners (e.g., by using blogs, microblogs, wikis; see McAfee 2009).

- Foster better internal relationships (e.g., by increasing employee productivity and satisfaction).
- Provide free advice to small enterprises by other enterprises and experts (e.g., via LinkedIn groups).
- Understand that it is usually not expensive to install and operate SC systems.
- Locate experts quickly, both internally and externally, whenever needed (e.g., see **guru.com**).
- Conduct market research quickly and inexpensively and get feedback from customers, employees, and business partners (see Chapter 10).
- Increase market share and margins (see survey results in Bughin and Chui 2010).
- Build brands through conversations and social media promotions.
- Micro segment for reaching very small markets with brand offerings at a low cost.
- Manage company and brand reputations online.
- Build brand communities for positive word of mouth online.
- Enhance customer service and support.
- Increase traffic and sales at the company website and at physical retailers.
- Facilitate market research by monitoring conversations online.
- Increase company and brand rankings on search engine results pages.

The potential benefits in the previous list may increase productivity and value (Chui et al. 2013) and could provide a *strategic advantage* (Bauer 2011) and they encourage companies to at least experiment with social commerce. Successful applications are introduced in Chapters 4, 5, 6, 7, 8, and a comprehensive list is available at Bazaarvoice (2011). Note that the use of social media and commerce is turning out to be a global phenomenon (e.g., see Ran 2012).

The Social Business: An IBM Approach

The previously noted benefits to enterprises make it desirable for enterprises to transform to what IBM calls a *social business*. A **social business** is "a business that embraces networks of people to create business value" (IBM 2011a). Many consider this term equivalent to social commerce and use the two interchangeably. However, IBM is more concerned with the structure and operations of enterprises. IBM and many other companies (notably Intel) are becoming social businesses. (For how to do this, see Troudt and Vancil 2011.) IBM (2011b) sees the following three goals for social businesses:

1. *Enable an effective workforce.* Functional departments can increase overall employee productivity and job satisfaction through improved knowledge capture, expertise, location, and collaboration. Travel, training, and teleconferencing expenses also can be reduced. In addition, better and faster recruitment can be done inexpensively.
2. *Accelerate innovation.* Product research and development teams can invoke and speed up internal idea generation, discovery, information, and strategy sharing, and gathering feedback from key customers and partners.
3. *Deepen customer relationships.* With immediate access to more content and expertise, customer service representatives can work more efficiently and provide higher-quality service. Marketing and sales teams can have more time to spend with customers and to dedicate that time to customer-focused initiatives thus strengthening relationships with customers.

In addition, IBM strategically integrates social media into various business processes (e.g., procurement) and is developing an organizational culture to support the integration process for delivering rapid and impressive outcomes. For details see IBM (2011a) and **ibm.com/social-business/us/en**.

New or Improved Business Models

A **business model** describes the method of doing business designed to meet the customer's needs, and by which a company generates revenue and creates value. Note that the January/February 2011 issue of *Harvard Business Review* is dedicated to business model innovations (5 articles), including several topics related to social commerce.

Social commerce provides innovative e-commerce business models. Some are new while others are improvements of regular EC models (e.g., group buying). A large number of SC models are in the area of social shopping as described in Section 7.4. Several other new models are in the area of enterprise commerce (Chapter 8). Here are some brief examples:

- Shopping business models include widgets on social media sites to "buy now."
- Online software agents that put buyers and sellers together, such as when TripAdvisor refers users to online travel sites to purchase hotel rooms.
- Content sponsorship–selling advertising on a site that supports content development (YouTube).
- Crowdsourcing models that allow companies to design their products or logos by involving their customers.
- Sales promotions conducted in social networks that drive traffic to the company's site, such as contests, discounts, and downloading free music and software.
- Location-based commerce as is offered by Foursquare, as illustrated in Section 7.5.
- Recruiting in social networks, as exemplified by LinkedIn.
- Collaboration models that are facilitated by blogs, wikis, and crowdsourcing (see examples in Chapter 8).

Many start-ups have invented these and other business models. For example, Webkinz (**webkinz.com**) created a huge business around virtual pets world for kids, and IZEA Inc. (**izea.com**; a pioneer of social sponsorship) created a marketplace for connecting advertisers with social media creators of content (e.g., bloggers).

Several of these start-up companies are so prosperous that they successfully went public with an IPO in the stock market. Well-known companies are Facebook, Pandora, LinkedIn, Renren, Yelp, TripAdvisor, Zillow, and Alibaba.

The potential for profitable social business models is very large. For example, **wikia.com** is using a crowdsourcing community in an attempt to develop a superior search mechanism. If it can create a successful one, Google may be in trouble. For the opportunities for business created by social commerce see Moontoast (2013). For new models in the fashion industry see Knopf (2012) and **businessfashion.com**. For a discussion of the strategic power of social media, see Bauer (2011).

Concerns and Limitations of Conducting Social Commerce

Although social commerce presents many opportunities for organizations, its implementation may involve some potential risks and possibly complex issues such as integration of new and existing information systems. Representative risk factors are difficulties in justification of SC initiatives to upper management, security and privacy issues, possibilities of fraud, legal concerns, quality of UGC, and time wasting by employees during work hours. Companies also risk loss of control over their brand images and reputations in social media conversations and product review sites, which can affect product sales. According to the Enterprise 2.0 Conference (2009), the major barriers to adoption of Enterprise 2.0 are resistance to change, difficulty in measuring ROI, and difficulties of integration with existing IT systems and security (see Chapter 10). A 2011 survey "Social Business Shifting Out of First Gear" reported by Burnham (2014) ranks the top concerns in deployment of social business as (1) security liability exposures, (2) doubts about ability to govern effectively, (3) poor systems integration, (4) doubts about ROI/value, and (5) poor organizational buy-in (technology adoption).

SECTION 7.3 REVIEW QUESTIONS

1. List the major benefits to customers.
2. List the major benefits to retailers.
3. List the major benefits to other companies than retailers.
4. Describe new or improved social commerce business models.
5. Describe some concerns and limitations of social commerce.

7.4   SOCIAL SHOPPING: CONCEPTS, BENEFITS, AND MODELS

Involvement in shopping is a natural area for social networks. Although shopping in social networks is only beginning to grow, it has enormous potential. In this section, we cover the essentials of social shopping.

Definitions, and Drivers of Social Shopping

Shopping is, by nature, a social activity. **Social shopping** (also known as *sales 2.0*) is online shopping with social media tools and platforms. It is about sharing shopping experiences with friends. Social shopping blends e-commerce and social media. Thus, social commerce takes the key features of social media (e.g., discussion groups, blogs, recommendations, reviews, etc.) and uses them before, during, and after shopping.

An overview of social shopping is provided by Shih (2011), and Turban et.al. (2015).

The Drivers of Social Commerce

The following are the major drivers of social shopping:

- A large number of people visiting social networks attracts advertisers
- The increasing number of recommendations/suggestions made by friends and the ease and speed of accessing them
- The need to compete (e.g., by differentiation) and to satisfy the social customer
- The emergence of social customers with knowledge and competence in using the Internet (e.g., in finding reviews and comparing prices)
- The need to collaborate with business partners
- The huge discounts provided by some of the new business models (e.g., flash sales)
- The socially-oriented shopping models (e.g., group buying)
- The ease of shopping while you are inside some social networks (e.g., from Facebook's 'Buy' button)
- The ease of communicating with friends in real-time using Twitter and smartphones

For more on social shopping, do a Google search for social shopping. Also see Kimball (2013) for an infographic and **webtrends.about. com/od/web20/a/social-shopping.htm**.

Concepts and Content of Social Shopping

Social shopping is done in social networks (e.g., Polyvore, Wanelo), in vendors' socially oriented stores, in stores of special intermediaries (such as Groupon.com). For an overview see Greenberg et al. (2011). The buyers are *social customers* that trust and/or enjoy social shopping. As will be seen later in this section, there is a wide range of social shopping models that utilize many of the Web 2.0 tools as well as social communities. The nature of shopping is changing, especially for brand name clothes and related items. For example, popular brands are sold by e-tailers such as Gap (**gap. com**), Shopbop (**shopbop.com**), and InStyle (**instyle.com**). In addition, fashion communities such as Stylehive (**stylehive.com**) and Polyvore (**polyvore.com**) help promote the season's latest fashion collections. Social shoppers are logging on to sites like Net-A-Porter (**net-a-porter.com**) to buy designer clothes online. They can also log on to sites such as ThisNext (**thisnext.com**), create profiles, and blog about their favorite brands. For practical issues of social commerce, see **digitalintelligencetoday.com/social-shopping-101-a-practitioners-prime**.

There are two basic practices for deployment of social shopping:

1. Add social software, apps and features (e.g., polling) to existing e-commerce sites.
2. Add e-commerce functionalities (e.g., e-catalogs, payment gateways, shopping carts) to social media and network sites, where many vendors offer their stores.

Why Shoppers Go Social

Many shoppers like to hear from others prior to purchasing. Therefore, they ask for recommendations from friends or use the concept of communal shopping.

Communal shopping (also known as *collaborative shopping*) is a method of shopping where shoppers enlist friends and other people they trust to advise them on what products to shop for. This results in more confidence in decisions made to buy or not to buy (a phenomenon known as the "bandwagon effect"). For examples watch the video "New Frontiers in the Communal Shopping Experience" (2:58 minutes) at **bloomberg.com/video/eden-s-communal-shopping-experience-ExvmRAIhTE2AZapKKd5aVA.html**.

The Roles in Social Commerce

Gartner Inc. conducted a study on social commerce (reported by Dubey 2010) in which it identified the following roles people play in social media and e-commerce:

- **Connectors.** These are the people with contacts that introduce people to each other. Connectors try to influence people to buy. Consultants and connected people play this role.
- **Salespeople.** Like their offline counterparts, salespeople's major effort is to influence shoppers to buy. They are well connected so they can impress buyers.

- **Seekers.** These consumers seek advice and information about shopping and services from experts, friends, and mavens.
- **Mavens.** Mavens are recognized, but are unofficial experts in certain domains that can provide positive or negative recommendations to advice seekers.
- **Self-sufficients.** These people work on their own and do not like to be influenced.
- **Unclassifieds.** Most people do not belong to any one of the above categories.

The major influencers are friends, other consumers, salespeople, connectors, and mavens (experts). For details see Dubey (2010) and McCafferty (2011).

Benefits of Social Shopping

Many of the benefits of social commerce (Section 7.3) apply to social shopping. Additional benefits are:

- You can socialize while shopping.
- You can discover products/services you never knew existed (e.g., see **thisnext.com**).
- You can interact with vendor (brand) representatives easily and quickly (e.g., feature available at the blog on **stylehive.com**).
- Your confidence and trust in online shopping may increase due to engagement and interactions with friends.
- You can get super deals via group buying, daily specials, and more. Join Groupon just to see the super daily deals.
- You can exchange shopping tips with your friends, fans, and others. Thus, you can learn from experiences of others.
- You can build and share wish lists.
- You can shop together with people like you.

For more benefits, including for sellers, see Turban et al. (2015). For an overview see an info-graphic at **guerillaconnection.com/wp-content/uploads/2012/06/Guerilla-Social-Media-Trends.pdf**.

Therefore, before you go shopping, consult social shopping sources.

Note that social shopping sites may generate additional revenue from advertising, commissions on actual sales, sharing customer information with retailers, and affiliate marketing.

Note: Both Pinterest and Twitter are providing activities with some or all of these models directly and indirectly. For Twitter, see **business.twitter.com/twitter-101**.

What Components to Expect in a Social Shopping Site

Depending on the social shopping model, on the products offered and related information, and on the supporting information systems, one may find a diversity of components in a site. The following are the major components help shoppers in making purchasing decisions:

- **Visual Sharing.** Photos, videos, and other images enable shoppers to visually share their product experiences.
- **Online discussions.** Ratings, reviews, interactions, recommendations, blogging, and comments facilitate discussions regarding features and benefits of products.
- **Journals of products and their use.** These demonstrate how to use products via videos, blogs, and step-by-step instructions.
- **Guides.** Guides are created by users who can be experienced consumers, experts, or employees. The guides are supported by case studies, testimonials, and videos. information.

Traditional E-Commerce Sites with Social Media Additions

In addition to pure social shopping sites, there are many traditional e-commerce sites that add social media tools. A prominent example is Amazon. com, which adds recommendations, reviews, ratings, and more. An example from Germany is presented next.

Example: Nestlé Interactive Social Commerce Site

The global food and beverage manufacturer launched an interactive online social commerce platform in Germany in September 2011 to engage with consumers while providing greater access to its products (see **nestle.com/media/newsandfeatures/nestle-marks-largest-ever-investment-germany**). The *Nestle Marketplace* ("Marktplatz") website, according to **fdbusiness.com/tag/germany**, was the first social commerce platform of its kind in Germany from a food and beverage manufacturer of Nestlé's size and range. Consumers can purchase products online (including foreign Nestlé's products that are not available in most of Nestlé's physical stores, or the stores of retailers who sell their products) and also review, rate, recommend, and ask questions about each product. The site supports two-way communication. According to **nestle.com/Media/NewsAndFeatures/Nestle-pilots-social-commerce-with-new-interactive-site-for-German-consumers**, people can leave ratings and comments about the products. Shoppers can submit suggestions for new products on the site. With more than 2,000 products (February 2014) and 75 different brands available online, Nestlé Germany experiences about 2 million visits to the site each year.

The company wants to enable its customers to engage and to help Nestlé Marketplace to prosper.

Visitors to the Nestlé Marketplace can search for products using a variety of detailed criteria including taste, packaging, color, specific occasions, or diet preferences. Nutritional information can also be found for each product. The Nestlé Marketplace website is supported by a Facebook page, which provides space for discussion about the company's brands, foods, and cooking. For details, see **nestle.com/Media/NewsAndFeatures/Pages/Nestle-pilots-social-commerce-with-new-interactive-site-for-German-consumers.aspx**. To learn about the company's strategies, expectations, and experiences, see **e-commercefacts.com:8080/background/2012/03/nestle-marketplace**.

The Major Types and Models of Social Shopping

A large number of social shopping models and strategies have appeared in recent years, many created by start-ups such as Groupon.com. Some are extensions of EC generic models; others are unique to social shopping. These models can be stand alone, combined, or used within social networks. We have grouped them into the following categories:

- Group buying
- Deal purchases (flash sales), such as daily special offers
- Shopping together in real-time
- Communities and clubs
- Marketplaces
- Innovative models
- Shopping for virtual products and services
- Location-based shopping (presented in Section 7.5; see also Zwilling 2011)
- Shopping presentation sites (e.g., on YouTube) and gaming sites
- Peer-to-peer models (e.g., money lending)
- Private online clubs
- B2B shopping

For these, there are several shopping aids which we describe after we elaborate on some of these categories.

Group Buying

The group buying B2C model that was introduced in Chapter 1 was unpopular and seldom used in many countries, including the United States. However, in other countries (e.g., China), group buying has had good success. The problem with this model was the difficulty in organizing the groups, even with an intermediary. Furthermore, even if a group was organized, the negotiations about discounts could have been difficult, unless a very large volume was negotiated. In order to rally shoppers, group-shopping sites like LivingSocial and BuyWithMe offer major discounts or special deals during a short time frame. These start-up companies act as intermediaries to negotiate the deals with vendors. Group buying is closely associated with daily deals (flash sales). The social commerce approach revived the not so successful original e-commerce model, and frequently is combined with flash sales.

Note: The model is not popular today (2015).

Example: Lot18

Lot 18 (**lot18.com**) offers access to fine wines at up to 60% off. Their team of curator works directly with producers around the world to bring high-quality, hard-to-find products directly to members. They showcase new wines daily, made available in limited quantities for a limited time, or until members have purchased all available quantity. Several new products appear on the site each day. Lot18 uses Facebook to advertise flash deals. Advertising flash sales on Facebook provides an ideal environment for recruiting friends into group-buy deals (members who invite friends to register are rewarded with a $25 Lot18 credit for future purchases after the friend's order ships). Each member receives a personalized link, which he or she can e-mail to friends or post on their Facebook or Twitter pages to share with friends. For related information see **mashable.com/2013/03/17/wine-ecommerce**.

Group Buying in China

Group buying is very popular in China ("tuangou" in Chinese). In December 2013, about 1,000 companies were active all over China with an estimated 140 million shoppers. For example, Lashou.com (**lashou.com**) operates in more than 100 cities. The process, however, is different from that of Western countries. See Yoon (2011).

The Process

For several years, according to Madden (2010), Chinese buyers were organizing groups to buy a product (e.g., a car). Then, the group leader bargained with potential sellers. Sometimes the leader brought the entire buying group to a face-to-face collective negotiation (e.g., see a video

[1:59 minutes] "Group Shopping Tuangou" at **vimeo.com/8619105**.

By 2014, all major Chinese Internet companies have launched, or plan to launch, group buying and flash deals. These includes **ir.baidu.com**, **sina.com**, **tencent.com**, and **alibaba.com**. For details, see Madden (2010) and watch the video titled 'Group Buying in China (2:10 minutes) at **cnn.com/video/data/2.0/video/business/2011/01/26/yoon.china.coupon.gen.cnn.html**.

Deal Purchases (Flash Sales)

Short period deals are practiced offline usually to attract people who are already in a store; or vendors advertise a sale for a day, or for several days (in a newspaper, radio and TV), or for "doorbuster" sales between certain hours on a certain day. There are several variations of this model when done online, and it is frequently offered together with other models.

The deal purchase may be offered only in one city or state. For example, LivingSocial asks people to sign up for a deal at a restaurant, spa, or an event in a given city. You can click on "today's deal" or on "past deals" (some are still active). The deals are e-mailed to anyone that signs up with LivingSocial or you can browse their site for a particular item. If you like it, you click on an icon and receive the deal the next day. After you buy the deal, you get a unique link to share with your friends. If you find three or more people willing to buy that specific deal using your link, then your deal is free. A common strategy of flash sale sites is to focus on an industry. For example, **gilt.com** focuses on designer apparel, jewelry, bags, and upscale home furnishings.

Woot.com (an Amazon.com company) offers community information related to its deals. For example, there is a "discussion about today's deal," a Woot blog, top past deals, deal news, and what percentage of community members bought which product and what quantities of the products. Testimonials by members are also available. Woot is known as a favorite place for gadget geeks. Thus, Woot is not only a brand, but also a culture. Other interesting flash sale companies are Jetsetter (a TripAdvisor company) and Rue La La. Flash sales may offer discounts up to 80%.

Shopping Together Online in Real-Time

Shoppers on social networks can invite their friends to shop online at the same time, while in different locations. Using Facebook e-mail (or other networks) or Twitter, they interact to discuss shopping-related subjects and provide opinions.

Some shopping providers use Facebook's *social graph* when integrating their shopping service into Facebook.

Shopping Together Sites

Dozens of sites facilitate shopping together models. For example, Select2gether allows you to join a conversation in a chat room; create a wish list; shop online in real-time with your friends; find inspirations, ideas, and advice; start a live showroom with your friends; and get access to the latest fashion-related products in which the site specializes. For details and explanations, see **www.select2gether.com/about/help**.

Coshopping

Coshopping is an IBM software tool that enables two online shoppers to browse a store, view products, chat together, all in real time. It also enables employees in customer care centers to conduct live interactions with customers.

Online Social Shopping Communities

According to **socialecart.com/category/stories**, "*shopping communities* bring like-minded people together to discuss, share, and shop. The community platforms and forums connect people with each other, with businesses and with other communities." To date, fashion communities are the most popular (e.g., Polyvore, Stylefeeder [a Time company], and ShopStyle). However, other shopping communities are organized around food, pets, toys, and so forth. For example, Listia (**listia.com**) is an online community for buying and selling used or new items, along with fashion, in online auctions using virtual currency. DJdoodleVILLE (**djdoodleville.com**) is an online shopping community specializing in arts and crafts.

For a summary about social shopping communities, see **digitalinnovationtoday.com/speed-summary-ijec-social-commerce-special-edition-social-shopping-communities**.

Common Features in Communities and Forums

Communities and forums share the following major features (per Marsden 2009b, Fisher 2010; see the slideshow with infographic there, and the authors' experiences):

- **User forums.** Forums are discussion places in social networks where people can meet to discuss issues or work together to solve problems raised by participants in discussion groups.
- **User galleries.** Galleries are usually hosted by vendors to display images and videos for discussion by viewers such as customers and business partners (e.g., Burberry's Art of the Trench; **artofthetrench.burberry.com**). In January 2013, Twitter added video to its user galleries and is now calling them "media galleries" (see **marketingland. com/twitter-adds-videos-to-user-media-galleries-32095**).
- **Idea boards.** These are usually inside enterprise networks (e.g., **mystarbucksidea.force.com**; "free crowdsourcing of product ideas"; Dell's **ideastorm. com**). This is a crowdsourcing mechanism (Chapter 8) for idea generation and idea evaluation.
- **Q&A forums.** Online groups where users (e.g., customers) can ask and answer questions about various topics (e.g., a company's products) and be helped by product experts and savvy customers (e.g., Bazaarvoice's "Ask & Answer;" PowerReviews' "AnswerBox"). Answers can be organized in Q&A format.
- **Brand communities.** Communities that are organized around a brand (e.g., Sony's MP3) to discuss a product or brand.
- **Comprehensive (multipurpose communities).** Kaboodle.com is probably the most well-known comprehensive community, while **polyvore.com** is the leading fashion (and related products) community. These communities started as fashion-related groups.

Examples of Shopping Communities

There are many sites that can be classified as pure shopping communities. A prime example is **polyvore.com**, which is presented in Case 7.1.

CASE 7.1: POLYVORE: A TRENDSETTER IN SOCIAL SHOPPING

According to Polyvore's website and Crunchbase **crunchbase.com**, **polyvore.com** is a community site for online fashion and style where users are empowered to discover and develop their style and possibly set fashion trends. Users do this by creating "sets" which are shared across the Web. The company collaborates with prominent brands such as Calvin Klein (**calvinklein.com**), Lancome (**lancome-usa.com**), and Coach (**coach.com**) and retailers such as Net-a-Porter, to drive product engagement; the user-generated fashion products on its site are then judged by community members and by celebrities such as Lady Gaga and Katy Perry. Today, the company is also using mobile technologies. For example, is has an app for iPad with many capabilities (see **blog.polyvore.com/2014/02/new-ipad-and-iphone-updates-clip-to.html**). Note: Some celebrities, such as Lady Gaga, post their own products for sale on the site.

The story of the now-profitable Polyvore is described in detail by Jacobs (2010) and Chaney (2011) as well as by Grant (2013; an Infographic). Users create "sets," of their wardrobe designs, using a special editor provided free on the site. These "sets" can then be posted and shared on Polyvore's site, Facebook, and Twitter. Merchants (e.g., designers) can use the site for free by (a) creating a profile, (b) uploading existing products, and (c) creating sets.

Once merchants create a profile and upload products, Polyvore encourages the merchants to engage with other community members by reviewing and evaluating the sets. Polyvore believes that the merchants' activity will be reciprocated. To facilitate actual shopping, the sets link to the creators' sites.

Polyvore can be viewed as a crowdsourcing fashion operation that reflects the creativity and opinion of many, thus it can be viewed as expressing current fashion trends, see Wang (2011) (they now do the same with interior design). According to Wang (2011), the site provides a new business model for both shopping and product and style discovery, as well as a venue for designers to hone their skills by introducing new fashion items.

As of December 2014, Polyvore had over 20 million unique visitors importing 2 million items to the site each month, creating about 2.4 million fashion sets per month, and viewing sets 1 billion times a month. Users spend hours browsing, following favorite taste streams, asking questions, and sharing ideas (see **corp.wishpond. com/blog/2013/02/05/understanding-poly- vore-for-business**). Polyvore is considered by many to be the best place to discover or evaluate fashion trends, which are facilitated by contests managed by the company. For more information, see **venturebeat.com/2012/12/20/polyvore- gets-a-cro**.

Polyvore can be used together with Pinterest to increase traffic to the site (see Mally 2012).

Sources: Based on Jacobs (2010), Wang (2011), **polyvore.com/cgi/about**, **polyvore.com/ cgi/about.press**, and **crunchbase.com/organiza- tion/polyvore** (all accessed May 2014).

Questions

1. How can one use the Polyvore Editor to create designs (see the short video (2:02 minutes) by Polyvore titled "How to Create a Set in the Polyvore Editor" at **vimeo.com/7800846**).
2. The company added supermodel Tyra Banks as an investor in 2013. Comment on the logic of such an addition.
3. Blogger Alexandra Jacobs (2010) writes, "Polyvore is a lot like playing paper dolls with pictures of real clothes." Discuss.
4. Read Jacobs (2010) and explain what and how people create at Polyvore. Also identify the critical success factors of this site.
5. Explain the statement made by Polyvore's vice president of product management: "Our mission is to democratize fashion."
6. Identify all the features of a shopping community in this case.

Kaboodle: A Unique Social Shopping Community

According to its website, Kaboodle (**kaboodle. com**) is a large comprehensive *social shopping community* and network. According to **crunch- base.com/organization/kaboodle**, "this free service lets users collect information from the Web and store it on a Kaboodle list that can be shared with others." The site's primary goal is to simplify shopping by making it easier for people to find items (of interest) in Kaboodle's catalog, and (then) allowing users to share recommendations with one another (about selected items), using Kaboodle *lists* and *groups*. Kaboodle lists, however, can serve a variety of other purposes besides just shopping. (For example), they can be used for planning vacations (or parties), sharing research for work or school, sharing favorite bands with friends, and basically anything else people might want to collect and share information about."

To learn more about how Kaboodle works, take the Kaboodle Tour at **kaboodle.com/zd/ help/getStarted.html**.

Some of Kaboodle's Capabilities

The "Add to Kaboodle" button simplifies the online shopping experience because, once inserted, the user can simply click on it whenever a product is selected from any website. Then, a snapshot of the selected item, its price, and other product information is automatically uploaded with a link about where to place it on Kaboodle lists. The user then can find any specific item in the future. Users can also discover deals, find new products, express their unique styles, connect with others, share their discoveries, blog, create shopping lists, and more.

Kaboodle allows the creation of "Top Picks" from the Kaboodle lists based on what members like (e.g., the "top 10 weird products").

Private Online Shopping Clubs

Vente-Price of France **us.vente-privee.com**) was the first private online shopping club. The club concentrates on designer products. In general, clubs run flash sale events featuring luxury brands at huge discounts (up to 80%). Luxury brands use the clubs to liquidate out of style items, overstock, or special samples. Consumers like the clubs due to the largest discounts.

The key to this business model's success is that in contrast with the Groupon model, *not* everyone is allowed to shop. The members-only model serves a myriad of purposes. Partially, it is a marketing device that makes members feel like VIPs; but it also helps the clubs manage a healthy growth.

Examples of Private Clubs

Some private (or "members only") clubs are: Beyond the Rack (**beyondtherack.com**; in the U.S. and Canada posts flash deals), Gilt Groupe (**gilt.com**), Rue La La (**ruelala.com**), Amazon's Buy VIP (**buyvip.com**; in Europe), Ideeli (**ideeli.com**), and BestSecret (**bestsecret.com**). Note that, to minimize conflict with department stores, luxury brands now offer select items at Internet prices in stores such as Target Inc. (**target.com**).

Other Innovative Models

There are hundreds of start-ups in social commerce. Here are some representative examples:

- **Find what your friends are buying.** This service was offered for example by **clubfurniture.com**, a site that sells online home furnishings from its factory. According to Fleenor (2010), users can log onto Facebook or other social network, and view a list of shoppers at Club Furniture via the See What Your Friends Are Buying, feature. Users can also find a list of repeat customers.
- **Wanelo.** This popular social shopping marketplace (especially with young shoppers) combines bookmarking and product sharing. Members can follow others to find trend y shopping. For details, see Leahey (2013). According to **pcmag.com/article2/0,2817, 2424709,00.asp**, the company's name is an abbreviation for the phrase 'Want, Need, Love.' Wanelo (**wanelo.com**) "is an online community-based e-commerce site that brings together products from a vast array of stores into one pinboard-style platform. You can browse, save, or buy products. Catering to

both brands and shoppers, members create collections – similar to Pinterest boards – from items onsite or external links." It also has an app on iTunes and Google Play as well as a Facebook Fan page. For more information about Wanelo, see **mashable.com/2013/11/05/ wanelo-social-shopping**.
- **Filtering consumers reviews.** TurboTax, a division of Intuit, launched a website called **turbotax.intuit.com/reviews** that allows consumers to describe their particular tax situation (own or rent a home, have children or not, previous tax prep method, etc.), and filter reviews on TurboTax products, to see only those written by "people like them" (similar tax and income situations); then, quickly find which TurboTax product best suits their needs. From **turbotax.com**, consumers can also click through to Facebook, Twitter, or MySpace and read reviews on TurboTax products written by members of their social network. In addition, anyone who reviews a TurboTax product, whether on the main company site or at **turbotax.intuit.com/reviews**, can automatically publish their reviews to any of those three social networks with one click.
- **RealGifts.** Facebook had a service called 'RealGifts' that allowed people to send real-life presents to their friends. People were getting together on Facebook to buy each other gifts. (Wrapp enables you to send giftcards from your smartphone.)
- **Virtual gifts.** Similar to trading in virtual properties and virtual gifts in Second Life, there is a rapidly increasing market on social networks for virtual gifts. Facebook sells virtual gifts in its marketplace.
- **Getting help from friends.** To get help from friends, you may go to sites such as **shopshocially.com**. You can post a question, share a purchase, and much more.
- **Shopping without leaving Facebook.** There are several ways to use Facebook Fan pages for shopping, so fans do not have to leave Facebook. Payment is one implementation issue, security is another (see **facebook.com/ auctionitems**).

- **Social auctions.** Facebook now has a Store App for eBay sellers, called Auction Items (previously "eBay items"), where members can send private invitations to their friends to invite them to their store. The Auction Items app is available in several languages. For more details see **facebook.com/ AuctionItems**. Facebook also offers an app for Etsy stores.
- In April 2010, Pampers offered its Pampers Cruisers at a big discount on its Facebook page. The offer of 1,000 units sold in less than one hour. The vendor (P&G) was willing to compensate the many thousands of people that missed the sale. This story demonstrates the power of Facebook marketing. For how you can shop on Facebook, see Solis (2010) and several other references.
- **Crowdsourcing shopping advice.** You can get advice from many people (the crowd), as is done by Cloud Shopper. According to Kessler (2011), Cloud Shopper allows users to organize the advice given by their friends. Users select products and start a conversation on Facebook about their items of interest. The company also provides price comparisons and price alerts about the selected items; see **cloudshopper.com** for details.
- **Helping sellers and bloggers sell products.** Etsy is socially-oriented marketplace which helps bloggers and sellers (mostly artists) monetize their businesses by making it easy for them to sell products directly to consumer.
- **Event shopping.** There are many sites that will help you shop for a special event (e.g., a wedding) with the assistance of your friends. Many variations of this model exist. For example, in 2010 Wendy's gave away gift cards for meals to the people who organized viewing parties on Wendy's Facebook page.

Social Shopping Aids: From Recommendations to Reviews, Ratings, and Marketplaces

In addition to the typical e-commerce shopping aids such as comparison engines and recommendations a la Amazon.com style (see Chapter 3), there are special aids for social commerce.

Recommendations in Social Commerce

Prior to making a purchase, customers tend to collect information that will help them, such as what brand to buy, from which vendor, and at what price. Online customers do this by using shopping aids (e.g., price comparison sites like **nextag.com**), looking at product review sites such as **epinions. com**, and researching other sources. Examining and participating in social networking forums is another way to compare prices and read product and service reviews. According to Gartner Inc. (reported by Dubey 2010), the majority of online customers already rely on social networks to guide them in purchase decisions. A variety of SC models and tools is available for this purpose (e.g., see Dugan 2010). We present two major categories here.

Ratings and Reviews

Ratings and reviews by friends, even by people that you do not know (e.g., experts or independent third-party evaluators), are usually available for social shoppers. In addition, any user has the opportunity to contribute reviews and participate in relevant discussions. The tools for conducting rating and reviews, which are presented here, are based on Fisher (2010), Rowan and Cheshire (2011), Shih (2011), **bazaarvoice.com/solutions/ conversations**, and the authors' experiences. The major types of tools and methods are:

- **Customer ratings and reviews.** Customer ratings are popular. They can be found on vendors' product (or service) sites such as Buzzillions, or on independent reviews sites, (e.g., TripAdvisor) and/or in customer news feeds (e.g., Amazon.com, Epinions). Customer ratings can be summarized by votes or polls.
- **Customer testimonials.** Customer experiences are typically published on vendors' sites, and third party sites such as **tripadvisor.com**. Many sites encourage discussion (e.g., **bazaarvoice.com/ solutions/conversations**).
- **Expert ratings and reviews.** Ratings or reviews can also be generated by domain experts and appear in different online publications.

- **Sponsored reviews.** These are written by paid bloggers or domain experts. Advertisers and bloggers find each other by searching through websites such as **sponsoredreviews.com**), which connects bloggers with marketers and advertisers.
- **Conversational marketing.** People communicate via e-mail, blog, live chat, discussion groups, and tweets. Monitoring conversations may yield rich data for market research and customer service (e.g., as practiced by Dell; see their social media command center). See Chapter 10 for additional information.
- **Video product review.** Reviews can be generated by using videos. YouTube offers reviews that are uploaded, viewed, commented on, and shared.
- **Bloggers reviews.** This is a questionable method since some bloggers are paid and may use a biased approach. However, many bloggers have the reputation to be unbiased. For a list of 50 bloggers see Sala (2012).

Example

Maui Jim (**mauijim.com**) is a designer of high quality polarized sunglasses. According to *Business Wire* (2010), the company is using Bazaarvoice Ratings & Reviews to enable customers to rate the company's sunglasses and accessories.

The company is relying on word-of-mouth marketing to advertise its products and help shoppers. Customers are invited to share their opinions on the style, fit, and quality of specific sunglass models. The invitations appear when customers are conducting a search. Maui Jim sends customers an e-mail asking them to review products and the company has reviews on its pages in selected social network sites.

Social Recommendations and Referrals

Recommendation engines allow shoppers to receive advice from other shoppers and to give advice to others.

Social shopping may combine recommendations in a social network platform with actual sales. Social recommendations and referrals are closely related to ratings and reviews and are sometimes integrated with them.

Traditional online product review companies such as Amazon.com and Bazaarvoice have helped traditional consumers, but today's customers like to receive advice from (and give advice to) friends and other shoppers. Sites such as CNET, Wired Reviews, Buzzillions, Epinons, Consumer Reports, and TheFind can be used for this purpose. Amazon.com also provides reviews on the products they sell.

Example

ThisNext (**thisnext.com**) is a social commerce site where community members *recommend* their favorite products so others can discover desirable or unique items and decide what to buy. ThisNext uses WOM, social experiences, and personalization to facilitate shopping. To assist with discovery and help finalize shopping decisions, the community includes experts, bloggers, style mavens, and trendsetters. ThisNext has also developed a set of shopping tools for bloggers, designers, and shoppers. For further description, see **thisnext.com/company/aboutus**.

It makes sense to combine recommendations with marketing communications and shopping. Sites in this category allow shoppers to receive and provide advice to specific friends, in contrast with traditional online product reviews that include advice provided by unknown shoppers. Furthermore, these sites sell ad space, provide coupons, and some offer automatic cash-back rewards for shopping with local merchants.

A new trend is to encourage conversations around purchases with a shopper's "real life" friends. The sites that include reviews from people one knows are logically more trustworthy than sites that include only the reviews made by strangers.

Sometimes, social recommendations are embedded in social shopping portals that offer shopping tools as well as bundling recommendations with ratings and reviews. A prime example is Kaboodle (described earlier as a shopping community).

Common recommendation methods are:

- **Social bookmarking.** Recommended products, services, etc. are bookmarked so members of social networks can easily find them.
- **Personal social recommendations.** These are based on finding people with similar profiles. By using these customers' actual purchases, conclusions can be reached about general and targeted recommendations (e.g., see Apple's Near Me [**getnearme.com**]; applications that are popular based on a user's current location), Amazon Recommendations, and Snoox (**snoox. com**; "your friends' recommendations on everything").
- **Referral programs.** Affiliate programs (e.g., Amazon Associates [**affiliate-program.amazon.com**], Apple's iTunes Affiliate Program [**apple.com/itunes/ affiliates**] pay people for referring new customers). For more about referral programs, see **slideshare.net/getAmbassador/building-an-effective-referral-program**.
- **Matching algorithms.** Consulting companies and vendors (e.g., Netflix) provide recommendations based on similarity algorithms (as described in Chapter 3).

For more on product reviews see: **mashable. com/2008/07/18/product-reviews**.

Illustrative Examples of Recommendation Sites

Recommendations, reviews, ratings, and other engagement activities can be done in online communities. However, the *major objectives* of communities (like Kaboodle) are different because they *concentrate* on recommendations, reviews, and ratings as important shopping aids. For a discussion, see **shopsmart.org**.

Crowdstorm

According to Chaney (2011), "Crowdstorm (**crowdstorm.com**) is a *shopping recommendation* website with two goals: (a) [being] a hub for product reviews and (b) being a source where shoppers can find the best online prices for consumer goods such as electronics, sporting equipment, clothing, and jewelry. This site is fueled by user-submitted product listings and product reviews. However it also includes expert reviews, buyer guides, and question-and-answer sessions. "The site promotes an open policy by allowing users to post their reviews to blogs, other review sites and online stores." The site claims to have over 300,000 visitors a month; however, it does not sell anything – it just aids shoppers. In addition, the site provides price comparisons. Crowdstorm is also a social shopping experience provider, where shoppers can ask other shoppers for recommendations about products they are looking to buy.

Buzzillions

Buzzillions (**buzzillions.com**) is a user-generated product review site. It gets reviews from its parent company, PowerReviews (acquired by Bazaarvoice), which provides customer review software to e-commerce sites. It also incorporates product reviews from companies that use other third-party providers, or have an in-house review system. The site provides several useful tools for tagging and researching the reviews. It also provides ranking.

Buzzillions' business model is based on selling traffic, or product leads, from Buzzillions right back to the merchant network that uses PowerReviews. In other words, Buzzillions' readers read reviews imported from many other sites, and they can then click on products of interest, giving them the opportunity to read more about these products and possibly purchase them at the seller's site.

The company is unique because:

1. The rankings are based on feedback from customers. The company provides the tools to narrow down the search, but the consumers have to read the reviews to see if the product is right for them.

2. Positive or negative, all reviews are encouraged on Buzzillions. Unless a review is profane or violates the company's terms, it will be shown on the site.
3. Buzzillions does not sell products, although the company has retail partners listed on the site for direct contact by consumers.

Example: How Intuit Corp. Helps Consumers with Recommendations

Intuit's TurboTax program is very popular, with about 20 million users. The company uses a social media recommendation system, called "Friends Like You Like TurboTax" (**turbotax. intuit.com/reviews**), where the customers, after completing the computation of their taxes, are asked to broadcast their opinion of their TurboTax experience. Friends Like You draws on social networks such as Facebook and Twitter. The program was so successful that TurboTax sales jumped 11% in 2011, compared to 2010.

According to **mashable.com/2011/01/10/ turbotax-twitter-feed-friendcasting**, "to further help the process, some 100,000 product reviews are segmented into tax-related categories like 'bought a house' or 'lost my job.' Intuit also made the search function on its site more prominent and easier to use. Intuit's program is unique because rather than (posting recommendations or "likes,") consumers broadcast a fairly neutral piece of information (about the tax computation they just finished) that others are likely to find beneficial, particularly around the tax submission period." From the Ratings & Reviews page (**turbotax.intuit.com/reviews/**), consumers can also click on TurboTax's Facebook or Twitter pages and read reviews about their products.

Concerns about Social Reviews and Recommendations

Some people raise the issue of how accurate the reported reviews and recommendations are. Fake reviews and claims are suspected to be 30–40% of the total reviews in some sites. For example, see the 'allegations against business owners' at **en.wikipedia.org/wiki/Yelp**. There is also a concern about businesses paying money to review sites to manipulate the reviews. Another concern is that in cases of small number of reviewers a bias (positive or negative) may be shown.

Other Shopping Aids and Services

In addition to recommendations and marketplaces, there are several sites that provide social shopping aids, as illustrated in the following examples.

Yelp: The Shoppers' Best Helper

Yelp (**yelp.com**) is company that operates a local guide for helping people find in a specific city services ranging from mechanics to restaurants based on reviews and recommendations of users. In this way, it connects people with great local businesses. Community members, known as "Yelpers," write reviews of the businesses and then rate them. Yelpers also find events and special offers and can "talk" with each other (e.g., see **yelp.com/talk**).

The site is also a place for businesses to advertise their products and services (paying fees to Yelp for posting a "Yelp Deal"). Yelp is also accessible via mobile devices. The site offers several social networking features such as discussion forums, photo posting, and creation of groups and have followers. Yelp has a company blog (**officialblog.yelp.com**), along with a community blog for Elite Yelpers worldwide (**communityblog.yelp.com**). Yelpers who frequently become actively involved and engage on the site, can apply to become an "Elite Squad" member (see **yelp.com/elite**).

Yelp operates in major metro cities in the United States, Canada, the United Kingdom, and other countries worldwide. As of Q3 2014, Yelp has over 138 million monthly visitors (as measured by Google Analytics) and Yelpers have written over 47 million reviews. According to Yelp (2014), Yelp's mobile application was used on approximately 11.2 million unique mobile devices on a monthly average basis during Q3 2013.

How Yelp Works

Users look for a business in a specific location. Yelp's search engine finds available businesses and presents them with ratings and reviews as well as with accessibility and directions.

Yelp connects with Google Maps to show the business location and further aids in discovering related businesses. (Google was negotiating to buy Yelp in November 2010, but the deal fell through in January 2011.)

Adding social features to user reviews creates a reputation system, whereby site visitors can see the good and the bad. For the topic of reputation management, see **seofriendly.com/tag/reputation-management**. Yelp became a major commercial success and was listed on the stock market in March 2012. Its stock price kept increasing until late 2014 when it began declining.

For more on Yelp's operation see 'How Yelp Works' at **computer.howstuffworks.com/internet/social-networking/networks/yelp.htm**. For further information, see **yelp.com/faq** and **en.wikipedia.org/wiki/Yelp**.

Note that some shopping aids can be used for both online and offline shopping. One such aid is the touch-screen PC available at kiosks in physical stores, (e.g., Kohl's) where you can examine catalogs and place your order to be shipped to your home, while you are in the store.

Collaborative Reviews

Sites such as ProductWiki (**productwiki.com**) are structured like a wiki; thus, every user can contribute to the site. The goal is to create a comprehensive resource collection. The companies believe that a need exists for unbiased, accurate, and community-based resources for product information. These sites use *collaborative reviews*, a collection of pros and cons about a product submitted by and voted on by the consumers. The result is a comprehensive review that takes the opinions of many people into account, and highlights the most important aspects of a product. A collaborative review is made up of two things – short statements and votes. Community members submit and vote on specific statements that are separated by pros and cons, making it easy to see what is good and bad about each product. For further information on collaborative reviews, see **productwiki.com/home/article/collaborative-reviews.html**.

In March 2013, ProductWiki merged with Bootic (**bootic.com**), known as a "wiki of products." (See **bootic.com/aboutus**.) The idea is for ProductWiki to offer a marketplace in addition to product reviews. Bootic is the first marketplace that allows shoppers to express themselves by editing, adding content, and enhancing the overall product description. As a result of this partnership, ProductWiki, like Bootic, will offer a marketplace in addition to product reviews. According to its website, vendors love Bootic's marketplace because "Bootic's e-commerce platform offers a free suite of easy-to-use Web-based tools and technology to help our vendors create their own individualized online shops. Unlike other marketplaces, we don't charge fees. On Bootic, storefronts can quickly get up and running without incurring any set-up costs, listing or on-going transaction fees. Bootic empowers small businesses to enhance their online brand while optimizing a new revenue stream."

Filtering Consumer Reviews

As described earlier, TurboTax, a division of Intuit, launched a ratings and reviews page on their website called "Friends Like You Like TurboTax" (**turbotax.intuit.com/reviews**). This page allows consumers to describe their particular tax situation, and then filter reviews on TurboTax products, then, they can quickly find which TurboTax product best suits their needs.

Dealing with Complaints

As seen earlier, customers have learned how to use social media to air their complaints. For a UK survey that shows that customers are more likely to complain via social media, see **xlgroup.com/press/new-survey-finds-customers-increasingly-likely-to-use-social-media-to-complain**. See also **wptv.com/dpp/news/science_tech/facebook-fb-twitter-twtr-used-to-complain-get-answers**.

Social Marketplaces and Direct Sales

The term **social marketplace** refers to a marketplace that uses social media tools and platforms and acts as an online intermediary between buyers and sellers. Ideally, a social marketplace should enable the marketing of members' own creations as Polyvore does.

Some examples of social marketplaces include:

- **Craigslist.** Craigslist (**craigslist.org**) can be considered a social network marketplace in that it provides online classified ads in addition to supporting social activities (meetings, dating, events). See Chapter 2.
- **Fotolia.** Fotolia (**fotolia.com**) is a social marketplace for royalty free photos, images, and video clips. In 2014 there were more than 31 million images available on the site. It serves a community of artists, designers, and other creative people who express themselves through images, forums, and blogs. Buyers can legally buy images (pay only one time for each or periodically) and then use these images and photos as they wish (e.g., resell them, modify them, etc.). For details see **us.fotolia.com/info/AboutUs**.
- **Flipsy.** Anyone can use Flipsy (**flipsy.com**) to list, buy, and sell books, music, movies, and games. It was created to fill the need for a free and trustworthy media marketplace. Flipsy does not charge commissions in order to increase the trading volume. Payment processing for items purchased is handled by a third party, such as PayPal.
- **Storenvy.** Storenvy (**storenvy.com**) is a marketplace for unique businesses and photos. At no cost to sellers, a simple way is made available (no programming experience is needed) to create personalized webstores. Sellers have the ability to make the sites as socially friendly as they wish, giving customers the chance to interact with the seller as well as other customers.
- **ShopSocially.** ShopSocially (**shopsocially. com**) is a consumer-to-consumer marketing communication and experience sharing platform for shopping. This platform also enables shoppers to recommend products to their friends. ShopSocially combines the concepts of online shopping and social networks, creating a new business model of online social shopping. Users can solicit shopping information from friends via Facebook, Twitter, and e-mail. A combination of shopping questions, their answers, and purchases shared by friends creates a powerful experience and shopping knowledge base. For details and benefits to retailers, see **shopsocially.com**.

Direct Sales from Within Social Networks

There is an increased volume of direct sales, mostly on Facebook. Here is an example:

Example: How Musicians Sell Online via Social Networks

Many musicians and other artists used to invest money to make their own CDs, T-shirts, and other items before they sold them. Now there is a free social commerce solution. Audiolife Inc. (an Alliance Entertainment Company) provides artists with webstores (one per artist), where artists (sellers) can directly interact with potential buyers. This arrangement also allows artists to "make-to-order" and sell merchandise.

To entice fans to order products, artists post their own Audiolife selection on any large social network site (e.g., Facebook). Each order, even for one item, is then forwarded to the artist for production. Audiolife arranges payment and shipping to the buyers. By 2012, Audiolife powered close to 100,000 webstores worldwide, serving 300,000 artists, including those who are already established. For details, see **www.audiolife.com/AboutUs.aspx** and Billingsley (2010).

Socially-Oriented Person to Person (P2P) Selling, Buying, Renting, or Bartering

When individuals trade online, they may do so with some social elements. For example, some consider **craigslist.org** to be a socially oriented virtual community and so is **www.altimetergroup.com**. Here are some more examples:

P2P Lending

P2P money lending is growing rapidly, enabling one person to lend money directly to another. In the process, they get to know each other. Another start-up created a community of people that rent goods to people in need, usually for the short term. **Snapgoods.com** helps these people connect over the Internet.

P2P Sharing (Also Known as *Collaborative Consumption*)

SnapGoods facilitates P2P sharing. Some other sites like SwapBabyGoods.com (**swapbabygoods.com**), Swapmamas (**swapmamas.com**), and Neighborhood Fruit (**neighborhoodfruit.com**; helps people share fruit that are growing in their yards or find fruit trees on public lands), have a niche market. The sharing and renting trend is booming, especially during the economic recession; and there is a "green" aspect as well – saving on the use of resources. There is also the social aspect of sharing, allowing people to make meaningful connections with others (see Walsh 2010 for details).

Several variations exist. Some people share cars, others invite travelers to stay free in their homes, or exchange homes (e.g., **4homex.com**) for a short periods and much more. LendingTree (**lendingtree.com**) is another company that allows prospective borrowers to get quick offers from multiple lenders. For a case study of P2P lending see Online File W7.1.

In May 2013, Google invested money in a P2P investment site **lendingclub.com** (see Hempel 2013). This company became a success in 2015.

Shopping for Virtual Goods in a Virtual Economy

An increasing number of shoppers purchase all kinds of virtual products and services online. **Virtual goods** are computer images of real or imaginary goods. These include, but are not limited to, properties and merchandise on Second Life (such as virtual mobile phones to equip your avatar), and a large number of items sold in multiplayer games in on social networks (e.g., FarmVille on Facebook). According to *eMarketer* (2011), U.S. social gaming virtual revenues were projected to grow almost 60%

from \$653 million in 2011 to \$792 million in 2012.

The Virtual Economy

A **virtual economy** is an emerging economy existing in several virtual worlds, where people exchange virtual goods frequently related to an Internet game or to a virtual business. People go there primarily for entertainment. However, some people trade their virtual goods or properties. A virtual property can be any resource that is controlled by virtual objects, avatars, or user accounts. For the characteristics of these properties, see **en.wikipedia.org/wiki/Virtual_economy**. For how payments are made for virtual goods, see Takahashi (2011), and for an overview of Facebook payments, see **developers.facebook.com/docs/payments/overview**.

Why People Buy Virtual Goods

There are several reasons why people buy virtual goods. For example, many people in China buy virtual properties because they cannot afford to buy properties in the real world. According to Savitz (2011), there are four major reasons for such purchases made in any country:

1. **Generating special experiences.** Studies found (e.g., see Markman 2010) that some people can maximize their happiness by spending money on the experience they get in a virtual world rather than when spending money on physical goods. Happiness from a dinner or a movie does not last for a long time, but it makes us happy in the moment. The same is true with virtual goods, but these can be very imaginative and beautiful, providing much more happiness.

2. **Generating emotions.** Purchases of virtual goods often fill emotional needs. In the virtual world, you can be whatever or whoever you always wanted to be, so people are willing to exchange real money for real emotions they find in the virtual goods.

3. **Small purchases make people happier.** Making small and frequent purchases of virtual goods (usually they do not cost much) make many (but not all) people happier than

infrequent purchases of larger physical goods.

4. **Virtual goods are low cost and low hassle.** There is no need to store virtual goods, maintain them, or be criticized about why you purchased them. In short – there is no hassle as long as one stays within one's budget.

In fact, several real world retailers are promoting their virtual goods in virtual games.

Real-Time Online Shopping

In real-time online shopping, shoppers can log onto a site and then either connect with Facebook or with another social network instantly from a smartphone or computer, or invite their friends and family via Twitter or e-mail. Friends shop online together *at the same time*, exchanging ideas and comparing experiences (e.g., see Dugan 2010).

Some real-time shopping platforms, are Facebook's social graph-based shopping platforms. Other players in this area are is BevyUP (see **bevyup.com/resources** and **samesurf.com/about.html**). These empower multiple users to share their experiences in real time.

Social Shopping in the Near Future

Imagine this scenario: A retailer will ask you to log in with Facebook on your mobile device as soon as you step into a physical store. Many of Facebook's partners have custom Facebook applications (Partner Apps) that users can download through their app stores, including Blackberry and Windows Phone (see **facebook.com/Mobile**).

In this way users can receive *customized recommendations* on their mobile phones. According to Appelo (2010), you can expect that your friends who have been in that store will indicate electronically, which clothes may be the best fit for you (e.g., using. "likes"), then walk in and find what to buy. What about the risks? Privacy is a concern to many, but less important to

"Millennials" who frequently share their experiences with others. In addition, sometimes people do not need to reveal their full identity on an in-store screen. See a related video titled 'The Future of Shopping' (48 seconds) at **youtube.com/watch?v=R_TAP0OY1Bk**.

For more on how Facebook "likes" and social plug-ins help business websites, see **searchengineland.com/by-the-numbers-how-facebook-says-likes-social-plugins-help-websites-76061**.

For example, according to Admin (2011), when you walk into a dressing room in a department store, the mirror reflects your image, but you also see the images of apparel items (you like and certain) celebrities wear, all on an interactive display. A webcam also projects an image of a consumer wearing the item on a website, for everyone to see. This creates an interaction between the consumers inside the store and their social network (friends) outside the store. The technology behind this system uses RFID (Radio Frequency Identification), and has already been tried by the Prada store in New York City for showing customers which shoes and purses would go with the clothes they are trying on in the dressing room. You can watch a video titled 'Future Store 'Smart Dressing Room' (2:53 minutes) of how a "smart" dressing room works at **youtube.com/watch?v=0VII-xdg5Ak&feature=related**. Note that due to privacy concerns, Prada (and others) discontinued their RFID experiments.

SECTION 7.4 REVIEW QUESTIONS

1. Define social shopping and describe its drivers.
2. List the major benefits of social shopping.
3. List the major models of social shopping. Briefly describe their functionalities.
4. Describe ratings, reviews, and recommendations.
5. Define group buying.
6. Define social communities and social clubs as they relate to marketing. How do they work?
7. Describe Kaboodle.
8. Define social marketplaces. What is going on there?

9. Describe the major shopping aids.
10. Describe shopping for virtual goods.
11. Describe social shopping in the near future.

7.5 SOCIAL ADVERTISING: FROM VIRAL ADVERTISING TO LOCATION-BASED ADVERTISEMENT/ MARKETING

The major current revenue source for many social commerce companies is advertising. The reason is that seeing the large number of members and visitors in the social networks, and the amount of time they spend there, has given advertisers the motivation and justification to pay a great deal for placing ads and running promotions in those networks. Like other SC activities, advertising is done both in public, as well as in private company-owned social networks.

Many advertisers are placing ads on Facebook, YouTube, LinkedIn, MySpace, Pinterest, or Twitter. Although social media campaigns may have a small impact on actual online retail sales, they may have huge benefits with regard to increasing *brand awareness*.

Social Ads and Social Apps

Most ads in social commerce are branded content paid for by advertisers. These come in two major categories: *social ads* and *social apps*.

1. **Social ads.** These display ads and banners and are placed in social games and discussion boards in social networks.
2. **Social apps.** These applications support social interactions and user contributions. These are more complex to implement than social ads.

Facebook features hundreds of thousands of third-party software applications on its site. One popular application area is travel. For example, one specific application is "Where I've Been," which includes a map of places where users have visited or hope to visit. You can plan trips, organize group travel, and find and rate free accommodations (e.g., at Couchswap). This information can be sold to travel-oriented vendors, who in turn advertise their products to Facebook members. Of special interest is Tripadvisor's "Cities I've Visited" with its interactive map.

Viral (Word-of-Mouth) Marketing and Social Networking

Viral marketing refers to electronic word-of-mouth (WOM) method by which people tell others (frequently their friends) about a product they like or dislike. Viral marketing and advertising has many variations (see Chapter 9) and it plays a major role in e-commerce and social commerce. For more see Logan (2014) and **learningmarketing.net**.

Young adults are especially good at viral marketing. If members like a certain product or service, word-of-mouth advertising will spread rapidly sometimes to millions of people at a minimal cost to companies' advertisers. For example, when YouTube first started up, the site conducted almost no traditional advertising in its first few months, but millions joined because of WOM. For the "power of WOM," see **bazaarvoice.com/research-and-insight/social-commerce-statistics** and Wilde (2013).

Viral Blogging

Many retailers are capitalizing on WOM marketing by using bloggers. See some examples at **viralbloggingsystem.com**. When viral marketing is done by bloggers, it is referred to as **viral blogging**. Viral blogging can be very effective with the use of tools such as Twitter. (e.g., do a Google search for "Dell Uses Twitter to Drive Sales").

Example

PayPerPost (**payperpost.com**) runs a marketplace where advertisers and bloggers, video bloggers, online photographers, and podcasters can connect with each other. Those who need services describe what they want and how much they are willing to pay for the services. Then providers bid on the jobs.

PayPerPost checks the reputation of the bloggers and matches them with the requirements of advertisers. PayPerPost also arranges payment to the bloggers. Note that the PayPerPost bloggers *are* required to disclose that they are being paid for their postings. (For details, see **payperpost.com/blogger/blogger-how-it-works**).

In addition, note that paid bloggers may be biased in favor of those that hire them. This could be a concern for the blogs' readers.

Other Viral Marketing Methods

Viral marketing is done in most social networks through internal e-mail, messaging, and forwarding of videos, stories, and special offers. In addition, there are other innovative ways to go viral (e.g., see Turban et al. 2015).

Location-Based Advertisements and Social Networks

In Chapter 6, we introduced the concept of location-based advertising and marketing as a business model for m-commerce. The model is based on knowing where a customer is via the GPS in her or his cell phone. Once the vendor knows that a person is near a certain business, the vendor of this business can send a text, e-mail, or even a telephone call offering discounted products, coupons, or services. This targeted ad-based business model was not too successful in traditional e-commerce. Customers were not interested, and those with GPS shut it off due to privacy concerns.

The situation changed with the introduction of social networks. The nature of location-based marketing changed to being social, entertaining, and rewarding; advertisement came as an add on service. According to Knight (2012), location-based ads generated nine times more interactions than non-targeted ads. The players in this area utilize are based on geolocation and geosocial networks.

Geosocial Networks

Geosocial networks are computer networks based on *geolocation.*

Geosocial Networking

Geosocial networking is social networking with location awareness capabilities. This enables social networks to connect users with local businesses, people, or events. The location of people is found by tracking their mobile phones or receiving text messages from them that provide their locations.

The Technology for Location-Based Social Networks

The basic idea is that users who have a GPS-enabled smartphone can let their friends know where they are. Users can also examine locations recommended by friends or "check in" with them remotely. Users may give permission for ads to be sent to them.

How LBS Works

Geolocation apps report a user's location (such as restaurants, parks, or events) to other users, and to participating vendors. According to Ionescu (2010), more significant information is given on mobile devices because the system follows your location.

Foursquare and Its Competitors

Several start-ups are competing fiercely in the geolocation market. However, the LBS model is not doing well.

How Foursquare Works

Foursquare works with all major smartphones. Alternatively one can use the Foursquare mobile website. Either way, Foursquare will find your location (with your permission) and provide a map, marking your location as "checking in." This information can be transmitted, with your permission, to your friends and to vendors. A detailed explanation of how Foursquare works and how to join is provided at **computer.howstuffworks.com/internet/social-networking/networks/foursquare.htm**.

You can check in at any participating location. When your friends are aware of your location, they can suggest what you visit or where to shop in the vicinity of your location.

Foursquare provides incentives to encourage users to digitally "check in" to specific locations. The check-ins show up on Twitter, Facebook, and other social networks.

Changes in the Business Model

In April 2014 Foursquare introduced a major change in its business model. The company changed its check-in capability to show users which of their friends are nearby (an app known as "Swarm"). The company also embarked on local recommendations, competing with Yelp (see Burnham 2014).

Competition: Facebook Places

Competitors try to clone Foursquare and provide some extra services. For example, Facebook created its own app called 'Locations'.

Strategy for Small Businesses in LBS

According to Van Grove (2010), a small business can offer the following location-based deals: (1) verified check-in rewards, (2) social bar codes, (3) group deals, (4) challenge-based rewards, and (5) opt-in deals. For details, see **mashable.com/2010/09/04/location-based-small-business-deals**. For an example, see Online File W7.2.

Privacy Concerns for LBS

There are some privacy concerns regarding finding the location of people or showing their profiles and shopping habits.

Opt-In Versus Op-Out

This can be allowed with opt-in or opt-out. An "opt-in" is a permission-based system that requires a user to join or sign up. Foursquare (or a similar company) is then given permission by friends or vendors to access the user's information and to contact him or her. An "opt-out" is an option which excludes the user from a group. Thus, users need to remove themselves from the system if they wish to be excluded.

Using YouTube and Other Social Presentation Sites for Advertising

As we will show in Chapter 9, using videos for advertising is becoming a major successful strategy. Sellers introduce new products or try to improve a brand image by attaching video clips to their product pages on social networks, or their corporate portal. Product images or videos of products can be effective in facilitating sales. Several vendors can help in video clip usage. The major motivation for such advertising is the potential viral effect.

Viral Videos

In Chapter 9 we will describe the use of videos for advertising, mostly via their viral impact. Here we briefly describe how viral videos work with social commerce. Social media can be most powerful when a video goes viral, because it is an attention grabber (e.g., funny). People forward videos to their friends and acquaintances, and as a result, many watch a video that may contain an ad or show a brand logo. Certain videos can receive several million hits in less than a week. Of course, big brands dominate here. For example, among the most well-known viral videos of 2012 were those produced by Nike, Visa, Mattel, and Samsung. However, there are many exceptions to this case. An excellent marketing campaign was produced in 2010 by the Australian Tourism Board (small organizations).

A **viral video** is any video that is forwarded rapidly from one person to others, sometimes with a recommendation to watch it. Social networks are an ideal place to disseminate such videos, which became popular due to Internet sharing (mostly through video sharing websites, e-mail, texting, blogs, etc.). This method is inexpensive.

Why It Works

Interesting videos seen on YouTube are usually shared through Facebook, Twitter, or e-mail. These posts are in turn shared through the same channels from the recipients.

Interesting examples are available at **blog.socialmaximizer.com/youtube-business-use-cases**.

Using Twitter as an Advertising and Marketing Tool

Twitter and some other microblogging sites have added social networking capabilities to their sites such as creating profiles and lists of fans and friends. Sellers can reach out to these friends to create strong WOM.

According to Learmonth (2011), Twitter is becoming a little more of a business. The company launched its first ad product – "promoted tweets" – in 2010 and netted $45 million in ad dollars. That was due in part because brands like Virgin America, Coke, Ford, and Verizon were willing to experiment with the idea. Bennett (2014) points out that an eMarketer report forecasts the ad revenue on Twitter will exceed $1 billion in 2014 up from $5.5 million in 2013. Companies can tweet about their business and product offerings, including promotions. This way, they can attract Twitter followers to visit their stores. Twitter may help disseminate ads resulting in increased sales. Twitter's software suites help merchants reach their Twitter followers by posting "tweets" when the merchants add new products or create promotions. For successful examples, do Google searches for 'twitter simply speakers,' and 'twitter SBLpublishing.' Twitter is already the world's second-largest social-networking platform (about 650 million registered users in December 2014) and may reach 1 billion followers in a few years, according to reports at **mediabistro.com**. This may help the microblogging site compete with Facebook in attracting advertisers.

As a matter of fact, Twitter began attracting many advertisers in September 2010 after a successful trial with a few leading brands.

Finally, here are some more ways one can do business or advertise on Twitter (based on **business.twitter.com**, Weber (2012), Gillette (2010), and Lincoln (2012):

- **Recruiting and finding jobs.** These can be facilitated by direct contacts, or contacts via an intermediary.

- **Brand display.** A company's blog, display ads, and marketing communications can be displayed on Twitter. Bloggers can display their capabilities.
- **Market research.** By listening to tweets, companies can learn what customers and competitors say. Also, companies can actively participate in discussions.
- **Delivering offers.** Companies can offer promotions, coupons, and discounts to those that opt-in. For example, American Express synchronized their customers' accounts with the customers' Twitter account to provide discounts from participating merchants.
- **Collaboration.** Twitter provides for efficient collaboration within and between organizations.
- **Customer service.** As will be described in Section 7.5, Twitter can facilitate CRM and customer service.
- **Using professionals to enhance company presence on Twitter.** Twitter is used by many professionals, some of who are social commerce influencers. Companies can interact with these professionals and with active bloggers. (For details see Weber 2012.)
- **Cost effectiveness.** Interacting with customers and business partners using Twitter is very cost-effective. An example is American Apparel, which is using Twitter to solicit and discuss ideas for ads.

Example: Mercedes-Benz

According to Heine (2011), Mercedes-Benz launched a "Tweet Race" as a promotion for its commercials being aired during the 2011 Super Bowl in Dallas, Texas. While driving cross country to the Super Bowl, four teams of two people earned points for each tweet and retweet about the event. The winning prize was a Mercedes Benz. See the video of the race at **vimeo.com/22300987**).

A major success factor is the mobility of Twitter. Most people tweet from mobile devices. As a matter of fact, the majority of its advertising revenue comes from mobile devices.

Other Innovative Ways to Advertise in Social Media

A major objective of social advertising is to increase traffic to the digital and or physical sites, as described in the Starbucks opening case in Chapter 1. There are many innovative ways to do this. 3dCart (**3dcart.com**) lists the following: Advertise your Facebook store on your company's Facebook Page, place a 'Like' button linked to a customer story to your product page, and use social e-mail marketing on Facebook; advertise your store using customer stories through Twitter; advertise in videos on YouTube; use mobile apps; and social bookmarking will improve communications from your product page.

- Use a Facebook Page for your company, and add a Facebook Store. Customers will become "fans" of your business to check on updates and meet others with similar interests.
- Tweet about the business and any promotions/ new products, etc.
- Blog to your customers to keep them updated about new products, etc.
- Integrate videos (e.g., YouTube) on your website.
- Add social bookmarking to your product's page for easy return.
- Embrace mobile apps.
- Add a Facebook "Like" button with its sponsored story to your product (e.g., Gatorade brand scored 1.2 million conversations in six months using their 'Mission Control' campaign).

For details on each of the above and more, see **blog.3dcart.com/7-social-commerce-tools-to-increase-traffic**.

The Changing Rules of Branding

The December 2010 issue of *Harvard Business Review* is dedicated to the new rules of branding introduced by social media. Four articles there discuss how social networks can help you build – or destroy – your brand.

Using Blogs

Blogs are Web 2.0 tools known as being an effective means of market communication, information dissemination, recommendations, and discussions about products (including upcoming ones). For example, merchants can post ideas about new products to start a discussion and collect opinions. Blogs can be added to a company's Facebook page (or pages of other social networks) as well as to the company's in-house webstore. In addition, companies can place click-on banners on bloggers' pages.

Using Coupons

Coupons can be distributed in several ways in social commerce. One solution is to distribute coupons by deploying LBS. Once a vendor knows your location and how to e-mail or text you, targeted coupons can be sent to you. Another way is to offer coupons on a company's Facebook Offers page. This is done via *Facebook Offers*.

Facebook Offers

This feature allows companies to post coupons on their Facebook page. Fans as well as other users can "claim" the offers (click on "get offer") that come as a mobile newsfeed. Any offer that is claimed is e-mailed to the person who claimed it for printing or sharing with friends. Offers can be daily deals and other promotions.

Mobile Advertising

Mobile advertising is a rapidly developing area. It refers to advertisements on smartphones and other mobile devices. The competition for mobile ad revenue is intensifying, especially with the increased use of smartphones. Advertisers are starting to attach ads to video clips (see Chapter 9). Finally, advertisers use microblogging, especially Twitter, to reach large audiences. According to Patel (2011), a Nielsen study of iPhone users compared Apple's iAds involving Campbell Soup Company as an advertiser against similar TV ads. The researcher found that those exposed to the iAd campaigns were more than twice as likely to recall it as compared to those who had seen similar TV ads. Those who were exposed to the iAd remembered the brand and the ads three times better than the TV viewers. For details about this study, see **adage.com/article/ digital/apple-campbell-s-iads-effective-tv/ 148630**.

SECTION 7.5 REVIEW QUESTIONS

1. Describe advertising in social commerce.
2. Define social ads and social apps.
3. Define viral marketing.
4. Describe viral blogging.
5. Define geolocation and geosocial networks.
6. How does location-based advertising work?
7. Describe how Foursquare works.
8. List some concerns of LBS advertising.
9. Describe viral videos.
10. How is Twitter used for advertising?
11. Describe mobile advertising.

7.6 SOCIAL CUSTOMER SERVICE AND CRM

The customer service landscape is undergoing significant transformation. The change is reflected both in the way that customers interact with organizations and the manner in which the company's employees interact with customers. For an overview see Lacy et al. (2013).

These changes resulted from the introduction of social media and; at first, one may think that not much of a connection exists between customer service and social commerce. However, the opposite is true. In a study published by Kiron et al. (2012), managing customer relationships was found to be one of two major business challenges related to social business implementation.

How Does Social Networking Empower Customers?

It is said that one angry tweet can torpedo a brand, but one sweet tweet can correct a problem (Bernoff and Schadler 2010). According to

Sysomos Inc. (2011), more than 65% of all customers have ended a relationship with vendors due to perceived poor customer service. Let's examine how Facebook helped change a policy for one company.

Example: How Facebook's Chorus Ended the Instrument Luggage Ban at Qantas Airways of Australia

Qantas Airways had a policy that required large musical instruments to be stored in the cargo hold, which would sometimes cause damage to the instruments. In Fall 2010, after suffering $1,200 in damages to her saxophone, Jamie Oehlers of Australia organized a Facebook campaign to persuade the airline to reverse the policy. When one person complains, the company's standard response is to send the customer a letter of apology, but usually the policies does not change. However, more than 8,700 people (including members of the country's symphony orchestras) joined forces on Facebook by posting similar incidents and pictures of damaged instruments and saying they would boycott Qantas if the airline did not change their policy. Qantas announced that they listened to their customers, and in December 2010, amended the policy, by allowing any instrument in a hard-shelled case on board, provided it falls within the airline's length and weight restrictions (based on a news item from Staff Writers 2010 and the *Taipei Times* 2011). Alternatively, one may purchase a seat for a large instrument and carry it as a bulky item. (For information about Qantas's new policy, see **qantas.com.au/travel/ airlines/carry-on-baggage/global/en**.

This story is not unique; similar stories appear in the media frequently. A well-known case is "United Breaks Guitars," which also is published in a book and a video that has been watched by over 14 million people as of November 2014, see **youtube.com/watch?v=5YGc4zOqozo**. In another example Olson (2009), reported that Maytag (appliances) only paid attention to a particular customer after she tweeted to her 10,000 followers about her nightmare experience with the company. Within a day, her problem was solved. In the past, customer complaints usually received little or no attention, even when customers threatened to publish their complaint on the Internet. But today, when you say, "I will organize a campaign against you on Facebook or Twitter," you can be sure that someone will pay attention. An empowered customer is a major driver of social CRM.

Social CRM

Customer relationship management (CRM) is a customer service approach that focuses on building long-term and sustainable customer relationships that adds value for both the customers and the merchants. When delivered online, it is referred to as e-CRM (Online Tutorial T1). A major area of e-CRM is social CRM.

Definition

According to Roebuck (2011), **social customer relationship management (SCRM)** (also known as **CRM 2.0**) is CRM supported by social media (e.g., Web 2.0 tools, social network sites), which are designed to engage the customer in conversations, sharing, and other interactions in order to provide benefits to all participants and increase trust. SCRM is based on social media, in support of companies' stated goals and objectives of optimizing the customer's experience, and building trust and loyalty. Success requires considering people, business processes, and technology associated with the interactions between customers and enterprises. Like CRM, a major goal of SCRM is building trust and brand loyalty (see Huba 2013).

SCRM is an extension of CRM, not a replacement. It adds two dimensions: social media and people. It is designed to engage customers in conversations using social media tools. An important goal of SCRM is to add benefits to the sellers (e.g., increased trust, loyalty, and sales from their customers) and to the customers (e.g., better, quicker service; more engagement; product improvements). SCRM is the segment of business strategy that addresses the issue of how companies adapt to the *social customers* and their expectations regarding the companies with which

they conduct business. SCRM evolved from CRM (and e-CRM). For a detailed presentation of this process and an overview of social CRM, download the free e-book by Fagan (2014). For comprehensive coverage of social CRM, see Fagan (2014), Roebuck (2011), and Lacy et al. (2013).

The Components of Social CRM

The major elements and characteristics of SCRM are shown in Figure 7.4. As the figure illustrates, these characteristics are the foundations of a social customer who is driven by social networking. The social customer's needs are different from those of the customer who does not use social media. Social customers, for example, want to communicate with vendors by using the Internet (e.g., see Metz 2011). This communication is provided by social media, which is the major element of social CRM. The social environment is also a major element of social CRM, since it is the source of interactions with the social customer.

How to Serve the Social Customers

Empowered customers are referred to as **social customers**. These are customers who usually are members in social networks, do social shopping, and understand their shopper's rights and how to use them to their advantage. Social customers select the mode of interaction with companies. These customers are influenced by friends, mavens, and family. Merchants must understand how social customers differ from conventional customers, and provide them with socially-based customer service.

Methods and Guidelines for Social Customer Service

How does a company serve the social media customer?

Companies are looking for an answer to this question not only because they are afraid of the negative comments posted by social network members, but also because they see an opportunity to involve customers in providing feedback

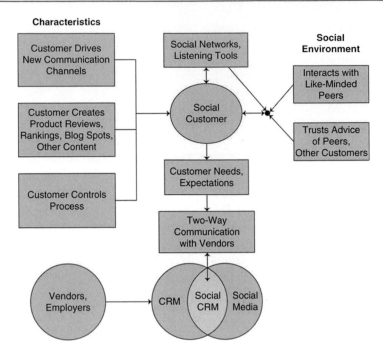

Figure 7.4 The elements of social CRM

and ideas on how to improve customer service and operations (Parature 2014). Furthermore, companies can solicit feedback from customers to improve customer loyalty and make their own customer service people more satisfied at work. For how this is done, see Parature (2014), Fagan (2014), Bernoff and Schadler (2010), and **mashable.com/2012/09/29/social-media-better-customer-service**. Procedures, guidelines, and software are available for social CRM.

The Benefits of Social CRM

This new breed of social customers places new demands on organizations. However, social media tools meet these demands nicely, usually at a low cost (except for staff time). Social media provides for engagement and collaboration that eventually results in a competitive advantage to the organization if implemented properly.

Social CRM offers the following potential benefits to customers ("c") and enterprise ("e"):

(Note: Several of these are illustrated in Case 7.2 (iRobot, presented later in this chapter). These benefits to iRobot are marked with an [I].)

- Drives quick resolution of customers' problems (c)
- Provides for effective and efficient business-customer collaboration (c), (e)
- Improves the reputation of companies (e), (I)
- Provides better understanding of customer needs and wants (e)
- Provides focused, intuitive, and easy-to-use CRM applications (e)
- Provides better marketing, better targeting, and improved products/services due to customers' creation of content, and WOM (e)
- Provides customer input for market research at a quicker rate and at a low cost for improving products and customer service (e)

- Provides customers with more information about products/services quickly (c), (I)
- Increases trust and loyalty (e)
- Provides a more complete view of the customer than what traditional CRM can provide (e)
- Decreases overall customer care costs (e.g., through self-helping communities) (e)
- Enables salespeople to find sales leads quickly and easily (e)
- Develops new revenue opportunities and turns new customers into repeat customers (c)
- Increases CRM staff productivity by teaching them to use analytics and collaboration 2.0 techniques (e)
- Improves employee performance by benefiting from knowledge sharing gained in social networks (e)
- Improves customer satisfaction by providing them with opportunities for engagement using social media platforms (c), (I)
- Converts leads to opportunities with more effective campaigns (e)

Petersen (2011) illustrates the benefits of social CRM in 16 case studies.

An article by Tiffany Brown (at **tiffanyabrown.wordpress.com/2011/10/26/social-CRM-as-a-holistic-marketing-tool**) includes a video which shows the essential elements of the SCRM process.

For additional benefits, see Fagan (2014), Shih (2011), and Ziff Davis (2012).

CASE 7.2: IROBOT USES SOCIAL MEDIA FOR MULTICHANNEL CRM

iRobot (**irobot.com**), which was founded in 1990 by three roboticists at MIT with the vision of making practical robots a reality, designs and builds some of the world's most important robots. According to their website, in 2013, iRobot gener-

ated $487 million in revenue and employed more than 500 of the robot industry's top professionals, including mechanical, electrical, and software engineers and related support staff. iRobot makes robots for the government, defense and security, military and civil defense forces worldwide, commercial applications, industry, and home use. The public is mostly familiar with the Roomba vacuuming robot (see Dignan 2013). Due to the technical nature of its products, the company's customers may require specialized support and service. On their customer care website, the company provides self-diagnosis, support videos, live chat, product FAQs go to 'customer help' and (type in a problem and receive automatic answers), and more (e.g., see **homesupport.irobot.com/app/answers/list/session/L3RpbWUvMTQwMDQzNjk4NS9zaWQvODJsX1ZBVWw%3D**). However, there are home market customers who may need more technical assistance since many are new at using robots. The company's objective is to expand the sale of home market products. Therefore, they must provide extensive assistance to inexperienced customers. The company supports a community and provides discussion boards, community search capability, and live chat.

Social CRM: Serve the Customers While Learning from Them

iRobot utilizes a CRM system with the help of Oracle RightNow Inc. (see Oracle Service Cloud at **oracle.com/us/products/applications/rightnow/overview/index.html**). The system enables customers to contact iRobot's service group via several different communication channels, including e-mail, live chat, social networks, and Web self-service. This way, iRobot can respond to any online customer communication in a timely manner, regardless of the channel used. All this needs to be done at a low cost; therefore, it is necessary to automate the services.

Specific Social Media Activities
iRobot customers can post service and support requests or complaints on **homesupport. irobot.com** or they can contact the help desk.

The company monitors these messages and tries to provide immediate responses. iRobot tries to find the identity of the customers that have problems by monitoring relevant conversations in the various social channels (e.g., in forums on social networks). Once identified, iRobot communicates with the customers privately to resolve the issues.

The social media-oriented activities are integrated with documents and videos in a knowledge base managed by RightNow. The company uses RightNow's monitoring tools to identify the customers who post the comments. Some customers may provide their real names. Anonymous customers are encouraged to contact iRobot directly. For how the company listens to social media, see **informationweek.com/software/social/roomba-robots-listen-to-social-media/d/d-id/1100404?**.

Responding to issues quickly is important because, as discussed earlier, customers can attract a considerable amount of attention using YouTube or Twitter (the company runs promotions, such as giveaways and games on Twitter), to publicize their complaints. In addition to problem resolution, the company gets valuable feedback from the customers so it can improve its products and services.

By 2013, iRobot achieved a 97% Web service rating, realized a 30% reduction in customer phone calls, and provided improved customer service at a 20% reduced cost.

iRobot has a presence on Facebook, Twitter, Pinterest, YouTube, and Tumblr. The company uses these sites to disseminate information and collect customer feedback and complaints.

Note: The social media activities supplemented the regular customer care activities. This is an example of multichannel services. In such a case, integration of the different types of care is necessary.

Sources: Based on Carr (2011), RightNow Technologies (2010), Dignan (2013), Oracle (2011), and **irobot.com** (accessed November 2014).

Questions
1. What is meant by the term *multichannel service support*? What is the benefit of multichanneling?
2. What are the activities related to social media at iRobot? What are their benefits?
3. Describe how the company listens to their customers' complaints, and how they resolve the problems.

The Evolution of Social CRM

Now that you have a basic understanding of CRM, e-CRM, and SCRM, we can look at the evolution of SCRM as well as some differences between SCRM and e-CRM. SCRM can be viewed as an extension of e-CRM. Most e-CRM software companies, such as Salesforce Inc. (**salesforce.com**), offer social media features in their products. However, there are some significant differences between e-CRM and SCRM. These differences can be seen at **slideshare.net/JatinKalra/e-crm-112520123741** and Cipriani's presentation (2008).

Cipriani's Multidimensional Presentation

Fabio Cipriani (2008) outlines the difference between CRM and SCRM (referred to as CRM 1.0 and CRM 2.0) along several dimensions. Figures 7.5, 7.6, 7.7, and 7.8 show some of these dimensions: landscape, customer touch points, business processing modeling, technology, and organizational mindset.

The Landscape
The landscape describes the difference between CRM 1.0 and CRM 2.0 in the structure, focus, relationship with the community, and value creation, as illustrated in Figure 7.5.

Notice that in CRM 2.0, the community is larger than in CRM, and it includes interconnections among the customers that were not present online in the early days of CRM.

Touch Points
The term *touch point* refers to any point of interaction a customer has with a brand or seller. Some points are company initiated (e.g., advertising or

CRM 1.0

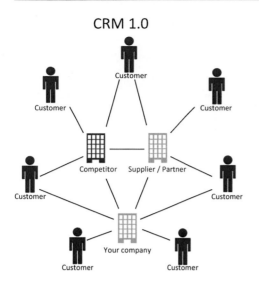

- Focus on individual relationship (company to customer, company to partner, etc.)
- Limited view of the customer and his community preferences, habits, etc.
- Targeted messages generate value

Figure 7.5 The landscape of CRM versus SCRM (**Source**: Courtesy of F. Cipriani, "Social CRM: Concept, Benefits, and Approach to Adopt," November 2008. **slide-**

CRM 2.0

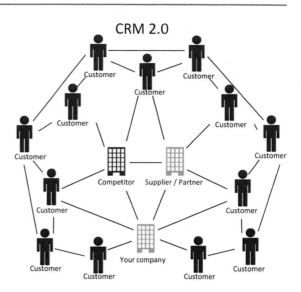

- Focus on collaborative relationship (engaging a more complex relationship network)
- Multiple connections allow better understanding of the customer and his community
- Conversation generates value

share.net/fhcipriani/social-crm-presentation-761225 (accessed November 2014). Used with permission)

CRM 1.0

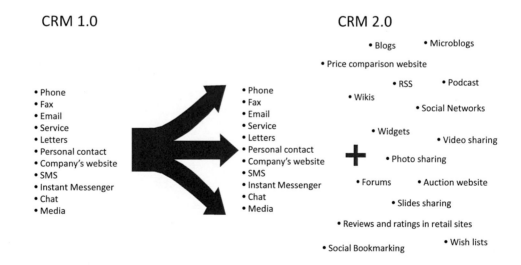

- Phone
- Fax
- Email
- Service
- Letters
- Personal contact
- Company's website
- SMS
- Instant Messenger
- Chat
- Media

CRM 2.0

- Phone
- Fax
- Email
- Service
- Letters
- Personal contact
- Company's website
- SMS
- Instant Messenger
- Chat
- Media

- Blogs
- Microblogs
- Price comparison website
- RSS
- Podcast
- Wikis
- Social Networks
- Widgets
- Video sharing
- Photo sharing
- Forums
- Auction website
- Slides sharing
- Reviews and ratings in retail sites
- Social Bookmarking
- Wish lists

- Single view of the customer based on the interactions history, customer profile data residing in the company's base and data integration with internal systems
- Company owns the data but it is limited to previous interactions

- Single view of the customer is far more complex to achieve. Besides internal information, the company must rely on external information such as customer profiles in social networks and his behavior when participating in a community.
- Customer and other web 2.0 sites own part of the precious data

Figure 7.6 Touch points in CRM versus SCRM (**Source**: Courtesy of F. Cipriani, "Social CRM: Concept, Benefits, and Approach to Adopt," November 2008. **slideshare.**

net/fhcipriani/social-crm-presentation-761225 (accessed November 2014). Used with permission)

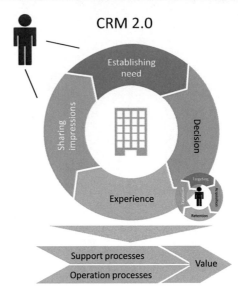

- Customer processes developed from the company standpoint (customer life cycle for the company)
- Process centric – adapt and optimize processes to support better customer interaction
- Focused on CRM processes

- Company processes developed from the customer standpoint (company life cycle for the customer)
- Conversation centric – include the conversation factor to establish brand community, enable idea capturing and better segmentation
- Focused on the evolution of CRM processes and resulting impacts in the value chain

Figure 7.7 The evolution of business processes in SCRM (**Source**: Courtesy of F. Cipriani, "Social CRM: Concept, Benefits, and Approach to Adopt," November 2008. **slideshare.net/fhcipriani/social-crm-presentation-761225** (accessed November 2014). Used with permission)

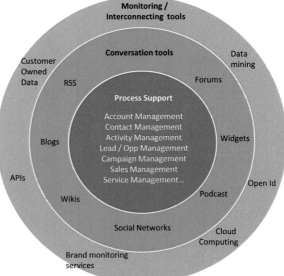

- CRM Solutions focused in automating and supporting internal business processes

- CRM Solutions focused in community creation internal and externally

Figure 7.8 The evolution of technology from CRM to SCRM (**Source**: Courtesy of F. Cipriani, "Social CRM: Concept, Benefits, and Approach to Adopt," November 2008. **slideshare.net/fhcipriani/social-crm-presentation-761225** (accessed November 2014). Used with permission)

e-mail interactions) and others are out of the company's control, such as word-of-mouth. CRM 2.0 adds additional touch points, as shown in Figure 7.6 (all the Web 1.0 tools + Web 2.0 tools). We can add crowdsourcing to this list.

Example: Get Satisfaction for CRM

Get Satisfaction (**getsatisfaction.com**) is a platform where customers can interact with one another and voice their opinions and complaints. Using a forum, they can quickly get resolutions to their problems. Each community is organized around four topics:

1. **Ask a question**. Customers can answer one another's questions.
2. **Share an idea**. Aggregated feedback is provided from customers (by topic, product, vendor).
3. **Report a problem**. Search to see if anyone posted a similar problem. Post yours.
4. **Give praise**. Customers can praise a product or vendor.

Get Satisfaction provides information on the customers' conversations to interested vendors at no charge.

For an example of a Get Satisfaction Support Community, see **getsatisfaction.com/ safarichallenge**.

Evolution of Business Processes in CRM

Traditional CRM was a part of a linear process that started with marketing that led to sales and then was followed by customer service (if needed). In CRM 2.0, the process starts with listening to customers' needs based on social media conversations rather than only on traditional market research through quantitative surveys or small scale qualitative research. The objective is to generate value for both the customer and the company. This difference is illustrated in Figure 7.7.

The Evolution of Technology

Traditional e-CRM focused on automating and supporting the internal business processes that relate to customer service. In CRM 2.0, an attempt is made to provide this same process support, but it is based on community creation and on improved interactions among customers and between vendors and customers, as illustrated in Figure 7.8.

Organizational Mindset

In CRM 1.0, there is a dialog between one customer service employee and one customer, or between a sales support team and one customer. Most interactions are routine, with limited innovations. In CRM 2.0, as shown in Figure 7.9, interactions occur among all employees (as in the Sony opening case) and several customers who also interact with each other (as in the iRobot case). This environment facilitates innovation and increases customer satisfaction.

Conclusions

Incorporating the previous five areas requires empowering the employees, which means that a new set of employee skills is needed. For a long time, marketers have said that everything starts with the needs of consumers. With social CRM and all the social media product discussions, marketers must now learn how to incorporate this philosophy in their strategies.

Implementation of Social Customer Service and CRM

There are several models and methods for implementing social customer service. First let us look at what Safeway is doing in this area.

Example: How Safeway Provides Social Customer Service

Safeway, a large grocery chain, has a virtual customer club. Members can get in-store discounts as well as e-mails with coupons and a description of what is on sale. An online newsletter with health news and recipes, shopping tips, etc. is also available to members. To extend this service, Safeway invites their customers to become Safeway Fans on Facebook and follow the company on Twitter. This allows customers/members to know about exclusive promotions. Also, members can connect and share information with other Safeway shoppers.

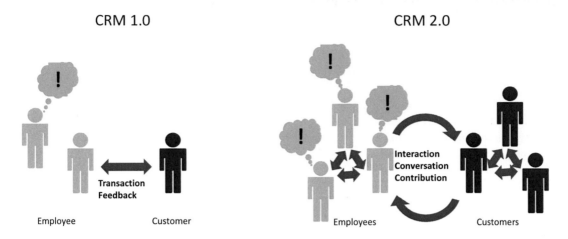

Figure 7.9 The organizational mindset for SCRM (**Source**: Courtesy of F. Cipriani, "Social CRM: Concept, Benefits, and Approach to Adopt," November 2008. **slide-share.net/fhcipriani/social-crm-presentation-761225** (accessed November 2014). Used with permission)

In their 'Just for U' program, shoppers can get digital coupons and personalized deals when they click on a certain coupon, say for milk; then, when they buy milk they get a 10–20% discount. There is no need to clip coupons anymore. For more information **safeway.com/ShopStores/Justforu-FAQ.page**.

Additionally, customers can visit the company's blog, *Today at Safeway!*, where the company's team members post items from Floral, Bakery, and other departments throughout the store. Safeway's experts also publish information about nutrition, environmental sustainability, and more. Members of the virtual customer club can comment on the blog and are asked to post original content only.

Some Recent Applications

There are many advanced applications to better serve customers.

Example: How Best Buy Uses Twitter to Provide Real-Time Customer Service

Best Buy is a large appliances retailer. The company uses their Twitter account @twelpforce to interact with customers.

Best Buy empowered its technical support service (called Geek Squad) and other corporate employees (total 4,000 participants). There, any employee who finds a relevant tweeted question can answer the customer. The answers are visible on the website, allowing other employees to add information.

For additional examples, see **thesocialcustomer.com/sites/thesocialcustomer.com/files/TheSocialContract.pdf**.

Social Networking Helps Customer Service in Small Companies

Most of the examples provided so far have dealt with large companies. What about the small ones? Obviously, there are some applications the

SMEs cannot afford. But many other applications can be deployed.

Example

Teusner Wines (**teusner.com.au**) is a small 3-person boutique winery in Australia. Using Twitter, the company's one-person marketing department:

- Initiates online conversations about wine with influential people in the wine industry.
- Sends tweets to people he finds talking online (e.g., in communities) about Teusner Wines, praising them for trying the wines.
- Starts to build trust with customers via online conversations.
- Invites people to tour the winery and taste the wines.
- Advises potential customers in the United States and Canada where they can buy the Australian wine.
- Monitors real-time online feedback from customers.
- Encourages customer-to-customer social media conversations.
- Posts customer reviews using Twitter.
- Shares all information with Twitter followers.

All this is done in a tiny company at virtually no cost. For details, see **dottedlinecollaborations. com/social-media/case-study-using-twitter-attract-new-customers**.

For large companies, it is necessary to integrate marketing, customer services, and social networks.

Reputation Management System

Not all postings in social networks are positive. The problem is what companies do when they see negative comments (see Christman 2014 for an overview). According to Carr (2010), when you create a Facebook business page, you may see negative posts by disgruntled customers or unethical competitors.

Companies cannot block people from posting negative comments on social platforms, including Facebook pages. If a company blocks such postings, it eliminates the potential positive comments from its fans, losing the positive WOM and customer feedback. If companies delete posts, the poster and others may retaliate. A possible solution for reputation management is to design the space for comments in a way that encourages positive ones. According to Dellarocas (2010) and Carr (2010), reputation systems should:

- Build trust in the sellers.
- Promote quality of the products and services.
- Sustain loyalty.

For comprehensive coverage, see Dellarocas (2010), Beal and Strauss (2008), and **reputation-institute.com**.

SECTION 7.9 REVIEW QUESTIONS

1. Define the social customer and describe their characteristics. (Consult Chapter 1.)
2. Why and how are customers empowered by social networks?
3. Define social CRM.
4. What are the needs of social customers?
5. List 5 to 8 benefits of social CRM.
6. How does social CRM differ from traditional CRM?
7. Describe a reputation management system.

MANAGERIAL ISSUES

Some managerial issues related to this chapter are as follows.

1. **How will social commerce influence businesses?** The impacts of social marketing can change the manner in which many shoppers make purchasing decisions. Social commerce will change both B2B and B2C by increasing interactions, engagement, and collaboration. The impact will change business processes, the manner in which companies treat customers and employees, and may even restructure some organizations. A strong impact will be felt in advertising, viral

marketing, collaboration, and brand recognition. The impact will also be strong on delivering customer service, conducting market research, and organizing collaboration.

2. **Do companies need to sponsor a social network?** Although sponsoring a social network might sound like a good idea, it may not be simple to execute. Community members need services, which cost money to provide. The most difficult task is to find an existing community that matches your business. In many cases, the cost of a social network may be justified by its contribution to advertising. However, social network service providers need to create various revenue models to maintain sustainable services. Creating revenue is the most challenging issue to social network service providers.

3. **Is it wise for a small business to be on Facebook?** The answer depends on the business and on what you are trying to achieve. It could be helpful for those that need to constantly reach customers and/or suppliers. Facebook, at present, may not be very helpful for direct sales. However, just having a presence costs little and therefore should be considered. A major issue for SMBs is the loose security in social networks. See **entrepreneur.com/article/239539** for comprehensive coverage of this topic.

4. **How to deal with false reviews and fake followers?** Unfortunately, there are many fake followers. Some are paid by companies to boost their image; others are paid by competitors. It is possible to use software to detect some fake accounts. These fictitious data can mislead companies when deciding, for example, where to advertise. This is issue is discussed in Chapter 8.

5. **Should we embark on selling via social networking?** For most cases the answer would be yes. Just view it as an additional channel to increase sales. Which model to use will depend on the product, the competition, and the potential risks. See Chapter 13 for strategy and Chapter 14 for implementation.

SUMMARY

In this chapter, you learned about the following EC issues as they related to the chapter's learning objectives.

1. **Social commerce definition and evolution.** Social commerce (SC) refers to conducting EC in the social media environment. It can be viewed as a subset of EC where activities are done in social networks and by using social media tools. It operates at the intersection of social media, EC, e-marketing, and supporting theories from several disciplines including social psychology, marketing, sociology, and information technology. SC is able to add value to the performance of organizations while at the same time increasing the satisfaction and added value to individuals. Social commerce's main activities and content are in the areas of social media marketing, social enterprise, and social games and entertainment.

2. **The scope, content, and drivers of social commerce.** Social commerce is a comprehensive field comprised mostly of social media marketing (advertising, market research, and customer service) and social enterprise (problem solving, recruiting, and collaboration). It also includes social entertainment, social games, and crowdsourcing. Social commerce is driven by the existence of giant social networks, Web 2.0 tools, and the emergence of social customers.

   The major models are: group buy, which is frequently combined with daily deals; providing reviews, recommendations, ratings, and conversations; shopping clubs and communities; location-based shopping; peer-to-peer trading and shopping using the support of Twitter. Groupon, Pinterest, Gilt, Kaboodle, and hundreds of other start-ups are active participants. Competition is getting strong, and success is visible mostly in Facebook, Tripadvisor, and Pinterest.

3. **Benefits and limitations of social commerce.** A large number of benefits are available for

customers, retailers, and other businesses. Customers can get better prices, improve customer service, and also receive social support (e.g., product recommendations) from friends. They can find new friends as well, and establish new contacts. Retailers can reach more customers, get quick feedback, improve relationships with customers, go global, and use free word-of-mouth marketing communication. There are also benefits to businesses. Businesses can conduct fast and inexpensive market research, recruit employees from all over the globe, innovate, collaborate, and locate experts when needed. Companies can receive help from other companies, sometimes with little or no cost. The major limitations are security, privacy, and changing user attitudes issues.

4. **Describe social shopping.** Social shopping refers to online shopping that is supported by social media and involves friends and online social media communities. The major drivers are the large number of people who are engaged in social networking, reliance on friends' recommendations, the potential of receiving large discounts for the buyers, the increase of sales volume for the sellers, the socially-oriented shopping models, and the rise of the social customer. The major models are group buying, daily flash sales, use of social communities and clubs, and the application of shopping aids such as reviews and recommendations.

5. **How advertisements and promotions are conducted in social networking.** The major driver of SC is the money spent by advertisers who see a huge potential market. Advertising can be done in many ways. Using word of mouth is almost free for companies, but it can be dangerous (e.g., negative comments). The use of banner ads and other paid advertisement and social search models generate billions for social networks (mostly to Google and Facebook). Large numbers of advertising apps exist. Also, bloggers can provide positive (but sometime negative) comments. LBS combines geolocation with advertisements and coupons (delivered in the right time and place). Many companies have developed special campaigns that engage community members in advertising-related activities (play games, vote, generate ideas, etc.). In addition, advertising on Pinterest, Twitter, and YouTube is becoming popular.

6. **Conducting social customer service and CRM.** When the CRM platform involves social media (e.g., Web 2.0 tools and social network sites), CRM is referred to as social CRM (SCRM). SCRM provides many benefits for customers, vendors, and public institutions that include an improved relationship between the empowered customers and the vendors, and service providers as well as providing better service to customers. The evolution to SCRM can be described along the following five dimensions: The landscape (e.g., structure and focus); the touch points (e.g., the use of social media tools); business processes (e.g., how to listen to customers); the technology (e.g., socially oriented tools); and the organizational mindset (e.g., patterns of interactions). This evolution is driven by the explosive use of social network sites, the rise of the social customer, and the importance buyers place on social recommendations. Customers are empowered by social networks so they can get attention quickly for problem resolution. Organizing a Facebook complaint blitz is not difficult. Customers can make suggestions for improvements and vote on them. Letting customers help themselves and each other is offered via social networking while reducing merchant expenses. Customers can become more loyal because they work closer with vendors. Social networking provides innovative ideas for improved and timely customer service (e.g., Twitter can be very helpful).

KEY TERMS

Business model
Communal shopping
Customer relationship management (CRM)

Enterprise 2.0
Geosocial networking
Social business
Social commerce (SC)
Social customer
Social customer relationship
management (SCRM; CRM 2.0)
Social marketplace
Social media marketing (SMM)
Social shopping
Viral blogging
Viral marketing
Viral video
Virtual economy
Virtual goods

DISCUSSION QUESTIONS

1. Compare social computing to traditional computing.
2. Discuss the social element in social media.
3. Discuss the contribution of social commerce to e-commerce.
4. Compare Polyvore to Pinterest.
5. Discuss the reasons why people buy virtual goods.
6. Discuss how traditional online vendors can add social networking capabilities to their sites.
7. Under what circumstances would you trust an expert's recommendation rather than a friend's?
8. How can marketers use social networks for viral marketing?
9. Why are advertisers so interested in social networks?
10. View the slide show "Altimeter Report: The 18 Use Cases of Social CRM, The New Rules of Relationship Management" by Owyang (2010) at **web-strategist.com/ blog/2010/03/05/altimeter-report-the-18-use-cases-of-social-crm-the-new-rules-of-relationship-management**. Discuss the major attributes of CRM. What are the major improvements since 2010?
11. Discuss the shortcomings of user generated reviews and recommendations.

TOPICS FOR CLASS DISCUSSION AND DEBATES

1. Debate the privacy dangers to social shoppers.
2. Debate: "Is the social media influence on purchasing overrated?" Start by viewing the slideshow titled "Social Media Influence on Purchase Overrated" (McCafferty 2011) at **baselinemag.com/c/a/Intelligence/Social-Media-Influence-On-Purchasing-Overrated-660095**.
3. Debate: One day all e-commerce will be social.
4. Daily deals are being offered today by many offline and online retailers and other organizations (e.g., newspapers). Only on the Internet are these offers common. Is there a need for intermediaries? Debate.
5. Discuss how trust is affected in social shopping. (Consult: Bazaarvoice.com).
6. Why do you think that Wanelo is popular?
7. Examine Facebook Offers. What is the potential of the viral service? What is the advantage of mobile newsfeeds? Explain the competition with Living Social.
8. Discuss Cipriani's five dimensions of social CRM.
9. Debate the viability of companies such as Groupon. Begin by reading the Amazon.com description. Also see Srinivasan's (2011) "To Group Coupon or Not?"
10. Clinique has a comprehensive customer service platform. They offer e-mail, phone service, and live chat. The live chat platform **clinique.com/customer_service/chatlivenow. tmpl** has regular live chat, live chat with your photo, and face-to-face live chat using webcam and speakers. Describe the multichannel service support concept. Comment on the different methods used.

INTERNET EXERCISES

1. Enter **smartmobs.com**. Go to the blogroll. Find three blogs related to social commerce, and summarize their major features.

2. Enter **thisnext.com**. What are the features of the site? What do you like? Dislike?

3. Enter **salesforce.com** and identify all SCRM activities supported by the company, especially those related to their Chatter product. View the slide show at: **slideshare.net/Salesforce/salesforce-customer-service best-practices-25640141**. Write a report.

4. Enter **salesforce.com/dreamforce/DF14**. Find topics that deal with SCRM. Write a summary.

5. Enter **bazaarvoice.com**. Summarize its major services. Examine SocialConnect.

6. Enter **thisnext.com**. What are the features of the site? What do you like? Dislike? Why?

7. Enter **tkg.com/social-media-marketing**. Prepare a list of information you can get there about social shopping.

8. Enter **select2gether.com**. What services can you get from this site?

9. Enter **kaboodle.com**. What are the major benefits can you derive from being a member there?

10. Enter **bristoleditor.co.uk** and find guidelines related to ethical and etiquette issues in social shopping.

11. Enter **powerreviews.com**. Compare their activities to those of similar sites.

12. Enter **deal-of-the-day-review.toptenreviews.com**, and summarize the lesson learned.

13. Enter **socialshoppingnetwork.org**. Find material related to this chapter. Write a report.

TEAM ASSIGNMENTS AND PROJECTS

1. **Assignment for the Opening Case**
   (a) What social media tools and platforms does Sony use?
   (b) How does each tool facilitate customer service?
   (c) What are the major benefits of social CRM to Sony?
   (d) Relate Sony's use of Pinterest to social CRM. (Start by entering **community. sony.com**.)
   (e) Find CRM-related activities. Summarize.
   (f) Go to Sony's community and ask a question. Get results. Summarize four experiences.

2. Facebook is increasingly offering marketing tools (e.g., Open Graph, Social Plug-ins). Identify all the tools offered. Each group concentrates on the business implications in one of the following areas: advertising and search engine optimization (SEO), shopping, market research, customer service, CRM, and others. Make a class presentation.

3. Each group adopts one or two of the following companies that actively advertise and engage on Facebook and Twitter: Coca-Cola, Starbucks, Ford, Pepsi, Levi's, Disney, Victoria's Secret, iTunes, Toyota, Sony, or P&G. Find and summarize what advertising methods they use and how they do their campaigns.

4. The class will investigate group buying in China and India. What is the prospect for group buying in Asia? (Start with Madden's article "China Pioneers Group Buying Discounts Without Groupon" at **adage.com/article/global-news/advertising-china-group-buying-discounts-groupon/147641**. Also check WoWo Ltd. in China.

5. Search for a group in a social network site or a community that is interested in social CRM. Join the group. Follow the discussions for one month. Each group member concentrates on one topic from this chapter and interacts with the group about this topic. Each member prepares a report, and the group gives a summary presentation for the class.

6. Shopping communities for fashion are exploding on the Internet. Make a list of the major sites (e.g., Polyvore, ShopStyle, Pinterest, My It Things, etc.). Investigate their activities and list their competitive advantage. Why is this industry a prime setting for social communities? How are they related to Facebook and Twitter? What are their business and revenue models? Write a summary report.

CLOSING CASE: GROUPON: WILL THE COMPANY PROSPER?

The name Groupon is a combination of *group* and *coupon*. Groupon was founded in November 2008 and has been considered the fastest-growing company ever by 2012 (in terms of sales). Initially, Groupon offered both *group buying* and *deal of the day* (one highly discounted deal per day) in selected metro areas in the United States. As of 2014, Groupon serves 500 markets worldwide, in 48 countries. According to Groupon's Q3 2014 financial report, the number of customers, that have purchased a Groupon deal within the last twelve months, grew by 25% year-over-year, to 53.5 million by September 30, 2013, with about 50% in North America, and the rest are all over the world. (See **grouponworks.com/merchant-resources/FAQs**). For statistics and facts about Groupon, see (**statista.com/topics/824/groupon**).

The Opportunity

Groupon is a start-up that offers special highly discounted deals, mostly via e-mail. The idea is that when subscribers hear about a big discount, they will forward the news to friends who may also place an order (the 'social' element). Initially, the more buyers who joined in the sale, creating a group buy, the larger the discount. However, this model has been changed as will be described next.

The Solution

To exploit the opportunity, Groupon developed a unique business model.

The Initial Business Model and the Strategy
According to Groupon (**groupon.com**), the company offers special sales, called "Groupons," in each city that the company serves. The advertised deal lasts for a limited time (usually between 24 and 72 hours) and becomes available to all registered members. According to Groupon's customer service department, in the past, Groupon's policy was to guarantee participating merchants a certain number of sales. In other words, the customer would only get the discount if enough people (hence, the "group" element) purchased that particular Groupon. If Groupon did not meet that promised quota, there was no need for the seller to honor the deal, nor was any commission paid to Groupon, and the customer was not charged.

Groupon charges advertising and promotions fees, usually a percentage of the revenue generated by the sellers. The retailers can use the system to promote their business, gain new customers, and run sales during their slow seasons (e.g., running a promotion such as liquidation during the late summer). The initial process, a combination of *group buys* and *flash deal models*, is illustrated in Figure 7.10. Today, it is basically a flash (daily) deal. The reason merchants are willing to offer a 50–80% discount to volume shoppers is that the merchants' marketing and overhead costs are lower, while their market share is increased.

Groupon's business strategy is to work with quality merchants who are willing to provide substantial discounts. Groupon uses both traditional e-mail and social networking (e.g., Facebook, Twitter, Pinterest, etc.) to promote the deals. Deals are e-mailed directly to members when available, but those interested in current daily deals can go to the Groupon website (Groupon Goods; **groupon.com/goods**). Groupon offers a "refer a friend" program, where the shopper can earn $10 for every friend they refer who buys their first deal (see **groupon.com/referral**).

Benefits and Expansion
The major benefits to customers are:

- Steep discounts (50–80%)
- Discovery of new/specialized services and products
- Deals related to the daily offer are presented by Groupon
- Useful recommendations provided to family and friends

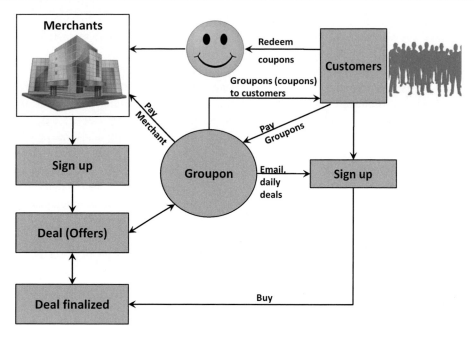

Figure 7.10 The business model and process of Groupon

The major benefits to merchants are:

- Can sell larger quantities and liquidate merchandise, quickly
- Save on advertising and marketing expenses (e.g., by using viral advertising)
- Get repeat customers (if they like the deal and the service, customers will come back)
- Lower customer acquisition cost
- Knowledge of and collaboration with vendors in a close geographical area

Limitations of the Model

Smaller vendors may not be able to fulfill large orders generated by Groupon. For example, according to Crum (2011), a restaurant in Tokyo, sold 500 Groupons for a traditional New Year's dinner, but the business was unable to process the orders in a timely fashion due to the overwhelming demand of the orders. Apparently, some of Groupon's deals became too large for vendors to fulfill, and customers complained about late deliveries and about orders arriving "in terrible conditions." A similar problem occurred in India when a high demand for onions caused the Groupon website to crash (see AOL On News 2013).

In response to such a problem, Groupon officials have created formulas to help vendors it partners with to determine how to meet consumer demand, and how many coupons to offer (capped the orders to a reasonable number).

Another limitation is that some businesses may not make money on the deal and may possibly even suffer a loss (e.g., see Phibbs 2011). Finally, although Groupon and similar companies can generate large revenues, they may have large expenses as a result, and actually lose money by offering more deals. Thus, the profitability of the model is questioned by many especially in light of the strong competition.

Groupon is attempting to become more than just a deal of the day business. As part of their branching out, in November 2013, Groupon opened an e-commerce "marketplace" (online retail site), known as Groupon Goods (**groupon.com/goods**), which focuses on slightly discounted products. These deals also have a time limit (ranging from 3 to 7 days). In Q2 of 2013, less than 40% of Groupon's

North America revenue came from the company's daily deal e-mails, suggesting the marketplace store (with over 60% of revenue) is getting to be successful. (See **usatoday.com/story/tech/2013/11/01/group- on-new-website-marketplace/3319943**).

In 2011, Groupon partnered with Expedia (**expedia.com**) to launch Groupon Getaways (**groupon.com/getaways**), which focuses on discounted travel (hotels, tours, etc).

Groupon also has a program called Groupon "Reserve" (**groupon.com/reserve**), where participating restaurants give diners discounts when they have empty tables. Unlike the usual daily deal where you buy a voucher, with Groupon Reserve, you make a reservation online and show up.

In March 2013, 45% of North American transactions were completed on mobile devices (see **groupon.com/mobile**), compared with nearly 30% in March 2012.

The Competition

As with any successful business, there are many companies that are attempting to clone Groupon. There are hundreds of Groupon clones (between 400 and 600 in the U.S. as of 2011, depending on the source), and that number is growing. Worldwide, there are thousands of similar sites. For example, there were over 1,000 similar companies in China alone, but many did not succeed. (For more about the top 10 daily deal sites in China as of 2013, see: **thenextweb.com/asia/2013/02/18/chinas-daily-deal-market-consolidates-as-top-10-sites-claim-90-revenue-share-report**.) Nevertheless, as of November 2013, Groupon's only *serious competitor* is LivingSocial (**livingsocial.com**), sponsored by Amazon.com, with competition from Google emerging. Google Offers (**google.com/offers**) which is available on Google+. Other notable competitors include Gilt City (**giltcity.com**), Gilt Groupe (**gilt.com**), Woot! (**woot.com**; an independent subsidiary of Amazon), HomeRun (**homerun.com**; available nationally and in limited cities along with 3 European countries). Yipit (**yipit.com**) is an e-mail-based "daily deal aggregator" that gathers deals (in your city) on products from daily deal sites such as Groupon. Tell Yipit what you want, and they

will alert you when there are deals that match. Groupon still controls more than 50% of all daily deals in the U.S.

Possible future competitors include Yahoo!, Amazon.com, Yelp, and local and national newspapers. Finally, some major retailers, manufacturers, and service providers (e.g., Walmart, Home Depot) offer daily deals independently.

In 2011, online retail giant Amazon.com jumped on the daily deals "bandwagon" with the launch of Amazon Local, a local daily deals website that offers savings on products and services. To learn more about AmazonLocal, go to **local.amazon.com**. Amazon itself offers deals of the day on its main web page. Amazon also has "Gold Box Deals," which are featured by accessing the "Today's Deals" link at the top of most Amazon.com pages or directly at **amazon.com/gp/goldbox**.

Factors in the Competition

It is challenging to compete with Groupon, given its large size and resources. Therefore, competitors use strategies such as concentrating on a niche market, which targets consumers in smaller demographics, such as one product, or one industry (e.g., tickets for sporting events; **crowdseats.com**, travel, food, and fashion). In addition, some sites concentrate on a small territory (e.g., a city) where they have a competitive advantage. (e.g., see **hotdealshawaii.com**). Similarly, deals for certain social or professional communities are getting popular (e.g., nurses, electrical engineers), deal sites geared toward mothers and their families (**plumdistrict.com**), deal sites geared towards men (**mandeals.com**), religion-based deals (**jdeal.com**), and dog lovers (**doggyloot.com** "Daily Deals for Dogs and Their People") may be very successful. For more about niche daily deal sites, see **business.time.com/2012/02/09/a-deal-just-for-you-niche-sites-with-deals-for-moms-dudes-jews-dog-lovers-the-military-more**.

Several sites have either folded (e.g., Facebook Deals) or were acquired by another company. For example, BuyWithMe was purchased by Gilt Groupe, Buy.com was purchased by the Japanese company Rakuten.com Shopping (**rakuten.com**), and private travel site Jetsetter (**jetsetter.com**) was acquired by TripAdvisor in 2013. As of March 2014, Groupon has acquired 30 sites, including the hotel booking site Blink (**blink-booking.com**), which is now known as "Blink by Groupon." In January 2014, Groupon announced that it had has acquired 'Ticket Monster,' a Korean e-commerce company (a subsidiary of LivingSocial).

The Results

In 2010, Groupon rejected a $6 billion buyout offer from Google. Instead, the company went public on November 4, 2011, raising $700 million. Share prices soared 31% the first day, bringing Groupon's valuation to about $16 billion. Since then, the share price has declined due to concerns about profitability. Groupon lost money until the first quarter of 2013, but each share price was not recovering as of May, 2014.

Sources: Based on Crum (2011), Sennett (2012), Phibbs (2011), **grouponworks.com/merchant-resources**, and **groupon.com** (both accessed April 2015).

Questions

1. It is difficult to do business with Groupon. Many merchant suggestions are dismissed by Groupon. Why do you think Groupon is so strict and how will this policy affect the competition?
2. Some claim that Groupon is an e-mail list that charges advertisers to send out their coupons (called Groupons). Comment.
3. Groupon is changing its business model again, moving from coupons to discount sales. Comment on this business model.
4. Write a short essay on Groupon's chance of survival in the intensely competitive environment. Examine its revenue model and expansion plans. Check stock market analysts' report about the company.
5. Learn more about Groupon's order fulfillment (e.g., ability to handle volume, control of

deliveries, and dealing with marketing and competitors). Write a report.
6. Research Groupon's global efforts. Start with Emma Hall's article "Groupon Clones in Europe Say They Offer Better Deals and Treatment of Merchants" at **adage.com/article/global-news/groupon-clones-europe-win-consumers-merchants/147689**. Write a report.
7. Groupon also deals in B2B. Search the Internet and find out how this is being done and how successful it is.
8. Read Phibbs's (2011) book (Kindle edition) and debate the following issues: "Are deep discounts good or bad for sellers?"

ONLINE FILES
available at **affordable-ecommerce-textbook.com/turban**

W7.1 Application Case: Social Money Lending: Zopa and Prosper
W7.2 Examples of Successful Location-Based Applications

COMPREHENSIVE EDUCATIONAL WEBSITES

socialtext.com/solutions/resources.php: A source for white papers, analyst reports, case studies and more regarding collaboration in the social setting.
mashable.com: A very comprehensive social media resource center.
dotmocracy.org: Download "Dotmocracy Handbook."
gauravbhalla.com: Insights on customer driven strategies.
darmano.typepad.com: In David Armano's personal blog; logic and emotion exist at the intersection of business, design, and the social Web.
wiki.secondlife.com/wiki/Second_Life_Work/FAQs: A comprehensive source of answers to questions.
slideshare.net/oukearts/transforming-retail-into-social-commerce-retail-ceo-briefing-strategy-boutique-thaesis: Comprehensive

slideshow (178 slides) about transforming retail into social commerce.

bloombergmarketing.blogs.com: Diva Marketing Blog.

socialmedia.org: Comprehensive collection of material, include case studies

awarenessnetworks.com: Webinars on social media, Web 2.0, ROI, and marketing.

digitalintelligencetoday.com: Comprehensive selection organized by sectors, news, solutions and directories. Free subscription.

socialtechnologyreview.com: *Social Technology Review* is the industry resource for all things social media and social commerce.

GLOSSARY

Business model The method of doing business that meets the customer's needs, and by which a company generates revenue and creates value.

Communal (collaborative) shopping A method of shopping where shoppers enlist friends and other people they trust to advise them on what products to shop for.

Customer relationship management (CRM) A customer service approach that focuses on building long-term and sustainable customer relationships that adds value for both the customers and the merchants.

Enterprise 2.0 "The use of social software platforms within companies, or between companies and their partners or customers." McAfee (2009)

Geosocial networking Social networking with location awareness capabilities. This enables social networks to connect users with local businesses, people, or events.

Social business "A business that embraces networks of people to create business value" (IBM 2011a).

Social commerce (SC) E-commerce transactions delivered via social media.

Social customers Customers who usually are members in social networks, do social shopping, and understand their shopper's rights and how to use them to their advantage.

Social customer relationship management (SCRM, CRM 2.0) The delivery of CRM by using social media tools and platforms.

Social marketplace A marketplace that uses social media tools and platforms and acts as an online intermediary between buyers and sellers.

Social media marketing (SMM) The application of marketing communication and other marketing tools using social media.

Social shopping (sales 2.0) Online shopping with social media tools and platforms. It is about sharing shopping experiences with friends. Social shopping is the combination of social media and e-commerce.

Viral blogging Viral marketing done by bloggers.

Viral marketing Word-of-mouth (WOM) method by which people tell others (frequently their friends) about a product they like (or dislike).

Viral video Any video that is forwarded from a person to others, sometimes with a recommendation to watch it.

Virtual economy An emerging economy existing in several virtual worlds, where people exchange virtual goods frequently related to an Internet game or to a virtual business.

Virtual goods Computer images of real or imaginary goods.

REFERENCES

Admin. "Social Shopping." January 15, 2011. **socialecart.com/social-shopping** (accessed May 2014).

AOL On News. "Groupon Website in India Crashes After Crazy Onion Deal." September 10, 2013. **on.aol.com/video/groupon-website-in-india-crashes-after-crazy-onion-deal-517928180** (accessed May 2014).

Appelo, J. "Social CommercDOUBLEHYPHENhat Are We Waiting For?" May 20, 2010. **slideshare.net/jurgenappelo/social-commerce-what-are-we-waiting-for** (accessed November 2014).

Baekdal, T. *Social Commerce…It Is a Completely New Playing Field!* Kindle edition. New York: Baekdal Plus, 2011.

Bauer, R. "Discover the Strategic Power of Social Media." *Information Management Newsletter*, August 2011.

Bazaarvoice.com. "Social Commerce Stories." 2011 (archived).

Beal, A., and J. Strauss. *Radically Transparent: Monitoring and Managing Reputations Online*, Indianapolis, IN: Sybex, 2008.

Bennett, S. "The Rise of Social Commerce [Infographic]." September 23, 2013, **mediabistro.com/alltwitter/rise-social-commerce_b49578** (accessed May 2014).

Bennett, S. "Twitter Ad Revenue Forecast to Exceed $1 Billion in 2014 [Stats]." March 21, 2104. **mediabistro.com/alltwitter/twitter-ad-revenue-growth_b56064** (accessed March 2015).

Bernoff, J., and T. Schadler. "Empowered: In a World Where One Angry Tweet Can Torpedo a Brand, Corporations Need to Unleash Their Employees to Fight Back." *Harvard Business Review* (July–August 2010).

Billingsley, E. "Cash-Strapped Musicians Empowered by Tech Company: Web: Portable Store Allows Artist to Sell Direct." *San Fernando Valley Business Journal*, March 29, 2010.

Bughin, J., and M. Chui. "The Rise of the Networked Enterprise: Web 2.0 Finds Its Payday." December 2010. **mckinsey.com/insights/high_tech_telecoms_internet/the_rise_of_the_networked_enterprise_web_20_finds_its_payday** (accessed May 2014).

Burnham, K. "Foursquare Splits into 2 Apps, Targets Yelp." May 3, 2014. **informationweek.com/software/social/foursquare-splits-into-2-apps-targets-yelp/d/d-id/1235048** (accessed May 2014).

Business Wire. "Maui Jim Sees Social Commerce Success with Bazaarvoice." Press Room News, April 5, 2010.

Carr, D. F. "Business Strategy on Facebook." *Baseline Magazine*, September 22, 2010.

Carr, D. F. "Roomba Robots Listen to Social Media." *Information Week*, September 28, 2011.

Chaney, P. "13 Social Shopping Sites for Ecommerce Merchants." August 1, 2011. **practicalecommerce.com/articles/2947-13-Social-Shopping-Sites-for-Ecommerce-Mechants** (accessed May 2014).

Christman, C. "Reputation Management through Social Media and Online Reviews." March 3, 2014. **smallbusiness.yahoo.com/advisor/reputation-management-social-media-online-reviews-212958979.html** (accessed May 2014).

Chui, M., M. Dewhurst, and L. Pollak. "Building the Social Enterprise." *McKinsey Quarterly*, November 2013. **mckinsey.com/insights/organization/building_the_social_enterprise**, (accessed November 2014).

Cipriani, F. "Social CRM." November 2008. **slideshare.net/Subbuinblr/social-crm-by-fabio-cipriani-presentation** (accessed May 2014).

Clifford, S. "Linking Customer Loyalty with Social Networking." *New York Times*, April 28, 2010.

Crum, C. "Groupon Apologizes for Deal Gone Bad in Tokyo." January 17, 2011. **webpronews.com/groupon-apologizes-for-deal-gone-bad-in-tokyo-2011-01** (accessed May 2014).

Cuccureddu, G. "Social Commerce to Rise Six Fold to $30 Billion in 2015, According to Booz & Company." February 3, 2011. **appmarket.tv/news/1021-social-commerce-to-rise-six-fold-to-30-billion-in-2015-according-to-booz-a-co.html** (accessed November 2014).

Dellarocas, C. "Online Reputation Systems: How to Design One That Does What You Need." *MIT Sloan Management Review* (Spring 2010). **sloanreview.mit.edu/article/online-reputation-systems-how-to-design-one-that-does-what-you-need** (accessed May 2014).

Dennison, G., S. Bourdage-Braun, and M. Chetuparambil. "Social Commerce Defined." IBM white paper #23747, November 2009. **www.ibm.com/tela/servlet/Asset/395425/Social Commerce Defined - ANZ.pdf** (accessed May 2014).

Dignan, L., "iRobot launches new Roomba: Five innovation lessons." November 12, 2013. **zdnet.com/irobot-launches-new-roomba-five-innovation-lessons-7000022993** (accessed May 2014).

Dubey, K. "Gartner Analyzes Social Networking Influence on Purchase Decisions." July 31, 2010. **techshout.com/internet/2010/31/gartner-analyzes-social-networking-influence-on-purchase-decisions** (accessed May 2014).

Dugan, L. "The Complete Guide to Social Shopping." October 27, 2010. **socialtimes.com/social-shopping-complete-guide_b25950**, (accessed March 2015).

Eckerle, C. "Social Email Integration: Sony Electronics Nets 3,000 Clickthroughs from Email to "Pin" on Pinterest." Case Study. April 23, 2013. **marketingsherpa.com/article/case-study/sony-nets-3000-clickthroughs-pinterest** (accessed May 2014).

eMarketer. "Marketers Are on Board with Virtual Goods." July 27, 2011. **emarketer.com/Article/Marketers-On-Board-with-Virtual-Goods/1008513** (accessed May 2014).

Enterprise 2.0 Conference. "Enterprise 2.0: What, Why and How." White Paper, May 2009. Boston, MA, June 22–25, 2009. Available for download at **informationweek.com/whitepaper/Internet/enterprise-2-0-what-why-and-hoDOUBLEHYPHENp1366879055?articleID=191708382** (accessed May 2014).

Fagan, L. "Free ebook: How Social CRM connects you to customers," April 3, 2014. **blogs.salesforce.com/company/2014/04/free-ebook-socialcrm.html** (accessed March 2015).

Fisher, S. "Social Commerce Camp: Creating a Killer Social Commerce Website Experience." February 22, 2010. **slideshare.net/stevenfisher/social-commerce-camp-killer-social-commerce-experience** (accessed May 2014).

Fleenor, G. "Friend-Powered Shopping." *StoreOnline*, September 2010.

Forrester Consulting Report. "Social Networking in the Enterprise: Benefits and Inhibitors." White Paper, June 2010.

Gillette, F. "Twitter, Twitter, Little Stars." *Bloomberg BusinessWeek*, July 19–July 25, 2010.

Grant, R. "A Look at Polyvore's 20M Users" An Infographic. February 21, 2013. **wearesocial.net/blog/2013/02/polyvores-20m-users** (accessed March 2015).

Greenberg, P., A. Seley, B. Komar, J. Dunn, J. Ahvenaine, and M. Dimaurizio. *The Art of Social Sales*. A comprehensive report sponsored by Oracle, March 2011.

oracle.com/us/products/applications/
Siebel/051270.pdf (accessed May 2014).

Heine, C. "Mercedes-Benz Rides Twitter to Super Bowl."
February 2, 2011. clickz.com/clickz/news/2023679/
mercedes-benz-rides-twitter-super-bowl (accessed
May 2014).

Hempel, J. "Google Takes Stake in Lending Club." May 2,
2013. tech.fortune.cnn.com/2013/05/02/lending-club
(accessed May 2014).

Holland, A. "How Sony Connects Social Media
Monitoring to ROI (and You Can, Too)." December 6,
2011. raventools.com/blog/how-sony-connects-
social-media-monitoring-to-roi-and-you-can-too
(accessed May 2014).

Huba, J. *Monster Loyalty: How Lady Gaga Turns
Followers into Fanatics.* New York: Portfolio
Hardcover, 2013.

IBM. The social business: Advent of a new age, White
Paper #EPW 14008-USEN-00, February 2011a. ibm.
com/smarterplanet/us/en/socialbusiness/overview/
index.html (accessed May 2014).

IBM. "The Compelling Returns from IBM Connections in
Support of Social Business: Five Stories." White
Paper. Somers, NY: IBM Corp. Software Group,
December 2011b.

Ionescu, D. "Geolocation 101: How It Works, the Apps,
and Your Privacy." March 29, 2010. techhive.com/
article/192803/geolo.html (accessed May 2014).

Jack, D. "2013 Forrester Groundswell Entry- Sony
Electronics: Support Channels Show Dramatic
Improvements in Consumer Engagement and Help
Boost Sales." *Lithium Technologies,* August 27, 2013
(ed. September 3, 2013). lithosphere.lithium.com/t5/
lithium-s-view-blog/2013-Forrester-Groundswell-
Entry-Sony-Electronics-Support/ba-p/100214
(accessed May 2014).

Jacobs, A. "Fashion Democracy." *The New Yorker*, March
29, 2010.

Kessler, S. "New Site Crowdsources Shopping Advice
from Your Facebook Friends." January 1, 2011. mash-
able.com/2010/12/30/cloud-shopper (accessed
January 2013).

Kimball, M. "Social Media: Changing the Way Your
Customers Shop Online [Infographic]." September 10,
2013. (Note: The Infographic was created by
MarketMeSuite on September 8, 2013.) mediabistro.
com/alltwitter/social-media-shopping_b50440
(accessed March 2015).

Kiron, D., D. Palmer, A. N. Phillips and, and N. Kruschwitz.
"What Managers Really Think About Social Business."
Sloan Management Review, Summer 2012.

Knight, K. "Why Travel Advertisers Need to Think
Mobile." *BizReport*, May 09, 2012. bizreport.
com/2012/05/why-travel-advertisers-need-to-
think-mobile.html (accessed November 2014).

Knopf, E. "E-Commerce Week/The Rise of New Business
Models." *E-Commerce Week,* January 18, 2012.

Lacy, K., et al. *Social CRM Dummies (For Dummies
(Business & Personal Finance)),* Hoboken, NJ: John
Wiley & Sons, 2013.

Leahey, C., "Why Your Teen Loves Wanelo." May 23,
2013. fortune.com/2013/05/23/tech-star-deena-
varshavskaya (accessed May 2014).

Learmonth, M. "Study: Twitter Ad Revenue Grow to
$150M in 2011." *Advertising Age*, January 24, 2011.

Leggatt, H. "Survey: Small Businesses Find Success with
Social Networking." July 9, 2010. bizreport.
com/2010/07/survey-small-businesses-find-suc-
cess-with-social-networking.html (accessed May
2014).

Liang, T.P., and E. Turban. "Introduction to the Special
Issue: Social Commerce: A Research Framework for
Social Commerce." *International Journal of Electronic
Commerce*, Winter 2011–12.

Lincoln, J. E. "How to Advertise on Twitter: Promoted
Tweets, Promoted Trends and Promoted Accounts."
SEO, Inc., August 22, 2012.

Little, K. "Models on Twitter: Tech Hits the Runway."
February 11, 2013. cnbc.com/id/100449013 (accessed
May 2014).

Logan, N. *Go Viral!: The Most Effective Viral Marketing
strategies to Launch Your Online Business* [Kindle
Edition]. Seattle, WA: Amazon Digital Services, Inc.,
2014.

Madden, N. "China Pioneers Group Buying Discounts
without Groupon." December 14, 2010. adage.com/
article/global-news/advertising-china-group-buy-
ing-discounts-groupon/147641 (accessed May
2014).

Mally, S. *How to Use the Social Media Sites Pinterest and
Polyvore Together to Drive Traffic to Your Website or
Blog*, Kindle edition, Seattle, WA: Simultaneous
Device Usage: Unlimited, 2012.

Markman, A. "Money Can Buy Happiness If You Spend
It Right." May 21, 2010. psychologytoday.com/blog/
ulterior-motives/201005/money-can-buy-happi-
ness-if-you-spent-it-right (accessed May 2014).

Marsden, P. "Simple Definition of Social Commerce."
November 17, 2009a. socialcommercetoday.com/
social-commerce-definition-word-cloud-definitive-
definition-list (accessed May 2014).

Mardsen, P. "Presentation: Social Commerce." Slide presentation, June 7, 2010a. digitalintelligencetoday.
com/presentation-social-commerce-what-are-we-
waiting-for (accessed March 2015).

Marsden, P. "Social Commerce: The Opportunity for
Brands," slide presentation, June 10, 2010b. slide-
share.net/paulsmarsden/social-commerce-the-
opportunity-for-brands (accessed May 2014).

Marsden, P. "The 6 Dimensions of Social Commerce:
Rated and Reviewed." December 22, 2009b. digital-
intelligencetoday.com/the-6-dimensions-of-social-
commerce-rated-and-reviewed (accessed May
2014).

Marsden, P., and P. Chaney. *The Social Commerce
Handbook: 20 Secrets for Turning Social Media Into
Social Sales*, New York: McGraw-Hill, 2012.

McAfee, A. P. "Enterprise 2.0: The Dawn of Emergent
Collaboration." *MIT Sloan Management Review*, vol.
47, no. 3, 2006.

McAfee, A. *Enterprise 2.0: New Collaborative Tools for Your Organization's Toughest Challenges.* Boston: Harvard Business School Press, 2009.

McCafferty, D. "Social Media Influence on Purchasing Overrated." September 7, 2011. **baselinemag.com/c/a/Intelligence/Social-Media-Influence-On-Purchasing-Overrated-660095** (accessed May 2014).

Metz, A. *The Social Customer: How Brands Can Use Social CRM to Acquire, Monetize, and Retain Fans, Friends, and Followers.* New York: McGraw-Hill, 2011.

Moontoast. *The Social Commerce Opportunity, How Brands can Take Advantage of the Next Evolution* (A free e-book). Boston, MA: Moontoast, 2013.

Olson, P. "A Twitterati Calls Out Whirlpool." *Forbes*, September 2, 2009.

Oracle. "With RightNow, iRobot's World-Class Social Contact Center Successfully Engages the Modern Consumer." 2011.

Owyang, J. "Altimeter Report: The 18 Use Cases of Social CRM, The New Rules of Relationship Management." March 5, 2010 **web-strategist.com/blog/2010/03/05/altimeter-report-the-18-use-cases-of-social-crm-the-new-rules-of-relationship-management** (accessed May 2014).

Parature. *Delivering WOW Social Customer Service* (Free). Herdon, VA: Parature (Microsoft Dynamics), 2014.

Patel, K. "Apple, Campbell's Say iAds Twice as Effective as TV." *Advertising Age*, February 3, 2011.

Petersen, R. "16 Case Studies That Prove Social CRM." January 13, 2011. **barnraisersllc.com/2011/01/19-case-studies-show-social-media-builds-1-to-1-sales-relationships** (accessed May 2014).

Phibbs, B. *Groupon Can't Afford It –Why Deep Discounts are Bad for Business and What to Do Instead*, Kindle edition, USA: Beyond the Page Publishing, 2011.

Ran, Y. "Social Networking Sends a Message to Business." *China Daily*, November 26, 2012.

Reevoo.com, "New Automated Translation Tool Brings Immediate International Social Commerce Benefits to Sony, 2014. **reevoo.com/pages/press_sony_international_reviews** (accessed March 2015).

RightNow Technologies. "RightNow Helps iRobot Successfully Pioneer a New Market by Listening and Responding to Its Customers." Case Study, 2010. **rightnow.virtuos.com/resources/case-studies/iRobot-Case-Study.pdf** (accessed May 2014).

Roebuck, K. *Social CRM: High-Impact Strategies - What You Need to Know: Definitions, Adoptions, Impact, Benefits, Maturity, Vendors.* Tebbo, 2011.

Rowan, D., and T. Cheshire. "Commerce Gets Social: How Your Networks Are Driving What You Buy." January 18, 2011. **wired.co.uk/magazine/archive/2011/02/features/social-networks-drive-commerce** (accessed May 2014).

Sala, K. "Top 50 Product Review Blogs." June 25, 2012. **cision.com/us/2012/06/top-50-product-review-blogs** (accessed March 2015).

Savitz, E. "Four Reasons Why Virtual Goods Make Us Happy." *CIO Network*, October 25, 2011. **forbes.com/sites/ciocentral/2011/10/25/four-reasons-why-virtual-goods-make-us-happy** (accessed May 2014).

Sennett, F. *Groupon's Biggest Deal Ever: The Inside Story of How One Insane Gamble, Tons of Unbelievable Hype, and Millions of Wild Deals Made Billions for One Ballsy Joker.* New York: St Martin's Press, 2012.

Shih, C. *The Facebook Era: Tapping Online Social Networks to Market, Sell, and Innovate,* 2nd ed. Reading, MA: Addison-Wesley Professional, 2011.

ShopSocially. "Social Commerce Is Making an Undeniable Impact in 2013." July 31, 2013. **prweb.com/releases/2013/7/prweb10980191.htm** (accessed March 2015).

Singh, S., and S. Diamond. *Social Media Marketing for Dummies,* 2nd ed. Hoboken, NJ: Wiley & Sons, 2012.

Solis, B. "The Business Guide to Facebook Part 2: From E-Commerce to F-Commerce." October 27, 2010. **briansolis.com/2010/10/the-business-guide-to-facebook-part-2-from-e-commerce-to-f-commerce** (accessed May 2014).

Srinivasan, R. To Group Coupon or Not: Quick Start Guide to Groupon, Kindle ed. (Amazon Digital Services, Seattle, 2011).

Staff Writers. "Facebook Chorus Prompts Qantas to Scrap Instruments Ban." December 30, 2010. **spacedaily.com/reports/Facebook_chorus_prompts_Qantas_to_scrap_instruments_ban_999.html** (accessed May 2014).

Stephen, A. T., and O. Toubia. "Deriving Value from Social Commerce Networks." *Journal of Marketing Research*, 47(2), 215–228 (April 2010).

Sysomos Inc. "Social Media: Leveraging Sentiment and Influence to Develop a Customer Service Strategy." A White Paper, 2011. **social-media-monitor.co.uk/resources/whitepapers/Sysomos-Leverage-Sentiment.pdf** (accessed May 2014).

Taipei Times. "Facebook Chorus Ends Instrument Luggage Ban." January 4, 2011. **taipeitimes.com/News/lang/archives/2011/01/04/2003492593** (accessed May 2014).

Takahashi, D. "PayPal: 12M Monthly Users Are Paying for Virtual Goods (Updated)." August 1, 2011. **venturebeat.com/2011/08/01/paypal-says-there-are-12m-monthly-users-paying-for-facebook-games-exclusive** (accessed May 2014).

Taylor, J. "Social CRM Case Study: Sony Europe Creates a Community of Super Fans." *OurSocialTimes*, May 14, 2013.

Troudt, E. and R. Vancil. "Becoming a Social Business: The IBM story." IDC White Paper, Doc #226706. January 2011.

Turban, E., et al. *Social Commerce.* New York: Springer, 2015.

Van Grove, J. "5 New Ways Small Business Can Offer Location-Based Deals." September 4, 2010. **mashable.com/2010/09/04/location-based-small-business-deals** (accessed May 2014).

Walsh, B. "Borrow, Don't Buy: Websites That Let Strangers Share." *Time Magazine*, December 5, 2010.

Wang, J. "How Polyvore Is a Trend-Setter in Social Shopping." *Entrepreneur,* May 24, 2011.

Wang, C., and Zhang P. "The Evolution of Social Commerce: The People, Management, Technology, and Information Dimensions." *Communications of the Association of Information Systems* (CAIS), November 2, 2012.

Weber, S. *Twitter Marketing: Promote Yourself and Your Business on Earth's Hottest Social Network.* Falls Church, VA: Weber Books, 2012.

Weblogs, Inc. "The Social Software Weblog." 2007. **socialsoftware.weblogsinc.com** (accessed June 2014).

Wilde, S. *Viral Marketing within Social Networking Sites: The Creation of an Effective Viral Marketing Campaign* (Google eBook). Munchen, Germany: Diplomica Verlag, 2013.

Wood, T. "The Marketers Guide to the Social Media Galaxy," (Infographic January 2, 2014. **business2community. com/infographics/marketers-guide-social-media-galaxy-infographic-0729381** (accessed May 2014).

Yelp. "Yelp Announces Date of Fourth Quarter and Full Year 2013 Financial Results." January 21, 2014. **yelp-ir.com/phoenix.zhtml?c=250809&p=irol-newsArticle&ID=1892381&highlight=** (accessed May 2014).

Yoon, E. "China's Latest Obsession: Group Buying." *CNN.com,* January 27, 2011. **business.blogs.cnn. com/2011/01/27/chinas-latest-obsession-group-buying** (accessed May 2014).

Ziff Davis. "Why Social CRM is Important to Business." A White Paper, 2012. **hosteddocs.itoolbox.com/zd_ wp_whysocialcrmimportanttobusiness_122812.pdf** (accessed May 2014).

Zwilling, M. "Location-Based Services Are a Bonanza for Startups." *Forbes*, January 31, 2011.

Social Enterprise and Other Social Commerce Topics

8

Contents

Learning Objectives

Upon completion of this chapter, you will be able to:

1. Understand the concept of the social enterprise and its variants.
2. Describe business-oriented public social networks, their characteristics and benefits.
3. Describe the major social commerce activities that can be conducted within and by enterprises and the characteristics of such private social networks.
4. Describe the commercial applications conducted in virtual worlds.
5. Review the social commerce activities and their relationship with e-entertainment and gaming.
6. Describe social gaming and gamification.
7. Define crowdsourcing and describe its use in social commerce.
8. Describe social collaboration and its benefits.
9. Comment of the future of social commerce.

Electronic supplementary material The online version of this chapter (doi: 10.1007/978-3-319-10091-3_8) contains supplementary material, which is available to authorized users

E. Turban et al., *Electronic Commerce: A Managerial and Social Networks Perspective*,
Springer Texts in Business and Economics, DOI 10.1007/978-3-319-10091-3_8,
© Springer International Publishing Switzerland 2015

OPENING CASE: HOW A PRIVATE ENTERPRISE NETWORK TRANSFORMED CEMEX INTO A SOCIAL BUSINESS

CEMEX (**cemex.com**) is a Mexico-based global building materials company known primarily for its cement and ready-mix concrete. They do business in over 58 countries, throughout the Americas, Europe, Africa, the Middle East, and Asia and maintain trade relationships in approximately 108 nations.

The Problem

The global economic slowdown of 2008–2012, and especially the drastic reduction in construction activities, drove CEMEX to try a host of traditional activities for cost reduction and increased productivity. However, this was not enough. In addition, top management was looking for ways to facilitate innovation. Given the company's global nature, top management realized that they needed to improve the company's internal and external collaboration to foster innovation.

The Solution

Recently, many companies have implemented Enterprise 2.0 platforms that include social media tools as well as mechanisms of social network services. CEMEX decided to follow this trend. The company wanted to fully utilize the institutional knowledge possessed by its thousands of employees worldwide and make it available to others whenever needed.

CEMEX created an internal private social collaboration platform called Shift (**cemex.com/whatisshift**), which facilitates innovation, efficiency, and collaboration by letting employees share information and jointly conduct problem solving. Shift integrates some of the best capabilities of social networks with knowledge management (KM) and collaboration techniques (using IBM Connection and its language translation feature). Shift includes many internal communities; each is composed of people with similar interests.

The Results

The main result was the major change in the way that people worked together. The workforce became more cooperative; employees helped each other, shared more information and knowledge, were more empowered, and were able to be more mobile. This led to better internal collaboration using in-house networking.

Projects started to move more quickly, with faster time to market; therefore, business processes improved. In short, the company successfully leveraged the collective talents and skills of its employees. One internal community, the "Construction for the 21st Century," was challenged to suggest the strategic topics that CEMEX should focus on to remain a leader in the construction industry. The 400 community members of this 21st Century group responded by proposing innovative ideas, tactics, and strategies addressing the challenge. Overall, Shift drew 5,000 users by the end of its first month. By 2013, there were 25,000 users of Shift and over 500 groups. By 2014 the company's stock price increased by over 300%.

For more results and discussion see: **slideshare.net/soccnx/shifting-the-way-we-work-at-cemex**.

Sources: Based on Garcia et al. (2011), Hinchcliffe (2012), and Donston-Miller (2012).

LESSONS LEARNED FROM THE CASE

The CEMEX case illustrates a successful private in-house social network whose major objectives were to foster collaboration among its thousands of employees worldwide and facilitate idea generation via internal crowdsourcing. Using Web 2.0 tools, collaboration became effective and efficient. A major result was idea generation and the evaluation and implementation of these ideas that facilitated innovation in the company. This chapter presents the major activities that private social networks support within enterprises and the structure and benefits of public business networks. This chapter also presents the issues of virtual worlds, social entertainment, gaming and gamification, crowdsourcing, and social collaboration.

8.1 SOCIAL BUSINESS AND SOCIAL ENTERPRISE

A major forthcoming trend in social commerce is its move to the enterprise level. This trend is related to the concept of social business. Let us define both terms.

Definitions: Social Business and Social Enterprise

The social enterprise concept has several names, definitions and explanations. The concept is sometimes confused with the related concept of social business. Generally, one can distinguish between the two concepts that often are used interchangeably. Let us explain.

Social Business
A **social business** is a name for a commercial for-profit or non-profit organization that is designed to achieve some social goal(s) such as improving human well-being, rather than just make a profit. SocialFirms UK (**socialfirmsuk.co.uk**) provide several other definitions (of what they call *social enterprise*). They cite the following UK government definition: "A social enterprise is a business with primarily social objectives whose surpluses are reinvested for that purpose in the business or in the community, rather than being driven by the need to deliver profit to shareholders and owners" (see details at **socialfirmsuk.co.uk/faq/faq-what-social-enterprise-and-what-types-are-**

there). About.com distinguishes between two types of social business: one type that describes companies that "aspire to social purposes more than to profit-making," and a second type that describes companies that "use social media to advance their business objectives." (See **webtrends.about.com/od/web20/a/social-media.htm.**)

The second type is the basis for the *social enterprise*. In summary, we view a *social business* as one that is built mainly around social objective(s), while a *social enterprise* uses social networking to facilitate its commercial objectives.

A major organization dedicated to social business (referring to itself as "social enterprise") is the *Social Enterprise Alliance* (see **se-alliance.org/what-is-social-enterprise**).

Social Employees
The successful social business needs to empower their employees (e.g., using IBM Connections). For how it is done in IBM, AT&T, and other large corporations, see Burgess and Burgess (2013).

The Social Enterprise (Enterprise 2.0)
Social enterprise refers to the use of social media tools and platforms and conducting social networking activities in organizations while its major objectives are either commercial or non-profit activities (e.g., the government). For an overview see Ridley-Duff and Bull (2011).

The concept of the social enterprise has become a buzzword in recent years. For an example see **se-alliance.org/what-is-social-enterprise**. Let us see what it is.

Social enterprise applications are growing rapidly. They appear under different names, mostly as social enterprises and Enterprise 2.0. According to Carr (2012), McKinsey (a management consultant company), predicts that the global revenue from social enterprise activities will reach $1 trillion in several years (two thirds of all social commerce value at that time).

Enterprise applications are conducted inside enterprises, on companies' private social networks or portals. They also are conducted on public social networks, both business-oriented (e.g., LinkedIn), and general networks, mostly Facebook and Twitter. Major applications are recruitment, collaboration, and problem solving. According to Kern (2012), enterprise social capabilities will facilitate a new type of collaboration, encourage business upgrades, and enable more vendor applications.

According to a 2009 IDC survey (reported by Businesswire 2010), 57% of all U.S. workers in 2010 used social media for business purposes at least once a week. Today that figure is higher. Corporations are rushing to get involved in several innovative ways, as will be described later in this chapter. Business networks are a core component in the social enterprise.

For additional definitions, characteristics, and discussion on social enterprise, see **centreforsocialenterprise.com/what.html**.

More Complex Definitions

In addition to the above definitions, there are some definitions that are more complex, as illustrated next.

The Social Business Forum's Definition

The Social Business Forum defines *social business* as "an organization that has put in place the strategies, technologies and processes to systematically engage all the individuals of its ecosystem (employees, customers, partners, suppliers) to maximize the co-created value" (**2012.socialbusinessforum.com/what-is-social-business**). The Forum also discusses the implications of this definition and its relevance, across and outside organizations. Note that an efficient creation of value using technology is emphasized.

IBM and IDC's Definition

IDC coined the term *social business* to refer to "those organizations that apply emerging technologies like Web 2.0 accompanied by organizational, cultural, and process changes to improve business performance in an increasingly connected global economic environment"(see IBM 2010; IDC 2010). The IBM effort concentrates on improved collaboration. The basic idea is that social customers require organizations to significantly change the way they operate so they can become social businesses. The new structure enables organizations to exploit the opportunities created by the social media environment. IBM is helping organizations become social businesses. (For an example of how this is done, see A Smarter Planet at **ibm.com/smarterplanet/us/en/?ca=v_smarterplanet**.) IBM also has an extensive "social business video library."

Three interesting videos are recommended for a better understanding of the concept:

1. "Social PHD Sandy Carter: How Do You Become a Social Business?"(1:05 minutes) at **youtube.com/watch?v=OZy0dNQbotg**
2. "How Do You Become a Social Business?" (3.27 minutes) at **youtube.com/watch?v=3Hov0l7SvAo**
3. "Social Business at IBM" – An Interview with Luis Suarez, Social Computing Evangelist (8:50 minutes), at (**youtube.com/watch?v=enudW2gHek0&feature=related**)

Notice that our definition of social enterprise is based on the use of social media tools and platforms. A related topic is *business networks*.

Business Networks

A *business network* refers to a group of people with a professional business relationship; for example, the relationships between sellers and buyers, buyers and suppliers, and professionals and their colleagues, such as the 21st Century Community at CEMEX. In this chapter, we use the term *buyers* to refer to agents buying something for a business (e.g., a purchasing agent). Such a network of people can form **business social networks**, which are business-oriented networks that are built on social relationships and can exist offline or online. For example, public places, such as airports or golf courses, provide opportunities to make new face-to-face business contacts if an individual has good social skills. Similarly, the Internet is also proving to be a good place to network and connect. In this book, we address online networks. The most well known network is LinkedIn (**linkedin.com**). For a discussion about business social networks, see Bughin and Chui (2013).

Types of Business Social Networks

There are three major types of business social networks: (a) *public networks*, such as LinkedIn, which are owned and operated by independent companies, and are open to anyone for business networking. The networks connect, for example, sellers and buyers or employers and potential employees; (b) *enterprise private networks*, which operate inside companies, like in CEMEX in the opening case. These usually restrict membership to employees and sometimes to business partners. An example is USAA that has an internal network for employees who can ask for help from their peers; and (c) *company-owned and hosted networks* that are controlled by a company but open to the public, usually for brand-related networking (e.g., Starbucks, Dell Computer).

The Benefits and Limitations of Enterprise Social Networking

Social networking appeals to business users for many reasons. For example, networking makes it easy to find people and discover information about companies, understands the relationships and communication patterns that make a company tick, and creates a common culture across large organizations.

The major reasons an organization becomes a social enterprise are the abilities to:

- Improve collaboration inside the enterprise and with business partners
- Facilitate knowledge management (increase access to specialized knowledge)
- Build better customer and employee relationships
- Facilitate recruiting and employee retention
- Increase business and marketing opportunities (e.g., meet new potential business partners and/or customers)
- Reduce operation, communication, and travel costs

- Increase sales and revenue (e.g., more sales leads)
- Improve customer satisfaction
- Reduce marketing and advertising costs
- Improve employee and organizational performance
- Foster internal and external relationships
- Collect feedback from employees
- Build an effective workforce
- Improve decision-making capabilities including forecasting
- "Spy" on competitors (intelligence gathering)
- Find experts and advice (internally and externally)
- Improve customer service and CRM
- Accelerate innovation and competitive advantage

For details of these and other benefits, see Carr (2012), Bughin and Chui (2013), and Section 8.2.

Enterprises that use social media extensively can reap the benefits found in the previous list and be transformed into social businesses. For details, see **ibm.com/social-business/us/en**.

Obstacles and Limitations

Some limitations, such as security of information and information pollution, slow down the growth of social enterprising. For details, see Forrester Consulting (2010), and **slideshare.net/norwiz/what-is-enterprise-20**.

How Web 2.0 Tools Are Used by Enterprises

Web 2.0 tools are used in different ways by various corporations. Typical uses are: Increasing speed of access to knowledge; reducing communication costs; increasing speed of access to internal exports; decreasing travel costs; increasing employee satisfaction; reducing operational costs; reducing time to market for products/services; and increasing the number of successful innovations for new products or services.

For statistics about which departments in the enterprise use the technology and what specific social media tools are used, see IDC's Social Business Survey (2011). Some of the uses outside the enterprises include recruitment, advice in problem solving, joint design, collaboration on supply chain issues, and marketing communication. For an example of how Balfour Beatty, a UK-based multinational corporation, is using several Web 2.0 technologies for substantial benefits, see Kelly (2011).

For a comprehensive slide presentation on Enterprise 2.0, see **slideshare.net/norwiz/what-is-enterprise-20**.

SECTION 8.1 REVIEW QUESTIONS

1. Define social business and relate it to the social enterprise.
2. How does IBM define social business?
3. What is a business network?
4. List five reasons why organizations want to become social enterprises.

8.2 BUSINESS-ORIENTED PUBLIC SOCIAL NETWORKING

Social networking activities are conducted in both public and/or private social networking sites. For example, LinkedIn is a business-oriented public network, whereas Facebook is primarily a public social network used for socially-oriented activities. Facebook, however, allows its members to conduct business-oriented activities. "My Starbucks Idea" (**mystarbucksi-dea.force.com**) is an example of a company-hosted social network that is open to the public. In contrast, CEMEX's internal social network, SHIFT (see opening case), is open only to the company's employees and is considered private. In this section, we will concentrate on public social networks.

The following are some examples of business-oriented public social networks.

- **Ryze.** Similar to LinkedIn, Ryze (**ryze.com**), according to its website and About.com, is a business social networking site with a focus on the entrepreneur. Individuals can use Ryze to help build up a personal network and find new jobs, while companies can use Ryze to create a business community. Ryze is especially liked by young professionals, by entrepreneurs, or by business owners who want to create a networking community for their employees (per **webtrends.about.com/od/profiles/fr/what-is-ryze.htm**).
- **Google+.** Google+ ("one Google account for everything"), which began operating in 2011, designated itself as a business-oriented social network. In its fourth year of operation, it has over 1.1 million users. For an overview, see **martinshervington.com/what-is-google-plus**.
- **LinkedIn.** Referred to as the premier business-oriented network, LinkedIn (**linkedin.com**) is known as the most popular network for business, as illustrated in the closing case of this chapter. Also see the infographic at **blog.hootsuite.com/social-network-for-work**.

  LinkedIn shows content and provides customer service in a multitude of languages, including English, Spanish, French, and Tagalog among others, with a plan for considering other languages in the future.

Several other networks similar to LinkedIn are Wealink (**wealink.com**) in China, Rediff (**rediff.com**) in India, International High Potential Network (iHipo) (**ihipo.com**) in Sweden, and Moikrug (My Circle) (**moikrug.ru**) in Russia.

There are many public business-oriented networks that focus on specific industries or types of professional specialties; one example is the Network of Entrepreneurial Women (**network-women.org**).

Entrepreneur Networks

Some business-oriented public networks concentrate on entrepreneurial activities. A few examples are listed next.

Ueland (2011) lists 18 social networks for entrepreneurs, such as PerfectBusiness (**perfectbusiness.com**), and Upspring (**upspring.com**).

- Biznik (**biznik.com**). Biznik is a community of entrepreneurs and small business owners dedicated to helping each other by sharing ideas and knowledge. Their motto is "collaboration beats the competition," (see **biznik.com/articles/collaboration-beats-the-competition**). According to **biznik.com**, their policy is that members must use their real names on the site and Biznik supplements its interactions with face-to-face-meetings.
- **EFactor** (**efactor.com**). The world's largest network of entrepreneurs (over 1 million members in 222 countries across 240 industries) provides members with people, tools, marketing, and expertise to succeed and make real, trustworthy, and lasting connections (2011 data). Members connect with like-minded people and with investors.
- **Startup Nation** (**startupnation.com**). Participants in this community of startup owners and experts are helping people start and operate new businesses. Sharing knowledge and ideas is the main objective.
- **Inspiration Station** (**inspiration.entrepreneur.com**). Inspiration Station is one of the best portals for small businesses and start-ups. It not only has a lot of useful information for business owners, it has a great community for you to take advantage of, and to connect with fellow business owners from around the globe.
- **SunZu** (**sunzu.com**). SunZu is a network for people doing business that lets you meet, share, learn, trade, and grow with other business owners. Joining SunZu gives members access to people, learning opportunities, news, updates, business opportunities, and insights (see **sunzu.com/pages/about-sunzu**).

SECTION 8.2 REVIEW QUESTIONS

1. Distinguish between private and public business-oriented networks.
2. List and briefly describe public business-oriented networks.
3. Define entrepreneur networks and list two examples.

8.3 ENTERPRISE SOCIAL NETWORKS

An increasing number of companies have created their own in-house, enterprise social networks. Some of these networks can be private, developed for use only by their employees, former employees, and business partners. Others are open to the public, although these are mostly used by their customers. Private networks are considered to be secured ("behind the firewall"), and are often referred to as *corporate social networks*. Such networks come in several formats, depending on their purpose, the industry, the country, and so forth. For the evolution of the networked enterprise, see Bughin and Chui (2013).

Taxonomy of Social Enterprise Applications

The following terms are frequently used in enterprise networking. Most will be discussed in this chapter.

1. **Networking and community building.** Conducting networking and community building involving employees, executives, business partners, and customers.
2. **Crowdsourcing.** Gathering ideas, insights, and feedback from crowds

(e.g., employees, customers, and business partners; see Section 8.2). Salesforce Success Community (**success.salesforce.com**) and My Starbucks Idea (**mystarbucksidea.force.com**) are examples.

3. **Social collaboration.** Collaborative work and problem solving using wikis, blogs, instant messaging, collaborative office documents, and other special purpose Web-based collaboration platforms such as Laboranova (**labo-ranova.com**).

4. **Social publishing.** This is the creation of user-generated content in the enterprise, which is accessible to all (e.g., **slideshare.net**, **youtube.com**).

5. **Social views and feedback.** Getting feedback and opinions from the enterprise's internal and external communities on specific issues.

Characteristics of Enterprise Social Networks

Enterprise social networks, like any social network, enable employees to create profiles and interact with one another. By encouraging interactions among members, a company can foster collaboration and teamwork, and increase employee satisfaction. For more benefits see **zdnet.com/blog/hinchcliffe.**

For additional information, see the *International Journal of Social and Humanistic Computing*. For additional tips and sources, see **socialcast.com**.

An Example of a Private Enterprise Network

In the opening case of Chapter 1, we introduced Starbucks' hosted enterprise network. We also described Sony's and iRobot's hosted enterprise social network in Chapter 7. Many other companies also have enterprise networks of all kinds. Here is an example of another private network:

Example: IBM'S Business and Professional Community

The Greater IBM Connection (**ibm.com/ibm/greateribm**) is an internal social networking site that gives IBM employees and former IBMers a rich connection to the people with whom they work, on both a personal and a professional level. The network helps employees make new connections, track current friends and coworkers, and renew contacts with people they have worked with in the past, including retirees. When employees join the network, they get a profile page. They can use the status message field and the free-form "About Me" section on their profile page to let other people at IBM know where they are, what they are doing, and even what they are thinking. In 2014, over 440,000 IBMers were connected to one another using IBM Connections platform.

Employees can also use the network to post photos, create lists, and organize events. If users are hosting an event, they can create an event page on the network and invite people to attend. The page can also be a place to spread the buzz about the event and get people talking about it through the comments feature.

The Greater IBM connection can also come in handy when preparing for conference calls. If users do not know some of the people on the conference call, they can check out the participants' profiles beforehand and find out if they have common interests, either work-related or recreational, or if they have colleagues in common.

In addition to the social goal, the network team created the site to help IBM employees meet the challenge of building professional relationships that are vital to working in large, distributed enterprises. The network can help IBM employees discover people with common interests or the right skills for a project. Learning more about someone – personally and professionally – facilitates making contacts and might entice people to learn about the ongoing projects and activities of other people. This network can also provide valuable insights for managers evaluating employees for promotion.

The IBM network is related to IBM's social business Innovation Projects, cited later in this chapter. It is also related to *IBM's Connections*, the company's social software platform.

How Enterprise Social Networking Helps Employees and Organizations

Enterprise social networking can help employees in one or more of the following ways:

1. **Quick access to knowledge, know-how, and "know-who."** As people list their skills, expertise, and experience, enterprise social networks can help simplify the job of locating people with specified knowledge and skills.
2. **Expansion of social connections and broadening of affiliations.** Enterprise social networks help managers and professionals to know people better by interacting with them in online communities, and by keeping up with their personal information. Such interaction and information about others can decrease the social distance in a company.
3. **Self-branding.** People can become creative in building their profiles the way they want to be known. It helps them promote their personal brand within the corporation.
4. **Referrals, testimonials, and benchmarking.** Enterprise social networks can help employees prepare and display referrals and testimonials about their work and also benchmark them with their colleagues.

Benefits to Organizations

The benefits to organizations, as well as to employees, were presented in Section 8.1. In addi-

tion, the benefits to employees can develop into benefits to organizations in the long run.

Support Services for Enterprise Social Networks

Businesses can use a variety of services and vendors to support their social networking. Two examples follow.

Example 1: Socialcast

Socialcast (**socialcast.com**), a VMware company, is an online vendor providing social network platforms that enterprises can deploy to let employees create their profiles and use them to facilitate collaboration and communication with coworkers. In 2014, the company had more than 30,000 customers in 190 countries. The platform connects people to knowledge, ideas, and resources. For details, see **socialcast.com/about**.

Example 2: Socialtext

Socialtext (**socialtext.com**) is a vendor of enterprise social software, providing an integrated suite of Web-based applications including social media tools and platforms. The company also provides Web security services. Businesses can benefit by keeping employees connected to the enterprise strategy and operations. For details, see **socialtext.com/about**.

Yammer: A Collaboration Platform

Yammer, Inc. (**yammer.com**), is a Microsoft company. According to its website, Yammer is a private social network that helps employees collaborate across departments, locations, and business apps in over 200,000 companies (in 2014). Yammer brings together people for conversations, content, and business data in a single location. With Yammer, you can easily stay connected to coworkers and information, collaborate with team members and make an impact at work. It is used for communication and collaboration within organizations, or between organizational members and pre-designated groups.

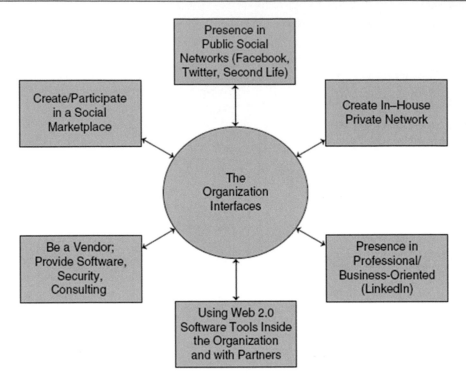

Figure 8.1 The major interfaces with social networking

Key Features (in Early 2014)

Yammer's social networks allow users to (compiled from Blair (2011) and from **about. yammer.com**):

- **Converse using enterprise microblogging.** Start a conversation, read posts, and actively collaborate with coworkers in real time using microblogging.
- **Create profiles.** Report your expertise, work experience, and contact information. You can upload photos, images, and documents. This will help you share information with others, and become easier to find.
- **Manage groups.** Create new groups or join private or public groups, and then discuss issues or collaborate with the group members. (Discover and join groups, invite team members to join and start collaborating.)
- **Conduct secure and private messaging.** Create a private dialog with one or multiple coworkers, similar to what you can do on Facebook. Secure the messages with Yammer's security features.
- **Create external networks.** Create external networks for working with business partners.

- **Create a company directory.** Create a directory of all employees.
- **Archive knowledge.** Archive all online conversations to be fully searchable.
- **Use administrative tools.** Keep the Yammer network running smoothly with a suite of features built to increase managerial control.
- **Employ tagging.** Tag the content and message in the company's network to make content easy to search for and to organize.
- **Integrate applications.** Install third-party applications into Yammer to increase the functionality of the company's network.
- **Deploy mobile capabilities.** Connect to the company's network from anywhere, at any time. Download free iPhone, Blackberry, Android, and Windows Mobile applications.

How Companies Interface with Social Networking

Enterprises can interface with public and/or private social networks in several ways. The major interfaces, which are shown in Figure 8.1, are described next.

- Use existing public social networks, such as Facebook or virtual worlds such as Second Life (**secondlife.com**), to create pages and microcommunities; advertise products or services; and post requests for advice, job openings, and so forth.
- Create an in-house private social network and then use it for communication and collaboration among employees and retirees or with outsiders (e.g., customers, suppliers, designers). Employees can create virtual rooms in their company's social networks where they can deploy applications to share information or to collaborate.
- Conduct business activities in a business-oriented or professional social network (e.g., LinkedIn or Sermo).
- Create services for social networks, such as software development, security, consulting services, and more (e.g., Oracle, IBM, Microsoft).
- Use Web 2.0 software tools, mostly blogs, wikis, workspaces, microblogging (Twitter), and team rooms, and create innovative applications for both internal and external users.
- Create and/or participate in a social marketplace (such as Fotolia; **us.fotolia.com**).

SECTION 8.3 REVIEW QUESTIONS

1. Define enterprise (private) social networks.
2. List the major characteristics of enterprise social networks.
3. Describe the enterprise social network within IBM.
4. List the benefits to organizations.
5. Describe Yammer and identify its connections with social networks.
6. List the different ways that companies interface with social networking.

8.4 SOCIAL COMMERCE: APPLICATIONS IN VIRTUAL WORLDS

Virtual worlds can be effective platforms for online social interactions, community building, conducting business transactions, and facilitating learning and training (e.g., education). As briefly described in Chapter 2, users can navigate and move around in a virtual world using their avatars, which they can also use for communication and other activities. Virtual worlds also may enable trading in virtual goods, and paying for them with virtual money. For the uses of virtual worlds, see **makeuseof.com/tag/what-are-virtual-worlds-what-are-their-uses-makeuseof-explains**. For a list of the major virtual worlds, see **arianeb.com/more3Dworlds.htm**. For using virtual worlds in education, see Angel Learning's 2008 White Paper titled "The Power of Virtual Worlds in Education: A Second Life Primer and Resource for Exploring the Potential of Virtual Worlds to Impact Teaching and Learning" (accessible at **soma.sbcc.edu/Users/Russotti/SL/PowerofVirtual%20WorldsEdu_0708.pdf**).

Businesses can make use of virtual worlds, not just for entertaining their customers and prospects, but also by engaging them in an experience that may be unavailable in the real world. Due to the use of multiple senses in a virtual world, users' experiences can be more fulfilling than in a 2D world, or sometimes even more than in a physical one. For instance, according to a Second Life's website posting (February 2011), Second Life had over 22 million registered user accounts (unique residents) who spent more than 115 million hours a month on the site. As of June 2013, the number of registered users has risen to over 36 million. (See the article and infographic by Reahard (2013) at **massively.joystiq.com/2013/06/20/seco-nd-life-readies-for-10th-anniversary-celebrates-a-million-a**.) Businesses can leverage features and spaces, as illustrated next, to exploit the opportunities in virtual worlds.

The Features of Virtual Worlds

Virtual worlds have a set of properties or features that provide the capabilities to conduct business there.

The Features That Businesses Can Leverage

- **Shared space.** The virtual world provides many users with the ability to participate simultaneously in activities, engage in discussions, and participate in collaborative activities.
- **3-D visualization (graphical user interface).** The virtual world depicts both 2-D and 3-D images.
- **Immediacy.** Interactions usually occur in real time, and users experience the results of their actions immediately.
- **Interactivity.** Participants can create or modify customized content. They may do so in collaboration with others.
- **Persistence.** Activities in virtual worlds are happening whether members are present or not.
- **Socialization and community formation.** A virtual world provides opportunities for socializing with other users and facilitates group formation of different types (e.g., work teams).

IBM, Walmart, Toyota, Sears, Wells Fargo, and other large companies have experimented with virtual worlds for testing new designs, customer service, employee training, and marketing communication.

The Major Spaces in Virtual Worlds
The following are brief descriptions of the major spaces used in virtual worlds:

1. **Social space.** Place where users' avatars (and their owners) can meet, discuss, share information and opinions, and socialize.

2. **Entertainment space.** Place where avatars (and their owners) can play games, watch movies, and attend concerts in a 3-D environment.
3. **Transaction space.** Marketplace where one can conduct business and financial transactions, sell and buy available virtual goods as well as some real goods at a virtual webstore.
4. **Experimental/demonstration space.** Place in the virtual world where real-world environments, products, and services can be simulated for experimentation, demonstration, training, and testing.
5. **Collaboration space.** Place for collaboration, innovation, and new product design and development.
6. **Smart agent space.** Place where software agents can seek information and engage with other agents to fulfil or facilitate transactions for their owners.
7. **Fantasy space.** A dream world where people can do things that are not feasible or not affordable in the real world (e.g., take trip to the moon or an expensive cruise).
8. **Educational Space.** Certain places in the virtual world are dedicated to educational activities such as teaching classes, doing projects, or learning by doing special projects.

One can arrange for the use of one or more of these eight spaces in innovative ways for business, education, medical, political, and other uses. Business applications of virtual worlds are varied and their use depends on the type of business in which a company is engaged, in the organizational objectives, and the target user profiles.

The Major Categories of Virtual World Applications

It is common to classify major applications into 18 categories (adapted from Ciaramitaro 2010; Murugesan 2008; Reeves and Read 2009).

1. **Webstores and online sales.** Companies have set up webstores in virtual worlds to enable customers to have a more immersive experience by trying out products, including clothes, cars, or jewellery before they buy them. This is done in a 3-D virtual salesroom. Potential buyers can also conduct research, dress avatars, and sometimes complete a purchase through links that lead them to a secure trading place. For details, see Second Life's 'Shop: Learn' page at **secondlife.com/shop/learn**.

2. **Front offices or help desks.** Virtual worlds can act as access points for customer service. The help desk is staffed by avatars (see Chapter 2 for avatars at airports). This service is available around the clock.

3. **Advertising and product demonstrations.** Marketers and advertisers can place 8D display ads and banners promoting products or services at various locations in virtual worlds to catch the attention of visitors. Consumers also can view demonstrations by avatars on how to install or assemble products such as washing machines or furniture. There are several advantages for using virtual worlds. Virtual stores allow businesses to reach a variety of demographically diverse customers. Furthermore, some real world constraints may be reduced or eliminated in virtual worlds. In addition, the cost of experimenting with virtual things is minimal and there is no cost of making errors. Restrictions and costs that are found in real world situations are further reduced.

4. **Content creation and distribution.** Virtual worlds can serve as channels for delivering music, games, art, and other forms of interactive content for engaging the participants.

5. **Meetings, seminars, and conferences.** Virtual worlds are being used as venues for individuals to virtually meet, participate, and interact through their avatars. Such interactions can reduce the cost and time of conducting meetings in the real world.

6. **Training.** Another promising use for virtual worlds is interactive and/or collaborative training. Trainees can learn by participating in simulations and role-playing. For example, one hotel chain is using virtual lobbies to train receptionists. Other organizations are developing applications that can help them train staff on how to deal with emergencies such as accidents and natural disasters. Another area where this can be used is military training (e.g., flight and battlefield simulations). For details, see Heiphetz and Woodill (2010).

7. **Education.** Universities are using virtual worlds as a new immersive and interactive platform that is useful for interacting with students, and even for teaching courses.

8. **Recruiting.** A growing number of organizations, including governments and the military, are recruiting employees via virtual worlds. All the activities of recruitment, ranging from providing job details to interviewing candidates, are conducted at the recruiter's virtual office. This mode of recruiting is gaining acceptance by technology-savvy graduates and job seekers.

9. **Tourism promotion.** Government tourist boards and tourist operators are using virtual worlds to promote their tourism destinations by providing tourists with 3-D virtual immersive experiences of real places and activities of interest.

10. **Museums and art galleries.** Many artists and agencies are setting up virtual

museums and galleries to display their creations and to promote sales. They also use virtual worlds to stage musicals and other performances.

11. **Information points.** Virtual worlds are used as sophisticated information kiosks. They can act as extremely powerful, interactive, and dynamic online resources or brochures.

12. **Data visualization and manipulation.** Interactive data visualization and manipulation in the virtual environment is an interesting new application of interest to enterprises and professionals. For instance, the software *Glasshouse* by Green Phosphor (**greenphosphor.com**) allows users to export data from either a spread sheet or database query to a virtual world and presents the user with a 3-D representation of the data in a virtual world environment for the user to explore interactively. A user's avatar can then manipulate the visualization of the data by drilling down into it, re-sorting it, or moving it around to view it from many different angles.

13. **Renting virtual world land and buildings.** One can earn virtual money by selling or renting buildings and lands in strategic locations in virtual worlds and by engaging in the "real estate" business in the virtual world.

14. **Platform for social science research.** Virtual worlds are also a good platform for conducting experimental social science research to observe how people behave or react (through their avatars) in structured and unstructured situations, and for studying customer behavior in virtual worlds.

15. **Market research.** Using virtual worlds as a platform enables companies to test new products by getting feedback from customers. These insights may give companies a competitive edge.

16. **Platform for design.** In order to receive feedback and opinions, many companies show images of virtual things such as parks and structures, furniture, and avatars to potential customers and designers in order to receive feedback and opinions.

17. **Providing CRM to employees and a platform for socialization.** Companies use virtual worlds for providing CRM to employees and/or customers. For example, several companies have created islands in Second Life dedicated to the sole use of their employees or for customer care.

18. **Virtual tradeshows.** Virtual tradeshows (sometimes called *virtual trade fairs*), take place in virtual worlds (see Yu 2010).

The Landscape of Virtual World Commercial Applications

The potential of virtual worlds, particularly when they are integrated with other IT and business systems, is large. A virtual world is particularly attractive to video game players, where sellers can build communities of fans and advertise. Other businesses are using virtual worlds for collaboration, design testing, learning, and relationship building.

Business Applications in Virtual Worlds

The following are examples of applications used in virtual worlds.

Example: Sony's Home for a Virtual Community of Gamers

Sony's Home virtual world (**us.playstation. com/psn/playstation-home**) is a large gathering place and marketplace for owners of PlayStation games. As of 2012, it has attracted about 25 million users worldwide who spend an average of 70 minutes per session (see **digiday. com/publishers/sonys-home-coming-back**). The community of gamers can play hundreds of games, attend different events, and buy many virtual goods.

Today, many organizations are looking for ways to conduct virtual meetings in Second Life, instead of in the real world.

For a review of other examples of how businesses and organizations are using virtual worlds to make the world greener, refer to *The Green Book: An Enterprise Guide to Virtual Worlds*, published by Association of Virtual Worlds (**associationofvirtualworlds.com**).

Representative Virtual World Applications Around the Globe

Here are a few other representative examples of virtual world applications (some of which have changed over time):

- **Hana City** (**hanacity.com**). Hana Bank of Korea uses a virtual world to educate its future customers, children ages 10 to 15. Its virtual world teaches children about home financing investment options.
- **MeetMe** (**meet-me.jp**). To make your retail shopping experience more exciting, this virtual world takes you shopping (virtually) in Japan.
- **New Belgium Brewing** (**newbelgium. com**). This brewery has added a virtual component to its regular website. In this virtual world, visitors can take an interactive tour of the brewery.
- **Aloft** (**starwoodhotels.com/alofthotels/index.html**). Aloft, the global brand of Starwood hotels and resorts, tested the design of its hotels on Second Life. The company used the feedback collected from more than a million visitors to create its final design for the hotels.

For additional examples and discussion see Reeves and Read (2009) and Knowledge at Wharton.

Trading Virtual Goods and Properties

There are many business opportunities for buying and selling virtual goods. Sales are conducted by using electronic catalogs, classified advertisements, and auctions (e.g., see **usd.auctions.secondlife.com**). Payments are made with virtual money ("Linden dollars") that can be converted to real money. The tax and contract/legal issues are not clear (e.g., see **secondlife.com/corporate/vat.php**). In 2013, the U.S. Government Accountability office released some guidelines and definitions for a virtual economy and currency, (see **cpa2biz.com/Content/media/ PRODUCER_CONTENT/Newsletters/ Articles_2013/Tax/VirtualEconomy.jsp**).

The major products/services in this category are: land, retail, manufacturing, scripting, fashion, and the adult entertainment industry.

The Major Drivers of Social Commerce in Virtual Worlds

The key factors that drive business applications in virtual worlds are:

- **Resemblance to the real-world environment.** Businesses can use the technology since it can simulate, and even conduct real-world activities (e.g., customer service) more promptly and a low cost (e.g., product design). Additionally, interactions with business partners are easy. It is also a place for attractive advertisements. Users can get a feel of the real world without cost and time constraints (e.g., buy properties, travel).
- **Shopping for virtual goods.** The major shopping activity is in real estate. Users can buy land, develop it, build on it and sell it. Millions of people who cannot afford their dream house (e.g., in developing countries) are satisfied with a virtual house. You can also shop for fascinating goods at Second Life at **secondlife.com/shop**.

- **Attractions for the younger generations.** Today's youth are tomorrow's shoppers. They grew up with computer applications and love games and online entertainment.
- **New means of navigation and discovery.** Virtual worlds enable the creation of visually attractive and unique products that visitors never knew existed.
- **The attributes and capabilities.** These are unique to virtual worlds. First, they are mostly 3D. Second, the worlds are populated with avatars. The virtual worlds are interactive and can be manipulated and changed by users at very low cost.
- **Better online meeting spaces and collaborative platforms.** Virtual worlds provide interesting platforms for collaboration, meetings, discussions, and chatting (e.g., try to chat in 3D at **imvu.com**).
- **Interactive environment for education and training.** Several activities, as shown in Table 8.1, can be used to facilitate training and learning.

Concerns and Limitations of Commercial Activities in Virtual Worlds

Although virtual worlds were expected to become a major platform for commerce, business, and social activities, they have not yet reached this level. Despite their promise, virtual worlds present several challenges and constraints of which developers, businesses, and individual users must be aware. Virtual worlds such as Second Life are not easy to use, and are expensive to build and operate. Software needs to be installed and updated, which for many users is too cumbersome. Additionally, substantial hardware is needed. There are also administrative issues such as legal, taxation, ethics, and reliability. Moreover, there are technology limitations, including reliability and accessibility, security, and some users experience difficulties in learning.

According to **en.wikipedia.org/wiki/Second_Life**, there is considerable fraud and violation of intellectual property in Second Life. Wikipedia provides examples of fraud and suggestions for protection. The Second Life Community also provides suggestions on dealing with abuse and harassment at **community.secondlife.com/**

Table 8.1 The use of virtual worlds to facilitate learning

Activity	Description
Simulation	Users can manipulate different scenarios and see results. Creating a virtual business is a popular activity
Distance learning	A virtual world can be used as a place for working, learning, and/or collaboration. It is also used for team-building, collaborative learning and collaborative problem solving
Class meetings	Learning institutions offer many virtual classes (mostly in Second Life). Students can explore, share, and work with teachers via their avatars
Exploration	The virtual world is a good platform for explorative learning. Learners can explore in a similar way to a real world exploration. The information is communicated by the environment to the user/avatar visually, by text or other media
Visualization	Visualization is a key learning enabler. The 3D virtual world provides an excellent opportunity to use images, videos, etc. to facilitate problem solving
Imaginative scenarios	People create fantasy objects and settings to entertain themselves and others
Information dissemination	Many organizations, governments, and universities provides updated interactive information, which can be used to learn topics such as geography, public administration, hospitality management, and technology

Sources: Based on Daden Ltd. (2010), Murugesan (2008), Terdiman (2008), and **secondlife.com** (accessed April 2014).

**t5/tkb/articleprintpage/tkb-id/English_KB@
tkb/article-id/283**.

Virtual worlds are targets for cybercriminals.
For instance, Second Life has been attacked not
only by outsiders, but also by groups of residents
who created objects that harass other residents, or
disrupted or damaged the system. Finally, virtual
worlds are full of adult entertainment activities,
some of which may not be legal. To protect the
users, Second Life has increased security.

For a comprehensive teaching case that demonstrates both the opportunities and challenges in
deploying Second Life, see Vitzthum et al. (2011).

For guidelines dealing with the major concerns regarding implementing virtual worlds, see
Mahar and Mahar (2009).

SECTION 8.4 REVIEW QUESTIONS
1. List the major features of virtual worlds.
2. List the major spaces of virtual worlds.
3. Select 5 categories of major application of the
   18 and describe them in detail.
4. Describe three business applications of virtual
   worlds in detail.
5. Describe trading of virtual properties.
6. List the major drivers of virtual worlds.
7. What are some of the concerns about the use
   of virtual worlds?

8.5   SOCIAL ENTERTAINMENT

The rich media capabilities of Web 2.0 technologies; the ability to engage millions of people who
congregate in social networks and who are interested in online entertainment; the availability of
innovative social media tools; and the creative and
collaborative nature of Web 2.0 all facilitate
social entertainment (e.g., *Gangnam Style* was
YouTube's most watched video in 2012 and 2013).
Web 2.0 tools also are aiding in the proliferation of
on-demand entertainment. The most well-known
entertainment application is streaming music (e.g.,
iTunes; **apple.com/itunes**). Also popular are
Spotify, Pandora, and Google's All Access (**play.
google.com/about/music**). The trend today is to
stream music on-demand usually for free, which
gives listeners the ability to enjoy whatever they
want, whenever they want. Jurgensen (2014)

provides a comprehensive coverage of digital
music today and tomorrow, including information
about providers and about players such as The
Entery Level. Finally, Facebook and Twitter
entered this area. This section describes some of
the entertainment-centered social networks, as
well as other issues related to entertainment in
social commerce. Note that a major issue with
such social networks is copyright violations, a
topic we discuss in detail in Chapter 15.

Entertainment and Social Networks

A large number of social networks are fully or
partially dedicated to entertainment. Well known
examples in 2014 are Vimeo, Netflix, and
MySpace. MySpace has a licensing agreement
with Sony BMG and other large media companies that gives its members free access to streaming videos, music, and other entertainment. The
following are representative examples of the use
of Web 2.0 applications for entertainment.

Mixi

In Japan, Mixi, Inc. (**mixi.jp**) is a highly visited
social networking service even though users must
be invited to join. Mixi's goal is to allow users to
build friendships with other users who share
common interests. As of March 2012, the site had
about 27 million members and over 1 million
small communities of friends and interests.

Last.fm

Last.fm (**last.fm**) is not just an Internet radio station. It also recommends music to its listeners.
Musical profiles are constructed when users listen to a personal music collection with a Last.fm
plug-in or when they listen to the Last.fm Internet
radio service. As of 2014, regular membership is
free; premium membership is $3 per month. The
site, which operates in 12 major languages (as of
2013), won the Digital Music Award for Best
Music Community Site in 2006.

Pandora

Similar to Last.fm, Pandora (**pandora.com**) is a site
for music lovers (see Chapter 3). It mostly acts as
a personal radio. The site is based on user-centered

music recommendations. Pandora can create a personalized "radio station" based on a user's search for a particular artist, song, or genre.

Web Series and Streaming Movies

Web series are similar to episodic series on TV (e.g., soap operas). The number of Web series is increasing, and some are already available on DVD. Examples include *Hemlock Grove*, *House of Cards*, and *Johnny Dynamo*. For more about Web series and other examples, see **webserieschannel.com/web-series-101**.

Hulu

Hulu (**hulu.com**) offers advertisement-supported streaming on-demand videos of TV shows and movies from NBC, Fox, Disney (including ABC programs), and other networks and studios. Due to copyright laws, Hulu offers videos only to users in the United States and a few other countries. Hulu provides video in Flash video format. In addition, Hulu offers some TV shows and movies in high definition in a manner similar to Google Sites, Fox Interactive Media, and Yahoo! Sites. Users can manually share videos they like on their Facebook pages by using the "Facebook" button. It is not necessary to connect their Hulu and Facebook accounts to do this. Hulu is one of the most popular Internet video sites (see **nielsen. com/us/en/newswire/2013/binging-is-the-new-viewing-for-over-the-top-streamers.html**). Hulu offers some of its services free, supported by advertising. It also offers Hulu Plus, which includes premium shows and the ability to watch on more devices for a monthly fee of $7.99. This service, however, also features limited advertising. For more about their offerings and difference between Hulu and Hulu Plus, click on the "frequently asked questions" tab at **hulu.com/plus**.

Advertising and subscriptions are the primary social commerce business models for most streaming entertainment sites.

Funny-or-Die and Cracked.com

According to their website, Funny or Die (**funnyordie.com**) is a comedy video website created by actor and comedian Will Ferrell, among others. Unlike other viral video sites, members of Funny or Die are encouraged to vote on videos that they view. If they think the video is funny, viewers cast a vote for "Funny." The video then gets a score of the total percentage of people who voted the video "Funny." If the video receives an 80% or greater "Funny" rating after 100,000 views, it gets an "Immortal" ranking. If the video receives a 20% or less "Funny" rating after 1,000 views, it "dies" and is relegated to the Crypt section of the site.

Cracked.com, another humor website (which includes videos), also uses crowdsourcing to solicit material from the Internet crowd.

Multimedia Presentation and Sharing Sites

Multimedia sharing can be done in several ways, and its purpose is entertainment, advertising, training, and socialization. The following are some representative types of sharing, and companies in each area:

- **Photography and art sharing.** Flickr, Instagram, Picasa, SmugMug, Photobucket
- **Video sharing.** YouTube, Vimeo, Metacafe, Openfilm, Japan's Niconico (**nicovideo.jp**; now available in English as well),
- **Livecasting.** Twitch.tv, Livestream, Skype, Ustream
- **Mobile Social Networks:** Path, Liveme
- **Music and audio sharing.** ccMixter, FreeSound, Last.fm, MySpace, ReverbNation, The Hype Machine (**hypem. com/popular**)
- **Presentation sharing.** SlideSnack, SlideShare, authorSTREAM
- **Media and entertainment platforms.** Kaltura Open Source Video (**corp.kaltura.com/Video-Solutions/Media-and-Entertainment**, Accenture (Media and Entertainment; **accenture.com/us-en/ industry/media-entertainment/Pages/ media-entertainment-index.aspx**)

- **Virtual worlds.** Second Life, The Sims, Activeworlds, IMVU
- **Game sharing.** Miniclip, Kongregate

Note that many of these have some features of social networks; therefore, they may be referred to as such. In addition, most of these generate revenue from advertising and/or subscriptions, including from mobile devices.

SECTION 8.5 REVIEW QUESTIONS
1. Relate social networks to streaming music.
2. Describe the ways you can watch videos on the Web (streaming videos on-demand).
3. Describe some of the multimedia presentation sites.

8.6 SOCIAL GAMES AND GAMIFICATION

A **social game** is a video multiplayer game played on the Internet, mostly in social networks or in virtual worlds. Gamers can play against computers or against each other. Many social games are "massively" multiplayer online games (known as MMOG or MMO), which are capable of supporting hundreds to many thousands of players simultaneously. MMOG players can compete, collaborate, or just interact with other players around the globe. Many game consoles, including the PSP, PlayStation 8, Xbox 860, Nintendo DSi, and Wii can be played on the Internet. Additionally, mobile devices and smartphones based on such operating systems as Android, iOS, webOS, and Windows Mobile are seeing an increase in the number of MMO available games. Social games are very popular. According to the 2018 State of Online Gaming Report, 44% of worldwide Internet users play online games (see the report and infographic at **auth-83051f68-ec6c-44e0-afe5-bd8902acff57. cdn.spilcloud.com/v1/archives/1384952861.25_ State_of_Gaming_2013_US_FINAL.pdf**), which is over 1.2 billion people (see **venture-beat.com/2013/11/25/more-than-1-2-billion-people-are-playing-games**). Although some games require fees for enhanced features, many are free (see Pearce et al. 2009).

Games on Social Networks

A **social network game** is a video game that is played in social networks, and usually involves multiplayers. Social (network) games may have little or nothing to do with how *social* the games are played. However, some games have social elements such as educating the public, gift-giving, and helping other or sharing playing strategies.

For a game to be more social, it should facilitate and encourage engagement and communication about the environment outside the game, run on or integrated with a social network, and use that network to enhance game play between players.

Example: Popular Games on Facebook
Players can choose from several thousands of games on Facebook. Some games are played by 50–150 million people each. The most popular games each attract tens of millions of players. Facebook's list of popular games for February 2014 includes Candy Crush Saga (most popular in 2014), FarmVille, FarmVille 2, CityVille, Bejeweled Blitz, Pet Rescue Saga, Criminal Case, Texas HoldEm Poker, Words with Friends, and Bubble Safari. (See **gamechitah.com/top-games-on-facebook.html**.)

As of September 2013, the major Facebook developers for games are King, Zynga, Social Point, and Pretty Simple. (See **beforeitsnews. com/science-and-technology/2013/10/top-9-facebook-developer-list-games-september-2013-2-2644806.html**.) Note that there is a trend to play more casino type games. To enhance the game experience, some platforms utilize the players' social graphs.

To learn more about social games, go to **museumstuff.com/learn/topics/Social_network_game**.

The Business Aspects of Social Games

To understand the variety of games and their properties and commercial possibilities, we suggest you watch the video "Social Media Games: Worldwide Gamification Is the New Paradigm for Life and Business" at **youtube.com/watch?v=xCWsgBHY_VU**. The video presents opportunities for advertising, marketing, and training, among others. Also, visit the site of Zynga (**zynga.com**), a major vendor in the field. During the 4th quarter of 2013 Zynga had about 298 million visitors. It took Facebook 4.5 years to reach the same level of visitors that Zynga reached in 2.5 years. However, Zynga's revenue was overestimated, causing the stock price to decline drastically. As far as revenues, Facebook games provide very little per person per month income. Electronic Arts, a Zynga competitor, has some games that generate three to five times more per game. Both companies have gone mobile. For example, FarmVille2 for iPad and iPhone are now available. For additional discussion, see Reeves and Read (2009).

Educational Social Games

Games can also be educational as the following examples show. Environmental apps for kids (e.g., for tablets) can be found at **usatoday.com/story/tech/columnist/gudmundsen/2013/09/01/ecology-learning-apps-kids/2700271**. See also **ecogamer.org/environmental-games.**

Example 1: Pollution Reduction Game
The Philippine-made Facebook game called Alter Space aims to educate the people on how to reduce pollution. Specifically, it educates the players about the concepts of carbon footprints and cleaner energy, and how people can help achieve a cleaner world. (Inactive now.)

Example 2: Economic and Finance Game – Empire Avenue
Empire Avenue (**empireavenue.com**) is a social media stock market simulation game where individuals and businesses buy and sell virtual shares

from each other. The shares can be of individuals, companies, etc. The share price is based on the shares' trading activity coupled with the players' influence on the major social networks. The trading is done with reward points called *Eaves* and *Vees*. In the game, there are financial data and decision-making capabilities about dividends, number of shares outstanding, and share prices, to name just a few. Empire has many variables within the game. The reward points can also be used as virtual currency to play the Social Market game. Players can interact via popular social networks (e.g., Facebook, Twitter, Instagram) across the Web. The more social the player is, the more virtual currency the player will earn, and the bigger the player's Empire will become. Several major brands are already using this site (e.g., Toyota, AT&T, Audi, and Ford). For details, see Empire Avenue at **businessesgrow.com/2014/01/08/how-empire-avenue-crushed-my-soul**.

Gamers Helped Scientists
For decades, scientists were unable to unfold the chemical chain of an enzyme of an AIDS-like virus. However, according to a September 19, 2011 article in the Balita Filipino News (**balita.com**), researchers at the University of Washington turned Foldit, a "fun for purpose" program created by the university, which transfers scientific problems into competitive computer games.

The gamers were divided into groups and were challenged to compete by using their problem-solving skills to build 3D models of a protein that scientists had been unable to find for years. The players solved the chemical chain problem accurately in just three weeks. (See **balita.com/online-gamers-crack-aids-enzyme-puzzle**.) For more about Foldit ("Solve Puzzles for Science"), see **fold.it/portal**.

Gamification

Some social games are designed so that players will connect with vendors or brands in the game environments. This is only one aspect of **gamification**, which refers to the introduction of gaming into social networking. Gamification can also be viewed as the introduction of social networking activities into online games. Our interest is in those applications that are related to social commerce and e-commerce. For more definitions and limitations, see the Gamification Wiki (**gamification.org**), and Duggan and Shoup (2013).

Social activities are not new to online gaming. For example, players collectively agree to the rules of the games. Also, gamers need trust between the players. What is new here is the integration of traditional multiplayer games and social networking. Given that so many people play online games, it is not surprising that vendors are encouraging players (e.g., via rewards) to engage in desired behavior (e.g., problem solving or collaboration). Vendors also use games as advertising platforms. For a gamification framework see Chou (2012).

According to a Lithium white paper (2011) and Florentine (2014), companies can use gamification to create winning social customer experiences such as increasing loyalty, building trust, accelerating innovation, providing brand engagement, and increasing relevant knowledge. For how to use gamification to engage employees, see Hein (2013).

For commercial possibilities and strategies of social games and gamification, see Radoff (2011), Dignan (2011), and Zichermann and Linder (2013).

For additional information, you can download the e-book titled "The Essential Social Playbook: 8 Steps to Turn Social into Sales," at **powerreviews.com/assets/new/ebooks/powerreviewsessential social playbook.pdf** and review Walter (2013).

SECTION 8.6 REVIEW QUESTIONS
1. Describe online games.
2. Describe games in social networks.
3. Discuss the business aspects of social games.
4. What is gamification? Relate it to social commerce.

8.7 CROWDSOURCING FOR PROBLEM SOLVING AND CONTENT CREATION

The essentials of crowdsourcing were described in Chapter 2. Listed there, as a major capability, was the facilitation of problem solving.

Crowdsourcing as a Distributed Problem Solving Enabler

Crowdsourcing actually describes a set of tools, concepts, and methodologies that deal with the process of outsourcing work, including problem solving and idea generation to a *community* of potential solvers known as the 'crowd.'

More than just brainstorming or ideation, crowdsourcing uses proven techniques to focus on the crowd's innovation, creativity, and problem-solving capacity on topics of vital interest to the host organization. An overview of crowdsourcing is provided in Jeff Howe's video titled "Crowdsourcing" (3:20 minutes) at **youtube.com/watch?v=F0-UtNg3ots**, **crowd-sourcing.org**, and in Brabham (2013). Also watch Brabham's video "Crowdsourcing As a Model for Problem Solving" (6.1 minutes) at **youtube.com/watch?v=hLGhKyiJ8Xo**.

Crowdsourcing Models
Howe (2008) has classified applications of crowd-sourcing into the following four categories:

1. **Collective intelligence (or wisdom).** Here, people are solving problems and providing new insights and ideas leading to product, process, or service innovations.
2. **Crowd creation.** Here, people are creating various types of content and sharing it with others (paid or for free). The content may be used for problem solving, advertising, or knowledge accumulation. This can be done by splitting large tasks into small segments (e.g., contributing content to create the Wikipedia).
3. **Crowd voting.** Here, people are giving their opinions and ratings on ideas, products, or services, as well as evaluating and filtering information presented to them. An example would be voting on American Idol.

4. **Crowd support and funding.** Here, people are contributing and supporting endeavors for social causes, which might include volunteering their effort and time, offering donations, and micro-financing.

Chaordix Corp. (**chaordix.com**) classifies crowdsourcing into the following three models:
1. **Secretive.** Individuals submit ideas, and the winner is selected by the company. Ideas are not visible to all participants.
2. **Collaborative.** Individuals submit ideas, the crowd evaluates the ideas, and the crowd picks the winners. Ideas are visible to all participants.
3. **Panel selects.** Individuals submit ideas, the crowd evolves ideas, a panel selects finalists, and the crowd votes for the winner.

A *crowdsortium* is a community of industry practitioners whose mission is to advance the crowdsourcing industry through best practices and education (see **crowdsortium.org**).

Crowdsourcing also has the potential to be a problem-solving mechanism for governments and nonprofit use via community participation. Urban and transit planning are prime areas for crowdsourcing. One project used crowdsourcing to encourage public participation in the planning process for the Salt Lake City transit system (from 2008 to 2009). Another notable application of crowdsourcing to government problem solving is the Peer to Patent Community Patent Review project for the U.S. Patent and Trademark Office, see **peertopatent.org**. (This project opens the patent examination process to public participation.)

Progressive companies and organizations now recognize the value of tapping into the wisdom of the crowd to capture the best answers and the most innovative ideas.

The Process of Crowdsourcing

The process of crowdsourcing, which was described briefly in Chapter 2, differs from application to application depending on the models of the specific problem to be solved and the method used. However, the following steps exist in most enterprise applications, even though the details of the execution differ. The major steps are based on the generic process described in Chapter 2. They are:

1. Identify the task (problem) you want to investigate or accomplish.
2. Select the target crowd.
3. Broadcast the task to the crowd. (Frequently to an unidentified crowd in an open call, as Starbucks and Dell do.)
4. Engage the crowd in accomplishing the task (e.g., idea generation).
5. Collect the user-generated content. (This may include a submission of solutions, voting, new ideas, etc.)
6. Evaluate the quality of submitted material—by the management that initiated the request, by experts, or by the crowd.
7. Accept or reject a solution.
8. Compensate the crowd.

The MIT Guide for Collective Intelligence

Malone et al. (2010) conducted a detailed analysis about the use of what they call **collective intelligence** (**CI**), which is an application of crowdsourcing for problem solving, idea generation, and innovation. The researchers attempted to answer the question: "How can you get the crowds to do what your business needs done?" Their major findings are provided in Malone et al. (2010).

Successfully Deployed Crowdsourcing Systems: Some Representative Examples

The following are some representative examples of implemented crowdsourcing systems.

- **Dell's IdeaStorm (ideastorm.com)** enables customers to vote on Dell's product features they prefer, including new ones. Dell is using a technically-oriented crowd, such as the Linux (**linux.org**) community. The crowd submits ideas and sometimes members of the community vote on them.
- **Procter & Gamble's** researchers post their problems at **innocentive.com**, and at **ninesigma.com**, offering cash rewards to problem solvers. P&G uses other crowdsourcing service providers such as **yourencore.com**.
- **Amazon Mechanical Turk (mturk. com)** is a marketplace for distributing large scale work that requires human intelligence. It is limited to large tasks that can be divided (known as HITs – human intelligence tasks) and is posted by companies that need assistance. Then, Amazon arranges workers (the "Mechanical Turk Workers"), each of whom is allocated a small subtask, and is paid when the work is completed. For details see **mturk.com**.
- **Facebook (facebook.com)** used crowdsourcing to translate its site into more than 65 different languages. The completion of the English to French translated by over 4,000 volunteers only took one day; however, Facebook had to hire a team of professional translators to oversee the whole crowdsourcing process to ensure that the resulting translations were accurate.
- **Goldcorp (goldcorp.com)**, a Canadian mining company, was unable to find sufficient gold. In 2000, the company initiated an open call to the public, providing geological data and a $575,000 in prizes to participants with the best methods. Using the submitted ideas, the company discovered $3 billion worth of gold.

- **Frito-Lay (fritolay.com)** used crowdsourcing for designing a successful annual Super Bowl advertising campaign.
- **Wikipedia (wikipedia.org)** is considered by many to be the "granddaddy" of crowdsourcing, and is certainly the world's largest crowdsourcing project.

Tools for Crowdsourcing

To launch crowdsourcing initiatives, businesses and developers can make use of crowdsourcing tools and platforms, such as NineSigma, InnoCentive, YourEncore, yet2, UserVoice, Get Satisfaction, and IdeaScale.

Crowdfunding and Kickstarter

Raising funds from the crowd for different purposes is gaining popularity with several start ups operating in this area. A notable company is Kickstarter. For how they help small businesses see the 2013 video **youtube.com/watch?v=xud OhEYIwyU**.

For tools for crowdfunding, see *2013*CF *Crowdfunding Market* report, or **crowd-sourcing.org** and **powerdecisions.com/faq-idea-generation-methods.cfm**.

Hypios: A Marketplace for Crowdsourcing

According to its website, Hypios (**hypios.com**) is a multinational social marketplace with over 950,000 registered experts across the world. As a problem-solving individual or research organization, one can create a profile, make professional contacts, and connect with colleagues (for a fee), peers, and friends. If you are a problem solver and only want to solve problems on Hypios, you choose what information you want to disclose and decide who can see it. In Hypios, users can share activities with their contacts on other social networks. You can develop your own networks or join one of the many networks that already exist on Hypios. Users can meet with people who share their interests and follow their friends' activities. After seeing what their friends are working on, people can decide to either compete or collaborate with their friends on problem solving. For more information, watch the video titled "Hypios Trailer" (0:46 minutes) at **youtube.com/ watch?v=WecFY6LI9Bk**. Problems to be solved are posted on **hypios.com/problems** (citing fees, solutions needed, time frame, etc.) and on their Facebook page (**facebook.com/hypios**). Solvers and solutions are ranked by peers. As a market organizer, Hypios provides a service to solution seekers as it combines intelligent crowdsourcing and expert identification. By applying advanced Semantic Web and machine-learning technologies, Hypios identifies problem solvers based on their publicly available data on the Internet. It then invites these solvers to compete to solve specific research and development (R&D) challenges in their areas of expertise.

Note: Crowdsourcing is used by thousands of volunteers to search disaster areas, such as typhoons in the Philippines and locating the missing MH370 Malaysian jet.

SECTION 8.7 REVIEW QUESTIONS
1. Define crowdsourcing.
2. List the seven crowdsourcing models.
3. List the major steps of the crowdsourcing process.
4. What are the capabilities of Kickstarter and Hypios?

8.8 SOCIAL COLLABORATION (COLLABORATION 2.0)

One of the major applications of Web 2.0 and social media in the enterprise is in the area of collaboration. Some even equate Web 2.0 with enterprise collaboration (e.g., McAfee 2009). Social collaboration is used for many purposes, an important one being product design.

Supporting Social Collaboration

Collaboration in business can be defined as people working with other people toward a common outcome or goal. For a comprehensive overview of collaboration supported by IT, see McCabe et al. (2009). For many images of social collaboration, search Google for: 'Images of social collaboration'.

Social collaboration refers to people's collaboration within and between communities enabled by social media tools and platforms. The processes help people interact and share information to achieve a common goal. It is also known as *Collaboration 2.0*. Collaboration 2.0 is recognized as a major element in social business that can provide considerable benefits (e.g., see examples in IBM Software Group 2011). For implementation of social collaboration, see Carr (2013).

Social Collaboration (Collaboration 2.0)

Collaboration drives business value up by enabling people to work together more efficiently. Wikis and other social software tools can be used effectively by all types and sizes of enterprises for a wide range of tasks and activities. Collaboration helps with solving business problems and uncovering new opportunities, especially with the help of social media tools (see details at Morgan 2012). Collaboration in social networking is done both internally, among employees from different units working in virtual teams, and externally, when working with suppliers, customers, and other business partners. For example, collaboration occurs in forums and other types of groups and by using wikis and blogs. For details on collaboration in social networks, see Coleman and Levine (2008). For the use of Collaboration 2.0 in the enterprise, see Dortch (2012) and Turban et al. (2015).

Social collaboration has several dimensions as illustrated in Figure 8.2.

Some believe that in the future, people will use mostly Web 2.0 tools, rather than e-mail, for collaboration. For a discussion, see **thefutureorganization.com**.

A large number of Web 2.0 tools are used to support social collaboration. The support is given to idea sharing, communication, working together on the same documents, and more. The Web 2.0 tools range from wikis to virtual worlds. For comprehensive coverage, see Coleman and Levine (2008). For the relationship between the

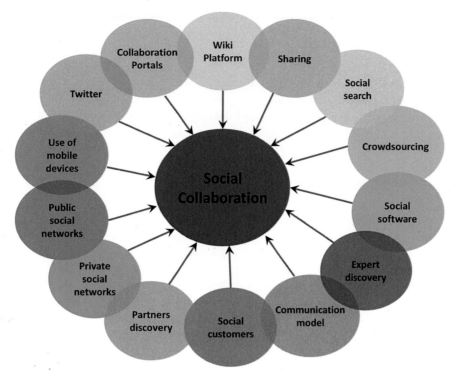

Figure 8.2   The various dimensions of social collaboration

different modes of collaboration and the appropriate tools, see Fauscette (2011).

Dunay (2014) describes in a webinar how to use enterprise social networks for internal collaboration.

The development of tools, philosophies, and procedures of social media support for collaboration allows employees and managers to engage much more fully in the collaboration process. Furthermore, social collaboration has improved the organizational culture.

Social collaboration is supported mainly by:

- Wikis, blogs, and microblogging (e.g., Twitter)
- Virtual worlds (see Heiphetz and Woodill 2010)
- Collaborative communities (forums and discussion groups)
- Early vintage Web 2.0 technologies
- Crowdsourcing
- Other tools (e.g., Yammer)

Most collaboration software vendors are adding Web 2.0 tools to their collaboration suites (e.g., Binfire Inc.).

Using Blogs and Wikis Inside the Enterprise

In Chapter 2, we provided some examples of blogs and wikis used within enterprises. The use of these tools is expanding rapidly. Companies use blogs and wikis for the following activities:

- Project collaboration and communication
- Process and procedure documentation
- FAQs
- E-learning and e-training
- Forums for new ideas
- Corporate-specific dynamic glossary and terminology
- Collaboration with customers

As you can see, most of the activities in the previous list relate to collaboration. For additional information, see **zdnet.com/blog/hinchcliffe** (several blogs), and Hinchcliffe (2011).

Using Twitter to Support Collaboration

Twitter already is used extensively in the enterprise to support collaboration. For example, Wagner (2009) describes the use of Twitter to facilitate the work of focus groups and other collaborative teams. Twitter is used extensively for interaction with customers and prospects as well as for conducting market research.

The Role of Mobile Commerce in Social Collaboration

As described in Chapter 6, mobile commerce is growing very rapidly. Most enterprise social applications can be done on wireless devices. This is particularly true for communication and collaboration.

Questions and Answers in Social Networks

In a Q&A "answer" function individuals and companies can post questions. For example, in LinkedIn community: go to the Help Forum and use the posting module on your home page to ask your network a question, and the community provides you with answers. You can also ask a question on the 'share box' on the home page. Many other professional networks and their internal groups provide advice and supporting material for helping in decision making. These services can be either paid or for free. For example, according to the medical social network 'Sermo' (**sermo.com**; "Social Media Meets Healthcare"), a large online community exclusive to physicians, "has an app that allows physicians to author and discuss urgent and interesting patient cases from any Web- or mobile-enabled device, and based on market tests, be almost assured feedback from multiple colleagues. Typical questions and responses include requested/suggested diagnoses and treatments with the best insights often resulting from collaboration among the doctors" (see **sermo.com/news/press-releases/54**).

Suites of Tools for Social Collaboration

Several companies offer suites of social collaboration tools, either as stand-alone products or as added tools in existing collaboration suites.

Example 1: IBM Connections

IBM Connections provides tools such as forums, wikis, and blogs, and new capabilities like advanced social analytics, which enable users to expand their network of connections and engagement. For details, see press release "IBM Launches New Software and Social Business Consulting Services" at **ibm.com/press/us/en/pressrelease/32949.wss**.

You can download many free white papers at the IBM Jam Events page (**collaborationjam.com**). According to Hibbard (2010), IBM has 17,000 internal blogs (used by 100,000 people), 53,000 members in SocialBlue (an internal clone of Facebook, called Connections today with over 70,000 members), 300,000 members on LinkedIn (January 2014), and over 500,000 participants in crowdsourcing. IBM also provides the tools needed to support innovation. Today these numbers are larger.

Example 2: Cisco WebEx Meeting Center (Formerly Cisco Quad)

Cisco WebEx, according to Cisco's website, is an enterprise collaboration platform, which is designed for today's workforce, is characterized by social, mobile, visual, and virtual features. WebEx connects people to the information and expertise they need, when they need it. Knowledge and ideas are easily shared across the enterprise, and teams collaborate across geographical and organizational boundaries. For details, see **webex.com/products/web-conferencing/mobile.html**.

WebEx Meetings is a universal app available for the Apple iPad, iPhone and Android phones. For other WebEx social features, see **webex.com/products/web-conferencing/mobile.html**.

Example 3: Laboranova

Under the European Union's Sixth Framework Programme, Laboranova (**laboranova.com**) assists professionals that take part in the management and development of innovations. Laboranova's tools and methodologies assist in the areas of team building, knowledge management, and the evaluation of innovations. It consists of a suite of Web 2.0 tools adopted for social innovation and collaboration. The tools include InnoTube (**laboranova.com/pages/tools/innotube.php?lang=DE**), which operates like a private YouTube for business; and Melodie (**laboranova.com/pages/tools/melodie.php?lang=DE**), which creates visual maps of concepts or idea submitted by its users, so that other users can comment or elaborate on the initial ideas.

For a list of vendors, the tools they use, and the type of collaboration/communication supported in the context of general use cases, see Fauscette (2011). For the benefits of social collaboration, see **web.esna.com/blog/social-collaboration-at-c-level**.

The Future of Social Commerce

In determining justification and strategy of social commerce, we need to look into the future. Many researchers and consultants are speculating on the future (e.g., **slideshare.net/YairCarmel1/e-commerce-trendsesenglish?related=3**). The predictions are diverse, ranging from "SC will dominate EC" to "it is a buzz word and will disappear soon." Given the popularity of Facebook, Twitter, Pinterest, YouTube, social games, social shopping, and social advertising, it is difficult to side with the pessimistic predictions. It looks as if mobile social commerce will be a major area of growth. Also, several of the social shopping and social collaboration models could be very successful. In the enterprise area, there is a trend to have a "social as a service" rather than as an application approach (due to the influence of cloud computing).

Conclusion: IBM's Watson and Social Commerce

There are many opinions on what the future of SC will be. Instead of presenting them, we decided to end this chapter by looking at IBM's Watson supercomputer. In February 2011, IBM's Watson won a *Jeopardy* 8-day tournament against two world champions. This was a great achievement for what IBM calls Social Business and Smart Computing. Aided by intelligent systems such as IBM's Pure Systems, Watson will be able to do much more. According to **research.ibm.com/smarterplanet/us/en/ibm**, Watson may assist people in the following social commerce-related tasks (for a full description see Lawinski 2011).

- **Personal investment advisor.** There is no need to conduct research any longer. All you have to do is to state your investment goals and Watson will make recommendations after checking all the needed input data. Given what goals you have, Watson can figure out what you need, recommending what to buy or sell. Upon your approval, Watson can conclude the deal for you.
- **Language translator.** In EC we sometimes need language translation for introducing websites to people who understand other languages, in order to exploit global opportunities. We need it also for translating a natural human language to a language that a computer can understand. Today's automatic machine translation is not optimal, but it is improving. Computer systems, such as IBM's Watson, have powerful natural language processors that are getting even better with time, and thus provide better machine translation.
- **Customer service.** Providing technical support is critical for success (e.g., see the iRobot case in Chapter 7). Watson's intelligence will enable automatic guides for people who need help, taking them through all the necessary steps. The service will be consistent, top quality, and available in real time.
- **Q&A service.** Watson will provide the best answers to any business, medical, legal, or personal question you have. It can answer any question and subsequent subquestions.

- **Matchmaking.** Watson can match sellers and buyers, products and markets, job seekers and job offers, partners to bartering, P2P lending participants or any other match you can think of. For example, Watson will be able to find you a partner who will fit your stated goals. IBM's Watson is related to IBM's Smarter plant activities (see **ibm.com/smarterplanet/us/en/ibmwatson/implement-watson.html**).

SECTION 8.8 REVIEW QUESTIONS

1. Define social collaboration.
2. List and describe the major benefits of social collaboration briefly.
3. List social collaboration tools.
4. What are the major points related to the future of social commerce?

MANAGERIAL ISSUES

1. **What are some of the ethical issues that may be involved in deploying social commerce?** Social commerce can lead to several ethical issues such as privacy and accountability. In addition, mistakes can cause harm to users as well as to the company. Another important ethical issue is human judgment, which is frequently a key factor in social commerce. Human judgment may be subjective or corrupt, and therefore, it may lead to unethical consequences. Companies should provide an ethical code for system builders and users. There are ethical issues related to the implementation of idea generation and other problem solving–related considerations. Some actions performed in a simulated virtual world can be unethical, or even illegal. One issue to consider is whether an organization should employ productivity-saving devices that are not ethical. Another ethical issue is the use of knowledge extracted from people in crowdsourcing. A further related issue is whether a company should compensate an employee when others use knowledge that he or she contributed. This issue is related to the motivation issue. It also is related to privacy. Should people be informed as to who contributed certain knowledge?

2. **How should we deal with social commerce risks?** There are several possible risks in implementing social commerce, depending on the applications. For example, to protect the security of the SC open source system, you need to consult your internal security experts and you may need some outside legal advice. There is also the risk of information pollution and biased or falsified user generated content. You may also need to use a consultant for large projects to examine and evaluate the associated risks. Weighing the benefits of social media against security and other potential risks is a major strategy issue (see Tucci 2010).

3. **Should we move to be a social business?** It depends on the estimated costs and benefits. Also, it is possible to introduce some, but not all, features of social enterprise. For example, using crowdsourcing, like CEMEX did by itself, can be very beneficial. Social collaboration may be cost-effective as well.

4. **What about a private, in-house social network?** Such a venture may bring many benefits and it can be combined with internal activities of crowdsourcing, as well as with social collaboration with business partners. Most successful in-house networks are used for idea generation, internal collaboration, recruitment, and public relations.

5. **Is it beneficial to engage in virtual worlds?** It depends on what you want to do there. See if any of your competitors in the virtual world. There are lots of opportunities (see the list of 18, Section 8.4). But, the success is questionable. This is not the place for SMEs. One needs a great deal of imagination and technical expertise.

6. **Shall we try gamification?** In most cases it is wise to wait and see the results of other companies. The deployment requires skilled employees. In certain applications the reward can be large. But in most cases we are not sure at this time. As one says: "Try it, you make like it."

SUMMARY

1. **The social enterprise.** Conducting social networking activities in the enterprise can result in substantial benefits. Two types of business

social networks exist, public and private. The private network is company owned; it may have restricted access, or it may be open to the public. The public network (e.g., LinkedIn) is used mainly for recruiting, connections, collaboration, and marketing communication. The private, in-house social enterprise uses Collaboration 2.0, social CRM, social marketing media, and more. You can even "spy" on your competitors (see **entre-preneur.com/article/229350**). All this translates to improved relationships with employees, customers, and business partners. Significant cost reduction, productivity increase, and competitive advantage can be achieved as well.

2. **Business-oriented public social networks.** Following the successful examples of LinkedIn and Xing, many public business-oriented networks were created. Notable networks are Viadeo (**us.viadeo.com/en**) and Google+. Applications vary from recruiting to market research and advertising. Most notable is f-commerce. One major activity in public networks is external collaboration. Several entrepreneurship networks also exist.

3. **Major enterprise social commerce activities.** Currently, collaboration and communication, as well as community building, are the major activities. In addition, problem solving via idea generation and finding expertise are becoming more and more important. Related to this is knowledge creation and management. Companies recruit, train, and conduct other HRM activities in enterprise networks. Several companies also use the enterprise social network for interactions with customers, suppliers, and other business partners.

4. **Commercial application of virtual worlds.** The major P2P commercial activity is trading or renting virtual goods. Companies conduct virtual meetings, training sessions, test designs, advertise, provide customer service (e.g., receptionists, call centers), recruit, organize trade shows, do market research, provide commercial games, and more.

5. **Social commerce, entertainment, and gaming.** Rich media, user-created content, and groups and subgroups with common interests have opened many possibilities for a second generation of online entertainment. Add to this the wireless revolution and the increased capabilities in mobile devices to support Web 2.0 tools and social networking activities, and you will discover a new and exciting world of online entertainment ranging from music and videos to comedy.

6. **Social gaming and gamification.** Many Internet-based games include some social activities. Players collectively agree to the rules and act as community members. Companies such as King and Zynga create the games which are played on Facebook and other social networks. This is one aspect of gamification. Another aspect is the introduction of social media into games.

7. **Crowdsourcing and social networking.** Crowdsourcing in the enterprise is used mostly for idea generation, voting, and problem identification. Content creation and updating projects, such as volunteers translating the Facebook website to French and German, falls into this category. Crowdfunding is an application for raising funds.

8. **Social collaboration.** Many see social collaboration (Collaboration 2.0) as the major activity that social media supports. Activities supported range from joint design to problem solving.

9. **The future of social commerce.** The general consensus is social commerce will grow rapidly; but some disagree. A major boost to social commerce is IBM's innovations (particularly the Watson Computer and Smarter Commerce).

KEY TERMS

Business social networks
Collective intelligence (CI)
Gamification
Social business
Social collaboration (Collaboration 2.0)
Social enterprise
Social Internet game
Social network game

DISCUSSION QUESTIONS

1. How do public business-oriented networks and private enterprise social networks differ?
2. Discuss the role of crowdsourcing in idea generation and in other enterprise activities.
3. Corporate social networking: Booster or time-waster? What are the pitfalls of enterprise social networking? Discuss.
4. How can crowdsourcing reduce risks to merchants?
5. What are some of the risks companies may face if they decide to use public social networks?
6. Review the features of Socialtext (**socialtext.com**). Discuss how you would make use of this platform in a small enterprise in retail, manufacturing, or financial services.
7. What real value do virtual worlds present to commercial users and businesses?
8. Read Smith (2012) and discuss how social collaboration can support talent management.
9. Discuss the social aspects of crowdsourcing and virtual worlds.
10. How can gamification be used in business?
11. Compare and contrast social collaboration and crowdsourcing.

TOPICS FOR CLASS DISCUSSION AND DEBATES

1. Debate: Should a crowd have professional knowledge of the task it has been given or not?
2. Some claim that using social collaboration may be slow and ineffective. Others disagree. Debate the issue.
3. Idea generation by the employees or customers using crowdsourcing is becoming popular. However, some say it is only an electronic suggestion box. Others disagree. Discuss.
4. What are the potential major legal issues that business applications in virtual worlds might encounter? Refer to online resources, including **socialgameslaw.com**.

5. Despite the attributes of virtual worlds, the technology has neither become popular nor is it being used widely. (Compare its use for example, with Facebook, Twitter, blogs, or wikis.) What aspects hinder their adoption? What are the critical success factors? Discuss.
6. Debate: Should companies build in-house social networks for external activities (e.g., marketing, CRM) or use existing public social networks?
7. Debate: Can knowledge be socialized?
8. Examine the Grand Theft Auto game. Why the game is so popular? Are there any social elements there?
9. Why does one needs a special entrepreneur network? What features make it effective?
10. What are some of the risks companies may face if they decide to use public social networks?
11. Review the features of Socialtext (**socialtext.com**). Discuss how you would make use of this platform in a small enterprise in (a) retail, (b) manufacturing, and (c) financial services.
12. Would you use **monster.com** or **linkedin.com** for recruiting top managers, or would you rather use a traditional agency? Why?
13. Crowdfunding is becoming very popular. Find recent information about its success. What are some of the implementation challenges?

INTERNET EXERCISES

1. Enter **xing.com** and **linkedin.com** and compare their functionalities (capabilities). Also, enter **youtube.com/watch?v=pBAghmYMG0M** and view the video "Ryze Business Networking Tutorial" (7:20 minutes). Compare Ryze's capabilities with those of LinkedIn.com. Write a report.
2. Enter **pandora.com**. Find out how you can create and share music with friends.
3. Enter **secondlife.com** and find the commercial activities of the following avatars: Fizik Baskerville, Craig Altman, Shaun Altman,

Flipper Peregrine, and Anshe Chung. Briefly describe, what they represent. Relate this to social commerce.

4. Enter **arianeb.com/more3Dworlds.htm**. View several worlds, and make a list of unique properties. Discuss the capabilities of virtual worlds.

5. Enter **innocentive.com**. Describe how this site works. List their major products and services. Identify benefits and challenges.

6. Enter **hulu.com/plus**. Why is it an online entertainment service? What are the benefits to viewers? Compare this site to **starz.com**.

7. Enter **gaiaonline.com** and find all socially oriented activities. Write a report.

8. Enter the **gillin.com/blog** and find information related to enterprise applications of social commerce technologies. Write a report.

9. Enter **brazencareerist.com/company** check the services Brazen provides. Compare services to the virtual event hosted at **expos2.com**.

10. Compare what **jobserve.com** and **aspiremediagroup.net** offer regarding solutions for recruitment. Differentiate services to employees from services to employers. Write a report.

11. Identify a difficult business problem. Post the problem on **linkedin.com**, and **answers.com**. Summarize the results or offers you received to solve the problem.

12. Enter **huddle.com** and take the interactive demo. (Registration required.) Also, view the video on the main page. Write a report on social collaboration activities.

TEAM ASSIGNMENTS AND PROJECTS

1. **Assignment for the Opening Case**
   Read the opening case and answer the following questions:
   (a) Describe the drivers of Shift at CEMEX.
   (b) Describe its major benefits.
   (c) Relate the case to Collaboration 2.0 and to crowdsourcing.
   (d) Enter Garcia et al. (2011) and view the supporting videos. Prepare a summary of one video.

2. The crowdsourcing model works with designers, like this: (1) A company outlines an area for which they need a design. (2) The company turns the design outline into a competition (e.g., among experts, among amateurs, or between amateur and professional designers). (3) A winner is selected by management, consultants, or by the crowd. This is done at little cost.
   (a) If this model becomes widespread, how will it affect the design industry?
   (b) What is the purpose of the competition?
   (c) Some believe that amateurs can do the best job. Others disagree. Find information and discuss.
   (d) Compare this situation to the Polyvore model. Discuss.

3. Some consider gamification to be a major social commerce technology of the future. Enter **badgeville.com/wiki/External_Resources**. Find additional resources. Also check Yu-Kaichou's framework at **yukaichou.com/gamification-examples/octalysis-complete-gamification-framework/#.UuzK8vldWSo**. Write a report on the existing and potential applications of gamification in e-commerce and social commerce.

4. All students register as members at LinkedIn.
   (a) Each team member joins two LinkedIn groups and observes their activities.
   (b) All join the EC group: (**group-digest@LinkedIn.com**). Follow some of the discussions there. Have a joint class presentation on the value of groups at LinkedIn.

5. Check the competition in the area of streaming music services (e.g., check Spotify, Amazon, Apple, Google, etc.). Write a report.

6. The crowdsourcing model works with designers as described in Team Assignment #2. Now, think about the future of the graphic design industry in general. What will be the fate of large design firms that are competing for the business of high-profile clients when the clients are now paying tiny, one-time fees to amateur designers? Is using crowdsourcing in your business (or a business you are familiar with) a viable model?

7. Yammer, Huddle, Chatter, and Jive Software are cloud-based social networking services. They are considered very useful, replacing traditional enterprise tools. Investigate the issue and write a report.

CLOSING CASE: EC APPLICATION: LINKEDIN: THE PREMIER PUBLIC BUSINESS-ORIENTED SOCIAL NETWORK

Let us look at LinkedIn (**linkedin.com**), the world's largest professional network. LinkedIn is a global business-oriented social networking site (has offered in 23 languages), used mainly for professional networking. By December 2013, it had about 259 million registered users spanning 200 countries and territories. By the end of 2013 there were 2.1 million different groups, each with a special interest. LinkedIn can be used to find jobs, people, potential clients, service providers, subject experts, and other business opportunities. The company became profitable in 2010 with revenue approaching $2.2 billion in 2014. The company filed for an initial public offering in January 2011, and its stock is one of the best performing on the stock market. A major objective of LinkedIn is to allow registered users to maintain a list of professional contacts (see **en.wikipedia.org/wiki/LinkedIn**), i.e., people with whom they have a relationship. The people in each person's network are called *connections*. Users can invite anyone, whether he or she is a LinkedIn user or not, to become a connection. When people join LinkedIn, they create a profile that summarizes their professional accomplishments. This profile makes it easier to be found by recruiters, former colleagues, and others. Members can also meet new people and find opportunitiesfor collaboration and marketing (see **brw.com.au/p/business/million_members_places_counting_Igi7nirJjn6NfV7KexTv0H**).

LinkedIn is based on the concept of "degrees of connections." A *contact network* consists of a user's direct connections (called first degree connections), people connected to their first-degree connections (called second degree connections),

and people connected to the second-degree connections (called third degree connections). Degree "icons" appear next to a contact's name. For more about degrees, see "Six Degrees of Separation – LinkedIn Style" at **thedigitalfa.com/d-brucejohnston/six-degrees-of-separation-linkedin-style**. The contact network makes it possible for a professional to gain an introduction, through a mutual, trusted contact, to someone he or she wishes to know. LinkedIn's administrators themselves are also members and have hundreds of connections each (see Elad 2014 and **linkedin.com**).

The "gated-access approach," where contact with any professional requires either a preexisting relationship or the intervention of a mutual contact, is intended to build trust among the site's users.

The searchable LinkedIn groups feature allows users to establish new business relationships by joining alumni, industry, professional, or other relevant groups. As of February 2014, it has approximately 2.1 million groups in its directory.

LinkedIn is especially useful in helping job seekers and employers find one another. According to Ahmad (2014), 94% of all U.S. recruiters use LinkedIn to examine potential candidates. Job seekers can list their résumés, search for open positions, check companies' profiles, and even review the profiles of the hiring managers. Applicants can also discover connections with existing contacts (people) who can introduce them to a specific hiring manager. They can even see who has viewed their profiles. For details see **linkedin.com/company/linkedin/careers** and **linkedin.com/directory/job.**

Companies can use the site to post available jobs and find and recruit employees, especially those who may not actively be searching for a new position.

Smart Ways to Use Linkedin

LinkedIn is known mostly as a platform for recruitment, job searches, and making connections. However, there are many opportunities in the network for marketing, advertising, sales, and more. Members can ask others to write recommendations (endorsements) for them. For a list of opportunities, see **linkedintelligence.com/ smart-ways-to-use-linkedin**.

In lieu of LinkedIn Answers that was discontinued in 2013, a new service is available, per **help.linkedin.com/app/answers/detail/ a_id/35227**.

In mid-2008, LinkedIn launched LinkedIn DirectAds (renamed "Ads" in 2011). Ads, which is their version of Google's AdWords, is a self-service, text-based advertising product that allows advertisers to reach a targeted professional audience of their choosing (see their FAQ's at **help.linkedin.com/app/answers/detail/ a_id/1015**). For a comparison between DirectAds and AdWords, see **shoutex.com/linkedin-directads-google-adwords-ppc-1** and **shoutex. com/linkedin-directads-vs-google-adwords-2**.

According to Ahmad (2014), LinkedIn has 3 times higher 'visitor-to-lead' conversion rate than Facebook and Twitter.

In 2008, LinkedIn joined forces with the financial news channel CNBC. The deal integrates LinkedIn's community and networking functionality into CNBC.com, allowing users to share and discuss financial and other news with their professional contacts. Communitygenerated content from LinkedIn, such as survey and poll results, are broadcast on CNBC, and CNBC provides LinkedIn with programming, articles, blogs, financial data, and video content. Because of this connection, CNBC is able to draw insights from LinkedIn's global user base to generate new types of business content for CNBC to broadcast. In 2014, LinkedIn could provide job matching to positions available, by using a computer algorithm that determines potential employee's fitness to potential jobs.

LinkedIn can also be used for several other marketing strategies such as creating special groups to promote interest in events, purchasing paid media space, and seeing what your competitors are doing (e.g., see Schaffer 2011 and **linkedin.com/about-us**). Note that about 75% of LinkedIn members are located outside the United States. For example, most users are in Brazil, India, the United Kingdom, and France. Over 1.5 million teachers are on LinkedIn and use the site for educational purposes.

As previously mentioned, LinkedIn is a public company. It was an instant success, as the share price almost tripled the first day of trading. In contrast, shares of Monster, a major online recruiting company, plunged more than 60% during 2011, mainly due to investors' fear that LinkedIn would take business away from Monster.

LinkedIn constantly adds capabilities to its site. For example, in 2014, the company launched features that help increase local relevance.

Mobile Applications

A mobile version of LinkedIn, launched in February 2008, offers access to most features in the site by using mobile devices. The mobile service is supported in many languages, including Chinese, English, French, German, Japanese, and Spanish (for mobile devices and supported languages, see **help.linkedin.com/app/answers/ detail/a_id/999**). A recent application is the ability to apply for jobs from smartphones and tablets.

Some Resources for Linkedin

The following are some useful resources on LinkedIn: **blog.linkedin.com**, **mylinkedinpowerforum.com**, and **linkedin.com/search**.

For LinkedIn success stories, see Elad (2014), Schaffer (2011), and **cbsnews.com/news/ linkedin-5-job-search-success-stories**

Sources: Based upon Elad (2014), Schaffer (2011), Gowel (2012), Ahmad (2014), **en.wikipedia.org/wiki/LinkedIn**, and **linkedin.com** (both accessed July 2015).

Questions

1. Enter **linkedin.com** and explore the site. Why do you think the site is so successful?
2. What features are related to recruiting and job search?

3. Conduct an investigation to find the company's revenue sources. Prepare a list.
4. Several companies have attempted to clone LinkedIn with little success. Why do you think LinkedIn is dominating?
5. Join the group called "eMarketing Association Network" on LinkedIn (free; it is a private group so you must request to join) and observe their group's activities regarding social media and commerce for one week. Write a report.

ONLINE FILES
available at **affordable-ecommerce-textbook.com/turban**

No online files are available for this chapter.

COMPREHENSIVE EDUCATIONAL WEBSITES

gamification.co/gabe-zichermann: A large collection of news, knowledge, videos and more.

crowdsortium.org: A crowdsourcing community with many resources.

darmano.typepad.com: In David Armano's personal blog, logic and emotion exist at the intersection of business, design, and the social Web.

ft.com/reports/the-connected-business: How businesses of all sizes use IT and IT services.

15inno.com/2012/08/09/oicrowdexamples 40 examples of open innovation and crowdsourcing for innovation.

what-is-crowdsourcing.com: An open source platform for sharing views and opinions on crowdsourcing.

c21org.typepad.com: Trends, thought leaders, and workable models for the 21st century organization.

jvwresearch.org: *Journal of Virtual Worlds Research*.

mashable.com: A comprehensive social media resource center.

socialtext.com/solutions/resources.php: Socialtext is an endless source of products/services.

socialbrite.org/sharing-center/glossary: A social media glossary.

GLOSSARY

Business social network A network that is built on social relationships, and can exist offline or online. Business social networking can take place in traditional corporate physical environments.

Collective intelligence (CI) An application of crowdsourcing for problem solving, idea generation, and innovation.

Gamification The introduction of gaming into social networking. Gamification can also be viewed as the introduction of social networking activities into online games.

Social business Is a name for a profit or nonprofit organization that is designed to achieve some social goal(s) rather than just make profit.

Social collaboration People's collaboration within and between communities enabled by social media tools and platforms.

Social enterprise The use of social media tools and platforms and conducting social networking in organizations while the major objectives are either commercial or nonprofit activities (e.g., the government).

Social Internet game A video multiplayer game played on the Internet, mostly in social networks or virtual worlds.

Social network game A video game that is played in social networks, and usually involves multiplayers.

REFERENCES

Ahmad, I. "How to Boost LinkedIn Engagement [Infographic]."*Social Media Today*, January 3, 2014.

Blair, K. "How to Use Yammer… And Why You Should Be Using It at Your Business." March 4, 2011. **social-times.com/how-to-use-yammer-and-why-you-should-be-using-it-at-your-business_b40658** (accessed November 2014).

Brabham, D. C. *Crowdsourcing*. Cambridge, MA: The MIT Press, 2013.

Bughin, J., and M. Chui. "Evolution of the Networked Enterprise: McKinsey Global Survey Results." *McKinsey Quarterly*, March 2013.

Burgess, C. and M. Burgess. *The Social Employee: How Great Companies Make Social Media Work.* New York: McGraw-Hill, 2013.

Carr, D. F. "McKinsey's Trillion-Dollar Social Prediction." *InformationWeek,* August 13, 2012.

Carr, D. F. *Social Collaboration for Dummies.* New York: For Dummies, 2013.

Chou, Y. "Octalysis: Complete Gamification Framework." October 2012. **yukaichou.com/gamification-examples/octalysis-complete-gamification-framework** (accessed November 2014).

Ciaramitaro, B. *Virtual Worlds and E-Commerce: Technologies and Applications for Building Customer Relationships.* New York: Business Science Reference, 2010.

Coleman, D., and S. Levine. *Collaboration 2.0.* Cupertino CA: Happy About Info, 2008.

Daden, B. "Virtual Worlds for Training and Education." A white paper, April 2010. **daden.co.uk/downloads/Virtual Worlds for Training and Education 01d2.pdf** (accessed November 2014).

Dignan, A. *Game Frame: Using Games as a Strategy for Success.* Florence, MA: Free Press, 2011.

Donston-Miller, D. "Social Business Leader Cemex Keeps Ideas Flowing." *Informationweek.com,* November 5, 2012. **informationweek.com/enterprise/social-business-leader-cemex-keeps-ideas-flowing/d/d-id/1107226** (accessed November 2014).

Dortch, M. E. "Working Social: Becoming a Collaborative Enterprise." February 2012. **s3.amazonaws.com/formcomposer/assets/asset/production/items/981/zd-cl-becoming-collaborative-enterprise_020811.pdf** (accessed November 2014).

Duggan, K., and K. Shoup. *Business Gamification for Dummies.* Hoboken, NJ: For Dummies, 2013.

Dunay, P. "Social Media Organization: What are the Best Practices for Internal Collaboration?" *Social Media Today,* January 23, 2014. **socialmediatoday.com/content/social-organization-what-are-best-practicesinternal-collaboration** (accessed November 2014)

Elad, J. *LinkedIn for Dummies.* Hoboken, NJ: Wiley & Sons, 2011.

Fauscette, M. "Communication and Collaboration in a Social Business World." April 17, 2011. **socialmediatoday.com/mfauscette/286789/communication-and-collaboration-social-business-world** (accessed November 2014).

Florentine, S. "How Gamification Makes Customer Services Fun." *Computer World,* March 3, 2014.

Forrester Consulting. "Social Networking in the Enterprise: Benefits and Inhibitors." June 2010.

Garcia, J. G., L. Martinez, and A. S. Vicente. "Shift Changes the Way CEMEX Works." A Winner Paper in the 2011 "Management Innovation eXchange Project." September 2, 2011. **managementexchange.com/story/shift-changes-way-cemex-works** (accessed November 2014).

Gowel, D. *The Power in a Link: Open Doors, Close Deals, and Change the Way You Do Business Using LinkedIn.* Hoboken, NJ: John Wiley & Sons, 2012.

Hein, R. "How to Use Gamification to Engage Employees." *CIO.com,* June 6, 2013. **cio.com/article/734521/How_to_Use_Gamification_to_Engage_Employees** (accessed November 2014).

Heiphetz, A., and G. Woodill. *Training and Collaboration with Virtual Worlds: How to Create Cost-Saving, Efficient and Engaging Programs.* New York: McGraw-Hill, 2010.

Hibbard, C. "How IBM Uses Social Media to Spur Employee Innovation." *Social Media Examiner,* February 2, 2010.

Hinchcliffe, D. "Social Business and Enterprise Usage: The Lessons." December 16, 2011. **zdnet.com/blog/hinchcliffe/social-business-and-enterprise-usage-the-lessons/1882** (accessed November 2014).

Hinchcliffe, D. "Social Business Success: CEMEX." February 1, 2012 **zdnet.com/blog/hinchcliffe/social-business-success-cemex/1927** (accessed November 2014).

Howe, J. *Crowdsourcing: Why the Power of the Crowd Is Driving the Future of Business.* New York: Crown Business, 2008.

IBM Software Group. "The Compelling Returns from IBM Connections in Support of Social Business: Five Stories." Thought Leadership White Paper, New York: IBM Corporation EPW 14010-USEN-00, 2011.

IBM. "IBM Launches New Software and Social Business Consulting Services." Press Room Release, November 8, 2010. **ibm.com/press/us/en/pressrelease/32949.wss** (accessed November 2014).

IDC. "Social Business Framework: Using People as a Platform to Enable Transformation." July 2010, IDC #223862, Volume 1 **idc.com/research/images/IDC-Social-Business-Framework-Download.pdf** (accessed November 2014).

IDC. "Social Business Survey." May 2011. **businesswire.com/news/home/20110714005194/en/IDCs-Social-Business-Maturity-Model-Outlines-Stages#.Urokh_RDuSo** (accessed November 2014).

Jurgensen, J. "An Ode to Joyful Streaming." *The Wall Street Journal,* January 4–5, 2014.

Kelly, D. A. "Social by Design." *Oracle Magazine,* May/June 2011. **oracle.com/technetwork/issue-archive/2011/11-may/o31webcenter-353502.html** (accessed November 2014).

Kern, J. "Social Determining Next Generation of Business Applications." *Information Management,* July 19, 2012.

Lawinski, J. "IBM's Watson Supercomputer Goes to Work for You: 11 Personal Apps." *CIOInsight,* February 22, 2011.

Lithium Report. "Gamification: Delivering Winning Social Customer Experiences." *Lithium Technologies Inc.,* White Paper, 2011.

Mahar, J., and S. M. Mahar. *The Unofficial Guide to Building Your Business in the Second Life Virtual World: Marketing and Selling Your Product, Services, and Brand In-World.* New York: AMACOM, 2009.

Malone, T. W., R. Laubacher, and C. Dellarocas. "The Collective Intelligence Genome." *MIT Sloan Management Review* (Spring 2010).

McAfee, A. P. *Enterprise 2.0: New Collaborative Tools for Your Organization's Toughest Challenge.* Boston: Harvard Business School Press, 2010.

McCabe, L., et al. *Collaboration for Dummies*, IBM Limited Edition. Hoboken, NJ: Wiley, 2009.

Morgan, J. *The Collaborative Organization: A Strategic Guide to Solving Your Internal Business Challenges Using Emerging Social and Collaborative Tools.* New York: McGraw-Hill, 2012.

Murugesan, S. S. "Harnessing the Power of Virtual Worlds: Exploration, Innovation, and Transformation—PART I & II." *Cutter Business Intelligence Executive Reports*, March and May 2008.

Pearce, C., et al., *Communities of Play: Emergent Culture in Multiplayer Games and Virtual Worlds.* Boston: The MIT Press, 2009.

Radoff, J. *Game On: Energize your Business with Social Media Games.* Hoboken. NJ: Wiley, 2011.

Reahard, J. "Second Life Readies for 10th Anniversary, Celebrates a Million Active Users Per Month." *Massively.Joystiq.com*, June 20, 2013. **massively.joystiq.com/2013/06/20/second-life-readies-for-10th...** (accessed November 2014).

Reeves, B., and L. Read. *Total Engagement: Using Games and Virtual Worlds to Change the Way People Work and Businesses Complete.* Boston: Harvard Business School Press, 2009.

Ridley-Duff, and M. Bull. *Understanding Social Enterprise: Theory and Practice.* Thousand Oaks, CA: Sage Publications, 2011.

Schaffer, N. *Maximizing LinkedIn for Sales and Social Media Marketing.* New York: Windmills Marketing, 2011.

Shih, C. *The Facebook Era: Tapping Online Social Networks to Market, Sell, and Innovate,* 2nd ed. Upper Saddle River, NJ: Prentice Hall, 2011.

Smith, M. A. "Enterprise Social is a Dream." *Information Management*, September 19, 2012.

Terdiman, D. *The Entrepreneur's Guide to Second Life.* Indianapolis, IN: Wiley & Sons, 2008.

Tucci, L. "Monitoring the Benefits of Social Media, and the Risks." April 15, 2010. **searchcio.techtarget.com/news/1510020/Monitoring-the-benefits-of-social-media-and-the-risks** (accessed November 2014).

Turban, E. et al. *Social Commerce.* New York: Springer 2015.

Ueland, S. "18 Social Networks for Entrepreneurs." *Practical eCommerce*, July 25, 2011.

Vitzthum, S., A. Kathuria, and B. Konsynski. "Toys Become Tools: From Virtual Worlds to Real Commerce." *Communication of the Association for Information Systems*, vol. 29, Article 21, 2011.

Wagner, M. "Opportunity Tweets." *Informationweek,* June 1, 2009.

Walter, E. "Gamification: Adding Stickiness to your Campaigns." September 9, 2013. **socialmediatoday.com/ekaterina/1723136/gamification-adding-stickiness-your-campaigns** (accessed November 2014).

Yu, R. "Companies Turn to Virtual Trade Shows to Save Money." January 5, 2010. **usatoday.com/travel/news/2010-01-04-virtual-trade-shows_N.htm** (accessed November 2014).

Zichermann, G., and J. Linder. *The Gamification Revolution: How Leaders Leverage Game Mechanics to Crush the Competition.* New York: McGraw-Hill, 2013.

Part IV

EC Support Services

Marketing and Advertising in E-Commerce

9

Content

Learning Objectives

Upon completion of this chapter, you will be able to:

1. Describe factors that influence online consumer behavior.
2. Understand the decision-making process of online consumer purchasing.
3. Discuss the issues of e-loyalty and e-trust in electronic commerce (EC).
4. Understand segmentation and how companies are building one-to-one relationships with customers.
5. Explain how consumer behavior can be analyzed for creating personalized services.
6. Understand consumer market research in e-commerce.
7. Describe the objectives and characteristics of Web advertising.
8. Describe the major advertising methods used on the Web.
9. Learn mobile marketing concepts and techniques.
10. Describe various online advertising strategies and types of promotions.
11. Understand some implementation issues.

Electronic supplementary material The online version of this chapter (doi: 10.1007/978-3-319-10091-3_9) contains supplementary material, which is available to authorized users

OPENING CASE: MARKET RESEARCH HELPS DEL MONTE IMPROVE DOG FOOD

The Problem

Del Monte operates in a very competitive global food industry. In addition to manufacturing canned fruits and vegetables for human consumption, Del Monte produces pet food such as Gravy Train, 9 Lives, and Meow Mix. Therefore, using market research, the company constantly looks for innovative ways to increase its competitive edge. The company noticed the fast growth of social media and decided to deploy social media projects. Their primary goal was to decide how best to use social media-based market research to support its diverse product line – in this case, dog food.

The Solution

The basic idea was first to connect and collaborate with dog lovers via social networks. The corporate IT department was unable to conduct social network research; therefore, the Pet Products Division of Del Monte Foods decided to leverage Insight Networks, an offering from MarketTools, Inc., a provider of on-demand market research.

Through previous research, Del Monte Pet Products Division identified one segment of the dog owner community as their target, and they wanted to understand that segment more in depth. In order to connect with millions of dog owners, Insight Networks provided Del Monte Pet Products Division with a direct, interactive connection to their consumers. Using their propriety software, Insight Networks monitors millions of relevant blogs in the blogosphere as well as forums in social networks, in order to identify key ideas in which consumers are interested. These ideas are then analyzed in order to predict consumer behavior trends. Such analysis is usually done by using computerized tools such as monitoring consumer interactions, analyzing consumer sentiments, and using social analytics (e.g., see Jayanti 2010).

By utilizing social media, Del Monte can conduct better market research. The conventional approach was using questionnaires or focus groups that were expensive and difficult to fill with qualified participants. Using social media, Del Monte can gather much of the same data faster and at a lower cost. All that is required now is to monitor customer conversations, collect the data, and analyze the vast amount of information. The software also facilitates subgroup creation, idea generation, and panel creation. The results of the analysis help Del Monte understand its customers and consequently plan its marketing activities, communication strategies, and customer service applications. The results also help evaluate the success of marketing campaigns, how well the business processes accomplished the goals, and better justify proposed new activities.

The Experiment

The first implementation of the above application was used to help improve the company's dog treat, Snausages Breakfast Bites. For guidance, Del Monte relied on its dog lovers' social community. By monitoring customer blogs and by posting questions to customers to stimulate discussions, Del Monte used text analysis methods to investigate the relationship between dogs and their owners. Del Monte concluded from the analysis that people who own small dogs would be the major purchasers of Snausages Breakfast Bites. The company also found differences of opinions based on the age of owners. Next, a small sample of the improved dog food was produced and tested in the physical market. As a result of both social media and traditional research, the product design decisions were revised. In addition, marketing promotions were modified. The product sells better because dogs love it. Finally, the new approach solidified the community of dog lovers who are happy that their opinions are considered.

The Results

Product cycle time was reduced by more than 50% to only six months, and Del Monte was able to develop a better marketing communication strategy. Furthermore, the analysis helped the company better understand customers and their purchasing activities, as well as predicting market trends and identifying and anticipating opportunities.

Sources: Based on Steel (2008), Greengard (2008), Jayanti (2010), Big Heart Pet Brands (2012), Wikinvest (2010), and MarketTools, Inc. (2008).

LESSONS LEARNED FROM THE CASE

The opening case illustrates that market research can be useful in a competitive market by providing insights for better product development and marketing strategy. In this case, the company collected data online from its socially-oriented customers. MarketTools, Inc. monitored over 50 million conversations on blogs, message boards, and online media sites to find the "voice of the customers." The collected data were then analyzed. The results of the analysis helped Del Monte improve its dog food and devise new marketing strategies. Online market research, as seen in the case, is related to consumer behavior, purchasing decision making, behavioral marketing, and advertising strategies. All these topics are addressed in this chapter.

9.1   LEARNING ABOUT ONLINE CONSUMER BEHAVIOR

Companies are operating in an increasingly competitive environment. Therefore, sellers try to understand customers' needs and influence them to buy their products and services. Customer acquisition and retention are key success factors, both offline and online. This is particularly important for online businesses, as most interactions with their customers are online. For a summary of factors affecting consumer behavior, see **aipmm. com/html/newsletter/archives/000434.php**.

A Model of Online Consumer Behavior

For decades, market researchers have tried to understand consumer shopping behavior, and develop various models to summarize their findings. A consumer behavior model is designed to help vendors understand how a consumer makes a purchasing decision. Through understanding the decision process, a business may be better able to influence the buyer's decision through improved product design or advertising.

Consumers can be divided into two groups: individual consumers and organizational buyers including governments, private corporations, resellers, and nonprofit organizations. These two types of buyers tend to have different purchasing behaviors and usually are analyzed differently. In this chapter, we focus on individual buyers. A discussion on organizational purchasing can be found in Chapter 4.

An individual consumer behavior model often includes *influential internal and external factors* that affect the buyer's *decision process* and the process for making a purchasing decision. Figure 9.1 shows a consumer behavior model.

- **Influential factors.** Factors influencing purchasing decisions fall into five major dimensions. They are *consumer factors, environmental factors, merchant and intermediary factors, product/service factors* (which include market stimuli), and *EC selling systems*. The first three dimensions are not controllable by the sellers, while the last two are mostly controlled by the sellers. The dimensions are shown in Figure 9.1. The influential factors affect the buyers' decision process.

- **The attitude-behavior decision process.** The second part in a consumer behavior model is the decision-making process, which usually starts with awareness of the situation and a positive attitude and ends with the buyer's decision to purchase and/or repurchase (see the oval part in Figure 9.1). A *favorable attitude* would lead to a stronger *buying intention*,

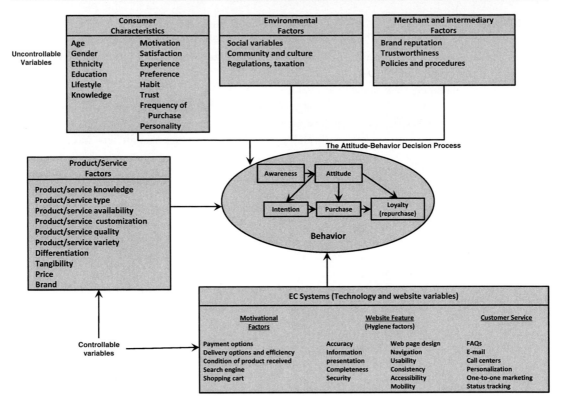

Figure 9.1 EC model of online consumer behavior

which in turn would result in the *actual buying behavior*. Previous research has shown that the links between attitude, purchase intention, and actual purchase behavior are quite strong.

The Major Influential Factors

Major influential factors of consumer purchasing behavior fall into the following categories:

Consumer Characteristics

Consumer (personal) characteristics, which are shown in the top-left portion of Figure 9.1, refer to demographic factors, individual preferences, and behavioral characteristics of the consumer. Several websites provide information on customer buying habits online (e.g., **emarketer.com**, **clickz.com**, and **comscore.com**). The major demographics that such sites track are gender, age, marital status, education level, ethnicity, occupation, and household income, which can be correlated with Internet usage and EC data. Both men and women have been found to perceive information differently

depending on their levels of purchase confidence and internal knowledge. Several studies show that shopping experience has a significant effect on consumer attitude and intention to purchase and repurchase online (e.g., Crespo and Rodriguez del Bosque 2010; Chiu et al. 2014).

Marketers also study the psychological variables such as personality and lifestyle characteristics. These variables are mentioned briefly in several places throughout the text. To read about the impact of lifestyle differences on online shopping, see Wang et al. (2006).

Merchant and Intermediary-Related Factors

Online transactions may also be affected by the merchant that provides the product/service. This group of factors includes merchant reputation, size of the transaction, trust in the merchant, and so on. For example, a customer may feel more secure when making a purchase from Amazon.com (due to its reputation) than from an unknown seller. Other factors such as marketing strategy and advertising can also play a major role.

Product/Service Factors

The second group of factors is related to the product/service itself. The consumer's decision to make a purchase is affected by the nature of the product/service in the transaction. These may include the price, quality, design, brand, and other related attributes of the product.

EC Systems

The EC platform for online transactions (e.g., security protection, payment mechanism, and so forth) offered by the merchant and the type of computing environment (e.g., mobile vs. desktop) may also have effects. EC design factors can be divided into payment and logistics support, website features, and consumer services. Liang and Lai (2002) classified them into *motivational* and *hygiene* factors and found motivational factors to be more important than hygiene factors in attracting online customers. Another factor that we include here is the type of EC. For example, consumer behavior in m-commerce may be unique and so is behavior during social shopping.

- **Motivational Factors.** Motivational factors are the functions available on the website to provide direct support in the purchasing process (e.g., search engines, shopping carts, multiple payment methods).
- **Hygiene Factors.** Hygiene factors are functions available on the website whose objective is to make the website functional and serviceable (e.g., ease of navigation, show items added to the cart); their main purpose is to protect consumers from risks or unexpected events in the transaction process (e.g., security breaching and site technical failure).

Environmental Factors

The environment in which a transaction occurs may affect a consumer's purchase decision.

As shown in Figure 9.1, environmental variables can be grouped into the following categories:

- **Social Variables.** People are influenced by family members, friends, coworkers, and current styles. Therefore, social variables (such as customer endorsements, word-of-mouth) play an important role in EC. Of special importance in EC are Internet communities and discussion groups, where people communicate via chat rooms, electronic bulletin boards, tweeting, and newsgroups. A study (by Liang et al. 2011–2012) shows that social support in online communities significantly enhances the intention to purchase online.
- **Cultural/Community Variables.** The influence of culture on buying behavior varies from country to country. It makes a big difference in what people buy if a consumer lives near Silicon Valley in California or in the mountains in Nepal. Chinese shoppers may differ from French shoppers, and rural shoppers may differ from urban ones. Bashir (2013) conducted a comprehensive study about online shopping for electronics in Pakistan.
- **Other Environmental Variables.** These include aspects such as available public information, government regulations, legal constraints, and situational factors. For example, tax rates (Chapter 15) may affect online shopping (see Einav et al. 2014).

Lately, attention has been given to customers' behavior in the mobile environment. For more information, see **mobilemarketer.com**.

SECTION 9.1 REVIEW QUESTIONS

1. Describe the major components of the model of online consumer behavior.
2. List some major personal characteristics that influence consumer behavior.
3. List the major environmental variables of the purchasing environment.
4. List and describe five major merchant-related variables.
5. Describe the relationships among attitude, intention, and actual behavior in the behavior process model.

9.2 THE CONSUMER PURCHASING DECISION PROCESS

The purchasing decision process is another major element in analyzing consumer behavior. It is composed of several steps, as discussed next. A generic model is introduced below.

A Generic Purchasing-Decision Model

From the consumer's perspective, a general purchasing-decision model consists of five major phases (Hawkins and Mothersbaugh 2010). The phases are discussed next.

- **Need identification**. The first step in the purchasing process is for a consumer to recognize a need. This occurs when a consumer is faced with a gap between the current state of what the customer has and the desired state (e.g., his mobile phone needs a useful new feature, such as a bigger screen). A consumer can recognize a need in different ways (e.g., by internal stimuli, hunger or thirst, or external stimuli, exposure to an advertisement).
- A marketer's goal is to get the consumer to recognize such a gap and then convince the consumer that the product or service the seller offers will fulfill the need.
- **Information search.** Once the need has been recognized, the consumer seeks information on how to fulfill that need. Here, we differentiate between two decisions: what product to buy (**product brokering**) and from whom to buy it (**merchant brokering**). These two decisions can be separate or combined. In the consumer's search for information, catalogs, advertisements, promotions, and reference groups could influence decision making. During this phase, online product searches and comparison engines can be very helpful. (See examples at shopping.com, pricegrabber.com, and mysimon.com, and 'decision aids' in Chapter 3.

- **Evaluation of alternatives.** The information search usually yields a few feasible options. From these, the would-be buyer will further evaluate the alternatives and, if possible, negotiate terms. In this phase, a consumer needs to generate and rank criteria for making the final choice. For online consumers, the criteria may include product prices and features.
- **Purchase and delivery.** After evaluating the alternatives, the consumer will make the final buying choice, arrange for payment and delivery, purchase warranties, and so on.
- **Post-purchase activities.** The final phase is the post-purchase phase, which consists of customer service and evaluation of the usefulness of the product. Customer service and consumer satisfaction will result in a positive experience and word-of-mouth (e.g., "This product is really great!" or "We really received good service when we had problems"). If the customer is satisfied with the product and services, loyalty will increase and repeat purchases will occur.

Although these phases offer a general guide to the consumer decision-making process, one should not assume that every consumer's decision-making process will necessarily proceed in this order. In fact, some consumers may proceed to a specific phase and then revert to a previous phase, or they may skip a phase altogether.

Several other purchasing-decision models also exist. A classic (1925) model for describing consumer message processing is the Attention-Interest-Desire-Action (AIDA) model. It is a handy tool for ensuring that your copy, or other writing, grabs attention. Advertising plays a major role in consumers' purchasing decisions. Some researchers add another letter, to form AIDA(S), where:

1. **A – Attention (Awareness).** The first step is to get the customer's attention (e.g., be quick and direct; use powerful words or phrases to catch the customer's eye).
2. **I – Interest.** By demonstrating features, advantages, and benefits, the customer becomes interested in the product (e.g., engage the customers by getting them interested).
3. **D – Desire.** After evaluation, the consumer generates a desire to acquire the product or service (e.g., build the reader's interest and create a desire in them – a motivation to act).
4. **A – Action.** Finally, the consumer will take action toward purchasing (e.g., take action on their desires and buy the product/service).
5. **S – Satisfaction.** Customer satisfaction will generate higher loyalty and lead to repurchase after using a product/service.

A recent version of AIDA is the AISAS model proposed by the Dentsu Group that is tailored to online behavior. The model replaces "*decision*" with "*search*" and adds "*share*" to show the increased word-of-mouth effect on the Internet. It indicates that consumers go through a process of *Attention-Interest-Search-Action-Share* in their online decision process. This model is particularly suitable for social commerce.

Players in the Consumer Decision Making Process

Several different people may play roles in various phases of the consumer decision process. The following are the five major roles:

1. **Initiator.** The person who recognizes and suggests the need to buy a specific product or service.
2. **Influencer.** The person who tries to convince other people to make a purchase.
3. **Decider.** The person who makes the final buying decision.
4. **Buyer.** The person who purchases the product or service and pays for it.
5. **User.** The customer that purchases and uses the product.

For more details, see **nptel.ac.in/courses/110105029/pdf%20sahany/Module4.(7)doc.pdf** and a SlideShare presentation titled "The Consumer Buying Decision Process and Factors That Influence It" at **slideshare.net/drafaraz/the-consumer-buying-decision-process**.

Shopping Cart Abandonment

The abandonment of online shopping carts by shoppers is of major concern to sellers. According to the Baymard Institute (reported by Li 2013), the results of 28 different studies showed that an average of about 68% of shoppers abandon their online shopping carts before payment (updated March 2015). The major reason discovered is: After filling the cart, buyers found that the shipping cost is too high (44%). Other reasons found are: (1) Not ready to purchase (41%); (2) high product price (25%); and (3) saving product for further consideration (24%). For an infographic and other statistics, see **salecycle.com/cart-abandonment-stats**.

SECTION 9.2 REVIEW QUESTIONS

1. List the five phases of the generic purchasing-decision model.
2. Use an example to explain the five phases in the generic purchasing-decision model.
3. Describe the AIDA and AISAS models and analyze their differences in illustrating online purchasing behavior.
4. Describe the major players in a purchasing decision and use buying a mobile phone as an example.
5. Describe why people abandon their online shopping carts. Do you have similar experiences while shopping online? Why or why not?

9.3 LOYALTY, SATISFACTION, AND TRUST IN E-COMMERCE

Effective online marketing activity can generate positive effects, which are generally observed as trust, customer satisfaction, and loyalty. Loyalty is the goal of marketing, while trust and customer satisfaction are factors that may affect customer loyalty.

Customer Loyalty

One of the major objectives of marketing is to increase *customer loyalty*. **Customer loyalty** refers to the chance that previous customers will continue to repurchase or repatronize a product/service from the same vendors over an extended period of time.

Increased customer loyalty can be accomplished by treating people in the way that they expected to be treated (or better). Loyalty can result in cost savings and increased revenue in various ways: lower marketing and advertising costs, lower transaction costs, and lower customer turnover expenses. The expense of acquiring a new customer can be more than $100; even for Amazon.com, which has millions of customers, the marketing cost to bring in a new customer is more than $15. In contrast, the cost of maintaining an existing customer at Amazon.com is $2 to $4.

Customer loyalty also strengthens a company's competitive advantage because loyal customers tend not to switch to competitors. In addition, customer loyalty can lead to an increase in favorable word of mouth. Obviously, most vendors are trying their best to find out what will make customers loyal (see eMarketer 2013).

Loyalty programs were introduced more than 100 years ago and are widely used among airlines, retailers, hotel chains, banks, casinos, car rentals, restaurants, and credit card companies. Now, however, loyalty programs have been computerized and expanded to all kinds of businesses. For example, the Hong Kong company Octopus Holdings (**octopuscards.com.hk**), a global leader in stored-value smart card payment systems, launched a reward program for members to use their membership card to shop at any Octopus Rewards Partners. Users get an automatic discount when they pay with their "Membership Octopus"; cumulative rewards can be used to spend at the establishment of any Rewards partners.

However, the introduction of social networking has the potential to undermine brands and reduce customer loyalty. Social media makes it easier to compare the price of products and evaluate the quality of vendors. In addition, consumers can get price quotes from several sellers, get honest opinions from friends, and switch to other vendors based on such information. Customers become less loyal to specific vendors because of the lower switching costs for them. They can take advantage of special online offers and promotions and exploit opportunities to try new products or services.

It is interesting to note that loyal customers end up buying more when they have the option to peruse and purchase items from a company's website. For example, W.W. Grainger (**grainger.com**), a large industrial-supply company, found that loyal B2B customers increased their purchases substantially when they began using Grainger's website rather than their voluminous paper catalog. (See Chapter 4 for more information.) In addition, loyal customers may refer other customers to a website, especially through communication in social networks. Therefore, it is important for EC companies to offer Web-based programs to increase customer loyalty.

E-Loyalty

E-loyalty refers to a customer's loyalty to an e-tailer or a manufacturer that sells directly online, or to online loyalty programs. Companies can foster e-loyalty by learning about their customers' needs, interacting with customers, and providing outstanding customer service. Another source of information is **colloquy.com**, which concentrates on loyalty marketing.

It is interesting to note that a percentage of positive customer reviews have a considerable impact on increased repurchase intention and e-loyalty (see Vora 2009 for details). For reviews and recommendations in social networks, see Chapter 7.

Many factors may affect customer loyalty and e-loyalty. A typical factor is the quality of the relationship between retailers and their customers. Customer loyalty is composed of trust, satisfaction, and commitment. Satisfaction and trust are particularly important because they will lead to commitment. For example, a study by Cyr (2008) found that e-loyalty is affected by satisfaction and trust across different cultures. The analysis of Sanz-Blas et al. (2014) showed how satisfaction, trust, and commitment can help strengthen customer loyalty toward websites selling accommodation services. For how to improve loyalty, build strong customer relationships, and persuade customers to share more information about themselves, see Pearson (2012).

Satisfaction in EC

Satisfaction is one of the most important success measures in the B2C online environment. Bashar and Wasiq (2013) found that customer satisfaction positively and significantly influences the e-loyalty of cyber consumers.

Satisfaction has received considerable attention in studies of B2C e-commerce. A few measurement indices have been developed. For example, the University of Michigan developed the American Customer Satisfaction Index (ACSI; **theacsi.org**), which measures customer satisfaction with the quality of various product and service sectors. The index is released quarterly. ForeSee (**foreseeresults.com**) developed customer satisfaction analytics to measure customer experience, and publishes the ForeSee Experience Index, ForeSee Government Satisfaction Index, and ForeSee Word of Mouth Index (WoMI). Several models were developed to explore satisfaction with online shopping. For example, Cheung and Lee (2005) proposed a framework for online consumer satisfaction by correlating the end-user satisfaction perspective with the *service quality, system quality,* and *information quality.*

Trust in EC

Trust in general conveys several meanings, yet it has been recognized as a major success factor in e-commerce that must be nurtured (e.g., see Salam et al. 2005). In general, **trust** means the willingness of one person to believe in the actions taken by another person. It is a perception variable. There are several definitions of trust in e-commerce since there are different types of trust. Examples are:

- Consumer trust in sellers.
- Consumer trust in the computerized system.
- Trust between buyers and sellers.
- Trust in foreign trading partners.
- Trust in EC intermediaries.
- Trust in online advertisements (e.g., Richter 2014).

Most studies of trust in EC concentrate on consumer trust.

EC Trust Models

Trust in e-commerce is often called **online trust**. Several models are available to explain the factors that may affect online trust. For example, comprehensive research by Lee and Turban (2001) examined the various aspects of EC trust and developed a cause-effect framework. According to this model, the level of trust is determined by three main categories of factors. They include trustworthiness of Internet merchants, shopping channels, and structural assurance associated with the business and regulatory environment.

How to Increase Trust in EC

Because consumer trust is fundamental to successful e-retailing, retailers are looking for ways to enhance the trustworthiness in e-commerce. The following are representative strategies for building consumer trust in EC.

Improve Your Website

A most important factor that affects online trust is the quality of the company's website. The ease of navigation, visual display, and information design of a website affects consumer trust. Gregg and Walczak (2010) reported a positive relationship between website quality and trust; based on a survey of 701 eBay users, they concluded that good website quality induces higher trust and price premium. Therefore, knowing how to design the EC website that delivers high-quality information and provides easy and effective navigation is a key to increased consumer trust in the sellers and their websites.

Objective Third-Party Seals

Webstores can be certified by third-party seals of approval such as TRUSTe (**truste.com**) and BBBOnline (**bbbonline.org**), the online version of the Better Business Bureau. Escrow providers and reputation finders (e.g., **cyberalert.com**) also are useful. These agencies provide business-critical intelligence such as how brands are being used on the Internet as well as research on businesses spying on their competitors.

Stories about fraud on the Internet, especially when unknown parties are involved, may reduce EC trust. Reputation systems that were described in Chapter 7 can affect trust either positively or negatively.

Establish Trustworthiness

Trustworthiness can be facilitated by the use of integrity, competence, and security.

Other Methods for Facilitating Trust

Several other methods are used to facilitate trust on the Web. For example, relating cognitive style to communication with customers (Urban et al. 2009) is designed to build trust. Smith (2014) believes that customers should know that they can trust a website (e.g., businesses should set up a trusted payment gateway, provide security and privacy, and provide a well-designed website with a short load time). Another method is to build reputation. Trust can be facilitated by positive word of mouth.

Reputation-Based Systems

A seller's reputation is important in online commerce. **Reputation-based systems** are used to establish trust among members of online trading systems where parties who have never done business with one another use feedback from others (e.g., reputations). For a comprehensive overview and how to manage online reputation systems, see Strauss and Frost (2014). For reputation management in agent mediated e-commerce (e.g., when the transaction is done by software agents, for example at Amazon.com or Expedia.com), see Gaur et al. (2013).

Reputation is often influenced by examining a website's rating. A major player in this area is Yelp.com, which aggregates reviews that contain highly subjective judgments. A Harvard study, using data from all Yelp, reviewed restaurants in Seattle, Washington from 2003 to 2009, concluded that a one-star increase in a restaurant's Yelp rating led to an increase of 5% to 9% in revenues (Luca 2011).

Online Word of Mouth

Due to the increase in online conversations and social networking, online word of mouth can influence the trust level and may impact reputation (positively or negatively).

Online word of mouth may occur in different forms, such as consumer online feedback or participation in social media forums. Hence, fostering positive word of mouth is an effective strategy to build stronger trust in a website. For more, see *viral marketing* in Section 9.8.

SECTION 9.3 REVIEW QUESTIONS

1. Describe the concept of customer loyalty and e-loyalty.
2. What are the key factors that affect customer satisfaction with a webstore?
3. Describe the issue of trust in EC.
4. What influences consumer satisfaction online? Why do companies need to monitor the satisfaction?
5. How can trust be increased in EC?
6. Define reputation-based systems and relate them to trust in EC.

9.4   MASS MARKETING, MARKET SEGMENTATION, AND RELATIONSHIP MARKETING

Online marketing is different from traditional marketing whereby online customers can be individually identified and targeted. This individually targeted marketing is called *one-to-one marketing or personalized marketing*. It is a part of the relationship marketing that treats each customer in a unique way to fit the profile and needs of that customer (e.g., personalized interactions). Let us first see how the one-to-one approach evolved from traditional marketing approaches.

From Mass Marketing to One-to-One Marketing

Three major marketing approaches have been widely adopted: mass marketing, market segmentation, and relationship (one-to-one) marketing.

Mass Marketing and Advertising

Traditionally, marketing efforts were designed to attract everyone in the market (the "masses"). For example, using a newspaper or TV ad usually means one-way communication from the message provider to the recipients. Such an effort may be effective for brand recognition or for introducing a new product or service to the public. Putting banner ads on an Internet portal so that everyone who accesses the website can see the message is a typical example of online mass marketing.

Example

In 2003, Ford Motor Company designed an online roadblock advertising campaign on the Internet to promote its F-150 trucks. A "roadblock" refers to running a commercial on all major TV or Internet channels at exactly the same time, so viewers cannot switch channels to escape the commercial. Ford advertised on the three major portals: AOL, MSN, and Yahoo! The campaign was a great success (see **clickz.com/clickz/ news/1712283/ford-f-150-drives-away-with-online-success**).

Market Segmentation

Market segmentation refers to the strategy that involves dividing a large group of consumers into smaller segments and then implementing suitable advertisements to target each segment. For example, cosmetics retailers may advertise in magazines geared mainly toward women. In this instance, the market is segmented by the gender

of consumers. The Internet enables more effective market segmentation, but it also improves relationship marketing, or one-to-one marketing.

Criteria for Market Segmentation

For effective market segmentation, the following are common criteria that companies use:

- *Geographic.* Region; size of city, county, or Standard Metropolitan Statistical Area (SMSA); population density; climate; language.
- *Demographic.* Age, occupation, gender, education, family size, religion, race, income, nationality, urban (or suburban or rural).
- *Psychological (lifestyle).* Social class, lifestyle, personality, activities, values, and attitudes (VALS; see **strategicbusinessinsights.com/vals/ustypes.shtml**).
- *Cognitive, affective, behavioral.* Attitudes, benefits, loyalty status, readiness stage, usage rate, perceived risk, user status, innovativeness, usage situation, involvement, Internet shopping experience.
- *Profitability.* Valued customers are placed in a special category.
- *Risk core.* High or low-risk customers are placed in a special category.

Statistical, data, and text mining methods are often used to identify valuable segments for promotion or advertising. Modern companies assign a variety of segments to their customers, often dynamically defining segments and temporarily regrouping customers for specific campaigns. By segmenting customers, companies can implement targeted communications about their products to cohesive groups. Much of this relies on the company understanding its business strategies to the extent that they know their most desirable segments.

Factor	 Mass Marketing	 Market Segmentation	 Relationship Marketing (One to One)
Interactions	Usually none, or one-way	Usually none, or with a sample	Active, two-way
Focus	Product	Group (segment)	Customer-focused (one)
Recipient	Anonymous	Segment profiles	Individuals
Campaigns	Few	More	Many
Reach	Wide	Smaller	One at a time
Market Research	Macro in nature	Based on segment analysis or demographics	Based on detailed customer behaviors and profiles

Figure 9.2 From mass marketing to segmentation to one-to-one

Relationship (One-to-One) Marketing

Relationship marketing is different from traditional marketing in that it focuses on building long-term relationships with customers. In order to do so, the seller must have a much deeper understanding of its customers on a one-to-one basis. Such information can be obtained faster, easier, and at a lower cost for online customers. When such information is analyzed, it becomes valuable for one-to-one marketing.

Although segmentation can focus on unified groups of customers, it may not be good enough because most competitors can adopt similar strategies. It may be advisable, therefore, to shift the target for marketing from a group of consumers to each individual customer. Instead of selling a single product to as many customers as possible, marketers are trying to sell as many products as possible to one customer – over a long period of time. To do this, marketers need to concentrate on building unique relationships with individual customers on a one-to-one basis.

One-to-one marketing is a way for marketers to get to know their customers more intimately by understanding their individual preferences and then providing them with personalized marketing communication.

One-to-one means not only communicating with customers as individuals, but also possibly providing customized products and tailored messages based on the customer's preferences. The major characteristics of one-to-one marketing as compared to those of mass marketing and market segmentation are illustrated in Figure 9.2.

How One-to-One Relationships are Practiced

Although some companies have implemented one-to-one marketing programs for years, it may be much more beneficial to institute a corporate-wide policy of building one-to-one relationships on the Web. Since one-to-one marketing strategies are applied directly to a specific consumer, marketers

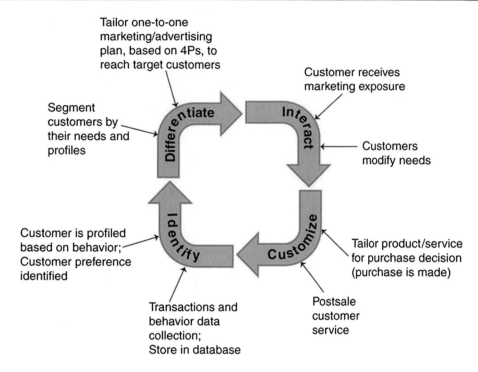

Tailor one-to-one
marketing/advertising
plan, based on 4Ps, to
reach target customers

Customer receives
marketing exposure

Segment
customers by
their needs and
profiles

Customers
modify needs

Customer is profiled
based on behavior;
Customer preference
identified

Tailor product/service
for purchase decision
(purchase is made)

Transactions and
behavior data
collection;
Store in database

Postsale
customer
service

Figure 9.3   The one-to-one marketing cycle (Sources: Compiled from Greenberg 2010 and the authors' experiences)

should apply a cyclical, four phase process in order to fulfill their goals of managing relationships with the individual customer. Figure 9.3 shows the four phases. The four phases are: *identification of customer preference*, *differentiation of customers, one from another*, *interaction with customers*, and *customization (personalized service)* (see **linkedin. com/today/post/article/20140103113441-17102372-building-customer-relationships-in-four-steps**).

A marketer can start the process at any point in the cycle, but usually the beginning is "identification." However, for new customers, it usually starts with "Customer receives marketing exposure" (top right side of figure). The customer then decides how to respond to the marketing exposure and makes the purchase decision (e.g., whether to buy the product online or offline; if online, whether to buy as an individual or to use group purchasing). After a sale is completed, customer information is collected (lower left corner) and then placed in a database. A customer's profile is developed, and then the so-called four P's of marketing (product, place, price, and promotion) are planned based on the profile, on a one-to-one basis. All of this can be done in the Web environment.

One of the benefits of one-to-one e-commerce is that companies can better interact with customers and understand their needs. These improvements, in turn, enable companies to enhance and frequently personalize their future marketing efforts. For example, Amazon.com can e-mail announcements of new books in the customers' areas of interest even before the books are published; Expedia.com asks consumers where they wish to travel, and then e-mails them information about special discounts to their desired destinations. Details on these key concepts that are part of personalization are discussed in Section 9.5.

SECTION 9.4 REVIEW QUESTIONS
1. Define and describe mass marketing.
2. Define market segmentation. How is segmentation done?
3. What is one-to-one marketing and what are its advantages?

4. Describe the major steps in the one-to-one marketing process.
5. How do advertisers use their knowledge about customer profiles?

9.5 PERSONALIZATION AND BEHAVIORAL MARKETING

As the Internet provides a huge amount of data for customer profiling, one-to-one marketing becomes effective. There are three generic strategies for one-to-one marketing: *personalization, behavioral targeting*, and *collaborative filtering*.

Personalization in E-Commerce

Personalization refers to the matching of advertising content and vendors' services with customers based on their preferences and individual needs. Personalized content on a website has been found to increase conversion rates (see **searchenginewatch.com/article/2334157/How-Personalizing-Websites-With-Dynamic-Content-Increases-Engagement**). The matching process is based on the *user profile*. The **user profile** describes customer preferences, behaviors, and demographics. It can be generated by getting information directly from the users; for example, observing what people are doing online through the use of tools such as a **cookie** – a data file that, frequently without the knowledge of users, is placed on their computers' hard drives. Alternatively, profiles can be built from previous purchase patterns. Profiles can be structured from market research or by making inferences from information known about similar consumers.

One-to-one matching can be done by methods such as *collaborative filtering* (discussed later in this section). Many vendors provide personalization tools that help with customer acquisition and retention. Examples of such vendors are Sidecar (**hello.getsidecar.com**) and Magnify360 (**magnify360.com**).

Web Cookies for Data Collection

Cookies are small files sent from a website and stored in a designated area in your computer. They allow companies to save certain information for future use. The use of cookies is a popular method that allows computers to look smarter and simplifies Internet access. According to Webopedia, "the main purpose of cookies is to identify users and possibly prepare customized Web pages for them" (per **webopedia.com/TERM/C/cookie.html**).

Are cookies bad or good? The answer is "both." When users revisit Amazon.com or other sites, they are greeted by their first name. Amazon.com knows the users' identity by using cookies. Vendors can provide consumers with considerable personalized information if they use cookies that signal a consumer's return to a site. Cookies can provide marketers with a wealth of information, which then can be used to target specific ads to them. Thus, marketers get higher rates of "click-throughs," and customers can view information that is relevant to them. Cookies can also prevent repetitive ads because vendors can arrange for a consumer not to see the same ad twice. Finally, advanced data mining companies (e.g., provided by SPSS and Sift), can analyze information in cookie files so companies can better meet their customers' needs.

However, some people object to cookies because they do not like the idea that "someone" is watching their activity on the Internet. Users who do not like cookies can disable them. On the other hand, some consumers may want to keep the "friendly" cookies. For example, many sites recognize a person as a subscriber by accessing their cookies so that they do not need to re-register every time they visit the site.

Cookies can be removed if the user does not like them. For instructions on deleting cookie files from your Internet browser (e.g., Internet Explorer, Google Chrome, Firefox), see **whitecanyon.com/delete-cookie**.

Using Personalized Techniques to Increase Sales

It has become a common practice for vendors to provide personalized services to customers in order to increase customer satisfaction and loyalty. A prime example is Amazon.com, which provides many personalized services where the most common activity is product recommendations. Amazon.com automatically generates such recommendations based on the buyers' purchasing and browsing histories, and upon the purchasing history of other customers with similar purchasing histories.

Personalized services can be facilitated when the companies know more about their customers. TowerData (**towerdata.com**) offers a service that helps businesses learn more about their customers, so they can personalize content (go to **intelligence.towerdata.com**). For a free e-book about the 40 best ways to personalize website, see **qubitproducts.com/content/40-best-ways-to-personalize**.

Behavioral Marketing and Collaborative Filtering

A major goal of marketing is to enhance customer value through delivering the right product or service to the customer. One of the most popular ways of matching ads with customers is *behavioral marketing*, which is identifying customer behavior on the Web and designing a marketing plan accordingly.

Behavioral Targeting

Behavioral targeting uses consumer browsing behavior information, and other information about consumers, to design personalized ads that may influence consumers better than mass advertising does. It also assumes that users with similar profiles and past shopping behavior may have similar product preferences. Google tests its "interest-based advertising" to make ads more relevant and useful. Representative vendors of behavioral targeting tools are **predictad.com**, **boomerang.com**, **criteo.com**, and **conversantmedia.com**. A major method of behavioral targeting is *collaborative filtering*.

Collaborative Filtering

When new customers come to a business, it would be useful if a company could predict what products or services are of interest to them without asking or viewing their previous records. A method that attempts to do just that is **collaborative filtering**. Using proprietary formulas, collaborative filtering automatically connects the preferences and activities of many customers that have similar characteristics to predict preferences of new customers and recommend products to them. For a free tutorial of 119 slides about collaborative filtering from Carnegie Mellon University, see Cohen (Undated). Many commercial systems are based on collaborative filtering.

Amazon's "Customers who bought this item also bought…" is a typical statement generated by collaborative filtering, which intends to persuade a consumer to purchase the recommended items by pointing to preferences of similar consumers.

Other Methods

In addition to collaborative filtering, a few other methods for identifying users' profiles are described below:

Rule-based Filtering

A company queries consumers about their preferences via multiple choice questions and uses the collected information to build patterns for predicting customers' needs. From this information, the collaborative filtering system derives behavioral and demographic rules such as, "If the customer's age is greater than 35, and the customer's income is above $100,000, show the Jeep Cherokee ad; otherwise, show the Mazda Protégé ad."

Content-based Filtering

This technique allows vendors to identify customer preferences by the attributes of the product(s) they buy or intend to buy. Knowing the customers' preferences, the vendor will recommend products with similar attributes to the user. For instance, the system may recommend a text-mining book to customers who have shown interest in data mining, or recommend more action movies after a consumer has rented one in this category.

Activity-based Filtering

Filtering rules can also be built by logging the user's activities on the Web. For example, a vendor may want to find potential customers who visit bookstores more than three times a month. This can be done by analyzing the website's visiting level and activities. For a comprehensive discussion and more information about data collection, targeted advertising, and 104 companies that catch data, and so forth (including an infographic), see Madrigal (2012).

Legal and Ethical Issues in Collaborative Filtering

A major issue in using collaborative filtering for personalization is the collection of information from users without their consent or knowledge. Such a practice is illegal in many countries (e.g., the U.S.) because of the violation of privacy laws. Permission-based practices solve this problem. (See Chapter 15 for more on privacy issues, and Section 9.10 for information about permission marketing.) In fact, empirical research indicates that permission-based practices are able to generate better positive attitude in mobile advertising (Tsang et al. 2004).

The negative effect of behavioral targeting can be seen in the Facebook case. In November 2010, Facebook announced the possibility of creating a Web-based advertising network that targets ads based on the recipients' behavior and the behavior of their Facebook friends. Privacy groups were unhappy and pressured Facebook to cancel the project. While there is an opt-out option, the practice is still in use and people are still unhappy.

Social Psychology and Morphing in Behavioral Marketing

Cognitive styles that define how people process information has become a subject of research in Internet marketing and advertising. The underlying rationale is that people with different cognitive styles have different preferences in website design and marketing messages. Specifically, an attempt is made to connect the Web with users in their preferred cognitive style. This can make one-to-one advertising messages more effective. MIT designed an empathetic Web that is utilized to figure out how a user processes information

and then responds to each visitor's cognitive style. For a comprehensive description, see Urban et al. (2009).

Use of Customer Database Marketing

Personalized services are often based on consumer information that the merchant gets from commercial database marketing services (e.g., see Strauss and Frost 2014). A unique example of such a service is TowerData (**towerdata.com**).

For how companies collect information, what they know about you, how they use the information, and what privacy concerns exist, see Steel (2010) and Madrigal (2012).

SECTION 9.5 REVIEW QUESTIONS

1. Define and describe the benefits and costs of personalization.
2. Define cookies and describe their values and drawbacks.
3. Define behavioral targeting and find a sample application on the Internet.
4. Define collaborative filtering and find a sample application on the Internet.
5. Explain how one-to-one advertising is done using cookies and behavioral targeting.

9.6   MARKET RESEARCH FOR E-COMMERCE

In order to sell more effectively, it is important to conduct proper market research to find information and knowledge about consumers and products. The market researcher's goal is to identify marketing opportunities and problems, to provide input for marketing planning, to find out how to influence the purchasing process, and to evaluate the success of promotions and advertisements. Market research aims to investigate the behavior of customers on the Web (see Strauss and Frost 2014). Market researchers gather information about competition, regulations, pricing, strategies, and consumer behavior. For the theoretical aspects of e-commerce market research, see the 2013 slide show presentation "E-Commerce Market: Theoretical Aspects and Market Research" at **slideshare.net/SellOnline Practive/e-commerce-market-research-26327400**.

Objectives and Concepts of Online Market Research

Investigation of EC markets can be conducted through conventional methods (e.g., in-person surveys; focus groups) or it can be done by using the Internet. Internet-based market research is frequently faster, allowing researchers to reach remote or diverse audiences. In addition, market researchers can conduct very large studies on the Web at a much lower price than using offline methods. Telephone surveys can cost as much as $50 per interview and their quality may be poor. Such cost can accumulate to thousands of dollars when several hundred respondents are needed. An online survey will cost a fraction of a similarly sized telephone survey and can expedite research considerably. On the other hand, the increased sample size in online surveys can increase the accuracy of the results. McDaniel and Gates (2012) provide a comprehensive review of online market research technologies, methods, tools, issues, and ethical considerations.

What are Marketers Looking for in EC Market Research?

By looking at a customer's personal profile that includes observed behaviors on the Web, it is possible for marketers to predict online buying behavior. For example, companies want to know why some customers are online shoppers, and why others are not. Major factors that are used for predicting customer online purchasing behavior are (in descending order of importance): product information requested, number of related e-mails, number of orders made, products/services ordered, and gender.

Typical questions that online market research attempts to answer are: What are the purchase patterns for typical individuals, and what are the patterns for specific groups? How can we identify those who are real buyers from those who are just browsing? What is the optimal Web page design? Knowing the answers to these questions can help a vendor advertise properly, price items, design a website, and provide appropriate customer service. Online marketing research can provide data to help answer these questions. More information about market research on the Web can be found in the tutorials at **webmonkey.com**.

Representative Market Research Approaches

To conduct online marketing, it is necessary to know what the customer wants or needs. Such information can be collected by:
- Soliciting information from customers online (e.g., via interviews, questionnaires, use of focus groups, or blogging).
- Observing what customers are doing on the Web by using transaction logs and cookies.
- Using data, text, and Web mining, or collaborative filtering techniques to analyze the available data.

Data Collection and Analysis

Specific methods for collecting online data include e-mail communication with individual customers, questionnaires placed on websites, monitoring conversations in social networks, and tracking customers' movements on the Web.

Online Surveys

An online survey is a major method for collecting EC data and it is considered the most cost-effective mode of survey research. It has several other advantages, including lower overall preparation and administration costs, better control of the process of filling out the questionnaire (which may lead to fewer response errors, and easier follow-up), and more flexibility in the questionnaire design. In addition, the cycle time can be much shorter. However, online surveys also have some limitations, including the lack of anonymity, data errors due to non-responses, reporting biases, and poor data privacy. For a comprehensive review, see Groves et al. (2009).

Web-Based Surveys

A special type of online survey is done by placing questions on selected websites and inviting potential consumers to reply. For example, Mazda North America used a Web-based survey to help design its Miata line. Web surveys may be passive (a fill-in questionnaire) or interactive (respondents download the questionnaires, add comments, ask questions, and discuss issues). The surveys may include both approaches. For online survey software and sample questionnaires see **surveymonkey.com**.

Online Focus Groups

Several research firms create panels of qualified Web visitors to participate in online focus groups. For example, see NPD Group, Inc. (go to **npd. com/wps/portal/npd/us/about-npd/consumer-panel**). This panel consists of 2 million consumers recruited online and verified by telephone to provide information for NPD's consumer tracking services. The use of preselected focus group participants helps to overcome some of the research limitations (e.g., small sample size and partial responses) that sometimes limit the effectiveness of Web-based surveys. See **us.toluna. com**. To create free online surveys, quizzes, and polls (a free to use online survey builder), see **kwiksurveys.com**.

Hearing Directly from Customers

Instead of using focus groups, a company may ask customers directly what they think about a product or service. Companies can use chat rooms, social network discussion groups, blogs, wikis, podcasts, and electronic consumer forums to interact with consumers. For example, toymaker LEGO used a market research company to establish a direct survey on an electronic bulletin board where millions of visitors read each other's comments and share opinions about LEGO toys. The researchers analyzed the responses daily and submitted the information to LEGO. Netflix is using this approach extensively by encouraging customers to report their likes and dislikes (see Online File W9.1). Software tools can facilitate obtaining input directly from customers. For examples, see **insightexpress.com**, a leading provider of media analytics and marketing solutions. Finally, as described in Chapter 7, social networks provide several methods to hear directly from customers.

Data Collection in Social Networks and Other Web 2.0 Environments

Collecting data in social networks and Web 2.0 environments provides new and exciting opportunities. Here are some methods:

- **Polling.** People like to vote (e.g., the U.S. television show *American Idol*), expressing their opinions on certain issues. People provide opinions on products, services, performances of artists and politicians, and so forth. Voting is popular in social networks.
- **Blogging.** Bloggers can raise issues or motivate others to express opinions in blogs.
- **Chatting.** Community members love to chat in public chat rooms. By following the chats, you can collect current data.
- **Tweeting.** Following what travels on Twitter can be enlightening.
- **Live chat.** Here, you can collect interactive data from customers in real time.
- **Chatterbots.** These can be partially interactive. You can analyze logs of communications. Sometimes people are more honest when they chat with an avatar.
- **Collective wisdom (intelligence).** This is a type of community brainstorming. It is used in crowdsourcing where communication is encouraged.
- **Find expertise.** Expertise is frequently found in the Web 2.0 environment; many times it is provided for free (e.g., Yahoo! Answers).
- **Folksonomy.** This social tagging makes data easier to find and access.
- **Data in videos, photos, and other rich media.** Places where these media are shared contribute to valuable data collection.
- **Discussion forums.** Subgroups in social networks use a discussion format where members exchange opinions on many topics.

Example: Xiaomi's Data Collection from Social Media in China

Xiaomi, Inc. (**mi.com/en**) is a Chinese company that designs and sells smartphones and consumer electronics. The company has grown unprecedentedly to become one of the top five smartphone brands in China in three years. It sold 18.7 million smartphones in 2013, only three years after its launch. A key to its success story is the effective use of social media as a marketing research tool. Xiaomi engages fans on social media sites. For example, the company organized a flash sale in 2014, using social media to notify their fans about their upcoming sale. According to the company's global director of marketing, social media is very important to Xiaomi, as it is the most direct and effective way to interact with its fans. Within a year, the market research website had enrolled over 6 million registered users (called Mi Fen). The company analyzed user contributions on the Xiaomi website to design a user interface called MIUI. Xiaomi's first smartphone model was released in August 2011, which received more than 300,000 pre-orders. Two years later, its sales reached US$ 5 billion in 2013 and started entering the market of other electronic products. Xiaomi's success story shows the importance of market research on social media. By November 2014, the Millet Forum (**bbs.xiaomi.cn**), called the Millet Community, had more than 221 million posts from its 30 million members. For more information about Xiaomi and its social media engagement, see **thenextweb. com/asia/2014/04/09/ xiaomis-social-media-strategy-drives-fan-loyalty-books-it-242m-in-sales-in-12-hours**.

Observing Customers' Movements Online

To avoid some of the problems of online surveys, especially the reporting bias that occurs when people give false or biased information, some marketers choose to learn about customers by observing their behavior rather than by asking them questions. Keeping track of consumer's online behavior can be done by using transaction logs (log files) or cookie files. This allows activity-based filtering to be done.

Transaction Logs

A **transaction log** (for Web applications) is a user file that records the user's activities on a company's website from the computer log. A transaction log can be further analyzed with log file analysis tools (e.g. from Oracle) to get a good idea about online visitors' activities, such as how often they visit the site.

Note that, as customers move from site to site, they establish their **clickstream behavior**, a pattern of their movements on the Internet, which can be seen in their transaction logs (see upcoming discussion of clickstream analysis).

Cookies and Web Bugs

Cookies and Web bugs can be used to supplement transaction-log methods. Cookies allow a website to store data on the user's personal device. When the customer returns to a site visited previously, the website can find what the customer did in the past from the cookie. The customer can be greeted by his(her)name, or a targeted ad can be sent to her(him). For a comprehensive description of cookies, including examples and privacy concerns, see the Indiana University Knowledge Base (**kb.iu.edu/d/agwm**). Cookies are frequently combined with **Web bugs** that are tiny (usually invisible) objects concealed in a Web page or in e-mail messages. Web bugs transmit information about the user and his or her movements to a monitoring site (e.g., to find out if the user has viewed certain content on the web page). Many believe that cookies and Web bugs are an invasion of a user's privacy.

Spyware

Spyware is software that enters your computer like a virus does, without your knowledge. It then enables an outsider to gather information about your browsing habits. Originally designed to allow freeware authors to make money on their products, spyware applications are typically bundled together with freeware that is downloaded onto users' computers. Many users do not realize that they are downloading spyware with the freeware. The best defense against spyware is to install anti-virus software, which should detect and remove any viruses or other harmful intrusions.

Web Analytics and Mining

Web analytics deal with the monitoring, collecting, measuring and evaluating, and reporting tasks related to Internet data and activities (e.g., see Provost and Fawcett 2013). Web analytics help us understand and optimize Web usage. Such analysis is done, for example, by retailers for market research. For example, see IBM Coremetrics (**ibm.com/software/marketing-solutions/core-metrics**; now part of IBM Enterprise Marketing Management). A company can also use Web analytics software to improve its website's look and operation. Web analytics can provide quick feedback from customers to help marketers decide which products to promote. For tutorials on data, text, and Web mining, see **mydatamine.com**, **tutorialspoint.com/data_mining/index.htm**, and the video 'Introduction to Data Mining 1/3' at **youtube.com/watch?v=EtFQv_B7YA8**.

For details and methods used, see Clifton (2012). A special type of Web Analytics is *clickstream analysis*, or just *click analysis*.

Clickstream Analysis

Clickstream data are data that describe which websites users visit, in what order, and the time spent on each. This is done by tracking the succession of "clicks" each visitor makes. By analyzing clickstream data, which can be maintained in a special database or data warehouse, a business can find out, for example, which promotions are effective and which population segments are interested in specific products.

Several companies offer tools that enable such an analysis. For example, Analytics 10 from Webtrends, Inc. (**analytics.webtrends.com**) features several advanced tools for analyzing clickstream data (**webtrends.com/solutions/digital-measurement/streams**). Finally, **clickstreamr.com** configures Google Analytics standards and can be used for such analysis.

Web Mining

Web mining refers to the use of data mining techniques for both Web content and usage in Web documents in order to discover patterns and hidden relationships. Web mining has the potential to change the way we access and use

the information available on the Web. For mining the social web, see Russell (2013).

Limitations of Online Market Research and How to Overcome Them

Online market research has technical and behavioral limitations. One technical problem with online market research is that there may be an abundance of data. To use data properly, one needs to organize, edit, condense, and summarize them. However, such a task may be expensive and time-consuming. One solution to this problem is to automate the process by using data warehousing and data mining. The essentials of this process, known as business intelligence, are provided in Online Tutorial T3 and in Sharda et.al. (2015).

Behavioral limitations of online research methods are responding biases, sample representatives that are hard to control, and the ethics and legality of Web tracking. As Web-based surveys often use an "open call" to recruit respondents, the response rate is hard to know and the respondent control is limited. Anonymity in Web-based surveys may encourage people to be more honest in their replies. However, anonymity may result in the loss of valuable information about the demographics, preferences, and behaviors of the respondents. To overcome some of the above limitations, online market research methods need to be designed carefully and rigorously. Small companies without proper expertise may outsource their market research to large and experienced companies that have specialized market research departments and expertise.

Privacy Issues in Market Research

Collecting data from customers, sometimes without their knowledge, may constitute an invasion of privacy. For an overview, guidelines, and standards, see **esomar.org/knowledge-and-standards/codes-and-guidelines.php**, and **marketing research.org/standards**.

Note: Stores may be tracking you through your phone: Some retailers are tracking their customers' shopping movements by monitoring shoppers' smartphones. While retailers are claiming that this is anonymous, consumer advocates disagree, claiming that this practice is spying, and shoppers who have their smartphone turned on while shopping should be given the option whether or not to being tracked. See Kerr (2014) and the accompanying video titled "Stores May be Tracking You through Your Phone" (1:11 minutes) at **landing.newsinc.com/shared/video.html?vcid=25637862&freewheel=90392&sitesection=jcntribune**. Retailers are using technology to track shoppers' location and movements in physical stores and malls by identifying the shoppers' smartphones (finding the MAC address). This information is used by advertisers and marketing planners. To avoid being monitored while at the mall, just turn off your smartphone. (For the opt-out website, see **smartstoreprivacy.org**).

Biometric and Smartphone Marketing Helps Market Research

Many households have several users; thus, the data collected may not represent any one person's preferences (unless, of course, we are sure that there is one user per device, as in the case of smartphones). Potential solutions are using biometric marketing or smartphones to access individuals.

A **biometric** is one of an individual's unique physical or behavioral trait that can be used to authenticate an individual (e.g., more precisely fingerprints; see list in Chapter 10). By applying the technology to computer users, we can improve security and learn about the user's profile. The question is how to do it. Indeed, there are programs by which users identify themselves to the computer by biometrics, and these are spreading rapidly. Note that utilizing the technology for market research involves social and legal acceptability.

Mobile market research is a method of collecting data though mobile devices including mobile phones, smartphones, and tablets. Typical methods for collecting information are through apps, short message systems (SMS), WAP, mobile Web, and location-based services. A major advantage of mobile market research is that it can be conducted virtually anywhere at any time. However, it does suffer from the limitation that it is hard to define the sampling frame and cannot access the sample without the users' mobile devices. Privacy protection is another key concern for conducting mobile market research. Hence, an organization called ESOMAR has released guidelines for conducting mobile market research (**esomar.org**).

SECTION 9.6 REVIEW QUESTIONS

1. Describe the objectives of market research.
2. Define and describe market segmentation.
3. Describe the role of transaction logs and clickstream analysis.
4. Define cookies, Web bugs, and spyware, and describe how they can be used in online market research.
5. Describe how the issue of privacy relates to online market research.
6. Describe the limitations of online market research.
7. Describe how biometrics and smartphones can improve market research.

9.7   WEB ADVERTISING

Advertising on the Web plays an extremely important role in e-commerce. Internet advertising is growing very rapidly, especially in B2C, and companies are changing their advertising strategies to gain a competitive edge. Since the Internet provides interactivity, online ads are also useful for brand building directly through response ads. Based on a 2014 IAB Internet Advertising Report conducted by the professional service network PricewaterhouseCoopers (**pwc.com**), online ad revenue reached a record high of $42.8 billion in 2013 in the United States alone, which is a 17% increase from the previous year, while mobile advertising increased by 110% to 7.1 billion in the United States in 2013 (see **about_the_iab/recent_press_releases/press_release_archive/press_release/pr-041014**). The Internet advertising revenue surpassed $40.1 billion of broadcast television and $34.4 billion of cable television.

Search, display/banner ads, and mobile ads are the three most popular types of Internet ads. Social media advertising is another fast growing area. A market research organization, eMarketer, reported social media advertising revenue in 2013 to be $4.4 billion, a 42.9% increase over 2012 and predicted a 30% increase in 2014. All these numbers indicate the fast growing trend in online and mobile advertising. In this section, we concentrate on generic Web advertising. We cover social media advertising in Chapter 7.

Overview of Web Advertising

Advertising is the delivery of ads to Internet users in order to influence people to buy a product or a service. Traditional advertising (also known as marketing communication) is an impersonal, one-way mass communication. Telemarketing and direct mail ads attempted to overcome the deficiencies of mass advertising, but they are expensive and their response rate was not too

high. For example, a direct mail campaign costs about $1 per person and has a response rate of only 1% to 3%. This makes the cost per responding person in the range of $20 (for a 5% response) to $100 for 1% response. Such an expense can be justified only for high-ticket items (e.g., cars).

One of the problems with direct mail advertising was that the advertisers knew very little about the recipients. Market segmentation by various characteristics (e.g., age, income, gender) helped a bit but did not solve the problem. The concept of **interactive marketing** enables marketers and advertisers to interact directly with customers.

On the Internet, a consumer can click an ad to obtain more information or send an e-mail to ask a question. The customer can chat live with the merchant (person or avatar), or with peers in a social network chat room. The Internet enables truly one-to-one advertising.

The Advertising Cycle
Many companies are treating advertising as a cyclical process, as shown in Figure 9.4. The

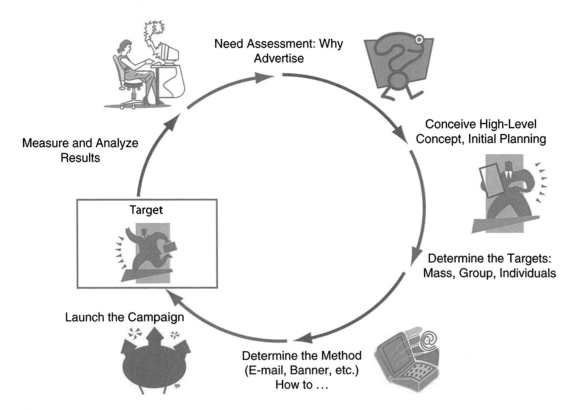

Figure 9.4 The advertising cycle

cyclical process requires a plan to determine the target audience of a campaign and how to reach that audience. Analyzing a campaign after its completion assists a company in understanding the campaign's success or failure. This knowledge is then used for planning future campaigns.

Before we describe the steps in the cycle as it is implemented in Web advertising, let us learn some basic Internet advertising terminology.

Basic Internet Advertising Terminology

The following terms and their definitions will be of use as you read about Web advertising.

- **Ad views**: The number of times users call up a page that has a banner on it during a specific period; known as *impressions* or *page views*.
- **Button**: A small banner that is linked to a website; may contain downloadable software.
- **Click (ad click)**: A count made each time a visitor clicks on an advertising banner to access the advertiser's website.
- **CPM (cost per mille, i.e., thousand impressions)**: The fee an advertiser pays for each 1,000 times a page with a banner ad is shown.
- **Conversion rate**: The percentage of clickers who actually make a purchase.
- **Click-through rate/ratio (CTR)**: The percentage of visitors who are exposed to a banner ad and click on it.
- **Hit**: A request for data from a Web page or file.
- **Landing page**: The page a viewer is directed to after having clicked on a link. In online marketing, this page is used to convert the person from a viewer to a buyer.
- **Page**: An HTML (Hypertext Markup Language) document that may contain text, images, and other online elements, such as Java applets and multimedia files; may be generated statically or dynamically.

Why Internet Advertising?

The major traditional advertising media are television, newspapers, magazines, and radio. However, the market is changing, as many consumers are spending more time on the Internet (about a 25% annual growth) and using mobile devices. Internet advertising is getting more attention. The advertising revenue of Internet advertising exceeded that of broadcast TV, cable TV and newspapers in 2013, and we can foresee this trend continuing. Hence, online advertising is a clear choice for the future.

Advertising Online and Its Advantages

The major advantages of Internet ads over traditional media advertising are the ability to interact one-to-one with customers and the ability to use rich media (e.g., videos) to grab attention. In addition, ads can be changed easily and campaigns are usually less costly. In comparison with traditional media, the Internet is the fastest growing communication medium by far. Worldwide, as of June 2014, the number of Internet users was getting close to 3 billion (see **internetworldstats.com/stats.htm**). Of course, advertisers are interested in such a fast growing community.

Other reasons why Web advertising is growing rapidly include:

- **Cost.** Online ads usually are cheaper than ads in traditional media.
- **Media richness.** Web ads can include rich and diversified media (e.g., videos, animation). In addition, ads can be combined with games and entertainment.
- **Easy updating.** Updating can be done quickly and inexpensively.
- **Personalization.** Web ads can be either one-to-one or addressed to population segments.
- **Location-based.** Using wireless technology and GPS, Web advertising can be location based (see Chapters 6 and 7).
- **Linking to shopping.** It is easy to link from an online ad to a vendor's webstore. Usually, it can be done in one click.

Traditional Versus Online Advertising

Each advertising medium, including the Internet, has its advantages and limitations. Pfeiffer and Zinnbauer (2010) compared traditional advertising against Internet advertising (including social networks). They concluded that, not only is Internet advertising more cost efficient, the business impact of Internet ads is larger than traditional ads. For a summary of a comparison, see Online File W9.2.

The synergy between TV and online advertising can help attract more attention than either medium on its own. It has been found that a TV campaign increases brand awareness by 27%, whereas a combined TV and online campaign increases it by 45%. A TV campaign increases intent to purchase by 2%, whereas a combined TV and online campaign increases it by 12%.

The impact of Internet ads on newspaper viability is devastating. Many newspapers are disappearing, merging, or losing money. One solution is to increase their digital ads, as the *New York Times* is doing (see Vanacore 2010).

Internet ads are subject to limitations such as screen size, space, and policies.

SECTION 9.7 REVIEW QUESTIONS

1. Define Web advertising and the major terms associated with it.
2. Describe the reasons for the growth in Web advertising.
3. Describe emerging Internet advertising approaches.
4. List the major benefits of Web advertising.
5. Draw and explain the advertising cycle.
6. What is the impact of online advertising on the viability of newspapers and TV?

9.8 ONLINE ADVERTISING METHODS: FROM E-MAIL TO SEO AND VIDEO ADS

A large number of online advertising methods exist. For a list and description, please see **en. wikipedia.org/wiki/Online_advertising**. Next, we discuss the three major categories of ads.

Major Categories of Ads

Ads can be classified into three major categories: *classified*, *display,* and *interactive*.

Classified Ads

These ads usually use text, but lately may include photos. The ads are grouped according to classification (e.g., cars, rentals). They are the least expensive.

Classified ads can be found on special sites (e.g., see classified ads at **craigslist.org** and **superpages.com**), as well as on online newspapers, e-markets, and portals. In many cases, posting regular-size classified ads is free, but placing them in a larger size, in color, or with some other noticeable features is done for a fee. For examples, see **traderonline.com** and **advertising. microsoft.com.**

Display Ads

These are illustrated advertisements that use graphics, logos, colors, or special designs. These ads are usually not classified, but they can be combined. Display ads are popular offline in billboards, yellow pages, and movies. They are becoming very popular on the Internet as well. All major search-based advertising companies (e.g., Google, Yahoo!, Microsoft, AOL) are leveraging their online positions in search advertising into the display ad business.

Interactive Ads

These ads use online or offline interactive media to interact with consumers and to promote products, brands, and services. This is most commonly performed through the Internet, often using video as a delivery medium.

There are several variations in each of these categories. The major methods are presented next.

Banners

A **banner** is a display that is used for advertising on a Web page (words, logos, etc. embedded in the page). A banner ad is frequently linked to an advertiser's Web page. When users "click" on the banner, they are transferred to the advertiser's site. A banner must be designed to catch a consumer's attention. Banners often include images, and sometimes video clips and sound. Banner advertising, including pop-up banners, is a popular advertising method on the Web.

There are several sizes and types of banners. The sizes, which are standardized by the Interactive Advertising Bureau (IAB) (**iab.net**), are measured in pixels. **Random banners** appear randomly, not as a result of some action by the user. Companies that want to introduce their new products (e.g., a new movie or CD) or promote their brand use random banners. **Static banners** stay on a Web page regularly. Finally, **pop-up banners** appear in a separate window when its affiliated Web page is activated.

If an advertiser knows something about a visitor, such as his/her user profile, or area of interest, the advertiser will try to match a specific banner with that visitor. Obviously, this kind of targeted, personalized banner is usually most effective. Such **personalized banners** that are tailored to meet the need of target customers are being developed, for example, by Conversant (**conversantmedia.com**).

Live banners are ads where the content can be created or modified at the time the ads pop up instead of being preprogrammed like banner ads. They usually are rich media. For details and examples, see **en.wikipedia.org/wiki/Live_banner**.

Benefits and Limitations of Banner Ads

The major benefit of banner ads is that, by clicking on a banner, users are transferred to an advertiser's site, frequently directly to the shopping page of that site. Another advantage of using banners is the ability to customize them for individual surfers or a market segment of surfers. In many cases, customers are forced to see banner ads while waiting for a page to load, or before they can get the page they requested (a strategy called *forced advertising*). Finally, banners may include attention-grabbing rich multimedia.

The major disadvantage of banners is their cost. If a company demands a successful marketing campaign, it will need to pay high fees for placing banners on websites with high traffic.

However, it seems that viewers have become somewhat immune to banners and simply ignore them. The click-through rate has been declining over time. Because of these drawbacks, it is important to decide where on the screen to place banners (e.g., right side is better than left side, top is better than bottom). Companies such as QQ.com and Taobao.com in China have built behavior labs to track eye movements of consumers to understand how screen location and Web page design may affect viewer attention. Ad blocking tools are also available to install on a browser to remove all banner ads when a Web page is accessed. This also reduces the number of click-throughs.

Banner Swapping and Banner Exchanges

Banner swapping means that company A agrees to display a banner of company B in exchange for company B's displaying company A's banner. This is probably the least expensive form of banner advertising, but it is difficult to arrange. A company must locate a site that will generate a sufficient amount of relevant traffic. Then, the company must contact the owner/Webmaster of the site and inquire if the company would be interested in a reciprocal banner swap. Because individual swaps are difficult to arrange, many companies use banner exchanges.

Banner exchanges are marketplaces that allow multiple websites to barter space for banners. Such an intermediary finds partners for such trades. A multi-company banner match may provide a better match, and it will be easier to arrange than a two-company swap. For example, company A can display B's banner effectively, but B displays A's banner with poor results. However, B can display C's banner, and C can display A's banner both successfully. Such bartering may involve many companies.

Pop-Up and Similar Type Ads

One of the most annoying phenomena in Web surfing is the increased use of pop-ups and similar ads. A **pop-up ad**, also known as *ad spawning*, appears due to the automatic launching of a new browser window when a visitor accesses or leaves a website, when a delay occurs. Pop-ups cover the user's current screen and may be difficult to close. They can gain a user's immediate attention, but their use is controversial. Many users strongly object to this advertising method, which they consider to be intrusive. Most browsers provide an option that allows the viewer to block pop-up windows. Legal attempts have also been made to control pop-ups because they are basically a form of spam.

Several other tactics, some of them very aggressive, are being used by advertisers, and their use is increasing. These tactics may be accompanied by music, voice, and other rich multimedia.

Pop-Up Videos

Along with the increase in popularity of free viral videos (e.g., on YouTube) comes the pop-up commercial before them. Some can be skipped; others cannot. These commercials usually last for 10 to 20 seconds. These pop-ups may or may not be related to the content of the video you want to watch. Sometimes, video ads come with an incentive, called *incentivized video ads*, which will be described later.

E-Mail Advertising

E-mail marketing refers to the use of e-mails for sending commercial messages to users. E-mail marketing may occur in different formats and for different purposes. Typical e-mail marketing formats are:

1. Using **e-mail advertising** means that ads are attached to e-mails.
2. Sending e-mail messages for facilitating vendor-customer relationships (CRM types).
3. Sending e-mail messages for attempting to acquire new customers.
4. Sending messages via microblogs or other social media platforms.

E-mail messages may be combined with brief audio or video clips to promote a product;

some messages provide links that users can click on to make a purchase. Sending coupons and special offers is done by all major retailers, including department stores and supermarkets. Airlines, banks, educational institutions, and anyone else who can get your e-mail will send you e-mail ads.

Major Advantages and Limitations of E-Mail Advertising

The major advantages of e-mail advertising are:

- It is a low-cost and effective method.
- Advertisers can reach a large number of consenting subscribers.
- Most Internet users check or send e-mail on a daily basis. Therefore, ads reach customers quickly.
- E-mail is an interactive medium that can combine advertising and customer service.
- E-mail ads can include a direct link to any website, so they act like banners.
- A consumer may be more likely to respond to relevant e-mail messages, especially when links to discounts or special sales are provided.

Using an infographic, Ellis (2013) explains the benefits of e-mail marketing for customer acquisition and retention, increased sales, and CRM.

Limitations

A major limitation of e-mail ads is that these messages are often treated as spam and are blocked by the user's spam control software. In general, using e-mail to send ads (sometimes floods of ads) without the receivers' permission is considered *spamming*.

As the volume of e-mail increases, consumers' tendency to screen and block messages is on the rise as well. Today, most e-mail services permit users to block messages from specific sources or automatically filter certain ads as junk mail.

Implementing E-Mail Advertising

A segmented list of e-mail addresses can be a very powerful tool for a company, helping it to target a group of people that share common characteristics. In many cases, the mailing list is based on membership and loyalty programs, such as an airline's frequent flyer program. For information on how to create a mailing list, consult **topica.com**.

E-mail can also be sent to mobile devices. Mobile phones, in particular, offer advertisers a real chance to advertise interactively and on a one-to-one basis with consumers – anytime, anyplace. Now e-mail ads are targeted to individuals based not only on their user profiles, but also on their physical location at any point in time.

E-Mail Hoaxes

E-mail hoaxes are very popular; some of them have been going on for years (e.g., Neiman Marcus's cookie recipe, the Nigerian Letters, the Homeland Security cashier check hoax). Some of these are scams. For details, see U.S. Federal Trade Commission (**ftc.gov**) and Chapter 10.

Fraud

Fraud may happen in e-mail ads. For example, a person may receive an e-mail stating that his or her credit card number is invalid or that his or her MSN service will be terminated unless another credit card number is provided by the recipient of the mail. For protection against such fraudulent practices, see **scambusters.org** and Chapters 10 and 15.

Search Engine Advertisement and Optimization

Search engines are a good mechanism for most people to find information, and therefore, a good platform for online advertising. Placing online ads on Web pages that show results from querying a search engine is known as **search advertising**. If the search result includes your company and product, it is a free advertisement for you. The problem is that the results of a search may include thousands of items, and your product may be not on the first or second page of the results. Note that, search advertising includes mobile search and social network search (see e.g., **wink.com**) or **pipl.com**). Two major forms of search engine advertising are *keyword advertising* and URL listing.

Keyword Advertising

Keyword advertising links the appearance of ads with keywords specified by the advertiser. It includes "pay per click." Businesses select the keywords to which they want their advertisements to be searched and matched. Advertisements appear on the screen along with the search results when the chosen keywords are searched. This can substantially increase the likelihood that the advertisement will be viewed and possibly acted on because of its high relevance to user interests. For an example of how this works, see **google.com/adwords/how-it-works/ads-on-google.html**. Google is using two major methods (to be described later) to implement its advertisement strategy. In fact, more than 90% of Google's revenue is generated from advertising (2014).

URL Listing

Most search engine companies allow businesses to submit their URLs for free, so that these URLs can be searched for by the search engines. Search engine spiders crawl through each site, indexing its content and links. The site is then included as a candidate for future searches. Because there are quite a few search engines, advertisers who use this method should register their URL with as many proper search engines as possible. In some cases, URLs may be searched even if they are not submitted to the search engines.

The major advantage of URL listing is that the listing can be very relevant to the subject of the search. This is the key to Google's success, as we will describe later. The second major advantage of using a search engine as an advertising tool is that it is free. Anyone can submit a URL to a search engine and be listed. People searching for a certain product will receive a list of sites that mention the products.

However, the URL method has several drawbacks. The major one is that it is difficult (or expensive) to get your ad to appear in a good location on the list generated by the search

engine. Search engines find a very large number of related Web pages for each inquiry made
by a user. The chance that a specific company's
site will be found and included at the top of a
search engine's display list (say, in the first
10 items) is very slim. Hence, many companies
provide a service to help advertisers improve
the location (usually targeting the first page) of
the search result. This is called *search engine
optimization.*

Search Engine
Optimization (SEO)

Search engine optimization (SEO) is a process
that improves the visibility of a company or
brands on the results page displayed by a search
engine. Ideally, the results should be in the top
five to ten on the first page. Companies hire
search optimizers or try to optimize by themselves. SEO can increase the number of visitors
to a website, and therefore companies are willing
to pay for this service. For how to do this, see
Harris (2014). SEO is performed in all types of
online searches, including video search, social

network search, and image search. According to
Google AdWords, "to get your ads to appear
when people search for your product or service,
the keywords you choose need to match the words
or phrases that people use, or should be related to
the content of the websites your customers visit."
Figure 9.5 shows the general process of SEO. For
further details, see Amerland (2015) and **blog.
kissmetrics.com/minimalist-seo**.

Sponsored Ads (Paid Inclusion)

In addition to optimizing your Web pages so that
they will appear on the first page of the search
results, you can buy keyword ads to appear on the
first page of the results. This is referred to as *paid
inclusion* or *sponsored ads*. Your ads will show
up on the first page of the results, at the top of the
page or on the right side based on the amount you
decide to spend. Google uses auctions (first page
bids) to sell the best locations to advertisers. For
how keywords work, see **support.google.com/
adwords/answer/1704371?hl=en**.

WebPosition (**webposition.com**) provides
such a service. More tips for improving a site's

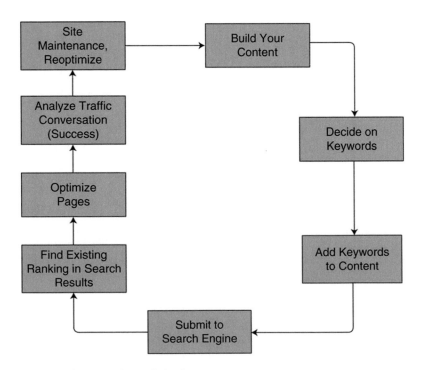

Figure 9.5 The process of search engine optimization

listing in various search engines can be found at **searchenginewatch.com**.

Google: The Online Advertising King

Google provides several methods of search engine advertising to their clients, generating most of its billions of dollars in revenue and profits from them. Google uses a behavioral marketing algorithm to determine users' interests while they search for information, and then targets (matches) advertisements to them. Google is continuously improving its matching algorithms (see Williams 2013).

Google's major advertising platform is composed of two programs: Google's AdWords and AdSense, and it can be supported by Google Analytics.

Google's Major Advertising Methods: AdWords and AdSense

The mechanisms of how AdWords and AdSense work are described below:

Google AdWords

AdWords is an advertising program for sponsored ads. Whenever you use Google to search for something, you will notice URLs with colored backgrounds, titled "sponsored links" on the right hand side or on the top of the page. These include Google AdWords participants. According to Google.com, these URLs are created by advertisers who select a few key terms related to their brands. They also choose how much they want to spend to "buy" these key terms (up to a daily dollar limit). Google uses ranking algorithms to match the advertisers' selected key terms with the searchers' search activities. Typically, if a searcher types in a selected keyword, a banner ad will appear in the sponsored links column. Then, if the searcher clicks on the ad (to go to the advertiser's page), the sponsor vendor is billed according to

---

the agreed upon rate (payments are made from the prepaid budget). For details and success stories, see **adwords.google.com**. Google AdWords is a "pay-per-click" type of advertising. You pay only if people click on your ads. How it works: You create your ads and choose your keywords (you can also target your ads); when someone searches on Google using your keyword, your ad may appear next to the search results; you gain more customers.

Since all advertisers like their ads to appear on the first page of the search results, Google devised a bidding system that determines which ads are shown where and how fees are calculated.

Despite its success, AdWords by itself does not provide the best one-to-one targeting. Better results may be achieved in many cases through a complementary program – AdSense (both are offered on mobile devices).

Google AdSense

Google's AdSense is an *affiliate program*. In other words, website publishers can earn money by displaying targeted Google ads on their website. In collaboration with Google, participating website owners (publishers) can add search engines to their own sites. Then, when someone is searching for a term related to the content of the affiliated websites, she(he) can see the Google ad and, if interested, will be directed to the advertisers' text, video, or image ads, which are crafted by Google.

The matching of the displayed ad to content of the affiliates is based on Google's proprietary algorithm. This matching algorithm is known to be fairly accurate. The key for success is the quality and appearance of both the affiliate's pages and the ads, as well as the popularity of the affiliate's sites. Hundreds of thousands of companies and individuals participate in the affiliate program. Google provides the affiliates with analytic tools and procedures that help convert visitors to customers (see the information at **google.com/adsense**). Google's affiliates earn money when visitors click on the ads. The advertisers pay Google. Google shares the revenue generated from advertisers with the affiliates.

AdSense has become a popular method of advertising on websites because the advertisements are less intrusive than in other programs, and the content is often better targeted. For an example of a site using AdSense, see **rtcmagazine.com**.

Google's success is attributed to the accuracy of the matches, the large number of advertisers in its network, the ability to use ads in many languages, and the clarity of the ads. Google offers several types of AdSense programs. See details at **webopedia.com/TERM/A/adsense.html**. Competing programs are offered by eBay and Yahoo! (see eBay AdContex at **affiliates.ebay.com.au/adcontext**; as of 2014, available only in select countries including Australia, the U.S., and the UK; also available only in few countries). For an overview on how AdSense works, see **google.com/adsense/start/how-it-works.html**.

Viral Marketing (Advertising)

Viral marketing (viral advertising) refers to electronic *word-of-mouth* (WOM) marketing – the spreading of a word, story, or some media. It is a marketing strategy where a company encourages the spreading of information and opinions from person to person about a product or service. This can be done by e-mails, text messaging, in chat rooms, via instant messaging, by posting messages on social network walls (e.g., Facebook), and in discussion groups or by microblogging (e.g., using Twitter). It is especially popular in social networks. Having people forward messages to friends, telling them about a good product is an

example of viral marketing. Viral marketing has been used offline for generations, but now, being online, its speed and reach are multiplied and is done at minimal cost to vendors, because the people who transmit the messages are usually paid nothing. The process is analogous to the spread of computer (or regular) viruses using a self-replication process. Viral messages may take the form of text messages, video clips, or interactive games.

An ad agency supplies Internet users with something of value for free, which encourages them to share with others, so as many people as possible can see the message. For example, advertisers might distribute a small e-game or a video embedded within a sponsor's e-mail sent to thousands of people hoping that they will forward it to tens of thousands of people. Viral marketing also was used at the pioneering of Hotmail (now closed), a free e-mail service that grew from zero to 12 million subscribers in its initial 18 months, and to more than 50 million subscribers in about four years. Each e-mail sent via Hotmail carried an embedded advertisement to the recipient to sign up for a free Hotmail account. Facebook's initial reputation was achieved in a similar way, but much faster. Viral marketing can be effective, efficient, and relatively inexpensive when used properly. eWOM can also influence consumer judgment about products. For further details, see **learnmarketing.net**. For six steps to an effective viral marketing strategy, see Wilson (2012). For a strategy see Wright (2014).

According to a 2010 survey conducted in Chinese markets, word of mouth has become an important factor in consumers' purchasing decisions. In 2010, 64% of respondents said that word of mouth influenced their purchasing decisions, while in 2008, only 56% of consumers preferred word of mouth advertising. Incidentally, researching a product or service online, rather than relying on traditional advertisements, was also found to be an important factor for people before they make the final purchase decision (see Atsmon and Magni 2010).

eWOM constitutes a multitude of activities, which can be divided into specific categories (see Wilde 2013). One category is a "higher degree" of e-word of mouth (e.g., viral marketing, e-referral marketing), and the other is "lower degree" marketing (e.g., social networks, brand communities).

One of the downsides of eWOM marketing is that many customers complain about receiving unsolicited e-mails, comparing them to telemarketing calls. Consumers may use spam blockers to filter out unsolicited e-mails, which may appear to be spam. For a comprehensive review, see Wilde (2013).

The messages circulated in viral marketing may be in different formats and serve different purposes. A typical one is a text message about a product or service sent for persuading consumers. Another format is video ads, a topic we will discuss next. Online videos are also discussed by Scott (2013) and in Chapter 7.

Line and Mobile Activities

Mobile messaging platforms such as LINE and WeChat have created a messaging app featuring cute and funny "chat stickers." These stickers are localized and tailored to the taste of individual markets. Line generates its revenue from in-app games (60%), followed by sticker purchases (20%), which are essentially big "emoticons" (Q3 2013 data). A sticker is downloaded from Line, which is a free download (available for Android and iPhones), and is attached as part of a text or chat message. Users can get stickers from the Line Store (**store.line.me**), and now the "Line Creators Market" is available for those who wish to design, create, and sell their own stickers in the shop.

Video Advertising

Video advertising refers to the insertion of video ads into advertisements or regular online contents. The Internet Advertising Bureau (IAB) believes in the importance of video ads, and created a guide to the topic; see **slideshare.net/hardnoyz/iab-guide-to-video-advertising-online** and the accompanying document transcript. Video ads are common in Internet TV programs.

Video ads are growing rapidly, mainly due to the popularity of YouTube and similar sites. Online video is growing nearly 40% annually while TV viewing continues to fall. For statistics, see **marketingcharts.com**.

Video ads appear all over the Web, both as unsolicited pop-ups, or when you give permission to see a demo or information about a product. Video ads have become very popular in the Web 2.0 environment and in social networking. The impact of video ads can be seen in Psy's "Gangnam Style" video, which the video was viewed more than 1.2 billion times within six months of its publication on YouTube. Any ad sponsor receives huge exposure in such a case. A 2013 IAB report shows a growth of digital video ads revenue from 721 million in 2012 to 807 million in 2013 in the United States.

The major reason for the popularity of videos is that almost everyone who uses the Internet now watches online videos. Videos are also viewed on all mobile devices (e.g., smartphones, tablets), and they can be posted on Twitter. Social media and the accessibility to increased broadband mobile access are also reasons for the growth of online video usage. Watching videos on mobile devices has become very popular on airplanes and other public transportation.

There are primarily two approaches to incorporating videos in Web advertising: (1) per-product videos that are embedded in regular product pages, adding product details; and (2) editorial-style videos that allow consumers to discover such products.. Many retailers are adding product-specific videos to their e-commerce sites. For a complete overview of video marketing and advertising, see **webvideomarketing.org/video-advertising** and Daum et al. (2012).

According to a Cisco survey, most large online retailers are using videos to help sell products. Forrester Research found that most major retailers are making product videos central to their marketing strategies. According to a comScore study (per McGee 2012), Americans watched more than 10 billion video ads in May 2012 and according to comScore, 28.7 billion in March 2014.

Some of the leading companies in this area are YouTube, Metacafé, VEVO, and Hulu. Figure 9.6 illustrates the IAB Model of video advertising. For information on Google's video advertising platform, see **google.com/ads/video**.

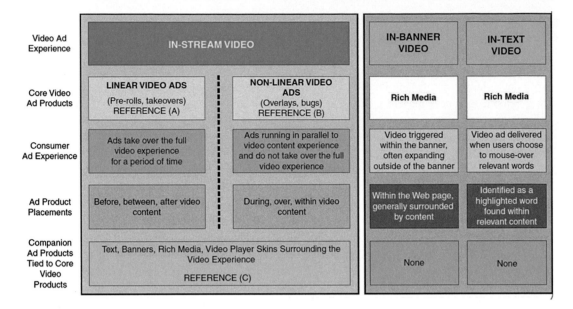

Figure 9.6 IAB model of video advertising (Source: Interactive Advertising Bureau. "A Digital Video Advertising Overview." January 2008. **iab.net/media/file/dv-report-v3.pdf** (accessed July 2014). Used with permission)

Almost any video that you click on is preceded by a 10 to 30 second commercial that can be skipped only some of the time. This kind of "forced view" commercial has been found to be effective because people are used to seeing commercials when watching TV programs. More TV shows are coming to the Internet, frequently with video ads.

Viral Videos

A **viral video** is a video that is spread rapidly through the process of online information sharing. These videos become popular when they are circulated via e-mail, SMSs, blogs, discussion forums, and so forth. This way, people share videos that receive more attention, sometimes drawing millions of viewers in a short time. Popular sites that are used for sharing viral videos include YouTube (**youtube.com**) and VEOH (**veoh.com**). For the top viral video ad campaigns, see **www.visiblemeasures.com/insights/charts/adage**.

Viral videos are liked (or disliked) so much that viewers send them to others, spreading the word about them quickly across the Internet. Marketers are using viral videos by inserting ads in videos or by using ads as pop-ups prior to the start of presentations; see **adage.com/section/the-viral-video-chart/674**. Note that, if the reactions to a video are positive, the buzz can be useful, but negative reactions can hurt the brand (see the discussion on reputation systems). *Baseline* magazine periodically provides a list of the 10 best viral marketing videos. For viral video marketing case studies (the best virals of 2013), see **digitalstrategy consulting.com/intelligence/2013/12/viral_video_marketing_case_studies_the_best_virals_of_2013.php**.

Consumer-Generated Videos

Many companies are utilizing user-generated videos for their online ads and even for their TV commercials.

YouTube is the largest advertising platform for video ads. It has billions of videos and is growing rapidly. YouTube permits selected marketers to upload videos with ads to the site. Google's AdSense ad distribution network also offers ad-supported video clips. Another way for advertisers to use viral video is by creating contests (see **onlinevideocontests.com** and **zooppa.com**).

Example: Crash the Super Bowl

Doritos runs an annual online contest, inviting fans to create their own Doritos ads. The winner gets a bonus prize of up to $1 million and their ad airs during that year's Super Bowl. In 2010, Doritos invited Pepsi Max to be a part of their fourth contest, receiving over 3,000 entries. In 2013, the contest was moved to Facebook, attracting over 3,500 submissions and over 100 million views. In 2013, for the first time, Doritos took its contest global, opening it to fans worldwide. This resulted in a huge advertising effect.

Interactive Videos

The term **interactive video** refers to a technique that is used to mix user interaction with videos. The interaction is controlled by a computer for entertainment, advertisement, or educational activities. Interactive videos are popular because:

- Increased bandwidth enables rapid downloading of videos
- Good search engines find videos that have been developed
- Both the media and advertisers have increased the use of videos
- Incentives such as contests and gifts are offered for the use of interactive videos

The following are representative types of interactive videos:

Video Click-Throughs

VideoClix.tv and Clickthrough.com have developed tools that allow people who watch videos to click on any person, place, banner ad, and so forth in the video.

Live Interactive Videos

In live interactive videos, you can see certain events in real time, and sometimes interact with those in the video. For example, GE presented the company's annual report in a banner ad during a live Webcast of its annual meeting. Viewers were able to interact with the presenters, asking questions or making comments.

Example: Interactive Dressing Room

Knickerpicker.com created an interactive online video dressing room (for lingerie). It is loaded with many designer brands. The animated models appear with your selected brands, and you can control their movements (e.g., turn them around). For details, see **knickerpicker.com**.

Advergaming and In-Game Advertising

Advergaming (in-game advertising) refers to the insertion of advertising into video games, especially computer-based ones, to advertise a product or a service. Such games are popular in social networks and give advertisers a chance to reach millions of players. Advergaming falls into one of three categories (per Obringer 2007):

1. A company places brand-related games on its website or Facebook page in order to attract players and introduce them to the brand. An example of in-game advertising is shown on Intel's gaming page (**itmanagerduels.intel. com**).
2. Games that are specifically designed to enable players to engage in certain activities can lead to brand exposure. Examples include PepsiCo brands partnering with leading video game platforms (**pepsico.com/Media/Story/ Winning-with-Video-Games041520141420. html**), and America's Army (**americasarmy. com**), which is intended to help boost U.S. Army recruitment.
3. With some free online games, advertising appears within the actual game (like banner ads). An example is the free version of online Monopoly (see **pogo.com/games/monopoly**) that contains ads. (Players can pay for an upgraded ad-free version.) Prizes are won in daily drawings.
4. For details on advergaming, see **adverblog. com/category/advergames**. Finally, Camaret (2013) provides several examples of serious and successful advergaming.

Augmented Reality in Advertising

Augmented reality (AR), which was introduced in Chapter 2, can be utilized by advertisers and marketers, especially in the fashion industry.

Examples of AR Applications

Several examples of interactive applications are provided at **en.wikipedia.org/wiki/Augmented_**

reality. These include real estate and architecture, product and industries design, tourism, and more. Companies such as Nissan, Best Buy, Walt Disney, and Burger King have experimented with using AR in advertising. For more examples, see Russell (2012).

Retailers in the clothing, fashion, and jewelry industries are using this technology, because in their industries, visualization is critical. For example, ClothiaCorp. combines AR and with real-time merchandise recommendations. It allows shoppers to "try on" clothing and share the 'how they look' with family and friends, in real time.

Virtual Dressing Rooms

These are becoming popular (e.g., see Amato-McCoy 2010). You can dress an avatar, or you can dress yourself when a Webcam is used to take your picture and upload it while you are in the dressing room. Zugara provides the technology for the latter application. According to its website, Zugara "leverage[s] the power of gestures, voice and Augmented Reality to create innovative and compelling experiences for retailers and brands" (watch the video titled "Zugara Virtual Dressing Room Technology: An Overview" at **youtube.com/watch?v=tNabSnBwBz0**).

Advertising in Chat Rooms and Forums

Chat rooms can be used for advertising. For example, Mattel Corp. sells about one-third of its Barbie dolls to collectors. These collectors use chat rooms to make comments or ask questions that are subsequently answered by Mattel's staff. The Xiaomi case in this chapter runs a smartphone forum for its product design and advertising.

Advertisers sometimes use online fantasy sports (e.g., available at Yahoo!, ESPN and more) to send ads to specific sports fans (e.g., fans of the National Football League or Major League Baseball). Online fantasy sports attract millions of visitors every month.

SECTION 9.8 REVIEW QUESTIONS

1. Define banner ads and describe their benefits and limitations.
2. Describe the difference between banner swapping and banner exchanges.
3. Describe the issues surrounding pop-ups and similar ads.
4. Explain how e-mail is used for advertising.
5. Describe the search engine optimization technique and what it is designed for.
6. Describe Google's AdWords and AdSense.
7. Describe video ads and their growing popularity.
8. Define advergaming and describe how it works.
9. Describe augmented reality advertising.

9.9   MOBILE MARKETING AND ADVERTISING

The rapid growth of mobile devices provides another arena for EC marketing and advertising. For example, the ratio of mobile handsets, including smartphones, to desktop and laptop computers is approximately 2 to 1 and growing. A 2013 estimation by eMarketer indicates that the global annual mobile ad spending has an increase of 105%, reaching US$18 billion in 2013 and is predicted to reach US$31.5 billion in 2014, a 75% growth. This represents a great opportunity for online mobile marketing and advertising. (See **emarketer.com/Article/Driven-by-Facebook-Google-Mobile-Ad-Market-Soars-10537-2013/1010690**.)

Mobile Marketing and Mobile Commerce

Mobile marketing and advertising are generally considered a subset of both mobile commerce (Chapter 6) and mobile marketing. Mobile marketing takes several forms, such as using SMS (e.g., Twitter), as well as games and videos. Their major elements are described next.

Defining Mobile Marketing

Mobile marketing is frequently defined as the use of mobile devices and wireless infrastructure as a means of marketing and advertising. The marketer intends to access potential customers through wireless information channels. The Mobile Marketing Association (**mmaglobal. com**) provides definitions of advertising, apps, messaging, m-commerce and CRM on all mobile devices, including smartphones and tablets. For a detailed description, see Krum (2010).

Mobile marketing includes sales, market research, customer service, and advertising, all supported by mobile computing. Companies can devise contests where customers describe the quality of a new product, and the sellers can post coupons and promotions. You can make ads interactive since mobile computing provides a direct link between vendors and consumers.

Mobile Advertising

Mobile advertising (m-advertising) is defined by the IAB (2014) as "Advertising tailored to and delivered through wireless mobile devices such as smartphones (e.g. Blackberry, iPhone, Android, etc.), feature phones (e.g. lower-end mobile phones capable of accessing mobile content), and media tablets (e.g. iPad, Samsung Galaxy Tablet, etc.)." Mobile advertising ranges from simple text messaging to intelligent interactive messaging on mobile devices. It involves several key players, such as the advertisers, mobile ad networks, mobile apps, and mobile devices.

Figure 9.7 shows how mobile ads work. A company hires a mobile advertiser to create a mobile ad and specifies the promotional criteria. The mobile ad is then sent to a mobile advertising network. The original network forwards these ads to multiple mobile networks and keeps track of the distribution and responses to these ads. The ad will reach the mobile user through proper mobile devices and apps. The user's response is then transmitted to the advertiser and the company through mobile networks.

Interactive Mobile Advertising

Interactive mobile advertising refers to the delivery of interactive marketing contents via mobile devices, mostly tablets and smartphones. The inclusion of the word "interactive" points to the fact that this is a two-way communication that may include a customer response (e.g., placing an order or asking a question). For a comprehensive guideline, see the IAB Mobile Web Advertising Measurement Guidelines at **iab.net/iab_products_and_industry_services/508676/guidelines/mobilewebmeasurement guidelines**.

Examples of Interactive iPad Ads

Econsultancy provides nine examples of great interactive iPads ads posted by D. Moth with a

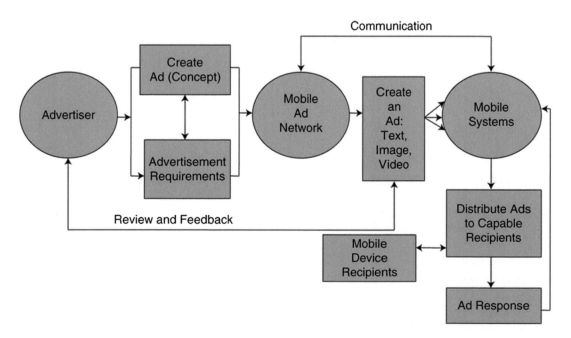

Figure 9.7 The process of mobile advertising

demonstration video for each (see **econsultancy. com/blog/10455-nine-examples-of-great-interactive-iPad-ads#i.1e2xw4r10pkflo**).

These include:

- VW ran an ad in the iPad version of *Auto Esporte* magazine (highlighting the VW Tiguan Park Assist feature). Users were engaged by being prompted to touch two targets on the screen and scroll through information about the VW cars.
- Visa presented users with a virtual wallet, enabling them to plan vacations, buy movie tickets, and so forth. By connecting to links on other sites, Visa added extra interactivity to its ads.
- Hyatt Hotel promoted its loyalty card using an iPad app. By visiting various virtual cities and finding more information about the city and the location of the nearest Hyatt, visitors were able to sign up for the loyalty card.
- Liberté of Canada created an interactive game within an ad to promote its blueberry Greek yogurt. Users rolled the blueberries around the screen and collected them in a yogurt pot.

An extension of interactive services is the use of Apple's iAds mobile advertising platform which is part of the iOs system. It facilitates integrating apps sold in the iOs App Store. It is developed for its iPhone, iPad, and iPod touch mobile devices, and allows third party developers to embed advertisements directly into their applications. For more information, see **advertising.apple.com**.

Types of Mobile Ads

Mobile ads may appear in different forms. The most popular one is short text messages. Other forms include rich media advertising, advergaming, and ads appearing during TV shows and movies on mobile devices.

Short Message Ads

SMS ads are commercial messages sent in the form of short text messages. They are quite popular and SMS mobile banner ads are growing rapidly due to the increased popularity of smartphones and 4G networks. Several major advertising portals have been launched by both private mobile advertisers and portals (e.g., D2 in Japan).

One advantage of SMS is that users can send them quickly and privately from any place and almost any time. A major drawback, however, is that short messages may interrupt and annoy the recipients.

Location-Based Ads

Delivering location-based ads to mobile devices was presented in Chapters 6 and 7. Location-sensitive businesses can take advantage of this feature to deliver location-based ads. A good example is a Google Map that can show nearby convenience stores, gas stations, hotels, and restaurants when a location is searched. Some of these are paid ads (see Chapter 7 for details).

Viral Mobile Marketing

Viral marketing can also be deployed to the mobile platforms. This is called viral mobile marketing. A typical approach is to develop and distribute apps for mobile devices. A successful example is provided by Malibu Bowling Game company. Their 2009 multi-channel campaign included a free bowling game called "Get Your Island On," available on iPhones and other smartphones. The game had over two million downloads the first six months. The managing director of the Great Works ad agency said that a phone app is a perfect way of branding, since the key to the product is the game (the bowling pins are replaced by Malibu rum bottles). For details, see **mobilemarketer.com/cms/news/advertising/3178.html**.

Mobile Marketing and Advertising Campaigns

There are basically four classes of online campaigns: Information, entertainment, raffles, and coupons. These classes focus on one or more of the following six objectives:

1. **Building brand awareness.** Increase customers' ability to recognize and recall a brand.
2. **Changing brand image.** Change the customers' perception of the brand.
3. **Promoting sales.** Stimulate quicker or greater purchase of products or services.

4. **Enhancing brand loyalty.** Increase consumers' commitment to repurchase the brand.
5. **Building customer databases.** Collect data about the mobile device, data network, or profiles of customers.
6. **Stimulating mobile word of mouth.** Encourage customers to share ads with other customers via their mobile devices.

Obviously, these are the same types of campaigns and objectives underlying traditional marketing approaches. Currently, SMS and e-mails are the principal technologies used to deliver advertisements to mobile devices. However, richer content and advertising is expanding with improved bandwidth.

Recent mobile marketing campaigns conducted by retailers have been very successful. For example, the "Singles Day" (November 11, 2014) sales resulted in over $9 billion, with 43% generating from mobile devices. (See **marketwatch.com/story/ alibabas-singles-day-bigger-than-black-friday-2014-11-10**.) Of these, over $5 billion were sold at Alibaba companies Tmail and TaoBao.

For interesting mobile ad case studies in 2014, involving Facebook, Coca-Cola, FOX's Family, Hotel Tonight and Oscar Mayer, see **moosylvania.com/tracker/category/mobile/mobile-ads**.

Mobile Marketing Implementation Guidelines

Although organizations such as the Direct Marketing Association have established codes of practice for Internet marketing, including the use of mobile media, most industry pundits agree that the codes are not well suited for the dynamic nature of mobile commerce. Therefore, the mobile media industry has established a set of guidelines and "best practices" for mobile advertising. The Global Code of Conduct from the Mobile Marketing Association (MMA; **mmaglobal.com**) is indicative of the types of practices

promoted by the industry. The basic principles of the code include four sections: Notice, choice and consent, customization and constraints, and enforcement and accountability. For practical tactics by large advertising companies, see Eslinger (2014). See also Rowles (2013).

Tools to Support Mobile Advertisement

A large number of applications, tools, and methods are available to support advertising in m-commerce. There are millions of applications (apps) that have been developed for iPhone and Android-based mobile devices that can be downloaded from app stores (e.g., Google Play and Apple store). Applications include features such as: finding products, places, or events. For details and a marketing glossary, see **where2 getit.com**.

Mobile Ad Trends

Several positive predictions have been made about the future of mobile ads. According to **mashable.com/2010/08/19/mobile-advertising-trends**, the following are the five important trends that advertisers need to watch:
1. Continued importance of SMS
2. Experimenting with rich media
3. Mobile sites vs. mobile apps
4. Interest in geolocation (see Chapters 6 and 7)
5. The growth of mobile video

Example: Innovative Sticker Advertising
In addition to these five trends, we also see the increasing importance of mobile social media, such as **whatsapp.com**, **wechat.com**, and **line. me/en/**. Creative advertising methods such as stickers offer new ways of advertising. A funny sticker is a small image (like an "emoticon") that can be used to show certain emotions such as great, love, hate, and so forth. It is very popular for Line users. Line allows a business to develop a set of eight sponsored fun stickers (with company logo or advertising messages) at a fixed

cost. Line users can download free chat stickers from Google Play and iTunes. For example, in the case of Tatung Electronics (of Taiwan), its *Boy character stickers and emoticons* generated more than one million active users within 24 hours of being introduced online.

Note: For a comprehensive collection of articles about mobile advertising, see **mashable. com/category/mobile-advertising** and Mobile Commerce Daily (**mobilecommercedaily.com**).

SECTION 9.9 REVIEW QUESTIONS

1. Define mobile marketing (provide at least three definitions). Why are there several definitions?
2. What drives mobile advertising?
3. What is the role of SMS in mobile ads?
4. Define interactive mobile advertising.
5. Describe the process of mobile advertising.
6. Define viral mobile marketing.
7. What are the similarities and differences between traditional media and mobile marketing/ad campaigns?
8. What are the trends in mobile advertising in the near future?

9.10   ADVERTISING STRATEGIES AND PROMOTIONS

Several advertising strategies can be used on the Internet. In this section, we present some major strategies and implementation concerns.

Permission Advertising

One solution to the flood of ads that people receive via e-mail that is used by advertisers is **permission advertising** or *permission marketing* (or the *opt-in approach*), in which users register with vendors and agree to accept advertisements (see **returnpath.com**). For example, one of the authors of this book agreed to receive a number of e-commerce newsletters via e-mail, knowing that some would include ads. This way, the authors of this book, for example, can keep abreast of what is happening in the field. The authors also agreed to accept e-mails from cer-

tain research companies, newspapers, travel agencies, and more. These include ads. The vendors publish and send valuable (and usually free) information to us. Note that, some vendors ask permission from consumers to send them other users' recommendations, but they do not ask whether they can use historical purchasing data to create the recommendations.

Other Advertising Strategies

Many advertising strategies exist both for wired and wireless advertisement systems. For examples, see **www.opentracker.net/article/online-advertising-strategies** and **ultracart.com/resources/articles/ecommerce-advertising.**

Affiliate Marketing and Advertising

In Chapters 1 and 3, we introduced the concept of *affiliate marketing* – the revenue sharing model in which an organization refers consumers to a seller's website. *Affiliate marketing* is a type of 'performance-based-marketing' used mainly as a revenue source for the referring organization and as a marketing tool for the sellers. Earlier in this chapter, we introduced Google's AdSense. This is an example of **affiliate marketing**. However, the fact that the vendor's logo is placed on many other websites is free advertising as well. Consider Amazon.com, whose logo can be seen on more than 1 million affiliate sites! Moreover, CDNow (a subsidiary of Amazon.com) and Amazon.com both are pioneers in the "get paid to view" or "listen to" commercials also used in affiliate marketing.

Affiliate Networks

A key to successful affiliate advertising is to have a good affiliate partner network. An **affiliate network** is a network created as a marketplace where publishers (affiliates) and merchants (affiliate programs) can collaborate. Examples of affiliate networks are: Rakuten LinkShare (**linkshare.com**) and CJ Affiliate by Conversant (**cj.com**). For the Top Affiliate Marketing Networks of 2014, see **monetizepros.com/blog/2014/the-top-affiliate-marketing-networks**.

Ads as a Commodity: Paying People to Watch Ads

In some cases, people are paid by advertisers (money or discounts) to view ads (also called "*ads as a commodity*"). This approach is used, for example, at Bing Rewards (get rewards for watching videos, playing games) at CreationsRewards searching the Web with Bing, net, and others. The HitBliss app pays you to watch commercials (but you must pay attention!). Consumers usually need to show some personal interest in the material viewed and then they receive targeted ads based on their personal interests. Each banner is labeled with the amount to be paid if the consumer reads the ad. If interested, the consumer clicks the banner to read it, and after he or she passes some tests to assure they read the content, the customer is paid for the effort. Readers can sort and choose what they read, and the advertisers can vary the payments to reflect the frequency and enthusiasm of the readers. Payments may be cash (e.g., 50¢ per banner), credit, or product discounts. This method is used with smartphones, too.

Selling Space by Pixels

The Million Dollar Homepage (**milliondollarhomepage.com**) was created by Alex Tew, a student in the United Kingdom. The website sold advertising spaces on one page (1 million pixels), similar to the way classified ads in a newspaper are sold. Once you clicked on a logo, you were taken to a website. The site sold out in five months (the last 1,000 pixels were auctioned on eBay). Within a short time, people in other countries started to sell pixels, cloning the idea (e.g., **millionaustraliandollarhomepage.com**, one of several Australian sites). Additionally, people who bought pixels at $1 each were selling them at higher prices through auctions. This is an innovative way of owning ad space because once you buy it, it remains there forever. Incidentally, The MillionDollarHomepage.com was the victim of a distributed denial-of-service (DDoS) attack (see Chapter 10) in January 2006. Malicious hackers tried to blackmail the site's owner. Mr. Tew ignored the demands, the site was eventually shut down.

Personalized Ads

Since the Internet contains too many irrelevant ads, customized ads can help. The heart of e-marketing is a customer database, which includes registration data and information gleaned from site visits. Companies use the one-to-one approach to send customized ads to consumers. Using this feature, a marketing manager can customize display ads based on user profiles.

Advertising as a Revenue Model

Many of the dot-com failures from 2000 to 2002 were caused by a revenue model that contained advertising income as the only or the major revenue source. Many small portals failed, but several large ones are dominating the field: Google, Facebook, AOL, and Yahoo!. However, even these heavy-traffic sites only started to show a significant profit after 2004. Too many websites are competing with limited advertising money. Thus, almost all portals are adding other sources of revenue.

However, if careful, a small site can survive by concentrating on a niche area. For example, NFL Rush (**nflrush.com**) is doing it well. It generates millions of dollars in advertising and sponsorship fees by concentrating on NFL fans, mostly kids 6 to 13 years old. The site attracts millions of visitors by providing comprehensive and interactive content and a chance to win prizes. It directs you to the NFL Shop for each team where sponsora such as Visa and U.S. Bank pay for the free games and the prize.

An important component in a revenue model is the *pay-per-click (PPC)* formula.

Pay per click (PPC) is a popular Internet advertising payment formula where advertisers pay sites only when someone clicks on their ad. Payments are made to search engines and other sites (e.g., affiliates). For tips on how to economize the cost of using PPC, see **advertise.com/ad-solutions/contextual/overview**. For further information, see **webopedia.com/TERM/P/PPC.html** and **wordstream.com/pay-per-click-campaign**.

Choose-Your-Own-Ad Format

AdSelector is a format created in 2010, which lets viewers choose their own ads. The AdSelector allows consumers to select what ads they like to view within the video clips (they are presented with 2 or 3 options). This model has been in use mostly for online videos with Hulu leadership. Users like this option and, according to research, are twice as likely to click on an ad. The AdSelector is used by publishers like Yahoo! For details, see Learmonth (2010).

Online Events, Promotions, and Attractions

In the winter of 1994, the term *EC* was hardly known, and people were just starting to discover the Internet. One company, DealerNet, which was selling new and used cars from physical lots, demonstrated a new way of doing business: It started a virtual car showroom on the Internet. The virtual showroom let people "visit" dozens of dealerships and compare prices and features. At that time, this was a revolutionary way of selling cars. To promote their website, DealerNet gave away a car over the Internet as the incentive for attracting viewers.

This promotion received a lot of offline media attention and was a total success. Today, such promotions are common on many websites. Contests, quizzes, coupons (see **coolsavings. com**), and giveaways designed to attract visitors are as much a part of online marketing as they are of offline commerce.

Live Web Events for Advertising

Live Web events (concerts, shows, interviews, debates, webcasts, videos), if done properly, can generate tremendous public excitement and drive massive traffic to a website. Some of the best practices for successful live Web events are:

- Carefully planning content, audiences, interactivity levels, and schedules
- Including as much rich media as possible
- Conducting appropriate promotions via e-mails, social media sites, and streaming media, as well as conducting proper offline and online advertisements
- Preparing for quality delivery

- Analyzing audience feedback so that improvements can be made

A global event can allow a product to debut in different locations.

Note: Web-based seminars, often called *webinars*, are becoming more popular to promote more knowledge-intensive products.

Localization in Advertising

The reach of Internet marketing is quite broad. An ad may be viewed around the world. This is an advantage, but could also be a drawback because culture differences may cause different interpretations of the same message in different communities. Hence, localization of ad messages is an important consideration for advertisers.

Localization in EC refers to the transformation and adaptation of Web content media products and advertising materials to fit the Web environment of a certain region or country (see Chapter 13). It is usually done following a set of international guidelines. An important aspect is that of language localization. Web page translation (see Chapter 13 and **lionbridge.com**) is just one aspect of localization. However, several other aspects, such as culture, are also important. For example, a U.S. jewelry manufacturer that displayed its products on a white background was astonished to find that this display might not appeal to customers in some countries where a blue background is preferred.

If a company aims at the global market where there are millions of potential customers, it must make an effort to localize its Web pages. This may not be a simple task because of the following factors:

- Many countries do business in English, but the English used may differ in terminology, spelling, and culture (e.g., United States versus United Kingdom versus Australia).
- Without a proper translation program, accented characters cannot be converted

to English and other languages. Thus, the translation may be inaccurate. If text includes an accented character, the accent will disappear when converted into English, which may result in an incorrect translation.

- Hard-coded text and fonts cannot be changed, so they will stay in their original format in the translated material.
- Graphics and icons look different to viewers in different countries. For example, a U.S. mailbox resembles a European trashcan.
- When translating into Asian languages, and so forth, significant cultural issues must be addressed; for example, how to address older adults in a culturally correct manner.
- Date formats that are written as mm/dd/yy (e.g., June 8, 2013) in the United States are written as dd/mm/yy (e.g., 8 June 2013) in many other countries. Therefore, "6/8" would have two meanings (June 8 or August 6), depending on the location of the writer.
- Consistency in document translation in several different documents can be very difficult to achieve. (For free translation in most languages, see **freetranslation. com**.)

Developing an Online Advertising Plan

Advertising online is a competitive necessity for most businesses these days. With so many different media and advertising methods available, a challenge is to develop an effective advertising plan within budget constraints. A life cycle process composed of six steps to build and maintain an advertising plan is illustrated in Figure 9.8.

(1) **Determine the goal of the advertising project:** The goal needs to be specific – is it for gaining brand awareness, traffic to the website, or higher revenue?

(2) **Identify the target customers:** A group of target customers must be determined for the advertising plan. As we have discussed in this chapter, customer segmetation is useful for reducing costs and increasing effectiveness. Depending on the nature of the campaign, segmentation may be based on demographics or other criteria.

(3) **Choose media and advertising tools:** Once the target customer is chosen, the advertising plan should select proper media and tools that can access the target customers. For instance, many firms use mobile social media to enhance their brand awareness in the younger generation in Taiwan.

(4) **Develop action and implementation plans:** After choosing media and tools, a number of implementation issues must be planned, such as budget, time frame for advertising, advertising designs (e.g., video), and so on.

(5) **Develop performance measurement and monitoring plans:** In order to ensure that the money spent on advertising is not wasted, performance measurement and monitoring plans must be developed before the plan is put into action. The performance measurement must be clearly defined and objectively measurable.

(6) **Execute plans and evaluate performance:** After the advertising plan is approved, attention must be given to its execution, and finally, its performance must be evaluated to see whether the originally planned goals are achieved. For preparing a promotion plan, see Sauer (2013), and for mobile marketing, see Brocato and Fairbrother (2013).

Advertising on Facebook

In 2012, Facebook began generating billions of dollars from advertising. For example, users' 'Likes' can appear in ads targeted to friends. For 45 'tips and tricks' see Marrs (2014). Note that other social networking sites such as Google+, Instagram, Twitter, and Pinterest also advertise. Advertising on social media is a trend in online marketing.

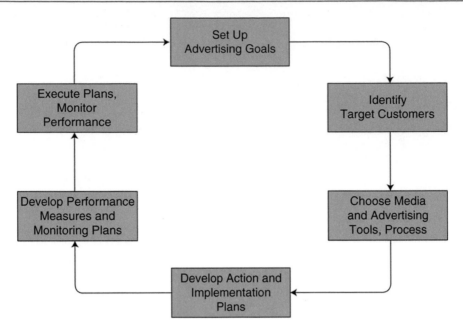

Figure 9.8 Life cycle of advertising plans

SECTION 9.10 REVIEW QUESTIONS

1. Describe permission advertising.
2. Describe video ads and their sudden increase in appearance.
3. Discuss the process and value of affiliate marketing.
4. How does the 'ads as a commodity' strategy work?
5. Describe other kinds of online advertising methods.
6. What is localization? What are the major issues in localizing Web pages?
7. Describe choose-your-own-ad format.
8. Describe the six-step process life cycle for an advertising plan.

MANAGERIAL ISSUES

Some managerial issues related to this chapter are as follows:

1. **Do we focus on value-creating customers?** Understanding customers, specifically what they need and how to respond to those needs, is the most critical part of consumer-centered marketing. This was not possible before the solutions for database marketing, one-to-one marketing, and customer relationship marketing became available. What tools do we use to satisfy and retain customers, monitor the entire process of marketing, sales, maintenance, and follow-up services? Do we focus resources effectively on VIP customers (e.g., giving them high priority)?

2. **Which Internet marketing/advertising channel(s) do we use?** An increasing number of online methods are available from which advertisers can choose. These include banners, search engines, video ads, blogging, social networks, and more. Angel (2006) proposed a methodology for Internet marketing channel selection with a matrix for selection and implementation that might be adopted to assess these alternatives.

3. **What metrics do we use to guide advertisers?** A large amount of information has been developed to guide advertisers as to where to advertise, how to design ads, and so on. Specific metrics such as CPM (cost per million impressions), click-through rate, stickiness, and actual purchase rate may be used to assess the effectiveness of advertising and

calculate the return on investment from an organization's online advertising campaign. The metrics can be monitored by third-party monitoring companies. For example, the Mobile Marketing Association and IAB developed the industry standards for measuring mobile ad delivery.

4. **What is our commitment to Web advertising?** Once a company has committed to advertising on the Web, it must remember that a successful program requires the collaboration of the marketing, legal, and IT departments. In addition, coordination with non-Web advertising as well as support from top management is needed.

5. **Should we integrate our Internet and non-Internet marketing campaigns?** Many companies are integrating their TV and Internet marketing campaigns. For example, a company's TV or newspaper ads direct the viewers/readers to their website, where short videos and sound ads, known as *rich media*, are used. With click-through ratios of banner ads down to less than 0.5% at many sites, innovations such as the integration of offline and online marketing are needed to increase click-through rates/ratios.

6. **Who will conduct the market research?** B2C requires extensive market research that may be costly and difficult to conduct. Thus, it may be necessary to outsource some or all of the marketing research activities. If a company owns a large-scale customer database, the research on the internal database itself can be an important market research activity, and data mining techniques may be helpful.

7. **Should we use mobile coupons?** Consumers and advertisers are curious about mobile coupons, but current usage is still low. Advertisers do not yet feel pressured to launch a nationwide coupon effort, but they should start to plan for it. Forrester Research Corp. claims that Instagram is the king of social engagement. Mobile coupons are gaining more popularity. The advantage of mobile coupons is that you can see them when you need them. Showing the coupon to a vendor may be sufficient to get the discount (there is

no need to print the coupons). In general, the benefits of mobile coupons are larger than their limitations.

Many large retailers (e.g., Walmart) offer coupons on their websites. Smaller companies may use intermediaries that have coupons of many companies in their database.

8. **What ethical issues should we consider in online marketing?** Several ethical issues relate to online advertising. One issue that receives a great deal of attention is spam (Chapters 9 and 15). Another issue is the selling of mailing lists and customer information. Some people believe that not only does a company need the consent of customers before selling a list, but that the company should also share the profits derived from the sale of such lists with the customers. Using cookies without an individual's consent is considered by many to be unethical. The negative impacts of advertising need to be considered.

SUMMARY

In this chapter, you learned about the following EC issues as they relate to the chapter's learning objectives.

1. **Factors influencing online consumer behavior.** Consumer behavior in EC is similar to that of any consumer behavior, but it has some unique features. It is described in a stimuli-based decision model that is influenced by factors that include the consumer's personal characteristics, environmental characteristics, product/service features, merchants and intermediaries, and the EC systems (logistics, technology, and customer service). All of these characteristics and systems interact to influence the decision-making process and produce an eventual buyer decision.

2. **The online consumer decision-making process.** The purchasing decision making process and purchasing online involves fairly standard steps that have been studied extensively. For each step in the process, sellers can develop appropriate strategies. The

Attention-Interest-Desire-Action (AIDA) model can help in designing ad and marketing efforts for different purposes. The Attention-Interest-Search-Action-Share (AISAS) model is tailored to the online behavior in the decision process. This model is particularly suitable for social commerce.

3. **Increasing loyalty and trust.** Customers can switch e-loyalty from one company to a competitor easily and quickly. Therefore, enhancing e-loyalty (e.g., through e-loyalty programs) is a must. Similarly, trust is a critical success factor that must be nourished. Creating loyalty is difficult when customers can easily switch to competitors with a few keystrokes. Building trust is very difficult since sellers and buyers usually do not know or cannot see each other. With the knowledge of factors that affect online trust, organizations should increase trust through website design and other actions.

4. **Market segmentation and building one-to-one relationships with customers.** In order to make online marketing and advertising more effective, customers are segmented so that attention can be focused on a subset of the population (e.g., female customers, young customers, or customers in a different country). EC provides companies with the chance to build strong one-to-one relationships with customers. In addition, advertising can be matched with customer profiles so that ads can be presented on a one-to-one basis.

5. **Online personalization.** Using personalized Web pages, customers can interact with a company, learn about its products or services in real time, or receive customized products or services. Companies can allow customers to self-configure the products or services they want. Customization also can be done by matching products with customer profiles. Personalization includes the recommendation of products (services) and delivering content that customers want.

6. **EC consumer market research.** Several fast and economical methods of online market research are available. The two major approaches to data collection are (1) solicit-

ing voluntary information from customers, and (2) using cookies, transaction logs, or clickstream data to track customer movements on the Internet and discover their interests. Understanding market segmentation by grouping consumers into categories is also an effective EC market research method. However, online market research has several limitations, including data accuracy and representation of the statistical population generated by using an incorrect sample.

7. **Objectives and characteristics of Web advertising.** Web advertising attempts to attract surfers to an advertiser's site. Once at the advertiser's site, consumers can receive information, interact with the seller (e.g., chat with an online representative), and in many cases, are given a chance to easily place an order. With Web advertising, ads can be customized to fit groups of people with similar interests (segmentation) or even individuals (one-to-one). In addition, Web advertising can be interactive, is easily updated, can reach millions at a reasonable cost, and offers dynamic presentation and rich multimedia.

8. **Major online advertising methods.** Banners are the most popular online advertising method. Other frequently used methods are pop-ups and similar ads, e-mail (including e-mail sent to mobile devices), classified ads, registration of URLs with search engines, and advertising in chat rooms. Some of these are related to search results obtained through search engines, such as keyword advertising (especially on Google). Social network communities provide new opportunities for marketing by enabling segmentation, viral marketing, user-generated ads, and more. Advertising in videos is gaining popularity as well.

9. **Mobile marketing.** With the increased use of mobile devices comes the opportunity to reach individuals wherever they are at any time. Despite the small screen size, advertisers use clever designs to show not only banners but video ads as well. Mobile ads are designed for the young generation and some

of these are interactive. The younger generation is especially active in viral advertising.

10. **Various advertising strategies and types of promotions.** The major advertising strategies are ads associated with search results (text links), affiliate marketing, monetary or other types of incentives for customers to view ads, viral marketing, ads customized on a one-to-one basis, and online events and promotions. Web promotions are similar to offline promotions. They include giveaways, contests, quizzes, entertainment, coupons, and so on. Customization and interactivity distinguish Internet promotions from conventional ones. It is also important that marketing projects are localized to meet the unique needs of different cultures.

11. **Implementation topics.** In permission marketing, customers are willing to accept ads in exchange for special (personalized) information or monetary incentives. Ad management deals with planning, organizing, and controlling ad campaigns and ad use. Ads can be localized to culture, country, and so forth. Market research can be facilitated by feedback from bloggers, chats in social networks, recommendations of friends, reading members' opinions, and so forth. Advertising is enhanced by user-generated ad content, viral marketing, and better segmentation.

KEY TERMS

Ad views
Advergaming (in-game advertising)
Affiliate marketing
Affiliate network
Banner
Banner exchange
Banner swapping
Behavioral targeting
Biometrics
Button
Click (ad click)
Clickstream behavior
Clickstream data
Click-through rate/ratio (CTR)
Collaborative filtering

Conversion rate
Cookie
CPM (cost per mille, i.e., thousand impressions)
Customer loyalty
E-loyalty
E-mail advertising
E-mail marketing
Hit
Interactive marketing
Interactive video
Landing page
Live banner
Localization
Market segmentation
Merchant brokering
Mobile advertising (m-advertising)
Mobile marketing
Mobile market research
One-to-one marketing
Online trust
Page
Pay per click (PPC)
Permission advertising
Personalization
Personalized banner
Pop-up ad
Pop-up banner
Product brokering
Random banners
Relationship marketing
Reputation-based systems
Search advertising
Search engine optimization (SEO)
Spyware
Static banner
Transaction log
Trust
User profile
Viral marketing (viral advertising)
Viral video
Web bugs
Web mining

DISCUSSION QUESTIONS

1. How can you describe the buying decision process when the customer is online and looking for an iPhone? What can a webstore

do to attract this customer to purchase from their store?

2. Why is personalization becoming an important element in EC? What techniques can be used to learn about consumer behavior? How can personalization be used to facilitate customer service? Give an example.

3. Watch the videos "Wherever You Want to Go" (from BMW; **youtube.com/playlist?list=PL53450A123A3ADCE2**), "One Million Heineken Hugs" (**youtube.com/watch?v=smO1onPkA3Q**), and Burger King's "Sign and Race" (**youtube.com/watch?v=qab5PH43sok**) and also find articles about them. Write a report on what made these videos so successful.

4. Discuss why banners are popular in Internet advertising. What kinds of products may or may not be suitable for banners?

5. Discuss the advantages and limitations of registering a company's URL with various search engines.

6. How might a chat room be used for advertising?

7. Explain why online ad management is critical. What are the major concerns for a company managing its own online ad program?

8. Explain the advantages of using chatterbots. Are there any disadvantages? Find information about their influence on online consumer shopping behavior.

9. Discuss the benefits of using software agents in marketing and advertising. Discuss whether a bargaining agent online (an agent that can interact with potential customers to settle a discount price) can help the webstore's sales.

10. Discuss SRI Consulting's VALS tool. Enter **strategicbusinessinsights.com/vals**. View their offerings and discuss how they can facilitate online market segmentation.

11. When you buy a banner ad, you actually lease space for a specific time period. On **million-dollarhomepage.com**, you buy space forever. Compare and discuss.

12. Discuss the advantages and limitations of three methods of data collection about individual online consumer behavior.

13. Discuss the benefits of video ads in the social networking environment.

TOPICS FOR CLASS DISCUSSION AND DEBATES

1. Discuss the similarities and differences between data mining, text mining, and Web mining for online market research. (Hint: To answer this question, you will need to read Online Tutorial T3.)

2. Some say that people come to social networks to socialize and they will disregard, disable, or not accept ads. Others say that people do not mind the ads, but they ignore them. Discuss.

3. What strategic implications do you see for companies that use videos, mobile devices, and social networks as platforms for advertising? Discuss.

4. Debate: Will traditional advertising (TV, newspapers, billboards) disappear in the future?

5. Debate: Netflix.com, Amazon.com, and others view historical purchases as input in their recommendation systems. Some believe that this is an invasion of privacy.

6. Debate: Do you think that it is ethical for a vendor to enter a chat room operated by a competitor and pose queries?

7. Some people claim that they trust traditional media advertising (e.g., newspaper) over online ads (e.g., Richter 2014). Others disagree. Debate the issue.

INTERNET EXERCISES

1. Enter **netflix.com/affiliates**. Write a report about the value of the affiliates program for Netflix as a marketing channel.

2. Surf **homedepot.com** and check whether (and how) the company provides service to customers. Look for their virtual designs. Particularly, check the "kitchen and bath design center" and other self-configuration assistance. Relate this to market research.

3. Examine a market research website (e.g., **nielsen.com**). Discuss what might motivate a consumer to provide feedback to market research questions used by this company.

4. Enter **mysimon.com** and share your experiences about how the information you provide might be used by the company for marketing in a specific industry (e.g., clothing).

5. Enter **marketingterms.com** and conduct a search by keywords and by category. Look at their marketing glossary. Check the definitions of any 10 key terms in this chapter.

6. Enter **2020research.com**, **infosurv.com**, and **marketingsherpa.com** and identify areas about market research on consumer behavior. Write a summary of your findings.

7. Enter **yume.com** and find their video ad activities and reports. Write a summary.

8. Enter **selfpromotion.com** and **nielsen-online.com**. What Internet traffic management, Web results, and auditing services are provided? What are the benefits of each service? Compare the services provided and their costs.

9. Enter **adweek.com**, **wdfm.com**, **ad-tech.com**, **adage.com**, and other online advertising websites to find new developments in Internet advertising. Write a report based on your findings.

10. Enter **clairol.com/en-US/virtual-makeover** to determine what hair color looks best on you. You can upload your own photo to the studio and see how different shades look on you. You can also try different hairstyles. (This site is for men also.) How can these activities increase branding? How can they increase sales?

11. Enter **clickz.com** and find its market research topics. Summarize your findings.

12. Enter **hotwire.com** and **espn.go.com**. Identify all the advertising methods used on each site. Can you find those that are targeted advertisements? What revenue sources can you find on the ESPN site? (Try to find at least seven.)

13. Enter **adobe.com/creativecloud.html**. How does this product help with site optimization? What other services does it provide?

14. What resources do you find to be most useful at **targetmarketingmag.com**, **clickz.com**, **admedia.org**, **marketresearch.com**, and **wdfm.com**? Describe useful information for online marketing that you have found from these websites.

15. Enter **zoomerang.com** and learn how it facilitates online surveys. Examine the various products, including those that supplement the surveys. Write a report.

16. Enter **pewinternet.org** and **pewresearch.org**. What research do they conduct that is relevant to B2C? To B2B? Write a report.

17. Enter **whattorent.com** and compare its recommendation system with the one Netflix uses. Write a brief report comparing the two.

TEAM ASSIGNMENTS AND PROJECTS

1. **Assignment for the Opening Case**
   Read the opening case and answer the following questions.
   a. What motivated Del Monte to advertise on social networks?
   b. Relate the capabilities of the social network sites to the market research activities (be specific on a one-to-one basis).
   c. Compare the methods used here to both computerized and noncomputerized focus groups.
   d. How can the data collected be used for EC justification?

2. Apple is encroaching onto Google's turf by buying Quattro Wireless, a mobile advertising company and by initiating the iAd mobile device platform. Research the reason for Apple's venture into the field and the Apple vs. Google battle. Give a presentation to the class.

3. The field of video ads is growing rapidly, with many companies introducing innovative models and services (e.g., see **yume.com**). The class examines the major models and services available, including mobile ads and video clips on Twitter. Write a report.

4. Each team will choose one advertising method and conduct an in-depth investigation of the major players in that part of the ad industry. For example, direct e-mail is relatively inexpensive. Visit **thedma.org** to learn about direct mail. Also visit **ezinedirector.com** and similar sites. Each team will prepare and present an argument as to why its method is superior.

5. In this exercise, each team member will enter **pogo.com** and a similar site to play games and win prizes. Relate the games to advertising and marketing. Write a report.

6. Watch the video of Google's past CEO Eric Schmidt delivering the opening keynote at the 2011 IAB Annual Leadership Meeting (8:19 minutes) at **iab.net/video/videos/view/431** and answer the following questions:
   a. What is the vision for the area of mobile videos?
   b. What is brand advertising? How can it change?
   c. What are the changes that mobile advertising brings to display ad advertising?
   d. What are the value-added benefits to customers?
   e. What is the vision for advertising?
   f. What are the major forthcoming changes?
   g. How does the mobile revolution contribute to closing the digital divide?

7. Enter **www.autonlab.org** and download tools for conducting data mining analysis (these downloads are free). Write a report about the capabilities of the tools.

8. Watch the video "Beginning Analytics: Interpreting and Acting on Your Data" at **youtube.com/watch?v=Hdsb_uH2yPU** and answer the following questions:
   a. To what metrics does the video refer?
   b. How can Google Analytics be used?
   c. What can analytics contribute to competitive intelligence?
   d. Why is the average time spent on a site so important?
   e. What decisions can be supported by analytics?
   f. What have you learned from this video?
   g. Compare Bing's Content Ads with Google's AdSense. Give a presentation.

CLOSING CASE: JOHNSON & JOHNSON USES NEW MEDIA MARKETING

The Problem

Johnson & Johnson is the world's largest medical and health care product company. In 2014, the company has more than 128,700 employees worldwide. A major problem facing the company is that their production and marketing must comply with strict global government regulations. In the Internet age, it is important for the company to use online communication tools to reach and support its customers. Moreover, the company has about 30,000 Internet domains. In the past several years, Johnson & Johnson has applied Internet media (called "new media" by the company) extensively and as a result, achieved significant performance improvement.

Using New Media Channels

Using new media, Johnson & Johnson (**jnj.com**) has grown in online activities and strategies over the years. Some of their strategies are introduced next:

- **Web 1.0 Stage.**
  In 1996, Johnson & Johnson had its first presence on the Internet and presented its products as a static brochure format. This grew to include about 30,000 domains in 2014.

- **Web 2.0 Stage.**
  1. *Kilmer House* (**kilmerhouse.com**; *Johnson & Johnson's First Blog*). In 2006, the company introduced its first Web 2.0 adverting tools after using Web 1.0 for over 10 years. The blog was a natural way for the company to enter the Web 2.0 era.
  2. *JNJ BTW (Second Blog Web 2.0).* In 2007, the company launched its second blog a year after launching Kilmer House. This blog promised to become "the voice for the company." JNJ BTW became a place for conversation about subjects related to Johnson & Johnson. It also offers public education about health care and JNJ's products.

3. *JNJ Health Channel on YouTube.* Johnson & Johnson is producing videos about health. In May 2008, the company launched two JNJ health test videos: "Ask Dr. Nancy – Prostate Cancer" and "Obesity and Gastric Bypass Options," which were watched by hundreds of thousands of viewers. Several hundred viewers posted their comments. For Johnson & Johnson, the site has turned out to be a great tool for interacting with consumers.

4. *Twitter and Facebook.* In March 2009, the company started a Twitter channel. In April 2009, the company created its first Facebook page. The page contains biographical information about the company. Twitter and Facebook also serve as a "bridging communicative tool" to integrate viewers into *JNJ BTW* for more detailed information about Johnson & Johnson.

- **Mobile Advertising Campaigns.**
  As of 2007, Johnson & Johnson has integrated several mobile advertising campaigns.
  1. *The company created a game called "Saving Momo"* for IM users working with Microsoft Digital Advertising Solutions.
  2. *Using a multichannel mobile campaign.* According to Butcher (2008), the company used in-call audio ads, SMS, and mobile websites to create a new way to send advertising messages to its target audiences in 2008.
  3. *Johnson & Johnson's Zyrtec and iPhone 2.0.* Zyrtec is a popular over-the-counter allergy medication. According to Butcher (2009), Zyrtec generated $315.9 million in sales in 2008. In 2009, Johnson & Johnson conducted a mobile advertising campaign together with The Weather Channel (TWC), putting an interactive Zyrtec banner ad on the TWC mobile app. Johnson & Johnson then extended to a new platform, TWC's upgraded iPhone application.

- **Social Media.**
  Johnson & Johnson is very active in the use of social media. For example, on the company's main Facebook page (**facebook.com/jnj**), the company provides a link to health information (on the J&J Channel). There are over 625,000 million 'Likes' in English and the most engaged city is Sao Paulo, Brazil (August 2014 data). J&J most active account on Twitter is its @JNNews. Finally, J&J is using social media to save lives (see Olenski 2013).

Results

The intensive campaigns that used various new media have resulted in significant performance improvements financially and managerially.

1. According to Ploof (2009), the company's reputation is one factor in figuring the ROI (return on investment) of using new media. YouTube provides usability metrics, such as views over time, trends, and viewer retention rates, which has helped the management team make better decisions.

2. Mobile advertising has shown to be very effective. In 2007, ACUVUE's one-month campaign promoted a new product by creating a shared game, called "Saving Momo," for Windows Live Messenger. The game was played 200,000 times, while approximately 300,000 personal expressions (for IM) were downloaded. The campaign drove sales, improved the target markets' connection to the brand, and had a positive viral impact on the brand. In 2008, Johnson & Johnson used the In-Call Network as another option to engage consumers, which made it easier for users to get a free trial of ACUVUE.

3. The Weather Channel remained the number one download for iPhone users in the Apple Store. The direct interaction between consumers and the brand illustrates the reach of mobile advertising.

Sources: Based on Butcher (2008), Butcher (2009), Microsoft (2009), and Ploof (2009).

Questions

1. Identify the online advertising actions adopted by Johnson & Johnson and relate them to the methods described in the chapter.

2. Search the Internet to find more details about Johnson & Johnson's marketing activities on YouTube.
3. Search the Internet to find more details about Johnson & Johnson's marketing activities on Facebook and Twitter.
4. Search the Internet to find more details about Johnson & Johnson's marketing activities on mobile devices.
5. Outline the major benefits from Johnson & Johnson's online marketing activities.

ONLINE FILES
available at **affordable-ecommerce-textbook.com/turban**

W9.1 Application Case: Netflix Increases Sales Using Movie Recommendations and Advertisements

W9.2 From Mass Advertising to Interactive Advertising; Advantages and Limitations

COMPREHENSIVE EDUCATIONAL WEBSITES

marketresearch.com: E-commerce market research reports (free).

ecommerce-guide.com: Comprehensive collection of resources.

internet.com: Many resources (for small businesses, in particular).

emarketer.com: Statistics, news, products, laws.

webmarketingtoday.com: Case studies, articles, tutorials, videos, and more; the research room may require fees.

lib.unc.edu: A collection of research books, articles, etc. on many different subjects from the University of North Carolina, Chapel Hill.

ecommercetimes.com: News and analysis on business, social media, e-commerce, and so forth.

ultracart.com: Resources, articles, etc. about EC advertising.

reelseo.com: Online video marketing guide; cases, news and more about video advertising.

clickz.com: Marketing news and expert advice; statistics and tools; articles on EC.

cio.com/resources: Index of white papers by topic.

scribd.com: Personal digital library with access to thousands of e-books and written works.

marketingdonut.co.uk: Comprehensive resources for a business, including topics such as marketing strategy, Internet marketing, customer care, and advertising.

GLOSSARY

Advergaming (in-game advertising) The insertion of an advertisement into video games, especially computer-based ones, to advertise a product or a service.

Ad views The number of times users call up a page that has a banner on it during a specific period; known as *impressions* or *page views*.

Affiliated marketing A type of 'performance-based-marketing' used mainly as a revenue source for the referring organization and as a marketing tool for the sellers.

Affiliate network A network created as a marketplace where publishers (affiliates) and merchant affiliate programs can collaborate.

Banner A display that is used for advertising on a Web page (words, logos, etc. embedded in the page).

Banner exchanges Marketplaces that allow multiple websites to barter space for banners.

Banner swapping Company A agrees to display a banner of company B in exchange for company B's displaying company A's banner.

Behavioral targeting Targeting that uses consumer browsing behavior information to design personalized ads that may influence consumers better than mass advertising does.

Biometric One of an individual's unique physical or behavioral trait that can be used to authenticate an individual precisely (e.g., fingerprints).

Button A small banner that is linked to a website; may contain downloadable software.

Click (ad click) A count made each time a visitor clicks on an advertising banner to access the advertiser's website.

Click-through rate/ratio (CTR) The percentage of visitors who are exposed to a banner ad and click on it.

Clickstream behavior A pattern of customer movements on the Internet, which can be seen in their transaction logs.

Clickstream data Data that describe which websites users visit, in what order and the time spent on each. This is done by tracking the succession of "clicks" each visitor makes.

Collaborative filtering A method that attempts to predict what products or services are of interest to new customers without asking or viewing their previous records.

Conversion rate The percentage of clickers who actually make a purchase.

Cookie A data file that, without the knowledge of users, is placed on their computer hard drives.

CPM (cost per mille, i.e., thousand impressions) The fee an advertiser pays for each 1,000 times a page with a banner ad is shown.

Customer loyalty The chance that previous customers will continue to repurchase or repatronize a product/service from the same vendors over an extended period of time.

E-loyalty A customer's loyalty to an e-tailer or a manufacturer that sells directly online, or to online loyalty programs.

E-mail marketing The use of e-mail for sending commercial messages to users.

E-mail advertising Ads are attached to e-mails.

Hit A request for data from a Web page or file.

Interactive marketing A marketing concept that enables marketers and advertisers to interact directly with customers.

Interactive video A technique used to mix user interaction with videos.

Landing page The page a viewer is directed to after having clicked on a link. In online marketing, this page is used to convert the person from a viewer to a buyer.

Live banners Ads where the content can be created or modified at the time the ads pop up instead of being preprogrammed like banner ads.

Localization The transformation and adaptation of Web content media products and advertising materials to fit the Web environment of a certain region or country.

Market segmentation The strategy that involves dividing a large group of consumers into smaller segments and then implementing suitable advertisements to target each segment.

Merchant brokering From whom to buy in the purchasing decision-making process.

Mobile advertising (m-advertising) "Advertising tailored to and delivered through wireless mobile devices such as smartphones (e.g. Blackberry, iPhone, Android, etc.), feature phones (e.g. lower-end mobile phones capable of accessing mobile content), and media tablets (e.g. iPad, Samsung Galaxy Tablet, etc.)" (IAB 2014).

Mobile marketing The use of mobile devices and wireless infrastructure as a means of marketing and advertising.

One-to-one marketing A way for marketers to get to know their customers more intimately by understanding their individual preferences and then providing them with personalized marketing communication.

Online trust Trust in e-commerce.

Page An HTML (Hypertext Markup Language) document that may contain text, images, and other online elements, such as Java applets and multimedia files; may be generated statically or dynamically.

Pay per click (PPC) A popular Internet advertising payment formula where advertisers pay sites only when someone clicks on their ad.

Permission advertising Advertising (marketing) strategy in which customers agree to accept advertising and marketing materials (known as *opt-in*).**personalization** The matching of advertising content and vendors' services with customers based on their preferences and individual needs.

Personalized banners Banners that are tailored to meet the need of target customers.

Pop-up ad An ad that appears due to the automatic launching of a new browser window when a visitor accesses or leaves a website, when a delay occurs; also known as *ad spawning*.

Pop-up banner Banners that appear in a separate window when its affiliated Web page is activated.

Product brokering Considering what product to buy in the purchasing decision-making process.

Random banners Banner ads that appear randomly, not as a result of some action by the user.

Relationship marketing Marketing method that focuses on building long-term relationships with customers.

Reputation-based systems Systems used to establish trust among members of online trading systems where parties who have never done business with one another use feedback from others (e.g., reputations).

Search advertising Placing online ads on web pages that show results from querying a search engine.

Search engine optimization (SEO) A process that improves the position of a company or brands on the results page displayed by a search engine. Ideally, the results should be in the top five on the first page of the results.

Spyware Software that enters your computer like a virus does, without your knowledge. It then enables an outsider to gather information about your browsing habits.

Static banner Banners that stay on a Web page regularly.

Sticker advertising Advertisers develop free funny stickers that include their messages for distribution in mobile social media (such as Line) to gain brand awareness.

Transaction log (for Web applications) A user file that records the user's activities on a company's website from the computer log.

Trust The willingness of one person to believe in the actions taken by another person.

User profile Customer preferences, behaviors, and demographics.

Viral marketing (viral advertising) Electronic word-of-mouth marketing (WOM) that spreads a word, story, or some media.

Viral video A video that is spread rapidly through the process of online information sharing. This way, people share videos that receive more attention, sometimes drawing millions of viewers in a short time.

Web bugs Tiny (usually invisible) objects concealed in a web page or in e-mail messages. Web bugs transmit information about the user and his or her movements to a monitoring site (e.g., to find out if the user has viewed certain content on the web page).

Web mining The use of data mining techniques for both Web content and usage in Web documents in order to discover patterns and hidden relationships.

REFERENCES

Amato-McCoy, D. M. "That's So You." *Stores,* April 2010.

Amerland, D. *Google Semantic Search: Search Engine Optimization (SEO) Techniques That Get Your Company More Traffic, Increase Brand Impact, and Amplify Your Online Presence (Que Biz-Tech Series),* New York: Que Publishing, 2015.

Angel, G. "The Art and Science of Choosing Net Marketing Channels." *CRM Buyer,* September 21, 2006. **crmbuyer.com/story/53141.html** (accessed July 2014).

Atsmon, Y., and M. Magni. "China's Internet Obsession." *McKinsey Quarterly* (March 2010).

Bashir, A., and M. Wasiq, "E-satisfaction and E-loyalty of Consumers Shopping Online." *Global Sci-Tech,* 5(1) January-March, 2013, 6-19.

Bashir, A., "Consumer Behavior towards Online Shopping of Electronics in Pakistan." *Seinäjoki University of Applied Sciences,* Thesis, Winter 2013. **theseus.fi/bitstream/handle/10024/53661/Thesis.pdf** (accessed July 2014).

Big Heart Pet Brands. "Cats Asked for It by Name: Meow Mix Jingle Returns!" March 13, 2012. **investors.bigheartpet.com/releasedetail.cfm?ReleaseID=66252** (accessed July 2014).

Brocato, C., and J. Fairbrother, *Mobile Marketing: Strategies for Mobile Consultants to Build a Profitable Local Marketing Business,* Seattle, WA: CreateSpace Independent Publishing Platform, 2013.

Butcher, D. "Johnson & Johnson Breaks Multichannel Mobile Campaign.", November 10, 2008. **mobilemarketer.com/cms/news/advertising/2075.html** (accessed July 2014).

Butcher, D. "Johnson & Johnson's Zyrtec Runs Mobile Banner Campaign on App." March 31, 2009. **mobilemarketer.com/cms/news/advertising/2938.html** (accessed July 2014).

Camaret, V. "Advergaming: The New Advertiser's Toy?" September 4, 2013. **digi-vibes.com/advergaming-new-advertisers-toy** (accessed July 2014).

Cheung, C. M. K., and M. K. O. Lee. "The Asymmetric Effect of Website Attribute Performance on Satisfaction: An Empirical Study." *e-Service Journal* 3, no. 3 (2005), 3(3) 65–86.

Chiu, C.-M., E. T. C. Wang, Y. H. Fang, and Y. H. Huang. "Understanding Customers' Repeat Purchase Intentions in B2C E-Commerce: The Roles of Utilitarian Value, Hedonic Value and Perceived Risk." DOI: 10.1111/j.1365-2575.2012.00407.x *Information Systems Journal,* Volume 24, Issue 1, (2014).

Clifton, B. *Advanced Web Metrics with Google Analytics,* 3rd edition, Hoboken, NJ: Sybex, 2012.

Cohen, W. W. "Collaborative Filtering: A Tutorial." *Carnegie Mellon University* (Undated). Available for download at **cs.cmu.edu/~wcohen/collab-filtering-tutorial** (accessed July 2014).

Crespo, A. H., and I. Rodriguez del Bosque. "The Influence of the Commercial Features of the Internet on the

Adoption of E-Commerce by Consumers." *Electronic Commerce Research and Applications*, 9 (2010).

Cyr, D. "Modeling Website Design Across Cultures: Relationships to Trust, Satisfaction, and E-Loyalty." *Journal of Management Information Systems* (Spring 2008).

Daum, K. et al. *Video Marketing for Dummies*. Hoboken, NJ: Wiley, 2012.

Einav, L., D. Knoepfle, J. Levin, and N. Sundaresan. "Consumer Behavior in Online Shopping Is Affected by Sales Tax." *London School of Economics and Political Science*, January 14, 2014. **blogs.lse.ac.uk/usappblog/2014/01/14/sales-tax-internet** (accessed July 2014).

eMarketer. "Online Retailers Move Past Discounts to Earn Deeper Customer Loyalty." March 11, 2013. **emarketer.com/Article/Online-Retailers-Move-Past-Discounts-Earn-Deeper-Customer-Loyalty/1009719** (accessed July 2014).

Ellis, D. "Why Every Company Needs Email Marketing [Infographic]." July 12, 2013. **socialmediatoday.com/debraellis/1591966/why-every-company-needs-email-marketing-infographic** (accessed July 2014).

Eslinger, T. *Mobile Magic: The Saatchi and Saatchi Guide to Mobile Marketing and Design*. Hoboken, NJ: Wiley, 2014.

Gaur, V., N. K. Sharma, P. Bedi. "Evaluating Reputation Systems for Agent Mediated e-Commerce." *CoRR*, *abs/1303.7377*, 2013..

Greenberg, P. *CRM at the Speed of Light: Social CRM Strategies, Tools, and Techniques for Engaging your Customers*, 4th ed. New York: McGraw-Hill, 2010.

Greengard, S. "Del Monte Gets Social. *Baseline Magazine*, July 30, 2008.

Gregg, D. G., and S. Walczak. "The Relationship Between Website Quality, Trust, and Price Premiums at Online Auctions." *Electronic Commerce Research*, 10 (2010).

Groves, R. M., et al. *Survey Methodology*, 2nd ed. New York: Wiley, 2009.

Harris, C. *SEO Top Secret: How to Get Top Ranking on the First Page of Google by Search Engine Optimization (Simple Online Marketing)*, [Kindle Edition]. Seattle, WA: Amazon Digital Services, 2014.

Hawkins, D. I., and D. L. Mothersbaugh. *Consumer Behavior: Building Marketing Strategy*, 11th ed. Boston: McGraw-Hill, 2010.

IAB. *IAB Internet Advertising Revenue Report: 2013 Full Year Results*. April 2014.

Jayanti, R. K. "A Netnographic Exploration: Listening to Online Consumer Conversations." *Journal of Advertising Research*, June 2010.

Kerr, J. C. "Stores Can See Where You Go by Tracking Your Phone." February 19, 2014. **bigstory.ap.org/article/stores-can-track-where-you-go-using-your-phone** (accessed July 2014).

Krum, C. *Mobile Marketing: Finding Your Customers No Matter Where They Are*. New York: Que Publishing Co., 2010.

Learmonth, M. "Vivaki Predicts $100M Market for Choose-Your-Own-Ad Format." *AdAge*, May 24, 2010.

Lee, M. K. O, and E. Turban. "Trust Model for Consumer Internet Shopping." *International Journal of Electronic Commerce*, 6, no. 1 (2001).

Li, J. "Study: Online Shopping Behavior in the Digital Era." May 10, 2013. **iacquire.com/blog/study-online-shopping-behavior-in-the-digital-era** (accessed July 2014).

Liang, T.-P., and H.-J. Lai. "Effect of Store Design on Consumer Purchases: An Empirical Study of Online Bookstores." *Information & Management*, 39, no. 6 (2002).

Liang, T.-P., Y. T. Ho, Y. W. Li, and E. Turban. "What Drives Social Commerce: The Role of Social Support and Relationship Quality." *International Journal of Electronic Commerce*, Winter 2011–2012.

Luca, M. "Reviews, Reputation, and Revenue: The Case of Yelp.com." Harvard Business School Working Paper, No.12-016, September 2011. **ssrn.com/abstract=1928601** (accessed July 2014).

Madrigal, A. C. "I'm Being Followed: How Google—and 104 Other Companies—Are Tracking Me on the Web." February 29, 2012. **theatlantic.com/technology/archive/2012/02/im-being-followed-how-google-151-and-104-other-companies-151-are-tracking-me-on-the-web/253758** (accessed April 2015).

MarketTools, Inc. "Del Monte Foods Turns to Dog Owners to Unleash Innovation." A case study, May 2008. **classmatandread.net/565media/DelMonte.pdf** (accessed July 2014).

Marrs, M. "45 Fabulous Facebook Advertising Tips & Magic Marketing Tricks."January 30, 2014. **wordstream.com/blog/ws/2014/01/30/facebook-advertising-tips** (accessed July 2014).

McDaniel, C. Jr., and R. Gates. *Marketing Research*, 9th ed. Hoboken, NJ: Wiley, 2012.

McGee, M. "Americans Watched More than 10 Billion Video Ads in May [Report]. June 18, 2012. **marketingland.com/americans-watched-more-than-10-billion-video-ads-in-may-report-14584** (accessed July 2014).

Microsoft Advertising. "Johnson & Johnson ACUVUE® Case Study." Compendium 2009. [Greater Asia Pacific] **advertising.microsoft.com/asia/WWDocs/User/Asia/ResearchLibrary/CaseStudy/GAP%20Case%20Study%20Compendium_2009_Final.pdf** (accessed April 2015).

Obringer, L. A. "How Advergaming Works." March 13, 2007. **money.howstuffworks.com/advergaming1.htm** (accessed July 2014).

Olenski, S. "How Johnson & Johnson is Using Social Media to Save Lives." July 10, 2013. **forbes.com/sites/steveolenski/2013/07/10/how-johnson-johnson-is-using-social-media-to-save-lives** (accessed July 2014).

Pearson, B. *The Loyalty Leap: Turning Customer Information into Customer Intimacy*. New York: Portfolio Hardcover, 2012.

Pfeiffer, M., and M. Zinnbauer. "Can Old Media Enhance New Media? How Traditional Advertising Pays Off for an Online Social Network." *Journal of Advertising Research*, (March 2010).

Ploof, R. *Johnson & Johnson Does New Media*. e-book, June 15, 2009. **ronamok.com/ebooks/jnj_case_study.pdf** (accessed July 2014).

Provost, F. and T. Fawcett. *Data Science for Business: What You Need to Know About Data Mining and Data-Analytic Thinking*. North Sebastopol, CA: O'Reilly Media, 2013.

Richter, F. "Consumers Still Trust Traditional Media Advertising Over Online Ads." January 8, 2014. **statista.com/chart/1473/consumer-trust-in-advertisin/** (accessed July 2014).

Rowles, D. *Mobile Marketing: How Mobile Technology is Revolutionizing Marketing, Communications and Advertising*. London, UK: Kogan Press, 2013.

Russell, M. "11 Amazing Augmented Reality Ads." January 28, 2012. **businessinsider.com/11-amazing-augmented-reality-ads-2012-1?op=1** (accessed July 2014).

Russell, M. A. *Mining the Social Web: Data Mining Facebook, Twitter, LinkedIn, Google+ GitHub, and More*, 2nd ed. North Sebastopol, CA: O'Reilly Media, 2013.

Salam, A.F., L. Iyer, P. Palvia, and R. Singh. "Trust in E-Commerce." *Communciations of the ACM*, February 2005.

Sanz-Blas, S., C. Ruiz-Mafé, and I. I. Perez. "Key Drivers of Services Website Loyalty., *Service Industries Journal*, Volume 34, Issue 5, 2014.

Sauer, J. "Planning Online Promotions in 15 Easy Steps." March 4, 2013. **jeffalytics.com/planning-online-promotions-15-steps** (accessed July 2014).

Scott, D. M. *The New Rules of Marketing & PR: How to Use Social Media, Online Video, Mobile Applications, Blogs, News Releases, and Viral Marketing to Reach Buyers Directly*, 4th ed. Hoboken, NJ: Wiley, 2013.

Sharda, R., et. al., *Business Intelligence and Analytics: Systems for Decision Support,* 10th ed. Upper Saddle River, NJ: Pearson Education, 2015.

Smith, G. "How E-Commerce Brands Can Build Trust Online." March 28, 2014. **sparksheet.com/how-e-commerce-brands-can-build-trust-online** (accessed July 2014).

Steel, E. "A Web Pioneer Profiles Users by Name." *Wall Street Journal*, Updated October 25, 2010. **online.wsj.com/news/articles/SB1000142405270 23044105045755560243259416072** (accessed July 2014).

Steel, E. "The New Focus Groups: Online Networks." January 14, 2008 (Updated). **online.wsj.com/news/articles/SB120027230906987357** (accessed July 2014).

Strauss, J., and R. Frost. *E-Marketing*, 7th ed. Upper Saddle River, NJ: Pearson Education, 2014.

Tsang, M. M., S-C. Ho, and T-P. Liang. "Consumer Attitudes toward Mobile Advertising: An Empirical Study." *International Journal of Electronic Commerce*, Spring 2004.

Urban, G. L., J. R. Hauser, G. Liberali, M. Braun, and F. Sultan. "Morph the Web to Build Empathy, Trust and Sales." *MIT Sloan Management Review*, (Summer 2009).

Vanacore, A. "Web Ad Sales Help New York Times Co. Halt Declines." *Associated Press,* July 22, 2010.

Vora, P. Chapter 9: "Social Applications." In *Web Application Design Patterns*. Mountain View, California: Morgan Kaufmann, 2009.

Wang, E. T. G., H.-Y. Yeh, and J. J. Jiang. "The Relative Weights of Internet Shopping Fundamental Objectives: Effect of Lifestyle Differences." *Psychology and Marketing,* 23, no. 5 (2006).

Wikinvest. "Del Monte Foods Company." 2010. **wikinvest.com/wiki/Del_Monte_Foods_Company_(DLM)** (accessed July 2014).

Wilde, S. *Viral Marketing within Social Networking Sites: The Creation of an Effective Viral Marketing Campaign* (Google eBook). Munchen, Germany: Diplomica Verlag, 2013.

Williams, A. *SEO 2014 & Beyond: Search Engine Optimization Will Never be the Same Again! (Version 2.0)*. Seattle, WA:, CreateSpace Independent Publishing Platform, 2013.

Wilson, R. F. "The Six Simple Principles of Viral Marketing." May 12, 2012. **webmarketingtoday.com/articles/viral-principles** (accessed July 2014).

Wright, T. *Fizz: Harness the Power of Word of Mouth Marketing to Drive Brand Growth*. New York: McGraw-Hill, 2014.

E-Commerce Security and Fraud Issues and Protections

10

Contents

Learning Objectives

Upon completion of this chapter, you will be able to:

1. Understand the importance and scope of security of information systems for EC.
2. Describe the major concepts and terminology of EC security.
3. Understand about the major EC security threats, vulnerabilities, and technical attacks.
4. Understand Internet fraud, phishing, and spam.
5. Describe the information assurance security principles.
6. Identify and assess major technologies and methods for securing EC access and communications.
7. Describe the major technologies for protection of EC networks.
8. Describe various types of controls and special defense mechanisms.
9. Describe consumer and seller protection from fraud.
10. Discuss enterprisewide implementation issues for EC security.
11. Understand why it is so difficult to stop computer crimes.

Electronic supplementary material The online version of this chapter (doi: 10.1007/978-3-319-10091-3_10) contains supplementary material, which is available to authorized users

E. Turban et al., *Electronic Commerce: A Managerial and Social Networks Perspective*,
Springer Texts in Business and Economics, DOI 10.1007/978-3-319-10091-3_10,
© Springer International Publishing Switzerland 2015

OPENING CASE: HOW STATE UNIVERSITY OF NEW YORK COLLEGE AT OLD WESTBURY CONTROLS ITS INTERNET USE

The State University of New York (SUNY) College at Old Westbury (**oldwestbury.edu**) is a relatively small U.S. university located in Long Island, New York. The college has 3,300 students and 122 full-time faculty. Internet access is essential for both faculty and students.

The Problem

The College does not regulate the types of devices people use in its network, such as laptops, tablets, and smartphones, nor the purposes for which the devices are used. Thus, students, faculty, and networks are vulnerable to a variety of security issues, many of which originate from social media websites such as Facebook and YouTube. The College encourages the use of social media as a collaborative, sharing, and learning environment.

Social media is also a leading target for malware writers. With the large number of downloads, social media has become an ideal place for cybercriminals to insert viruses and hack into systems. Phishers use social engineering techniques to deceive users into clicking on, or downloading, malware.

Because of the various devices used by the students and faculty, the College's attempts to manage network security were unsuccessful. Specifically, the attempt to use intelligent agents (which some students objected to having on their computers) as guards failed.

The College had computer-use policies in place, but these were established in the past for older computing environments. Since the old policies were not effective, the university decided to transform its old usage policy to meet the needs of current technology.

Bandwidth usage was a problem due to the extensive downloading of videos by faculty and students. The high level usage for non

educational related activities sometimes interfered with classroom or research needs.

The Solution

All students, faculty, and staff received a user ID for computer utilization. Next, a new usage policy was implemented. This policy was communicated to all users and was enforced by monitoring the usage for each ID, watching network traffic, and performing behavioral analysis.

The policy covered all users, all devices, and all types of usage, including mobile devices and the Internet. According to SUNY College at Old Westbury (2014), the policy states that users should not expect full privacy when it comes to their e-mail messages or other online private information, including Internet usage records and sets forth what information is collected by the university. Given that the IDs identify the type of users (e.g., student or faculty), management was able to set priorities in allocating bandwidth.

Old Westbury is not alone in utilizing a policy to control Internet usage. Social Media Governance (**socialmediagovernance.com**) is a website that provides tools and instructions regarding the control of computing resources where social media is concerned.

The Results

The new system monitors performance and automatically sends alerts to management when deviations from the policy occur (e.g., excessive usage). Also, it conducts behavioral analysis and reports behavioral changes of users.

The users are contacted via e-mail and alerted to the problem. The system may even block the user's access. In such an event, the user can go to the student computer lab for problem resolution.

Bandwidth is controlled only when classes are in session.

Sources: Based on Goodchild (2011), SUNY (2014), and **oldwestbury.edu** (accessed May 2014).

10.1   THE INFORMATION SECURITY PROBLEM

Information security refers to a variety of activities and methods that protect information systems, data, and procedures from any action designed to destroy, modify, or degrade the systems and their operations. In this chapter, we provide an overview of the generic information security problems and solutions as they relate to EC and IT. In this section, we look at the nature of the security problems, the magnitude of the problems, and introduce some essential terminology of information security.

What Is EC Security?

Computer security in general refers to the protection of data, networks, computer programs, computer power, and other elements of computerized information systems. It is a very broad field due to the many methods of attack as well as the many modes of defense. The attacks on and defenses for computers can affect individuals, organizations, countries, or the entire Web. Computer security aims to prevent, or at least minimize, the attacks. We classify computer security into two categories: *generic topics*, relating to any information system (e.g., encryption), and *EC-related issues*, such as buyers' protection. Attacks on EC websites, *identify theft* of both individuals and organizations, and a large variety of fraud schemes, such as phishing, are described in this chapter.

Information security has been ranked consistently as one of the top management concerns in the United States and many other countries. Figure 10.1 illustrates the major topics cited in various studies as being the most important in information security.

The Status of Computer Security in the United States

Several private and government organizations try to assess the status of computer security in the United States annually. Notable is the annual CSI report, which is described next.

No one really knows the true impact of online security breaches because, according to the Computer Security Institute (CSI; **gocsi.com**), 2010/2011 Computer Crime and Security Survey, only 27.5% of businesses report computer intrusions to legal authorities. The survey is available at **scadahacker.com/library/Documents/ Insider_Threats/CSI%20-%202010-2011%20 Computer%20Crime%20and%20Security% 20Survey.pdf**. Comprehensive annual security surveys are published periodically by IBM, Symantec, and other organizations.

In addition to organizational security issues, there is also the issue of personal security.

Personal Security

Fraud on the Web is aimed mostly at individuals. In addition, loose security may mean danger of personal safety due to sex offenders who find their victims on the Internet.

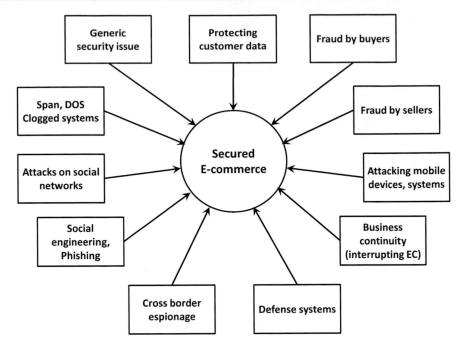

Figure 10.1 Major EC security management concerns for 2011

National Security

Protection of U.S. computer networks is handled by the Department of Homeland Security (DHS). It includes the following programs:

cials to use the Internet to collaborate and share sensitive information with one another in a secure environment.

- **Cyber Security Preparedness and the National Cyber Alert System.** Computer users can stay up-to-date on cyberthreats through this program.
- **United States Computer Emergency Readiness Team (U.S.-CERT Operations).** Provides information about vulnerabilities and threats, proactively manages cyber risks to the nation, and operates a database to provide technical descriptions of vulnerabilities.
- **National Cyber Response Coordination Group (NCRCG).** Comprised of representatives from 13 federal agencies, it reviews threat assessments and recommends actions to incidents, including allocation of federal resources.
- **CyberCop Portal.** A portal designed for law enforcement and government offi-

According to Goldman (2013), hackers are increasingly attacking the most critical infrastructures of the U.S. (e.g., power, nuclear, and water facilities). In 2012, a group of unidentified hackers broke into the corporate systems of some natural gas pipeline companies and stole data on how their control systems work. Goldman also states that according to industry researchers, many companies choose not to report cyberattacks.

On February 17, 2013, President Obama issued an executive order for combatting cyberwars. This order gave "federal agencies greater authority to share 'cyber threat' information with the public sector."

Security Risks for 2014 and 2015

According to IBM (2014) and EMC/RSA (2014), and security vendors, the major security risks for the near future are:

- Cyberespionage and cyberwars (discussed below) are growing threats.
- Attacks are now also against mobile assets, including on smartphones, tablets, and other mobile devices. Enterprise mobile devices are a particular target.
- Attacks on social networks and social software tools. User-generated content is a major source of malware.
- Attacks on BYOD ("Bring Your Own Device").
- Identity theft is exploding, increasing the criminal use of the stolen identities.
- Profit motive – as long as cybercriminals can make money, security threats and phishing attacks, will continue to grow.
- Social engineering tools such as phishing via e-mail are growing rapidly.
- Cybergang consolidation – underground groups are multiplying and getting bigger, especially in Internet fraud and cyberwars.
- Business-oriented spam (including image-based spam).
- Attacks using spyware (e.g., using Denial-of-Service method).
- Attacks on new technologies such as cloud computing and virtualization.
- Attacks on Web and mobile applications (apps).

We cover all the major topics on the above list in the rest of this chapter. According to Lawinski (2012), the major attacks on corporations are on executives (25%), shared mailboxes (23%) and sales (12%). While most of the attacks are against large enterprises (50%), hackers attack medium (32%) and small companies (48%) as well. Additionally, 93% of companies affected are in the health care or IT industries. We assume the 2014 to 2015 data will be similar.

For more information, see **sans.org**, **baselinemag.com/security**, **enisa.europa.eu/activities/risk-management**, and the Information Systems Security Certification Consortium (isc2.org).

Security Risks in Mobile Devices

According to Davis (2012b), the major mobile devices security concerns are: loss of devices that include sensitive information (66%); mobile devices infected by malware (60%); theft of data from the device (44%); users downloading malicious apps (33%); identity theft; and other user personal loss (30%).

Cyberwars and Cyberespionage Across Borders

Using computers as a tool to attack information systems and computers is growing rapidly and becoming more and more dangerous.

Cyberwarefare

According to the UN Crime and Justice Research Institute (Unicri), *Cyberwarefare* or (*Cyberwar*) refers to any action by a nation-state or international organization to penetrate another nation's computer networks for the purpose of causing damage or disruption. However, broader definitions claim that cyberwarfare also includes acts of 'cyberhooliganism,' cybervandalism or cyberterrorism. The attack usually is done through viruses, DoS, or botnets.

- Cyberwarfare, which is an illegal activity in most countries, includes the following major threats: Online acts of espionage and security breaches – which are done to obtain national material and information of a sensitive or classified nature through the exploitation of the Internet (e.g., exploitation of network flaws through malicious software).
- Sabotage – the use of the Internet to disrupt online communications with the intent to cause damage.
- Attacks on SCADA (Supervisory Control and Data Acquisition) network and NCIs (National Computational Infrastructure).

Cyberespionage

Cyberespionage refers to unauthorized spying using a computer system. Espionage involves obtaining secrets without the permission of the holder of the information (individual, group, or organization). Cyberespionage is an illegal activity in most countries.

Attacking Information Systems

The GhostNet attack cited earlier was not an isolated case of cross-border cyber attacks. In February 2011, the U.S. security firm McAfee, Inc. reported that Chinese hackers had stolen sensitive data from oil companies in the United States and several other countries. These attacks started in November 2009, and, as of 2011, are continuing. The attacks are done via e-mails containing a virus sent to tens of thousands of people (see **csmonitor.com/USA/2011/0210/Report-Chinese-hackers-targeted-big-oil-companies-stole-data**). The U.S. Congress is working on legislation to protect the country from what some call the 'Cyber Pearl Harbor' attack (however, others say it will not happen), or a digital 9/11 (Cowley 2012). In May 2014, the U.S. government named five military people in China as responsible for stealing data and spying on several thousand companies in the U.S. stealing trade secrets (Kravets 2014).

Types of Attacks

Cyber attacks can be classified into two major interrelated categories:

1. **Corporate espionage.** Many attacks target energy-related companies because their inside information is valuable (see McAfee 2011). According to a 2010 report by McAfee (as reported by News24 2011), almost half of all power plants and other infrastructures surveyed have been infiltrated by "sophisticated adversaries," with extortion being a common motive. For example, Nakashima (2011) reported that in November 2011, foreign hackers targeted a water plant control system in Illinois, causing the pump to fail. The attackers also gained unauthorized access to the system database. The Internet address used was tracked back to Russia. According to the *Wall Street Journal* of April 23, 2012, there were suspected cyber attacks against Iranian oil production and refineries. Cyber attackers hacked into 30,000 of Saudi Aramco's computers in 2012, and crippled the national oil company's networks, but failed to disrupt gas or oil output (Constantin 2012).

   Finally, in 2013, documents leaked from the whistleblower Edward Snowden revealed that Belgacom, a Belgian telecom company, was hacked into by a British spy agency (see **spiegel.de/international/europe/british-spy-agency-gchq-hacked-belgian-telecoms-firm-a-923406.html**).

   According to Esposito and Ferran (2011), in 2011, cyber thieves (known as the "Rove group") based in Eastern Europe hijacked at least four million computers in more than 100 countries before they were caught. The attackers used malware and rerouted Internet traffic illegally. The cyber thieves stole $14 million before they were captured. The hackers also attacked U.S. government agencies and large corporations.

   The Chinese cyber attacking network not only installed malware to send and receive classified data from the compromised computers, but also gave them the ability to spy on people by using installed audio and video devices to monitor the rooms where the computers were located (however, investigators could not confirm whether the audio/visual had been used). In 2013, Chinese hackers allegedly attacked the *New York Times*' computers to intimidate the American news media into not reporting on China's negative image and the journalists' sources of this information.

2. **Political espionage and warfare.** Political espionage and cyberwars are increasing in magnitude. Sometimes, these are related to corporate espionage. In 2014, U.S. hackers in Illinois used DDoS malware to attack the official website of the Crimean referendum. A few days later, major Russian government Web resources and state media websites were also attacked by DDoS malware. For information about the Crimean website cyber attack, see **rt.com/news/crimea-referendum-attack-website-194**.

Example 1

In December 2010, the Iranian nuclear program was attacked via computer programs rumored to have been created by the United States and Israel. The attack was successful, causing major physical damage to the nuclear program, delaying it by months or possibly even years. The attack was perpetrated using a sophisticated computer worm named Stuxnet. This is an example of a weapon created by a country to achieve a goal that otherwise may have been achieved only by physical weapons. In apparent retaliation, Iranians and pro-Palestinian hackers attacked El-Al (Israel's national airline) and the country's stock exchange. Iran is believed to have been behind a November 2012 attack on U.S. banks (see Goldman 2012).

Example 2

A suspected cyberespionage network known as GhostNet, compromised computer systems in 103 countries, including computer systems belonging to the Dalai Lama's exile network, embassies, and foreign ministries. The attacks allegedly came from China.

Example 3

One of the most complex cyberespionage incidents that has ever occurred (2014) is the suspected Russian spyware Turla, which was used to attack hundreds of government computers in the U.S. and Western Europe (see Apps and Finkle 2014).

The above incidents illustrate the ineffectiveness of some information security systems. For an overview of how cyberwarfare works, see **forbes.com/sites/quora/2013/07/18/how-does-cyber-warfare-work**.

For the implications of such warfare, see Dickey et al. (2010). For the U.S. Senate Homeland Security Committee's concerns and proposed legislation (e.g., the Cybersecurity Act of 2012, which failed), see Reske and Bachmann (2012).

The Drivers of EC Security Problems

There are many drivers (and inhibitors) that can cause security problems to EC. Here, we describe several major ones: the *Internet's vulnerable design*, the *shift to profit-induced crimes*, the *wireless revolution*, the *Internet underground economy*, the *dynamic nature of EC systems, and the role of insiders*, and the *sophistication of the attacks*.

The Internet's Vulnerable Design

The Internet and its network protocols were never intended to protect against cybercriminals. They were designed to accommodate computer-based communications in a *trusted community*. However, the Internet is now a global place for communication, search, and trading. Furthermore, the Internet was designed for maximum efficiency without regard for security. Despite improvements, the Internet is still fundamentally insecure.

The Shift to Profit-Induced Crimes

There is a clear shift in the nature of the operation of computer criminals (see IBM Corporation 2012). In the early days of e-commerce, many hackers simply wanted to gain fame or notoriety by defacing websites. Online File W10.1 illustrates a case of a criminal who did not attack systems to make a profit. There are many more criminals today, and they are more sophisticated and technical experts. Most popular is the theft of personal information such as credit card numbers, bank accounts, Internet IDs, and passwords. According to Privacy Rights Clearinghouse (**privacyrights.org**), approximately 250 million records containing personal information were involved in security breaches between April 2005 and April 2008 (reported by Palgon 2008). Today, the number is much higher. Criminals today are even holding data for ransom and trying to extort payments from their victims. An illustrative CNN video posted on October 8, 2012 (2:30 minutes) titled "Hackers Are Holding Data for Ransom" is available at **money.cnn.com/video/technology/2012/10/08/t-ransomware-hackers.cnnmoney**. CryptoLocker is a new ransomware Trojan used for such crimes (see **usatoday.com/story/news/nation/2014/05/14/ransom-ware-computer-dark-web-criminal/8843633**).

Note that laptop computers are stolen for two reasons: selling them (e.g., to pawn shops, on eBay) and trying to find the owners' personal information (e.g., social security number, driver's license details, and so forth). In January 2014, a former Coca-Cola employee stole laptops containing information on 74,000 individuals belonging to current and past employees of the company. The company did not have a data loss prevention program in place, nor were the laptops encrypted (see **infosecurity-magazine.com/view/36627/74000-data-records-breached-on-stolen-cocacola-laptops**).

A major driver of data theft and other crimes is the ability to profit from the theft. Today, stolen data are sold on the black market, which is described next.

The Increased Volume of Wireless Activities and the Number of Mobile Devices

Wireless networks are more difficult to protect than wireline. For example, many smartphones are equipped with near-field communication (NFC) chips, which are necessary for mobile payments. Additionally, BYOD (Chapter 6) may create security problems. Hackers can exploit the features of smartphones and related devices (e.g., Bluetooth) with relative ease; see Drew (2012) for details.

The Globalization of the Attackers

Many countries have cyberattackers (e.g., China, Russia, Nigeria and India). See Fowler and Valentino-DeVries (2013) for cyberattacks originating in India.

The Darknet and the Underground Economy

The **darknet** can be viewed as a separate Internet that can be accessed via the regular Internet and a connection to the TOR network (TOR is a network of VPNs that allows privacy and security on the Internet). The darknet has restricted access to trusted people ("friends") by using non standard protocols (IP addresses are not listed). Darknet allows anonymous surfing. For a tutorial, see Kalomni (2012). The darknet's contents are not accessible through Google or other search engines. The TOR technology is used in file sharing (e.g., see the Pirate Bay case in Chapter 15). The darknet is often used for political dissent and conducting illegal transactions, such selling drugs and pirating intellectual property via file sharing. The latter activity is known as the *Internet underground economy*.

In November 2014, law enforcement authorities in Europe and the U.S. shut down many of TOR websites. But it seems they have not cracked TOR encryptions yet (Dalton and Grossman 2014).

The Internet Underground Economy

The **Internet underground economy** refers to the e-markets for stolen information made up of thousands of websites that sell credit card numbers, social security numbers, e-mail addresses, bank account numbers, social network IDs, passwords, and much more. For details, see the Symantec Report on the Underground Economy: July 07-June 08 (2008) and, their Fraud Activity Trends (2009–2010) at **symantec.com/threatreport/topic.jsp?id=fraud_activity_trends&aid=underground_economy_servers**. Stolen data are sold to spammers or criminals for less than a dollar a piece to several hundred dollars each. The purchasers use them to send spam or conduct illegal financial transactions such as transferring other people's money into their own accounts, or paying their credit card bills. It is estimated that about 30% of all the transactions in the underground market are made with stolen credit cards. Symantec estimates the potential worth of just the credit cards and banking information for sale was $7 billion. Forty-one percent of the underground economy is in the United States, while 13% is in Romania. The Symantec report also covers the issue of software piracy, which is estimated to be more than $100 million annually. Criminals use several methods to steal the information they sell. One popular method is *keystroke logging.*

The Internet Silk Road

This is one of the underground sites where hundreds of drug dealers and other 'black market' merchants conduct their business. In October 2013, law enforcement authorities in the U.S. shut down the site and arrested its founder. However, shortly thereafter, Silk Road was "resurrected" as Silk Road 2.0.

Transactions on Silk Road are paid only by *bitcoins* (Chapter 11). In February 2014, hackers stole over 4,400 bitcoins that were held in escrow (between buyers and sellers); over $2.7 million value of bitcoins are gone forever (see Pagliery 2014). The owner of the Silk Road site declared bankruptcy. However, by May 2014 the site was back in business.

Keystroke Logging in the Underground Economy

Keystroke logging (keylogging) is the process of using a device or software program that tracks and records the activity of a user in real time (without the user's knowledge or consent) by the keyboard keys they press. Since personal information such as passwords and user names are entered on a keyboard, the keylogger can use the keystrokes to obtain them. A keylogger can also be a malware Trojan installed to infect the user's computer with viruses and steal confidential information. Keylogging methods and their tutorials are available free on the Web. For more information, see **pctools.com/security-news/what-is-a-keylogger**. The more sophisticated the underground economy is, the more criminals will use keylogging to obtain users' personal information to sell in underground marketplaces.

The Explosion of Social Networking

The huge growth of social networking and the proliferation of platforms and tools make it difficult to protect against hackers. Social networks are easy targets for phishing and other social engineering attacks.

The Dynamic Nature of EC Systems and the Acts of Insiders

EC systems are changing all the time due to a stream of innovations. Security problems often accompany change. In recent years, we have experienced many security problems in the new areas of social networks and wireless systems (some will be explored later in this book). Note that insiders (people who work for the attacked organizations) are responsible for almost half of the security problems. New employees are being added frequently to organizations, and they may bring security threats with them.

The Sophistication of the Attacks

Cybercriminals are sharpening their weapons continuously, using technological innovations. In addition, criminals are getting organized in very powerful groups, such as LulzSec and Anonymous. According to IBM Corporation (2012), cybercriminals change their tactics because of improved security in a certain area (i.e., they are adapting quickly to a changing environment). See Acohido (2011).

The Cost of Cyber Crime

It is not clear how much cybercrime costs. Many companies do not disclose their losses. However, HP Enterprise Security's "2013 Cost of Cyber Crime Study: Global Report" (independently conducted by Ponemon Institute) found that the average annualized cost of cybercrime per company surveyed was $7.2 million per year, which is an increase of 30% from the previous year's global cyber cost study. Data breaches can be very costly to organizations (see Kirk 2013). For how organizations can be devastated by cyberattacks, see Kavilanz (2013b).

SECTION 10.1 REVIEW QUESTIONS
1. Define computer security.
2. List the major findings of the CSI 2010/2011 survey.
3. Describe the vulnerable design of the Internet.
4. Describe some profit-induced computer crimes.
5. Describe the Internet underground economy and the darknet.
6. Describe the dynamic nature of EC systems.
7. Relate security issues to social networks and mobile computing.

10.2 BASIC E-COMMERCE SECURITY ISSUES AND LANDSCAPE

In order to understand security problems better, we need to understand some basic concepts in EC and IT security. We begin with some basic terminology frequently related to security issues.

Basic Security Terminology

In Section 10.1, we introduced some key concepts and security terms. We begin this section by introducing alphabetically the major terms needed to understand EC security issues:

Business continuity plan
Cybercrime
Cybercriminal
Exposure
Fraud
Malware (malicious software)
Phishing
Risk
Social engineering
Spam
Vulnerability
Zombie

Definitions of these terms are provided later in the chapter glossary and at **webopedia.com/TERM**.

The EC Security Battleground

The essence of EC security can be viewed as a battleground between attackers and defenders and the defenders' security requirements. This battleground includes the following components, as shown in Figure 10.2:

- The attacks, the attackers, and their strategies
- The assets that are being attacked (the targets) in vulnerable areas
- The security defense, the defenders, and their methods and strategy

The Threats, Attacks, and Attackers

Information systems, including EC, are vulnerable to both unintentional and intentional threats. (For a discussion, see IBM Corporation 2012).

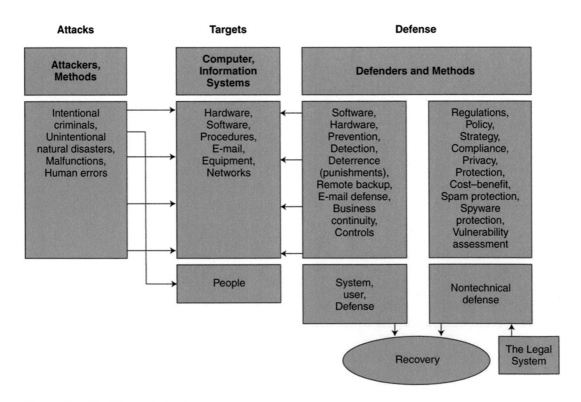

Figure 10.2 The EC security battleground

Unintentional Threats

Unintentional threats fall into three major categories: human error, environmental hazards, and malfunctions in the computer system.

Human Error

Human errors can occur in the design of the hardware, software, or information systems. It can also occur in programming (e.g., forgetting to factor in leap year), testing, data collection, data entry, authorization, and instructions. Errors can occur because of negligence, outdated security procedures or inadequate employee training, or because passwords are not changed or are shared with others. According to the 2013 *Cost of Breach Study: Global Analysis* by Symantec and Ponemon Institute, human error accounted for over half of data breaches in 2012 (see HP Enterprise Security 2013).

Environmental Hazards

These include natural disasters and other environmental conditions outside of human control (e.g., Acts of God, large scale acts of nature and accidents such as earthquakes, severe storms, hurricanes, blizzards, or sand storms), floods, power failures or strong fluctuations, fires (the most common hazard), explosions, radioactive fallout, and water-cooling system failures. Computer resources also can be damaged by side effects such as smoke and water. Damages during wars or property vandalism are a special kind of environmental hazards.

Malfunctions in the Computer System

Defects can be the result of poor manufacturing, defective materials, memory leaks, and outdated or poorly maintained networks. Unintentional malfunctions can also happen for other causes, ranging from lack of user experience to inadequate testing. For example, in March 2012, a computer glitch (related to United Airlines switching over to the computer system used by Continental Airlines after their merger) overloaded United Airlines' phone lines and caused flight delays, causing frustration for customers, and the problem continues. According to the *Sydney Morning Herald Traveller* (January 13, 2014), United Airlines "is still struggling to integrate Continental Airlines more than three years after their merger" (see **smh.com.au/travel/travel-essentials/travel-news/united-airlines-computer-glitch-strands-pilots-20140113-30q4d.html**). In the early part of 2014, United was still having problems with their computer system, with hundreds of flights being cancelled and thousands being delayed. United's computer problems extended to printing boarding passes, checking in passengers, and getting baggage tags. According to United, most of the problems were due to the computer glitches. (For the problems United is facing due to computer glitches in 2014, see **dailymail.co.uk/wires/ap/article-2562268/Flight-delays-soar-winter-storm-United-glitch.html**.)

Another example is Amazon's Cloud (EC2), which hosts many major websites (e.g., Reddit, Airbnb, Foursqure). In June and October 2012, the cloud hosting service crashed due to problems with the company's data centers. The system also crashed in July 2012, taking down Netflix, Foursquare, Dropbox, Instagram, and Pinterest due to severe weather hitting the North Virginia data center.

Intentional Attacks and Crimes

Intentional attacks are committed by cybercriminals. Types of intentional attacks include theft of data; inappropriate use of data (e.g., changing it or presenting it for fraudulent purposes); theft of laptops and other devices and equipment and/or computer programs to steal data; vandalism or sabotage directed toward the computer or its information system; damaging computer resources; losses from malware attacks; creating and distributing viruses; and causing monetary losses due to Internet fraud. Most of these are described in Sections 10.3 and 10.4.

For a 2013 state of the art study including all threats, see Suby (2013).

The Criminals and Methods

Intentional crimes carried out using computers and the Internet are called *cybercrimes*, which are done by *cybercriminals* (*criminals* for short), that includes *hackers and crackers*. A **hacker** describes someone who gains unauthorized access to a computer system. A **cracker**, (also known as *"black hat" hacker*), is a *malicious hacker* with extensive computer experience who may be more damaging. According to PC Tools, "hackers build things while crackers break things. Cracker is the name given to hackers who break into computers for criminal gain…Crackers' motivations can range from profit, a cause they believe in, general maliciousness or just because they like the challenge. They may steal credit card numbers, leave viruses, destroy files or collect personal information to sell." (See **pctools. com/security-news/crackers-and-hackers** for the differences between crackers and hackers.) Some hacker groups (such as the international group Anonymous) are considered unstoppable in penetrating organizations of all kinds (many U.S. government agencies, including the U.S. Army and the Department of Energy). The danger is that some companies may not take even minimal precautions to protect their customer information if they can place the blame for the attacks on the cybercriminals (see Murray 2011).

Unlike "black hat" hackers, "white hat" hackers can be Internet security experts who are hired by companies to find vulnerabilities in their computer systems.

Criminals use a variety of methods for the attacks. Some use computers as a weapon; some attack computing assets depending on the targets. For a short history of hacking (with an infographic) see **i-programmer.info/news/149-security/3972-a-short-history-of-hacking.html**.

Hackers and crackers may recruit unsuspecting people, including company insiders, to assist in their crimes. For example, according to Malware Bytes Unpacked, a "money mule" is a person who is local to the compromised account, who can receive money transfers with a lesser chance of alerting the banking authorities.

"These money mules retrieve the funds and then transfer them to the cyber criminal." Since the mules are used to transfer stolen money, they can face criminal charges and become victims of identity theft. Notorious hacker Kevin Mitnick, who served jail time for hacking, used social engineering as his primary method to gain access to computer systems.

For 10 tips to keeping your EC website protected against hacking and fraud, see **tweak yourbiz.com/technology/2014/01/20/10-tips-to-protect-an-ecommerce-website-against-hacking-and-fraud**.

The Targets of the Attacks in Vulnerable Areas

As seen in Figure 10.2, the targets can be people, computers, or information systems. Fraud usually aims to steal money or other assets such as real estate. Computers are also used to harass people (e.g., cyberbullying), damage their reputation, violate their privacy, and so forth.

Vulnerable Areas Are Being Attacked

Any part of an information system can be attacked. PCs, tablets, or smartphones can easily be stolen or attacked by viruses and/or malware. Users can become victims of a variety of fraudulent actions. Databases can be attacked by unauthorized intruders, and data are very vulnerable in many places in a computerized system. For example, data can be copied, altered, or stolen. Networks can be attacked, and information flow can be stopped or altered. Computer terminals, printers, and any other pieces of equipment can be damaged in different ways. Software programs can be manipulated. Procedures and policies may be altered, and much more. *Vulnerable* areas are frequently attacked.

Vulnerability Information

A *vulnerability* is where an attacker finds a weakness in the system and then exploits that weakness. Vulnerability creates opportunities for attackers to damage information systems. MITRE Corporation publishes a dictionary of publicly known security vulnerabilities called *common vulnerabilities and exposures (CVE)* (**cve.mitre. org**). In a December 27, 2006 article in *SC Magazine*, MITRE reported that four of the top five reported vulnerabilities were within Web applications. *Exposure* can result when a cybercriminal exploits a vulnerability. See also Microsoft's guide to threats and vulnerabilities at **technet. microsoft.com/en-us/library/dd159785.aspx**.

Attacking E-Mail

One of the easiest places to attack is a user's e-mail, since it travels via the unsecured Internet. One example is the ease of former candidate for U.S. Vice President Sarah Palin's e-mail that was hacked in March 2008.

Attacking Smartphones and Wireless Systems

Since mobile devices are more vulnerable than wired systems, attacking smartphones and wireless systems is becoming popular due to the explosive growth of mobile computing.

The Vulnerability of RFID Chips

These chips are embedded everywhere, including in credit cards and U.S. passports. Cards are designed to be read from some distance (contactless), which also creates a vulnerability. When you carry a credit card in your wallet or pocket, anyone with a RFID reader that gets close enough to you may be able to read the RFID information on your card. For a presentation, watch the video "How to Hack RFID-Enabled Credit Cards for $8 (BBtv)" at **youtube.com/ watch?v=vmajlKJlT3U**.

The Vulnerabilities in Business IT and EC Systems

Sullivan (2009) divided the vulnerabilities into *technical weaknesses* (e.g., unencrypted communications; insufficient use of security programs

and firewalls) and *organizational weaknesses* (e.g., lack of user training and security awareness, and an insider who steals data and engages in inappropriate use of business computers).

Many areas can be vulnerable, some of which we do not even think about (e.g., RFID). A related topic is that of intellectual property piracy.

Pirated Videos, Music, and Other Copyrighted Material

It is relatively easy to illegally download, copy, or distribute music, videos, books, software, and other intellectual property when it is on the Web. Online piracy occurs when illegal software is downloaded from a peer-to-peer network. An example is the pirating of live sports events. At stake are millions of dollars in lost revenue to sports leagues and media companies. These institutions are joining forces in lobbying for stronger copyright legislation and by filing lawsuits against violators (see Chapter 15 for details). For a comprehensive discussion, see Stone (2011). For facts and statistics about online piracy, see **articles.latimes.com/2013/sep/17/business/ la-fi-ct-piracy-bandwith-20130917**.

EC Security Requirements

Good security is a key success factor in EC.

The following set of security requirements are used to assure success and to minimize EC transaction risks:

- **Authentication. Authentication** is a process used to verify (assure) the real identity of an EC entity, which could be an individual, software agent, computer program, or EC website. For electronic messages, authentication verifies that the sender/receiver of the message is who the person or organization claims to be. (The ability to detect the identity of a person/entity with whom you are doing business.)
- **Authorization. Authorization** is the provision of permission to an authenticated

person to access systems and perform certain operations in those specific systems.

- **Auditing.** When a person or program accesses a website or queries a database, various pieces of information are recorded or logged into a file. The process of maintaining or revisiting the sequence of events during the transaction, when, and by whom, is known as *auditing*.
- **Availability.** Assuring that systems and information are available to the user when needed and that the site continues to function. Appropriate hardware, software, and procedures ensure availability.
- **Nonrepudiation.** Closely associated with authentication is **nonrepudiation**, which is the assurance that online customers or trading partners will not be able to falsely deny (repudiate) their purchase, transaction, sale, or other obligation. Nonrepudiation involves several assurances, including providing proof of delivery from the sender and proof of sender and recipient identities and the identity of the delivery company.

Authentication and non-repudiation are potential defenses against phishing and identity theft. To protect and ensure trust in EC transactions, *digital signatures*, or *digital certificates*, are often added to validate the senders and the times of the transactions so buyers are not able to deny that they authorized a transaction or that it never occurred. Section 10.6 provides a technical overview of digital signatures and certificates and how they provide verification in EC. Unfortunately, phishers and spammers have devised ways to compromise certain types of digital signatures.

The Defense: Defenders, Strategy, and Methods

Everybody should be concerned about security. However, in a company, the information systems department and security vendors provide the technical side, while management provides the administrative aspects. Such activities are done via security and strategy procedures that users need to follow.

EC Defense Programs and Strategy

An **EC security strategy** consists of multiple layers of defense that includes several methods. This defense aims to deter, prevent, and detect unauthorized entry into an organization's computer and information systems. **Deterrent methods** are countermeasures that make criminals abandon their idea of attacking a specific system (e.g., a possible deterrent is a realistic expectation of being caught and punished). **Prevention measures** help stop unauthorized people from accessing the EC system (e.g., by using authentication devices and firewalls or by using *intrusion prevention* which is, according to TechTarget "a preemptive approach to network security used to identify potential threats and respond to them swiftly"). **Detection measures** help find security breaches in computer systems. Usually this means to find out whether intruders are attempting (or have attempted) to break into the EC system, whether they were successful, whether they are still damaging the system, and what damage they may have done. This needs to be done as early as possible after a criminal attempt is made and can be done with an *intrusion detecting system*.

Information Assurance

Making sure that a customer is safe and secure while shopping online is a crucial part of improving the online buyer's experience. **Information assurance (IA)** is measures taken to protect information systems and their processes against all risks. In other words assure the systems' availability when needed. The assurance includes all tools and defense methods.

Possible Punishment

A part of the defense is to deter criminals by punishing them heavily if they are caught. Judges now are giving more and harsher punishments than a decade ago. For example, in March 2010, a federal judge sentenced 28 year old TJX hacker Albert Gonzalez to 20 years in prison for his role in stealing millions of credit and debit card numbers and selling them. Such severe sentences send a powerful message to hackers and help the defense. Unfortunately, in many cases the punishment is too light to deter the cybercriminals (see Jones and Bartlett Learning LLC 2012).

Defense Methods and Technologies

There are hundreds of security defense methods, technologies, and vendors and these can be classified in different ways so their analyses and selection may be difficult. We introduce only some of them in Sections 10.5, 10.6, 10.7, 10.8, and 10.9.

Recovery

In security battles, there are winners and losers in each security episode, but it is difficult to win the security war. As we will discuss in Section 10.9, there are many reasons for this. On the other hand, organizations and individuals usually recover after a security breach. Recovery is especially critical in cases of a disaster or a major attack, and it must be speedy. Organizations need to continue their business until the information systems are fully restored, and they need to restore them fast. This is accomplished by activating *business continuity and disaster recovery plans.*

Because of the complexity of EC and network security, comprehensive coverage requires an entire book, or even several books. Here we cover only selected topics. Those readers interested in a more comprehensive discussion should see the *Pearson/Prentice Hall Security Series* of security books and also conduct a Google search.

SECTION 10.2 REVIEW QUESTIONS

1. List five major EC security terms.
2. Describe the major unintentional security hazards.
3. List five examples of intentional EC security crimes.
4. Describe the security battleground, who participates, and how. What are the possible results?
5. Define hacker and cracker.
6. List all security requirements and define authentication and authorization requirements.
7. What is non-repudiation?
8. Describe vulnerability and provide some examples of potential attacks.
9. Describe deterring, preventing, and detecting in EC security systems.
10. What is a security strategy, and why it is needed?

10.3 TECHNICAL MALWARE ATTACK METHODS: FROM VIRUSES TO DENIAL OF SERVICE

There are many ways criminals attack information systems and users (see Suby 2013 for a survey). Here, we cover some major representative methods.

It is helpful to distinguish between two common types of attacks – *technical* (which we discuss in this section) and *nontechnical* (or *organizational*), which we discuss in Section 10.4.

Technical and Nontechnical Attacks: An Overview

Software and systems knowledge are used to perpetrate *technical attacks*. Insufficient use of antivirus and personal firewalls and unencrypted communication are the major reasons for technical vulnerabilities.

Organizational attacks are those where the security of a network or the computer is compromised (e.g., lack of proper security awareness training). According to Sullivan (2009), "Organizational vulnerability is the improper use of computers and network services." We consider *financial fraud, spam, social engineering,* that includes *phishing,* and other fraud methods as nontechnical. The goals of social engineering are to gain unauthorized access to systems or information by persuading unsuspecting people to disclose personal information that is used by criminals to conduct fraud and other crimes. The major nontechnical methods are described in Section 10.4.

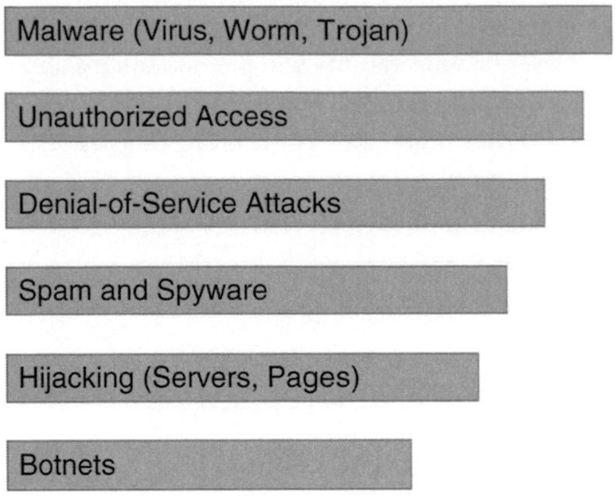

Malware (Virus, Worm, Trojan)

Unauthorized Access

Denial-of-Service Attacks

Spam and Spyware

Hijacking (Servers, Pages)

Botnets

Figure 10.3 The major technical security attack methods (in descending order of importance)

The Major Technical Attack Methods

Hackers often use several software tools (which unfortunately are readily and freely available over the Internet together with tutorials on how to use them) in order to learn about vulnerabilities as well as attack procedures. The major technical attack methods are illustrated in Figure 10.3 and are briefly described next. Note that there are many other methods such as "Mass SQL Injection" attacks that can be very damaging.

Malware (Malicious Code): Viruses, Worms, and Trojan Horses

Malware (or *malicious software*) is software code, that when spread, is designed to infect, alter, damage, delete, or replace data or an information system without the owner's knowledge or consent. Malware is a comprehensive term that describes any malicious code or software (e.g., a virus is a "subset" of malware). According to Lawinski (2011), malware attacks are the most frequent security breaches, affecting 22% of companies. Computer systems infected by malware take orders from the criminals and do

things such as send spam or steal the user's stored passwords.

Malware includes computer viruses, worms, botnets, Trojan horses, phishing tools, spyware tools, and other malicious and unwanted software. For an overview, see "malware and the malicious web" at IBM Corporation (2012).

Viruses

A **virus** is programmed software inserted by criminals into a computer to damage the system; running the infected host program activates the virus. A virus has two basic capabilities. First, it has a mechanism by which it spreads. Second, it can carry out damaging activities the once it is activated. Sometimes a particular event triggers the virus's execution. For instance, Michelangelo's birth date triggered the infamous Michelangelo virus. On April 1, 2009, the entire world was waiting for a virus named Conficker (see Brooks 2009). In 2014, a virus by the name of "Pony" infected hundreds of thousands of computers to steal bitcoins and other currencies (see Finkle 2014). Finally, Finkle reports that a virus named Agent BTZ attacked over 400,000 computers in Russia, the U.S., and Europe. The big attack was not successful, but viruses continue to spread all the time. For how computer viruses work, see **computer.howstuffworks.com/virus.htm**. Some viruses simply infect and spread, causing only minor damage. Others do substantial damage (e.g., deleting files or corrupting the hard drive).

According to Kaspersky Lab (a major Russian Internet crime fighting company), malware-based crime is growing very rapidly.

Web-based malware is very popular today. Virus attacks are the most frequent computer attacks. The process of a virus attack is illustrated in Figure 10.4.

Viruses are dangerous, especially for small companies. In 2013, the CryptoLocker virus was used to blackmail companies after seizing their computer files and threatening to erase their content.

For tutorials on, and information about, viruses, see Scott (2014) and Dawn Ontario (undated). For symptoms of, and diagnosis tips for PC

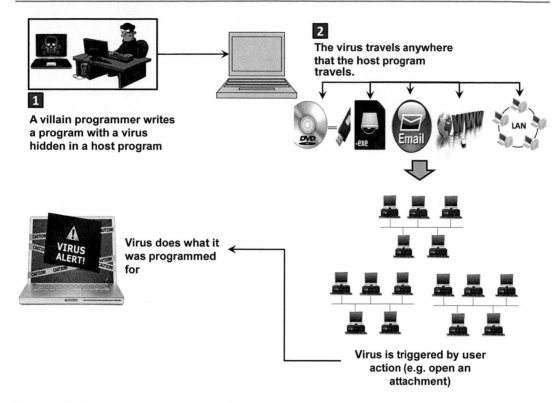

Figure 10.4 How a computer virus can spread

viruses, see Worley (2012). Note that in Microsoft tutorials, you will learn how to identify a computer virus, how to know if you are infected, and how to protect yourself against viruses (see the Microsoft Safety and Security Center at **microsoft.com/security/default.aspx**). Computer programs that are very similar to viruses are worms and Trojan horses.

Worms

Unlike a virus, a **worm** can replicate itself automatically (as a "standalone" – without any host or human activation). Worms use networks to propagate and infect a computer or handheld device and can even spread via instant messages or e-mail. In addition, unlike viruses that generally are confined within a target computer, a worm can infect many devices in a network as well as degrade the network's performance. According to Cisco, "worms either exploit a vulnerability on the target system or use some kind of social engineering to trick users into executing them." Because worms spread much more rapidly than viruses, they may be more dangerous.

Macro Viruses and Microworms

A **macro virus (macro worm)** is a malware code that is attached to a data file rather than to an executable program (e.g., a Word file). According to Microsoft, macro viruses can attack Word files as well as any other application that uses a programming language. When the document is opened or closed, the virus can spread to other documents on the computer's system. For information about Word macro viruses, see Microsoft Support at **support.microsoft.com/kb/187243/en**.

Trojan Horse

A **Trojan horse** is a program that seems to be harmless or even looks useful but actually contains a hidden malicious code. Users are tricked into executing an infected file, where it attacks the host, anywhere from inserting pop-up windows to damaging the host by deleting files, spreading malware, and so forth. The name is derived from the Trojan horse in Greek mythology. Legend has it that during the Trojan War, the city of Troy was presented with a large wooden horse as a gift to the goddess Athena. The Trojans hauled the horse inside the city gates. During the night, Greek soldiers who were hiding in the hollow horse opened the gates of Troy and let in the Greek army. The army was able to take the city and win the war.

Trojans spread only by user interaction (e.g., such as opening an under the guise of an e-mail allegedly sent by Verizon), and there are many variants of Trojans (e.g., Zeus, W32) that will be discussed later.

Example 1: Trojan-Phisher-Rebery

In 2006, a variant of a Trojan horse program named *Trojan-Phisher-Rebery* was used to steal tens of thousands of identities from people in 125 different countries. The Rebery malicious software is an example of a **banking Trojan**, which is programmed to create damage when users visit certain online banking or e-commerce sites. For an infographic describing the state of financial Trojans see Symantec (2014).

Example 2: The DDOS Attacks on WordPress

In March 2014, hackers used a botnet to attack more than 162,000 WordPress sites. Given that WordPress powers about 17% of the world's blogging websites, any attack can be devastating (see BBC News Technology 2013).

Some Recent Security Bugs: Heartbleed and Crytolocker

Two dangerous computer bugs were discovered in 2013 and 2014.

Heartbleed

According to Russel (2014) "Heartbleed is a flaw in OpenSSL, the open-source encryption standard used by the majority of websites that need to transmit the data that users want to keep secure. It basically gives you a secure line when you're sending an e-mail or chatting on IM."

Encryption works by making it so that the data sent looks like nonsense to anyone but the intended recipient. Occasionally, one computer might want to check that there's still a computer at the end of its secure connection, and it will send out what's known as a heartbreak, a small packet of data that asks for a response.

Because of a programming error in the implementation of OpenSSL, researchers found that it was possible to send a well-disguised packet of data that looked like one of these heartbeats to trick the computer at the other end into sending data stored in its memory.

The potential damage may be large. In theory, any data kept in the active memory can be pulled out by the bug. Hackers can even steal encryption keys that enable them to read encrypted messages. About 650 million websites may be affected. The only advice provided by experts is to change the online passwords. The Mashable Team (2014) provides a list of popular websites that are affected.

Cryptolocker

Discovered in September 2013, Cryptolocker is a ransomware Trojan bug. This malware can come from many sources including e-mail attachments, can encrypt files on your computer, so that you cannot read these files. The malware owner then offers to decrypt the data in exchange for a Bitcoin or similar untraceable payment system.

For information on what to do if you are being blackmailed and how to protect yourself see Cannell (2013).

Denial of Service

According to Incapsula, Inc., a **denial-of-service (DoS) attack** is "a malicious attempt to make a server or network resource unavailable to users, usually by temporarily interrupting or suspending the services of a host connected to the Internet." This causes the system to crash or become unable to respond in time, so the site becomes unavailable. One of the most popular types of DoS attacks occurs when a hacker "floods" the system by overloading the system with "useless traffic" so a user is prevented from accessing their e-mail, websites, etc.

Note: A DoS attack is a malicious attack caused by one computer and one Internet connection as opposed to a DDos attack, which involves many devices and multiple Internet connections (to be discussed later). An attacker can also use spam e-mail messages to launch a similar attack on your e-mail account. A common method of launching DoS attacks is by using *zombie (hijacked) computers*, which enable the hijacked computer to be controlled remotely by a hacker without the knowledge of the computer's owner. The zombie computer (also known as a 'botnet') launches an overwhelming number of requests toward an attacked website, creating the DoS. For example, DoS attackers target social networks, especially Facebook and Twitter. An example of such an attack is described in Online File W10.1.

DoS attacks can be difficult to stop. Fortunately, the security community has developed tools for combating them. For comprehensive coverage, see **us-cert.gov/ncas/tips/ST04-015**.

Web Server and Web Page Hijacking

Page hijacking, *or pagejacking*, is illegally copying website content so that a user is misdirected to a different website. Social media accounts are sometimes hijacked for the purpose of stealing the account holder's personal information. For example, Justin Bieber's 50 million followers fell victim to this when Bieber's Twitter account was hijacked in March 2014 (see Lyne 2014). The account was embedded with a malicious link to an application that was used to hijack accounts and retweeted to their friends.

Botnets

According to the Microsoft Safety and Security Center, a **botnet** (also known as "zombie army"), is malicious software that criminals distribute to infect a large number of hijacked Internet connected computers controlled by hackers. These infected computers then form a "botnet," causing the personal computer to "perform unauthorized attacks over the Internet" without the user's knowledge. Unauthorized tasks include sending spam and e-mail messages, attacking computers and servers, and committing other kinds of fraud, causing the user's computer to slow down (**microsoft.com/security/resources/botnet-whatis.aspx**).

Each attacking computer is considered *computer robot*. According to Prince (2010a), a botnet made up of 75,000 systems infected with

the Zeus Trojan contaminated computers within 2,500 companies worldwide in 2010. Among its targets were the login credentials for Facebook, Yahoo!, and other popular sites, including financial and e-mail systems.

For the six most dangerous cyberattacks, including the Timthumb attack, see Kavilanz (2013a). Botnets are used in scams, spams, frauds, or just to damage systems (as in the hospital case described in Online File W10.1). Botnets appear in different forms and can include worms or viruses. Famous botnets include Zeus, Srizbi, Pushdo/Cutwail, Torpig, and Conficker.

Example

Rustock was a botnet made up of about one million hijacked PCs, which evaded discovery for years. The botnet, which sent out up to 30 billion spam messages per day, placed "booby trapped" advertisements and links on websites visited by the victims. The spammers camouflaged the updates to PCs to look like comments in discussion boards, which made them hard to find by security software. In March 2011, Microsoft was one of the companies that helped shut down Rustock (reported by BBC News Technology 2011). In 2013, Microsoft and the FBI "disrupted" over 1,000 botnets used to steal banking information and identities. Both Microsoft and the FBI had been trying to take down the malware "Citadel," which affected millions of people located in more than 90 countries, since early 2012 (see Albanesius 2013). For an analysis of malicious botnet attacks, see Katz (2014).

Home Appliance "Botnet"

The Internet of Things (IoT) can also be hacked. Since participating home appliances have a connection to the Internet, they can become computers that can be hacked and controlled. The first home attack, which involved television sets and at least one refrigerator, occurred between December 2013 and January 2014, and was referred to as "the first home appliance 'botnet' and the first cyberattack from the Internet of Things." Hackers broke into more than 100,000 home appliances and used them to send over 750,000 malicious e-mails to enterprises and individuals worldwide (see Bort 2014; Kaiser 2014).

Malvertising

According to Techopedia, *malvertising* is "a malicious form of Internet advertising used to spread malware." Malvertising is accomplished by hiding malicious code within relatively safe online advertisements (see **techopedia.com/definition/4016/malvertising**).

Note that hackers are targeting ads at accelerating rates. For example, in 2013, Google disabled ads from over 400,000 sites that were hiding malware (see Yadron 2014). A final word: If you get an e-mail that congratulates you on winning a large amount of money and asks you to "Please view the attachment," don't!

SECTION 10.3 REVIEW QUESTIONS

1. Describe the difference between a nontechnical and a technical cyber attack.
2. What are the major forms of malicious code?
3. What factors account for the increase in malicious code?
4. Define a virus and explain how it works.
5. Define worm and Trojan horse.
6. Define DoS. How are DoS attacks perpetrated?
7. Define server and page hijacking.
8. Describe botnet attacks.

10.4 NONTECHNICAL METHODS: FROM PHISHING TO SPAM AND FRAUD

As discussed in Section 10.1, there has been a shift to profit-related Internet crimes. These crimes are conducted with the help of both technical methods, such as malicious code that can access confidential information that may be used to steal money from your online bank account, and nontechnical methods, such as social engineering.

Social Engineering and Fraud

As stated earlier, *social engineering* refers to a collection of methods where criminals use human psychology to persuade or manipulate people into revealing their confidential information so they can collect information for illegal activities. The hacker may also attempt to get access to the user's computer in order to install malicious software that will give them control over the person's computer. The major social engineering attacks are: phishing (several sub-methods; typically, a phisher sends an e-mail that appears to come from a legitimate source), pretexting (e.g., an e-mail allegedly sent from a friend asking for money), and diversion theft (when a social engineer convinces a courier company that he is the real recipient of the package but it should be "rerouted" to another address, whereupon the social engineer accepts the package). Once information is obtained from a victim (e.g., via phishing), it is used for committing crimes, mostly for financial gain, as shown in Figure 10.5. The growth rate of unpatched vulnerabilities and the volume of e-mail scam/phishing activities are increasing rapidly.

As you can see in the figure, phishers (or other criminals) obtain confidential information by using methods ranging from social engineering to physical theft. The stolen information (e.g., credit card numbers, users' identity) is used by the thieves to commit fraud for financial gain, or it is sold in the underground Internet marketplace to another set of criminals, who then use the information to conduct financial crimes themselves. For details see Goodchild (2012). In this section, we will describe how phishing, which is a subset of social engineering, is used.

Social Phishing

In the field of computer security, **phishing** is a fraudulent process of acquiring confidential information, such as credit card or banking details, from unsuspecting computer users. According to Teller (2012), "a phisher sends an e-mail, IM, comment, or text message that appears to come from a legitimate, popular company, bank, school, or institution." Once the user enters the corrupted website, he or she may be tricked into submitting confidential information (e.g., being asked to "update" information). Sometimes phishers install malware to facilitate the extraction of information. For an interesting novel that "cries out an alarm about cyber security," read

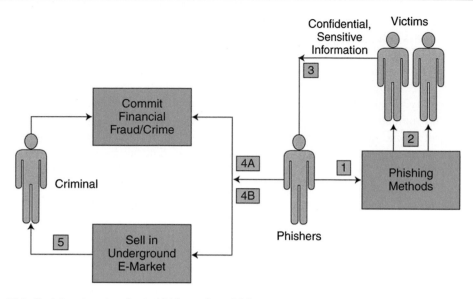

Figure 10.5   Social engineering: from phishing to financial fraud and crime

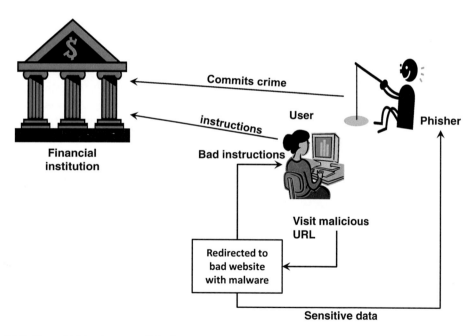

Figure 10.6   How phishing is accomplished

"Marlins Cry A Phishing Story" by Swann (2012). The process of Web-based phishing is illustrated in Figure 10.6.

For a discussion of what phishing is and how to recognize it, see **ehow.com/how_7350964_recognize-phishing.html**. EMC/RSA (2014)

provides a comprehensive coverage of phishing with statistics and forecasts. Casti (2014a) describes a phishing scam on Netflix where users were tricked into contacting phony customer service representatives and handing over personal account data. Scammers have now targeted other companies, such as AT&T and Comcast, by drawing users to fake websites via phony sponsored ads (Casti 2014b).

Selling stolen information, like selling any stolen goods, can be profitable and unstoppable. Unfortunately, potential e-commerce customers list "the potential risk of fraud," and "the mistrust of online merchants that you do not know" as their primary reasons for not shopping online.

Notes that as companies try to expand their e-businesses in countries where the legal systems are underdeveloped, opportunities for fraud expand, making it difficult to conduct EC.

There are several different kinds of phishing. *Spear phishing* is when attackers target specific individuals by gaining personal data about them through information they share on the Internet, such as on social networks. Spear phishing is more dangerous than regular phishing because the e-mails are targeting specific people or organizations, rather than to millions of unknown recipients.

Example: The Target Security Breach

The Target Corp. 2013 security breach, where millions of customers had their debit and credit card data stolen, started as a phishing attack (see Schwartz 2014). Hackers used the credentials of an employee of one of Target's vendors to gain access to Target's security system and install malware for the purpose of accessing the data of every card used. A Target employee would swipe the customer's card and the installed malware would "capture the shopper's credit card number, and store it on a server commandeered by the hackers" (see Riley et al. 2014). Once the hackers gained access to the data, they were able to steal 40 million credit and debit card numbers – and 70 million addresses, phone numbers, and other pieces of personal information. To see an infographic of how the hackers broke in, and how Target could have prevented the hack, see Smith (2014).

For an overview of phishing, its process, techniques, and the damage it can cause, see Mandalia (2011), and the *Symantec Monthly Intelligence Report* at **symantec.com**.

Pharming

Similarly to phishing, **pharming** is a scam where malicious code is installed on a computer and used to redirect victims to a bogus websites without their knowledge or consent. Pharming can be more dangerous than phishing since users have no idea that they are have been redirected to a fake website. Pharming is directed towards large groups of people at one time via *domain spoofing*. Pharming can be used for identity theft scams (discussed later in this section). For details, see Pattison (2012) and **en.wikipedia.org/wiki/Pharming**.

Fraud and Scams on the Internet

Phishing is the first step that leads to many fraud schemes. The EC environment where buyers and sellers cannot see each other facilitates fraud. There are many types of fraud on the Internet (see CyberSource 2012 and **fbi.gov/scams-safety/fraud/internet_fraud**). Fraud is a problem for online retailers and customers alike. Fortunately, even though actual losses per incident increase, there are fewer incidents; and thus the total monetary damage may be declining. Note that online merchants reject roughly 4% of submitted credit card-based shopping orders because of suspicion of fraud. Yet, only an estimated 1% of accepted online orders turn out to be fraudulent.

Internet fraud has grown very rapidly since 2005. The following examples demonstrate the scope of the problem. In addition, visit **dmoz.org/Society/Issues/Fraud/Internet** for a comprehensive collection of fraud resources.

Examples of Typical Online Fraud Attacks

The following are some characteristic fraud attacks perpetrated on the Internet.

• In March 2011, Google removed over 50 apps from its Android marketplace due to malware infections. Users who downloaded the infected apps, which contained malware called "DroidDream" may have had their data compromised. The infected apps included Spider Man, Photo Editor, and other popular apps. Luckily, Google was quickly able to remove the infected apps from the market.

- When one of the authors of this book advertised online that he had a house to rent, several "doctors" and "nurses" pretending to be from the United Kingdom and South America applied. They agreed to pay a premium price for a short-term lease and said they would pay with a cashier's check. They asked if the author would accept a check from $6,000 to $10,000 and send them back the balance of $4,000 to $8,000. When advised that this would be fine, but that the difference would be returned only after their check had cleared, none of the would-be renters followed up.
- Extortion rings in the United Kingdom and Russia have extorted hundreds of thousands of dollars from online sports betting websites. Any site refusing to pay "protection fees" has been threatened with DoS attacks.

For a video titled "How Hackers Can Invade Your Home" (2:26 minutes) showing how hackers can invade your home, see **money.cnn.com/video/ technology/2013/08/14/t-hack-my-baby-monitor- and-house.cnnmoney**. For a comprehensive discussion of fraud, see CyberSource (2013).

More examples of Internet fraud and typical scams are provided by Pattison (2012) and in **voices.washingtonpost.com/securityfix/web_ fraud_20**. For a discussion on social engineering, phishing, and other methods of fraudulently obtaining confidential information online, see Pontrioli (2013).

Types of Scams
The following are some representative types of current scams (per Spamlaws see **spamlaws.**

com/scams.html): Literary scams, jury duty scams, banking scams, e-mail scams, lottery scams, Nigerian scams (or "419" fraud), credit cards scams (several types), work at/from home scams, IRS e-mail scams, and free vacation scams. Many more can be found at fbi.gov (see **fbi.gov/scams-safety/fraud/internet_fraud**).

E-Mail Scams
E-mail scams are the most popular type of scam since they are so easy to commit. Dog Breed Info Center (**dogbreedinfo.com**; undated) posts common examples at (**dogbreedinfo.com/internet- fraud/scamemailexamples.htm**). The examples are both educational and entertaining. The most dangerous are e-mails scams that look like they come from well-known organizations (banks, telecommunication companies) that tell you that you must provide information in order to keep your account active. An example of an e-mail purportedly sent by Yahoo! is provided below.

Yahoo Account Verification Alert!!! (KMM69467VL55834KM)
Dear Valued Member,
Due to the congestion in all Yahoo Accounts, Yahoo would be shutting down all unused Accounts. You will have to confirm your E-mail by filling out your Login Information below after clicking the reply button, or your account will be suspended within 24 hours for security reasons.

Yahoo! ID Card
Name: . . . .
Yahoo! ID: . . . .
Yahoo! Mail Address: . . . .
Password: . . . .
Member Information
Gender: . . . .
Birth Date: . . . .
Occupation: . . . .
Country: . . . .
If you are a Yahoo! Account Premium subscriber, we will refund the unused por-

tion of your Premium subscription. The refund will appear as a credit via the billing method we have on file for you. So please make sure that your billing information is correct and up-to-date. For more information, please visit billing.yahoo. com.

After following the instruction on this sheet your account will not be interrupted and will continue as normal.

We appreciate your being a Yahoo! Account user.

Sincerely,

Yahoo! Customer Support

Any e-mail you receive asking for personal details is most likely a scam or phishing attempt since a legitimate organization will already have all your personal information. For tips from Yahoo! on how to protect yourself online, see Yahoo! Safely (**safely.yahoo.com/safety-tips**).

Everyone can be a victim of e-mail scams, as shown in Case 10.1.

How it happened: Hackers hacked into your e-mail accounts, finding who your contacts are and their e-mail addresses. They then sent out an e-mail to you from people on the list.

Alternatively, hackers get into your friend's e-mail account and find that you are one of their contacts. Then they send you the request for help.

LESSONS LEARNED FROM THE CASE

1. In general, make sure you log off of your e-mail account when you are away from home. Change your password often, especially after travelling, and have a complex password.
2. Have an additional (secondary) password to communicate with e-mail servers (e.g., Yahoo! Gmail) to advise them of the security breach.
3. Remember, many scammers are smart and experienced. Read examples given by the Dog Breed Info Center and the FTC.

CASE 10.1: ANYONE CAN BE A VICTIM (FROM STUDENTS TO LAWYERS TO TEXTBOOK AUTHORS)

How a scammer attacked an author of this book:

Example

The "Stranded Traveler" scam is still going strong. How it works: An individual receives an e-mail purportedly sent from a real friend that goes something like this (these come in variations of countries, amounts of currency needed, etc.):

I'm writing this e-mail with tears in my eyes, I came down to London for a program unfortunately, I was mugged at the park of the hotel where I stayed, all cash, credit, and cell were stolen off me but luckily for me I still have my passport with me, I have no access to my account. I have been to the embassy and the police here but they are not helping issue at all and my flight leaves tomorrow night but I am having problems settling the hotel bills and the hotel manager won't let me leave until I settle the bills. I'm freaked out at the moment. I need about £2,250 or any amount you can lend me to sort-out the bills, I will repay you as soon as I get back home.

Questions

1. Find information on the different methods scammers can use to hijack e-mail account and what a possible defense may be.
2. What is the process used by the scammer?
3. It looks as if this attack method is very popular. Why it is used so frequently, and why are so many e-mail accounts being hijacked?

Top 10 Attacks and Remedies

IT security site Secpoint.com provides a list of the top 10 security-related attacks on the following topics: Top viruses, spyware, spam, worms, phishing, hacker attacks, and hackers and social engineering tactics. In addition, the site provides related pages on IT security resources such as the top 10 top hackers; top 10 security tips and tools; pages relating to Anti phishing, Anti DOS, Anti spam, and more. For SecPoint IT resources for top 10 spam attacks, see **secpoint.com/Top-10-Spam-Attacks.html**.

Identity Theft and Identify Fraud

Identity theft, according to the United States Department of Justice website, is a crime. It refers to wrongfully obtaining and using the identity of another person in some way to commit crimes that involve fraud or deception (e.g., for economic gain). Victims can suffer serious damages. In many countries, it is a crime to assume another person's identity. According to the U.S. Federal Trade Commission (**ftc.gov**), identity theft is one of the major concerns of EC shoppers. According to the FTC statistics, identity theft affects over 12 million Americans each year, for a loss of over $55 billion, and is growing about 20% annually. For an entertaining comedy, see the 2013 movie "Identity Thief."

Identity Fraud

Identity fraud refers to assuming the identity of another person or creating a fictitious person and then unlawfully using that identity to commit a crime. Typical activities include:

- Opening a credit card account in the victim's name
- Making a purchase using a false identity (e.g., using another's identity to buy goods)
- Business identity theft is using another's business name to obtain credit or to get into a partnership
- Posing as another to commit a crime
- Conducting money laundering (e.g., organized crime) using a fake identity

For additional information, see Nuerm (2012). For information and protection, see **idtheftcenter.org** and **fdic.gov/consumers/theft**.

Cyber Bank Robberies

Cyberattacks can happen to individuals and organizations, including banks.

Example

According to Perez (2010), a global computer gang stole about $70 million (possibly up to $220 million) from bank accounts of businesses, municipalities, and churches, mostly in the U.S. In October 2010, over 100 people in four countries were detained or charged. According to the FBI, the hacking ring included computer-code writers who were located in the Ukraine. A network of "mules" (people recruited to move stolen funds via bank accounts opened with fake names) were located in several countries.

The thieves used different versions of Zeus malware, a popular tool of cyber bank robbers (a variant Trojan horse). The thieves concentrated on small and medium businesses, because those usually have technologically limited computer security systems.

In 2011, criminals combined old-fashioned "con artistry" with "newfangled technology" to rob banks in London. Two cases where the thieves entered the bank posing as IT technicians are reported by Nugent (2013).

In addition to stealing bank accounts, criminals commit check fraud as well.

Example

Secureworks.com uncovered the following check fraud operations (per Prince 2010b): Russian cybercriminals used "money mules" (people who thought they were signing up for a legitimate job), 2,000 computers, and sophisticated hacking methods to steal archived check images from five companies, and wire the collected money overseas.

Next, the scammers printed counterfeit checks, which the money mules deposited in their own accounts. Then, the mules were ordered to wire (transfer) the money to a bank in Russia. The "mules," as usual, were innocent people who were hired and paid to do the transfer. Some of the mules became suspicious and reported the scam to the authorities.

Spam Attacks

E-mail spam, also known as *junk e-mail* or just *spam,* occurs when almost identical messages are e-mailed to many recipients in bulk (sometimes millions of unsolicited e-mails). According to Symantec (as reported by McMillan 2009), in April 2009, over 90% of messages on corporate networks were e-mail spam. Nearly 58% of spam came from botnets, the worst called *Dotnet*. The situation is better today (2014) due to improved filtering of junk mail. Spammers can purchase millions of e-mail addresses, and then using a program such as MS Word, format the addresses, cut and paste the messages and press "send." Mass e-mail software that generates, sends, and automates spam e-mail sending is called *Ratware*. The messages can be advertisements (to buy a product), fraud-based, or just annoying viruses. For current statistics on spam, see **securelist.com/en/ analysis/spam?topic=199380272**. Securelist is a comprehensive site that also provides descriptions of spam and viruses, a glossary, and information on threats. See Gudkova (2013) for the evolution of spam in 2013. Spam annoys e-mail users and therefore legislators are attempting to control it (see discussion of the CAN-Spam Act in Chapter 15). More than 130 billion spam e-mails are sent each day as of 2013, but this growth rate has stabilized. Note that approximately 80% of all spam is sent by fewer than 200 spammers. These spammers are using spyware and other tools mostly for sending unsolicited advertising. The spammers are getting more and more sophisticated. (e.g., see Kaiser 2014).

An example of how spam is used for stock market fraud is provided in Case 10.2.

CASE 10.2: INTERNET STOCK FRAUD AIDED BY SPAM

A study reported by Lerer (2007) concluded that stock market spam could influence stock prices. The results show that on average, the investors influenced by the spam lost about 5.5%, while the spammers made a 5.79% return. Spammers send out a massive amount of e-mails telling the recipients that a certain stock is "too good to miss," and if many people are influenced into buying it, the shares rise and the spammers can sell at a big profit.

In March 2007, the federal government cracked down on dozens of such stock sites. The success of *Operation Spamalot*, conducted by the Securities and Exchange Commission (SEC), helped, but did not eliminate this kind of fraud. By 2014, the practice spread all over the Internet (see Gandel 2014).

There are two reasons that such spam will not go away: It *works* and it is *profitable*.

However, unlucky spammers may end up in jail. For example, Ralsky and Bradley advertised Chinese penny stocks via e-mail and then, when the demand drove the share price up, sold them at a profit. Both people, together with their accomplices, were sentenced to several years in prison.

Sources: Based on Lerer (2007) and Gandel (2014).

Questions

1. Why might people buy the penny stocks promoted in an e-mail message from an unknown source?
2. Use Google or Bing to find out what can be done to better filter spam.

Secure Computing Corporation saw a 50% increase in spam. In 2012, spam accounted for nearly 90% of all e-mail. The amount of image spam, which today accounts for 30% of all spam, tripled between 2010 and 2011. According to Gudkova (2013), the percentage of spam sent in 2013 was 73.26, while the percentage of spam in Q 1 of 2014 was approximately 66%.

Typical Examples of Spamming

Each month Symantec provides a report titled "The State of Spam: A Monthly Report." The report provides examples of current popular scams, categories of spam, originating countries, volume, and much more.

Spyware

Spyware is tracking software that is installed by criminals or advertisers, without the user's consent, in order to gather information about the user and direct it to advertisers or other third parties. Once installed the spyware program tracks and records the user's movements on the Internet. Spyware may contain malicious code redirecting Web browser activity. Spyware can also slow surfing speeds and damage a program's functionality. Spyware usually is installed when you download freeware or shareware. For more on spyware, see Harkins (2011) and Gil (2013). For news and a video titled "Ethiopian Government Spying on U.S.-Based Journalists" (2:23 minutes) of how some regimes use spyware against journalists, see Timberg (2014).

Social Networking Makes Social Engineering Easy

Social networking sites are a vulnerable and fertile area for hackers and con artists to gain a user's trust, according to a study by Danish-owned IT security company CSIS.

The CSIS Security Group Research (csis.dk)

Dennis Rand, a security and malware researcher at CSIS designed the following experiment:

1. Under the fake name of John Smith, he created a profile on LinkedIn.com.
2. He selected thousands of people at random, inviting them to join his network.
3. He targeted several companies and posed on their enterprise social network as an ex-employee.
4. Many existing employees of these companies, who were included in the randomly selected sample, accepted the invitation, creating a network of over a thousand trusted members for Rand.
5. Rand communicated with the members, thus collecting their e-mail addresses. He harvested confidential data from some of the members. He also sent links (e.g., recommendations for videos), and some were clicked on by the receivers.

The objective of the experiment was to study the potential security risks in using social networks. For example, messages may include links to malware and these attachments may be opened since they come from trusted friends. Some networks do not even encourage users to select strong passwords and to change them periodically. At the end of the experiment, Rand sent an e-mail to all participating members, explaining the purpose of the experiment. Then he closed the "John Smith" network. See Rand (2007).

How Hackers Are Attacking Social Networks

Hackers are exploiting the trusted environment of social networks that contain personal information (especially Facebook) to launch different social engineering attacks. Unfortunately, many social network sites have poor track records for security controls. There is a growing trend to use social networking sites as platforms for stealing users' personal data.

Examples

Here are some examples of security problems in social networking:

- Users may unknowingly insert malicious code into their profile page, or even their list of friends.
- Most anti-spam solutions cannot differentiate between real and criminal requests to connect to a network. This enables criminals to obtain personal information about the members in a network.
- Facebook and other popular social networking sites offer free, useful, attractive applications. These applications may have been built by developers who used weak security.
- Scammers may create a fake profile and use it in a phishing scam.

Spam in Social Networks and in the Web 2.0 Environment

Social networks attract spammers due to the large number of potential recipients and the less secure Internet and social network platforms. Spammers like to attack Facebook in particular. Another problem area is blog spam.

Automated Blog Spam

Bloggers are spammed by automatically generated commercials (some real and some fake) for items ranging from herbal Viagra to gambling vendors. Blog writers can use tools to ensure that a human, and not an automated system, posts comments on their blogs.

Search Engine Spam and Splogs

Search engine spam, is technology that enables the creation of pages called **spam sites** that trick search engines into offering biased search results so that the ranking of certain pages is inflated. A similar tactic involves the use of **splogs** (short for *spam blog sites*), which are blogs created by spammers solely for advertising. The spammer creates many splogs and links them to the sites of those that pay him (her) to increase certain page ranking. As you may recall from Chapter 9, companies are looking for search engine optimization (SEO), which is conducted unethically by the above techniques.

Sploggers assume that some Web surfers who land on their site will click on one or more linked advertisements. Each of these clicks earns a few cents for the splogger, and because any one splogger can create millions of splogs, this kind of spam can be very profitable.

Examples

Some examples of spam attacks in social networks (social spam) are:

- In January 2009, Twitter became a target for a hacker who hijacked the accounts of 33 high-profile users (including President Obama), sending out fake messages.
- Instant messaging in social networks is frequently vulnerable to spam attacks.
- Cluley (2014) describes how Twitter users are attacked by phishing attacks and spammers.

Data Breach (Leak)

A **data breach** (also known as *data leak* or *data loss*) is a security incident in which data are obtained illegally and then published or processed. For an overview, see Thomson (2012). There are many purposes for data breaches. Data leaks received considerable publicity between 2010 and 2012. For instance, one person in the U.S. military used a USB to download classified information and then posted the stolen informa-tion on the Internet. For drivers of data breaches and how to protect yourself, see Goldman (2014) and Section 10.7.

The discussion so far has concentrated on attacks. Defense mechanisms, including those related to spam and other cybercrimes, are provided in Sections 10.6, 10.7, 10.8, and 10.9. First, let us examine what is involved in assuring information security.

SECTION 10.4 REVIEW QUESTIONS

1. Define phishing.
2. Describe the relationship of phishing to financial fraud.
3. Briefly describe some phishing tactics.
4. Define pharming.
5. Describe spam and its methods.
6. Define splogs and explain how sploggers make money.
7. Why and how are social networks being attacked?
8. Describe data breaches (data leaks).

10.5 THE INFORMATION ASSURANCE MODEL AND DEFENSE STRATEGY

The *Information Assurance (IA) model,* known as the **CIA security triad**, is a point of reference used to identify problem areas and evaluate the information security of an organization. The use of the model includes three necessary attributes: *confidentiality*, *integrity*, and *availability.* This model is described next. (For a discussion, see **whatis.techtarget.com/definition/Confidentiality-integrity-and-availability-CIA**.)

Note. The assurance model can be adapted to several EC applications. For example, securing the supply chain is critical.

Confidentiality, Integrity, and Availability

The success and security of EC can be measured by these attributes:

1. **Confidentiality** is the assurance of data secrecy and privacy. Namely, the data is disclosed only to authorized people. Confidentiality is achieved by using several methods, such as encryption and passwords, which are described in Sections 10.6, 10.7, 10.8, and 10.9.
2. **Integrity** is the assurance that data are accurate and that they cannot be altered. The integrity attribute needs to be able to detect and prevent the unauthorized creation, modification, or deletion of data or messages in transit.
3. **Availability** is the assurance that access to any relevant data, information websites, or other EC services and their use is available in real time, whenever and wherever needed. The information must be reliable.

Authentication, Authorization, and Nonrepudiation

Three concepts are related to the IA model: *authentication, authorization*, and *nonrepudiation*. These important concepts are:

- *Authentication* is a security measure making sure that data information, ECD participants and transactions, and all other EC related objects, are valid. *Authentication* requires verification. For example, a person can be authenticated by something he knows (e.g., a password), something he possesses (e.g., an entry token), or something unique to that person (e.g., a fingerprint).
- *Authorization* requires comparing information provided by a person or a program during a login with stored information associated with the access requested.
- *Nonrepudiation* is the concept of ensuring that a party in an EC transaction can-

not repudiate (or refute) the validity of an EC contract and that she or he will fulfill their obligation in the transactions. According to the National Information Systems Security (INFOSEC)'s glossary, Nonrepudiation is the "[a]ssurance the sender of data is provided with proof of delivery and the recipient is provided with proof of the sender's identity, so that neither can later deny having processed the data."

Note: See the list of Key Terms in Section 10.2. Some sources list more concepts (e.g., Techopedia).

To assure these attributes, e-commerce applies technologies such as encryption, digital signature, and certification (Section 10.6). For example, the use of a *digital signature* makes it difficult for people to deny their involvement in an EC transaction.

In e-commerce, new or improved methods to ensure the confidentiality of credit card numbers, the integrity of transaction-related messages, the authentication of buyers and sellers, and nonrepudiation of transactions need to be constantly updated as older methods become obsolete.

E-Commerce Security Strategy

EC security needs to address the IA model and its components. In Figure 10.7, an EC security framework that defines the high-level categories of assurance and their controls is presented. The major categories are regulatory, financial, and marketing operations. Only the key areas are listed in the figure.

The Phases of Security Defense
The security defense process includes the following phases:
1. **Prevention and deterrence (preparation).** Good controls may prevent criminal activities as well as human error from occurring.

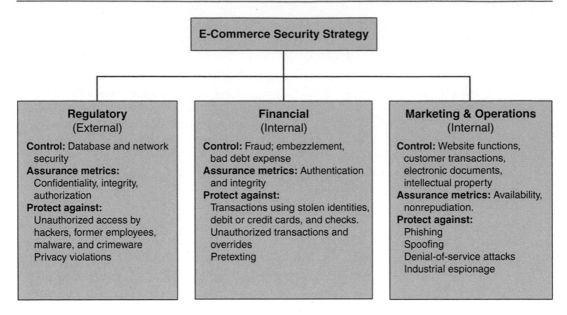

Figure 10.7 E-commerce security strategy framework

Controls can also deter criminals from attacking computerized systems and deny access to unauthorized human intruders. Also, necessary tools need to be acquired.

2. **Initial Response**. The first thing to do is to verify if there is an attack. If so, determine how the intruder gained access to the system and which systems and data are infected or corrupted.

3. **Detection.** The earlier an attack is detected, the easier it is to fix the problem, and the smaller amount of damage is done. Detection can be executed by using inexpensive or free intrusion detecting software.

4. **Containment (contain the damage).** This objective is to minimize or limit losses once a malfunction has occurred. It is also called *damage control*. Damage control can be done, for example, by using *fault-tolerant* hardware and software that enable operation in a satisfactory, but not optimal, mode until full recovery is made.

5. **Eradication.** Remove the malware from infected hosts.

6. **Recovery.** Recovery needs to be planned for to assure quick return to normal operations at

a reasonable cost. One option is to replace parts rather than to repair them. Functionality of data should also be restored.

7. **Correction.** Finding the causes of damaged systems and fixing them will prevent future occurrences.

8. **Awareness and compliance.** All organization members must be educated about possible hazards and must comply with the security rules and regulations.

Security Spending Versus Needs Gap

A major concern in information security management is how to match the security defense efforts (money, labor, time) against the major security threats. This is a difficult task since the EC threat landscape is constantly changing. Therefore, in any defense strategy one should explore the following issues (examples of each are available in Chickowski 2008):

1. What are the most critical current data security issues?

2. Where are the greatest risks of exposure?

3. Where do you spend the money? How is spending matched with risk exposure?

4. What are the benefits (including intangible) that you can derive from money spent on security project tools?
5. What are the losses due to security incidents (in your organization and in general)?
6. What are the major security technologies that reduce security losses (e.g., firewall, encryption, and antiviruses are usually at the top)?
7. What guidelines will be used for the upcoming security budget?

The Defense Side EC Systems

We organize the defense into seven categories:

1. **Defending access to computing systems, data flow, and EC transactions.** In Section 10.6, we present three topics: Access control (including biometrics), encryption of contents, and public key infrastructure (PKI).

    This line of defense provides comprehensive protection when applied together. Intruders that circumvent the access control will face encrypted material even if they pass a firewall.

2. **Defending EC networks.** In Section 10.7, we recognize the protection provided by firewalls. The firewall isolates the corporate network and computing devices from the Internet that are poorly secured. To make the Internet more secure, we can use virtual private networks. In addition to these measures, it is wise to use intrusion-detecting systems. A protected network means securing the incoming e-mail, which is usually unencrypted. It is also necessary to protect against viruses and other malware that are transmitted via the networks.

3. **General, administrative, and application controls.** These are a variety of safeguards that are intended to protect computing assets by establishing guide-

lines, checking procedures, and so forth. They are discussed in Section 10.8.

4. **Protection against social engineering and fraud.** In Section 10.8, we describe defense methods against spam, phishing, and spyware.

5. **Disaster preparation, business continuity, and risk management.** These topics are managerial issues that are supported by software and described in Section 10.9.

6. **Implementing enterprisewide security programs.** To deploy the previously mentioned defense methods, one needs to use appropriate implementation strategy, as described in Section 10.9.

7. **Conduct a vulnerability assessment and a penetration test.** (See the following text.)

For a comprehensive coverage of all aspects of information protection, see Rhodes-Ousley (2013).

To implement the above defense, first conduct some assessment and then plan and execute. Two possible activities are *vulnerability assessments* and *penetration tests*. For the concepts of information systems security fundamentals as applied to an IT infrastructure, see Jones and Bartlett Learning LLC (2012).

Assessing Vulnerabilities and Security Needs

A key task in security strategy is to find the weaknesses and strengths of the existing security strategies and solutions. This is part of a risk assessment and can be accomplished in different ways. Here are two representative suggestions:

1. Conduct a vulnerability assessment of your EC systems. A **vulnerability assessment** is a process of identifying and evaluating problem areas that are vulnerable to attack on a computerized system. The assessment can also predict the potential effectiveness of implemented countermeasures and evaluate their effectiveness after they are applied. The EC system includes online ordering,

communication networks, payment gates, product database, fraud protection, and so forth. The most critical vulnerabilities are those that can interrupt or shut down the business. For example, a DoS can prevent order taking; a virus attack can prevent communication. The assessment will determine the need for, and priority of, the defense mechanisms. For an overview of vulnerability assessment including the process, see **searchmidmarket-security.techtarget.com/definition/vulnerability-analysis**. For a method of conducting Web vulnerability analysis at a reasonable cost, see Symantec (2011).

2. Conduct *penetration (pen) tests* (possibly implemented by hiring ex-hackers) to find the vulnerabilities and security weaknesses of a system. These tests are designed to simulate outside (external) attacks. This is also called "black-box" testing. In contrast, software development companies conduct intensive "white-hat" testing, which involves a careful inspection of the system – both hardware and software. Other types of pen testing include targeted texting, blind testing, and double blind testing.

For more information, see Talabis and Martin (2013) and **searchsoftwarequality.techtarget.com/definition/penetration-testing**.

Penetration Test

A **penetration test (pen test)** is a method of assessing the vulnerability of a computer system. It can be done manually, by allowing experts to act as hackers to simulate malicious attacks. The process checks the weak (vulnerable) points that an attacker may find and exploit. Any weakness that is discovered is presented to management, together with the potential impact and a proposed solution. A pen test can be one step in a comprehensive security audit.

Several methods can be used to execute pen tests (e.g., automated process). In addition, many software tools are available for this purpose. For a review and a tutorial, see **pen-tests.com** and **coresecurity.com/penetration-testing-overview**.

SECTION 10.5 REVIEW QUESTIONS

1. What is Information Assurance? List its major components.
2. Define confidentiality, integrity, and availability.
3. Define authentication, authorization, and nonrepudiation.
4. List the objectives of EC strategy.
5. List the seven categories of defense in EC systems.
6. Describe vulnerability assessment.
7. What is a penetration test?

10.6 THE DEFENSE I: ACCESS CONTROL, ENCRYPTION, AND PKI

In this section, we describe several popular methods that deal with protection of EC information assets inside organizations, from both outside and inside attacks. For new malware mitigation tools and techniques, see Snyder (2014), who also discusses firewalls, sandboxing, and reputation services.

Access Control

Access control determines who (person, program, or machine) can legitimately use the organization's computing resources (which resources, when, and how). A resource refers to hardware, software, Web pages, text files, databases, applications, servers, printers, or any other information source or network component. Typically, access control defines the rights that specific users with access may have with respect to those resources (i.e., read, view, write, print, copy, delete, execute, modify, or move).

Authorization and Authentication

Access control involves *authorization* (having the right to access) and *authentication*, which is also called *user identification* (user ID), i.e., proving that the user is who he or she claims to be. Each user has a distinctive identification that differentiates it from other users. Typically, user identification is used together with a password.

Authentication

After a user has been *identified*, the user must be *authenticated*. *Authentication* is the process of verifying the user's identity and access rights. Verification of the user's identity usually is based on one or more characteristics that distinguish one individual from another.

Traditionally, authentication has been based only on passwords. Passwords by themselves may be ineffective because people have a habit of writing them down and putting them where they can be easily found, choosing values that are guessed easily (e.g. "password"), and sharing their passwords with others.

Two-Factor Authentication

This type of authentication system is a security process that requires two different types of identification (more than just your password). For example, one mechanism is physical (something a person *has*), such as a token card, and the other is something that a person *knows* (usually a password or an answer to a security question, or a combination of variations of both). Companies use RSA's Security ID to manage systems that require high security. However, in 2011 hackers breached the RSA code. Therefore, companies must enforce password discipline, which will protect the system even when the RSA code is hacked.

Biometric Systems

A **biometric authentication** is a technology that measures and analyzes the identity of people based on measurable biological or behavioral characteristics or physiological signals.

Biometric systems can *identify* a previously registered person by searching through a database for a possible *match* based on the person's observed physical, biological, or behavioral traits, or the system can *verify* a person's identity by matching an individual's measured biometric traits against a previously stored version.

Examples of biometric features include fingerprints, facial recognition, DNA, palm print, hand geometry, iris recognition, and even odor/scent. Behavioral traits include voice ID, typing rhythm (keystroke dynamics), and signa-

ture verification. A brief description of some of these follows:

- **Thumbprint or fingerprint.** A thumb- or fingerprint (finger scan) of users requesting access is matched against a template containing the fingerprints of authorized people.
- **Retinal scan.** A match is sought between the patterns of the blood vessels in the retina of the access seekers against the retinal images of authorized people stored in a source database.
- **Voice ID (voice authentication).** A match is sought between the voice pattern of the access seekers and the stored voice patterns of the authorized people.
- **Facial recognition.** Computer software that views an image or video of a person and compares it to an image stored in a database.
- **Signature recognition.** Signatures of access seekers are matched against stored authentic signatures.

Other biometrics types are: thermal infrared face recognition, hand geometry, and hand veins. For details, comparisons with regard to human characteristics, and cost–benefit analyses, see **findbiometrics.com/solutions** and Rubens (2012).

To implement a biometric authentication system, the physiological or behavioral characteristics of a participant must be scanned repeatedly under different settings. The scans are then used to produce a biometric template, or identifier. The template is encrypted and stored in a database. When a person enters a biometric system, a live scan is conducted, and the scan is converted to the encrypted template and compared to the stored one. Biometric methods are improving, but they have not yet replaced passwords (see Duncan 2013). In addition, for stronger security you need to use encryption.

Encryption and the One-Key (Symmetric) System

Encryption is the process of encoding data into a form (called a *ciphertext*) that will be difficult, expensive, or time-consuming for an unauthorized person to understand. All encryption methods have five basic components: *plaintext, ciphertext*, an *encryption algorithm*, the *key,* and *key space*. **Plaintext** is a human-readable text or message. **Ciphertext** is an encrypted plaintext. The **encryption algorithm** is the set of procedures or mathematical algorithms used to encrypt or decrypt a message. Typically, the algorithm is not the secret piece of the encryption process. The **key (key value)** is the secret piece used with the algorithm to encrypt (or decrypt) the message. The **key space** is the total universe of possible key values that can be created by a specific encryption algorithm. Today, both encryption and trying to break the encryption codes (i.e., decrypting the messages) are done by powerful computers. However, it may be difficult to decide which data to encrypt, how best to manage encryption, and how to make the process as transparent as possible. For how encryption works, see **computer.howstuffworks.com/encryption.htm**.

According to Davis (2012a), encryption is more important today than ever, especially when cloud computing and other methods are being added to the defense system. Many databases are still unprotected, and very few companies encrypt information on company mobile devices. This is because of the attributes and benefits of encryption.

The major benefits of encryption are:

- Allows users to carry data on their laptops, mobile devices, and storage devices (e.g., USB flash drives).
- Protects backup media while people and data are offsite.
- Allows for highly secure virtual private networks (VPNs; see Section 10.7).
- Enforces policies regarding who is authorized to handle specific corporate data.

- Ensures compliance with privacy laws and government regulations, and reduces the risk of lawsuits.
- Protects the organization's reputation and secrets.

For the top 10 benefits of encryption, including how to safeguard data stored in the cloud, see Pate (2013).

Encryption has two basic options: he *symmetric system*, with one secret key, and the *asymmetric system*, with two keys.

Symmetric (Private) Key Encryption

In a **symmetric (private) key encryption**, the same key is used to encrypt and decrypt the plaintext (see Figure 10.8). The sender and receiver of the text must share the same key without revealing it to anyone else – making it a so-called *private* system. For a symmetric encryption to succeed, it needs a strong key. The strength is measured by bits used. For example, a 4-bit key will have only 16 combinations (i.e., 2 raised to the fourth power). However, a 64-bit encryption key has 2 raised to the 64th power combinations, which would take even a powerful computer years to enumerate.

A strong key is only one requirement. Transferring the key between individuals and organizations may make it insecure. Therefore, in EC, a PKI system is used.

Public Key Infrastructure

A **public key infrastructure (PKI)** is a comprehensive framework for securing data flow and information exchange that overcomes some of the shortcomings of the one-key system. For example, the symmetric one-key encryption requires the writer of a message to reveal the key to the message's recipient. A person that is sending a message (e.g., vendor) may need to distribute the key to thousands of recipients (e.g., buyers), and then the key probably would not

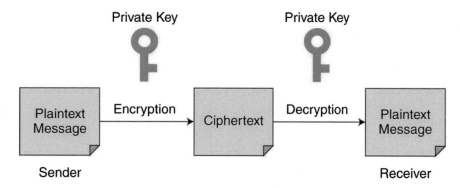

Figure 10.8 Symmetric (private) key encryption

remain secret for long unless the vendor has a different key for each buyer. If the electronic transfer of the key is intercepted, the key may be stolen or changed. The PKI solution overcomes this problem by using two keys, public and private, as well as additional features that create a highly secured system. In addition to the keys, PKI includes digital signatures, hash digests (function), and digital certificates. Let us see how the system works.

Public (Asymmetric) Key Encryption

Public (asymmetric) key encryption uses two keys – a **public key** that is known to all and a **private key** that only its owner knows. The two keys must be used together. If a message is encrypted with a public key, then only the associated private key can decrypt the message (and vice versa). If, for example, a person wants to send a purchase order to a vendor and have the contents remain private, the sender encrypts the message with the buyer's public key. When the vendor, who is the *only one able* to read the purchase order, receives the order, the vendor decrypts it with the associated private key.

The most common public key encryption algorithm is RSA (sold by RSA Security acquired by EMC Corporation; **emc.com**). The RSA algorithm uses keys ranging in length from 1,024 bits to 4,096 bits. The main problem with public key encryption is speed. Symmetrical algorithms are significantly faster than asymmetrical key algorithms. Therefore,

public key encryption cannot be used effectively to encrypt and decrypt large amounts of data. In theory, a combination of symmetric and asymmetric encryption should be used to encrypt messages. Public key encryption is supplemented by *digital signatures* and *certificate authority*.

The PKI Process: Digital Signatures and Certificate Authorities

Digital signatures are the electronic equivalent of personal signatures on paper. They are difficult to forge since they authenticate the identity of the sender that uses the public key. According to the U.S. Federal Electronic Signatures in Global and National Commerce Act of 2000, digital signatures are legally treated as signatures on paper. To see how a digital signature works, go to **searchsecurity.techtarget.com/definition/digital-signature**.

Figure 10.9 illustrates how the PKI process works. Suppose a person wants to send a financial contract to a vendor (the recipient) via e-mail. The sender wants to assure the vendor that the content is secure. To do so, the sender takes the following steps:

1. The sender creates the e-mail message that includes the contract in plain language.

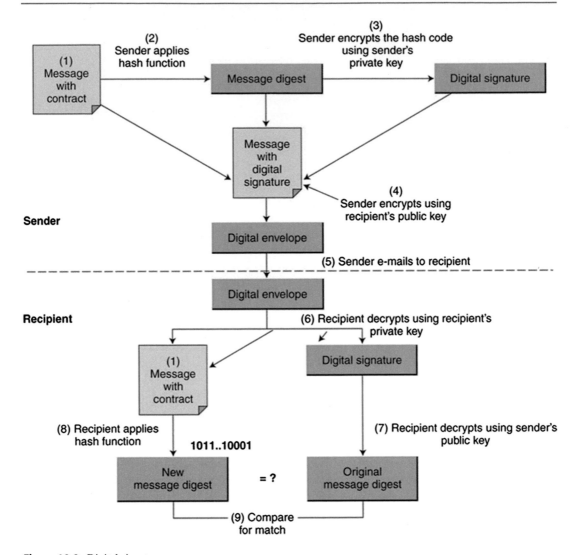

Figure 10.9 Digital signature

2. Using special software, a secured mathematical algorithm called a **hash function** is applied to the message, which results in a special summary of the message converted into a string of digits that is called a **message digest**.

3. The sender uses his or her private key to encrypt the hash. This is the sender's *digital signature*. No one else can replicate the sender's digital signature because it is based on the sender's private key, which no one else knows.

4. The sender encrypts with the recipients' public key, both the original message and the digital signature. This pair together form a **digital envelope**.

5. The sender e-mails the digital envelope to the vendor.

6. Upon receipt, the vendor uses his or her private key to decrypt the contents

of the digital envelope. This produces a copy of the message and the sender's digital signature. No one else can do it since there is only one copy of the of the vendor's private key.

7. The vendor uses the sender's public key for decrypting the content of the digital signature, resulting in a copy of the original message digest.

8. Using the same hash function employed in step 2, the vendor then creates a message digest from the decrypted message.

9. The vendor then compares this digest with the original message digest.

10. If the two digests match, then the vendor can conclude that the message is authentic.

Thus, the receiver is assured that the sender really sent the e-mail, because the sender is the only one with access to his private key. The receiver knows that the message has not been tampered with because if it had been, the two hashes would not have matched.

Certificate Authority

Independent agencies called **certificate authorities (CAs)** issue digital certificates or SSL certificates, which are electronic files that uniquely identify individuals and websites and enable encrypted communication. The certificate contains personal information and other information related to the public key and the encryption method, as well as a signed hash of the certificate data. There are different types of certificates. The major types are: *site certificates*, *personal certificates*, and *software publisher certificates*.

There are several third-party CAs. VeriSign (a Symantec company) is the most well-known of the CAs (see **verisign.com**).

Secure Socket Layer (SSL)

PKI systems are further secured with SSL – a protocol for e-commerce. The PKI with SSL make e-commerce very secure but cumbersome for users. Fortunately, Web browsers and Web servers handle many of the PKI's activities in a transparent fashion. Given that different companies, financial institutions, and governments in many countries are involved in e-commerce, it is necessary to have generally accepted protocols for securing e-commerce transactions. One of the major protocols in use today is Secure Socket Layer (SSL). SSL has been succeeded by Transport Layer Security (TLS), which is based on SSL. For further details, see **searchsecurity.techtarget. com/definition/Transport-Layer-Security-TLS**.

Other Topics and Methods of Defense

There are many other methods to combat malware and improve computer security in general.

- Use of antivirus tools. Hundreds of these are marketed by Internet security companies (e.g., Norton from Symantec and virus removing tools from Kaspersky Inc.).
- The U.S. Federal government has a website that provides information on how to avoid, detect, and eliminate malware (see **onguardonline. gov/articles/0011-malware**). The site provides a list of resources about combating spyware, spam, viruses, adware, and more. See also Wang (2013).
- Cloud-based security is advocated by many as a successful method to fight cybercriminals (e.g., Fisher 2014 and Kaplan et al. 2013). Cloud computing security includes a broad set of technologies, controls, and policies deployed to protect computer resources (see Fisher 2014).
- Integrated suites of tools. Some vendors provide an integrated set of tools in one package. This combination can be especially useful for a small company. An example is Symantec's *Endpoint Protection Small Business Edition* (**symantec. com/endpoint-protection-small-business-edition**). This integrated suite includes most of the products discussed in Sections. 10.6 and 10.7.

- Innovation. The more new methods are used by cyber criminals, the more innovative defense methods need to be developed (e.g., see Kontzer 2011).

In the next section, the focus is on the company's digital perimeters – the networks.

SECTION 10.6 REVIEW QUESTIONS
1. Define access control.
2. What are the basic elements of an authentication system?
3. Define biometric systems and list five of their methods.
4. Define a symmetric (one-key) encryption.
5. List some of the disadvantages of the symmetric system.
6. What are the key components of PKI?
7. Describe the PKI process.
8. How does a digital signature work?
9. Describe digital certification.

10.7 THE DEFENSE II: SECURING E-COMMERCE NETWORKS

Several technologies exist that ensure that an organization's network boundaries are secure from cyber attack or intrusion, and that if the organization's boundaries are compromised, the intrusion is detected quickly and combated. Different types of cyber attacks (e.g., viruses and other malware, DoS, and other botnet attacks) can arrive via the organization's communication networks. Companies need to detect intrusions as quickly as possible, diagnose the specific type of attack, and fix the problem. The major tools for protecting against attacks that arrive via the networks are described next.

Firewalls

Firewalls are barriers between an internal trusted network (or a PC) and the untrustworthy Internet. A firewall is designed to prevent unauthorized access to and from private networks, such as intranets. Technically, a firewall is composed of hardware and a software package that separates a private computer network (e.g., your LAN) from a public network (the Internet). On the Internet, the data and information exchanged between computers are broken into segments called **packets**. Each packet contains the Internet address of the computer sending the data, as well as the Internet address of the computer receiving the data. A firewall examines all data packets that pass through it and then takes appropriate action based on its diagnosis – to allow or not to allow the data to enter the computer. Firewalls are designed mainly to protect against any remote login, access by intruders via backdoors, spam, and different types of malware (e.g., viruses or macros). Firewalls come in several shapes and formats (search Google Images for 'firewalls'). A popular defense system is a DMZ. The DMZ can be designed in two different ways, using a single firewall or with dual firewalls. The one that includes two firewalls is illustrated in Figure 10.10.

The Dual Firewall Architecture: The DMZ

In the simplest case, there is one firewall between the Internet and the internal users. In the DMZ architecture (DMZ stands for demilitarized zone), there are two firewalls between the Internet and the internal users. One firewall is between the Internet and the DMZ (border firewall) and another one is between the DMZ and the internal network. All public servers are placed in the DMZ (i.e., between the two firewalls). With this setup, it is possible to have firewall rules that allow trusted partners access to the public servers, but the interior firewall can restrict all incoming connections. Using internal firewalls at various intranet boundaries also can limit damage from *threats* that have managed to penetrate the border firewalls.

Personal Firewalls

The number of users with high-speed broadband (cable modem or digital subscriber lines; DSL) has increased the number of Internet connections to homes or small businesses. The connections that are always "on" are much more vulnerable to attack than simple dial-up connections.

Personal firewalls protect desktop systems by monitoring all incoming traffic to your computer.

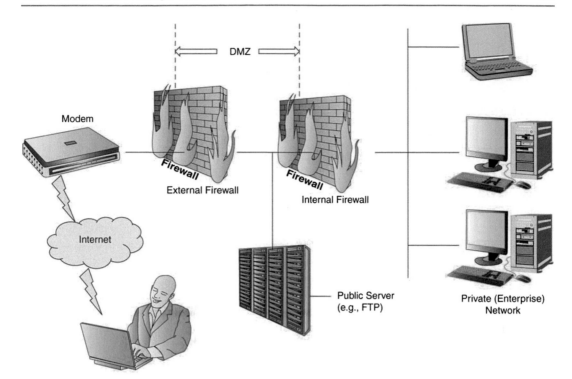

Figure 10.10 The two firewalls: DMZ architecture

Virtual Private Networks (VPNs)

Suppose a company wants to establish a B2B application, providing suppliers, partners, and others access not only to data residing on its internal website, but also to data contained in other files (e.g., Word documents) or in legacy systems (e.g., large relational databases). Traditionally, communications with the company would have taken place over a secure but expensive *value-added private leased line* or through a dial up line connected to modems or a remote access server (RAS). Unfortunately, using the Internet instead, which is free, may not be secure. A more secure use of the Internet is provided by using a VPN.

A **virtual private network (VPN)** refers to the use of the Internet to transfer information, but in a more secure manner. A VPN behaves like a private network by using encryption and other security features to keep the information secure. For example, a VPN verifies the identity of anyone using the network.

VPNs can reduce communication costs dramatically. The costs are lower because VPN equipment is cheaper than other communication solutions; private leased lines are not needed to support remote access; and a single access line can be used to support multiple purposes.

To ensure the confidentiality, integrity, and availability of the data transmitted, a VPN uses *protocol tunneling*. With **protocol tunneling**, data packets are first encrypted and then encapsulated into packets that can be transmitted across the Internet. Cisco Systems, Inc. (**cisco.com**) provides several types of VPNs. For details on VPNs, see **searchenterprisewan.techtarget.com/definition/virtual-private-network.**

Intrusion Detection Systems (IDS)

No matter how protected an organization is, it still can be a target for attempted security attacks. For example, most organizations have antivirus software, yet they are subjected to virus attacks by new viruses. This is why an organization must continually monitor for attempted, as well as actual, security breaches. The monitoring can be done by using intrusion detectors.

An **intrusion detection system (IDS)** is a device composed of software and/or hardware designed to monitor the activities of computer networks and computer systems in order to detect and define unauthorized and malicious attempts to access, manipulate, and/or disable these networks and systems. An IDS inspects all inbound and outbound flows of information and is used for detecting specific types of malicious activities (e.g. viruses, DoS) that have already occurred. For example, the IDS checks files on a regular basis to see if the current digital signatures match the previous signatures. If the signatures do not match, security personnel are alerted. For details, the technology, benefits, and limitations, see **searchsecurity.techtarget.com/ guidesIntroduction-to-IDS-IPS-Network-intrusion-detection-system-basics**.

Dealing with DoS Attacks

DoS attacks, as described earlier, are designed to bombard websites with all types of useless information, which clogs the sites. The faster a DoS attack is discovered, the easier is the defense. DoS attacks grow rapidly. Therefore, detecting an intrusion early can help. Since there are several types of DoS attacks (e.g., DDoS), there are several defense methods. For examples, see **learn-networking.com/network-security/how-to-prevent-denial-of-service-attacks**. Intrusion detecting software also identifies the DoS type, which makes the defense easier and faster.

Cloud Computing Prevents DoS Attacks
In 2011, it was demonstrated that cloud computing was effective against distributed denial-of-service (DDoS). For examples, see Fisher (2014).

Honeynets and Honeypots

Honeynets are another technology that can detect and analyze intrusions. A **honeynet** is a network of *honeypots* designed to attract hackers, just as bees are attracted to honey. In this case, the **hon-**eypots** are simulated information system components such as EC servers, payments gates, routers, database servers, and even firewalls, that look like real working systems. When intruders enter the honeypot, their activities are monitored. Security experts then analyze why and how the hackers attack, and what they do during and after the system is compromised.

Project Honeypot consists of thousands of security professionals from around the world (see **projecthoneypot.org**). The project runs its own honeynet traps, but also helps others with running theirs. Honeynet's volunteers investigate the latest attacks and help create new tools to improve Internet security.

E-Mail Security

E-mail exhibits several of the security problems discussed in Sections 10.3 and 10.4. To begin with, we get viruses from e-mail attachments and software downloads. Spam and social engineering attacks arrive via e-mail. Unfortunately, firewalls may not be effective in protecting e-mail, and therefore one should use an antivirus program as well as anti-spam software (available from dozens of vendors). E-mail encryption is advisable and available from many vendors. Finally, a technique called *outbound filtering* may be used. A brief description of each of these methods follows:

- **Antivirus and antispam.** Detects and quarantines messages that contain viruses, worms, spam, phishing attacks, or other unwanted content.
- **E-mail encryption.** Scrambles sensitive data in messages and attachments so they can be read only by intended recipients.
- **Outbound filtering.** Scans for unauthorized content, such as a user's Social Security number, included in outgoing e-mail or other communications.

Cloud Computing May Help
As of 2008, there has been increased interest in using cloud computing to improve e-mail security. Furthermore, this can be done by cutting

costs 50 to 80% (per Habal 2010). One reason is that there are dozens of vendors that offer cloud solutions, ranging from Oracle and Microsoft to small vendors.

SECTION 10.7 REVIEW QUESTIONS

1. List the basic types of firewalls and briefly describe each.
2. What is a personal firewall? What is DMZ architecture?
3. How does a VPN work and how does it benefit users?
4. Briefly describe the major types of IDSs.
5. What is a honeynet? What is a honeypot?
6. Describe e-mail security.

10.8   THE DEFENSE III: GENERAL CONTROLS, SPAM, POP UPS, FRAUD, AND SOCIAL ENGINEERING CONTROLS

The objective of IT security management practices is to defend information systems. A defense strategy requires several *controls*, as shown in Figure 10.11.

The major types of controls are: (1) **General controls**, which are designed to protect all system applications. (2) **Application controls** guard applications. In this and the following sections, we discuss representative types of these two groups of

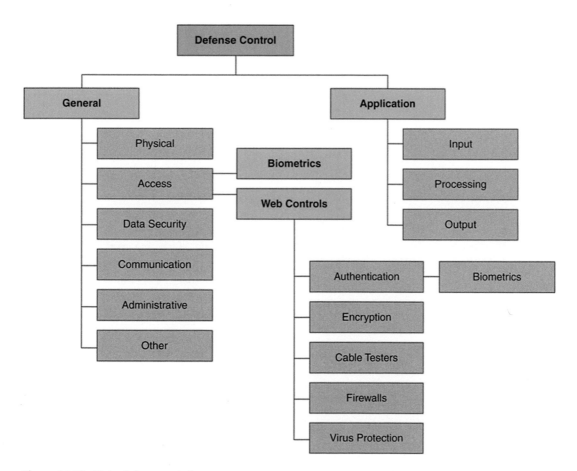

Figure 10.11   Major defense controls

information system controls. Later in the section, we cover spam and fraud mitigation.

General, Administrative, and Other Controls

The major categories of general controls are physical controls, administrative controls, and other controls. A brief description of general controls is provided next.

Physical Controls

Physical controls protect computer facilities and resources, including the physical area where computing facilities are located. The controls provide protection against natural hazards, criminal attacks, and some human error. Typical physical controls could include:

- A properly designed data center. For example, the site should be air conditioned, noncombustible, and waterproof.
- Protection against electromagnetic fields (e.g., against lightning).
- Comprehensive fire management (i.e., fire prevention, detection, containment, and extinguishment).
- Emergency (back up) power generators and automatic shut off power devices, if needed.
- Motion detectors that can detect physical intrusion and activate alarms.

Network access control software is offered by all major security vendors (e.g., see **symantec.com/endpoint-protection**).

Administrative Controls

Administrative controls are defined by management and cover guidelines and compliance issuing and monitoring. Table 10.1 gives examples of such controls.

Table 10.1   Representative administrative controls

- Appropriately selecting, training, and supervising employees, especially in accounting and information systems
- Fostering company loyalty
- Immediately revoking access privileges of dismissed, resigned, or transferred employees
- Requiring periodic modification of access controls (such as passwords)
- Developing programming and documentation standards (to make auditing easier and to use the standards as guides for employees)
- Insisting on security bonds or malfeasance insurance for key employees
- Instituting separation of duties; namely, dividing sensitive computer duties among as many employees as economically feasible in order to decrease the chance of intentional or unintentional damage
- Holding periodic random audits of the system

Protecting Against Spam

Sending spam that includes a sales pitch and looks like personal, legitimate e-mail and may bypass filters, is a violation of the U.S. Controlling the Assault of Non-Solicited Pornography and Marketing (CAN-SPAM) Act of 2003. However, many spammers hide their identity by using hijacked PCs or spam zombies to avoid detection and identification. For protecting your system against botnet attacks, which also spread a huge volume of spam, see MessageLabs (2009).

The "Controlling the Assault of Non-Solicited Pornography and Marketing Act," **CAN-SPAM Act** makes it a crime to send commercial e-mail messages with spam. The following are other provisions of the law, extracted from the United States Federal Trade Commission (FTC) Bureau of Consumer Protection Business Center (**business.ftc.gov/documents/bus61-can-spam-act-compliance-guide-business**), which provides "The CAN-SPAM Act: A Compliance Guide for Business.

- Companies must offer an opt-out link in each message and marketing campaigns.
- Allows heavy penalties for spamming (each separate e-mail is subject to penalties of up to $16,000).

- Requires marketers to report their physical postal address in e-mail messages.
- Carries other penalties – those found guilty of certain criminal acts (e.g., accessing someone else's computer to send spam; using false information to register multiple e-mail addresses, etc.) may face up to five years in prison.
- Enables the FTC, certain other federal agencies, and state attorneys general to bring lawsuits under certain sections of the Act. Although individuals are prohibited from suing spammers, individuals may be able to sue as ISPs but this may be cost prohibitive.

In 2008, the FTC added four new provisions to the CAN-SPAM Act of 2003, intending to clarify the Act's requirements. For details, see **ftc.gov/news-events/press-releases/2008/05/ftc-approves-new-rule-provision-under-can-spam-act**.

Protecting Your Computer from Pop-Up Ads

As discussed in Chapter 9, the use of pop-ups and similar advertising methods is growing rapidly. Sometimes it is even difficult to close these ads when they appear on the screen. Some of these ads may be part of a consumer's permitted marketing agreement, but most are unsolicited. What can a user do about unsolicited pop-up ads? The following tools help minimize pop-ups.

Tools for Stopping or at Least Minimizing Pop-Ups

It is possible to install software that blocks pop-up ads. Several software packages offer pop-up stoppers. Some are free (e.g., Panicware, Inc.'s Pop-Up Stopper Free Edition **pop-up-stopper-free-edition.software.informer.com**), Softonic's Pop up Blocker (**pop-up-blocker.en.softonic.com/download**), and AdFender (**adfender.com**); others are available for a fee. For a list, see

snapfiles.com; and for a list of blocker software for Windows, see **download.cnet.com/windows/popup-blocker-software**. Many ISPs and major browser makers (e.g., Google, Microsoft, Yahoo!, Mozilla) offer tools to stop pop-ups.

However, adware or software that is bundled with other popular applications, like person-to-person file sharing, is able to deliver the pop-up ads.

Protecting Against Other Social Engineering Attacks

With the increasing number of social engineering attacks via websites and in social networks comes the need for better protection. The open source environment and the interactive nature of the technology also create risks (see Chapter 7 and Section 10.4). Thus, EC security becomes a necessity for any successful social networking initiative.

Social networking spans many different applications and services. Therefore, many methods and tools are available to defend such systems. Many of the solutions are technical in nature and are outside the scope of this book.

For discussion on security in social media and social networking, see Sarrel (2010).

Protecting Against Phishing

Because there are many phishing methods, there are many defense methods as well. Illustrative examples are provided by Symantec (2009) and the FTC Consumer Information at **consumer.ftc.gov/articles/0003-phishing**. For risk and fraud insights, see **sas.com/en_us/insights/risk-fraud.html**.

Protecting Against Malvertising

According to TechTarget, *malvertising (malicious advertising)* "is an advertisement on the Internet that is capable of infecting the viewer's computer with malware." Microsoft combats malvertising by taking legal action against malvertisers.

Protecting Against Spyware

In response to the emergence of spyware, a large variety of antispyware software exists. Antispyware laws, available in many jurisdictions, usually target any malicious software that is installed without the knowledge of users. The U.S. Federal Trade Commission advises consumers about spyware infections. For details and resources, see **ftc.gov/news-events/media-resources/identity-theft-and-data-security/spyware-and-malware**.

Protecting Against Cyberwars

This is a difficult task since these attacks usually come from foreign countries. The U.S. government is developing tools that will mine social media sites to predict cyber attacks. The tools will monitor all Facebook, Twitter, and other social networks sites to interpret content. The idea is to automate the process.

Fraud Protection

As we will see in Chapter 15, it is necessary to protect both the sellers and buyers (consumers) against fraud they may commit against each other. In a special annual online fraud report, CyberSource (2012, 2013) describes the issue of payment fraud committed by buyers, which cost merchants several billions of dollars annually. The reports cover the areas of detection, prevention, and management of online fraud. The report also list tools for automatic screening of credit cards.

Business Continuity, Disaster Recovery, and Risk Management

A major building block in EC security for large companies or companies where EC plays a critical role (e.g., banks, airlines, stock brokerages, e-tailers) is to prepare for natural or man-made disasters. Disasters may occur without warning. A prudent defense is to have a *business continuity plan*, mainly consisting of a *disaster recovery* plan. Such a plan describes the details of the recovery process from major disasters such as loss of all (or most) of the computing facilities. Moreover, organizations may need to have a satisfactory disaster prevention and recovery plan

in order to obtain insurance for their computer systems or even for the entire business operation. The comprehensiveness of a business recovery plan is shown in Figure 10.12. The details are presented in Online File W10.2.

Risk-Management and Cost-Benefit Analysis

It is usually not economical to prepare protection against every possible threat. Therefore, an EC security program must provide a process for assessing threats and their potential damages, deciding which threats to protect against first, and which threats to ignore or provide only reduced protection. For details, see Online File W10.2.

SECTION 10.8 REVIEW QUESTIONS
1. What are general controls? List the various types.
2. What are administrative controls?
3. How does one protect against spam?
4. How does one protect against pop-ups?
5. How does one protect against phishing, spyware, and malvertising?
6. Describe protection against cyberwars.
7. Define business continuity and disaster recovery.

10.9   IMPLEMENTING ENTERPRISEWIDE E-COMMERCE SECURITY

Now that you have learned about both the threats and the defenses, we can discuss some implementation issues starting with the reasons why it is difficult, or even impossible, to stop computer crimes and the malfunction of information systems.

The Drivers of EC Security Management

The explosive growth of EC and SC, together with an increase in the ever-changing strategies of cybercriminals (Jaishankar 2011), combined with regulatory requirements and demands by insurance companies, drive the need for comprehensive EC security management. Additional drivers are:

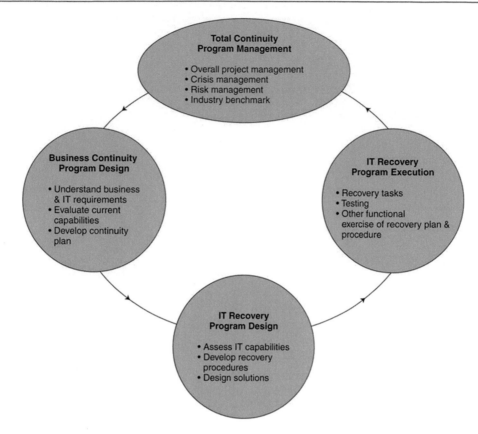

Figure 10.12 Business continuity services and IT recovery process

- The laws and regulations with which organizations must comply.
- The conduct of global EC. More protection is needed when doing business with a foreign country.
- Information assets have become critical to the operation of many businesses.
- New and faster information technologies are shared throughout organizations. Organizational collaboration is needed.
- The complexity of both the attacks and the defense require an organization-wide collaboration approach.

Senior Management Commitment and Support

The success of an EC security strategy and program depends on the commitment and involvement of senior management. Many forms of security are unpopular because they are inconvenient, restrictive, time-consuming, and expensive. Security practices may not be a top organizational priority unless they are mandated.

Therefore, an EC security and privacy model for effective enterprisewide security should begin with senior management's commitment and support, as shown in Figure 10.13. The model views EC security (as well as the broader IT security)

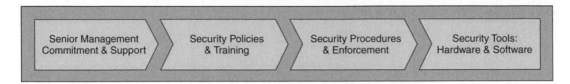

Figure 10.13   Enterprisewide EC security and privacy model

as a combination of commitment and support, policies and training, procedures and enforcement, and tools, all executed as a continuous process.

EC Security Policies and Training

An important security task is developing an organizational EC security policy, as well as procedures for specific security and EC activities such as access control and protecting customer data. These include roles, responsibilities, and enforcement. The policies need to be disseminated throughout the organization and necessary training needs to be provided (see Bailey et al. 2012). For example, to protect privacy during data collection, policies need to specify that customers should:

- Know that data is being collected, and when it is done.
- Give their permission for the data to be collected.
- Have knowledge and some control over how the data is controlled and used.
- Be informed that the information collected is not to be shared with other organizations.

Similarly, to protect against criminal use of social media, you can:

- Develop policies and procedures to exploit opportunities but provide customer protection.
- Educate employees and others about what is acceptable and what is not acceptable.

Cyber Threat Intelligence (CTI)
As part of policies and training, companies can deploy cyber intelligence. According to **sans.org**, it is an important defense tool.

EC Risk Analysis and Ethical Issues

EC security procedures require an evaluation of the digital and financial assets at risk – including cost and operational considerations. To calculate the proper level of protection, managers responsible for a digital asset need to assess its risk exposure.

A related assessment is the *business impact analysis*. **Business impact analysis (BIA)** refers to an analysis of the impact of losing the functionality of an EC activity (e.g., e-procurement, e-ordering) to an organization. Once such risks are computed, the organization should focus its defense strategy on the largest risks. This analysis may include the use of cyber-risk insurance against data breaches and other cybercrimes (see Willhite 2013).

Ethical Issues
Implementing security programs raises several ethical issues. First, some people are against the monitoring of any individual's activities. Imposing certain controls is seen by some as a violation of freedom of speech or other civil rights. A survey by the Gartner Group found that even after the terrorist attacks of September 11, 2001, only 26% of Americans approved a national ID database. Many consider using biometrics to be a violation of privacy.

Handling the privacy versus security dilemma is difficult. There are other ethical and legal obligations that may require companies to "invade the privacy" of employees and monitor their actions. In particular, IT security measures are needed to protect against loss, liability, and litigation. Losses are not just financial, but also include the loss of valuable information, customers, trading partners, brand image, and the inability to conduct business as usual due to the actions of hackers, malware, or employees.

Why Is It Difficult to Stop Internet Crime?

The following are the major reasons Internet crime is so difficult to stop.

Making Shopping Inconvenient
Strong EC security may make online shopping inconvenient and may slow shopping as well. Therefore, shoppers may not like some security measures.

Lack of Cooperation by Business Partners
There is a potential lack of cooperation from credit card issuers, suppliers, local and especially foreign ISPs, and other business partners. If the source ISP would cooperate and suspend the hacker's acccss, it would be very difficult for hackers to gain access to the systems.

Shoppers' Negligence
Many online shoppers are not taking the necessary (but inconvenient) precautions to avoid becoming victims of identity theft or fraud.

Ignoring EC Security Best Practices
Many companies do not have prudent IT security management or employee security awareness. For example, in a 2008 study, the *Computing Technology Industry Association* (CompTIA 2008) found that the most widespread threats in the United States stem from the lack of user awareness and malware attacks. The situation is somewhat better today.

Design and Architecture Issues
It is well known that preventing vulnerability during the EC design and preimplementation stage is far less expensive than mitigating problems later; unfortunately, such prevention is not always made. Even minor design errors can increase hacking. Note that, almost every element in an EC application may be subject to some sort of security threat. Designers may not consider all the elements.

Lack of Due Care in Business Practices
Another reason for the difficulty is the lack of due care in conducting many business processes (e.g., in crowdsourcing). The **standard of due care** is the minimum and customary practice that a company is reasonably expected to take to protect the company and its resources from possible risks. Managers may ignore the standard of due care (e.g., they hire criminals, outsource to fraudulent vendors), placing their EC business security at risk. For a description of the Payment Card Industry (PCI) standard and its requirements, see **pcistandard.com**. For a major survey see PWC (2013).

Protecting Mobile Devices, Networks, and Applications

With the explosive growth of mobility and m-commerce comes the task of protecting these systems from the security problems described earlier in this chapter and from some new ones. While the challenges, attacks, and defenses described earlier relate both to the wireline and wireless environments, there are certain challenges that are unique to the mobile/wireless environment.

Mobile Security Issues
Cooney (2012) lists the 10 major security issues that range from wireless transmissions not being encrypted, to lack of firewalls or passwords on mobile devices, or connecting to an unsecured WiFi network. The article offers many solutions, most of which are discussed in Sections 10.6 and 10.7 (e.g., conduct risk assessment, install firewalls).

Reisinger (2014) lists additional security issues such as data theft and unlocked jailbreaking devices. The proliferation of BYOD (Chapter 6) also brings threat to the enterprise (see Westervelt 2013 and Phneah 2013).

The Defense

To defend mobile systems it is necessary to implement tools and procedures such as those described in Sections 10.6 and 10.7, and modify them for the mobile environment. A practical checklist for reducing security risks is offered by Lenovo (2013). See also, LabTech (2012). Finally, a major problem is the theft of mobile devices. Two solutions are at work: First, automatic security that enables only the owners to use their devices and second, make a kill switch a mandatory feature in all smartphone (scheduled for 2015).

SECTION 10.9 REVIEW QUESTIONS

1. If senior management is not committed to EC security, how might that impact the e-business?
2. What is a benefit of using the risk exposure method for EC security planning?
3. Why should every company implement an acceptable use policy?
4. Why is training required?
5. List the major reasons why it is difficult to stop computer crimes.

MANAGERIAL ISSUES

Some managerial issues related to this chapter are as follows.

1. **What steps should businesses follow in establishing a security plan?** Security management is an ongoing process involving three phases: asset identification, risk assessment, and implementation. By actively monitoring existing security policies and procedures, companies can determine which of them are successful or unsuccessful and, in turn, which should be modified or eliminated. However, it also is important to monitor changes in business processes and business environments and adjust the plans accordingly. In this way, an organization can keep its security policies and measures up-to-date.

2. **Should organizations be concerned with internal security threats?** Except for malware, breaches committed by insiders are much more frequent than those done by outsiders. This is true for both B2C and B2B sites. Security policies and measures for EC sites need to address the insider threats. For a guideline, see Schwartz (2012). In addition, insiders can be victims of security crimes. Therefore, organizations need to be aware of social engineering schemes. Companies should educate employees, especially new hires, about such threats.

3. **What is the key to establishing strong e-commerce security?** Most discussions about security focus on technology, with statements like, "all messages should be encrypted." Although technologies are important, no security solution is useful unless it is adopted by the employees. Determining business requirements is the first step in creating a security solution. Business requirements, in turn, determine information requirements. Once information requirements are known, it is possible to assess their value, and then a plan can be made for how to protect the most valuable and most vulnerable information assets.

SUMMARY

In this chapter, you learned about the following EC issues as they relate to the chapter's learning objectives.

1. **The importance and scope of EC information security.** For EC to succeed, it must be secure. Unfortunately, this is not an easy task due to many unintentional and intentional hazards. Security incidents and breaches interrupt EC transactions and increase the cost of doing business online. Internet design is vulnerable, and the temptation to commit computer crime is increasing with the increased applications and volume of EC. Criminals are expanding operations, creating an underground economy of valuable information that was stolen.

A strategy is needed to handle the costly defense technology and operation, which includes training, education, project management, and the ability to enforce security policy. EC security will remain an evolving discipline because threats are changing continuously. Therefore, e-business needs to adapt. An EC security strategy is needed to optimize EC security programs for efficiency and effectiveness. There are several reasons why. EC security costs and efforts, when implemented as a reaction to crises is greater than if organizations had an EC security strategy and acts accordingly. The Internet is still a fundamentally insecure infrastructure. There are many criminals whose major motive is to profit by stealing information.

2. **Basic EC security issues.** The security issue can be viewed as a battleground between attackers and attacks and defenders and defense. There are many variations on both sides and many possible collision scenarios. Owners of EC sites need to be concerned with multiple security issues: authentication, verifying the identity of the participants in a transaction; authorization, ensuring that a person or process has access rights to particular systems or data; and auditing, being able to determine whether particular actions have been taken and by whom.

3. **Threats, vulnerabilities, and technical attacks.** EC sites are exposed to a wide range of attacks. Attacks may be nontechnical (social engineering), in which a criminal lures people into revealing sensitive personal information. Alternatively, attacks may be technical, whereby software and systems expertise are used to attack networks, databases, or programs. DoS attacks bring operations to a halt by sending a flood of data to target specific computers and websites. Malicious code attacks include viruses, worms, Trojan horses, or some combination of these. Over the past few years, new malware trends have emerged, such as Blackhole and ZeroAccess (see Wang 2013). The new trends include an increase in the speed and volume of new attack methods; and the shorter time between the discovery of a vulnerability and the release of an attack (to exploit the vulnerability). Finally, the new trends include the growing use of bots to launch attacks; an increase in attacks on mobile systems, social networks, and Web applications; and a shift to profit-motivated attacks.

4. **Internet fraud, phishing, and spam.** A large variety of Internet crimes exist. Notable are identify theft and misuse, stock market frauds, get-rich-quick scams, and phishing. Phishing attempts to obtain valuable information from people by masquerading as a trustworthy entity. Personal information is extracted from people (or stolen) and sold to criminals, who use it to commit financial crimes such as transferring money to their own accounts. A related area is the use of unsolicited advertising or sales via spam.

5. **Information assurance.** The information assurance model represents a process for managing the protection of data and computer systems by ensuring their confidentiality, integrity, and availability. Confidentiality is the assurance of data privacy. Integrity is the assurance that data is accurate or that a message has not been altered. Availability is the assurance that access to data, the website, or EC systems and applications is available, reliable, and restricted to authorized users whenever they need it.

6. **Securing EC access control and communications.** In EC, issues of communication among trading partners are paramount. In many cases, EC partners do not know their counterparts, so they need secured communication and trust building. Trust starts with the authentication of the parties involved in a transaction; that is, identifying the parties in a transaction along with the actions they are authorized to perform. Authentication can be established with something one knows (e.g., a password), something one has (e.g., an entry card), or some physical characteristic (e.g., a fingerprint). Biometric systems can confirm a person's identity. Fingerprint

scanners, iris scanners, facial recognition, and voice recognition are examples of biometric systems. A special encryption system for EC is the PKI. Public key infrastructure (PKI), which is the cornerstone of secure e-payments and communication, also can authenticate the parties in a transaction. For the average consumer and merchant, PKI is made simple by including it in Web browsers and services. Such tools are secure because security is based on SSL (or TSL) communication standards.

7. **Technologies for protecting networks.** Firewalls, VPNs, and IDSs have proven extremely useful on EC sites. A firewall is a combination of hardware and software that separates an enterprise private network from the Internet. Firewalls are of two general types – packet-filtering routers or application-level proxies. IDSs monitor activities done on a network or inside a computer system. The IDSs watch for intruders and automatically act whenever a security breach or attack occurs. In the same vein, some companies are installing honeynets and honeypots in an effort to gather information on intrusions and to analyze the types and methods of attacks being perpetrated.

8. **The different controls and special defense mechanisms.** The major controls are general (including physical, access controls, biometrics, administrative controls, application controls, and internal controls for security and compliance). Each type has several variations.

9. **Protecting against fraud.** Given the large number of ways to commit Internet fraud, it is difficult to protect against all of them. Fraud protection is done by companies, security vendors, government regulations, and perhaps most important, consumer education. Knowing the most common methods used by criminals is the first step of defense. Remember, most criminals are very experienced. They are able to invest in new and clever attack methods.

10. **Enterprisewide EC security.** EC security procedures are inconvenient, expensive, tedious, and never ending. Implementing a defensive in-depth model that views EC security as a combination of commitment, people, processes, and technology is essential. An effective program starts with senior management's commitment and budgeting support. This sets the tone that EC security is important to the organization. Other components are security policies and training. Security procedures must be clearly defined. Positive incentives for compliance can help, and negative consequences need to be enforced for violations. The last stage is the deployment of hardware and software tools based on the policies and procedures defined by the management team.

11. **Why is it so difficult to stop computer crimes?** Responsibility or blame for cybercrimes can be placed on criminals, victimized people, and organizations. Online shoppers fail to take necessary precautions to avoid becoming victims. Security system designs and architectures are still incredibly vulnerable. Organizations may fail to exercise due care in business or hiring and practices, opening the doors to security attacks. Every EC business knows that there are threats of stolen credit cards, data breaches, phishing, malware, and viruses that never end – and that these threats must be addressed comprehensively and strategically.

KEY TERMS

Access control
Application controls
Authentication
Authorization
Availability
Banking Trojan
Biometric authentication
Biometric systems
Botnet
Business continuity plan
Business impact analysis (BIA)
CAN-SPAM Act
Certificate authorities
CIA security triad (CIA triad)

Ciphertext
Confidentiality
Cracker
Cybercrime
Cybercriminal
Darknet
Data breach
Denial-of-service (DoS) attack
Detection measures
Deterring measures
Digital envelope
Digital signature
EC security strategy
E-mail spam
Encryption
Encryption algorithm
Exposure
Firewall
Fraud
General controls
Hacker
Hash function
Honeynet
Honeypot
Identity theft
Information assurance (IA)
Information security
Integrity
Internet underground economy
Intrusion detection system (IDS)
Key (key value)
Key space
Keystroke logging (keylogging)
Macro virus (macro worm)
Malware (malicious software)
Message digest (MD)
Non-repudiation
Packet
Page hijacking
Penetration test (pen test)
Personal firewall
Pharming
Phishing
Plaintext
Prevention measures
Private key
Protocol tunneling
Public key

Public key infrastructure (PKI)
Public (asymmetric) key encryption
Risk
Search engine spam
Social engineering
Spam
Spam site
Splog
Spyware
Standard of due care
Symmetric (private) key encryption
Trojan horse
Virtual private network (VPN)
Virus
Vulnerability
Vulnerability assessment
Worm
Zombies

DISCUSSION QUESTIONS

1. Consider how a hacker might trick people into divulging their user IDs and passwords to their Amazon.com accounts. What are some of the specific ways that a hacker might accomplish this? What crimes can be performed with such information?

2. B2C EC sites and social networks continue to experience DoS and DDoS attacks. How are these attacks executed? Why is it so difficult to safeguard against them? What are some of the things a site can do to mitigate such attacks?

3. How are botnets, identity theft, DoS attacks, and website hijackings perpetrated? Why are they so dangerous to e-commerce?

4. Discuss some of the difficulties of eliminating online financial fraud.

5. Enter **zvetcobiometrics.com**. Discuss the benefits of these products over other biometrics.

6. Find information about the Zeus Trojan virus. Discuss why it is so effective at stealing financial data. Why is it so difficult to protect against this Trojan? Hint: See Falliere and Chien (2009).

7. Find information about the scareware social engineering method. Why do you think it is so effective?

8. Visit the National Vulnerability Database (**nvd. nist.gov**) and review five recent CVE vulnerabilities. For each vulnerability list its published date, CVSS severity, impact type, and the operating system or software with the vulnerability.

9. Report on the status of using biometrics in mobile commerce. (Start **nxt-id.com**.)

TOPICS FOR CLASS DISCUSSION AND DEBATES

1. Read McNeal (2012) and take the multiple choice quiz there. Discuss the results.

2. A business wants to share its customer data with a trading partner, and provide its business customers with access to marketing data. What types of security components (e.g., firewalls, VPNs, etc.) could be used to ensure that the partners and customers have access to the account information while those who are unauthorized do not? What types of network administrative procedures will provide the appropriate security?

3. Why is it so difficult to fight computer criminals? What strategies can be implemented by financial institutions, airlines, and other heavy users of EC?

4. All EC sites share common security threats and vulnerabilities. Do you think that B2C websites face different threats and vulnerabilities than do B2B sites? Explain.

5. Why is phishing so difficult to control? What can be done? Discuss.

6. Debate this statement: "The best strategy is to invest very little and only in proven technologies such as encryption and firewalls."

7. Debate: Can the underground Internet marketplace be controlled? Why or why not?

8. Debate: Is taking your fingerprints or other biometrics to assure EC security a violation of your privacy?

9. Body scans at airports have created controversy. Debate both points of this issue and relate it to EC security.

10. Debate: The U.S. government has signaled that it would view a computer attack from a foreign nation as justification for military action. Do you agree or not?

11. Discuss the issue of providing credit card details on Facebook. Would you do it?

12. Examine the identity theft and identity crime topics from the FBI site **fbi.gov/about-us/investigate/cyber/identity_theft**. Report the highlights.

INTERNET EXERCISES

1. Your B2C site has been hacked with a new, innovative method. List two organizations where you would report this incident so that they can alert other sites. How do you do this and what type of information do you have to provide?

2. Determine the IP address of your computer by visiting at least two websites that provide that feature. You can use a search engine to locate websites or visit **ip-adress.com** or **whatismyipaddress.com**. What other information does the search reveal about your connections? Based on this finding, how could a hacker use that information?

3. Conduct a Google search for 'Institutional Identity Theft.' Compare institutional identity theft with personal identity theft. How can a company protect itself against identity theft? Write a report.

4. The National Strategy to Secure Cyberspace (**dhs.gov/national-strategy-secure-cyberspace**) provides a series of actions and recommendations for each of its five national priorities. Download a copy of the strategy (**us-cert.gov/sites/default/files/publications/cyberspace_strategy.pdf**). Select one of the priorities and discuss in detail the actions and recommendations for that priority.

5. The Symantec Annual Internet Security Threat Report provides details about the trends in attacks and vulnerabilities in Internet security. Obtain a copy of the latest report and summarize the major findings of the report for both attacks and vulnerabilities.

6. Conduct a Google search for examples of underground Internet activities in five different countries. Prepare a summary.

7. Enter **consumer.ftc.gov/features/feature-0014-identity-theft**, **idtheftcenter.org**, and **fbi.gov/about-us/investigate/cyber/identity_theft**. Find information about the prevention of and protection against identity theft. Also look for cases of companies that survived identity theft. Write a report.

8. Enter **verisign.com** (a Symantec company) and find information about PKI and encryption. Write a report.

9. Enter **hijackthis.com**. What is offered in the site? Write a report.

10. Enter **blackhat.com**. Find out what the site is about. Describe some of the site's activities.

11. Conduct a Google search for articles on 'Fort Disco' and other botnets used to attack WordPress. Discuss the attacks and possible defenses.

TEAM ASSIGNMENTS AND PROJECTS

1. **Assignment for the Opening Case**
   Read the opening case and answer the following questions:
   (a) Why did the college have security problems? What types of problems?
   (b) What is the security problem concerning social media applications?
   (c) Why was the automation (agent-based) solution unsuccessful?
   (d) Why were the computer-use policies ineffective?
   (e) What was the problem with the bandwidth?
   (f) Describe the new security policy. Why does it work?
   (g) Discuss the issue of privacy as it applies to this case.

2. Assign teams to report on the latest major spam and scam threats. Look at examples provided by **ftc.gov**, the latest Symantec report on the State of Spam, and white papers from IBM, VeriSign, McAfee, and other security firms.

3. Enter **symantec.com/security_response/publications/whitepapers.jsp** and find the white papers: (1) "The Risks of Social Networking" (available at **symantec.com/content/en/us/enterprise/media/security_response/whitepapers/the_risks_of_social_networking.pdf**) and (2) "The Rise of PDF Malware" (available at **symantec.com/content/en/us/enterprise/media/security_response/whitepapers/the_rise_of_pdf_malware.pdf**). Prepare a summary of both and find how they relate to each other.

4. Watch the video "Cyberattacks and Extortion" (13:55 minutes) at **searchsecurity.techtarget.com/video/Cyberattacks-and-extortion**. Answer the following questions:
   (a) Why are there more extortions online today? How are they accomplished?
   (b) What is involved in targeted e-mail attacks?
   (c) What is an SQL injection attack?

5. Data leaks can be a major problem. Find some major defense methods. Check some major security vendors (e.g., Symantec). Find white papers and Webinars on the subject. Write a report.

6. Each team is assigned one method of fighting against online fraud. Each method should involve a different type of fraud (e.g., in banking). Identify suspicious e-mails, dealing with cookies in Web browsers, credit card protection, securing wireless networks, installing anti-phishing protection for your browser with a phishing filter, and so forth.

7. Find information on the Target data breaches and other physical stores that have been affected. Identify the methods used by the hackers. What defense strategies are used?

CLOSING CASE: HOW ONE BANK STOPPED SCAMS, SPAMS, AND CYBERCRIMINALS

Some say that as many as 90% of phishers are targeting financial institutions. Let us see how one bank is protecting its customers.

BankWest of South Dakota (bankwest-sd.com)

As a privately owned entity, a bank can disregard short term profit. Instead, a bank provides the utmost in customer care and employee educational programs. However, one problem is challenging:

the increasing number of incidents of social engineering experienced by customers. A few examples of scams that were noticed by the BankWest staff reported by Kitten (2010) are:

- **Sweetheart schemes.** There may be long term online relationship between a bank's customer and an overseas user. The overseas user tries to convince the customer to wire funds, share bank account information, and open joint accounts.
- **Letters, postal service, or e-mail.** A bank customer is notified by an e-mail that he or she has won a large amount of money (e.g., a sweepstakes). Hackers ask for some processing money to release the prize money to the customer.
- **Telephone scams.** A customer is asked to provide personal information from a government check and receives repeated telephone calls, each asking for different personal information (e.g., Social Security Number). Phone scams usually target elderly customers and depend on the social engineer's ability to develop a rapport with the customer.
- **Cell phone scams.** A customer is told that his or her debit card has been compromised and the customer is asked to provide card details for replacement.

The bank now provides information about social engineering schemes on its website (see **bankwest-sd.com/etc.htm**). Employees direct customers to the site and provide information about fraudulent schemes when the customers come into a branch. The bank also instituted an "Employee Rewards Program" (to be described later).

It is critical to combat social engineering attempts in order to increase customer confidence in Internet security. According to Kitten (2010), "the bank's information security team regularly attend workshops and participate in forums related to social engineering and other fraud schemes. The information collected is immediately shared with the staff in order to keep the entire bank team abreast of new and emerging fraud threats. All staff members also are required to complete online training in scheme detection that is designed by the bank."

Also according to Kitten (2010), the training program includes:

- Ability to identify phone scams, especially automated ones (e.g., *vishing attempts*) that lure customers into divulging sensitive information.
- Ability to identify *phishing e-mails* and use caution when clicking on links or opening file attachments.
- Conduct monthly training and employee-oriented demonstrations on face-to-face personal social engineering schemes.

Employee Rewards

Employees who identify scams are rewarded with certificates and small monetary rewards; their manager is notified and employees can take pride in the acknowledgement.

The Results

According to the bank's information security administrator, although the number of schemes has not decreased, the number of employees reporting such schemes has increased significantly.

To read BankWest's tips on how to protect yourself against identity theft, phishing, and so forth, see **bankwest-sd.com/etc.htm**.

Sources: Based on Kitten (2010) and BankWest (2014).

Questions

1. List the major security problems faced by BankWest and relate them to the attack methods described in Sections 10.2, 10.3, and 10.4.
2. In what ways is BankWest helping to stop scams before they cause damage?
3. Given the problems of BankWest and its solutions, can you suggest an even better defense mechanism?

ONLINE FILES
available at **affordable-ecommerce-textbook.com/turban**

W10.1 Application Case: How Seattle's Hospital Survived a Bot Attack

W10.2 Business Continuity and Disaster Recovery

COMPREHENSIVE EDUCATIONAL WEBSITES

cert.org: A comprehensive site, listing many resources.

csrc.nist.gov: Computer Security Resource Center.

eseminarslive.com: Webinars, events, news on security.

ic3.gov/crimeschemes.aspx: A comprehensive list of Internet crime schemes and descriptions.

itworld.com/security: A comprehensive collection of information security news, reviews and analysis, blogs, and white papers, and so forth.

nvd.nist.gov: National Vulnerability Database; a comprehensive cybersecurity and vulnerability database.

onguardonline.gov: A U.S. government comprehensive guide for online security.

sans.org/security-resources: Information security resources, glossary, and research.

spamlaws.com: Providing up-to-date information on issues affecting Internet security. News, cases, legal information, and much more; information on spam, scams, security, and so forth.

darkreading.com: *InformationWeek*'s security website. News and commentary; blogs; top stories and information on many different aspects of security.

technet.microsoft.com/en-US/security/bb291012: Microsoft Security TechCenter. Security updates, bulletins, advisories, updates, blogs, tools, and downloads.

microsoft.com/security/default.aspx: Microsoft Internet Safety and Security Center. Download updates and security essentials; tips on online security and how to avoid scams and hoaxes; resources.

technologyevaluation.com: Research articles and reports; white papers, etc. on software and security.

techsupportalert.com/best_computer_security_sites.htm: A detailed directory of computer security sites.

computer-protection-software-review. toptenreviews.com: 2014 Best computer software comparisons and reviews.

ddosattackprotection.org/blog/cyber-security-blogs: Top 100+ cyber security blogs and information security resources.

GLOSSARY

Access control A defense mechanism that determines who (person, program, or machine) can legitimately use the organization's computing resources (which resources, when, and how).

Application controls Controls that guard applications.

Authentication A process to verify (assure) the real identity of an EC entity, which could be an individual, software agent, computer program, or EC website.

Authorization The provision of permission to an authenticated person to access systems and perform certain operations in those specific systems.

Availability The assurance that access to any relevant data, information websites, or other EC services and their use is available in real time, whenever and wherever needed.

Banking Trojan Malicious software programmed to create damage when users visit certain online banking or e-commerce sites.

Biometric authentication A technology that measures and analyzes the identity of people based on measurable biological or behavioral characteristics or physiological signals.

Biometric systems A system that can *identify* a previously registered person by searching through a database for a possible *match* based on the person's observed physical, biological, or behavioral traits, or the system can *verify* a person's identity by matching an individual's measured biometric traits against a previously stored version.

Botnet Malicious software that criminals distribute, usually to infect a large number of computers.

Business continuity plan A plan that keeps the business running after a disaster occurs. Each function in the business should have a valid recovery capability plan.

Business impact analysis (BIA) An analysis of the impact of losing the functionality of an EC activity (e.g., e-procurement, e-ordering) to an organization.

Certificate authorities (CAs) Independent agencies that issue digital certificates or SSL certificates, which are electronic files that uniquely identify individuals and websites and enable encrypted communication.

CIA security triad (CIA triad) A point of reference used to identify problem areas and evaluate the information security of an organization that includes *confidentiality*, *integrity*, and *availability*.

Ciphertext An encrypted plaintext.

Controlling the assault of non-solicited pornography and marketing (CAN-SPAM) act Law that makes it a crime to send commercial e-mail messages with spam.

Cracker A malicious hacker who may be more damaging than a hacker.

Confidentiality The assurance of data secrecy and privacy. Namely, the data is disclosed only to authorized people.

Cybercrime Intentional crimes carried out on the Internet.

Cybercriminal A person who intentionally carries out crimes over the Internet.

Data breach A security incident in which data are obtained illegally and then published or processed.

Denial-of-service (DoS) attack "A malicious attempt to make a server or network resource unavailable to users, usually by temporarily interrupting or suspending the services of a host connected to the Internet." (Incapsula, Inc.)

Detection measures Methods that help find security breaches in computer systems. Usually this means to find out whether intruders are attempting (or have attempted) to break into the EC system, whether they were successful, whether they are still damaging the system, and what damage they may have done.

Deterrent methods Countermeasures that make criminals abandon their idea of attacking a specific system (e.g., a possible deterrent is a realistic expectation of being caught and punished).

Digital envelop The pair of encryptions that occurs the sender encrypts with the recipients' public key, both the original message and the digital signature.

Digital signatures The electronic equivalent of personal signatures on paper. They are difficult to forge since they authenticate the identity of the sender that uses the public key.

EC security strategy Multiple layers of defense that includes several methods. This defense aims to deter, prevent, and detect unauthorized entry into an organization's computer and information systems.

E-mail spam Occurs when almost identical messages are e-mailed to many recipients (sometimes millions of unsolicited e-mails).

Encryption The process of encoding data into a form (called a *ciphertext*) that will be difficult, expensive, or time-consuming for an unauthorized person to understand.

Encryption algorithm The set of procedures or mathematical algorithms used to encrypt or decrypt a message.

Exposure The estimated cost, loss, or damage that can result if a threat exploits a vulnerability.

Firewalls Barriers between an internal trusted network (or a PC) and the untrustworthy Internet. Technically, it is composed of hardware and a software package that separates a private computer network (e.g., your LAN) from a public network (the Internet).

Fraud Any business activity that uses deceitful practices or devices to deprive another of property or other rights.

General controls Controls designed to protect all system applications.

Hacker Someone who gains unauthorized access to a computer system.

Hash function A secured mathematical algorithm applied to a message.

Honeynet A network of honeypots designed to attract hackers, just as bees are attracted to honey.

Honeypot Simulated information system components such as EC servers, payments gates, routers, database servers, and even firewalls that look like real working systems.

Identity theft Wrongfully obtaining and using the identity of another person in some way to commit crimes that involve fraud or deception (e.g., for economic gain).

Information assurance (IA) The performance of activities (steps) to protect information systems and their processes against all risks. The assurance includes all tools and defense methods.

Information security Measures taken to protect information systems and their processes against all risks.

Integrity The assurance that data are accurate and that they cannot be altered.

Internet underground economy E-markets for stolen information made up of thousands of websites that sell credit card numbers, social security numbers, e-mail addresses, bank account numbers, social network IDs, passwords, and much more.

Intrusion detection system (IDS) A device composed of software and/or hardware designed to monitor the activities of computer networks and computer systems in order to detect and define unauthorized and malicious attempts to access, manipulate, and/or disable these networks and systems.

Key (key value) The secret piece used with the algorithm to encrypt (or decrypt) the message.

Key space The total universe of possible key values that can be created by a specific encryption algorithm.

Keystroke logging (keylogging) The process of using a device or software program that tracks and records the activity of a user in real time (without the user's knowledge or consent) by the keyboard keys they press.

Macro virus (macro worm) A malware code that is attached to a data file rather than to an executable program (e.g., a Word file).

Malware (malicious software) A generic term for malicious software.

Message digest The results of the hash function that is a special summary of the message converted into a string of digits.

Nonrepudiation The assurance that online customers or trading partners cannot falsely deny (repudiate) their purchase, transaction, sale, or other obligation.

Packet Segment of the data and information exchanged between computers over the Internet.

Page hijacking Illegally copying website content so that a user is misdirected to a different website.

Penetration test (pen test) A method of assessing the vulnerability of a computer system, which is done by allowing experts to act as malicious attackers.

Personal firewall A firewall that protects desktop systems by monitoring all incoming traffic to your computer.

Pharming A scam where malicious code is installed on a computer and used to redirect victims to a bogus websites without their knowledge or consent.

Phishing A fraudulent process of attempting to acquire sensitive information by masquerading as a trustworthy entity.

Plaintext A human-readable text or message.

Prevention measures Ways to help stop unauthorized people from accessing the EC system (e.g., by using authentication devices and firewalls or by using *intrusion prevention* which is, according to TechTarget "a preemptive approach to network security used to identify potential threats and respond to them swiftly").

Private key A key that only its owner knows.

Protocol tunneling Method used to ensure confidentiality and integrity of data transmitted over the Internet by encrypting data packets, and then encapsulating them in packets that can be transmitted across the Internet.

Public key A key that is known to all.

Public (asymmetric) key encryption An encryption method that uses two keys: public key and private key.

Public key infrastructure (PKI) A comprehensive framework for securing data flow and information exchange that overcomes some of the shortcomings of the one-key system.

Risk The probability that a vulnerability will be known and used.

Search engine spam The technology that enables the creation of spam sites.

Social engineering A type of nontechnical attack that uses some ruse to trick users into revealing information or performing an action that compromises a computer or network.

Spam The electronic equivalent of junk mail.

Spam site Pages that trick search engines into offering biased search results such so that the ranking of certain pages is inflated.

Splog Blogs created by spammers solely for advertising.

Spyware Tracking software that is installed by criminals or advertisers, without the user's consent, in order to gather information about the user and direct it to advertisers or other third parties.

Standard of due care The minimum and customary practice that a company is reasonably expected to take to protect the company and its resources from possible risks.

Symmetric (private) key encryption A scheme in which the same key is used to encrypt and decrypt the plaintext.

Trojan horse A program that seems to be harmless or even looks useful but actually contains a hidden malicious code.

Virtual private network (VPN) A network that uses the Internet to transfer information in a secure manner.

Virus Programmed software inserted by criminals into a computer to damage the system; running the infected host program activates the virus.

Vulnerability Weakness in software or other mechanism that threatens the confidentiality, integrity, or availability of an asset (recall the CIA model). It can be directly used by a hacker to gain access to a system or network.

Vulnerability assessment A process of identifying and evaluating problem areas that are vulnerable to attack on a computerized system.

Worm A software code that can replicate itself automatically (as a "standalone" – without any human intervention). Worms use networks to propagate and infect a computer or handheld device and can even spread via instant messages.

Zombies Computers infected with malware that are under the control of a spammer, hacker, or other criminal.

REFERENCES

Acohido, B. "Black Hat Shows Hacker Exploits Getting More Sophisticated." *USA Today*, August 3, 2011 (updated August 9, 2011).

Albanesius, C. "Microsoft, FBI Take Down 'Citadel' Botnet Targeting Bank Info." *PCMag.com*, June 6, 2013. **pcmag.com/article2/0,2817,2420046,00.asp** (accessed May 2014).

Apps, P., and J. Finkle. "Suspected Russian Spyware Turla Targets Europe, United States." *Reuters.com U.S. Edition*, March 7, 2014. **reuters.com/article/2014/03/07/us-russia-cyberespionage-insight-idUSBREA260YI20140307** (accessed May 2014).

Bailey, T., J. Kaplan, and A. Weinberg. "Playing War Games to Prepare for a Cyberattack." *McKinsey Quarterly*, July 2012.

BankWest. "About Us." **bankwest-sd.com/about.htm** (accessed May 2014).

BBC News Technology, Wordpress website targeted by hackers. April 15, 2013. **bbc.com/news/technology-22152296** (accessed December 2013).

BBC News Technology. "Spammers Sought After Botnet Takedown." March 25, 2011. **bbc.com/news/technology-12859591** (accessed May 2014).

Bort, J. "For the First Time, Hackers Have Used a Refrigerator to Attack Businesses." *Business Insider*, January 16, 2014.

Brooks, J. "Conficker: What It Is, How to Stop It and Why You May Already Be Protected." *eWeek*, March 31, 2009.

Cannel, J. "Cryptolocker Ransomware: What You Need to Know." October 8, 2013. **blog.malwarebytes.org/intelligence/2013/10/cryptolocker-ransom** (accessed June 2014).

Casti, T. "Phishing Scam Targeting Netflix May Trick You With Phony Customer Service Reps." *The Huffington Post Tech*, March 3, 2014a. **huffingtonpost.com/2014/03/03/netflix-phishing-scam-customer-support_n_4892048.html** (accessed May 2014).

Casti, T. "Scammers are Targeting Netflix Users Again, Preying on the Most Trusting among Us." *The Huffington Post Tech*, April 17, 2014b. **huffingtonpost.com/2014/04/17/netflix-comcast-phishing-_n_5161680.html** (accessed May 2014).

Chickowski, E. "Closing the Security Gap." *Baseline*, June 2, 2008. **baselinemag.com/c/a/Security/Closing-the-Security-Gap/** (accessed May 2014).

Cluley, G. "Phishing and Diet Spam Attacks Hit Twitter Users." *Cluley Associates Limited*, January 9, 2014. **grahamcluley.com/2014/01/phishing-diet-spam-attacks-hit-twitter-users** (accessed May 2014).

CompTIA. "Trends in Information Security: A CompTIA Analysis of IT Security and the Workforce." 2008.

Constantin, L. "Kill Timer Found in Shamoon Malware Suggests Possible Connection to Saudi Aramco Attack." *PC World*, August 23, 2012.

Cooney, M., "10 Common Mobile Security Problems to Attack." *PC World*, September 21, 2012

Cowley, S. "Former FBI Cyber Cop Worries about a Digital 9/11." July 25, 2012. **money.cnn.com/2012/07/25/technology/blackhat-shawn-henry** (accessed May 2014).

CyberSource. *13th Annual 2012 Online Fraud Report*, CyberSource Corporation (2012).

CyberSource. *14th Annual 2013 Online Fraud Report*, CyberSource Corporation (2013).

Dawn Ontario. "Virus Information: Guide to Computer Viruses." Undated. **dawn.thot.net/cd/206.html** (accessed May 2014).

Dalton, M., and A. Grossman. Arrests signal breach in 'darknet' sites, November 7, 2014. **online.wsj.com/articles/illegal-websites-seized-by-eu-u-s-authorities-1415368411** (Accessed November 2014).

Davis, M. A. "Data Encryption: Piling On." *Information Week Reports*, January 30, 2012a.

Davis, M. A. "2012 Strategic Security Survey." *Information Week*, May 14, 2012b.

Dickey, C., M. Bahari, R. Bergman, and J. Barry."The Covert War against Iran's Nuclear Program." *Newsweek*, December 13, 2010.

Dog Breed Info Center. "Examples of Scam E-Mails." Undated. **dogbreedinfo.com/internetfraud/scamemailexamples.htm** (accessed May 2014).

Drew, S. GPS loophole could allow mass smartphone hacking. August 16, 2012. **geoawesomeness.com/gps-loophole-could-allow-mass-smartphone-hacking** (accessed December 2014).

Duncan, G. "Why Haven't Biometrics Replaced Passwords Yet?" *Digital Trends*, March 9, 2013. **digitaltrends.com/computing/can-biometrics-secure-our-digital-lives/#!Qebtp** (accessed May 2014).

EMC/RSA. "2013 A Year in Review." Report # JAN RPT 0114, January 2014. **emc.com/collateral/fraud-report/rsa-online-fraud-report-012014.pdf** (accessed May 2014).

Esposito, R., and L. Ferran. "Feds: Cyber Criminals Hijacked 4 Million Computers." November 9, 2011. **abcnews.go.com/Blotter/feds-cyber-criminals-hijacked-million-computers/story?id=14915648** (accessed May 2014).

Falliere, N., and E. Chien. "Zeus: King of the Bots." Security Response White paper, Symantec, November 2009.

Finkle, J. "'Pony' Botnet Steals Bitcoins, Digital Currencies: Trustwave." *Reuters.com US Edition*, February 24, 2014. **reuters.com/article/2014/02/24/us-bitcoin-security-idUSBREA1N1JO20140224** (accessed May 2014).

Fisher, R. *The Book on Networks: Everything You Need to Know about the Internet, Online Security and Cloud Computing.* Seattle, WA: CreateSpace Independent Publishing Platform, 2014.

Fowler, G. A., and J. Valentino-DeVries. "Spate of Cyberattacks Points to Inside India." *The Wall Street Journal*, June 23, 2013.

Gandel, S. "At Financial News Sites, Stock Promoters Make Inroads." March 20, 2014. **fortunewallstreet.wordpress.com/author/stephengandelfortune/page/6** (accessed June 2014).

Gil, P. "Spyware-Malware 101: Understanding the Secret Digital War of the Internet." July 2013. **netforbeginners.about.com/od/antivirusantispyware/a/malware101.htm** (accessed May 2014).

Goldman, D. "Hacker Hits on U.S. Power and Nuclear Targets Spiked in 2012." January 9, 2013. **money.cnn.com/2013/01/09/technology/security/infrastructure-cyberattacks** (accessed May 2014).

Goldman, D. "The Real Iranian Threat: Cyberattacks." November 5, 2012. **money.cnn.com/2012/11/05/technology/security/iran-cyberattack** (accessed May 2014).

Goldman, J. "Data Breach Roundup: January 2014." February 14, 2014. **esecurityplanet.com/network-security/data-breach-roundup-january-2014.html** (accessed May 2014).

Goodchild, J. "Policy-Based Security and Access Control." April 5, 2011. **csoonline.com/article/2128022/mobile-security/case-studDOUBLEHYPHENolicy-based-security-and-access-control.html** (accessed June 2014).

Goodchild, J. "Social Engineering: The Basics." December 20, 2012. **csoonline.com/article/2124681/security-awareness/social-engineering-the-basics.html** (accessed May 2014).

Gudkova, D. "Kaspersky Security Bulletin. Spam Evolution 2013." *Kaspersky Lab.* 2014. Available for download at **securelist.com/en/analysis/204792322/Kaspersky_Security_Bulletin_Spam_evolution_2013** (accessed May 2014).

Habal, R. "How to Assess Cloud-Based E-Mail Security Vendors." *eWeek*, September 28, 2010.

Harkins, J.M. *Spyware.* Charleston, NC: CreateSpace, 2011.

HP Enterprise Security. "2013 Cost of Cyber Crime Study: Global Report." A Ponemon Institute Research Report. October 2013. (Available for download at **hpenterprisesecurity.com/register/thank-you/2013-fourth-annual-cost-of-cyber-crime-study-global**) (accessed May 2014).

IBM. "IBM X-Force Threat Intelligence Quarterly 1Q 2014." February 2014. **public.dhe.ibm.com/common/ssi/ecm/en/wgl03045usen/WGL03045USEN.PDF** (accessed June 2014).

IBM Corporation. "IBM X-Force 2012 Mid-year Trend and Risk Report." *IBM Security Systems*, White Paper # WGE03019-USEN-00, September 2012. **public.dhe.ibm.com/common/ssi/ecm/en/wgl03014usen/WGL03014USEN.PDF** (accessed May 2014).

Jaishankar, K. (Ed.). *Cyber Criminology: Exploring Internet Crimes and Criminal Behavior.* Boca Raton, Florida: CRC Press, 2011.

Jones and Bartlett Learning LLC. "Fundamentals of Information Systems Security: Unit 1 – Information Systems Security Fundamentals." 2012. **ccahs.net/Fundamentals.U1.pdf** (accessed May 2014).

Kaiser, T. "Hackers Use Refrigerator, Other Devices to Send 750,000 Spam Emails." January 17, 2014. **dailytech.com/Hackers+Use+Refrigerator+Other+Devices+to+Send+750000+Spam+Emails+/article34161.htm** (accessed May 2014).

Kalomni, R. "Dark Net 101." *Ask The Computer Guy*, June 13, 2012. **askthecomputerguy.com/opinions/dark-net-101** (accessed May 2014).

Kaplan, J., C. Rezek, and K. Sprague. "Protecting Information in the Cloud." *McKinsey Quarterly*, January 2013.

Katz, O. "Analyzing a Malicious Botnet Attack Campaign through the Security Big Data Prism." January 6, 2014. **blogs.akamai.com/2014/01/analyzing-a-malicious-botnet-attack-campaign-through-the-security-big-data-prism.html** (accessed May 2014).

Kavilanz, P. "6 Most Dangerous Cyberattacks." (Last updated November 21, 2013a). **money.cnn.com/**

gallery/smallbusiness/2013/11/21/dangerous-cyberattacks/index.html (accessed May 2014).

Kavilanz, P. "Cyberattacks Devastated My Business!" (Last updated May 28, 2013b). money.cnn.com/gallery/smallbusiness/2013/05/28/cybercrime/index.html?iid=Lead (accessed May 2014).

Kirk, J. "Security Company Scours 'Dark Web' for Stolen Data." Computerworld, September 30, 2013.

Kitten, T. "Case Study: How to Stop Scams." July 14, 2010.bankinfosecurity.com/case-study-how-to-stop-scams-a-2748 (accessed May 2014).

Kontzer, T. "Cyber-Attacks Spur Innovative Security Approaches." Baseline, May/June 2011.

LabTech. "Mobile Security: Controlling Growing Threats with Mobile Device Management." LabTech Software, White Paper #1866272, 2012. thinkhdi.com/~/media/HDICorp/Files/White-Papers/LabTech-Mobile-Security.pdf (accessed May 2014).

Kravets, D. "How China's Army Hacked America." May 19, 2014 arstechnica.com/tech-policy/2014/05/how-chinas-army-hacked-american-companies (accessed June 2014).

Lawinski, J. "Companies Spend on Security Amid Mobile and Social Threats." Baseline, September 14, 2011.

Lawinski, J. "Security Slideshow: Malicious Attacks Skyrocket as Hackers Explore New Targets." CIO Insight, May 7, 2012.

Lenovo. "Lenovo Recommends 15 Steps to Reducing Security Risks in Enterprise Mobility." White Paper, August 2013. Available for download in .pdf format at techrepublic.com/resource-library/whitepapers/lenovo-recommends-15-steps-to-reducing-security-risks-in-enterprise-mobility/post (accessed May 2014).

Lerer, L. "Why the SEC Can't Stop Spam." Forbes, March 8, 2007.

Lyne, J. "What Justin Bieber's Twitter Hack Teaches Us about Social Media Security." March 12, 2014. forbes.com/sites/jameslyne/2014/03/12/what-justin-biebers-twitter-hack-teaches-us-about-social-security (accessed May 2014).

Mandalia, R. "Spammers, Phishers Increasingly Targeting Users of Social Networking Sites." December 27, 2011. itproportal.com/2011/12/27/spammers-phishers-increasingly-targeting-users-social-networking-sites/ (accessed May 2014).

Mashable Team. "The Heartbleed Hit List: The Password You Need to Change." April 9, 2014. mashable.com/2014/04/09/heartbleed-bug-websites-affected (accessed June 2014).

McAfee. "Global Energy Cyberattacks: 'Night Dragon.'" White paper. Santa Clara, CA: McAfee Foundstone Professional Services and McAfee Labs, February 10, 2011. mcafee.com/us/resources/white-papers/wp-global-energy-cyberattacks-night-dragon.pdf (accessed May 2014).

McMillan, R. "90 Percent of E-Mail Is Spam, Symantec Says." PCWorld, May 26, 2009. pcworld.com/article/165533/article.html (accessed May 2014).

McNeal, A. "What's Your Fraud IQ?" Journal of Accountancy, August 2012. journalofaccountancy.com/Issues/2012/Aug/20125443.htm (accessed May 2014).

MessageLabs. "How to Defend Against New Botnet Attacks." A MessageLabs (Now Part of Symantec) White paper, 1011979. 2009.

Murray, A. C. "Omnipotent Hacker Myth Lets Business Off the Hook." InformationWeek, June 27, 2011. informationweek.com/it-leadership/omnipotent-hacker-myth-lets-business-off-the-hook/d/d-id/1098580 (accessed May 2014).

Nakashima, E. "Foreign Hackers Targeted U.S. Water Plant in Apparent Malicious Cyber Attack, Expert Says." Washington Post, November 18, 2011. washingtonpost.com/blogs/checkpoint-washington/post/foreign-hackers-broke-into-illinois-water-plant-control-system-industry-expert-says/2011/11/18/gIQAgmTZYN_blog.html (accessed May 2014).

News24. "Hackers Hit Western Oil Firms." News24.com, February 11, 2011. news24.com/SciTech/News/Hackers-hit-Western-oil-firms-20110211 (accessed May 2014).

Nuerm, J. Identity Theft Manual: Practical Tips, Legal Hints and Other Secret Revealed. Seattle, WA: Amazon Digital Services, Inc., 2012.

Nugent, J. "Classical Bank Robbery with a Cyber Twist." Forbes.com, November 11, 2013. forbes.com/sites/riskmap/2013/11/08/classical-bank-robbery-with-a-cyber-twist (accessed May 2014).

Pagliery, J. "Drug Site Silk Road Wiped Out by Bitcoin Glitch." CNN Money, February 14, 2014. money.cnn.com/2014/02/14/technology/security/silk-road-bitcoin (accessed May 2014).

Palgon, G. "Simple Steps to Data Protection." Security Management, June 2008. (No longer available online.)

Pate, S. "Encryption as an Enabler: The Top 10 Benefits." April 30, 2013. networkworld.com/news/tech/2013/042613-encryption-269183.html?page=1 (accessed May 2014).

Pattison, III, W. B. Attack of the Internet: Phishing Attempts, Pharming Scams, Swindles and Frauds. Seattle, WA: Amazon Digital Services, Inc., 2012.

Perez, E. "Hackers Siphoned $70 Million." Wall Street Journal, Updated October 2, 2010.

Phneah, E. "Five Security Risks of Moving Data in BYOD Era." February 4, 2013. zdnet.com/five-security-risks-of-moving-data-in-byod-era-7000010665 (accessed May 2014).

Pontrioli, S. "Social Engineering, Hacking the Human OS." December 20, 2013. blog.kaspersky.com/social-engineering-hacking-the-human-os (accessed May 2014).

Prince, B. "Kneber Botnet Highlights Trend of Social Networking Data Being Used by Hackers." eWeek, February 18, 2010a.

Prince, B. "Massive Check Fraud Operation Run by Hackers Revealed at Black Hat." eWeek, July 28, 2010b.

PWC. "Key Findings from the 2013 US State of Cybercrime Survey." June 2013. **pwc.com/en_US/us/increasing-it-effectiveness/publications/assets/us-state-of-cybercrime.pdf** (accessed June 2014).

Rand, D. "Threats When Using Online Social Networks." CSIS Security Group, May 16, 2007. **csis.dk/downloads/LinkedIn.pdf** (accessed May 2014).

Reisinger, D. "10 Mobile Security Issues that Should Worry You." *eWeek*, February 11, 2014.

Reske, H. J., and J. Bachmann. "Lieberman Worried that Cyber Attack 'Could be Imminent.'" July 24, 2012. **newsmax.com/TheWire/cyber-attacklieberman-bill/2012/07/24/id/446429** (accessed May 2014).

Riley, M., B. Elgin, D. Lawrence, and C. Matlack. "Missed Alarms and 40 Million Credit Cards Numbers: How Target Blew It." *Businessweek.com*, March 13, 2014. **businessweek.com/articles/2014-03-13/target-missed-alarms-in-epic-hack-of-credit-card-data** (accessed May 2014).

Rhodes-Ousley, M. *Information Security the Complete Reference*, 2nd edition. New York: McGraw-Hill, 2013.

Rubens, P. "Biometric Authentication: How it Works." August 17, 2012. **esecurityplanet.com/trends/biometric-authentication-how-it-works.html** (accessed May 2014).

Russell, K. "Here's How to Protect Yourself from the Massive Security Flaw That's Taken over the Internet." *Business Insider*, April 8, 2014.

Sarrel, M. "Stay Safe, Productive on Social Networks." *eWeek*, March 28, 2010.

Schwartz, M. J. "10 Best Ways to Stop Insider Attacks." *Information Week Dark Reading*, March 12, 2012. **darkreading.com/attacks-and-breaches/10-best-ways-to-stop-insider-attacks-/d/d-id/1103321?**(accessed May 2014).

Schwartz, M. J. "Target Breach: Phishing Attack Implicated." *Information Week Dark Reading*, February 13, 2014. **darkreading.com/attacks-and-breaches/target-breach-phishing-attack-implicated/d/d-id/1113829** (accessed May 2014).

Scott, W. *Information Security 249 Success Secrets- 249 Most Asked Questions on Information Security- What You Need to Know*. Brisbane, Queensland, Australia: Emereo Publishing, 2014.

Smith, C. "It Turns Out Target Could Have Easily Prevented Its Massive Security Breach." March 13, 2014. **bgr.com/2014/03/13/target-data-hack-how-it-happened** (accessed May 2014).

Snyder, J. "Staying One Step Ahead of Modern Hackers." *BizTech Magazine*, March 14, 2014.

Stone, B. "Sports Leagues Battle Video Pirates Showing Bootleg Live Games on Internet." February 24, 2011. **bloomberg.com/news/2011-02-24/sports-leagues-battle-video-pirates-showing-bootleg-live-games-on-internet.html** (accessed May 2014).

Suby, M. "The 2013 (ISC)² Global Information Security Workforce Study." Mountain View, CA: Frost and Sullivan, 2013.

Sullivan, D. "The Shortcut Guide to Business Security Measures Using SSL." Symantec White paper, Realtime Publishers, 2009. Available for download at **realtimepublishers.com/chapters/1562/sgbsmus-2.pdf** (accessed May 2014).

SUNY College at Old Westbury. "Website Privacy Policy Statement." 2014. **oldwestbury.edu/policy/privacy_policy.cfm** (accessed May 2014).

Swann, C. T. *Marlins Cry a Phishing Story*. Spokane, WA: Cutting Edge Communications, Inc., 2012.

Symantec. "Infographic: The State of Financial Trojans 2013." Updated January 8, 2014. **symantec.com/connect/blogs/state-financial-trojans-2013** (accessed June 2014).

Symantec. "Reducing the Cost and Complexity of Web Vulnerability Management." White Paper, Symantec Corp., 2011. **verisign.com/ssl/ssl-information-center/ssl-resources/vulnerability-management-white-paper.pdf** (accessed May 2014).

Symantec. *Symantec Report on the Underground Economy: July 07–June 08*. Symantec Corp., November 2008, Report #14525717. **eval.symantec.com/mktginfo/enterprise/white_papers/b-whitepaper_underground_economy_report_11-2008-14525717.en-us.pdf** (accessed May 2014).

Symantec. "Web-Based Attacks." White paper, #20016955, February 2009. **symantec.com/content/en/us/enterprise/media/security_response/whitepapers/web_based_attacks_02-2009.pdf** (accessed May 2014).

Talabis, M., and J. Martin. *Information Security Risk Assessment Toolkit: Practical Assessment through Data Collection and Data Analysis*. Maryland Heights, MO: Syngress, 2013.

Teller, T. "Social Engineering: Hacking the Human Mind." *Forbes*, March 29, 2012.

Thomson, L. (Ed.) *Data Breach and Encryption Handbook*. Chicago, IL: American Bar Association, 2012.

Timberg, C. "Foreign Regimes Use Spyware against Journalists, Even in U.S." February 12, 2014. **washingtonpost.com/business/technology/foreign-regimes-use-spyware-against-journalists-even-in-us/2014/02/12/9501a20e-9043-11e3-84e1-27626c5ef5fb_story.html** (accessed May 2014).

Wang, R. "Malware B-Z: Inside the Threat from Blackhole to Zero Access." A Sophos White Paper, Sophos Ltd., January 2013. **sophos.com/en-us/medialibrary/Gated%20Assets/white%20papers/sophos_from_blackhole_to_zeroaccess_wpna.pdf** (accessed May 2014).

Westervelt, R. "Top 10 BYOD Risks Facing the Enterprise." July 26, 2013. **crn.com/slide-shows/security/240157796/top-10-byod-risks-facing-the-enterprise.htm** (accessed May 2014).

Willhite, J. "On Alert against Cybercrime." *The Wall Street Journal Blogs – CFO Journal*, August 13, 2013. **blogs.wsj.com/cfo/2013/08/13/on-alert-against-cybercrime** (accessed May 2014).

Worley, B., "Does Your PC Have a Virus? Or Is It Just Slow?" April 4, 2012. **news.yahoo.com/blogs/ upgrade-your-life/does-pc-virus-just-slow-181117610.html** (accessed May 2014).

Yadron, D. "Newest Hacker Target: Ads." *The Wall Street Journal Tech*, **January 31, 2014. online.wsj. com/news/articles/SB10001424052702303743604579 350654103483462 (accessed May 2014).**

Electronic Commerce Payment Systems

11

Contents

Learning Objectives

Upon completion of this chapter, you will be able to:

1. Describe the situations where micropayments are used and alternative ways to handle these situations.
2. Discuss the different payment cards used online and processing methods.
3. Discuss the different categories and potential uses of smart cards.
4. Discuss stored-value cards and identify under what circumstances they are used best.
5. Describe micropayments online.
6. Describe the processes and parties involved in e-checking.
7. Understand the major types and methods of mobile payments.
8. Describe payment methods in B2B EC, including payments for global trade.
9. Describe emerging EC payment systems.

Electronic supplementary material The online version of this chapter (doi: 10.1007/978-3-319-10091-3_11) contains supplementary material, which is available to authorized users

E. Turban et al., *Electronic Commerce: A Managerial and Social Networks Perspective*,
Springer Texts in Business and Economics, DOI 10.1007/978-3-319-10091-3_11,
© Springer International Publishing Switzerland 2015

OPENING CASE: PAY-PER-PAGE: ALTERNATIVES TO E-MICROPAYMENTS

The Problem

The e-book market is booming while the brick-and-mortar book market is rapidly declining. In 2013, Amazon.com released the 6th generation Kindle reader – the "Kindle Paperwhite" (also known as 'Paperwhite 2'). Kindle books can also be read on virtually any PC or tablet device. Barnes & Noble has a Kindle competitor called the Nook. The result is that some categories of books in digital format sell better than their hardcover and paperback counterparts, as described in Chapter 5.

For the most part, e-books are sold as "digital replicas" of their print counterparts. This approach may be fine for works of fiction, true crime, and so forth. Most fiction readers are primarily interested in purchasing the entire book, not individual pages or chapters. This may not be the case for nonfiction readers. Many nonfiction readers do not need, nor do they want, a complete book. For example:

- A reader is traveling to Rome, Italy on his or her next vacation and only wants a couple of chapters from Fodor's holiday travel guide to Italy, not the whole guide.
- A software programmer faces a perplexing problem and discovers a solution in a particular chapter of a well-known programming book. The book sells for $80, but the programmer needs only 5 pages from the 600-page edition.
- A professor would like to assign his students one chapter from a noncourse textbook without violating copyright laws or requiring the students to spend a small fortune purchasing the entire book.

Selling books online – either hard copies or electronic – is straightforward. Selling pages, chapters, or any other sections of a book or journal online for under $5 is another story. There are two barriers, neither of which is technical. The first barrier is that publishers are hesitant to cannibalize their profits by selling parts of a book rather than the book as a whole. This was the same viewpoint the music industry held before iTunes and Amazon.com began selling individual songs in addition to complete CDs.

The second barrier is that merchants incur transaction costs that are too high when they allow customers to use credit or debit cards to make purchases for less than $5. In the online world, the vast majority of consumers use credit cards to make purchases. The financial institutions issuing credit cards charge merchants a fixed percentage and a fixed fee for each credit card purchase. Merchants who accept credit cards typically must pay a minimum transaction fee that ranges from 25¢ to 35¢, plus 2% to 3% of the purchase price. The same is true for debit cards, even though the fee is lower. These fees are reasonable for card purchases over $10–$12, but can be cost-prohibitive for smaller transactions.

The same problem occurs when a customer tries to make a credit or debit card purchase in each of the following situations:

- Buying a song on iTunes for $1.29, or an application from the App store for $1.99.
- Purchasing a copy of an archived newspaper article from a leading newspaper or news journal (such as *Forbes* or *BusinessWeek*) for $1.50.
- Selecting an online game and buying 30 minutes of playing time for $3.00 or buying an accessory or weapon while playing the game.
- Purchasing a couple of digital images from an online clip art store for 80¢ each.

In 2005, Amazon.com tried to remedy this problem. Amazon announced a plan called "Amazon Pages" that would allow readers to purchase sections of books online. The plan was supplemented by the release of the Kindle e-book reader and the opening of the Kindle Store. Similarly, in February 2008, Random House began testing the idea of selling individual chapters online for $2.99. In 2011, the first, and only, title offered was Chip and Dan Heath's *Made to Stick* (which was given away free in 2013).

The Solution

Small online payments, usually $10–12 each ($10 per PayPal), are called *micropayments*. In the offline world, these small purchases are usually made with cash because credit card companies charge merchants exorbitant fees to make the transactions profitable. Because cash cannot be used in the online world, there have been several efforts aimed at producing digital surrogates. As far back as 2000, a number of companies offered micropayment solutions designed to circumvent the fees associated with credit and debit cards. For the most part, the history of these companies is one of unfulfilled promises and outright failure. Digicash, First Virtual, Cybercoin, Millicent, and Internet Dollar are some of the micropayment companies that went bankrupt during the dot-com crash. Bitpass is an example of a company that failed in 2007. A number of factors played a role in their demise, including the fact that early users of the Internet thought that digital content should be free.

While some digital currencies have been a resounding failure, there are a series of micropayment models that do not depend solely or directly on credit or debit cards and have enjoyed some success.

The Results

In 2012, Apple announced that consumers had downloaded over 20 billion songs and 10 billion applications from the iTunes Store. The vast majority of these songs and applications cost less than $2.00 each. Consumers downloaded over $150 million worth of 46 different applications on a single day in December 2011. Clearly, Apple has been able to overcome the micropayment problem, using the "aggregation" payment model (described later in this chapter). In particular, any consumer who wants to purchase items from iTunes or the App store creates an account that is associated with a credit or debit card. When she or he makes a purchase, the purchase amount is added to the prior totals until the new total exceeds a value that makes it cost-effective for Apple to submit the payment to the credit or debit card issuer. Naturally, other vendors and particularly Amazon.com could follow Apple's lead and use the same sort of system to sell book pages, chapters, and articles on demand, assuming the publishers are willing to collaborate.

Credit and debit card companies are well aware of the difficulties associated with using cards for online micropayments; therefore, they have lowered their fees in an effort to entice online (and offline) vendors to permit credit and debit card micropayments. Even with the new fee structure, purchases of less than $10 are still cost-prohibitive for the average merchant. PayPal also has enhanced their payment system to handle micropayments (described in Section "Nontechnical Methods: from Phishing to Spam and Fraud" in Chapter 10).

Sources: Based on Analysys Mason (2010), Tsotsis (2011), and **en.ecommercewiki.info/payment/micro_payment** (accessed June 2014).

LESSONS LEARNED FROM THE CASE

Almost since the inception of e-commerce, credit and debit cards have ruled the world of e-payments. Virtually all B2C purchases are made using payment cards. As noted in the opening case, many electronic money clones have tried to solve the problem but virtually all failed. The only major company to succeed is PayPal (**paypal.com**), which is discussed in Section "The Information Security Problem" in Chapter 10. A similar situation exists in B2B where several methods were attempted, but only a few succeeded.

While the majority of B2C e-payments are made with credit and debit cards, there are a number of new situations where other alternatives are making inroads (although they still tend to be linked to cards somewhere in the payment chain). One of these is the micropayment scenario discussed in the opening case. Another is in the mobile arena. Smartphones and other mobile devices are being used to make payments both online and offline. Over time, the mobile payments may actually end up on our phone bills, not on our credit card statements. Note that globally there are big differences in the way that e-payments are made. For an overview, see yStats.com (2014).

In this chapter, we discuss the evolution of e-payments in B2C and B2B and the increased importance of mobile devices for e-payments. The chapter also explores the players and processes associated with the various payment alternatives along with the underlying reasons why some have been widely adopted while others have not.

11.1   THE PAYMENT REVOLUTION

The year 2003 was a turning point in the use of cash, checks, and credit cards for in-store purchases. In that year, for the first time, the combined use of credit and debit cards exceeded the combined use of cash and checks in the U.S. Since then, debit and credit cards have accounted for over 50% of in-store payments, with cash and checks constituting the rest. This trend is continuing. The growth in the use of cards is correlated with the decline in the use of cash. In addition, in recent years, debit card use has been spurred by a change in the U.S. Electronic Funds Transfer Act, which eliminated the requirement for merchants to issue receipts for debit purchases of $15 or less. For a reflection on e-commerce in Europe (2013), see **www.ecommerce-europe.eu/news/reflecting-on-2013-e-payments**.

Similar trends have occurred in recurring bill payments. For example, in 2001, over 75% of all recurring bill payments were made by paper-based methods (e.g., paper checks), whereas less than 25% of these payments were made electronically. Today (2014), the percentage of recurring bills paid electronically is over 55% and growing.

For decades, people have been talking about a cashless society. Although the demise of cash and checks is certainly not imminent, many individuals can live without checks or cash. Today, almost 100% of online B2C payments are made electronically. Throughout developed countries, the vast majority of online purchases are made by using credit cards, although there are some countries where other payment methods prevail. For instance, consumers in Germany prefer to pay with either direct debit or bank cards, whereas Chinese consumers rely mainly on debit cards and making PayPal type arrangements. As will be described later, payments for e-commerce in developing countries are being made with new methods such as PayPal. For example, according to Zawya (2014), the Cairo Amman Bank is introducing PayPal services in Jordan to promote e-commerce.

For online B2C merchants, the implications of these trends are straightforward. In most countries, it is difficult to operate an online business without supporting credit and debit card payments, despite the costs. For merchants who are interested in international markets, there is a need to support a variety of e-payment mechanisms, including bank transfers, COD, electronic checks, private-label cards, gift cards, instant credit, and other non-card payment systems, such as PayPal. Merchants who offer multiple payment types have a higher percentage of conversion of clicks to purchases resulting in increased revenues.

The short history of e-payments is littered with the remains of companies that have attempted to introduce nontraditional payment systems. One of the more recent attempts is Bitcoin (**bitcoin.org**). Bitcoin is a peer-to-peer, encrypted digital currency powered by the company's special software. The currency is for simple use and only by its owner. To date, Bitcoin is used fairly extensively but it has some problems (see Section 11.8). Bitcoin may be used for micropayments in the future (see **ciondesk.com**). For details, see links at **weusecoins.com**. It takes years for any payment system to gain widespread acceptance. For example, credit cards were introduced in the 1950s but did not reach widespread use until the 1980s. A crucial element in the success of any e-payment method is the "chicken-and-egg" problem: How do you get sellers to adopt a payment method when there are few buyers using it? Further, how do you get buyers to adopt a method when there are few sellers using it?

The competition for e-payment systems is fierce (see Jing 2013). The success of any e-payment system depends on factors such as those listed below (based on Evans and Schmalensee (2005), Roth (2010), and the authors' experiences.

- **Independence.** Most forms of e-payment require the merchant to install specialized software and hardware to authorize and process a payment. Specialized methods may be cumbersome and costly.
- **Interoperability and portability.** An e-payment method must be integrated with existing information systems.
- **Security.** How safe is the money transfer? What if the money transfer is compromised? Only safe systems will succeed.
- **Anonymity.** Some buyers want their identities and purchase records to be anonymous. This can be done only when cash is used. To succeed, special payment methods, such as e-cash, have to maintain anonymity.
- **Divisibility.** Since most merchants accept credit cards only if the purchase price is over a certain amount, it is necessary for a successful EC transaction to address the issue of small payments.
- **Ease of use.** Credit cards are used for B2C and B2B e-payments because of their ease of use. E-payments must complement the trading methods.
- **Transaction fees.** When a credit card is used, the merchant pays processing fees. These fees make the use of credit cards for small payments cost prohibitive for the seller. Thus, a solution for a small amount of money is necessary.
- **International support.** EC is a worldwide phenomenon. An e-payment method must be easily adapted to fit buying needs and local legal requirements before it can be widely adopted.
- **Regulations.** A number of international, federal, and state regulations govern all payment methods. Any changes or new methods need approval of the regulators. PayPal, for instance, faced several lawsuits brought against them by several U.S. states for alleged violations of banking regulations.

The PayPal Alternative

While credit and debit cards dominate e-commerce payments, one alternative that has succeeded is PayPal (and its clones). PayPal was formed in the late 1990s from the merger of two small startup companies, Confinity and X.com. Their initial success came from providing a payment system that was used for eBay transactions (PayPal is now an eBay company). How did the system work? Essentially, eBay sellers and buyers opened up PayPal accounts that were secured by a bank or credit card account. At the completion of an auction, the payment transactions were conducted via the seller's and buyer's PayPal accounts. In this way, the bank or credit card accounts remained confidential. It is important to remember that in those days, buyers were often wary of revealing their credit card numbers online. For the seller, it also eliminated the transaction fees charged by the credit card companies, although PayPal eventually began charging similar, though somewhat lower, transaction fees.

Even though eBay had a payment system called Billpoint, PayPal became so successful that eBay eventually decided to close Billpoint and acquired PayPal in October 2002. For details see **news.cnet.com/eBay-picks-up-PayPal-for-1.5-billion/2100-1017_3-941964.html**.

Why was PayPal more successful than Billpoint? This is a tough question that has generated of multitude answers. PayPal had a better user interface, better marketing, a better mix of services, and is user friendly for both buyers and sellers. Regardless, neither Billpoint nor PayPal had to find the market of potential buyers and sellers; eBay had already done this. What Billpoint and PayPal had to do was convince eBay consumers and merchants to use their systems. PayPal was more successful than Billpoint.

As of December 2014, PayPal operates in 203 global markets and has 157 million active accounts (see **paypal-media.com/about and paypal-media.com/assets/pdf/fact_sheet/paypal_fastfacts_Q4_2013.pdf**). PayPal supports payments in 26 currencies. In 2013, their revenue was about $7 billion, half of which came from their global trading and approximately 65% of which was generated by their Merchant Services unit. PayPal's revenue figures increased about 26% in one year, representing close to 40% of eBay's total revenue. PayPal's overall success is the result of a three-phase approach to e-payments that has unfolded over time. First, they concentrated on expanding services provided to eBay users in the U.S. Next, they increased the size of their market by opening the system to eBay's international sites and users. Finally, they decided to build PayPal's operations to non-eBay businesses. One such initiative was a system designed to support person-to-person payments (the online equivalent of a wire transfer service between individuals). More importantly, in 2003 they created a new business unit called Merchant Services (serving e-commerce merchants) independent of the eBay community. The analysis of revenues reveals that the growth of PayPal's international business along with the growth of the Merchant Services unit is the reasons why PayPal continues to be so successful.

Over the years, PayPal has had a handful of competitors – none of which has posed a serious threat. Today, there is a new cast including:

- Google Wallet (formerly Google Checkout; **google.com/wallet**). The payment processing is incorporated in the user's Google Account. Note that Google Wallet is not accepted by eBay. Google Wallet allows you to shop and pay with your cell phone.
- Wirecard AG (**wirecard.com**). Wirecard AG offers cashless payment and other services on a one-stop basis as well as offering a vast range of e-commerce industries worldwide. This system competes with PayPal and Western Union.
- Skrill (formerly Moneybookers; **skrill.com**). Skrill is a British e- payment, storage, and money transfer system owned by Investcorp Technology Partners. Operationally, it is similar to PayPal. However, Skrill's transaction fees are lower. Skrill is not as popular as PayPal, but is a convenient electronic payment system to use with Forex brokers. It is also accepted on eBay.
- Popmoney (formerly ZashPay; **popmoney. com**). Popmoney (a subsidiary of Fiserv, Inc.)

is an online person-to-person payment service that allows people to send and receive money directly from their bank account using text messaging or e-mail.

For more on PayPal, see Valentine (2012).

Person-to-Person (P2P) Payments

A considerable number of EC transactions are conducted between individuals. Payments from unknown buyers are critical to the success of EC where transactions are conducted online and the participants are in different places and do not know each other. Additionally, money lending between individuals is becoming more popular, as discussed in Chapter 3.

The following are some of the methods used in P2P payments:

- Using PayPal (described earlier)
- Using prepaid cards
- Using the clearXchange (CXC) network (**clearxchange.com**). This network serves customers of participating banks (Wells Fargo and Bank of America as of 2014). Customers can transfer funds from their existing checking accounts directly to any other customer in any participating bank (see Valentine 2012)
- Using Bitcoin and other digital currencies

Digital Currencies

How much is a Linden Dollar worth in U.S. dollars? How about Farm Cash? What about a Mahalo Dollar? What are these things?

These are all examples of digital (or virtual) currencies. A **digital (virtual) currency** is a medium of payment that is electronically created, stored, and used in e-commerce. It can be used to pay for either physical goods or virtual ones. Some of the better known examples of virtual currencies include:

- *Linden Dollars.* Second Life is a virtual world. It has its own economy and in turn its own currency called the Linden Dollar (L$). The L$ can be used to pay for any transaction made in Second Life such as purchasing land or furniture. Services include wage labor, entertainment, custom content creation, and the like. The L\$ is purchased on the Second Life site.

- *Game Playing Currencies.* Most of the massively multiplayer online games (MMOGs) have their own virtual currencies. For example, FarmVille has Farm Cash, Habbo (previously Habbo Hotel) has Habbo Coins, Whyville has Pearls, and World of Warcraft has WOW Gold. In each case, the currency can be used to purchase whatever goods and services are pertinent to the specific game. Like L\$ and Facebook Payments, game currencies cost *real-world money*.
- *Bitcoin.* One of the most discussed global currencies is Bitcoin. It has both successes and problems. For a presentation of Bitcoin and other emerging digital currencies, see Section 11.8.

Unlike other forms of digital currencies, virtual currencies of this sort have managed to take hold primarily because of the tremendous growth experienced in social networks and social games. In both of these cases, virtual currencies represent a major source of revenue, especially in the social network and gaming worlds.

E-payments are classified depending upon their nature (prepaid, real time, and post-paid), protocols (credit, debit, check, and cash), size of payment (regular payment and micropayment), payment entities (individual and business), and platform (smart card and mobile payment). Finally, there are real world and virtual currencies. Virtual currencies are part of the coming currency revolution and its virtual social currency. For an overview, watch the video "The Coming Currency Revolution" (7:08 minutes) at **youtube.com/watch?v=ITKJoCLP9Z0**.

SECTION 11.1 QUESTIONS

1. What types of e-payments should B2C merchants support?
2. What is the "chicken-and-the-egg" problem in e-payments?
3. Describe the factors that are critical for an e-payment method to achieve critical mass.
4. What is PayPal? What business strategy did they use to build their payment services? Who are some of PayPal's current competitors?
5. What is a virtual currency? What are some examples?
6. What is virtual social currency? (Hint: watch the video "The Coming Currency Revolution" also check VEN Commerce Ltd. **ven.com**).

11.2 USING PAYMENT CARDS ONLINE

Payment cards are electronic cards that contain payment-related data. They come in three forms:

1. **Credit cards.** A credit card enables its holder to charge items (and pay later), or obtain cash up to the cardholder's authorized limit. With each purchase, the credit card holder receives a loan from the credit card issuers. Most credit cards do not have an annual fee. However, holders are charged interest if the balance is not paid in full by the due date. Several cards where you accumulate loyalty points (e.g., frequent flyer programs) charge annual fees. Visa, MasterCard, and American Express are prime examples of credit cards.
2. **Charge cards.** These are special credit cards where the balance must be paid in full by the due date and usually have annual fees. Examples of issuers are American Express and Diner's Club (they both offer regular credit cards as well).
3. **Debit cards.** Payments made with a debit card are withdrawn from the holder's checking or savings account. The actual transfer of funds usually takes place in real time from the holder's account (if an ATM card is used). However, a settlement to a merchant's checking account may take place within one to two days. MasterCard and Visa are examples of debit card issuers. For security risks of debit cards, see Bell (2011). For four places where not to use a debit card, see **usatoday.com/story/tech/columnist/komando/2014/04/11/4-places-you-should-not-swipe-your-debit-card/7436229**.

Processing Cards Online

The processing of credit card payments has two major phases: *authorization* and *settlement*. **Authorization** determines whether a buyer's card is valid (e.g., not expired) and whether the customer has sufficient credit or funds in his or her account. Authentication is the first step of authorization, as described in Chapter 10. **Settlement** involves the transfer of money from the buyer's account to the merchant's. The way in which these phases actually are performed varies somewhat depending on the type of payment card used. The settlement also varies by the configuration of the system used by the merchant to process payments.

The following are the processing options. The EC merchant may:

1. **Own the payment software.** A merchant can purchase a payment-processing module and integrate it with its other EC software. This module communicates with a payment gateway run by an acquiring bank or another third party.

2. **Use a point-of-sale (POS) system operated by a card acquirer.** Merchants can redirect cardholders to a POS system run by an acquirer. The POS handles the complete payment process and directs the cardholder back to the merchant's site once payment is complete. In this case, the merchant's system deals only with order information. In this configuration, it is important to find an acquirer that handles multiple cards and payment instruments. If not, the merchant will need to connect with a multitude of acquirers.

3. **Use a POS system operated by a payment service provider.** Merchants can rely on **payment service providers (PSPs)**, which are third-party companies that provide services to merchants so they can accept all kinds of electronic payments. The PSPs connect all participants in the electronic transactions. See an example at **usa.visa.com/download/merchants/new-payment-service-provider-model.pdf**.

Many point of sale terminals are becoming contactless. For example, in June 2013, MasterCard deployed 410,000 contactless terminals in Japan.

For any given type of payment card and processing system, the processes and participants are essentially the same for offline (card present) and online (card not present) purchases as depicted in Figure 11.1. The major parties in processing card payments online are:

- **Customer.** The individual possessing the card.
- **Merchant.** The vendor that sells goods or services.
- **Issuing bank.** The issuer (usually a bank) of the credit (debit) card to people (or businesses).
- **Acquiring bank.** The financial institution offering a special account called an *Internet Merchant Account* that enables payment authorization and processing.
- **Credit card association.** The financial institution providing card services to banks (e.g., Visa and MasterCard).
- **Payment service provider.** The company that provides electronic connections and transaction services among all the parties involved in electronic payments (including authorizations). A payment service provider is also called a *payment gateway provider.*

Table 11.1 compares the steps taken in making an online credit card purchase with the steps taken in making an offline purchase. As the table demonstrates, there is very little difference between the two.

Credit Card Reading

When paying with a credit card, it is necessary for merchants to read the content of the card and then transfer the content for approval and processing. This must be done in almost real time.

Several methods are available.

Figure 11.1 Credit card payment procedure (Drawn by J. K. Lee)

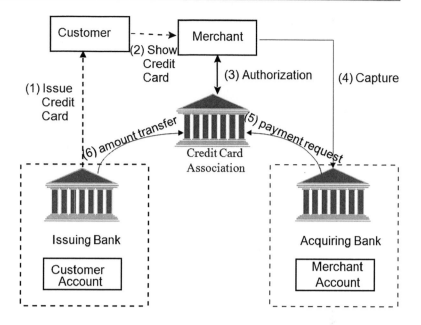

Fraudulent Card Transactions

- **Stationary card readers.** The most common readers available are physical POS in stores. They are wirelined to the authorization and processing system.
- **Portable card readers.** These are used in places where wirelines do not exist (e.g., on airplanes). They may be connected wirelessly to the processing system, or may be stand-alone systems (sellers then take risks, usually for small payments).
- **Mobile readers.** These systems enable payments from mobile devices. They include credit card readers, which are plugged in to the smartphones. The Square Reader (**squareup.com**), which has a "swiper" that plugs into the smartphone's headphone jack and reads the information from the magnetic strip of the customer's card, is such a device (see Section 11.6).
- **Image readers.** These new systems use smartphone scanning and imaging capabilities to read the cards, thus eliminating the need for a card reader (e.g., see Clancy 2012).

Although the processes used for authorizing and settling card payments offline and online are very similar, there is one substantial difference between the two. In e-commerce, the merchants usually are liable for fraudulent transactions. In addition to the cost of lost merchandise and shipping charges, merchants who accept fraudulent or unauthorized cards for payments may have to pay penalties to the credit card companies. However, these are not the only costs. There also are the costs associated with combating fraudulent transactions. These include the costs of tools and systems to review orders, the costs of manually reviewing orders, and the revenue that is lost from erroneously rejecting valid orders. According to CyberSource's twelfth annual survey of fraudulent online card transactions, online fraud results in a significant and growing expenditure for merchants (CyberSource 2011). However, since 2011, merchants have improved their fraud management systems (some are using 'CyberSource Fraud Management Solutions'). Over the years, the CyberSource surveys (CyberSource is a subsidiary of Visa) also have monitored the steps taken by merchants to combat fraud. The results show that relative to earlier years, merchants have

Table 11.1 Credit card purchases: online versus offline

Online purchase	Offline purchase
1. The *customer* decides to purchase a CD on the Web, adding it to the electronic shopping cart and going to the checkout page to enter his or her credit card information	1. The *customer* selects a CD to purchase, takes it to the checkout counter, and hands a credit card to the cashier
2. The *merchant's* site receives the customer's information and sends the transaction information to its *payment processing service (PPS)*	2. The *cashier* swipes the card and transfers the transaction information to a *point-of-sale (POS)* terminal (usually via a computer keyboard)
3. The PPS routes the information to the *processor* (a large data center for processing transactions and settling funds to the merchant)	3. The POS terminal routes the information to the card *processor* via wireline or other connection
4. The processor sends the information to the *bank* that issued that credit card	4. The processor transmits the credit card data and sales amount, requesting payment
5. The issuing bank either authorizes authorizing the payment or not	5. The issuing bank authorizes (or declines) the transaction
6. The processor routes the transaction result to the PPS	6. The processor sends the transaction code (if authorized) to the POS
7. The PPS passes the results to the merchant	7. The POS shows the outcome to the merchant
8. The merchant accepts or rejects the transaction	8. The merchant tells the customer the outcome of the transaction (i.e., you are approved or not)

Sources: Based on PayPal (2004) and Whitman (1996)

increased the number of fraud detection tools that they regularly use. The key tools used in combating fraud are:

> • **Certificate and Digital Signature**. *Certificates* are used for public key encryption; a *digital signature* is used for authentication that is the electronic equivalent of a personal signature, as described in Chapter 10. Some countries, such as Korea, require that all electronic financial transactions have both a digital certificate and a digital signature to enhance security.
>
> • **Address verification.** A vast majority of merchants use the **Address Verification System (AVS)**, which detects fraud by comparing the address provided by the buyer at checkout with the address on file. Unfortunately, this method may result in a number of false positives, meaning that the merchant may reject a valid order. Cardholders may have a new address or simply make mistakes in inputting numeric street addresses or zip codes. AVS is available only in the United States and Canada.
>
> • **Manual review.** Around 70% of all merchants use the manual review method, which relies on staff to manually review suspicious orders. For small merchants with a small volume of orders, this is a reasonable method. For larger merchants, this method does not scale well, is expensive, and influences customer satisfaction. Over the past few years, large merchants have begun to recognize the limitations of this method and have substantially reduced manually reviewed orders.
>
> • **Fraud screens and automated decision models.** Larger merchants (those generating over $25 million in revenue) often use fraud screens and automated decision models. These tools are based on automated rules that determine whether a transaction should be accepted, rejected, or suspended. A key element of

this method is the merchant's ability to change the rules easily in order to combat changing fraud methods used by criminals (see discussions in Chapters 10 and 15).

- **Card verification number (CVN).** More than 70% of all merchants use the **card verification number (CVN)** method, which detects fraud by matching the 3-digit verification number printed on the signature strip on the back of the credit card (or the 4-digit number on the front of the card, such as American Express cards) to the number stored by the cardholder's issuing bank. However, if a fraudster possesses a stolen card, the number is in plain view and verification becomes difficult. Attempts are made to check the habits of the card user (e.g., to check unusually large purchases or purchases made overseas). In such cases, a cardholder may get a telephone call from the card issuer or the credit card company, asking for verification of identity. In such a case, the verification may be done by intelligent software agents automatically.
- **Card association payer authentication services.** In the last couple of years, card companies have developed a new set of payer identification services (e.g., Verified by Visa and MasterCard SecureCode).
- **Negative lists.** Approximately half of all merchants use *negative lists*. According to "Understanding Credit Card Frauds" (**popcenter.org/problems/credit_card_fraud/PDFs/Bhatla.pdf**), a negative list is a database of card numbers that could potentially be used by fraudsters. It is also a database of card numbers used to avoid further fraud from repeat offenders. The merchants can match each customer's card against this database to find customers and cards with known problems.

The overall impact of these tools is that merchants are still rejecting a significant number of orders due to a suspicion of fraud. The problem with these rejection rates is that a number of the rejected orders are valid, resulting in lost revenue.

SECTION 11.2 REVIEW QUESTIONS

1. Describe the three types of payment cards.
2. What options does a merchant have in setting up an e-payment system?
3. Describe P2P payments.
4. List the major participants in processing cards online.
5. Describe credit card readers.
6. What costs does an online merchant incur if it accepts a fraudulent card transaction?
7. What steps are often taken by online merchants to combat fraudulent orders?

11.3 SMART CARDS

A **smart card** is a plastic payment card that contains data in an embedded microchip. The embedded chip can be a microprocessor combined with a memory chip or just a memory chip with nonprogrammable logic. Information on a microprocessor card can be added, deleted, or otherwise manipulated; a memory-chip card is usually a "read-only" card, similar to a magnetic stripe card. The card's programs and data must be downloaded from, and activated by, some other device (such as an ATM). The smart card can perform the multiple functions of a credit card, debit card, stored-value card (e.g., to pay for transportation and telephone calls), and various loyalty cards. It can also be used as a security and ID card.

In 2010, the global market for smart cards grew to record levels. Approximately 6 billion smart cards were shipped in 2010, as compared to 4 billion in 2008. In 2015, the number is expected to reach approximately 10 billion units. The biggest driver underlying the smart card growth is its application in the financial services market where smart cards are used mostly as credit and debit cards. The largest demand for smart cards continues to come from transportation cards in the Asia-Pacific region and Europe.

Types of Smart Cards

There are two distinct types of smart cards. The first type is a **contact card**, which is activated when it is inserted into a smart card reader. The second type of card is a **contactless (proximity) card**, meaning that the card only has to be within a certain proximity of a smart card reader to process a transaction. On the front or back of the contact smart cards there is a small gold (or silver) plate about one-half inch in diameter that contains a chip. When the card is inserted into the card reader, the plate makes electronic contact and data are transferred to and from the chip. A contactless card has an embedded antenna that facilitates data transfer to another antenna (e.g., attached to another device). Contactless cards are especially useful where data must be processed (e.g., paying toll road fees, bus or train fares) or when contact may be difficult. Most proximity cards work at short range (just a few inches). For some applications, such as payments at highway tollbooths, longer range proximity cards are available.

With both types of cards, *smart card readers* are crucial to the operation of the system. Technically speaking, a smart card reader is actually a read/write device. The primary purpose of the **smart card reader** is to act as a mediator between the card and the host system that stores application data and processes transactions. Just as there are two basic types of cards, there are two types of smart card readers – *contact* and *proximity* – that match the particular type of card. Smart card readers can be transparent, requiring a host device to operate, or stand alone, functioning independently. Smart card readers are a key element in determining the overall cost of a smart card application. Although the cost of a single reader is usually low, the cost can be quite high when they are used with a large population of users (e.g., passengers traveling on a metropolitan mass transit system).

Hybrid cards and *combi cards* combine the properties of contact and proximity cards into one card. A hybrid smart card has two separate chips embedded in a card: contact and contactless. In contrast, a combi card (dual-interface) smart card has a single chip that supports both types of interfaces. The benefit of either card is that it eliminates the need of carrying both contact and contactless cards to use with different applications. In addition, you need only one card reader.

Stored-Value Cards

The **stored-value card** is a card where a monetary value is prepaid and can be loaded on the card once or several times. From a physical and technical standpoint, a stored-value card is indistinguishable from a regular credit or debit card. In the past, the money value was stored on the magnetic strip, but recently, most stored-value cards use the technology of smart cards. With stored-value cards, the chip stores the prepaid value. Consumers can use stored-value cards to make purchases, offline or online, in the same way that they use credit and debit cards – relying on the same networks, encrypted communications, and electronic banking protocols. What is different about a stored-value card is there is no need for authorization, but there is a limit set by how much money is stored on the card. The most popular applications of stored-value cards are the transportation cards that are very popular in the large cities in Asia. It is a necessity for the citizens in Seoul, Hong Kong, and Singapore to hold smart cards that pay for subways, buses, taxis, and other applications. The transportation cards do not require any fees, but the bank that initiates prepaid cards may require fixed monthly fees or a registration fee. Stored-value cards are also popular to pay for telephone calls and texting.

Stored-value cards come in two varieties: *closed loop* (single purpose) and *open loop* (multiple purposes). Closed-loop cards are issued by a specific merchant or merchant group (e.g., a shopping mall) and can be used to make purchases only from the card issuer. Mall cards, refund cards, some toll-pay cards, prepaid telephone cards, and Internet use cards are all examples of closed-loop cards. Among closed-loop cards, gift cards have traditionally represented the largest growth area, especially in the United States. However, over the past few years, gift card purchases have been declining. In 2011, gift card spending rebounded to reach a five-year high, comprising close to 18% of total holiday expenditures.

An open-loop card is a multipurpose card that can be used for transactions at several retailers or service providers. Open-loop cards also can be used for other purposes, such as a prepaid debit card or for withdrawing cash from an ATM. Financial institutions with card-association branding, such as Visa or MasterCard®, issue some open-loop cards. They can be used anywhere that the branded cards are accepted. *Full open-loop cards* (e.g., the MasterCard Mondex® card) allow the transfer of money between cards without the bank's intervention.

Stored-value cards may be acquired in a variety of ways. Employers or government agencies may issue them as payroll cards or benefit cards in lieu of checks or direct deposits. Merchants or merchant groups sell and load gift cards. Various financial institutions and nonfinancial outlets sell prepaid cards by telephone, online, or in person. Cash, bank wire transfers, money orders, cashier's checks, other credit cards, or direct payroll or government deposits fund prepaid cards.

Stored-value cards have been, and continue to be, marketed heavily to people who do not use credit cards. Approximately 100 million adults in the United States do not have credit cards or bank accounts (2013) – low-income people or those who have declared bankruptcy, young adults, people with bad or no credit history, and others. Among those with credit cards, 40% are close to their credit limits. The expectation is that these groups will be major users of prepaid cards in the future.

Applications of Smart Cards

In many parts of the world, smart cards with magnetic stripes are used as credit cards for retail purchases and paying for transportation. They also are used to support nonretail and nonfinancial applications. A general discussion of all types of smart card applications can be found at **globalplatform.org**.

Retail Purchases

Credit card companies and financial institutions are transitioning their traditional credit and debit cards to multi-application smart cards. In many parts of the world, smart cards have reached mass-market adoption rates. This is especially true in Europe, where the goal was to have all bank cards be smart cards with strong authentication and digital signature capabilities by 2010.

In 2000, the European Commission established an initiative known as the Single Europe Payment Area (SEPA), encompassing 33 European countries. To bring this initiative to fruition, all the EU banks agreed to use the same basic bank card standard, enabling the use of credit and debit cards throughout the EU. The standard (EMV) is named after the four card associations that developed it (AmEx, MasterCard, JCB, and Visa). It is based on smart cards with a microprocessor chip. The chip is capable of storing not only financial information, but other applications as well, such as strong authentication and digital signatures. Originally, the 33 countries agreed to convert all their magnetic strip cards to EMV smart cards by December 2010. However, by the first quarter of 2011, only 40.1% of the total payment cards in circulation, 71% of the point of sale (POS) terminals globally, and 93% of ATMs had been converted (Capgemini 2010; Gemalto 2013).

One benefit of smart cards versus standard cards is that they are more secure. Because they are often used to store more valuable or sensitive information (e.g., cash or medical records), smart cards often are secured against theft, fraud, or misuse. In contrast, if someone steals a regular payment card, he (she) can see the card's number, the owner's signature, and the security code. In many cases only the card number and the security code are required to make a purchase. However, criminals can use the cards up to the authorized value, which is a loss to the bank and Visa or MasterCard.

On the other hand, if someone steals a smart card, the thief is usually out of luck (with the major exception of contactless, or "wave and go," cards used for retail purchases). Before the smart card can be used, the holder may be required to enter a PIN. The other benefit of smart cards versus standard payment cards is that they can be widened to include other payment services. In the retail arena, many of these services are aimed at those establishments where payments are usually made in cash, and speed and convenience are important. These include convenience stores, gas stations, fast food or quick-service restaurants, and cinemas. Contactless payments exemplify this sort of value-added service.

A few years ago, card companies began piloting contactless payment systems in retail operations where speed and convenience are crucial. All these systems utilize the existing POS and magnetic strip payment infrastructure used with traditional credit and debit cards. The only difference is that a special contactless smart card reader is required. To make a purchase, a cardholder simply waves his or her card near the terminal, and the terminal reads the financial information on the card. Despite their convenience and speed, the overall uptake of contactless payment cards in retail stores has been relatively slow, although the number is steadily increasing. For instance, in 2009, MasterCard issued around 66 million PayPass cards (over 100 million in 2013) that are EMV-compatible, supporting both magnetic strip and contactless payments. Again, it is the same "chicken-and-the-egg problem" facing any new payment system.

Transit Fares

In the U.S., several European countries, and large Japanese cities, commuters need to drive to a parking lot near a train station, board a train, and then change to one or more subways or buses to arrive at work. The entire trip may require several payments. Many major transit operators in the United States and Asia have introduced smart card fare-ticketing systems to help these commuters. The transit systems in Washington, D.C., Seoul, Hong Kong, San Francisco Bay area, Singapore and most other major cities all use

smart card payment systems. In addition to handling transit fares, the public transport smart cards and other e-payment systems (e.g., smartphones) are being used for paying parking fees and even for purchasing certain goods. For an example, see the Philadelphia Parking Authority (**philapark. org**). Similarly, many of the major toll roads in the United States and elsewhere accept electronic payments rendered by devices called *transponders* that operate much like contactless smart cards but from a much larger distance. Singapore's ERP (Electronic Road Pricing) system, shown in Figure 11.2, monitors the roads in downtown Singapore to control traffic, especially during rush hour, by using remote transponders in the car.

SECTION 11.3 REVIEW QUESTIONS

1. What is a smart card? Contact card? Contactless card?
2. What is a smart card operating system?
3. What is a closed-loop stored-value card? What is an open-loop card?
4. Identify the major markets for stored-value cards.
5. Describe the use of smart cards in metropolitan transportation systems.

11.4   MICROPAYMENTS

Micropayments or **e-micropayments** are small online payments made online, usually under $10. From the viewpoint of many vendors, credit cards are too expensive for processing small payments. The same is true for debit cards, where the fixed transaction fees are greater, even though there are no percentage charges. These fees are relatively small (in percentage) only for card purchases over $10. Regardless of the vendor's point of view, there is substantial evidence, at least in the offline world, that consumers are willing to use their credit or debit cards for small value purchases. In the online world, the evidence suggests that consumers are interested in making small-value purchases, but not with credit or debit card payments. For example, as noted in the opening case, Apple's iTunes music store celebrated its 20 billionth download in 2012.

Figure 11.2 Singapore electronic road pricing system (Source: Photo taken by J. K. Lee March 2013)

A substantial percentage of these were downloads of single songs at $1.29 apiece. Although most of iTunes' customers paid for these downloads with a credit or debit card, the payments were not on a per-transaction basis. Instead, iTunes customers created accounts and Apple then aggregated multiple purchases before charging a user's credit or debit card. Other areas where consumers have shown a willingness to purchase items under $5 using a credit card are cell phone ringtones, ring-back tones, and online games. The annual market for ringtones and ring-back tones is in the billions of dollars. The download of both types of tones is charged to the consumer's cell phone bill. Similarly, the annual market for online games is in the billions of dollars. Like songs and tones, downloading a game is usually charged to the consumer's account, which is paid by a credit or debit card.

Currently, there are five basic micropayment models that do not depend solely or directly on credit or debit cards, and that have enjoyed some amount of success. Some of these are better suited for offline payments than online payments, although there is nothing that precludes the application of any of the models to the online world.

The models include the following (based in part on D'Agostino 2006 and the authors' experiences):

- **Aggregation.** Payments from a single consumer are accumulated and processed periodically (e.g., once a month), or as a certain level is reached (e.g., $100). This model fits vendors with a high volume of repeat business. Both Apple's iTunes and App stores use this model. The transportation card used in Seoul, Korea and many other places is of this nature.
- **Direct payment.** In this case an aggregation is used but the micropayments are processed with an existing monthly bill (e.g., a mobile phone bill). Service providers of this type are PayOne (**pay-one.com**), M-coin (**mcoin.com**), and Boku (**boku.com**; formerly Paymo). Boku is a global company. For mobile micropayments, we note Zong (**zong.com**; a PayPal service), which is used

for social network games and virtual goods (e.g., Facebook, Habbo).

- **Stored value.** Funds are loaded into a debit account from which the money value of purchases is deducted when purchases are made. Offline vendors (e.g., Starbucks) use this model, and music-download services use variants of this model. This system is being used by several online gaming companies and social media sites.
- **Subscriptions.** A single payment (e.g., monthly) provides access to content. Online gaming companies and a number of online newspapers and journals (e.g., *Wall Street Journal*) often use this model.
- **À la carte.** Payments are made for transactions as they occur; volume discounts may be negotiated. This model is used in stock trading, such as at E-Trade.

In the past few years, micropayments have come to represent a growth opportunity for credit card companies, because credit cards are being used increasingly as a substitute for cash. In response, both Visa and MasterCard® have lowered their fees, especially for vendors with high transaction volumes, such as McDonald's. In August 2005, PayPal also entered the micropayment market when it announced an alternative fee structure of 5% plus 5¢ per transaction. This was economical only for micropayments. In the long run, credit card companies and PayPal will dominate this market. There are a number of new micropayment start-ups that are focused solely on social networks (e.g., **zong.com**).

SECTION 11.4 REVIEW QUESTIONS
1. What is a micropayment?
2. List some circumstances where micropayments can be used.

3. In addition to using credit or debit cards, what are some alternative ways that an online merchant can process micropayments?

11.5   E-CHECKING

As noted in Section 11.1, in the United States, the paper check is the only payment instrument that is being used less frequently today than several years ago (see Online File W11.1). The reason for this is the availability of paying over the Internet and with e-checks. An **electronic check (e-check)** is the electronic clone of a paper check (containing the same information). E-checks are a legal payment method in many countries. They work in a process similar to that of a paper check, but their processing is more efficient because several steps are automated. With an online e-check purchase, the buyer simply provides the merchant with his or her account number, the nine-digit bank ABA routing number, the bank account type (e.g., checking, savings, etc.), the name of the account holder, and the amount to be paid. The account number and routing number are provided as magnetic ink character recognition (MICR) numbers and characters.

E-checks rely on current business and banking practices and can be used by any business that has a checking account, including small and mid-size businesses that may not be able to afford other forms of electronic payments (e.g., credit and debit cards). E-checks or their equivalents also can be used with in-person purchases. In this case, the merchant takes a paper check from the buyer at the point of purchase, uses the MICR information and the check number to complete the transaction, and then voids and returns the check to the buyer.

Most businesses rely on third-party software to handle e-check payments. Fiserv (**fiserv.com**), Chase Paymentech (**chasepaymentech.com**), and Authorize.Net (**authorize.net**) are some of the major vendors of software and systems that enable an online merchant to accept and process e- checks directly from a website. For the most part, these software offerings work in the same way regardless of the vendor. For details, see

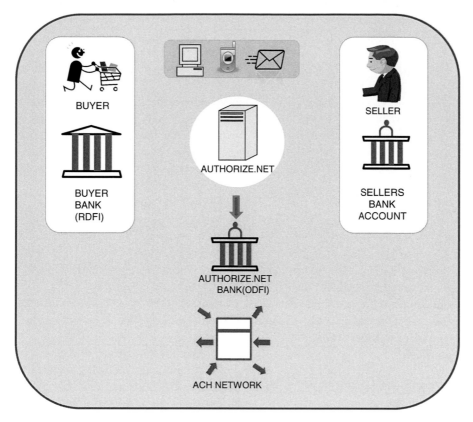

Figure 11.3   Processing e-checks with authorize.net (Drawn by J. K. Lee)

support.quickbooks.intuit.com/support/arti-cles/how16416.

The system shown in Figure 11.3 is based on Authorize.Net and is typical of the underlying processes used to support e-checks. It is a seven-step process.

(Step 1) First, the merchant receives authorization from a customer to charge his or her bank account, including the amount.

(Step 2) Next, the merchant securely transmits the above information to the Authorize.Net Payment Gateway server.

(Step 3) If the transaction is authorized, then its information is sent as an ACH transaction to the Originating Depository Financial Institution (ODFI).

(Step 4) From there, this information is passed to the Automated Clearing House (ACH) Network for settlement. The ACH Network identifies the government institution that governs the customer's bank account (known as the Receiving Depository Financial Institution (RDFI).

(Step 5) The ACH Network instructs the RDFI what to transact. Then, the RDFI transfers money from the customer's account to the ACH Network.

(Step 6) The money transfer authorization goes to the ACH and to the ODFI, and then to Authorize.Net.

(Step 7) The merchant's account is now credited.

As the figure illustrates, the processing of e-checks in the United States relies quite heavily on the **Automated Clearing House (ACH) Network**. According to the U.S. Government Accountability Office (**gao.gov**), the ACH Network is a processor of paper checks by converting them to electronic format via the government's electronic funds transfer (EFT) system (see **fms.treas.gov/ach/index.html**).

E-check processing provides a number of benefits:

> - It expedites the checkout time during shopping.
> - It reduces the merchant's processing costs.
> - Merchants receive funds more quickly.
> - It is more secure than a paper system with less probability of fraud.
> - It reduces the processing time of bounced checks.
> - There are fewer errors.

In 2014, an electronic services provider called MyECheck, Inc. (**myecheck.com**) launched a G2G payment platform for real-time transfers between government accounts (see **pymnts. com/news/2014/myecheck-launches-g2g-payments-platform**).

SECTION 11.5 REVIEW QUESTIONS

1. What is an e-check?
2. Briefly describe how third-party e-check payment systems work.
3. What is the ACH?
4. List the benefits of e-checking.

11.6   MOBILE PAYMENTS

The term **mobile payment** refers to payment transactions initiated or confirmed using a person's mobile device, usually a smartphone. Mobile payments are replacing some traditional nonelectronic payment methods, such as the purchasing of products (services), money transfers, bill payments, and proximity purchases (see Fishman, Part I 2014a).

Among wireless carriers, smartphone vendors, and mobile operators, there is a strong belief that mobile payments will emerge as a primary way to pay, potentially eliminating dependence on credit and debit cards, as well as cash. A study by *Juniper Research* (2008) supports this belief. The study estimated that the value of mobile payments will reach approximately $670 billion by 2015, which is about a 45% increase from the previous

estimate for 2013. While the bulk of the market involves the sale of digital goods (e.g., music, tickets, and games), the growth of mobile payments for physical goods is strong and will reach $170 billion by 2015. The rapid growth in mobile payments is the result of the increased use of smartphones, the increased usage and availability of apps, the increasing use of mobile payments for railway and other transportation tickets, and the increase in online shopping at webstores such as Amazon Mobile apps.

Overall, the study concluded that:
- Mobile payments are used extensively in East Asia, Africa, China, Western Europe, and North America.
- In 2015, digital goods may account for about 70% of mobile payments.
- Greater collaboration among involved stakeholders is needed to assure even greater success.

Mobile payments come with a variety of features and methods, including mobile proximity, remote, and POS payments. Each of these is described in the sections that follow.

Mobile Proximity Payments

Mobile proximity payments are used for making purchases in physical stores, vending machines, transportation services, and much more. Proximity payments are frequently done via mobile phones equipped with an integrated chip or a smartcard, a specialized reader that recognizes the chip when the chip comes within a short distance from the reader, and a network for handling the payment. Essentially, a buyer waves the specially equipped mobile phone near a reader to initiate a payment. For this reason, proximity payments are also called *contactless payments*. Rarely is additional authentication (e.g., a PIN) required to complete a contactless transaction. The payments are accumulated and debited to a mobile phone monthly account, or charged to a debit card account. Such payments are made from a **mobile (digital) wallet**, an electronic account, such as Google Wallet, which enables payments as well as processing loyalty programs and performing target promotions all from one mobile device.

The Near Field Communication Standards

Over the years, a number of protocols and technologies have been proposed to support proximity payments (e.g., from mobile devices). Currently, the most promising protocol is *Near Field Communication* (NFC). It is used in a number of non-payment, contactless applications (e.g., access control to buildings or secured rooms, paying toll fees without stopping). Estimates indicate the usage of NFC for proximity payments will increase rapidly in the next few years, going from $50 billion in 2014 to $670 billion in 2015 (e.g., estimates found at **thefonecast.com/News/tabid/62/ArticleID/4337/ArtMID/541/Default.aspx**). For details, see **nearfieldcommunication.org**.

While there seems to be an agreement among many firms and organizations that NFC will play a major role in the future of EC mobile payments, there is still disagreement about the specific handsets, chips, readers, and networks to be used. At the moment, only a few of these NFC participants seem to be in agreement on a standard. Instead, various players have introduced their own proprietary systems which are being field tested in a number of pilot programs. The following describes two of these attempts:

1. *Google Wallet* (**google.com/wallet**). Google Wallet is an application that lets a mobile device be used for payments. It was launched to the public in September 2011. It stores digital versions of credit and loyalty cards. In 2013, Google Wallet had a fixed set of operational partners (Sprint, Citibank, MasterCard, and FirstData), and was available only on the Sprint Nexus S 4 G handset, supporting two credit cards (Citibank MasterCard and Google Prepaid cards). Currently, it only works with one reader (MasterCard PayPass terminals). However, the fact that it works with PayPass means that it is accepted by many PayPass merchants (e.g. McDonald's, CVS Pharmacy, and Best Buy). Eventually, Google plans to expand the partnership so that other companies can participate. Square Wallet (**squareup.com/wallet**) performs similar functions. For more on Google Wallet, see Fishman, Part I (2014a).

2. *ISIS* (**paywithisis.com**). According to *Business Wire* (2011), in November 2010, three of the major U.S. wireless service providers, namely, AT&T, T-Mobile USA, and Verizon Wireless joined forces to build a nationwide mobile commerce network, called Isis, using NFC technology. Its major function is to support electronic payments. The Isis system works with major U.S. card issuers, financial institutions, and merchants offering them NFC-based services. Tests were conducted in Salt Lake City and in Austin. The ISIS mobile payment system was released in 2012. For more information, see *Business Wire* (2011).

The Bluetooth Low Energy

Bluetooth low energy (BLE) wireless technology, marketed as Bluetooth Smart, is an alternative to NFC. A comparison between the two is provided in an infographic by Fishman, Part II (2014b) along 16 dimensions. For more about Bluetooth Smart technology, see **bluetooth.com/pages/bluetooth-smart.aspx**.

Mobile Remote Payments

A number of initiatives have been launched to support mobile remote payments. In addition to Internet shopping, these initiatives offer services that enable clients and consumers to use their mobile devices to pay their monthly bills, transfer funds to other individuals (P2P payments), and add money to their prepaid mobile accounts without having to purchase prepaid phone cards.

Example: M-Pesa in Kenya

While Google Wallet and similar systems in the U.S. are growing slowly, M-Pesa in Kenya is used by about of 19 million out of a population of 44 million. The system is used to pay micro-loans and to transfer money from urban to rural centers. The receivers can use M-Pesa to buy products and services, thus eliminating cash. In a developing country where only 40% of the population have bank accounts, a mobile service of this nature is extremely useful and revolutionary. The system is now replicated by other developing countries. For details see Fishman, Part I (2014a).

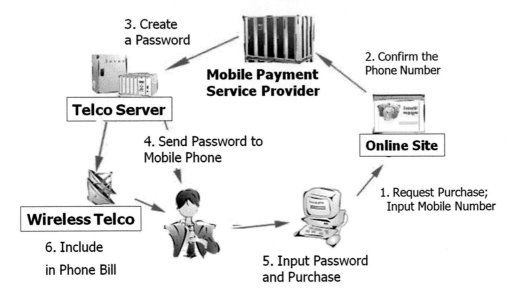

Figure 11.4 Process of mobile payment service (Drawn by J. K. Lee)

Online File W11.2 provides an example of how remote mobile payments are being used in developing countries like India to service loans to those on the economic margins of the country.

Often, because of the need to support the lowest common denominator cell phones, SMS text messaging has been used to handle these tasks. Prior to starting transactions, the customer needs to establish an account with a mobile payment service provider such as Boku or Gamalto that handles the payment transaction for the merchant. The following six steps demonstrated in Figure 11.4 show how a customer can pay a bill using SMS.

1. To make the payment, the merchant's website requests the customer's mobile phone number.
2. The merchant sends a text message to the managed service provider (MPSP) that includes the dollar amount, phone number, and the merchant's account number.
3. The MPSP receives the information, and sends a message to the mobile telecommunication company requesting that a one-time password be created.

4. The mobile telecommunication company sends the password to the customer.
5. The customer inputs the password to authenticate himself.
6. The telecommunication company includes the fee in the next month's phone bill.

If the online shopping takes place on mobile phones, as illustrated in the Crutchfield case (Case 11.1), companies may count on a third party mobile payment service such as PayPal Mobile Express Checkout (**paypal.com/us/webapps/mpp/mobile-checkout**).

CASE 11.1: EC APPLICATION: CRUTCHFIELD GOES MOBILE

The Problem

Crutchfield Corporation (**crutchfield.com**) is a successful consumer electronics retailer headquartered in Virginia. They began in 1974 as a print "magalog" – a cross between a magazine and a catalog (see **books.infotoday.com/books/casinwitcon/sample.pdf**). What distinguished their catalog from others was the inclusion of information designed to educate potential buyers.

Cruthchfield sells a wide range of electronic products – televisions, digital cameras, stereo equipment, and the like. It is a multichannel retailer providing sales and service through their mail order catalog, call centers, and their website that includes live chat. Crutchfield has won BizRate's "Circle of Excellence Platinum" award for fourteen consecutive years (**twice.com/articletype/news/crutchfield-earns-top-bizrate-honors-again/108515**).

Crutchfield recognized the growing importance of mobile technology as new sales and service channels. Goldman Sachs' March 2014 forecast $626 billion in sales by 2018 would be accounted for by mobile online shopping globally. This number represents about 98% of the total of mobile shopping in 2013 (reported by Severt 2014). Crutchfield concluded that they needed a payment solution that was built specifically for mobile transactions and could run on a variety of mobile devices. In addition, the solution needed to support their Canadian call center and the Web, as well as servicing other international buyers outside the U.S. and Canada and could be implemented quickly.

The Solution

As noted earlier, most e-payments are made with credit and debit cards. This is true for both non-mobile and mobile purchases. However, the number of steps and the total amount of information required to complete a card transaction with a mobile device can be a bit more because of the smaller design and the time delay in mobile responses. For this reason, Crutchfield decided to implement an alternative solution that could support a range of mobile devices. They chose PayPal Mobile Express Checkout.

In October 2010, PayPal introduced their Mobile Express Checkout system (**paypal.com/us/webapps/mpp/mobile-checkout**), which is a mobile version of their Express Checkout service. Before the introduction, they had approximately 5 million members using mobile devices to place orders. It was a cumbersome process

requiring a number of steps. They tried to simplify the process with a pay-by-text service, but were unsuccessful. The Express Checkout is a comprehensive, streamlined, and highly secure service that expedites checkouts.

Crutchfield decided to employ Usablenet Inc. (**usablenet.com**), which built Crutchfield's mobile site, to help integrate Mobile Express Checkout with their existing website. Usablenet has over 400 clients worldwide, and has been named by *Fast Company* magazine as one of the top 10 innovative companies in mobile computing. They have lived up to their billing. They took only two weeks to get the system up and running, just in time for the holiday season.

The Results

Crutchfield's ROI from their new mobile system was substantial. First, testing revealed that the Mobile Express system increased conversion by 33.7%. In this case, conversion refers to the number of unique visitors to a site who actually made a purchase. More importantly, testing also revealed that 65% of the PayPal mobile users were new to Crutchfield. Not only did the system result in improved sales, but it also attracted new customers. (The case study is available at **paypalobjects.com/webstatic/mktg/docs/Crutchfield_case_study.pdf**.)

Sources: Based on Severt (2014), O'Dell (2010), Hachman (2010), Hamblen (2011), and McMillian (2011).

Questions
1. Why was Crutchfield interested in implementing a mobile payment solution?
2. What solution did Crutchfield select?
3. What were the outcomes of the mobile payment implementation?

Mobile Payment Participants and Issues

The major participants in mobile payments as shown in Figure 11.4 are: The *shoppers*, the *sellers*, the *network operators* (wireless Telco and

Telco servers), and the *financial institutions* (mobile payment service providers). To successfully implement mobile payments, it is necessary to overcome the following issues:

For Buyer: Security (fraud protection), privacy, ease of use, choice of mobile device.

For Seller: Security (getting paid on time), low cost of operations, adoption by sufficient number of users, improved speed of transactions.

For Network Operator: Availability of open standards, cost of operation, inter-operability, and flexibility and roaming.

For Financial Institutions: Fraud protection and reduction, security (authentication, integrity, non-repudiation; see Chapter 10), and reputation.

Mobile POS Payments

Similar steps are used to enable merchants or service providers the opportunity to conduct POS transactions without the need for special POS terminals. These payments have been labeled *mobile POS* (*mPOS*) transactions. With mPOS transactions, the merchant utilizes a special mobile service to send a payment request to the customer's mobile device. Once the request is received, the customer enters his or her PIN. At this point, the service sends a confirmation to both the merchant and the customer. The transactions are completed by debiting the customer's account and crediting the merchant's account. The cost to the merchant is substantially less than a POS credit card–based transaction. These services are aimed at small businesses and independent operators such as doctors, dentists, delivery companies, taxis, and repair people.

Innovative POS Mobile Payments Systems

E-payments in physical stores and other places (e.g., taxis) are improving with time. Several methods exist and several companies are competing in this growing field. Here are some examples:

Example: Carmen's Best Ice Cream (carmensbest.com)

This small business in the Philippines became successful due to a mobile POS that allows it to move payments to its suppliers faster and at significantly less cost. It also collects money from its business buyers faster and less expensively. The mPOS is managed by Globe Telecom. The system uses a smartphone attached to a credit card reader. For details see Estopace (2014).

Example: Square (squareup.com)

Square Inc. developed a mobile *card reader* that enables merchants to accept payments made with credit cards by using a card reader attached to a smartphone or a tablet. The credit card is inserted into the reader for processing by the company. Square charges less than Visa and other card processors, and promises next day deposit into the merchant's account.

The merchants get a free reader and the customer gets the free Square Wallet smartphone application (**squareup.com/wallet**). For example, Square partnered with Whole Foods in 2014 to make shopping easier for customers at the coffee, juice, wine and beer bar in-store venues. The iPad-based checkout system enables cashiers to swipe the customers' credit cards using Square Wallet (which is connected to customers' credit cards system). The system reads the QR-code and deducts the money from the customer's account. For more about the partnership, see **media.wholefoodsmarket.com/news/square-and-whole-foods-market-partner-to-create-faster-easier-payment-and-c**.

The reader is distributed at **squareup.com**. Users input the payment amount, swipe the credit card through the reader, sign, and receive a receipt on their mobile phone or tablet. The Square Card Reader is used by major vendors such as AT&T, Walgreens, FedEx Office, and Walmart. Square Readers are provided for free. For more details, see Chen (2013) and the description in the Starbucks case in Chapter 1.

Example: PayPal's Card Reader

PayPal offers a similar device called PayPal Here™ (**paypal.com/webapps/mpp/credit-card-reader**) that works with PayPal's processing system. The company charges a 2.7% transaction fee (in the U.S.) compared to Square's 2.75% (and

3% or more charged by traditional credit card companies). PayPal allows merchants to accept payments, including credit card payments, on their website or on eBay. For details, see **paypalbusinesscenter.com** and **paypal.com/webapps/mpp/merchant**. Note: Several other companies offer similar services. Examples are Brain Tree Payments (**braintreepayments.com**; a division of PayPal, Inc.), Bank of America Mobile Pay on Demand (**mobilepay.bankofamerica.com/bams/mobilepay/home.html**), Intuit Payments (**payments.intuit.com/**), Phone Swipe (**phoneswipe.com**) and Capital One Spark Pay (**sparkpay.com**).

MasterPass™: Automating the Shopping and Payment Processes

When you buy at Amazon.com you can use the 1-Click system that stores all your necessary data, including a credit card number and shipping address; therefore, you can complete a transaction easily and quickly. A similar concept has been developed by MasterCard® in their *MasterPass™* innovation. The basic idea is to streamline the entire shopping process using mobile devices.

MasterPass™ in an extension of the PayPass Wallet service that is provided by MasterCard® as a checkout system to several hundred thousand merchants. The system enables customers easy and fast shopping from any Internet connected mobile devices, using the PayPass NFC terminals at participating merchants, or clicking on a button for an online purchase. MasterPass™ allows you to go one step further. For example, you can scan a product barcode with your smartphone in a store, show your smartphone receipt at the checkout and take the item with you or request shipment to your home. Alternatively, you can shop online in a similar manner as you would on Amazon.com. MasterPass™ also works with Quick Response (QR) codes and tags.

Eliminating Credit Cards

MasterPass is an example of an effort to eliminate the use of physical credit cards for payments.

Participating merchants can accept any major credit or debit card as well as prepaid cards (stored value) for payments. Therefore, there is no need to swipe a credit card—just use your mobile device. There are many possible applications. Imagine you are in a store and like a product but your size is not available. You can click to pay and the store will ship the right size to you, or you can be transferred to the manufacturer's site to complete the purchase. For more details, see Bonnington (2013), Trinh (2013), and MasterCard® (2013).

Innovative Social Commerce Payments

In Chapter 7, we introduced several social commerce models. Here are few examples of related innovative systems for mobile payment readers.

Groupon Breadcrumb (Formerly Groupon Payments)

Breadcrumb by Groupon (**breadcrumb.groupon.com/payments**) is a POS app for businesses. Breadcrumb Payments offers a mobile credit card reader, which is attached to an iPhone or other mobile device. To compete with similar companies, Groupon offers lower processing rates to Groupon's partners. The system is available to other merchants, but at higher processing fees. For details, see Boorstin (2012) and Purewal (2012).

Placecast

Placecast (**placecast.net**) is a pioneer in location-based marketing. According to their website, Placecast's *Card-Linked ShopAlerts* service (**shopalerts.com**) is a mobile management monetization solution that sends offers from participating merchants to customers. Offers are delivered via mobile devices by a location-based service. When customers receive an offer in a targeted area, they can redeem it by making their purchase, swiping their linked card at the store, and receiving the discount on their bank statement (see Rao 2012 and **placecast.net/press/releases/PR_card_linked_offers.pdf** for details). A related product by Placecast is *ShopAlerts Wallet*; see Lunden (2012) and **placecast.net/shopalerts/payments.html** for details.

Apple and Mobile Payment Processing

In early 2014, there were continuous rumors that Apple was going to enter the mobile payment market. For a discussion on this speculation and Apple's strategic advantages, see LowRiskValue (2014). In late 2014 Apple introduced its Apple Pay system.

SECTION 11.6 REVIEW QUESTIONS

1. Discuss proximity-based wireless payments. What is NFC? Give some examples of where it is used.
2. What are the basic processes used in handling SMS mobile remote payments?
3. How can the Square Card Reader process credit card transactions via smartphones?
4. How does MasterPass™ work? What are its advantages?

11.7   B2B AND INTERNATIONAL ELECTRONIC PAYMENTS

B2B payments usually are much larger and significantly more complex than payments made by individual consumers. The dollar values often are in the hundreds of thousands, the purchases and payments involve multiple items and shipments, and the exchanges are much more likely to create disputes that require significant work to resolve. Simple e-billing or EBPP (i.e., electronic bill presentment and payment) systems lack the precision and security to handle these B2B situations. This section examines the processes of EBPP.

B2B Payment Practices in the Financial Supply Chain

B2B payments are part of a company's financial supply chain that includes procurement, contract administration, fulfillment, financing, insurance, credit ratings, shipment validation, order matching, payment authorization, remittance matching, and general ledger accounting. Unlike the larger (physical) supply chains, inefficiencies still characterize the financial supply chains of many companies. A number of factors create these inefficiencies, including:

- The need for tight security
- The time needed for handling the necessary paper documents
- The supply chain segments may not work together in an efficient manner
- There are too many human errors that result in disputes
- The need for reconciliation of documents
- The lack of transparency of cash flow when goods are in transit

These inefficiencies are evident especially with A/P (accounts payable) and A/R (accounts receivable) processes where payments are still made with paper.

The world of B2B payments continues to be slow to change. A large portion of B2B payments are still made by paper checks and the barriers to electronic payments remain essentially the same. However, there is increasing evidence that companies are beginning to move to B2B e-payments. For example, according to NACHA, in 2013, the number of B2B transactions on the ACH network grew to almost 22 billion, an increase of 4% over 2012 volume. This rate continues at about the same level (see **nacha.org/news/ach-volume-grows-nearly-22-billion-payments-2013**).

Enterprise Invoice Presentment and Payment

The procedures and processes by which companies present invoices and get paid for these invoices over the Internet is known as **Electronic Invoice Presentment and Payment (EIPP)**. For many firms, presentment and payment used to be costly and time consuming. This means that millions of dollars of B2B were tied up in floats. This reduces the recipients' cash flow and increases the amount they must borrow to cover the float. In the same vein, manual billing and remittance can result in errors, which in turn can result in disputes that delay payments. In electronic systems, the cost is much lower and the transfer is faster. Given that most firms handle thousands of invoices and payments yearly, any reduction in time, cost, or errors can result in millions of dollars in savings. Improved cash flow, customer service, and data quality, along with reduced processing costs, are the primary reasons companies turn to EIPP.

The EIPP Models

EIPP automates the workflow surrounding presentment and payment. Like EBPP, there are three EIPP models: seller direct, buyer direct, and consolidator.

Seller Direct

This solution electronically links one seller to many buyers for invoice presentment. Buyers sign up for the seller's EIPP program. The seller posts the invoices and informs the buyers when the invoices are ready to view on its website. The buyers review and analyze the invoices. The buyers may authorize invoice payment or communicate any disputes to the sellers. Once payment is authorized and made, the seller's account is credited.

Buyer Direct

In this model, there is one buyer for many sellers. Sellers enroll in the buyer's EIPP system. Sellers generate invoices and post them at the buyer's EIPP. Once an invoice is posted, the buyer's staff is notified. The buyer checks and approves (or rejects) the invoices. Once an invoice is approved, the buyer authorizes payment, which the buyer's financial institution processes. Companies such as Walmart are in a strong position to institute buyer-direct EIPPs.

Consolidator

This is a many-to-many model with an intermediary consolidator. Consolidators generally are third parties who not only provide EIPP services but also offer other financial services (e.g., insurance, escrow). In this model, the sellers and buyers register with the consolidator's EIPP system. The sellers generate and transfer invoice information to the EIPP system. The consolidator notifies buyers when to inspect a bill. Then, the buyers can view the bills. Once a buyer authorizes the invoice payment, the consolidator arranges for payment.

The consolidator model eliminates the hassles associated with implementing and running an EIPP. The model has been adopted in those industries where multiple buyers rely on the same suppliers. The Global eXchange Services (GXS) Trading Grid (**gxs.com**), which is now operating under the name of Open Text, is an example of a third-party consolidator linking thousands of suppliers and buyers. GXS's Trading Grid supported online trading for 40,000 customers in over 20 countries in 2013. This network eliminates the need for point-to-point connections between suppliers and buyers, and automates most of the administrative tasks. Finally, the GXS network complements and integrates the suppliers' and buyers' existing purchasing and procurement systems. In addition, Paymode-X (**paymode-x.com**) provides a settlement network for global payment that enables electronic invoicing and payment, and PAY.ON (**payon.com**) and Syncada (**usbpayment.com/syncada**; now a part of U.S. Bank Payments Group) provide global payment networks respectively. Sage Exchange (**sageexchange.com**) provides a mobile payment portal for small businesses when they have multiple physical locations that accept credit and debit card payments. See Sage Software (**na. sage.com**) for details.

EIPP Options

A variety of online options are available for making payments in an EIPP system. They differ in terms of cost, speed, accessibility, and control. The selection of a particular mechanism depends on the requirements of the buyers and sellers. Some frequently used B2B payment options follow.

ACH Network

The Automated Clearing House (ACH) Network is the same network that underlies the processing of e-checks (described in Section "The Information Assurance Model and Defense Strategy" in Chapter 10). The difference is that there are three types of B2B payments that vary by the amount of remittance information that accompanies the payments. The remittance information enables a buyer or seller to examine the details of a particular invoice or payment. The three types of ACH entries for B2B transactions are: (1) Cash Concentration and Disbursement (CCD), which is a simple payment, usually for a single invoice that has no accompanying remittance data and typically is initiated by the buyer, who credits the seller's account; (2) CCD + (which is CCD with a small amount of remittance data, called Addenda); and (3) Corporate Trade Exchange (CTX), for paying multiple invoices.

The ACH Network does not require any special hardware. The cost of the software needed to initiate ACH transactions depends on the volume of CTX transactions. In addition to hardware and software costs, the buyer's and the seller's financial institutions charge handling fees for ACH transactions.

Purchasing Cards

While credit cards are the most popular for B2C payments, this is not the case in the B2B marketplace. In the B2B marketplace, the major credit card companies and associations have encouraged businesses and government agencies to rely on *purchasing cards*, instead of checks, for repetitive, low-value transactions. **Purchasing cards (p-cards)** are payment cards issued to a company's employees. They are used to pay for unexpected purchases of goods and services, usually MROs (e.g., stationery, office supplies, and computer supplies) up to a certain limit (usually $1,000–$5,000). These purchases often represent the majority of a company's payment transactions, but only a small percentage of the dollars spent. Purchasing cards are similar to regular credit cards and are used for both offline and online purchases. The major difference between a credit card and a purchasing card is that the latter is a non-revolving account, meaning that it needs to be paid in full each month, usually within five days of the end of the billing cycle. For additional information, see **purchsinginsight.com/resources/what-is/what-is-a-purchasing-card**.

Purchasing cards enable a company or government agency to consolidate the purchases of multiple cardholders into a single account and, thus, issue a single invoice that can be paid through EDI, EFT, or an e-check (e.g., authorization, placing the orders). This has the benefit of freeing the purchasing department from day-to-day procurement activities and from the need to manage the reconciliation of individual invoices. With a single invoice, accounts can be settled more quickly, enabling a company or agency to take advantage of discounts associated with faster payments and large volumes. A single invoice also enables a company or agency to more easily analyze the spending behavior of its cardholders. Finally, the spending limits make it easier to control unexpected purchases. Some estimates suggest that benefits resulting from the use of purchasing cards can reduce transaction costs by 50 to 90%. To learn more about purchasing cards, see the National Association of Purchasing Card Professionals (**napcp.org**).

Fedwire or Wire Transfer

Among the forms of online B2B payments, Fedwire (**frbservices.org/fedwire/index.html**) is second only to ACH in terms of frequency of use. Fedwire, or wire transfer, is a U.S. government (Federal Reserve Bank Services) funds transfer system. It typically is used with larger dollar payments and/or where time is a critical element. The settlement of real estate transactions, the purchase of securities, and the repayment of loans are all examples of situations where Fedwire is likely to be used. All Fedwire payments are immediate and irrevocable. For more information about Fedwire Funds Services, see **federalreserve.gov/payment systems/fedfunds_about.htm.**

International Payments

Cross border payments, both B2C and B2B, can be complicated due to country-specific regulations, import/export requirements, and global attempts to control money laundering. Several of the methods cited earlier can be used for global payments. Another common method is letters of credit.

Letters of Credit for Global Payments

Letters of credit often are used in global B2B trading. A **letter of credit (L/C)**, also known as a *documentary credit*, is issued by one bank to another bank (usually in another country) on behalf of a buyer (e.g., importer). It guarantees a seller (e.g., exporter) that sufficient payment for goods or services will be made on time, provided the conditions of the L/C are met by the exporter. L/C arrangements usually involve a series of steps that can be conducted much faster online than offline.

For sellers, the main benefit of an L/C is reduced risk – the bank assures the creditworthiness of the buyer. For those global situations where the buyer is a resident in a country with political or financial instability, the risk can be reduced if the L/C is confirmed by a bank in the seller's country. Reduced risk also is beneficial to buyers.

Digital River's World Payment

Digital River Inc. (**digitalriver.com**) partnered with Meridian Global Services (**meridianglobalservices.us**; a company that provides merchants with international value-added tax (VAT) and Travel and Expense compliance and consulting services) to offer a comprehensive payment service. The combined service enables buyers to use locally preferred payment methods. The partnership offers online merchants about 170 types of transactions in more than 180 international and local payment options. Small and medium companies that do not have personnel who specialize in global payments may find this service especially helpful.

SECTION 11.7 REVIEW QUESTIONS

1. Describe the financial supply chain.
2. Describe the current state of B2B e-payments.
3. What is Electronic Invoice Presentment and Payment (EIPP)?
4. Describe the three models of EIPP.
5. Describe the basic EIPP options.
6. What is a purchasing card?

11.8 EMERGING EC PAYMENT SYSTEMS AND ISSUES

In this section we present several emerging systems, starting with Bitcoin.

Bitcoin: Ups and Downs, but Alive

Earlier, we described Bitcoin briefly and described how it was hacked (Chapter 10). **Bitcoin** is a digital currency managed by a group of individuals and companies who own the computing power and process (called mining) of creating Bitcoins. The individuals and companies who are known as "miners" verify and record transactions in a public ledger, assuring the credibility of the currency.

Bitcoin is very secure, protected by the two key encryption method described in Chapter 10 (public and private keys; the private key is used to authorize transactions).

Here are some facts about Bitcoin. (Derived from Patel 2014, **bitcoin.org/en/vocabulary**, and **money.cnn.com/infographic/technology/what-is-bitcoin/?iid=HP_Highlight**.)

- *Advantages:*
  1. Buyers remain anonymous
  2. Simple international transactions (no regulations)
  3. No transaction fees
  4. Can be used for micropayments
- *Trading*: Done in marketplaces (exchanges) such as in Mt. Gox in Japan. BTC of China is the world's largest exchange. Ownership is transferred to buyers.
- *Valuation*: Prices between 2011 and 2013 were in the range of $5 to $1, 242. The price has been fueled by demand in China.
- *Illegal activities*: Bitcoin is the currency of choice for drug dealers and other illegal traders (e.g., used in the Internet drug site "Silk Road," see Chapter 10).
- *Taxation*: The Internal Revenue Service in the U.S. and some other countries treat Bitcoin

like property, not like currency; owners may have to pay property tax (see Green 2014).

- *Bitcoin exchange*: BitInstant used is Silk Road's online site for money laundering. In January 2014, U.S. government agents arrested its CEO.
- *Biocoins are illegal* in certain countries (e.g., Russia).
- *Litecoin*, a cheaper version of Bitcoin, is "silver to Bitcoin's gold" (see **businessinsider. com/introduction-to-litecoin-2013-11**).
- *Bitcoins are produced* by users running computers in many places in the world utilizing software that solves mathematical problems.
- *There are* only 21 million Bitcoin units that will ever be created.
- *Bitcoin wallet*. The wallet secures the Bitcoins using strong encryption.
- *Bitcoin is being accepted as a universal currency* by an increasing number of legal business in many countries (e.g., Texas-based gun company TrackingPoint; **tracking-point.com**). For how you can live on Bitcoin alone when you travel, see Vigna (2013). According to *Business Wire* (April 2, 2014), the average daily business Bitcoin transactions in February 2014 totaled $68 million (a 10 fold increase since February 2013) compared with the popular PayPal's $492 million in 2013. See **businesswire.com/news/ home/20140402006189/en/Fitch-Bitcoin- Remains-Small-Comparison-Payment- Processors#.U1tpH_mICm5** for details.
- *Bitcoin bypasses banks and regulations.* Many people use Bitcoins for illegal transactions for this reason.
- *Bitcoin has a monthly magazine. Bitcoin Magazine* (**bitcoinmagazine.com**).
- *Mt. Gox* exchange has been raided by the U.S. authorities, sued by CoinLab, hacked by cybercriminals, and had to file for temporary bankruptcy protection in March 2011. The company closed in February 2014.
- *Banking regulators* in New York sent subpoenas to 22 companies that have had some involvement with Bitcoin in August 2013 (see **dealbook.nytimes.com/2013/08/13/officials- broaden-inquiries-into-oversight-of-bitcoin- and-other-currencies/?_php=true&_ type=blogs&_r=0**).

Other Interesting Systems

We present here only a few of the many other emerging systems.

Coin (The "All in One" Credit Card)

Coin (**onlycoin.com**) is the name of an electronic device that contains the information of all your credit and debit cards on one "coin." The mobile app allows you to add or delete cards you wish to store on the device. You swipe your card through a small device on your smartphone, then choose which card you wish to use. The merchants swipe Coin just as they would a regular card (see Pepitone 2013). For more information on how Coin works, compatible mobile devices, and so forth, see **onlycoin.com/support/faq**).

Also watch the video titled "Why Coin Is the Future of Payments" (3:10 minutes) at **money. cnn.com/video/technology/2013/12/05/ t-coin-ceo-kanishk-parashar-app-start-up. cnnmoney/index.html**.

The device is planned to debut in summer 2014, and reached its pre-order goal in November 2013. However, there are issues with the product. According to Pepitone (2013), the device has three disadvantages. First, it "locks up" if you are away from your smartphone for more than 10 minutes or if your battery has run out. Second, Coin has not received approval from any credit card companies; Coin does not know if the credit card companies will even welcome the idea. Finally, merchants may be confused since Coin does not look like a "regular" credit card (with raised numbers and hologram).

A competitor, NXT-ID, is also releasing a mobile digital wallet, called the Wocket™ (described later).

TrialPay (trialpay.com)

TrialPay is an EC payment system using the "Get It Free" payment model. According to Wikipedia, based on Kim (2008), "TrialPay's payment platform presents online shoppers with advertising offers as a way to pay for goods or services. Shoppers sign up for a trial or purchase a product from an advertiser to receive a free product. The system tries to provide benefits to each party: online stores make more sales from their current traffic, advertisers acquire new customers on a pay-for-performance basis and shoppers get a free product with every purchase."

Amazon Payments

Amazon Payments (**payments.amazon.com**) is a comprehensive set of online payment tools. These tools are for businesses, individual consumers, and developers. The objective is to make payments easy, fast, and secure.

For Consumers

Users make a purchase from any online store featuring the "Pay with Amazon" link and pay from their existing Amazon.com account. Consumers can also send or receive money, using the payment information stored in their Amazon.com account.

For Businesses

Businesses can accept payments from buyers and provide payment processes and order management capabilities ('Checkout by Amazon'). 'Amazon Simple Pay' allows an easy way to accept payments or donations online. For example, customers can pay participating vendors using the secure information in their Amazon accounts. For more about Amazon Payments for businesses, see **payments.amazon.com/business/asp**.

M-Payment

Amazon has a mobile payment method with their subsidiary GoPago. According to Amazon, mobile shoppers are buying, not just browsing. Customers can now buy from a merchant using a mobile-optimized checkout flow hosted by Amazon, or by using a touchscreen widget installed by the merchant embedded on their site. This simplifies the payment process for the customers, since they do not have to re-enter their payment information (see **payments.amazon. com/business/mobile/overview**).

Kindle Checkout System

Amazon is planning to offer brick-and-mortar retailers a checkout system using Kindle tablets to process payments. The system, which will be offered to SMBs first, could include a combination of Kindle tablets and card readers. For details, see **smartplanet.com/blog/bulletin/amazon-develops-kindle-based-checkout-system-for-smbs**.

Miscellaneous Systems

The following are some other payment systems.

- A *cash-payment kiosk* for marijuana users functions like an ATM, recording each transaction, tracking payments, ensuring that the accounting is accurate and the proper taxes are collected. This solves the problem of marijuana-related cash that many banks refuse to handle.
- *Google Wallet* Sent Money feature lets Gmail users send money to anyone in the U.S. with an e-mail address. The service works with the Google Wallet app. See **google.com/wallet/send-money**.
- *NXT-ID.* Their digital wallet system, the Wocket™ (**nxt-id.com/products/wocket**; **wocketwallet.com**), is scheduled to launch in 2014. Similar to Coin, this product aggregates up to 100 credit cards, coupons, gift cards, loyalty cards, and more. In addition, it works only with a biometric system (e.g., face, voice, fingerprint) that eliminates the need for a password structure (see **nxt-id.com/wocket-hopes-replace-wallet**).
- *Alipay of Alibaba Group* (see Chapter 4) partnered with the Chinese microblogging site Sina Weibo (**weibo.com**) to launch Weibo Payment ("Weibo Zhifu"), an online payment platform where users can connect their Alipay and Weibo accounts and shop and purchase directly using their Weibo app. According to *Global Times* (January 7, 2014), "Weibo users can buy things and pay bills online easier just by inputting passwords." (See **globaltimes. cn/content/836256.shtml#.U17DR_ldWSo**.)
- *Apple is moving closer to m-payments.* In early 2014, it was rumored that Apple was laying the groundwork for an expanded mobile payment service (see Del Rey 2014).

SECTION 11.8 REVIEW QUESTIONS

1. Describe Bitcoin and list its benefits to buyers and sellers.
2. Describe the functions of the Bitcoin exchanges.
3. Why do governments want to make Bitcoin and similar currencies illegal?

4. Find the status of Coin and NXT-ID Wocket ™.
5. Review Amazon.com's payment systems from the points of view of buyers and sellers.

MANAGERIAL ISSUES

Some managerial issues related to this chapter are as follows:

1. **What payment methods should your B2C site support?** Most B2C sites use more than one payment gateway to support customers' preferred payment methods. Companies that only accept credit cards exclude a number of potential segments of buyers (e.g., customers under the age of 18, customers who do not have or do not want to use credit cards online). EFT, e-checks, stored-value cards, and PayPal are some possible alternatives to credit cards. The e-check is barely used in some countries because it is not considered an efficient enough method in the electronic era there; thus, selecting a globally acceptable payment method is important for the globalization of EC. For solutions in Asia, see **asiapay.com**.

2. **What micropayment strategy should your e-marketplace support?** If your EC site sells items priced less than $10, credit cards are not a viable solution. Many digital content products cost less than $1. For small-value products, micropayments should be supported. Fees may be taken from a prepaid account that is connected to the buyer's bank account or credit card, or the fee may be charged to the buyer's cell phone bill. The use of stored-value smart cards on the Internet has emerged, but has not widely penetrated the market because buyers need to install the card reader/writer. Companies should support multiple options so that customers can choose their preferred payment method.

3. **Which mobile systems could influence your business?** Over the next few years, mobile payments will emerge as a primary, if not the primary, way that people will pay for digital and physical goods, both online and off. Mobile payments have the potential to replace the direct use of credit and debit cards, as well as cash. At the present time, mobile payment technologies and protocols are in a state of flux, making it difficult to decide which systems to adopt. The key is to determine which forms of mobile payment are required for a particular business – remote or proximate – and, in the short term, rely on those vendors and organizations that are ready to have a strong presence in the online world (for instance, PayPal or the protocols and systems supported by major credit card vendors).

4. **Should we outsource our payment gateway service?** It takes time, skill, money, software, and hardware to build and maintain a comprehensive self-payment system. For this reason, even a large online business usually outsources its e-payment service. Many third-party vendors provide comprehensive payment gateways. Furthermore, if a website is hosted by a third party (e.g., Yahoo! Stores), an e-payment service may be provided by the host.

5. **How secure are e-payments?** Security and fraud continue to be major concerns in different online e-payments. This is especially true with regard to the use of credit cards for online purchases. B2C merchants are employing a wide variety of tools (e.g., address verification and other authentication services) to combat fraudulent orders. These need to be an integral part of the business security program (Chapter 10). For more on payment security, see Morphy (2012).

6. **What B2B payment methods should we use?** Several methods are available. Electronic transfers are very popular. Some customers pay with e-checks while small amounts are paid with credit cards. For MROs, consider using purchasing cards. For global trade, electronic letters of credit are popular. With all these methods, a key factor is determining how well they work with existing accounting and ordering systems and with business partners.

SUMMARY

In this chapter, you learned about the following EC issues as they relate to the chapter's learning objectives.

1. **Payment revolution and micropayments.** Cash and checks are no longer kings. Debit and credit cards now rule – both online and offline. This means that online B2C businesses need to support debit and credit card purchases. In international markets outside of Western Europe, buyers often favor other forms of e-payment (e.g., bank transfers). With the exception of PayPal, virtually all the alternatives to charge cards have failed. None have gained critical mass to overcome the "chicken-and-the-egg" problem.

   A major area of development is the payment of small amounts (micropayments) in EC. Several different methods are being developed ranging from PayPal to prepaid cards.

   Note: Due to security problems with credit cards (see Chapter 10), many people are using cash. However, as the problems are solved, we anticipate the return to credit cards.

2. **Using payment cards online.** The processing of online card payments is essentially the same as it is for brick-and-mortar stores and involves essentially the same players and the same systems – banks, card associations, payment processing services, and the like. This is one of the reasons why payment cards are predominant in the online world. The major difference is that the rate of fraudulent orders is much higher online. Surveys, such as those conducted annually by CyberSource, indicate that over the past few years, merchants have adopted a wide variety of methods including address verification, manual review, fraud analysis, card verification services, authentication services, and negative pay files to combat fraudulent orders. In the same vein, some consumers have turned to virtual or single-use credit cards to avoid using their actual credit card numbers online.

3. **Smart cards.** Smart cards resemble credit cards but contain microprocessors for manipulating data and have a large memory capacity. Some cards have memory chips for read/write data. Smart cards can be rechargeable. Applications include contactless retail payments, paying for mass transit services, identifying cardholders for government services, securing physical and network access, storing healthcare data, and verifying eligibility for healthcare and government services. Given the sensitive nature of much of the data on smart cards, public key encryption and other cryptographic techniques are used to secure their contents.

4. **Stored-value cards.** A stored-value card is similar in appearance to a credit or debit card. The monetary value of a stored value card is housed in a magnetic strip on the back of the card. Closed-loop stored-value cards are issued for a single purpose by a specific merchant (e.g., a Starbucks gift card). In contrast, open-loop stored-value cards are more like standard credit or debit cards and can be used for multiple purposes (e.g., a payroll card). Those segments of the population without credit cards or bank accounts – people with bad credit, no credit history, problems with immigration status, or another reason – are driving the substantial growth of stored-value cards. Specialized cards, such as BB&T EasySend (**bbt.com/bbtdotcom/banking/cards/easysend.page**), make it simple to send money internationally. MasterCard® offers a variety of prepaid cards, such as the MuchMusic Prepaid MasterCard®, where the user loads the card with cash and can use it online or anywhere. For a list of the different prepaid cards offered by MasterCard®, see **mastercard.ca/prepaid-card.html**.

5. **Micropayments.** In the online world, most purchases are made with credit and debit cards. When the value of a purchase is under $10, it is called a micropayment. The problem is that the fees associated with card purchases make these low value transactions cost prohibitive. Today, as an alternative, most merchants rely on one of five methods such as aggregation, stored-value card, and subscription to avoid the individual transaction costs. Aggregation adds the value of a number of purchases before submitting the transaction to the card companies; a stored-value card enables up-front payments to a debit account from which purchases are deducted as they are made; and a subscrip-

tion is a single payment that covers access to content for a defined period of time. More recently, card companies have lowered their transaction fees in order to encourage their use in these situations. Similarly, PayPal has introduced support for micropayments at a reduced transaction costs.

6. **E-checking.** E-checks are the electronic equivalent of paper checks. They are handled in much the same way as paper checks and rely quite heavily on the ACH Network. E-checks offer a number of benefits, including a potential reduction in processing time, reduced administrative costs, a more efficient deposits process, reduced float period, and fewer checks returned for non-sufficient funds. These factors have resulted in the rapid growth of e-check usage. The rapid growth is also being facilitated by the use of e-checks for in-store purchases. Purchase Order Processing (POP) and Back-Office Order Conversion (BOC) are two systems established by NACHA (The Electronic Payments association), that enable retailers to convert paper checks used for in-store purchases to ACH debits (i.e., e-checks) without the need to process the checks using traditional procedures.

7. **Mobile payments.** Wireless and smartphone companies are rapidly enabling their customers to initiate or confirm payments and other financial transactions via their mobile devices. These transactions are one of two types: mobile proximity payments or mobile remote payments. With mobile proximity payments, also known as "contactless" payments, a cell phone or smartphone is outfitted with a special chip that allows users to swipe their phones near a payment device (e.g., POS reader), much like a contactless smart card or credit card. With mobile remote payments, the mobile handset can be used to make person-to-person, person-to-business, and business-to-business payments. The uptake of mobile proximity payments is currently hindered because vendors cannot agree on the chip, reader, or network standards to be used.

8. **B2B electronic payments.** B2B payments are the financial part of a company's supply chain that encompasses the range of processes from procurement to payment and from ordering to cash flow. Today, the vast majority of B2B payments are still made by check, although many organizations are moving to Electronic Invoice Presentment and Payment (EIPP) that has three models: seller direct (buyers go to the seller's website), buyer direct (sellers post invoices on the buyer's website), and consolidator (many buyers and many sellers are linked through the consolidator's website). One of the largest consolidators is GXS Trading Grid. In addition to these services, there are several EIPP payment options, including the ACH Network, purchasing cards, wire transfers, and letters of credit (L/C). The move to EIPP is being inhibited by the shortage of IT staff, the lack of integration of payment and accounting systems, the lack of standard formats for remittance information, and the inability of trading partners to transfer payments electronically with all the necessary accompanying information and procedures.

9. **Emerging EC payment systems.** A large number of new payment systems are emerging. Most notable is the controversial Bitcoin that is popular in the underground economy as digital currency. Coin is an 'all-in-one' credit/debit card competing with NXT-ID. Amazon Payments is a comprehensive set of payment tools aimed at providing payment flexibility to shoppers. Of special interest is Alipay from the Alibaba Group that caters to millions of Chinese shoppers.

KEY TERMS

Address Verification System (AVS)
Authorization
Automated Clearing House
(ACH) Network
Bitcoin
Card verification number (CVN)
Contact card

Contactless (proximity) card
Digital (virtual) currency
Electronic check (e-check)
Electronic Invoice Presentment
and Payment (EIPP)
Letter of credit (L/C)
Micropayments (e-micropayments)
Mobile payment
Mobile wallet
Payment cards
Payment service provider (PSP)
Purchasing cards (P-cards)
Settlement
Smart card
Smart card reader
Stored-value card

DISCUSSION QUESTIONS

1. Boku (**boku.com**) launched a mobile payment service with the 2009 acquisition of Paymo and MobileCash (two leading providers in the global mobile payment industry) that enables buyers to make online purchases with their mobile phones. How does the Boku payments service work? Who are some of the companies supporting Boku? Do you think the Boku mobile payments system will succeed? What factors will play a major role in its success or failure? Start by reading the press release at **www.boku.com/boku-launches-new-online-payments-service-for-mobile-consumers-acquires-paymo-and-mobillcash-businesses-pr**.

2. Criminals may use fake or stolen credit cards to pay merchants. What steps should the merchants take to combat the fraud?

3. A retail clothing manufacturer is considering e-payments for both its suppliers and its buyers. What sort of e-payment method should it use to pay for office supplies? How should it pay suppliers of raw materials? How should its customers – both domestic and international clothing retailers – pay?

4. A metropolitan area wants to provide users of its public transportation system with the ability to pay transit fares, and make retail purchases, using a single contactless smart card. What sorts of problems can it encounter in setting up the system, and what types of problems could the riders encounter by using the cards?

5. Discuss the probability that Ven (**ven.vc**) will become an acceptable global digital currency.

6. Discuss the role of e-checking. Does it have a future?

7. Discuss the different methods of global payments.

TOPICS FOR CLASS DISCUSSION AND DEBATES

1. If you were running an online retail store, would you permit purchases with e-checks? Why or why not?

2. Why is the marketplace for electronic payment systems so volatile? Is there a need for some other form of electronic payment?

3. Debate: Why was PayPal able to succeed where other e-payment alternatives were not? Does the company present a threat to the banking industry?

4. Several years ago Facebook declared that all Facebook applications, including games, would have to use Facebook Credits as their currency. A short time later they rescinded this policy. Why would Facebook issue such a policy? Why did they rescind it? Do you agree with their actions?

5. Besides e-books and online music, what are some of the other places where micropayments could be used?

6. Which would you prefer, paying for goods and services with a physical debit or credit card or paying with your cell phone? What are some of the benefits and limitations of each?

7. Several companies are trying to enter the e-textbook business. Debate: Which company, Apple or Amazon.com, has the best chance of building and dominating this market in the long run? Explain.

8. Some question the viability of MasterPass™. Find pro and con information and debate the issue.

9. Some say (e.g., former U.S. Congressman Ron Paul) that Bitcoin could destroy the dollar. Investigate and discuss.

10. Research VeriFone Systems (**verifone.com**) and discuss its role in the e-payment field.

11. Debate the future of credit cards.

12. Discuss the differences between digital currency and virtual currency.

INTERNET EXERCISES

1. In 1999, eBay purchased a payment system called Billpoint, which was a head-to-head competitor of PayPal. Use online sources to research why PayPal succeeded and Billpoint failed. Write a report based on your findings.

2. Select a major retail B2C merchant in the United States and one outside of North America. Detail the similarities and differences in the e-payment systems they offer. What other payment systems could the sites offer? Write a short report.

3. A small number of companies are providing digital (mobile) wallet systems. What is a digital wallet? Make a list of these companies and their products. Compare their various capabilities. Do you think any of these products will be popular in the near future? Why or why not?

4. Read the White Paper titled "Transit and Contactless Financial Payments" at **smartcardalliance.org/resources/pdf/Transit_Financial_Linkages_WP_102006.pdf**. What are the key requirements for an automated fare-collection system? Based on the report, what type of payment system did the New York City Transit Authority pilot use? What factors helped determine the type of system to be piloted? How did the pilot program work?

5. Go to **nacha.org**. What is NACHA? What is its role? What is the ACH Network? Who are the key participants in an ACH e-payment?

6. Both Walgreens and Kohl's utilize Solutran's SPIN for their BOC systems. Based on information provided at **solutran.com** and information found in online articles about the system, what kinds of capabilities and benefits does the system provide? What is unique about the system? If you were running a large retail operation, would you focus on POP or BOC?

7. Read about Starbucks' mobile payment alternatives at **mashable.com/category/starbucks card-mobile** and find other sources. Write a summary.

8. Find current information about **authorize.net**, which is now a CyberSource Solution. Write a report.

9. Enter **placecast.net/shopalerts/brands.html** and find information about the capabilities of ShopAlerts. What is ShopAlerts Wallet? Write a report.

10. Enter fiserv.com. Find what this company is doing worldwide in financial services. Also check its Popmoney division. Write a report.

TEAM ASSIGNMENTS AND PROJECTS

1. **Assignment for the Opening Case**
   Read the opening case and answer the following questions.
   Suppose Amazon decided to resurrect its Amazon Pages program.
   (a) What sort of micropayment system should it use in order to run this business profitably?
   (b) What types of business and legal issues would it encounter?
   (c) Besides the book and music businesses, describe some other online business where micropayments are, or would be, critical to its success.

2. The competition within the mobile payment reader industry is very intense. Each team selects a company in this field (e.g., Square, PayPal, Groupon) and presents the company's capabilities and weaknesses.

3. Write a report comparing smart card applications in two or more European and/or Asian countries. In the report, discuss whether those applications would succeed in North America. Start with 'Payment Methods in Peru' at **emarketservices.com/start/Home/Intro/prod/Payment-methods-in-Peru.html?xz=0&cc=1&sd=1&ci=2129** (November 15, 2012).

4. Have one team represent MasterCard® *Pay Pass™* (**mastercard.us/paypass.html**) and another represent Visa payWave (**usa.visa. com/personal/security/card-technology/ visa-paywave.jsp**). The task of each team is to convince a company that its product is superior to the other.

5. Have each team member interview three to five people who have made a purchase or sold an item via an online auction. Find out how they paid. What security and privacy concerns did they have regarding the payment? Is there an ideal payment method?

6. AT&T, Verizon, T-Mobile, and Discover Financial Services released a mobile commerce platform called *Isis Mobile Wallet* (**paywithisis.com**) that resulted in a new cell phone–powered payment system. How does this system work? What are some of the competing systems that have been proposed or implemented? Which system has the best chance of success and why? Research and write a report.

7. Go to the NACHA site for the Council for Electronic Billing and Payment (**cebp.nacha. org**). The site provides information (see the "Current Initiatives" section) about various forms of EIPP and EBPP. Compare and contrast two of the forms it details.

CLOSING CASE: INNOVATIVE CREDIT CARD MICROPAYMENTS FOR THE KOREAN METROPOLITAN UNIFIED FARE SYSTEM

Boram, a banker in Seoul, Korea commutes by MRT and public buses. She uses a credit card that allows her to pay for both MRT and buses, not only in Seoul, but also in other major Korean cities without having to recharge the card. The accumulated monthly charges are automatically paid by the bank. Boram recalls the days when she had to carry two different transportation cards in addition to credit cards.

In the past, Boram used to pay for the subway by using a Seoul MRT Card, which is a stored-value card. The card is issued by the city-owned Seoul MRT Corporation and could be recharged only at MRT stations. To ride a bus, she had to use a Seoul Bus Card that is another stored-value card issued by the private Seoul Bus Transport Association (SBTA). The Seoul Bus Card was introduced in 1996 as the first RF-type bus card in the world. Thus, she had to recharge both cards individually because they could not be used interchangeably. Other cities have similar governance structures. Therefore, to take the subway in another city, Boram had to buy one-time subway tickets at the subway station.

Credit cards, as described in this chapter, are not cost-effective enough to be used for the micropayment of transportation because the card company could not justify its service fee. Therefore, as described earlier, Boram needed to carry at least one credit card and two transportation cards in her wallet.

Large cities in Asia such as Seoul, Hong Kong, and Singapore have adopted similar types of stored-value transportation cards. As such, credit cards and stored-value cards coexist as two major card services. The two types of card issuers compete to expand their application territory. The transportation card company wants to extend the card's application so users can pay for parking fees, various toll fees, and at restaurants and stores. However, the users have to load the cards for prepayment.

At the same time, for credit cards issuers to expand their application to include payments for transportation, they need to simplify the authorization process and reduce the service fee for the participating transporters. The question is: which business model will eventually win? In Seoul, it is the credit card issuer that includes payments for transportation.

In order to pay transportation fares quickly, credit card payments for subways and buses must be processed without the full authorization procedure. This risk is tolerable because the frequency and amount of micropayment abuse is low in Korea. Therefore, the transportation ticket gate merely automatically checks whether the card is valid and not on a "blacklist." The gate displays not only the fare, but also the charges incurred during the current month as shown in Figure 11.5. The first credit- based MRT card was adopted by Kookmin Bank in 1998. Today, several issuers support this type of card.

Figure 11.5 The credit-based transportation card displays the fare and accumulated charges for the current month at the ticket gate (Photos by J. K. Lee)

The credit-based transportation card has revolutionized the recharge service process. In the early stage, both MRT cards and bus cards had to be recharged at manned booths. To reduce the expense of the recharge service, unmanned booths were installed at MRT stations. However, with the credit card, recharge booths can be eliminated altogether and users do not have to spend time recharging their cards. Therefore, both the users and the city transportation authority benefit.

Another benefit of the smart transportation card is that it can restructure the city's transportation system by aligning and coordinating the routes of subways and buses. In the past, bus routes were designed in consideration of the departure and destination points of citizens' trips. This approach intended to make it convenient for citizens to take only one bus to reach their destination. However, too many buses created bottlenecks in busy streets, causing traffic jams. To avoid such congestion, the MRT and main bus companies planned to design the transportation system so that bus branch routes are connected to the subway and to the main bus routes. However, if citizens are required to pay an additional fee for branch routes, they may resist the new structure. Therefore, the transportation fare card should be interconnected.

To solve this problem, the transportation card, credit or stored-value, is designed to memorize the departure time from the MRT station so that the connecting buses do not charge passengers again if the elapsed time is less than 30 minutes. Taking a branch bus is regarded as a transfer for single trip. This means that the owners of transport systems need to agree on about how to allocate the collected fees. Therefore, the city of Seoul adopted the Metropolitan Unified Fare System in 2009.

Due to the national standardization and integration effort, nationwide transportation cards are now unified using smart cards. Credit card companies do not really make enough money through transportation payment services, but this service is essential for them to gain new customers and retain existing ones.

The city also can collect data about commuters so that additional buses can be dispatched depending upon the passenger load by route and time. Note that, at midnight, regular bus services stops. For midnight bus service, the control center analyzes the frequency of mobile phone usage in certain areas to estimate the number of potential commuters and dynamically determine the routes of midnight buses.

Another lesson that can be learned from Korea's experience is the C2C payment system use of credit cards. In C2C auction markets, escrow services that are based on credit cards allow individual buyers to pay eBay Korea directly. The sellers can receive payment through eBay Korea if delivery is confirmed by the buyer. Therefore, there is no need for an e-mail payment system such as PayPal that charges high service fees. The function of a debit card, combined with a credit card, has also virtually replaced the function of electronic checks, so e-checks are no longer needed. In this manner, payments by credit cards in Korea are electronically integrated for e-commerce, physical stores, and micropayments for transportation.

Sources: Case written by Jae K. Lee, Seoul –Korea.

Questions

1. How can credit cards be processed as quickly as stored-value cards at the ticket gate?
2. What is the major benefit of owning a credit-based transportation card for commuters?
3. What is the major benefit of credit-based transportation cards to the city government?
4. How can the Metropolitan Unified Fare System enable the restructuring of public transportation infrastructure?

ONLINE FILES
available at **affordable-ecommerce-textbook.com/turban**

W11.1 To POP or BOC Digital Checks
W11.2 Application Case: Closing the Digital Divide with Mobile Microfinance in Bangalore, India

---

COMPREHENSIVE EDUCATIONAL WEBSITES

afponline.org: Website of the Association for Financial Professionals.

agents.umbc.edu: Large collection of information about intelligent agents.

paymentssource.com: Comprehensive site for reports, news, events, technologies, and vendors.

cybersource.com: A Visa company for payment security and management, digital wallets, reports, and news.

globalplatform.org: GlobalPlatform provides information and guides on smart cards and their infrastructure and security.

nacha.org: NACHA – The Electronic Payments Association. They manage the development and governance of the ACH Network.

paymentsnews.com: Website maintained by Glenbrook Partners offering daily news about e-payment innovations and other financial services.

glenbrook.com: A payments industry strategy consulting and research firm. Monitors the news of the day across the wide-ranging field of electronic payments, including mobile payments.

smartcardalliance.org: A nonprofit association for smart card-related issues.

GLOSSARY

Address Verification System (AVS) System that detects fraud by comparing the address provided by the buyer at checkout with the address on file.

Authorization First phase of processing a credit card transaction that determines whether a buyer's card is valid (e.g., not expired) and whether the customer has sufficient credit or funds in his or her account.

Automated Clearing House (ACH) Network A processor of paper checks by converting them to electronic format via the government's electronic funds transfer (EFT) system. Bitcoin A digital currency managed by a group of individuals and companies who own the computing power and process of creating Biocoins.

Card verification number (CVN) Method for detecting fraud by matching the 3-digit verification number printed on the signature strip on the back of the credit card (or the 4-digit number on the front of the card, such as American Express cards) with the number stored by the cardholder's issuing bank.

Contact card A smart card that is activated when it is inserted into a smart card reader.

Contactless (proximity) card A smart card that only has to be within a certain proximity of a smart card reader to process a transaction.

Digital (virtual) currency A medium of payment that is electronically created, stored, and used in e-commerce. It can be used to pay for either physical goods or virtual ones.

Electronic check (e-check) An electronic clone of a paper check, containing the same information.

Electronic Invoice Presentment and Payment (EIPP) The procedures and processes by which companies present invoices and get paid for these invoices over the Internet.

Letter of credit (L/C) Letter issued by one bank to another bank (usually in another country) on behalf of a buyer (e.g., importer). It guarantees a seller (e.g., exporter) that sufficient payment for goods or services will be made on time, provided the conditions of the L/C are met by the exporter.

Micropayments (e-micropayments) Small online payments, usually under $10.

Mobile (digital) wallet Proximity payments that are debited to a mobile phone account as a monthly fee or to a debit card account. The technology enables payments as well as processing loyalty programs and performing target promotions all in one mobile device.

Mobile payment Payment transactions initiated or confirmed using a person's mobile device, usually a smartphone.

Payment cards Electronic cards that contain payment-related data. They include credit cards, charge cards, and debit cards.

Payment service providers (PSPs) Third-party companies that provide services to merchants so they can accept all kinds of electronic payments. The PSPs connect all participants in the electronic transactions.

Purchasing cards (p-cards) Payment cards issued to a company's employees used to pay for unexpected purchases of goods and services, usually MROs (e.g., stationery, office supplies, and computer supplies) up to a certain limit (usually $1,000 to $5,000).settlement Second phase of processing a credit card transaction that transfers money from the buyer's account to the merchant's account.

Smart card A plastic payment card that contains data in an embedded microchip.

Smart card reader A read/write device that acts as a mediator between the card and the host system that stores application data and processes transactions.

Stored-value card A card where a monetary value is prepaid and can be loaded on the card once, or several times.

REFERENCES

Analysys Mason. "Final Report for PhonepayPlus: The Marketplace for and Regulation of Micropayment Services in the UK." [Ref: 18615–503] December, 2010. **phonepayplus.org.uk/~/media/Files/Phonepay Plus/Research/Analysys_Mason_The_marketplace_ for_and_regulation_of_micropayment_services_ in_the_UK.pdf** (accessed April 2014).

Bell, C. "4 Risky Places to Swipe Your Debit Card." *Bankrate*, December 22, 2011. **bankrate.com/ finance/checking/risky-places-swipe-debit-card-1. aspx** (accessed June 2014).

Bonnington, C. "MasterCard MasterPass Augments Your Digital Shopping Experience." *Wired*, February 25, 2013.

Boorstin, J. "Groupon Gambles Big on Mobile Payments." *CNBC*, September 19, 2012. **cnbc.com/id/49078709** (accessed June 2014).

Business Wire. "ISIS Advances Mobile Commerce with First Market." April 4, 2011. **businesswire.com/news/ home/20110404007248/en/Isis-Advances-Mobile-Commerce-Market#.VIIlHjHF-So.** Accessed Dec 2014

Capgemini. "World Payments Report 2010." 2010. **euro. ecom.cmu.edu/resources/elibrary/epay/ WPR_2010.pdf** (accessed April 2014).

Chen, B. X. "Now on Sale at Starbucks: Square's Credit Card Reader." January 3, 2013. **bits.blogs.nytimes. com/2013/01/03/starbucks-square-mobile-credit-card-reader** (accessed April 2014).

Clancy, H. "Mobile Payment Apps Eliminates Card Reader." November 21, 2012. **zdnet.com/mobile-payment-apps-eliminates-card-reader-7000007747** (accessed April 2014).

CyberSource. "12th Annual Online Fraud Reports." 2011. **cybersource.com** (accessed April 2014).

D'Agostino, D. "Pennies from Heaven." *CIO Insight*, January 2006. **allbusiness.com/company-activities-management/financial-performance/13443526-1. html** (accessed June 2014).

Del Rey, J. "PayPal Wants Role in Apple's Mobile Payments Dreams." *Re/code*, January 30, 2014. **recode.net/2014/01/30/paypal-wants-in-on-apples-mobile-payments-dreams/** (accessed April 2014).

Estopace. E. "Ice Cream Maker Makes a Difference with Mobile POS." *Enterprise Innovation*, May 21, 2014.

Evans, D. S., and R Schmalensee. *Paying with Plastic: The Digital Revolution in Buying and Borrowing*, 2nd ed., Cambridge, MA: MIT Press, 2005.

Fishman, J. "The Future of Mobile Payments: Part I." *Seeking Alpha*, February 18, 2014a. **seekingalpha. com/article/2028491-the-future-of-mobile-payments-part-i** (accessed June 2014).

Fishman, J. "The Future of Mobile Payments: Part II." *Seeking Alpha*, February 19, 2014b. **seekingalpha. com/article/2030631-the-future-of-mobile-payments-part-ii** (accessed June 2014).

Gemalto, N. V. "EMV in the United States." 2013. **gemalto.com/emv** (accessed April 2014)

Green, J. "IRS Deems Bitcoins Taxable Property." *Pymnts.com*, March 26, 2014. **pymnts.com/in-depth/2014/irs-deems-bitcoins-taxable-property/#. U1tg4_mICm4** (accessed April 2014).

Hachman, M. "PayPal Launches Mobile Express Checkout." *PCMag.com*, October 26, 2010. **pcmag. com/article2/0,2817,2371519,00.asp** (accessed April 2014).

Hamblen, M. "Crutchfield Sees Benefits from Speedy Mobile Checkout." *Computerworld*. June 3, 2011.

Jing, M. "Internet Finance: Golden Goose for Nest Eggs?" *China Daily USA*, November 28, 2013 (Updated). **usa. chinadaily.com.cn/epaper/2013-11/28/content_17138252.htm** (accessed April 2014).

Juniper Research. "Mobile Payment Transaction Values for Digital and Physical Goods to Exceed $300bn Globally Within 5 Years, According to Juniper Research." July 1, 2008. **juniperresearch.com/view-pressrelease.php?pr=97** (accessed April 2014).

Kim, R. "TrialPay Offers Double the Savings for Valentine's Day." *San Francisco Chronicle*, February 11, 2008.

LowRiskValue. "Evidence that Apple Intends to Start Mobile Payment Processing." *Seeking Alpha*, February 27, 2014. **seekingalpha.com/article/2053153-evidence-that-apple-intends-to-start-mobile-payment-processing** (accessed April 2014).

Lunden, I. "More Mobile Wallets Incoming: Placecast Launches White Label ShopAlerts Wallet." *TechCrunch*, June 27, 2012. **techcrunch.com/2012/06/27/more-mobile-wallets-incoming-placecast-launches-white-label-shopalerts-wallet** (accessed February 2013 April 2014).

MasterCard. "MasterCard Introduces MasterPass – The Future of Digital Payments." A Press Release, February 25, 2013. **newsroom.mastercard.com/press-releases/mastercard-introduces-masterpass-the-future-of-digital-payments** (accessed April 2014).

McMillian, J. "Crutchfield Drives High Mobile Conversion with PayPal." June 26, 2011. Available at **archive-ca.com/page/165097/2012-07-19/https:// www.paypal-blog.ca/2011/06/crutchfield-drives-high-mobile-conversion-with-paypal-2** (accessed April 2014).

Morphy, E. "Troubles Multiply for Global Payments." *E-Commerce Times*, April 3, 2012. **ecommercetimes. com/story/74771.html** (accessed April 2014).

O'Dell, J. "PayPal Debuts Mobile Express Checkout." *Mashable*, October 26, 2010. **mashable.com/2010/ 10/26/paypal-mobile-express-checkout** (accessed April 2014).

Patel, C. "Decoding Virtual Currencies and Bitcoin for Beginners, List of Terms and Definitions." *Let's Talk Payments*, March 26, 2014. **letstalkpayments.com/ decoding-virtual-currencies-bitcoin-beginners-list-terms-definition** (accessed April 2014).

PayPal. "Business Guide to Online Payment Processing." 2004. No longer available online.

Pepitone, J. "Hot Startup Coin Has 3 Big Problems." *CNN Money*, November 17, 2013. **money.cnn. com/2013/11/17/technology/innovation/coin-startup-credit-card** (accessed April 2014).

Purewal, S. J. "Groupon Introduces Mobile Payments System.", *PC World*, September 20, 2012.

Rao, L. "Placecast Debuts Location-Based, Credit Card-Linked ShopAlerts Offers." *TechCrunch*, October 18, 2012. **techcrunch.com/2012/10/18/placecast-debuts-location-based-credit-card-linked-shopalerts-offers** (accessed April 2014).

Roth, D. "The Future of Money: It's Flexible, Frictionless and (Almost) Free." *Wired*, February 22, 2010. **wired. com/magazine/2010/02/ff_futureofmoney/all/1** (accessed April 2014).

Severt, N. "Goldman Sachs: M-Commerce Sales Forecast to Hit $626 Billion by 2018." March 12, 2014. **evigo. com/12038-goldman-sachs-m-commerce-sales-forecast-hit-626-billion-2018** (accessed June 2014).

Trinh, T. "MasterCard Rolls Out MasterPass Mobile Payment System." February 25, 2013. **abcnews. go.com/blogs/technology/2013/02/mastercard-rolls-out-masterpass-digital-wallet** (accessed April 2014).

Tsotsis, A. "Kindle Books Overtake Paperback Books to Become Amazon's Most Popular Format." January 27, 2011. **techcrunch.com/2011/01/27/kindle-books-overtake-paperback-books-to-become-amazons-most-popular-format** (accessed February 2013 April 2014).

Valentine, L. "Payment Innovations: Are You In?" *ABA Banking Journal*, July 2012.

Vigna, P. "Bitcoin Couple Travels the World Using Virtual Cash." *Wall Street Journal*, November 20, 2013.

Whitman, D. "Credit Card Transactions: Real World and Online." *VirtualSchool.edu*, 1996. **virtualschool.edu/ mon/ElectronicProperty/klamond/credit_card.htm** (accessed April 2014).

yStats.com. "Global Alternative Payment Methods 2014." *GmbH & Co. KG*, May 23, 2014. **ystats.com/en/ reports/preview.php?reportId=1085&backtosearc h=true** (accessed June 2014).

Zawya."Cairo Amman Bank Introduces PayPal Services to Promote Electronic Commerce in Jordan." April 23, 2014. **zawya.com/story/Cairo_Amman_Bank_introduces_PayPal_services_to_promote_Electronic_Commerce_in_Jordan-ZAWYA20140423103516** (accessed June 2014).

Order Fulfillment Along the Supply Chain

12

Contents

Learning Objectives

Upon completion of this chapter, you will be able to:

1. Define EC order fulfillment and describe the EC order fulfillment process.
2. Describe the major problems of EC order fulfillment.
3. Describe various solutions to EC order fulfillment problems.
4. Describe RFID supply chain applications.
5. Describe collaborative planning and the CPFR model.
6. Describe other EC support services.
7. Discuss the drivers of outsourcing support services.

OPENING CASE: HOW AMAZON.COM FULFILLS ORDERS

The Problem

With traditional retailing, customers go to a physical store and purchase items that they then take home. Large quantities are delivered to each store or supermarket; there are not too many delivery destinations. With e-tailing, customers want the goods quickly and to have them shipped to their homes. Deliveries of small quantities need to go to a large number of destinations. Also, items must

Electronic supplementary material The online version of this chapter (doi: 10.1007/978-3-319-10091-3_12) contains supplementary material, which is available to authorized users

be available for immediate delivery. Therefore, maintaining an inventory of items becomes critical. Maintaining inventory and shipping products costs money and takes time, which may negate some of the advantages of e-tailing. Let us see how Amazon.com, the "king" of e-tailing, handles the situation.

Amazon started with "virtual retailing" as a business model – no warehouses, no inventory, and no shipments. The idea was to take orders and receive payments electronically and then let others fill the orders. It soon became clear that this model, although appropriate for a small company, would not work for the world's largest e-tailer.

The Solution

Amazon.com decided to change its business model and handle its own inventory and logistics. Furthermore, for a fee the company provides logistics services to any seller even its competitors. The company spent billions of dollars to construct their own warehouses around the country and became a world-class leader in warehouse management, warehouse automation, packaging, and inventory management. For a description see Harkness (2013).

How is Amazon.com able to efficiently fulfill many millions of orders every month?

- **Step 1.** When you place an order at Amazon.com and designate a destination, the computer program knows from where it is going to be shipped. It is usually shipped from Amazon's fulfillment center, or from the sellers' locations. Sellers have an option to ship their merchandise to Amazon.com for storage and processing. Amazon lists the products in its online catalog and may advertise the product(s). When an order arrives, a computer program will route the order to where it will be fulfilled. Amazon.com has dozens of distribution centers. In general, a typical Amazon.com distribution center operates in the follow way:
- **Step 2.** All orders received are routed electronically by the dispatcher to specific parts pickers for fulfillment.

- **Step 3.** The items (such as books, games, and CDs) are stocked in the warehouse in bins. Each bin is equipped with a red light. When an item in the bin needs to be picked up, the red light turns on. Pickers then pick up the items from the bins with red lights and then turn off the lights.
- **Step 4.** Each picked item is placed in a basket with a barcode designating the order number. The baskets are placed on a 10-mile long winding conveyor belt in the warehouse. Each basket is directed automatically to a specific destination point guided by barcode readers.
- **Step 5.** Each full basket is checked to assure that the barcodes are matched with a specific order. Then the items are moved to appropriate chutes, where they slide into delivery boxes. The system arranges for multiple items to reach this same box if there are several items in one order.
- **Step 6.** The boxes are then sealed for delivery. If gift wrapping was selected, this is done by hand.
- **Step 7.** The full boxes are then taped, weighed, labeled, and routed to one of the truck bays in the warehouse for shipment; some are owned by UPS, the U.S. Postal Service (USPS), and other shippers.

Del Rey (2013) provides a photo slideshow of the operation of one of Amazon.com's largest centers located in Phoenix, AZ.

Amazon.com also rents out space in its warehouse and provides logistics services to other companies. It takes orders for them, too. How does this work?

1. Sellers label and ship items in bulk to Amazon.com.
2. When Amazon.com receives sellers' items, it stores them until an order is placed.
3. When an order is placed, Amazon.com will pick, pack, and ship the items to individual customers and may combine several items in the same order.
4. Amazon.com manages after-ordering customer service and handles returns as needed.

Until a couple of years ago, Amazon.com outsourced the actual shipment of products to UPS and the USPS. This enabled them to locate their warehouses and distribution centers in low-cost states in order to ship to high-cost states with larger populations. It also limited their shipments to next day or two-day service. In mid-2012 Amazon.com decided to offer "same day" delivery service in a select group of cities (Manjoo 2012). A number of EC companies tried out "same day" service before and failed. In order to deliver this service Amazon.com spent millions of dollars to construct distribution centers in major metropolitan areas in California, Texas, Virginia, Tennessee, and New Jersey. In these cases shipments are handled by other third-party delivery services.

Some Recent Innovations

Amazon is a great innovation company. Some recent innovations that will be discussed later in this chapter are: same day delivery (e.g., Amazon Fresh), the use of robots in warehouses, and the use of drones (in planning) for delivery within 30 minutes. Amazon also delivers in some cities in one hour!

The Results

In the beginning, Amazon.com's warehouses were only able to deliver 1 million pieces a day, creating delays during peak periods. Today, the average warehouse can deliver hundreds of thousands of pieces a day. During the peak holiday season, their warehouses must handle millions of pieces per day. The current system gives Amazon.com the ability to offer lower prices and stay competitive, especially because the company is becoming a huge online marketplace that sells thousands of items.

To increase efficiency, Amazon.com combines several items into one shipment if they are small enough. Shipping warehouses do not handle returns of unwanted merchandise – the Altrec.com warehouse in Auburn, Washington, handles returns.

More recently, Amazon.com created "Pantry," a pilot program providing same day delivery of a number of the non-perishable items found in a grocery store (e.g., detergent). The program is aimed at Amazon's Prime members and is designed to compete with Costco and Walmart's Sam's Club. The program is described in Barr (2013).

Sources: Barr (2013), Del Rey (2013), Harkness (2013), Manjoo (2012), and **services.amazon. com/fulfillment-by-amazon/how-it-works.htm** (accessed April 2015).

LESSONS LEARNED FROM THE CASE

The Amazon.com case illustrates the complexity and benefits of the overall order fulfillment process used by a large e-tailer. This chapter provides a detailed overview of the fulfillment process in EC, focusing on the major problems associated with this EC support service, as well as the solutions used to overcome those problems.

12.1   ORDER FULFILLMENT AND LOGISTICS: AN OVERVIEW

Comparatively speaking, taking orders over the Internet may be the easy part of B2C. Fulfilling orders and delivering the ordered items to the customers' doors can be the tricky part. For example, as the open case showed, Amazon.com initially started out as a totally virtual company accepting orders and payments but relying on third parties to fulfill and deliver the orders. Eventually, they came to realize that they needed physical warehouses with thousands of employees in order to expedite deliveries and substantially reduce order fulfillment costs. In order to understand the importance of order fulfillment and delivery in EC, as well as the complexities and problems associated with each, you first have to have a general understanding of these concepts.

Basic Concepts of Order Fulfillment and Logistics

Regardless of the type of product and the type of commerce involved – online or off, **order fulfillment** refers to all the operations a company undertakes from the time it receives an order to the time the items are delivered to the customers, including all related customer services. For example, a customer must receive assembly and operation instructions with a new appliance. This can be done by including a paper document with the product or by providing the instructions on the Web. In addition, if the customer is dissatisfied with a product, an exchange or return must be arranged.

Order fulfillment encompasses a number of *back-office operations*, which are the activities that support the fulfillment of orders, such as packing, delivery, accounting, inventory management, and shipping. It also is strongly related to the *front-office operations*, or *customer-facing activities*, such as advertising and order taking, that are visible to customers.

Obviously, the overall objective of order fulfillment is to deliver the right product, to the right customer in a timely, cost effective, and profitable manner. The way these objectives are achieved varies between e-tailing and offline retailing because e-tailers are focused on delivering smaller numbers of items directly to the individual consumer, while many retailers are focused on delivering volumes of products to the store shelf. Of course, these days e-tailing and conventional retailing are intertwined because most retailers have multiple sales and services channels – Web, mobile, in store, call center, etc. This requires them to integrate the various channels, enabling customers to order anywhere and

pick up or receive anywhere. The closing case in this chapter discusses the issues, use, and benefits of this multichannel integration.

Overview of Logistics

Logistics encompasses activities required to efficiently and effectively control and manage the movement and storage of items, services, and information across the entire supply chain to the consumer and potentially back. Logistics can be viewed as a major activity in order fulfillment.

Traditional Versus EC Logistics

EC logistics, or **e-logistics**, refers to the logistics of EC systems mainly in B2C. The major difference between e-logistics and traditional logistics is that the latter deals with the movement of large amounts of materials to a few destinations (e.g., to retail stores). E-logistics shipments typically are small parcels sent to many customers' homes. Other differences are shown in Table 12.1.

The EC Order Fulfillment Process

In order to understand why there are problems in order fulfillment, it is beneficial to look at a

Table 12.1 How e-logistics differ from traditional logistics

Characteristic	Traditional knowledge	EC logistics
Type, quantity	Bulk, large volume	Small parcels
Destinations	Few	Large number, highly dispersed
Demand type	Push	Pull
Value of shipment	Very large, usually more than $1,000	Very small, frequently less than $50
Nature of demand	Stable, consistent	Seasonal (holiday season), fragmented
Customers	Business partners (in B2B), usually repeat customers (B2C), not many	Usually unknown in B2C, many
Inventory order flow	Usually unidirectional, from manufacturers	Usually bidirectional
Accountability	One link	Through the entire supply chain
Transporter	Frequently by the company, sometimes outsourced	Usually outsourced, sometimes by the company
Warehouse	Common	Only very large shippers (e.g., Amazon.com) operate their own

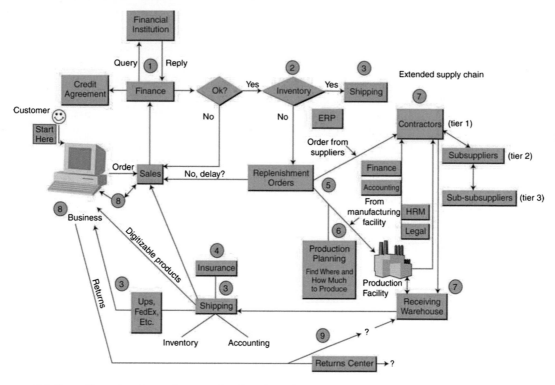

Note: Demand forecasts and accounting are conducted at various points throughout the process.

Figure 12.1   Order fulfillment and the logistic process

typical EC fulfillment process, as shown in Figure 12.1. The process starts on the left, when an order is received, and after verification that it is a real order, several activities take place, some of which can be done simultaneously; others must be done in sequence. These activities include the following steps:

- **Activity 1: Making sure the customer will pay.** Depending on the payment method and prior arrangements, the validity of each payment must be determined. In B2B, the company's finance department or a financial institution (i.e., a bank or a credit card issuer, such as Visa) may do this. Any holdup may cause a shipment to be delayed, resulting in a loss of goodwill or a customer. In B2C, in many countries, the customers usually prepay, frequently by credit card or by using services such as PayPal (Chapter 11). In other countries the customer may go to a payment station (e.g., a convenience store) and prepay there.

- **Activity 2: Checking for in-stock availability.** Regardless of whether the seller is a manufacturer or a retailer, as soon as an order is received, an inquiry needs to be made regarding stock availability. Several scenarios are possible that may involve the material management and production departments, as well as outside suppliers and warehouse facilities. In this step, the order information needs to be connected to the information about in-stock inventory availability or manufacturing capability.

- **Activity 3: Arranging shipments.** If the product is readily available, and it is paid for, it can be shipped to the customer right away (otherwise, go to activity 5). Products can be digital or physical. If the item is physical and it is readily available, packaging and shipment arrangements need to be made. It may involve both the packaging and shipping department and internal shippers or outside logistics services. Digital items are usually available because their "inventory" is not depleted. However, a digital product, such as software, may be under revision, and unavailable for delivery at certain times. In either case, information needs to flow among several partners.

- **Activity 4: Insurance.** Sometimes the contents of a shipment need to be insured. This could involve both the finance department and an insurance company, and again, information needs to flow, not only inside the company, but also to and from the customer and insurance agent.

- **Activity 5: Replenishment.** Customized orders will always trigger a need for some manufacturing or assembly operation. Similarly, if standard items are out of stock, they need to be produced or procured. In both cases, production can be done in-house or by suppliers. The suppliers involved may have their own suppliers (sub-suppliers or tier-2 suppliers).

- **Activity 6: In-house production.** A plan is needed for in-house production. Production planning involves people, materials, components, machines, financial resources, and possibly suppliers and subcontractors. In the case of assembly, manufacturing, or both, plant services may be needed, including possible collaboration with business partners. Services may include scheduling of people and equipment, shifting other products' plans, working with engineering on modifications, getting equipment, and preparing content. The actual production facilities may be in a different country than the company's headquarters or retailers. This may further complicate the flow of information, collaboration, and communication. All this needs to be done efficiently and effectively.

- **Activity 7: Use contractors.** A manufacturer may opt to buy products or subassemblies from contractors. Similarly, if the seller is a retailer, such as in the case of Amazon.com or Walmart.com, the retailer must purchase products from its manufacturers. Several scenarios are possible. Warehouses can stock purchased items, which is what Amazon.com does with its best-selling books, toys, and other commodity items. However, Amazon.com does not stock books for which it receives only a few orders. In such cases, the publishers or intermediaries must make special delivery arrangements. In either case, appropriate receiving and quality assurance of incoming materials and products must take place. Once production (activity 6) or purchasing from suppliers (activity 7) is completed, shipments to the customers (Activity 3) can be arranged.

- **Activity 8: Contacts with customers.** Sales representatives need to keep in constant contact with customers, especially in B2B, starting with notification of orders received and ending with notification of a shipment or a change in delivery date. These contacts are usually done via e-mail and are frequently generated automatically. For typical services that customers need, see Online File W12.1.

- **Activity 9: Returns.** In some cases, customers want to exchange or return items. Such returns can be a major problem, as billions of dollars in North American goods are returned each year for both online and offline situations. The movement of returns from customers back to vendors is called **reverse logistics.**

Order fulfillment processes may vary, depending on the product and the vendor. The order fulfillment process also differs between B2B and B2C activities, between the delivery of goods and services, and between small and large products. Furthermore, certain circumstances, such as in the case of perishable materials or foods or pharmaceuticals, require additional steps, administrative activities, and legal constraints and obligations.

The opening case describes how Amazon.com fulfills its orders. Complex processes, such as those used by Amazon.com, may have problems (see Section 12.2) that are often minimized or eliminated through automation (as the slideshow in Del Rey 2012 demonstrates).

The Importance of Order Fulfillment

Order fulfillment is considered a critical success factor for e-commerce. Wozniak (2013) lists the following five keys order fulfillment issues that are critical for profitability and customer satisfaction.

- *Correct product delivery*. Customers abandon shopping from a vendor that delivers even one incorrect item (295 of all shoppers).
- *On time delivery*. 42% of customers will change vendors that do not ship as promised.
- *Order tracking*. Order tracking and e-mail notifications are a must now.
- *Speedy delivery*. Retailers must meet customer expectations.
- *Free shipping*. Helps a lot. Common for expensive items, also see Amazon's Prime membership.

Order Fulfillment and the Supply Chain

The nine-activity order fulfillment process is an integral part of the *supply chain*. The flows of orders, payments, information, materials, and parts need to be coordinated among all the company's relevant department participants, as well as with and among all relevant external partners. The procedures of supply chain management (SCM) must be considered when planning and managing the order fulfillment process, which due to its complexity may have problems.

SECTION 12.1 REVIEW QUESTIONS

1. Define order fulfillment and logistics.
2. Compare traditional logistics with e-logistics.
3. List the nine activities of the order fulfillment process.

12.2 PROBLEMS IN ORDER FULFILLMENT ALONG SUPPLY CHAINS

During the 2011 holiday season online sales increased 15% from the previous year. Some retailers were caught off guard (Hayes 2012). For example, the large demand for some products from BestBuy.com led to problems in fulfilling orders made in November and December 2011. As a consequence, Best Buy was unable to fulfill many of these orders. The reason was that the supply chain management system was unable to

detect problems before they occurred. The problem resulted in bad publicity for Best Buy.

A similar situation arose during the 2013 holiday season in the U.S., although the fulfillment and delivery problems were much more widespread among e-tailers. While online sales increased a little over ten percent from the previous year, last minute orders were up close to 50%. Many of these last minute orders were no doubt predicated on the promise of one to two day deliveries. As a result of this last minute flood of requests, the major carriers – UPS and FedEx – were unable to handle the massive volume, resulting in a substantial percentage of orders failing to be delivered in time for Christmas (Heller 2013). A number of retailers had to offer gift coupons or other forms of remuneration to make up for the missed deliveries.

The inability to deliver products on time is a typical supply chain problem in both offline and online commerce. Several other problems have been observed along the supply chain: Some companies grapple with high inventory costs; shipments of wrong products, materials, and parts occur frequently; and the cost to expedite operations or shipments is high. The chance that such problems will occur in EC is often higher because of the mismatch between standard supply chain structures and processes and the special nature and requirements of EC. For example, most manufacturers' and distributors' warehouses are designed to ship large quantities to a set number of stores; they are not designed to optimally pack and ship small orders to a large number of customers' doors. Improper inventory levels are typical in EC, as are poor delivery scheduling and mixed-up shipments.

Uncertainties in Demand

Many problems along the EC supply chain stem from demand uncertainties and the difficulties that ensue across the supply chain in trying to meet this uncertain demand. This is where demand forecasting comes into play. The major goal of demand planning is to forecast at a very detailed level the number of products of a certain type that will be needed to meet the demand at specific locations at particular points or time intervals in the future. For instance, a virtual retailer might want to estimate the number of smartphones of a particular model that will be needed to fulfill potential orders for a particular city or area of a city during the upcoming holiday season.

Usually, demand forecasts rest on statistical (time series) estimates from historical patterns and trends in sales or order data. The estimates try to incorporate a number of factors in understanding what produced these historical patterns and trends so these factors can be taken into account when making the estimates. Some of the factors might include economic conditions, prices, seasonal adjustments, weather conditions, estimates of consumer confidence, and the impact of promotions of various types. Obviously, anyone of these factors can change very quickly, as well as the fact that consumers tastes can change quite radically, which is why demand forecasting is as much an art as it is a science.

The problem is that demand planning is probably the most critical planning process in the supply chain because it determines many of the other processes in the chain. Among other things, it drives the plans of how many orders can be filled from inventory, how much a retailer will buy, how much manufacturers will need to build, what raw materials are needed, how much factory capacity is needed, how much will have to be shipped, and when and where it will have to be shipped, and so forth. Inaccurate estimates of demand ripple throughout the supply chain. This is why the demand forecast should be conducted frequently, and adjustments need to be made to plans in collaboration among the business partners along the supply chain. Companies attempt to achieve accurate demand forecasts by methods such as information sharing using collaborative commerce.

Inadequate Logistical Infrastructure

Pure play EC companies are likely to have more problems because they do not have a logistics infrastructure already in place and are forced to use external logistics services rather than in-house departments for these functions. These external logistics services are often called **third-party logistics suppliers (3PL)**, or *logistics service providers*. Outsourcing logistics services can be expensive, and it requires more coordination and dependence on outsiders who may not be reliable. For this reason, large virtual retailers usually have their own physical warehouses and distribution systems. Other virtual retailers are creating strategic alliances with logistics companies or with experienced mail-order companies that have their own logistics systems.

Inefficient Financial Flows

Note that supply chain problems and improvements refer not only to the flow of goods but also to the flow of information and money. Money flow includes invoicing, payment, collection, and so forth.

In spite of the availability of computer-based systems, many suppliers, manufacturers, distributors and retailers rely on manual and paper-based systems to conduct financial transactions. These inefficient financial processes not only slow the flow of cash across the supply chain but halt the flow of goods and services and put the various partners at a competitive disadvantage. To succeed in today's global economy trading partners need to rely on automated systems to speed their financial transactions. For solutions to such problems, see Crossgate Inc. (2010).

Lack of Information Sharing

In today's world the flow of information across the supply chain is almost as critical as the flow of goods and services. Information systems support this flow, enabling communication and coordination of the various players and systems in the chain. Without these systems and the information sharing they support, the supply chain could not exist or survive.

Virtually every world-class company has a variety of information systems designed to support both supply chain planning and execution.

Included are some combination of integrated capabilities designed to support network design, demand, supply, and logistics planning along with systems enabling supply, transportation, warehousing, labor, and return logistics management.

One of the most persistent order fulfillment problems is the *bullwhip effect*. Basically, it refers to the mismatch between the actual demand for goods and the inventory supplied upstream in the supply chain to meet the assumed demand. The mismatch results in excess inventory and safety stock that is used as a buffer against underestimated demand. In practice the mismatch grows as you move up the chain from the retailer to the distributor to the supplier to the manufacturer so that variability in inventory and safety stock increases along the way. One way to reduce the mismatch is to ensure that information and, thus visibility, about demand flows to all the parties involved, so that there is only "one version of the truth" instead of each party either producing its own estimate from different data sources or only working with the previous link in the chain, rather than all parties relying on common data that is close to the actual point of sale.

The effect is described in Online File W12.2.

SECTION 12.2 REVIEW QUESTIONS

1. List some problems along the EC supply chain.
2. Explain how uncertainties create order fulfillment problems. List some of these problems.
3. What problems may exist in financial supply chains?
4. Describe the role of 3PLs.
5. Why is information sharing needed along the end-to-end supply chain?

12.3 SOLUTIONS TO ORDER FULFILLMENT PROBLEMS ALONG THE SUPPLY CHAIN

Many EC logistics problems are generic; they can be found in the non-Internet world as well. Therefore, many of the solutions that have been developed for these problems in brick-and-mortar companies also work for e-tailers. IT and EC technologies facilitate most of these solutions. They also provide for automation of various operations along the supply chain that usually improve its operation. In this section, we will discuss some of the specific solutions to EC order fulfillment problems along the supply chain.

Improvements in the Order-Taking Activity

One way to excel in order fulfillment is to improve the order-taking activity and its links to fulfillment and logistics. Order taking can be done via e-mail or on a webstore and it may be automated. For example, in B2B, orders can be generated and transmitted automatically to suppliers when inventory levels fall below a certain threshold. It is a part of the *vendor-managed inventory* (VMI) strategy described in Chapter 5. The result is a fast, inexpensive, and more accurate (no need to rekey data) order-taking process. In B2C, Web-based ordering using electronic forms expedites the process, making it more accurate (e.g., automated processes can check the input data and provide instant feedback), and reduces processing costs for sellers. When EC order taking can interface or integrate with a company's back-office system, it shortens cycle times and eliminates errors.

Order-taking improvements also can take place within an organization, for example, when a manufacturer orders parts from its own warehouse. When delivery of such parts runs smoothly, it minimizes disruptions to the manufacturing process, reducing losses from downtime.

Warehousing and Inventory Management Improvements

A popular EC inventory management solution is a **warehouse management system (WMS)**. On the surface, WMS refers to a software system that helps in managing warehouses. Behind the scenes, any market-leading WMS provides:

- **Inbound functions** such as yard management, appointment scheduling, multi-method receiving, cross-docking, put-to-store, quality assurance, staging, and put-away

- **Inventory functions** such as inventory visibility, lot-serial control, multi-level holds, counts, replenishments, value-added services (VAS) processing, work order processing, internationalization, and slotting
- **Resource management** such as dynamic pick location assignment, equipment utilization, facility utilization, task management, automation interfaces, and workforce management
- **Outbound functions** such as shipment order management, multi-method order picking, retail in-store and dark-store picking and processing of e-commerce orders, cartonization, shipping and parcel manifesting, sequenced staging and loading, and compliance of shipping documents.
- **3PL/divisional support** such as multi-client architecture, client billing, client-based process modeling, cross-client optimization, client visibility and reporting

See, for example, **jda.com**, for a description of the detailed capabilities of a WMS.

A WMS is useful in reducing inventories and decreasing the number of out-of-stock incidents. Such systems also are useful in maintaining an inventory of repair items so repairs can be expedited; picking items out of storage bins in the warehouse; receiving items at the receiving docks; and automating the warehouse operations. For example, introducing a make-to-order production process and providing timely and accurate demand information to suppliers can minimize inventories and out-of-stock incidents. In some instances, the ultimate inventory improvement is to have no inventory at all; for products that can be digitized (e.g., software), order fulfillment can be instantaneous and can eliminate the need for inventory.

Changing the Structure and Process of the Supply Chain

An efficient solution to many supply chain problems is to change the supply chain structure from a linear to a hub structure as illustrated in Figure 12.2. Notice that in a hub structure connection between supply chain partners and elements is much shorter. Also, coordination and control is done at the center of the hub, making the management more efficient, and the structure increases visibility. Long supply chains are usually more susceptible to problems. Also, the hub structure management is usually fully digital, making order fulfillment faster, less expensive, and less problematic.

Speeding Up Deliveries: From Same Day to a Few Minutes

As discussed earlier, a major success factor in EC is the speed within which shoppers receive their orders. And indeed, the competition for fast delivery is intensifying.

FedEx initiated the concept of "next day" delivery in 1973. It was a revolution in door-to-door logistics. A few years later, FedEx, introduced its "next-morning delivery" service. In the digital age, however, even the next morning may not be fast enough. Today, we talk about same-day delivery and even delivery within an hour. Deliveries of urgent materials to and from hospitals, shipping auto parts to car service shops, and delivering medicine to patients are additional examples of such a service. The opening case to this chapter described Amazon.com's recent implementation of their "same-day" delivery service. Two other newcomers to this area are eFulfillment Service (**efulfillmentservice.com**) and OneWorld Direct (**owd.com**). These companies have created networks for the rapid distribution of products, mostly EC-related ones. They offer national distribution systems across the United States in collaboration with shipping companies, such as FedEx and UPS.

Delivering groceries is another area where speed is important, as discussed in Chapter 3. Quick pizza deliveries have been available for a long time (e.g., Domino's Pizza). Today, many pizza orders can be placed online. Also, many restaurants deliver food to customers who order online. Examples of this service can be found at **gourmetdinnerservice.com.au** and the

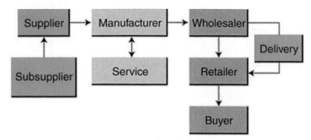

Traditional Linear Supply Chain

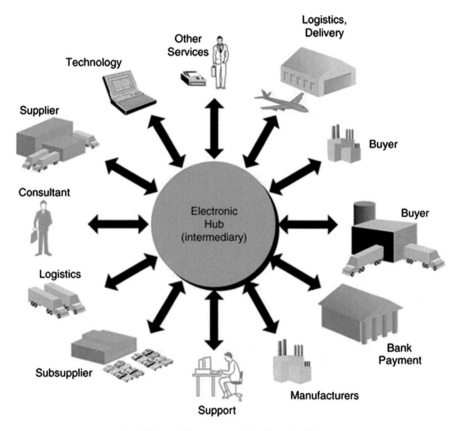

Hub-Based Structure of the Supply Chain

Figure 12.2   Changes in the supply chain

GrubHub company. Some companies even offer aggregating supply services, processing orders from several restaurants and then making deliveries (e.g., **dialadinner.com.hk** in Hong Kong).

Supermarket deliveries are often done same day. Arranging and coordinating such deliveries may be difficult, especially when fresh or perishable food is to be transported. Buyers may need to be home at certain times to accept the deliveries.

Delivery by Drones

Ideally, e-tailers want to deliver faster than you can get products by going to a store and buying then. The futuristic solution is delivery of packages by drones in minutes. A dream? Amazon.com believes that the dream will come true in 2015. However, this may take much longer due to legal, technological (sensors' capabilities) and other constraints, see Black (2014).

Example: Amazon Prime Air

One day we will see a fleet of Prime Air vehicles in the sky, delivering packages to customers' doors. For how the delivery is envisioned see the video and text at **amazon.com/b?node=8037720011**. The technology is available today, the cost is declining and the Federal Aviation Administration is working on the regulations. According to a lobbying registration filing, Amazon Prime Air hired Akin Gump Strauss Hauer & Feld to lobby regarding testing and operation of unmanned aerial vehicles.

Amazon is not the only company that banks on delivery by drones. For example, QuiQui is a startup that plans to deliver medicine in the San Francisco Bay Area with delivery time of 8–12 minutes (see Segall 2014).

Same Day Delivery

We covered this topic in Chapter 3 as it related to groceries. Also cited there is the increased competition. In addition to Amazon Fresh many other companies are active in the market. Notable are Instacart, Postmates, and Google Express (see Pisani 2014). But, same day delivery does not only apply to groceries. Amazon is starting same day delivery of everything in several large cities. Google Shopping Express is active too, and so are eBay, Uber Rush and others (Bowman 2014). For one hour delivery see Halkias (2015).

Partnering Efforts and Outsourcing Logistics

An effective way to solve order fulfillment problems is for an organization to partner with other companies. For example, several EC companies have partnered with UPS or FedEx.

Logistics-related partnerships can take many forms. For example, marketplaces may be managed by one of many freight forwarders such as A & A Contract Customs Brokers, a company that helps other companies find "forwarders." Forwarders help prepare goods for shipping and work with carriers to determine the optimal way to ship. Forwarders can also find the least expensive prices on air carriers, and the carriers bid to fill the space with forwarders' goods that need to be shipped.

Example

SkyMall (**skymall.com**; a subsidiary of Gemstar-TV Guide International), is a retailer that sells from catalogs on airplanes, over the Internet, and by mail order. It relies on its suppliers to fill the orders. For small suppliers that do not handle their own shipments and for international shipments, SkyMall contracts the appropriate distribution centers owned by Sykes Enterprises. Note: The company went out of business in 2015.

Instead of a joint venture or equity ownership with partners, many companies simply outsource logistics with comprehensive logistics service providers like UPS and FedEx. Their services cover all forms of EC including B2C, B2B, and G2B. See Case 12.1 for a description of the broad EC services that UPS provides. One advantage of outsourcing is that it is easy to change the logistics provider. Outsourcing is especially appealing to small companies.

CASE 12.1: UPS PROVIDES BROAD EC SERVICES

In 2013 United Parcel Service (**ups.com**) delivered close to 17 million packages with the help of over 395,000 employees, each day, all over the globe, using a network of hundreds of planes and thousands of vans. This represents a volume of 4.3 billion packages per year, an increase of over a 4% increase in volume from the prior year, due in large part to increases in deliveries for EC. UPS is the undisputed leader in packages delivery worldwide. Towards this end, they provide customers with tools and applications for tracking packages, examining shipping histories, figuring time-in-transit, and verifying on time arrival.

In their annual financial reports UPS describes their business as being divided into three segments: U.S. Domestic Package, International Package, and Supply Chain and Freight. For the past few years, these segments have represented around 62%, 22%, and 16%, respectively. While package delivery represents the major part of their business, they also provide expertise, infrastructure, and technology for managing global logistics services. These logistics services include "transportation, distribution, forwarding, ground, ocean and air freight, brokerage and financing" (UPS 2014). In essence, for customers who utilize these services, UPS runs major parts of their supply chains.

A major component of their Supply Chain and Freight business segment is their worldwide network of distribution centers. For example, in China they have over 130 centers for supporting the distribution of goods to customers in close to 90 cities in the country. The centers manage receiving, storage, order processing, and shipment. The centers are also used to provide post-sales services including planning, fulfillment, testing, reporting, refurbishing, and reverse logistics for critical parts. These latter capabilities, for example, are utilized by the manufacturers and suppliers of automobile parts.

Even Experts Can Encounter Problems

As noted in Case 12.1, in spite of UPS' supply chain expertise and infrastructure, they were still unable to handle the peak in demand and the surge in last minute orders experienced during the 2013 holiday season. The overall volume of orders throughout December, as well as the number of last minute orders spurred by retailers guaranteeing next day delivery, even for orders placed at 11 PM on Christmas Eve, far exceeded UPS's projections and, consequently, the ability of their supply chain networks to

process and handle the orders. In response, UPS is focusing on:

- **Improved Forecasts**. Online retail is growing rapidly – faster than many companies have anticipated. The methods used for forecasting demand and the impacts of this demand upstream on the supply chain no longer work in this environment. Greater collaboration is required with large customers in order to estimate the impact of evolving consumer behavior and promotions (like guaranteed free delivery).
- **Network Throughput**. Investments are required to update the infrastructure of a number of UPS' distribution centers and to improve the routing capabilities of their delivery systems. Increased automation is critical to the improvement of the distribution centers, while the rollout of their On-Road Integrated Optimization and Navigation (ORION) system is key to improved routing. ORION optimizes the routes taken by delivery vehicles resulting in shortened overall distances for a given delivery cycle, improved delivery times, and more efficient fuel consumption (see Konrad 2013). It also supports better tracking of packages.
- **Shipment Visibility**. With the growth of their Supply Chain and Freight business, there has been a substantial increase in the number of truck trailers that customers leave at their distribution centers. UPS has limited visibility to the contents in these trailers.
- **Improved Communication**. Better communication between shippers and receivers is needed during peak periods and when disruption occur in the network. Better communications will enable their customers to not only respond to disruptions but also to proactively plan for the peaks.

Impact of Ship from Store

Many of the EC orders that UPS handles involve shipments that travel long distances from one of their or the retailer's distribution center to the customer. Obviously, this results in a higher cost to either the customer or the retailer or both. Although UPS has adjusted their shipment costs so that the margin percentage is essentially the same regardless of distance, longer distances mean higher revenues.

In an effort to reduce shipping costs, some of the specialty retailers like the Gap, are servicing online orders by shipping directly from the store to the customer (Nilsson 2013). Similarly, larger retailers, who have been shipping directly from their stores for quite some time, have substantially increased these shipments. For example, in the past year Walmart has doubled the number of their stores using direct from store shipments. In essence, the store nearest the customer becomes a distribution center. While UPS and their main competitor FedEx are still used for a majority of these deliveries, the fact that the distances are shorter means that their revenues are also reduced.

In the short run this is not likely to have a major impact on UPS's overall revenues. However, over the next few years, as alternative EC distribution methods emerge (e.g., order online and ship from store and pick up in store), and as Amazon.com's distribution network expands (see opening case), UPS and FedEx will have to come up with alternative strategies to address the potential revenue impacts.

Sources: Based on Nilsson (2013), Konrad (2013), UPS (2014), and **ups.com** (accessed April 2015).

Questions
1. What sort of outsourcing services does UPS provide besides package delivery?
2. Why would a shipper, such as UPS, expand to other logistics services?
3. What changes is UPS contemplating to avoid the problems encountered during the 2013 holiday season?
4. Why does "ship from store" EC delivery represent a threat to UPS' business?

Using Robots in Warehouses
Robots have been used in warehouses to fetch parts stored in bins for many years. What is new

is using them on a large scale in EC. According to Lobosco (2014) Amazon planned to use 10,000 robots in its warehouses by the end of 2014. You can watch the video titled "Robot Army Helps Run Warehouse" (3:10 minutes), cited by Lobosco (2014), to see what the robots are doing. In 2015 Amazon was using over 20,000 robots.

Integrated Global Logistics Program

An increase in global trading created a need for an effective global logistics system. Order fulfillment problems described earlier tend to be even larger in longer supply chains that cross country borders. The number of partners in such situations is usually larger than in domestic logistics (e.g., customs brokers, global carriers), and so is the need for coordination, communication, and collaboration. Furthermore, such systems require a high level of security, especially when the Internet is the centric technology platform. Integrating separate segments of the supply chain can be very beneficial for minimizing problems in long global chains.

Order Fulfillment in Make-to-Order and Mass Customization

As you may recall from Chapter 1, one of the advantages of EC is the ability to easily customize products and personalize services. Although taking customized orders is easily done online, the fulfillment of such orders may not be simple. Mass production enabled companies to reduce the price per unit. Customization is usually expensive, since each item must be handled separately. Customization also requires time, especially for large products like cars. However, consumers usually want customized products to be delivered in a timely fashion at price points that are not much higher than those of a similar product that is mass produced. So, the question is: how does a supplier, manufacturer or retailer do this at a reasonable cost to themselves and in a reasonable time for their customers?

Fulfilling Orders

Dell was a pioneer in providing customized products to end consumers in a timely and cost effective fashion. They were able to do this using mass produced components that were assembled to meet the customized orders of their customers. This approach has been adopted by many other manufacturers. Most customized cars, shoes, toys, textbooks, and wedding rings are made this way. Of course, when you talk about millions of computers at Dell, the supply chain, the logistics, and the delivery of components become critical (see EC Case 12.2 p. 578 for a discussion of Dell supply chain practices). You also need to closely collaborate with your suppliers. In addition, you need to have flexible production lines where changes are made quickly and inexpensively (e.g., painting cars at Toyota), and you need tools that enable quick and not-so-expensive changes (usually driven by computerized systems). This is usually a part of *intelligent factories* or production lines.

For sources on intelligent factories and mass customization, see the *International Journal of Mass Customization* and Smart Factory KL (**smartfactory.eu**).

Here, we present examples of how customization is accomplished by these methods.

Example 1: Intelligent Factories

These factories work on totally integrated automation that enables mass customization to be executed at a reasonable cost and speed. Major developers are Siemens AG, IBM, and General Electric.

Example 2: Distributed Mass Customization

Etsy (**etsy.com**) is a market maker for handmade goods, many of which are customized and sold online. Thousands of small producers custom produce on demand. Etsy aggregates them into one electronic marketplace.

Handling Returns (Reverse Logistics)

Allowing for the return of defective or unsatisfactory merchandise and providing for product exchanges or refunds, are necessary to maintaining customers' trust and loyalty. Some time ago, it was found that the absence of a good return mechanism was the number two reason for shopper reluctance to buy online. A good return policy is a must in EC.

Dealing with returns is a major logistics problem for EC merchants. Several options for handling returns are:

- **Return the item to the place of purchase.** This is easy to do with a purchase from a brick-and-mortar store, but not a virtual one. To return a product to a virtual store, a customer needs to get authorization, pack everything up, pay to ship it back, insure it, and wait up to two billing cycles for a credit to show up on his or her credit card statement. The buyer is not happy and neither is the seller, who must unpack, check the paperwork, and resell the item, usually at a loss. This solution is workable only if the number of returns is small or the merchandise is expensive (e.g., Blue Nile). Some vendors, (e.g., Amazon.com), enable customers to print prepaid UPS or USPS shipping labels that make returns easier for the customers.
- **Separate the logistics of returns from the logistics of delivery.** With this option, returns are shipped to an independent returns unit and are handled separately. This solution may be more efficient from the seller's point of view, but it does not ease the return process for the buyer.
- **Completely outsource returns.** Several outsourcers, including UPS and FedEx, provide logistics services for returns. The services deal not only with delivery and returns but also with the entire logistics process. FedEx, for example, offers several options for returning goods.
- **Allow the customer to physically drop the returned item at a collection station or at a physical store of the same**

vendor. Offer customers locations (such as a convenience store or the UPS Store) where they can drop off returns. In Asia and Australia, returns are accepted in convenience stores and at gas stations. For example, BP Australia Ltd. (gasoline service stations) teamed up with **wishlist.com.au**, and Caltex Australia is accepting returns at the convenience stores connected to its gasoline stations. The accepting stores may offer in-store computers for ordering and may also offer payment options, as at Japanese 7-Elevens (**7dream.com**). In Taiwan and some other countries, you can order merchandise (e.g., books), pay, pick up the item ordered, and return unwanted items, at a 7-Eleven store. Click-and-mortar stores usually allow customers to return merchandise that was ordered online to their physical stores (e.g., **walmart.com** and **eddiebauer.com**).

- **Auction the returned items.** This option can go hand-in-hand with any of the previous solutions.

For strategy, guidelines, and other information on returns, see The Reverse Logistics Executive Council.

Order Fulfillment in B2B

According to recent forecasts by Forrester Research (reported by Sheldon and Hoar 2013), online revenues for B2B EC in 2013 were substantially higher than online revenues for B2C EC. The figures were close to $570 billion versus $250 billion, respectively. In spite of the sizeable difference, B2B EC is far less developed than B2C EC. The differences are found not only in the front-end experience but also in the back-office functionality including information management, Web content management and order management.

Some of the major differences in order management capabilities were pinpointed in another survey sponsored in 2013 by Honeywell and conducted by Peerless Research Group (2013) for *Logistics Management* and *Supply Chain Management Review*. Based on responses from 469 supply chain managers, most of whom were responsible for either B2B or a combination of B2B and B2C EC systems across a range of industries, the survey revealed that:

- The most important missions for their systems were increasing the volume and speed of fulfillment while reducing costs per order, increasing profitability, and improving customer service.
- Many of the inefficiencies and increased costs in order fulfillment were due to increased transportation, packaging, and materials costs.
- The keys to addressing the inefficiencies and costs rest with improved supply chain software applications, re-engineered (fulfillment) operations, and adoption of supply chain analytics.

B2B fulfillment tends to be more inefficient than B2C because it is usually more complex. Typically, the shipments are larger, there are multiple distribution channels, the shipment frequency is more varied, the breadth of the carrier services is more uneven, there are fewer EC carrier offerings, and the EC transaction paths are much more complicated. The types of improvements in applications and re-engineering of processes needed to resolve these sorts of complications revolve around the automation of physical systems, as well as the use of business process management (BPM) software to automate processes.

Using E-Marketplaces and Exchanges to Ease Order Fulfillment Problems in B2B

In Chapter 4, we introduced a variety of e-marketplaces and exchanges. One of the major objectives of these entities is to improve the operation of the B2B supply chain. Let's see how this works with different business models.

- A company-centric marketplace can solve several supply chain problems. For example,

CSX Technology developed an extranet-based EC system for tracking cross-country train shipments as part of its supply chain initiative, and was able to effectively identify bottlenecks and more accurately forecast demand.

- Using an extranet, Toshiba America provides an ordering system for its dealers to buy replacement parts for Toshiba's products. The system smooths the supply chain and delivers better customer service.
- HighJump Software suggested taking into account a number of key elements for optimal order fulfillment including the automation of picking, packing and shipping, the transformation of paper-based processes, and the inclusion of sales and marketing input into various supply chain processes.

For additional discussion on how fulfillment is done in B2B, see **fedex.com/us/supply-chain/services/fulfillment-services** and Demery (2012).

Order Fulfillment in Services

Thus far, we have concentrated on order fulfillment with physical products. Fulfilling service orders (e.g., buy or sell stocks, process insurance claims) may involve additional information processing, which requires more sophisticated EC systems.

Other Solutions to Supply Chain Problems

- *Visibility* increases along the supply chain. It is critical to know where materials and parts are at any given time. This is referred to as **visibility**. Such knowledge can help in solving problems such as delays, combining shipments, and more. Visibility is provided by several tools, such as bar codes, RFID, collaborative devices, and collaborative portals that provide access to information required to manage various aspects of the supply chain. Visibility enables the efficient coordination of supply chain activities in spite of rapid changes in the market.
- *Order fulfillment* can become instant if the products can be digitized (e.g., software). In other cases, EC order taking interfaces with the company's back-office systems, including

logistics. Such an interface, or even integration, shortens cycle time and eliminates errors.

- *Managing risk* to avoid supply chain breakdown can be done in several ways. Carrying additional inventories is effective against the risk of stock-outs, and hence, poor customer service, but it can be expensive. Also, in certain cases the risk increases because products may become obsolete. (Managing inventories was described in Chapter 4.)
- *Inventories can be minimized* by introducing a build-to-order manufacturing process as well as by providing timely and accurate information to suppliers. By allowing business partners to electronically track in route orders and production activities, inventory management can be improved and inventory levels and the expense of inventory management can be minimized. Inventories can be better managed if we know exactly where parts and materials are at any given time (e.g., by using RFID). Retailers' inventories can be managed electronically by their suppliers.
- *Self-service* can reduce supply chain problems and costs. Some activities can be done by customers, business partners, or employees. For example, customers can self-track the status of their orders (e.g., at FedEx, UPS, USPS, etc.); using FAQs, customers and business partners may solve small problems by themselves. Customers can self-configure details of orders (e.g., for a computer at HP, Dell, and Apple), and finally, employees can update personal data online.
- *Collaboration* among members of the supply chain can shorten cycle times, minimize delays and work interruptions, lower inventories, and lower administrative costs. A variety of tools exists ranging from collaborative hubs and networks to collaborative planning.

Innovative E-Fulfillment Strategies

Several innovative e-fulfillment strategies exist. For example, supply chain partners can transmit information flows and hold off shipping physical goods until a point in time when they can make more direct shipments. An example of logistics postponement is merge-in-transit.

Merge-in-transit is a model in which components for a product need to arrive from two or more physical locations. For example, in shipping a desktop PC, the monitor may come from the East Coast of the United States and the CPU from the West Coast. Instead of shipping the components to a central location and then shipping both together to the customer, the components are shipped directly to the customer and merged into one shipment by the local deliverer (so the customer gets all the parts in one delivery), reducing unnecessary transportation.

One of the most innovative logistics systems is that of Dell Computers, as described in Case 12.2.

CASE 12.2: DELL'S WORLD-CLASS SUPPLY CHAIN AND ORDER FULFILLMENT SYSTEM

Since 2004, AMR Research, now part of Gartner, has been publishing an annual Supply Chain Top 25 Ranking. The ranking is based on a combined assessment from Gartner's supply chain experts along with votes from external supply chain peers. Since its inception, Dell has appeared on this list every year, reaching as high as number 2 in 2011.

Direct-to-Consumer and Configure-to-Order

One of the key reasons for their continued high ranking has been the quality of their logistics and order fulfillment systems. Dell was a pioneer in the direct-to-order consumer business model, as well as the configure-to-order method of manufacturing. For much of the time period between 2004 and present day, this business model and manufacturing method served them well. Dell was able to automate the order taking and fulfillment processes, enabling them to coordinate with their suppliers to produce the specific components and finished products required to fill the various customer orders.

This system enabled Dell to handle the overwhelming majority of their purchase orders online through an Internet portal. The portal was used by suppliers to view the requirements of various orders and to work with Dell on forecasted requirements and delivery dates. In this way, only those components required to fulfill current orders were shipped to Dell's factories. The result was a substantial reduction in the flow of parts, the warehouse space required to manage the parts, and idle inventory. Compared to other competitors, Dell had less than 4 days of inventory at any given time, while their competitors had more than 30 days of inventory on hand.

In both the B2C and B2B world of computer electronics, components and models have a short lifespan. Today's computer models are rapidly becoming obsolete. Dell's automated system enabled them to avoid this problem, as well as helping their suppliers respond rapidly to changing demand.

Segmented Supply Chain

In 2008, things began to change for Dell. Dell found that their online configure-to-order system was too inflexible and resulted in configurations that were too expensive for its other, faster growing business segments – their retail stores, enterprise customers, and high-volume consumer products. In each case, fewer, cheaper configurations were required. Because of the mismatch between their supply chain model and the expectations of their newer customers in newer channels, Dell's competitors were able capture significant market share. In response, Dell decided to transform its supply chain into a segmented model with different policies for different types of customers. The result was four supply chain segments, each focused on a different type of customer. The four segments are displayed in Table 12.2 along with their distinguishing characteristics.

Table 12.2 Dell's segmented supply chain

SC production policy	**Build-to-order:** built when configured order received	**Build-to-plan:** built in anticipation of forecasted demand	**Build-to-stock:** built and stocked in anticipation of demand	**Build-to-spec:** built in short time period according to corporate specs with no inventory stocks
SC segment	Online	Retail	Online	Corporate
Volume	Low	High	High	Med-high
Product batch size	One	Large	Large	Med-large
Finished goods inventory	No	Yes, at retailer	Yes, at Dell	No
Lead time	Short	Long	Long	Long

Source: Based on Simchi-Levi et al. (2012) and Thomas (2012)

The Results

Dell's shift to a segmented supply chain substantially impacted the efficiencies and effectiveness of their supply chain. Some of the major benefits included:

- Improved product availability
- Reduced order-to-delivery times
- Fewer configurations required to meet customer demand
- Improved forecast accuracy
- Reduced transportation and manufacturing costs.

Up until 2011, these improvements served Dell's bottom line well. In 2011 they were ranked number 2 on the Supply Chain Top 25; in 2012 they were number 4, and in 2013, number 11. The shift in rankings was primarily a function of the declining revenues in their PC business and had little to do with the performance of their supply chain. Dell's overall business model was built on providing PC systems for businesses and consumers. This business has been severely impacted by the rapid increase in smartphones and tablets, which has eroded the demand for PCs. It will take more than improvements in the supply chain to address the declining demand.

Sources: Based on Hofman et al. (2013), Simchi-Levi et al. (2012), and Thomas (2012).

Questions

1. If Dell was ranked number 11 in 2013, what companies were ranked 1 through 3? Were these the same companies ranked 1 through 3 in 2012?
2. What type of supply chain did Dell originally have? What were its benefits?
3. Why did Dell encounter supply chain problems around 2008?
4. What is a segmented supply chain?
5. Describe Dell's segmented supply chain.

Integration and Enterprise Resource Planning

If you review Figure 12.1 (p. 565) for the order fulfillment process, you will notice that certain activities involve interfacing with other information systems, such as finance, inventory management, production schedule, vendor and customer contact, and logistics. Most of these interfaces are internal, but some are external (most with suppliers and customers). For the sake of effectiveness and efficiency, such interfaces need to be done quickly and without errors. The fewer manual interfaces we need to make, the better. How wonderful it would be if we used only one interface, and if it was automated! This is exactly what an enterprise resource planning (ERP) system does.

The Supply Chains of Tomorrow

According to a comprehensive study done at MIT, tomorrow's supply chains will have to deliver various degrees six outcomes (reported by Melnyk et al. 2010), each with a corresponding set of specific design traits. The outcomes that drive the supply chains are:

1. Monitoring cost, quality, and on-time delivery
2. Safety and security of goods delivered
3. Eliminating waste, reducing pollution, improving the environment
4. Resilience, quick recovery from disruptions of all kinds
5. Responsiveness – change quickly to adapt to changing conditions
6. Innovation – using the supply chain as a source of new processes and products, both internally and with business partners

These outcomes will assure effective and efficient order fulfillment.

SECTION 12.3 REVIEW QUESTIONS

1. List the various order-taking solutions.
2. List solutions for improved delivery.
3. Describe same-day shipments.
4. Describe some innovative e-strategies for order fulfillment.
5. Describe how to effectively manage the return of items.
6. Describe issues in B2B fulfillment.
7. List three outcomes of tomorrow's supply chain.

12.4   RFID AND CPFR AS KEY ENABLERS IN SUPPLY CHAIN MANAGEMENT

Two major technologies were found to be effective for improving and reducing problems along the end-to-end supply chains: RFID and CPFR.

The Essentials of RFID

Radio frequency identification (RFID) is a tag technology in which RFID (electronic) tags are attached to or embedded in objects (including people) and employ wireless radio waves to communicate with RFID readers so that the objects can be identified, located, or can transmit data. Tags are similar to barcodes, but they contain much more information. Also, they can be read from a longer distance (up to 50 feet).

Theoretically, RFID can be utilized and read in many places along the supply chain, as illustrated in Figure 12.3. Over the long run, RFID tags will be attached to most items flowing through the supply chain and tracked and monitored at most of the places depicted in Figure 12.3. To date, cost has been a major inhibitor to the uptake of RFID technology. However, costs are coming down to the point where companies will be willing to invest in RFID because they can be more certain of achieving an ROI on their RFID investments. Even if costs are reasonable, organizations still need to learn how to effectively use RFID technologies with their back-office systems and how to redesign and retool their business processes so they can accrue solid business benefits from these technologies.

Given these developments, what effect will RFID have on supply chains? Let's look at Figure 12.4, which shows the relationship between a retailer (Walmart), a manufacturer (such as P&G), and P&G's suppliers. Note that the tags are read as merchandise travels from the supplier to the retailer (steps 1 and 2). The RFID transmits real-time information on the location of the merchandise. Steps 3 through 6 show the use of the RFID at the retailer, mainly to confirm arrivals (step 3) and to locate merchandise inside the company, control inventory, prevent theft, and expedite processing of relevant information (steps 4 through 6). It is no longer necessary to count inventories, and all business partners are able to view inventory information in real time. This transparency can go several tiers down the supply chain. Additional applications, such as rapid checkout, which eliminates the need to scan each item, will be provided by RFID in the future.

According to Reyes (2011), RFID can help improve supply chain visibility, asset visibility and capital goods tracking, returnable asset tracking, work-in-process tracking, as well as managing internal supply chains. Examples of several applications are presented next.

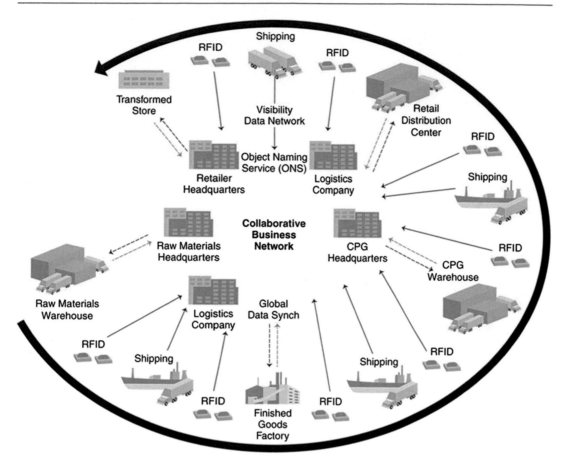

Figure 12.3 Digital supply chains (Source: Intel, "Building the Digital Supply Chain: An Intel Perspective." Intel Solutions White Paper, January 2005, Figure 5, p. 9. Reprinted with permission from Intel Corporation)

RFID Applications in the Supply Chain Around the Globe

Many potential and actual applications exist in enterprises using RFID (e.g., see *RFID Journal*). The following are examples of how RFID is used in the supply chain. For a comprehensive review see Reyes (2011) and the *RFID Journal* (**rfidjournal.com/case-studies**).

RFID at Starbucks

As Starbucks expands its range of fresh foods (such as salads, sandwiches, and the like) available at its stores, the complexity and demands of managing this supply chain increases. Keeping the food fresh depends on keeping it at a steady

cool state and in ensuring timely delivery. Starbucks is requiring its distributors to employ RFID tags to measure the temperature in the delivery trucks. These tags are programmed to record the temperature inside the truck every few minutes, and on return to the depot, this temperature data can be downloaded and analyzed carefully. If there are unacceptable readings (e.g., the temperature is deemed to have risen too high), efforts are made to determine the cause and remedy the problem. This can then cause a redesign of critical business processes with regard to the transportation and handling of food. As RFID technology matures, it is conceivable that in the future, the tags themselves will be able to detect variations in temperature and send a signal to a

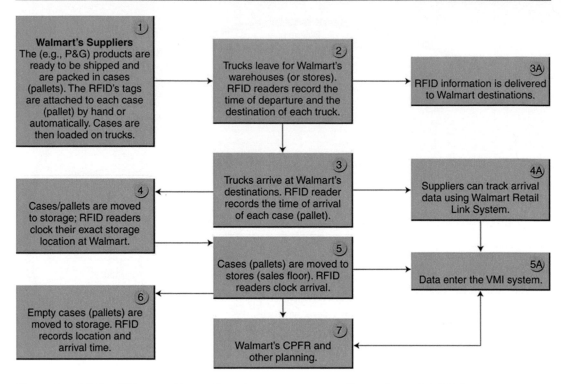

Figure 12.4   RFID at Walmart and its suppliers: the seven-step process (Source: Drawn by E. Turban)

thermostat to activate refrigeration fans within the truck. For details, see Xue (2010).

RFID at Deutsche Post (Germany)

Deutsche Post owns six million shipping containers that it uses to hold and transport about 70 million letters and other items that pass through its distribution centers daily. In order to process these crates, Deutsche Post prints in excess of 500 million thick paper labels, all of which are thrown away after a single use. It was environmental concerns, rather than purely economic ones, that drove Deutsche Post's RFID initiative.

Deutsche Post uses passive RFID tags with a bi-stable display, meaning that the text displayed remains on-screen after the power is removed and does not change until power is restored and the text is rewritten by an RFID interrogator. Tags on the crates must be readable from all angles and in all types of weather, requiring a

robust tag. Furthermore, the tags need to last about five years in order for the application to be financially viable.

Deutsche Post developed a custom tag and RFID reader, and uses specialized software in this innovative application. Several other post offices around the world use RFID (e.g., Canada).

RFID at Atlantic Beef Products (Ontario, Canada)

Cow's ears are tagged with RFID tags. After a cow is slaughtered, its ear tags are scanned for food traceability. The carcass goes onto two leg hooks, each equipped with an RFID chip. They are synced to each animal's database record. The RFIDs replace barcodes, which could get contaminated with *E. coli* on the slaughter house. The RFID helps track the movement of each cow and the meat produced at any time. The system won a gold medal from the Canadian IT organization. For details, see Makepolo (2014).

Collaborative Planning, Forecasting, and Replenishment

As you may recall, a major problem in order fulfillment is the demand forecast. A related problem is the bullwhip effect. A possible solution to both problems is CPFR.

Collaborative planning, forecasting, and replenishment (CPFR) refers to the practice of suppliers, manufacturers, and retailers collaborating on the planning and forecasting of demand so that the supply of goods and services matches customer demand at the retailer's shelf. The goal of CPFR is to minimize the inefficiencies in the supply chain that result from the mismatch of supply and demand, both in the amount of goods that flow as well as in the timing of the flow. Large manufacturers of consumer goods, such as P&G, have superb supply chains resulting from their use of CPFR.

For the essentials of CPFR "Google Images of CPFR model." This figure is based on the guidelines originally conceived and approved by the Voluntary Interindustry Commerce Solutions (VICS) committee in 1998. The guidelines prescribe a cyclical process in which sellers, buyers, and end customers are considered. The process starts with strategy and planning, followed by demand and supply management, which results in execution. The results are analyzed, leading to a reexamination of the strategy.

CPFR can be used with company-centric B2B and with sell-side or buy-side marketplaces. The major benefits that follow from CPFR include: faster adjustments to consumer demand; more precise sales forecasts; reduced out-of-stock resulting in improved sales; reduced safety stock resulting in reduced inventory; and reduced handling and administrative costs. There have been a number of case studies detailing the realized benefits of CPFR. Many of these case studies have involved consumer packaged goods (CPG), companies like Kraft Foods, Kimberly Clark, Proctor & Gamble, and Johnson & Johnson to name a few (see Sadhu et al. 2011 for a summary of these cases).

In spite of its long history and a relatively large number of success stories, acceptance and use outside the CPG arena is not widespread. As Jakovljevic (2010) highlights, the gap between reality and hype is attributable to a number of factors, including:

- There is a general reluctance and lack of trust among trading partners to share data.
- The overall approach is complicated and involves a number of steps and processes. This makes it difficult to start and maintain the intertwined processes.
- The approach overlooks the fact that the different parties have different goals and objectives. As a result, they tend to focus on those parts of the approach that directly impact their goals and ignore those parts of the approach that don't.
- Existing technologies are incapable of handling the breadth of processes and/or the volumes of data required to support the required planning, forecasting, and replenishment.

Since 2012, a special Voluntary Interindustry Commerce Solutions (VICS) advisory committee (VICS 2013) has been focusing on one of the key elements of CPFR – store-level Distribution Resource Planning (DRP). The use and benefits of DRP are discussed in EC Case 12.3.

CASE 12.3: STANLEY BLACK & DECKER'S COLLABORATIVE SUCCESS WITH LOWE'S AND HOME DEPOT

In today's retail world, consumers are in the driver's seat. They expect a "seamless" experience across all the shopping channels that a retailer offers. This has put a strain not only on retailers to deliver the right products to the right channel at the right time, but also on every other node in the supply chain, particularly their suppliers. This strain has resulted in a renewed interest on collaboration focused on optimizing inventory and order fulfillment.

One of the key technologies supporting this renewed collaboration is store – level DRP. **Store-Level Distribution Resource Planning (DRP)** is a collaborative approach that utilizes the retailer's POS data to produce a model that yields a bottoms-up, time-phased forecast of consumer sales, shipments, receipts, and inventories at all stores or channels and distribution centers (DCs) for all items usually over a 12-month period. Typically, the forecasts are for daily periods in the near-term (say the next 3 months) and weekly for the remaining time. These forecasts are then used by the suppliers (manufacturers) to calculate – not forecast – what should be produced and delivered, where it should be produced and delivered, and when it should be produced and delivered. In this way, supply is tied directly to demand on the (real or virtual) shelf. If there are changes in the demand at a store or channel, then the model is used to adjust production and delivery.

The model for a single forecast provides visibility across the supply chain with a number of attendant benefits (VICS 2013):

- Improved availability at the shelf, in-stocks, service levels, forecast accuracy and productivity.
- Reduced safety-stock, product costs, transportation costs and lead times.

In alliance with the superstore retailers Lowe's and Home Depot, Stanley Black & Decker has been one of the strongest proponents of DRP. Stanley Black & Decker was built in 2010 from the merger of The Stanley Works with Black & Decker. According to their latest financial reports, today they are a global provider of power and hand tools, products and services for industrial applications, mechanical access solutions (e.g. door locks), and electronic security and monitoring systems. In 2013, their revenues were approximately $11 billion with close to 50% coming from North America. Within North America two of their largest customers are Lowe's and Home Depot.

A few years back, before the merger, Black & Decker established dedicated demand forecasting teams for one of their three divisions (Hardware and Home Improvement) that worked directly with Lowe's and Home Depot in the same cities where the two retailers were located. The focus was on matching supply levels with consumer demand while maintaining the high fill rates and delivery schedules required by the two retailers. The overall process, which rested on spreadsheets, proved too cumbersome, inflexible and time consuming. The result was increased overtime costs, unfulfilled demand, and problematic inventory levels.

After a thorough review, the process and system was replaced by a 3rd party software demand forecasting system which provided the means to use POS data from Lowe's and Home Depot to model item level demand at the store level across time. In this way they had a centralized process for conducting line reviews, as well as determining the impacts of price changes and promotions. Later they added a system for master planning at the plant level and for fulfillment which improved operating efficiency and improved fill rates and optimized the multi-level replenishment process. All of the systems were provided by JDA Software Group, Inc. (**jda.com**).

In 2010, Stanley Black & Decker and Lowe's were nominated for the VICS CPFR Implementation Excellence award for their DPR implementation. The nomination noted the joint improvements in fill rates to 98% percent levels, in-stock improvements to 98%, reduction in excess inventory, and a 10% improvement in forecast accuracy, along with reduced transportation costs.

Sources: Based on Ackerman and Padilla (2009), Fiorletta (2013), Pappas (2013), VICS (2013), and **stanleyblackanddecker.com** (access April 2014).

Questions
1. What is DPR?
2. What are the benefits of DPR?
3. Describe the DPR system established by Stanley Black and Decker in collaboration with Lowe's and Home Depot.
4. What benefits did Stanley Black & Decker and Lowe's realize with their DPR system?

SECTION 12.4 REVIEW QUESTIONS
1. What is RFID?
2. How can RFID improve supply chain visibility?
3. Describe three RFID supply chain applications.
4. What is CPFR?
5. How can CPFR improve supply chain operations of an e-commerce retailer?
6. What are some of the reasons that CPFR has not enjoyed widespread use?

12.5   OTHER E-COMMERCE SUPPORT SERVICES

Depending on the nature and magnitude of its EC initiatives, a company may require several other support services. The services range from consulting to directory services, newsletters, specialized search engines, a number of value-added services, and outsourced EC services.

Consulting Services

How does a firm learn how to do something that it has never done before? Many firms, both start-up and established companies, rely on outside consulting firms. Some of these firms have established a reputation in one area of expertise, whereas others are generalists. Some consultants even take equity (ownership) positions in the firms they advise. Some consultants will build, test, and deliver a working website and may even host it and maintain it for their clients. There are three broad categories of consulting firms.

The first type of consulting firm includes those that provide expertise in the area of EC but not in traditional business. In the past there were a number of larger consulting firms specializing in EC services. Many of these firms were acquired or changed direction. Today, this expertise is provided by smaller firms such as Candid software (**candidinfo.com**), Holbi (**holbi.co.uk**), and Lounge Lizard (**loungelizard.com**). These firms were all started prior to the dot-com bubble and are still in operation today.

The second type of consulting firm is a traditional consulting company that maintains organizational units that focus on EC. These firms leverage their existing relationships with their corporate clients and offer EC value-added services. Representative companies are Accenture, Boston Consulting Group, Deloitte & Touche, Ernst & Young, McKinsey, and PricewaterhouseCoopers.

The third category of consulting firms is EC hardware and software vendors that provide technology-consulting services. These include SAP, IBM, HP, Oracle, Microsoft, Cisco, Intel, and many more.

Directory Services, Newsletters, and Search Engines

The EC landscape is huge, with hundreds of thousands of companies selling products and services online. How can a buyer find all the suitable sellers? How can a seller find all the suitable buyers? In B2B, vertical exchanges can help with this matching process, but even vertical exchanges include only a limited number of potential partners, usually located in one country. To overcome the problem of finding buyers or sellers online, a company may use directory services.

Directory Services

There are several types of *directory services*. Some simply list companies by categories; others provide links to companies. In many cases, the data are classified in several different ways for easy search purposes. In others, special search engines are provided. Finally, value-added services, such as matching buyers and sellers, are available. The following are some popular directories:

- B2B-Today.com (**b2b-today.com**) is an e-business portal aimed at small to medium enterprises and providing B2B directory services to Chinese suppliers of goods and services across a wide variety of industries ranging from automotive to medical to office supplies just to name a few. The portal supports the RFQ process (Request for Quotation from buyers to suppliers), as well as a number of other related activities.
- Websters (**webstersonline.com**) is a large business directory organized by location and by product or service. In addition, it provides listings by industry and subindustry (according to SIC and NAICS codes).
- ThomasNet (**thomasnet.com**) provides a directory of several hundred thousands of manufacturers of industrial products and services in about 70,000 categories.

Newsletters

There are many B2B newsletters to choose from. Several are e-mailed to individuals free of charge. Examples of B2B newsletters are shown at **savvyb2bmarketing.com/home/newsletters magazines**. Many companies (e.g., Ariba) issue corporate newsletters and e-mail them to people who request them.

Directories and newsletters are helpful, but they may not be sufficient. Therefore, one may need specialized search engines.

Search Engines and News Aggregators

Several search engines can be used to discover B2B-related information. Some of these are embedded in the directories. Here are some examples:

- iEntry (**ientry.com**) provides B2B search engines, targeted "niche engines," and several industry-focused newsletters. iEntry operates a network of websites and e-mail newsletters that reaches more than two million unique opt-in subscribers. Newsletters are available in each of the following categories: Web Developers, Advice, Technology, Professional, Sports & Entertainment, Leisure & Lifestyles, and Web Entrepreneurs. Click on a newsletter to get a brief description and view sample content.
- Sourcetool (**sourcetool.com**) is a search engine that locates information and aggregates B2B (and other business) news.

More EC Support Services

Many other service providers support e-commerce in different ways. Each service provider adds a unique value-added service. This section describes only several representative examples.

Trust Services

Chapter 13 introduced the role of trust in B2C. Trust also is important in B2B because one cannot touch the seller's products and because buyers may not be known to sellers. Trust-support services such as TRUSTe and BBBOnline (Better Business Bureau) are used both in B2C and B2B.

Trademark and Domain Names

A number of domain name services are available. Examples are **mydomain.com**, **register.com**, **easyspace.com**, and **whois.net**.

Digital Photos

Companies such as IPIX (**ipix.com**), which is part of Minds-Eye-View, Inc., provide innovative pictures and video capabilities for websites.

Access to Commercial Databases

Subscribers to ProQuest Dialog (**dialog.com**) can access about 900 databases, including those containing patents, trademarks, government reports, and news articles.

Knowledge Management

IBM Domino offers the capability to integrate social knowledge with IBM's Websphere Portal software, providing enhanced team collaboration and networking.

Client Matching

TechRepublic (**techrepublic.com**) matches business clients with firms that provide a wide variety of IT services. It works like a matchmaking service. Clients define what they want, and TechRepublic performs the searching and screening, checking against some general parameters and criteria. This reduces the risk of clients making bad choices. Buyers also save time and have greater exposure to a larger number of IT service providers.

E-Business Rating Sites

A number of sites are available for businesses to research rankings of potential partners and suppliers. **Bizrate.com**, **forrester.com**, **gomez.com** (now part of Compuware), and **consumersearch. com** all provide business ratings.

Security and Encryption Sites

An example of security/encryption sites is VeriSign (**verisign.com**). The company provides valuable encryption tools for all types of EC organizations. It also provides domain site registration and several security mechanisms.

Table 12.3 Other B2B services

Category	Description	Examples
Marketplace concentrator (aggregator)	Aggregates information about products and services from multiple providers. Purchasers can search, compare, shop, and sometimes complete the purchase transaction	Internet Mall, Insweb, Industrial Marketplace
Information brokers (infomediaries)	Provide product, pricing, and availability information. Some facilitate transactions, but their main value is the information they provide	Travelocity, Autobytel
Transaction brokers	Buyers can view prices and terms, etc. but the primary business activity is to execute the transaction	E*TRADE, TD Ameritrade
Digital product delivery	Sells and delivers software, multimedia, and other digital products over the Internet	Most software and media vendors. Also **sandowl.com**
Content provider or publisher	Creates revenue by providing content	Most publishers
Online service provider	Provides service and support for hardware and software users	CyberMedia.com, TuneUp.com
Specialized directories	Provide leads to a variety of B2B services categories	Business.com, KnowledgeStorm, Searchedu.com

Web Research Services

A number of Web research providers help companies learn more about technologies, trends, and potential business partners and suppliers. Some of these are **idc.com**, **zdnet.com**, and **forrester.com**.

Coupon-Generating Sites

A number of vendors help companies generate online coupons. **Q-pon.com** and **centsoff.com** are a couple of examples.

Table 12.3 presents additional services available for B2B operations.

Outsourcing EC Support Services

Most companies do not maintain in-house EC support services. Instead, they outsource many of these services.

Why Outsource EC Services?

In general, outsourcing has many benefits and only few limitations and risks. For a comprehensive list of benefits, see **outsource2india.com/why_outsource/articles/benefit_outsourcing.asp**.

To show the importance of outsourcing, we will look briefly at the typical process of developing and managing EC infrastructure and applica-

tions. The process includes the following major steps:

1. EC strategy initiation, formulation, and implementation (Chapter 13)
2. Systems design (Chapter 14)
3. Building (or buying) the systems (Chapter 16)
4. Hosting, operating, and maintaining the EC site (Chapter 16)

IT Outsourcing and Application Service Providers

In the past many outside contractors focused on serving SMEs with few IT staff and smaller IT budgets. Today, enterprises of all sizes rely on outside contractors to service a substantial part of their EC system requirements. The list of large companies who rely on third-party vendors to run their B2C websites is extensive. Examples include sites such as **eddiebauer.com**, **1800flowers.com**, and **lenovo.com**. Several types of providers offer services for creating and operating electronic webstores.

SECTION 12.5 REVIEW QUESTIONS

1. Describe the role of EC consultants and list their major types.
2. Describe the value offered by directory services. Provide three examples of what value they add.

3. Explain why specialized search engines are needed.
4. List some other EC support services.
5. List the major reasons why companies outsource EC support services.

MANAGERIAL ISSUES

Some managerial issues related to this chapter are as follows:

1. **If you are an EC vendor, what is the bottleneck in the order fulfillment process?** Order fulfillment is an important task, especially for e-tailers. The problem is not only the physical shipment, but also the efficient execution of the entire order fulfillment process, which may be complex along a lengthy supply chain. To enhance the order fulfillment process, the vendor needs to identify the bottleneck that needs improvement. Potential issues are delayed delivery date, high return rate, high inventory cost, high shipping cost, and poor integration along the supply and demand chains. The EC vendor should identify its own problem first.

2. **For which items should we keep our own inventory?** As Amazon.com has experienced, online vendors try to avoid keeping inventory because it is expensive. However, we should not neglect the fact that retailing with appropriate inventory is a source of extra profit as well. In addition, for certain items, it is not possible to assure on-time delivery without having controllable inventory; the no-inventory policy is not always the best policy. A company has to design the portfolio plan of inventory and distribution centers for the items that have a positive effect of having inventory. A CPFR program may be adopted to minimize the burden of holding inventories. The plan for distribution centers must be balanced with the plan of outsourced items through partners.

3. **What is the alliance strategy in order fulfillment?** Partnerships and alliances can improve collaboration and increase the efficiency of the supply chain. We need to decide in which part of order fulfillment we should count on partners. The typical activities that may be outsourced are shipping, warehousing, inventory holding, return management, and so on. Decide on the appropriate third-party logistics supplier that can provide reliable service for these activities. For certain items that you cannot supply well, a partner may take care of the entire merchandising as well as order fulfillment, especially if you have leverage on the online brand image. An example is Fulfillment by Amazon (FBA) sellers.

4. **How should we manage returns?** Dealing with returns is important for CRM, yet may not be simple. Reverse logistics is very costly, and most companies cannot continue online business if the return rate is too high. Use the CRM system to identify the items with higher return rates and resolve the reason or stop the online sales of these items. A company should estimate its percentage of returns and plan a process for receiving and handling them. The logistics of returns may be executed through an external logistics service provider.

5. **What logistics information should we provide to customers?** Customers, particularly business customers, want to know the availability of inventory and delivery date at the time of order. To meet these needs, the EC system should be integrated with the back-end information system. Customers may also want to trace the status of order processing, which should be managed by more than one company along the order fulfillment process. To provide seamless information beyond the boundary of the vendor, the partners should collaborate while developing their information systems.

6. **Should we use RFID for the order fulfillment?** If your buyer requires you to use RFID tags, there is no choice but to follow the request; however, the expertise and equipment of RFID are not always available within a company. Some third-party logistics service providers support the tagging service. One question is who pays for the cost and who gets the benefit? So far, big buyers such as Walmart

and the Department of Defense get the benefit, while the suppliers pay the cost. In the long run, suppliers may be able to share the benefit in inventory management. However, it will take time until the penetration becomes pervasive enough to maximize the benefit of RFID technology.

7. **Can we use CPFR in SMEs?** CPFR is a conceptual model for working with business partners and is usually effective and efficient with for large organizations. However, since it is basically a conceptual model of collaborative planning, it may work in some SMEs where collaborative planning is critical. A visit to **gs1us.org/industries/apparel-general-merchandise**, and an examination of some of the applications there, can help identify places where CPFR can help SMEs.

SUMMARY

In this chapter, you learned about the following EC issues as they relate to the chapter's learning objectives.

1. **The order fulfillment process.** Large numbers of support services are needed for EC implementation. Most important are payment mechanisms and order fulfillment. On-time delivery of products to customers may be a difficult task, especially in B2C. Fulfilling an order requires several activities ranging from credit and inventory checks to arranging shipments. Most of these activities are part of back-office operations and are related to logistics. The order fulfillment process varies from business to business and also depends on the products to be delivered. Generally speaking, the following steps are recognized: payment verification, inventory checking, shipping arrangement, insurance, production (or assembly), plant services, purchasing materials, customer contacts, and return of defective or unwanted products.

2. **Problems in order fulfillment.** It is difficult to fulfill B2C orders due to difficulties in forecasting demand and potential delays in supply and deliveries. Problems also result from insufficient coordination and information sharing among business partners.

3. **Solutions to order fulfillment problems.** Automating order taking (e.g., by using forms over the Internet) and smoothing the supply chain are two ways to solve order fulfillment problems. Several other innovative solutions exist, most of which are supported by software that enables more accurate inventories, coordination along the supply chain, and appropriate planning and decision making.

4. **RFID tags.** Replacing barcodes with RFID can greatly improve locating items along the supply chain quickly. This technology has many other benefits, which will soon outweigh the major limitations. The major applications are improving supply chain visibility, expediting tracking, speeding up inventory counting, speeding up deliveries, and reducing errors.

5. **Collaborative planning and CPFR.** Collaborative planning concentrates on joint demand forecasting and on accurate resource and activity planning along the supply chain. Collaborative planning tries to synchronize partners' activities. CPFR is a business strategy that attempts to develop standard protocols and procedures for collaboration. Its goal is to improve demand forecasting by collaborative planning in order to ensure delivery of materials when needed. In practice there are a number of successful implementations, although there is not widespread use. Recently, VICS has focused on another collaborative process – store-level DPR – which provides detailed demand forecasts used to calculate inventory and distribution requirements from sourcing to the retail shelf or channel.

6. **Other support services.** EC support services include consulting services, directory services, infrastructure providers, and many more. One cannot conduct EC without some of them. These support services need to be coordinated and integrated. Some of them can be done in-house; others must be outsourced.

7. **Outsourcing EC services.** Selective outsourcing of EC services is usually a must. Lack of resources, time and expertise forces

companies of all sizes to outsource, despite the risks of doing so. Using ASPs is a viable alternative, but they are neither inexpensive nor risk-free.

KEY TERMS

Collaborative planning, forecasting, and replenishment (CPFR)
Distribution Resource Planning (DRP)
E-logistics
Logistics
Merge-in-transit
Order fulfillment
Radio frequency identification (RFID)
Reverse logistics
Third-party logistics suppliers (3PL)
Visibility
Warehouse management system (WMS)

DISCUSSION QUESTIONS

1. Discuss the problem of reverse logistics in EC. What types of companies may suffer the most from this problem?
2. Explain why UPS views itself as a "technology company with trucks" rather than as a "trucking company with technology."
3. Under what situations might the outsourcing of EC services not be desirable?
4. UPS and other logistics companies also provide financial services. What does this mean and what is the logic behind this?
5. Differentiate order fulfillment in B2C from that of B2B.
6. Discuss the motivation of suppliers to improve the supply chain to customers.
7. Describe the advantages of RFID over a regular barcode in light of supply chain management.
8. Discuss how CPFR can lead to more accurate forecasting and how it can resolve the bullwhip effect.
9. Describe the importance of providing a single demand forecast for improving control along the entire supply chain.

10. Investigate and discuss how artificial intelligence can be used to pick and pack orders faster and more accurately. Begin with McGown (2010).

TOPICS FOR CLASS DISCUSSION AND DEBATES

1. Chart the supply chain portion of returns to a virtual store. Check with an e-tailer to see how it handles returns. Prepare a report based on your findings.
2. Discuss how CPFR can solve order fulfillment problems along the supply chain. Use any image from Google of the CPFR model to relate the elements of the figure to your proposed solutions.
3. Identify the major concerns about using RFID by companies. Discuss the validity of these concerns.
4. Should a B2B EC company outsource its delivery of ordered goods?
5. Some say outsourcing B2B services may hurt the competitive edge. Others disagree. Discuss.
6. Which activities are most critical in order fulfillment of B2C (check Table 12.1)? Which are for B2B? Discuss the differences.
7. Debate the issue of outsourcing EC order fulfillment. Consult Johnson (2010).
8. Debate: Should companies use RFID or not?
9. Find the status of Amazon.com's same day delivery project. Write a report.

INTERNET EXERCISES

1. The U.S. Postal Service (USPS) is also in the EC logistics field. Examine its shipping services and tracking systems at **usps.com**. What are the potential advantages of these systems for EC shippers?
2. Enter **xpertfulfillment.com**, **shipwire.com**, and **infifthgear.com**. Compare their EC order fulfillment services. Write a report.
3. Visit **freightquote.com** and the sites of two other online freight companies. Compare the

features offered by these companies for online delivery.

4. Enter **efulfillmentservice.com**. Review the products you find there. View the video about their operation. How does the company organize the network? How is it related to companies such as FedEx? How does this company make money?

5. Enter **cerqa.com** and find information about products that can facilitate order fulfillment. Write a report.

6. Enter **kewill.com**. Find the innovations offered there that facilitate order fulfillment. Compare it with **shipsmo.net**. Write a report.

7. Visit **b2b-today.com**. Go to the B2B Communities area and identify the major vendors there. Then select three vendors and examine the services they provide to the B2B community.

8. Go to **ariba.com**. Who is Ariba and what supply chain solutions do they provide? Prepare a report describing the solutions they offer in the procurement arena.

9. Investigate the status of CPFR. Start at **gs1us.org/industries/apparel-general-merchandise**, conduct a search. Also enter **apics.org/sites/apics-supply-chain-council** and find information about CPFR. Write a report on the status of CPFR.

10. Enter **future-store.org** and find the progress on the use of RFID and other tools in supply chain improvements in retailing.

11. Enter **reverselogistics.com** and summarize the differences between reverse and forward logistics.

12. Discuss the difficulties in fulfilling orders for fresh food. Start with Thau (2010).

13. Enter **freshdirect.com** and examine the methods it uses to improve order fulfillment of online grocery items. Also explain how they do an eco-friendly fulfillment.

14. Visit **alice.com**. What type of business is it? What supply chain services do they provide? Describe their relationship with OHL. What services does OHL provide and why are they critical to Alice.com's operation?

15. Enter **corporate.sifycorp.com** and study their enterprise services. Specifically find what support services they provide. Write a report.

TEAM ASSIGNMENTS AND PROJECTS

1. **Assignment for the Opening Case**
   Read the opening case and answer the following questions:
   (a) What were the drivers of the centralized warehousing?
   (b) Amazon.com is using third-party companies for delivery. Can you guess why?
   (c) Can Amazon.com use RFID in its warehouses? If yes, where and when? If no, why not?
   (d) Find how Amazon.com handles returned merchandise.
   (e) Draw Amazon.com's supply chain for books.
   (f) Where do you think there are intelligent (software) agents in Amazon.com's order fulfillment/logistics?

2. Each team should investigate the order fulfillment process offered at an e-tailer's site, such as **barnes-andnoble.com**, **staples.com**, or **walmart.com**. Contact the company, if necessary, and examine any related business partnerships. Based on the content of this chapter, prepare a report with suggestions for how the company can improve its order fulfillment process. Each group's findings will be discussed in class. Based on the class's findings, draw some conclusions about how companies can improve order fulfillment.

3. FedEx, UPS, the U.S. Postal Service, DHL, and others are competing in the EC logistics market. Each team should examine one such company and investigate the services it provides. Contact the company, if necessary, and aggregate the team's findings into a report that will convince classmates or readers that the company is the best. (What are its best features? What are its weaknesses?)

4. Enter Ingram Micro's resources site (**ingram-micro.com**). Use the case studies and articles there to write a report on the importance and benefits of Web fulfillment. Include both order fulfillment and reverse logistics.

5. Watch the video titled "Marks and Spencer Expands RFID to All Its Stores" (22:50 minutes)

at **rfidjournal.com/videos/view?1282**. Write a report describing who M&S is, how they have and are going to use RFID in retail, and the benefits they hope to achieve.

6. Read about the warehouse management systems provided by JDA (RedPrairie) and Manhattan Associates (including some of their warehouse case studies) and answer the following:

   (a) What supply chain processes are supported by both systems?
   (b) What are the major benefits of each system?
   (c) What are the major differences in the capabilities provided?

7. The competition on 'same day delivery' is intensifying with more and more competitors enter the race. Investigate the status of the competition including delivery by drones (e.g., FAA's approval). Start with Bowman (2014). Write a report.

CLOSING CASE: MULTICHANNEL RETAILERS – EXPERIENCES OF NORDSTROM AND REI

Retail channels such as store, Web, catalog, call center, or kiosk cannot satisfy the expectations of today's consumers alone. In today's consumer-centric world, customers want to buy what they want, at a price they want, where and when they want, and all these with same day delivery or easy pickup. The result is that many online and offline retailers are providing customers multiple channels for satisfying these demands. For example, a multi-channel retailer might offer customers the means to purchase online and pick up their purchase in the physical stores. Or, a retailer with stores might provide in-store kiosks that enable customers to search online for merchandise that is not in the store, locating the merchandise at either a nearby store, or offering the ability to purchase it online and have it delivered to the customers homes or to a store location of their choice. One retailer who has long history of providing multi-channel sales and service is Nordstrom.

Multichannel Evolution at Nordstrom

Founded in 1901 in Seattle, WA, Nordstrom, Inc. is a high end fashion retailer offering clothing, shoes, and accessories for men, women, and children. They have 117 full-line stores in 44 countries. Additionally, they have 119 Nordstrom Rack stores, 2 Jeffrey boutiques, one clearance store, a private subsidiary called HauteLook, a NYC boutique called Treasure & Bond, and their online site, **nordstrom.com**.

Nordstrom began their online presence in 1998 with **nordstromshoes.com**. In 2000 this was enhanced to include their entire catalog but did not incorporate the inventory in the stores. In the same vein, the merchandising, marketing, and accounting systems used to run their online and offline stores were different. Around 2004, Nordstrom began to look at the possibility of combining the systems and providing online customers with the same experience they got in the store. From the customer's perspective, the key to providing a similar experience across multiple channels: in store, Web, catalog, call center, mobile, etc. – is providing access to inventory information and the capability to fulfill an order from any point in the system – ship to home, ship to store, or pick up in store.

It took 4 to 5 years to combine the online and in store experience into an integrated multichannel system. By 2009, Nordstrom had aggregated its inventory and was providing visibility to in-store inventory on its website. Basically, stores were treated as warehouses or distribution centers for online customers. Under this scheme, customers were able to pick up online purchases in stores.

Nordstrom's Multichannel Systems

The technical underpinning for these multichannel capabilities was provided by Sterling Commerce's Selling and Fulfillment Suite which included Sterling Catalog and Offer Management, as well as their Order Management capabilities. At the core of the Suite is a centralized order hub that synchronizes orders and provides access to inventory across all the channels. In today's terminology, this sort of system is called a "Distributed

Order Management" (DOM) system. Today, there are a variety of software vendors that provide DOM capabilities including Oracle, Manhattan Associates, IBM Sterling, and JDA Software. All of these DOMs offer a baseline of capabilities including:

- System-wide views of inventory across the entire supply chain, anticipating shortages and delivery problems
- Optimized fulfillment across the system taking into account, transportation cost, labor, and service level
- Determination of fulfillment location for ship to home, ship to store, or pick up in store.
- Support order lifecycle management including creation, modification, and cancellation
- Availability of information about items, prices, and promotions across the supply chain
- Full financial functionality including authorization, fraud management, invoicing, and settlement.

Multichannel Impact at Nordstrom

From the inception, Nordstrom's multichannel integration had immediate effects. Same-store sales went from declining to an increase close to 10%. At the same time, the percentage of customers who completed purchases after searching for an item almost doubled. Inventory turns improved from 4.8 in 2005 to 5.4 in 2009. Finally, overall sales reached $8.3 billion in 2009.

Multichannel Experiences at REI

Even today, the various sales and marketing channels of most retailers are managed as separate silos rather than as an integrated whole. Like Nordstrom, another well-known exception is Recreational Equipment, Inc. (or REI for short). REI was started in 1938 and is headquartered in Kent, WA. They have 129 stores in 22 states and are the largest consumer co-op with over 10 million members. Since the late 1990s, REI has provided a number of multi-channel options for customer sales and service including:

- Web-Based Kiosks – Like many other retailers, REI got its online start in the late 1990s. However, unlike most retailers, they brought web-based kiosks into their stores shortly after that. In this way, customers can order from their portfolio of over 40,000 products. Obviously, this is many more items than are stocked in the average store.
- In-Store Pickup – Customers can shop online and have the item shipped to a local store of their choice. The main benefit of this service is that once customers are in the store they are much more likely to purchase other products.
- Gift Registry – Many retailers provide online gift registries. Like their other services, REI's registry can be established, followed, and updated online, in the store, or through their call center.

REI's multi-channel capabilities are built on top of IBM's WebSphere Commerce platform. Over the years this platform has enabled REI to integrate the disparate systems from the individual channels into a set of cohesive supply chain capabilities, such as order fulfillment or the product catalog, that are uniformly available to all the channels.

Like Nordstrom, REI has enjoyed strong revenue growth since the inception of its integration multichannel capabilities. In 2011, revenues were around $1.7 billion making it one of the leaders in outdoor equipment and apparel. In addition to their bottom line growth, all of the multi-channel capabilities enjoyed immediate growth and rapid payback. Customers who participated in two channels spent 114% more and those using three channels spent 48% more. Also, REI's In-Store Pickup capabilities increased sales by 1% within the first year of operation.

What Nordstrom and REI have recognized is that the key to multichannel support is the customer. Retailers need to concentrate on providing uniform sales and services to customers where, how, and when they want them, regardless of the channel.

Sources: Based on Banker (2011), Clifford (2010), Friedman (2011), Lynch (2012), Taylor (2012), **nordstrom.com** and **rei.com** (both accessed February 2014).

Questions

1. How would you define multichannel retail?
2. What multichannel capabilities does Nordstrom support?
3. What multichannel capabilities does REI have?
4. What are some of the major features of a distributed order management (DOM) system?
5. What are some of the benefits that arise from integrated multichannel sales and services?

ONLINE FILES
available at **affordable-ecommerce-textbook.com/turban**

W12.1 What Services Do Customers Need?
W12.2 The Bullwhip Effect

COMPREHENSIVE EDUCATIONAL WEBSITES

rfid.org: News, videos, cases.
rfidjournal.com: Comprehensive collection of articles, cases, videos.
vics.org: Business guidelines, collaboration (CPFR).
apics.org: Association for Operations Management.
cscmp.org: Council of Supply Chain Management.
asuscma.org: Supply Chain Management Association.
reverselogisticstrends.com: News, trade shows, cases, etc.
agents.umbc.edu: Large collection of information about intelligent agents.
silicon.com/white-papers: Publications on enterprise planning and supply management.

GLOSSARY

Collaborative planning, forecasting, and replenishment (CPFR) The practice of suppliers, manufacturers and retailers collaborating on the planning and forecasting of demand so that the supply of goods and services matches customer demand on the retailer's shelf.

E-logistics The logistics of EC systems, typically involving small parcels sent to many customers' homes (in B2C).

Logistics Activities required to efficiently and effectively control and manage the movement and storage of items, services and information across the entire supply chain to the consumer and potentially back.

Merge-in-transit Logistics model in which components for a product may come from two (or more) different physical locations and are shipped directly to the customer's location.

Order fulfillment All the operations a company undertakes from the time it receives an order to the time the items are delivered to the customers, including all related customer services.

Radio frequency identification (RFID) Tag technology in which RFID (electronic) tags are attached to or embedded in objects (included people) and employ wireless radio waves to communicate with RFID readers so that the objects can be identified, located, or can transmit data.

Reverse logistics The movement of returns from customers to vendors.

Store-level distribution resource planning (DRP) A collaborative approach that utilizes a retailer's POS data to produce a model that yields a bottoms-up, time-phased forecast of consumer sales, shipments, receipts and inventories at all stores or channels and DCs for all items, usually over a 12-month period.

Third-party logistics suppliers (3PL) External, rather than in-house, providers of logistics services.

Visibility The knowledge about where materials and parts are at any given time, which helps in solving problems such as delay, combining shipments, and more.

Warehouse management system (WMS) A software system that helps in managing warehouses.

REFERENCES

Ackerman, A. and A. Padilla. "Black & Decker HHI Puts CPFR to Action." 2009. **consumergoods.edgl.com/case-studies/Black---Decker-HHI-Puts-CPFR-to-Action51135** (accessed April 2015).

Banker, S. "Nordstrom Profits from Improved Multichannel Capabilities." February 2011. **logisticsviewpoints.com/2011/02/07/nordstrom-profits-from-improved-multichannel-capabilities** (accessed April 2015).

Barr, A. "Amazon Said to Launch Pantry to Take on Costco, Sam's." *USA Today*, December 13, 2013. **usatoday.com/story/tech/2013/12/12/amazon-pantry/4001707** (accessed April 2015).

Black, T. "Amazon Drones Set Off Air Delivery Race." June 9, 2014. **stuff.co.nz/technology/gadgets/60094928/amazon-drones-set-off-air-delivery-race** (accessed June 2014).

Bowman, R. "Will Google Shopping Express Help Retailers Fend Off Challenge from Amazon?" *Forbes*, June 7, 2014.

Clifford, S. "Nordstrom Links Online Inventory to the Real World." August 23, 2010. **nytimes.com/2010/08/24/business/24shop.html?_r=0** (accessed April 2015).

Crossgate Inc. "Crossgate Reducing Aging Account Receivables with E-Invoicing." Crossgate whitepaper, 2010. **prnewswire.com/news-releases/crossgate-to-offer-e-invoicing-services-in-collaboration-with-sap-ag-57464437.html** (accessed April 2015).

Del Rey, J. "This Is What It Looks Like Inside an Amazon Warehouse (Photos)." December 23, 2013. **allthingsd.com/20131223/this-is-what-it-looks-like-inside-an-amazon-warehouse-slideshow/#slideshow-1-3** (accessed April 2015).

Demery, P. "UPS Ties Technology to Bridgeline Digital's E-Commerce Software." June 12, 2012. **internetretailer.com/2012/06/12/ups-ties-technology-bridgeline-digitals-e-commerce-software** (accessed April 2015).

Fiorletta, A. "Kraft Taps JDA Flowcasting To Maximize Retailer-Supplier Collaboration." July 26, 2013. **retailtouchpoints.com/in-store-insights/2734-kraft-taps-jda-flowcasting-to-maximize-retailer-supplier-collaboration** (accessed May 2015).

Friedman, L. "12 for 2012." June 2011. **e-tailing.com/content/wp-content/uploads/2011/06/Acquity Group_Whitepaper_12for2012.pdf** (accessed April 2015).

Halkias, M. "Amazon's One-Hour Delivery Now Available in Dallas; Find your ZIP Cose." *The Dallas Morning News*, March 26, 2015.

Harkness, G. *Making a GREAT Living with Fulfillment by Amazon: Specific Answers to 30 Questions Every Newbie Asks.* Ridgefield Park, NJ: Pro-Count Inc., 2013.

Hayes, B. "Order Fulfillment: Potential Source of Embarrassment." January 20, 2012. **enterpriseresilienceblog.typepad.com/enterprise_resilience_man/2012/01/order-fulfillment-potential-source-of-embarrassment.html** (accessed April 2015).

Heller, L. "How Shipping Stole Christmas." December 27, 2013. **forbes.com/sites/lauraheller/2013/12/27/how-shipping-stole-christmas** (accessed April 2015).

Hofman, D., S. Aronow, and K. Nilles. "The Gartner Supply Chain Top 25 of 2013." May 2013. **gartner.com/imagesrv/summits/docs/na/supply-chain/Gartner-2013-SupplyChain-Top25.pdf** (accessed April 2015).

Johnson, R. "Three Reasons to Outsource Fulfillment." May 25, 2010. **infifthgear.com/clientuploads/Press/3%20Reasons%20to%20Outsource%20Fulfillment.pdf** (accessed April 2015).

Jakovljevic, P. "Linking S&OP and CPFR (For Retailers' and Manufacturers' Sakes): An Executive Panel Discussion." October 19, 2010. **technologyevaluation.com/research/article/Linking-SampOP-and-CPFR-For-Retailers-and-Manufacturers-Sakes-An-Executive-Panel-Discussion.html** (accessed April 2015).

Konrad, A. "Meet ORION, Software That Will Save UPS Millions By Improving Drivers' Routes." *Forbes*, November 1, 2013.

Lobosco, K. "Army of Robots to Invade Amazon Warehouse."(including video 3:10 minutes.) May 22, 2014. **money.cnn.com/2014/05/22/technology/amazon-robots** (accessed June 2015).

Lynch, E. "Nordstrom: Retailers Need a Focus on Customer Engagement." September 2012. **multichannelmerchant.com/crosschannel/nordstrom-retailers-need-a-focus-on-customer-engagement-13092012** (accessed April 2015).

Makepolo. "Canadian Beef Processor Touts RFID Computer Hardware & Software." January 11, 2014. **madeinchinasuppliers.com/canadian-beef-processor-touts-rfid-computer-hardware-software.html** (accessed April 2015).

Manjoo, F. "I Want It Today: How Amazon's Ambitious New Push for Same-Day Delivery Will Destroy Local Retail." July, 2012. **slate.com/articles/business/small_business/2012/07/amazon_same_day_delivery_how_the_e_commerce_giant_will_destroy_local_retail_.html** (accessed April 2015).

McGown, A. "Artificial Intelligence." *Retailer Magazine*, January 2010. **connection.ebscohost.com/c/articles/48294897/artificial-intelligence** (accessed April 2015).

Melnyk, S., E. W. Davis, R. E. Spekman, and J. Sandor. "Outcome-Driven Supply Chains." *MIT Sloan Management Review*, Winter 2010. **sloanreview.mit.edu/article/outcome-driven-supply-chains** (accessed April 2015).

Nilsson, J. "UPS, FedEx Threatened by New E-Commerce Strategies." *Reuters*. July 15, 2013. **dailyfinance.com/2013/07/15/ecommerce-threat-ups-fedex-package-delivery** (accessed April 2015).

Pappas, L. "Nestlé Purina PetCare: A Supplier's View Of Collaboration." February 25, 2013. **retailtouchpoints.com/in-store-insights/2325-nestle-purina-petcare-a-suppliers-view-of-collaboration** (accessed April 2015).

Pisani, J. "What's Better for Grocery Delivery: Google, Instacart, or Postmates?" *San Jose Mercury Business*, June 19, 2014.

Peerless Research Group. "Aligning Order and Fulfillment Channels." June 2013. **honeywellaidc.com/Catalog Documents/honeywell-multichannel-fulfillment-white-paper.pdf** (accessed April 2015).

Reyes, P. *RFID in the Supply Chain.* New York: McGraw-Hill Professional, 2011.

Segall, L. "Meet QuiQui, the Drug-Delivering Drone." June 19, 2014. **money.cnn.com/2014/06/19/technology/innovation/quiqui-drone-drugs** (accessed June 2015)

Sheldon, P. and A. Hoar. "The Forrester Wave: B2B Commerce Suites, Q4 2013." October 7, 2013.

forrester.com/The+Forrester+Wave+Enterprise+B
usiness+Intelligence+Platforms+Q4+2013/fulltext/-
/E-RES108103 (accessed April 2015).

Sadhu, O., P. Petkar, M. Jaju, and K. Singh. "Study of Collaborative Planning, Forecasting and Replenishment:
Opportunities and Challenges in India." October 22,
2011.   slideshare.net/kunal2k3/cpfr-oppotunities-
challenges (accessed May 2015).

Simchi-Levi, D., A. Clayton, and B. Raven. "When One
Size Does Not Fit All." (December 2012). *Operations
Management and Research*, December 2010.

Taylor, H. "Nordstrom VP Warns Retailers 'Put Customers
in the Driver's Seat or be Dead by 2020.'" September
2012. **econsultancy.com/blog/10736-nordstrom-vp-
warns-retailers-put-customers-in-driver-s-seat-or-
be-dead-by-2020** (accessed April 2015).

Thau, B. "Out-of-the-Box Solution." *Stores*, February
2010.   **stores.org/stores-magazine-february-2010/
out-box-solution** (accessed April 2015).

Thomas, K. "Supply Chain Segmentation: 10 Steps to
Greater Profits." Quarter 1, 2012. **supplychainquar-
terly.com/topics/Strategy/201201segmentation**
(accessed April 2015).

UPS. "United Parcel Service's CEO Discusses Q4 2013
Results - Earnings Call." January 30, 2014. **finance.
yahoo.com/news/united-parcel-services-ceo-dis-
cusses-165012497.html** (accessed April 2015).

VICS. "The Ultimate Retail Supply Chain Machine:
Connecting the Consumer to the Factory." January 2013.

Wozniak, C. "5 Keys to Maximizing Ecommerce
Profitability & Customer Satisfaction." *Rakuten*
(formerly *Webgistics*), July 30, 2013. **webgistix.
com/blog/5-keys-to-maximizing-ecommerce-
profitability-customer-satisfaction** (accessed April
2015).

Xue, H. "Starbucks Supply Chain Model." December 5, 2010.
**blogs.ubc.ca/hanbinxue/2010/12/05/starbucks-
supply-chain-model** (accessed April 2015).

Part V

E-Commerce Strategy and Implementation

EC Strategy, Globalization, and SMEs

13

Contents

Learning Objectives

Upon completion of this chapter, you will be able to:

1. Understand the essentials of online business competition and strategy and how the Internet and EC influence Porter's Five Forces model.
2. Describe the performance and strategy cycle.
3. Describe the strategy initiation phase.
4. Understand the activities of strategy formulation.
5. Understand the strategy implementation phase.
6. Describe strategy assessment, including the role of metrics.
7. Describe performance improvements and innovations in EC.
8. Evaluate the issues involved in global EC.
9. Describe how small and medium-sized businesses can use EC.

OPENING CASE: PROCTER & GAMBLE'S E-COMMERCE STRATEGY

Procter & Gamble Company (P&G) is the world's largest multinational company of consumer goods. With over 121,000 employees and over $84 billion in sales (in 2014), the company is considered one of the world's best. Its products include some of the most well-known brands such as Tide, Crest, Pampers, Old Spice, Gillette, and Charmin. The company is known as a global innovator,

Electronic supplementary material The online version of this chapter (doi: 10.1007/978-3-319-10091-3_13) contains supplementary material, which is available to authorized users

E. Turban et al., *Electronic Commerce: A Managerial and Social Networks Perspective*,
Springer Texts in Business and Economics, DOI 10.1007/978-3-319-10091-3_13,
© Springer International Publishing Switzerland 2015

introducing revolutionary products and excelling in marketing communication.

The Problem

P&G operates in a very competitive industry where other large global companies are extremely active (e.g., Unilever, Johnson & Johnson). Brand recognition is a critical success factor, and extensive advertisement is necessary. P&G is known for being a pioneer in the radio and TV production of soap operas (the term "soap opera" is based on P&G's detergents and soaps). P&G sponsors music, TV shows, movies, and sporting events (including the London Olympics in 2012 and the Sochi Winter Olympics in 2014). As of 2000, the company is active on the Internet, sponsoring numerous online communities and operating dozens of websites (one for each brand).

The rise of the social customer (Chapters 1 and 7) contributes to a more intense competition. The customers now can share information and experiences, compare prices, get coupons online, learn about the ingredients in products and their environmental impact, recommend, evaluate, and trash the brands that they do not like. All these make customers less loyal to some brands and more loyal to others. Sales of some of P&G's brands (e.g., Pepto-Bismol) had been flat or even declining, since 2000. In 2010, P&G noticed that Pepto-Bismol users had been discussing the stomach pain reliever online, especially on weekend mornings, after they had overindulged the night before. Therefore, the marketers decided to entice customers to use Pepto-Bismol before they began eating and drinking. Their strategy was to advertise on Facebook by posting the catchy slogan "Celebrate Life." This resulted in an 11% market-share gain in the following 12 months through fall 2011 (see Coleman-Lochner 2012).

The Solution

P&G has been active online since the late 1990s, and they began using social media in 2005. According to Coleman-Lochner (2012), social networking is taking central stage at P&G.

In addition to their traditional marketing research of what customers are doing at home, P&G is now monitoring customers' conversations on the Web, knowing that potential buyers spend a considerable amount of time on Facebook and other social networks. Coleman-Lochner (2012) provides the following examples of P&G advertising on social media: Pepto-Bismol on Facebook and Twitter (see above), Secret Deodorant's anti-bullying drive on Facebook, Cover Girl on Facebook and Twitter, and Iams Pet food on Facebook and in blogs.

P&G's strategy in 2012 was to test the viral effect of social media. The idea was that promotions in social media can be much more cost effective than TV promotions. The company selected Old Spice as their brand for testing social media ads.

The Old Spice Brand

The Old Spice brand includes dozens of products for both men and women: deodorants, body wash, cologne, and more. The brand is known for its successful social media campaigns. We distinguish between the permanent presence on social networks and social networking and special advertising campaigns.

The Major Social Media Presence

Old Spice Website (**oldspice.com**). This site includes product information, videos, photos, display ads, a webstore, and downloads (e.g., ringtones, screensavers, wallpaper).

- *Presence on Facebook* (**facebook.com/old Spice**). Similar information as on the brand's website and 'Likes' (over 2,600,000 as of June 2014), comments (posts) by fans, and special campaigns.
- *Presence on Twitter* (**twitter.com/OldSpice**). Old Spice has over 221,000 followers on Twitter, who tweet their questions, requests, and opinions to be answered by Old Spice and shared by other followers.
- *Presence on YouTube*. A large number of related videos (many featuring "The Old Spice Guy") are available (**youtube.com/user/Old Spice**). These videos are popular (over 231 million video views as of June 2014). P&G was recognized for its social media presence at

the 2014 Winter Olympics. P&G was the most "buzzed-about brand" with over 27 million YouTube views during the first week of the Games (Horovitz 2014).

- *Using Pinterest.* In 2012, P&G began pinning material onto a Pinterest board (Edwards 2012). Since then, the company is actively pinning material for many of its brands.

The 2010 Campaign

In order to appeal to the younger generation, Procter and Gamble wanted to get both men and women talking about Old Spice. The Widen + Kennedy advertising agency began with a viral marketing campaign during the 2010 Super Bowl, starring "The Old Spice Guy," who became "The Men Your Men Could Smell Like."

According to Ehrlich (2010), within 24 hours, there were 5.9 million video views and 22,500 comments posted. According to Lipp (2010), Old Spice became the most-viewed sponsored channel on YouTube. Old Spice gained 80,000 Twitter followers in two days and 740,000 Facebook fans. The campaign's success made it a continuous one. According to Bullas (2011), the number of YouTube views increased to 236 million a month and the sales figures increased by 107%.

For additional results, see a video case study of Wieden + Kennedy's Old Spice Media Social Campaign (posted August 10, 2010), at **wearesocial.net/blog/2010/08/wieden-kennedys-spice-case-study**.

The Results

As indicated by the results of the Old Spice social media campaign, people's reactions to well organized campaigns via social media can be overwhelming. The number of viewers and interactions reached record highs and sales volume increased as well. Overall, the company is doing well with the new strategy. P&G now advertises heavily on the Internet (e.g., their YouTube channel), but still advertises on TV.

While some are afraid that the social media activities will sink P&G's innovation program (e.g., Baskin 2012), others think that the opposite is true. As described in Chapter 8, crowdsourcing and collaboration facilitate innovation. Additionally, CEO Robert McDonald (as reported by Chui and Fleming 2011), sees improvement in innovations. He wants to make P&G "the most technologically enabled business in the world."

Related to social media is the use of analytics for strategy assessment. To read the case study, see Effie Awards (2011) and P& G Innovations (undated).

In 2014, P&G is shifting from a presence in social media to a convergence of e-commerce and social media; see Cooper (2014) for details.

Sources: Based on Chui and Fleming (2011), Cooper (2014), Coleman-Lochner (2012), Brady (2013), Bullas (2011), Ehrlich (2010), and **pg. com/en_US/downloads/innovation/factsheet_ OldSpice.pdf** (accessed June 2014).

LESSONS LEARNED FROM THE CASE

Appropriate IT and EC strategies, can help companies survive and excel. For global companies such as P&G, digitization is becoming an essential strategy. Lately, using social media has helped increase sales. For such large company, a formal strategy is necessary.

The case illustrates an advertising campaign that was planned by a consultant (an advertising agency), was implemented first on an experimental basis (the Super Bowl), was enhanced (the "Response Campaign"), and then was evaluated for success. We distinguish four major steps in strategy development.

First is *strategy initiation*, this is when P&G decided to use social media; then strategy *formulation*, which included the design of the campaign and the plan of the strategy (e.g., the selection of the brand). The third phase, *strategy implementation* was the detailed plan for how to 'go social' (e.g., how to utilize YouTube, Facebook, and Twitter). Finally, in *strategy assessment*, the results were measured using several metrics.

The focus of this chapter is on the basic steps in the creation of strategic planning as influenced by the Internet and used in EC companies. The chapter also presents and discusses issues related to creating an e-strategy to engage in global EC and the opportunities that EC creates for small and medium-sized enterprises (SMEs).

13.1 ORGANIZATIONAL STRATEGY: CONCEPTS AND OVERVIEW

An organizational **strategy** is a comprehensive framework for expressing the manner in which a business plans to achieve its mission, what goals are needed to support it, and what plans and policies will be needed to accomplish these goals. Strategy also is about making decisions on what activities not to pursue and trade-offs between strategic alternatives. An organization's strategy (including EC and IT strategies) starts with understanding where the company is today with respect to its goals, and where it wants to be in the future. The economic/financial crisis of 2008–2014 has made it even more important to have effective EC and IT strategies as sales continue to grow and global competition intensifies.

Strategy in the Web Environment

Many strategies depend on the goals of increasing revenues, profitability, and shareholder values. An example is Amazon.com's strategy to defer profitability in the short run and instead increase revenue and market share. The data considered by a company are included in the value proposition of the business model, especially concerning customers.

Today, a strategy formulation process must include the Internet, which is more important than ever before. According to Porter (2001), "Many have argued that the Internet renders strategy obsolete. In reality, the opposite is true . . . it is more important than ever for companies to distinguish themselves through strategy. The winners will be those that view the Internet as a complement to, not a cannibal of, traditional ways of competing" (p. 2).

Porter's Five Forces Model and Strategies as Influenced by the Internet and EC

Porter's "Five Forces" model has been used by companies to better compete in their industry. It also illustrates how EC can facilitate a company's competitive advantage (see Hanlon 2013).

The model recognizes the following five major forces in an industry that affect the degree of competition and, ultimately, the level of profitability. They are:

1. Threat of entry of new competitors
2. Bargaining power of suppliers
3. Bargaining power of customers or buyers
4. Threat of substitute products or services
5. Rivalry among existing firms in the industry

The strength of each force is determined by the industry's structure, government regulations, size of the industry, and the global competition. Existing companies in an industry need to protect themselves against newcomers and the five forces. Alternatively, they can use the forces to improve their position, to fight newcomers or to challenge the leaders in the industry. The relationships between the forces are shown in Figure 13.1. The definitions and details are provided by Porter (1980) and Hanlon (2013).

Strategies for Gaining Competitive Advantage

While implementing Porter's model, companies can identify the forces that influence competitive advantage in their marketplace and then develop a defensive or offensive strategy. Porter (1985) proposed three such classical strategies: *cost leadership*, *differentiation*, and *niche strategies*.

In Table 13.1, we list seven strategies for gaining competitive advantage. Each of these strategies can be enhanced by EC, as shown throughout the book.

A popular strategy of gaining competitive advantage is to learn what your competitor is doing. For methodology and tools, see Rayson (2014).

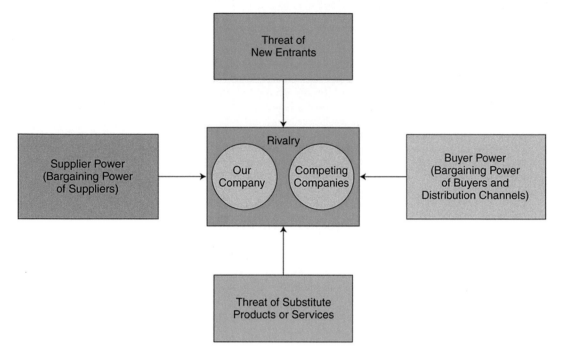

Figure 13.1   Porter's five forces model

Table 13.1   Strategies for competitive advantage

Strategy	Description
Niche	Select a market niche and be the best in quality, speed, or cost in that market
Growth	Increase market share, acquire more customers, or sell more types of products
Alliance	Work with business partners in partnerships, alliances, joint ventures, or virtual companies
Innovation	Introduce new products/services; put new features in existing products/services; develop new ways to produce products/services
Time	Treat time as a resource, then manage it, and use it to the firm's advantage
Entry barriers	Create barriers to entry. By introducing innovative products or using EC business models to provide exceptional service, companies can create entry barriers to discourage new entrants
Customer or supplier lock-in	Persuade suppliers or customers to remain loyal to a company instead of switching to the competition. Reduce customers' bargaining power by locking them to a supplier

The Impact of the Internet

Porter (2001) has identified several ways that the Internet can influence each of the five forces of competitiveness. These five forces and associated Internet impacts are shown in Table 13.2.

Example

Facebook, Google, and others compete for social-network advertising dollars. Google, for example created Google+ to compete with Facebook. In 2014, Facebook paid $19 billion to buy the cross-platform messaging app "WhatsApp." It is recognized as a "strategy to gain both a mobile interface that is not only more user-friendly than anything Facebook created, but that also has certain monetizable features that come along with P2P application use" (ActiveVest 2014).

Many companies are examining the impact of the Internet and EC today and tomorrow on their business. For these firms, an *e-commerce*

Table 13.2 Impacts of e-commerce and social commerce on industry competition

Competitive force	Impacts
Bargaining power of suppliers	**Decreases.** Due to e-procurement, availability of more suppliers and competitors (global), increased use of e-auctions, Internet procurement tends to give all buyers equal access to suppliers. There is more product standardization and reduction of differentiation among suppliers. Not much difference in prices. Finally, the cost of customers switching to other sellers is low
Bargaining power of customers	**Increases.** Due to the ability to compare prices, buy online, use group buying and daily deals (e.g., Groupon), use more recommendations (including from friends), get more power due to social networking, customers are more knowledgeable (e.g., global directories such as Alibaba.com) and have more information, see Brownell (2013). Customers can buy in global markets, reducing switching costs. Customers can negotiate via new models (e.g., Priceline's name-your-own-price model)
Barriers to entry	**Decreases.** Due to the ease of starting online businesses, there is faster access to information that is more accurate, reduced start-up and fixed costs, and new business reputation can spread fast online via word of mouth. It gets easier to clone competitors. Many new startups appear online. New brands can get good reputations quickly
Threat of substitute products and services	**Increases.** New products/services can be developed and advertised quickly on a global basis. Customers (and B2Bs) can find substitutes faster and easier. They also can get reviews and recommendations rapidly. EC and SC facilitate new business models that can create alternative products/services (e.g., e-books, are replacing hardcover books)
Rivalry among existing competitors	**Increases.** Markets are more efficient, and it is easy to get competitive information in a timely manner. However, companies have more competitors to contend with and there is less localization advantage. Global players gain access to local markets, increasing competition. More SMEs are competing. Increased online business facilitates competition. Amazon.com has caused competitors to reduce prices and close stores (e.g., Best Buy; see Dignan 2012). Fierce competition is evidenced in the travel and fashion industries as well as in jewelry. Many competitors are declaring bankruptcy

strategy (e-strategy or EC strategy) can be very helpful.

The process of building an EC strategy will be explained in detail later in this chapter. First, though, we continue our overview of organizational and IT strategies, of which e-commerce strategy is a component.

Strategic Planning for IT and EC

Developing EC strategy requires creativity, planning, resources, good technological skills, and overcoming technical limitations. Technical limitations can often be resolved by spending additional capital, whereas nontechnical limitations involve things such as people's lack of trust in computers or resistance to change, and they are not as easy to overcome.

As time passes, the limitations, especially the technological ones, are becoming less of an issue. In addition, careful planning can minimize the negative impact of some of them, and hopefully, the information provided in this chapter will help

you avoid some of the pitfalls associated with e-commerce. The major challenges associated with developing an EC strategy are shown in Table 13.3.

As companies become more experienced with e-commerce and the technology continues to improve, the benefits of EC will far outweigh the limitations. In general, total EC sales are growing 15 to 18% annually. Thus, companies need to have some EC strategy to be able to compete. In the next section, we will discuss the process, tools, and techniques that companies typically use to plan their strategy effectively.

SECTION 13.1 REVIEW QUESTIONS

1. What is strategy?
2. Describe strategy in the Web environment.
3. Describe Porter's Five Forces model.
4. Describe strategies for gaining competitive advantage.
5. Understand the influence of the Internet and EC on each of Porter's forces.
6. Relate EC strategy to organizational IT strategies.

Table 13.3 E-commerce challenges

Technological	Non-technological
Software standards: lack of universally accepted standards for quality, security, and reliability	**Distrust:** skeptical buyers and sellers. Lack of trust in "virtual" companies
Integration: difficult to integrate new e-commerce applications and software with existing applications and databases	**Regulations:** lack of national and international government regulations and industry standards
Cost to customers: expensive and/or inconvenient Internet access (in some areas)	**Measurement:** immature methodologies for measuring benefits of, and justifying, e-commerce
	Legal: unresolved legal issues
	Security: perception that e-commerce locations are not secure

13.2   THE STRATEGY AND PERFORMANCE CYCLE AND TOOLS

The major objective of a strategy is to improve organizational performance. Therefore, strategy development and performance are interrelated and described here as a five phase cyclical process.

Strategy and Performance Cycle

A strategy is important, but the *process* of developing a strategy can be even more important. No matter how large or how small the organization, the strategic planning process leads managers to assess the current performance of the firm, then determine where the performance should be, and plan how to get from where a company is to where it wants to be.

Any strategic planning process has five major phases, *initiation, formulation, implementation, assessment,* and *performance improvement*, as shown in Figure 13.2. The major phases of the strategic planning process, and some identifiable activities and outcomes associated with each phase, are discussed briefly in the following text. The phases are then discussed more extensively in Sections 13.3, 13.4, 13.5, 13.6, and 13.7. Note that the process is cyclical and continuous. A brief description of the five phases follows.

Strategy Initiation

In the **strategy initiation** phase, an organization is setting its vision, goals, and objectives. Looking at its environment, strategy initiation includes an assessment of a company's strengths and weaknesses, and examines the external factors that may affect the business. Additionally, a company may undertake a competitive and competitor analysis to determine its strategy. All these activities need to be related to the Internet and e-commerce.

Specific outcomes from this phase include a *company analysis.* One key outcome from this analysis should be a clear statement of the company's *value proposition* (see discussion in Chapter 1). For a description and examples, see Davis (2012) and Skok (2013).

Example: Amazon.com

Amazon.com recognizes that besides selling books, there is also value in providing customers with information about books, personalized services, and outstanding customer care. Amazon is continuously expanding its product line (e.g., adding the grocery same day delivery service; increasing its App store to include 200 countries). This increases the value proposition to its customers. Moreover, since Amazon's inception in 1995, the company frequently changes its business model.

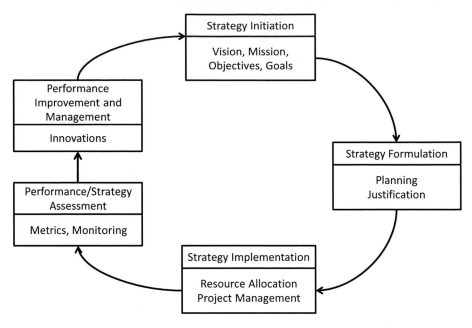

Figure 13.2 The strategy-performance cycle

Typical goals and objectives of EC include:

> - Improved performance
> - Gain competitive advantage
> - Increased sales and revenue
> - Improved customer and partner service and relationships
> - Generation of new business models and facilitating innovation

These goals are based on the following concepts and activities:

Core Competencies

A *core competency* refers to the unique capabilities of companies, which are difficult to imitate. For example, Google's core competency is its expertise in information search technology, and eBay's core competency is in conducting online auctions. VeriSign's expertise is in Internet security and Priceline concentrates on travel and hospitality.

- **Forecasts.** *Forecasting* means predicting future behavior and trends of factors that may impact the business.

- **Market Research: Competitor and Industry Analyses.** *Competitor analysis* involves scanning the business environment to assess the strategy, strengths, and weakness of all types of competitors. Several methodologies are available to conduct such an analysis, including strengths, weaknesses, opportunities, threats (SWOT) analysis and competitor analysis (see 'competitor analysis' at **tutor2u.net/business/strategy/competitor_analysis.htm**).

Strategy Formulation

Once the goals and objectives are known and prioritized, a company can start to formulate its strategy.

Strategy formulation refers to the development of specific strategies and tactics to exploit opportunities and manage threats in the business environment in light of corporate strengths and weaknesses. In an EC strategy, the result is likely to be a list of EC applications or projects to be implemented (e.g., e-procurement, e-auctions). For details, see Section 13.4.

Specific activities and outcomes from this phase include:

- **Business opportunities.** The strategy initiation may point to future opportunities.
- **Cost–benefit analysis.** Each proposed opportunity must be assessed and justified. More information about conducting a cost–benefit analysis is included in Chapter 14.
- **Risk analysis, assessment, and management.** The risks of each proposed EC initiative (project) must be analyzed and assessed. If a significant risk is suspected, then a risk management plan is required. Of particular importance in an EC strategy are business risk factors such as a transition risk.
- **Business plan.** Many of the outcomes from these first two phases – goals, competitor analysis, strategic opportunities, risk analysis, and more are components of a business plan. The business plan should consider the necessary resources and the budget. The business plan should contain a value proposition section (see Skok 2013).

Strategy Implementation

In this phase, the emphasis is on "How do we do it?" The **strategy implementation** phase includes tactics, plans, schedules, deployment strategies, resource allocation, and project management.

The major specific activities and outcomes from this phase include:

- **Project planning.** Project planning includes setting project objectives, metrics, a project schedule, and EC initiatives.
- **Resource allocation.** All internal and external resources need to be properly planned and allocated.
- **Project management.** Each project needs to be managed during the implementation phases. Activities here range from purchasing parts to developing an Internet security system.

Strategy Assessment

Strategy assessment refers to the continuous performance monitoring, the comparison of actual to desired performance, and the evaluation of the progress toward the organization's goals, resulting in corrective action and, if necessary, in strategy reformulation (see Section 13.7). In strategy assessment, EC metrics are used as a standard against which the performance level of the strategy is compared using analytics. For large EC projects, *business performance management* tools can be employed.

Performance Improvement and Innovations

Obviously, if the analysis shows a negative result, it is necessary to take some corrective action. A key activity here is to improve the performance. However, even if the results are good, the organization may take actions that range from providing bonuses for the best performers identified in the analysis, to raising the desired levels of performance in the future. A key activity here is being innovative, because even good performance can be improved by innovation. In addition, techniques such as competitive analysis can be useful. For details, see Section 13.7.

At times, the strategic planning process requires reassessment of today's strategy, while preparing a new strategy for tomorrow, as demonstrated in Case 13.1.

CASE 13.1: WARNER MUSIC GROUP'S DIGITAL STRATEGY

In 2008, Warner Music Group (WMG) designated Michael Nash as the executive vice president of digital strategy. His responsibilities included key initiatives such as EC applications, social commerce, and innovative online new music-based services and products.

The Opportunity

Nash played a major role in the corporate strategy, strategic partnership relations, and expansions (e.g., new projects) for WMG since 2000. The partnership portfolio includes AT&T, Amazon.com, Google, Microsoft, Motorola, Verizon, and Sony Ericsson.

WMG, an independent spinoff of AOL, was one of the first brands to team up with YouTube. WMG was also a pioneer in licensing their products to other subscription and ad-supported music services. Nash's early assessment of music distribution via the Internet was that, by having numerous partners to sell a product, WMG would increase its profits.

WMG is acquiring companies all over the world (e.g., in June 2013 it acquired Russia's Gala Records Group).

By implementing this strategy, WMG focused on mobile services and online music sites. The company started with a small group known as Outrigger. The purpose was to see how well Outrigger could sell ads on WMG videos on YouTube, and on social networks, blogs, or the artist's website. Thus, the strategy was to sell ads through Outrigger and share the revenue with the video site. This strategy differed from that of other companies in the industry who had licensing agreements with distributors or collected royalties when videos were played.

The Results

WMG's revenue grew substantially between 2005 and the first fiscal quarter of 2009. Digital revenues increased to $184 million, equalling 20% of the company's total revenue. International recorded music revenue climbed 12.7% from the prior year quarter, and U.S. recorded music revenue reached 35%. WMG is and has been at the forefront in digital leadership among the major music companies since 2005, showing the advantage of e-commerce over physical stores. **Sources:** Based on Learmonth (2009), Warner Music Group (2008), and **wmg.com** (accessed June 2014).

Questions

1. Why did WMG change their distribution strategy?
2. Why did it develop a deal with YouTube? Is this a strategic alliance?
3. Why did WMG start its digital-oriented strategy?
4. Explore the ad arrangement with Outrigger. Does it make sense? Why?
5. Identify the activities in strategy initiation and strategy formulation in this case.

Major Tools for Strategic Planning

This section describes a few of the most popular tools used by strategists. The following are the major generic tools: (1) Strategy maps, (2) SWOT analysis, (3) Competitor analysis grid (including competitive intelligence), (4) Scenario planning, (5) Balanced scorecard, (6) Business plan and business case, and (7) Value proposition analysis.

Notes: (a) To learn how to build a business case for social media, see the video "How to Build a Business Case for Social Media" at **youtube.com/watch?v=_59iJrYanw0**.

SECTION 13.2 REVIEW QUESTIONS
1. Describe the strategy-performance cycle.
2. Describe the strategy initiation phase.
3. Describe the strategy formulation phase.
4. What is involved in strategy implementation?
5. What is strategy assessment?
6. Describe the phase of performance improvement.

13.3   E-COMMERCE STRATEGY INITIATION

In the strategy initiation phase, the organization prepares the initial steps needed for starting the strategy development cycle, such as collecting information about the company, its competitors, and its business environment. The steps in strategy initiation include a review of the organization's vision and mission; an analysis of the industry, company, competitive position; and various initiation-related issues.

Representative Issues in E-Strategy Initiation in E-Commerce

With a company, competitors, and trend data in hand, a strategist faces a number of questions about its approach to, and operation of, its EC strategy that need to be explored prior to strategy formulation. These activities are generic. The "how to" can be found in many strategy books. Here we describe some issues in strategy initiation relevant to EC.

First-Mover Advantage

The business, IT, and e-commerce worlds all have examples of companies that have succeeded with first-mover advantage. However, some companies have failed, despite their first-mover advantage. Generally, the advantages of being first include an opportunity to make a first and lasting impression on customers, to establish strong brand recognition, to lock in strategic partners, and to increase switching costs for customers.

Example

Amazon.com operated the first major online bookstore, and laid the groundwork for brick-and-mortar bookstores such as Barnes & Noble to follow suit. Two strategies Amazon used to maintain its first-mover advantage were (1) to partner with Borders (a competitor, now defunct) and (2) to expand its product line to include housewares, apparel, electronics, and toys that attracted customers who were looking for more than just books.

In some cases, being the first mover can have some disadvantages. The risks of being a first mover include the high cost of pioneering EC initiatives, making mistakes, the chance that a second wave of competitors will eliminate a first mover's lead through lower cost and innovation, and the risk that the move will be too early. Although the advantage of a speedy market entry cannot be ignored, followers can be more profitable than first can movers in the long run.

Example

One of the first large-scale social networks was GeoCities (acquired by Yahoo! in 1999). However, Yahoo! shut down the site after 10 years of huge losses. On the other hand, Facebook was not a first mover, but it succeeded and replaced MySpace, which was a leader. LinkedIn, Groupon, Foursquare, and Pinterest are also successful first movers.

So what determines whether a first mover succeeds or fails? It has been suggested that the following factors are important determinants of EC success: (1) the size of the opportunity (i.e., the first-mover company must be big enough for the opportunity, and the opportunity must be big enough for just one company); (2) the nature of the product (i.e., first-mover advantage is easier to maintain in commodity products in which later entrants have a hard time differentiating their products); (3) whether the company can be the best and most innovative in the market.

- Does the company have to spend capital (and how much) to be a first mover?
- What is the optimal way to conduct market timing should an opportunity present itself?
- From which of the three types of benefits listed above will the first entrant in the market most likely achieve success?
- Can the company afford sufficient resources to maintain its first mover position?
- Will it be difficult to follow someone else that is a first mover?
- What are the advantages of following the first mover?
- Will technology be better or cost less, or will customer needs be easier to determine?

Since a company cannot determine if and when they will gain a first-mover advantage, the following questions should be answered when deciding EC strategies:

Company strategists can examine the answers to these questions and determine the appropriate approach that has the highest potential for long-term benefits.

Managing Channel Conflict and Disintermediation

As discussed in Chapter 3, channel conflict may arise when an existing company adds an online distribution channel. In general, the strategy today is to add EC as an *additional* marketing and sales channel. This may create a channel conflict. Selling online may result in disintermediation.

Disintermediation refers to the removal of intermediaries in the EC supply chain. This occurs, for example, when consumers buy directly from manufacturers. When a company adds EC as a distribution channel, it may undercut its existing intermediaries who serve the other channels. Here are some possible strategies that sellers can use to ease disintermediation:

- Let the regular distributors fulfill the e-business orders, as the auto industry is usually doing. Buyers can order online, and then receive directions to go to distributors where they can pick up their orders.
- Provide online services to intermediaries (e.g., by building portals for them) and encourage them to re-intermediate themselves in innovative ways.
- Sell some products only online, such as LEGO (**lego.com**) is doing. Other products may be advertised online, but sold only offline.
- Avoid channel conflict entirely by not selling online. In such a case, a company could still have an EC presence by offering promotions and customer service online, as BMW (**bmw.com**) is doing.

Example

To eliminate channel conflict, companies can use a B2B2C model. For examples of two companies that took their B2B business into the world of B2B2C e-commerce, see Taddonio (2011).

E-commerce may require that new intermediaries are added to the distribution chain (e.g., aggregator, e-payments, escrow services), which may add to the problem of channel conflict. For example, delivery to the customer's home is a key to customer satisfaction, leading many e-tailers to hire a delivery company.

Price Conflict and Its Management

Price conflicts may occur when the same product is priced differently when it is sold online (usually lower) than when it is sold in the physical stores of the same company. This is a common practice in selling airline tickets. For a discussion, see Section 13.4.

Both price and channel conflicts can be minimized or eliminated if the EC business is separate from the non-EC business.

Separating Online and Offline Operations

Converting a company's online operations into a separate new company makes sense when: (1) the volume of anticipated e-business is very large; (2) a new business model needs to be developed; (3) the subsidiary can be created without dependence on current operations and legacy information systems; and (4) the online company is given the freedom to form new alliances, attract new talent, set its own prices, and raise additional funding. Barnes & Noble, Halifax in the United Kingdom (online banking), and ASB Bank in New Zealand are a few examples of companies that have established separate companies or subsidiaries for their online operations.

Brand Independence

A company faces a similar decision when deciding whether to create a separate brand for its online offerings.

Strategy in the Web 2.0 Environment and in Social Networking

Social networks and Web 2.0 tools and platforms are being used extensively by organizations today. Reported benefits included the ability to provide more innovative products and services, market their products and services more effectively, gain better access to knowledge, maintain lower costs, and raise revenues. For example, because of the current recession, companies are investing heavily in Web 2.0.

Shuen (2008) offers four major reasons why companies should create and use in-house social networks: (1) immediate access to knowledge, expertise, and human connections; (2) growth of social relationships and expansion of affiliations; (3) self-branding through a personal digital identity and reputation; and (4) viral distribution of knowledge through referrals, testimonials, benchmarking, and RSS updating. In 2008, Deloitte, IBM, and Best Buy began seeing benefits from early adoption of internal social networking.

A popular strategy is to start EC projects with small groups of employees to test their response to the Web 2.0 tools. For example, Dell first launched internal blogs before creating IdeaStorm, which is offered to customers to submit ideas, engage in dialog with company representatives, and so forth.

More than ever, marketers are using social networking tools in a wide range of activities, as illustrated in the following examples.

Example

The importance of social media as critical to merchants' e-commerce success was discussed by GoECart (**goecart.com**; 2010), in an interview with the company's CEO. GoECart is an e-commerce vendor that provides retailers with innovative, on-demand e-commerce solutions ("software as a service"). The company helps retailers develop personalized CRM based on data available in social networks (e.g., a florist who has access to a customer's birthdate can send a personalized message, including a promotion or coupons).

It is important to consider the following issues when planning a successful online EC strategy that includes social media:

- Develop an overall e-commerce strategy with clearly defined business and EC goals.
- Develop an innovative, online, and offline brand strategy involving social networks
- Plan for customer engagement activities
- Leverage the top social commerce platforms (e.g., Facebook, Twitter) by creating merchant pages
- Use LinkedIn to create vendor profiles (corporate profile)
- Leverage social networks for mobile strategy
- Create surveys and two-way communication mechanisms to solicit feedback from customers regarding products and services. This will help in strategy formulation.

Shuen (2008) provides a comprehensive guide to Web 2.0 strategy, and Gold (2008) provides a strategic guide for mobilizing applications and modifying them to fit a company's specific needs.

SECTION 13.3 REVIEW QUESTIONS

1. Describe the advantages, risks, and success factors that first movers face.
2. What are the advantages and disadvantages of creating a separate online company?
3. Why might an existing company decide to create a new brand for its e-commerce site?
4. What strategic benefits are associated with using social networks?
5. Distinguish between social strategy and digital strategy.

13.4   E-COMMERCE STRATEGY FORMULATION

The outcome of the strategy initiation phase should be a number of potential EC initiatives that can exploit opportunities on one hand and mitigate threats on the other. In the strategy formulation phase, the firm must decide which initiatives to implement and in what order. Strategy formulation activities include evaluating specific EC opportunities and conducting cost–benefit and risk analyses associated with those opportunities. Specific outcomes include a list of approved EC projects or applications, risk management plans, pricing strategies, and a business plan. These will be used in the next phase of strategy implementation. The following are the major activities in this phase.

Selecting E-Commerce Opportunities

There are many potential ways to get involved in EC (e.g., see Pantic 2013).

Selecting an appropriate EC project(s) involves a justification, ranking, and cost-benefit analysis. Best results can be achieved with input solicited from both internal and external participants. One approach is to use a strategy driven by existing factors. For example, a problem-driven strategy may help a company if its EC strategy can solve an existing, difficult problem (e.g., using forward e-auctions via e-auctioneers such as Liquidation. com to dispose of excess equipment). As noted earlier, a late-mover strategy can be effective if the company can use its brand, technology, superior customer service, or innovative products and strategies to overcome any potential deficiencies resulting from not being the first mover. Examples are Internet Explorer's emergence as the leading browser, and Facebook becoming the top social network.

However, most times it is best to use a systematic methodology that determines which initiatives to pursue.

Determining an Appropriate EC Application Portfolio Mix

For years, companies have tried to find the most appropriate portfolio (group) of EC (or other) projects among which an organization should share its limited resources. The classic *portfolio strategy* attempts to balance investments with different characteristics.

The BCG Model and an Internet Portfolio Map

Boston Consulting Group (BCG) implemented a well-known matrix (called a BCG matrix; also known as a "Boston" matrix or "growth-share" matrix) for cash allocation among projects. The matrix is based on the observation that a company's business units can be classified into four categories. Each business unit can be classified as a star, wild card (or "unknown" or "question marks"), cash cow, and dog. The two levels of the matrix are: "market growth rate" and "market share." Each can be either "low" or "high." The results are placed into four cells, into which the corporation would classify its projects (or business units): stars (high growth, high share), cash cows (high share, low growth), wild cards (high growth, low share), and dogs (low growth, low share). Money can then be moved within the budget, for example, from the business units classified as "cash cows" to projects in stars and wild cards that have the highest upside potential. The model can be used to prioritize EC projects. For details, see **netmba.com/strategy/matrix/bcg**.

The Viability-Fit Model

Tjan (2001) adapted the BCG approach to create what he calls an "Internet portfolio map," which is based on a potential fit between the culture of companies and the project viabilities. The viability area includes success factors such as projected sales, justification, and use of resources. Similarly, metrics such as alignment with core capabilities, alignment with other company initiatives, fit with organizational culture and structure, and ease of technical implementation can be used to evaluate fit. Together, these create an Internet portfolio map (see Figure 13.3).

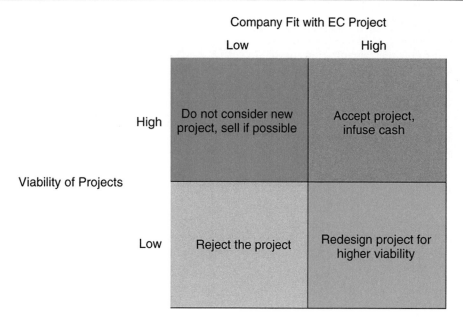

Company Fit with EC Project

	Low	High
High	Do not consider new project, sell if possible	Accept project, infuse cash
Low	Reject the project	Redesign project for higher viability

Viability of Projects

Figure 13.3 The internet portfolio map (**Sources:** Based on Tjan (2001), Sones (2001); and the authors' experiences)

Each company can determine criteria to be used to assess viability and fit. Senior managers and outside experts evaluate each proposed EC initiative (e.g., a B2B procurement site, a B2C webstore, an enterprise portal) on each of these criteria, typically on quantitative (e.g., 1 to 100) or qualitative (e.g., high, medium, low) scales. If some criteria are more important than others are, these can receive more weight. The scores are combined, and average fit and viability scores are calculated for each initiative. Initiatives in which there is high agreement on rankings can be considered with more confidence.

The candidate initiatives are then placed on the portfolio map. If both viability and fit are low, the project is rejected. If both are high, the project is adopted. If fit is high but viability is low, the project is redesigned (to get higher viability). Finally, if the fit is low but the viability is high, the project is not adopted. Senior management must also consider factors such as cost–benefit and risk (discussed next) in making the final decision about what initiatives become funded and in what order.

In addition to the above more well-known strategy methods, there are many special models (some of which are properties). For example, Egol et al. (2014) presents four new models for e-marketing.

Risk Analysis in Strategy Formulation

While Web 2.0 enables new business opportunities, it also may create substantial risks because of the open computing and interactive nature of the technology. **E-commerce risk** is the likelihood that a negative outcome will occur in the course of developing and operating an e-commerce initiative. Risk on the Internet and in EC environments is different from those faced by offline companies. For example, an EC auction company may face unique Internet security threats and vulnerabilities. As a result, a robust Web 2.0 security strategy is essential for fraud protection.

The most dangerous risk to a company engaged in e-commerce is business risk – the possibility that developing and operating a new e-commerce business could negatively impact the well-being of the organization itself. In Online File W13.1, attention is given to additional business and EC risks.

Collaborative Efforts in Strategy Formulation

Strategy formulation is considered a highly secretive process, which is done by a small team that only seldom involves outsiders (e.g., a consultant). However, this situation is changing, mostly due to the trend of companies transforming into social businesses. The basic idea is to open the planning process to be more participatory. According to Gast and Zanini (2012), companies that are experimenting with this approach see two major benefits. One benefit is "improving the quality of strategy by pulling in diverse and detailed frontline perspectives that are typically overlooked but can make the resulting plans more insightful and actionable." The second benefit involves "building enthusiasm and alignment behind a company's strategic direction – a critical component of long-term organizational health, effective execution, and strong financial performance." Such participation usually helps in strategy implementation.

Gast and Zanini (2012) provide the following examples of collaborative (sometimes outsourced) strategy formulation:

- Wikimedia (the owner of Wikipedia) used over 1,000 volunteers to generate ideas (a kind of crowdsourcing) for the company's future direction. The volunteers generated about 900 proposals and participated in task forces in the evaluation of the suggestions submitted and in the formulation of specific aspects of the strategy.
- Red Hat (**redhat.com**), a major provider of open-source software, formed teams that used wikis and other online tools to generate and organize ideas for strategy development; this "idea generation phase" has restructured the way Red Hat conducts strategic planning (see Case 13.2).

CASE 13.2: RED HAT: COLLABORATIVE STRATEGIC PLANNING

This major, open source software company operates in a very competitive global market. Strategic planning is critical for its success; therefore, the company embarked on the following collaborative strategic process:

Step 1: Generated a set of priorities of issues based on the company's mission, objectives, and goals.

Step 2: For each high priority issue, the company created a team. The leaders of each team were top executives who were given tasks that were not related to their areas of expertise, with the hopes that they would generate fresh ideas.

Step 3: Each team used traditional, as well as Web 2.0 collaboration tools (e.g., blogs, wikis), to reach any and all Red Hat employees, providing background information on each issue, and requesting ideas and feedback. The ideas were collected, organized and evaluated by all the participants. For a period of five months, there were discussions, online chats, and debates. At the end of the "idea generation phase," the best ideas were combined into nine strategic priorities.

Step 4: The company created new teams, one for each strategic priority. The teams identified initiatives for each priority (again using feedback from employees). The teams included people who were involved in strategy implementation and were empowered to plan and implement the one or two most important strategic initiatives.

This process resulted in the identification of some innovative ideas. It encouraged creativity commitment for implementation. In addition, there was an increased understanding of others' work and better collaboration. Those who were involved in strategy implementation also participated in strategy initiation and formulation.

Because of the success of the project, Red Hat now updates and evaluates strategy on an ongoing basis, rather than refreshing strategy yearly.

Despite the economic downturn, the company's earnings have grown consistently since the initiation of the process. The stock price increased by over 500% between 2009 and 2013.

For a detailed description of the process, its benefits, lessons learned, a supporting video ("Jim Whitehurst on Red Hat Strategy"), and the corporation's financial results, see Yeaney (2011).

Source: Based on Yeaney (2011), Gast and Zanini (2012), and Bort (2012).

Questions

1. Red Hat is an open source company. Why was it more likely to use Web 2.0 tools?
2. Relate the case to crowdsourcing (Chapter 8).
3. Identify strategy formulation activities in the process.
4. View the video "Jim Whitehurst on Red Hat Strategy" (2:26 minutes; at **youtube.com/watch? v=64V6nV0WnHE**) cited in Yeaney (2011), and summarize the drivers and motivations.
5. Summarize the benefits and the critical success factors in the case.

Security Issues to Consider During Strategy Formulation

Some security issues that need to be considered when setting up an EC strategy include:

- Malware and other technological attack methods.
- Human error and natural disasters.
- Botnet DoS attacks that shut down order taking, or slow it down considerably.
- Extortion, using DoS and DDoS as blackmail platforms.
- Business interruption due to any security attack.
- Relevant penalties and legal expenses due to litigation.
- Damages caused by disgruntled employees.
- Damage to intellectual property (e.g., stolen or reproduced trade secrets).

Other Issues in E-Commerce Strategy Formulation

Different types of issues exist in e-strategy formulation, depending on the company, industry, nature of the applications, and so forth. Here we discuss some representative issues.

Managing Conflict Between the Offline and Online Businesses

In a click-and-mortar business, it may be difficult to allocate limited resources between offline and online activities. The two activities can be viewed as competitors, especially in sell-side projects. In this case, personnel in charge of offline and online activities may behave as competitors. This conflict may cause problems when the offline side needs to handle the logistics of the online side, or when prices need to be determined. The ability of top management to introduce change properly, and the use of innovative processes that support collaboration, will all determine the degree of collaboration between offline and online units in a business. It is essential to have strong support by top management for both the offline and online operations and a clear strategy of "what and how" each unit operates.

Pricing Strategy

Traditional methods for determining price are the *cost-plus* and *competition-based models*. **Cost-plus** means determining the expenses associated with producing a product (production cost) by adding up all the costs involved – materials, labor, rent, overhead, and so forth – and adding an additional amount to generate a profit margin (a percentage mark-up). The *competition-based model* determines price based on what competitors are charging for similar products in the marketplace. For a comprehensive presentation see **netmba.com/marketing/pricing**.

Pricing products and services for online sales changes these pricing strategies in the following ways:

- **Price comparison is easier.** In traditional markets, either the buyer, or more often the seller, has more information than the other party does, and the seller uses this information to determine a product's price. Price comparisons help create the 'perfect market' – one in which both the buyer and the seller have ubiquitous and equal access to all relevant information, frequently in the buyer's favor. On the Internet, search engines, and price comparison sites (e.g., **mysimon.com, kelkoo.co.uk**) make it easy for customers to find out who offers the product they want at the lowest price.
- **Buyers sometimes set the price.** Name-your-own-price models, such as Priceline. com and auction sites, provide buyers with the option to set their own prices.
- **Online and offline goods are priced differently.** Pricing strategy may be especially difficult for a click-and-mortar company. Setting online prices lower than those offered by the offline side of the same business may lead to internal conflict, whereas setting prices at the same level might hurt the competitive advantage of the online business.
- **Differentiated pricing can be a pricing strategy.** For decades, airline companies have maximized revenues with *yield management* models – charging different customers different prices for the same product or service. In the B2C EC marketplace, one-on-one marketing can provide price differentiation to a segment of customers (e.g., those buying an airline seat early).

The consumer's buying power is increasing due to Internet technologies that provide easy access to pricing information. Sellers need to implement smarter pricing strategies in order to be profitable and competitive, particularly using the Internet to optimize prices. This can be done by setting prices more competitively, adapting to changing prices, and segmenting customers for differentiated pricing.

Multichannel Strategy

One of the most popular strategies in EC is offering several marketing channels to consumers, including online and m-commerce. This is known as *multichannel or omnichannel* strategy. In some cases, companies need a policy of how to integrate the several channels, in order to avoid channel conflicts cited earlier. In addition, several pure EC companies have opened physical locations. For example, Expedia (**expedia.com**) opened Expedia Local Desks, located in select cities. In addition, it was rumored that in 2014, Amazon opened physical stores (called "Pantry") where they will sell about 2,000 items that would normally be found in a grocery store. Pantry will be competing with warehouse stores like Costco and Walmart's Sam's Club. For details, see **usatoday. com/story/tech/2013/12/12/amazon-pantry/4001707**. In February 2015, Amazon opened its first physical store. The strategy of opening physical stores by pure online companies can be complex. For example, Vaish (2011) describes the need to create a maturity model with different levels. The levels range from limited presence (Maturity Level 0) to optimization and innovation (Maturity Level 4). For each level, a company needs different strategy initiation, formulation, implementation and assessment. For more on multichannel e-commerce, see Lee (2013).

Acquisitions, Partnerships, Joint Venture, and Multi EC Model Strategy

In contrast with early EC companies, which were not diversified with one website, many EC companies today have multiple online divisions and websites. Furthermore, many collaborate with other companies in joint ventures or other kinds of partnership. For example, Alibaba Group (Chapter 4) includes nine companies (e.g., Alipay, Alibaba.com, Tmall), and Amazon.com is in the business of selling hardware and software in addition to e-tailing. In 2014, China's Tencent Holdings purchased a percentage of Leju Holdings Ltd., an online real estate services company. Tencent wants to broaden their range of online services that can be connected to the popular smartphone messaging application WeChat, which they own. Facebook, Google, Apple and Amazon are aggressively seeking access to a broad range of online services. Google is even investing in robotics and Facebook purchased the virtual reality company Oculus VR in 2014. Alibaba Group purchased a Silicon Valley startup called TangoMe, and the list goes on and on. Many of these acquisitions are purchased at such a high price, like the $19 billion that Facebook paid for WhatsApp. Do all the acquisitions make sense? For example, many wonder if Facebook's acquisition of Oculus VR for $2 billion is a visionary or crazy acquisition (e.g., see Ortutay and Liedtke 2014).

SECTION 13.4 REVIEW QUESTIONS

1. Describe how a company should and should *not* select EC applications.
2. Explain Tjan's Internet portfolio map.
3. List four sources of business risk in EC. What questions exemplify each source of risk?
4. Discuss three strategies for smarter online pricing.
5. Describe the multichannel issues and strategy.
6. Describe the acquisition strategy and its benefits.

13.5 E-COMMERCE STRATEGY IMPLEMENTATION

The execution of the strategic plan takes place during the strategy implementation phase, where EC systems are deployed. Decision makers evaluate options, establish specific milestones, allocate resources, and manage the projects.

In this section, we examine some of the topics related to this implementation process.

E-Commerce Strategy Implementation Process

Typically, the first step in e-strategy implementation is to find a champion and establish an EC team, which then initiates and manages the execution of the plan. As EC implementation continues, the team is likely to introduce changes in the organization. Thus, during the implementation phase, it also becomes necessary to develop an effective *change management* program, including the possibility of utilizing the *business process management* approach. For a comprehensive case study on implementing social media at IBM, see Chess Media Group (2012).

Find a Champion

Every Web project and every Web team requires a project champion. The **project champion** is the person who ensures that the team is ready to move forward and understands its responsibilities. The project champion is responsible for activities such as identifying the project's objectives, prioritizing phases, and allocating resources to ensure completion of the project, and so forth. The project champion may be the Web team leader or a senior executive. In his study of e-strategy in 43 companies, Plant (2000) found that a strong project champion was present in every e-commerce project that was successful, and that the champion was either a senior executive or someone who was able to demonstrate the benefits the project would bring to the organization. Similarly, "top management championship" was identified as a critical success factor for organizational assimilation of Web technologies.

Start with a Pilot Project

A clever way to implement EC is to begin with one or a small number of EC pilot projects. Problems can be determined during the pilot stage, allowing plans to be modified before it is too late.

Allocate Resources

The resources required for EC projects depend on the information requirements, the capabilities of the performers, and the requirements of each project. Some resources – software, computers, warehouse capacity, staff – could be new and unique to the EC project. A project's success depends upon an effective allocation and utilization of shared resources to the project such as databases, the intranet, and possibly an extranet. A variety of tools can assist in resource allocation.

Manage the Project

Project management tools, such as Microsoft Project, assist in determining specific project tasks, milestones, and resource requirements. Standard system design tools (e.g., data flow diagrams) can help in executing the resource-requirement plan.

E-Commerce Strategy Implementation Issues

There are several e-strategy implementation issues, depending on the circumstances. Here we describe some representative ones.

Build, Buy, or Rent EC Elements

Implementation of an EC application requires access to the construction of the company's website and integration of the site with the existing corporate information systems (e.g., front end for order taking, back end for order fulfillment). At this point, a number of decisions of whether to build, buy, or outsource various components or an entire project needs to be made. Some of the more specific decisions include the following:

> • Should site development be done internally, externally, or by a combination of the two?
> • Is it necessary to build the software application or will the commercially available software be satisfactory?
> • If a commercial software package will fit, should it be purchased or rented from an application service provider (ASP)? Should it be modified?
> • Will the company or an external ISP (Internet service provider) host the website?
> • If hosted externally, who will be responsible for monitoring and maintaining the information and system?

Each option has its strengths and weaknesses, and the correct decisions will depend on factors such as the strategic priority of the application, the existing skills of the company's technology group, and when the EC application is needed.

Outsource: What? When? To Whom?

Outsourcing can deliver strategic advantages for firms in that it provides access to highly skilled or low-cost labor, and provides potential market opportunities. **Outsourcing** is the process of contracting (farming out) the company's products, services, or work to another organization that is willing and able to do the job. Alternatively, the company's own employees could carry out these projects in-house. In the context of EC, outsourcing means the use of external vendors to acquire EC applications.

Example

An interesting tool to help the 'go or no go' outsourcing decisions is *Gartner's Magic Quadrant*. It analyzes companies (providers) along two scales: the *ability to execute* and the *completeness of vision*. Vendors are then placed in one of four resulting quadrants (e.g. high ability to execute and full vision make *leaders*, while low ability to execute and high vision make *visionaries*). Companies can use the quadrant to find the right outsourcers. For details, see (**gartner.com/technology/research/methodologies/magic-Quadrants.jsp#m**).

Successful implementation of EC projects often requires careful consideration of outsourcing strategies, which involves: (1) evaluating when outsourcing should take place; (2) deciding which part(s) of the EC projects to outsource and which to keep in-house; and (3) choosing an appropriate vendor(s).

Software-as-a-Service

In considering outsourcing, a company should look at both software-as-a-service and cloud computing (see Online Tutorial T2) as outsourcing options.

Table 13.4 In-house development versus outsourcing

Criteria	In-house development	Outsourcing
Accessibility to the project	Greater	Limited
Knowledge of the system and its development	More	Less
Retention of staff's knowledge and skills	Higher	Lower
Ownership cost	Higher	Lower
Self-reliance for maintenance, update, and expansion	Greater	Lower
Development times	Longer	Shorter
Experienced staff with technical know-how and specialized areas	Less	More

Outsourcing decisions are often made during EC project implementation. Companies may choose outsourcing when they want to experiment with new EC technologies without spending too much money.

A comparison of the in-house and outsourcing approaches is provided in Table 13.4. Sometimes, after an evaluation of both approaches, a hybrid approach is taken to leverage the benefit of both.

ISPs, ASPs, and consultants are external vendors (business partners) that are commonly involved in EC application developments.

It is important not to overestimate the advantages of outsourcing, since it also can involve a number of risks such as the vendor going out of business. When the vendor is a foreign company, there may be additional risks such as shifts in the political stability and the legal environment. In addition, an organization's lack of experience with outsourcing and contract negotiations in a different culture may create problems.

Chapter 16 discusses several of these options in more detail – build or buy, in-house or outsource, host externally or internally. In many such decisions, one needs to consider partners' strategy and business alliances as described in Online File W13.2.

Redesigning Business Processes: BPR and BPM

During the implementation stage, many firms face the need to change business processes to accommodate the changes an EC strategy brings. Sometimes these changes are incremental and can be managed as part of the project implementation process (e.g., see Harvard Business School Press 2010). In other cases, the changes are so dramatic that they affect the manner in which the organization operates. In this instance, business process reengineering or business process management is needed.

Business Process Reengineering (BPR)

Business process reengineering (BPR) is a methodology for conducting a one-time comprehensive redesign of an enterprise's processes. BPR may be needed for the following reasons:

- To fix poorly designed processes (e.g., processes that are not flexible or scalable)
- To change processes so that they fit commercially available software (e.g., ERP, e-procurement)
- To produce a fit between systems and processes of different companies that are partnering in e-commerce (e.g., e-marketplaces, ASPs)
- To align procedures and processes with e-services such as logistics, payments, or security

For an overview, see Johnston (2012). For a case study about Mary Kay using e-commerce strategies to revamp its business model, see Online File W13.3.

Business Process Management

The term **business process management (BPM)** refers to activities performed by businesses to improve their processes. While such activities usually are not new, software tools called *business process management* systems have made the execution of such activities faster and cheaper. BPM systems monitor the execution of the business processes so that managers can analyze and change processes whenever needed. BPM differs from BPR in that it deals not just with a one-time change to the organization, but also with long-term-consequences and repetitive actions. Business process management activities can be grouped into three categories: monitoring, execution, and design. For details on value-driven BPM, see Franz and Kirchmer (2012).

Change Management

Implementing large scale EC or social commerce projects may require change management approaches, especially if the processes of the business have changed. A business can use a generic change management approach. For how IBM is conducting change management for Enterprise 2.0 applications, see Chess Media Group (2012). For an additional description, see Chapter 14.

SECTION 13.5 REVIEW QUESTIONS

1. Describe a Web (project) team and its purpose.
2. What is the role of a project champion?
3. What is the purpose of a pilot project?
4. Discuss the major strategy implementation issues of application development and BPR.
5. Describe BPM and the need for it in EC development.

13.6   E-COMMERCE PERFORMANCE ASSESSMENT

The last phase of EC strategy development begins as soon as the deployment of the EC project is complete. Strategy assessment includes both the continual assessment of the performance of the implemented systems, and the periodic formal evaluation of progress toward the organization's strategic goals. Based on the results, corrective actions are taken and, if necessary, the strategy is reformulated.

The Objectives of Assessment

Strategic assessment has several objectives. The most important ones are:

- Measure the extent to which the EC strategy and projects are delivering what they are supposed to deliver.
- Determine if the EC strategy and projects are still viable in the current changing business environment.
- Reassess the initial strategy in order to learn from mistakes and improve future planning.
- Identify failing or lagging projects as soon as possible, and determine why they failed or lagged to avoid the same problems in the future.

Web applications often grow in unexpected ways, expanding beyond their initial plan. For example, Genentec, Inc. (**gene.com**), a biotechnology giant, wanted to replace a home-grown online bulletin board system (BBS). It started the project with a small budget but soon found that the corporate intranet had grown rapidly and had become very popular in a short span of time, encompassing many applications. Taking corrective action is part of performance management, a topic we describe in Section 13.7. For a guideline and framework for performance management, see Gosselin (2010).

The Performance Assessment Process

The performance assessment is a process that is based on the stated strategy, tactics, and implementation plans. The process involves the following steps:

1. Set up performance metrics.
2. Monitor the performance of the business.
3. Compare the actual performance to the metrics.
4. Conduct an analysis using analytics, including Web analytics.
5. Combine the analysis with the methodology of the *Balanced Scorecard*.
6. Present the results to management in the form of reports, tables and dashboards.

Figure 13.4 The performance assessment process

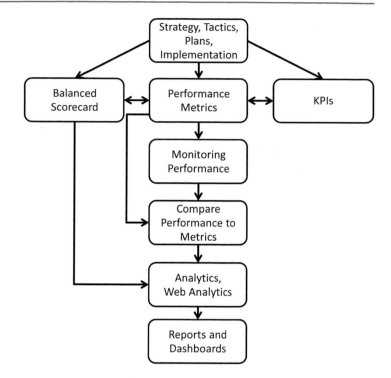

The process is illustrated in Figure 13.4.

This process is part of the larger cyclical process that starts with strategy initiation and formulation and ends with taking corrective action. The major steps of the process are described in the remainder of this section.

Establish and Use Metrics

The first issue to address here is "what to assess?" The answer to this is to identify the major activities listed in the strategy and plans. For example, if one of the corporate objectives is to improve customer service, it is necessary to find the strategy, tactics, and plans to do so. Then one needs to establish metrics.

A **metric** is a specific, measurable standard against which actual performance is compared. A metric can be an absolute number or a ratio, and it can be tangible or intangible. For example, if the strategy includes the development of an e-auction system for increasing sales, a metric can be the resultant sale volume.

A business metric is a quantifiable measure that is used to track the performance of a business process (see Klubeck 2011 and **klipfolio.com/resources/articles/what-are-business-metrics**). Establishing and measuring performance and comparing it against the metrics is an important key success factor.

Metrics can produce positive results in organizations by driving behavior in a number of ways. Metrics can:

- Be the basis for establishing and assessing specific goals and plans.
- Structure the value proposition of business models.
- Communicate a business strategy to the workforce through performance targets.
- Increase accountability when metrics are linked with performance appraisal programs and rewards.

- Align the objectives of individuals, departments, and divisions to the enterprise's strategic objectives.
- Track the performance of EC systems, including usage, types of visitors, page visits, conversion rate, and so forth.
- Assess the health of companies by using tools such as balanced scorecards and performance dashboards (see Person 2013).

Table 13.5 2012 E-strategy measurement challenges

Description	% of companies concerned
Attracting new customers or clients to the site	40
Improving online marketing effectiveness	38
Retaining existing customers and clients	31
Finding the right staff	25
Managing technology innovation	16
Analyzing and understanding how to optimize performance	13
Planning an international strategy	7
Engaging social media channels	5

Measurements in Performance Metrics

Metrics need to be defined properly, with a clear way to measure them. For example, revenue growth can be measured in total dollars, in percentage change over time, or in percentage growth as compared to that of the entire industry. *Cost avoidance*, for example, can be achieved in many ways. Defining the specific measures is critical; otherwise, what the metrics actually measure may be open to interpretation. Each metric can be expressed by one or several measures, known as *indicators*. The most important indicators are called *key performance indicators*.

A **key performance indicator (KPI)** is a quantifiable measurement that reflects the critical success factors of a company, department, or project. KPIs are used to measure performance in terms of meeting the company's goals and objectives. There could be several KPIs for one metric or one goal. Different companies measure success or failure by different sets of KPIs. (See Francis 2013 for a discussion.)

Examples

Hayes (2013) provides some examples of goals and 32 suggested e-commerce KPIs. For example, for sales KPIs, he suggests monitoring daily or weekly sales, traffic to the website, and customers' order size. For customer service KPIs, he suggests counting e-mails and service-related chats.

Table 13.5 lists the measurement challenges that companies are facing.

In measuring performance KPIs, some companies may realize that their initial goals were unrealistic, that their Web servers are inadequate to handle demand, or that expected cost savings have not been realized. This calls for some adjustments.

Assessing EC is difficult because of the many real life configurations and impact variables involved in what is being measured. In addition, it is important that the Web team address both the evaluation of project performance and the assessment of a changing environment.

Intangible Variables

When dealing with KPIs and their assessment, one should also pay attention to intangible variables. For dealing with intangible variables, see Hubbard (2010).

E-Commerce Metrics in Action

An example of using metrics in strategy management is provided in the case of Axon of New Zealand (see Online File W13.4). To capitalize on this opportunity and retain its reputation, Axon launched Quality Direct, an online procurement service for small and medium-sized companies, to give them the same service as large companies. The case lists several Web-related metrics.

Performance Metrics

Performance metrics are measures of an organization's performance. They are a subclass of general metrics.

Metrics are closely related to performance management systems and to the balanced scorecard.

Monitoring Performance

Given the diversity of EC activities and websites, it is no wonder there are so many ways companies conduct performance monitoring. The monitoring covers the activities occurring on websites, customers' conversations in social media, financial and marketing success, and more. Hundreds of vendors provide tools and services; therefore, it is not possible to list all of them. For example, AlertSite, a product of Smartbear Software (**smartbear.com**), provides 24/7 website monitoring and provides an alert if there is an issue with the site. For resources on website monitoring, network performance, etc., see **blog.monitor.us**. One major area of monitoring occurs in social media. For instructions on how to monitor your family's Internet use, see Miller (2012).

Monitoring the Social Media Field

The amount of social media data on the Web is increasing exponentially with billions of videos, photos, and endless tweets and other conversations. The problem that companies face is how to monitor the Web for data that are relevant to them. Furthermore, companies need to do this quickly and at a low cost. The solution is selecting appropriate metrics and automating data collection. Companies can set up an automated monitoring system on their own using e-mail, RSS feeds, or special software. For comprehensive coverage see Turban et al. (2015), and for tips for brand marketers, see **forbes.com/sites/cherylsnappconner/2014/03/04/top-online-reputation-management-tips-for-brand-marketers**.

Google offers e-mail *alerts* for any keywords of a user's choice, such as a brand name, or a competitor's brand name, and so forth. Users can set up e-mail alerts for the entire Web, blogs, etc. (e.g., see Beal and Strauss 2008).

Social Media Monitoring Tools

A large number of tools are available for social media monitoring. For a comprehensive list, see **wiki.kenburbary.com**, and Paine (2011).

A number of social media monitoring services provide data to businesses (e.g., **actionly.com**, Radian 6; **salesforcemarketingcloud.com/products/social-media-listening**, **visibletechnologies.com**, and **twelvefold.com**). Most of these services track online content and then feed summaries and other statistics into dashboards. Fee-free services to conduct monitoring are available for smaller companies. For example, Google News, Moreover Technologies, and Yahoo! track news about companies and whole industries. Technorati (**technorati.com**) specifically tracks social media sites. Some of the social media monitoring tools provide analytics as well.

The Balanced Scorecard (BSC)

One of the best-known and most widely used performance management systems is the *Balanced Scorecard* (see **balancedscorecard.org**). Kaplan and Norton first articulated this methodology in their *Harvard Business Review* article "The Balanced Scorecard: Measures That Drive Performance" (see Kaplan and Norton 1992). For an overview, see Person (2013), and for resources, including white papers, examples, basics, and infographics, etc., see **balancedscorecard.org/Resources/AbouttheBalancedScorecard/tabid/55/Default.aspx**. The major objective of the Balanced Scorecard is to monitor the execution of EC strategy-related activities. For details, see Online File W13.5.

Analyzing Performance Data

Once data are collected, they can be compared to metrics and KPIs. Both the performance data and the deviations from the targets are analyzed. Analyzing e-commerce data and information is a comprehensive field that includes many methods and tools. We cover only the major ones in this chapter.

Defining EC Analytics

EC analytics is an umbrella term that includes a number of specialized analysis techniques. For example, in the social media area, one can use social filtering, social network analysis, sentiment analysis, and social-media analytics. In general, *e-commerce analytics* describes the process of measuring, analyzing, and interpreting the results of what we monitor (e.g., interactions and associations among people).

EC analytics is crucial for obtaining a strategic understanding of what is taking place in EC. EC analytics is a subcategory of *Web analytics* (described later).

Major Types of Analysis

Analysis can be done on marketing data, financial data, behavioral data, and on other data. The major types of analysis are text and Web mining, optimization, forecasting and predictions, and sentiment analysis.

Web Analytics and Its Major Tools

One large and growing area of EC strategy assessment is **Web analytics**, which, according to the Web Analytics Association, "is the measurement, collection, analysis, and reporting of Internet data for the purposes of understanding and optimizing Web usage." It also can be used to facilitate market research and performance assessment. Web analytics begins by identifying data that can assess the effectiveness of the site's goals and objectives (e.g., too many visitors to a site map may indicate site navigation problems). Web analytics concentrates on Web traffic patterns and people's behavior online. Next, analytics data are collected, such as the location of site visitors, what pages they view, time spent visiting the site, and the manner in which they interact with the site's content. The data can reveal the impact of search engine optimization or an advertising campaign, the effectiveness of website design and navigation, and, most important, visitor conversion. Because the goal of most EC websites is to sell products, the most valuable

Web analytics are those related to the conversion rate, from a visitor to a buyer.

Information about Web analytics is available from **emetrics.org** and **jimnovo.com**. Two of the many Web analytics tools providers are WebTrends (**webtrends.com**) and Google Analytics (**google. com/analytics**).

Example: Google Analytics

This comprehensive tool conducts many statistical activities (e.g., time-series analysis, cross-sectional analysis, scatter diagrams, trend analysis, ROI, and much more. For seven Google Analytics metrics to watch, see **prdaily.com/ Main/Articles/7_Google_Analytics_metrics_ you_should_monitor_13939.aspx#**).

To learn about the new features of the Google Analytics system and how to use them for optimization, see Cutroni (2014). Several companies have created tools to supplement Google Analytics. Examples are: Agency Platform, Argyle Social, Unilyzer, Social Commerce Insights by Bazaarvoice, and Visible Intelligence from **trucast.net**.

Other Web analytic tools include: Yahoo! Web analytics (**web.analytics.yahoo.com**). Watch the video "SAS® Social Media Analytics" (3:49 minutes) at **youtube.com/playlist?list=PLED82 1CEF3DF6AB33**.

Social Media Activities

There are many ways to analyze social media. Generic e-commerce tools such as Web mining and text mining can be used in social media too. There are several other tools for data, texting, and Web mining that are useful in social media. For comprehensive coverage of social media platforms, tools to use to find customers, and much more, see Sponder (2012). Following are some examples of analytical tools.

Example 1

IBM SPSS Modeler (**ibm.com/software/analytics/spss/products/modeler**) is a predictive analytics software tool that measures trends in consumer views of products and services that are collected from Web 2.0 tools (e.g., blogs and social networks). The upgraded versions of

Modeler also analyze emoticons and common texting jargon terms. The software covers 180 variables and 400,000 industry-specific terms that can be analyzed.

Example 2

Wendy's International uses software to analyze over 500,000 text-based customer messages collected each year. Using Clarabridge text analytics software, Wendy's analyzes comments from its Web-based feedback forms, e-mails, receipt-based surveys, and social media. Before the emergence of social media, the company used a combination of spreadsheets and keyword searches to review comments in a slow and manual approach.

Example 3

Nielsen Social offers Twitter TV analytics and an engagement platform.

Other major vendors that provide analytic tools are **clarabridge.com**, **attensity.com**, **sas.com**, and **sap.com**.

Sentiment Analysis

Sentiment analysis or **opinion mining** refers to a type of analysis that aims to determine the attitude of a person with respect to a particular issue as expressed in online conversations. For details, see Pang and Lee (2008). It is measured by techniques such as natural language processing (NLP), computational linguistics, and text analysis to automatically identify and extract subjective information found in social media.

Automated sentiment analysis is a process of training a computer to identify sentiments within content using NLP. Various sentiment measurement platforms employ different techniques and statistical methodologies to evaluate sentiments while some use a hybrid system.

IBM Social Sentiment Index

IBM developed an index that aggregates and gauges public opinion from a range of social media sources. For example, the software identifies the emotional context of the conversation (e.g., between sarcasm and sincerity), and discovers which conversations are important and should be monitored. For details, see **ibm.com/analytics/us/en/conversations/social-sentiment-steampunk.html**.

For success in sentiment analysis, see Valentine (2014). For how Thomson Reuters is incorporating sentiment analysis gained from Twitter to use in their market analysis and trading platform, see Lunden (2014).

SECTION 13.6 REVIEW QUESTIONS

1. Describe the need for assessment.
2. Define metrics and describe their contribution to strategic planning.
3. Describe the corporate performance management approach to strategy assessment.
4. What is the Balanced Scorecard?
5. Describe Web analytics.
6. Describe sentiment analysis.
7. What is the IBM sentiment analysis index?

13.7 PERFORMANCE IMPROVEMENT AND INNOVATION

The final step in the cycle is to determine, based on the results of Phase 4, how to improve performance, or how to change the strategy.

Most organizations are consistently trying to improve their performance, which in many cases, is necessary to do in order to stay competitive or even to survive.

In this section, we discuss the following topics: overview, dashboards, and performance improvement via innovation. We also provide examples of innovative strategies.

An Overview of Performance Improvement

There are many ways and tools to improve the performance of organizations and individuals. Which approach to use depends on a diagnosis of what the performance assessment reveals. One approach is to do restructuring by using BPM and

BPR (Section 13.5). Large companies are using *competitive intelligence* (CI; see **whatis.techtarget.com/definition/competitive-intelligence-CI**). This includes the analysis of competitive markets, competitors, and the business environment. Using the Balanced Scorecard to check the 'health' of companies has been recommended by Kaplan and Norton (1996). Kaplan et al. (2010) suggest using the balanced scorecard to avoid failures of partnerships. The field of Industrial Engineering is dedicated to performance improvement, as are several other disciplines. Today, there are tens of thousands of apps that can be used to improve the performance of EC; many of the apps are for smartphones. Therefore, it is impossible to list all the techniques available for performance improvement. Consequently, we have elected to cover only two topics here: *dashboards* and *innovations*.

Dashboards in E-Commerce

Once data are analyzed and summarized in tables and charts, they need to be presented to management for decision making. One popular tool to do just that is a *dashboard.*

What Is a Dashboard?

A dashboard is a control panel. Its most well-known application is the instrument panel in front of a driver of an automobile, or in front of an airplane pilot. It usually involves many gauges and indicators. An **information dashboard** (referred to as a "dashboard" in this chapter) is a visual presentation of data organized in a way that is easy to read and interpret. It is popular user interface. The information is presented through gauges, charts, maps, tables, etc., to reveal the direction and velocity of the measured metrics. Dashboards are very popular business tools for use by executives and managers since they visually summarize and track the important information (usually the status of KPIs and metrics) and point to any deviations from targets using alerts (e.g., red colors), indicating where action needs to be taken. Dashboards are usually interactive and integrate information from multiple sources. Dashboards may be customized.

There are many types of dashboards and they can be very colorful. Over 100 examples

can be seen when you use Google to search "photos (or images) of dashboards." For information on getting started with dashboards, a dashboard gallery, articles, and more, see **dashboardinsight.com**, and for a comprehensive guide to dashboards, including infographics and case studies, see **klipfolio.com/guide-to-business-dashboards**.

Innovation for Performance Improvement

Innovation in e-commerce is similar to any other innovation activity. It is the key to improving performance and may determine the success of e-commerce projects as well as the success of the entire organization, and possibly its survival. What is unique today is the development of philosophy, strategy, and tools for both management and employees to engage much more fully in the innovation process. Social media also provides management with new methods of innovation, such as the use of crowdsourcing for idea generation and listening to customers' suggestions (and complaints) as input for product design or redesign.

1. Spigit, Inc. (**spigit.com**; now part of Mindjet Corporation) provides nine keys to innovation in the social media environment (Spigit 2011). A summary of some of the continually changing nine key points is: Treat innovation as a discipline.
2. Create common community space to give everyone in the organization a chance to contribute ideas.
3. Innovation benefits from a diversity of perspectives (e.g., in the composition of crowdsourcing participants).
4. Employees' ideas should be free and unrestricted.
5. Create a culture of constant choices since the markets are constantly changing.
6. Recognize that for innovation to take place, ideas must go through an evaluation process; however, realize the power of rejected ideas.

The innovations must to be measured in order to be managed. Here are few innovation strategies:

- IBM helps their clients innovate their EC business model by enabling the clients to better manage and redefine their value chain and use e-commerce technology (see **ibm.com/smarterplanet/us/en/smarter_commerce/overview**).
- Communication technologies and Web 2.0 tools enable employees to work off site. The virtual office (see Violino 2011) can help increase performance.
- Many companies are integrating war games in their innovations to study strategies for improving their products. By simulating the thoughts and actions of their competitors (to see how their innovations compare with their rivals), they will be able to better seize opportunities (see Capozzi et al. 2012).
- A large number of innovations are related to m-commerce.

Computerized creativity tools can facilitate innovation both for individuals and for groups. For a list of individual and group creativity support tools, see Shneiderman (2007). Note that several Web 2.0 tools are on the list. For many innovation-related cases, strategies, and articles, visit **enterpriseinnovation.net**.

Common ways to improve innovations are: (1) Foster openness to innovation, (2) expand the pipeline of new ideas, (3) triage the most promising ideas, and (4) adopt a 'test and learn' approach.

Innovative Strategies: Some Illustrative Examples

The following are several illustrative examples of strategic EC decisions:

- Target Corporation (**target.com**) matched certain online retailers' prices during the 2012 holiday season to compete with other stores for shoppers. They first decided to match prices until December 24, but in 2013, they decided to offer online price matching year-round. Target is matching prices offered by Amazon.com, Walmart.com, BestBuy.com,

and ToysRus.com. Target stores are also price matching items found on Target.com. For details, see Wohl (2012). Toys "R" Us is matching prices at their Babies "R" Us store against competitors.

- Best Buy (**bestbuy.com**) is facing competition from all sides, mostly from Amazon.com and GameStop.com, which provides a serious threat to Best Buy's sales. Best Buy's physical stores have become a showroom for people who visit the stores, use their smartphones to scan product barcodes to compare prices, and then buy the same items at a cheaper price on Amazon.com or other online stores. Due to its losses, Best Buy was forced to close many of their low level of sell stores. Best Buy's strategy now is to sell more products from its online store, but it is still struggling. Best Buy has improved its customer service as well as its loyalty program and is offering free shipping for its loyalty card members. For details, see Dignan (2012).
- Travelzoo Inc. (**travelzoo.com**) operates in a competitive online environment. Their strategy is to increase their reach, expand the sales force and develop new products, especially in the mobile and hotel categories. eBay (**ebay.com**) competes with Amazon, Etsy, Bonanza, and others by helping clothing start-up companies put their webstores on eBay's site.
- Facebook (**facebook.com**) sells game cards that are redeemable only for Facebook games.
- Apple (**apple.com**) and Facebook (**facebook.com**) have teamed up to counter Google by bringing "Facebook Integration" through Apple's iOS 6. With Facebook Integration, users can sign in to Facebook and update their status, share links in Safari, and post photos, with an option to allow Facebook to access their Contacts and Calendar. Apple also introduced Apple Maps (an unsuccessful attempt to compete with Google Maps). However, in an attempt to better Maps, in 2014, Apple purchased Spotsetter, a social search and mapping startup.
- Cars.com (**cars.com**) uses a differentiation strategy by making its website a secure display for all makes and models of cars. It

serves both consumers and dealers for new and used cars. The site enables consumers to compare features, read recommendations, and obtain quotes from dealers. By using Web 2.0 tools and platforms through sites such as Facebook, Twitter, and Google+. For details, see (**cars.com**).

- Google+ is a social network launched in 2011; it uses differentiation to advance its network, building upon its search capabilities. Google+ is offering branding pages in its effort to take advertising business away from Facebook. (Facebook has a huge competitive advantage due to the large number of members and visits.) However, Google's strategy seems to have worked. By August 2011, it became the fastest growing (in percentage) social network.

- To support its Smarter Commerce strategic initiative, IBM acquired several EC companies at high prices (Coremetrics, Sterling Commerce, Unica). IBM's strategy is to meet the demand for social media products and services by tying mobile, social, analytics, and cloud computing together, for both online and offline shopping. For details, see Guinn et al. (2011). In April 2012, Facebook bought Instagram for $1 billion. Many wondered why the company paid so much for a company with no revenue. The answer is: It is a strategic acquisition. Hill (2012) provides 10 reasons for the acquisition. (See discussion questions at the end of this chapter.)

SECTION 13.7 REVIEW QUESTIONS

1. Why do organizations need to improve performance even if their performance is already good?
2. Define dashboards and explain their usage in the strategy-performance cycle.
3. Is it wise for big companies to pay so much money to acquire small EC-related companies?

13.8 A STRATEGY FOR GLOBAL E-COMMERCE

Deciding whether to "go global" is a strategic issue. In a June 30, 2010 report on world Internet use, Miniwatts Marketing Group reported that nearly 2 billion people worldwide are regular Internet users. In the second quarter of 2012, approximately 248 million people were in North America, more than 800 million were in Asia, and nearly a half billion were in Europe (**internetworldstats.com/stats.htm**). These statistics illustrate the enormous potential that exists for companies to expand their market share globally using EC. Today the figures are much higher.

The decision to go global is made for many reasons, both reactive and proactive. Reactive reasons include factors such as competitors that are already selling internationally. Proactive reasons include sellers that are seeking economies of scale, looking for new international markets, gaining access to sufficient or new resources, cost savings, and local government incentives. Regardless of the reasons, expanding globally to realize a company's strategic objectives requires extensive planning and responding quickly to opportunities.

A global electronic marketplace can be an attractive opportunity in an EC strategy. Going global means access to larger markets, opportunity to minimize taxes, and flexibility to employ a less expensive workforce anywhere. However, going global is a complex and strategic decision process for several reasons. Geographic distance is an obviously important issue in conducting business globally; however, frequently, it is not the most important issue. Cultural differences and political, legal, administrative, and economic issues must be considered. This section briefly examines representative opportunities, problems, and solutions for companies that are going global with EC. For an overview of globalization, see Prahalad and Krishnan (2008).

Benefits and Extent of Global Operations

A major advantage of EC is the ability to conduct business at any time, from anywhere, and at a reasonable cost. These are also the drivers behind global EC, and there have been some incredible success stories in this area. For example:

- eBay conducts auctions in hundreds of countries worldwide.
- Alibaba.com (Chapter 4) provides B2B trading services to hundreds of thousands of companies worldwide.
- Amazon.com sells books and millions of other items to individuals and separate retail websites for 13 countries, including the U.S., UK, France, and Brazil.
- Small companies, such as ZD Wines (**zdwines.com**), sell to hundreds of customers worldwide. HotHotHot (**hothothot.com**), a tiny Internet pioneering company reported its first international trade only after it went online; within two years, global sales accounted for 25% of its total sales. Global sales now are done via HotSauce.com service.
- Major corporations, such as GE and Boeing, have reported an increasing number of international vendors participating in their electronic RFQs. These electronic bids have resulted in a 10 to 15% cost reduction and more than 50% reduction in cycle time.
- In 2013, the NFL opened an e-commerce shop for the Chinese market (**nfl. tmall.com**), which partners with 25 regional TV broadcasters and digital media outlets across China (see *PR Newswire* 2013).
- By recruiting online via social networks (e.g., **xing.com** and **linkedin.com**), many international corporations have considerably increased their success in recruiting employees to work in international locations.

Globalization and Social Networking

Globalization of EC has benefitted greatly from social networking. For example, there are about four times more international Facebook members than in the U.S. Furthermore, companies such as Amazon.com, Google, Groupon, and Yahoo! are very active globally. For insights about going global in the social environment, see Adobe (2012).

Barriers to Global E-Commerce

Despite the benefits and opportunities offered by globalization, there are several barriers to global EC. Some of these barriers face any EC venture but become more difficult when international impacts are considered. These barriers include authentication of buyers and sellers (Chapter 10), generating and retaining trust (Chapter 9), order fulfillment and delivery (Chapter 12), security (Chapter 10), and domain names (Chapter 16). Others are unique to global EC. In this chapter, we will discuss some of these barriers.

iGlobal stores (**iglobalstores.com**) offers suggestions on what to offer international customers: country-specific checkout experience, up-to-the minute currency conversion and foreign settlement, global fraud and risk and its protection, calculation of duty and tax, and integration with existing information systems. (Note: The offerings keep changing.)

Cultural Differences

The Internet is a multifaceted marketplace made up of cross-cultural users. The multicultural nature of global EC is important because cultural attributes (such as social norms, local habits and spoken languages) determine how people interact with companies, agencies, and with each other. Cultural and related differences include spelling differences (e.g., American versus British spelling), information formatting (e.g., dates can be mm/dd/yy or dd/mm/yy), graphics and icons (e.g., mailbox shapes differ from country to country), measurement standards (e.g., metric versus imperial system), and so forth. Many companies are globalizing their websites by creating different sites for different countries, taking into account site design elements, pricing and payment infrastructures, currency conversion, customer support, and language translation.

Language Translation

Although the world population is over 7 billion (2014), only about 1 billion people speak English as their native or second language. In contrast, more than 1.4 billion people speak Chinese. In their study of 1,000 top websites, Sargent and Kelly (2010) found that more than 72% of consumers would be more likely to purchase a product with the description in their native language, and 56.2% agreed that price is not as important as being able to access information in their native language. In order to reach 80% of the world's population, a website would have to be translated into 83 of the world's 6,912 languages. Therefore, a website offered in only one language can only reach 20 to 30% of the total online population at the most.

Clearly, these single language websites are severely limiting their customer base. It is not surprising then, that language translation is one of the most obvious and most important aspects of creating and maintaining global websites. Sargent and Kelly (2010) also reported that 23 was the average number of languages supported by the 250 sites who participated in their survey. The top 25 global websites support an average of 58 languages. In 2014, Byte Level Research reviewed 150 corporate global websites, identifying the 25 top "amazing global gateways" – leaders, laggards, and best practice companies (**bytelevel.com/reportcard2014/#25top**).

The number one global website in 2011 was Facebook. It replaced Google, which was number one in 2010. (In 2014, Google was back to number one.) Facebook's representative innovations include multilingual plug-ins, an improved global gateway, and multilingual user profiles. The primary problems with language translation are speed and cost. It may take a human translator a week to translate a medium-sized website into another language. For large sites, the cost can be more than $500,000, depending on the complex-ity of the site and the number of languages for translation and can be a lengthy process.

Machine Translation

Some companies address the cost and time problems by translating their Web pages into different languages through what is called *machine translations*. A list of free translation programs can be found at **xmarks.com/site/www.humanitas-international.org/newstran/more-translators.htm** and **websites.translations.com**. For examples on how Lionbridge Technologies, Inc. uses machine translation to help their clients, see **lionbridge.com/clients**. For example, in November 2013, Lionbridge was selected by Net-A-Porter (Case 1.1, Chapter 1) to develop and maintain translated content for Net-A-Porter's global websites. Net-A-Porter ships its luxury fashion products to 170 countries and operates several non-English sites (e.g., Mandarin, French, German). For details, see Sklair (2009).

Example: Ortsbo, Inc.

The company that enables real-time global communication, claims more than 212 million unique users in over 170 countries. Telus International teamed up with Ortsbo in a customer care program to enable Telus's customer service agents to chat in real time online to almost anyone in their native language (as of 2013, the software is available in 66 languages). Telus can offer multilingual support at a lower cost because they do not have to hire additional agents for each language. (See Bach 2013 for details.)

The Droid Translator app, launched in June 2014, offers the capabilities to transform personal and business chat by translating phone, video, and text chat in 29 languages (see Petroff 2014).

Legal Issues

One of the most contentious areas of global EC is the resolution of international legal issues (Chapter 15). An ambitious effort to reduce differences in international law governing EC is the United Nations Commission on International Trade Law (UNCITRAL) Model Law on

Electronic Commerce. Its purpose is to provide national legislators with a set of guidelines that are internationally acceptable, which specify how to overcome some of the legal constraints in the development of e-commerce. It also provides for a safer legal platform to be constructed through the design of fair, current, and consistent guidelines in e-commerce transactions (see **uncitral. org**).The Model Law has been adopted in some form or another in many countries and legal jurisdictions, including Singapore, Australia, Canada, Haiti, and the United States.

International trade organizations, such as the World Trade Organization (WTO) and the Asia-Pacific Economic Cooperation (APEC) forum, have working groups that are attempting to reduce EC trade barriers in areas such as pricing regulations, customs, import/export restrictions, tax issues, and product specification regulations.

Geographic Issues and Localization
Barriers posed by geography differ based on the transportation infrastructure between and within countries and the type of product or service being delivered. For example, geographic distance is almost irrelevant with online software sales.

Example: Clarins Group
Clarins Group (**clarinsusa.com**), a major player in the skin care, makeup, and fragrance business sector, is significantly increasing its global online presence and its e-commerce analytics to optimize online performance of its trading platform. Its brands, such as Clarins, and Azzaro, are advertised and sold on websites using the EC vendor Intelligent Trader, in more than 15 countries, while the challenges of multichannel, multilanguage, and multicurrency are addressed.

Web Localization
Many companies use different names, colors, sizes, and packaging for their overseas products and services. This practice is referred to as *localization*. In order to maximize the benefits of global e-commerce, the localization approach also should be used in the design and operation of the supporting information systems. For example, many websites offer different language or currency options, as well as special content. Europcar (**europcar.com**), for example, has a global presence in over 150 countries, each with an option for one of 10 languages. The company has a free iPhone app, which is available in eight languages.

Payments in Global EC Trades
The issues facing global payments vary from fraud to banking regulations. Some solutions were discussed in Chapter 11. Companies such as Elavon (**elavon.com**) provide global EC gateway solutions (see *Business Wire* 2012).

Economic and Financial Issues
Economic and financial issues encompassing global EC include government tariffs, customs, and taxation. In areas subject to government regulation, tax and regulatory agencies have attempted to apply the rules used in traditional commerce to e-commerce, with considerable success. Exceptions include areas such as international tariff duties and taxation. Software shipped in a box would be taxed for duties and tariffs upon arrival. However, software downloaded online may rely on self-reporting and voluntary payment of tax by the purchaser, something that does not happen very often. Note that Amazon.com and other e-tailers have started charging sales tax in many U.S. states for digital downloads (see **taxes.about.com/od/ statetaxes/a/sales-tax-for-digital-downloads. htm**; updated April 28, 2014).

A major financial barrier to global EC is electronic payment systems. To effectively sell online, EC firms must have flexible payment methods that match the ways people in different countries pay for their online purchases. Although credit cards are used widely in the United States, many European and Asian customers prefer to complete online transactions with offline payments. Even within the category of offline payments, companies must offer different options depending on the country. For example, French consumers prefer to pay with a check, Swiss consumers expect an invoice by mail, Germans commonly pay for products only upon delivery, and Swedes are accustomed to paying online with debit cards.

Pricing is another economic issue. A vendor may want to price the same product at different prices in different countries based upon local prices and competition. However, if a company has one website, differential pricing will be difficult or impossible. Similarly, what currency will be used for pricing? What currency will be used for payment?

E-Commerce in Developing Countries

Economic conditions determine the degree of the development of countries. Some developing countries are using EC as a springboard to improve their economies (e.g., China, Malaysia, India). Other developing countries are making strides. For a discussion, see Sanayei (2011).

Breaking Down the Barriers to Global E-Commerce

A number of international organizations and experts have offered suggestions on how to break down the barriers to global EC. Some of these suggestions are:

- **Be strategic.** Follow the entire strategy life cycle. A company must consider what countries to target and which languages, and how the users in the target countries will react. These considerations need to be included in the strategy.
- **Know your audience.** Consider cultural issues and legal constraints, which vary around the world.
- **Localize.** Websites need to be localized, as described in Chapter 8. In certain countries (e.g., Japan, China, Russia), local languages are essential (e.g.,

Yahoo! has a specific website for Japan: "Yahoo! Japan;" **yahoo.co.jp**); products are priced in local currencies; and local terms, conditions, and business practices are based on local laws and cultural practices.

- **Think globally, act consistently.** An international company with country-specific websites should be managed locally and must make sure that areas such as brand management, pricing, ad design, and content creation and control are consistent with the company's strategy.
- **Value the human touch.** Human translators are preferred over machine translation programs. The quality of translation is important because even a slight mistranslation may drive customers away.
- **Clarify, document, explain.** Pricing, privacy policies, shipping restrictions, contact information, and business practices should be well documented, located on the website, and visible to the customer.
- **Offer services that reduce trade barriers**. It is not feasible to offer prices and payments in all currencies, so provide a link to a currency exchange service (e.g., **xe.com**) for the customer's convenience. In B2B e-commerce, integrate EC transactions with the accounting/finance information system of the major buyers.

SECTION 13.8 REVIEW QUESTIONS

1. Describe globalization in EC and the advantages it presents.
2. Describe the major barriers to global EC.
3. What can companies do to overcome the barriers to global EC?
4. Discuss the pros and cons of a company offering its website in more than one language.

13.9   E-COMMERCE STRATEGY FOR SMALL AND MEDIUM-SIZED ENTERPRISES

E-commerce can be one of the most effective business tactics for small and medium-sized enterprises (SMEs). The potential for SMEs to expand their markets and compete with larger firms through EC is enormous. Some of the first companies to take advantage of Web-based e-commerce were small and medium-sized enterprises (SMEs). While larger, established, tradition-bound companies hesitated, some forward-thinking SMEs initiated online presence and opened webstores because they realized there were opportunities in marketing, business expansion, cost-cutting, procurement, and a wider selection of partner alliances. An example of an active SME is: The Mysterious Bookshop (**mysteriousbookshop. com**).

Clearly, SMEs are still finding it difficult to formulate or implement an EC strategy, mainly because of their inability to handle large volumes of inventory, limited use of EC by suppliers, lack of knowledge or IT expertise in the SME, and limited awareness of the associated opportunities and risks. As a result, many SMEs create static websites that are not used for selling. However, a growing number of SMEs are adopting the EC strategy. Arceo-Dumlao (2012) provides an overview of how digital marketing helps small businesses to grow.

In her article, Burke (2013) describes how a 15 year old girl created a successful business inventing special flip-flops, which are now sold online, in various offline boutiques, and at Nordstrom. For the future of EC for small businesses, see Mills (2014).

Choosing an EC approach is a strategic decision that must be made in the context of the company's overall business strategy. On the positive side, the nature of EC lowers the barriers to entry, and it is a relatively inexpensive way of reaching a larger number of buyers and sellers who can more easily search for, compare prices, and negotiate a purchase. However, there are also some inherent risks associated with the use of EC in SMEs. Table 13.6 provides a list of major advantages and disadvantages of EC for SMEs.

Table 13.6   Advantages and disadvantages of EC for small and medium-sized businesses

Advantages/benefits	Disadvantages/risks
• Inexpensive sources of information. A Scandinavian study found that over 90% of SMEs use the Internet for information search (OECD 2001)	• Lack of funds to fully exploit the potential of EC
• Inexpensive ways of advertising and conducting market research. Banner exchanges, newsletters, chat rooms, and so on are frequently cost-free ways to reach customers	• Lack of technical staff or insufficient expertise in legal issues, advertising, etc. These human resources may be unavailable or prohibitively expensive to an SME
• Competitor analysis is easier. A Finnish study found that Finnish firms rated competitor analysis third in their use of the Internet, after information search and marketing	• Less risk tolerance than a large company. If initial sales are low or the unexpected happens, the typical SME does not have a large reserve of resources to fall back on
• Inexpensive ways to build (or rent) a webstore. Creating and maintaining a website is relatively easy and cheap (see Online Chapter 16)	• When the product is not suitable or is difficult for online sales
• SMEs are less locked into legacy technologies and existing relationships with traditional retail channels	• Reduced personal contact with customers
• Image and public recognition can be generated quickly. A Web presence makes it easier for a small business to compete against larger firms	• There is an inability to afford entry, or purchase enough volume, to take advantage of digital exchanges
• An opportunity to reach worldwide customers. Global marketing, sales, and customer support online can be very efficient	

If Judy Can – You Can Too!: The Story of Blissful Tones Webstore

Blissful Tones **blissfultones.com** sells antique Tibetan Singing Bowls, Nepali jewelry, and meditation items such incense, mala, tingsha, and prayer wheels. It is a tiny online business, hosted by Shopify.com. Creating the website on Shopify involved the following process:

1. Creating a welcoming home page for the site, with a description about the company and products.
2. Uploading all product images and descriptions (see Figure 13.5).

3. Setting the retail price for each item.
4. Grouping the products into "collections." These are pages that hold similar products, such as large singing bowls, medium bowls, and small bowls.
5. Creating additional pages for customer service, "about" Judy the store owner, and educational videos and other material about the history and use of singing bowls.

Another task involved setting the shipping prices for various items, so that the shipping cost is automatically added to the item price when a buyer checks out. The choice for Blissful is USPS

Antique singing bowls were first made about 480 – 560 B.C. They were originally used for eating! They are made from an alloy of nickel, copper, silver, iron and 8 other precious metals found in the Himalayan region. We use the bowls for meditation, relaxation, chakra balancing and to assist the body in physical healing. The overtones created by these ancient bowls are amazing and cannot be experienced with the new singing bowls. Try it!

Figure 13.5 Screen shot of BlissfulTones.com

Priority Flat-Rate shipping boxes in small, medium, and large sizes. Free shipping is offered for all orders over $100.

For marketing the site, Judy is using the Constant Contact e-mail database with nearly 1,500 names. Judy occasionally sends occasional discount offers and notifications of new products. In addition, Google Ad Words is used to promote the site, which has proven to be a great success. Judy is currently planning marketing campaigns using social media.

When a customer places an order, the Shopify system offers several payment options: PayPal, credit cards, or cash on delivery. Judy opted to use the first two options so the income would be credited quickly. A small fee is deducted from the customer's payment for credit card or PayPal fees. Shopify deposits the payments directly into Judy's bank account.

When a customer places an order, Shopify sends an e-mail alert to Judy's e-mail address. This way, she can go online and find the customer's specific order and mailing address.

Order fulfillment is a more difficult task. The packaging involves using bubble wrap and Styrofoam peanuts to protect the merchandise. Shopify has a special page for "orders" where the customer's order, address, and e-mail address are kept. Judy labels the package with the customer's address and her return address, adds a special thank you note inside, and takes the packages to the post office. Once Judy sends the package, she logs into Shopify and hits the "fulfill" button, and types in the package tracking number. Then, the customer automatically receives an e-mail notification that the product is in the mail.

Note: After the book was printed Judy decided to close Blissful Tones.

Globalization and SMEs

In addition to increasing their domestic market, EC opens up a vast global marketplace for SMEs, but only a small percentage of them conduct a significant part of their business globally. However, a growing number are beginning to use EC to tap into the global marketplace in some way, but even then, SMEs are more likely to purchase globally than to sell globally. In the June 2010 "The State of Small Business Success" (was available at **networksolutions.com/small-business/wp-content/files/Network_Solutions_Small_Business_Success_Index.pdf**), the incidence of global purchasing by SMEs showed an increase in the first six months of 2010 from 11 to 18%. On the other hand, global selling of products and services by SMEs decreased in the same time period. Despite this, SMEs doing business globally report that EC has a "major impact" on their ability to operate on a broader scale. EC activities that SMEs engage in globally include communicating with global customers (41%), buying supplies (31%), and selling their products globally online (27%).

Resources to Support SME Activities in EC

SME owners often lack strategic management skills and consequently are not always aware of changes in their business environment with respect to emerging technologies. Fortunately, SMEs have a variety of private and public support options (e.g., **sba.gov**, **business.gov.au**).

In addition, vendors realize that the large number of small businesses means an opportunity for acquiring more customers. Thus, many vendors have created service centers that offer both free information and fee-based support. Examples are IBM's Small and Medium Business Solutions (**ibm.com/midmarket/us/en**) and Microsoft's Business Hub (**microsoftbusinesshub.com**). Professional associations, Web resource services (e.g., **smallbusiness.yahoo.com**) and small organizations that are in the business of helping other small businesses, go online today.

Resources to assist SMEs in going global are also emerging as helpful tools for SMEs that want to expand their horizons. For example, the Global Small Business Blog (GSBB) (**globalsmallbusinessblog.com**) was created in 2004 by Laurel Delaney to help entrepreneurs and small business owners expand their businesses internationally.

A good source regarding SMEs' use of e-markets to conduct international business is **emarketservices. com/start/Case-studies-and-reports/index.html**.

SMEs and Social Networks

Social commerce is one of the fastest growing EC technologies that is being adopted by SMEs.

Small businesses can utilize social network sites to interact with peer groups outside their immediate geographical area in order to exchange opinions about topics of mutual interest and help each other solve problems. SMEs can find websites that are dedicated to small businesses. These sites provide SMEs with opportunities to make contacts, get start-up information, and receive advice on e-strategies. Not only can sites such as LinkedIn be used to garner advice and make contacts, they can be used in B2B to develop networks that can connect SMEs with other small businesses or foster relationships with partners.

Table 13.7 lists 10 steps to success when using social media in SMEs. Note that, social networks facilitate interactions and relationship building, which are very important for SMEs. For tips on how to use YouTube to promote the online content of SMEs, see **masternewmedia.org/online_ marketing/youtube-promote-content- viral-marketing/youtube-video-marketing- 10-ways-20070503.htm**.

SMEs are following the growing popularity of social networking sites and using social media to build connected networks, enhance customer relationships, and gather feedback about their services and products (e.g., see Knight 2012).

For implementation issues of social commerce, see Chess Media Group (2012).

SECTION 13.9 REVIEW QUESTIONS

1. What are the advantages or benefits of EC for small businesses?
2. What are the disadvantages or risks of EC for small businesses?
3. What are the advantages and disadvantages for small businesses online?
4. How can social networks help SMEs become more competitive?

Table 13.7 Ten steps to a successful social media strategy

Step	Description
1	Understand what social media is and what the benefits of using it are
2	Identify the audience you want to reach
3	Identify the resources you currently have available for use
4	Identify the most appropriate technologies to use
5	Start a blog and create a social culture in your business
6	Build social media profiles for your business on Facebook, LinkedIn, Twitter, and YouTube
7	Make your blog social media friendly
8	Build relationships with your target market
9	Turn friends and followers into customers
10	Decide how you will monitor and measure the performance of your social media initiatives

Sources: Based on Gallagher (2010) and Ward (2009).

MANAGERIAL ISSUES

Some managerial issues related to this chapter are as follows:

1. **What is the strategic value of EC to the organization?** It is important for management to understand how EC can improve marketing and promotions, customer service and sales, and the supply chain and procurement processes. More significantly, the greatest potential of EC is realized when management views EC from a strategic perspective, not merely as a technological advancement. Management should determine the primary goals of EC, such as new market creation, cost avoidance and reduction, and customer service enhancement.

2. **How do you relate the EC activities to business objectives and metrics?** Companies first must choose objectives and design-appropriate metrics to measure the goals and actual achievement. The companies need to exercise with caution, because the metrics may accidentally lead employees to behave in the opposite direction of the intended objectives. The Balanced Scorecard is a popular framework adopted to define objectives, establish performance metrics, and then map them. EC planning needs to identify what the role

of EC is in achieving the goals in BSC metrics.

3. **Should the EC activities in a brick-and-click company be organized as a separate entity?** This is a debatable issue. Sometimes it is useful in eliminating conflicts of prices and strategy. Additionally, using the spin-off as an IPO can be rewarding. Lotte Department Store in Korea spun off their e-commerce business because of its unique growth opportunity. In other cases, the spin-off can create problems and administrative expenses. Walmart, Barnes & Noble, and Sears have suffered from their spin-offs and have merged them back into the offline part of their companies.

4. **How should the e-business scope evolve?** A selling company may handle only one or few items at the beginning stage. However, the number of items will expand with time, as was the case of Amazon.com. As the scope of items expands, the order fulfillment plan has to evolve accordingly, considering an alliance with partners who have strong sourcing capability. Note that the key competitors will change as the scope of business evolves. Management has to envision the prospect of e-business that can create justifiable revenue and profit so that investors can contribute to the funding and wait patiently for success. The community in the social network eventually needs to be linked with the revenue creation.

5. **What are the benefits and risks of EC?** Strategic advantage has to be weighed carefully against potential risks. Identifying CSFs for EC and doing a cost–benefit analysis is an important step in developing an EC strategy. Benefits can be derived not only from the adoption of EC, but also from the reengineering of traditional business processes. Benefits often are difficult to quantify, especially because gains tend to be strategic. In such an analysis, risks should be addressed with contingency planning (deciding what to do if problems arise).

6. **Why do we need an EC planning process?** A strategic plan is both a document and a process. Former U.S. President Dwight D. Eisenhower once said, "Plans are nothing, planning is everything." A planning process

that includes management, employees, business partners, and other stakeholders not only produces a planning document that will guide a business into the future, but also describes to the participants about where the company is going and how it intends to get there. The same can be said for e-business planning – the process is as important as the plan itself.

7. **How can EC go global?** Going global with EC is a very appealing proposition for companies of all sizes, but it may be difficult to do, especially on a large scale or for SMEs that lack the necessary resources. Companies need to identify, understand, and address the barriers to globalization such as culture, language, and law, as well as customers and suppliers. An e-business needs to decide on a localization strategy. Some companies, such as eBay, acquire or establish local companies to support local customers, whereas other companies only support the English language site. In B2B, a business may create collaborative projects with partners in other countries.

8. **How do you manage the EC project?** Forming an effective team is critical for EC project success. The team's leadership, the balance between technical and business staff, getting the best staff representation on the team, and having a project champion are essential for success. Reconciling the business objectives and system design is critical. IT sourcing needs to be considered, particularly for SMEs.

SUMMARY

In this chapter, you learned about the following EC issues as they relate to the chapter's learning objectives:

1. **Strategy concepts and competitiveness.** Implementing EC projects requires a strategy. A common approach is the use of Porter's Five Forces model and his suggested strategies. The Internet affects the competitive forces and the strategies to deal with them.

2. **The strategy-performance cycle and strategy tools.** The five major phases of developing a business strategy are: initiation, formulation,

implementation, assessment, and performance improvements. The major generic tools for strategic management are: the strategy map, SWOT analysis, competitor analysis, scenario planning, and business plan.

3. **Strategy initiation.** The strategy initiation phase involves understanding the company, the industry, and the competition. Companies must consider questions such as "Should we be a first mover?" "Should we go global?" "Should we create a separate company or brand?" and "How do we handle channel conflict?" With the proliferation of Web 2.0 tools, companies should also consider strategies related to Web 2.0 and social networking.

4. **Strategy formulation.** In this phase, the strategic and tactical planning are executed. Planning issues deal with the portfolio of EC projects to use, the viability of these projects, and the potential benefits, costs, and risks involved. Issues such as security, pricing strategy, and channel and pricing conflicts are considered in this phase.

5. **Strategy implementation.** Creating an effective Web team and ensuring that sufficient resources are available initiate the implementation phase. Other important implementation issues are whether to outsource various aspects of the system development and the need to redesign existing business processes. Assessment begins immediately after implementation.

6. **Strategy assessment.** To assess the success of a strategy, companies establish metrics against which actual performance is compared. To do this, companies need to create a performance monitoring system and establish a system of analytics for the evaluation. Generic tools such as scorecards can be used, as well as special tools developed for different EC categories. Of special interest is the assessment of social media applications.

7. **Performance improvement and innovation.** Once performance is recorded and assessed, it is communicated to management (e.g., via dashboards). Management needs to take action, not only about increasing inferior performance, but also to take advantage of superior performance. Appropriate corrections and rewards can be used. In general, companies should improve any performance level over time. One approach is by introducing innovation into the organization. Innovation can be enhanced by several methods such as crowdsourcing.

8. **Issues in global EC.** Going global with EC can be done quickly and with a relatively small investment. However, businesses must deal with a number of different issues in the cultural, administrative, geographic, legal, and economic dimensions of global trading.

9. **Small and medium-sized businesses and EC.** Depending on the circumstances, innovative small companies have a tremendous opportunity to adopt EC at little cost and expand rapidly. Being in a niche market provides the best chance for small business to succeed. A variety of Web-based resources are available for small and medium-sized business owners to get help to ensure success.

KEY TERMS

Business process management (BPM)
Business process reengineering (BPR)
Cost-plus
Disintermediation
E-commerce (EC) risk
Information dashboard
Key performance indicator (KPI)
Metric
Outsourcing
Project champion
Sentiment analysis (opinion mining)
Strategy
Strategy assessment
Strategy formulation
Strategy implementation
Strategy initiation
Web analytics

DISCUSSION QUESTIONS

1. How would you identify competitors of your small business who want to launch an EC project?

2. How would you apply Porter's five forces and Internet impacts in Figure 13.1 to the Internet search engine industry?

3. Why must e-businesses consider strategic planning to be a cyclical process?

4. How would you apply the SWOT approach to a small bank in your town that is considering e-banking services?

5. Offer some practical suggestions as to how a company can include the impact of the Internet in all levels of planning.

6. Discuss the pros and cons of going global online to sell a physical product.

7. Find some SME EC success stories and identify the common elements in them.

8. Submit three questions regarding EC strategy for small businesses to **linkedin.com** and **answers.yahoo.com**. Get some answers and summarize your experience.

9. After viewing the video "FiftyOne Global E-commerce Demo" (2:08 minutes) at **youtube.com/watch?v=2YazivwAm2o& fea-ture=related**, consider the following: FiftyOne Global E-Commerce (now called Borderfree; **borderfree.com**), claims to address all major issues associated with global EC. Check what they do.

   (a) Discuss how a company embarking on global e-commerce would approach each challenge such as payments or logistics, without the assistance of a company like Borderfree.

   (b) Would these challenges be insurmountable? For each challenge, explain why or why not.

   (c) Would the type or size of a business affect whether it could successfully navigate these challenges to global e-commerce? Explain your conclusions.

10. Find information about Travelzoo's strategy of accelerating its audience growth by expanding its sales force, enhancing product offerings, launching local deals in new markets, and conducting long-term EC projects at the expense of short-term profits. Discuss this strategy.

TOPICS FOR CLASS DISCUSSION AND DEBATES

1. Has the availability of EC affected the way we assess industry attractiveness? Develop new criteria for assessing the attractiveness of pure online industries.

2. Consider the challenges of a brick-and-mortar company manager who wants to create an integrated (online/offline) business. Discuss the challenges that he or she will face.

3. As the principal in a small business that already has an effective Web presence, you are considering taking your company global. Discuss the main issues that you will have to consider in making this strategic decision.

4. Examine the seven strategies of Facebook and Twitter at **socialmediatoday.com/chris-tinegallagher/165536/top-7-facebook-and-twitter-strategies** and comment on them.

5. Debate: Is Google Translate effective for the translation of EC websites?

6. Is Amazon.com eBay's biggest competitor? What about Walmart.com? What about Alibaba group?

7. Read the paper by Hill (2012) and discuss the 10 reasons cited there for Facebook's acquisition of Instagram. Which of the reasons make sense to you? Which ones do not?

8. Apple has a strategy of having an alliance with Facebook to integrate the social network into its products. Find the status of this alliance and discuss its value.

9. Google is trying to counter Facebook by offering branding pages through Google+. Discuss the value of this strategy.

10. Amazon.com is considering opening physical stores. Find the status of this strategy and discuss its logic.

11. Apple created its own music streaming service (iTunes Radio), similar to Pandora. Is this a good or bad strategy? Discuss.

INTERNET EXERCISES

1. Survey several online travel agencies (e.g., **travelocity.com**, **orbitz.com**, **cheaptickets.com**, **priceline.com**, **expedia.com**, **hotwire.com**), and compare the business strategies of three of them. How do they compete against brick and mortar travel agencies?

2. Enter **digitalenterprise.org/metrics/metrics.html**. Read the material on Web analytics and prepare a report on the use of Web analytics for measuring advertising success.

3. Check Internet retailers specializing in the sale of CDs, music, and movies (e.g., **cduniverse.com**). Do any of these companies focus on specialized niche markets as a strategy?

4. Enter **ibm.com/procurement/proweb.nsf/ContentDocsByTitle/United+States~e-Procurement**. Prepare a report on how IBM's Supplier Integration Strategy can assist companies in implementing an EC strategy.

5. One of the most global companies is Amazon.com. Find stories about its global strategies and activities (try **forbes.com**) and conduct a Google search. What are the most important lessons you learned?

6. Visit **business.com/guides/startup** and find some of the EC opportunities available to small businesses. Also visit the website of the Small Business Administration (SBA) office in your area. Summarize recent EC-related topics for SMEs.

7. Find out how websites such as Nexus and Tradecard (now one company available at **gtnexus.com**) facilitate the conduct of international trade over the Internet. Prepare a report based on your findings.

8. Conduct research on small businesses and their use of the Internet for EC. Visit sites such as **microsoftbusinesshub.com** and **uschamber.com**. Also enter **google.com** or **yahoo.com** and type "small businesses + electronic commerce." Use your findings to write a report on current small business EC issues.

9. Enter **lwshare.languageweaver.com** and locate its product for language translation for multinational corporations. Write a report.

10. Enter **compete.com** and identify all the services it provides. Also identify all lists, ranking, marketing performance, and competitive intelligence reports it provides. Prepare a list of the services and comment on their value to merchants.

TEAM ASSIGNMENTS AND PROJECTS

1. **Assignment for the Opening Case**
   Read the opening case and answer the following questions.
   (a) Why did P&G decide to use a social media strategy?
   (b) Does the strategy of moving from TV to the Internet make sense?
   (c) In what ways do viral videos work?
   (d) Can the large number of video views, comments, and interactions really increase sales?
   (e) View one or two videos of Isaiah Mustafa regarding Old-Spice on YouTube. What makes them so attractive? Write a comment.
   (f) Why is P&G's campaign called "the most popular interactive campaign in history?"

2. Have three teams represent the following units of one click-and-mortar company: (1) an offline division, (2) an online division, and (3) top management. Each team member represents a different functional area within the division. The teams will develop an EC strategy in a specific industry (a group of three teams will represent a company in one industry). Teams will present their strategies to the class.

3. The relationship between manufacturers and their distributors regarding sales on the Web can be very strained. Direct sales may cut into the distributors' business. Review some of the strategies available to handle such channel conflicts. Each team member should be assigned to a company in a different industry.

Study the strategies, compare and contrast them, and derive a proposed generic strategy.

4. Each team needs to find the latest information on one global EC issue (e.g., cultural, administrative, geographic, economic). In addition, check how leading retailers, such as Levi's, serve different content to local audiences, both on their websites and on their Facebook pages. Each team prepares a report based on their findings.

5. Google is trying to compete with Amazon.com by opening Google Shopping Express (**google.com/shopping/express**) in selected cities in collaboration with Target and other retailers (see Santos 2013). Find the status of this strategy. Examine the capabilities of Google and Amazon in the various activities of EC. Conduct a competitor analysis and prepare a report on the possible results of this venture.

6. Compare the services provided by Yahoo!, Microsoft, and Web.com to SMEs in the e-commerce area. Each team should take one company and give a presentation.

7. Research the topic of going 'global in the social world.' Start with Adobe (2012). Identify the issues and the practices. Write a report.

8. Read the white paper by dynaTrace (2011). Identify all the suggestions for EC performance improvement. View the demo at **compuware.com/en_us/application-performance-management/products/purepath-technology.html**. Prepare a report.

CLOSING CASE: INNOVATIVE WEB AUCTION STRATEGY NETS HIGHER PRODUCTIVITY FOR PORTLAND FISH EXCHANGE

The Problem

In 2009, the Portland Fish Exchange, owned by the city of Portland, Maine, was losing some of its fish-buying wholesalers due to the downturn in the economy. To add to this decline in business, stricter federal regulations to protect the ocean population caused the average annual volume of fish handled through the Exchange to drop by almost 50% from roughly 30 million pounds of fish a few years ago to the current 10 million pounds per year.

There were several reasons the Exchange suffered from this economic distress. Although demand for good, fresh seafood is usually high, the economic downturn had reduced consumers' dining out budgets. Furthermore, commercial fishing is complex and expensive. In addition, rising expenses, increasing competition for the limited pool of wholesale fish buyers, and fewer boat landings due to the stricter government regulations alerted Bert Jongerden, the general manager of the Portland Fish Exchange. He recognized the need to reconsider his existing business strategy to reduce administrative overhead and increase sales. The need to increase sales was the driving factor for Jongerden to invest between $300,000 and $400,000 in an IT including e-auctions. Jongerden also believed that the convenience of barcoding and an online auction system were appealing to customers, would save administrative overhead, and increase sales. He wanted to create more opportunity for customers to buy fish, leading to his decision to invest in IT/EC solutions.

The Solution

A Portland Fish Exchange website with an online auction system was developed.

The company began using a warehouse management system from SeaTrak (built with Progressive Software's application development tools and customized by developer DC Systems) that was customized to the company's business. The Fish Exchange staff designates barcodes to containers of fresh fish directly on the docks. Using the dock's PC, the staff prints labels that include details on each container of fish (date caught, weight, the boat that brought it in). Previously, while the Exchange staff sorted and weighed the fish each morning, one staff member wrote paper tags to stick on boxes, while a second employee keyed in the data at the end of the auction. The barcoding was the first step in eliminating "soggy paper." There was no longer a need for an auctioneer.

The second step in implementing the improved e-strategy was to deploy an online auction system. The new system uses a private virtual network (see Chapter 10), so wholesalers, seafood processors, and other interested buyers can place bids directly on the secure Web-based auction system remotely. The website lists available fish lots with weights, prices, grades, and current bidders in a simple table format using no images or graphics. Buyers and sellers are now connected more efficiently.

The Results

Revenues are up at the Portland Fish Exchange. Buyers who previously found it too expensive to fly in from Boston or New York to buy fish in Maine can now purchase from the comfort of their restaurants and offices. Others have increased the amount of their purchases and, due to the laws of supply and demand, the increase in demand means that prices are rising.

At the Portland Fish Exchange, three positions have been eliminated – two on the docks and the job of auctioneer. The cost savings of labor amount to approximately $80,000 per year, thus offsetting the cost of implementing the barcoding and online auction system.

The types of fish handled at the Portland Fish Exchange are not subject to as many federal traceability regulations as shellfish are. However, this situation may change. The barcodes and online auction system already provide the company with data that will be necessary to show compliance whenever needed.

Sources: Based on Nash (2009) and **pfex.org/auction** (accessed June 2014).

Questions

1. What were the drivers for Jongerden's e-strategy?
2. What makes the e-commerce strategy at Portland Fish Exchange effective?
3. Which strategic tools might have been used when formulating his e-business solution?
4. In implementing the e-strategy, what issues needed to be considered?
5. What risks might have been involved in setting up the online auctions at Portland Fish Exchange?

ONLINE FILES
available at **affordable-ecommerce-textbook.com/turban**

W13.1 Security Risks in E-Commerce and Social Commerce and Mitigation Guidelines
W13.2 Partners' Strategy and Business Alliances
W13.3 Application Case: Mary Kay Combines E-Commerce Strategies to Revamp Its Business Model
W13.4 Application Case: Performance at AXON Computer (Now Datacraft)
W13.5 The Balanced Scorecard

COMPREHENSIVE EDUCATIONAL WEBSITES

bizauto.com/net.htm: Business Automation's five-step approach to success on the Internet.
net-strat.com/portfolio.htm: Company offering website design, Internet marketing, online marketing services, and search engine optimization.
monitus.com/internet.htm: Company offering Web design and Internet strategy.
sazbean.com/2008/10/06/creating-an-internet-business-strategy-implementation: Comprehensive coverage on developing an Internet strategy and implementation.
tutorialized.com/tutorials/eCommerce/Strategy/1: Tutorials on how e-commerce affects hosting services, businesses, online marketing strategies, and more.
ecommerce-digest.com/strategy.html: A detailed guide to successful online strategy and implementation.
informationweek.com: A large collection of related material, articles, cases, and videos.
blogs.hbr.org/cs/2011/05/introducing_the_hbrmckinsey_m-.html: HBR/McKinsey M-Prize for Management Innovation.

sba.gov/content/ecommerce-resources: A large collection of resources on many topics (e.g., technology, e-commerce, advertising, etc.).

GLOSSARY

Business process management (BPM) Activities performed by businesses to improve their processes.

Business process reengineering (BPR) A methodology for conducting a one-time comprehensive redesign of an enterprise's processes.

Cost-plus A pricing strategy that determines the expenses associated with producing a product (production cost) by adding up all the costs involved – materials, labor, rent, overhead, and so forth – and adding an additional amount to generate a profit margin (a percentage mark-up).

Disintermediation The removal of intermediaries in the EC supply chain. This occurs, for example, when consumers buy directly from manufacturers.

E-commerce (EC) risk The likelihood that a negative outcome will occur in the course of developing and operating an e-commerce initiative.

Information dashboard A visual presentation of data organized in ways easy to read and interpret. It is popular user interface. The information is presented through gauges, charts, maps, tables, etc., to reveal the direction and velocity of the measured metrics.

Key performance indicator (KPI) A quantifiable measurement that is considered a critical success factor of a company, department or project.

Metric A specific, measurable standard against which actual performance is compared.

Outsourcing The process of contracting (farming out) the company's products, services, or work to another organization that is willing and able to do the job.

Project champion The person who ensures that the team is ready to move forward and understands its responsibilities. The project champion is responsible for activities such as identifying the project's objectives, prioritiz-

ing phases, and allocating resources to ensure completion of the project, and so forth.

Sentiment analysis (opinion mining) Analysis that aims to determine the attitude of a person with respect to a particular issue as expressed in online conversations.

Strategy A comprehensive framework for expressing the manner in which a business plans to achieve its mission, what goals are needed to support it, and what plans and policies will be needed to accomplish these goals.

Strategy assessment The continuous performance monitoring, comparison of actual to desired performance, and evaluation of the progress toward the organization's goals, resulting in corrective actions and, if necessary, in strategy reformulation.

Strategy formulation The development of specific strategies and tactics to exploit opportunities and manage threats in the business environment in light of corporate strengths and weaknesses.

Strategy implementation The "How do we do it?" phase that includes tactics, plans, schedules, deployment strategies, resource allocation, and project management.

Strategy initiation The initial phase of strategic planning in which the organization is setting its vision, goals and objectives. Looking at its environment, strategy initiation includes an assessment of a company's strengths and weaknesses, examining the external factors that may affect the business.

Web analytics "The measurement, collection, analysis, and reporting of Internet data for the purposes of understanding and optimizing Web usage." (per Web Analytics Association)

REFERENCES

ActiveVest. "After WhatsApp Buy, Facebook Faces Stiff Competition from Tencent's WeChat." *Seeking Alpha*, March 10, 2014. **seekingalpha.com/article/2078843-after-whatsapp-buy-facebook-faces-stiff-competition-from-tencents-wechat** (accessed June 2014).

Adobe. "Going Global in a Social World: Promoting Global Brands Using the Facebook Page Structure." A white paper by Adobe Systems Inc., #91069096, March 2012. **marketingpedia.com/Marketing-**

Library/Social%20Media/Adobe_Going_Global_ Social_World.pdf (accessed June 2014).

Arceo-Dumlao, T. "Small Traders Urged to Enhance Online Presence as Growth Strategy." *Philippine Daily Inquirer*, December 14, 2012.

Bach, J. "Telus International and Ortsbo Deliver Real-Time Language Translation for Online Chat Customer Service." *Telus International Blog*, August 29, 2013. **web.telusinternational.com/blog/telus-international-and-ortsbo-deliver-real-time-language-translation-for-online-chat-customer-service** (accessed June 2014).

Baskin, J. S. "P&G's Social Media Orthodoxy Could Sink Its Innovation Progress." *Forbes*, November 17, 2012.

Beal, A., and J. Strauss. *Radically Transparent: Monitoring and Managing Reputations Online.* Indianapolis, IN: Wiley & Sons, Inc., 2008.

Bort, J. "The Secret to Red Hat's Billion-Dollar Success: Everyone's the Boss." *Business Insider*, February 7, 2012.

Brady, D. "Game On: Super Bowl Ads Are Already Playing Online." *Bloomberg Businessweek*, February 1, 2013.

Brownell, M. "Get the Best Prices, Period: 10 Must-Have Tools for Every Shopper." *Daily Finance*, January 9, 2013. **dailyfinance.com/2013/01/09/best-prices-apps-tools-comparison-shopping-showrooming** (accessed June 2014).

Bullas, J. "11 Social Media Marketing Lessons from the Old Spice Campaign." August 31, 2011. **jeffbullas. com/2011/08/30/11-social-media-marketing-lessons-from-the-old-spice-campaign** (accessed June 2014).

Burke, A., "How a 15 Year-Old Entrepreneur Got Her Product into Nordstrom." *Yahoo! News*, May 30, 2013. **news.yahoo.com/blogs/profit-minded/15-old-entrepreneur-got-her-product-nordstrom-233738356. html** (accessed June 2014).

Business Wire. "Elavon Introduces Global E-Commerce Gateway Solution." Elavon Press release, February 21, 2012.

Capozzi, M. M., J. Horn, and A. Kellen. "Battle-Test Your Innovation Strategy." *McKinsey Quarterly*, December 2012.

Chess Media Group. *Implementing Enterprise 2.0 at IBM.* Enterprise 2.0 Case Study Series, No. 9, May 2012.

Chui, M., and T. Fleming. "Inside P&G's Digital Revolution." *McKinsey Quarterly Insights and Publications*, November 2011.

Coleman-Lochner, L. "Social Networking Takes Center Stage at P&G." *Bloomberg Businessweek*, March 29, 2012.

Cooper, J. "SMG's Lead on P&G Wants to See a Shift from Social Media to Commerce." *AdWeek*, March 2, 2014

Cutroni, J. *Google Analytics: Understanding Visitor Behavior*, 2nd ed. Sebastopol, CA: O'Reilly Media, 2014.

Davis, A. "50 Value Propositions for Ecommerce Retailers." *CPC Strategy Blog*, July 12, 2012. **cpcstrategy.com/blog/2012/07/50-value-propositions-for-ecommerce-retailers** (accessed June 2014).

Dignan, L. "Best Buy Feels Amazon Squeeze, to Close 50 Big-Box Stores." *CNET*, March 29, 2012. **news.cnet. com/8301-1001_3-57406388-92/best-buy-feels-**

amazon-squeeze-to-close-50-big-box-stores (accessed June 2014).

dynaTrace. "Increase Your E-Commerce Revenue with Continuous Application Performance Management." A white paper by dynaTrace Software (a division of Compuware Corporation), Waltham, MA: August 2011. **i.zdnet.com/whitepapers/dynaTrace-Increase_ Your_eCommerce_Revenue_with_Continuous_ Application_Performance_Management.pdf** (accessed June 2014).

Edwards, J. "Pinterest just Solved All Procter & Gamble's Social Media Problems." *Business Insider*, March 19, 2012.

Egol, M., M. Peterson, and S. Stroh. "How to Choose the Right Digital Marketing Model" *Strategy+Business*, January 27, 2014

Effie Awards. "2011 Gold Effie Winner: 'The Man Your Man Could Smell Like.'" *Effie.org*, 2011. **apaceffie. com/docs/default-source/resource-library/old-spice_case_pdf.pdf?sfvrsn=2** (accessed June 2014).

Ehrlich, B. "The Old Spice Social Media Campaign by the Numbers." *Mashable*, July 15, 2010. **mashable. com/2010/07/15/old-spice-stats** (accessed June 2014).

Francis, C. "The Importance of KPIs in Measuring Sales Success." *Social Media Today*, May 5, 2013. **socialmediatoday.com/colleenfrancis/1437546/importance-kpi-measuring-sales-success** (accessed June 2014).

Franz, P., and M. Kirchmer. *Value-Driven Business Process Management: The Value-Switch for Lasting Competitive Advantage.* New York: McGraw-Hill, 2012.

Gallagher, C. "Small Business Social Media…6 Steps to Success." March 4, 2010. **socialmediatoday.com/ christinegallagher/102866/small-business-social-media6-steps-success** (accessed June 2014).

Gast, A. and M. Zanini. "The Social Side of Strategy." *McKinsey Quarterly Insights & Publications*, May 2012.

GoECart. "GoECart CEO Provides Social Networking Tips for Online Merchants During WGCH Business Radio Interview." *GoECart Ecommerce Blog*, September 28, 2010. **blog.goecart.com/index.php/ goecart-ceo-provides-social-networking-tips-during-interview** (accessed June 2014).

Gold, J. E. "E-Guide: A Strategic Approach to Enabling MobileBusinessApplications."*SearchMobileComputing. com*, Sponsored by BlackBerry, 2008. **meritalk.com/ uploads_legacy/whitepapers/RIM_231_ sMCom.3.13.pdf** (accessed June 2014).

Gosselin, M. "Designing and Implementing a Performance Measurement System." *CMA Management*, November 2010.

Guinn, S., L. Hand, S. Ellis, M. Fauscette, M. Wardly, and K. Knickle. "IBM Synchronizes Its Commerce 2.0 Strategy with 'Smarter Commerce' Initiative." *IDC* Research Document #227526, Volume 1, March 2011.

Hanlon, A. "How to Use Porter's 5 Forces." November 18, 2013. **smartinsights.com/marketing-planning/ marketing-models/use-porters-5-forces/** (accessed June 2014).

Harvard Business School Press. *Improving Business Processes (Pocket Mentor Series)*. Boston: Harvard Business Review Press, 2010.

Hayes, M. "32 Key Performance Indicators (KPIs) for Ecommerce." *Shopify.com Blog (Posted in "How to Sell Online")*, February 21, 2013. **shopify.com/blog/7365564-32-key-performance-indicators-kpis-for-ecommerce#axzz2OfDB15gb** (accessed June 2014).

Hill, K. "10 Reasons Why Facebook Bought Instagram." *Forbes*, April 11, 2012.

Horovitz, B. "P&G Holds Early Gold in Olympic Social Media." *USA Today*, February 14, 2014.

Hubbard, D. *How to Measure Anything: Finding the Value of "Intangibles" in Business, 2nd Ed*, Hoboken, NJ: Wiley, 2010.

Johnston, G. *Business Process Re-Engineering: A Simple Process Improvement Approach to Improve Business Performance (The Business Productivity Series) [Kindle Edition]*. Seattle, WA: Amazon Digital Services, 2012.

Kaplan, R. S., and D.P. Norton. "The Balanced Scorecard: Measures that Drive Performance." *Harvard Business Review,* January–February, 1992.

Kaplan, R. S., and D. P. Norton. *The Balanced Scorecard: Translating Strategy into Action.* Boston: Harvard Business School Press, 1996.

Kaplan, R.S., D. P. Norton, and B. Rugelsjoen. "Managing Alliances with the Balanced Scorecard." *Harvard Business Review*, January-February, 2010.

Klubeck, M. *Metrics: How to Improve Key Business Results.* New York: Apress, 2011.

Knight, K. "New Mobile Options Give SMBs Foothold into Mobile, Social." *BizReport*, February 16, 2012. **bizreport.com/2012/02/new-mobile-options-give-smbs-foothold-into-mobile-social.html** (accessed June 2014).

Learmonth, M. "Warner Music Group Launches Web Strategy 2.0." *Ad Age*, October 8, 2009.

Lee, S., *It's Time for E-Commerce to Grow Up.* [Kindle edition], Cambridge, MA: Simon-Kucher & Partners, 2013.

Lipp, J. "Social Media Case Study: Old Spice." *SlideShare*, August 2, 2010. **slideshare.net/josephinelipp/social-media-case-study-old-spice** (accessed June 2014).

Lunden, I. "Thomson Reuters Taps into Twitter for Big Data Sentiment Analysis." February 3, 2014. **techcrunch.com/2014/02/03/twitter-raises-its-enterprise-cred-with-thomson-reuters-sentiment-analysis-deal** (accessed June 2014).

Miller, A. *Monitoring the Internet: A Guide to Watching your Family's Computer Activity* [Kindle edition]. Amazon Digital Services: Seattle, WA, 2012.

Mills, I. "The Future of Ecommerce for Small Business." *Huffington Post*, March 3, 2014. **huffingtonpost.com/ian-mills/future-of-ecommerce-for-small-business_b_4862514.html** (accessed June 2014).

Nash, K. S. "How Portland Fish Exchange Won Back Customers Through Automation." *CIO Magazine,* August 24, 2009.

OECD (Organization for Economic Cooperation and Development). Enhancing SME Competitiveness:

The OECD Bologna Ministerial Conference, Bologna, 14–15, June 2000. (2001). **browse.oecd-bookshop.org/oecd/pdfs/product/9201051e.pdf** (accessed June 2014).

Ortutay, B., and M. Liedtke. "$2B Oculus Deal: Is Facebook Visionary, or Crazy?" *The Seattle Times*, March 26, 2014 (modified March 27, 2014).

Paine, K. D. *Measure What Matters: Online Tools for Understanding Customers, Social Media, Engagement, and Key Relationships.* Hoboken, N.J.: John Wiley, 2011.

Pang, B., and L. Lee. "Opinion Mining and Sentiment Analysis." *Foundations and Trends in Information Retrieval*, vol. 2, nos. 1–2, 2008.

Pantic, M. "How to Make Money from a Website- 55 Ways to Bring in the Cash." *Business2 Community*, August 31, 2013.

Person, R. *Balanced Scorecards and Operational Dashboards with Microsoft Excel*, 2nd ed. Hoboken, NJ: Wiley & Sons, 2013.

Petroff, A. "Want to Chat in 29 Languages?" *CNN Money*, January 2, 2014. **money.cnn.com/2014/01/02/technology/translation-service-app** (accessed June 2014).

Plant, R. *eCommerce: Formulation of Strategy.* Upper Saddle River, NJ: Prentice Hall, 2000.

Porter, M. E. *Competitive Strategy: Techniques for Analyzing Industries and Competitors.* New York: The Free Press, 1980.

Porter, M. E. *Competitive Advantage: Creating and Sustaining Superior Performance.* New York: The Free Press, 1985.

Porter, M. E. "Strategy and the Internet." *Harvard Business Review* (March 2001).

PR Newswire. "NFL Opens E-Commerce Shop in Chinese Market." October 28, 2013. **prnewswire.com/news-releases/nfl-opens-e-commerce-shop-in-chinese-market-229541851.html** (accessed June 2014).

Prahalad, C. K., and M. S. Krishnan. *The New Age of Innovation: Driving Co-Created Value through Global Networks.* New York: McGraw-Hill, 2008.

Rayson, S. "SMToolbox: Gain a Competitive Edge with Insights from Rival IQ." March 16, 2014. **socialmediatoday.com/SMToolbox/rivaliq-gain-competitive-edge-insights** (accessed June 2014).

Sanayei, A. (Ed.). *E-Business in Developing Countries.* London: Koros Press Ltd., 2011.

Santos, P. "Google Shopping Express Draws Closer." *Seeking Alpha*, March 5, 2013. **seekingalpha.com/article/1249341-google-shopping-express-draws-closer** (accessed June 2014).

Sargent, B. B., and N. Kelly. *Gaining Global Web Presence: Common Practices from 1,000 Top Websites.* Lowell, MA: Common Sense Advisory, Inc., 2010. **commonsenseadvisory.com/Portals/_default/Knowledgebase/ArticleImages/101130_R_Global_Web_Presence_Preview.pdf** (accessed June 2014).

Shneiderman, B. "Creativity Support Tools: Accelerating Discovery and Innovation." *Communication of the ACM*, December 2007.

Shuen, A. *Web 2.0: A Strategy Guide: Business Thinking and Strategies Behind Successful Web 2.0 Implementations.* Sebastopol, CA: O'Reilly Media, 2008.

Sklair, S. "Technical Translation Services–What Is Machine Translation?" *Lionbridge Technologies, Inc.*, December 16, 2009. **blog.lionbridge.com/translation/2009/12/16/technical-translation-services-what-is-machine-translation** (accessed June 2014).

Skok, M. "4 Steps to Building a Compelling Value Proposition." *Forbes.com*, June 14, 2013.

Sones, R. "Resolving the Complexity Dilemma in E-Commerce Firms Through Objective Organization." *Logistics Information Management*, (January 2001).

Spigit. "Nine Keys to Innovation Management 2.0: How Organizations Are Taking Advantage." A white paper by Spigit Inc., May 2011. **neccf.org/whitepapers/whitepaper-nine-keys.pdf** (accessed June 2014).

Sponder, M., *Social Media Analytics: Effective Tools for Building, Interpreting, and Using Metrics*, New York: McGraw-Hill, 2012.

Taddonio, L. "B2B2C Success: Two Unique Ecommerce Strategies." May 19, 2011. **insitesoft.com/blog/b2b2c-success-two-unique-ecommerce-strategies** (accessed June 2014).

Tjan, A. K. "Finally, a Way to Put Your Internet Portfolio in Order." *Harvard Business Review* (February 2001).

Turban, et al. *Social Commerce*, New York: Springer, 2015.

Vaish, N. "Creating an Integrated Multichannel Strategy." *Baseline*, September/October 2011.

Valentine, S. *Sentiment Analysis 19 Success Secrets- 19 Most Asked Question on Sentiment Analysis- What You Need to Know.* Australia: Emereo Publishing, 2014.

Violino, B. "Virtual Tech Powers Mobile Workers." *Baseline Innovation*, July/August, 2011. **baselinemag.com/c/a/Mobile-and-Wireless/Virtual-Tech-Powers-Mobile-Workers-212957** (accessed June 2014).

Ward, A. S. "5 Steps to a Successful Social Media Strategy." August 18, 2009. **amysampleward.org/2009/08/18/5-steps-to-a-successful-social-media-strategy** (accessed June 2014).

Warner Music Group. "Warner Music Group Announces Transition in Digital Strategy Team." *Investor Relations News Release*, February 25, 2008. **investors.wmg.com/phoenix.zhtml?c=182480&p=irol-newsArticle&ID=1111672&highlight=**(accessed June 2014).

Wohl, J. "Target Holiday Push Includes Matching Online Prices." *Reuters*, October 16, 2012. **reuters.com/article/2012/10/16/us-target-meeting-idUSBRE-89F1QY20121016** (accessed June 2014).

Yeaney, J. "Democratizing the Corporate Strategy Process at Red Hat." *Management Innovation eXchange*, November 10, 2011. **managementexchange.com/story/democratizing-corporate-strategy-process-red-hat** (accessed June 2014).

Implementing EC Systems: From Justification to Successful Performance

14

Contents

Learning Objectives

Upon completion of this chapter, you will be able to:

1. Describe the major components of EC implementation.
2. Describe the need for justifying EC investments.
3. Understand the difficulties in measuring and justifying EC investments.
4. Recognize the difficulties in establishing intangible metrics.
5. List and describe traditional and advanced methods of justifying EC investments.
6. Describe some examples of EC justification.
7. Describe the role of economics in EC evaluation.
8. Discuss the steps in developing an EC system.
9. Describe the major EC development strategies.
10. List the various EC development methods along with their benefits and limitations.
11. Discuss the major outsourcing strategies.
12. Describe EC organizational structure and change management.
13. Understand how product, industry, seller, and buyer characteristics influence the success of EC.

Electronic supplementary material The online version of this chapter (doi: 10.1007/978-3-319-10091-3_14) contains supplementary material, which is available to authorized users

E. Turban et al., *Electronic Commerce: A Managerial and Social Networks Perspective*,
Springer Texts in Business and Economics, DOI 10.1007/978-3-319-10091-3_14,
© Springer International Publishing Switzerland 2015

OPENING CASE: TELSTRA CORPORATION HELPS ITS CORPORATE CUSTOMERS JUSTIFY EC INITIATIVES

Telstra Corp. is Australia's major telecommunication company, which provides fixed line and mobile communications as well as digital TV and Internet access services. The company operates in a competitive market (e.g., against Vodafone and Optus Corp.). Telstra has expanded its services to several countries in Asia and Europe.

The Problem

The company is very active in the e-commerce and social media markets, mainly through Telstra Digital and its wireless units. For example, it provided its corporate customers with Facebook apps so they can manage their Telstra accounts. One area where the company saw an opportunity but had some marketing difficulties was m-commerce. In particular, the company offered its corporate customers applications that had many intangible benefits. The customers had difficulty getting approval from their own top management for paying for Telstra's services without detailed justification.

Telstra was interested in promoting the following four lines of applications:

1. **Fleet and field service management.** This topic, involving enterprise mobility applications, was described in Chapter 6.
2. **Video conferencing.** This application uses video conferencing in order to save on travel expenses to meeting places, and helps expedite decision making. Both fixed line and mobile services can support this initiative.
3. **Web contact centers.** This application is designed to improve CRM as described in Chapter 8 and in Online Tutorial T1.
4. **Teleworking.** Allows employees to work offsite. *Teleworking* (also known as telecommuting) requires sophisticated technology to enable effective communication, collaboration, and collaborative commerce activities (Chapters. 5, 8, and Online Tutorial T5).

Both the infrastructure and the software for the above applications is expensive. Many Telstra customers were interested in learning about to justify the investment, but they did not know how to go about it.

The Solution

Telstra developed a white paper to illustrate the use of ROI calculators in each of the above four lines of applications. The unique property of the calculators is that they compute benefits to the users' organizations, to the employees, and to society. Examples of some calculators are available in Saddington and Toni (2009). Here, we provide some of the highlights.

Justifying Video Conferencing

Benefits include reduction in travel expenses, work time lost by employees, and so forth. This calculator uses the Net Present Value (NVP) approach.

The cost-benefit analysis calculates the savings to a company (seven variables), some of which are intangible (such as faster decision making). The benefits are compared with both the fixed and variable costs. The benefits to employees are measured by five variables, some of which are intangible (e.g., better job satisfaction). Finally, benefits to society include variables such as reduced car emissions and traffic congestion.

Justifying Teleworking

The benefits to the companies range from reduced office footprints to higher employee retention. Again, some benefits are intangible. The costs are detailed (e.g., cost of equipment). Employees save travel time when they work at home but they need to pay for the energy used at home. Society enjoys reduced vehicle emissions when people telecommute.

Justifying Web Contact Centers

The above approach is used here, too: The calculator includes savings, benefits, and costs to the company, employees, and society. Both tangible and intangible variables are considered in the calculations.

Justifying Fleet and Field Force Management

The structure of this calculator is similar to those above: Savings, benefits, and costs to the company, employees, and society.

The white paper provides comprehensive calculations with sample data for a hypothetical company.

Telstra offers other calculators including one for data usage for mobile devices.

The Results

Telstra believes that Australian companies have an opportunity to develop a sustainability strategy using the above technologies that need to be justified. Telstra provides proof of substantial cost-benefits. While the savings to companies are substantial in many cases, the benefits to employees and society should not be ignored.

As far as Telstra itself, the introduction of the calculators in 2009 helped the company increase its market share and profitability between 2011 and 2013. Also the market value of Telstra almost doubled from 2010 to 2014.

LESSONS LEARNED FROM THE CASE

The Telstra case demonstrates the need for organizations to justify EC-related projects and the fact that this may not be easy to do. Telstra provided calculators to their clients to help them with the justification of IT and EC investments. The case points to intangible benefits, which are difficult to measure and quantify. It also raises the issue of sharing costs among several projects, and the need to consider the benefits to employees and to society. These are only some of the topics presented in this chapter. Other topics deal with traditional and advanced methods of cost-benefit analysis, use of EC metrics, economic theories of EC, and methods for developing or acquiring EC systems. This chapter also describes some organizational issues of implementation and it ends with a discussion of successes and failures in e-commerce.

Sources: Based on Saddington and Toni (2009) and AIIA Report (2009).

14.1 THE IMPLEMENTATION LANDSCAPE

Now that you know about e-commerce benefits and applications, you may wonder what to do next. First you need to ask questions such as: "Do I need EC?" and then "How am I going to do it?" The answers to these two and other questions can be very complex since they depend on many factors that we will discuss in this chapter. We refer to these factors as *implementation factors*.

The Major Implementation Factors

Many factors can determine the need and success of e-commerce projects. We organize them in the following categories.

Justification/Economics

The first issue is to find out if you need to get involved in an EC project(s). This issue can be very complex for large-scale projects. We call it EC project justification. This issue is covered in Sections 14.2, 14.3, 14.4, 14.5, and 14.6.

Acquire or Self Develop Your E-Commerce System

This issue is not simple either, especially when medium- and large-scale projects are involved. We cover this issue in Sections 14.7, 14.8, and 14.9.

Organizational Readiness and Impacts of E-Commerce

How to organize your EC unit within the organization and how to deal with changing business processes and other changes brought by e-commerce are all part of the implementation considerations. In addition, potential impacts on marketing, manufacturing, and people need to be addressed. Finally, some technical issues such as

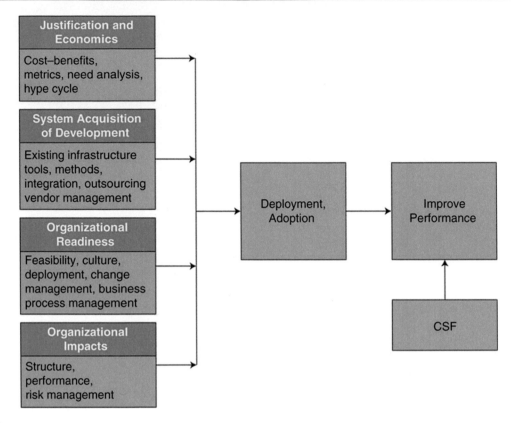

Figure 14.1 The elements in EC implementation

connecting to other information systems need to be considered. These are all described briefly in Section 14.10.

How to Succeed

The last part of this chapter (Section 14.10) addresses some of the critical success factors of implementing EC projects.

We have organized the above factors into a framework, which is shown in Figure 14.1.

On the left side of the figure, we placed the major factors that impact implementation. They all may affect the adoption and deployment of the EC projects. A successful deployment and adoption will lead to improved performance.

SECTION 14.1 REVIEW QUESTIONS

1. Why is the implementation of EC so complex?
2. What are the major elements of EC implementation (see Figure 14.1)?
3. What factors determine deployment and adoption (see Figure 14.1)?

14.2 WHY JUSTIFY E-COMMERCE INVESTMENTS? HOW CAN THEY BE JUSTIFIED?

Companies need to justify their EC investments for a number of different reasons.

Increased Pressure for Financial Justification

Once upon a time, or so the story goes, the beggars of New York City decided to conduct a competition to find out who could collect the most money in one day. Many innovative ideas were employed, and several beggars collected almost $1,000 each. The winner, however, collected $5 million. When asked how he did it, the beggar replied, "I made a sign that said 'EC experts need funding for an innovative electronic marketplace' and put the sign in front of the New York Stock Exchange."

This story symbolizes what happened from 1995 through 2000, when EC projects and start-up companies were funded with little or no analysis of their business viability or finances. The result of the rush to invest without analysis was the 2001 to 2003 "dot-com bust," when hundreds of EC start-ups went out of business and the stock market crashed. Some companies and individual investors lost more than 90–100% of their investments. Furthermore, many companies, even large ones such as Disney, Merrill Lynch, and Sears, terminated some EC projects after losing considerable amounts of money and realizing few benefits from huge investments. The positive result of the crash was the "back-to-basics" movement, namely, a return to carefully checking and scrutinizing any request for EC funding.

Today, companies are more careful with EC expenses and budgets. Technology executives feel the pressure for financial justification and planning from top executives. However, there is still a long way to go as demonstrated by the following data:

- Most companies lack the knowledge or tools to do ROI calculations for EC projects.
- The vast majority of companies have no formal processes or metrics in place for measuring ROI for EC projects.
- Many companies do not measure how completed EC projects compare with their promised benefits.

At the same time, the demand for expanding or initiating e-business projects is high. Therefore, it is recommended to calculate the projected value of proposed EC projects in order to gain approval for them. For further discussion, see Keen and Joshi (2011) and TeamQuest (2014).

Note that in some cases, following the competitors is the major reason to embark on EC projects. In such cases, you still need to do a formal justification, but it may be more of a qualitative in nature.

Other Reasons Why EC Justification Is Needed

The following are some additional reasons for conducting EC justification:

- Companies now realize that EC is not necessarily the solution to all problems. Therefore, EC projects must compete with other internal and external projects for funding and resources. The answer usually is provided by ROI, which we discuss in Section 14.4.
- Some large companies and many public organizations mandate a formal evaluation of requests for funding.
- Companies are required to assess the success of EC projects after their completion.
- The pressure by top management for better alignment of EC strategy with the business strategy.
- The success of EC projects may be assessed in order to pay bonuses to those involved with the projects.

EC Investment Categories and Benefits

Before we look at how to justify EC investments, let us examine the nature of such investments. One basic way to categorize different EC investments is to distinguish between investments in infrastructure and investments in specific EC applications.

IT infrastructure provides the foundation for EC applications in the enterprise. IT infrastructure includes servers, intranets, extranets, data centers, data warehouses, knowledge bases, and so forth. In addition, it is necessary to integrate the EC applications with other applications throughout the enterprise that share the infrastructure. Infrastructure investments are made for the long term.

EC applications are specific projects and programs for achieving certain objectives. The number of EC applications can be large. They may be in one functional department, or several departments may share them, which makes the assessment of their costs and benefits more complex.

Note: Cloud computing may provide a low cost IT infrastructure and EC applications and must be considered.

The major reasons that companies invest in IT and EC are to improve business processes, lower costs, increase productivity, increase customer satisfaction and retention, increase revenue and market share, reduce time-to-market, and gain a competitive advantage.

How Is An EC Investment Justified?

Justifying an EC investment means comparing the costs of each project against its benefits in what is known as a **cost–benefit analysis**. To conduct such an analysis, it is necessary to define and measure the relevant EC benefits and costs. Cost–benefit analysis is frequently assessed by *return on investment (ROI)*, which is also the name of a specific method for evaluating investments.

A number of different methods are available to measure the *business value* of EC and IT investments. Traditional methods that support such analyses are *net present value (NPV)* and ROI (see **nucleusresearch.com/research**).

Cost–Benefit Analysis and the Business Case

The cost–benefit analysis and the business value are part of a *business case*. The business case's cost benefit includes three major components: *Benefits* (e.g., revenue increase, cost reduction, customer satisfaction), *costs* (investment and fixed variables) and *risks* (e.g., obsolescence, employee resistance). Several vendors provide templates, tools, guidelines, and other aids for preparing the business case in specific areas. For example, IT Business Edge (**itbusinessedge. com**) provides a Business Case Resource Kit (see **itbusinessedge.com/downloads**).

What Needs to Be Justified? When Should Justification Take Place?

Not all EC investments need to be justified formally. In some cases, a simple one-page qualitative justification is sufficient. The following are cases where formal evaluation may not be needed:

- When the value of the investment is relatively small for the organization.
- When the relevant data are not available, are inaccurate, or are too volatile.

When the EC project is mandated – *it must* be done regardless of the costs involved (e.g., when mandated by the government, or when it is necessary to match the competition).

However, even when formal analysis is not required, an organization should conduct at least some qualitative analysis to explain the logic of investing in the EC project.

Using Metrics in EC Justification

EC metrics were described in Chapter 13. Metrics can be used to designate the ratio between costs and benefits or the total costs themselves. They are used not only for justification but also for other economic activities (e.g., to compare employee performance in order to reward those who do the best job). Metrics can produce very positive results in organizations by driving behavior in a number of ways. Metrics can:

- Be the basis for setting up specific goals and plans.
- Describe and measure the value proposition of business models (Chapter 1).
- Align the goals of individuals to teams, departments, and other organizational units to the enterprise's objectives.
- Track the performance of EC systems, including usage, types of visitors, page visits, conversion rate, and so forth.
- Assess the health of companies by using tools such as *balanced scorecards* and *performance dashboards*.

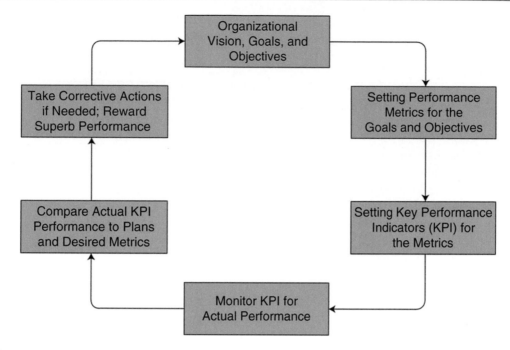

Figure 14.2 How metrics are used in performance management

Metrics, Measurements, and Key Performance Indicators

Metrics need to be defined properly with a clear way to measure them. Figure 14.2 shows the process of using metrics. The cyclical process begins with setting up goals and objectives for organizational and EC performance, which is then expressed by a set of metrics. The metrics are expressed by a set of **key performance indicators (KPIs)**, which are the quantitative expressions of critically important metrics. Often one metric has several KPIs.

The KPIs are continuously monitored by the organization, (e.g., via Web analytics, financial reports, marketing data, and so forth). As shown in Figure 14.2, the KPIs that reflect actual performance are compared to the desired KPIs and planned metrics. If a gap exists, corrective actions take place and then goals, objectives, and metrics are adjusted if necessary.

Another example of metrics is shown in the *balanced scorecard method* (see Chapter 13). This method uses four types of metrics: *customer, financial, internal businesses processes*, and *learning growth*.

We limit our discussion here mainly to individual EC projects or initiatives. EC projects deal most often with the automation of business processes, and as such, they can be viewed as capital investment decisions. Many tools help in the performance monitoring and measurement of e-commerce and the application of metrics (as shown in Figure 14.2). One of the most useful tools for EC is Web analytics, which was briefly introduced in Chapter 13. Web analytics are closely related to metrics (e.g., via Google Analytics; see Clifton 2012).

Web Analytics

Web analytics refers to tools and methods that are used to measure, analyze, and optimize Web usage and other Internet activities. A common usage of Web analytics is to evaluate website traffic, but it can also be used as a tool for EC market research. The outcomes of advertising campaigns can also be assessed with Web analytics. For additional information, see Kaushik (2010) and Beasley (2013).

Now that we understand the need for conducting EC justification and the use of metrics, let us see why EC justification is difficult to accomplish.

SECTION 14.2 REVIEW QUESTIONS

1. List some of the reasons for justifying an EC investment.
2. Describe the risks of not conducting an EC justification study.
3. Describe how an EC investment is justified.
4. List the major EC investment categories.
5. When is it unnecessary to formally justify EC investments?
6. What are metrics? What benefits do they offer?
7. Describe KPI.
8. Describe the cyclical use of metrics as it relates to organizational performance.
9. What is Web analytics, and what role does it play in the justification of EC projects?

14.3 DIFFICULTIES IN MEASURING AND JUSTIFYING E-COMMERCE INVESTMENTS

Justifying EC (and IT) projects can be complex, and therefore, difficult to justify. Let us see why.

The EC Justification Process

The EC justification process varies depending on the situation and the methods used. However, in its extreme, it can be very complex. As shown

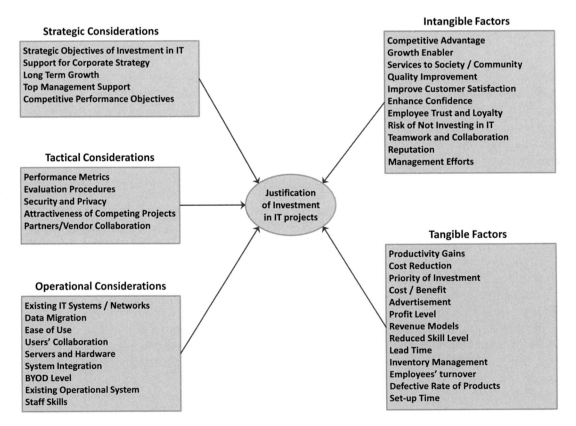

Figure 14.3 A model for IT project justification (Sources: Based on Gunasekaran et al. (2001) and Misra (2006); and the authors' experience.)

in Figure 14.3, five areas must be considered in the justification of IT projects. In this section, we discuss the intangible and tangible areas. In Chapter 13, we discussed some strategic and tactical considerations.

In addition to the complex process, one may face other difficulties in conducting justification.

Difficulties in Measuring Productivity and Performance Gains

One of the major benefits of using EC is increased productivity. However, productivity increases may be difficult to measure for a number of reasons.

Data and Analysis Issues

Data, or the analysis of data, may hide productivity gains. Why is this so? In manufacturing, it is easy to measure outputs and inputs. For example, Toyota produces motor vehicles – a relatively well-defined product that shows gradual quality changes over time. It is not difficult to identify the resources used to produce these vehicles with reasonable accuracy. However, in service industries, such as education, social services, or health care delivery, it is more difficult to define what the products are, how they differ in quality, and how they may be related to corresponding benefits and costs.

Other generic factors are:
- EC productivity gains in one area may be offset by losses in other areas
- Hidden costs and benefits
- Incorrectly defining what is measured

Relating EC and Its Expenditures to Organizational Performance

It may be difficult to find the relationship between EC investment and organizational performance. The reason is that the relationship between investment and performance may be indirect; factors such as shared EC and IT assets and how they are used can impact organizational performance and make it difficult to assess the value of an investment.

Other Difficulties

The long time lags between investment and profit realization may throw off productivity measurements.

Intangible Costs and Benefits

In many cases EC projects generate intangible benefits, such as faster time-to-market, and increased employee and customer satisfaction. These are very desirable benefits, but it may be difficult to place an accurate monetary value on them. For example, it is generally known that e-mail improves communications, but it is difficult to measure the value of this improvement.

Tangible Costs and Benefits

The costs involved in purchasing hardware, software, consulting, and support services usually are tangible, as are the costs of telecommunication services, maintenance, and direct labor. These costs can be measured through accounting information systems (e.g., from the general ledger). Similarly, tangible benefits, including increased profitability, improved productivity, and greater market share can be measured with relative ease.

Intangible Costs and Benefits

When it comes to *intangible* costs and benefits, organizations must develop innovative metrics to track these as accurately as possible. Intangible costs may range from the inclusion of some vague costs, such as those resulting from the learning curve during of the incorporation of an EC system, to better respond to customer inquiries. Another intangible cost may result from the need to change or adapt to certain business processes such as building and operating an inventory tracking system. An additional difficulty is separating EC costs from the costs of routine maintenance of inventory and other relevant IT systems.

Managing Intangible Benefits

The first step in managing intangible benefits is to define them (see the opening case of Telstra), and if possible, specify how they are going to be measured.

A simple solution is to make *rough estimates* of the monetary values of all the intangible benefits and then conduct an ROI or similar financial analysis. The simplicity of this approach is appealing, but in many cases, the simplification assumptions used in these estimates are questionable. If the estimates were too high, a wrong investment may have been made. An estimate that is too low may result in disregarding a good investment and potentially losing a competitive advantage. Intangible costs and benefits may be approached in a number of different ways. Several of the methods presented in Section 14.4 also can be used to evaluate intangible benefits. For more on intangible costs and benefits, see Ritter and Röttgers (2008).

One way to deal with intangible benefits is to develop a balanced scorecard (Chapter 13) for the proposed investments. This approach requires listing both tangible and intangible goals and their measurements. For an example of how this works, see Asefeso (2014).

These difficulties can cause many companies not to measure the value of IT and EC projects, which can be a risky approach. For those companies that conduct a formal justification, we present a number of methods in Sections 14.4 and 14.5.

The Process of Justifying EC and IT Projects

Justifying large-scale investments is not only about selecting a method; it is also about executing it. The appropriate process is not simple. The major steps of this process, according to *Baseline* (2006) and the authors' experience are:

1. Establish an appropriate basis for analysis with your vendor, and then conduct your ROI.

2. Investigate what metrics to use (including internal and external metrics) and be sure about their accuracy.
3. Justify the cost-benefit under appropriate assumptions. (See the references provided in the opening case.)
4. Verify all data used in the calculation.
5. Include strategic benefits, including long-term ones. Find contributions to competitive advantage. Make sure not to underestimate costs and overestimate benefits (a tendency of many managers).
6. Make data as realistic as possible, and include cost avoidance and risk analysis.
7. Commit all business partners, as well as suppliers and major customers.

The Use of Gartner's Hype Cycle

Before we introduce the specific methods used in justification, we present briefly the concept of the *hype cycle*. Organizations can use this tool to assess the maturity level of specific EC technologies so they can develop a strategy before they invest efforts and money in conducting cost–benefit and justification analysis.

What Is Gartner's Hype Cycle?

A **hype cycle** is a graphic representation of the life cycle of specific IT and EC technologies (e.g., cloud computing, 3D printing, e-payment). The term was coined by the information technology research and advisory company, Gartner, Inc. The hype cycle provides a snapshot of the relative maturity of different categories of technologies, IT methodologies, and management-related disciplines overtime. The hype cycle highlights the overhyped technologies versus those that are matured and already have high usage in industry. The hype cycle also provides estimates of how long technologies and trends will take to reach maturity. The methodology and details are presented at **gartner.com/technology/research/**

methodologies/hype-cycle.jsp. Hype cycles can be customized (by Gartner Inc., for a fee) to fit certain industries and companies. Gartner revises the hype cycles once a year.

Each hype cycle has five stages that reflect the basic adoption path any technology follows, starting with a trigger point, through over-enthusiasm hype, and then enduring disillusionment, before finally becoming accepted. (Note that Gartner developed the hype cycle to replace the *product life cycle*, which includes four stages.) The five stages of the hype cycle are:

1. **Technology trigger.** The generation of media interest and industry exposure in new IT or EC technology, which includes publicity events (such as product launch parties, public demonstrations, or press releases), that result in considerable attention to the technology.
2. **Peak of inflated expectations.** This is the phase of exuberance and overenthusiasm, and too much publicity and overestimation of the technology's potential. In 2013, augmented reality and the Internet of Things were in this stage. The technology performance may not be able to keep up with the promises made by technology leaders, consultants, and financial analysts.
3. **Trough of disillusionment.** A point where the media no longer care about the technology because its results were disappointing.
4. **Slope of enlightenment.** The usefulness, risks, and benefits of the technology are understood because of the combined good results and best efforts and practices of many organizations.
5. **Plateau of productivity.** The technology has shown to have actual benefits. Now in their second or third generation, the methodologies and tools are more stable and consistent. The location of

the plateau of the technology depends on whether the technology is specifically for a niche market or is universal.

Application of the Hype Cycle

Gartner, Inc. provides an annual report that covers about 102 different hype cycles evaluating over 2,000 different technologies across 75 industries (e.g., see Gartner 2013). For information, including a video, see **gartner.com/technology/research/hype-cycle**. Gartner Inc. charges fees for providing its reports, which include technology trends. The 2011 and 2014 reports cover many EC technologies such as mobile commerce and devices, microblogging, augmented reality, green IT in data centers, social analytics, cloud computing, context-aware computing, Internet of Things, virtual worlds, location-based applications, security, RFID, video telepresence, and collective intelligence.

An example of how EC technologies were placed on the hype cycle in the past is available at **gartner.com/newsroom/id/2575515**. The press release provides interesting information about several emerging EC technologies. Examination of the hype cycle can be useful to any organization that seriously considers the emerging tools of e-commerce, m-commerce, and social commerce.

SECTION 14.3 REVIEW QUESTIONS

1. How do organizations measure performance and productivity? What are the difficulties in measuring performance and productivity?
2. Why is it difficult to relate EC (IT) investments to organizational performance? List the major reasons.
3. Define tangible costs and benefits.
4. Define intangible costs and benefits and explain why they must be considered when justifying an EC investment.
5. How should management handle the intangibles and uncertainties of benefits?
6. Define the hype cycle and describe its five stages.
7. Describe how the hype cycle is used in e-commerce.

14.4 METHODS AND TOOLS FOR EVALUATING AND JUSTIFYING E-COMMERCE INVESTMENTS

At their core, all economic justification approaches attempt to account for the costs and benefits of investments. They differ in their ability to account for the tangible and intangible costs and benefits of EC, particularly when compared to other corporate investments.

Opportunities and Revenue Generated by EC Investments

In preparing the business case for EC investments, as we will describe later, one should examine the potential *additional revenues* created by the EC investments. Chapter 1 presented the typical revenue models generated by EC and the Web. Additional examples are:

- Companies that allow people to play games for a fee, or watch a sports competition in real time for a fee (e.g., see **espn.go.com**)
- Increased revenues via selling goods and services online in other countries (e.g., NFL in China)
- By using less expensive business processes, the profitability increases
- Ability to sell from mobile devices
- Using social networking for advertising and marketing
- Selling data collected with Web analysis to other companies
- Selling space for ad display on one's website
- Commissions generated from affiliate marketing

Companies use a variety of commercially available tools or develop in-house tools.

Methodological Aspects of Justifying EC Investments

Before presenting the specific methods for EC justification, let us examine the cost issue that is common to most of the justification methods.

Types of Costs

Although costs may appear to be the simple side of a cost–benefit analysis, they may be complex at times. Here are a few things to consider:

- **Distinguish between initial (up-front) costs and operating costs.** The initial costs may be a one-time investment or they may spread over several months or years. In addition, system operating costs need to be considered.
- **Direct and indirect shared costs.** Direct costs can be related directly to a specific EC project. Indirect costs usually are shared infrastructure-related costs. In addition, the costs may be related to several EC and IT projects. Therefore, one needs to allocate these costs for the specific project(s). Such allocation may not be easy to perform; a number of approaches to cost allocation are available (consult an accountant).
- **In-kind costs.** Although it is easy to track monetary payments, costs also may be of the in-kind type; for example, costs of the efforts of a manager working on an EC project and on other projects at the same time, and so on. These frequently are indirectly shared costs (e.g., overhead), which complicates their allocation to specific projects.

Traditional Methods for Evaluating EC Investments

The following are the most popular methods for evaluating IT and EC investments. For details, see Nucleus Research (2014). The major ones follow.

The ROI Method

The *ROI method* uses a formula that divides the total net benefits (revenue minus costs, for each year) by the initial cost. The result is a ratio that measures the ROI for each year or for an entire period; see Fell (2013) and Keen and Joshi (2011). In calculating ROI, one should consider the following techniques.

Payback Period

With the *payback-period* method, the company calculates how long it will take for the initial investment to be paid back from the profits.

NPV Analysis

In an *NPV analysis*, analysts convert future values of benefits to their present-value equivalents using an interest rate that equals what the company paid to obtain funding. The analyst then can compare the present value of the future benefits with the present value of the costs required to achieve those benefits to determine whether the benefits exceed the costs. In this case one needs to also consider the intangible benefits. For guidelines that are more specific and decision criteria on how NPV analysis works, consult Nucleus Research (2014).

Internal Rate of Return (IRR)

For an investment that requires and/or produces a number of cash flows over time, it is common to use the *internal rate of return (IRR)* method. The IRR is the discount rate that makes the NPV of those cash flows equal to zero.

Break-Even Analyses

A *break-even point* is the point at which the benefits of a project are equal to the costs. Firms use this type of analysis to determine the point at which the EC investment starts to pay for itself.

The Total Costs and Benefits of Ownership

The costs of an EC system may accumulate over many years. An important factor in an EC cost evaluation is the *total cost of ownership*. **Total cost of ownership (TCO)** is a formula for estimating the direct and indirect cost of owning, operating, and controlling an EC system, over the entire life of the project. The cost includes acquisition costs (hardware and software), operation costs (maintenance, training, operations, etc.),

and any other related cost. The TCO may be 100% higher than the cost of the hardware, especially for PCs.

By considering TCO, organizations can make more accurate cost–benefit analyses. Boardman et al. (2011) offer a methodology for calculating TCO. They also provide a detailed example of the items to include in TCO calculations. A similar concept is **total benefits of ownership (TBO)**. The TBO calculation includes both tangible and intangible benefits. By calculating and comparing TCO and TBO, one can compute the payoff of an IT investment (i.e., payoff = TBO – TCO).

Economic Value Added

Economic value added (EVA) attempts to quantify the net value added by an investment. It is the return on invested capital (i.e., after-tax cash flow) generated by a company, minus the cost of the capital used in creating the cash flow.

Using Several Traditional Methods for One Project

Some companies use several traditional methods to be cautious. Each of these methods provides us with a different aspect of the analysis.

Business ROI Versus Technology ROI

When implementing ROI, one should look at both the business side and the technology side of the project to be justified. For details, see Fell (2013). Related to this is the issue of measuring the quality of EC projects.

ROI Calculators

The traditional methods of calculating ROI involve simple formulas and are available as Excel functions or other calculators. Calculators are also available for complex and proprietary formulas, as illustrated in the opening case.

Practitioners' experiences and theories are embedded in **ROI calculators** to evaluate investments using metrics and formulas. Recently, companies specializing in ROI also have developed ROI calculators, some of which are available for free.

The Offerings from Baseline Magazine

One of the major sources of simple calculators is *Baseline* (**baselinemag.com**). It offers several dozen Excel-based calculators (for free or for a fee). Examples of calculators offered include:

- Calculating ROI in general
- Figuring the ROI of RFID
- Comparing smartphones and laptops
- Figuring the ROI of application performance management
- Determining the true total cost of ownership (TCO)
- Calculating the ROI of VoIP
- Determining the cost of videoconferencing solutions

In addition, *Baseline* offers tutorials, guides, statistical data, and more, related to these calculators.

Other Calculators

Nucleus Research Inc. (**nucleusresearch.com**) offers several ROI calculators. Nucleus Research believes that if an EC justification includes intangible costs and benefits, then a customized calculator will be needed. ROI calculators for e-services are also available.

Example

A few organizations have attempted to assess the ROI on e-learning. For example, **elearningindustry.com** provides resources such as ROI calculators, methodologies, infographics, articles, and online communities to support the assessment of e-learning (see **elearningindustry.com/free-elearning-roi-calculators**).

ROI calculators also are available from various other companies, such as Phoenix Technologies (**phoenix.com**), and Citrix's XenDesktop (**citrix.com/products/xendesktop/overview.html**). CovalentWorks Corporation (**covalentworks.com**) specializes in B2B calculators. For more examples of ROI calculators, see ROI-Calc, Inc. (**roi-calc.com**), Money-Zine (**money-zine.com**), and Microsoft (**microsoft.com**).

Advanced Methods for Evaluating IT and EC Investments

Traditional methods that are based only on tangible financial factors may not be sufficient for many IT and EC justifications. Therefore, new methods have evolved with time and now include intangible factors such as customer satisfaction. These methods may supplement the ROI traditional methods or replace them.

Renkema (2000) presents a comprehensive list of more than 60 different appraisal and justification methods for IT investments. Most justification methods can be categorized into the following four types:

1. **Financial approaches.** These methods consider only financial factors. ROI, IRR, and payback period are examples of financial methods.
2. **Multicriteria approaches.** These methods consider both financial impacts and non-financial impacts that cannot be (or cannot easily be) expressed in monetary terms. These methods employ quantitative and qualitative decision-making techniques. Examples include information economics, balanced scorecards, and value analysis.
3. **Ratio approaches.** Several ratios can be used in these methods to aid in the evaluation of EC investments. The ratios used frequently are financial in nature, but other types of metrics can be used as well. An example of this would be EC expenditures divided by annual sales or EC expenditures as a percentage of the operating budget.
4. **Portfolio approaches.** These methods plot a group of investment alternatives against decision-making criteria. Portfolio methods can be very complex.

Table 14.1 Advanced methods for EC justification and evaluation

- **Information economics.** Using the idea of critical success factors, this method focuses on key organizational objectives and the potential impacts of the proposed EC project on each of them and on economic decisions
- **Scoring methodology.** This method assigns weights and scores to various aspects of alternative evaluated projects (e.g., weights to each metric) and then calculates a total (or weighted average) score. Information economics theories are used to determine the factors to include in the scoring
- **Benchmarks.** This method is appropriate for evaluating EC infrastructure. Using industry standards (or indices), for example, the organization can determine what the industry is spending on e-CRM on the average. The organization can decide then how much it should spend. Benchmarks may be industry metrics or best practices recommended by professional associations or consultants
- **Management by maxim.** An organization may use this method to determine how much it should invest in large EC (and IT) infrastructures. It is a combination of brainstorming and consensus-reaching methodologies
- **Real-options valuation.** This is a complex assessment method, and is used infrequently. It can be accurate only in certain situations. The idea behind this method is to look at future opportunities that may result from the EC investment and then place monetary values on those opportunities
- **Balanced scorecard.** This method evaluates the health or performance of the organization by looking at a broad set of factors, not just financial ones. It is becoming a popular tool for assessing EC projects
- **Performance dashboard.** This is a variant of the balanced scorecard that is popular in e-business investment situations. A dashboard is a single view that provides the status of multiple metrics on one chart
- **Activity-based costing and justification.** This method considers costs that occur when certain activities are performed. This managerial accounting concept was adapted by some companies for assessing EC investments, and has proven to be successful

Table 14.1 summarizes representative advanced methods useful in evaluating EC investments.

Unfortunately, none of these methods is perfect or universal. Therefore, you need to look at the advantages and disadvantages of each. Justification methods usually are included in a business plan or business case. Business case software for EC is available from BPlans (**bplans. com**) and Palo Alto Software (**paloalto.com**).

SECTION 14.4 REVIEW QUESTIONS

1. Briefly define ROI, NPV, payoff period, IRR, and break-even methods of evaluation.
2. What are ROI calculators?
3. Describe the four major justification approaches.

14.5 EXAMPLES OF E-COMMERCE METRICS AND PROJECT JUSTIFICATION

The methods and tools described in the previous section can be used alone, in a combination, or with modifications to justify different EC projects. Here, we provide a few examples of how these methods and tools can be used to justify different types of EC projects.

Justifying E-procurement

E-procurement includes the supporting administrative processes of procurements (e.g., selecting suppliers, submitting formal requests for proposals, processing purchase orders, and organizing payments).

Setting metrics for e-procurement is difficult especially when procurement is done in B2B exchanges. An example of e-procurement metrics is provided next.

Example: E-procurement Metrics

The following performance on the designated metrics signifies success of e-procurement.

- Increased on-time deliveries of purchased goods
- Decreased purchase order processing time
- Decreased prices of items procured due to increased supplier availability, improved interactions, and use of order aggregation (volume discount)
- Decreased ratio of transportation and handling costs to purchasing costs

Indirect metrics include minimizing costs, such as:

- Reduced inventory handling costs
- Reduced damage in-transit costs
- Reduced raw material costs
- Reduced rework costs (of defective items)
- Reduced operating and administrative costs
- Reduced transportation and handling costs

E-procurement can directly or indirectly affect these and similar metrics. Measuring and monitoring e-procurement activities is crucial to identifying both problematic and successful areas. The evolution from basic online purchasing to the use of exchanges is shown in Online File W14.1.

Justifying Social Networking and the Use of Web 2.0 Tools

Justifying social networking initiatives and the use of Web 2.0 tools can be difficult due to the intangible benefits and the potential risks. However, in many cases, the cost is relatively low and so companies embark on such projects without formal justification, especially in cases where project is just experimenting with the technology. The major issue could be that of risk assessment. Some of the tools are available for free or are being added by vendors to communication and collaboration tools. For a comprehensive e-book, see Petouhoff (2012). For a white paper on the business case for making business processes social, see Ziff Davis (2012). Also, watch two videos from Salesforce.com: "How to Build a Business Case for Social Media" (**youtube.com/watch?v=_59iJrYanw0**) and "How to Measure Social Media ROI" (**youtube.com/watch?v=UhUO30VRN1M.com**). For a comprehensive coverage see Turban et al. (2015).

Justifying an Investment in Mobile Computing and in RFID

Justifying the cost of mobile computing may be difficult due to cost sharing infrastructure and the many intangible benefits of mobile applications. **Baselinemag.com** offers tutorials and several calculators to help companies do the following:

- Calculate the ROI on the wireless workforce
- Calculate the ROI on outsourcing mobile device management
- Calculate the cost of the wireless networks

Vendors of wireless and mobile hardware, software, and services offer tutorials and calculators, as well (e.g., Symbol Technologies [**symboltech.net**]; now a Motorola company, Sybase [**sybase.com**]; a SAP company, and Intel [**intel.com**]). For a comprehensive discussion of the justification of mobile computing, see *MobileInfo.com* (2011).

Justifying Investing in RFID

Many medium and large corporations are considering implementing RFID systems to improve their supply chain and warehousing operations (see Chapter 12). Although such systems offer many tangible benefits that can be defined, metrics are difficult to develop because the technology is new and legal requirements (for privacy protection) are still evolving.

An example of justifying an investment in wireless computing is provided in Online File W14.2.

Justifying Security Projects

More than 85% of viruses enter business networks via e-mail. Cleaning up infections is labor intensive, but antivirus scanning is not. ROI calculators are available for investing in security software and employee training at **baselinemag.com**.

Justifying Buying Products or Services from Vendors

Google developed a methodology and calculators that enable organizations to justify the investment in some of Google's major products, notably "Search." See the 2009 white paper by Google titled: "Maximizing Website ROI: The Crucial Role of High Quality Search" at **static.google-usercontent.com/media/www.google.com/en/us/enterprise/search/files/Google_Maximizing WebsiteROI.pdf**.

SECTION 14.5 REVIEW QUESTIONS
1. List five success factors for e-procurement.
2. List five performance metrics for e-procurement.
3. List some metrics that can justify social networking.
4. List some metrics for justifying the installation of a wireless network in a restaurant.

14.6   THE ECONOMICS OF E-COMMERCE

The economic environment of e-commerce is broad and diversified. In this section, we present only representative topics that relate to the traditional microeconomic theory and formula. For a theoretical paper, see Prieger and Heil (2009).

Reducing Production Costs

Production costs are the costs to produce the product or service a company is selling. E-commerce makes a major contribution to lowering production costs. For example, e-procurement may result in cost reduction for purchasing. Much of intrabusiness EC consists of cost reduction. The following economic principles express these reductions.

Product Cost Curves

The *average variable cost (AVC)* represents the behavior of average costs as quantity changes. The AVC of many physical products and services is U shaped (see Figure 14.4). This curve indicates that, at first, as quantity increases, the more the cost declines (Part A). The more the quantity increases, the cost starts to go back up, due to increasing variable costs (especially marketing costs) and fixed costs (because more management is needed) in the short run. In contrast, the variable cost per unit of digital products is very low in most cases, and almost fixed once the initial investment is recovered. Therefore, as Figure 14.4

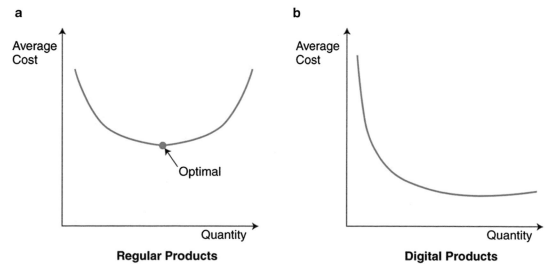

Figure 14.4 Average cost curve of (**a**) regular and (**b**) digital products

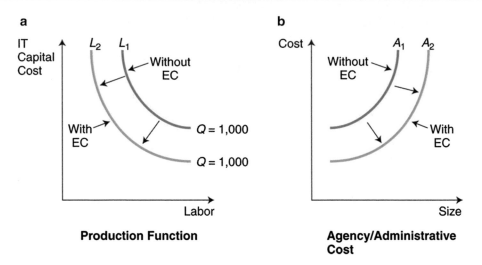

Figure 14.5 The economic effects of EC: the production function and agency costs

(Part B) shows, with digital products the average cost per unit declines as quantity increases, because the fixed costs are spread (prorated) over more and more units. This relationship results in increasing returns with increased sales. It provides a competitive advantage, because EC users can sell their products at lower prices.

Production Function

The **production function**, shown in Figure 14.5 (Part A), represents a mathematical formula that indicates that for the same quantity of production, Q, companies either can use a certain amount of labor or invest in more automation (e.g., they can substitute IT capital for labor). For example, for a quantity Q 1,000, the lower the amount of labor needed, the higher the required IT investment (capital costs). When EC enters the picture, it *shifts* the function inward (from L_1 to L_2), lowering the amount of labor and/or capital needed to produce the same Q 1,000. Again, EC provides a competitive advantage, allowing companies to sell at lower prices than the competition.

Agency Costs

Figure 14.5 (Part B) shows the economics of the firm's **agency costs** (or *administrative costs*).

These are the costs incurred in ensuring that certain support and administrative tasks related to production are performed as intended (e.g., by an agent). In the "old economy," agency costs (A_1) grew with the size (and complexity) of the firm, quickly reaching a high level of cost. This frequently prevented companies from growing to a very large size. In the digital economy, the agency costs curve shifts outward, to A_2. This means that EC, companies can significantly expand their businesses without too much of an increase in administrative costs. Again, this is a competitive advantage for rapidly growing EC companies.

Transaction Costs

Transaction costs describe a wide range of expenses that are associated with commercial transactions, including the bartering of products and services. Transaction costs according to **businessdictionary.com**, cover a wide range: communication charges, legal fees, information cost of finding the price, quality, and durability, and so forth, and may also include transportation costs, which are a critical factor in justifying EC investment. Many economists (e.g., Chen 2005) divide these costs into the following six categories:

1. **Search costs**
2. **Information costs**
3. **Negotiation costs**
4. **Decision costs**
5. **Monitoring and policing costs**
6. **Legal-related costs**

As we have seen throughout the book, e-commerce can reduce all these costs. Reducing transaction costs benefits merchants by providing them a competitive advantage and enabling them to deliver better customer service. For example, search engines and comparison bots can reduce search costs and information costs. EC also can drastically reduce the costs of monitoring, collaborating, and negotiating.

Figure 14.6 reflects one aspect of transaction costs. As seen in the figure, there is a trade-off between transaction cost and size (volume) of business. Traditionally, in order to reduce transaction costs, firms had to grow in size (as depicted in curve T_1). In the digital economy, the transaction cost curve shifts downward to position T_2. This means that EC makes it possible to have low transaction costs, even with smaller firm size, and to enjoy much lower transaction costs as firm size increases.

Increased Revenues

Throughout the text, we have demonstrated how an organization can use EC to increase revenues through webstores, auctions, cross-selling opportunities, multichannel distribution arrangements, and so on. EC also can be used to increase revenues by improving reach and richness.

Reach Versus Richness

Another economic issue of EC is the trade-off between the number of customers a company can reach (called *reach*) and the amount of interactions and information (e.g., advertisement) it can provide to them (called *richness*). For a given amount of cost (resources), there is a trade-off between reach and richness. For a given amount of expenses, the more customers a company wants to reach the fewer services it can provide to them. Figure 14.7 depicts this economic relationship.

The case of investment and brokerage company Charles Schwab illustrates the implementation of the reach versus richness trade-off. Initially, Schwab attempted to increase its reach. To do so, the company went downward along the curve (see Figure 14.7), reducing its richness. However, using its website (**schwab. com**), Schwab was able to drastically increase

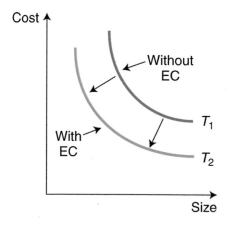

Figure 14.6 The economic effects of EC: transaction costs

Figure 14.7 Reach versus richness

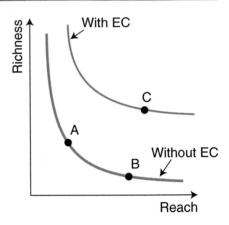

its reach (moving from point A to B) and at the same time provide more richness in terms of customer service and financial information to customers (moving from point B to point C). For example, by using Schwab's Mutual Fund Screener, customers can build investment portfolios comprised of several mutual funds. Providing such services (richness) allows Schwab to increase the number of customers (reach), as well as charge higher fees than competitors who provide few value-added services. In summary, the Internet pushes the curve outward toward the upper right-hand corner of the chart, allowing more reach at the same cost. For additional details, see Jelassi and Enders (2008).

Facilitating Product Differentiation

Organizations can use EC to provide **product differentiation** – products with special features. For example, McAfee allows users of its VirusScan (a virus detection software) to update the latest security patches online automatically, differentiating itself from competing software that require manual upgrades. Differentiation does not necessarily require a physical product; it can also be done for services. EC can provide differentiation through Web-based product information, informing users how to use the product, how to replenish it, and how to provide feedback.

EC Increases Agility

EC can provide firms with the *agility* needed to monitor, report, and quickly respond to changes in the marketplace and the business environment. Companies with agile systems can respond to customer requests quickly, improving customer service. FedEx, UPS, and other delivery companies can provide location information because they use EC to connect with customers and make package tracking information available. EC systems enable companies to learn more about customers and understand their buying habits. This enables a company to better predict trends for better planning and quickly introduce changes when needed. Similarly, e-procurement has given firms the ability to swiftly locate sellers and place orders with them online. Sellers, in turn, use e-fulfillment to rapidly locate products in their warehouses and fill customer orders.

Valuation of EC Companies

Valuation is the process of trying to determine the value or worth of a company. It is done for the purpose of selling a company or determining its value for going public (an IPO) or for a proposed merger. In the EC context, valuation often is conducted to determine a reasonable IPO price when a start-up company goes public or is acquired by another company. For example, in 2014 Facebook paid $19 billion to acquire messaging service What'sApp Inc.

The three most common valuation methods, according to Rayport and Jaworski (2004), are the *comparable method*, the *financial performance method*, and the *venture capital method*:

- **The comparable method.** Using this method, analysts compare the company with similar companies based on as many factors as possible (e.g., size, industry, customer base, products, growth rate, book value, debt, sales, financial performance). In addition, they may look at performance trends, management teams, and other features. A major difficulty with this method is finding such information for privately held companies. Another difficulty is a lack of such data for start-ups.
- **The financial performance method.** This method uses projections of future earnings (usually 5 years), cash flows, and so on, to find the NPV of a company. The major problem with this method is in determining the discount rate.
- **The venture capital method.** Venture capital (VC) firms invest in start-ups and usually take them through to their IPOs. They may use a combination of the first two methods or their proprietary formulas. The VC firm may use a very high discount rate (e.g., 30–70%). When companies pay using their stock, they tend to agree to a higher valuation. An example is Apple's acquisition of Instagram in 2012.

Let us look at one of the most successful IPOs of an EC company – Google. Google floated its IPO in fall 2004, targeting it at $85 per share. Within a few weeks, the share price more than doubled, reaching over $450 in late 2005, $500 in 2006, more than $700 in 2007, and over $1,100 in 2014, giving Google a market capitalization of $350 billion. Facebook went public in 2013 at a price of $38 per share. Making its valuation in 2014 estimated at over $200 billion. The increase in share price indicated that investors were willing to pay huge premiums for anticipated future performance and valuation. Many acquisitions and mergers from 1996 through 2001 involved unrealistically high valuations, and so did the acquisition of social networks from 2005 to 2014. For example, note that, when EC companies acquire other EC companies, they frequently pay in the form of stock, not cash, so such high valuations are more appropriate. Google used this same strategy to acquire other companies. In 2010, Groupon refused Google's offer of $6 billion. It went public as an IPO in the stock market in 2011 with $20 billion valuation. However, in May 2014 the valuation decline to about $4.5 billion.

In summary, the economics of EC enables companies to be more competitive and more profitable. EC economics also enables them to grow faster, collaborate better, provide excellent customer service, and innovate better. As in any economic environment, here, too, those who capitalize on these opportunities will excel; the rest are doomed to mediocrity or failure.

Once EC projects are justified, these systems need to be developed.

SECTION 14.6 REVIEW QUESTIONS

1. How does EC impact the production cost curve?
2. Define transaction costs. List the major types and explain how EC can reduce such costs.
3. How can EC increase revenue?
4. How can EC increase the competitive advantage for a firm?
5. What are the benefits of increasing reach? How can EC help?
6. Explain the impact of EC on product differentiation and agility.
7. Define valuation. Why is it so high for some EC start-ups?

14.7   A FIVE-STEP APPROACH TO DEVELOPING AN E-COMMERCE SYSTEM

Once it has been determined that a business can benefit from a specific EC initiative, it is time to establish detailed plans of what and how to do it,

Table 14.2 Capabilities needed by webstore users

Buyers need the ability to	Sellers need the ability to
• Discover, search for, evaluate, and compare products for purchase using e-catalogs	• Provide access to a current catalog
• Select products to purchase and compare their price and terms	• Allow price comparisons
• Place an order for desired products using a shopping cart	• Provide an electronic shopping cart
• Pay for the ordered products, usually by credit card or e-payment	• Verify a customer's credit card or accept PayPal (or similar) e-payments
• Confirm an order, ensuring that the desired product is available	• Process orders (back-end services)
• Track orders once they are shipped	• Arrange for product fulfillment and delivery
	• Track shipments to ensure that they are delivered
	• Provide the means for buyers and visitors to register at the site, to make comments and recommendations, or to request additional information
	• Answer customers' questions or pass queries and requests on to a Web-based call center
	• Provide the ability to customize products/services
	• Provide Web-based post-sale support
	• Create the capability for cross-selling and up-selling
	• Provide language translation if needed
	• Measure and analyze the traffic at the site to improve services and operations

and to design the components and the capabilities of the EC system. It is wise to start with the identification of the users' needs. Some typical capabilities needed by a webstore are shown in Table 14.2.

Next, one should consider all the elements that can be used in a comprehensive EC system. These include hardware, software, networks, site design, capabilities, people involved, and interactions with other systems.

It is also important that a firm choose the correct development strategy to obtain the greatest return on its investment. The diversity of e-business models and applications, which varies in size from small webstores to global exchanges, requires a variety of development methodologies and approaches.

Building medium to large applications requires extensive integration with existing information systems, such as corporate databases, intranets, enterprise resource planning (ERP), and other application programs. Therefore, although the process of building EC systems can vary, in many cases, it tends to follow a standard format, such

as using the systems development life cycle (SDLC; described next). Before we present the SDLC, it is worthwhile to look at the life cycle of a typical EC system. This life cycle is illustrated in Figure 14.8, and it is self-explanatory.

Building a large EC system can be a very complex process, as is illustrated in Figure 14.9. The SDLC organized this process.

The Essentials of the SDLC: An EC Application

The traditional *systems development life cycle (SDLC)* systematically leads developers through several analysis and design stages: problem identification, analysis, logical design, physical design, implementation, and maintenance. The SDLC is the basis for the development of the majority of traditional business systems (see Kendall and Kendall 2013 for more details on this approach). However, innovative new software and hardware are enabling a move to a more streamlined approach to e-commerce development.

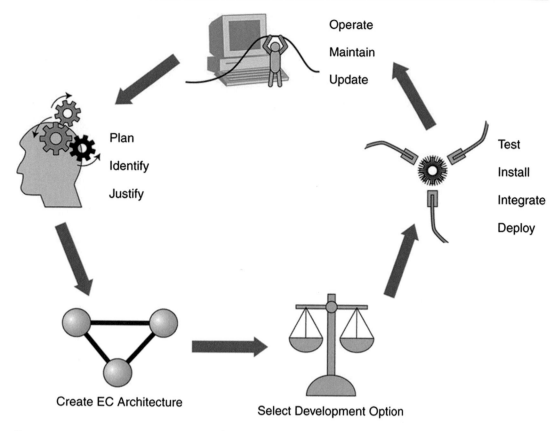

Figure 14.8 E-commerce system life cycle

The Five Traditional Steps

These steps are:

- **Step 1:** Identifying, justifying, and planning EC systems
- **Step 2:** Creating an EC architecture
- **Step 3:** Selecting a development option
- **Step 4:** Installing, testing, integrating, and deploying EC applications
- **Step 5:** Operations, maintenance, and updates

Managing the Development Process

The development process can be complex and must be managed properly. For medium-to-large applications, a project team is usually created to manage both the process and the vendors. Collaboration with business partners also is critical. Some e-business failures are the result of a lack of cooperation by business partners. For example, a firm can install an effective e-procurement system, but if its suppliers do not use it properly, the system will collapse. Projects can be managed with project management software. Best practice management also includes periodic evaluations of system performance. Standard project management techniques and tools are useful for this task. Finally, do not rule out the possibility that implementing an EC project may require restructuring one or more business processes.

SECTION 14.7 REVIEW QUESTIONS

1. Examine 10 different websites and choose your five favorites. Explain why you like each site. Relate your answers to the content of this chapter.
2. Go to the website of each of the developers/Webmasters of your five favorite websites. What expertise do they profess to have? What projects have they completed? Would you feel comfortable hiring their services?

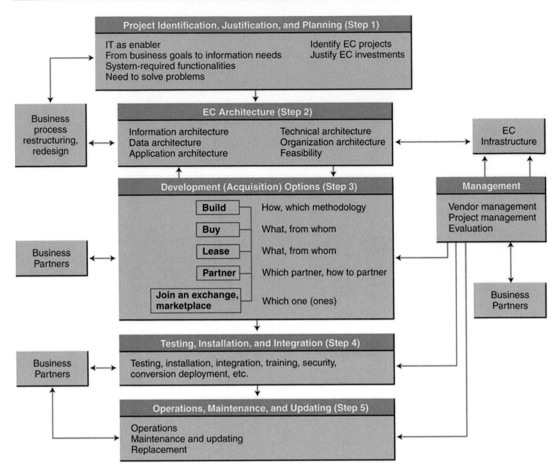

Figure 14.9 The EC application development process

3. List the major steps in developing an EC application.
4. Comment on the management of the development process.

14.8 DEVELOPMENT STRATEGIES FOR E-COMMERCE PROJECTS

If a company does not want to acquire a website or an EC system it could build one in-house. However, before deciding on self-building a website, a company should ask itself a few questions: Is the firm capable of developing the site (e.g., having qualified staff)? Does the firm have access to the proper tools to build the EC system and so forth? If the firm does not have these capabilities, it usu-ally is best to hire a qualified contractor (e.g., see the closing case about Memphis Invest). A useful directory of vendors is **webdesigners-directory. com**. The Microsoft Small Business Center (**microsoft.com/business/en-us/resources/technology/ecommerce/ecommerce-website-design-mistakes.aspx?fbid=oQfmmYZYpzu**) offers some tips for avoiding common e-commerce site developing mistakes. There are four popular options for developing an EC website:

1. **Develop the site in-house** either from scratch or with off-the-shelf components.
2. **Buy a packaged application** designed for a particular type of EC activity (e.g., e-procurement).

3. **Outsource the system development** to a vendor(s) either completely, or partially.
4. **Lease the application** from a third party (e.g., use *software as a service* or another cloud-based approach).

Each of these approaches has its benefits and limitations, and it is important to remember that the development options are not mutually exclusive. That is, two or more options may be used in one EC project. Each of these development options is discussed next.

In-House Development: Insourcing

The first generation of EC development was accomplished largely through proprietary programming and in-house development that is widely referred to as **insourcing**.

Although insourcing can be time-consuming and costly, it may lead to EC applications that best fit an organization's strategy and needs, and differentiate the company from its competition. The in-house development of EC applications, however, can be lengthy and expensive. Furthermore, the system's maintenance and updating may require considerable resources in the future.

Buy the Applications (Off-the-Shelf Approach)

A number of software packages provide many features that are required by EC applications. These packages are ready to turn on and operate. Therefore, this option is also known as a **turnkey approach** — the packages are ready to use with minimal installation and testing efforts.

Because one package can rarely meet all of an organization's requirements, it is sometimes necessary to acquire multiple packages. In this case, the packages need to be integrated with each other and with other software and data.

Advantages and Limitations of Ready Made Packages

The following are the major advantages of purchasing ready-made EC systems:

- A large variety of off-the-shelf software packages is available.
- It saves time and money (compared to in-house development).
- The company does not need to hire programmers with EC programming skills.
- The company knows the system's capabilities before it invests in it.
- The company is neither the first nor the only user of the package.
- Updating is done by the vendor with little or no cost to the users.

This option also has some major disadvantages:

- Software may not exactly meet the company's needs.
- Software may be difficult or impossible to modify, or it may necessary to modify the company's business processes.
- The using company has little control over software improvements and new versions.
- Off-the-shelf applications can be difficult to integrate with existing software systems.
- Vendors may discontinue a product or go out of business (risk factor).

Outsourcing EC Systems Development and Applications

The use of vendors for EC system acquisition or development is one type of *outsourcing*. In many cases, the systems need to be built quickly, (e.g., in a week or two), and special expertise of outside contractors and software vendors is necessary. Therefore, outsourcing is used.

Outsourcers can perform any or all tasks in EC applications development. For example, they can plan, program, and build applications and integrate, operate, and maintain them. It is useful for firms to develop good relationships with outsourcers.

Types of Outsourcing Options

Several types of vendors offer services for creating and operating EC applications:

- Software houses.
- Outsourcers and others.
- Telecommunications companies.

Leasing EC Applications: Cloud Computing and Software as a Service (SaaS)

An option in EC acquisition is to lease systems rather than to buy or build them. This includes ready to use applications and tools/components for system development.

Companies may choose leasing when they want to experiment with new EC technologies without a great deal of up-front investment. Leasing also allows firms to protect their internal networks and gain expert advice. Small firms with limited IT expertise and tight budgets also may find leasing advantageous.

Leasing eliminates the users' need to buy software, install it, run it, and maintain it. Furthermore, users can start utilizing leased systems very quickly. (Remember that "time is money.") Finally, since all users have the same software, they can connect to each other in an expeditious fashion.

In recent years, leasing has become very popular, appearing under several variations and names. The most well-known are *utility computing*, *software-as-a-service*, and *on-demand computing*. As of 2009, these are bundled under the concept of *cloud computing*.

Cloud Computing

Cloud computing refers to the delivery of computational assets and services required by users and systems when needed (on demand). The delivery is done via the Internet or other computer networks. Users only pay for actual usage. It is the same as the supply of metered utilities, such as water or electricity. Therefore, cloud computing is also called utility computing. The details and internal structures of cloud computing are simplified to the point where they can be ignored by computer application developers and users. A large number of companies provide cloud computing products and services (e.g., Salesforce, Inc., Oracle, Microsoft).

Cloud computing includes cloud platforms, cloud infrastructure, cloud applications, cloud storage, and more. For details, see Online Tutorial T2 and Kavis (2014).

Advantages of Cloud Applications

The major advantages for the users are:

- Accessible from anywhere. All you need is an Internet (or intranet) connection
- No need for an onsite server or the installation of a local server
- Pay per use or per time period (e.g., monthly, like for cable TV)
- Rapid scalability – provides a strategic advantage due to the ability to change in a timely manner
- Shorter time-to-market (TTM)
- Often includes system maintenance (security, updates, backup, etc.) in the service
- The possibility of improved security; however, users that require a high level of security (e.g., financial institutions) may see SaaS as a security concern
- Dependability of the systems that incorporate the technology

For other benefits, see **intel.com/content/www/us/en/cloud-computing/intel-cloud-based-solutions.html** and **ibm.com/marketplace/cloud/**

us/en-us. For detailed benefits and limitations see Viswanathan (undated).

Other Development Options

Several additional options are currently available for developing EC applications. Some popular ones are:

- **Join an e-marketplace.** With this option, the company can be connected to an e-marketplace. For example, a company can place its catalogs in Yahoo!'s marketplace. Visitors to Yahoo! Shopping will find the company's products and will be able to make purchases. The company pays Yahoo! a monthly space-rental fee . In such a case, Yahoo! is a hosting service for the company as well. As for development, the company will use templates to build its webstore, and it can start to sell after only a short time of preparation.
- **Join a consortium.** This option is similar to the previous one, except that the company will be one of the e-market owners. Thus, the company may have more control over the market operations.
- **Join an auction or reverse auction third-party site.** Joining a third-party site is another alternative. A plug-in can be created quickly. Many companies use this option for e-procurement activities.
- **Form joint ventures.** Several different joint-venture partnerships may facilitate e-business applications development. For example, in Hong Kong, four small banks developed a joint e-banking system. In some cases, a company can team up with another company that already has an application in place.
- **Use a hybrid approach.** A hybrid approach combines the best of what the company does internally with an outsourced strategy.

Selecting a Development Option

Before choosing an appropriate development option, you need to consider the following factors (given here as questions):

- **Customers.** Who are the target customers? What are their needs? What kind of marketing tactics should a business use to promote the webstore and attract traffic? How can a business enhance customer loyalty? How can a business engage the customers and make them happy so they will return?
- **Merchandising.** What kinds of products or services will the business sell online? Are soft (digitized) goods or hard goods sold? Are soft goods downloadable?
- **Sales service.** Can customers order online? How? Can they pay online? Can they check the status of their order(s) online? How are customer inquiries handled? Are warranties, service agreements, and guarantees available for the different products? What are the refund procedures?
- **Promotion.** How are the products and services promoted? How will the traffic to special events be organized? Are coupons, manufacturer's rebates, or quantity discounts offered? Is cross-selling possible?
- **Transaction processing.** Is transaction processing done in real time? How are taxes, shipping and handling fees, and payments processed? What kinds of shipping methods will the site offer? What kind of payment method(s) will the site accept? How will the site conduct order fulfillment?
- **Marketing data and analysis.** What information, such as sales, customer data, and advertising trends will the site collect? How will the site use such information for future marketing? How is the information secured?
- **Branding.** What image should the webstore reinforce? How is the company's webstore different from the competition webstore?

The initial list of requirements should be as comprehensive as possible. It is preferable to validate the identified requirements through focus group discussions or surveys with potential customers. The business can then prioritize the requirements based on customer preferences.

SECTION 14.8 REVIEW QUESTIONS

1. List the major e-commerce development and acquisition options.
2. Define insourcing.
3. List some of the pros and cons of using packaged EC applications.
4. Compare the buy option against the lease option. What are the benefits and risks associated with each option?
5. Compare the other development options. If you were the owner of a small company trying to establish a new webstore, which would you choose?
6. How can cloud computing be used as an option for acquiring a system?
7. What is SaaS?
8. What are the advantages of building with templates? What are the disadvantages?
9. List the typical features of a webstore.
10. What are some of the selection criteria for a software option?
11. Describe cloud computing technology as a leasing option.

14.9   ORGANIZATIONAL IMPACTS OF E-COMMERCE

Only limited statistical data or empirical research on the full organizational impact of EC is available because the field is so new. Therefore, the discussion in this section is based primarily on expert opinions, logic, and only limited empirical data.

Existing and emerging Web technologies provide companies with a chance to reconsider business models, relationships, and business processes. These e-opportunities can be divided into three categories: e-marketing (Web-based initiatives that improve the marketing of existing products) e-operations (Web-based initiatives that improve the creation of existing products); and e-services (Web-based initiatives that improve service industries and customer service). The discussion here is also based in part on the work of Bloch et al. (1996), who approached the impact of e-marketplaces on organizations from a value-added point of view. Their model, divides the impact of e-marketplaces into three major categories: *improving direct marketing*, *transforming organizations*, and *redefining organizations*. This section examines each of these impacts.

Improving Direct Marketing and Sales

Brick-and-mortar direct marketing is done by mail order (from catalogs) and by telephone (telemarketing).

For digital products – software, music, and videos – the changes brought by e-markets is dramatic. Already, digital products are downloadable from the Internet. The ability to transfer digitized products electronically eliminates the need for packaging and shipping, and greatly reduces the need for specialized distribution services.

New sales and distribution models for digitized goods such as downloading music, videos and software, shareware, freeware, social shopping, and pay-as-you-use are emerging. In certain cases, all of these impacts of EC on direct marketing provide companies with a competitive advantage over those that use only traditional direct-sales methods, as illustrated in the Blue Nile case in Chapter 2 (p. 59) and described in Chapter 3 (Section 3.9). Furthermore, because the competitive advantage is so large, e-markets are likely to replace many non-direct marketing channels. Some people predict the "fall of the shopping mall," and label many retail stores and full-service brokers (e.g., stocks, real estate, and insurance) as a soon-to-be-endangered species.

Transforming Organizations and Work

A second impact of e-marketplaces is the transformation of organizations. Here, we look at four key topics: *organizational learning*, *changing the nature of work*, *disintermediation and reintermediation*, and the *structure of the EC unit*.

Technology and Organizational Learning

Rapid progress in EC will force a Darwinian struggle: To survive, companies will have to learn and adapt quickly to the new technologies. An example is the newspaper industry, where losses, bankruptcies, and consolidations are regular events. For example, the *New York Times* developed its electronic version and products to compensate for the reduction in advertising income from its print version. These changes may transform the way in which business is conducted. EC may have a significant impact on the strategies of many organizations and industries. New technologies may lead to new organizational structures and procedures. Problems with traditional bookstores and record stores, and the struggle of companies such as Best Buy and Blockbuster to survive, illustrate what is occurring in some industries.

The Changing Nature of Work

Certain EC applications, and especially social commerce, could change the way people work. Changes are occurring, for example, in man–machine interactions and in sharing Web material and online activities. Another area is that of collaboration. Web 2.0 tools as well as m-commerce are changing the way people collaborate (e.g., a joint design). Innovations in e-payments are changing the manner in which cashiers work in supermarkets, and much more.

Disintermediation and Reintermediation

Intermediaries are agents that mediate between sellers and buyers. Usually, they provide two types of services: (1) they provide relevant information about demand, supply, prices, and requirements and, in doing so, help match sellers and buyers; and (2) they offer value-added services such as transfer of products, escrow, payment arrangements, consulting, or assistance in finding a business partner. In general, the first type of service can be fully automated and thus is likely to be performed by e-marketplaces, infomediaries, and portals that provide free or low-commission services. The second type requires expertise, such as knowledge of the industry, the products and technological trends, and it can only be partially automated.

Intermediaries that provide only (or mainly) the first type of service can be eliminated; this phenomenon is called *disintermediation*. An example is travel agents in the airline industry. The airlines are advocating electronic tickets. Most airlines require customers to pay $25 or more per ticket if they buy the ticket from a travel agent or by phone, which may be equivalent to the agent's commission. Online transactions results in the *disintermediation* of travel agents from the purchasing process. In another example, traditional stockbrokers who only execute trades manually, are disappearing. However, brokers who manage electronic intermediation are not only surviving, but may also be prospering (e.g., E*TRADE). This phenomenon, in which disintermediated entities or newcomers take on new intermediary roles, is called *reintermediation* (see Chapters 3 and 4).

Disintermediation is more likely to occur in supply chains involving several intermediaries, as illustrated in the Blue Nile case in the jewelry industry (Chapter 2).

Restructuring Business Processes

We stated earlier that to use over-the-counter software packages may lead to a change in some business processes. The same is true for implementing some of the new business models introduced by EC. For the topic of restructuring business processes, as well as the techniques used see Lymbersky (2013).

Redefining Organizations

The following are some of the ways in which e-markets redefine organizations.

New and Improved Products and Services

E-commerce allows for new products to be created and for existing products to be changed (e.g., to customized). Such changes may redefine organizations' strategies, products, and services. Also, the more powerful and knowledgeable customers are demanding new or improved products and services.

Mass Customization and On-Demand Manufacturing

Mass customization, also known as **on-demand manufacturing**, enables manufacturers to create specific products for each customer based on the customer's preferences. We described this topic in Chapters 3, 12, and 13. There are many examples of mass customization ranging from customizing shoes at Nike and toys at LEGO to designing engagement rings at Blue Nile. In an effort to save billions in inventory reduction, the automobile industry is producing customized cars where the orders and configurations are made online. Today you can design your own T-shirt, Swatch watch, and many other products and services online. Configuring the details of the customized products is done online. Also known as *build-to-order*, customization can be done on a large scale, in which case it is called *mass customization*. With the use of mass-customization methods, the cost of customized products is at, or slightly above, the comparable retail price of standard products. Figure 14.10 shows how customers can order customized Nike shoes.

The technology of 3D is expected to enable companies to manufacture customized products at a competitive cost. For a comprehensive discussion see Gandhi et al. (2014).

The On-Demand Revolution

EC is changing manufacturing systems from mass production to mass customization, which is demand-driven. These new production systems need to be integrated with finance, marketing, and other functional systems, as well as with business partners and customers. In fact, the entire supply chain is changing (see discussion in Chapter 12).

In what Flynn and Vencat (2012) call "Custom Nation," a growing number of scholars and practitioners predict that the on-demand phenomena, which drives manufacturing and is facilitated by e-commerce, will significantly change both businesses and manufacturing. Many successful brands, e.g., Netflix, Pandora, Nike, and Chipotle are already mostly on-demand companies. Other companies incorporate customization into their businesses in a larger volume. For a strategy on

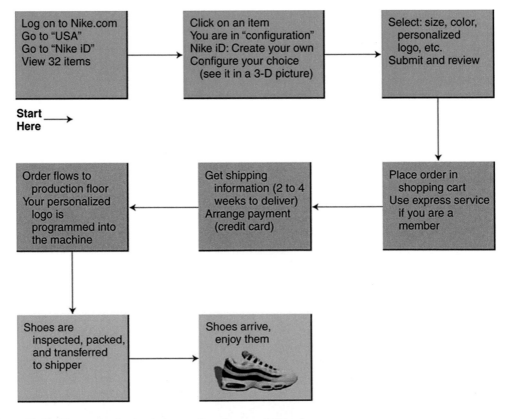

Figure 14.10 How customization is done online: the case of Nike shoes

how to do this, consult Flynn and Vencat (2012). One technology that may revolutionize on-demand manufacturing is 3D printing.

3D Printing
3D printing, also known as *additive manufacturing*, is a computer-driven manufacturing process for making parts (from plastic, metals, or other material), by producing one layer at a time and as many layers as needed. The process, which saves time and money, is done directly from computer-aided manufacturing (CAD) blueprints. For the current and future impact of 3D printing on on-demand manufacturing and factories, see Hausman and Horne (2014) and Winnan (2012). 3D printing is already changing manufacturing processes (e.g. Autodesk Corp.). The *Economist* calls the use of 3D printing "A Third Industrial Revolution."

Change Management

Deploying an EC project, especially if it involves major restructuring, introduces changes to organizations that must be managed properly.

Change management in business is a process of managing the administrative and behavioral issues related to a change in people's jobs, work areas, relationships, procedures, and so forth. The process, which includes an analysis of the need for change and feasibility, is intended to encourage employees to adopt such changes. For details see *Harvard Business Review* (2011) and Kotter (2012).

How to Organize an EC Unit in a Company

If a company is engaged in EC, it will usually have employees in this area. The question is how to organize the EC unit of these employees. The best structure depends on many variables such as:
- The size of the EC workforce
- The nature of the EC projects (e.g., e-tailing, e-procurement, e-training)
- The existing organizational structure of the company
- Is the company pure-play EC?

- The types of products/services delivered by the company
- The internal politics of the organization
- The number of active EC projects
- The budget of the EC workforce

These factors need to be considered. The major options available are discussed next.

Options for Organizing the EC Workforce
The major options are as follows.

Report to the Marketing Department
This is a viable solution for the case where e-tailing is the major EC activity.

Report to the Finance Department
This happens in cases where EC involves repeated RFQ, outsourcing, and other finance-related activities.

Report to the Chief Operating Officer
This could be a good solution if the major EC activity is e-procurement.

Distribute the EC Workforce in Several Departments
This can be a suitable solution when EC activities are independent of each other and closely related to specific departments.

Report to the IT Department
This makes sense when EC is continuously engaged in the technical aspects of EC.

Create a New, Possibly Autonomous EC Department
This solution can vary for a large EC workforce.

No Formal Structure for EC Exists

Create an Autonomous Division or a Separate Online Company
When the volume of an e-business is large, the temptation to create a separate company increases, especially if it goes public (undertaking an IPO). Barnes & Noble did just that.

The advantages of creating a separate company are:

- Reducing or eliminating internal conflicts.
- Providing more freedom for the online company's management in pricing, advertising, and other decisions.
- Creating a new brand more quickly.
- Taking the e-business to an IPO, and if successful, making a fortune.

The disadvantages of creating an independent division are:

- It may be very costly and risky.
- Collaboration with the offline business may be difficult.
- You lose the expertise of the offline business (e.g., marketing, finance, distribution), unless you get true and committed collaboration.

Note that some spin-offs of this nature, such as Barnes & Noble (**barnesandnoble.com**), were not doing so well, and Grainger, Inc. (**grainger. com**) ceased to be a separate company. However, several spin-off online companies have succeeded as independent entities.

SECTION 14.9 REVIEW QUESTIONS

1. Describe how EC improves direct marketing.
2. Describe how EC transforms organizations.
3. Describe how EC redefines organizations.
4. Discuss the need for change management in deploying EC projects to e-businesses.
5. Describe the position and structure of the EC unit in organizations.

14.10 OPPORTUNITIES FOR SUCCESS IN E-COMMERCE AND AVOIDING FAILURE

Now that EC has been around for about 20 years, it is possible to observe certain patterns that contribute to the success or failure of EC projects. By examining these patterns, one can find indications of the opportunities that lie ahead and avoiding pitfalls along the way.

Factors that Determine E-Commerce Success

The economic capabilities of EC described earlier influence some industries more than others do. The success factors of EC depend on the industry, the sellers and buyers, and the products sold. Furthermore, the ability of sellers to create economic value for consumers will also determine EC success. When deciding to sell online, looking at the major factors that determine the impact of EC can assist in evaluating the chances for success.

Four categories of e-market success factors exist: *product*, *industry*, *seller*, and *consumer* characteristics.

E-Commerce Failures

By examining the economic history of previous innovations, the failure of EC initiatives and EC companies should come as no surprise. Three economic phenomena suggest why this is the case (e.g., see the description of the hype cycle in this chapter).

Chapters 3 and 13 provide some of the specific reasons for failure in B2C EC: lack of profitability, excessive risk exposure, the high cost of customer acquisition, poor performance, and static website design. Two additional financial reasons are lack of funding and incorrect revenue models. An example of a failure is the Webvan case – an express delivery company that lost $1.2 billion – the largest of any other bankrupt dot-com. Another bankrupt company is Kozmo, whose story is available in Online File W14.3.

E-Commerce Successes

Despite the failure of hundreds of start-ups and thousands of EC projects, EC is alive and well, and continues to grow rapidly (after a short pause from 2000 through 2002), as discussed throughout the text.

Table 14.3 Critical success factors: old economy and EC

Old Economy CSFs	EC CSFs
Vertically integrate or do it yourself	Create new partnerships and alliances; stay with core competency
Deliver high-value products	Deliver high-value service offerings that encompass products
Build market share to establish economies of scale.	Optimize natural scale and scope of business; look at mass customization.
Analyze carefully to avoid missteps	Approach with urgency to avoid being left out; use proactive strategies
Leverage physical assets	Leverage intangible assets, capabilities, and relationships – unleash dormant assets
Compete to sell product	Compete to control access to markets, and build relationships with customers; compete with other websites

EC success stories abound, primarily in the specialty and niche markets. One example is Puritan's Pride Inc., (**puritan.com**), a successful vitamin and natural health care product store. Another is GrubHub, Inc. (**grubhub.com**), which allows people to order food online for either pickup or delivery (previously CampusFood. com). Also doing very well are travel sites, such as Expedia, Trip Advisor or Priceline.

Alloy Apparel (**alloy.com**) is a successful shopping and entertainment portal for young adults. As pointed out in Chapter 3, online services such as stock trading, travel and hospitality, online banking, and more are commanding a major part of the transactions in their industries. For a comparison of how these and other thriving online businesses have translated critical success factors (CSFs) from the old economy into EC success, see Table 14.3. EC successful companies such as Priceline, Netflix, Amazon. com, Facebook, and Google are becoming major players in their industries, making their shareholders very rich.

Following are some of the reasons for EC success and suggestions from EC experts and consultants on how to succeed in EC.

Strategies for EC Success
- Thousands of brick-and-mortar companies are adding online marketing and/or procurement channels with great success. Examples are Uniglobe Travel (**uniglobetravel.com**), Staples (**staples.com**), Home Depot (**homedepot. com**), Walmart (**walmart.com**), FIS (**fisglobal.**

com/products-retailpayments-ecommerce), 1-800-Flowers.com (**1800flowers.com**) and Southwest Airlines (**southwest.com**). Existing firms can use organizational knowledge, brand recognition, infrastructure, and other "morphing strategies" to migrate from the offline marketplace to the online marketspace. The following are strategies and critical success factors that can help EC succeed. A group of Asian CEOs recommend the following EC CSFs: select proper business models, project, predict, and prepare for the EC company, encourage e-innovation, co-brand marketing, and focus on younger customers (e.g., see **alloy.com** and **bolt3.com**).

- For an EC exchange to be successful, it has to create value for *all* participants. A vivid example is Alibaba.com.

- Pricing in EC has continued to be a challenge for sellers because of shipping and handling costs. Often, the seller and market maker will see the potential for profits and ignore the fact that the buyers will subscribe to EC only if they see a benefit in price or product variety. For example, Amazon.com decided to absorb delivery costs for orders above a certain amount (e.g., $25). Free shipping is also available at Dell, Newegg, and many other e-tailers.

- New technologies can boost the success of EC. For example, RFID has great potential for improving the supply chain (Chapter 12); however, it will take a large investment in EC infrastructure and applications to realize its full potential.

Additional Guidelines for EC Success

A number of experts and consultants have proposed many more keys to success. Several studies identified success factors such as:

* Effective marketing and advertising
* User-friendly website
* Good relationships between customers and merchants
* Proper supply chain management and order fulfillment
* Integration with internal and external information systems
* Use of appropriate business models (including revenue models)
* Effective and efficient infrastructure
* Organization culture regarding becoming an e-business and social business

At this still-early stage of the EC revolution, success cannot be guaranteed, and failure rates remain high. However, if companies learn from the mistakes of the past and follow the guidelines offered by experts and researchers, their chances for success are greatly enhanced.

In the remainder of this section, we will discuss important strategies and factors that should be considered to ensure EC success.

Cultural Differences in EC Successes and Failures

In Chapter 13, we discussed the need to understand cultural issues such as differences in social norms, measurement standards, and nomenclature. Here, we add the issue of *cultural differences* so that appropriate strategies can be developed when doing business globally.

One of the strengths of EC is the ease with which sellers and buyers can reach a global population of consumers or suppliers. However, they must recognize existing cultural differences and act upon them. Even the content of online ads can mean different things in different cultures. Due to these differences, the transaction costs, including coordination costs, may vary among the consumer base.

EC success factors as well as adoption strategies differ among countries (see Online File W14.4).

Can EC Succeed in Developing Economies?

Similar to cultural differences, developed and developing economies vary in how EC is used and whether the economics favor electronic commerce. Developing economies struggle with various issues taken for granted in developed economies.

Developing economies often face power blackouts, unreliable shipments, unstable political and social environments, lack of regulations that protect customers and insufficient payment options. Such limitations make it difficult for firms to predict whether EC investments will pay off, and when. However, developing economies, such as in China and India, represent a significant opportunity for EC to connect businesses to customers, as well as other businesses. The potential volume of transactions in developed countries can make EC investments more attractive for established firms. This is because much of the cost of EC systems development would have already been recovered because EC initiatives frequently can use existing IT infrastructures.

The traditional EC assumption is that every computer user has the ability to own a computer and afford Internet connection, as is the case in developed economies. In developing economies, this assumption will have to be revised to include the existence infrastructure, poverty levels, and technology availability and affordability. The payoffs from EC use in developing countries are likely to go beyond financial returns. Enabling people to take advantage of EC technology without disrupting their traditions may be the most valuable, yet intangible, return.

A major booster for EC in developing countries is the increasing use of low-cost laptop computers and tablets in a wireless environment. With simple computers costing less than $100 (and declining in 2014), and the widespread use of cell phones with Internet access and free access in public places, it is likely that EC use will increase significantly in developing countries. For comprehensive coverage of e-commerce in developing countries, see Sanayei (2010).

As discussed in Chapter 6, the mobile revolution enables developing countries to leap frog EC deployment, especially in the areas of mobile banking (finance) and mobile marketing.

SECTION 14.10 REVIEW QUESTIONS

1. Describe product characteristics in EC.
2. What are industry characteristics in EC?
3. What are seller characteristics in EC?
4. What are consumer characteristics in EC?
5. List three reasons why EC failure should not come as a surprise.
6. What are some reasons for EC success?
7. Relate EC to cultural differences.
8. Discuss some factors of implementation in developing countries.

MANAGERIAL ISSUES

Some managerial issues related to this chapter are as follows:

1. **How should the value of EC investments be justified?** EC investments must be measured against their contribution to business objectives. The best justification may come from the behavior of competitors. If EC has a strategic value to customers, there is no choice but to invest as long as competitors provide EC services. EC investments will involve direct and indirect costs as well as tangible and intangible benefits. The impact of EC on restructuring existing processes and systems must not be ignored.

   Automated transactions in EC may replace human roles in sales, procurement, and services. However, in some applications like customer service and knowledge management, EC may only supplement the human element. To identify the intangible benefits, refer to the business performance indicators in the balanced scorecard, which may not be measured easily with tangible metrics.

2. **Which investment analysis method should we adopt for EC justification?** The precise estimation of total cost of ownership is a good starting point for financial investment analysis. If an intangible benefit, such as enhanced customer service and quality assurance of purchased material is the primary contributor to productivity increase, management has to include it in the analysis. However, if the benefit can be measured quantitatively, such as creation of new revenue and/or reduced purchase cost, the net present value and ROI can be computed with tangible benefits and costs. Based on the investment analysis, the intangible factors may be considered additionally for managers' multicriteria judgments. Since there is high uncertainty in estimating future revenue creation, the best or worst case analysis may supplement the most likely analysis.

3. **Who should conduct the justification?** For small projects, the project team, possibly in cooperation with the finance department, can do the analysis. For a large or complex project, an unbiased outside consultant may be used, although it may be expensive. The justification should include both tangible and intangible benefits and costs. However, some vendors may provide ROI calculators as part of a proposal that might fit with your application without extra charge.

4. **Should we use the hype cycle?** The hype cycle can be extremely useful in determining EC strategy. Small organizations may use some of the free material (e.g., one year old; no details). For specific advice, it may benefit the company to pay Gartner for the detailed charts and analysis.

5. **Should we embark on cloud computing products for our EC initiatives?** According to the hype cycle, you probably should wait for a while. However, companies do report successful implementation in EC system development, security, e-CRM, and e-procurement. Given that it takes only a few years to move from hype to maturity, it is wise to at least experiment with some projects.

6. **Which strategy should we choose for vendor selection: the inside-out or outside-in approach?** The success of the EC application depends on appropriate selection of vendors and software packages (e.g., using Gartner's

Magic Quadrant). Also, consider using one vendor against using several.

7. **What kinds of organizational changes may be needed?** Companies should expect organizational changes in all functional areas once e-commerce reaches momentum. Change is particularly evident in the financial services sector, where many services can be replaced by the Internet. Social marketing and shopping is another area with major potential changes (especially f-commerce). Electronic procurement changes the purchasing business processes, and affiliate programs change the paradigm of marketing and business partnerships. Finally, the trends toward build-to-order and demand-driven manufacturing will continue to expand and may require restructuring of some business processes.

8. **Is it possible to predict EC success?** The more comprehensive the analysis, the more accurate the justification of the EC project. Furthermore, the project's chances for approval will be greater even though management cannot precisely know the future success of the project. Procurement innovation using EC is almost risk free in achieving the goals. Using EC for sales may involve uncertainties. Opening new independent e-marketplaces may require a high investment and is very risky because the entry barriers may be very high. This kind of EC investment may fail. The risk depends on the type of EC being used.

SUMMARY

In this chapter, you learned about the following EC issues as they relate to the chapter's learning objectives.

1. **The major components of EC implementation.** Four major categories exist for implementation: justification and economics (cost–benefit); acquiring and/or developing EC systems; assurance of organizational readiness and performance of necessary restructuring, training, and so forth; and cultivating the necessary success factors while avoiding mistakes.

2. **The need for EC justification.** Like any other investment, EC investment (unless it is small) needs to be justified. Many start-up EC companies have crashed because of incorrect or no justification. In its simplest form, justification looks at revenue minus all relevant costs. Analysis is done by defining performance and comparing actual performance to the desired metrics and KPI related to organizational goals.

3. **The difficulties in justifying EC investment.** The nature of EC makes it difficult to justify due to the presence of many intangible costs and benefits. In addition, the relationship between investment and results may be complex, extending over several years. Several projects may share both costs and benefits; and several different organizational areas may feel the impacts (sometimes negatively).

4. **Difficulties in establishing intangible metrics.** Intangible benefits may be difficult to define. Some of these benefits change rapidly; others have different values to different people or organizational units. Therefore, metrics that are based on intangible benefits have qualitative measures that are difficult to compare. One solution is to quantify the qualitative measures.

5. **Traditional methods for evaluating EC investments.** Evaluating EC involves a financial analysis, usually the ROI analysis, as well as an assessment of the technology and its architecture. Future costs and benefits need to be discounted, using the NPV method, especially if the costs and benefits will extend over several years. A payback period describes how long it will take to recover the initial investment. However, financial ROI alone can lead to an incomplete and misleading evaluation. Tools to integrate the various ROI aspects of EC investments include the balanced scorecard (BSC), which also emphasizes learning and growth in EC. ROI should take into account the risk of reducing possible failures or adverse events that can drain the financial ROI. No method is universal or perfect, so selecting a method (or a mix of methods) is critical.

6. **Describe the justification of representative EC projects.** The justification of an EC project starts with a need analysis and then involves listing all the costs and benefits. Examples of EC projects are the justification of e-procurement and m-commerce. All EC projects include intangible and tangible benefits and costs that must be identified. At that time, a method(s) must be selected to match the particular characteristics of the EC application.

7. **EC economic evaluation.** Economic fundamentals must be kept in mind when evaluating an EC investment. With non-digital products, the cost curve shows that average per unit costs decline as quantity increases. However, with digital products, the variable cost per unit usually is low, and thus, the evaluation will be different. Similar differences are evident in EC's ability to lower transaction costs, agency costs, and transaction risks. EC can also enable the firm to be agile in responding faster to changing market conditions and ensure increasing returns to scale, regardless of the volume involved. Finally, EC enables increased reach with multimedia richness at a reasonable cost.

8. **The major steps in developing an EC system.** Because of their cost and complexity, some EC sites need to be developed in a well-planned manner. The development of an EC site should proceed in steps. First, an EC application portfolio is defined based on an organization's strategy. Second, the EC architecture is created. Third, a decision is made whether to build, buy, or outsource the development. Fourth, the system is installed, tested, and deployed. Fifth, the system goes into maintenance mode, with continual changes being made to ensure the system's continuing success.

9. **The major EC development strategies, along with their advantages and disadvantages.** EC sites and applications are rarely built from scratch. Instead, enterprises buy a packaged EC suite and customize it to suit their needs (if possible), or they outsource the development to a vendor. A new generation of Web tools including social software, enables more "do it yourself" activities.

10. **The variety of EC application development methods, along with their benefits and limitations.** Numerous development methods can be used to develop an EC system. These include Web 2.0, cloud computing, software as a service (SaaS), and several other methods listed and detailed within the chapter. Depending on the resources available to the organization developing the EC system and the requirements of the system, one or more of the different development methods will be chosen to create the most efficient and effective solution.

11. **EC application outsourcing strategies.** Many enterprises elect to outsource the development and maintenance of their EC sites and applications. The most common type of EC applications outsourcing is the use of cloud computing. An enterprise can also rely on an existing e-marketplace or exchange. A webstore can be hosted by an Internet mall, or an enterprise could enter into a joint development agreement with a venture partner or a consortium. Again, the choice depends on the functional requirements of the EC site or application, the costs involved, the period, and the available IT resources.

12. **Organizational structure and change management.** All functional areas of an organization can be affected by e-markets. E-markets improve direct marketing and transform and redefine organizations. Direct marketing (manufacturers to customers) and one-to-one marketing and advertising are becoming the norm, and mass customization and personalization are thriving. Production is moving to build-to-order models, changing supply chain relationships, and reducing cycle time. Business process management (BPM) allows organizations to be more effective, more efficient, and more proficient in adapting to change. Change management is a process of managing the administrative and behavioral issues related to a change in people's jobs, work areas, relationships, procedures, and so forth; employees are encouraged to accept the

change. The process includes an analysis of the needs for the change and its feasibility.

13. **Reasons for EC success and failure.** Products, industries, sellers, and consumer characteristics require different metrics of EC value. With the growing worldwide connectivity to the Internet, EC economics will play a major role in supporting buyers and sellers. Like other innovations, EC is expected to go through the cycle of enormous success, followed by speculation and then disaster before the reality of the new situation sets in. Some EC failures are the result of problematic website design, lack of sustained funding, and weak revenue models. Success in EC has come through automating and enhancing familiar strategies, such as branding, morphing, building trust, and creating value for all trading partners by enriching the human experience with integrated and timely information. EC investments can go beyond the traditional business models by creating digital options. To ensure success, complementary investments must be made in managing change and responding to cultural differences among EC users.

KEY TERMS

3D printing
Agency costs
Change management
Cloud computing
Cost–benefit analysis
Hype cycle (of Gartner)
Insourcing
Key performance indicator (KPI)
Mass customization (on-demand manufacturing)
Product differentiation
Production function
ROI calculator
Total benefits of ownership (TBO)
Total cost of ownership (TCO)
Transaction costs
Turnkey approach
Valuation
Web analytics

DISCUSSION QUESTIONS

1. Your state government is considering an online vehicle registration system. Develop a set of EC metrics and discuss how these metrics differ from that of the existing manual system.
2. Discuss the advantage of using several methods (e.g., ROI, payback period) to justify investments.
3. Enter **businesscase.com** and find material on ROI analysis. Discuss how ROI is related to a business case.
4. A craftsperson operates a small business making wooden musical instruments in a small U.S. town. The business owner is considering using EC to increase the business's reach to the nation and the world. How can the business owner use EC to increase richness to make the products more attractive to consumers?
5. A company is planning a wireless-based CRM system for its customers. Almost all the benefits are intangible. How can you justify the project to top management?
6. An enterprise wants to modify its EC site so that it conforms more closely to the company's overall business strategies. What types of online data are available for this purpose? How can these data be collected? What types of business strategy questions can be addressed by these data?
7. Discuss product and industry characteristics as they affect EC success.
8. Discuss the need to restructure business processes and suggest how it can be accomplished.

TOPICS FOR CLASS DISCUSSION AND DEBATES

1. Discuss the logic of outsourcing the combination of Web hosting and site construction. What are some of the disadvantages?
2. Enter **broadvision.com/en/products/clearvale/ #clearvale-overview** and find the free products that businesses can easily use to offer social networking capabilities to their employees. Examine the capabilities provided and discuss instances for which such an offer could be attractive.

3. Debate: A cost–benefit analysis may be inaccurate, so why should we conduct it?

4. Debate the use of cloud computing (leasing) against the purchase of a merchant suite by a retailer.

5. Debate: An airline offers extensive travel services online including hotels, car rentals, vacations, and so forth all over the globe. Its online business should be autonomous.

6. The stock market success of e-commerce and social commerce companies vary greatly from very successful (e.g., Google, LinkedIn) to poor (Groupon, Zynga, Facebook). Examine the IPOs of 2011 through 2014 and try to explain the CSF. Write a report.

INTERNET EXERCISES

1. Enter **idc.com** and find how it evaluates ROI on intranets, supply chains, and other EC and IT projects. Summarize your findings in a report.

2. Enter **salesforce.com/form/roi**. Register and download the free ROI kit. Summarize one case study. View two demos. Write a report.

3. Enter **schwab.com**. Examine the list of online services available for planning a retirement, and for advised investment services. Relate them to *richness* and *reach*.

4. Go to **google.com** and search for articles about the ROI of RFID. List the key issues in measuring the ROI of RFID.

5. Go to **alinean.com/value_selling** and follow the walk-through of the calculators. Find the capabilities of the calculators. Calculate the ROI of a project of your choice as well as the TCO.

6. Enter **sas.com**, **rocketsoftware.com/brand/rocket-corvu**, **balancedscorecard.org**, and **cio.com**. Find demos and examples of how to use the various tools and methods to evaluate EC projects. Write a report.

7. Enter **roi-calc.com**. View the demos. What investment analysis services does the company provide?

8. Enter **zebra.com/us/en/solutions/research-and-learn/roi-calculators.html**. What kind of analyses can the calculators do?

9. Design a pair of shoes at **nike.com** and **ralphlauren.com**. Compare all three sites.

10. Enter **sap.com** and use the "business case builder and ROI calculator" for a hypothetical (or real) EC project. Write a report on you experience.

11. Enter **baselinemag.com** and find free ROI analysis tools. Download a tool of your choice and identify its major components. Write a report.

TEAM ASSIGNMENTS AND PROJECTS

1. **Assignment for the Opening Case**
   Read the opening case and answer the following questions:
   (a) What motivated Telstra to prepare the calculators?
   (b) Why do the calculators include benefits to employees and to the community?
   (c) Download the e-book at AIIA (2009), and examine the list of benefits in all four cases. Which benefits are intangible?
   (d) The case cites the use of NPV. Explain how it works in this case.
   (e) Find the appendices cited in AIIA (2009) case, and comment on the detailed examples.

2. Explore the business value of EC. Each member enters a different site (e.g., Nicholas G. Carr (**nicholasgcarr.com**), Baseline (**baselinemag.com**), Strassmann, Inc. (**strassmann.com**), etc.). Prepare a presentation on issues, value, and directions.

3. This project requires reading the free White Paper by Saddington and Toni (2009). Each team concentrates on one of the following calculators: video conferencing, telecommuting, Web contact center, and Fleet and field force management. Examine the variables included for measuring costs and benefits. Analyze the savings. Add any missing variables, including intangible ones. Each team gives a presentation.

4. Several vendors offer products for creating webstores. The websites of these vendors usually list those webstores that currently use their software (customer success stories). Assign

each team a number of vendors. Each team should prepare reports comparing the similarities and differences among the vendors' sites and evaluating the customers' success stories. Are the customers taking advantage of the functionality provided by the various products?

5. Enter **youtube.com/watch?v=qh1drAg1jdg** and watch the video titled "Gartner Hype Cycle." Write a summary of the major points. Do the assignment provided there.

6. The class will set up a webstore on Facebook. You can use the application from **ecwid.com/pavvment** or from **bigcommerce.com**. Have several members place products there while others shop. Write a report on your experience.

CLOSING CASE: MEMPHIS INVEST EXCELS THANKS TO E-COMMERCE

Memphis Invest (**memphisinvest.com**) is a small, family-owned real estate investment company. Most of its clients live more than 100 miles away from Memphis. Therefore, the Internet plays a major role in the company's success.

The Problem

In 2009, the company was very small and barely able to stay in a static condition. All it had on its website was a simple brochure, with no interaction with customers or any marketing or Web strategies. The online and offline activities were not connected, and there was no analysis of what was occurring on the website. Management realized that a change was needed.

The Solution

The first step was to set up a marketing department. However, being a small business of 8 people at that time, in-house expertise was lacking about what to do, especially with respect to e-commerce strategy. Therefore, the company collaborated with HubSpot Inc. (**hubspot.com**), a company that makes inbound marketing software that allows

businesses to conduct marketing online. Memphis Invest initiated a Web strategy (see steps in Chapter 13). Among the initial EC initiatives was the creation of a blog. The owner posted news, commentaries, and tutorials regarding the real estate investment business. The site was optimized for SEO (Chapter 9) to have better exposure. On the revitalized website, the company provided the investors with *investor kits* and generated opportunities for conversations with potential customers. All this increased the company's visibility, traffic, and marketing skills.

The company created interesting content on the website that facilitated conversations. The more conversations initiated, the more buyers appeared. The company also introduced metrics for strategy assessment. The company created a page on Facebook (**facebook.com/meminvest**), and uses video ads on its own website and on pages in other social networks.

Note: Real estate investment provides opportunities for people to make money from buying, remodelling, renting out, exchanging, and managing real estate. To learn what to do and how to avoid the pitfalls, consult the free Jump Start Success Package provided by Memphis Invest.

The Results

According to HubSpot, Inc. (2012), sales increased 260% in 24 months, reaching 30.4 million in 2011. In 2013, the company now has over 40 employees. All this was achieved, despite the economic problems in the real estate industry between 2008 and 2012.

The company was ranked #1355 in the top 5,000 Real Estate Companies in 2014, by Inc. (**inc.com/inc5000/list/2014/industry/real-estate**). Different rankings by other institutions improved dramatically. The company's reputation and trust level are at an all-time high and increasing. Finally, the organizational climate improved dramatically and employees care much more about the business and the customers.

Sources: Based on HubSpot, Inc. (2012), **memphisinvest.com/about.php**, **inc.com/profile/Memphis-invest**, and **memphisinvest.com** (all accessed November 2014).

Questions

1. Identify the success factors of Memphis Invest.
2. Describe the development of Web analysis.
3. Enter **youtube.com/watch?v=00JMdY-dBuA** and watch the video titled "Than Merrill Visits Memphis Real Estate Company Memphisinvest. com." Summarize the critical success factors of Memphis Invest.
4. Why is reputation and trust so important for the company, and how did they increased it using e-commerce?
5. Why was the collaboration with HubSpot so successful?
6. Go to **youtube.com/user/MemphisInvest** and describe the use of video ads on the site.

ONLINE FILES
available at **affordable-ecommerce-textbook.com/turban**

W14.1 E-Procurement Complexities in Marketplaces

W14.2 Application Case: Cost–Benefit Justification of Wireless E-Commerce at Paesano Restaurant of Australia

W14.3 Application Case: The Rise and Fall of Kozmo.com

W14.4 Application Case: The Success Story of E-Choupal

COMPREHENSIVE EDUCATIONAL WEBSITES

mmv.vic.gov.au/ecommerce: Tips and case studies.

nucleusresearch.com: Metrics, ROI.

roi-calc.com: Calculators, metrics.

baselinemag.com: Calculators, metrics.

strassmann.com: ROI, justification.

fstc.org: Financial Services Technology Consortium.

gartner.com/technology/research/methodologies/magicQuadrants.jsp: The Gartner Magic Quadrant for E-Commerce.

wiki.secondlife.com/wiki/Video_tutorials: Video tutorials for distance learning providers.

vectec.org/resources: Research resources into the various aspects of e-business.

allthingsweb2.wordpress.com: Open directory of Web 2.0 tools and so forth.

GLOSSARY

3D printing Computer driven manufacturing process of making parts (from plastic, metals, or other materials), by producing one layer at a time, and as many layers as needed.

Agency costs Costs incurred in ensuring that certain support and administrative tasks related to production are performed as intended (e.g., by an agent). (Also called *administrative costs*.)

Change management A process of managing the administrative and behavioral issues related to a change in people's jobs, work area, relationships, procedures, and so forth. The process is intended to encourage employees to adopt such changes.

Cloud computing The delivery of computational assets and services required by users and systems when needed (on-demand).

Cost–benefit analysis A comparison of the costs of each project against its benefits.

Hype cycle (Gartner, Inc.) A graphic representation of the life cycle of specific IT and EC technologies (e.g., cloud computing, 3D printing, e-payment).

Insourcing In-house development of applications.

Key performance indicators (KPIs) The quantitative expression of critically important metrics.

Mass customization (on-demand manufacturing) A method that enables manufacturers to create specific products for each customer based on the customer's preferences.

Product differentiation Products with special features.

Production function A mathematical formula that indicates that for the same quantity of production, Q, companies either can use a certain amount of labor or invest in more automation (e.g., they can substitute IT capital for labor).

ROI calculator Calculator used to evaluate investments using metrics and formulas.

Total benefits of ownership (TBO) This calculation includes both tangible and intangible benefits.

Total cost of ownership (TCO) A formula for estimating the direct and indirect cost of owning, operating, and controlling an IT system, over the entire life of a product or system.

Transaction costs Costs that cover a wide range of expenses that are associated with commercial transactions, including the bartering of products and services.

Turnkey approach Software packages that are ready to use with minimal installation and testing efforts.

Valuation The process of trying to determine the value or worth of a company.

Web analytics Tools and methods that are used to measure, analyze, and optimize Web usage and other Internet activities.

REFERENCES

AIIA. *Greening Your Business Through Technology*, (an e-Book). Section 4.3.1 case study: Telstra-Cost-Benefit Analysis Calculators (Business Innovation). November 2009, Download at **witsa.org/news/newsletter_Q210/img/AIIA_GreenIT_eBook.pdf** (accessed July 2014).

Asefeso, A. *Balanced Scorecard*. Seattle, WA: CreateSpace Independent Publishing Platform, 2014.

Baseline. "How to Calculate ROI." September 6, 2006.

Beasley, M. *Practical Web Analytics for User Experience: How Analytics Can Help You Understand Your Users*. Burlington, MA: Morgan Kaufmann, 2013.

Bloch, M., Y. Pigneur, and A. Segev. "Leveraging Electronic Commerce for Competitive Advantage: A Business Value Framework." *Proceedings of the Ninth International Conference on EDI-IOS*, June 1996, Bled, Slovenia.

Boardman, A., et al. *Cost-Benefit Analysis*, 4th edition, (Pearson Series in Economics). New York: Pearson/Prentice Hall 2011.

Chen, S. *Strategic Management of E-Business*, 2nd ed. West Sussex, England: John Wiley & Sons, Ltd., 2005.

Clifton, B. *Advanced Web Metrics with Google Analytics,* 3rd ed. Hoboken, NJ: Sybex, 2012.

Flynn, A., and E. F. Vencat. *Custom Nation: Why Customization Is the Future of Business and How to Profit From It*. Dallas, TX: BenBella Books, 2012.

Fell, G. J. *Decoding the IT Value Problem: An Executive Guide for Achieving Optimal ROI on Critical IT Investments*. Hoboken, NJ: Wiley, 2013.

Gandhi, A., C. Magar, and R. Roberts. "How Technology Can Drive the Next Wave of Mass Customization." *McKinsey & Company*, February 2014, **mckinsey.com/insights/business_technology/how_technology_can_drive_the_next_wave_of_mass_customization** (accessed July 2014).

Gartner. Gartner's Hype Cycle Special Report for 2014. **gartner.com/technology/research/hype-cycles** (accessed November 2014).

Gunasekaran, A., P. Love, F. Rahimi, and R. Miele. "A Model for Investment Justification in Information Technology Projects." *International Journal of Information Management*, 21 349–364 (2001).

Harvard Business Review. HBR's 10 Must Reads on Change Management. Boston, MA: Harvard Business Review Press, 2011.

Hausman, K. K., and R. Horne. *3D Printing For Dummies*, [Kindle Edition]. Hoboken, NJ: For Dummies, 2014.

HubSpot, Inc. (2012), Memphis invest sees 260% increase in sales with inbound marketing. **hubspot.com/customers/memphis-invest** Accessed November 2014.

Jelassi, T., and A. Enders. *Strategies for E-Business: Concepts and Cases,* 2nd ed. Harlow, England: Prentice Hall, 2008.

Kaushik, A. *Web Analytics 2.0: The Art of Online Accountability and Science of Customer Centricity*. Hoboken, NJ: Sybex, 2010.

Kavis, M. J. *Architecting the Cloud: Design Decisions for Cloud Computing Service Models (SaaS, PaaS, and IaaS)*. Hoboken, NJ: Wiley, 2014.

Keen, J. M., and R. Joshi. *Making Technology Investments Profitable: ROI Road Map to Better Business Cases*, 2nd ed. Hoboken, NJ: Wiley, 2011.

Kendall, K. E., and J. E. Kendall. *Systems Analysis and Design*, 9th ed. Upper Saddle River, NJ: Prentice Hall, 2013.

Kotter, J. P. *Leading Change*. Boston, MA: Harvard Business Review Press, 2012.

Lymbersky, C. *International Turnaround Management Standard: A Guided System for Corporate Restructurings and Transformation Processes*. Seattle, WA: CreateSpace Independent Publishing Platform, 2013.

Misra, R. B. "Evolution of the Philosophy of Investments in IT Projects." *Issues in Informing Sciences and Information Technology*, 399-409 (2006).

MobileInfo.com. "Mobile Computing Business Cases." 2011. **mobileinfo.com/business_cases.htm** (accessed May 2014).

Nucleus Research, "ROI Tools and Case Studies." **nucleusresearch.com/research** (accessed July 2014).

Petouhoff, N. L. Radian6 Community "EBook: ROI of Social Media: Myths, Truths and How to Measure." February 2012. **digitalintelligencetoday.com/documents/Radian6_2012.pdf** (accessed May 2014).

Prieger, J. E., and D. Heil. "The Microeconomic Impacts of E-Business on the Economy. *Social Science Research Network*, May 20, 2009. **papers.ssrn.com/sol3/papers.cfm?abstract_id=1407713** (accessed May 2014).

Rayport, J., and B. J. Jaworski. *Introduction to E-Commerce*, 2nd ed. New York: McGraw-Hill/Irwin, 2004.

Renkema, T. J. W. *The IT Value Quest: How to Capture the Business Value of IT-Based Infrastructure*. Hoboken, NJ: Wiley, 2000.

Ritter, J., and F. Röttgers. *The Definitive Guide to Getting Your Budget Approved- Measure Intangibles to Calculate Your ROI Business Case*. Boston, MA: Solution Matrix, 2008.

Saddington, H. and P. Toni. "Using ICT to Drive Your Sustainability Strategy." A white paper, April 2009. **awsassets.wwf.org.au/downloads/fs004_using_ict_to_drive_sustainaibility_strategy_telstra_1apr09.pdf** (accessed Nov 2014).

Sanayei, A. (Ed.) *E-Commerce in Developing Countries.* London, UK: Koros Press Ltd., 2010.

TeamQuest. "The Business Value of IT." Special Report, *Computer Weekly*, October 2013, Reprinted as a White Paper on April 23, 2014. **teamquest.com/pdfs/white-paper/understanding-real-value-it-proving-it-to-business.pdf** (accessed Nov 2014).

Turban, E., et al. *Social Commerce.* New York: Springer, 2015.

Viswanathan, P. "Cloud Computing- Is It Really All That Beneficial?" Undated **mobiledevices.about.com/od/additionalresources/a/Cloud-Computing-Is-It-Really-All-That-Beneficial.htm** (accessed Nov 2014).

Winnan, C. D. *3D Printing: The Next Technology Gold Rush-Future Factories and How to Capitalize on Distributed Manufacturing*, Kindle edition. Seattle, WA: Amazon Digital Services, 2012.

Ziff Davis. "The Business Case for Making Business Processes Social." White Paper # 131012, 2012. Available for download at **itmanagement.com/research/the-business-case-for-making-business-processes-social-28785** (accessed July 2014).

E-Commerce: Regulatory, Ethical, and Social Environments

15

Contents

Learning Objectives

Upon completion of this chapter, you will be able to:
1. Understand the foundations for legal and ethical issues in EC.
2. Describe intellectual property law and understand its adjudication.
3. Explain privacy and free speech issues and their challenges.
4. Describe types of fraud on the Internet and how to protect against them.
5. Describe the needs and methods of protecting both buyers and sellers.
6. Describe EC-related societal issues.
7. Describe Green EC and IT.
8. Describe the future of e-commerce.

OPENING CASE: WHY WAS DISNEY FUNDING CHINESE PIRATES?

In 2006, Disney's funding arm, Steamboat Ventures, invested $10 million in one of the largest Chinese video- and file-sharing site called 56.com (**56.com**). The site is very popular in China, Taiwan, Singapore, and Hong Kong.

The Problem

In May 2008, The Walt Disney Company released its animated film *Wall-E*; the film was released on DVD in November 2008. However, immediately

Electronic supplementary material The online version of this chapter (doi: 10.1007/978-3-319-10091-3_15) contains supplementary material, which is available to authorized users

after the movie release in May, the robot love story was available to download and watch for free on the Chinese video site 56.com. In other words, Disney was funding a Chinese site that bootlegs its own work.

A major reason that pirated movies are difficult to detect is that the same movie may appear under different names. Although 56.com managed to remove some of the full-length bootlegged copies, many others still remain. The 56.com site is often referred to as a Chinese version of YouTube. However, unlike YouTube, 56.com and similar sites like Youku Tudou Inc. (China's leading Internet television company) do not impose 15-minute limits on uploaded videos, which makes them a haven for illegally uploaded videos, including full-length movies and TV episodes. Note, it is possible today to upload videos longer than 15 minutes by using special procedures.)

If 56.com were located in the United States, we would expect the Motion Picture Association of America (MPAA) and similar organizations in other countries to pressure the "bootlegging" company to remove copyrighted materials. However, China has not had a very solid record of enforcing intellectual property rights. Therefore, the Chinese government is turning to harsher punishments for piracy of copyrighted material. In 2011, they discovered over 2,000 cases of copyright infringement and arrested 4,000 people. The government has vowed to create harsher punishments to combat the problem (see Billboard Biz 2011).

The Solution

Before Disney's affiliate, Steamboat Ventures, invested in 56.com, they knew they faced a battle preventing pirated movies and TV shows from being shown on the 56.com site. However, Steamboat Ventures said that they were attracted to the site's 'refined, controlled, and effective technology platform,' as well as its large user base. Although Steamboat was aware of the piracy issue, they thought that they "could promote legal content on the site and work towards eliminating pirated materials" (see McBride and Chao 2008).

In the United States, you can take legal action against companies such as 56.com for copyright violations. For example, in 2007, Viacom sued YouTube for $1 billion, requesting access to the viewing habits of YouTube users On March 18, 2014, Google (owner of YouTube) and Viacom settled out of court, finally resolving the seven-year long *Viacom v. YouTube* litigation.

Note that, in China, the government, which in the past provided only warnings to violators, is increasing penalties for violations of copyright infringement. In November 2013, several Chinese video companies, including Youko Tudou and Tencent Video, along with the Motion Picture Association of America (MPAA), joined together in Beijing to fight against video online infringement and piracy in China. Legal action had already been taken against Baidu and QVOD (see **marketwatch.com/story/joint-action-against-online-video-piracy-in-china-2013-11-13**). In 2013, Chinese authorities closed the largest piracy website and arrested 30 employees.

The Results

56.com allowed the downloading of free movies, video games, and the like until about 2010. Disney did not seem to be too concerned with this. Its investment provides 56.com with a distribution channel for its Disney products that may provide a strategic advantage to Disney in China. In March 2009, Disney allowed YouTube to run short videos as well as full episodes of its ABC (a television station) and ESPN (Internet and television sports channel) networks under an ad-revenue sharing arrangement.

In August 2009, 56.com launched 'Kankan 56' (**kankan.56.com**), a fee-based innovative video content platform that provides user-paid benefits to original video authors, video makers, and copyright owners in exchange for video sharing. Video uploaders charge users for viewing and set their own prices, with 56.com taking a 10% commission; the video can be viewed for 15 days only. By 2014, 56.com was purchased by the social network RenRen.

Sources: Based on *56.com* (2009), Albanesius (2008), and McBride and Chao (2008).

LESSONS LEARNED FROM THE CASE

Copyright violation on the Internet is a major problem for creators and distributors of intellectual property such as software, movies, music, and books. The problem arises not only because it is difficult to monitor millions of users and their posts, but also because in many countries there is not a great deal of legal protection of copyrighted material; and even if there is, it is difficult and very expensive to enforce.

Protection of intellectual property is one of the major EC legal issues presented in this chapter. An overview of other intellectual property topics, and especially privacy, are also presented. A full analysis of legal and ethical issues is far beyond the scope of one chapter. For comprehensive treatment and case studies, see Mann and Winn (2008). This chapter also covers several societal issues related to EC, especially the potential environmental impacts from what is known as *"Green EC,"* and how societal issues may affect individual privacy and enjoyment of life.

Note: For a collection of free e-books, slide shows, and files and documents about ethical, social, and political issues in e-commerce, see **pwebs.net/i/internet-ethics**.

15.1   ETHICAL CHALLENGES AND GUIDELINES

Ethics is a set of moral principles or rules of how people are expected to conduct themselves. It specifies what is considered by society to be right or wrong.

Issues of privacy, ownership, control, and security must be confronted in implementing and understanding the ethical challenges of EC.

Ethical Principles and Guidelines

Public law embodies ethical principles, but the two are not the same. Acts that generally are considered unethical may not be illegal. Lying to someone may be unethical, but it is not illegal. Conversely, the law is not a collection of ethical norms, and not all ethical codes are incorporated into public law. Online File W15.1 shows a framework for ethical issues.

One example of an ethical issue is the Facebook class action lawsuit of 2009, described next.

Example: Who Owns User-Generated Content?

In August 2009, five Facebook users filed a class action lawsuit against Facebook, claiming that Facebook violated privacy laws by gathering online users' activity and providing their personal information to third parties without the users' permission. They also alleged that Facebook engages in data mining, without informing the users.

The objective of the data collection was to enable Facebook to sell their users' data to advertisers because Facebook needed more revenue sources. The Electronic Privacy Information Center filed a complaint with the FCC, alleging that Facebook's changes in privacy settings made users' information publicly available without giving the users the option to opt out. Facebook was found to be liable for violating the privacy of their users and amended their rules (see ComputerWeekly. com 2009). Facebook has continuously been modifying and changing its privacy settings, letting its users decide how much they want to share with the public.

Business Ethics

Business ethics (also known as *corporate* or *enterprise ethics*) is a code of values, behaviors, and rules, written or unwritten, for how people should behave in the business world. These ethics dictate the operations of organizations. For details, see Ferrell et al. (2012). For implementation considerations, see Business for Social Responsibility (**bsr.org**).

The Issues of Internet Abuse in the Workplace

In 2009, 24/7 Wall St. (**247wallst.com**) conducted a workplace study about how people spend time online. Their findings revealed that actual time wasted and productivity losses were staggering; about one-fourth of the hours spent online during the workday were spent on personal matters (per blog by Mike Plitzer; **plixer. com/blog/2010/10/page/4** October 6, 2010). In general, employees spent more than one hour per week on social media alone, followed by online games and e-mails. A majority of companies have banned access to social networks such as Facebook, Twitter, MySpace, and LinkedIn. In 2013, *SFGate* (per Gouveia 2013) conducted a survey in which they found that 69% of the employees were wasting time for 30 minutes to several hours per day. The top five employee "time wasters" were: checking news (37%), social networking (14%); online shopping (12%), and online entertainment (11%). For an article see **salary.com/2014-wasting-time-at-work**.

Managing Internet Abuse

Instead of banning the use of social networks in the workplace, some employers are following less draconian measures by setting the following policies in place: employees are encouraged to check their social networks only once or twice a day, consolidate their social networking streams, develop a clear social networking policy, and utilize technology made for consolidation. A social networking policy should communicate clear guidelines from employers to employees. For example, employees should not spend more than 20 minutes per day of company time browsing social networks.

Monitoring Employees: Is It Ethical?

Google and several other software application providers have incorporated new spyware on company smartphones given to employees, which enables employers to monitor the whereabouts of their employees using the smartphones' built-in GPS tracking systems. Google's Latitude enables companies to know their employees' location at all times. The ethical question is, whether this new power will be used by governments to invade the privacy of an individual's real-time whereabouts. In other words, rules and procedures for ethical behavior are needed for business people practicing EC. Two major risks are criminal charges and civil suits. Table 15.1 lists examples of safeguards to minimize exposure to those risks (also see Yamamura and Grupe 2008).

EC Ethical and Legal Issues

There are many EC- and Internet-related ethical issues that are related to legal issues (Himma and Tavani 2008). These issues are often categorized into intellectual property rights, privacy, free speech versus censorship, and fraud protection methods.

Table 15.1 Typical safeguards to minimize exposure to risk of criminal or civil charges

1. Does the website clearly post shipping policies and guarantees? Can the selling company fulfill its policies and guarantees? Does it comply with Federal Trade Commission (FTC) rules?
2. Does the website clearly articulate procedures for customers to follow when returning a shipment or when seeking a refund for products or services not received, or received in bad or damaged condition?
3. Has the company checked partners' backgrounds before entering into agreements with third-party vendors and supply chain partners? Do those agreements include protection of the company against all possible risks?
4. Is there sufficient customer support staff, and are they knowledgeable and adequately trained to process customers' inquiries?

- **Intellectual property rights.** Owner-ship and value of information and intel-lectual property. Intellectual property is difficult to protect on the Web. Owners are losing a substantial amount of money due to piracy (see Section 15.2).
- **Privacy.** Because it is so difficult to pro-tect the privacy of individuals on the Web, there are some countries that do not regulate privacy issues while others have strict anti-invasion rules (Section 15.3).
- **Free speech versus censorship.** Free speech on the Web may result in offensive and harmful attacks on individuals and organizations (Section 15.4). Therefore, some countries have decided to censor material on the Internet.
- **Consumer and merchant protection against fraud.** For e-commerce to suc-ceed, it is necessary to protect all trans-actions and participants against fraud (Section 15.5).

Examples of ethical issues discussed elsewhere in this book are channel conflict (Chapters 3 and 13), pricing conflict (Chapter 3), disintermedia-tion (Chapters 3, 4, and 13), and trust (Chapter 9). Two additional EC-related ethical issues are Internet use that is not work-related and code of ethics. See also **investopedia.com/terms/c/code-of-ethics.asp**.

Internet Use that Is Not Work-Related

As described earlier, a majority of employees use e-mail and surf the Web for purposes not related to work. The use of company property (i.e., com-puters, networks) for e-mail and Internet use may create risk and waste time. The degree of risk depends on the extent to which the company has implemented policies and procedures to prevent and detect illegal uses. For example, companies may be held liable for their employees' use of e-mail to harass other employees, participate in illegal gambling, or distribute child pornography (Gray 2010).

Code of Ethics

A practical and necessary approach to limiting Internet surfing that is not work-related is an Internet Acceptable Use Policy (AUP) to which all employees must conform. It includes EC, social networks, and any IT-related topics. Without a for-mal AUP, it is much more difficult to enforce acceptable and eliminate unacceptable behaviors and reprimand violators. Whenever a user signs on to the corporate network, the user should see a reminder of the AUP and be notified that online activities are monitored. Such notification should be a part of a code of ethics.

A corporate *code of ethics* sets out the rules and expected behaviors and actions of a company. Typically, the code of ethics should address the use of offensive content and graphics, as well as proprietary information. It should encourage employees to think about who should and who should not have access to information before they post it on the company's website. The code should specify whether the company allows employees to set up their own Web pages on the company intranet and provide policies regarding private e-mail usage and surfing during working hours. A company should formulate a general idea of the role it wants websites to play in the workplace. This should guide the company in developing an AUP and provide employees with a rationale for that policy. Finally, do not be surprised if the code of ethics looks a lot like simple rules of etiquette – it should. Table 15.2 lists several useful guidelines for a corporate Web policy. For a list of website quality guidelines, see Online File W15.2. For business ethics case studies, see **harpercollege. edu/~tmorris/ekin/resources.htm**.

SECTION 15.1 REVIEW QUESTIONS

1. List seven ethical issues related to EC.
2. List the major principles of ethics.
3. Define business ethics.
4. Give an example of an EC activity that is unethical but not illegal.
5. How can employees abuse the Internet? How do small companies handle this?
6. Describe the issues of monitoring employees.
7. List the major issues that should be included in a code of ethics.

Table 15.2 Corporate web policy guidelines

Issue written guidelines regarding employee use of the Internet, including e-mail, instant messaging and social network sites
Make it clear to employees that they cannot use copyrighted or trademarked material without permission
Post disclaimers concerning Web content that the company does not support
Post disclaimers of responsibility concerning content of online forums and chat sessions
Make sure that Web content and activity comply with the laws in other countries (if you are conducting business there), such as those governing intellectual property and privacy
Make sure that the company's Web content policy is consistent with your company's other policies
Appoint someone to monitor Internet legal and liability issues and have that person report to a senior executive or to a legal counsel
Have attorneys with cyberlaw expertise review Web content to make sure that there is nothing unethical or illegal on the company's website and that all required statements and disclaimers are properly included

15.2   INTELLECTUAL PROPERTY LAW AND COPYRIGHT INFRINGEMENT

The legal system is faced with the task of maintaining a delicate balance between preserving social order and protecting individual rights. Keep in mind that, when used in law, the term *individual* is broadly defined to mean a person, group of people, or other legal entity, such as an organization or corporation. In this section, we explain some types of intellectual property laws and the issues arising from EC.

Intellectual Property in E-Commerce

Intellectual property (IP) refers to property that derives from the creative work of an individual, such as literary or artistic work. Intellectual property can be viewed as the ownership of intangible assets, such as inventions, ideas, and creative work. It is a legal concept protected by patents, copyrights, trademarks, and trade secret law (known as **Intellectual Property Law**).

Intellectual property law also may be concerned with the regulation of thought-related products, including creativity. It affects such diverse subjects as the visual and performing arts, electronic databases, advertising, and video games. Creativity is a critical success factor in the business world, and is the foundation of innovation. See the World Intellectual Property Organization website (go to **wipo.int**).

There are various intellectual property law specialties, as shown in Table 15.3. Those specialty laws are interrelated and may even overlap.

Recording Movies, Shows and Other Events

A common method of infringement is to bring video cameras and video-capable cell phones to movie theaters and record the performances. PirateEye (**pirateeye.com**) is one of the companies that manufacture devices that discover and identify the presence of any digital recording device, monitor remotely in real time, and much more.

Copyright Infringement and Protection

Numerous high-profile lawsuits already have been filed regarding online copyright infringement related to EC and the Web (e.g., see the closing case in this chapter). A **copyright** is an exclusive legal right of an author or creator of intellectual property to publish, sell, license, distribute, or use such work in any desired way. In the United States, content is automatically protected by federal copyright laws as soon as a work is produced in a tangible shape or form. A copyright does not last forever; it is good for a set number of years after the death of the author or creator (e.g., 50 years in the United Kingdom). After the copyright expires, the work reverts to the public domain (or becomes publicly available). See **fairuse.stanford.edu/overview/public-domain** and **thepublicdomain.org**. In many cases, corporations own copyrights. In such a case, the copyrights will last 120 years, or even

Table 15.3 Intellectual property laws and the protections of intellectual property

Laws	Protection provided by the law
Intellectual property law	Protects the creative work of people
Patent law	Protects inventions and discoveries
Copyright law	Protects original works of authorship, such as music and literary works, artistic design and writing computer codes
Trademark law	Protects trademarks, logos, etc.
Trade secret law	Protects proprietary business information
Law of licensing	Enables owners of intellectual property to share it via licensing.
Law of unfair competition relating to counterfeiting and piracy	Protects against those who use illegal or unfair methods, or methods not available to others. Also against those pirating intellectual property

longer. The legal term for the use of a work without permission or contracting for payment of a royalty is **copyright infringement**.

File Sharing

One of the major methods of violating copyrights is *file sharing*. File sharing became popular in the late 1990s through facilitating companies such as Napster. One of the players in this area is The Pirate Bay (see the closing case to this chapter). The loss to copyright holders is estimated to be several billion dollars annually. The Recording Industry Association of America (RIAA) is fighting back.

Examples

The file sharing business is a major target of the RIAA, which shut down popular sites LimeWire LLC and Kazaa. Additionally, another popular file sharing site, Megaupload.com, was shut down in January 2012 (see Barakat 2012). However, the site was re-launched in January 2013 under the domain name **mega.co.nz**.

Legal Aspects of Infringement

In November 2010, the U.S. Senate Judiciary Committee approved the controversial Combating Online Infringement and Counterfeits Act (COICA) that provides the Attorney General with the power to shut down websites without a trial or court order if copyright infringement is considered to be the "central activity of the site" (see Gustin 2010). The problem is that, under this bill, most business websites are considered publishers (e.g., even when publishing an online sales brochure), and may be subject to disruptive investigations. (e.g., see Fogarty 2010). Note, this bill was still in debate as of May 2015.

The RIAA Industry Versus the Violators

To protect its interests, the RIAA uses selective lawsuits to stamp out rampant music piracy on the Internet. The RIAA spent more than $58 million in pursuit of targeted infringers between 2006 and 2008, yet collected less than $1.4 million (less than about 2%) from judgments (Frucci 2010).

However, since 2009, the number of lawsuits has been declining for several reasons. For example, see Bambauer (2010). Another example is Google's victory against Viacom's $1 billion copyright violation lawsuit. In 2013, Viacom lost its case against YouTube (the appellate court ruled in favor of Google). Finally, pending copyright infringement lawsuits are not favored because they are lengthy and very costly. As an alternative to direct lawsuits, the entertainment industry has begun developing digital rights management (DRM) policies to be enforced through the court system as well through federal legislation.

Globalization

Much of the media piracy occurs in other countries (e.g., Russia, China, and Sweden, as per the closing case of Pirate Bay), and therefore it is difficult to regulate. According to Doctorow (2012), most piracy occurs in developing countries.

Digital Rights Management (DRM)

Digital rights management (DRM) describes a system of protecting the copyrights of data circulated over the Internet or digital media. These arrangements are technology-based protection measures (via encryption or using watermarks). Typically, sellers own the rights to their digital content. In the past, when content was analog in nature, it was easier to buy a new copy of a copyrighted work in the form of a physical medium (e.g., paper, film, tape) than to produce such a copy independently. The quality of most copies often was inferior. Digital technologies make it possible to produce and distribute a high-quality duplicate of any digital recording with minimal effort and cost. The Internet virtually has eliminated the need for a physical medium to transfer a work, which has led to the use of DRM systems for protection. For details, see **eff.org/issues/drm**. However, DRM systems may restrict the *fair use* of material by individuals. In law, **fair use** refers to the limited use of copyrighted material, without paying a fee or royalty, for certain purposes (e.g., reviews, commentaries, teaching).

All is not simple when implementing DRM system applications. For example, Apple has a controlled ecosystem called 'jailbreaker.' In Apple's losing argument, the company claimed that jailbreaking should not be considered fair use, even though it provides great value to consumers (see Kravets 2010 and Anderson 2010).

Patents

According to Fedcirc.us, a **patent** is "an exclusive right to a particular invention. Patents are granted by states or governments to the creator of an invention, or to someone who has been designated by them to accept the rights over the invention. The holder of the patent has sole rights over the invention for a specified period of time" (e.g., 20 years for applications filed on or after June 8, 1995 in the United States and 20 years in the United Kingdom). Patents serve to protect the idea or design of the invention, rather than any tangible form of the invention. (For details, see **money.howstuffworks.com/question492.htm**, **internetpatentscorporation.net**, and the United States Patent and Trademark office (**uspto.gov**).

There is some discrepancy between the U.S. and Europe over the way certain patents are granted. For example, in 1999, Amazon.com successfully obtained a U.S. patent for its "1-Click" ordering and payment procedure. Using this patent, Amazon.com sued Barnes & Noble in 1999, alleging that its rival had copied its patented technology. Barnes & Noble was enjoined by the courts from using their "Express Lane" payment procedure. However, on May 12, 2006, the USPTO ordered a reexamination of the "1-Click" patent. In March 2010, the Amazon patent was rewritten in the U.S. to include only a shopping cart, and was approved as such. Nevertheless, Expedia and many other e-tailers use similar "checkout" systems today. See **en.wikipedia.org/wiki/1-Click**.

There is a big debate about granting patents for *business methods*. Companies may unknowingly use a business method, unaware that there is already a patent for that method. An example of a business method that was involved in litigation is Amazon's '1-click' ordering system. More than 13 years after Amazon's patent application, the patent was approved in Canada. For a discussion, see Kalanda (2012).

In legal cases involving business methods, some companies were allowed to avoid paying royalties, because they were unaware a patent for the business method already existed. The business methods patent is meant to protect new ways of doing business. In 2010, the Supreme Court ruled that patents cannot cover abstract ideas.

Another example of a legal case involving patents is when Canadian firm i4i Corporation sued Microsoft, for patent infringement, alleging that Microsoft had infringed i4i's patent relating to text manipulation software. Microsoft wanted the standard changed by which patents would be deemed invalid. Microsoft took the case all the way to the U.S. Supreme Court and lost. For details, see Greene (2011).

Oracle Versus Google

In following its legal right of enforcement, Oracle has been mining its newly acquired patent portfolio and actively seeking and suing infringers. In 2012, Oracle sued Google over its Android product for using Oracle's Java technology (copying Java code) without a license. While the trial court ruled that APIs are not subject to copyright, the appeals court disagreed, holding that Java's API packages were copyrightable, although it sent back the case to the trial court to determine whether or not Google's copying was a violation of the Fair Use Doctrine. As of June 2014, Google has not appealed this decision to the U.S. Supreme Court.

Trademarks

According to the USPTO, a *trademark* is "a word, phrase, symbol, and/or design that identifies and distinguishes the source of the goods of one party from those of others." A trademark is used by individuals, business organizations, or other legal entities to notify consumers of a unique source, and to tell the difference between a company's products or services and those of others. Although federal registration it is not necessary, there are several advantages, such as informing the public that the trademark belongs to the registrants, and giving them exclusive right of use (see **uspto. gov/trademarks/basics/definitions.jsp**.)

Trademark dilution is the use of a "famous" trademark by a third party, which causes the lessening (or dilution) of the 'distinguishing quality' of the mark (see **bitlaw.com/trademark/dilution.html**). In 1996, the Federal Trademark Dilution Act (FTDA) was enacted to safeguard well-known trademarks from third-party users. In 2006, the Trademark Dilution Revision Act (TDRA) was passed, which amended the earlier law. For details and a comprehensive discussion on trademark dilution, see Owens (2011).

In 2008, eBay won a landmark trademark case against Tiffany, a leading jewelry retailer, who had sued eBay alleging that many of the items being advertised on eBay as Tiffany merchandise were actually fakes. The U.S. court ruled in 2008 that eBay cannot be held liable for trademark infringements "based solely on their generalized knowledge that trademark infringement might be occurring on their websites" (Savitz 2008).

Fan and Hate Sites

Fan and hate websites are part of the Internet self-publishing and user-generated content (UGC) phenomena that includes blogging. Fan sites may violate intellectual property rights. For example, some people illegally obtain copies of new movies or TV shows and create sites that compete with the legal sites of the movie or TV producer, even before the legal site is activated. Although the producers can get a court order to shut such sites down, new sites can appear the next day. In contrast with fan websites, there are *hate websites* that disseminate negative comments about corporations and individuals, and can cause problems for them.

Many hate sites are directed against large corporations (e.g., Walmart, Microsoft, Nike).

Cyberbashing

Associated with hate sites is **cyberbashing**, which is the registration of a domain name that criticizes (normally maliciously) an organization, product, or person (e.g., **paypalsucks.com**, **walmartsucks.org**, **verizonpathetic.com**).

SECTION 15.2 REVIEW QUESTIONS

1. What is intellectual property law? How is it helpful to creators and inventors?
2. Define DRM. Describe one potential impact on privacy and one drawback.
3. What is meant by "fair use"? How does the "jailbreaking" of iPhones fall under "fair use"?
4. Define trademark infringement and discuss why trademarks need to be protected from dilution.
5. Describe fan and hate sites. How do they benefit society? Should they be more regulated?
6. Define cyberbashing. Should attempts to expose unscrupulous corporate activities be banned?

15.3 PRIVACY RIGHTS, PROTECTION, AND FREE SPEECH

Privacy has several meanings and definitions. In general, privacy is the state of not being disturbed by others, being free from others' attention, and having the right to be left alone and not to be intruded upon. (For other definitions of privacy, see the Privacy Rights Clearinghouse at **privacy-rights.org**.) Privacy has long been a legal, ethical, and social issue in most countries.

The reason for privacy concerns stems from the fact that in using the Internet, users are asked to provide some personal data in exchange for access to information (such as getting coupons, other downloads, etc.). Data and Web mining companies receive and gather the collected data. As a result, users' privacy may be violated (e.g., Stein 2011; and a slide presentation titled "Your Data, Yourself" by Justyne Cerulli at **prezi.com/ fgxmaftxrxke/your-data-yourself**).

Privacy rights protection is one of the most debated and frequently emotional issues in EC and social commerce. According to Leggatt (2012), in a survey conducted by TRUSTe, 90% of Internet users "were found to worry about their online privacy." Here we explore the major aspects of the problem as it relates to social networking. Many EC activities involve privacy issues ranging from collection of information by Facebook to the use of RFID. Here is an example.

Example: Google Glass
In May 2013, eight lawmakers, concerned about Google Glass (and other smart glasses), wrote a letter to Google asking what the company planned do to protect people's privacy. See Guynn (2013) for a description.

Social Networks Changing the Landscape of Privacy and Its Protection

Today's youth seem to be less concerned about privacy than they were in the past. The younger generations are more interested in blogs, photos, social networking, and texting. Attitudes about what constitutes private information are changing. As a result, there are new opportunities for marketers and marketing communication, mainly in offering experiences that are better personalized, which do not violate Internet user privacy. See Bhargava (2010) for a discussion.

This problem has been articulated by Andrews (2012), who studied privacy protection in social networks and concluded that very little privacy protection exists (e.g., college applicants are being rejected because of what they posted on the social networks; criminals read posts about vacations to know when to break into an empty house).

However, in May 2014, Facebook announced the addition of the 'Anonymous Login' feature and changes in login procedures, which allow users to try apps without sharing personal information from Facebook.

Information Pollution and Privacy
Information pollution (presented in Chapter 14), the adding of irrelevant, unsolicited information, may raise privacy issues such as the spreading of misinformation about individuals. In addition, polluted information used by decision makers or by UGC may cause invasion of privacy.

Global View
Note that the issue of privacy on the Internet is treated differently in different countries. For example, in November 2009, Google was sued in Switzerland over privacy concerns regarding its Street View application (Pfanner 2009). In 2012, the Swiss highest court ruled that Google may document residential street fronts with its Street View technology, but imposed some limitations on the kinds of images the company can take (e.g., lowering the height of its Street View cameras so they would not peer over garden walls and hedges). For more about the court's decision and the reaction of the parties, see O'Brien and Streitfeld (2012). In June 2013, the European Union highest court determined that government agencies cannot force Google to remove links to personal material. However, in May 2014, Europe's highest court ruled that people should have the right to say what information is available when someone Googles them. The ruling applies to 28 nations and all search engines (Google, Bing) in Europe. The decision does not apply to the U.S. or any other country outside Europe (see Sterling 2014).

Privacy Rights and Protection

Today, virtually all U.S. states and the federal government (and many other countries) recognize the right to privacy, but few government agencies actually follow all the statutes (e.g., citing reasons of national security). One reason is that the definition of privacy can be interpreted quite broadly. However, the following two rules have been followed closely in past U.S. court decisions: (1) the right to privacy is not absolute. Privacy must be balanced against the needs of society; (2) the public's "right to know" is superior to the individual's right to privacy. The vagueness of the two rules shows why it is sometimes difficult to determine and enforce privacy regulations.

Section 5 of the Federal Trade Commission Act protects privacy. For an explanation of the FTC Act, see **ftc.gov/news-events/media-resources/protecting-consumer-privacy**. Those practices extend to protecting consumer privacy, including the "do not track" option, protecting consumers' financial privacy, and the Children's Online Privacy Protection Act (COPPA).

Opt-In and Opt-Out

Privacy concerns have been overshadowed by post-9/11 counterterrorism activities, but consumers still want their data protected. One way to manage this issue is the *opt-in* and *opt-out* system, generally used by direct marketing companies. **Opt-out** is a method that gives consumers the choice to refuse to share information about themselves, or to avoid receiving unsolicited information. Offering the choice to opt-out is good customer practice, but it is difficult to opt out in some industries, either because consumer demand for opting out is low or the value of the customer information is high.

In contrast, **opt-in** is based on the principle that consumers must approve in advance what information they receive from a company, or allow a company to share their information with third parties. That is, information sharing should not occur unless customers affirmatively allow or request it.

See also the Direct Marketing Association (**thedma.org**) for information and resources on consumers' ad choices, opt-in and opt-out, privacy, identity theft, and more.

According to IBM (2008a), the following six practices for implementing a successful privacy project are:

1. **Get organized.** This can be done by creating a cross-functional privacy team for guidance.
2. **Define the privacy protection needs.** Decide what needs to be protected.
3. **Conduct inventory of data.** List and analyze all data that need protection.
4. **Select solution(s).** Choose and implement a solution that protects privacy.
5. **Test a prototype system.** Create a prototype of the system and test it under different conditions.
6. **Expand the project scope.** Expand the project to encompass other applications.

For further information on privacy protection, see IBM (2008a) and the International Association of Privacy Professionals (**privacyassociation.org**).

Some Measures of Privacy Protection

Several government agencies, communities, and security companies specialize in privacy protection. Representative examples in the U.S. include the Consumer Privacy Guide (**consumerprivacyguide.org/law**), Privacy Protection (**privacyprotect.org/about-privacyprotection**), Privacy Choice (**privacychoice.org**), and Home PC Firewall Guide (**firewallguide.com/privacy.htm**). Finally, Cagaoan et al. (2014) describe the issue of privacy awareness in e-commerce. Other issues are reported by Shah et al. (2013).

Free Speech Online Versus Privacy Protection

Although the First Amendment of the U.S. Constitution grants the right to free speech, as with many rights, the right to free speech is not unlimited. The First Amendment does not give citizens the right to say absolutely anything to anyone. Defamation laws (including privacy violations), child pornography, fighting words, and terrorist threats are some of the traditional restrictions on what may be said freely. For example, it is illegal to scream "fire" in a crowded theater or make bomb threats in an airport, but there is no law against taking pictures in public places. Free speech often conflicts with privacy, protection of children, indecency, and so forth. For a discussion of the First Amendment and the ten rights it does not grant, see **people.howstuffworks. com/10-rights-first-amendment-does-not-grant.htm#page=1**.

Even in the United Kingdom, there is an increasing risk of police stopping citizens for taking photographs in a public place. In 2010, police questioned amateur photographer Bob Patefield under "anti-terrorist legislation," and later arrested him for "antisocial behavior" (e.g., taking pictures of Christmas decorations, which the police deemed to be "suspicious behavior"). Patefield videotaped his arrest and posted it on the Internet for public viewing (see Lewis and Domokos 2010 for the video and **theguardian. com/uk/2010/feb/21/photographer-films-anti-terror-arrest** for the story).

Example

Anthony Graber, a motorcyclist in Maryland was stopped by a plainclothes state police officer driving an unmarked car. He filmed his own traffic stop by using a camera attached to his motorcycle helmet. He posted his video on YouTube in March 2010, and as a result, was charged with violating state wiretap laws for audio recording the officers and posting the video on the Internet without police consent. Graber was arrested and faced up to 16 years in prison for this undisclosed recording. He pled guilty to speeding, but fought the charge of illegal monitoring, citing Freedom of Speech as a defense. The court ruled that the state trooper had "no legal expectation of privacy," and that videotaping is protected under the First Amendment. The court dismissed all of Graber's charges, except for the traffic violations.

See **youtube.com/watch?v=QNcDGqzAB30&f eature=related**.

Free Speech Online Versus Child Protection Debate

The debate over free speech versus child protection began in December 2000, after the *Children's Internet Protection Act (CIPA)*, which mandated the use of filtering techniques in libraries and schools that receive federal funding, was signed into law. For details of the debate regarding public libraries, see ACLU of Washington State (2006). In June 2003, the Supreme Court handed down a ruling that the CIPA was constitutional, allowing Congress to require some kinds of blocking, but the filters must not block too much material. Their review represented the third time justices had heard arguments pitting free speech against attempts to protect children from offensive online content. In 2001, the FCC issued rules implementing CIPA, and updated those rules in 2011. (For background and requirements of CIPA, see the FCC Children's Internet Protection Act at **fcc.gov/ guides/childrens-internet-protection-act**.)

The Price of Protecting an Individual's Privacy

In the past, gathering information about individuals, that was residing in government agencies' databases, was difficult and expensive to do, which helped protect privacy. The Internet, in combination with powerful computers, and targeting algorithms with access to large-scale databases, have in all practical terms, eliminated the barriers of protecting citizens' privacy.

In the UK in 2010, Heathrow airport security officials were caught circulating printouts of a Bollywood star's full naked body scans downloaded from the full-body security scanners. However, authorities feel that the scanning process is necessary for airport security. Today's technology even enables monitoring people's activities from a distance, which may be considered a violation of their privacy, as shown in Case 15.1.

CASE 15.1: SCHOOL ADMINISTRATORS USED WEBCAMS TO SPY ON STUDENTS AT HOME

Unbeknownst to the students in a Pennsylvania high school, administrators were caught spying on the activities of the underage students. The administrators did this by remotely activating webcams built into each laptop that was issued to the students by the Lower Merion School District, without the permission or knowledge of the students or their parents.

The continued surveillance of the students, even while they were at home, by school officials at Harriton High School revealed that one student was conducting what the school defined as "improper behavior." Based on the video taken at his home, the student was confronted at the school by the assistant principal, and shown "photographic evidence." The school told the parents that they can do such monitoring. As a result, one student filed a class action lawsuit representing all the students who received laptops, for invasion of privacy and illegal interception of private information. The case was settled in October 2010 and the school district paid $610,000. In 2011, the same school district was sued by a former student over the secret monitoring of laptops in 2009.

Sources: Based on Hill (2010), Schreiber (2010), Lattanzio (2010), and **courthousenews. com/2010/02/18/Eyes.pdf** (accessed June 2014).

Questions

1. What legitimate excuse could be made to justify this behavior? Why should the school's actions be stopped?
2. What federal laws were broken? What rights in the U.S. Constitution were violated?
3. What precedent did this decision set? Can you see a way that schools will be allowed to continue this behavior for a narrowly construed purpose?
4. Find other similar cases.

Here is another example of freedom of speech on the Internet conflicting with public safety.

Example: Sheriff Sues Craigslist to Curb Prostitution

The Sheriff of Cook County, Illinois, filed a federal lawsuit in March 2009, alleging that Craigslist had become the top provider of prostitution services in the United States.

The sheriff wanted Craigslist to shut down the erotic services category of its website and compensate his department for the cost of prosecuting website-related prostitution cases. However, advocates for free speech on the Web argued that existing laws insulate Craigslist from any illegal activities related to its ads, and they predicted the sheriff's legal action would not prevail. For details, see San Miguel (2009). Nonetheless, in May 2009, Craigslist removed the "erotic services" category altogether. Craigslist then developed an "adult services" section where they vetted all material before allowing it to be posted. Moreover, in September 2010, Craigslist closed all adult services ads on its site (Miller 2010).

How Information About Individuals Is Collected and Used Online

An individual's private data can be gathered in a number of ways over the Internet. Representative examples of the ways that the Internet can be used to find information about an individual are provided next; the first three are the most common ways of gathering information on the Internet.

- By a user completing a registration form including personal data
- By tracking users' movement on the Web (e.g., by using cookies)
- By using spyware, keystroke logging, and similar methods
- By website registration
- By reading an individual's blog(s) or social network postings
- By looking up an individual's name and identity in an Internet directory or social network profile

- By reading an individual's e-mail, IM, or text messages (hacking)
- By monitoring employees in real time
- By wiretapping conversations over communication lines
- By using wearables such as smart glasses (Chapter 6), including invisible ones (see Leonhard 2014).

We describe some of the above issues next.

Website Registration

Virtually all B2C sites, marketing websites, online magazines, vendors, government sites, and social networks ask visitors to fill out registration forms. During the process, individuals voluntarily provide information such as their name, address, phone number, e-mail address, hobbies, likes or dislikes, and other personal information in order to participate in some free activity, download a paper or read an article, win a lottery, or receive some other benefit. The site might use the information it collected to improve customer service, or it might sell the information to third parties (e.g., other businesses), where it is possible that the information could be used inappropriately.

Internet users are not too happy about giving such information to online businesses. Most people dislike registering at websites they visit and 15% refuse to register. Many do not trust companies that request such information and do not want to share their personal information. In 2012, Facebook was accused by a German advocacy group of allegedly violating privacy laws in Germany. The group wanted Facebook to stop giving to third parties Facebook users' private information until Facebook receive explicit consent from the users. Although Facebook did not admit any wrongdoing, they agreed to cooperate.

Cookies

A popular way for a website to gather information about an individual is by using cookies. As described in Chapter 9, *cookies* enable websites to keep track of users' online movements without asking the users for permission.

Originally, cookies were designed to help with personalization and market research; however, cookies can also be used to disseminate unsolicited commercial information. Cookies allows vendors to collect detailed information about a user's online behavior. The personal data collected by cookies often are more accurate than information provided by users, because users have a tendency to falsify information while filling out registration forms. Although the ethical use of cookies is still being debated, concerns about cookies reached a peak in 1997 at the U.S. FTC hearings on online privacy. Following those hearings, Netscape and Microsoft introduced options enabling users to *block cookies*. Since that time, the uproar surrounding cookies has subsided because most users accept cookies or know how to delete them. The problem with deleting or disabling cookies is that the user will have to keep reentering information each time she or he return to a website, because of not being recognized and, in some instances, may be blocked from viewing useful pages.

Cookies can be successfully deleted by informed users with programs such as: Cookie Monster and CCleaner; to delete and manage flash cookies, see **flashcookiecleaner.com**. By setting the privacy levels on Web browsers very high, cookies from all websites are blocked, and existing cookies cannot be read.

Spyware as a Threat to Privacy and Intellectual Property

In Chapter 10, we discussed **spyware** as a tool that some merchants use to gather information about users without their knowledge. Spyware infections are a major threat to privacy and intellectual property.

Spyware may enter the user's computer as a virus or as a result of the user clicking some innocent looking, but harmful, links. Spyware is effective in illegally tracking users' Internet surfing habits. Using spyware clearly is an invasion of the computer user's privacy and may be illegal. It can also slow down computer performance. While specific spyware can harvest data, it can also be used to take pictures from an unsuspecting user's Webcam and e-mail or post the photos all over the Internet.

Sophisticated tracking technology is being installed into the computers of unsuspecting Internet users. While most are innocuous, some tools include malware, which can cause major damage. The information collected on individuals by spyware is frequently exchanged or sold on the online black market (Chapter 10).

Unfortunately, antivirus software and Internet firewalls cannot always detect all spyware; therefore, extra protection is needed. Many free and low-cost antispyware software packages are available. Representative free antispyware programs are Lavasoft's Ad-Aware (**lavasoft.com**), Microsoft security essentials (**windows.microsoft.com/en-us/windows/security-essentials-download**), and AVG (**avg.com**). Programs that charge a fee include Trend Micro (**trendmicro.com**) and Kaspersky Lab (**usa.kaspersky.com**). Upgraded versions of free programs are also available for a fee. Symantec and other companies that provide Internet security services also provide anti-spyware software.

Even if you use antispyware on your home computer, your smartphone and your PC or tablet that use public Wi-Fi connections may be giving out your personal information by transmitting your location back to your cell phone/Internet provider about every seven seconds. Government supercomputers are capable of reading every e-mail sent, listening to every mobile conversation, reading every text message, knowing every user's location (e.g., GPS), and following every credit card purchase besides tracking every website visited by Internet users around the globe. Records about when you are at church, school, work, a political rally, or a hospital or clinic are stored for months or even years.

RFID's Threat to Privacy

Although several states have mandated or are considering legislation to protect customers from loss of privacy due to RFID tags, as mentioned in Online Tutorial T2 and in Chapter 12, privacy advocates fear that the information stored on RFID tags or collected with them may violate an individual's privacy.

Other Methods

Other methods of collecting data about people are:

- **Site transaction logs.** These logs show what users are doing on the Internet.
- **EC ordering systems and shopping carts.** These features permit sellers to know buyers' ordering history.
- **Search engines.** Search engines can be used to collect information about users' areas of interest.
- **Web 2.0 tools.** Blogs, discussion groups, chatting, social networks, etc. contain a wealth of information about users' activities and personalities.
- **Behavioral targeting.** Using tools to learn people's preferences (Chapter 9).
- **Polling and surveys.** People's demographics, thoughts, and opinions are collected in surveys.
- **Payment information and e-wallets.** These may include sensitive information about shoppers.

Monitoring Employees

There are several issues concerning Internet use at work and employee privacy. In addition to wasting time online, employees may disclose trade secrets and possibly make employers liable for defamation based on their actions on the corporate website. In response to these concerns, many companies monitor their employees' e-mail and Web surfing activities. One tool that enables companies to monitor their employees is Google Location, which works in combination with a compatible device (e.g., Android, iOS).

Example: The Ontario Versus Quon Case

In 2003, a police sergeant named Jeff Quon and three other officers sued the City of Ontario, California, alleging Fourth Amendment violations. The case involved text messages sent and received by Sergeant Quon and his colleagues on pagers issued to them by the City. Because Quon exceeded the allotted number of messages allowed by the City, the City conducted an audit by reviewing the text messages and found that the vast majority of Quon's messages (as many as 80 per day while he was on duty) were not work-related, and many were sexually explicit. However, the City claimed that since the text messages fell under the City's public information policy, they would be eligible for auditing. While a lower court in California sided with the City, in 2008, the appellate court reversed the decision, ruling that the search was unreasonable. However, the City appealed to the U.S. Supreme Court, which issued a ruling in 2010, holding that the City's review of the text messages did not violate Quon or his co-plaintiffs' Fourth Amendment rights (see Sager et al. 2010 and **oyez.org/ cases/2000-2009/2009/2009_08_1332**).

The issue of monitoring employees is complex and debatable because of the possibility of invasion of privacy. For comprehensive coverage, see PRC (2014). For more about employers and Internet usage monitoring, see **wisegeek.org/ how-do-employers-monitor-internet-usage-at-work.htm**.

Privacy Protection by Information Technologies

Dozens of software programs and IT policies and procedures are available to protect your privacy. Some were defined in Chapter 10. Representative examples are:

- **Platform for Privacy Preferences Project (P3P).** Software that communicates privacy policies (described later in this chapter).
- **Encryption.** Software programs such as PKI for encrypting e-mail, payment transactions, and other documents.
- **Spam blocking.** Built into browsers and e-mail; blocks pop-ups and unwanted mail.

- **Spyware blocking.** Detects and removes spyware and adware; built into some browsers.
- **Cookie managers.** Prevents the computer from accepting cookies; identifies and blocks specific types of cookies.
- **Anonymous e-mail and surfing.** Allows you to send e-mail and surf without leaving a history.

Privacy Policies

A useful practice for companies is to disclose their privacy policies to their customers. For an example, see **arvest.com/pdfs/about/arvest_bank_privacy_notice.pdf.**

Privacy Issues in Web 2.0 Tools and Social Networks

The rise in social network use raises some special issues of privacy and free speech. Here are a few examples.

Presence, Location-Based Systems, and Privacy

Establishing real time connections in the social networking world is an important activity. For example, Facebook offers Nearby Friends, an app that enables users to know where their friends are.

IBM has presence capabilities in its Lotus Software Connections (now called IBM Connections; **ibm.com/software/products/en/conn**), while Microsoft offers similar capabilities with Share-Point (**office.microsoft.com/en-us/sharepoint**). Apple, Google, and other companies offer similar features. Several social networks enable people to share their location with others. What are the privacy implications of such capabilities if used by businesses to locate customers and goods? Who will be held responsible or legally liable for unforeseen harm resulting from so much awareness and connectivity?

Obviously, clear policies are needed to govern what social networks can do with all the data they collect about people.

Privacy Protection by Ethical Principles

Some ethical principles that exist for the collection and use of personal information also apply to information collected in e-commerce. Some of these principles were discussed in Sections 15.1 and 15.2. Examples are: proper notification about the possible use of personal data, option of opting-in and/or opting-out, accessibility to stored data, keeping consumers' data secured, and the ability to enforce related policies.

The broadest law in scope is the Communications Privacy and Consumer Empowerment Act (1997), which requires, among other things, that the FTC enforces online privacy rights in EC, including the collection and use of personal data. For the status of pending legislation in the United States, see **govtrack.us/congress/bills/subjects/right_of_privacy/5910**.

The USA Patriot Act Versus Privacy

The USA PATRIOT Act (abbreviation of 'Uniting and Strengthening America by Providing Appropriate Tools Required to Intercept and Obstruct Terrorism') was passed in October 2001, in the aftermath of the 9/11 terrorist attacks. Its intent is to give law enforcement agencies broader capabilities in their efforts to protect the public. However, the American Civil Liberties Union (ACLU), the Electronic Freedom Foundation (EFF), and other organizations have raised grave concerns, including (1) expanded surveillance with reduced checks and balances, (2) overbreadth with a lack of focus on terrorism, and (3) rules that would allow U.S. foreign intelligence agencies to spy on Americans more easily.

A report by the U.S. Department of Justice (DOJ) in March 2007 found that the FBI had misused the Act to obtain thousands of telephone, business, and financial records from Americans without prior judicial approval. The result was that Congress amended some parts of the Act to require judicial approval prior to the FBI accessing sensitive information.

For highlights of the USA Patriot Act, see the U.S. Department of Justice website (go to **justice.gov/archive/ll/highlights.htm**).

Government Spying on Its Citizens

At issue here is the proper balance between personal privacy and national security, whereby innovation and commerce is not stifled. The claim is that social networking sites have technology that has outpaced government law enforcement capabilities. The laws on the books do not cover new communication methods (i.e., texting and social networking). Opponents see this as nothing more than unbridled government eavesdropping (Nakashima 2010). For other aspects, see Mercola (2012). During 2013 and 2014, it was found that the U.S. government did spy on its citizens. In 2014, efforts were taken to minimize such government surveillance.

P3P Privacy Platform

The **Platform for Privacy Preferences Project (P3P)** is a protocol for privacy protection on the Web developed by the World Wide Web Consortium (W3C). According to W3C, an international standards organization for the Web, the "Platform for Privacy Preferences Project (P3P) enables websites to express their privacy practices in a standard format that can be retrieved automatically and interpreted easily by user agents" (per **w3.org/P3P**). The W3C also explains that P3P is useful because "P3P uses machine readable descriptions to describe the collection and use of data. Sites implementing such policies make their practices explicit and thus open them to public scrutiny." This exposure can increase users' trust and confidence in e-commerce sites and vendors. Figure 15.1 shows the process of P3P.

Privacy Protection in Countries Other than the United States

In 1998, the European Union passed a privacy directive (EU Data Protection Directive) reaffirming the principles of personal data protection in the Internet age. This directive protects privacy more than U.S. protection laws do.

In many countries, the debate about the rights of the individual versus the rights of society continues. In some countries, like China, there is little protection of an individual's Internet privacy.

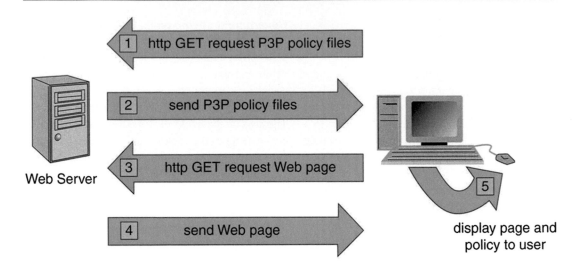

A Simple http Transaction with P3P Added   Source: U.S. Department of Commerce (2009).

Figure 15.1 How P3P Works

SECTION 15.3 REVIEW QUESTIONS

1. Define privacy and free speech. Do your definitions depend on technology?
2. List some of the ways that the Internet can collect information about individuals.
3. What are cookies and spyware, and what do they have to do with online privacy?
4. Describe information pollution and privacy.
5. List four common ethical principles related to the gathering of personal information.
6. Describe privacy issues in social networks. What are the dangers?
7. Define P3P and describe its objectives and procedures.

15.4 OTHER EC LEGAL ISSUES

During the last 10 years, a large number of laws dealing with EC and the Internet have been enacted. Representative major issues are listed in Online File W15.3.

Note that we discussed some of these issues in previous sections. Note also that legal issues are country or even state-dependent. For comprehensive coverage of these, see Davidson (2009) and Mallor et al. (2009). You can find a comprehensive e-commerce law blog at **ecommercelaw. typepad.com.**

Selected Legal and Regulatory Environment: E-Discovery and Cyberbullying

The legal and regulatory environment related to EC is very broad (e.g., see Alghamdi 2011).

Here, we briefly describe two issues: e-discovery and cyberbullying.

E-Discovery

Electronic discovery (e-discovery) refers to the process of finding any type of electronic data (e.g., text, images, videos) by using computerized systems. A major application of e-discovery is its use of finding evidence in legal cases. For details, see **en.wikipedia.org/wiki/Electronic_discovery**.

E-discovery deals frequently with e-mail archives. E-mail is the prime target of e-discovery requests. E-discovery must have features such as full-content index, keyword search, and metadata index. For e-discovery tools for aiding compliance and saving money, see Kontzer (2012).

E-Discovery and Social Networks

Speaking of discovery, should families of the recently deceased get access to their loved one's social network(s) after they die? How do you manage privacy in the afterlife?

Several social networks have developed policies for such cases. For example, Facebook has developed several policies for the accounts of its users who have passed away. A useful tool is Deathswitch (**deathswitch.com**), an automated system that sends you password requests on a regular schedule to make sure you are still alive. Also see the password manager, PasswordBox.

Cyberbullying

According to **stopybullying.gov**, **cyberbullying** is "bullying that takes place using electronic technology. Electronic technology includes devices and equipment such as cell phones, computers and tablets as well as communication tools including social media sites, text messages, chat, and websites." Examples of cyberbullying include mean text messages or e-mails, rumors sent by e-mail or posted on social networking sites, and embarrassing pictures, videos, websites, or fake profiles (per **stopbullying.gov/cyberbullying/what-is-it/index.html**). Bullying means "unwanted, aggressive behavior among school aged children that involves a real or perceived power imbalance." Examples of bullying are "actions such as making threats, spreading rumors, attacking someone physically or verbally, and excluding someone from a group on purpose" (per **stopbullying.gov/what-is-bullying/definition/index.html**). Unfortunately, adults can also be victims of bullying (see **bullyingstatistics.org/content/adult-bullying.html**).

The National Science foundation (**nsf.gov**) published a series titled "Bullying in the Age of Social Media," which describes how cyberbullying is done, its possible damage to people (some commit suicide), and how to manage it. For legislation and awareness campaigns see **cyberbullying.us** and **stopcyberbullying.org**.

A Sample of Other Issues

Here is a list of other EC legal issues:
- Legalizing Internet gambling (Parry 2013)
- Web monopoly by giant companies (Google, Tencent in China).
- Use of social media sites for prostitution
- Regulating online P2P money lenders.

Protection is needed not only for buying goods, but also from buying services. In Chapter 3, we describe online stock trading as an example.

SECTION 15.4 REVIEW QUESTIONS

1. List some of the issues that EC will face in the coming years that will affect your daily life.
2. Define e-discovery. How is it related to the law? To e-commerce?
3. Define cyberbullying. What damages can it cause?

15.5 CONSUMER AND SELLER PROTECTION FROM ONLINE FRAUD

The 2013 Internet Crime Report issued by the FBI Internet Crime Complaint Center (IC3) (**ic3.gov/media/annualreport/2013_IC3Report.pdf**) revealed that in 2013, the IC3 received 262,813 complaints, with a total adjusted dollar loss of about $781 million.

It is necessary to protect EC consumers, which the IC3 attempts to do, by informing the public about Internet scams by publishing public service announcements. Auction fraud is also developing into a major issue, and is one of the main sources of overall Internet fraud (see Gavish and Tucci 2008).

Consumer (Buyer) Protection

Consumer protection is critical to the success of any commerce, especially electronic, where transactions between buyers and sellers are not face-to-face. The Federal Trade Commission (FTC) enforces consumer protection laws in the United States (see **ftc.gov**). The FTC provides a list of common online scams (see **onguardonline.gov/articles/0002-common-online-scams**). In addition, the European Union and the United States are attempting to develop joint consumer protection policies. For details, see the Trans Atlantic Consumer Dialogue website at **tacd.org**.

Representative Tips and Sources for Your Protection

Protecting consumers is an important topic for government agencies, vendors, professional associations, and consumer protection organizations. These agencies provide many tips on how to protect consumers online. A representative list follows:

- Users should make sure that they enter the real website of well-known companies, such as Walmart, Disney, and Amazon. com, by going directly to the site, rather than through a link.
- Check any unfamiliar site for an address and telephone and fax numbers. Call and quiz a salesperson about the company and the products.
- Investigate sellers with the local chamber of commerce, Better Business Bureau (**bbb.org**), or TRUSTe (**truste.com**).
- Investigate how secure the seller's site is and how well it is organized.
- Examine the money-back guarantees, warranties, and service agreements before making a purchase.
- Compare prices online with those in regular stores – prices that are too low may be too good to be true.
- Ask friends what they know about the websites. Find testimonials and endorsements (be careful, some may be biased).
- Find out what remedy is available in case of a dispute.
- Consult the National Consumers League Fraud Center (**fraud.org**).
- Check the resources available at **consumerworld.org**.
- Amazon.com provides comprehensive protection. See **webstore.amazon.com/Fraud-Protection-Power/b/9437355011.**

In addition to these tips, consumers and shoppers also have rights on the Internet, as described in the following list of sources:

- The Federal Trade Commission (**ftc. gov**): Protecting America's Consumers. Abusive e-mail should be forwarded to spam@uce.go. For tips and advice see **ftc.gov/tips-advice**.

- National Consumers League Fraud Center (**fraud.org**).
- Federal Citizen Information Center (**gsa.gov/portal/category/101011**).
- U.S. Department of Justice (**justice.gov**).
- Internet Crime Complaint Center (**ic3. gov/default.aspx**).
- The American Bar Association provides online shopping tips at **safeshopping.org.**
- The Better Business Bureau (**bbb.org**).
- The U.S. Food and Drug Administration provides information on buying medicine and medical products online (**www. fda.gov/forconsumers/protectyourself/default.htm**).
- The Direct Marketing Association (**thedma.org**).
- Privacy Rights Clearinghouse (**privacyrights.org**): Provides information on different types of privacy, including online privacy and technology, identity theft, and junk mail.

Disclaimer: This is general information on consumer rights. It is not legal advice on how any particular individual should proceed. If you require specific legal advice, consult an attorney.

Third-Party Assurance Services
Several public organizations and private companies also attempt to protect consumers. The following are just a few examples.

Protection by a Third-Party Intermediary
Intermediaries who manage electronic markets try to protect buyers and sellers. A good example is eBay, which provides an extensive protection program (see eBay Money Back Guarantee (**pages.ebay.com/coverage/index.html**) and a Dispute Resolution Center).

TRUSTe's "Trustmark."
TRUSTe (**truste.com**) is a for-profit company whose mission is to ensure that "businesses adhere to best practices regarding the collection

and use of personal information on their website" (see **truste.com/about-TRUSTe**). Exhibiting the TRUSTe Advertising Affiliate "Trustmark" (a seal of quality) facilitates consumer confidence in business conducted online. The TRUSTe seal identifies sites that have agreed to comply with responsible information-gathering guidelines. In addition, the TRUSTe website provides its members with a "privacy policy wizard," which helps companies create their own privacy policies. The site offers several types of seals for different purposes such as for privacy, children, e-health, wireless, e-mail services, and international services.

The TRUSTe program is voluntary. The licensing fee for use of the Trustmark is paid by sellers, depending on the size of the online business. Many websites are certified as TRUSTe participants, including AT&T, IBM, The Walt Disney Company, AOL, Infoseek, the *New York Times,* and eBay. However, some merchants fear that signing with TRUSTe could expose them to litigation from third parties if they fail to comply exactly with TRUSTe rules, and that fear is likely to deter some companies from joining the program.

Better Business Bureau

The Better Business Bureau (BBB), a private non-profit organization supported largely by membership, collects and provides reports on businesses that consumers can review before making a purchase. The BBB responds to millions of inquiries each year. The BBB also handles customer disputes against businesses. Its BBBOnLine program (**bbb.org/online/customer/default.aspx**) is similar to TRUSTe's Trustmark. The goal of the program is to promote confidence on the Internet through two different seals. Companies that meet the BBBOnLine standards for the Reliability Seal are members of the local BBB and have good truth-in-advertising and consumer service practices. Those that exhibit the BBBOnLine Privacy Seal on their websites have an online privacy protection policy and standards for handling consumers' personal information. In addition, consumers are able to click on the BBBOnLine seals and instantly get a BBB report on the participating company.

Which?

Supported by the European Union, Which? (**which.co.uk**) gives consumers protection by ensuring that online traders under its Which? Web Trader scheme abide by a code of proactive guidelines. These guidelines outline issues such as product information, advertising, ordering methods, prices, delivery of goods, consumer privacy, receipting, dispute resolution, and security.

WebTrust Seal

The WebTrust seal program is similar to TRUSTe. The American Institute of Certified Public Accountants (**cpawebtrust.com**) sponsors it.

Evaluation by Consumers

A large number of sites include product and vendor evaluations offered by consumers. For example, on Yelp!, community members rate and comment on businesses.

The Computer Fraud and Abuse Act (CFAA)

The **Computer Fraud and Abuse Act (CFAA)**, passed in 1984 and amended several times, is an important milestone in EC legislation. Initially, the scope and intent of CFAA was to protect government computers and financial industry computers from criminal theft by outsiders. In 1986, the CFAA was amended to include stiffer penalties for violations, but it still only protected computers used by the federal government or financial institutions. As the Internet expanded in scope, so did the CFAA. In 1994 and 1996, there were significant revisions of the CFAA that added a civil law component and civil charges to this law that had previously applied to criminal offenses only. In 2001, it was modified by the USA PATRIOT Act, adding sections relating to cyberterrorism and adding crimes that are considered to be "Federal Acts of Terror." In 2008, the CFAA was amended again by the Identity Theft Enforcement and Restitution Act to address the malicious use of spyware to steal sensitive personal information, eliminating the financial loss requirement, and creating harsher penalties for those who intentionally access or conspire to access, computers without authorization. See the manual titled "Prosecuting Computer Crimes" at **justice.gov/criminal/cybercrime/docs/ccmanual.pdf**.

Seller Protection

The Internet makes it easier for buyers and sellers engaging in EC to commit fraud. Sellers must be protected against:

> - Customers who deny that they placed an order.
> - Customers who download copyrighted software and sell it to others.
> - Customers who give fraudulent payment information (false credit card or a bad check) for products and services that they buy.
> - Imposters – sellers using the name of another seller (see the CyberSource Annual Reports).
> - Other sellers using the original seller's names, trademarks, and other unique features, and even their Web addresses (or similar to it).
> - Payment fraud by consumers and by criminals.

Sellers also can be attacked illegally or unethically by competitors.

Example
A class action lawsuit was filed against McAfee in the United States District Court for the Northern District of California (Case No. 10-1455-HRL) alleging that after the plaintiffs purchased McAfee software from McAfee's website, a deceptive pop-up ad (from one of McAfee's partners) that looks like a McAfee page appeared, and thanked the plaintiffs for their software purchase. The pop-up ad asked them to click on a "Try it Now" button, which they assumed would download the software they had just purchased, but unbeknownst to them,

they received a 30-day trial subscription to Arpu, Inc. (a non-McAfee product). They found out later that McAfee transmits customer credit/debit card and billing information to Arpu (customers are charged $4.95 per month after the trial period) and collects an undisclosed fee for each customer who "tries" Arpu via the McAfee website (ClassActionLawsuitsInTheNews.com 2010). See also **courthousenews.com/2010/04/08/McAfee.pdf**.

What Can Sellers Do?
Companies like Chargeback Stopper (**chargebackstopper.com**) and Chargeback Protection (**chargebackprotection.org**) provide merchants with a database of credit card numbers that have had 'chargeback orders' recorded against them. Sellers who have access to the database can use this information to decide whether to proceed with a sale. In the future, the credit card industry is planning to use biometrics to manage electronic shoplifting. In addition, sellers can use PKI and digital certificates, especially the SET protocol, to help prevent fraud (see Chapter 11).

Other possible solutions include the following:
- Use intelligent software to identify questionable customers (or in small companies, do this identification manually). One technique, for example, involves comparing credit card billing and requested shipping addresses.
- Identify warning signals – i.e., red flags – for possible fraudulent transactions.
- Ask customers whose billing address is different from the shipping address to call their bank and have the alternate address added to their bank account. Retailers will agree to ship the goods to the alternate address only if this is done.
- Ask the customer to disclose the credit card verification code.
- Delay shipment until money is received.

For further discussion of what merchants can do to protect themselves from fraud, see Litle & Co. (2014) and CyberSource (2012). For 10 measures to reduce credit card fraud for Internet Merchants (a FraudLabs.com White Paper), see **fraudlabs.com/docs/fraudlabs_white_paper.pdf**.

Protecting Both Buyers and Sellers: Using Electronic Signatures and Other Security Features

One method to help distinguish between legitimate and fraudulent transactions is electronic signatures.

An **electronic signature** is "the electronic equivalent of a handwritten signature" (per **pcmag.com/encyclopedia/term/42500/electronic-signature**; see Chapter 10). Electronic signatures provide high level of security and are recognized by most legal entities as being equivalent to handwritten signatures. All electronic signatures are represented digitally. Signed electronic documents and contracts are as legally binding as paper-based documents and contracts. For details, see **en.wikipedia.org/wiki/Electronic_signature**. See also **e-signature.com**.

Authentication

In the online environment where consumers and merchants do not have physical contact with one another, proving the authenticity of each person is necessary since buyers and sellers do not see each other. However, if one can be sure of the identity of the person on the other end of the line, there could be more e-commerce applications. For example, students would be able to take exams online from anywhere without the need for proctors. Fraud among recipients of government payments would be minimized. Buyers would be assured who the sellers are, and sellers would know, with a very high degree of confidence, who the buyers really are. Online job interviews would be accurate because it would be almost impossible for an applicant to impersonate another person. Overall, trust in online transactions and in EC in general would increase significantly. Authentication can be achieved in several ways, including the use of biometrics (see Chapter 10).

Fraud Detecting Systems

There are a large number of fraud detection systems such as the use of data mining for credit card fraud. For other methods, see Parks (2010). CyberSource also has developed several tools for detecting fraud. For details, see Cyber Source (2012) and **authorize.net/resources/files/fdswhitepaper.pdf**.

SECTION 15.5 REVIEW QUESTIONS

1. Describe consumer protection measures.
2. Describe assurance services.
3. What must a seller do to protect itself against fraud? How?
4. Describe types of electronic signatures. Who is protected? Why?
5. Describe authentication.

15.6 PUBLIC POLICY, TAXATION, AND POLITICAL ENVIRONMENTS

In this chapter, we include four topics of public policy that are closely related to e-commerce.

Net Neutrality

Internet neutrality (also *network neutrality, net neutrality,* or *NN*) has been a hotly debated topic that may shape the future of the Internet (see **businessinsider.com/net-neutralityfor-dummies-and-how-it-effects-you-2014-1**). It became a high-profile topic when telecommunications network operators AT&T and Verizon announced that they wanted to charge an extra fee to deliver content on the Internet at a faster rate of speed. Currently, all Internet traffic is being treated equally (or "neutrally") by telecommunication providers. In response, numerous groups have tried to stop the extra fee. The problem here is that 5–10% of the users occupy 80–90% of the available bandwidth, partially because of the heavy peer-to-peer (P2P) traffic.

On December 21, 2010, the Federal Communications Commission (FCC) approved net neutrality. **Net neutrality** is a network design principle stating that basic protocols of the Internet should enable users to utilize the Web without being discriminated against by Internet service providers. In other words, there should be net equality. Net providers cannot dictate the types of content you see, they must treat all Internet traffic sources equally, and consumers can access anything they want at no extra charge (see **businessinsider. com/net-neutralityfor-dummies-and-how-it-effects-you-2014-1**). Net neutrality puts in place three high-level rules for service providers (see Woyke 2010 for details). For more on net neutrality and its impact, see Gross (2014). Note that implementation of net neutrality is not simple; it involves Web companies, lawmakers and government agencies, fiber-optics owners, content providers, mobile carriers, and consumers. Opponents are fighting the authority of the FCC to enforce net neutrality by circulating and signing petitions, protesting, and so forth. For how net neutrality, or lack thereof, can affect a business, see **entrepreneur.com/article/233991**. For a discussion on the net neutrality debate, and an infographic, see **wired.com/2014/06/net_neutrality_missing**. In January 2014, a federal appeals court struck down the FCC's net neutrality rule.

In April 2014, the FCC announced new rules that may abolish net neutrality (see Mayton 2014). However, in May 2014, the FCC generated a new *proposal* that is intended to uphold net neutrality. The FCC's proposal includes keeping the Internet open and holding Internet providers to higher levels of transparency. Also in question is how the FCC plans to regulate ISPs. The FCC plans on adopting a new set of rules by the end of 2014 (see Anthony 2014). Well, it sure keeps changing!

Taxation of EC Transactions

Several types of taxes are related to e-commerce. The most debatable one is the Internet sales tax, which is imposed by individual states on products sold in their jurisdictions. See **en.wikipedia. org/wiki/Internet_taxes**.

When Internet commerce started in the mid-1990s, it was declared free of taxation in the United States at the federal, state, county, and city levels in order to encourage e-commerce. However, not imposing taxes on the Internet was seen as discriminatory against mail-order businesses and traditional retailers who must collect taxes. Over the years, there were several court challenges and modifications. You can read about the history at **taxbrain.com**. One development was the 1998 Internet Tax Freedom Act that placed a moratorium on special taxation on the Internet for one year. This meant that Internet access could not be taxed by state and local governments. The Act has been renewed by Congress periodically, with a few changes (see **money.howstuffworks.com/personal-finance/personal-income-taxes/internet-tax-freedom-act1.htm**). A bill to permanently extend the Internet Tax Freedom Act was introduced in 2013, and was passed by the House Committee on the Judiciary in June 2014. To read about the bill and track its progress, see **govtrack.us/congress/bills/113/hr3086#overview**.

Therefore, the states' budget and taxing authorities have placed the issue of collecting Internet taxes high on their agendas as a potential means of generating state revenues. Some states are suing online vendors for not collecting sales taxes. It appears that there is a consensus forming among state lawmakers that Internet taxes are inevitable. Obviously, there is consumer resistance.

A major player in the conflict between consumers that are used to not paying taxes and states that need money is Amazon.com. In 2011, California passed a tax collection bill for the Internet, and started to pressure Amazon into collecting the sales tax. In 2012, Amazon agreed to collect sales tax from its buyers in California as well as in some other states.

In 2013, the U.S. Senate passed the Marketplace Fairness Act (**marketplacefairness.org**), a law that will require all online and catalog sellers in the U.S. to collect sales tax at the time of an online transaction. However, states must simplify their sales tax laws. The bill was sent to the House Subcommittee and as of June 2014, is still being reviewed.

In addition to sales tax, there are several other taxes related to e-commerce.

For example, in July 2010, in a move to legalize Internet gambling, the United States House Committee on Financial Services approved a bill that lays the groundwork for a multibillion-dollar online gambling tax.

Internet Censorship by Countries

Internet censorship refers to restrictions on what can be seen, published, or accessed on the Internet. Internet restrictions can be imposed domestically (e.g., big businesses and corporations restricting employee Internet access), and in foreign countries. Censorship is done using different methods, ranging from blocking access to certain websites to the creation of a whole alternative Internet, as was done in Iran. A popular method of censorship is content filtering. Filtering can be based on a blacklist of offensive website content providers, or by other methods. When blacklisted, a website will have all or part of its content censored by a government agency that sees the website's content as offensive to citizens or to the government. For comprehensive information on the different types of Internet censorship in the U.S. and other countries, see **computer. howstuffworks.com/internet-censorship.htm**. In 2010, Google decided not to do business in China because the Chinese government had asked Google to block certain websites and information in Google searches. Google refused and withdrew from China.

In early 2009, President Obama appointed Cass Sunstein as the White House's "Regulatory Czar." Sunstein is an advocate for Internet censorship, having written several white papers promoting the idea (see *WorldNetDaily* 2009). For examples and an infographic of censorship in countries around the world, see **safervpn.com/blog/mapping-internet-censorship-worldwide-infographic**.

SECTION 15.6 REVIEW QUESTIONS

1. What is net neutrality and how will it affect the Internet?
2. Why is net neutrality such a hotly debated issue? Find the legal status of this issue.
3. Describe how taxes relate to e-commerce.
4. What is Internet censorship?

15.7 SOCIETAL ISSUES AND GREEN EC

At this point in the chapter, our attention turns to several societal issues of EC. The first societal topic is one that concerns many – the *digital divide*.

The Digital Divide

Despite the factors and trends that contribute to future EC growth, since the inception of the Internet, and e-commerce in particular, a gap has emerged between those who have and those who do not have the ability to engage in e-commerce. This gap is referred to, in its generic format, as the **digital divide**. According to Internet World Stats, the digital divide "is a social issue referring to the differing amount of information between those who have access to the Internet (especially broadband access) and those who do not have access" (see **internetworldstats.com/links10.htm**). The gap exists both *within* and *between* countries. The U.S. federal and state governments are attempting to close this gap within the U.S. by encouraging training and supporting education and infrastructure. The gap between countries, however, may be widening rather than narrowing. For an overview and statistics, see **en.wikipedia.org/wiki/Digital_divide**. Many government and international organizations, including the United Nations and Citizens Online, are exploring this issue.

Overcoming the Digital Divide

Governments, companies, and nonprofit organizations are trying to reduce the digital divide. One example is the "One Laptop per Child" project (**one.laptop.org**), a non-profit organization whose mission is to provide children in low-income communities and developing nations with low-cost "XO" brand laptops.

For a short video, see **laptop.org/en/video/brand/index.html**. The current cost of each laptop (2014) is around $35. For more information about the program and the capabilities of the laptops, see **one.laptop.org/about/faq**.

In Online File W11.2, we provided an example of how underprivileged farmers in India use smartphones to make payments on bank loans and to receive farm-related information.

Telecommuting

One activity of e-commerce is **telecommuting**, which is working at home using a PC, tablet, smartphone, and the Internet. Telecommuting is on the rise in the United States and in several

Table 15.4 Potential benefits of telecommuting or virtual work

Individuals	Organizational	Community and society
Reduces or eliminates travel-related time and expenses	Reduces office space needed	Conserves energy and lessens dependence on foreign oil
Improves health by reducing stress related to compromises made between family and work	Increases labor pool and competitive advantage in recruitment	Preserves the environment by reducing traffic-related pollution and congestion
Allows closer proximity to and involvement with family	Provides compliance with the Americans with Disabilities Act	Reduces traffic accidents and resulting injuries or deaths
Allows closer bonds with the family and the community	Decreases employee turnover, absenteeism, and use of sick leave	Reduces the incidence of disrupted families; telecommuters may be able to keep their job and work from home if a family member needs to relocate for business reasons, etc.
Decreases involvement in office politics	Improves job satisfaction and productivity	Increases employment opportunities for the homebound
Increases productivity despite distractions		Allows the transfer of jobs to areas of high unemployment

developing countries. For a list of potential benefits, see Table 15.4. For example, one benefit of working from home is that people who live in the suburbs can save one to two hours of time per day by not having to commute to work (Enviro Boys 2010).

Example

Ascend One Corporation, a consumer debt management business, decided to change their networking strategies in order to expand. Ascend One's success was substantially burdened by having to provide its call center agents with daily cumbersome support and application updates on their desktop computers. The company increased productivity and satisfaction of customer care employees by combining telecommuting with virtualization technology. The company stored and managed applications on virtual desktops instead of on remote computers. Call center agent productivity increased by 10%. By allowing telecommuting, there was an increase in employee productivity and a reduction in attrition rates. The technology also allowed the company to maintain high levels of communication with mobile employees. Training programs are accessible 24 hours per day to remote workers (see Park 2009 for details).

Note: Some companies do not like their employees to work from home. In 2013, Yahoo's CEO banned the work-from-home policy. For a debate on this policy, see Bercovici (2013) and

Ascharya (2013). Although the ban on telecommuting is still enforced, the CEO extended Yahoo's parental leave policy.

Green EC and IT

There are many opportunities to go EC green, and here we are representative ones.

Operating Greener Businesses, Eco-Friendly Data Centers, and Cloud Computing

The growing power consumption of computing technology and high energy costs are having a direct negative impact on business profitability. Enterprises are trying to reduce energy costs and increase the use of recyclable materials. **Green computing** refers to the eco-friendly use of computing resources (e.g., see **searchdatacenter. techtarget.com/definition/green-computing**). In this section, we focus on how EC is *going green* by adopting environmentally friendly practices.

For example, energy use in data centers is a major concern to corporations. Green EC/IT is a growing movement (see Nelson 2008) that also includes data centers. According to Gartner Inc., Green IT initiatives are expanding to many other areas (see **enterpriseinnovation.net/article/ gartner-green-data-center-means-more-energy-efficiency**). For guidelines on how to go green, see Table 15.5.

Table 15.5 Turning IT green: guidelines for energy-efficient computer use

Use the computer's power management options, such as setting all computers to hibernate and using the standby option
Instruct all personnel to turn off computer monitors when not in use
Shut down all computers automatically after hours or when not in use
Encourage telecommuting whenever possible
Follow the manufacturers' recommendations on all energy-related equipment
Embrace cloud computing. Replace existing servers with virtualization, as money permits
Increase cooling efficiency

For practices, see "Cooling Data Center Costs" in *Baseline*, August 13, 2010 (available online at **baselinemag.com/infrastructure/Cooling-Data-Center-Costs** (accessed June 2014).

The efforts to improve the use of EC (and IT) by minimizing damage to the environment, and at the same time saving money, are major objectives of **Green IT**. Company data center servers are also known to be both power hungry and heat generating. PC monitors consume about 80 to 100 billion kilowatt hours of electricity every year in the United States. Both Intel and AMD are producing new chips aimed at reducing this amount of energy usage. Turning off PCs when they are not in use can save a company money and add to good corporate social health by reducing the damage caused by excessive carbon dioxide release. Finally, discarded PCs and other computer equipment can cause serious waste disposal problems. An important issue is how to recycle old computing equipment and whose responsibility it is to take care of the problem (the manufacturers? the users? the government?). *Green software* assists companies save energy and/or comply with EPA requirements.

A comprehensive coverage of Green IT is provided by Murugesan and Gangadharan (2012), who distinguish between making EC (and IT) greener and using IT and EC as enabling tool to improve environmental sustainability (i.e., make it greener). They also cover implementation and strategy issues. For a guide to green IT strategy, see IBM (2008b).

How to Operate Greener Businesses, Data Centers, and Supply Chains

Chief information officers (CIOs) who are looking to operate greener businesses, data centers, and supply chains should focus on: (1) virtualiza-

tion, (2) software management, and (3) harnessing the "cloud." *Virtualization* provides energy saving solutions, resulting in both energy and monetary savings. Companies seeking advice, tools, and processes can turn to software management outsourcing to help them achieve their software needs and licensing management needs. Finally, cloud computing is predicted to be included in 45% of all IT applications by 2017.

Gaining energy efficiency in business requires managing these issues: the computers, computing power of the data center, data center power/cooling, and data center storage. Many organizations are turning to server virtualization, such as cloud computing, to cut their energy costs. For more details on green computing, see Online File W15.4.

Example 1

Wells Fargo (**wellsfargo.com**) is a large financial institution that offers a wide range of banking services online. The company is data-dependent and known for its eco-friendliness. The company decided to "go green" in its two data centers. Data centers must ensure security and availability of their services, and when they are planned from scratch, they can be energy efficient with low power consumption. The two new facilities had more than 8,000 servers. After major virtualization efforts, the data centers were using significantly less power compared to the previous year.

Wells Fargo introduced several energy saving devices (see Clancy 2010). Wells Fargo constantly expands and renovates its data centers, yet shows high consideration to the environment. Wells Fargo is also eco-friendly in other ways. (For more about "green banking" at Wells Fargo, see **bankrate.com/financing/banking/green-banking-at-wells-fargo**.)

Example 2

Google aimed to reduce the power consumption of its data centers by 30%. This was done by reducing overhead costs: improving the cooling system, lighting, and the power infrastructure. Google closely followed the strategies and recommendations of the company's "Green Energy Czar." Google, whenever possible, embraces free cooling – such as cooling towers and use of fresh air. Google also purchases clean energy from several sources. For details, see Samson (2010).

Global Green Regulations

Global regulations also are influencing green business practices. Sustainability regulations such as the Restriction of Hazardous Substances Directive (RoHS) in the European Union (EU) will increasingly impact how supply chains function regardless of location (see **ec.europa.eu/ environment/waste/rohs_eee** and **rohs.gov.uk**).

Eco-friendly practices reduce costs and improve public relations in the long run. Not surprisingly, demand for green computing is on the rise. A tool to help companies find greener computers and other electronics is the Electronic Product Environmental Assessment Tool (EPEAT).

The Electronic Product Environmental Assessment Tool

Maintained by the Green Electronics Council (GEC), the **Electronic Product Environmental Assessment Tool (EPEAT)**, according to their website, rate electronic products against a range of environmental performance criteria. They are a comprehensive global rating system for greener electronics. For more on e-commerce for a better environment, see **rainforestagencies.com.au/ egreen.html**.

Telecommuting, which was discussed earlier, also offers several green benefits, including reducing rush-hour traffic, improving air quality, improving highway safety, and even improving health care by reducing pollution.

Other Societal Issues

Many other societal issues can be related to EC. Three in which EC has had a generally positive impact are mentioned here: education, public safety, and health.

Education

E-commerce has had a major impact on education and learning. Virtual universities are helping to reduce the digital divide. Companies can use the Internet to help retrain employees, enabling them to defer retirement.

Public Safety, Surveillance, and Homeland Security

With increased concerns about public safety after September 11, 2001, many organizations and individuals have started to look at technologies that will help deter, prevent, or detect criminal activities of various types. Various e-commerce tools can help increase both safety at home and in public places. These include e-911 systems; global collaborative commerce technologies (for collaboration among national and international law enforcement units); e-procurement (of unique equipment to fight crime); e-government efforts at coordinating, information sharing, and expediting legal work and cases; intelligent homes, offices, and public buildings; and e-training of law enforcement officers.

An issue to consider is whether the financial, functional, and social impact of surveillance systems is worth the public's perceived intrusion of privacy. The fact remains that most cities that use the surveillance cameras do so more for the retrieval of images rather than for active monitoring. Thus, as a crime deterrent, these cameras make little financial sense since only one person can effectively monitor 10 cameras at one time. The City of Chicago, for example, has installed more than 10,000 cameras. For real time monitoring, the city would need to hire an additional 1,000 city employees, which is impossible with budget shortages and lower tax revenues (per Gallio 2010). Machine interpretation of videos, which is getting more and more accurate, will make surveillance a more cost-effective tool in the future. However, Chicago is adding more surveillance cameras. As of 2014, Chicago has 24,000 cameras, which is raising privacy concerns with citizens and the ACLU (see **foxnews.com/politics/2014/05/12/ security-camera-surge-in-chicago-sparks-concerns- massive-surveillance-system**).

Health Aspects

Is EC a health risk? Generally speaking, it is probably safer and healthier to shop from home than in a physical store. However, some believe that exposure to cellular mobile communication radiation may cause health problems. It may take years before the truth of this claim is known. Even if communication's radiation may cause health problems, the damage would probably be insignificant due to the small amount of time most people spend on wireless shopping and other m-commerce activities. However, given the concern of some about this issue, protective devices are now available that would minimize this problem (e.g., see **safecell.net**).

Another health-related issue is the addiction to online games, social networks, and EC/Internet-related applications. Several countries (including the U.S.) have begun prevention and re-education programs and some have opened inpatient treatment and recovery centers (e.g., see Geranios 2009 and **netaddiction.com**).

EC technologies such as collaborative commerce can help improve health care. For example, using Web technologies during the review process and the approval process of new drugs has been shortened, saving lives and reducing suffering. Wireless computing helps in the delivery of health care (see Chapter 6). Intelligent systems facilitate medical diagnoses. Health care advice can be provided from a distance. Finally, intelligent hospitals, doctors, and other health care facilities use EC tools. In 2009, the major social networks and Twitter were tracking the outbreak of the Swine Flu Pandemic, advising people where not to travel and how to protect themselves. Finally, in Israel and Europe, an ongoing major multinational, collaborative research project called "MOBIGuide" combines monitoring patients from a distance and generating medical decisions according to the data collected. For details, see **newmedia-eng.haifa.ac.il/?p=5593**.

Make Cities More Livable

In Chapter 6, we described smart cities. The objective is to make cities more livable. Chia (2012) discusses research on how to make cities like Singapore more intelligent. Gaylord (2013) describes the use of big data and government transparency in big cities.

SECTION 15.7 REVIEW QUESTIONS

1. Define the digital divide.
2. Describe the One Laptop per Child project.
3. Describe how EC can improve safety and security.
4. Describe the impact of EC on health services.
5. What is green computing?
6. List three examples in which green computing can help protect the environment or conserve resources.
7. What is a green supply chain? Give one example.
8. How do the new data centers help us "go green"?
9. How does telecommuting or virtual work conserve the environment?

15.8   THE FUTURE OF E-COMMERCE

Generally speaking, the consensus is that the future of EC is positive. EC will become an increasingly important method of trading, reaching customers, providing services, and improving organizations' operations. In addition, EC facilitates collaboration, innovation, and people-to-people interactions. Analysts differ in their predictions for the anticipated growth rate of EC and the length of time it will become a substantial portion of the economy. There is also disagreement about the identification of industry segments that will grow the fastest. However, there also is a consensus about the direction of the field: full speed ahead! Companies such as Amazon.com, eBay, Alibaba Group, Priceline, and Newegg.com are growing rapidly.

The Enterprise Innovation Editors (2013) made predictions regarding EC for 2014 and beyond. These include many topics cited in this book, ranging from mobility to medical information systems and security. Gerber (2013) made 10 predictions about the future of EC, ranging from comprehensive customer-engagement to custom design.

Integrating the Marketplace with the Marketspace

Throughout this book, we have commented on the relationship between the physical marketplace and the online marketspace. We have pointed out conflicts in certain areas, as well as successful applications. The fact is that, from the point of view of the consumer, as well as of most of the merchants and suppliers, these two entities exist, and will continue to exist, together.

Probably the most noticeable integration of the two concepts is in the click-and-mortar organization. In the near future, the click-and-mortar organization will be the most prevalent model (e.g., see Sears.com, Target.com, Costco.com, and Walmart.com), although the model may take different forms. Some organizations will use EC as just another sales channel, as most large retailers, airlines, and banks are doing today. Others will use EC only for some products and services, and sell other products and services the conventional way (e.g., LEGO Group).

M-Commerce

There is almost a 100% consensus that the role of m-commerce in e-commerce will increase significantly. There already are millions of innovative mobile apps and their numbers are growing rapidly. The area where we will see the fastest growth in EC is the proliferation of apps. Many m-commerce start-ups are entering the field.

Social Commerce

Recently, the use of mobile social networks has been accelerating. The increasing number of new wireless Web 2.0 services have assisted many social networks to go wireless, enabling more interactions between people. Nielsen's September 2012 release of its *Social Media Report* indicated four out of five active Internet users visit social networks and blogs. The report also shows that nearly 82% of social media users access these websites using their mobile phones (Nielsen 2012). These numbers continue to grow.

Social commerce is growing rapidly on Facebook, Twitter, Google, and many other companies. Mobile advertising and promotions are major areas of growth.

Future Technological Trends that May Accelerate the Speed of E-Commerce

The following are a few examples that will facilitate the use of e-commerce:

- Much wider broadband of technologies and faster networks
- More powerful search engines (intelligent agent-based)
- Better batteries for mobile devices
- Development in quantum computing and the semantic Web
- The arrival of flexible computer screens
- Better cloud applications
- Wide use of smartphones and tablets
- Increased use of wearable devices
- Possibility of free Internet access

Future Trends That Are Limiting the Spread of EC

The following trends may slow down the growth of EC and Web 2.0, and may even cripple the Internet:

- **Security concerns.** Both shoppers and users of e-banking and other services worry about online security. The Web needs to be made safer.
- **Lack of net neutrality.** If the big telecom companies are allowed to charge more for faster access, small companies that cannot pay extra may be at a disadvantage.

- **Copyright violations.** The legal problems of YouTube, Wikipedia, and others may result in a loss of vital outlets of public opinion and creativity.
- **Lack of standards.** There is still a lack of standards for EC, especially for global trade.

In conclusion, many people believe that the impact of EC on our lives will be as much as, and possibly more profound than, that of the Industrial Revolution. No other phenomenon since the Industrial Revolution has been classified in this category. It is our hope that this book will help you move successfully into this exciting and challenging area of the digital revolution.

Enjoy Some Interesting Videos About the Future of E-Commerce

The following are some suggested videos about e-commerce:

1. "E-Commerce's Future Ain't What It Used to Be; It's Even Better" (7:48 minutes) at **youtube.com/watch?v=mJtw1027FYs**
2. "Future of E-Commerce: Trends, Challenges, and Opportunities for Telecom and the Mobile Industry" (7:41 minutes) at **youtube.com/watch?v=wCZXif3MUEw**

SECTION 15.8 REVIEW QUESTIONS

1. How is EC related to traditional commerce?
2. Describe the role of mobility in the future of EC.
3. How will social networks facilitate EC?
4. Which future trends will help EC?
5. Which trends slow down the growth of EC?

MANAGERIAL ISSUES

Some managerial issues related to this chapter are as follows:

1. **What legal and ethical issues are of concern in an EC initiative?** Key issues to consider include the following: (1) What type of proprietary information should we allow and disallow on our site? (2) Who will have access to information that visitors post on our site? (3) Do the content and activities on our site comply with laws in other countries? (4) What disclaimers do we need to post on our website? (5) Are we using trademarked or copyrighted materials without permission? Regardless of the specific issues, an attorney should periodically review the website content, and someone should be responsible for monitoring legal and liability issues.

2. **What are the most critical ethical issues?** Negative or defamatory articles published online about people, companies, or products on websites or blogs can lead to charges of libel – and libel can stretch across countries. Issues of privacy, ethics, and legal exposure may seem tangential to running a business, but ignoring them puts the company at risk of fines, customer dissatisfaction, and disruption of an organization's operations. Privacy protection is a necessary investment.

3. **How can intellectual property rights be protected when it comes to digital content?** To protect intellectual property rights such as video, music, and books online, we need to monitor what copyrights, trademarks, and patents are infringed upon over the Internet. Portal sites that allow pirated video and music files should be monitored. This monitoring may require a vast amount of work, so software agents should be employed to continually inspect any pirated material. The risk to the business that can be caused by the infringement and the possibility of legal protection as well as technical protection by current regulation and potential new common law should be analyzed. Consider settling any suit for damages by negotiation.

4. **How can a patent in EC be purchased?** Some people claim that patents should not be awarded to businesses or computer processes related to EC (as is the case in some European countries). Therefore, investing large amounts of money in developing or buying EC patents may be financially unwise in cases where patents may not be granted or protected properly. Some companies that own many business

model patents have been unable to create business value out of these patents.

5. **What is the ethical principle of protecting the privacy of customers?** To provide personalized services, companies need to collect and manage customers' profile data. In practice, the company has to decide whether to use spyware to collect data. Collecting data may make customers unhappy (as in the cases of Google Street View or Facebook privacy settings). The company needs well-established principles of protecting customer privacy: Notify customers before collecting their personal information; inform and get consent on the type and extent of disclosures; allow customers to access their personal data and make sure the data are accurate and securely managed; and apply some method of enforcement and remedy to deter privacy breaches. In this manner, the company can avoid litigation and gain the long-term trust of customers.

6. **How can a company create opportunities in the global trend toward green EC?** Reducing carbon emissions and saving energy are global issues. (1) EC can save carbon emissions by reducing the need for transportation. This is a generic contribution of EC. (2) EC can provide an electronic exchange platform for trading CO_2 emission rights. This is a new business opportunity. (3) The IT hardware manufacturers may try to earn the Energy Star Excellence Award from the Environmental Protection Agency to prove that their products are contributing to the protection of the environment.

SUMMARY

In this chapter, you learned about the following EC issues as they relate to the chapter's learning objectives.

1. **Understanding legal and ethical challenges and how to contain them.** The global scope and universal accessibility of the Internet create serious questions as to which ethical rules and laws apply. Ignoring laws exposes companies to lawsuits or criminal charges that are disruptive, expensive, and damaging to customer relations. The best strategy is to avoid behaviors that would expose the company to these types of risks. Important safeguards are a corporate code of ethics stating the rules and expected behaviors and actions and an Internet acceptable use policy.

2. **Intellectual property law.** EC operations are subject to various types of intellectual property (IP) laws, some of which judges have created in landmark court cases. IP law provides companies with methods of compensation for damages or misuse of their property rights. IP laws passed by Congress are being amended to better protect EC. These protections are needed because the theft or replication of intellectual works on the Internet is both simple and inexpensive. These actions violate or infringe upon copyrights, trademarks, and patents. Although the legal aspects seem clear, monitoring and catching violators remains difficult.

3. **Privacy, free speech, defamation, and their challenges.** B2C companies use CRM and depend on customer information to improve products and services. Registration and cookies are two ways to collect this information. The key privacy issues are who controls personal information and how private it should remain. Strict privacy laws have been passed recently that carry harsh penalties for any negligence that exposes personal or confidential data. There is ongoing debate about censorship on the Internet. The proponents of censorship feel that it is up to the government and various ISPs and websites to control inappropriate or offensive content. Others oppose any form of censorship; they believe that control is up to the individual. In the United States, most legal attempts to censor content on the Internet have been found unconstitutional. The debate is not likely to be resolved any time soon.

4. **Fraud on the Internet and how to protect consumers against it.** Protection is needed because there is no face-to-face contact between buyers and sellers; there is a great possibility of fraud; there are insufficient legal constraints; and new issues and scams appear constantly. Several organizations, private and

public, attempt to provide the protection needed to build the trust that is essential for the success of widespread EC. Of note are electronic contracts (including digital signatures), the control of gambling, and what taxes should be paid to whom on interstate, intrastate, and international transactions. The practice of no sales tax on the Internet is changing. States are starting to collect sales tax on Internet transactions.

5. **Protection of buyers and sellers.** Many procedures are used to protect consumers. In addition to legislation, the FTC tries to educate consumers so they know the major scams. The use of seals on sites (such as TRUSTe) can help, as well as tips and measures taken by vendors. Sellers can be cheated by buyers, by other sellers, or by criminals. Protective measures include using contacts and encryption (PKI, see Chapter 10), keeping databases of past criminals, sharing information with other sellers, educating employees, and using artificial intelligence software.

6. **Societal impacts of EC.** EC brings many societal benefits, ranging from improved security, transportation, and education to better healthcare delivery and international collaboration. Although the digital divide still exists between developed and developing countries, the advent of mobile computing, especially through smartphones, is beginning to close the gap.

7. **Green EC.** EC requires large data centers, but these data centers waste energy and create pollution. Users of large data centers (e.g., Google) are using innovative methods to improve the situation. Other environmental concerns are also caused by the use of EC. There are several ways to make EC greener, including working from home (telecommuting).

8. **The future of EC.** EC is growing steadily and rapidly, expanding to include new products, services, business models, and countries. The most notable areas of growth are the integration of online and offline commerce, mobile commerce (mostly due to smartphone apps), video-based marketing, and social media and networks. Several emerging technologies, ranging from intelligent applications to wearable devices, are

facilitating the growth of EC. On the other hand, several factors, are slowing down the spread of EC such as security and privacy concerns; limited bandwidth, and lack of standards in some areas of EC.

KEY TERMS

Business ethics
Computer Fraud and Abuse Act (CFAA)
Copyright
Copyright infringement
Cyberbashing
Cyberbullying
Digital divide
Digital rights management (DRM)
Electronic discovery (e-discovery)
Electronic Product Environmental Assessment Tool (EPEAT)
Electronic signature
Ethics
Fair use
Green computing
Green IT
Intellectual property (IP)
Intellectual property law
Internet censorship
Net neutrality
Opt-in
Opt-out
Patent
Platform for Privacy Preferences Project (P3P)
Spyware
Telecommuting
Trademark dilution

DISCUSSION QUESTIONS

1. What can EC websites and social networks do to ensure the safeguarding of personal information?
2. Privacy is the right to be left alone and free of unreasonable personal intrusions. What are some intrusions that you consider "unreasonable"?
3. Who should control minors' access to "offensive" material on the Internet – parents, the government, or ISPs? Why?

4. Discuss the conflict between freedom of speech and the control of offensive websites.

5. Discuss the possible insufficient protection of opt-in and opt-out options. What measures would satisfy you?

6. Clerks at some convenience stores enter their customers' data (gender, approximate age, and so on) into the computer. These data are then processed for improved decision making. Customers are not informed about this, nor are they being asked for permission. (Names are not keyed in.) Are the clerks' actions ethical? Compare this with the use of cookies.

7. Why do many companies and professional organizations develop their own codes of ethics? After all, ethics are generic and "one size may fit all."

8. Cyberpromotions, Inc. attempted to use the First Amendment in defense of its flooding AOL subscribers with junk e-mail, which AOL tried to block. A federal judge agreed with AOL that unsolicited e-mail is annoying, a waste of Internet time, and often inappropriate and, therefore, should not be sent. Discuss some of the issues involved, such as freedom of speech, how to distinguish between junk and non-junk e-mail, and the similarity to regular mail. Cyberpromotions is no longer in business.

9. What contribution does TRUSTe make to e-commerce?

TOPICS FOR CLASS DISCUSSION AND DEBATES

1. Discuss what the RIAA hopes to achieve by using lawsuits against college students for copyright infringement. Research the issue of how will the proposed Copyright Enforcement Bill, if enacted, support further RIAA lawsuits? Find the status of the bill. Write a report.

2. The proposed Copyright Enforcement Bill defines everyone that creates a website as a publisher and is liable under the Act. Enforcement under this proposed bill for unintentional use or distribution of copyrighted content on business websites could result in the confiscation of a company's domain name or server, which in turn could potentially disable the company's e-mail capability – substantially killing commerce. What steps should a business take to minimize the risk? Discuss.

3. The IRS buys demographic market research data from private companies. These data contain income statistics that could be compared with tax returns. Many U.S. citizens feel that their rights within the realm of the Electronic Communications Privacy Act (ECPA) are being violated; others say that this is unethical behavior on the part of the government. Discuss.

4. Many hospitals, health maintenance organizations, and federal agencies are converting, or plan to convert, all patient medical records from paper to electronic storage (using imaging technology) in compliance with the Patient Protection and Affordable Care Act (PPAC), also known as "Obamacare." The PPAC mandates that all medical records shall be freely disseminated to insurance companies, the U.S. government, and government-approved third-party vendors. Once completed, electronic storage will enable expeditious access to most records anytime and from anywhere. However, the availability of these records in a database or on networks or smart cards may allow people, some of whom are unauthorized, to view another person's private medical data. To protect privacy fully may cost too much money or may considerably slow down the speed of access to the records. What policies could healthcare administrators use to prevent unauthorized access? Discuss.

5. The Communications Decency Act (CDA), which was intended to protect children and others from pornography and other offensive material online, was approved by the U.S. Congress but then was ruled unconstitutional by lower courts. In 2015, it is still being debated. Discuss the implications of this Act. Also, check the Supreme Court ruling.

6. Debate the pros and cons of the Marketplace Fairness Act.

7. Debate the pros and cons of net neutrality.

8. Research the potential impact of online gambling on physical casinos.

9. Erotic services advertising on Craigslist amounted to a significant portion of the total revenue before being taken down following national publicity over the robbery and murder of a Boston massage therapist, who had advertised on Craigslist. Craigslist denied responsibility, citing the 1996 Federal Communication Act, since Craigslist does not create the content published on its website. Later, Craigslist voluntarily removed the erotic services from its regular pages. Address the following topics in a class discussion:

(a) Craigslist may have chosen to voluntarily remove its erotic-related advertising for political reasons, even though no laws were being broken. Discuss free speech versus public safety. Take an issue and support the pros and cons of Craigslist's action.

(b) Do you agree that self-governing Web content is the most effective means of providing public safety or should the federal government step in to enact tougher laws?

(c) Take the position of an erotic dancer. Determine an argument in favor of reversing Craigslist's decision to remove "erotic services" advertisements. (Use free speech and right to earn money through employment.)

10. Many sports-related leagues, including the NFL and UK Football Association, restrict the players' use of social networks. The NFL prohibits any use of social networks 90 minutes before and 90 minutes after games. Debate the issue.

11. Debate Yahoo's "no work from home" policy. Start by reading Ascharya (2013).

12. Have two groups debate the issue of ownership of user-generated content (the Facebook example). One group should be for and one against.

13. Debate: Neutrality on the Internet is good for EC.

14. Debate: Should the exchange of songs between individuals, without paying royalties, be allowed over the Internet?

15. Debate: Is the Patriot Act too loose or too tight?

16. Debate: It may be too expensive for some companies to "go green." If they "go green," they may not be able to compete against companies in countries that do not practice green EC. Should the government subsidize green EC?

17. Debate: Who should own content created by employees during their regular work hours?

18. Debate: Are privacy standards strict enough to protect electronic health records?

INTERNET EXERCISES

1. You want to set up an ethical blog. Using sites such as CyberJournalist.net: A Bloggers' Code of Ethics at **cyberjournalist.net/news/000215.php**, review the suggested guide to publishing a blog. Make a list of the top 10 ethical issues for blogging.

2. You want to set up a business-oriented website. Prepare a report summarizing the types of materials you can and cannot use (e.g., logos, graphics, etc.) without breaking copyright laws. (Consult some free legal websites.)

3. Conduct a Google search for industry and trade organizations involved in various computer privacy initiatives. One of these groups is the World Wide Web Consortium (W3C). Describe its Platform for Privacy Preferences Project (P3P) (**w3.org/P3P**). Prepare a table with 10 initiatives and describe each briefly.

4. Enter **symantec.com**. Review the services offered to topics discussed in this chapter.

5. Enter **calastrology.com**. What kind of community is this? Check the revenue model. Then enter **astrocenter.com**. What kind of site is this? Compare and comment on the two sites.

6. Enter **nolo.com**. Find information about various EC legal issues. Find information about international EC issues. Then go to **legalcompliance.org** or **cybertriallawyer.com**. Find information about international legal aspects of EC. Conduct a Google search for additional information on EC legal issues. Prepare a report on the international legal aspects of EC.

7. Find the status of the latest copyright legislation. Try **fairuse.stanford.edu** and **wipo.int/**

copyright/en. Is there anything new regarding the international aspects of copyright legislation? Write a report.

8. Enter **ftc.gov** and identify some of the typical types of fraud and scams on the Internet. List 10 of them.

9. Enter **www.usispa.org** and **ispa.org.uk**, two organizations that represent the ISP industry. Identify the various initiatives they have undertaken regarding topics discussed in this chapter. Write a report.

10. Enter **scambusters.org** and identify and list its anti-fraud and anti-scam activities.

TEAM ASSIGNMENTS AND PROJECTS

1. **Assignment for the Opening Case**
   Read the opening case and answer the following questions:
   (a) Discuss the issue of preventing movies and TV shows from being streamed online for free.
   (b) Was it ethical for Disney to invest in 56.com?
   (c) What are the business benefits to Disney if it is not in conflict with 56.com?
   (d) Discuss the global considerations of this case.
   (e) Find the status of the $1 billion lawsuit Viacom brought against YouTube.

2. The number of lawsuits in the United States and elsewhere involving EC has increased. Have each team prepare a list of five recent EC legal cases on each topic in this chapter (e.g., privacy, digital property, defamation, patents). Prepare a summary of the issues of each case, the parties, the courts, and dates. What were the outcomes of these cases? What was (or might be) the impact of each decision?

3. Form three teams. Have two teams debate free speech versus protection of children. The third team acts as judges. One team is for complete freedom of speech on the Internet; the other team advocates protection of children by censoring offensive and pornographic material.

After the debate, have the judges decide which team provided the most compelling legal arguments.

4. It is legal to monitor employees' Internet activity, e-mail, and instant messages? Note that it is legal to open letters addressed to individuals sent to the company's address. Why is the monitoring necessary? To what extent is it ethical? Are employees' rights being violated? Have two teams debate these issues.

5. Amazon.com is disputing several states that are trying to force the company to collect state taxes ("Amazon laws"). Amazon cancelled its affiliate program in certain states (e.g., Colorado, Minnesota) when the sales tax for online retailing was imposed (however, they reinstated their program in California). Check the status of this law (requiring Amazon to collect taxes) and its relationship to Federal law. Start at **illinoisjltp.com/timelytech/ongoing-taxation-disputes-between-amazon-and-state-governments.**

6. Smart computer programs enable employers to monitor their employees' movements online. The objective is to minimize wasting time and computing resources, and reduce theft by employees. These actions may invade privacy, and reduce confidence and loyalty. Find the various methods used to monitor employees (list their approaches) and list all possible negative aspects. Find case studies about the benefits (including increasing productivity) and the limitations and dangers. Relate monitoring to telecommuting and debate the issue.

CLOSING CASE: THE PIRATE BAY AND THE FUTURE OF FILE SHARING

What had been considered a landmark 2009 copyright law case involving the Motion Picture Association of America (MPAA) against illegal file sharing in Sweden appears to not have significantly deterred online file sharing. In fact, just the opposite may have occurred.

An Overview

The Pirate Bay (TPB) site was launched in 2003 by hackers and computer activists as a BitTorrent tracker, make it possible to get free access to most media content (including copyrighted material) using BitTorrent peer-to-peer (P2P) file-sharing protocol services (see **en.wikipedia.org/wiki/ BitTorrent**). The Pirate Bay site includes links to websites where you can download movies, TV shows, music e-books, live sport games, software, and more. TPB has been ranked as one of the most popular websites in the world. The site generates revenue by advertisements, donations, and sales of merchandise. The site is probably the most well-known among dozens of other sites that provide free access to copyrighted content.

The Legal Situation

The Pirate Bay has been involved in a number of lawsuits, both as a defendant and as a plaintiff. For an overview, see **torrentfreak.com/the-pirate-bay-turns-10-years-old-the-history-130810**. Here are some examples. In Sweden, The Pirate Bay company was raided by the Swedish police in 2006. The site was shut down, but reappeared a few days later with servers hosted in different countries. In 2008, the Swedish government began a criminal investigation against the founders of TPB for copyright theft. Three founders and a financier were charged with promoting copyright infringement by facilitating other people's breach of copyright law by using TPB BitTorrent technology. For 34 cases of copyright infringement, the damage claims could have exceeded US$12 million. The trial started on February 16, 2009, and ended on March 3, 2009, with a guilty verdict that carried a one-year prison sentence and a fine of US$3.5 million. The four founders lost on appeal in 2010 but succeeded in getting reduced prison time; however, the copyright infringement fine was increased. The site is now blocked by several countries. The U.S. government considers TPB (together with the Chinese sites Baidu and Taobao Marketplace) a top market for pirated and counterfeit goods.

Current Operation

As of June 2014, TPB continues to offer torrent files and magnet links to facilitate file sharing for those using the BitTorrent system. The site also offers downloading, watching videos, and searching for all types of media. In fact, much public support for TPB was noted. In 2003, Piratbyrån ("The Pirate Bureau"), a Swedish organization, was established to support the free sharing of information (however, they disbanded in 2010). Political parties in many European countries have adopted the label "The Pirate Party," after a party in Sweden, which was formed in 2006. Other countries followed suit, creating their own Pirate Parties. The party supports the reform of copyright and patent laws, government transparency, and net neutrality. In 2006, the International Pirate Party Movement was formed as an umbrella organization. In 2009, the Swedish Pirate Party won a seat in the European Parliament and in 2013, Iceland gained three similar seats. The Pirate Bay advocates copyright and patent law reform and a reduction in government surveillance. In the meantime, in Sweden, TPB's founders have worked on several other decentralized peer-to-peer file-sharing websites, which have flourished in filling the enormous global demand for P2P file sharing. TPB has plenty of defenders. In 2014, the supporters of TPB's jailed founder planned an online campaign to bring more attention to his situation.

All along, file-sharing technology has been one step ahead of enforcement. Since some countries block access to TPB, there are several proxy URLs now that provide indirect access to TPB website.

Despite losing its November 2010 appeal, TPB has kept growing. In 2011, TPB's founders launched a new website, called IPREDator, offering IP address anonymity to registered users by tunneling traffic into a secure server, which reassigns fake IP addresses to registered users so that they may access TPB or other BitTorrent tracking sites on the Web for file sharing without revealing their true IP addresses. Although TPB continues to thrive today as one of the most popular websites on the Internet, many countries are enacting new stricter copyright protection laws aimed directly at stopping this illegal activity.

Note that Facebook blocks all shared links to TPB in both public and private messages (however, TPB does have a Facebook page). In 2012, a UK court ordered a blockade on TPB in the UK because of its violation of copyright law (see Dragani 2012). Some countries are allowing access to TPB. For example, in 2014, the Netherlands court ordered the ban on TPB lifted (see **bbc.com/news/technology-25943716**).

In 2012, The Pirate Bay, to protect itself from raids, moved its operation from physical servers to the cloud. Serving its users from several cloud hosting providers makes it impossible to raid because there are no physical locations; the site is more portable and thus makes it more difficult to shut down. Other benefits include reducing downtime, ensuring better uptime, and cutting costs (see Van Der Sar 2012).

Discussion

The Pirate Bay is one of a multitude of websites that specializing in pirated and counterfeit content. The Pirate Bay does not host content, in contrast to sites, which allow people to upload videos, included pirated ones. The Pirate Bay only provides links to possible illegal downloads. This strategy did not help the site much in its legal battles.

The Pirate Bay case is only one part of a much broader issue of protecting intellectual property on the Internet. An interesting related issue is the hosting of content by sites such as YouTube and Justin.tv, which is more complicated.

Note that one aspect of this case is that the U.S. government is pushing the Swedish government to take a stronger stand against pirating.

Sources: Based on Stone (2011), Dragani (2012), Martin (2012), and **medlibrary.org** (accessed June 2014).

Questions

1. Compare TPB's legal problems to those of Napster between 2000 and 2005, and to those of Kazaa (file sharing companies).
2. Debate the issue of freedom of speech on the Internet against the need to protect intellectual property.

3. What is The Pirate Bay's business model? What are its revenue sources? (Find more information; start with Wikipedia.)
4. Explore the international legal aspects of this case. Can one country persuade another country to introduce stricter laws?
5. Read the Stone (2011) article and identify all the measures used to battle piracy of live sporting events. Which of these measures can be used in The Pirate Bay case? Which cannot? Why?
6. Find the status of the TPB website.

ONLINE FILES
available at **affordable-ecommerce-textbook.com/turban**

W15.1 Framework for Ethical Issues
W15.2 Website Quality Guidelines
W15.3 Summary of Important EC Legal Issues
W15.4 How to Go Green in a Data Centers

COMPREHENSIVE EDUCATIONAL WEBSITES

ftc.gov: Major source on consumer fraud and protection.
dmoz.org/Society/Issues/Fraud/Internet: Comprehensive resources on Internet fraud.
fraud.org: The National Consumers League Fraud Center.
ic3.gov: The FBI's Internet Crime Complaint Center.
www.fda.gov/ForConsumers/ProtectYourself/default.htm: Food and Drug Administration center for resources, recalls, safety, regulatory information, etc. about food, drugs, vaccines, cosmetics, and more.
business.usa.gov: A single platform to make it easier for businesses to access programs and services.
sba.gov/advo/laws/law_modeleg.html: Small Business Administration's advocacy site to stay current with federal regulations.
law.com: A comprehensive source for legal news and analysis.

lawbrain.com: A comprehensive collection of law–related material; users can share opinions and knowledge by adding to and editing existing pages.

bna.com/legal-business-t5009: Bloomberg Inc. legal and business portal that includes blogs, events, news, and more.

privacy.org: A comprehensive source of information on privacy.

epic.org: Electronic Privacy Information Center; a non-profit research center to protect privacy, freedom of expression, and more.

privacyrights.org: Privacy Rights Clearinghouse; a non-profit organization educating and empowering individuals to protect their privacy. An online clearinghouse.

www.itworld.com/green-it: A comprehensive source for green IT-related news and analysis.

digitaldivide.org: The Digital Divide Institute. A comprehensive collection material related to the digital divide.

techworld.com/green-it: A comprehensive collection of green IT-related material.

epolicyinstitute.com: A comprehensive collection of EC policy development resources.

eff.org/issues/bloggers/legal: A legal guide for bloggers.

thegreengrid.org: Comprehensive resources on efficiency in IT and data centers.

GLOSSARY

Business ethics (corporate or enterprise ethics) A code of values, behaviors, and rules, written or unwritten, for conducting business. These ethics dictate the operations of organizations.

Computer Fraud and Abuse Act (CFAA) An important milestone in EC legislation that protects government computers and other Internet-connected computers.

Copyright An exclusive legal right of an author or creator of intellectual property to publish, sell, license, distribute, or use such work in any desired way.

Copyright infringement The use of a work without permission or contracting for payment of a royalty.

Cyberbashing The registration of a domain name that criticizes (normally maliciously) an organization, product, or person (e.g., **paypalsucks.com**, **walmartsucks.org**, **verizonpathetic.com**). Usually associated with hate sites.

Cyberbullying "Bullying that takes place using electronic technology. Electronic technology includes devices and equipment such as cell phones, computers and tablets as well as communication tools including social media sites, text messages, chat, and websites." (per **stopybullying.gov**)

Digital divide The gap that has emerged between those who have and those who do not have the ability to engage in e-commerce.

Digital rights management (DRM) A system of protecting the copyrights of data circulated over the Internet or digital media. These arrangements are technology-based protection measures (via encryption or using watermarks).

Electronic discovery (e-discovery) The process of finding any type of electronic data (e.g., text, images, videos) by using computerized systems.

Electronic Product Environmental Assessment Tool (EPEAT) A comprehensive global rating system for greener electronics based on a range of environmental performance criteria.

Electronic signature "The electronic equivalent of a handwritten signature" (per **pcmag.com/encyclopedia/term/42500/electronic-signature**).

Ethics A set of moral principles or rules of how people are expected to conduct themselves.

Fair use The limited use of copyrighted material, without paying a fee or royalty, for certain purposes (e.g., reviews, commentaries, teaching).

Green computing The eco-friendly use of computing resources.

Green IT The efforts to improve the use of EC (and IT) by minimizing damage to the environment, and at the same time saving money.

Intellectual property (IP) Property that derives from the creative work of an individual, such as literary or artistic work.

Intellectual property law Area of the law concerned with the regulation of thinking-related products, including creativity that are protected by patents, copyrights, trademarks, and trade secret law.

Internet censorship Restrictions on what can be seen, published, or accessed on the Internet.

Net neutrality A network design principle stating that basic protocols of the Internet should enable users to utilize the Web without being discriminated against by Internet service providers.

Opt-in The principle that consumers must approve, in advance, what they are willing to see. That is, information sharing should not occur unless customers affirmatively allow or request it.

Opt-out A method that gives consumers the choice to refuse to share information about themselves, or to avoid receiving unsolicited information.

Patent "An exclusive right to a particular invention. Patents are granted by states or governments to the creator of an invention, or to someone who has been designated by them to accept the rights over the invention. The holder of the patent has sole rights over the invention for a specified period of time." (per Fedcirc.us)

Platform for Privacy Preferences Project (P3P) A protocol for privacy protection on the Web developed by the W3 Organization (W3C).

Spyware A tool that some merchants use to gather information about users without their knowledge.

Telecommuting Working at home using a PC, tablet, smartphone, and the Internet.

trademark dilution The use of a "famous" trademark by a third party, which causes the lessening (or dilution) of the 'distinguishing quality' of the mark.

REFERENCES

56.*com*. "56.com Launch Content C-C Platform '56 Kan Kan'." August 18, 2009. **56.com/v/about/en/intro_press_en.html** (accessed June 2014).

ACLU of Washington State. "Libraries, the Internet, and the Law: Adults Must Have Unfiltered Access." November 15, 2006. **aclu-wa.org/news/libraries-internet-and-law-adults-must-have-unfiltered-access** (accessed June 2014).

Albanesius, C. "Viacom Will Know What You've Watched on YouTube." July 3, 2008. **pcmag.com/article2/0,2817,2324635,00.aspml** (accessed June 2014).

Alghamdi, A. M. *The Law of E-Commerce: E-Contract, E-Business.* UK: AuthorHouse UK, 2011.

Anderson, N. "Apple Loses Big in DRM Ruling: Jailbreaks Are Fair Use." July 26, 2010. **arstechnica.com/tech-policy/2010/07/apple-loses-big-in-drm-ruling-jailbreaks-are-fair-use** (accessed June 2014).

Andrews, L. *I Know Who You Are and I Saw What You Did: Social Networks and the Death of Privacy.* Florence, MA: Free Press, 2012.

Anthony, S. "The FCC's Net Neutrality Proposal: What Does It Mean for You, and the Internet?" May 16, 2014. **extremetech.com/computing/182572-the-fccs-net-neutrality-proposal-what-does-it-mean-for-you-and-the-internet** (accessed June 2014).

Ascharya, K. "Marissa Mayer and the Telecommuting Debate." March 26, 2013. **2machines.com/articles/178412.html** (accessed June 2014)

Bambauer, D. "Tenenbaum and Statutory Damages." *Info/ Law*, July 11, 2010. **blogs.law.harvard.edu/infolaw/2010/07/11/tenenbaum-and-statutory-damages** (accessed July 2014).

Barakat, M. "Popular File-Sharing MegaUpload Shut Down." January 20, 2012. **news.yahoo.com/popular-file-sharing-website-megaupload-shutdown-232101369.html** (accessed June 2014).

Bercovici, J. "Yahoo Spins No-Work-From-Home Policy as Morale Booster. Seriously." *Forbes*, March 6, 2013.

Bhargava, R. "Social Media and the Axe Murderer: How Privacy Is Evolving Online." February 7, 2010. **socialmediatoday.com/rohitbhargava/111773/social-media-axe-murderer-how-privacy-evolving-online** (accessed June 2014).

Billboard Biz. "China Arrests 4,000, Vows Tougher Punishments for Copyright Piracy in Advance of U.S. Trade Talks." January 11, 2011. **billboard.com/biz/articles/news/global/1179729/china-arrests-4000-vows-tougher-punishments-for-copyright-piracy-in** (accessed June 2014).

Cagaoan, K.A.A, M. J. A. V. Buenaobra, A. T. M. Martin, and J. C. Paurillo. "Privacy Awareness in E-Commerce." *International Journal of Education and Research*, January 2014. Vol. 2, No. 1, **ijern.com/journal/January-2014/19.pdf** (accessed Nov 2014).

Chia, E. "City 2.0: Technology to Make Cities More Liveable." March 22, 2012. **enterpriseinnovation.net/article/city-2-0-technology-make-cities-more-liveable** (accessed June 2014).

Clancy, H. "Virtualization Core to Wells Fargo Green IT Initiative." July 6, 2010. **zdnet.com/blog/green/virtualization-core-to-wells-fargo-green-it-initiative/12852** (accessed June 2014).

ClassActionLawsuitsInTheNews.com. "McAfee Class Action Lawsuit Filed over Arpu Pop Up Advertisements." April 9, 2010. **classactionlawsuitsinthenews.com/class-action-lawsuits/mcafee-class-action-lawsuit-filed-over-arpu-pop-up-advertisements** (accessed June 2014).

ComputerWeekly.com. "Privacy Lawsuit Filed Against Facebook." August 18, 2009. **computerweekly.com/news/1280090498/Privacy-lawsuit-filed-against-Facebook** (accessed June 2014).

CyberSource. "13th Annual 2012 Online Fraud Report." CyberSource Corporation, 2012.

Davidson, A. *The Law of Electronic Commerce*. Melbourne, Australia: Cambridge University Press, 2009.

Doctorow, C. "The Curious Case of Internet Piracy." *MIT Technology Review*, June 6, 2012.

Dragani, R. "UK Court Orders Blockade on Pirate Bay." *E-Commerce Times*, May 1, 2012.

Enterprise Innovation Editors. "A Whole Host of Prediction for 2014 and Beyond." December 31, 2013. **enterpriseinnovation.net/article/whole-host-predictions-2014-and-beyond-1771618066** (accessed June 2014).

Enviro Boys. "Is Telecommuting on the Rise?" November 14, 2010. **enviroboys88.blogspot.com/2010/11/telecommuting-on-rise.html** (accessed June 2014).

Ferrell, O.C., et al. *Business Ethics: Ethical Decision Making & Cases*, 9th ed., Boston, MA: South-Western Cengage Learning, 2012.

Fogarty, K. "Copyright Infringement Bill Could Bring the FBI to Your Intranet." November 22, 2010. **www.itworld.com/legal/128550/copyright-infringement-bill-could-bring-fbi-your-intranet?page=0,0** (accessed June 2014).

Frucci, A. "RIAA Spent $58 Million Suing File Sharers, Got 2% Back." July 14, 2010. **gizmodo.com/5587306/the-riaa-spent-58-million-suing-file-sharers-got-2-back** (accessed June 2014).

Gallio, L. "Surveillance Camera: Big Brother and Big Sis are Watching!" August 29, 2010. **examiner.com/article/surveillance-cameras-big-brother-and-big-sis-are-watching** (accessed June 2014).

Gavish, B., and C. L. Tucci. "Reducing Internet Auction Fraud." *Communications of the ACM*, vol. 51 no. 5, 89–97 May 2008.

Gaylord, C., "How Big Data Helps Big Cities." *The Christian Science Monitor*, June 7, 2013.

Geranios, N. K. "Internet Addiction Center Opens in U.S." *USA Today* (by Associated Press) September 3, 2009.

Gerber, S., "10 Predictions About the Future of Ecommerce." October 1, 2013. **mashable.com/2013/10/01/future-e-commerece/** (accessed June 2014).

Gouveia, A. "2013 Wasting Time at Work Survey." July 28, 2013. **sfgate.com/jobs/salary/article/2013-Wasting-Time-at-Work-Survey-4374026.php** (accessed June 2014).

Gray, B. R. "Bullying and Harassment in the Workplace." October 13, 2010. **ezinearticles.com/?Bullying-And-Harassment-In-The-Workplace&id=5200849** (accessed June 2014).

Greene, J. "Supreme Court Rules Against Microsoft in i4i Patent Case." June 9, 2011. **cnet.com/news/supreme-court-rules-against-microsoft-in-i4i-patent-case** (accessed June 2014).

Gross, D. "Pay to Play on the Web? Net Neutrality Explained." January 15, 2014. **cnn.com/2014/01/15/tech/web/net-neutrality-explained** (accessed May 2015).

Gustin, S. "Web Censorship Bill Sails through Senate Committee." November 18, 2010. **wired.com/2010/11/coica-web-censorship-bill** (accessed June 2014).

Guynn, J., "Lawmakers ask Google's Larry Page to address Glass privacy issues." *Los Angeles Times*, May 16, 2013

Hill, K. "Lawsuit of the Day: Hey Teacher, Leave Them Kids Alone! (Or: Activating Laptop Webcams to Spy on Students at Home is Not Cool)." February 18, 2010. **abovethelaw.com/2010/02/lawsuit-of-the-day-hey-teacher-leave-them-kids-aloneor-activating-laptop-webcams-to-spy-on-students-at-home-is-not-cool** (accessed June 2014).

Himma, K. E., and H. T. Tavani (Eds.). *The Handbook of Information and Computer Ethics*. Hoboken, NJ: Wiley-Interscience, 2008.

IBM. "Data Privacy Best Practices: Time to Take Action!" A white paper (#IMW14072-USEN-00), September 2008a. *IBM Information Management Software* (see Enterprise data management solutions).

IBM. "IBM Software: A Green Strategy for Your Entire Organization." A white paper, June 2008b. New York: IBM Software Group.

Kalanda, R. "Does Amazon's 'One-Click' Success Mean Business Method Patents for All?" *E-Commerce Times*, March 31, 2012. **ecommercetimes.com/story/74719.html** (accessed June 2014).

Kontzer, T. "E-Discovery Tools Aid Compliance, Save Money." *Baseline*, July 11, 2012.

Kravets, D. "U.S. Declares iPhone Jailbreaking Legal, Over Apple's Objections." July 26, 2010. **wired.com/threatlevel/2010/07/feds-ok-iphone-jailbreaking** (accessed June 2014).

Lattanzio, V. "2nd Lawsuit Filed Over WebcamGate." July 28, 2010. **nbcphiladelphia.com/news/politics/2nd-Lawsuit-Filed-Over-Webcam-Gate-99368474.html** (accessed June 2014).

Leggatt, H. "Online Privacy Real Concern for 90% of U.S. Internet Users." February 14, 2012. **bizreport.com/2012/02/90-percent-of-online-adults-worry-about-their-online-privacy.html** (accessed June 2014).

Leonhard, G. "Is Your Wearable Tech Helping You—or Watching You?" April 29, 2014. **edition.cnn.com/2014/04/29/business/is-your-wearable-tech-helping-you----or-watching-you/** (accessed June 2014).

Lewis, P., and J. Domokos. "Caught on Camera: Lancashire Police Arrest Amateur Photographer." *The Guardian*, February 21, 2010.

Litle & Co. "Fraud Detection & Mitigation Strategies." May 2014. **litle.com/downloads/resources/Fraud-Detection-Mitigation-Strategies.pdf** (accessed June 2014).

Mallor, J., et al. *Business Law: The Ethical, Global and E-Commerce Environment,* 14th ed. New York: McGraw-Hill/Irwin, 2009.

Mann, R. J., and J. K. Winn.Electronic Commerce (Law in Commerce), 3rd ed. New York: Aspen Publishers, 2008.

Martin, R. "Supreme Court Denies Pirate Bay Right to Appeal."February 1, 2012. **thelocal.se/20120201/38844#.UWTQh5M27Sg** (accessed June 2014).

Mayton, J. "RIP Net Neutrality? FCC Backs New Rules That Permit Pay-Based Internet 'Fast Lane.'" April 26,

2014. **techtimes.com/articles/6062/20140426/rip-net-neutrality-fcc-backs-new-rules-that-permit-pay-based-internet-fast-lane.htm** (accessed June 2014).

McBride, S., and L. Chao. "Disney Affiliate Is Besieged by Pirates." November 21, 2008 (Updated). **online.wsj.com/news/articles/SB122722555475645951** (accessed June 2014).

Mercola, J. "If You See This Google Warning, Act Fast: Big Brother is Watching." August 5, 2012. **articles.mercola.com/sites/articles/archive/2012/08/05/internet-security-virus.aspx** (accessed June 2014).

Miller, C. C. "Craigslist Says It Has Shut Its Section for Sex Ads." *New York Times Business,* September 15, 2010.

Murugesan, S., and G. R. Gangadharan (Eds.) *Harnessing Green IT: Principles and Practices.* Hoboken, NJ: Wiley, 2012.

Nakashima, E. "U.S. Seeks Ways to Wiretap the Internet." *The Washington Post*, September 28, 2010.

Nelson, N. "How to Estimate Energy Efficiency as Part of a Server Upgrade." *eWeek*, April 28, 2008. **eweek.com/it-management/How-to-Estimate-Energy-Efficiency-as-Part-of-a-Server-Upgrade/** (accessed June 2014).

Nielsen. "State of the Media: The Social Media Report 2012." 2012. **nielsen.com/us/en/reports/2012/state-of-the-media-the-social-media-report-2012.html** (accessed June 2014).

O'Brien, K.J. and Streitfeld, D. "Swiss Court Orders Modifications to Google Street View." June 8, 2012. **nytimes.com/2012/06/09/technology/09iht-google09.html?_r=0** (accessed June 2014).

Owens, D. "What is Trademark Dilution." May 3, 2011. **smartbusinessrevolution.com/trademark-dilution** (accessed June 2014).

Park, H. S. "Empowering Employees with Technology." *Baseline*, May 27, 2009.

Parks, L. "Just the Ticket: Detection System Helps New Era Virtually Eliminate Online Fraud." *Stores,* April 2010.

Parry, W. "Casinos Brace for Impact of Internet Gambling." May 3, 2013. **bigstory.ap.org/article/casinos-brace-impact-internet-gambling** (accessed June 2014).

Pfanner, E. "Swiss Say Google's Street View Is Too Revealing." *New York Times Technology*, November 13, 2009. **nytimes.com/2009/11/14/technology/companies/14google.html** (accessed June 2014).

PRC. "Workplace Privacy and Employee Monitoring." (Revised May 2014). **privacyrights.org/workplace-privacy-and-employee-monitoring** (accessed June 2014).

Sager, K., J. Fisher, R. Wilcox, and J. Eastburg. "City of Ontario v. Quon: United States Supreme Court Rejects Police Officer's Lawsuit Claiming That City's Review of His Personal Text Messages Was an Illegal Search." June 18, 2010. **dwt.com/advisories/City_of_Ontario_v_Quon_United_States_Supreme_Court_Rejects_Police_Officers_Lawsuit_Claiming_That_Citys_Review_of_His_Personal_Text_Messages_Was_an_Illegal_Search_06_18_2010** (accessed June 2014).

Samson, T. "GreenNet 2010: Google Shares Its Green Data Center Secrets." *InfoWorld*, April 29, 2010.

San Miguel, R. "Sheriff Sues Craigslist to Curb Prostitution." *E-Commerce Times*, March 6, 2009.

Savitz, E. "eBay Wins Tiffany Trademark Case." July 14, 2008. **blogs.barrons.com/techtraderdaily/2008/07/14/ebay-wins-tiffany-trademark-case** (accessed June 2014).

Schreiber, J. "Big Brother Is Here, Families Say." February 18, 2010. **courthousenews.com/2010/02/18/24789.htm** (accessed June 2014).

Shah, M.H., R. Okeke, and R. Ahmed. "Issues of Privacy and Trust in E-Commerce: Exploring Customers' Perspective." *Journal of Basic and Applied Scientific Research*, 3 (3) 571–577, 2013.

Stein, J. "Data Mining: How Companies Know Everything About You." *Time*, March 21, 2011, Vol. 177, No. 11.

Sterling, T. "European Court: Google Must Yield on Personal Info." May 13, 2014. **bigstory.ap.org/article/european-court-upholds-right-be-forgotten-says-google-must-edit-some-search-results** (accessed June 2014).

Stone, B. "Pro Sports versus the Web Pirates." February 24, 2011. **businessweek.com/magazine/content/11_10/b4218066626285.htm** (accessed June 2014).

Van Der Sar, E. "Pirate Bay Moves to the Cloud, Becomes Raid-Proof." October 17, 2012. **torrentfreak.com/pirate-bay-moves-to-the-cloud-becomes-raid-proof-121017** (accessed June 2014).

WorldNetDaily. "U.S. Regulatory Czar Nominee Wants Net 'Fairness Doctrine.'" April 27, 2009. **wnd.com/2009/04/96301** (accessed June 2014).

Woyke, E. "FCC Tips Net Neutrality Passage but Questions Remain." *Forbes*, December 20, 2010.

Yamamura, J. H., and F. H. Grupe. "Ethical Considerations for Providing Professional Services Online." May 2008. **nysscpa.org/cpajournal/2008/508/essentials/p62.htm** (accessed June 2014).

Launching a Successful Online Business and EC Projects

16

Contents

Learning Objectives

Upon completion of this chapter, you will be able to:

1. Understand the fundamental requirements for initiating an online business.
2. Describe the process of initiating and funding a startup e-business or large e-project.
3. Understand the process of adding EC initiatives to an existing business.
4. Describe the issues and methods of transforming an organization into an e-business.
5. Describe the process of acquiring websites and evaluate building versus hosting options.
6. Understand the importance of providing and managing content and describe how to accomplish this.
7. Evaluate websites on design criteria such as appearance, navigation, consistency, and performance.
8. Understand how search engine optimization may help a website obtain high placement in search engines.
9. Understand how to provide some e-commerce support services.
10. Understand the process of building a webstore.
11. Know how to build a webstore with templates.

Electronic supplementary material The online version of this chapter (doi: 10.1007/978-3-319-10091-3_16) contains supplementary material, which is available to authorized users

E. Turban et al., *Electronic Commerce: A Managerial and Social Networks Perspective*, Springer Texts in Business and Economics, DOI 10.1007/978-3-319-10091-3_16, © Springer International Publishing Switzerland 2015

OPENING CASE: I AM HUNGRY: CHEAP EATS IS NOT THE SOLUTION

There are many e-commerce startup success stories such as Facebook (the closing case) and Alibaba (Case 16.2), among others. However, failure can constitute a large part of entrepreneurship. According to di Stefano (2010), over 70% of online businesses fail within 10 years. I Am Hungry is not a success story and the company is not in operation any longer. However, there are lessons to be learned from the creative Web 2.0 project.

The Problem and Opportunity

One of the major issues that e-commerce has been dealing with is local relevance. It is an attempt to offer EC services that are relevant to users based on their location. For example, Groupon offers restaurant discounts in specific cities. I Am Hungry was created as a result of an observation that it was difficult to find information about local eateries and cafes, and advertisers were not offer the type of information that users were looking for (Lowman 2010). This means that there was a market gap between what consumers wanted (real-time, local information about good food availability, coupons when you need them and recommendations created by actual visitors), and what online marketing and advertising were offering (generic information). Note: today Yelp and several other companies have closed the above gap.

The Solution

I Am Hungry was a Facebook and iPhone app that provided detailed information about restaurants, cafes, and other eateries in the Boston area (Lowman 2010). However, the app went beyond simply advertising the presence of restaurants. Instead, it offered specific deals, including coupons and limited time only specials, through its app-based platform. The app, which had over 80 member restaurants in 2010, also had other offerings such as notifications of expiring deals. Once again, Groupon and others closed this gap.

The Startup

I Am Hungry, Inc. was founded in January 2010 by young entrepreneurs Alex Kravets and Mike Markarian, who had been developing the idea for three years prior to launching the company (Lowman 2010). The two men performed most of the management and operational activities (Zinsmeister and Venkatraman 2011). Angel investors initially funded the company, offering $150,000 in order to finance the development of the app. Markarian was in charge of most of the capital raising activities, while Kravets performed most of the other management duties.

There were eight additional employees in the operation, including six salespeople (all undergraduate students) and two system developers. These two activities operated under the direction of Kravets, with the sales staff focusing on signing up more restaurants to offer deals, and the development team was working on improving the apps. There were no marketing or advertising professionals on the team. The main advertising activities were performed through university events like CollegeFest (**collegefest.com**), which offered a low-cost opportunity to reach the core audience of the app.

In 2010, they had 400 users. The company had two main groups who took advantage of the app: restaurant patrons (who used the app) and restaurants (that advertised through it). The main restaurant patron group that the app targeted was college students, who eat at different hours. To target this group of customers, the firm advertised at venues such as CollegeFest, and had some success, attracting around 17,000 end users in its first six months of marketing. The other set was restaurants, which offered deals and advertised through the app in order to reach the hungry customers. Thus, I Am Hungry was essentially an advertising platform, allowing restaurants to reach app users.

The Revenue Models

The company used three distinct revenue models during its operation (Zinsmeister and Venkatraman 2011). All three of these models concentrated on the restaurant as the main revenue source. Initially, the company allowed restaurant owners to sign up to the program for a fee, so they were able to offer their deals to the consumer. However, this was very difficult to sell to restaurant owners, who did not understand the potential benefits of the model and only considered it as another method of advertising. In order to overcome this resistance, I Am Hungry offered, another model, a limited-time no subscription fees to restaurant owners, who eventually would switch to a paid subscription. Yet, a third model that the company considered was a redemption model that would allow restaurants to list offers for free, and then pay I am Hungry promised to generate operating capital to significant operating income.

All above three revenue models were problematic. As previously noted, the app did not attract sufficient interest from restaurant owners in its initial subscription form. While the trial free subscription had promise, it did not have enough conversion potential at the company's current sign-up rate to generate operating capital – even if 500 restaurants signed up (or six times the initial subscription number), it would not be sufficient. While the redemption model could have been potentially lucrative for the company, it would not be possible to implement since it required technological integration with the restaurant's POS. The failure of all three of the revenue models explored by the firm meant that there was no realistic way that the company could have met its revenue requirements.

The Results

As expected, given the inability of the company to monetize its services, I Am Hungry no longer exists as an ongoing business. Little information is available about the firm's failure. Its social media presence was originally robust (including Facebook and Twitter). However, this has not been updated since 2010. The I Am Hungry app is no longer available on Facebook. Despite the company's ambitions, the app was abandoned shortly after its initial announcement, and it never expanded beyond the Boston market.

Since the app is no longer alive, I Am Hungry is out of business. Competitors such as Groupon and Living Social have demonstrated that the advertising model offered by I Am Hungry is viable only if a business can find a way to monetize its services. If the app were to re-emerge, the most important strategic need would have been to find a way to attract restaurant owners who would be willing to pay enough money to support the app.

Sources: Based on Lowman (2010), Zinsmeister and Venkatraman (2011), and di Stefano (2010).

LESSONS LEARNED FROM THE CASE

The case of I Am Hungry offers a key strategic lesson for e-commerce businesses and startups. This lesson is that any company must have a business model that allows for a generation of revenues in a sufficient amount to support development and operations, preferably even before it begin to seek external funding. In order to do this, the company needs a firm idea of who its customers are and what its value proposition is, and understand the competitive market and the needs of its customers (see Chapter 13). Without this information, a good idea may not translate into a money-making opportunity.

This chapter addresses the basic requirements for launching an e-commerce business, including the financing foundations. It provides a guide on how to convert a bright idea into a sustainable e-business and how to implement a business plan. These, as well as the description of how to turn ideas into realities and how to provide the necessary support services, are the major topics of the chapter.

16.1 GETTING INTO E-COMMERCE AND STARTING A NEW ONLINE BUSINESS

As described in Chapter 1 and throughout the book, it is great to be an e-entrepreneur. The availability of inexpensive computing resources, smartphones, and other mobile devices with Internet access and high-speed bandwidth, has created a powerful infrastructure for launching a new e-business or adding e-commerce capabilities to existing organizations. Belew and Elad (2011) and Holden (2013) provide complete guides on how to start an online business. This chapter describes some of the major steps involved in setting up an e-business.

Getting into E-Commerce

Now that you are familiar with EC and its potential, you may want to know how to get started in EC yourself. You can start an e-commerce venture in any number of ways; your only limit is your imagination. Specifically, this chapter presents the following topics:

- Starting a new online business (a startup; see Section 16.1)
- Adding e-commerce initiative(s) to an existing traditional business (i.e., becoming a click-and-mortar organization; see Section 16.2)
- Transforming to a complete e-business (Section 16.2)
- Opening a webstore (Section 16.8)

Almost any e-commerce initiative will require support activities and services, as well as plans for attracting visitors to a website. This chapter presents the following with regard to these types of activities:

- Developing a website (Section 16.3)
- Hosting the website and selecting and registering a domain name (Section 16.4)

- Developing, updating, and managing the content of a website (Section 16.5)
- Designing a website for maximum usability (Section 16.6)
- Providing support services (Section 16.7)

Starting a New Online Business

Having an online marketplace does not guarantee success. Just like brick-and-mortar business, many startups will fail. The questions to ask are: Why do so few online companies succeed while many others fail? What do entrepreneurs need to know to launch a profitable online business?

Online businesses may be pure-play companies or click-and-mortar companies that add online projects. Projects can be, for example, e-procurement, or selling online.

An E-Startup Is a Startup

Before we start our discussion, we need to emphasize that an e-startup is basically a regular startup and, as such, we must consider the same issues facing a physical startup and some more. Many books, magazines, and articles are dedicated to describing the startup of a new business. Magazines such as *Entrepreneur* are fully dedicated to startups. Nagy (2010) provides some practical guidelines to avoid e-commerce failures. Specifically, he suggests looking at: (1) easy navigation website design, (2) customer loyalty and trust, (3) easy and logical order processing, and (4) appropriate method of payment.

Remember that it is advisable for new business owners to seek the guidance of a professional tax consultant, accountant, and/or an attorney to verify that all legal and other requirements have been met before starting and operating a business.

One of the major steps in launching any startup is finding a feasible product (service). This may take a long time, especially for a new product, because the concept comes first, followed by a prototype, and then a market test.

In addition, finding the correct *business model* is critical but not easy (see the opening case). A **business model** as defined in Chapter 1 expresses the manner in which the business from the website is done to generate revenue and create value. This value is usually revenue that hopefully results in profit. A well-defined business strategy picks up where the model leaves off. All of this is designed to help a business thrive.

Peterson et al. (2013) and Holden (2013), among others, provide practical guidelines for initiating and implementing a successful e-business. They cover topics such as setting up the website, getting a domain name, managing the website, initiating accounting, and running the online business. For a free 14-session guide to starting a business, see **myownbusiness.org/course.html**. Several centers for information technology startups exist; some are sponsored by major software companies.

Creating a New Company or Adding an Online Project

Most new businesses – brick-and-mortar, pure play, or click-and-mortar – begin in a similar manner. The following three typical steps describe the process:

1. **Identify a consumer or business need in the marketplace.** Successful businesses must begin with a good idea. A magazine article, a personal observation, an unsolved marketing problem, or a friend's suggestion may trigger an idea for an online business. The entrepreneur then examines if there is a gap between what people need and what is available on the market. If there is such a gap, an assessment is made to see if e-commerce can fill this gap. In addition, an idea can be derived from new technology, such as in the case of Amazon.com (Case 16.1). Note that the key here is *innovation.*

2. **Investigate the opportunity.** The idea needs to be realistic. Namely, there should be enough potential to attract customers as soon as the business starts to run. In addition, the cost of manufacturing, marketing, and distributing the product or providing the service cannot be excessive. This requires appropriate pricing of the product or services. For example, online grocery shopping would seem like a wonderful opportunity – relieving busy people from having to spend time leaving the house to shop. Unfortunately, many have tried to provide large- and small-scale online grocery ventures, but most have failed or continue to lose money because they misjudged the logistical problems associated with grocery warehousing and delivery (see discussion in Chapters 3 and 12). This is why it is so important to develop a business plan. One of the purposes of a *business plan* is to determine the viability of a business opportunity in the marketplace.

3. **Determine the business owner's ability to meet the need.** Assuming that a realistic business opportunity exists, does the prospective business owner have the ability to convert the opportunity into success? First, the availability of resources needs to be checked. Second, the personal qualities are important: Is the business in an industry that the prospective entrepreneur knows well and likes? Business skills in recruitment, planning, management, negotiation, marketing, and financial management are required, as well as entrepreneurial attitudes such as innovation, risk taking, and being strategic. Finally, government regulations must be considered.

The process for developing EC projects in existing companies is similar, except Step 3 changes to: "Determine the organization's ability to meet the need."

CASE 16.1: INNOVATION AND CREATIVITY AT AMAZON.COM

It is well known that having the right person with the right idea at the right place and time is a key success factor for any new business. At the start of e-commerce, Jeff Bezos, with his creative mind, was the key to the success of Amazon.com (see opening case in Chapter 3).

As a young entrepreneur, Bezos promoted a summer camp for exchanging new ideas in old areas.

Bezos graduated from Princeton University with a degree in computer science, and his first job was building a financial EDI network for cross-border transactions. A few years later, he became senior vice president at a stock market fund firm D. E. Shaw, responsible for exploring new Internet-related business opportunities. Using his intelligence, entrepreneurial talents, computing education, and e-commerce experience and after titles led him to the idea of selling products online. He then made a list of possible products to sell. Books were #1 on the list since a virtual bookstore could offer millions of different titles and books are a standard commodity. He then decided to create his own company (selling books). Several years later, he added dozens of other products. Today millions of different products are available on Amazon.com.

Why did Bezos decide to sell books? Bezos was willing to bet that many people who buy books would be willing to give up the browsing environment of the local bookstore and the attached coffee shop if he could offer them a huge selection of books at significantly discount prices. In addition, it would be less expensive to offer outstanding customer service and features that one would not find at a physical bookstore, such as book reviews by customers and experts, author interviews, and personalized services such as book recommendations. Bezos wanted to establish a "virtual community" where visitors could "hang out." Bezos also knew that in 1992 the Supreme Court had ruled in *Quill Corp. v. North Dakota* that retailers were exempt from charging sales tax in states where they did not have a physical presence.

Bezos started by writing the Amazon.com business plan. He built the website in his home garage (similar to the way Microsoft and Apple Computer started). When Amazon.com was launched in July 1995, it was nothing more than a few people in the garage, packing books on a table. When Amazon opened its "virtual doors," it offered millions of titles (books). Today, Amazon.com sells millions of items each week.

In the late 1990s and early 2000s, Amazon. com invested $2 billion in physical logistic system, including warehouses. This was in line with Bezos's broader vision for Amazon.com and its strategy to sacrifice short term profit as an investment for the long run.

After years of substantial losses, Amazon.com announced its first small profit in the fourth quarter of 2001. In 2009, Amazon.com was one of the few companies to report increased sales and earnings. Amazon.com's revenue reached $74 billion in 2013, and it is growing rapidly.

Since its inception, Amazon.com has changed its business model several times, adding innovative ideas. It also has acquired other companies took stakes in different companies in several countries (e.g., **amazon.cn** – a large e-tailer of books, music, and videos in China, but without Kindle). Amazon Instant Viewing offers users the ability to watch videos and Internet TV shows on compatible devices (e.g., TV, any Internet-connected computer, Kindle Fire, iPad). In 2007, Amazon.com released the Kindle (1st generation) and began selling downloadable books (recall the Kindle e-book reader in Chapter 5), music, and movies. A major change in the company occurred when Bezos decided to go into the cloud computing business (AWS), providing cloud-based computing to hundreds of thousands of companies (e.g., the U.S. Department of Defense).

Bezos is indeed an innovator. His most original idea is his vision of Blue Origin (**blueorigin. com**), a futuristic center for suborbital spaceships. During the last few years, he has worked on commercializing space travel. The most recently publicized timetable states that Blue Origin was being tested for flight in July 2012. Other interesting 2013/2014 innovations are the use of thousands of robots in the company's warehouses (Chapter 12), the use of drones for order fulfilment, and the creation of the first 3D smartphone.

Sources: Based on Quittner (2008), press releases during 2013 and 2014, and **amazon.com** (accessed June 2014).

Questions
1. What were the opportunities and needs in the consumer market that inspired Bezos to create Amazon.com?
2. What factors, at both personal and business levels, led Bezos to his brilliant idea?
3. Describe some recent innovations from Amazon. com.

Some Tips for Success

Many people provide tips on how to succeed in EC (for examples, see Condra 2014). A good source for EC ideas is *Practical Commerce*, **practicalcommerce.com**, where you can find articles and commentaries (and a free e-book) to help online merchants.

There are some requirements and constraints that an owner of an online business must consider. The first requirement is to understand the culture of the Internet. For example, the correct use of graphics in website design attracts visitors, while intrusive pop-ups are counter-productive. Additionally, there is a need to consider the characteristics of the products and services you plan to sell. For example, digital products (e.g., information, music, software), services (e.g., stock brokering, travel ticket sales), and standard item commodities (e.g., books, CDs) have been quite successful. In contrast, grocery products, such as fresh vegetables and ice cream do not sell well online. One of the greatest opportunities the Internet offers is niche marketing. Unique concepts, such as antique Coke bottles (**antiquebottles.com**), gadgets for left-handed individuals (**anythinglefthanded. co.uk**), and toys for cats and dogs (**cattoys.com** and **dogtoys.com**), would rarely succeed doing business a physical storefront (due to not having enough customers), but the Internet offers the owners of these sites an opportunity to reach much larger markets.

Cloning

Entrepreneurs all over the globe try to clone or copy the Web's most successful websites, such as Facebook, Twitter, eBay, Pinterest, and Amazon.com. Examples are Amazon.gr (no longer live), which called itself "Greece's Biggest Bookstore," and had much the same look and feel as Amazon.com's site at the time when Amazon.com referred to itself as the "Earth's Biggest Bookstore."

Planning Online Businesses

Planning an online business is similar to planning for any startup venture in that it centers on a business plan (see Berry undated).

Business Plan

Every new online business needs at least an informal *business plan*. Medium and large businesses, or those seeking external funding, must have a formal business plan. A **business plan** is a written, formal document that specifies a company's goals, and outlines how the company intends to achieve these goals. The plan describes the nature and characteristics of the business. It includes both strategic elements (e.g., mission statement, business model, value proposition, and competitive positioning analysis) and/or operational elements (e.g., production and operation plans, financial projections) of how a new venture intends to do business. For details, see Peterson et al. (2013) and the U.S. Small Business Administration(**sba.gov/content/what-business-plan-and-why-do-i-need-one**).

The primary reason an entrepreneur writes a business plan is to use it to secure funding from a bank, an angel investor or a venture capitalist. Similarly, in an existing business, a *business case* needs to be written for any new large EC project. For all aspects of business plans for start-up companies, see HJ Ventures International (**hjventures.com**).

For a sample of business plan software, see PlanWare (**planware.org**), PlanMagic Corporation (**planmagic.com**), and Atlas Business Solutions, Inc. (**abs-usa.com**). Palo Alto Software (**paloalto. com**) offers online access to more than 500 sample business plans, in their LivePlan, for a monthly fee of US$19.95. For more on getting started with writing a business plan for a small company, see **smallbusiness.yahoo.com**. See also Session 2: The Business Plan at My Own Business, Inc. (**myownbusiness.org/outline.html**).

The Business Case

An existing brick-and-mortar business looking to move online (either to add EC projects or to

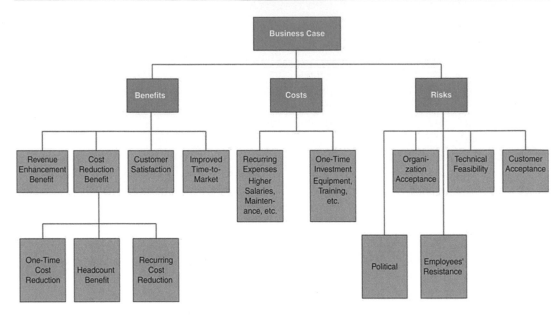

Figure 16.1   The cost-benefit elements of a business case

transform itself to an e-business) needs a **business case** – a document that is used to convince management to approve the investment of organizational resources in specific EC or other projects (see Figure 16.1). A business case supports the decision to go or not to go with an EC project. For a large, resource-intensive EC project, a business case resembles a business plan. For a small or medium-sized project, the business case can be much simpler and less formal. If a business is considering several initiatives, there should be a separate business case for each one.

The Major Advantages of Business Case

Business cases develop a systematic financial justification for projects; they assist in organizing and not forgetting all the necessary data; they point to drawbacks, constraints and risks; assist in collaboration with relevant partners, and help determine who needs a business case and how to use one. The business case structure is assisted by templates.

Business Case Templates

Several business case templates are available online. In general, they include the elements listed in Figure 16.1. For examples of business case templates, see **score.org/resources/business-planning-financial-statements-template-gallery**. Free templates and tutorials are available at **projectmanagementdocs.com/project-initiation-templates/business-case.html**. For more on business cases, see **know.about.com/Business_Case**.

Funding a New Online Business

Launching an online business can be expensive. The entrepreneur is expected to invest personal funds from savings, personal lines of credit, or taking a second mortgage on his or her house, but these sources of "bootstrap funding" may not be sufficient. Entrepreneurs should "bootstrap" as long as possible, before tapping into the venture capital market. If the new venture involves a significant risk, traditional sources of debt financing, such as a bank loan, can be difficult or impossible to obtain. See Rutgers (2014) for financing a startup business. For an introduction to sources of e-business funding, see the Business Partners Network (**businesspartners.com**).

First Round of Initial Funding: Angel Investors and Incubators

When an entrepreneur's personal funds are insufficient, he or she will go to friends, family members, or to *angel investors*. An **angel investor** is a wealthy individual who contributes personal funds and possibly advice at the earliest stage of business development usually in exchange of equity in the business. Angel investors can be found through organizations such as the Angel Capital Association (**angelcapitalassociation. org**), newspapers, magazines, and business-oriented social networks (e.g., LinkedIn).

Another important source of support, if not direct funding, for pre-venture-capital firms is an *incubator*. An **EC incubator** is a company, university, or nonprofit organization that supports promising EC businesses in their initial stages of development. Although some incubators offer startup funding, the primary purpose of most incubators is to offer a variety of support services – office space, accounting services, group purchasing programs, reception services, coaching, and information technology consulting – at little or no cost. In return, the incubator receives a modest fee, startup equity in the company, or both.

A special case of angel investors is using crowdfunding.

Crowdfunding

A new approach to the financing of startups and small businesses is *crowdfunding*.

Crowdfunding, also known as *crowd financing*, is based on using investors to fund startups. Each individual invests a small amount of money; the collection channels are Internet-based social networks (see Young 2013).

The concept is implemented via online portals, which connect small investors with entrepreneurs. For details, see Neiss et al. (2013). There are numerous companies that manage such portals (e.g., Kickstarter, and Spot.us). For an overview, see Prive (2012).

Second Round Financing: Venture Capital

One major source of funding new ventures is *venture capital*. **Venture capital (VC)** is money invested in a business by an individual, a group of individuals (venture capitalists), or a funding company in exchange for equity in the business.

The downside for the startup business to acquire VC is minimal; it loses some control over the business in return for funds it is unlikely to acquire from any other source. The more difficult problem is finding VC. Due to the many dot-com failures since 2000, many VC sources have disappeared, and competition for venture capital is fierce. However, currently there is a surge in VC financing social media and social commerce companies.

Some well-known VC companies are vFinance, Inc. (**vfinance.com**), Westlake Securities (**westlake securities.com**), and Garage Technology Ventures (**garage.com**). For more information, see the National Venture Capital Association (**nvca.org**), Venture Capital (**v-capital.com.au**), and VC Fodder (**vcfodder.com**).

Additional Funding: A Large Partner

As part of a VC investment or after the depletion of VC money, one or more large companies may offer financial assistance. For example, Yahoo!, IBM, eBay, Microsoft, Facebook, Motorola, Google, Time Warner News Corp., and Oracle have invested in hundreds of EC startup companies. Eventually, they may acquire the startup completely. Such investments are done frequently in complementary or competing areas. For example, Yahoo! is a major investor in Alibaba.com. Microsoft purchased a stake in Facebook in 2008, and eBay owns 25% of Craigslist.

The closing case discusses the management challenges faced by Facebook as it has grown. A major dilemma of a startup is: Should it collaborate with larger partners or should it stay independent? Facebook eventually went public in June 2012. It is important for a startup to make the right decision at the right time. Some EC startups like Friendster waited too long and saw disastrous results.

The Initial Public Offer (IPO)

Once a company is well known and successful, it will go to a stock exchange to raise money via an *initial public offering* (IPO). In such offerings, investors will pay a much larger amount of money per share than would be paid by an initial and secondary funding source, sometimes 5 or 10 times more per share. A well-known example is the launch of Alibaba.com (see Case 16.2); its IPO was valued in the billions of dollars on the Hong Kong stock exchange in October 2007. Then the owners repurchased all the publically traded shares. In 2014, Alibaba group went public on the New York Stock Exchange, raising its valuation to $150 billion. In 2011, several social commerce startups took the IPO route (e.g., LinkedIn, Groupon, and Pandora). Finally, in 2012, Facebook went public. Some successful recent IPOs are Yelp, Tripadvisor, and HomeAway.

SECTION 16.1 REVIEW QUESTIONS

1. List the major steps in the process of building an online business.
2. What special requirements must an online business consider in its formation? In e-business planning?
3. Describe a business plan.
4. What is a business case and how does it contribute to the success of a business?
5. Describe initial, secondary, and IPO funding options available to a startup.
6. What is an angel investor? An incubator?
7. Define crowdfunding and describe how it works.
8. How does a VC company support a startup?

16.2   ADDING E-COMMERCE INITIATIVES OR TRANSFORMING TO AN E-BUSINESS

Creating an e-business startup certainly is exciting, but it also is very risky. As with any other new business, the failure rate is very high. However, in cyberspace the risks and uncertainties, plus lack of experience, may result in an even higher rate of failure. Nevertheless, hundred thousands of new, mostly small, online businesses have been created since e-commerce started in 1995.

Another common strategy to get involved in EC is adding one or several EC initiatives to an existing business.

Adding EC Initiatives to an Existing Business

Almost all medium-to-large organizations have added or plan to add EC initiatives to their existing business. The most common additions are:

- **A webstore.** Adding an online sales channel is common in both B2C (e.g., **godiva.com**, **walmart.com**) and B2B (e.g., **ibm.com/us/en**). The required investment is low, because inexpensive webstore hosting and software is available from many vendors (see Sections 16.4 and 16.6). A webstore can be built quickly, and the damage in case of failure may not be too great. Because the required investment is usually not too large, it may not be necessary to expend the time and money in developing a formal business case. This is a practical strategy for a *small- and medium-sized enterprise* (SME). For a large-scale webstore, a company will need to follow the steps suggested in Section 16.1, especially the preparation of a business case, in order to secure internal funding from the top management. For further details on developing webstores, see the Yahoo! Small Business site (go to **smallbusiness. yahoo.com/advisor/getstarted**). A major issue in developing a webstore is deciding what support services to offer and how to provide them.
- **A portal.** There are several types of corporate portals. Almost all companies today have one or several portals that they use for external and/or internal collaboration and communication. A webstore for employees or for external customers will include a portal. Adding a portal (or several portals) may be a necessity. Issues of content and design, as well as security, are of utmost importance. Because many vendors offer

portal-building services, vendor selection might be an important issue.

- **E-procurement.** This EC initiative is popular with large companies, as described in Chapter 4. E-procurement frequently requires a business plan and extensive integration (both internally and externally with business partners), so EC architecture must be in place.
- **Auctions and reverse auctions.** Large corporations need to consider building their own auction or reverse auction (for e-procurement) sites. Although forward auctions can be added to a webstore at a reasonable cost, a reverse auction usually requires more integration with business partners, and, consequently, a larger investment and a business case. You can learn more about reverse auctions at **whatisareverseauction.com.**
- **M-commerce.** Many companies are embarking on the usage of internal wireless applications as well as on selling and advertising via m-commerce technologies. The resounding effect of this policy can be seen in sites that have gone wireless. With the increasing popularity of tablets and smartphones, posts on Twitter, LinkedIn, and Facebook are effective tactics and strategies for e-commerce.
- **Social commerce.** Many large companies now offer blogs and wikis; others (e.g., Toyota, Coca-Cola and Starbucks) operate enterprise social networks, and social CRM is offered by Best Buy. For more, see Chapter 7. Learn about the explosive growth of social commerce from **bazaarvoice.com/research-and-insight/social-commerce-statistics** and in Turban et al. (2015).

Organizations may consider many other EC initiatives, following the business models presented in Chapter 1. For example, Qantas Airways (**qantas.com.au**) sells tickets online directly from its website. From a B2B exchange, Qantas buys supplies and services by using e-procurement; provides e-training for its employees; operates several corporate portals; offers online banking services to its employees; provides eCRM and e-PRM; manages its frequent-flyer program; supports a wireless notification system to customers; and so forth. Large companies, such as GE and IBM, have hundreds of active EC projects.

Transformation to an E-Business and Social Business

As a brick-and-mortar organization implements more EC projects, it becomes a click-and-mortar organization, and eventually an e-business. Being an e-business does not imply that the organization is a pure-play company; it just means that it conducts as many processes as possible online. A rapid or large-scale change from brick-and-mortar to e-business involves organizational transformation.

What Is Organizational Transformation?

Organizational transformation is a comprehensive concept that implies a major organizational change. A *transformation* is not only a major change, but also a sharp break from the past. The key points in understanding organizational transformation are as follows:

- The organization's thinking is fundamentally modified.
- There are major changes to processes and business models.
- The change makes organizations completely different from the past practices.
- The behavior of management and employees is completely changed.
- The change will create new organizational structures and possibly different chains of command.

How an Organization Can Be Transformed into an E-Business

An e-business transformation is not solely about new technology. Technologies must be integrated with possible changes in business strategy, processes, organizational culture, and infrastructure. For details, see Gloor (2011). A discussion regarding transformation to e-business is provided in Chapter 1.

Transforming an organization, especially a large company, into an e-business can be a very complex endeavor. For an organization to transform itself into an e-business, it must transform several major processes, such as procurement, sales, customer relationship management (CRM), and manufacturing, as well as handle *change management* efforts.

It is suggested that companies spin off EC activities as part of the transformation process.

Software Tools for Facilitating the Transformation to E-Business

Several vendors offer methodologies and tools to facilitate the transformation to e-business. IBM is one, but there are many others, such as Cisco and Oracle. Using special methodologies, organizations in the public sector can achieve significant cost and cycle time reductions.

Change Management

Transforming an existing business into an e-business or adding a major e-commerce initiative means a manager must change business processes and the manner in which people work, communicate, and are promoted and managed (see Kotter 2012 for details).

SECTION 16.2 REVIEW QUESTIONS

1. Which EC initiatives are brick-and-mortar organizations most likely to add?
2. Describe the steps in becoming an e-business and the major activities involved in the process.
3. List some of the issues involved in transforming to an e-business.
4. Describe the major characteristics (key points) of organizational transformation.

16.3 BUILDING OR ACQUIRING A WEBSITE

Every online business needs a website. A website is the primary mechanism where any firm doing business on the Internet advertises its products or services and attracts customers. Many websites also sell products and services. The website may be a webstore, a portal, an auction site, and so on (See Rutgers 2014). How can an organization build or acquire such a site? First, let us examine the major types of websites.

Classification of Websites

Websites can be classified according to the level of functionality of the site. Here are the most common levels:

- An **informational website** provides information about the business and its products and services. The major purpose is to have a *presence* on the Web.
- An **interactive website** provides opportunities for the customers and the business to interact, converse and present information (as in information website). It may include an e-newsletter, search engine, video product demonstrations, wikis, blogs, feedback from customers, discussion forums and value added features.
- **Attractors** are websites with features that do more than the previously described sites do. Attractors include puzzles, competitions, and prize giveaways. They are designed so that visitors will like them so much that they will visit again, and recommend the site to their friends. For example, Ragú's website (**ragu.com**; an easy name to remember) does not sell Ragú products, but the recipes and customer interaction provided attract visitors

and contributes to the brand recognition. Coca-Cola, Whole Foods Market, and Disney have similar sites.

- A **transactional website** sells products and services. These websites also include information and interactive features, but they concentrate on selling mechanism features (Chapter 2), such as shopping carts.
- A **collaborative website** is a site that allows business partners to interact and collaborate (i.e., it includes many supportive tools; see Chapter 5). B2B *exchanges* may also provide collaboration capabilities.
- A **social-oriented website** is a site that provides users with online tools for communication and sharing information on common interests. It empowers consumers to utilize their time around the converged media experience for social participation. Social-oriented websites like Facebook (see the closing case) have emerged as one of the most powerful marketing channels.

Building a Website

Once a business completes all preliminary tasks, it can construct the website.

Steps in Building a Website

These are the typical steps in building a website:

1. **Select a Web host.** One of the first decisions that an online business will face is where to place its website on the Internet. The website may be included in a virtual shopping mall, such as **3d-berlin.com**, **the-virtualmall.com**, or **pointshop.com/mall**. Alternatively, a webstore can be hosted in a marketplace that is a collection of independent webstores like Yahoo! (**smallbusiness.yahoo.com**), Amazon.com, Etsy, or eBay (even if it is not an auction business). However, many medium and large-sized businesses build their own websites with either an independent hosting service or through self-hosting arrangements (see Chapter 14).

2. **Register a domain name.** In a mall or webstore, the business's name may be an extension of the host's name. A stand-alone website will need its own domain name, and decisions will have to be made about which top-level domain name to use and whether the domain name includes the business name or only some aspect of branding. Registering domain names is essential to a business (see **iregistry.com/what-is-a-domain.html**).

3. **Create and manage content.** The website also needs content – the text, catalog, images, sound, and video – that delivers the information that visitors need and expect. Content can come from a variety of sources, but getting the right content in place, making it easy for viewers to find, delivering it effectively, and managing the content so it remains accurate and up-to-date are critical success factors (see discussion in Section 16.5). Hosting services may provide advice and services (Section 16.4). Table 16.1 lists the major criteria website visitors use to evaluate the content of a website. More criteria are provided in Section 16.4.

4. **Design the website.** This important task is described in Section 16.6. Stores in a mall or those using storebuilders may have limited options, but the stand-alone websites have many options. Table 16.1 lists the primary criteria that visitors use to evaluate the usefulness of a website.

5. **Construct the website and test.** Businesses must also decide whether to design and construct the website internally, contract it out to a Web design firm, or a combination of both. When the business owners are satisfied with the website, it is transferred to the website host. At this point, the website is open for business, but it requires final testing to ensure that all the links work and that the processes function as expected (e.g., acceptance of credit cards).

6. **Market and promote the website.** At this stage, the business promotes the location of the website, both online and offline. A business can use any of the advertising strategies discussed in Chapter 9 – banner exchanges, e-mail, chat

Table 16.1 How website visitors evaluate websites

How website visitors evaluate content	
Criteria (and related subcriteria)	**Explanation**
Relevance (applicable, related, clear)	What is the relevancy, clarity, and quality of the information?
Timeliness (current, continuously updated)	How current is the information?
Reliability (believable, accurate, consistent)	How accurate, dependable, and uniform is the information?
Personality	Is there any personalized content? Is it pleasing to the customer?
Scope (sufficient, complete, covers a wide range, detailed)	What extent of information, range of information, and amount of detail does the website provide?
Perceived usefulness (informative, valuable, instrumental)	What is the likelihood that the website's information will facilitate a visitor's purchasing decision?
How website visitors evaluate website design	
Criteria (and related subcriteria)	**Explanation**
Access (responsive, loads quickly) (see **w3.org/WAI**)	How long does it take to access the website, and is it always available?
Usability (simple layout, easy to use, well organized, visually attractive, fun, clear design)	Is the website visually appealing, reliable, and easy to use?
Navigation	Are the links to needed information appropriate and active on the website?
Interactivity (customized product; search engine; ability to create list of items, change list of items, and find related items)	Is there an ability to utilize the search engine and the personalized features of the website?
Attractiveness, Appearance	Are multimedia and colors used properly?

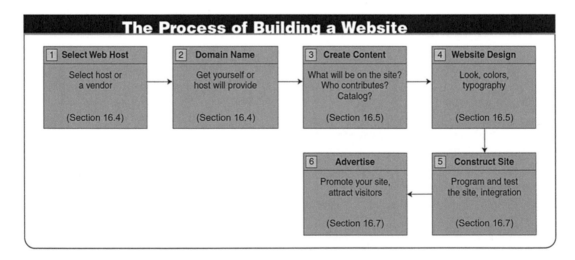

Figure 16.2 The process of building a website

rooms, viral marketing, and so forth. The process of building the site is illustrated in Figure 16.2. Templates are available at **smallbusiness.yahoo. com/ecommerce**. The forthcoming sections discuss each of the steps illustrated in Figure 16.2.

SECTION 16.3 REVIEW QUESTIONS

1. Distinguish among informational, interactive, transactional, collaborative, and social-oriented websites.
2. List the six steps in building a website.

16.4 WEBSITE HOSTING AND OBTAINING A DOMAIN NAME

Selling online requires a webstore. An e-business either owns, or rents the webstore in a mall, or at an independent location. The decisions about whether to own (self-host) or rent, where to host the website (e.g., storebuilder service, ISP, use a pure Web hosting service, or self-hosting), and the site's domain name are some of the initial decisions an e-business owner has to make. This section discusses the considerations in making these decisions. For details, see Rutgers (2014), and Holden (2013).

Web Hosting Options

The following are the major Web hosting options.

Storebuilder Service
A **storebuilder service** (also called a *design-and-host service*) provides Web hosting as well as storage space, templates, and other services to help small businesses build a website expeditiously and inexpensively. An example of a company that offers comprehensive storebuilding services is Yahoo! (**smallbusiness.yahoo.com/webhosting**). However, using a storebuilding service has certain disadvantages, one being the lack of certain functionalities (e.g., accepting payments through PayPal may not be possible). In addition, the client's website tends to look like other sites because everyone is using the same set of templates. Despite the disadvantages, storebuilder services are popular. However, today's storebuilders offer services similar to those offered by dedicated hosting services, which are the leading choice of small and sometimes medium-sized businesses. These services are usually inexpensive unless you want them upgraded (to a premium level).

A Dedicated Hosting Service
A **Web hosting service** is a type of hosting service that allows individuals and organizations to make their website accessible on the Web (providing websites with space on the Internet). Companies such as Go Daddy, iPage, Shopify, Web.com, and BlueHost offer more and better services than a storebuilder service offers. Almost all Web hosting companies also have internal Web design departments to help the clients. In addition, features such as shipping, tax calculators, and comprehensive site statistics are likely to be available. Comprehensive services are also offered by large vendors such as Microsoft (see-**microsoftbusinesshub.com**), IBM (**ibm.com/us/en**), and Adobe's Dreamweaver (**adobe.com/devnet/dreamweaver.html**). For a list of the top 10 Web hosting companies for 2014 and for a discussion on how to select one, see **top10bestwebhosting.com**. For a comprehensive site offering resources and references, articles and newsletters on Web hosting, website design, domain names, etc., see **thesitewizard.com** (to see a list of categories and a topical index, go to **thesitewizard.com/topics/index.shtml**).

Self-Hosting
With **self-hosting**, a company is doing the job in-house (build your own website). For this purpose, it needs hardware, software, IT staff, and dedicated telecommunications services. Self-hosting is beneficial when a business has special requirements, or a large and complex site. Some of the disadvantages of self-hosting are the high cost and the low speed of construction. The other Web hosting options enable the hosting company to share the costs of site hosting among many of their customers.

Free Web Hosting Services
Several companies offer free web hosting, but they do not offer the many features offered by the dedicated web hosting companies (e.g., Google "sites" is used to support the website of this book). For a comparison of some free Web hosting services, see **en.wikipedia.org/wiki/Comparison_of_free_web_hosting_services**. With these sites, you can get free hosting, a free domain name, and build your website very quickly.

Selecting and Registering a Domain Name

A **domain name** is a name-based Internet address (owned by a person or an organization) that identifies a specific website and its Internet-connected server. It is an "online identity," which allows users to identify one or more IP addresses. Most domain names are assigned by an agency called Domail Name Systems, or DNS. Usually, a domain name is designated by the portion of the address that comes right before the ".com" or ".org" (or other top level designation), and it includes the ".com" or ".org" portion.

For more information and details about Web hosting, domain names, and website builders, see **midphase.com/website-hosting/what-is-web-hosting.php**.

Selecting a domain name is an important marketing and branding consideration for any business (an example is Alibaba.com, as presented in Case 16.2).

CASE 16.2: ALIBABA.COM OPENS DOORS TO E-COMMERCE ENTREPRENEURS

We presented the case of Alibaba Group and its B2B subsidiary, Alibaba.com, in Chapter 4. Here we describe a few additional topics related to the content of this chapter.

Alibaba.com has grown into a global provider of online trading solutions, initially serving only small- and medium-sized enterprises in China, but is now serving many types of companies and individuals worldwide. Founded in 1998 by Jack Ma, it has successfully adapted to the challenges of e-commerce and seized opportunities brought by technological innovation over the years. Its name is derived from the classic Arabian story "Alibaba and the Forty Thieves." Ma deliberately chose this name, believing in its potential for brand recognition, as he envisioned the company's international expansion. In addition, people associate the name with the saying "Open Sesame!" (per **usatoday.com/story/money/2014/05/07/alibaba-name/8805805**). Perhaps more profoundly, the story of Alibaba.com reflects the type of success that results from practicing honesty and integrity similar to that depicted in the fairy tale.

Where Technology Meets Business

The Alibaba Group is committed to supporting the growth and success of SMEs. Alibaba.com is a B2B site where small companies can conduct transactions. As superior technology with advanced security features is essential to such dealings, the website utilizes TrustPass, a certificate given to companies assuring that they are a real and legitimate business (see **img.alibaba.com/hermes/trustpass.html**).

The details of Alibaba.com are provided in the opening case to Chapter 4. In addition, the site provides an efficient search engine and members can subscribe to news alerts on the latest products. Alibaba members can join online forums that discuss relevant issues in online global trading. Additionally, the Alibaba instant messaging tool TradeManager (**trademanager.alibaba.com**) allows real-time chat between buyers and suppliers online.

The website interface is simple and user-friendly, designed to attract even non-technical users.

An Inspiration to SMEs

Now a household name in e-commerce, Alibaba.com proves the importance of brand recognition, especially with the large number of companies competing for customer attention. The site is popular among SMEs, owing to the customized membership packages that it provides in exchange for a minimal membership fee. This approach stands in stark contrast to the complex and costly maintenance of a self-maintained company website. Member firms gain access to the advanced technology utilized by Alibaba.com, yet they can choose only certain features within their limited budget. Furthermore, members can benefit from the extensive network of trading partners. Alibaba emphasizes popular issues on trading and offers helpful advice through discussion groups or forums. Alibaba.com empowers SMEs to contribute to China's economic growth.

Despite its enormous success, Alibaba.com, which began as a small start-up company, has maintained its goal: to support SMEs. With its wide community of buyers and sellers today, Alibaba.com not only boosts e-commerce but also serves as an inspiration to other start-up companies, urging them to aim for global success.

Sources: Based on Lai (2010b), Farhoomand and Lai (2010), and **alibaba.com** (accessed July 2014).

Questions

1. Alibaba.com has a strong commitment to assist small and medium enterprises (SMEs) in B2B e-commerce. What are the advantages and disadvantages of this strategy to Alibaba Group and to the network member?
2. Go to **alibaba.com** and examine the layout and features of the site. Do you think the interface design is appropriate for SME users? Why or Why not? Explain.
3. Compare and contrast the business model of Alibaba.com with other B2B business models (e.g., of Ariba.com).
4. What lessons does the Alibaba.com case offer to e-commerce startups and entrepreneurs?

The Essentials of Domain Names

A domain name should be easy to remember. The *domain name system* (DNS) maps a domain name to a corresponding IP address (e.g., 211.180.338). Each domain name must include a top-level domain (TLD) (e.g., .com, .net, .org), or a country-code top-level domain (ccTLD; e.g., .au for Australia, .jp for Japan). Most ccTLDs also have a *second-level domain name* that indicates the type of organization (e.g., **yahoo.co.jp**). On the left side of the domain name is the organization's name (e.g., **ibm.com**), or a brand name (e.g., **cadillac.com**).

A useful resource for learning more about domain names and the registration process is Domainmart (**domainmart.com**), which offers "guides and resources for successful Internet presence," including a domain name glossary and a registration FAQ file. See also, "How to

Register a Domain Name" at **2createawebsite. com/prebuild/register_domain.html**. You can also get a domain name at **smallbusiness.yahoo. com/domains** and other hosting services.

SECTION 16.4 REVIEW QUESTIONS

1. What are the advantages and disadvantages of the different Web hosting options?
2. What is a domain name? Why is selecting a domain name an important step for creating an online business?

16.5   WEB CONTENT CREATION AND MANAGEMENT

Web content is content (the text, images, sound, and video) that is included on a Web page. Creating and managing content is critical to website success because it presents the company and its products to customers. In Web design, "Content is king!" This section describes the essentials of Web content. For details, see Rutgers (2014). For more about the importance of content, including an infographic, see **simplycompelling. com/content-is-king**.

Categories and Types of Content

Providing content to EC sites may be a complex job due to the variety and quantity of the contributing sources. In addition, content may include foreign languages and must be updated frequently. Content may include all types of media. Finally, content may involve security, quality, privacy protection, and permission issues.

Frequently changing content (e.g., weather news) is referred to as **dynamic Web content**, which is constant and may updated infrequently (standard HTML pages) as distinguished from *static Web content*.

Up-to-the-minute dynamic content is what attracts new and returning customers ("eyeballs") and makes them stay longer ("stickiness"). Therefore, dynamic Web content contributes to customer loyalty.

Primary and Secondary Content

Content should include more than just information about the product itself (the *primary content*). A website also should include *secondary content* that offers marketing opportunities, such as the following:

- **Cross-selling.** Using content for **cross-selling** means offering complementary or related products and services to increase sales. Amazon. com offers people who read personalized recommendations such as "customers who bought this book also bought…" and items "frequently bought together." Accessories, add-on products, extended warranties, and gift wrapping are examples of cross-selling opportunities that companies can offer to buyers on the product pages or in the purchase process. Another example of cross-selling is if you buy a car online, you may be offered insurance and financing.

- **Up-selling.** Creating content for **up-selling** means offering an upgraded version of the product in order to boost sales and profit. Amazon.com offers "great buy" book combinations (buy two related books for slightly more than the price of one). (It also practices *down-selling* by offering visitors used copies of a book at a cheaper price than the new book.) Up-selling activities usually include offering products with a different design, color, fabric, or size.

- **Promotions.** A coupon, rebate, discount, or special service is secondary content that can increase sales or improve customer service. Amazon.com frequently offers reduced or free shipping charges, (e.g., to Prime members or with a purchase of $35 or more).

- **Comments.** Reviews, testimonials, recommendations, or 'how to use the product' supplement content. Amazon.com book pages always have editorial and customer reviews of the book, and the "look inside this book" feature sometimes allows website visitors to preview some book chapters.

Content Management and Maintenance

Content management is the process of collecting, publishing, revising, updating, and removing content from a website to keep content fresh, accurate, compelling, and credible. Almost all sites begin with a high level of relevant content, but over time material becomes dated, irrelevant, or incorrect. Content management makes sure a site remains relevant and accurate long after it was placed on the site.

Content Management Software (System)

Content management software enables nontechnical contributors to create, edit, and delete content on a company's website. This way, companies empower and induce content owners to manage their own content. There are numerous software packages available on the market that help with content management. For more information, see-**slideshare.net/abelsp/content-quality-management-using-software-to-manage-quality-and-track-metrics**.

Catalog Content and Its Management

Much of the content in B2B and B2C sites is catalog based. Chapter 2 discussed the benefits of electronic catalogs. Although there are many positive aspects of e-catalogs, poorly organized ones may deter buyers. Companies need to make sure that their catalog content is well created and managed.

For B2B internal catalog creators (Chapter 4), who aggregate suppliers' catalogs on their own websites, content management begins by interacting with suppliers and then collecting their relevant content. That is no small task, considering that most large buying organizations have hundreds, or even thousands, of suppliers, each of which may use different data formats and nomenclature to describe their catalog items.

SECTION 16.5 REVIEW QUESTIONS

1. What is website content? Dynamic content? What are the major categories of content?
2. How can a business use content for cross-selling? For up-selling? For promotion?
3. What is the purpose of content management?

16.6   WEBSITE DESIGN

The website owner's next task is website design, which includes information architecture, navigation design, use of colors and graphics, and maximizing site performance. The purpose of this section is to enable users to understand and possibly contribute to the design of a website when working with Web designers. For details, see Rutgers (2014) and Jenkins (2013).

Successful website design is about meeting the customers' expectations and enabling the selling of the products or services. Design starts with identifying the customer's needs, expectations, and problems. A site is then designed to meet those needs and expectations. Jenkins (2013) and

McNeil (2013) provide some practical guidelines for a successful website. For a comprehensive collection of tutorials, templates, articles, and more, see Web Design Library (**webdesign.org**). For elements of a successful business website, including a discussion on content, SEO, and website design, see **businessexposuregroup. wordpress.com/2012/07/25/elements-of-a-successful-business-website**.

Table 16.2 shows a list of important website design criteria, with relevant questions. For a large collection of images, click on 'web design' in a Google image search.

Examples of well-designed sites are those of Intel, Sears, HP, Express Scripts, Whole Foods, Procter & Gamble, Johnson & Johnson, IBM, Pfizer, and Bank of America.

Information Architecture for a Website

A website's **information architecture** describes how a site is organized. It lists all the components of a site and how they are connected together. The most common site structure is *hierarchical* (see Figure 16.3). Most hierarchical websites are built

Table 16.2 Website design criteria

Navigation	Is it easy for visitors to find their way around the site?
Consistency	Are design elements, especially look, terminology, icons, and users' feeling, consistent across all pages? Does everything match?
Response time	How long does it take to access the site?
	Does the site comply with efficient rules (e.g., the 12-second rule?)
Appearance	Is the site aesthetically pleasing? Are the colors visually pleasing? Does the site's look express the company's desired image? Is the content easy to read, easy to navigate, and easy to understand?
Quality assurance	Are the site's calculators, navigation links, visitor registration processes, search tools, etc. in working order?
Availability	Are all broken links fixed promptly? Is the site always available to access?
Interactivity	Does the site encourage the visitor to play an active role in learning about the business's products or services? Are all appropriate contact details available on the website for visitors to submit feedback and ask questions? Is the information (contact names, e-mails, addresses, telephone numbers, etc.) current?
Content	How much multimedia is on the site? How current and relevant is the content? Is it easy to read? Informative?
Usability	How easy is it to use the site? How easy is it to learn to use the site?
Security	Is the customer's information protected? Does the customer feel safe accessing and using the site and, for example, submitting credit card information?
Scalability	Does the site design provide an easy format for future updates? Will the site's growth and increased usage protect the initial investment in site construction?

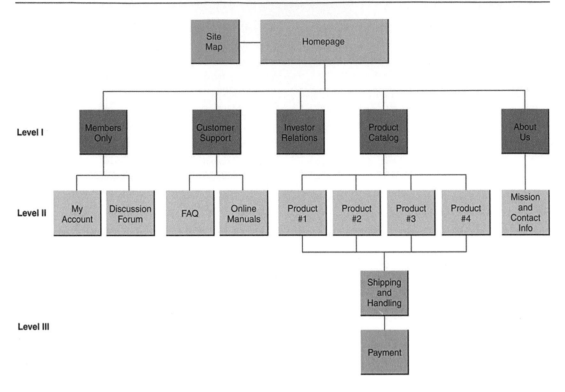

Figure 16.3   A simple hierarchical website structure

with wide and shallow structures, putting 3–10 components in level II (see figure) and limiting the components in most other levels. Other, less frequently used structures are circular and linear. A circular structure is useful for presenting training materials. A linear structure is useful for tutorials.

A website typically includes a *homepage* that welcomes visitors and introduces the site; *help* pages that assist the visitor in using or navigating through the site; *company* pages that give the visitor information about the e-business; *transaction* pages that lead the customer through the purchase process; and *content* pages that deliver information about products, services, and related topics.

Site Navigation

The purpose of **site navigation** is to help visitors quickly and easily find the information they need on a website. Among the questions considered in the creation of site navigation are: How will visitors access a site? How will visitors use the site? How will they find what is available at the site?

How will they go from one page to another and from one topic to another? How will visitors find what they are looking for? Site navigation has to help visitors find information efficiently, because visitors do not want to take the time to figure out how to access a site.

A simple navigation aid is a navigation bar. A navigation bar (see Figure 16.4) provides the visitor with an opportunity to link to frequently accessed destinations (e.g., homepage, "about us") and major sections of the website (e.g., product catalog, customer support).

Site Map and Navigation

A navigation bar usually appears at the top of the page where it will load first in the browser window and be visible "above the fold." However, if the page contains banner ads, then the navigation bar may be placed below the ads. Why? Frequent Web users develop "banner ad blindness" and they ignore banner ads. A duplicate navigation bar may appear at the bottom of every page.

Figure 16.5 summarizes the major concepts discussed here.

Figure 16.4 A typical navigation bar

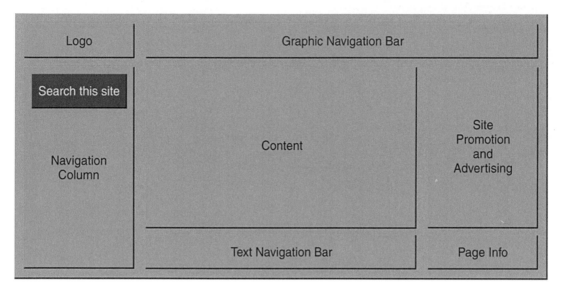

Figure 16.5 Web page layout grid

Performance (Speed)

Speed is a major design success factor. Visitors who have to wait more than a few seconds for a Web page to load might leave the site.

A number of factors affect the page speed, some of which are out of the control of the Web designer (e.g., the visitor's modem speed). The factors that are under the control of the Web designer relate to the content and design of the page. For example, videos and large images should be minimized.

Colors and Graphics

Rich media that includes colors, images, sound, and videos can improve the attractiveness of websites. Therefore, designers try to find what visitors like in rich media and give it to them.

For example, dashboards need to use multiple colors, and so do maps and videos.

Website Usability

According to **usability.gov/what-and-why/index. html**, **usability** refers to how well users can learn and use a product to achieve their goals. It also refers to how satisfied users with that process. Usability measures the quality of a user's experience when interacting with a product or system, including:

- Websites
- Software applications
- Mobile technologies
- Any user-operated device

Usability Is a Combination of Factors

It is important to realize that usability is not a single, one-dimensional property for visitors to the website. Usability factors include:

- **Intuitive design**: a nearly effortless understanding of the architecture and navigation of the site
- **Ease of learning**: how fast a user who has never seen the user interface before can accomplish basic tasks
- **Efficiency of use**: how fast an experienced user can accomplish tasks
- **Memorability**: after visiting the site, if a user can remember enough to use it effectively in future visits
- **Error frequency and severity**: how often users make errors while using the system, how serious the errors are, and how users recover from the errors
- **Subjective satisfaction**: if the user likes using the system

For additional concepts, see Nielsen (2012).

On the Web, usability is a necessary condition for success. If a website is difficult to use, visitors will leave. For further details, templates, guidelines, and methods, see **usability.gov**. Usable sites need to meet customer demands.

Software for Helping Web Designers

Several companies provide software to facilitate Web designs. Some are free. One example is Google Web Designer (free download). If you want to design your own website, you can do a Google search and find information about ideas, templates, tips for success, images, and more. Several tutorials are available as well.

What Annoys EC Customers?

One approach to a good Web design is to eliminate things that annoy site visitors, such as: pages loading too slowly, pop-up ads, the need to install extra software, mandatory complex registration requirements, confusing navigation, out-of-date content, and poor search tools. For details, see Kyrnin (undated). For important criteria for a quality website, see Clay (undated).

SECTION 16.6 REVIEW QUESTIONS

1. Describe 10 criteria used to judge a website design.
2. Name four site navigation aids.
3. Why is performance a key design criterion? What slows performance? What can decrease download time?
4. What is usability? List the major criteria used to determine usability.
5. Describe five EC annoyances.

16.7 PROVIDING E-COMMERCE SUPPORT SERVICES

Determining how the website actually will be built and by whom are the implementation parts of website construction. Website construction can be done in one of the following options: In-house development, outsourcing, and partnering. In addition, construction is done during both start up and maintenance.

Who Builds the Website?

The online business owner has to decide among the above-cited options or some combination(s) of them. This involves considerations such as available resources, urgency, budget, and existing computing systems.

Payments: Accepting Credit Cards

Another important service is payment (see Chapter 11). No business can exist without a payment system. Thus, every online business has to make decisions about electronic payment systems. The dominant form of B2C payment is accepting credit cards over the Internet. Paying for goods and services in the physical world is moving to mobile devices, including conducting micropayments.

Chapter 11 described the process for accepting credit card payments. As noted there, processing credit card payments on the Internet differs only slightly from the process in traditional, face-to-face transactions.

Website Promotion

Chapter 9 discussed website promotion through advertising (e.g., banner ads, pop-up ads) and marketing strategies (e.g., banner swapping, use of video ads, use of blogs, chat rooms, or groups in social networks and virtual worlds). This section focuses on internal website promotion, i.e., conducting marketing communications on the site itself. The related topic of search engine optimization also was described in Chapter 9.

Internal Website Promotion
Internal website promotion begins by including content to attract customers so that they will return and refer others to the site. To do this, the website needs compelling content, useful links to other websites, and features that will make customers want to return (e.g., provide entertainment).

The results derived from Web analytics are used to plan promotions and ads. *Web analytics* is defined and described in Chapter 14. Web analytics vendors include IBM, Oracle, Microsoft, MicroStrategy, SAS, and Webtrends.

Search Engine Optimization (SEO)
How do customers find a specific website in cyberspace? How does a new e-business get noticed and beat established competitors? In addition to promotional and advertising strategies discussed in this and other chapters, perhaps the most important and cost-effective way to attract new customers is *search engine optimization. Search engine optimization (SEO),* as defined in Chapter 9, is the use of strategies intended to position a website at the top of Web search engine results.

Several SEO services, such as **webposition. com** and **searchsummit.com** will manage the entire SEO process for a website. However, SEO requires constant monitoring to be effective. For comprehensive coverage of SEO, see Harris (2014).

An Example: How Does Baidu Succeed?

Case 16.3 describes the rise of Baidu (**baidu. com**) from a small startup to the top search engine in China.

CASE 16.3: EC APPLICATION: BAIDU'S STRATEGIES FOR SUCCESS

Baidu is a Chinese language Internet search provider, offering a Chinese-language search platform on its website. It provides Chinese language Internet search services to enable users to find relevant information online (e.g., images, news, Web pages). Founded in 2000 by software developers Robin Li and Eric Xu, Baidu.com is known as "China's Google." However, it has differentiated itself from Google by targeting Chinese users. Chinese Internet users search for content in a different way than the way people do in the West (see **clickz.com/clickz/column/2288982/search-in-china-how-baidu-is-different-from-google**).

According to Li, the name of the company "Baidu," meaning "hundreds of times," is from a Chinese poem written during the Song Dynasty. The company initially relied on financing provided by venture capitalists. In August 2005, Baidu went public in the U.S. (debuting at $27/share).

The Business Model

Baidu's strategy of focusing on the local market has allowed it to dominate the Chinese market for search engine users. Its revenues increased by 76.4% in 2010, with its share of Chinese search traffic reaching 73% compared with Google's 21% (China Daily 2010). In Q1 2014, Baidu led the search engine market with 77.1% market share (channel revenue included), compared with Google China's 11% (per **chinainternetwatch. com/7375/china-search-engine-market-q1-2014**). For Baidu's annual revenue from 2007 to 2013, see **statista.com/statistics/269032/annual-revenue-of-baidu**. For the company's annual revenue and other statistics, see their financial reports at **ir.baidu.com/phoenix.zhtml?c = 188488&p = irol-reportsAnnual**.

A leading formula for Baidu's success is its focus on several search services, which are geared to the Chinese culture and to mobility. Other strategies likewise have proven effective for Baidu. The company offers paid search, where the client chooses keywords that their customers may use to search for their products. Their ads then appear at the top of the related search results page. In terms of advertising, Baidu uses in addition to PPC ads, third parties to sell ads, unlike Google, which sells only PPC ads directly.

Google's withdrawal from the Chinese market in 2010, due the Chinese Government's refusal to stop censoring Google's content, further improved Baidu's customer base. Its stock price in May 2010 doubled the level it was trading at in January of the same year (see Wells 2010), and in 2014 it was much higher. Because Google could not afford to miss out on the world's biggest Internet market, it began its push to return to the Chinese market in 2012. As of June 2014, Google is intermittently available in China.

Note: Google (including YouTube) is frequently blocked in China (e.g., in June 2014, ahead of the anniversary of Tiananman).

In 2013, Baidu began promoting its mobile advertising, recognizing that this is the area of most growth. In 2014, net profit was up more than 24% in Q1 2014 and average revenue, and their CEO anticipates that within the year, the company's mobile traffic will surpass its PC-based traffic (see **pcworld.com/article/2148260/baidus-profit-boosted-by-mobile-ad-revenue.html**).The company has been acquiring EC companies or a stake in EC and IT companies in mobile ads and related fields.

Competitiveness and Constraints

Baidu was awarded the "China Internet Self-Discipline Award" in 2009, due to its strict monitoring and censorship of online information. Despite this recognition, Baidu was not spared lawsuits for copyright infringement. In June 2005, the company was sued by Shanghai Busheng Music and Culture Media Company for allegedly allowing downloads of pirated music. Likewise, popular film companies presented similar charges against Baidu for unauthorized downloading of movies. These lawsuits were settled.

Despite being initially recognized as "China's Google," Baidu has adopted several strategies to differentiate itself from the competition. Over the years, its range of services has expanded to include news, multimedia, and image searching. By stressing its competitive advantage – use of the Chinese language – Baidu has effectively reached and gained the loyalty of Chinese users.

In 2014, Baidu was in stiff competition with Alibaba Group's companies and other large Chinese EC companies.

For an overview of Baidu, including its products and services for users and customers, see **reuters.com/finance/stocks/company Profile?rpc = 66&symbol = BIDU.O**.

Sources: Based on Lai (2011b), Wells (2010), China Daily (2010), and **baidu.com** (accessed July 2014).

Questions

1. Baidu is also known as "China's Google." How is Baidu's business model different from Google's?
2. Baidu offers paid search placement. Do you think such website ranking services will promote unfair competition?
3. Baidu's strategy that uses Chinese language for its search engine is considered its biggest competitive advantage. Explain why (start by reading Lai 2011b).
4. What lessons does the Baidu case offer to e-commerce startups and entrepreneurs?
5. Investigate Baidu's activity in using mobility and m-commerce.

Customer Relationship Management (CRM)

Customer relationship management (CRM) refers to a customer service approach that focuses on building long-term and sustainable customer relationships that add value for both the customer and the company (see Online Tutorial T1). In building an EC website or an EC project, one needs to consider CRM. This section focuses on what every startup e-business needs to know in order to initiate an effective CRM program.

In EC, we concentrate on eCRM, as described in Online Tutorial T1.

Using Content to Build Customer Relationships

The first step in building customer relationships is to give customers good reasons to visit and return to the company's website. In other words, the site should be rich with information, provide entertainment whenever appropriate, and have more content than a visitor can absorb in a single visit. Online Tutorial T1 lists some ways in which online businesses can build customer relationships through content.

SECTION 16.7 REVIEW QUESTIONS

1. List the three options for website construction.
2. What factors are more suitable when considering internal development of a website? What factors are suitable for external development considerations?
3. List four types of website content that can promote the website internally.
4. What is search engine optimization (SEO)? Why is it important?
5. List some ways websites can use content to manage customer relationships.

16.8 OPENING A WEBSTORE

The most common EC project on the Internet is the *webstore*. Millions of webstores exist on the Internet, mostly those of small businesses. However, large corporations, as well as many individuals, including students, also have webstores. As we have seen throughout the book, most online entrepreneurs, such as the initiators of GrubHub.com, Amazon.com, CatToys.com, and JetPens.com, started with a small website or a webstore. Webstores vary in appearance, and their construction and operating expenses vary greatly. Webstores primarily sell products or services, yet their functionalities differ considerably.

Options For Acquiring Webstores

Webstores can be acquired in several ways:

- **Build them from scratch.** Pioneering webstores, such as **hothothot.com**, **wine.com**, and **amazon.com**, built their initial stores from scratch. Specifically, they designed them and then hired programmers (if they did not had their own) to program all the necessary software. The major advantage of this approach is that the site owner can customize the site to his or her liking. The disadvantage is that the process is slow, expensive, error prone, and requires constant maintenance. Consequently, today, only large corporations build their webstores from scratch. Most companies use other alternatives, as described next.
- **Build them from components.** This option is faster and less expensive than building from scratch. The site owner purchases off-the-shelf components (or sometimes obtains them for free), such as a shopping cart, an e-catalog, and a payment gate, and then assembles them into a website. The site owner needs to replace the components if they become obsolete; therefore, the site owner can save on maintenance (replace rather than repair). The downside is that the resulting site may not fit the online business owner's needs very well.
- **Build with templates (storebuilders and dedicated Web hosting).** As described earlier in the chapter, using storebuilders is one of the most viable options for starting an online business. Several vendors provide storebuilding templates. Some provide them free of charge, free for 30 days, or for a nominal monthly fee

that includes hosting the site on their servers. Using this approach is especially attractive for small- and medium-sized businesses because the cost is relatively low, the business can construct the webstore in a few hours or a few days, and it does not require extensive programming skills. The site owner uses templates, fills out forms, and attaches pictures. Another major benefit of this approach is that Web hosting and support services such as payment collection, shipping, and security are usually provided (see the "Judy's store" example in Chapter 13). Furthermore, the vendor will update its templates.

- Many vendors also offer store and inventory management as well as other capabilities, as described later in this section. Finally, and perhaps most important, if the site owner uses a vendor such as Yahoo!, eBay, or Amazon. com, the site will be included in that vendor's e-marketplace, which provides a great deal of exposure. The downside of this approach is that it limits the site owner to the available templates and tools. However, some vendors provide, for a fee, a professional version that allows customization and other advanced services. Representative vendors that provide templates are:
  - Yahoo! Small Business offers Yahoo! Merchant Solutions (**smallbusiness. yahoo.com/ecommerce**)
  - Hostway (**hostway.com**)
  - GoEmerchant (**goemerchant.com**)
  - StoreFront eCommerce (**storefront.net**)
  - 1&1 Hosting (**1and1.com**)
  - Go Daddy (**godaddy.com**)
  - Amazon.com ProMerchant (**services. amazon.com**)
  - ShoppingCartsPlus (**shoppingcartsplus. com**)
  - Shopify (**shopify.com**)
  - iPage (**ipage.com**)

For a comparison and evaluation of these vendors and others, see **ecommerce-software-review. toptenreviews.com**. The major criteria used for comparison are: ease of use, ease of installation, ease of setup, available capabilities, documentation, and fraud protection.

Identifying Requirements and Selecting a Development Option

Before choosing the appropriate development option, you need to consider a number of issues in order to generate a list of requirements and capabilities. The following is a list of representative questions that need to be addressed when defining requirements:

- **Customers.** Who are the target customers? What are their characteristics? What are their needs? What kind of marketing tactics should a business use to attract customers to its website? How can a business increase customer loyalty and trust?
- **Merchandising.** What kinds of products or services can be sold online? Which products or services can be digitized?
- **Sales service.** How easy is it to order and pay online? Can customers track their orders? How are customer inquiries and complaints handled? What kind of service agreements and guarantees are available? What are the return and refund procedures?
- **Promotions.** How are the products and services promoted? How will the site attract and keep customers? Are there coupons, manufacturer rebates, or quantity discounts available? Is cross-selling, upselling, and so forth possible? Is it beneficial?
- **Transaction processing.** How are taxes, shipping and handling fees, and payments processed? What kinds of shipping methods will the site offer? What kind(s) of payment methods will the site accept? How will the site manage order fulfillment? How it will deal with returned items?
- **Marketing data and analysis.** What information, such as sales, customer data, and advertising trends will the site collect? How will the site process and use such information for future marketing?

> • **Branding.** Compare and contrast the webstore with the competitors' webstores. How does the online brand relate to the offline brand?

The initial list of requirements should be as comprehensive as possible. It is advisable to validate the list using experts. The business can then prioritize the requirements based on the customers' preferences.

In the remainder of this section, we will introduce the Yahoo! Small Business Web Hosting service.

Yahoo! Small Business

Yahoo! offers one of the most popular e-commerce plans at **smallbusiness.yahoo.com**. It offers three levels of merchant solutions: starter, standard, and professional. The features and fees of each plan are available at **smallbusiness.yahoo. com/ecommerce**. Yahoo! offers a step-by-step guide that explains how Yahoo! Merchant Solutions works and how you can use it to build, manage, and market an online business. Yahoo! also offers related services such as Web hosting and sponsored advertising. The essentials of how to develop a webstore are provided next.

Take a Tour and See the Videos

To see all the features that Yahoo! Merchant Solutions has to offer, take a tour at **smallbusiness.yahoo.com/ecommerce**. Notable features (in July 2014, they keep changing) include the following: Web hosting and domain name registration; e-mail; EC tools (shopping cart, payment processing, inventory management); business tools and services (site design, marketing, site management); order processing tools; site development tools (site editor, templates, uploading content, for example, with Yahoo! SiteBuilder); finding and keeping customers; payment acceptance tools; tax calculators; order notification and confirmations; and performance-tracking tools

(statistics, drill-downs, measuring the effectiveness of marketing campaigns). Finally, read the success stories of small businesses that now use Yahoo! Merchant Solutions.

Using the Templates

You can build your webstore in several ways. Your primary tool is the easy-to-use Store Editor. You can create a homepage, set up various store sections, and add to them. You can upload content developed in Microsoft Expression Web (**msdn.microsoft.com/en-us/expression/jj712700.aspx**), Adobe Dreamweaver (**adobe.com/products/dreamweaver.html**), or Yahoo! SiteBuilder (**secure.webhosting.yahoo.com/ps/sb/index.php**).

SECTION 16.8 REVIEW QUESTIONS

1. List the various options for acquiring a webstore.
2. What are the advantages of building with templates? What are the disadvantages?
3. List the typical features of a webstore.
4. What are some of the website building selection criteria?

MANAGERIAL ISSUES

Some managerial issues related to this chapter are as follows:

1. **What does it take to create a successful online business?** The ability of a business to survive and thrive depends on the strength of the business model, the capabilities of the entrepreneur, and successful execution of the business plan. Creativity, entrepreneurial attitudes, and management skills represent a human capital investment that every potentially successful business needs. This is true for both online and offline businesses. However, to succeed in online business, management needs to consider additional factors, such as e-business models, revenue models, synergy and conflict between the online and offline channels, website management, and integration of information systems for EC and back-end systems.

2. **Is creating a website a technical task or a management task?** It is both. Although somewhat expensive, the technical skills required to build a website are readily available in the marketplace. The prerequisite managerial skills are somewhat more difficult to find. In order to be able to hire and work with information architects, Web designers, and website hosting services, online business owners need to possess traditional business skills as well as understand the technical aspects of building a website. Management should be able to map the business goals with a combination of solution sets, such as e-marketplaces, CRM, SCM, and ERP. The integration policy should connect the internal entities and enable collaboration with external partners.

3. **How do we attract visitors to the website?** Search engine optimization is important, but the key to attracting visitors, getting them to return, and encouraging them to tell others about the site is to offer credible content that fulfills a value-exchange proposition. That is, both the site owner and the customer must receive value from the visit. Web design delivers content in a compelling manner that enhances the readability of the content and the quality of the customer experience. Personalized support services are important in order to provide relevant information and to motivate users to revisit.

4. **How do we turn visitors into buyers?** Getting people to visit the website is only half the battle. Visitors become buyers when a website offers products and services that they need. A website could also offer promotions and bargains that entice visitors to buy at that site rather than shop elsewhere. Customer service for complaint resolution will contribute to retaining the customer and generating repurchases. A well-designed CRM system needs to support the services.

5. **Are best practices useful?** For an inexperienced EC person or company, the best practices of others can be extremely useful. The experiences of vendors, buyers, companies, academics, and others are most useful. Free advice is available from many sources, including E-Commerce Partners (**ecommercepartners.net**).

6. **What should my new business submit to money suppliers?** It depends on the stage of the business life cycle. In the early stage, funders are concerned about the sales growth rate and market share. Losses may be tolerated as long as the growth is high and the vision of future profit is clear. However, the eventual concern will be the realized profit and stock price. The important thing is to maintain control, with the company retaining 51% of the shares (at least up to the time of the IPO).

7. **What are important factors for successful website management?** To manage the website successfully, the e-business owner needs to select an appropriate Web hosting service, maintain up-to-date and useful content, and promote the website so that new customers will visit, and existing one will revisit. The alternatives to Web hosting are storebuilder services, dedicated hosting, ISP hosting services, and self-hosting. To maintain the quality of the site's content, a policy for acquiring, testing, and updating content should be established. Personalization is also important. Social networking may be adopted as an important source of interactions and feedback from users.

SUMMARY

In this chapter, you learned about the following EC issues as they relate to the chapter's learning objectives.

1. **Fundamental requirements for initiating an online business.** A good idea becomes a successful online business when owners with the required skills, attitudes, and understanding of Internet culture execute a powerful business plan.

2. **Funding options for a startup online business.** Incubators usually provide support services, whereas angel investors and venture capitalists provide funds for a prospective online business. The business and business owners usually benefit greatly from these arrangements, but the funding sources are scarce and competition for funds is formidable.

3. **Adding e-initiatives.** Adding e-initiatives (or projects) is common. A large project requires a business case. Additions are made gradually that eventually make the business a click-and-mortar. Common projects are e-procurement, eCRM, and a webstore.

4. **Transformation to e-business.** In an e-business, all possible processes are conducted online. Achieving such a state in a large organization is a complex process involving change management.

5. **Website hosting options for an online business.** Storebuilder services, ISPs, dedicated website hosting services, and self-hosting give online business owners a range of options in deciding how and where to host the website. A well-chosen domain name is an "address for success," a way of making the site easy to find and remember. Choosing a domain name is an important step in setting up the hosting site.

6. **Provide content that attracts and keeps website visitors.** Content is a major factoring attracting visitors to website. Content can be created, purchased, or acquired for free and used for site promotion, sales, and building customer relationships. Successful websites offer content that the site's target audience wants and expects.

7. **Design a visitor-friendly site.** Although text is content rich and inexpensive, a text-only site is a boring and unmemorable site. Select graphics and colors with the site's business goals and visitors' needs in mind. Website owners and designers should never misjudge the attention span of the site visitor, so it is best to include small graphics that can load fast and add attractions. The key to visitor-friendly navigation is to project a visitor's mental map on the website: where they are, where they were, where they should go next, and how to get to where they want to be.

8. **Search engines optimization is a critical success factor.** It is necessary to design strategies for search engine optimization. The higher the placement of your brand in a search result, the more traffic to your site.

9. **Provision of support services.** Like offline businesses, online businesses need support services. These include payment, security, content creation, website design, advertisement (promotion), search engine optimization, and CRM.

10. **The process of building a webstore.** Assuming that you know what you want to sell, you need to obtain a domain name and arrange for hosting. The next step is to design the site and fill it with appropriate content. Your webstore needs to have support services (such as payment) and be secure. You must also promote the site in order to attract buyers.

11. **Using templates to build a webstore.** Small sites can be built expeditiously, easily, and inexpensively using templates. The disadvantages are that the site will look like many others that use the same templates and it might not fit the needs of the company.

KEY TERMS

Angel investor
Attractors
Business case
Business model
Business plan
Collaborative website
Content management
Cross-selling
Crowdfunding
Domain name
Dynamic Web content
EC Incubator
Information architecture
Informational website
Interactive website
Self-hosting
Site navigation
Social-oriented website
Storebuilder service
Transactional website
Usability (of a website)
Up-selling
Venture capital (VC)
Web content
Web hosting service

DISCUSSION QUESTIONS

1. Compare and contrast setting up a traditional brick-and-mortar business and an online business. Consider factors such as entrepreneurial skills, facilities and equipment, and business processes.
2. How is an e-business plan different from a traditional business plan?
3. Describe organizational transformation and discuss some of the difficulties involved.
4. How would you decide which website hosting option an online business should use? List and briefly explain factors to consider in your decision.
5. Who should be on a website development team for a small business? For a large business?
6. Why is a webstore such as **cattoys.com** not economically feasible offline?
7. What are the advantages and disadvantages of using templates to build a webstore?
8. Yahoo! provides many services, including website hosting, storebuilding tools, and an online marketplace that hosts many independent vendors. List the benefits of these services. What are the drawbacks, if any?
9. How is usability related to website design?

TOPICS FOR CLASS DISCUSSION AND DEBATES

1. Compare and contrast the creation of a new online business and the establishment of an online initiative in an existing company. Consider factors such as resource acquisition, startup processes, and competitor analysis.
2. Enter **shopify.com** and find out what they do. Compare it to Google Analytics. Write a report.
3. What are the potential conflicts and trade-offs in giving the customer everything possible (e.g., personalized content, high-resolution graphics, a feature-full site) and the fundamental rules of website design?
4. What are the merits and drawbacks of taking a startup public (initial public offering [IPO])?

When is a good time for entrepreneurial startups to go public? You may refer to the cases of Alibaba.com (Case 16.2), Baidu (Case 16.3) and Facebook (the closing case) for your discussion.
5. Debate: Could the success of Facebook (the closing case), Amazon.com (Case 16.1), Alibaba.com (Case 16.2) and Baidu (Case 16.3) be traced to the entrepreneurial attitudes of their founders? Would it be possible for other EC entrepreneurs to duplicate Zuckerberg, Bezos, Ma, and Li's success on the strength of similar traits and characteristics?
6. Debate: Should a small business maintain its own website? Why or why not? Should a large business maintain its own website? Why or why not?
7. Discuss the benefits of crowdfunding and its limitations.

INTERNET EXERCISES

1. Go to **vfinance.com** and **nvca.org** and identify any trends or opportunities in acquiring startup funding for an e-business.
2. Go to a Yahoo! category, such as tourist agencies or insurance companies, and pick 10 sites. Classify them as informational, interactive, transactional, or social-oriented websites. Make a list of any informational, interactive, transactional, or social features.
3. Many individuals try to make a living simply by buying and selling goods on eBay. Visit **ebay.com** and make a list of the ways in which these entrepreneurs use cross-selling and up-selling in their sales activities.
4. Visit the **webmaster-forums.net**. Register (for free). Compare the design rules offered in this chapter with some of the websites offered the site. Provide at least one design suggestion to a Webmaster who is soliciting feedback.
5. Enter **1and1.com**. Examine its hosting, development, and other tools. Compare it with services offered by **shopify.com**. Write a report.

6. Enter **willmaster.com**. View its tutorials and comment on its usefulness to EC website builders.

7. Go to **google.com/wallet** and find the services offered to buyers.

8. Log on to **facebook.com** and socialize on the website. Compare and contrast Facebook with other social networking sites such as Google+, Hi5, and LinkedIn.

9. Enter **godaddy.com/design/web-design.aspx** and view the tutorials there. Summarize your findings.

10. Enter Kickstarter (**kickstarter.com**) and other crowdfunding portals. Compare their functionalities. Write a report.

TEAM ASSIGNMENTS AND PROJECTS

Assignment for the Opening Case

1. Read the opening case and answer the following questions.
   (a) What benefits could I Am Hungry offer to end-users and restaurants?
   (b) Using I Am Hungry as an example, discuss the business values of geolocation applications.
   (c) What are the three revenue models of I Am Hungry? Explain the pros and cons of each model.
   (d) Using I Am Hungry as an example, discuss the importance of revenue generation to small startups.
   (e) What lessons does the I Am Hungry experience offer to e-commerce startups and entrepreneurs?

2. Identify a product or service that is suitable for marketing on Facebook. Draft a promotion plan. Present your plan to the class.

3. Enter **entrepreneurs.about.com**. Each team member should select two or three of the "browse topics" (on the left side of the page) and relate them to online businesses. Give a presentation to the class.

4. Enter **myownbusiness.org/s2/index.html**. Obtain a template and design a business plan for your class EC project.

5. Form two teams: a client team and a Web design team. After suitable preparation, both teams meet for their first website planning meeting. Afterward, both teams critique their own and the other team's performance in the meeting.

6. Enter **secure.webhosting.yahoo.com/ps/sb/index.php** and download the SiteBuilder. As a team, build a webstore for your dream business. You can try it for free for 30 days. Use the design features available. Have visitors check out the site. The instructor and class will review the sites for design and usability. Awards will be given to the best webstores. Alternatively, you may use the equivalent tools from another sitebuilder.

7. Many companies offer software for e-commerce. Each team takes one of the following companies (you can find other ones), lists their offering and gives a presentation to the class. Then the class votes for the best site. The suggested companies are: Netsuite (**netsuite.com**), Volusion (**volusion.com**), ZippyCart (**zippycart.com**), Vendio (**vendio.com**; an Alibaba company), Vcommerce (**vcommerce.com/vc-econnect**), and Demandware (**demandware.com**). Distinguish between B2B and B2C software. Consult: "Top 10 Ecommerce Software Vendors Revealed" from **business-software.com/ecommerce.**

8. Compare some of the free website hosting services. Start with Google sites and Wix.com. In your comparison, develop five major criteria for evaluation. Each team will build a sample site.

CLOSING CASE: FACEBOOK: A COLLEGE PROJECT THAT TOOK THE WORLD BY STORM

When Facebook CEO Mark Zuckerberg was named Time Magazine's "Person of the Year" in 2010, it reflected both his incredible achievement and the global impact of Facebook. Today, Facebook has radically changed the ways by which hundreds of millions of people interact and socialize online.

The Startup

Facebook started under the name of Facemash in 2003. The name was changed to The Facebook, and then to Facebook. Facebook (**facebook.com**) has evolved from a simple social networking site for Harvard University students to the world's largest portal for social networking. Mark Zuckerberg and his friends, then in college, started the site, which served as a platform that allowed their fellow Harvard students to interact with one another online. Enjoying instant success, they expanded the site to include students from Columbia, Stanford, and Yale Universities. Purchasing the domain name **facebook.com** for $200,000, Zuckerberg and his partners officially adopted the name "Facebook" for the site in August 2005.

The Solution

Similar to most start-up companies, Facebook faced funding and infrastructure challenges to support its expansion. In August 2004, private investor Peter Thiel was granted 10% ownership for infusing $500,000 into the site's expansion. With the help of this funding, the number of site users climbed rapidly, reaching 1 million by the end of 2004. In April 2005, another venture capitalist provided more funding, in exchange for a 13% stake. Facebook needed additional investments for its continued growth. They decided to look for venture capital. Venture capital firms invested $27.5 million in April 2006. Within the same month, Facebook expanded its reach to include members from high technology companies. Finally, in September 2006, the site was opened to all users worldwide. Based on 2012 data, more than two-thirds of its users are non-students. Of these, those belonging to the over-35 age group comprise the fastest growing segment of users. As of October 2014, the number of active users had exceeded 1.35 billion, with 180 million logging in at least once each day, each spending 20 minutes per visit on the average. In late 2012, the rate of photos being uploaded to the site reached 3,600 per second.

The Business Model

Facebook offers various on-site features, many of which are being copied by other platforms such as Google. Facebook invites developers to build applications and allows them to earn advertising revenues. Zuckerberg believes that Facebook should not employ a strategy that is just about "winning all the content or owning all the applications." Instead, Facebook earns revenues from its sponsors and from banner advertisements (for an infographic, see **ritholtz.com/blog/2014/02/how-does-facebook-make-its-money**). The site charges ads based on cost per mille (CPM) or cost per 1,000 impressions, CPC or cost per click, CPA or cost per action, and CPI or cost per impression. In 2014, Facebook was exploring new advertising models. Facebook also receives money from Zynga's gamers and from Facebook Gifts (now only gift cards and digital gifts). For details, see Cutler (2013) and **market-realist.com/2014/01/facebook** (Parts 1–9).

Facebook IPO

In June 2012, Facebook released public shares, and its initial public offering was valued at approximately $60 billion (in June 2014 the value was $165 billion). Going public was evidently a smart move, especially since Microsoft previously offered to buy the site for only a quarter of the amount. Facebook's total revenue in 2014 exceeded $10 billion, around $3 billion of which was earned from ad sales. The IPO was not too successful during the first few months, but as of mid-2013, the price of the stock increased about 400% from its bottom.

LESSONS LEARNED FROM THIS CASE

Facebook's success can be attributed largely to its ability to connect users, and provide users with many effective ways to interact with their friends. This innovative form of connections is the major reason why Facebook founder and CEO Mark Zuckerberg was named Time's "Person of the Year" in 2010.

Initially a college project, Facebook has now grown into a world-renowned site for social networking and commerce. Facebook does not just aim to provide innovative technology, it also responds to customer demands. Currently, it focuses on developing its own ad platform and operating system, as well as providing wireless services to enhance overall user experience.

Sources: Based on Kirkpatrick (2011), Lai (2010a, 2011a), Cutler (2013), Crager et al. (2014), Grossman (2010), and **facebook.com** (accessed July 2014).

Questions

1. What are the factors that have contributed to the rapid growth of Facebook's loyal user base for the past few years?
2. What tools does Facebook provide to promote selling and buying activities? Can Facebook be used as a marketing tool? How?
3. Do you agree that Facebook should open its internal operations to external developers? Why or why not?
4. Identify all of Facebook's sources of income and elaborate on the revenue models of social networking sites using Facebook as an example. (Consult Cutler 2013.)
5. What lessons can e-commerce startups and entrepreneurs learn from Facebook's experience?
6. Find out how many servers Facebook uses and how they are managed.

Note: Wikipedia provides extensive discussion about Facebook. Some of it may be inaccurate or incomplete.

ONLINE FILES
available at **affordable-ecommerce-textbook.com/turban**

No online files are available for this chapter.

COMPREHENSIVE EDUCATIONAL WEBSITES

bplans.com: Sample business plans.
libguides.rutgers.edu/ecommerce: A comprehensive EC guide.

smallbusiness.yahoo.com/ecommerce/#design: Yahoo! Small Business e-commerce webstore features.
entrepreneur.com: Information on starting a business, social media, small business management, marketing, and more.
onlinebusiness.about.com: A guide for beginners.
entrepreneur.com/startingabusiness/startup basics/index.html: All about starting a business (e.g., articles, videos).
webdesign.org: Tutorials, articles, news, templates, and examples.
sba.gov: The U.S. Small Business Administration; resources and information on loans and grants to help small businesses.
thesitewizard.com: Comprehensive guide to website design, promotion, web hosting, and more; topical index; free Web Wizards.
marketingdonut.co.uk: Provides reliable information and resources to help business owners. Includes free advice, tools, and marketing for small businesses.

GLOSSARY

Angel investor A wealthy individual who contributes personal funds and possibly advice at the earliest stage of business development usually in exchange of equity in the business.

Attractors Websites that include puzzles, competitions, and prize giveaways. They are designed so that visitors will like them so much that they will visit again, and recommend the site to their friends.

Business model The manner in which business is done to generate revenue and create value.

Business plan A written, formal document that specifies a company's goals, and outlines how the company intends to achieve these goals.

Business case A document that is used to convince management to approve the investment of organizational resources in specific EC or other projects.

Collaborative website A website that allows business partners to interact and collaborate (i.e., it includes many supportive tools).

Content management The process of collecting, publishing, revising, updating, and removing content from a website to keep content fresh, accurate, compelling, and credible.

Crowdfunding A funding method based on using investors to fund startups. Each individual invests a small amount of money; the collection channels are Internet-based social networks.

Cross-selling Offering complementary or related products and services to increase sales.

Domain name A name-based address (owned by a person or an organization) that identifies a specific website and its Internet-connected server.

Dynamic Web content Frequently changing content that continuously needs to be kept up-to-date.

EC incubator A company, university, or nonprofit organization that supports promising EC businesses in their initial stages of development.

Information architecture How a site is organized. It lists all the components of a site and how they are connected together.

Informational website A website that provides mostly information about the business and its products and services.

Interactive website A website that provides opportunities for the customers and the business to interact converse and present information (as in information website).

Self-hosting When a business acquires the hardware, software, staff, and dedicated telecommunications services necessary to set up and then manage its own website.

Site navigation Aids that help visitors quickly and easily find the information they need on a website.

Social-oriented website A site that provides users online tools for communication and sharing information on common interests.

Storebuilder service A service that provides Web hosting as well as storage space, templates, and other services to help small businesses build a website expeditiously and inexpensively.

Transactional website A website that sells products and services.

Up-selling Offering an upgraded version of the product in order to boost sales and profit.

Usability (of a website) Refers to how well users can learn and use a product to achieve their goals. It also refers to how satisfied users are with that process. It measures the quality of a user's experience when interacting with a product or system.

Venture capital (VC) Money invested in a business by an individual, a group of individuals (venture capitalists), or a funding company in exchange for equity in the business.

Web content Content (the text, images, sound, and video) that is included on a Web page.

Web hosting service A type of hosting service that allows individual and organizations to make their website accessible on the Web (providing websites with space on the Internet).

REFERENCES

Belew, S., and J. Elad. *Starting an Online Business: All-In-One Desk Reference for Dummies*, 3rd ed. Hoboken, NJ: Wiley & Sons, 2011.

Berry, T. "A Simpler Plan for Startups." *BPlans* (Undated). **articles.bplans.com/writing-a-business-plan/a-simpler-plan-for-start-ups/39** (accessed July 2014).

China Daily. "Baidu Gains More Search Market Share in Q3." (Updated) October 19, 2010. **chinadaily.com.cn/business/2010-10/19/content_11430298.htm** (accessed July 2014).

Clay, B. "Quality Site Criteria." *Bruce Clay, Inc.* (undated). **bruceclay.com/design/web_crit.htm** (accessed July 2014).

Condra, C. "Top 5 Tips: How to Succeed in Ecommerce: Online Merchants Wear Many Hats." 2014. **ecommerce.about.com/od/eCommerce-Basics/a/How-to-Succeed-in-eCommerce.htm** (accessed July 2014).

Crager, J., et al. *Facebook All-in-One for Dummies (For Dummies (Computer/Tech))*, 2nd edition, Hoboken, NJ: Wiley/For Dummies, 2014.

Cutler, K-M. "Facebook's Q4 Revenue Rises 40% to $1.59B, Shares Down Slightly in After-Hours." January 30, 2013. **techcrunch.com/2013/01/30/facebooks-q4-revenue-rises-40-to-1-59b-shares-decline-7-percent-in-after-hours** (accessed July 2014).

di Stefano, T.F. "What Makes So Many Startups Fail." *E-Commerce Times*, November 11, 2010.

Farhoomand, A., and R. Lai. "Alibaba's Jack Ma: Rise of the New Chinese Entrepreneur." *Asia Case Research Centre*, University of Hong Kong, 2010.

Gloor, P. *Making the e-Business Transformation*. New York: Springer (softcover reprint of the original 1st ed. 2000 edition), 2011.

Grossman, L. "Person of the Year 2010." *Time,* December 2010.

Harris, C. *SEO Top Secret: How to Get Top Ranking on the First Page of Google by Search Engine Optimization (Simple Online Marketing)* [Kindle Edition]. Seattle, WA: Amazon Digital Services, 2014.

Holden, G. *Starting an Online Business for Dummies*, 7th ed. Hoboken, NJ: Wiley/For Dummies, 2013.

Jenkins, S. *Web Design All-in-One for Dummies*, 2nd edition, New York: Wiley/For Dummies, 2013.

Kirkpatrick, D. *The Facebook Effect: The Inside Story of the Company That Is Connecting the World*. New York: Simon & Schuster, 2011.

Kotter, J.P., *Leading Change, With a New Preface by the Author.* Boston: Harvard Business Review Press, 2012.

Kyrnin, J. "Ecommerce Annoyances." *About.com Web Design.* Undated. **webdesign.about.com/od/ecommerce/qt/ecom_annoyances.htm** (accessed July 2014).

Lai, L. S. "Facebook Lessons for E-Business Startups." *World Academy of Science, Engineering and Technology*, Issue 60, 5(12), 774–778, 2011a.

Lai, L. S. "In Search of Excellence – Google vs Baidu." *World Academy of Science, Engineering and Technology*, 60, 5(12), 1108–1111, 2011b.

Lai, L. S. "Social Commerce – E-Commerce in Social Media Context." *World Academy of Science, Engineering and Technology*, Issue 48, 4(12), 39–44, 2010a.

Lai, L. S. "Chinese Entrepreneurship in the Internet Age: Lessons from Alibaba.com." *World Academy of Science, Engineering and Technology*, 4(12), 405–411, 2010b.

Lowman, M. "I Am Hungry: Your Geolocated Ticket to Cheap Eats in Boston." July 2, 2010. **bostinno.streetwise.co/2010/07/02/i-am-hungry-your-geolocated-ticket-to-cheap-eats-in-boston** (accessed July 2014).

McNeil, P. *The Web Designer's Idea Book, Volume 3: Inspiration from Today's Best Web Design Trends, Themes and Styles.* Blue Ash, OH: HOW Books, 2013.

Nagy, S. "What Is E-Commerce Failure—The Six Main Reasons." July 14, 2010. **ezinearticles.com/?What-is-E-commerce-Failure—The-Six-Main-Reasons&id=4667530** (accessed July 2014).

Neiss, S., et al. *Crowdfunding Investing for Dummies.* Hoboken, N.J.: For Wiley/Dummies, 2013.

Nielsen, J. "Usability 101: Introduction to Usability." January 4, 2012. **nngroup.com/articles/usability-101-introduction-to-usability** (accessed July 2014).

Peterson, S.D., et al. *Business Plans Kit For Dummies.* Hoboken, NJ: Wiley/For Dummies, 2013.

Prive, T. "What is Crowdfunding and How Does It Benefit the Economy." November 27, 2012. **forbes.com/sites/tanyaprive/2012/11/27/what-is-crowdfunding-and-how-does-it-benefit-the-economy/** (accessed July 2014).

Quittner, J. "The Charmed Life of Amazon's Jeff Bezos." *Fortune Magazine*, Last updated) April 15, 2008.

Rutgers. *Rutgers University Libraries: Electronic Commerce 2013.* (Last Updated June 21, 2014.) **libguides.rutgers.edu/ecommerce** (accessed July 2014).

Turban, E., et al., *Social Commerce.* New York: Springer, 2015.

Wells, T. "Baidu Profits from Google's China Exit." July 19, 2010. **seochat.com.au/c/a/Search-Engine-News/Baidu-Profits-From-Googles-China-Exit** (accessed July 2014).

Young, T. E. *The Everything Guide to Crowdfunding: Learn How to Use Social Media for Small-Business Funding (Everything Series).* Holbrook, MA: Adams Media, 2013.

Zinsmeister, S., and M. Venkatraman. "I Am Hungry: Cheap Eats in Cyberspace." *The CASE Journal*, 8(1), Fall 2011. **caseweb.org/docs/TCJfrontVol8Issue1.pdf**. Accessed Dec 2014

Index